Business Ethics

Policies and Persons

Business Ethics

Policies and Persons

Fourth Edition

Kenneth E. Goodpaster

College of Business
University of St. Thomas

Laura L. Nash

Harvard Business School

Henri-Claude de Bettignies

Euro-Asia and Comparative Research Centre
INSEAD

Boston Burr Ridge, IL Dubuque, IA Madison, WI New York San Francisco St. Louis
Bangkok Bogotá Caracas Kuala Lumpur Lisbon London Madrid Mexico City
Milan Montreal New Delhi Santiago Seoul Singapore Sydney Taipei Toronto

BUSINESS ETHICS: POLICIES AND PERSONS

Published by McGraw-Hill/Irwin, a business unit of The McGraw-Hill Companies, Inc., 1221 Avenue of the Americas, New York, NY, 10020.

This book is printed on acid-free paper.

1 2 3 4 5 6 7 8 9 0 QPD/QPD 0 9 8 7 6 5

ISBN 0-07-299690-0

Editorial director: *John E. Biernat*
Senior sponsoring editor: *Kelly H. Lowery*
Editorial assistant: *Kirsten Guidero*
Senior marketing manager: *Lisa Nicks*
Project manager: *Bruce Gin*
Senior production supervisor: *Sesha Bolisetty*
Senior designer: *Mary E. Kazak*
Media project manager: *Lynn M. Bluhm*
Developer, Media technology: *Brian Nacik*
Cover design: *David Seidler*
Cover image: *© Benjamin Rondel/CORBIS*
Typeface: *10/12Palatino*
Compositor: *SR Nova Pvt Ltd., Bangalore, India*
Printer: *Quebecor World Dubuque Inc.*

Library of Congress Cataloging-in-Publication Data

Goodpaster, Kenneth E., 1944-
Business ethics: policies and persons / Kenneth E. Goodpaster, Laura L. Nash, Henri-Claude de Bettignies.— 4th ed.
p. cm.
Rev. ed. of: Policies and persons. 3rd. ed. 1998.
Includes bibliographical references.
ISBN 0-07-299690-0 (alk. paper)
1. Business ethics–Case studies. I. Nash, Laura L. II. Bettignies, Henri Claude de. III. Goodpaster, Kenneth E., 1944-. Policies and persons. IV. Title.
HF5387.M385 2006
174'.4–dc22

2004061061

www.mhhe.com

In fond memory of John B. Matthews (1922–1991): teacher, mentor, colleague, friend

John B. Matthews was the coauthor of the first two editions of this casebook. Until his death in December 1991, he was the Joseph C. Wilson Professor of Business Administration at the Harvard Business School, where he taught since 1949. He held an A.B. and an honorary LL.D. from Bowdoin College, and received his MBA and D.C.S. degrees from the Harvard Business School. Professor Matthews taught a course entitled "Ethical Aspects of Corporate Policy" in the school's Advanced Management Program and the Program for Management Development, and "Managerial Decision Making and Ethical Values: An Introduction" in the first-year MBA program. He also taught in a number of executive programs and served as Faculty Chairman of the Advanced Management Programme at Oxford University's Templeton College. He served as a consultant to a number of companies and on the boards of directors of Ampco-Pittsburgh Corporation, Guest Services Inc., and Johnson Partners. Professor Matthews wrote a number of books in addition to his contributions to this volume.

About the Authors

Kenneth E. Goodpaster holds the David and Barbara Koch Chair in Business Ethics at the University of St. Thomas in St. Paul, Minnesota. He received his Ph.D. in philosophy at the University of Michigan and holds an A.M. in philosophy from that school and an A.B. in mathematics from the University of Notre Dame. Professor Goodpaster taught graduate and undergraduate philosophy at Notre Dame before joining the faculty of the Harvard Business School in 1980, where he taught both MBA candidates and business executives until 1990. His research in applied philosophy, focusing on the dynamic relationships among three levels of ethical analysis—the person, the organization, and the capitalist system—has led to course development, numerous journal publications, encyclopedia articles, and other books including *Ethics in Management* (Harvard Business School, 1984), *Managerial Decision Making and Ethical Values* with Thomas R. Piper (Harvard Business School, 1989), and *Conscience and Corporate Culture* (Blackwell Publishers, 2005). Goodpaster is on the editorial boards of many professional journals in business ethics and consults with corporations and educational institutions around the world.

Laura L. Nash is a Senior Research Fellow at Harvard Business School. She earned her Ph.D. in classics under a Danforth Fellowship at Harvard University. Professor Nash has taught at Brown, Brandeis, and Boston University in addition to her consulting work with many of the nation's top corporations. She has also been an ongoing consultant to The Conference Board. Nash writes on a variety of topics in business ethics including corporate ethics programs, executive values, corporate social benefits, and desegregation. She is a frequent contributor to *Across the Board* and other publications. Among her books are *Good Intentions Aside: A Manager's Guide for Resolving Ethical Problems* (Harvard Business School Press, 1990) and *Believers in Business* (Thomas Nelson Publishers, 1994) and *Just Enough: Tools for Creating Success in Your Work and Life* (John Wiley & Sons, 2004).

Henri-Claude de Bettignies holds the AVIVA Chair in Leadership and Responsibility at INSEAD where he is Professor of Asian Business and Comparative Management. He is also—since 1988—Visiting Professor of International Business at Stanford University. Educated at the Sorbonne and at the Catholic University of Paris, he spent two years at the Harvard Business School (ITP) and at the University of California (Berkeley) before working in Japan and Asia for five years. At INSEAD he initiated the development of the Organizational Behavior group and was the founder and director general of the Euro-Asia Centre, before launching the ethics initiative and the AVIRA programme for chief executives. Both at INSEAD (in Fontainebleau and Singapore) and Stanford he teaches in the MBA programme and in executive education. His books are on Asia (China, Japan) and his publications are on change management and social responsibility. H. C. de Bettignies is on the editorial board of a number of journals, including *The International Journal of Business Governance and Ethics, Corporate Governance, New Academy Review, Finance and Common Good, Journal of Asian Business, Asian Business and Management*, and *International Studies of Management & Organization.*

Table of Contents

Preface

Our goal in this book is to provide a flexible learning tool, containing high-quality case research on topics useful to both today's managers and students of management. The approximately 60 primary cases (and 45 secondary cases) are grouped into four categories: (1) personal values, (2) corporate values: looking inward, (3) corporate values: looking outward, and (4) corporate values: international business. Thus, they are organized to take the reader from individual decisions made on a personal level to corporate policies decided on the global scale.

The topics of the cases were chosen sometimes for their timeliness or fertility, and sometimes simply because they reflected important realities of the business environment. We do not claim that they exhaust the field of business ethics, but we do believe that they illustrate the main types of issues encountered in management practice. New to this edition are well over two dozen cases and background notes, covering such issues as the corporate scandals of 2002 and the Sarbanes-Oxley Act, corporate responsibilities for privacy, product safety, and employees with disabilities. Other new issues include the responsibilities of business media, responsibilities for marketing products and services to young people, and the ethical challenges presented by globalization in relation to child labor, questionable payments, human rights abuses, and environmental pollution.

We and the other contributors to this collection developed most of the cases over a 25-year period (1980–2005) in the field rather than in the library. Some are short, only a few pages. Others are fairly lengthy. Still others are divided into parts to provide "sequenced" learning opportunities. The shades of gray that are characteristic of ethical decision making often require attention to depth and detail in a case. We have been guided by our sense of how much information was needed to achieve learning objectives, not by any predetermined standards of length or format.

The cases have been classroom-tested at the Harvard Business School (both in the MBA program and in programs for middle- and upper-level managers), at INSEAD in Fontainebleau, France, and in the College of Business at the University of St. Thomas in Minneapolis, Minnesota. The first, second, and third editions found acceptance in academic programs in colleges and universities in the United States and abroad. Sometimes they were supplemented by other readings, role-played, or used for written assignments and examinations. For the most part, however, they have been used just as they are, to stimulate vigorous dialogue and self-discovery.

We have chosen not to accompany the cases with very many texts and readings. There is good reason for this decision. It has been our experience that as the field of business ethics has evolved, the variety of educators with an interest in the field has expanded. Academics schooled in business administration have undertaken studies in ethics; philosophers and humanists have pursued studies in business management; and managers have undertaken both. As a result, business ethics courses have proliferated in schools of business, departments of philosophy, colleges of arts and letters, and corporate in-house education programs. It would be difficult to make accurate assumptions about the kinds of discourse with which educators in these various fields would feel comfortable. The permutations of this basic problem convinced us in the end that the case studies were the principal items of value that we wished to convey.

Included in this edition is a new Introduction that provides some background on the case method for the student and teacher, elaborates the goals of the method, and shows how the method applies in the field of ethics. The instructors and students who have read this Introduction will be well versed in the rationale for the case method and will have some useful tools for ethics-related case analysis.

Given the diversity in background and interest of those using the book, we believe the items in the appendixes are important: "Bridging East and West in Management Ethics" offers a discussion of certain basic similarities between Asian and Western ethical ideals, along with a statement of the Caux Roundtable *Principles for Business,* a set of shared norms for global business that has been accepted widely by corporate leaders in North America, Europe, and Japan. "A Baldrige Process for Ethics?" describes and illustrates a self-assessment tool for corporate leaders and boards of directors aimed at increasing ethical awareness and avoiding potential threats to an organization's reputation. "The Self-Assessment and Improvement Process: Executive Survey" presents the first-stage version of that tool.

An Instructor's Manual accompanies this text. In addition to teaching notes for each of the cases, it includes follow-up cases, sample syllabi for shorter and longer courses, and a summary matrix indicating topics or themes in each of the cases.

It is our hope that this book can be used not only in advanced undergraduate and graduate courses in schools of business but also in departments of philosophy and religious studies, in other humanities programs, and in corporate management education. It is also our hope that the cases are themselves important and interesting enough to merit a more general readership both inside and outside the academy. There are, frankly, many thoughtful people who underestimate the complexity of the decisions—economic and ethical—that confront business executives.

Acknowledgments

This book of cases draws heavily upon two types of sources. First are the companies, other organizations, and people that furnished information for the cases. Second are the people who made possible the processes by which the cases were gathered and gave support and encouragement to the processes and to us. We wish here to acknowledge, with deep gratitude, those many contributions.

Each situation in this book is taken from the "real world." Though the names of many companies and people have been disguised, the fact of disguises has, in no way, we believe, lessened the reality of the case situations. We are grateful to the companies and individuals—disguised or not—who contributed time, information, and thought to the cases. We cannot thank each individually, but a modest measure of our gratitude may be conveyed by acknowledging that without those contributions, there would be no casebook.

Most of the cases in this book are Harvard Business School, INSEAD, and St. Thomas cases. We thank former HBS colleagues Norman Berg for "Environmental Pressures" and Bart van Dissel for "Martha McCaskey." But friends from other schools and organizations have added to the quality of the book and reduced our burden by giving us permission to use cases prepared by them. We are grateful to the following for permissions: Professors Linda Ginzel (of the University of Chicago) for "Playskool Travel-Lite Crib," and John

Hennessey (formerly of Dartmouth College) for "Viking Air Compressor, Inc." We thank the National Council on Foundations for "Dayton Hudson Corporation: Conscience and Control."

To acknowledge new contributors, we wish to thank Professors Olivier Cadot, H. Landis Gabel, Daniel Traça (as well as their Assistant Sara McDonald) of INSEAD in Fontainebleau, France for the Monsanto case; Professors Olivier Cadot and Daniel Traça (as well as their Research Associate Robert Crawford) for the case "Soccer Balls Made for Children by Children"; INSEAD Visiting Professor Marc Le Menestrel (and Senior Research Fellow Mark Hunter) for "Business e-Ethics: Yahoo! on Trial"; Professor Marc Le Menestrel (and Research Fellow Dr. Sybille van den Hove) for "The Oil Industry and Climate Change."

We are grateful to Professor Thomas Holloran of the University of St. Thomas (and his Research Assistant Beth Goodpaster) for "Northwest Airlines," "The Bush Foundation," and "Exxon *Valdez*: Corporate Recklessness on Trial." Further thanks go to Professor Norman Bowie of the University of Minnesota, John Swanson, and Research Assistant Charles Sellers for their contributions to "Dow Corning Corporation: The Breast Implant Controversy." Professors Mary S. Daugherty, Mark Spriggs and William Estrem of the University of St. Thomas were coauthors of the "FBS," "Joe Camel's Mom," and "Minnesota Bank" cases, respectively.

In terms of case preparation we would indeed be remiss were we not to acknowledge our debt to Charlotte Butler, Randel S. Carlock, Dekkers Davidson, Anne Delehunt, Liana Downey, Robert G. Kennedy, Aaron Macke, T. Dean Maines, Richard Post, Linda Swenson, and Hassan Valji who wrote or contributed to the writing of several of the cases.

Many others at the Harvard Business School, INSEAD, and the University of St. Thomas have helped to make this book possible. Directors of the division of research made time and funds available for case-writing purposes. Special mention should be made of Professor Thomas Piper, who continues the Harvard Business School's commitment to education in corporate responsibility and business ethics. Mention should also be made of former Deans of the College of Business at the University of St. Thomas, Michael Evers and Theodore Fredrickson, as well as the current Dean, Christopher Puto, who have supported the second, third, and fourth editions of this book.

Manuscripts require typing, editing, retyping, proofreading and a variety of things both substantive and procedural. Many people at the University of St. Thomas have helped in these regards. For this fourth edition, Liz Nelson and Michelle Rovang deserve mention for initial work, while Nancy Bruggeman deserves very special mention as Administrative Assistant seeing the project through myriad final preparations. Thanks, too, to Marie Klein and Terri Hastings for their patient and generous help in proofing the manuscript. T. Dean Maines has been a Research Associate *extraordinaire* and occasional coauthor. His contributions to this volume and to the Instructor's Manual are considerable. We are also grateful to Andy Winston, Amy Luck, Kelly Lowery, Kirsten Guidero, and Bruce Gin at McGraw-Hill for their editorial support.

We dedicated the first and second editions of this book to our spouses. We owed them much then and we owe them much now. We particularly wish to thank Margaret Matthews for her generous support of the third and fourth editions—which we have dedicated to the memory of her husband, John B. Matthews.

Kenneth E. Goodpaster

Laura L. Nash

Henri-Claude de Bettignies

Introduction: *Teaching and Learning Ethics by the Case Method*

Preface: A Philosopher's Odyssey

When I joined the Harvard Business School faculty in 1980, a wayward philosopher seeking to connect ethical theory with management education, I confronted an enormous intellectual and cultural gap. I discovered that philosophers were trained to think differently from professional managers. They usually *zigged* when managers *zagged*. They *ascended* the ladder of reflection toward premises and assumptions when managers *descended* the ladder toward pragmatics and action; they often insisted on *examining* a goal or purpose while managers often cared more about *implementing* it.

The effect was, at first, exasperating. Both the substance and the style of my training ran counter to the distinctive practical orientation of business administration. Nevertheless, I was convinced that philosophy—specifically *moral* philosophy, or *ethics*—had as much to offer as to gain from a "joint venture" with management education.

On the *gain* side, there was the practice-oriented pedagogy of the case method. Moral philosophy in the 20th century had been preoccupied with conceptual analysis. Questions about the meanings of terms like "right" and "good" had dominated the philosophical landscape to the exclusion of questions about what *actions* are right and what *things* are good. Conceptual analysis had run amok in many ways, and a return to "applied" ethics (that would-be redundancy) was needed.

What philosophy had to *offer* was an inheritance and a talent. The inheritance was a body of thought about the nature of ethics and the human condition that had developed over more than two millennia. The talent was an eye and an ear for distinguishing cogent reasoning from its counterfeits. At a time when the ethical aspects of professional management were coming under increasing scrutiny, this seemed like a valuable resource.

Learning aimed at integrating ethics and management education called for a different pedagogy. Professor Donald Schön of MIT once suggested (in a working paper shared with me in 1984) an image that may have special meaning in this context:

> In the varied topography of professional practice, there is a high, hard ground which overlooks a swamp. On the high ground, manageable problems lend themselves to solution through the use of research-based theory and technique. In the swampy lowlands, problems are messy and confusing and incapable of technical solution. The irony of this situation is that the problems of the high ground tend to be relatively unimportant to individuals or to society at large, however great their technical interest may be, while in the swamp lie the problems of greatest human concern. The practitioner is confronted with a choice. Shall he remain on the high ground where he can solve relatively unimportant problems according to his standards of rigor, or shall he descend to the swamp of important problems and non-rigorous inquiry?

I found myself departing the high ground and entering the swamp. In the process, I came to believe that if the field of business ethics were to have a future, a new kind of discipline would have to be formed that did not yet exist. A generation of educators was needed that could think and teach using the skills of management

Reprinted with permission from "Teaching and Learning Ethics by the Case Method," by Kenneth E. Goodpaster, *The Blackwell Guide to Business Ethics*, Norman Bowie, ed. (Blackwell Publishers, 2002), pp. 117–141.

education *and* the reflectiveness of moral philosophy at the same time.

On the advice of several Harvard colleagues, therefore, I learned business policy by the case method. Never mind that I was on the instructor's side of the desk. I considered myself a learner. I had to relinquish my "expertise" to learn. It was like starting a second career after having become established in a first. But my students and faculty colleagues helped.

I learned the hard way and the only way: *from teaching and from practice.* At first, I could not appreciate the so-called administrative point of view—how competent managers think about problems; the way they identify issues, formulate and implement strategy, generate action plans. This appreciation was neither part of my experience nor part of my background in moral philosophy. I had to walk in the moccasins of the general manager. I had to puzzle over the strategic, organizational, and interpersonal challenges that general managers face. And I had to do it *case by case.*

I gained a new respect for the vocation of the manager, charting a course amidst the uncertainties of physical events and human nature: trying to motivate others, remaining loyal to providers of resources, setting goals, imposing new structures, monitoring progress and performance, achieving purpose through cooperation and the exercise of authority. I listened and I learned how different was the mind of the manager from the mind of the philosopher. Not better or worse. *Different.*

There were challenges on the other side of the desk too. My first classes in business ethics, using the case method, were no small challenge to my students. On some days, looks of glazed incomprehension were a relief from looks of irritation. What had Plato or John Stuart Mill to do with this marketing strategy and these accounting practices? What was the point of comparing and contrasting utilitarian and social contract theories of justice? But they learned, often in spite of their professor, that questioning *ends* was healthy and that questioning *means* to ends was healthy too; that moral reasoning was more than shooting from the hip; and that their fellow students were actually following certain tried and true patterns in the way they joined their realism with their idealism.

The "joint venture" eventually began to happen. It happened as I acknowledged that the frameworks and concepts that are the stock-in-trade of philosophy often blush in the face of the complexity and concreteness of management decisions. What was needed was an ethical *point of view,* not an ethical *algorithm.* I had believed this many years ago, but had forgotten it. I began to change, to think differently. Outer dialogues became inner dialogues. A case method teacher had joined the philosopher in me, and slowly the case method had become my philosophy of moral education.

Part I. Can Ethics Be Taught?

Some questions have staying power, and this question from Plato's dialogue, the *Meno,* is certainly one of them: "Can you tell me, Socrates, whether virtue is acquired by teaching or by practice; or if neither by teaching nor practice, then whether it comes to man by nature or in what other way?" It is a question that invites us to probe not one but two profound ideas in tandem: teaching and virtue. In this essay, I will follow Plato's classical lead, as I explore the meaning of the case method (a learner-centered form of teaching) in the context of business ethics (an organizational and commercial opportunity for virtue).

Teaching is perhaps less mysterious when it is not practical, just as *virtue* is less mysterious when the challenge does not include passing it on. We understand reasonably well how to communicate information and intellectual skills in an educational environment (information about history or skills like computer programming or factoring in algebra). And we understand reasonably well that ethics is about cultivating the moral point of view (and habits of the heart such as prudence, courage, benevolence, and fairness). But when we move education into the ethical arena, or ethics into the educational arena, our understanding seems to weaken.

I propose to discuss not just the case method in isolation—others have done this with distinction.[1] Nor do I propose to discuss the field of business

[1] See Laurence E. Lynn, Jr., *Teaching & Learning with Cases* (Chatham House Publishers, Seven Bridges Press, LLC, New York and London, 1999). Also see C. Roland Christensen, "Teaching with Cases at the Harvard Business School," in *Teaching by the Case Method* (Cambridge, MA: Harvard

ethics in general, something I have done on several previous occasions.[2] Instead, my focus will be on *the case method as a form of pedagogy particularly suited to the subject matter of business ethics.* If the answer to the question of Socrates is that ethics *cannot* be taught, it will not be for lack of trying the most promising (Socratic) pedagogy available: the case method.

In this section, I shall sketch some key features of the case method in action. In Parts II and III, the focus will be on the power of the case method as a pedagogy for ethics.

What Is the Case Method—in Aspiration and in Action?

The term "case study" is used differently in different contexts. It can mean an anecdote or a clipping from the *Wall Street Journal* used by a professor to illustrate an idea discussed in the classroom (a "case in point"). It can mean a report on a topic or an event describing the empirical results of a study of that topic or event (a "study"). It can mean a summary description of the issue, arguments, and verdict of a judicial proceeding (Harvard Law School "cases"). Or it can mean a narrative designed and written to provide learners with an occasion for engaging one another in a dynamic classroom environment (Harvard Business School "case method"). This essay is about the pedagogy surrounding the last-mentioned meaning of "case" or "case study."

In the words of a classic essay on the case method by Charles I. Gragg:

> A case typically is a record of a business situation that *actually* has been faced by business executives, together with surrounding facts, opinions, and prejudices upon which executive decisions had to depend. These real and particularized cases are presented to students for considered analysis, open discussion, and final decision as to the type of action that should be taken. (Gragg, 1940)

The idea behind the case method in the *ethical* arena is to offer the learner a vicarious decision-making opportunity so that both moral and managerial judgment can be exercised, indeed actively *practiced*. For this reason, cases are sometimes presented in sequenced parts to simulate decisions in one part (e.g., the "A" case) that give rise to new decisions in subsequent parts (e.g., the "B" and "C" cases). To quote Gragg again:

> The outstanding virtue of the case system is that it is suited to inspiring activity, under realistic conditions, on the part of the students; it takes them out of the role of passive absorbers and makes them partners in the joint process of learning and furthering learning. (Gragg, 1940)

Given this understanding of the "virtue of the case system," the role of the instructor in the process is crucial. For the instructor guides the special "partnership" in the classroom using various techniques, among them structured questioning, instructor feedback, role playing, breakout team activities, and written case analysis assignments. More recently, Internet technology has enhanced case method teaching and learning through threaded discussions in "virtual" classrooms.

Structured Questioning

The Socratic character of the case method is nowhere more evident than in the structured questioning that the instructor brings to the material for the day. Questions must be aimed at eliciting the learners' analysis of the important problems, the key decision maker, and a defense of the preferred course of action. Questions can be addressed to *specific* students in the class, especially at the opening of the discussion, which eventually widens out to *any* participant with a comment on the topic at hand. These "first tier" questions are followed up by questions that probe deeper or seek to clarify the student's meaning. Typically, questions will have either a diagnostic or a therapeutic backdrop. That is, the class will seek either to understand more fully the nature of the presenting problem or will explore a solution in the

---

Business School Publishing Division, 1987); Kenneth R. Andrews, "The Role of the Instructor in the Case Method," in Malcolm P. McNair, ed., *The Case Method at the Harvard Business School* (New York: McGraw-Hill, 1954); and the classic article by Charles I. Gragg, "Because Wisdom Can't Be Told," *Harvard Alumni Bulletin*, October 19, 1940.

[2] See Kenneth E. Goodpaster, "Business Ethics" and "Stakeholder Analysis" in the expanded second edition of the *Encyclopedia of Ethics* (Garland Publications, 2000) and "Business Ethics" in the *Oxford Companion to Christian Thought* (Oxford University Press, 2000). Also four articles entitled "Business Ethics," "Teleopathy," "Principle of Moral Projection," and "Stakeholder Paradox" in Blackwell's *Encyclopedia of Management* and *Dictionary of Business Ethics* (Oxford: Blackwell's, 1997).

form of a sequence of action steps. Sometimes the instructor will want to elicit more detail from students about the circumstances in the case—and this will call for "When?" "Where?" "What?" and "Who?" questions. At other times, the instructor will be looking more for explanations or justifications—escalating the conversation using "Why?" questions. A thoughtful outline of the various paths of questioning to be explored during the discussion period is important preparation for structured questioning.

Instructor Feedback

Instructor responses to the learner after a question has been posed and answered are critical variables in case method discussion. Feedback can have several purposes, among them clarification, assessment, reinforcement, and transition. Rephrasing a student's comment in order to clarify it—always inviting the student to accept or reject the rephrasing—can be an effective tool in guiding discussion. Sometimes it can exhibit *more starkly* the implications of the student's remarks, leading to more energetic engagement from the rest of the group. ("You said we should *discipline* Mr. West. Do you really mean *fire* him?") Feedback can also involve assessing a student's remark, applauding it for insight or pointing out that it is inconsistent with certain facts in the case. Using a chalkboard, flip chart, or overhead transparency to record visually the unfolding of the discussion provides another opportunity for feedback. Students notice whether and how their comments are recorded as affirmations of their relevance and significance. Feedback can also provide the instructor an opportunity to shift the focus of the discussion or to segue to another topic entirely. ("In the wake of that comment, I think we can now shift from our diagnosis of the problem to an action plan.")

Role Playing

Addressing structured questions and feedback to individuals or subgroups in the class by casting them into *roles* can be a very effective discussion tool. ("I'd like the left side of the room to take the shareholders' point of view on this management decision, and the right side of the room to play the role of the customers who are looking for more safety features in the product.") Role playing leads the students to take on points of view they might not have appreciated during their preparation of the case, and it models a kind of stakeholder awareness that instructors usually want to encourage, especially in ethics (see Part II below).

Breakout Team Activities

Often small-group breakout activities can energize case discussion and enhance learning, especially when the class is sizable (25–75). Students have more opportunity to speak in small groups, learn team-building and representation skills, and simulate real-life decision making. ("Let's break into five groups, each charged with the following two questions as the product liability jury was in the case study; then report back to the full class after 20 minutes.") The instructor will benefit greatly from silently listening in on the small-group discussions, often discerning student behaviors that are different from those in the full class.

Written Case Analysis Assignments

Individual student learning and feedback opportunities are best provided through written case analysis assignments. These need not be lengthy assignments (3 to 5 pages often suffice), but they provide a window for the instructor on student progress and a gateway for intervention if remedial study is needed.

Threaded Discussions in "Virtual" Classrooms

During the mid-1990s, online technology became more widely available which allows for asynchronous, threaded discussions among students (and between students and instructors) outside the physical and temporal confines of the classroom. This technology, while perhaps less personal than classroom communication, makes it possible for interactive discussion to continue "outside of class" (usually before the time of the next class). For large classes in which "air time" for student participation is relatively scarce, and especially for students who for various reasons are less verbally active in the regular classroom, the virtual classroom provides a convenient enhancement to case method learning.

The above-mentioned features of case method interaction between instructor and learner illustrate the *dynamics* of this pedagogy, beyond the written document (the "case") that provides the essential substrate for the process. A good case method instructor who researches and writes cases for classroom use will also prepare a second document—called a *teaching note*—not for the student audience but for other instructors considering the case for *their* classes. (Goodpaster and Nash, 1998)

The Teaching Note: Slowing Down Time

Teaching notes can take many forms, but typically they are pedagogical essays, several pages in length, which contain an abstract of the case or case series in question, learning objectives, specific teaching questions and subquestions with observations about the direction of discussion. Some teaching notes also include suggestions about classroom process, timing and case preparation, design layouts for chalkboards or flip charts that help organize the discussion, and summary bullet points for the instructor to use in winding up the case discussion.

The function of the teaching note is to provide a reflective guide for instructors who might wish to include the case (or cases) in question within their courses. There can, of course, be more than one teaching note for a given case, especially if the case has versatility in the curriculum. Teaching notes serve as formal reminders of the spirit of case method pedagogy as it empowers (with an "inside view") teachers who might be new to the specific facts of a given case narrative.

Teaching notes help put into practice one of the principal learning opportunities afforded by the case method: *slowing down time*. Comedian George Carlin, commenting on the paradoxes of our time in history, once remarked that "we have bigger houses and smaller families; more conveniences, but less time; we have more degrees, but less sense; more knowledge, but less judgment; more experts, but more problems; more medicine, but less wellness."

We can view the case method as a device for slowing time in a decision-making situation, so that learners are able to build habits of discernment otherwise hindered by the sheer velocity of business life. Like a football team viewing and discussing videotapes in slow motion after key games, management students prepare for their futures by practicing on realistic decision situations with minimal urgency.

Properly *processed* in the classroom, cases offer learners the opportunity to think through the details of a decision situation slowly, "try out" ideas on their peers, and debate the merits of decisions and action plans. This means that learners must expect and be responsible for the kind of *preparation* necessary for such a process. These learners are most often professionals, such as MBA students, but they can also be younger (high school, college) or older (life-long learners).

Limitations of Case Method Pedagogy

Case method pedagogy also has important *limitations*. The classroom and the case study are not replacements for reality and experience. No matter how true-to-life the situations are, they are not decided in a real-life setting. Student decision makers are subject to no risks from amateurish or unreasoned actions, nor can their conclusions be easily tested by subsequent developments in the business situation. As Gragg comments, "It is too much to expect that anything except experience can be exactly like experience" (Gragg, 1940).

Another limitation is that a case can never present all the facts in a situation. Facts in the narrative must of necessity be selected by the case writer, who generally has a particular expository purpose in mind. Some "facts" are personal reports of events from interviews with the parties involved, and this can introduce evaluation and possible bias. Some cases use press reports as a source of information, but the media sometimes have axes to grind in their accounts of corporate action (or inaction). Neutral and complete factual accounts are virtually impossible in case narratives, but then it is well to remember that real-life situations seldom present themselves in factually neutral and complete ways.

In summary, as we view the question "Can ethics be taught?"—mindful of the aspiration and practice of the case method—we see that certain prerequisites must be in place for success:

- Well-written and well-researched case narratives.
- Instructional techniques (including new forms of online technology) that encourage active learning by "slowing down time."
- Clear expectations about preparation to learners.

- Carefully written teaching notes for the preparation of instructors.
- A recognition of the inevitable limitations of the case method.

Let us now focus more directly on our principal quarry—the learning of *ethics* through case method pedagogy.

Part II. Business Ethics and the Case Method

In the context of business ethics, the case method aims at *moral insight*—the ability to discern right and wrong, good and bad, virtue and vice as they pertain to persons within organizations or organizations within the wider society. Harvard philosopher Josiah Royce defined the *moral insight* in his book *The Religious Aspect of Philosophy* (Royce, 1865):

> The moral insight is the realization of one's neighbor, in the full sense of the word realization; the resolution to treat him unselfishly. But this resolution expresses and belongs to the moment of insight. Passion may cloud the insight after no very long time. It is as impossible for us to avoid the illusion of selfishness in our daily lives, as to escape seeing through the illusion at the moment of insight. We see the reality of our neighbor, that is, we determine to treat him as we do ourselves. But then we go back to daily action, and we feel the heat of hereditary passions, and we straightway forget what we have seen. Our neighbor becomes obscured. He is once more a foreign power. He is unreal. We are again deluded and selfish. This conflict goes on and will go on as long as we live after the manner of men. Moments of insight, with their accompanying resolutions; long stretches of delusion and selfishness: That is our life.

The moral insight lies at the foundation of the Golden Rule, the oldest and most widely shared ethical precept known to us. The moral insight is about reciprocity between self-love and love of "one's neighbor" (or more generally, "stakeholders"). Understanding and appreciating the moral insight as the *aim* of case teaching, then, is essential for linking this *insight* with the *method.*

Also essential is understanding the *attitude* with which the case method instructor pursues the moral insight of the learner. Let us take up this attitudinal point first. Then we shall look at a case method tool for approaching the moral insight.

Teaching Ethics with an Attitude: Making or Doing?

Some years ago, I wrote an article for the *Hastings Center Report* (Goodpaster, 1982) in which I argued that the teaching of ethics was not an attempt to *produce* something, to intervene in the lives of learners for the sake of *results* which can be measured at the end of the process. Instead, I said (and still believe) that "the teacher seeks to foster a certain kind of growth, but more as a leader of active inquiry than as a therapist or physician." I concluded that:

> The subtle contract between teacher and student, especially in the context of adult ethics education, carries in most instances a provision that might read something like this, if it were ever written down: "The teacher is here to work *with* you, not *on* you." One wonders whether the psychological model of moral development, freighted with the discourse of the laboratory and human subjects, would not undermine the very effort it seeks to foster, a kind of moral version of Heisenberg's Uncertainty Principle. This is not to imply that impartiality and objectivity in student evaluation are impossible or undesirable. But the impartiality of the educator is distinguishable from the detachment of the experimenter—and the teacher's effectiveness can be lost by not paying heed to that distinction. (Goodpaster, 1982)

The convictions defended in this passage are born of years of personal experience teaching ethics by conventional methods at the University of Notre Dame, and then by the case method at both the Harvard Business School and the University of St. Thomas. The role of the educator in the context of the case method is implied in the Latin roots of the word *educate,* that is, to *lead out, to elicit*. The wisdom and ethical awareness being sought lie *in the learner*, and it is the mission of the instructor to lead it out. Wisdom "can't be told" in Gragg's memorable phrase, because it does not reside in the instructor to be *conveyed* by some mechanism (like *telling*) to the learner.

Case Method Pedagogy and Moral Epistemology

For many philosophers, some of whom are strangers to the case method in the context of ethics education, the foregoing observations are not free of controversy. An occupational hazard of philosophy teaching may be a posture that emphasizes content and rigor, minimizing the importance of a learner-centered process. For this reason, we philosophers are well advised to recall the eloquent reflection of William James in his 1891 essay entitled "The Moral Philosopher and the Moral Life."

> The philosopher is just like the rest of us non-philosophers, so far as we are just and sympathetic instinctively, and so far as we are open to the voice of complaint. His function is in fact indistinguishable from that of the best kind of statesman at the present day. His books upon ethics, therefore, so far as they truly touch the moral life, must more and more ally themselves with a literature which is confessedly tentative and suggestive rather than dogmatic,—I mean with novels and dramas of the deeper sort, with sermons, with books on statecraft and philanthropy and social and economic reform. Treated in this way, ethical treatises may be voluminous and luminous as well; but they never can be final, except in their abstractest and vaguest features; and they must more and more abandon the old-fashioned, clear-cut, and would-be "scientific" form.

An attentive observer in a successful case method ethics classroom, therefore, would see that "what's going on" is less often dogmatic presenting and more often questioning aimed at *forming habits that lead to moral insight*. Critical thinking in ethics is essential, of course, but our understanding of critical thinking must be compatible with the circumstantial realities of human decision makers. For all decisions seem in the end to be a matter of *balancing* by the parties involved. This is a philosophical point, not an accidental side constraint. Inevitably, it means an approach to moral knowledge that is *pluralistic*, that permits several basic methods or principles to be in tension or conflict with one another.

Some fear that the ultimate destination of such a pluralistic approach is some form of relativism or subjectivism. But this is certainly not evident and does not follow from the absence of a moral framework based on a single principle. We must not fall into the trap of identifying moral *pluralism* with moral *relativism*. Moral pluralism is the view that (singular) decision procedures or algorithms are not available to resolve moral arguments. Moral relativism is the view that moral argument is hopelessly fated to lead us in diverse directions, and consequently that a common vision, a moral community, is impossible. The two are not the same, conceptually or practically. One can, and probably should, embrace pluralism with discipline and reject its relativistic counterfeit.

As James implies, studying on a case-by-case basis the challenges of decision making under conditions of uncertainty and personal and institutional imperfection can raise difficult questions for philosophers. Try as they might to achieve positions variously described as archangelic, original, and ideal, decision makers whose problems set the agenda in applied ethics usually "can't get there from here." Neither can the rest of us. But there are some ways to be practical about the limitations of ethical theory.

The C.A.T. Scan

An approach to an ethics case that avoids both too much and too little analytical rigor involves doing what I call a "C.A.T. Scan." "C.A.T." is an acronym for <u>c</u>ase <u>a</u>nalysis <u>t</u>emplate, a matrix for the ethical analysis of cases that is described (and displayed) in Figure 1 on page 8. When learners are presented with an administrative situation calling for analysis and judgment, certain questions suggest themselves naturally as an initial inventory:

- Are there ethically significant *issues* in this case and do they call for a decision?
- Do I understand the *genesis* of the problems in the case—how they came to be?
- Can I *discern* amidst the sometimes complex issues in the case situation those that are the keys to the resolution of all the others? Is there a most *salient* moral challenge?
- What are several realistic *alternatives* or options from which the decision maker in the case must choose in responding to the most salient challenge? How does each option look through the principal normative lenses of ethical reasoning?
- What is my recommended *decision* and my suggested *action plan* for implementing it?
- Can I give myself and others a reasonable *justification* for the selection of this alternative or option from among those available? If each

FIGURE 1 Case Analysis Template ("C.A.T. Scan")

"C.A.T. Scan"
[Case Analysis Template]

Case Analysis Steps (5 Ds)	Interest-Based Outlook	Rights-Based Outlook	Duty-Based Outlook	Virtue-Based Outlook
Describe	How did the situation come about? What are the key presenting issues? Who are the key individuals and groups affected by the situation, the *stakeholders*?			
	Identify interests.	Identify rights.	Identify duties.	Identify virtues.
Discern	What is the most significant of the "presenting issues"—the one that might lie underneath it all? And who are the core stakeholders involved in the case?			
	Are there conflicting interests with respect to this issue, and how basic are they?	Are there rights in conflict with interests or with other rights? Are some weightier than others?	Does duty come into the picture—and are there tensions with rights or interests? Can I prioritize?	Is character an issue in this case—habits that bring us to this point or that will be reinforced later?
Display	What are the principal realistic *options* available to the decision maker(s) in this case, including possible branching among suboptions—leading to a set of action plans?			
Decide	What is my *considered judgment* on the best option to take from those listed above?			
Defend	Which of the avenues predominates in my choice of options above, and can I give *good reasons* for preferring the ethical priorities I have adopted in this case that are consistent with other such cases? What would an imaginary jury of the four "voices" decide and why? What is my moral framework?			

normative lens represents a moral "voice," are the voices in harmony or are they in discord?

- If harmony, does this fit with my moral common sense?
- If discord, which "voice" should prevail or override? Can I explain why?
- Am I prepared to see this *kind* of resolution in similar cases when the normative lenses appear to be in conflict?

In order to apply the above inventory of questions more directly and to make them easier to remember, we can organize them first into a five-step case analysis sequence (the *5 Ds*):

- *Describe*—the key factual elements of the situation.
- *Discern*—the most significant ethical issues at stake.
- *Display*—the main options available to the decision maker.
- *Decide*—among the options and offer a plan of action.
- *Defend*—your decision and your moral framework.

These "Ds" order the case analysis process from beginning to end, naming the *rows* of an analytical matrix or template. The *columns* of the matrix are based on what I have elsewhere called the four principal normative lenses (or "avenues") leading to the moral insight (Goodpaster, 1998).

A comprehensive review of the many ways in which philosophers, past and present, have identified the principal normative lenses of ethics is beyond the scope of this essay. It is possible, however, to sketch briefly the recurrent normative views that have been proposed.

Interest-Based Avenues

One of the most influential types of ethical reasoning, at least in the modern period, is *interest-based*. The fundamental idea here is that the moral assessment of actions and policies depends solely on their practical consequences, and that the only consequences that really matter are the interests of the parties affected (usually human beings). *On this view, ethics is all about harms and benefits to identifiable parties*. Moral common sense is governed by *a single dominant objective*, maximizing net expectable utility (happiness, satisfaction, well-being, pleasure). Critical thinking, on this type of view, amounts to testing our ethical instincts and rules of thumb against the yardstick of social costs and benefits. (Problems and questions regarding interest-based thinking are several: How does one *measure* utility or interest satisfaction? For *whom* does one measure it [self, group, humankind, beyond]? What about the *tyranny of the majority* in the calculation?)

Rights-Based Avenues

A second influential type of thinking is *rights-based*. The central idea here is that moral common sense is to be governed not (or not only) by interest satisfaction but by rights protection. And the relevant rights are of two broad kinds: rights to fair distribution of opportunities and wealth (contractarianism) and rights to basic freedoms or liberties (libertarianism). Fair distribution is often explained as a condition that obtains when all individuals are accorded equal respect and equal voice in social arrangements. Basic liberties are often explained in terms of individuals' opportunities for self-development, work rewards, and freedoms including religion and speech. (Problems and questions regarding this avenue include: Is there a trade-off between equality and liberty when it comes to rights? Does rights-based thinking lead to *tyrannies of minorities* that are as bad as tyrannies of majorities? Is this type of thinking excessively focused on individuals and their entitlements without sufficient attention to larger communities and the *responsibilities* of individuals to such larger wholes?)

Duty-Based Avenues

Duty-based thinking is perhaps the least unified and well-defined. The governing ethical idea is *duty* or *responsibility* not so much to other *individuals* as to *communities* of individuals. Critical thinking depends ultimately on individuals conforming to the legitimate norms of a healthy community. Ethics is about playing one's role as part of a larger whole, either a web of relationships (like the family) or a community (communitarianism). This line of thinking was implicit in John F. Kennedy's inaugural address: "Ask not what your country can do for you, ask what you can do for your country." In management, duty-based thinking appears in appeals to principles like fiduciary obligation. (Problems and questions regarding this type of thinking include the concern that individualism might get lost in a kind of collectivism [under a socialist or communitarian banner]. Also, how are our various duties to be prioritized when they come into conflict?)

Virtue-Based Avenues

In *virtue-based* thinking actions and policies are subjected to scrutiny not on the basis of their *consequences* (for individuals or for communities) but on the basis of their *genesis*—the degree to which they flow from or reinforce a virtue or positive trait of character. The traditional short list of basic (or "cardinal") virtues includes prudence, temperance, courage, and justice. "Love, and do what you will," Augustine is supposed to have said, indicating that the virtue of love was ethically more basic and more directly practical than attempts at determining "the right thing to do." (Problems or questions associated with the virtue-based thinking include: What are the central virtues and their relative priorities in a postmodern world that does not appear to agree on such matters? Are there timeless character traits that are not culture-bound, so that we can recommend them to anyone, particularly those in leadership roles?)

The resulting case analysis template for preparing and discussing ethics-related cases can then be constructed as displayed in Figure 1. (A *blank* version of the template used by students is included as Exhibit 1. It can be detached and copied for use in class preparation and for case analysis assignments.)

It is important to emphasize that the four "avenues" for ethical reasoning depicted in the template represent what philosophers often call *prima facie* moral guidelines. That is, each avenue gives a first approximation to an ethical conclusion, but no one avenue, *by itself*, is ethically definitive. If the application of three or all four avenues gives a positive or a negative assessment for a given option, learners may take this as *a strong case* for or against that option.

If and when avenues *conflict*, however, learners must think through the nature of the conflict—asking whether they are prepared to affirm the positives and override the negatives in comparable cases. Learners are not *encouraged* to conclude in such cases that *moral insight* is unattainable—or that the *moral point of view* is subjective, arbitrary, or self-contradictory. A legitimate conclusion, instead, is that *moral insight* in this case is more elusive and must continue to be sought through further reflection and dialogue.

In "Avenues for Ethical Reasoning in Management" (Goodpaster, 1998) the idea of the *moral point of view* was introduced as a perspective that "governs and disciplines what we take to be the central virtues . . . good and bad reasons, sound and unsound arguments, principles, intuitions." The *moral point of view* was further described as "a mental and emotional standpoint from which all persons have a special dignity or worth, from which the Golden Rule gets its force, from which words like 'ought,' 'duty,' and 'virtue' derive their meaning."

As the instructor works with cases, applying each of the four avenues of ethical reasoning, he or she must remember that the ultimate purpose of the analysis is *to seek the insight of the moral point of view* in the case situation. Each avenue represents an important *voice* in the conversation—so important that one should be uncomfortable when the voices are not unanimous.

An Imaginary Jury

Instructors might imagine this process within each learner as analogous to a *jury* of deliberative voices from which the learner seeks a verdict. The jury includes interest-based, rights-based, duty-based, and virtue-based voices. Each hopes that his or her jury will speak with unanimity and strong conviction.

The class as a whole is a kind of jury also, with the voices belonging to each of the learners. And as with a more conventional jury in the context of judicial proceedings, case method instructors are dealing with ordinary human beings, not gods. Consequently, they may expect different levels of dispassionate reflection, with appropriate diversity in their approaches to ethical conclusions.

Now most of us do not believe that a jury is immune from error and misjudgment—that what a jury says must, even if unanimous, be correct *just because the jury said so*. But many (if not most) of us *do* believe that the jury system is the best systematic alternative we have for reaching a fair and just outcome. As the judgments of juries are usually our best approximations to *justice* in matters of *law*—the voices represented in the four avenues are our best approximations to the *moral point of view* in matters of applied *ethics*.

Searching out the insight provided by the *moral point of view* is no small task, partly because the voices involved may not always agree, but also because decision makers can "fall back" into other tempting ways of thinking, using *surrogates* for ethical reflection rather than the real thing. Such surrogates include personal self-interest, preoccupation with market competition, existing law and regulation, or any one of the four avenues taken alone without input from the others. Thus the case method instructor must, as part of his or her teaching plan, include questions aimed at eliciting from each of the learners the perspectives of the imaginary jury, questions like:

- Whose interests are at stake for each of the decision maker's realistic options in this case?
- Are there legitimate rights that need attention associated with each option?
- What duties does the decision maker have and to whom?
- What virtues or character traits would be reinforced by alternative options available to the decision maker (including traits of individuals and policy precedents for the organization)?
- Which option available is *most responsive* to the four avenues we have identified?

Is there a "normative bias" in the use of this approach to teaching and learning ethics by the case method? To some extent, yes, although "bias" need not be the operative word. "Conviction" may be a better word. Value-neutral education is a myth and always has been, despite postmodern attempts to embrace it. Real education (whether by the case method or not) inevitably conveys ethical content, by omission or commission. Emory University president James T. Laney put it nicely some years ago:

> In many academic disciplines, there has been a retreat from the attempt to relate values and wisdom to what is being taught. Not long ago, Bernard Williams, the noted British philosopher, observed that philosophers have been trying all this century to get rid of the dreadful idea that philosophy ought to be edifying. Philosophers are not the only ones to appreciate the force of that statement. . . . How can society survive if education does not attend to those qualities which it requires for its very perpetuation? (Laney, 1985)

Good business ethics case studies are carefully researched true narratives of managerial challenges in value-laden situations. They represent the stuff of the moral life in business. Some present situations may seem impossible to resolve; but they can at least serve the purpose of showing how such dilemmas might be avoided through better management. Cases provide an essential empirical basis for normative and conceptual inquiry. They can be used as dynamic tools to test our generalizations and our moral frameworks, just as our generalizations and our moral frameworks can be used to test our judgment in individual cases. John Rawls refers to this as "reflective equilibrium."

In summary, the case method as it relates to business ethics calls for analytical tools that are philosophically rigorous but epistemologically realistic as well. The case method instructor in the ethics arena needs to understand the Socratic character of the interaction more practically than other instructors.

Let us now turn to the third part of our discussion, the place of the case method in the business school curriculum. Case method teaching and learning requires a curricular setting that is friendly to this pedagogy. There must be resources and incentives for linking cases into modules, modules into courses, and for putting curricular unity into course sequences. This does not mean that a business school curriculum needs to be fully dedicated only to case method teaching—even in ethics. But it does mean that support for teaching ethics by case method is essential if students (and faculty) are not to get conflicting messages.

Part III. Ethics, Cases, and the Curriculum

Efforts were made at many academic institutions during the 1970s and 1980s by management and philosophy departments to "team teach" business ethics. Implicit in these efforts was a belief that the two sides of the house—management and ethics—needed somehow to be joined. Most of these efforts met with limited success, however, because the integration that was needed was simply *reassigned* to the students rather than *modeled* by the faculty. The marriage of management and moral philosophy would take more than this if it were not to end as so many marriages do today.

I am convinced that a deeper kind of integration is needed. The natural tendency in our society of professionals is to call in the experts when we experience some degree of dissonance over a problem. When the problem is how to relate ethics to business decision making, that tendency leads us to call in ethics specialists much as we would call in specialists in international relations when faced with a question about the U.S. balance of trade. But in business ethics, it does not work that way. The field of ethics does not lend itself to an "external application," despite the best efforts of philosophers to rise to the occasion. A better way is for teachers of business administration to learn some moral philosophy and for moral philosophers to learn some business administration. In this way, the educator can avoid the problem described in an old Latin aphorism: *Nemo dat quod non habet* ("Nobody gives what he/she doesn't have").

Curricular support for joining management education and ethics education manifests itself institutionally in two broad arenas: (a) integration *within* the curriculum and (b) emphasis from what we might call the *"extracurriculum."*

Ethics within the Curriculum: A Strategy

A curricular strategy that involves teaching ethics by the case method must start with a commitment by administration and faculty to the importance of the task. Without such a commitment, any strategy is doomed to failure. At the University of St. Thomas, administrators and faculty sought (and succeeded) in 1990 to formulate a mission-like document, which we called a "Preamble," that articulated the institution's commitment to the importance of ethics in the curriculum:

> Business education is commonly aimed at the knowledge needed to perform effectively and efficiently in the business world. We at the University of St. Thomas are committed to that objective and more: encouraging serious consideration and application of ethical values in business decision making.
>
> Since business ethics can mean different things to different people, we want to specify the assumptions that guide our efforts. Responsibility for one's actions and respect for the dignity of others are fundamental, both for the content of our approach to ethics and for the process by which we teach it. In this approach, dogmatism is as inappropriate as relativism.
>
> Our emphasis, therefore, is on the importance of dialogue for developing mature moral

> judgment both personally and in group decision making. In our view, this maturity includes the exercise of certain virtues in the workplace, such as honesty, fairness, empathy, promise keeping, prudence, courage, and concern for the common good. It also includes interaction between the cognitive and emotional dimensions of conscience (i.e., both "head" and "heart") and the need for congruence between judgment and action. We believe such moral development is a life-long process.
>
> Our goal in the Graduate School of Business and in the Division of Business is to encourage this development in the context of sound policies and practices. We affirm the legitimacy and centrality of moral values in economic decision-making because without them, business relationships and strong communities are impossible.

This statement has served the institution well for over a decade now, providing the "north" on our curricular compass when occasionally we lost our way in either the graduate or the undergraduate schools of business. In the spirit of this "Preamble," there is a *curricular strategy* for the integration of business ethics into these two schools—a strategy that avoids the false dilemma of "Should we have a special course or should ethics be in every course?" This strategy consists of four principal steps in a cycle, each called for by the step preceding and each leading to the step following. The steps are:

- *Initiation*, an introductory module or "half-course" to foster a common language among students in addressing ethical aspects of business.
- *Inclusion* of ethics cases and readings in the main functional courses in the curriculum, for example, marketing, finance, accounting, management, business law and entrepreneurship.
- *Consolidation* of functional applications of ethics in the business capstone.
- *Feedback* from alumni of the program to improve methods and teaching materials for the next generation of students, returning us to the initiatory stage.

We *initiate* through a deliberately incomplete, required module at both graduate and undergraduate levels. *Inclusion* is sought through course design workshops with departments, including Marketing, Finance, Accounting, Management, Business Law, and Entrepreneurship. The goal of working with each of the departments is to develop specific cases and readings in the core offerings of each department, linking to the required initiation module and reinforcing students' understanding of the relevance of ethical thinking to their chosen area of specialization in business. One of the notable advantages of including ethics in the curriculum using the case method is that it can enable the teacher to add ethical themes into an already content-packed course, permitting the analysis of conventional business problems that also have significant ethical dimensions. We might call this "curricular multitasking."

Consolidation is implemented by working with the capstone course faculty. The hope is to offer the students who are completing the business curriculum in the capstone course a significant exposure to ways of blending strategic and ethical considerations in strategic decision making.

Feedback includes (a) holding alumni workshops and (b) tapping graduates (after they have had substantial business experience) for contributions to ethics-related case development. This represents a generous investment on their part in future St. Thomas students, and it completes the circle, bringing us back to initiation again as we constantly revitalize the opening module.

The initiatory module offers a set of cases and readings aimed at joining ethical reflection to business decision making. Several criteria guide the selection and organization of these materials: *topical relevance* to the modern manager, *curricular relevance* to the required core courses that will follow, and *conceptual relevance* to applied ethics.

Topically, the idea is to examine current and significant management challenges such as product safety, honesty in marketing, environmental protection, and international business in diverse cultures. From the perspective of *curricular* relevance, the course materials display breadth and richness of a different kind. The principal subject areas in the curriculum should be represented: management (human resources, operations, strategy), marketing, finance, accounting, entrepreneurship, and business law. The third criterion—*conceptual* relevance in applied ethics—draws attention to several levels at which ethical concepts can be applied to business activity: the level of the individual (managerial decisions and virtues), the level of the organization (policy formulation and implementation), and the level of the society as a whole (democratic capitalism nationally and globally). Other conceptual questions in the background include: What is the moral point of view? What avenues are available for making responsible decisions? Do ethical principles and values transcend cultural boundaries?

The search for *excellence* in such a course calls for a team effort by the faculty. The *flow* of the course, after some introductory material, goes from "Ethics and the Individual," to "Ethics and the Organization," to "Ethics and Capitalism as a System." In each of these parts of the course—and thus at each of these three levels of analysis—instructors and learners examine cases and readings with attention not only to "stakeholder" thinking but also virtue-based (or culture-based) thinking. Course objectives are:

- To enhance learner awareness of the importance of ethical values for individual and organizational effectiveness.
- To stimulate a positive attitude in learners toward incorporating virtue-based and stakeholder analysis throughout business decision making.
- To provide a process for thinking through the economic and noneconomic implications of strategies and implementation plans in realistic business situations.

Ethical awareness and sound moral judgment are not, of course, substitutes for basic business skills in the functional areas (marketing, finance, accounting, etc.). But it is becoming increasingly clear that the exercise of basic managerial skills in an atmosphere of uncritical moral and social premises leads not only to expanding external regulation and adversarialism but to a widespread and reasonable lack of trust in institutional forms of all kinds: economic, political, academic, and even religious.

Students need to engage in case method dialogue, allowing their preparation, energy, and willingness to learn from peers to produce genuine moral insight. They can then take what they have learned and carry it into each of the courses that make up their business curriculum. Ultimately, students must be *challenged* to go beyond specific issues and courses to develop a responsible business philosophy of their own.

The Extracurriculum

Beyond the regular curriculum itself, wrapped around it in concentric circles as it were, there can be many "extracurricular" activities that support a *culture of relevance* for ethics and the case method. In addition to core courses, there are elective courses, guest speakers, colloquia, alumni seminars, and various Internet-based enhancements to learning.

Elective Courses

Making all ethics-related courses in the curriculum *required* courses is probably unwise, never mind that it would be politically impossible in most colleges and universities. The menu of elective courses in a business curriculum that relate in various ways to business ethics (e.g., a seminar on *spirituality and management* or a *great books* seminar for graduate students and alumni or a *case research* practicum) carries an important message to teachers and learners alike about the importance the institution assigns to the ethics agenda.

Guest Speakers

Regular guest speakers addressing ethics-related themes are also a powerful signal of an institution's commitment, especially if the audience is "town and gown," that is, not only faculty and students but also businesspersons in the college or university community.

Colloquia

Another type of extracurricular integration of ethics—and case method learning—is the systematic dialogue of colloquia. Colloquia can involve student participants and/or faculty participants and/or executives. Individual and panel presentations can include prepared papers or case studies.

Alumni Seminars

While alumni are natural participants in both guest speaker events and colloquia, events held especially for alumni provide an opportunity for both alumni and their *alma mater* to share important information. Lifelong learning for alumni is increasingly valuable to them, of course, but less noticed is an *institution's* need for lifelong learning by sharing the experiences of its alumni, often in the form of case studies. Without the latter information, an institution risks lack of currency and eventually irrelevance in its professional education programs.

Internet-Assisted Learning

Virtual classrooms were mentioned earlier in this essay as new techniques for case method learning. Other e-learning opportunities that relate to an institution's "extracurriculum" include Internet-based *case studies* and distance learning case method *courses* in ethics (among other subjects). Internet-based case studies, often available on CD-ROMs, provide more than conventional case text. They also provide audio-visual examples of case facts and hyperlinks to relevant case information on various Internet sites. Distance learning case method courses in ethics are a very recent development, but they will be a growing pedagogical form. Geographical dispersion and asynchronous delivery can be seen as limitations on the case method—but they can also provide new opportunities. A case discussion in ethics is never richer, for example, than when the participants come from different cultural backgrounds, as the Internet makes possible. In a new distance course that this writer has recently developed, the "C.A.T. Scan" (discussed above) has been automated as a learning tool for participants and as a way for instructors to regularly monitor participants' understanding of ethics case material.

In summary, the case method is most effective in the ethics arena if it is supported and used widely in an institution. This reinforces the expectations of learners and permits quality control on cases and classroom process. But the responsibility for ethics in the business school curriculum must be borne by the entire business faculty, not outsourced or handled by one or two specialists or "gurus." The risk of both outsourcing (e.g., from a philosophy department) and special gurus is the risk of *compartmentalization*. Compartmentalization means that ethical issues that arise in other parts of the business curriculum are "referred to the experts," sending the wrong message to students as future ethical decision makers.

FIGURE 2 Teaching and Learning Ethics by the Case Method

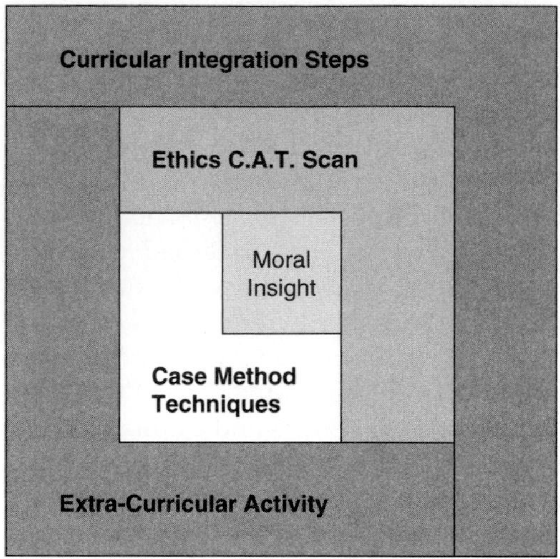

Summary and Conclusions

I have portrayed teaching and learning ethics by the case method as an activity which, when undertaken with certain epistemological, analytical, and curricular convictions, provides a powerful approach to professional education. Joining learner-centered techniques with philosophical analysis (the "C.A.T. Scan"), the case method offers as clear an answer as possible to the question that spurred our inquiry at the outset: "Can you tell me, Socrates, whether virtue is acquired by teaching or by practice; or if neither by teaching nor practice, then whether it comes to man by nature or in what other way?" The answer seems to be this: "Virtue is acquired by teaching *and* by practice, assuming an honest desire by all parties to seek moral insight."

Works Cited

Gragg, Charles I. "Because Wisdom Can't Be Told," *Harvard Alumni Bulletin*, October 19, 1940.

Goodpaster, Kenneth E. "Is Teaching Ethics Making or Doing?" *Hastings Center Report*, vol. 12, no. 1, February 1982. © 1982 by the *Institute of Society, Ethics and the Life Sciences*. This article appeared in tandem with *"A Psychologist Looks at the Teaching of Ethics"* by James R. Rest.

Goodpaster, Kenneth E. "An Agenda for Applied Ethics," in *Social Responsibility: Business, Journalism,*

Law, Medicine, volume XI, Lexington, VA: Washington and Lee University, 1985.

Goodpaster, K., and Nash, L. *Policies and Persons* (3d edition, McGraw-Hill, 1998).

Goodpaster, Kenneth E. "Avenues for Ethical Analysis in Management," in Goodpaster and Nash, *Policies and Persons* (3d edition, McGraw-Hill, 1998).

Laney, James T. "The Education of the Heart," *Harvard Magazine,* September–October 1985, pp. 23–24.

Royce, Josiah. *The Religious Aspect of Philosophy.* First published in 1865. Reprinted 1965 by Harper & Row, Publishers, p. 155.

Selected Bibliography

Books

Christensen, C. Roland, with Abby J. Hansen. *Teaching and the Case Method.* Boston: Harvard Business School Press, 1987.

Lynn, Jr., Laurence E. *Teaching and Learning with Cases: A Guidebook.* London: Chatham House Publishers, 1999.

Lundeberg, Mary A., ed. *Who Learns What from Cases and How? The Research Base for Teaching and Learning with Cases* (2000).

Articles

Campbell, Elizabeth, "Connecting the Ethics of Teaching and Moral Education." *Journal of Teacher Education,* vol. 48, no. 4, pp. 255–63 (Sept.–Oct. 1997).

Brisin, Tom, "Active Learning in Applied Ethics Instruction." *Journal on Excellence in College Teaching,* vol. 6, no. 3, pp. 161–67 (1995).

Stevens, Betsy, "Teaching Communication with Ethics-Based Cases." *Business Communication Quarterly,* vol. 59, no. 3, pp. 5–15 (Sept. 1996).

Websites

www.virginia.edu/~trc/casemeth.htm Useful articles on case method teaching and sample cases from the *Teaching Resource Center* at the University of Virginia.

www.agecon.uga.edu/~wacra/wacra.htm *World Association for Case Method Research & Application.* Comprehensive site for case method educators, based in Needham, Massachusetts.

www.stanford.edu/class/ee353/case.htm Nice statement from a *Stanford University* course on the nature of the case method.

www.abo.fi/instut/hied/case.htm Very good online source of links to case method sites and current events related to the case method from *Higher Education Development International.*

EXHIBIT 1 Case Analysis Template

Type your answers to each question after "Type answer here" or "Start list here" in each table cell.

C.A.T. Scan: Case Analysis Template				
Aspects of the Moral Point of View (Avenues = ethical basis)	**Interests**	**Rights**	**Duties**	**Virtues**
Case Analysis Steps (5 D's sequence)				
Describe Identify the facts.	How did the situation come about? Type answer here.			
	What are the key presenting issues? Type answer here.			
	Who are the key individuals and groups affected by the situation (i.e., the stakeholders)? Type answer here.			
	Who is the key decision maker? Type answer here.			
	Identify interests. Are there interests in-volved? If yes, identify further. Make a list. Start list here.	Identify rights. Are there rights involved? If yes, whose are they? Make a list. Start list here.	Identify duties. Are there duties involved? If yes, identify further. Make a list. Start list here.	Identify virtues. Are there precedents? If yes, what are they? Make a list. Start list here.
Discern Identify the ethical issues. Select the issue to debate.	What are the three most significant of the "presenting issues"—the ones that might lie under-neath it all? Describe which issue is the most important. Type answer here.			
	Are there conflicting interests with respect to this issue, and how basic are they? Can you rate them in order of importance? Type answer here.	Are there rights in conflict with interests or with other rights? Are some weightier that others? Type answer here.	Does duty come into the picture—and are there tensions with rights or interests? Can I prioritize these claims? Type answer here.	Is character an issue in this case—are there habits that bring us to this point or that will be reinforced later? Type answer here.
Display Based on facts and ethical issues, identify options you can consider.	What are the principal realistic options available to the decision maker(s) in this case, including possible branching among suboptions—leading to an array of action sequences or plans? Type answer here.			
Decide Based on all the options, choose one and create a plan of action to implement it.	What, finally, is my considered judgement on the best option to take from those listed above? The Moral Point of View is here joined to the Administrative or Managerial Point of View. Type answer here.			
Defend Justify your choice from the perspective of each avenue.	Which of the avenues predominates in my choice of options above, and can I give good reasons for preferring the ethical priorities I have adopted in this case that are consistent with other such cases? Type answer here.			

Part 1

Personal Values

Individuals bring personal values to their jobs and to the real or perceived problems of moral choice that confront them. Moral choices must be made because of tensions within individuals, between individuals, or between individuals and what they believe to be the values that drive their organizations. The series of case situations in Part 1 involve such moral decisions for people at different levels in organizations and at different stages of their careers. Those who study and discuss these cases have an opportunity to think about how the people involved in the case situations might or should solve the problems that they encounter—and also, we hope, to think introspectively and perhaps share with other discussants the ethical standards that they intend to bring to their professional work.

"Answers" to these case problems will not often come easily, nor will they be susceptible of proof as problems are in, say, geometry. But decisions must be made, for decisions are an inescapable part of life in a business career.

"Peter Green's First Day" is a short case. On his first day on the job, Peter Green is told to do something that the company's training program has not prepared him for, something that his moral standards would clearly define as wrong. The decision seems an easy one, but is it? And after Green makes his decision—whatever it may be—what should he do next?

The second case, "Dilemma of an Accountant," is more difficult; issues of right and wrong appear cloudier from the start. Daniel Potter thinks he knows what is right but seems less certain than Peter Green did. A number of issues confront him and his superiors. Matters of judgment are involved, both for Potter and for his more experienced superiors. What is at stake for Daniel as he responds to his situation, and what trade-offs may be involved? Does one "go along" in order to "get along"?

Going along and getting along are also on the mind of Martha McCaskey in the third case. Not only is Martha faced with a personal choice about how she will behave in the gray area between industrial espionage and competitor analysis, but she must also consider the implications of her actions for the value system in her company.

In a case classic—"Viking Air Compressor, Inc."—George Ames has been given a mission having to do with Viking's corporate responsibility activities. As he works at it, he discovers that the mission and the contribution expected from him are less than clear. As the case ends, Ames finds himself being chastised by the president of the company, John Larsen. At issue are seeming value differences between him and Larsen, questions as to what the phrase "corporate responsibility" means, and the personal question of how he should react to Larsen's tirade.

Part 1 closes with "Joe Camel's Mom: RJR and Youth Marketing." A midwestern MBA graduate in marketing progresses in her career at RJR and eventually becomes the originator of the successful "Joe Camel" cigarette advertising campaign. The case traces her personal decision making as well as her 1999 trial testimony in which she has to defend the campaign against the charge that it markets cigarettes to children and underage youth.

The Viking case and the Joe Camel case are useful in and of themselves as examples of personal decision making, but they also serve as links to organizational decision making in Parts 2 and 3.

Peter Green's First Day

Peter Green came home to his wife and new baby a dejected man. What a contrast to the morning, when he had left the apartment full of enthusiasm to tackle his first customer in his new job at Scott Carpets. And what a customer! Peabody Rug was the largest carpet retailer in the area and accounted for 15% of the entire volume of Peter's territory. When Peabody introduced a Scott product, other retailers were quick to follow with orders. So when Bob Franklin, the owner of Peabody Rug, had called District Manager John Murphy expressing interest in "Carpet Supreme," Scott's newest commercial-duty home carpet, Peter knew that a $15,000–$20,000 order was a real probability, and no small show for his first sale. And it was important to do well at the start, for John Murphy had made no bones about his scorn for the new breed of salespeople at Scott Carpet.

Murphy was of the old school: in the business since his graduation from a local high school, he had fought his way through the stiffest retail competition in the nation to be District Manager of the area at age fifty-eight. Murphy knew his textiles, and he knew his competitors' textiles. He knew his customers, and he knew how well his competitors knew his customers. Formerly, when Scott Carpet had needed to fill sales positions, it had generally raided the competition for experienced personnel, put them on a straight commission, and thereby managed to increase sales and maintain its good reputation for service at the same time. When Murphy had been promoted eight years ago to the position of District Manager, he had passed on his sales territory to Harvey Katchorian, a sixty-year-old mill rep and son of an immigrant who had also spent his life in the carpet trade. Harvey had had no trouble keeping up his sales and had retired from the company the previous spring after forty-five years of successful service in the industry. Peter, in turn, was to take over Harvey's accounts, and Peter knew that John Murphy was not sure that his original legacy to Harvey was being passed on to the best salesperson.

Peter was one of the new force of salespeople from Scott's Sales Management Program. In 1976 top management had created a training program to compensate for the industry's dearth of younger salespeople with long-term management potential. Peter, a college graduate, had entered Scott's five-month training program immediately after college and was the first graduate of the program to be assigned to John Murphy's district. Murphy had made it known to top management from the start that he did not think the training program could compensate for on-the-job experience, and he was clearly withholding optimism about Peter's prospects as a salesperson despite Peter's fine performance during the training program.

Peter had been surprised, therefore, when Murphy volunteered to accompany him on his first week of sales "to ease your transition into the territory." As they entered the office at Peabody Rug, Murphy had even seemed friendly and said reassuringly, "I think you'll get along with Bob. He's a great guy—knows the business and has been a good friend of mine for years."

Everything went smoothly. Bob liked the new line and appeared ready to place a large order with Peter the following week, but he indicated that he would require some "help on the freight costs" before committing himself definitely. Peter was puzzled and unfamiliar with the procedure, but Murphy quickly stepped in and assured Bob that Peter would be able to work something out.

After the meeting, on their way back to Scott Carpets' district office, Peter asked Murphy about freight costs. Murphy sarcastically explained the procedure: Because of its large volume, Peabody regularly "asked for a little help to cover shipping costs," and got it from all or most suppliers. Bob Franklin was simply issued a credit for defective merchandise. By claiming he had received second-quality goods, Bob was entitled to a

10%–25% discount. The discount on defective merchandise had been calculated by the company to equal roughly the cost of shipping the 500-lb. rolls back to the mill, and so it just about covered Bob's own freight costs. The practice had been going on so long that Bob demanded "freight assistance" as a matter of course before placing a large order. Obviously, the merchandise was not defective, but by making an official claim, the sales representative could set in gear the defective-merchandise compensation system. Murphy reiterated, as if to a two-year-old, the importance of a Peabody account to any sales rep, and shrugged off the freight assistance as part of doing business with such an influential firm.

Peter stared at Murphy. "Basically, what you're asking me to do, Mr. Murphy, is to lie to the front office."

Murphy angrily replied, "Look, do you want to make it here or not? If you do, you ought to know you need Peabody's business. I don't know what kind of fancy thinking they taught you at college, but where I come from you don't call your boss a liar."

From the time he was a child, Peter Green had been taught not to lie or steal. He believed these principles were absolute and that one should support one's beliefs at whatever personal cost. But during college the only even remote test of his principles was his strict adherence to the honor system in taking exams.

As he reviewed the conversation with Murphy, it seemed to Peter that there was no way to avoid losing the Peabody account, which would look bad on his own record as well as Murphy's—not to mention the loss in commissions for them both. He felt badly about getting into a tiff with Murphy on his first day out in the territory, and knew Murphy would feel betrayed if one of his salespeople purposely lost a major account.

The only out he could see, aside from quitting, was to play down the whole episode. Murphy had not actually *ordered* Peter to submit a claim for damaged goods (was he covering himself legally?), so Peter could technically ignore the conversation and simply not authorize a discount. He knew very well, however, that such a course was only superficially passive, and that in Murphy's opinion he would have lost the account on purpose. As Peter sipped halfheartedly at a martini, he thought bitterly to himself, "Boy, they sure didn't prepare me for this in Management Training. And I don't even know if this kind of thing goes on in the rest of Murphy's district, let alone in Scott's eleven other districts."

Dilemma of an Accountant

In 1976 Senator Lee Metcalf (D-Mont.) released a report on the public accounting industry which rocked the profession. Despite a decade of revisions in rules and regulations (variously established by the Securities and Exchange Commission, Accounting Principles Board, and Financial Accounting Standards Board), public accounting firms were still perceived by many on Capitol Hill as biased in favor of their clients, incapable of or unwilling to police themselves, and at times participants in coverups of client affairs. Senator Metcalf even went so far as to suggest nationalizing the industry in light of these activities.

Just prior to the Metcalf report, Daniel Potter began working as a staff accountant for Baker Greenleaf, one of the Big Eight accounting firms. In preparation for his CPA examination, Dan had rigorously studied the code of ethics of the American Institute of Certified Public Accountants (AICPA), and had thoroughly familiarized himself with his profession's guidelines for morality. He was aware of ethical situations which might pose practical problems, such as maintaining independence from the client or bearing the responsibility for reporting a client's unlawful or unreasonably misleading activities, and he knew the channels through which a CPA was expected to resolve unethical business policies. Dan had taken the guidelines very seriously: they were not only an integral part of the auditing exam, they also expressed to him the fundamental dignity and calling of the profession—namely, to help sustain the system of checks and balances on which capitalism has been based. Daniel Potter firmly believed that every independent auditor was obligated to maintain professional integrity, if what he believed to be the best economic system in the world was to survive.

Thus, when Senator Metcalf's report was released, Dan was very interested in discussing it with numerous partners in the firm. They responded thoughtfully to the study and were concerned with the possible ramifications of Senator Metcalf's assessment. Dan's discussions at this time and his subsequent experiences during his first year and a half at Baker Greenleaf confirmed his initial impressions that the firm deserved its reputation for excellence in the field.

Dan's own career had been positive. After graduating in Economics from an Ivy League school, he had been accepted into Acorn Business School's accountant training program, and was sponsored by Baker Greenleaf. His enthusiasm and abilities had been clear from the start, and he was rapidly promoted through the ranks and enlisted to help recruit undergraduates to work for the firm. In describing his own professional ethos, Dan endorsed the Protestant work ethic on which he had been raised, and combined this belief with a strong faith in his own worth and responsibility. A strong adherent to the assumptions behind the profession's standards and prepared to defend them as a part of his own self-interest, he backed up his reasoning with an unquestioning belief in loyalty to one's employer and to the clients who helped support his employer. He liked the clear-cut hierarchy of authority and promotion schedule on which Baker Greenleaf was organized, and once had likened his loyalty to his superior to the absolute loyalty which St. Paul advised the slave to have towards his earthly master "out of fear of God" (Colossians 3:22). Thus, when he encountered the first situation where both his boss and his client seemed to be departing from the rules of the profession, Dan's moral dilemma was deep-seated and difficult to solve.

The new assignment began as a welcome challenge. A long-standing and important account which Baker had always shared with another Big Eight accounting firm needed a special audit, and Baker had reason to expect that a satisfactory performance might secure it the account exclusively. Baker put its best people on the job, and Dan was elated to be included on the special assignment team; success could lead to an important one-year promotion.

Oliver Freeman, the project senior, assigned Dan to audit a wholly-owned real estate subsidiary (Sub) which had given Baker a lot of headaches in the past. "I want you to solve the problems we're having with this Sub, and come out with a clean opinion (i.e., confirmation that the client's statements are presented fairly) in one month. I leave it to you to do what you think is necessary."

For the first time Dan was allotted a subordinate, Gene Doherty, to help him. Gene had worked with the project senior several times before on the same client's account, and he was not wholly enthusiastic about Oliver's supervision. "Oliver is completely inflexible about running things his own way—most of the staff accountants hate him. He contributes a 7:00 A.M. to 9:00 P.M. day every day, and expects everyone else to do the same. You've *really* got to put out, on his terms, to get an excellent evaluation from him." Oliver was indeed a strict authoritarian. Several times over the next month Dan and Oliver had petty disagreements over interpretive issues, but when Dan began to realize just how stubborn Oliver was, he regularly deferred to his superior's opinion.

Three days before the audit was due, Dan completed his files and submitted them to Oliver for review. He had uncovered quite a few problems but managed to solve all except one: one of the Sub's largest real estate properties was valued on the balance sheet at $2 million, and Dan's own estimate of its value was no more than $100,000. The property was a run-down structure in an undesirable neighborhood, and had been unoccupied for several years. Dan discussed his proposal to write down the property by $1,900,000 with the Sub's managers, but since they felt there was a good prospect of renting the property shortly, they refused to write down its value. Discussion with the client had broken off at this point, and Dan had to resolve the disagreement on his own. His courses of action were ambiguous, and depended on how he defined the income statement: according to AICPA regulations on materiality, any difference in opinion between the client and the public accountant which affected the income statement by more than 3% was considered material and had to be disclosed in the CPA's opinion. The $1,900,000 write-down would have a 7% impact on the Sub's net income, but less than 1% on the client's consolidated net income. Dan eventually decided that since the report on the Sub would be issued separately (although for the client's internal use only), the write-down did indeed represent a material difference in opinion.

The report which he submitted to Oliver Freeman contained a recommendation that it be filed with a subject-to-opinion proviso, which indicated that all the financial statements were reasonable subject to the $1.9 million adjustment disclosed in the accompanying opinion. After Freeman reviewed Dan's files, he fired back a list of "To Do's," which was the normal procedure at Baker Greenleaf. Included in the list was the following note:

1. Take out the pages in the files where you estimate the value of the real estate property at $100,000.
2. Express an opinion that the real estate properties are correctly evaluated by the Sub.
3. Remove your "subject-to-opinion" designation and substitute a "clean opinion."

Dan immediately wrote back on the list of "To Do's" that he would not alter his assessment since it clearly violated his own reading of accounting regulations. That afternoon Oliver and Dan met behind closed doors.

Oliver first pointed out his own views to Dan:

1. He (Oliver) wanted no problems on this audit. With six years of experience he knew better than Dan how to handle the situation.
2. Dan was responsible for a "clean opinion."
3. Any neglect of his duties would be viewed as an act of irresponsibility.
4. The problem was not material to the client (consolidated) and the Sub's opinion would only be used "in house."
5. No one read or cared about these financial statements anyway.

The exchange became more heated as Dan reasserted his own interpretation of the write-down, which was that it was a material difference to the Sub and a matter of importance from the standpoint of both professional integrity and legality. He posited a situation where Baker issued a clean opinion which the client subsequently used to show prospective buyers of the property in question. Shortly thereafter the buyer might discover the real value of the property and sue for damages. Baker, Oliver, and Dan would be liable. Both men agreed that such a scenario was highly improbable, but Dan continued to question the ethics of issuing a clean opinion. He fully understood the importance of this particular audit and expressed his loyalty to Baker Greenleaf and to Oliver, but nevertheless believed that, in asking him to issue knowingly a false evaluation, Freeman was transgressing the bounds of conventional loyalty. Ultimately a false audit might not benefit Baker Greenleaf or Dan.

Freeman told Dan he was making a mountain out of a molehill and was jeopardizing the client's account and hence Baker Greenleaf's welfare. Freeman also reminded Dan that his own welfare patently depended on the personal evaluation which he would receive on this project. Dan hotly replied that he would not be threatened, and as he left the room, he asked, "What would Senator Metcalf think?"

A few days later Dan learned that Freeman had pulled Dan's analysis from the files and substituted a clean opinion. He also issued a negative evaluation of Daniel Potter's performance on this audit. Dan knew that he had the right to report the incident to his partner counselor or to the personnel department, but was not terribly satisfied with either approach. He would have preferred to take the issue to an independent review board within the company, but Baker Greenleaf had no such board. However, the negative evaluation would stand, Oliver's arrogance with his junior staff would remain unquestioned, and the files would remain with Dan's name on them unless he raised the incident with someone.

He was not at all sure what he should do. He knew that Oliver's six years with Baker Greenleaf counted for a lot, and he felt a tremendous obligation to trust his superior's judgment and perspective. He also was aware that Oliver was inclined to stick to his own opinions. As Dan weighed the alternative, the vision of Senator Metcalf calling for nationalization continued to haunt him.

Martha McCaskey

Martha McCaskey felt both elated and uneasy after her late Friday meeting with Tom Malone and Bud Hackert, two of the top managers in Seleris Associates' Industry Analysis Division (IAD). Malone, the division's de facto chief operating officer (COO), had assured her that upon successful completion of the Silicon 6 study, for which McCaskey was project leader, she would be promoted to group manager. The promotion would mean both a substantial increase in pay and a reprieve from the tedious field work typical of Seleris's consulting projects. However, completing the Silicon 6 project would not be easy. It would mean a second session with Phil Devon, the one person who could provide her with the vital information required by Seleris's client. Now, McCaskey reflected, finishing the project would likely mean following the course of action proposed by Hackert and seconded by Malone: to pay Devon off.

Seleris's client, a semiconductor manufacturer based in California, was trying to identify the cost structure and manufacturing technologies of a new chip produced by one of its competitors. McCaskey and the others felt certain that Devon, a semiconductor industry consultant who had worked in the competitor's West Coast operation some 12 years earlier, could provide the detailed information on manufacturing costs and processes required by their client (see Exhibit 1 for a summary of the necessary information). Her first interview with Devon had caused McCaskey to have serious doubts about both the propriety of asking for such information and Devon's motivation in so eagerly offering to help her.

Malone suggested that she prepare an action plan over the weekend. Ty Richardson, head of IAD, would be in town on Monday to meet with Malone and the two group managers, Hackert and Bill Davies. McCaskey could present her plan for completing the Silicon 6 project at that meeting. Malone made it clear that the group would be primed to hear her ideas.

Silicon 6 was turning out to be a crucial project. The client currently accounted for close to 20% of the division's revenues. In a meeting earlier that day, the marketing manager representing the client had offered to double the fee for the Silicon 6 project. He had also promised that if they could come through on Silicon 6, equally lucrative projects would follow.

By Saturday afternoon, McCaskey had worked up several approaches for finishing the Silicon 6 project. With the additional funds now available from the client, she could simply have Devon provide analyses of several alternatives for manufacturing state-of-the-art chips, including the one used at the competitor's Silicon 6 plant. While the extra analyses would be expensive and time-consuming, Devon most likely would not suspect what she was after. Another option was to hand the project over to Chuck Kaufmann, another senior associate. Kaufmann handled many of the division's projects that required getting information that a competitor, if asked, would consider proprietary.

McCaskey felt, however, that no matter which option she chose, completing the Silicon 6 project would compromise her values. "Where do you draw the line on proprietary information?" she wondered. Was she about to engage in what one of her friends at another consulting firm referred to as "gentleman's industrial espionage"? McCaskey reflected on how well things had gone since she joined IAD. She had been an exemplary performer and, until the Silicon 6 project, she felt that she had always been able to maintain a high degree of integrity in her work.

This case is a revised version of "Martha McCaskey," HBS Case No. 488-021 (Boston: Harvard Business School Publishing, 1988), prepared by Professor Bart J. Van Dissel. Professor Joshua Margolis and Research Associate Ayesha Kanji updated this case as the basis for class discussion. The circumstances described in this case are reported entirely from Martha McCaskey's point of view and do not necessarily reflect the perceptions of others involved. All names, places, and companies have been disguised. Cases are not intended to serve as endorsements, sources of primary data, or illustrations of effective or ineffective management.

Now, McCaskey wondered, would the next step to success require playing the game the way everyone else did?

Seleris Associates

Seleris was a medium-sized consulting firm based in Chicago, with offices in New York, Los Angeles, and San Francisco. Founded in 1962 by three professors who taught accounting in Chicago-area universities, the firm had grown to nearly 500 employees by 1996. Throughout its history, Seleris had enjoyed a reputation of high technical and professional standards and had maintained its informal, think-tank atmosphere. Seleris had expanded its practice into four divisions: Management Control and Systems (which had been the original practice of the firm), Financial Services, General Management, and Industry Analysis.

Industry Analysis was the youngest and smallest of Seleris's four divisions. It had been created in 1987 in response to increasing demand for industry and competitive analysis by clients of the firm's Financial Services and General Management divisions. Unlike the other three divisions, IAD was a separate, autonomous unit operating exclusively out of San Francisco. The other divisions were headquartered in Chicago, with branch operations in New York and Los Angeles. IAD had been located in San Francisco for two reasons: (1) much of Seleris's demand for competitive analysis came from clients based in California, and particularly in Silicon Valley; and (2) Ty Richardson, the person hired to start the division, was well connected in Northern California and had made staying in San Francisco part of his terms for accepting the job. Richardson reported directly to Seleris's executive committee. Richardson had also insisted on hiring all his own people. Unlike the rest of Seleris's divisions, which were staffed primarily by people who were developed internally, IAD was staffed entirely with outsiders.

The Industry Analysis Division

IAD consisted of 15 professionals, 12 analysts (called associates), and 6 support staff. In addition to Richardson, (who was a senior vice president) the division had one vice president (who served as Richardson's chief of operations) and two group managers. The remaining 11 professionals formed two groups of senior associates who reported to the two group managers. (See Exhibit 2 for a complete chart showing the names and positions of members of both groups.)

The two groups of senior associates were distinctly different. The senior associates who reported to Hackert were referred to as the "old guard." Several years earlier, they had all worked for Richardson when he had run his own consulting firm in Los Angeles. The senior associates reporting to Davies all had MBAs from top-tier schools and, not surprisingly, this "new guard" had significantly higher starting salaries. Another difference between the two groups was that while members of the new guard tended to spend their time equally between individual and team projects, the old guard worked strictly on individual projects.

Senior associates and group managers received their project assignments from Malone, Richardson's chief of operations. For the most part, however, roles and reporting relationships among the professional staff were loosely defined. Senior associates often discussed the status of their projects directly with Malone or Richardson rather than with the group managers. Both group managers and senior associates served as project leaders. On team projects, it was not unusual for the group manager to be part of a team on which a senior associate was project leader. The assignment of associates to projects, determined by a process of informal bargaining among associates and project leaders, served to further blur the distinction between senior associates and group managers.

Executive Leadership

Malone and the two group managers also had previously worked with Richardson. Hackert and Richardson met when Richardson, who had a Ph.D. in business administration, left academia to join the Los Angeles branch of a well-known consulting firm. Richardson left shortly thereafter to start his own firm in Los Angeles, consulting to high-tech industries. Malone had managed Richardson's Los Angeles operation.

Clients and employees alike described Richardson as an exceptional salesman. Very sharp in all his dealings, he had a folksy way with people that was both disarming and charismatic.

Richardson was also a highly driven person who rarely slept more than four hours a night. He had taken major risks with personal finances, making and losing several fortunes by the time he was 35. By the time he turned 40, the demands of being an entrepreneur and running his own consulting business had wrecked havoc with Richardson's personal life. At his wife's insistence, Richardson switched careers and moved to San Francisco, where his wife started her own business and he accepted a high-level job with a major international consulting firm. But within the year, Richardson had grown restless. When Seleris agreed to let Richardson run his own show in San Francisco, he left the consulting firm, taking Davies and several of the new guard with him.

Martha McCaskey

Martha McCaskey, 29 years old and single, had been with Seleris for 18 months. She joined the firm in 1995, shortly after completing her MBA at Harvard. Prior to business school, McCaskey had worked at a major consumer electronics firm for three years after graduating from CalTech with a degree in electrical engineering. In the summer between her two MBA years, McCaskey worked as a consultant to a fledgling biomedical firm in Massachusetts that specialized in self-administered diagnostic tests. While there, she developed product strategy and implementation plans for a supplement to one of the product lines and assisted in preparation of the firm's second equity offering. McCaskey thoroughly enjoyed the project orientation of the summer work experience and her role as consultant. The biomedical firm indicated a strong interest in hiring her upon completion of the MBA. McCaskey, however, had decided to pursue a career in consulting. In addition, she had grown up in the Bay area and wanted to return there if possible.

Seleris was one of several consulting firms with which McCaskey interviewed. Her first interview at the San Francisco branch was with Malone, the division's vice president. Malone told her that IAD was a wonderful place to work, especially emphasizing the collegial, think tank environment. He said that they were experiencing tremendous growth. He also said they were just beginning to get involved in some very exciting projects. The interview ended before McCaskey could push him on specifics, but she wasn't sure that such questions would have been appropriate. Malone had impressed her as very dynamic and engaging. Instead of interrogating her, as she expected, he had made her feel like she could be a major contributor to the team, McCaskey commented later, and that felt good.

The rest of her interviews were similar. Although she grilled the other people she met, they all told her what a terrific place IAD was. In one of the interviews, McCaskey was also surprised to see Jeff McCollum, an acquaintance who was a former classmate at CalTech.

Upon returning to Boston, McCaskey had a message from Richardson, who had called to say he would be in town the following night and was wondering if she could meet him. Over dinner at one of Boston's most expensive restaurants, Richardson told her he was quite impressed with what he had heard about her. They were looking for people like her to help the business grow and to handle their exciting new projects. He also said that, for the right candidates, IAD offered rapid advancement—more so than she would likely find at the other firms with which she was interviewing.

The next day Richardson called McCaskey with a generous offer. Later that afternoon she received a call from McCollum, who once again told her what a great place Seleris was, citing, as an example of the firm's culture, how Richardson often would take everybody out for drinks Friday afternoon when he was around.

After weighing the Seleris offer, McCaskey called Richardson early the next week to accept.

Working in the Industry Analysis Division

McCaskey's First Assignment

McCaskey's first day at work started with a visit from Malone. He explained that the division was experiencing a bit of a crunch just then, and they needed her help on a competitive analysis study. In fact, she would have to do the project by herself. It was unusual to give a new person his or her own project, Malone continued, but he had arranged for Davies, her group manager, to provide backup support if she needed it. McCaskey reflected on her first project:

> It was relatively easy and I was lucky; it was a good industry to interview in. Some industries are tough to interview in because they tend to be very closemouthed. Some industries are easier. The consumer electronics industry, for example, is pretty easy. Other industries, like the electronic chemicals area, can be really tough. People making chips are very secretive.

Although it was her first assignment, McCaskey gave the client presentation and wrote a formal report detailing her analysis and recommendations. A few days later, Richardson dropped in on a working lunch among Davies's group to compliment McCaskey on her handling of the project. He went so far as to say that both he and Malone felt that her analysis was the best they had yet seen by anyone in the division.

McCaskey's Second Assignment

Two weeks later, McCaskey was assigned to a major project involving a competitive analysis for a company that made printed circuit boards. As with her first assignment, she was to work alone on the study, consulting Davies if and when she needed help. It was during this period that Malone began suggesting that she talk with two members of the old guard, Dan Rendall and Chuck Kaufmann, about sources of information. The project involved gathering some fairly detailed information about a number of competitors, including one Japanese and two European firms. The old guard handled many of the projects that involved gathering sensitive information on target firms (i.e., the client's competitors). This was always information that was not publicly available—information that a target firm would consider proprietary. It appeared to McCaskey that Rendall and Kaufmann were the real producers in this group, often taking on projects when other members of the old guard had difficulty obtaining sensitive information.

Rendall was the recognized leader of the old guard. He could often be seen coming and going from Richardson's office on the infrequent occasions that Richardson was in town. Recently, Richardson had been spending about 80% of his time on the road. When McCaskey approached Rendall, however, she felt him to be difficult and uncooperative. Subsequent attempts to talk with Rendall proved equally unproductive. Kaufmann was out of town on assignment for two weeks and thus unable to meet with McCaskey.

Given her difficulty in following through on Malone's recommendation to work with the old guard, McCaskey developed her own approach to the printed circuit board project. The project turned out to be extremely difficult. Over a period of six months, McCaskey conducted nearly 300 telephone interviews; attended trade shows in the United States, Japan, and Europe; and personally interviewed consultants, distributors, and industry representatives in all three places. Toward the end, McCaskey remembered working seven days a week, 10 to 15 hours a day. Her European contacts finally came through with all the necessary information just three days before the client presentation. Despite the results that her efforts produced, McCaskey felt that Richardson and Malone disapproved of how she handled the project—that it could have been completed with less time and effort:

> The presentation went really well. Toward the end, I began to relax and feel really good. I was presenting to a bunch of guys who had been in the business for 30 years. There were a few minor follow up questions but mostly a lot of compliments. I was really looking forward to taking a break. I had been with the company at this point for nine months and had never taken a day of vacation, and I was exhausted. And then, Richardson got up and promised the client a written report in two weeks.
>
> Davies was very good about it. We got in the car to go back to the airport, and he asked me wasn't I planning to take a vacation in the near future? But it went right by Richardson. Davies didn't press it, of course. Even though he had an MBA from Stanford, he was a really laid-back California type. That sometimes made for problems when you needed direction on projects or firm policy.
>
> The next day, I was a basket case. I should have called in sick, I really should have. I managed to dictate about one page. Richardson came by at the end of the day and said, "Well, what's the delay?" I was so livid I finished the report in 10 days.

The rate at which McCaskey wrote the report was held up as an example by Malone as a new standard for IAD projects.

McCaskey's handling of the written report on her next project led to an even tighter standard for the division's projects. Seeking to avoid a similar bind on the project, McCaskey planned to write the report before the client presentation. Malone had told her she would not have any other responsibilities while on the project because the deadline was so tight. Two weeks later, however, Richardson asked her to join a major project involving the rest of Davies's group. McCaskey explained:

> He kind of shuffled into my office and said something like: "You know, Martha, we really admire you. I'd really like to have you on this team. We're a little behind schedule and we could really use your expertise. I've also asked Chuck Kaufmann to join the team and I'd like the two of you to work on a particularly challenging piece of the project."

Despite the dual assignment, McCaskey managed to complete the report on her original project before the client presentation. That also became a standard within the division.

The Environment at IAD

In mid-1996, several senior associates left the firm. Bill Whiting and Cory Williamson took jobs with competing firms. Doug Forrest was planning to take a job with one of Seleris's clients. McCollum left complaining that he was burnt out and planned to take several months off to travel before looking for work. Over the previous six months there also had been high turnover among the associates. It had become a running joke that Tuesday's edition of *The Wall Street Journal*, which carried the job advertisements, should be included in the set of industry journals that were circulated around the office.

While some of the turnover could be attributed to the increasing workload and performance expectations, a number of people had also been upset over the previous year's bonuses. Richardson and Malone had met with each senior associate prior to Christmas and explained that the division was going through a growth phase and was not the cash generator everybody seemed to think it was. They were all given the same bonus and told how valuable they were to the firm, regardless of the length of time they had been with the firm or what they had accomplished. But, as McCaskey recalled, what really got to people was when Richardson and Malone showed up at the New Year's office party, each in a brand new Mercedes.

Kaufmann had gone to see Malone about the personnel situation. He warned Malone that unless something was done to improve the situation, more people would leave. Malone responded that he could put an ad in the paper and get 10 new people any time he wanted. Kaufmann was shocked. McCaskey, however, was not surprised. In the lighter moments of working on team projects, conversation among members of the new guard had naturally drifted to views on Richardson and Malone and on what made them so successful:

> Malone was married with two kids and usually drove a Ferrari instead of the Mercedes. He looked the part of a consultant. He was very aggressive. You could hear this man all over the building when he was on the phone. We decided he was just really driven by money. That's all there was . . . he'd go whip someone and tell them to get work out by the end of the month so we could bill for it—and have no qualms about doing it because he's counting his bucks. He was also a very smart man. If you spent a couple of hours with him in the car or on a plane explaining a business to him, he'd have it. The man had amazing retention.
>
> Both he and Richardson were great salesmen. Malone could be an incredible talker. At times, though, you wondered how much credibility you could put in these people. They kept saying they wanted you to be part of the management team. But then they'd turn around and wouldn't even tell us where or when they would go on a client call, so you really couldn't make a contribution.

Kaufmann's shock at Malone's response to the personnel question was also typical. McCaskey had worked with Kaufmann on a number of team projects and found him to be different from most of the old guard. He was working on his MBA in the evening program at Berkeley and really seemed to enjoy being with the new guard. McCaskey knew that Kaufmann also had a reputation for working on what were referred to as the "sleaze" projects in the office: projects that involved questionable practices in contacting and interviewing people who could provide very detailed information about target companies. Even so, McCaskey felt that he did this work mainly out of a sense of loyalty to Richardson and Malone.

> Kaufmann was always torn between doing the job and feeling, "These guys need me to help them run their business, because I'm going to be a group manager someday and they really need me." He was torn between that and trying to be objective about his situation, saying, "They're paying me less than anybody else but look what these guys are asking me to do." He wanted to do good in the eyes of people he looked up to, whether it's Richardson and Malone, or peers like Dan or myself, because he has that personal attachment and can't step back and say, "They're taking advantage of me." He just could not make that distinction.

Kaufmann had been fun to work with, though. McCaskey had observed that many of their team projects had required increasingly detailed information about a client's competitors. These projects had given rise to discussions among McCaskey and her colleagues about what constituted proprietary information and what, if anything, they should do if they found they had to obtain such information. While there was some discussion about the appropriateness of such projects, McCaskey recalled a particular conversation that characterized how the issue was typically handled:

> We were on a quick coffee break and Linda Shepherd said she really needed to get psyched up for her next call. Linda was a member of the new guard whom I liked and respected. She had an MBA from Berkeley and had been at IAD approximately a year longer than I had. We became good friends soon after I arrived and ended up working together a lot on team projects.
>
> I said, "I know what you mean. I tried to get some discounting information from a marketing manager this morning and all he would give me was list price. As usual, I started out with general questions but as soon as I tried to get specific he was all over me. Like pulling teeth. Invariably, they slap it back at you. What information do you have? You know, and you don't want to give away the plot because then he'd know what you're doing."
>
> Kaufmann's advice was pretty funny. He said that he was working on a project that was so slimy he had to take a shower every time he got off the phone, and maybe that's what we ought to do, too.

As was the norm on most of the division's projects, McCaskey usually identified herself as a representative of a newly formed trade journal for the particular industry in which she was interviewing. To McCaskey, that was not nearly as dishonest as visiting a target company on the pretense of interviewing for a job, as a friend of hers who worked for another consulting firm had done.

All in all, McCaskey felt that she had been given the freedom to do her work with integrity. It was also clear that her performance was recognized by Richardson. Of the senior associates, Richardson spent the most time with Rendall, McCaskey, and Kaufmann. While Rendall often could be seen in Richardson's office, Richardson seemed to make a point of dropping in on Kaufmann and McCaskey.

At the end of 1996, McCaskey received a substantial increase in pay. She also received a $25,000 bonus. Most of the other senior associates had received much smaller bonuses—in many cases equivalent to what they had received the previous year.

The Silicon 6 Project

In January 1997, both Richardson and Malone met with McCaskey to talk about a new assignment. The project was for one of Seleris's oldest clients in the high-tech electronics field. Since its inception, IAD had done a lot of work for this client. The project involved a new type of computer chip being produced by one of the client's prime competitors—a company that had also once been one of Seleris's major clients. The project had originally been assigned to Lee Rogoff, a senior associate who reported to Hackert. The client was interested in obtaining detailed information about manufacturing processes and costs for the new computer chip. Although Rogoff had made numerous calls to the target company's clients and distributors, he had been largely unsuccessful in obtaining any of the required information.

Normally, Rendall would have been asked to take over the project if it had previously been handled by a member of the old guard. Instead, Malone explained, he and Richardson had decided to approach McCaskey because of her background in electrical engineering. (McCaskey had in fact done some coursework on chip design at CalTech.) Malone also told her they had been impressed with her creativity and success in obtaining difficult, detailed information on previous projects. Malone added that there was one constraint on the project: the client had insisted that Seleris not contact the target company to avoid potential allegations of price fixing.

The project was code-named Silicon 6 after the plant at which the chip was produced—the sixth building of an industrial cluster in Silicon Valley. McCaskey began by contacting the Silicon 6 plant's equipment manufacturers. They were unusually closemouthed. She was unable to get them even to say what equipment the plant had ordered, never mind its operating characteristics. McCaskey also contacted raw materials suppliers to semiconductor manufacturers. Again, she faced an impasse. She held meetings nearly every day with Malone (standard operating procedure for problem projects). For McCaskey, the meetings soon became monotonous, following the same pattern: "How's it going? Well, OK. Let's retrench. Did you try this tack? Did you try that tack? Did you try this customer base? Did you try this group of calls?"

Malone was especially interested in whether she was having any luck identifying ex-employees. For several of the projects on which McCaskey had worked, particularly those requiring detailed data, the best source of information had been ex-employees of target companies. McCaskey had generally found these people quite willing to talk, sometimes out of vengeance, but also at times because there was a sympathetic, willing listener available. People love to talk about their "expertise," she often thought.

Industry consultants had been another good source of detailed information. It was not unusual for IAD to hire consultants for $4,000 or $5,000 a day on specific projects. McCaskey felt that some of the senior associates had been rather creative in their use of this practice. Several months earlier, Kaufmann had confided to her that he had hired an ex-employee of a target company as a "consultant" to provide him with a list of software contracts for that target company. He said that this was something that Rendall had done regularly on his projects. In one case, Rendall had paid an ex-employee of a target company a "consulting" fee of $5,000 for a business plan and spreadsheets of a target company's upcoming new product introduction. Hackert was there when Kaufmann had asked Rendall if such information was proprietary. Hackert had a reputation as a tough, no-nonsense manager who prided himself on running a tight shop and on his ability to get the job done, no matter what it took. Hackert said that if someone was willing to talk about it, then it wasn't proprietary.

McCaskey had mentioned this incident to Shepherd. They both agreed that Rendall's behavior, and Hackert's response, only confirmed what they had suspected all along about the old guard: they routinely paid ex-employees of target companies to obtain highly sensitive information for Seleris's clients. Shepherd ended the conversation with a comment that, given such behavior, the old guard wouldn't last long when the division really took off and headquarters became more interested in the San Francisco operation.

Many consulting firms had formal, written policies regarding the solicitation and performance of contracts. For example, some consulting firms required that their employees identify themselves as working for the firm before beginning an interview. IAD did not have any such written, formal policies. Richardson occasionally had given lunchtime talks concerning the division's policies, but, as McCaskey recalled, these tended to be quite vague and general. For example, for McCaskey, the bottom line in Richardson's "ethics" talk was quite simply, we do not do anything unethical. Besides, McCaskey knew from her friends at highly reputable firms that people occasionally broke the rules even when formal, written policies existed. After her discussion with Shepherd, McCaskey considered raising the old guard's use of ex-employees with Richardson but he was out of the office for a couple of weeks. By the time he returned, she was in the middle of several large projects and had all but forgotten about it.

McCaskey's only lead on the Silicon 6 project occurred through a seemingly random set of events. Working through a list of academics involved in semiconductor research, she found a professor at a small East Coast engineering school who actively consulted with several European manufacturers of semiconductors. When she called him, McCaskey found that he could not provide her with any of the information on the list. Malone had suggested, however, that she fly out and interview him because he might have some gossip on the new chip. The interview served to clarify McCaskey's understanding of the manufacturing processes involved but, as she had suspected, did not provide her with any new information. He did suggest, however, that she get in touch with Phil Devon, a consultant in southern California. He did not know Devon personally but knew that Devon recently had been involved in the design and start-up of a plant for one of the European firms.

Upon returning to San Francisco, McCaskey called Devon to set up an interview. During the call she learned that he had been a vice president at the target company some 12 years earlier. When she told Malone about Devon, he was ecstatic. He congratulated her on once again coming through for the division, letting her know that both he and Richardson felt she was the one person they could always count on.

McCaskey Meets with Devon

McCaskey met with Devon the following Friday. He was in his mid-40's, distinguished looking, and relaxed in his manner. McCaskey's first impression of Devon was that he was both professional and warm. Even before getting into the interview, she began to have qualms about asking for detailed information on the Silicon 6 plant. Feeling uneasy, McCaskey opened the interview by saying that she represented an international concern that was interested in building a semiconductor manufacturing plant in the United States. Devon responded by saying that he could not understand why anybody would want to build another plant, given the current global overcapacity for semiconductor production. He added, however, that he was willing to help her in whatever way he could.

McCaskey then suggested that they talk about the cost structure for a plant that would be employing state-of-the-art technology. Devon responded that he would need more information to work with if he was going to be of help to her. He explained that there were several new technologies available or under development, and it would make a difference which one they chose. It briefly crossed McCaskey's mind that this was an opportunity to talk about the Silicon 6 plant. Instead, she suggested that they might try to cover each of the options. Devon responded that it would involve an awful lot of work, and that it would be helpful if she could narrow things down. He then asked what kind of chips they intended to produce and whether there would be several products or just a single line. He added that if he knew whom she was representing, it would help him to determine what type of facility they might be interested in.

McCaskey felt increasingly uncomfortable as the interview progressed. She felt that Devon was earnestly trying to help her. He seemed to have an excellent technical background and knew what he was doing. It was clear that Devon took pride in doing what he did and in doing it well. By midmorning, McCaskey began to feel nauseated with herself and the prospect of asking Devon to give her proprietary information on the Silicon 6 plant. As she talked with him, she couldn't help thinking, "This is a guy who's trying to do good in the world. How can I be doing this? I have an EE degree from CalTech, an MBA from Harvard, and here I am trying to sleaze this guy."

At this point, McCaskey settled on a scheme to end the interview but keep open the option of a second interview with Devon. From the morning's discussion, she was convinced that he had access to the information she needed to complete the Silicon 6 project. Instead of probing for the information, she told Devon that her client had not supplied her with adequately detailed information to focus on a specific technology and plant cost structure. She added that his questions had helped her learn a lot about what she needed to find out from her client before she came back to him. She suggested, however, that if they could put together a representative plant cost structure, it would be useful in going back to her client. Once again, Devon said that he was willing to help her in whatever way he could. He said he had recently helped set up a state-of-the-art facility in Europe that might be similar to the type of plant her client was considering. At this point, McCaskey began to feel that perhaps Devon was being too helpful. She wondered if he might be leading her on to find out who she was working for.

As the morning progressed, Devon provided her with background on the European plant, including general information about its cost structure and other items on McCaskey's list. McCaskey was so uncomfortable about deceiving him about the purpose of her visit that she barely made it through lunch, even though she had contracted with him for the full day. After lunch, she paid Devon the full day's fee and thanked him. McCaskey said that she would get in touch with him after meeting with her client to see if they could focus on a particular plant design. Devon thanked her, said that he wished he could have been more helpful, and that he looked forward to seeing her again.

McCaskey Meets with Malone

A meeting on the Silicon 6 project was scheduled with the client for the following Friday. McCaskey worked over the weekend and through the early part of the next week putting together her slides and presentation.

As she worked, she continued to reflect on her meeting with Devon. He had seemed so professional. She was not really sure how he would have responded to specific questions about the Silicon 6 plant, but she felt sure he could have provided her with all the information they needed. On the other hand, although it sounded far-fetched, it seemed just possible that Devon was so straight he might have called the police had she asked him for the information. Or, given his prior employment at the target company, Devon might have called someone there about McCaskey's interest in the Silicon 6 plant.

On Wednesday, McCaskey met with Malone to update him on her meeting with Devon and with her presentation. She told Malone that she had been unable to get the information. To her surprise, Malone did not press her to try to get more information from Devon. Instead, he asked McCaskey to go through her presentation. When she came to a slide titled "Representative Plant Cost Structure," Malone stopped her, saying that the title should read "Plant Cost Structure." When McCaskey asked him what he meant, Malone told her to cross out the word "Representative." They would conduct the presentation as if this was data they had gathered on the actual Silicon 6 plant. When McCaskey objected, Malone pointed out that the analysis was general enough that no one would know the difference.

McCaskey Meets with the Client's Plant Managers

Going into the presentation Friday morning, McCaskey had only 30 slides. On other projects she typically had used in excess of 100 slides. To McCaskey's surprise, all of the client's senior plant managers were present for the presentation. She had been under the impression that the meeting was to be a dry run for a more formal presentation later on. The plant managers were courteous, but stopped her 15 minutes into the presentation to say that she was not telling them anything new. If this was all she had, they said, it would be pointless to meet with senior management on the Silicon 6 project, although such a meeting was scheduled for the following month. They then asked her to identify all the sources she had contacted. McCaskey did not mention Devon but the plant managers seemed satisfied with her efforts. Malone then explained that the lack of detailed information was due to the constraint of not being able to contact the target company.

The marketing manager in charge of the Silicon 6 project then asked his secretary to take McCaskey and Malone to his office, while he held a brief meeting with the plant managers. Upon joining McCaskey and Malone, the marketing manager expressed his disappointment with Seleris's handling of the Silicon 6 project. Specifically, he said that his firm had never had any trouble getting such information before. Further, he pointed out how much business they provided for IAD and that he hoped the relationship could continue. Given their progress on the Silicon 6 project, however, he had doubts. Malone then brought up the possibility of still being able to successfully complete the project. Without mentioning Devon's name, he said that they had just made contact with an ex-employee who could provide them with the necessary information if provided with the proper incentives.

McCaskey was struck by how the marketing manager immediately brightened and told them that he didn't care how they got the information, as long as they got it. He then doubled the original fee that IAD would be paid upon completion of the project, adding that the additional funds should provide their source with an adequate incentive. He also told them that if they could come through on Silicon 6, he had 10 more projects just like it for them that would be just as lucrative.

As they climbed into Malone's Ferrari for the ride back to the office, McCaskey felt stunned by the turn of events. First, there had been the unexpected importance of the presentation; then, the marketing manager's proposition; and, now, Malone's enthusiasm for it. Malone could barely contain himself, delighting in how Richardson would react upon hearing how things had worked out. McCaskey just looked at him, shook her head, and said, "You're amazing!" Malone agreed with her, complimented McCaskey in return, and promised her she would be promoted to group manager as soon as she completed Silicon 6.

When they got back, Malone called Hackert into his office with McCaskey and briefed him on the meeting. Hackert's response was that it would be a "piece of cake." All they'd have to do is figure out how to handle Devon. Hackert then suggested that, given the importance of the project, Devon be offered a per diem consulting fee of $7,000 instead of the standard $4,000. Malone responded that he was unsure if that was how they should approach it, but did agree they should make it worthwhile to Devon to provide the necessary information. He then turned to McCaskey and suggested she think about how to proceed with Devon. He also told her not to overlook the option of having someone else, such as Kaufmann, meet with Devon. She could still manage the overall project. He said it would be good training for her upcoming promotion.

EXHIBIT 1 **Summary of Information Required by Seleris's Client**

Source: Company Documents

Develop a competitive profile, in detail, of the Silicon 6 semiconductor manufacturing facility, obtaining:

1. Detailed cost information per 1,000 chips
   - Utilities
   - Scrap
   - Depreciation
   - Other materials
2. Salaries for professionals
3. Number of people in each category of hourly workers
4. How overhead is split out between the different chips
5. Equipment
   - Description, including capacities
   - Operating temperatures
   - Actual production rates and expenses
   - Do they use the same lines for different chips?
6. Raw materials
   - Source
   - Price
   - Long-term contracts?
   - How to account for captive raw materials—transferred at cost or cost plus?
7. Marketing and service expenses

EXHIBIT 2 **Seleris Associates-Staffing in the San Francisco Office**

Source: Company Documents

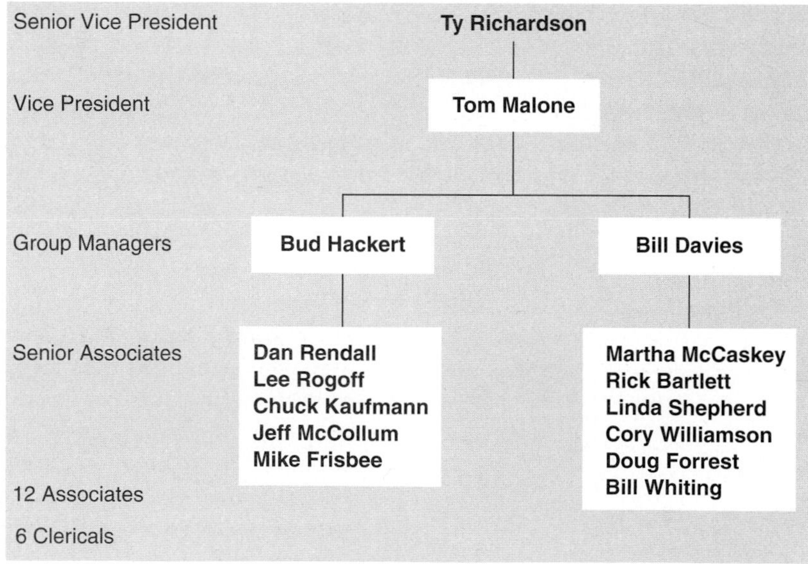

Viking Air Compressor, Inc.

As he left the president's office, George Ames[1] wondered what he ought to do. His impulse was to resign, but he knew that could be a costly blot on his employment record. Moreover, there was the possibility that he was seeing things in a distorted way, that he might later regret leaving Viking before he really knew all the facts bearing on his position and its future. He decided to wait for another week before making up his mind, and in the meantime he made an appointment with Professor Farnsworth of the Amos Tuck School of Business Administration at Dartmouth College to get his advice. Mr. Ames had received his MBA degree from the Tuck School the previous June.[2]

The Viking Air Compressor Company was founded in Bradley, Connecticut, in 1908 by Nels Larsen, an inventor and engineer who left the Westinghouse Electric Company to start his own organization. Mr. Larsen had both a successful design for a new type of air compressor and a talent for management. He led Viking to steadily increasing successes in the air compressor industry.

In 1971 Viking held a 25% share of the air compressor business in the United States, with total annual sales of $180 million. Mr. John T. Larsen, grandson of the founder, was chairman of the board and chief executive officer. Three other descendants of the founder were officers of the company, and the rest of the management team had been developed from Viking employees who rose through the ranks. The ownership of Viking was substantially in the Larsen family hands.

In March 1971 Mr. Oscar Stewart, vice president for personnel administration of Viking, visited the Amos Tuck School to talk with MBA candidates interested in a new position to be created in the Viking structure the following June. Mr. Stewart explained to Dean Robert Y. Kimball, Tuck's Director of Placement, that Viking had never hired MBAs directly from business schools, but wanted to experiment in 1971 with this method of bringing fresh ideas and new techniques into the firm.

The corporate officers had decided, according to Mr. Stewart, to begin to test the effectiveness of the recruitment of MBAs by hiring a business school graduate to become Director of Public Affairs, with the assignment of coordinating the relationships between Viking and outside agencies seeking financial contributions from the company.

As Mr. Stewart described the job to the students he interviewed at Tuck in March 1971, it would contain such tasks as (a) proposing to the Board of Directors the best criteria to use in deciding how to make corporate gifts to charitable organizations of all kinds, (b) supplying the chief officers of the company with information about the participation of Viking employees in public service activities, (c) recommending future strategy for Viking in the employment of women and members of minority groups, and (d) serving as secretary to the newly formed Committee on Corporate Responsibility, which consisted of five members of the Board of Directors.

George Ames accepted the post of Director of Public Affairs at Viking. He had been chosen by Vice President Stewart as the most promising of the five attractive Tuck applicants for the new position. After a short vacation, Mr. Ames reported for work on July 1, 1971, and immediately plunged into the difficult task of gathering information about his new assignment. It soon became clear that his primary task would be to work with the Board Committee on Corporate Responsibility, mainly to propose new policy guidelines to the Board at its September 10th meeting. Mr. Stewart said there were two other areas of high priority: (1) the Corporation's attitude toward public service of employees, and (2) developing criteria for corporate philanthropic giving.

This case was prepared by John W. Hennessey, Jr., and is intended solely for instructional purposes.

[1] Most of the names in this case have been disguised.

[2] Mr. Ames received his B.A. from the University of Michigan in June 1966. He spent three years as an Army officer, concluding as a Captain in Vietnam, before entering Tuck in September 1969. He was married in June 1971.

As Vice President Stewart explained to George in early July, the Committee on Corporate Responsibility was created at the January meeting of the Viking Board after unanimous endorsement of the suggestion made by Dr. Thomas A. Barr, pastor of the local Congregational Church and one of the four outside members of the twelve-man Board. Reverend Barr's major support for his recommendation was the observation that the General Motors Corporation had taken a similar step, under some pressure, and that corporate responsibility was an idea whose time had come on the American scene. In response to the question "What will such a committee do?" Reverend Barr replied that there need be no hurry in defining the detailed responsibilities of the Committee, but that furthermore there could not possibly be any harm or drawbacks from setting it up as soon as possible. He added that the public relations value of such a gesture should not be underestimated. In establishing the Committee on Corporate Responsibility, the Board voted to require the first progress report from the Committee in September 1971.

The Committee on Corporate Responsibility met following the February meeting of the Board of Directors and decided to delay any definite action until an Executive Secretary could be hired. Vice President Stewart was asked to keep this post in mind as he interviewed MBA graduates of several of the leading business schools, and so he did.

George Ames met with the Chairman of the Committee on Responsibility at a luncheon on July 21, 1971, arranged by Vice President Stewart. The Committee Chairman was Mr. Paul Merrow, one of the most respected lawyers in Northern Connecticut and the son of one of the first Board members of Viking when the company was incorporated in the 1920s. Mr. Merrow expressed his pleasure that George Ames was working on the corporate responsibility question and asked him to prepare a report that might be reviewed by the Committee just prior to the September Board meeting. What he wanted, he explained to Mr. Ames, was an analysis of the three or four possible approaches to corporate responsibility which the Directors ought to consider. He asked for a listing of the pros and cons of these various approaches. He said that Mr. Ames should consider this very much like an assignment in a course at the Tuck School. He would be performing a task which none of the Board members had the time or academic background to do, and thus he would substantially improve the decision making of the Board of Directors.

Mr. Merrow concluded the luncheon by saying that he would like Mr. Ames to proceed on his own during the summer, but that he would be glad to confer with him in early September. Mr. Merrow explained that he was leaving the next day for a legal conference in Europe and would be on an extended vacation until September 6th. He said that he had "the proxies" of the other committee members and that they would prefer not to get involved in working on the committee tasks until after the September Board meeting.

George Ames worked assiduously during August, reading all the articles and books he could find in the area of corporate responsibility, including the background of developments in the General Motors situation. He decided not to talk about this particular assignment with other officers of the company, primarily because of Mr. Merrow's injunction that the committee itself would prefer not to engage in substantive talk about the issues until the September Board meeting. George feared he would do more harm than good by talking before he knew his subject well.

In early September John Larsen asked George to see him and the following conversation took place:

John Larsen: I've asked you to see me this morning and tell me what progress you have been making in developing background materials for the work of the Committee on Corporate Responsibility. Mr. Merrow told me he had asked you to do some digging and that you would have a brief report to make at the September 10th meeting of the Board. I know Mr. Merrow hoped he would be back from Europe in time to talk with you before the Board meeting, but it now appears he will be lucky to make the meeting at all. He expects to arrive in town about noon on the tenth.

George Ames: Mr. Larsen, I appreciate the opportunity I have been given to help Viking by developing recommendations about possible strategies for the company to follow in the area of corporate responsibility. Mr. Merrow told me

I ought to develop alternative proposals for recommendations to the Board and I have as recently as yesterday finally been able to narrow the field so that I can make four recommendations with confidence.

I realize the Board may prefer to consider them one at a time, at different meetings, but I would like to tell you about all four so that you will know what my report will contain.

I have decided that the most important issue in the area of corporate responsibility is equal-opportunity hiring. I have been able to develop statistics from the personnel records which show that Viking is rather far behind most major national corporations in the percentage of blacks and women now employed, and, although I am sure conscientious efforts have been made by all officers to remedy this, I cannot stress too strongly how much of a time bomb the present situation is. There will be wide ramifications if we do not improve our record.

The second item of priority which I see is the development of corporate sanctions for public service activities of employees. I believe the company should grant paid leaves of absence for employees who wish to accept public service posts. At present we have done that only for two vice presidents who have been in charge of the Northern Connecticut United Fund. In each case the man was lent to the charitable organization for two full weeks. What I have in mind is a much wider program which would grant employees leaves of absence to work in poverty programs in urban ghettos, or in VISTA projects in Connecticut or neighboring states.

It seems to me a third priority is to develop a committee of consumers who will monitor the safety features and other quality items having to do with our products. If we do not do this we will have Ralph Nader breathing down our necks as has already happened in the automotive industry and some others.

Finally, I strongly recommend that we close our sales contact in Capetown, South Africa, and establish policies which will avoid our being embarrassed as a corporation by discriminatory or dictatorial policies of foreign governments which become critically important political and social issues here in this country.

I feel sure these are great issues of our times and I hope the Board will be willing to debate them at the September 10th meeting. I know I could learn a great deal in my position if such a debate could take place.

Mr. Larsen: Young man, I want to congratulate you on how articulately you have told me about some of the things you have learned in the MBA program at the Tuck School. I envy fellows of your generation who go through MBA programs because you get an opportunity to think about policy problems at a much earlier age than my generation ever did. Indeed my only complaint is that the business schools go too far to educate young men to think they know how to run a company long before they have enough real experience to be even a first-line supervisor.

Now, I think you have your assignment all backwards as secretary to the Committee on Corporate Responsibility and I will tell you why I think that. The Committee hasn't even met yet and your remarks make it sound as if you have written the final report. Worse than that it sounds like the final report of the Committee on Corporate Responsibility of the General Motors Company, not Viking. Everybody knows we've done as good a job as we can to hire blacks and women. There just aren't many such people in the work force in our part of Connecticut who could fit our talent standards, and we are going to follow our historical policy of nondiscrimination as we hire the best people to do Viking jobs. We owe it to our stockholders to make a profit, and if we don't do that we don't have the right to do anything else.

Your remarks on public service activities for our employees are equally off target. The first obligation of our employees is to give a fair day's work for a fair day's pay. All public service activities are extracurricular activities, and that's the way they must be. In order for us to sponsor public service on company time we would have to discriminate between good and bad activities and that would get us into partisan politics and preoccupy all of our executive time. How would the company have done if I had been a part-time chief executive officer in the last five years? That is a preposterous idea! At the same time by working harder on my regular job I have been able some evenings and some weekends to work in fund-raising activities for the Boy Scouts, YMCA, and heaven knows how many other charitable organizations. I would expect every employee to do the same and not to expect the corporation to subsidize activities in their roles as private citizens. As far as public service is concerned, "Live and let live" should be our corporate motto. If we encourage public service activities and include them as part of our compensation and promotion system we will be bogged down in a fantastic collection of information about private lives which will lead to chaos. Even the most superficial examination of this question should have led you to see the problems with the route your theory took you.

As far as the safety of our products and other demands consumers might make, that's all done through the marketplace, as you will come to understand. If our products were not safe or durable they wouldn't sell. You could have found this out had you talked with our production and marketing people as you certainly should have done by now. It's our responsibility to decide after careful market research what the air-compressor needs of America are and will be in the future. We don't need a special panel of bleeding hearts to lead us along paths where we are already expert.

As for our selling operations in South Africa, I'm afraid you just don't know what you are talking about. As long as there is no plank of American foreign policy or Federal law which tells corporations where they can and where they can't sell their products, American businesses must depend on the free market system. President Nixon is talking about opening the trade doors to mainland China. Do you think for one moment the practices of the Chinese government are any less nefarious in some respects than the practices of the South African government? Of course not. And yet you would probably urge me in your liberal way to establish a selling office in Peking just to go along with the new liberal ideas of our President, and I call that kind of pragmatism ridiculous.

Come to think of it, how could you miss this opportunity to lecture the Board on our responsibilities for pollution control and our obligations to get out of the military-industrial complex by canceling all of our air-compressor contracts with the Federal Government!

Young man, you have shown yourself to be a wooly-minded theoretician and I want to tell you that bluntly now so that you will not think me hypocritical at any later point. I will tell the Committee on Corporate Responsibility that you have not had time to prepare your first briefing of the Board of Directors and then I want to have a meeting with you and the Chairman of the Corporate Responsibility Committee on Monday morning September 20th.

That's all I have time for now. I'll see you later.

Joe Camel's Mom: *Marketing at R.J. Reynolds Tobacco Company (A)*

Late Friday afternoon, April 24, 1998, Lynn Beasley took a deep breath as she looked out the window of her office, still reliving the week's events. She had testified at a trial in St. Paul, Minnesota, on Monday and had been wading through dozens of e-mails, voice mails, letters, and meetings since her return to Winston-Salem, North Carolina. The intensity of the cross-examination echoed in her memory. The lead plaintiffs' attorney had pressed her hard with what one observer referred to as his "trademark question":

> Would you agree ma'am that when you put a product into the marketplace that's reported to kill over 400,000 people a year, that you should ascertain whether the marketing campaign that you're going to utilize would appeal to the youth of America? Do you think you have a responsibility to do that?

Her reply had been defiant:

> No. I think that if advertising caused children to start smoking, which it doesn't, then that would be different. But advertising affects brand choice and that's been well documented. And we only do research among adult smokers, we develop the campaigns among adult smokers and we screen ads for appeal among adult smokers.

This case was prepared from public sources by Research Assistant Linda Swenson under the supervision of Kenneth E. Goodpaster, Koch Professor of Business Ethics, and Mark Spriggs, Assistant Professor of Marketing, University of St. Thomas as a basis for class discussion rather than to illustrate either effective or ineffective handling of an administrative situation.

Camel filtre. Une Camel plus douce à 3.60 F

When Beasley joined R.J. Reynolds Tobacco Company 16 years before, she wouldn't have believed that before age 40 she would become an executive vice president of marketing, reporting to RJR's president and CEO. Neither would she have guessed that she would be nicknamed "Joe Camel's Mom" during her testimony in an historic trial.

Lynn Beasley

Beasley had been born Lynn Breininger, one of nine children raised on a dairy farm in Richland Center, Wisconsin, a small town near Madison. During her high school years, she worked as a grocery store clerk. After graduating from high school, she worked in a sewing factory for a year while she earned an associate degree at the local community college. She then transferred to the University of Wisconsin–Madison, where she earned a bachelor's degree in business in 1981. She attended graduate school with the help of a fellowship and earned an MBA in marketing in 1982.

At this point, Beasley had planned to accept a job offer from General Mills, but RJR called in the middle of winter and invited her to North Carolina for an interview at company headquarters. "It was March . . . and I had never been to the South . . . Once I got there, I was really pleased because the people were so nice and I felt like I would really fit in. My ingoing impression was: a *cigarette* company! But the company explained its philosophy on how it marketed cigarettes and how it viewed them, and I felt good about it. And I came back home and I talked to my parents and the marketing professors and I ultimately made the decision to go with R.J. Reynolds."[1]

During Beasley's career at RJR, begun in July 1982 as a marketing assistant, she received training in advertising and marketing. By October 1984 she had risen to assistant brand manager responsible for promoting Camel cigarettes. In 1987, she was promoted to senior brand manager, overseeing all Camel's advertising, promotions, and packaging. Ten years later, in 1997, she would end the "Joe Camel" campaign—her brainchild—as part of a settlement in a California lawsuit alleging RJR's targeting of minors with its advertising.[2]

The Tobacco Industry

Tobacco may have been discovered by Christopher Columbus when he landed in the Bahia Bariay in the Oriente Province of Cuba (not the East Indies as he imagined) in 1492. One of his landing parties met a walking party of Taino Indians traveling "with a firebrand." The Tainos relit the cigar at every stop, passing it around so all could inhale the smoke.[3]

Tobacco had been introduced in Europe by the Spanish and later formed the economic basis of the first successful English Colonies in North America. Around 1612, Virginia colonist John Rolfe used seeds from Trinidad and Orinoco to replace the more bitter Virginia tobacco. As new varieties spread up and down the East Coast, tobacco became the lifeblood of the colonies.

Spanish soldiers introduced "pepelete"—the forerunner of the cigarette—to fellow Russian, French, and British soldiers during the Crimean War (1854–1856). Less than a century later, an entire generation of Americans would receive free cigarettes when they were distributed to soldiers during World War II (1939–1945). Tobacco companies considered this their contribution to the war effort.

By the 1950s, however, smoking and tobacco had come under fire from the scientific community. One of the first salvos came from the *Journal of the American Medical Association (JAMA)*, which linked smoking to lung cancer and chronic obstructive pulmonary disease. Subsequent studies linked tobacco to heart disease and fetal abnormalities.

Smoking became a national health concern in 1964 when the Surgeon General's Report first linked smoking and lung cancer. These findings were endorsed by the American Medical Association, the American Cancer Society, the American Heart Association, and the American Lung Association.[4] In 1965, Congress passed the Federal Cigarette Labeling and Advertising Act requiring the Surgeon General's warnings on cigarette packs. Tobacco ads were banned from TV and radio in 1971, and tobacco sales dropped 10 percent. In 1985 Congress mandated that the warnings required on cigarette packages be rotated to one of four statements.[5] In 1993 the EPA issued a report identifying secondhand smoke as a Class A carcinogen.[6]

Despite the negative press, according to one source, in any given year fewer than 10 percent of the one-third of U.S. smokers who tried to quit actually succeeded. Tobacco's "staying power in the marketplace" made the business of selling cigarettes very profitable. In 1994, global operating profits on tobacco for the six U.S. cigarette manufacturers totaled approximately $10 billion.[7]

[1] *MN Trial Transcript*, April 20, 1998: *State of Minnesota and Blue Cross Blue Shield of Minnesota v. Philip Morris. Inc., et al.*, defendants *(A.M., *3)*.

[2] See below, Mangini case history.

[3] *A Brief History of Tobacco Use and Abuse*, Online Patient Education, Walter Reed Army Medical Center, www.wramc.amedd.army.mil/education.

[4] D. Kirk Davidson, *Selling Sin: The Marketing of Socially Unacceptable Products*, Quorum Books 1996, p. 22.

[5] "Smoking reduces life expectancy"; "Smoking is the major cause of lung cancer"; "Smoking is a major cause of heart disease"; or "Smoking during pregnancy can harm the baby."

[6] Davidson, pp. 25–26.

[7] Davidson, pp. 28–29.

Tobacco remained a significant cash crop in at least 21 states (see Table 1), providing significant revenues for local, state, and federal governments. Excise and sales taxes totaled $15 billion in 1996. Some critics of tobacco claimed that its economic impact was one reason elected officials were reluctant to further regulate its marketing and sale.[8]

By 1996, Philip Morris dominated its competitors in market share, with 47.8 percent of industry sales from Marlboro, Basic, Virginia Slims, and several other brands. In second place was R.J. Reynolds with 24.6 percent (primarily Winston, Camel, and Salem), followed by Brown & Williamson at 17.2 percent (Kool, GPC, Capri), Lorillard at 8.4 percent (Newport, Kent, Old Gold, True), and Liggett at 1.9 percent (Chesterfield, L&M).[9] All of these companies spent heavily on advertising and promotion. (See Exhibit 1.)

Advertising and promotion of cigarettes had grown to almost $4 billion by 1990, despite bans on television and radio advertising. This made cigarettes the second-most-promoted consumer product (after automobiles) in the United States.[10] According to a 1993 Federal Trade Commission report on overall advertising and promotional spending for tobacco companies from 1990 to 1993, spending on coupons and retail value-added such as buy-one-get-one-free promotions totalled $2.5 billion or 42.4 percent of total U.S. advertising and promotion expenditures. Another 25.8 percent or $1.5 billion of spending went for promotional allowances paid to retailers. Tobacco companies used these promotions to try to keep customers from switching to reduced-price brands.

Notwithstanding the large dollar amounts the tobacco industry was spending on advertising, other industries were spending more as *a percentage of sales*. An August 8, 1994, report in *Advertising Age* compared advertising-to-sales ratios for various products.[11] Compared with the tobacco industry, the following categories of products spent a larger percentage of net sales on advertising: bakery products, beverages, dolls and stuffed toys, educational services, greeting cards, household furniture, miscellaneous chemical products, motion pictures, videotapes, pens and pencils and office materials, phonograph records, audiotapes, radio broadcasting stations, retail stores, shoe stores, soap, and sugar.

TABLE 1 Tobacco Crop Cash Receipts (in millions) Top Ten States, 1996

Source: *Tobacco Industry Profile*, 1997, www.tobaccoresolution.com/industryfacts.

North Carolina	$1,076	Virginia	194
Kentucky	768	Florida	36
Tennessee	217	Indiana	28
South Carolina	214	Pennsylvania	25
Georgia	205	Ohio	24

R.J. Reynolds Tobacco Company

The R.J. Reynolds Tobacco Company dated to the post-Civil War era, when Richard Joshua Reynolds began trading in tobacco, first in Virginia and then in Winston, North Carolina. In 1899, RJR was incorporated, and the following year it entered the giant tobacco trust known as the American Tobacco Company. In 1911, the company again became independent when a Supreme Court ruling dissolved the trust. In 1913, RJR introduced a new cigarette, a blend of American and Turkish tobaccos, called *Camel*.[12]

RJR was the nation's leading cigarette manufacturer from 1958 to 1983. Company headquarters were located in Winston-Salem, North Carolina. The company began diversifying into foods and other nontobacco businesses in the 1960s. By 1970, the corporation formed a new parent company called R.J. Reynolds Industries. In 1985 the parent company was renamed RJR Nabisco. For the fiscal year ending December 1997, RJR revenues were more than $17 billion and gross profits were $9.2 billion.[13] (See Exhibit 2.) As the second-largest U.S. cigarette manufacturer in 1998, RJR employed about 8,000 people.

[8] Napoleon Bonaparte once said, "This vice brings in 100 million francs each year. I will certainly forbid it at once—as soon as you can name a virtue that brings in as much revenue." Op. cit., *A Brief History of Tobacco Use and Abuse*.

[9] *Wall Street Journal*, Sept. 23, 1997, A3, from *Market Up*.

[10] *1994 Surgeon General's Report*.

[11] *MN Tobacco Document Depository*. Box D2; MN Trial Exhibit 50005.

[12] "Reynolds Tobacco Company," *Encyclopedia Britannica Online*.

[13] R.J. Reynolds Tobacco Holdings Inc. 10-year 10K history, Disclosure Global Access.

RJR's market research practices had been consistent with those used by other companies in the consumer goods industry. The company used focus groups of eight to ten people to gather information for marketing campaigns. A trained interviewer would ask participants what they liked, didn't like, and what they would change about the brand they smoked as well as competitive brands. Members of RJR's marketing team would watch the focus groups on a monitor. "You might do three to four groups a day for two days in different cities so you hear what people have to say across the country," Beasley said.

The marketing department would review focus group research and then brainstorm about product, packaging, and campaign. From one to five advertising agencies would be asked to submit proposals; then focus groups would be asked if they would switch brands based on the proposed advertising. The process would be repeated and could take from months to years until a feasible idea would emerge.

Most marketing executives used the trade publication *Advertising Age* to follow new products and ad campaigns. Advertising-to-sales ratios were used to gauge competitiveness. Between 1983 and 1994, RJR spent more than $6.1 billion for advertising, marketing, and promotion.[14] Critics were quick to compare this figure with the $19 million the company spent on youth smoking prevention programs.

The Antismoking Movement and the Mangini Lawsuit

By the mid-1980s and into the 1990s an antismoking movement was gaining ground and being reflected in national publications. In July 1986, syndicated columnist Ellen Goodman assailed Scott Stapf of the *Tobacco Institute*, a joint lobbying organization for the cigarette companies, for his rejection of the idea that ads enticed consumers into trying a product. Stapf had called the idea "complete baloney!" Goodman's response: "What are they doing wasting all that money if Stapf is right, if ads are not crucial in getting customers to draw their first breath of smoke? Why do they go to the trouble of creating campaigns and slogans? According to Stapf . . . the tobacco companies are merely trying to lure people who already smoke from one brand to another."[15]

Articles also reflected the public ire over tobacco advertising campaigns targeting youth, and especially RJR's Joe Camel campaign. In February 1990, the *Washington Post* reported: "One hour after being sworn in as New York City's consumer affairs commissioner, Mark Green assailed RJR Nabisco Inc. . . . for an advertising campaign for Camel cigarettes . . . aimed primarily at adolescents. In a letter, Green urged RJR Chairman Louis V. Gerstner Jr. to end the campaign saying, 'there are few, if any, marketplace abuses worse than inducing children to smoke.' Green told reporters that the *Camel* campaign is 'little better than commercial child abuse.'"[16] (See Exhibit 3.)

In 1991, San Francisco family-law attorney Janet Mangini brought suit to end the Joe Camel campaign.[17] While the Mangini case was in pretrial discovery during 1994, the Federal Trade Commission considered a complaint against the Joe Camel campaign but closed its investigation without taking action. A joint statement by the FDA commissioners explained:

> Although it may seem intuitive to some that the Joe Camel advertising campaign would lead more children to smoke or lead children to smoke more, the evidence to support that intuition is not there. Our responsibility as commissioners is not to make decisions based on intuition but to evaluate the evidence and determine whether there is reason to believe that a proposed respondent violated the law.
> The Commission has spent a great deal of time

[14] The company spent slightly less on traditional advertising and slightly more on discounting than other tobacco companies.

[15] "Time Is Right for a Ban on Cigarette Ads," *Newsday*, July 15, 1986, p. 54, from *Viewpoints*.

[16] "Camel Ad Campaign Accused of Targeting Youth," *Washington Post*, Feb. 21. 1990, A3.

[17] "Case History—*Mangini v. R.J. Reynolds Tobacco Company.*" *Tobacco Control Archives: Mangini Collection*, www.library.ucsf.edu/tobacco/mangini/history.html. The California Supreme Court, in supporting Mangini's standing to sue, stated that "the targeting of minors is oppressive and unscrupulous, in that it exploits minors by luring them into unhealthy and potentially life-threatening addiction before they have achieved the maturity necessary to make an informed decision whether to take up smoking despite its health risks."

> and effort reviewing the difficult factual and legal questions raised by this case, including a comprehensive review of relevant studies and statistics. Because the evidence in the record does not provide reason to believe that the law has been violated, we cannot issue a complaint.[18]

In 1997, however, the FTC reversed its position and voted to file a formal complaint that claimed the R.J. Reynolds Tobacco Company had created the "Joe Camel" theme advertisements "to reposition the Camel brand to make it attractive to younger smokers, and that the campaign was successful in appealing to many children and adolescents under the age of 18." The complaint ordered RJR to cease advertising Camel cigarettes to children by using themes relating to Joe Camel.[19]

But before either the Mangini or the FTC cases were actually heard, RJR terminated the Joe Camel campaign and settled the Mangini suit. The company statement at the time acknowledged that the "Mangini action . . . was an early significant and unique driver of the overall legal and social controversy regarding underage smoking [and] led to the decision to phase out the Joe Camel Campaign." The settlement also provided for the public release of confidential documents about youth marketing and the Joe Camel campaign.[20]

The Minnesota Tobacco Trial

During the mid-1990s, a number of individual states were also initiating legal actions against the tobacco industry. Minnesota Attorney General Hubert "Skip" Humphrey and health care insurer *Blue Cross Blue Shield of Minnesota* filed a joint lawsuit August 17, 1994, alleging antitrust conspiracy and consumer fraud. The defendants were Philip Morris, R.J. Reynolds Tobacco Co., Brown & Williamson Tobacco Corp., B.A.T. Industries, British-American Tobacco Co. Ltd., BAT (UK & Export) Ltd., the American Tobacco Co., Liggett Group Inc., the Council for Tobacco Research, and the Tobacco Institute. As one observer put it, "Instead of blaming tobacco companies for causing Uncle Ned's cancer, the Minnesota case would charge that the tobacco companies knew their product was dangerous for Uncle Ned to use, and lied about it."[21]

Pretrial discovery for the Minnesota trial began in June 1995 and document depositories—one in Minneapolis, another outside London for the British defendants—were created for the tens of millions of pages of material that would come in over time.

In 1997, Humphrey broke with his attorney general colleagues, refusing to join a negotiated settlement that eventually would grow to $368.5 billion. Humphrey's reasons: "absence of full FDA regulation on tobacco, an inadequate $300 billion settlement figure, and lack of full disclosure of corporate documents."[22]

The Minnesota trial began in January 1998 in the city of St. Paul, Ramsey County. After three months of testimony, the defense called Lynn Beasley as a witness. In the words of two journalists who followed the trial closely:

> Lynn Beasley was the Betty Crocker of the tobacco industry. Petite, attractive, and ani-

[18] Joint Statement of Commissioners Mary L. Azcuenaga, Deborah K. Owen and Roscoe B. Starek III in R.J. Reynolds File No. 932-3162, 1994.

[19] But one of the commissioners dissented firmly: "As was true three years ago, intuition and concern for children's health are not the equivalent of—and should not be substituted for—evidence sufficient to find reason to believe that there is a likely causal connection between the Joe Camel advertising campaign and smoking by children." Dissenting Statement of Commissioner Roscoe B. Starek III in *RJ Reynolds Tobacco Co., Docket No. 9285*, 1997.

[20] As quoted in "Case History—*Mangini v. R.J. Reynolds Tobacco Company*." *Tobacco Control Archives: Mangini Collection*. www.library.ucsf.edu/tobacco/mangini/history.html.

[21] Patrick Kessler of WCCO-TV in his September 1998 "Forward" to Deborah Caulfield Rybak and David Phelps, *Smoked: The Inside Story of the Minnesota Tobacco Trial*, MSP Books, 1998.

[22] Ibid., p. 37. The charge against the tobacco companies in the negotiated settlement was "wrongful conduct and smoking-related illnesses." Said Humphrey at a press conference announcing the lawsuit: "Previous lawsuits have said the tobacco companies should pay because their products are dangerous. This suit says they should pay because their conduct is illegal" (p. 25). In his opening argument, lead plaintiffs' attorney Michael Ciresi put it this way: "The purpose of this lawsuit is to hold the industry accountable, accountable for its own illegal actions. This, the evidence will show, is a case of corporate irresponsibility in which an entire industry, in a half-century-long combination of conspiracy, of willful and intentional wrongdoing, violated the consumer protection and antitrust statutes of the state of Minnesota" (p. 91).

> mated, she was wholesome in appearance and the only female defense witness to take the stand. She had deep Midwestern roots and a Horatio Alger background. She was executive vice president of marketing for R. J. Reynolds Tobacco Company and had never before testified in a tobacco trial. RJR attorney Robert Weber wanted to put a human face on the industry. Lynn Beasley provided the perfect visage. Through Beasley's enthusiastic sincerity, Weber would attempt to dispel the state's allegations that cigarette manufacturers marketed their products to kids.[23]

During her testimony, Beasley had explained her role in developing the Joe Camel marketing campaign. She reviewed R.J. Reynolds' policies against advertising and promotions aimed at buyers under age 18. And she withstood an aggressive cross-examination by Michael Ciresi, the lead attorney for the plaintiffs.

Beasley's Views on Youth Marketing and RJR's Policies

Tobacco companies built their customer bases by attracting new smokers, discouraging smokers from quitting, reacquiring lapsed smokers, and persuading smokers to switch brands and maintain brand loyalty. As smokers aged, they became "brand loyal."[24] RJR's 1990–1992 Strategic Plan stated that loyalty, not switching, drove cigarette sales. According to the report, brands almost never gained market share through switching. Most switching occurred because of "problems" such as tar (1970s), price (1980s), or personal/social reasons (1990s). The low incidence of switching was attributed to high brand loyalty (only 2–3 percent switch per year), the presence of more than 60 competing brands, and consumers' diverse wants.[25]

Beasley recalled that when she was hired by RJR in 1982, the company's views on marketing had been consistent with the government's interpretation that an "adult" smoker was age 18 and older. More than once, she had asserted that she didn't believe advertising caused kids to smoke.

The company had been studying groups of smokers, aged 18 and older. A February 1984 RJR Strategic Research Report, "Younger Adult Smokers: Strategies and Opportunities," concluded that by the time smokers reached age 18, they were extremely brand loyal, so that efforts to shift their brand preference would be quite expensive and/or unsuccessful. The report recommended that RJR commit substantial resources to the younger adult market segment.[26] The report also stated:

> Younger adult smokers have been the critical factor in the growth and decline of every major brand and company over the last 50 years. They will continue to be just as important to brands/companies in the future. . . . The renewal of the market stems almost entirely from 18-year-old smokers. No more than 5 percent of smokers start after age 24.

From 1983 to 1992, the company marketed tobacco to 18-, 19-, and 20-year-olds. In 1992 that changed. "We felt we were receiving a lot of criticism [for] marketing to kids—and we weren't," Beasley explained. She added that if the team created a buffer—studying and developing promotions only for smokers aged 21 and older—it would assure critics that the aim was adults and not underage smokers. "That's why we changed [the marketing] to 21."[27]

A 1992 memo from RJR's executive vice president of marketing and sales outlined how the company's advertising policy would change to compensate for the perception that RJR marketed to people aged 18 and older while other companies restricted marketing to the 21-and-older group. (See Exhibit 4.)

[23] Ibid., p. 353. "Associated Press reporter Steve Karnowski, one of the trial media's master nicknamers, found his peg for Beasley. 'She's Joe Camel's mother,' he marveled, chuckling" (p. 360). Rybak and Phelps commented later that Joe Camel's mother turned out to be an *Eclipse* smoker, RJR's super-low-nicotine brand (p. 363).

[24] Rybak and Phelps.

[25] *MN Tobacco Document Depository*. Bates # TE 8 00001-00033; MN Trial Exhibit 13004.

[26] *MN Tobacco Document Depository*. Bates # TE 7 00602-00616, TE 7 00665-00666; *MN Trial Exhibit* 12579.

[27] *MN Trial Transcript*, April 20, 1998 (*A.M., *22*). "People were assuming that our intent was to market to younger smokers when it wasn't," Beasley had testified during the trial. "We said, yes, the government makes it legal to buy and purchase and smoke cigarettes at the age of 18, but rather than developing marketing programs for 18-, 19- and 20-year-olds, we'll move it to 21" (*P.M., *11*).

RJR had voluntarily adhered to standards such as the *Cigarette Advertising and Promotion Code.* Company policy prohibited advertising on billboards located less than 500 feet from schools or playgrounds as well as paying for the use of products in movies. To receive promotional offers, participants had to certify they were 21 years of age. If the company learned that someone under age 21 had signed a certification, he or she would be denied future promotional products. To receive product samples at promotional events, people had to present an ID. Promotional T-shirts and jackets were produced only in adult sizes.

During her testimony, Beasley recounted an instance in which a sales manager had instructed salespeople to give special attention to placing promotions in the stores around high schools—a clear violation of RJR policy. He was reprimanded in writing and asked to correct the misperception with all his salespeople. Yancey Ford, executive vice president of sales, subsequently sent all RJR salespeople a letter emphasizing the importance of adherence to company policies.[28] (See Exhibit 5.)

RJR and other tobacco companies also participated in industry efforts to educate retailers about underage sales. Government statistics had reported that 2 percent of cigarette sales were made to underage buyers. In 1992, RJR initiated a youth smoking prevention program called "It's the Law," which evolved into the "We Card" program. The latter program supplied retailers with a video and employee handbook as well as "We Card" signs.

Reynolds tracked its share of smokers in the market through *RJR Tracker,* a system which measured adult smokers, aged 18 and older, by asking them which brand they bought most often. RJR's research group routinely had tracked brand preferences among smokers age 14 to 17, comparing market shares for the company's Winston and Salem brands with Philip Morris' Marlboro and Kool brands. The information about underage smokers, however, came from secondary sources such as *National Family Opinion,*[29] a private research organization, or government agencies such as the *U.S. Department of Health, Education, and Welfare,* not from RJR's internal research department.

As to why people started smoking, a July 1974 internal RJR memo cited research identifying one or more of the following as the essential reasons for smoking cigarettes:

- Conformance.
- Support, or to gain confidence in stressful (often social) situations.
- Enjoyment, taste, or other physiological benefits (after an initial learning period).
- To show off.

Initial brand selection was believed to relate directly to why young people smoked. The strongest influence was a smoker's friends or peer group, but smokers also identified closely with the brand image portrayed in advertising. At the time of this report, younger smokers usually chose either Marlboro or Kool. These two brands enjoyed a 50 percent share of smokers 18–20 years of age versus a share of 6 percent and 5 percent, respectively, among smokers age 35–49. Some people credited the strong market share of Marlboro to the highly successful (and long-running) Marlboro Man campaign.[30]

Beasley had explained to Ciresi in her testimony that "if you wanted to actually market to 14–17-year-olds, you'd need to do the focus groups and the quantitative surveys; you'd need to know what they think of the brands, develop ideas for them, show them the ideas. . . . That's how we develop advertising and that's how you find out if you have an idea that works."[31]

Camel's 75th Anniversary Campaign

At the time Beasley was named senior brand manager for Camel in 1987, the company was looking for a new ad campaign to reverse Camel's sliding sales trend and to change Camel's image as a "nonfiltered, harsh" product used by older

[28] *MN Tobacco Document Depository*. Bates TE 14 00836; *MN Trial Exhibit* AM002637.

[29] Memorandum "Teenage Smokers (14–17) and New Adult Smokers and Quitters." Source: *Tobacco Control Archives: Mangini Collection*, www.library.ucsf.edu/tobacco/mangini.

[30] Memorandum "What Causes Smokers to Select their First Brand of Cigarette?" Source: *Tobacco Control Archives: Mangini Collection*, www.library.ucsf.edu/tobacco/mangini.

[31] *MN Trial Transcript (A.M., *28).*

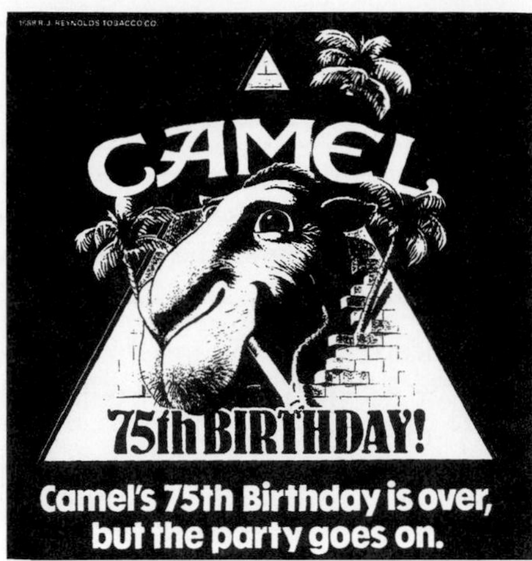

males. Camel's current "Bob Beck" campaign (Beck was the model with the curly blond hair used in the ads), seen as a bad imitation of Marlboro's Marlboro Man campaign, lacked appeal for the targeted young adult smoker.

In 1986, the Camel brand team recommended a new target market—18- to 24-year-old male smokers. These smokers were more brand loyal than older smokers and were also the core market for Marlboro. The strategy for the new Camel campaign would be to leverage the positive and distinctive aspects of Camel's product user heritage: full authentic smoking satisfaction, masculinity, and nonconformist, self-confident user perceptions. The aim was to use "peer acceptance [and] influence to provide the motivation for target smokers to select Camel." The campaign would emphasize male smokers because RJR felt that a masculine theme would attract male Marlboro smokers. Forty percent of Marlboro smokers were female.[32] This would make it difficult for Marlboro to counter Camel's efforts to attract male smokers without alienating a significant portion of their current market. Camel's 75th anniversary campaign would be the first step in repositioning the Camel brand to reach this target market.

The marketing team that worked on the 75th anniversary campaign developed several potential themes and presented them to focus groups. The most popular was a humorous theme featuring a picture of a camel with a cigarette in its mouth based on a French poster.[33] Focus group participants loved this humorous approach, saying it reflected the rich heritage of the brand and was "contemporary" in the minds of the target consumers.[34]

Beasley and her team came up with the name "Joe Camel" for the image taken from the French poster. "I envisioned him as an average kind of guy that the average smoker could relate to . . . Camel originally was created with a camel on the pack. They had taken a photograph of a camel in a circus and the name of the animal was Joe. It was part of the history and it represented 'the average Joe.' We created an ad in which this camel was wearing a blue work shirt embroidered with the name *Joe*."[35] The phrase "smooth character" was added to the Joe Camel image to portray him as being cool while sending the message that Camel cigarettes were smooth in taste.

"We put four agencies to work on it," Beasley recalled. "I gave them this poster as a starting point and said . . . 'Give him human characteristics and think of him as someone who is 75 years old but that you really like and is fun and you'd like to be around. . . . Treat Camel as a fun and exciting brand.' The line we used in the advertising was *'75 years and still smokin,'* to say the brand had been around for 75 years and still was modern."[36]

As the campaign developed, Beasley said, steps were taken to be sure that the Joe Camel campaign did not appeal to minors. "When we conducted focus groups, we asked people if the ads would appeal to people their age, or to people older or younger. When we showed them a Joe with pink punk hair standing on end, they said it was for younger people. So we eliminated it and made sure no one was developing ideas with that look." A singing birthday card also was nixed because when focus groups saw ads that included party hats and favors, they said it would make the

[32] *MN Tobacco Document Depository*. Bates # TE 7 00846-00850; *MN Trial Exhibit* 12761, "March 1986 Camel New Advertising Campaign Development."

[33] The poster is reproduced on the opening page of this case; the "birthday" poster above was based on it.

[34] *MN Tobacco Document Depository*. Bates # TE 12 01147; *MN Trial Exhibit* 24348.

[35] *MN Trial Transcript (A.M., *38)*.

[36] Ibid. *(A.M., *28)*.

ads appeal to people younger than those to which RJR was marketing.

"The ad agencies all came back with ideas and we did more focus groups to see how smokers would react to them," Beasley recalled. "But when I approached management for approval on the campaign, the head of marketing was concerned Camel smokers would think the company was poking fun at their brand. So I asked people age 40 and older who worked on the Camel production line if we should run the Joe Camel campaign. They loved the idea. We asked focus groups of Camel smokers age 18 and older the same thing and found they liked the idea very much."[37] With management's final approval, the campaign was launched.

The 75th Anniversary Campaign and the debut of Joe Camel were enormously successful. Camel's market share among 18- to 24-year-olds increased from 3 to 10 percent between 1987 and 1994, while increasing 3 to 5 share points among smokers 25 to 34, and 2 to 3 points for those 35 to 49.[38] A single market share point in this industry could be worth hundreds of thousands of dollars.

Challenges to Beasley's Business Judgment

During his cross-examination, Michael Ciresi asked Beasley whether studies had been conducted for the Joe Camel 75th birthday campaign to measure its appeal to people under age 18. Beasley replied: "We have a very firm policy; we do not do any research among those under 18. . . . If advertising caused children to start smoking, which it doesn't, then that would be different. But advertising affects brand choice and that's been well-documented. And we only do research among adult smokers, we develop the campaigns among adult smokers and we screen ads for appeal among adult smokers."

RJR did not have research aimed at determining what would appeal to, motivate, and influence an 18-year-old as opposed to a 17-year-old. Beasley had told Ciresi, "18-year-olds are moving out on their own. That's why they have the right to vote and the right to smoke and the right to join the military; I think 18-year-olds are different than 17-year-olds."

Ciresi questioned Beasley intensely about a March 1986 memo, entitled "Camel New Advertising Campaign Development," that her predecessor had written to RJR's director of marketing:[39]

> Ciresi: "And it is stated that [the dynamics of brand loyalty and peer influence] strongly suggest that repositioning Camel as the relevant brand choice for younger adult smokers will be critical to generating sustained volume growth; correct?"
>
> Beasley: "Yes."
>
> Ciresi: "And then it talks about the fact that in directing your market to that new repositioning, you've still got to take care of the folks that are outside of that prime prospect group; correct?"
>
> Beasley: "Yes. . . ."
>
> Ciresi: "And it talks about employing universal cues and symbols; doesn't it?"
>
> Beasley: "Yes, it does. . . ."
>
> Ciresi: "Now do you know of any type of investigation that RJR did to determine what would attract, influence and motivate an 18-year-old as opposed to a 17-year-old?
>
> Beasley: ". . . No. We don't do any research among 17-year-olds. . . ."
>
> Ciresi: "So you had no idea [whether] what would appeal [to], motivate and influence an 18-year-old also would appeal [to], motivate and influence a 17-year-old? Did you?" [Ciresi continued:] "Are youth influenced by peers? . . . Are teenagers influenced by peers? . . . And nothing was done to determine whether or not what appealed to this 18-year-old would also appeal to a broader group which would be younger, correct?"
>
> Beasley: "No. We do not do research among those under the age of 18. We only market to adults."

The memo said ads would create the perception that Camel smokers were self-confident non-conformists who projected a "cool" attitude "admired by peers." Research had shown these

[37] *MN Tobacco Document Depository*. Bates # TE 7 00982-01002; MN Trial Exhibit 12811, *Camel Younger Adult Smoker Focus Groups, Feb. 1, 1985*, RJR Marketing Research Report.

[38] *MN Trial Transcript (P.M., *39)*.

[39] *MN Tobacco Document Depository*. Bates # TE 7 00846-00850; MN Trial Exhibit 12761.

to be attributes of Camel smokers, Beasley explained. "Camel smokers like to stand out from the crowd . . . we have a higher share out on the West Coast where there are more non-conformists," she told Ciresi.

Ciresi had cited statistics from the *California Tobacco Survey*, a telephone survey of adults and teenagers conducted from 1989 to 1994.[40] The study claimed that during this period Camel's market share for children under age 18 had surged from 8.1 to 13.3.[41] Ciresi also referred to a U.S. Department of Health and Human Services report on focus groups held during October and November 1995.[42] The participants—12–17-year-old males and females, both smokers and nonsmokers—said smoking was addictive and a matter of need, not choice. Focus group members were familiar with the cigarette ads they were shown, and many were aware of incentive programs that offered clothing or other products for "Camel dollars" or "Marlboro miles."

Referring to the HHS report, Ciresi said to Beasley: "The focus groups said that they felt the primary target of cigarette ads were teens and young adults and that the ads show people having a good time so that kids will think that their lives will improve if they smoke." Beasley replied: "Yes. And they also said they didn't think advertising was why they started smoking."

Joe Camel was not the only cartoon character being used to sell an adult product, Beasley had pointed out. "These characters often are used for adult products because it makes it more memorable and you can recall the ads better, and so a lot of adult products use these characters. . . . The Minnesota State Lottery used Bullwinkle the Moose for its advertisements."

The testimony of Cheryl Perry, a professor in the division of epidemiology at the University of Minnesota and scientific editor for the 1994 Surgeon General's Report focusing on tobacco use among young people, provided a different view of Joe Camel. Perry didn't see a cartoon camel—she saw a subliminal manipulative creature designed to appeal to teenagers' need for peer approval: "You can see Joe Camel with his peer group. He's part of the 'in' group. And you can see that there's some card playing going on; it's slightly risky. But primarily, this is an advertisement that would appeal to wanting to be part of a peer group. An adolescent would see smoking as associated with the peer group."[43] Studies published in JAMA and in several prestigious marketing/advertising journals had also examined the issue of using cartoon characters to advertise adult products and the effect on youth. (See Exhibit 6.)

Marketing and Morality

Beasley believed that she had been a good witness and that the jury had accepted her testimony favorably. She had spoken her mind on youth smoking: "We definitely do not want underage sales at all. . . . First of all, of course, it's wrong. I don't want kids to smoke. I don't think any responsible adult wants kids to smoke. That's why our society has set the legal age for smoking at 18 years old—that's when we think someone can make an informed choice about the risks. . . . Every time a kid lights up, especially if it's one of our brands, then it becomes harder and harder for me to market to adults. . . . because we become more limited in what we can do. So if the kids didn't smoke, if they weren't experimenting with smoking, it would have almost no volume impact, and we would be able to market more freely, which is what we need to be able to do to move people to our brand."[44]

Although Ciresi had introduced company documents revealing the importance of underage smokers to market share and future sales at RJR, he had been unable to undermine Beasley's credibility. Still, her experience in the witness chair that week had left her with a kind of "ethical vertigo." Her day in court kept replaying in her mind. She didn't believe that RJR's marketing practices were unethical, but it was clear that many people did. Her judgment had been questioned for not researching youth and for deliberately targeting youth. *Could* she or *should* she have done something differently to shape RJR marketing?

[40] The survey was commissioned by the California Department of Health and carried out under the direction of John P. Pierce, Ph.D., University of California–San Diego.

[41] *MN Trial Transcript (P.M., *39).*

[42] *MN Tobacco Document Depository*. Bates # TE 15 00096-00100; *MN Trial Exhibit* AT000507. Also published in *The Federal Register*, December 1995.

[43] Rybak and Phelps, p. 252.

[44] *MN Trial Transcript (AM., *18)*

EXHIBIT 1 Percentage Share of Total U.S. Market for Selected Brands (all ages)

Sources: 1985–1990: *Mangini v. R.J. Reynolds, Share Trend Memo,* June 19, 1991; 1991–1995: *Market Share Reporter*, Gale Research, Detroit, Washington D.C., and London.

Brands	1985	1986	1987	1988	1989	1990	1991	1992	1993	1994	1995
Marlboro (PM)	22.1	23.0	23.9	25.0	25.3	25.5	25.8	24.5	23.5	28.1	30.1
Winston (RJR)	11.6	11.3	11.1	10.7	10.0	8.9	7.5	6.8	6.7	5.8	5.8
Salem (RJR)	8.1	7.8	7.7	7.3	6.9	6.2	5.4	4.8	3.9	3.8	3.7
Kool (B&W)	6.8	6.4	6.1	5.9	4.0	4.9	4.6	4.3	3.0	3.6	3.6
Newport (L)	3.4	3.7	4.0	4.4	4.6	4.8	4.7	4.8	4.8	5.1	5.6
Camel (RJR)	4.4	4.3	4.2	4.3	4.3	4.4	4.0	4.1	3.9	4.0	4.4
Benson & Hedges (PM)	4.6	4.4	4.3	4.0	3.7	3.4	3.2	3.1	2.5	2.4	2.3
Merit (PM)	4.1	4.0	3.9	3.0	3.4	3.4	3.1	2.8	2.6	2.4	2.3
Doral (RJR)	1.0	2.0	3.0	3.4	3.8	4.3	4.6	4.4	4.6	5.1	5.7
Virginia Slims (PM)	2.7	2.9	3.1	3.1	3.1	3.0	2.8	2.8	2.6	2.4	2.4
Vantage (RJR)	3.4	3.2	3.1	2.9	2.8	2.4	2.0	NA	NA	NA	NA
Other Misc. Brands	27.8	27.0	25.6	26.0	28.1	28.8	32.3	37.6	41.9	37.3	34.1
Total	100.0	100.0	100.0	100.0	100.0	100.0	100.0	100.0	100.0	100.0	100.0

Corporate Parent of Brand, Philip Morris (PM) R.J. Reynolds (RJR), Brown & Williamson (B&W), Lorillard (L).

EXHIBIT 2 Financial Information, R.J. Reynolds Tobacco Holdings, Fiscal Years 1989–1997

RJR Annual Financial Information—Fiscal Years December 1989–December 1997 ($000s)									
Fiscal year ending	12/31/89	12/31/90	12/31/91	12/31/92	12/31/93	12/31/94	12/31/95	12/31/96	12/31/97
Total assets	36,376,000	32,675,000	32,100,000	32,010,000	31,272,000	31,393,000	31,508,000	31,260,000	30,657,000
Income taxes	713,000	471,000	72,000	300,000	234,000	248,000	302,000	235,000	243,000
Net sales	12,114,000	13,879,000	14,989,000	15,734,000	15,104,000	15,366,000	16,008,000	17,063,000	17,057,000
Cost of goods	5,241,000	5,652,000	6,088,000	6,326,000	6,640,000	6,977,000	7,468,000	7,973,000	7,847,000
Gross profit	6,873,000	8,227,000	8,901,000	9,408,000	8,464,000	8,389,000	8,540,000	9,090,000	9,210,000
Net income	110,000	–171,000	349,000	319,000	–139,000	517,000	622,000	666,000	433,000
Nonoperating income	169,000	–844,000	–876,000	–710,000	–1,462,000	–750,000	–811,000	–1,191,000	–767,000

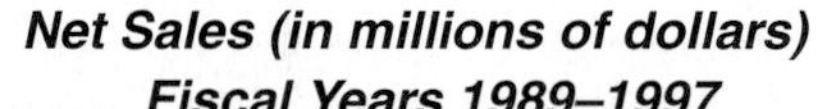

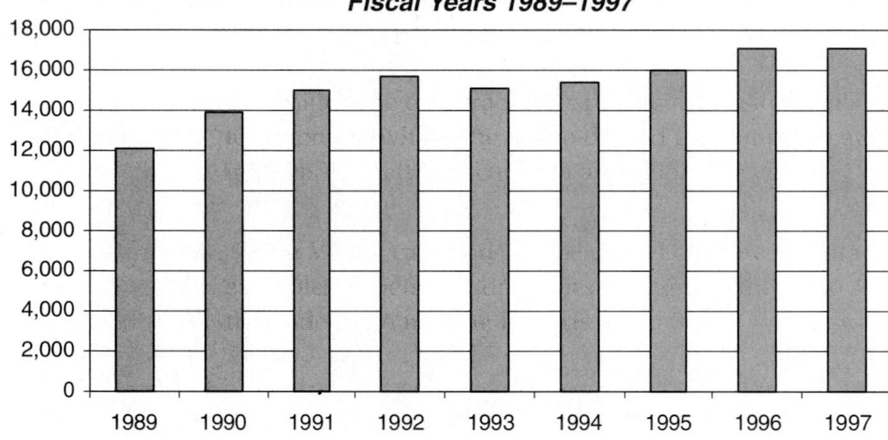

Net Income, Nonoperating Income (in millions of dollars)
Fiscal Years 1989–1997

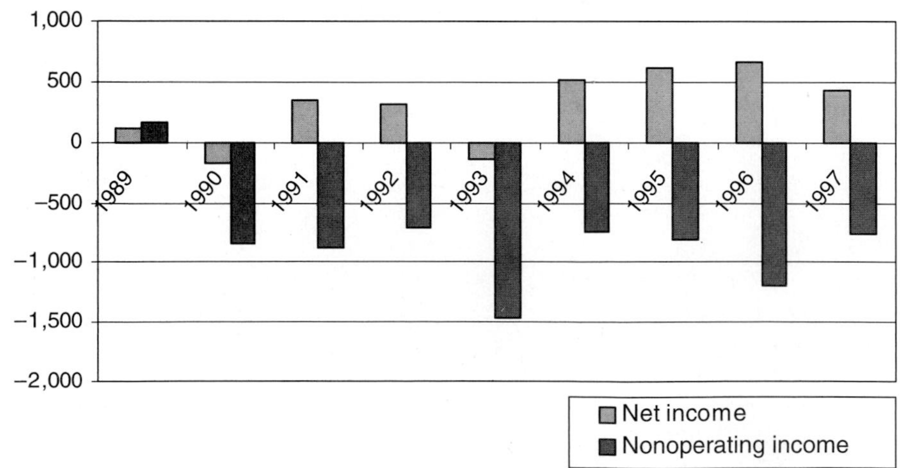

EXHIBIT 3 **News Coverage of Camel Marketing**

The Wall Street Journal, April 1990: "Both liquor and cigarette makers are increasingly under attack for allegedly targeting young people in their advertising. The criticism is part of a growing attack on targeted marketing of all types by liquor and tobacco companies."[a]

The San Diego Union-Tribune, August 1990: "R.J. Reynolds has drawn criticism that its new, cartoon-like 'Joe Camel,' symbol of its oldest brand, is intended to appeal to youngsters. But Maura Payne, a Reynolds' spokeswoman, contended the heavily promoted Camel brand is an attempt to reach adults. 'Owens-Corning uses a pink panther to sell insulation, and I don't think there are a whole lot of 8-year-olds buying insulation,' Payne said. 'He (the camel) is a fun-loving kind of guy who goes out with friends and finds himself in social settings. It was a way of giving the brand a personality that the previous camel did not give it.'"[b]

USA Today, November 1990: "Sparks were flying Thursday after the release of a federal drug report critical of the alcohol and tobacco industries. The National Commission on Drug-Free Schools, a 26-member blue-ribbon panel set up by Congress in 1988, took harsh aim at the industries for targeting youth in their ads."[c]

USA Today, December 1990: "We've waited long enough for tobacco pushers to voluntarily clean up their act and leave children alone. Truth: While the *Tobacco Institute* campaign urges parents to talk with children about smoking, the tobacco industry aggressively markets tobacco to children by glamorizing smoking in ads and sponsoring sporty events and rock concerts. Ads and posters featuring the Joe Camel smooth character cartoon are clearly aimed at kids."[d]

The Washington Post, October 1991: "Brown & Williamson Tobacco Corp. has re-ignited the smoldering controversy over cigarette and alcohol 'target' marketing by introducing the colorful penguin as the spokes-symbol for its Kool cigarette brand. . . . The nation's two top health officials, Secretary of Health and Human Services Louis W. Sullivan and Surgeon General Antonia C. Novello, echoed the criticisms of anti-smoking organizations that say the introduction of the irreverent cartoon character is a blatant attempt to hook youngsters on smoking."[e]

[a] "Riunite Isn't Afraid to Target the Young," *The Wall Street Journal*, April 4, 1990, B6.

[b] "Anti-Tobacco Forces, Anti-Smokers Start Taking Aim at Tobacco Ads, Promotion," *The San Diego Union-Tribune*, August 26, 1990, A1.

[c] "Drug Panel: Alcohol, Cigarette Ads Prey on Youth," *USA Today*, November 16, 1990, 3A.

[d] "Anti-smoking Effort Is Just a Cynical Ploy," *USA Today*, December 14, 1990, 12A.

[e] "Kool's Penguin Draws Health Officials Heat; Surgeon General HHS Claim Ad Campaign Is Aimed at Minors," *The Washington Post*, October 23, 1991, C1.

EXHIBIT 4 RJR Internal Memo on Advertising Practices

Source: *MN Tobacco Document Depository*. Bates TE 514763119-514763120.

RJReynolds Tobacco Company

May 28, 1992

JAMES C. SCHROER
Executive Vice President
Marketing and Sales

Winston-Salem, NC 27102
919-741-2202

TO:

L.J. Beasley	R.E. Evans	E.M. McAtee
J.W. Best	Y.W. Ford, Jr.	G.C. Pennell
L. Birlin	S.G. Hanes	M.R. Savoca
E.M. Blackmer	R.S. Hendrix	R.M. Sanders
P.J. Cundari	D.A. Krishock	S.R. Strawsburg

RE: Advertising Practices

As you are well aware, our long-standing policy and that of the entire industry has been that we advertise and promote our brands only to adult smokers because we firmly believe that smoking is an adult activity and that children should not smoke.

We define adults as those being 18 years of age or older and continue to support industry efforts to enact and enforce laws prohibiting the sale of cigarettes to persons under 18 years of age as well as a wide variety of other programs intended to discourage underage smoking.

We have been very candid in our public statements to the effect that we advertise certain of our brands to smokers 18 years of age and older. This is entirely consistent with our view (and the law of most states) that 18-year-olds are adults for purposes of the purchase of cigarettes.

The Cigarette Advertising and Promotion Code, as it has evolved over time, contains a number of provisions which are age-specific. For example, models must be and appear to be 25 or older; we do not advertise in publications directed primarily to those under 21; and our direct mail and sampling activities are restricted to smokers 21 or older. These provisions in our voluntary code have been the source of some confusion outside the Company because they have been misinterpreted to prohibit <u>any</u> marketing activities directed to persons under 21.

None of our competitors in their public statements admit that they advertise or promote their products to anyone under 21. The fact that our public statements on this issue differ from our competitors' and, on the surface might appear inconsistent with elements of the Cigarette Advertising and Promotion Code, has not gone unnoticed by our adversaries. In fact, a similar issue was raised recently by an apparently well-intentioned shareholder at our annual meeting.

"We work for smokers."

(continued)

EXHIBIT 4 RJR Internal Memo on Advertising Practices—Continued

May 28, 1992
Page 2

Under these circumstances, Jim Johnston, Dave Iauco, Ernie Fackelman and I have concluded that it would be in our long-term best interests to join the ranks of our competitors and limit our advertising and marketing efforts to smokers 21 years of age and older. We don't believe for a minute that this will silence our adversaries in their attempts to misrepresent our motives or the effect of our advertising. We do feel that it will blunt this point of attack and provide us with a three year "cushion" that can be used in response to claims that we're after the underage market.

Since all of our direct marketing, sampling and most of our promotional activities are already limited to 21 and above, what this means, as a practical matter, is the following:

1. All brand positioning statements that currently reflect audiences below the age of 21 should be revised to reflect audiences which are 21 or older.

2. All of our advertising agencies that are currently working on brands/styles with audiences below 21, should be promptly advised that the audience has been revised to 21 or above and that any work-in-progress should, to the extent necessary, be revised to reflect this repositioning.

3. Marketing Research conducted with the purpose of developing our marketing elements (product, packaging, promotion, advertising) or enhancing the appeal of these elements will be conducted only among smokers 21 and above.

4. Research conducted to understand and track the cigarette category and the performance of our brands and those of our competitors can continue to be conducted among all adult (18+) smokers.

5. Our internal advertising review panel should be advised of this policy immediately and instructed to factor it into its work.

6. While our policy already prohibits our advertising in publications directed primarily to those under 21, I would suggest that we also take this opportunity to review our media list.

Please ensure that all our marketing materials/activities conform with this policy as soon as practicable.

James C. Schroer

:jt

cc: J.W. Johnston
E.J. Fackelman
D.N. Iauco

EXHIBIT 5 RJR Internal Memo on Advertising Practices, April 10, 1990

Source: *MN Tobacco Document Depository. Bates TE 14 00836; MN Trial Exhibit AM002637.*

April 10, 1990

TO: All Field Sales Employees

It is our long-standing and firmly-held view at R.J. Reynolds Tobacco Company that smoking is an adult custom. Our policy is to promote and market our products only to adult smokers, primarily those who smoke competitive brands.

It has come to our attention that our current sales strategy against Marlboro was misinterpreted in one of our 166 sales divisions. As a result, our sales representatives in that division were apparently asked to identify retail calls near high schools for the purpose of maintaining ongoing promotions in these stores.

Actions of this nature are in clear violation of our policy and will not be tolerated. Corrective action has been taken in the involved division. Once again, I want to reinforce our policy that we promote our products only to adult smokers.

Retail stores near high schools should be given no special emphasis and should be worked with the normal course of frequency and with the same programs you would give any other similar outlet, regardless of location.

Please give this matter your immediate attention and high priority.

Sincerely,

Yancey W. Ford, Jr.
Executive Vice President – Sales

EXHIBIT 6 **Research on the Use of Cartoon Characters to Advertise Adult Products and Their Effect on Children and Youth**

Journal of the American Medical Association (JAMA)

Pierce et al., 1991. "Does Tobacco Advertising Target Young People to Start Smoking? Evidence from California." In this study, a telephone survey of adults and teenager asked, "What brand do you usually buy?" and "Think back to the cigarette advertisements you have seen recently on billboards or in magazines. What brand of cigarette was advertised the most?" Both the adults and teenagers said Marlboro was the most advertised followed by Camel. Marlboro and Camel purchases dominated sales for 12- through 17-year-old male smokers, but the study found market share for these brands declined steadily with increasing age. The study concluded that changes in market share resulting from advertising occur mainly in younger smokers and that cigarette advertising encourages youth to smoke and should be banned.

Fisher et al., 1991. "Brand Logo Recognition by Children Age 3 to 6 Years—Mickey Mouse and Old Joe the Camel." In this study, children were shown brand logos for children's products, cigarette brands, and adult brands. The highest recognition was for the Disney Channel (91.7 percent). Joe Camel was recognized by 51.1 percent of children, about the same as for Chevrolet and Ford. In addition, recognition of Joe Camel was positively correlated with age. The study concluded that even though cigarettes were not being advertised on TV and although the children studied were prereaders, environmental tobacco advertising such as billboards and movie placements still influenced children.

DiFranza et al., 1991. "RJR Nabisco's Cartoon Camel Promotes Camel Cigarettes to Children." In this study high school students and adults were shown pictures and ads containing Joe Camel and asked to identify the product being advertised. Children were more likely than adults to recognize Joe Camel. Children also were more likely to think the advertisements looked "cool" and want to be friends with Joe Camel. When asked for their brand preference, Camel was given as the preferred brand by 32.8 percent of children up to age 18 who smoked versus 23.1 percent for ages 19 and 20 and 8.7 percent of smokers 21 and over. The study concluded that the Joe Camel cartoon ads succeeded far better at marketing Camel cigarettes to children than to adults.

Journal of Advertising

Henke, 1995. "Young Children's Perceptions of Cigarette Brand Advertising Symbols: Awareness, Affect and Target Market Identification." This study assessed whether recognition of cigarette brand symbols was related to children's liking and evaluation of cigarettes. When asked whether they liked or disliked the product, 96 percent of the children reported they disliked cigarettes. When asked whether cigarettes were "good for you" or "bad for you," 97 percent said cigarettes were "bad for you."

Journal of Marketing

Mizerski, 1995. "The Relationship between Cartoon Trade Character Recognition and Attitude toward Product Category in Young Children." In this study, 3- to 6-year-old children were asked to match cartoon trade characters such as Joe Camel and Tony the Tiger with products; then were asked if they liked or disliked the products. Mizerski found that recognition increased with age but liking of cigarettes decreased with age. For children's products in contrast, recognition and liking both increased with age.

Part 2

Corporate Values: Looking Inward

Moving from the personal values which are brought to bear in a business context, Parts 2 and 3 introduce a broader platform of moral concerns as we focus on the values and responsibilities of corporations as entities.

The issue of corporate values and social responsibility is not new. Ever since Adam Smith speculated on the possible social benefits which might result from the butcher's, brewer's, and baker's pursuit of self-interest, the moral responsibility that should be attached to economic activity has remained problematic for society. Managers and the general public alike continue to ask such questions as what constitutes the ethical way of doing business, what constraints should properly be imposed on self-interest and by whom, and how far a corporation should extend the range of constituencies to whom it is held responsible.

To complicate matters further, the unit of economic activity has shifted fundamentally since Smith's day—from the individual to the institution—and a host of laws and internal policies concerning the responsibility of and for economic activity has been generated to respond to this organizational reality. From a legal standpoint, the corporation is regarded as an entity whose actions are subject to civil and criminal sanctions. From a managerial standpoint, the corporation's several responsibilities can be generalized and therefore articulated into policy. On this view, the corporation is capable of personification and of having a set of values in much the same way that an individual businessperson has certain standards of conduct for daily work life.

In Parts 2 and 3, we present two series of cases in which corporations as entities have embraced, either implicitly or explicitly, values and responsibilities to guide the decisions of all their members. The moral questions that arose in Part 1 with regard to personal values have not disappeared, but a new level of moral inquiry—the institutional level—is introduced.

The cases in Part 2 involve corporate values of an *inward-looking sort*, in which individual responsibility and institutional pressures are brought into sharp focus around such questions as the following: From where should the values that influence managerial discretion come? How do institutional values relate to the individual rights and responsibilities of employees? Can meaningful distinctions be drawn between an executive's personal and professional life? Is the corporation, like Emerson's vision of institutions, "the lengthened shadow of one man," or should it accommodate a variety of personal philosophies and styles? It is the nature and legitimacy of moral authority within corporations that is often at stake in these cases.

We have subdivided the cases in Part 2 under two headings, those dealing primarily with corporate governance issues and those dealing primarily with employee rights and interests.

The four cases that comprise "The Corporate Scandals of 2002," as well as "An Introduction to the Sarbanes-Oxley Act," provide a gateway into a number of corporate governance challenges posed by Enron, Arthur Andersen, WorldCom, Tyco, and others during the first few years of the new millennium. "A Brief Note on Corporate Ethics Officers" helps the reader understand a relatively young profession in the realm of corporate governance: the ethics officer. This profession came into existence with the November 1991 Federal Sentencing Guidelines for Organizations, which were revised in 2004. This note also includes a summary of the 1977 Foreign Corrupt Practices Act, which is also a key piece of business legislation for senior leaders.

"American Refining Group, Inc. (A)" is a case that challenges the ethical leadership skills of the reader through the eyes of the CEO and chief operating officer of a medium-sized Pennsylvania oil refining company. They have decided to do a companywide self-assessment using the tools described in an article in Appendix B, "Corporate Self-Assessment and Improvement: A Baldrige Process for Ethics?"

A look at the interplay between individual integrity and corporate policy is provided in "H. J. Heinz Company: The Administration of Policy (A) and (B)." These two cases take up a problem of questionable or illegal financial reporting practices and explore the manner in which corporate policies can affect executives' behavior. Implicit in the Heinz cases, again, is the impact of the corporation's culture on individual decision makers.

"The Individual and the Corporation" opens the second set of cases in Part 2 focusing on employee issues—where the employee in this case is a senior manager. Nowhere is the issue of individual rights versus a manager's responsibility to protect the well-being of the corporation more starkly presented than in this classic case. The narrative describes an article, written by an executive, concerning the assassination of John F. Kennedy and the possible impact of that article on its author's company. Although the case was written almost 40 years ago, the issues that it raises continue to be important today.

The Lex case series ("Developing the Guidelines," "Closing Portsmouth Depot," "Work Conditions at Inglesby Shipyard," and "The Reading Pallets Theft") moves from corporate governance issues to employee issues as it examines the development of a set of ethical guidelines for top management. The first case in the series presents the historical and cultural rationale for such an undertaking, the guidelines themselves, and some of the conflicting opinions which Lex's senior managers have about the whole idea. The follow-up cases present three management problems that occurred during the first year after the guidelines were adopted.

"Reell Precision Manufacturing, Inc.: A Matter of Direction (A)" presents us with one of the most difficult conundrums in American social life as we embrace the 21st century. Reell has been successful for years partly because it was built on a strong culture, a culture that takes seriously values normally associated with Judeo-Christian faith. But its very success has led to growth, and growth has led to the presence of a number of employees who do not share the company's core beliefs. How do the leaders (and founders) of the company maintain its "soul" while being respectful of the consciences of all employees? In matters of maintaining culture and avoiding discrimination, must the common denominator prevail?

Employee issues continue to be examined in "FBS, Incorporated: Ethics and Employee Investments" as the HR director of the firm must decide how much education employees deserve as they move to a defined contribution retirement plan from a defined benefit retirement plan. Is the company obligated to provide support when retirement funds are managed by the employees themselves?

Employee Internet privacy and employee rights under the 1990 Americans with Disabilities Act are the themes in two case modules: "Waterbee Toy Company (A)" and "Webster Health Systems (A)." The first case is accompanied by "Note on E-Mail, Internet Use, and Privacy in the Workplace," the second by "Note on the Americans with Disabilities Act." In the Waterbee case, a tension develops between privacy and sexual harassment. In the Webster case, the ADA seems to clash with employee discipline when alcohol is a central factor.

These cases and notes provide a fitting conclusion to Part 2—on the inward-looking dimensions of corporate values—and at the same time a transition to Part 3, in which the outward-looking dimensions of those values in society are the primary focus.

The Corporate Scandals of 2002 (A): *Enron, Inc.*

The tragic consequences of the related-party transactions and accounting errors were the result of failures at many levels and by many people: a flawed idea, self-enrichment by employees, inadequately-designed controls, poor implementation, inattentive oversight, simple (and not so simple) accounting mistakes, and overreaching in a culture that appears to have encouraged pushing the limits.

"Report of Investigation,"
Special Investigative Committee,
Board of Directors of Enron Corp.,
William C. Powers, Jr., Chair,
February 1, 2002

Company History

Enron was formed in 1985, the product of a merger between Houston Natural Gas and Omaha, Nebraska–based InterNorth, Inc. The merger integrated the companies' natural gas networks, yielding a system of nearly 37,000 miles of pipeline. Kenneth L. Lay, the former head of Houston Natural Gas, was named Enron's chairman and chief executive officer in 1986.

Aided by market deregulation, Enron quickly expanded beyond natural gas transmission. While continuing to enlarge its pipeline system and building power plants around the world, Enron began trading natural gas commodities in the late 1980s. In 1994 it entered the electricity trading business, eventually becoming the largest marketer of wholesale electricity in the United States. Enron established a broadband services division in 1999 that would come to manage over 14,000 miles of fiber optics lines across the United States. That same year it created an Internet-based trading floor for commodities. It quickly became the largest e-business site in the world, handling more than $880 billion worth of transactions.[1] Enron also formed Azurix, a water management firm, and a division that provided energy management services to corporate customers.

By the end of the 1990s, more than 80 percent of Enron's earnings were generated from what it termed "wholesale energy operations and services." The firm's revenues and profits skyrocketed during the decade. In 1990, Enron recorded revenues of $5.5 billion and a net income of $202 million. By 2000 it had become the seventh largest corporation in the United States, booking revenues of roughly $101 billion—more than double that of the year before—and $979 million in profits. The company's 2000 annual report highlighted the cumulative total returns from its stock, which over the previous ten years were nearly four times those attained by the S&P 500.

Enron's success in radically changing the energy industry, coupled with its impressive financial performance, earned it numerous accolades from the popular business press. For example, *Fortune* magazine named it America's most innovative company six consecutive years. In summer 2001, one observer praised Enron as the paradigmatic "new economy" company:

> A quote from Gary Hamel and C.K. Prahalad's book *Competing for the Future* provides a useful framework for new economy companies like Enron . . . "To be a leader, a company must take charge of the process of transformation." Enron has been at the forefront of change in the energy industry since its formation in 1985—and more recently it has been an active agent for change in the broadband communications and the global e-commerce industries.[2]

This note was prepared from public materials by Research Associate T. Dean Maines under the supervision of Kenneth E. Goodpaster, Koch Professor of Business Ethics, University of St. Thomas.

[1] Rebecca Smith and John R. Emshwiller, "Enron Replaces Fastow as Finance Chief," *Wall Street Journal* 25 Oct. 2001: A3. *Dow Jones Factiva*, Charles J. Keffer Library, Minneapolis, MN, 3 Mar. 2003 (global.factiva.com).

[2] Margaret M. Carson, "Enron and the New Economy," *Competitiveness Review* 11,2 (2001): 1.

Jeffrey Skilling and Andrew Fastow

Enron provided young managers with the opportunity to quickly assume high-profile, highly compensated positions. In February 2001, 48-year-old Jeffrey Skilling, Enron's president since 1997, succeeded Lay as chief executive. A graduate of Harvard Business School, Skilling had joined Enron in 1990 after previously advising the firm as a consultant with McKinsey & Company. Tom Peters, a former McKinsey colleague, described Skilling as someone "who could out-argue God."[3] Andrew Fastow, Skilling's long-time colleague and friend, served as Enron's chief financial officer (CFO). Named CFO at the age of 36, Fastow had obtained an MBA from the Kellogg School of Management at Northwestern University in 1986, joining Enron shortly after Skilling. In 1999 *CFO* magazine awarded Fastow their CFO Excellence Award for capital structure management.

Skilling envisioned Enron as a nimble, "asset-light" organization, where hard assets like pipelines and power plants would take a backseat to intellectual capital and risk management. Fastow engineered Enron's transformation into a service and trading-based company by developing a financial engine that would spur the company's growth:

> As CFO, Fastow became a master of off-balance-sheet financing, a tactic that companies in capital-intensive industries use to avoid carrying debt on their books. For years, the energy industry had used partnerships to finance drilling and build pipelines. For example, an oil company that wanted to drill a group of wells would form a partnership. Investors would put money into the partnership in exchange for a share of the profits from the wells. The company, as general partner, would contribute the leases and oversee the drilling and completion of the wells. The arrangement enabled oil companies to drill wells without taking debt onto their books for the financing. . . .
>
> Enron needed capital as it expanded internationally and tried to exploit deregulated energy markets. In 1990, it had been primarily a regulated pipeline company with about $3.5 billion in assets. By 1999, its assets were worth $35 billion. . . . Taking on debt would have jeopardized the company's credit rating and impaired its ability to grow. . . . Fastow's solution was to establish partnerships that would hold and sell such assets as power plants and pipelines. In some cases, Enron capitalized the partnerships with notes that were convertible into shares of Enron stock. Enron would get the cash up front and continue managing the assets.[4]

Skilling and Fastow were highly intelligent, confident to the point of cockiness, inventive, and impatient with traditional business disciplines. Skilling was known to deride fund managers and analysts who would question the firm's performance during investor conference calls, and in the late 1990s he reportedly told a conference of utility executives that Enron was preparing to "eat their lunch."[5] While Fastow maintained a much lower profile than Skilling, he had a reputation for prickliness and for bullying Enron executives who disagreed with his positions. Investment bankers bristled at his condescending attitude and the "we're smarter than you guys" attitude projected by members of his finance organization.[6]

The Enron Culture

As Skilling and Fastow rose within the company, they remade the organization in their image. A banner hanging in the lobby of its Houston headquarters proclaimed Enron "The World's Leading Company." There was a sense of excitement within the firm as Skilling's self-described pioneers looked for new ways to make money in energy and commodity markets. One former employee described Enron as a company filled with people "energized to change the world"; the ambiance was "electric."[7] Another recalled the firm's atmosphere as "intoxicating . . . if you loved business,

[3] April Witt and Peter Behr, "Dream Job Turns into a Nightmare," *Washingtonpost.com* 29 July, 2002, 2 July, 2004 (www.washingtonpost.com/ac2/wp-dyn/A14229-2002jul28).

[4] Loren Steffy, "Andrew Fastow, Mystery CFO," *Bloomberg Markets* Jan. 2002: 41.

[5] Bethany McLean, "Why Enron Went Bust," *Fortune* 24 Dec. 2001: 58. *Expanded Academic ASAP Plus*, Charles J. Keffer Library, Minneapolis, MN, 14 Feb. 2003 (web2.infotrac.gale group.com).

[6] "The Fall of Enron," *BusinessWeek* 17 Dec. 2001: 30. *Expanded Academic ASAP Plus*, Charles J. Keffer Library, Minneapolis, MN, 14 Feb. 2003 (web2.infotracgalegroup.com).

[7] Jodie Morse and Amanda Bower, "The Party Crasher," *Time* 30 Dec. 2002: 52. *Expanded Academic ASAP Plus*, Charles J. Keffer Library, Minneapolis, MN, 14 Feb 2003.

and loved being challenged and working with unique, novel situations . . . it was the most wonderful place."[8]

Yet there was a shadow side to the company's culture. While Enron invested heavily in young talent, hiring over 200 high-potential MBAs each year, internal competition was harsh. It was exacerbated by a forced ranking system—informally referred to as "rank and yank"—in which those rated in the bottom 20 percent were moved out of the company. The process damaged morale and led employees to undermine one another. "People tried to take work away from you," one employee remembered. "There was a Darwinism for ideas, for projects." One utility executive described Enron's culture as "kill-and-eat."[9]

Compensation practices were so lucrative that one former executive described Enron as "giddy with money."[10] Some employees reaped tremendous bonuses under a program that paid them up to 3 percent of the value of major commercial transactions they engineered. In 2000 alone Enron paid $750 million in cash bonuses, or nearly 72 percent of its reported earnings for the year. Since the bonuses were payable when the deal was struck, deal makers were effectively encouraged to inflate projected returns. Furthermore, such transactions were treated as sacrosanct. While legal, accounting, and risk management reviews were mandated for proposed ventures, the oversight system frequently was circumvented. At times Enron employees and employees of the firm's external auditor, Arthur Andersen, would attempt to slow the review process, to permit appropriate vetting. Those who did so regularly found themselves reassigned to other duties.[11]

[8] Peter Behr and April Witt, "Visionary's Dream Led to Risky Business," *Washingtonpost.com* 28 July 2002, 2 July 2004 (www.washingtonpost.com/ac2/wp-dyn/A9783-2002jul27).

[9] David Barboza, "Victims and Champions of a Darwinian Enron," *New York Times on the Web* 12 Dec. 2001:C5.

[10] Behr and Witt, "Visionary's Dream."

[11] Tom Fowler, "The Pride and Fall of Enron," *Houston Chronicle* 20 Oct. 2002, 18 Feb. 2003 (www.chron.com/cs/CDA/printstory.hts/special/enron/1624822).

A Resignation . . . and Questions

In August 2000, Enron's stock price reached an all-time high of $90.56. One year later, on August 14, 2001, Jeff Skilling abruptly resigned as CEO. At the time of Skilling's resignation, Enron stock was trading under $40. Share price had eroded steadily throughout 2001, the result of several factors. First, the end of the technology boom had impacted Enron's performance. The company's broadband unit failed to grow as predicted, a situation exacerbated by the March cancellation of a proposed venture with Blockbuster to provide on-demand home video services. Second, confidence in the firm's prospects wavered when Enron disclosed in April that bankrupt Pacific Gas & Electric owed it $570 million. Third, investors were troubled by the deteriorating quality of Enron's earnings. Enron's operating margin had fallen from approximately 5 percent in early 2000 to under 2 percent one year later, and its return on invested capital hovered at just 7 percent.[12] Fourth, concerns about the firm's financial health were heightened by aggressive employee stock sales. Enron executives still held a large portion of the firm's equity; however, key insiders disposed of over 1.75 million shares during the first nine months of 2001, selling even as the stock's value fell.[13] Finally, the complexity of Enron's finances and its lack of transparency also contributed to its diminished stature among analysts and investors. A *Fortune* article published after Skilling's resignation described their growing impatience:

> Enron's financials are on the dim side of opaque. While Wall Street was once willing to take the company's word on financial performance, it no longer is. And because Enron gives analysts so little to work with, building independent models is next to impossible. Enron's major business, the trading and marketing of energy, is relatively new and extremely complicated. Seemingly basic questions—like the effects of lower natural gas prices and less volatility in the energy markets on Enron's profits—are still unanswered. And there's confusion about the relationship between Enron's reported earnings, which reflect changes

[12] McLean, "Why Enron Went Bust."

[13] Bethany McLean, "Enron's Power Crisis," *Fortune* 17 Oct. 2001:48. *Expanded Academic ASAP Plus*, Charles J. Keffer Library, Minneapolis, MN, 14 Feb. 2003 (web2.infotrac.galegroup.com).

> in the value of its energy-trading portfolio, and the actual cash coming in. In the first half of the year, Enron reported net income of $810 million and cash flow from operations of negative $1.3 billion.[14]

Ken Lay immediately reclaimed Enron's chief executive office in the wake of Skilling's departure. To bolster morale, Lay planned an all-employee meeting for August 16, asking firm members to submit comments and questions beforehand. His request prompted Sherron Watkins, a 41-year-old Enron vice president, to pen an anonymous one-page memorandum (Exhibit 1). Watkins had worked for a time within Enron's broadband division. When that organization was downsized in spring 2001, she accepted a position working for Fastow, helping identify Enron assets that were candidates for divestment. Her memorandum to Lay addressed aggressive accounting practices associated with unconsolidated entities designated "Condor" and "Raptor." Watkins noted that Skilling's resignation would place a spotlight on Enron, and the company's handling of some partnership transactions might cause it to "implode in a wave of accounting scandals."

Special-Purpose Entities and the Raptors

The Raptors continued a financial strategy pioneered by Enron in 1999. During the late 1990s, the company invested $10 million in an organization called Rhythms NetConnections. Enron's stake in the firm inflated to $300 million in the second quarter of 1999. Securities restrictions prevented Enron from immediately selling the stock. But it could—and did—treat the paper gain as a profit, a windfall that exceeded Enron's net income from operations for the period. Skilling wanted to protect the gain. Wall Street firms could provide such protection; however, the stock was so risky that no company would offer a hedge on acceptable terms.

Skilling's and Fastow's solution was to form a special-purpose entity (SPE) in the Cayman Islands. The SPE would contain capital from both Enron and external investors. To qualify as an independent entity—and thus remain off Enron's books—outside parties needed to hold a minimum 3 percent stake in the partnership. If the value of the Rhythms NetConnections stock fell, the SPE would issue payments to cover Enron's loss. This permitted Enron to "lock in" the gain from its investment and exempted it from a mandated disclosure of any subsequent deterioration in the value of its Rhythms NetConnections stake. The arrangement called for Fastow to serve as the SPE's general manager. He named the partnership LJM1, after his wife and two children. Enron's board approved the proposed plan in late June 1999 and ratified a determination by the Office of the Chairman that Fastow's role as LJMl's general manager would not adversely affect Enron's interests. Fastow eventually raised $15 million from outsiders and contributed $1 million of his own money to LJM1. Enron contributed $276 million in stock.

The success of LJM1 prompted Skilling and Fastow to propose the formation of LJM2. LJM2 would provide a large reserve of private equity. Enron could tap this fund to quickly create partnerships that would purchase assets held by its business units or hedge risky investments. As with LJM1, Fastow would serve as LJM2's general manager. Enron's board considered the proposal in October 1999. It stipulated two conditions for approval. First, Enron and LJM2 would not be obliged to do business with one another. Second, LJM2's transactions with Enron would be subject to special scrutiny. Each transaction had to be approved by Richard Causey, Enron's chief accounting officer, and Richard Buy, its chief risk officer. In addition, the board's Audit and Compliance Committee would annually review all transactions completed in the prior year. Obtaining agreement on these conditions, the board authorized Fastow to form LJM2, waiving relevant portions of the company's code of ethics. A later company investigation would conclude that the controls mandated by the board "were not rigorous enough, and their implementation and oversight was inadequate at both the Management and Board levels."[15]

Fastow obtained external capital commitments to LJM2 of nearly $400 million. Limited partners in LJM2 included American Home Assurance Co., the Arkansas Teachers Retirement System, and the McArthur Foundation. Fastow also encouraged

[14] McLean, "Enron's Power Crisis."

[15] William C. Powers, Jr., Raymond S. Troubh, and Herbert S. Winokur, Jr., "Report of Investigation by the Special Investigative Committee of the Board of Directors of Enron Corp.," 1 Feb. 2002: 10.

Enron's Wall Street banking partners to invest in LJM2; J.P. Morgan Chase & Co., Citigroup Inc., and Merrill Lynch & Co all did so. It later would be revealed that Fastow had made future Enron business contingent upon these placements.[16]

The Raptors were four SPEs formed in spring 2000. They hedged Enron's investments in two "new economy" companies: Avici, a network-equipment supplier, and New Power, an energy retailer. If Avici's or New Power's stock dropped in value, payments from the Raptors would make up Enron's losses. LJM2 fulfilled the outside funding requirement for the Raptors by placing $120 million with the entities.[17] Enron contributed $2 billion in stock.

The Raptors protected nearly $1 billion in profit that Enron had already reported.[18] Enron had repaid LJM2's initial investment in the Raptors within six months, supplemented by $40 million in profit. This left only Enron stock or stock pledges in the partnership. As a result, the Raptors were not truly independent and thus should have been consolidated into Enron's financial statements. The repayment also meant that Enron was hedging itself and bearing the entire risk of the investments in Avici and New Power. If Enron's share price fell below $20, its obligation to the Raptors would become so great that Enron could not afford to sustain the partnerships.

A few insiders voiced concerns about the Raptors and Fastow's involvement with the LJM partnerships. Jeff McMahon, Enron's treasurer, complained to Skilling about Fastow's conflict of interest. Soon thereafter, Fastow confronted McMahon. Fastow told McMahon that he "should have known anything said to Skilling would get back to him."[19] A week later, Skilling encouraged McMahon to assume a new role within Enron. When McMahon accepted, Skilling appointed Ben Glisan, one of Fastow's closest aides, to the treasury post. Stuart Zisman, a relatively new member of Enron's legal department, reviewed the Raptors in mid-2000 to develop a legal risk assessment. Zisman described Enron's transactions with Raptor as "cleverly designed." He concluded the Raptors represented a significant risk for Enron, and they "might lead one to believe that the financial books at Enron are being manipulated." After consulting with more senior Enron attorneys and receiving a reprimand from his boss for the critical language in his report, Zisman shifted his position.[20]

Quarterly and annual reports by Enron acknowledged the existence of the LJM partnerships. However, the disclosures were confusing and failed to communicate the substance of the transactions between the partnerships and the company. One analyst complained that "we read the disclosures over and over and over again, and we just didn't understand it—and we read footnotes for a living."[21] Enron did not explicitly report Fastow's involvement with the partnerships. For example, its 2000 annual report simply noted that the company had "entered into transactions with limited partnerships . . . whose general partner's managing member is a senior officer of Enron."[22] Nor was mention made of Fastow's financial interest in the partnerships. However, an offering memorandum for LJM2 identified Fastow as its general manager and noted that his interests would be aligned with investors' because the "economics of the partnership would have significant impact on the general partner's wealth."[23]

Two of the Raptors began to falter in late 2000, as Avici's stock price fell and payments to Enron came due. Enron accountants restructured the entities so that the solvent Raptors covered the debt of the failing ones. This prevented the company from having to book a loss in excess of $500 million. However, the solution provided only temporary relief. By March 2001 the Raptors' instability had been compounded by Enron's falling stock price. This led to a second restructuring and the infusion of an additional $800 million of Enron stock. Neither Enron's

[16] Behr and Witt, "Visionary's Dream."

[17] Witt and Behr, "Dream Job."

[18] Behr and Witt, "Concerns Grow amid Conflicts," *Washingtonpost.com* 30 July 2002, 2 July 2004 (www.washingtonpost.com/ac2/wp-dyn/A18876-2002jul29).

[19] Behr and Witt, "Visionary's Dream."

[20] Behr and Witt, "Visionary's Dream."

[21] Cassell Bryan-Low and Suzanne McGee, "What Enron's Financial Reports Did—and Didn't—Reveal," *Wall Street Journal* 5 Nov. 2001: Cl. *Dow Jones Factiva*, Charles J. Keffer Library, Minneapolis, MN, 14 Mar. 2003 (global.factiva.com).

[22] Enron Corporation, *2000 Annual Report*, 48.

[23] John Emshwiller and Rebecca Smith, "Enron Jolt: Investments, Assets Generate Big Losses," *Wall Street Journal* 17 Oct. 2001: Cl. *Dow Jones Factiva*. Charles J. Keffer Library, Minneapolis, MN, 19 Feb. 2003 (global.factiva.com).

board nor the investment community was notified of the actions.[24]

As concerns about Fastow's role in the LJM partnerships mounted during early 2001, Skilling moved to address the issue. Skilling gave Fastow the choice of being Enron's CFO or running LJM, but told him he could not continue in both positions. Fastow chose Enron and in July sold his interest in LJM to a close Enron associate, Michael Koppers. Koppers left Enron to take over as the leader of the partnership.[25]

"Enron Prep"

Enron's external auditor, Arthur Andersen, enjoyed close ties with the company. A number of Andersen partners were housed within Enron's Houston headquarters. Approximately 90 Andersen employees had left the firm to work for Enron since 1989, earning the auditor the nickname "Enron Prep." Causey, himself an ex-Andersen staffer, characterized the relationship as a collaboration in which Andersen "gets all the documents and they walk down the path with Enron all the way."[26]

When the Raptors got into trouble in March 2001, the Andersen audit team for Enron had approved their restructuring. In doing so, it had overruled Andersen's Professional Service Group, an internal review board whose rulings on complex or questionable transactions were supposed to carry the day. After examining the proposed solution, this senior panel had concluded the restructuring violated accounting rules.[27]

Investigating an Employee's Concerns

Sherron Watkins did not have a complete portrait of the Raptors' history when she penned her anonymous note to Lay on August 15, 2001. However, she was aware that some Enron employees, including McMahon, had voiced concerns and that the company would need to inject an additional $250 million in the third quarter of 2001 to keep the Raptors solvent. Soon after composing the anonymous note, Watkins identified herself as its author and requested a meeting with Lay. The two conferred on August 22.

At that meeting, Watkins presented the CEO with a six-page memorandum detailing her concerns. This longer document dwelled at length on the Raptor transactions. In discussing one of the Raptors, Watkins stated the "basic question" she could not answer:

> The related party has lost $500 mm in its equity derivative transactions with Enron. Who bears that loss? I can't find an equity holder that bears that loss. Find out who will lose this money. Who will pay for this loss at the related party entity . . . If it's Enron, from our shares, then I think we do not have a fact pattern that would look good to the SEC or investors.

Lay promised to review the Raptors. However, he ignored Watkins's advice and chose Vinson & Elkins, a law firm headquartered in Houston, to perform the review. Like Andersen, Vinson & Elkins had developed a close working relationship with Enron. Members of the Houston business community joked that the firm's real name was "Vinson & Enron." A number of former Vinson & Elkins attorneys now practiced as members of Enron's internal legal staff.[28] More importantly, Vinson & Elkins had worked on some of the Raptor transactions.[29]

A team of Vinson & Elkins attorneys interviewed a number of people connected to the Raptors, including Watkins, Fastow, and David Duncan, the Arthur Andersen partner in charge of the Enron audit team. Fastow dismissed the concerns raised by Watkins. Duncan assured the investigators that while some of the accounting that had troubled Watkins looked questionable, it satisfied technical requirements and "unique control features" were in place to protect Enron.[30]

On October 15, the day before Enron was to announce its third quarter results, Vinson & Elkins issued a nine-page report on its investigation. It concluded that "the facts disclosed through our

[24] Tom Fowler, "Partnerships' Practices May Have Been Illegal," *Houston Chronicle* 9 Feb. 2002, 5 Mar. 2003 (www.chron.com/cs/CDA/printstory.hts/special/enron/1247866).

[25] Behr and Witt, "Visionary's Dream."

[26] Behr and Witt, "Concerns Grow."

[27] Behr and Witt, "Concerns Grow."

[28] Michael Sean Quinn, "Enron, Andersen, and the Temptations of the Byzantinely Clever," Energy Law Institute for Attorneys and Landmen, South Texas College of Law, 15–16 Aug. 2002: E-24.

[29] Michael Duffy, "What Did They Know and . . . When Did They Know It?" *Time* 28 Jan. 2002: 16. *Expanded Academic ASAP Plus.* Charles J. Keffer Library, Minneapolis, MN, 14 Feb. 2003 (web2.infotrac.galegroup.com).

[30] Behr and Witt, "Concerns Grow."

preliminary investigation do not, in our judgment, warrant a further widespread investigation by independent counsels and auditors."[31] However, the report noted that Raptor transactions suffered from "bad cosmetics"—that is, there would be a "serious risk of adverse publicity and litigation" if they became the subject of a "*Wall Street Journal* exposé or class action lawsuit."[32]

Cleaning the Raptors' Nest

The terrorist attacks on September 11, 2001, killed more than 3,000 people and forced Wall Street to suspend trading until September 17. When the markets reopened, stock prices plummeted. On September 18, Enron shares closed at $28.08, just $8 above the $20 level at which the Raptors would become unsustainable. That day Lay acted on the advice of Causey and decided to shut down the Raptors. The decision required Enron to take an after-tax charge of $544 million for its third quarter, which would end September 30. Enron also needed to take special charges for Azurix and its broadband services group. These expanded the total write-off for the quarter to $1.01 billion after taxes.

The company also needed to announce a $1.2 billion reduction in shareholder equity, the result of an accounting error. The fault had been Andersen's. When Enron had injected additional stock into the partnership in March 2001, it had received a note in return. Andersen had wrongly advised Enron to treat the note as shareholder equity.[33] The error had come to light during an Andersen review of the Raptors' restructuring that had been conducted in August. The restatement would reverse this mistake.

Enron was scheduled to announce its quarterly results on October 16. On October 12, company officials sent an advance copy of its press release to Andersen for review.[34] The draft did not mention the equity reduction. It referred only obliquely to the Raptors and LMJ, mentioning "certain structured finance arrangements with a previously disclosed entity." It also characterized the $1.01 billion in losses as a one-time, "non-recurring charge." Andersen partners objected to this phrasing:

> In their view, some of the losses were just the opposite—indications that core parts of Enron's business were not doing well. Shareholders had to be told, the auditors maintained. Duncan warned Causey that the SEC had taken action against companies for similarly misleading statements.[35]

Duncan wrote a memo to the file on October 16 outlining his conversation with Causey and documenting his warning.[36] The press release was unchanged.

Lay gave an upbeat prognosis for Enron during a conference call with analysts on October 16. Consistent with the press release, he emphasized that, aside from the special charge, profits for the quarter had risen 26 percent compared with the previous year. Lay described the $1.01 billion write-off as part of an effort to "find anything and everything that was a distraction and was causing a cloud over the company." He mentioned the reduction in shareholder equity but provided no details. The analysts who participated in the call seemed satisfied with Lay's explanations. Enron's stock rose in trading on Wall Street, ending the day at nearly $34.

The next morning, the *Wall Street Journal* ran an article highlighting that Enron's losses were connected to partnerships run by Fastow and raising questions about Fastow's conflicting roles.[37] A second article about Enron's third quarter results appeared in the *Journal* on October 18. It focused on the reduction in shareholder equity, which, in response to reporters' questions, the company had explained as a decision to repurchase 55 million of its shares:

> Enron downplayed the significance of the share-reduction exercise. Mark Palmer, an Enron spokesman, described it as "just a balance-sheet issue" and therefore wasn't deemed "material" for disclosure purposes.
>
> Jeff Dietrat, an analyst for Simmons & Co. in Houston, said that a large reduction in equity could be "a flag for the rating agencies" because it could adversely affect a company's debt-to-equity ratio. Enron said yesterday that as a

[31] Vinson & Elkins, LLP, "Preliminary Investigation of Allegations of an Anonymous Employee," 15 Oct. 2001: 8.

[32] Vinson & Elkins, LLP, "Preliminary Investigation," 8.

[33] April Witt and Peter Behr, "Losses, Confiicts Threaten Survival," *Washingtonpost.com* 31 July 2002, 2 July 2004 (www. washingtonpost.com/ac2/wp-dyn/A23653-2002jul30).

[34] Witt and Behr, "Losses, Conflicts."

[35] Witt and Behr, "Losses, Conflicts."

[36] Witt and Behr, "Losses, Conflicts."

[37] Emshwiller and Smith, "Enron Jolt."

> result of the equity reduction its debt-to-equity ratio rose to 50 percent from 46 percent previously.
>
> On Tuesday, after Enron reported its big quarterly loss, Moody's Investors Services Inc. put Enron's long-term debt on review for a possible downgrade . . . Enron, which as of June 30 had $33.6 billion in current liabilities and long-term debt, has lately been attempting to shed assets to pay down debt.[38]

A third *Journal* article appeared on Friday, October 19. Drawing on a recent quarterly report sent to LJM2 investors, the story reported that Fastow had earned millions as the general partner for LJM. His total earnings, including capital gains, were unclear. The article also pointed to evidence in the quarterly report that some transactions had helped LJM2 at Enron's expense.[39] Enron's stock price dropped for the third consecutive day, closing at just over $26 a share. The company had lost nearly $6 billion of market value since October 17.

The Death Spiral

The following week opened on a sour note for Enron. On Monday, October 22, the company disclosed that it was the subject of a preliminary inquiry launched by the Securities and Exchange Commission (SEC) into Fastow's apparent conflict of interest. The company's stock price fell an additional 20 percent on the news, ending the day at $20.65.

Two days later, Lay announced that Jeff McMahon had replaced Fastow as Enron's chief financial officer. The announcement came just 24 hours after Lay had given Fastow votes of confidence during a conference call with securities analysts and at a large meeting of Enron employees. A press release stated that Fastow had been placed on a leave of absence. According to the release, the move had been prompted by discussions with investors and analysts. What it failed to mention was that Enron's board had finally discovered how much Fastow had earned from his involvement with the LJM partnerships. In an interview with the head of the board's compensation committee, Fastow admitted to making $45 million.[40]

Wall Street reacted to the news by dropping Enron's share price an additional 17 percent, to $16.41. Trading volumes suggested that institutional investors were taking steps to reduce their holdings in the company.[41] Concerns about an Enron death spiral were now beginning to be heard within the financial community. One Goldman Sachs analyst suggested that Enron needed to disclose more information about its transactions with related partnerships and entities. He noted that Enron was facing a problem of "trust and credibility. It's not easy to regain something as basic as trust."[42]

On October 25 Enron drew $3 billion from its credit lines. That same day, the credit rating agency Fitch announced that it was reviewing Enron for a possible downgrade, while Standard & Poor's changed Enron's credit outlook from stable to negative.[43] A *Wall Street Journal* article noted that Enron's involvement with energy trading required the firm to carefully manage liquidity. It also pointed out that should the company's credit rating ever fall below investment grade, the company would default on obligations involving billions of dollars of borrowings.[44]

A week later, Enron disclosed that the SEC had upgraded its inquiry to a formal investigation.[45] This meant that the SEC's enforcement branch had obtained formal subpoena power to pursue its review of Enron's dealings with various

[38] Rebecca Smith and John R. Emshwiller, "Partnership Spurs Enron Equity Cut," *Wall Street Journal* 18 Oct. 2001: Cl. *Dow Jones Factiva*, Charles J. Keffer Library, Minneapolis, MN, 19 Feb. 2003 (global.factiva.com).

[39] Rebecca Smith and John R. Emshwiller, "Enron's CFO's Partnership Had Millions in Profit," *Wall Street Journal* 19 Oct. 2001: Cl. *Dow Jones Factiva*. Charles J. Keffer Library, Minneapolis, MN, 14 Mar. 2003 (global.factiva.com).

[40] Witt and Behr, "Losses, Conflicts."

[41] Rebecca Smith and John R. Emshwiller, "Enron Replaces Fastow as Finance Chief," *Wall Street Journal* 25 Oct. 2001: A3. *Dow Jones Factiva*. Charles J. Keffer Library, Minneapolis, MN, 14 Mar. 2003 (global.factiva.com).

[42] Smith and Emshwiller, "Enron Replaces."

[43] John R. Emshwiller, Rebecca Smith, and Jathon Sapsford, "Enron Taps $3 Billion from Bank Lines in Pre-emptive Move to Ensure Liquidity," *Wall Street Journal* 26 Oct. 2001: C1. *Dow Jones Factiva*, Charles J. Keffer Library, Minneapolis, MN, 14 Mar. 2003 (global.factiva.com).

[44] Emshwiller, Smith and Sapsford, "Enron Taps."

[45] John Emshwiller and Rebecca Smith, "Enron Partnerships Led by Fastow Face a Formal SEC Investigation," *Wall Street Journal* 1 Nov. 2001: A4. *Dow Jones Factiva*, Charles J. Keffer Library, Minneapolis, MN, 14 Mar. 2003 (global.factiva.com).

parties. Enron also announced that it had added the dean of the University of Texas Law School, William Powers, to its board of directors, and that Powers would head a board committee charged with investigating company transactions with the partnerships headed by Andrew Fastow.

On November 1, Enron secured $1 billion in new credit lines from J.P. Morgan Chase and Citigroup, pledging its prime gas-pipeline assets as collateral. However, Standard & Poor's also announced that it was following an earlier action by Moody's and downgrading the company's debt.[46] Enron's stock price dropped 14 percent on the news, to $11.91.

In a filing submitted to the SEC on November 8, Enron admitted that it had improperly accounted for dealings with additional partnerships run by company officers. These partnerships, named Chewco and Joint Energy Development Investments (JEDI), had recently become the focus of investigative reporters: Three days earlier, the *Wall Street Journal* ran an article describing the partnerships and the involvement of both Fastow and Michael Koppers with them.[47] Enron's filing stated that Chewco should have been consolidated into Enron's financial statement beginning November 1997; that JEDI should have been consolidated beginning January 1997; and a third entity, related to LJM1, should have been consolidated beginning in 1999. In each case, the consolidation was required because the stake of external investors had fallen below the 3 percent threshold. Their retroactive inclusion required Enron to lower its reported net earnings since 1997, eliminating $586 million, or nearly 20 percent of its profits. In addition, it necessitated an increase in the company's debt for the same period by hundreds of millions and a reduction of shareholder equity by an incremental $1 billion. The filing also stated that Enron had discharged Ben Glisan, the company's treasurer, and Kristina Mordaunt, general counsel of Enron's North America unit, in connection with their investments in one of the partnerships. By the close of trading, Enron shares had fallen to $8.41.

On November 9, both Moody' s and Standard & Poor's downgraded Enron's debt to one notch above junk-bond status. That same day, Enron and Dynergy, Inc., announced an agreement to merge the two companies.[48] Dynergy was a Houston-based independent power producer and energy trading company. It had long operated in Enron's shadow, and was little known outside the energy industry. The merger would combine the two organizations under the Dynergy name. Chuck Watson, Dynergy's founder and chief executive, would head the new firm. Since the proposed merger would require a lengthy regulatory review, Dynergy and its major investor, ChevronTexaco Corp., had pledged to infuse $1.5 billion into Enron. In return, Enron pledged a large pipeline network as collateral. The merger agreement also included a $60 million buyout of Lay's contract. However, Lay announced he would forgo the buyout after it was made public on November 13.

Enron filed its third quarter financial report with the SEC on November 19. The report contained two significant revelations. First, Enron disclosed that a $690 million loan, due to be settled in two years, might now have to be paid within weeks because of the downgrading of its credit rating ten days earlier. This obligation was incremental to the nearly $3.9 billion in debt whose repayment would accelerate if Enron's credit rating dropped to junk status. Second, Enron's filing showed that the company had run through more than $1.5 billion in cash since announcing the merger with Dynergy. Part of this outflow had resulted from Enron's energy trading contracts. Contract provisions required the trading parties to make up-front cash deposits if their credit rating was lowered. In the past, the stipulation had worked in Enron's favor; it now worked against the company.[49]

Watson was surprised by both the disclosure of the $690 million debt and Enron's heavy cash outflow. He met with Lay to discuss the revelations, but announced that he had come away

[46] Rebecca Smith, "Enron Gets $1 Billion New Credit Line, But Must Pledge Top Gas-Pipeline Assets," *Wall Street Journal* 2 Nov. 2001: A4. *Dow Jones Factiva*, Charles J. Keffer Library, Minneapolis, MN, 14 Mar. 2003 (global.factiva.com).

[47] John R. Emshwiller, "Enron Transaction with Entity Run by Executive Raises Questions," *Wall Street Journal* 5 Nov. 2001. *Dow Jones Factiva*. Charles J. Keffer Library, Minneapolis, MN, 24 Nov. 2004 (global.factiva.com).

[48] Peter Behr and April Witt, "Hidden Debts, Deals Scuttle Last Chance," *Washingtonpost.com* 1 Aug. 2002, 2 July 2004 (www.washingtonpost.com/ac2/wp-dyn/A28822-2002jul31).

[49] Behr and Witt, "Hidden Debts, Deals."

unsatisfied with Lay's answers.[50] Enron disputed Watson's account of the conversations, but by November 21 it was clear that Dynergy was seeking to renegotiate the terms of the $7 billion merger. Enron shares closed that day at $5.

Over the next week, Dynergy and Enron officials met outside New York City to attempt to rescue the merger. As time passed, reports on their discussions grew increasingly pessimistic. On November 28, Standard & Poor's reduced Enron's credit rating to non-investment graded.[51] Later that day, Dynergy announced that the merger was off. Enron shares dropped from $4.11 to 61 cents. On December 2, Enron filed for bankruptcy protection from its creditors under Chapter 11.

The Toll

One legacy of the company's implosion was the toll it took on its shareholders and employees. Measured from the pinnacle of a share price of $90 in August 2000, Enron's fall destroyed more than $60 billion in investment value, $19 billion alone in the 24-day period between October 16 and November 8. Much of what was wiped out had been held by middle-class Americans in mutual funds and retirement accounts. Enron's employees lost an estimated $1.2 billion in retirement funds. In the immediate wake of the bankruptcy, over 25 percent of its 20,000-person workforce was laid off. Enron's failure also helped catalyze the demise of Arthur Andersen, which put thousands of Andersen employees on the street in 2002.

Another legacy was the serial legal saga that began in 2002 as criminal charges were brought against the lead players in the drama. Michael Koppers pleaded guilty to conspiracy charges on August 21, 2002, admitting he had funneled millions of dollars to Andrew Fastow through an intricate set of financial schemes. Fastow himself was indicted on 78 counts in October 2002 and an additional 20 counts seven months later. In January 2004 he pleaded guilty to two charges, and agreed to serve ten years in prison. Fastow also agreed to forfeit approximately $24 million and claims on an additional $6 million held by third parties. On September 10, 2003, Ben Glisan pled guilty to one count of conspiracy. He became the first Enron executive to be jailed. In February 2004 Richard Causey pleaded not guilty to five counts of security fraud and one count of conspiracy. That same month Jeff Skilling was indicted on 35 counts, including wire fraud, securities fraud, conspiracy, insider trading, and making false statements on financial reports. He pleaded not guilty to all charges. And in late June 2004 reports began to surface that federal prosecutors would shortly press charges against Ken Lay.[52]

[50] Behr and Witt, "Hidden Debts, Deals."

[51] Behr and Witt, "Hidden Debts, Deals."

[52] Mary Flood, "Prosecutors Seeking Lay Indictment," *Houston Chronicle* 20 June 2004, 2 July 2004 (www.chron.com/cs/CDA/printstory.mpl/front/2635540).

EXHIBIT 1 Sherron Watkin's Anonymous Memorandum to Kenneth Lay (August 15, 2002)

Source: Houston Chronicle.

Dear Mr. Lay,

Has Enron become a risky place to work? For those of us who didn't get rich over the last few years, can we afford to stay?

Skilling's abrupt departure will raise suspicions of accounting improprieties and valuation issues. Enron has been very aggressive in its accounting—most notably the Raptor transactions and the Condor vehicle. We do have valuation issues with our international assets and possibly some of our EES MTM positions.

The spotlight will be on us, the market just can't accept that Skilling is leaving his dream job. I think that the valuation issues can be fixed and reported with other goodwill write-downs to occur in 2002. How do we fix the Raptor and Condor deals? They unwind in 2002 and 2003, we will have to pony up Enron stock and that won't go unnoticed.

To the layman on the street, it will look like we recognized funds flow of $800 mm from merchant asset sales in 1999 by selling to a vehicle (Condor) that we capitalized with a promise of Enron stock in later years. Is that really funds flow or is it cash from equity issuance?

We have recognized over $550 million of fair value gains on stocks via our swaps with Raptor, much of the stock has declined significantly—Avici by 98 percent, from $178 mm to $5 mm, the New Power Co by 70 percent, from $20/share to $6/share. The value in the swaps won't be there for Raptor, so once again Enron will issue stock to offset these losses. Raptor is an LJM entity. It sure looks to the layman on the street that we are hiding losses in a related company and will compensate that company with Enron stock in the future.

I am incredibly nervous that we will implode in a wave of accounting scandals. My 8 years of Enron work history will be worth nothing on my résumé, the business world will consider the past successes as nothing but an elaborate accounting hoax. Skilling is resigning now for "personal reasons" but I think he wasn't having fun, looked down the road and knew this stuff was unfixable and would rather abandon ship now than resign in shame in 2 years.

Is there a way our accounting guru's can unwind these deals now? I have thought and thought about how to do this, but I keep bumping into one big problem—we booked the Condor and Raptor deals in 1999 and 2000, we enjoyed a wonderfully high stock price, many executives sold stock, we then try and reverse or fix the deals in 2001 and it's a bit like robbing the bank in one year and trying to pay it back 2 years later. Nice try, but investors were hurt, they bought at $70 and $80/share looking for $120/share and they're at $38 or worse. We are under too much scrutiny and there are probably one or two disgruntled "redeployed" employees who know enough about the "funny" accounting to get us in trouble.

What do we do? I know this question cannot be addressed in the all employee meeting, but can you give some assurances that you and Causey will sit down and take a good hard objective look at what is going to happen to Condor and Raptor in 2002 and 2003?

The Corporate Scandals of 2002 (B): *Arthur Andersen LLP*

Audit failure has an illustrious history that long precedes Enron and long precedes consulting. The problem is and ever was the audit relationship itself . . . Unlike the other Big Five, [Andersen] allowed partners working directly with clients to overrule the accounting cardinals in the home office on matters of accounting theology. Unlike the other Big Five, it had gone through a messy and costly divorce with its own consulting arm, now known as Accenture, and had reason to cling more desperately to its auditing clients . . . instead of doing what any smart firm would have done and sending a SWAT team to take over the Houston office soon after Enron erupted, it satisfied itself with sending ambiguous memos reminding staff of the firm's "document retention" policies. Voila, an accounting scandal compounded by document shredding.

Holman W. Jenkins,
"Too Bad for Andersen,
but Good for Accounting,"
Wall Street Journal, May 1, 2002

Origins

The firm that would become Arthur Andersen & Co. opened for business on December 1, 1913, in Chicago, Illinois. Its founder, the 28-year-old son of Norwegian immigrants, was a professor of accounting at Northwestern University. Arthur Andersen envisioned an organization that would move beyond routine bookkeeping and provide "the designing and installing of new systems of financial and cost accounting and control."[1] He also envisioned a firm whose defining characteristic would be ethical integrity.

Andersen set the tone for the company during its infancy. Just months after launching his new venture, he was confronted by the president of a local railroad. The executive angrily demanded the approval of a transaction that would inflate the railroad's profits by improperly recording expenses. Andersen, struggling to meet the next payroll, responded that there was "not enough money in the city of Chicago to make him approve the bad bookkeeping."[2] The president fired Andersen. A few months later the railroad went bankrupt, vindicating Andersen's stance and gaining his firm a reputation for courage and independence.

Andersen preached that auditors ultimately were responsible to the investing public, and independent thinking was crucial to the fulfillment of this trust. "To preserve the integrity of the reports, the accountant must insist upon absolute independence of judgment and action," he insisted in a lecture on ethics at Northwestern's School of Commerce.[3] Andersen's emphasis upon honest accounting and the elimination of conflicts of interest helped restore the American public's

This note was prepared from public materials by Research Associate T. Dean Maines under the supervision of Kenneth E. Goodpaster, Koch Professor of Business Ethics, University of St. Thomas.

[1] Delroy Alexander, Greg Burns, Robert Manor, Flynn McRoberts, and E. A. Torriero, "The Fall of Andersen," *Chicago Tribune Online Edition* 1 Sept. 2002, 26 July 2004 (www.chicagotribune.com/business/showcase/chi-0209010315sep01, 1,1676300.story).

[2] Alexander, Burns, Manor, McRoberts, and Torriero, "Fall of Andersen."

[3] Alexander, Burns, Manor, McRoberts, and Torriero, "Fall of Andersen."

trust in business after the stock crash of 1929 and the ensuing economic depression.

Andersen also believed that auditors who did not sugarcoat their opinions would gain clients' respect.[4] His approach was epitomized by an old Scandinavian saying he had learned from his mother: "Think straight, talk straight." Over time, generations of new Andersen accountants would repeat this phrase as they learned "the Andersen way." They also were schooled in the firm's four cornerstones: Provide good service to clients; produce quality audits; manage staff well; and produce profits for the firm.[5]

Auditors *and* Consultants, Auditors *versus* Consultants

Arthur Andersen died in 1947. In 1950, his vision of a company that both audited and sold solutions to accounting problems was realized when his namesake firm introduced a small computer called the "Glickiac." Developed by an Andersen engineer named Joseph Glickauf, the Glickiac demonstrated the advantages of automated bookkeeping. Glickauf used the device to convince General Electric to automate its payroll. Now Andersen was not only auditing ledgers, but also showing companies how to use technology to strengthen their accounting and control systems. Glickauf's three-person administrative services team proved to be the forerunner of Andersen's consulting practice.

In 1979, Andersen became the world's largest professional services firm. That year 42 percent of Andersen's $645 million in worldwide revenues came from consulting and tax work; in the United States, more than half of its fees came from nonaudit services.[6] But the growth of Andersen's and other accounting firms' consulting practices raised concerns: Regulators worried that consulting income would compromise auditor independence, making it more difficult for them to reject questionable accounting practices uncovered within companies that were also consulting customers. That same year the Securities and Exchange Commission (SEC) implemented a directive requiring publicly traded companies to disclose the amount and percentage of their auditor's fees that came from consulting.[7]

The success of the Andersen's consultants further accelerated during the 1980s. This exacerbated tensions within the partnership:

> Under rules set by the auditors who ran the firm, all of the profits from all the practice areas had to go into one big pot to be divided among partners. But since the average consultant brought in more money than the average auditor, the consulting side complained the arrangement was unfair.
>
> The week after New Year's Day in 1989, at a world-wide meeting of the firm in Dallas, the consultants finally made their break. They won an agreement to separate into two units—Arthur Andersen and Andersen Consulting—under a Geneva-based parent company known as Andersen Worldwide SC. But more importantly, the accounting side agreed to make the profit-sharing more equitable.[8]

The new profit sharing formula bred fierce competition between the accounting and consulting units. For the former, the overarching goal became maintaining high auditing standards while aggressively boosting sales and profits. However, cost-cutting led to numerous early retirements, resulting in fewer accounting partners to oversee audits. Furthermore, accounting partners increasingly were pushed to "develop practice," that is, to win new clients or elicit new fees from established clients.[9] A split developed within the audit practice between "merchants"—the partners skilled in bringing in revenues—and "samurai"—partners with a strong sense of professional honor and duty. Many audit employees balked at the emerging culture, which seemed to promote "auditor-salespeople":

> J. Paul Boyer, the former marketing director for the Columbus office of Arthur Andersen,

[4] Alexander, Burns, Manor, McRoberts, and Torriero, "Fall of Andersen."

[5] Ken Brown and Ianthe Jeanne Dugan, "Andersen's Fall from Grace Is a Tale of Greed and Miscues," *Wall Street Journal*, 7 June 2002: A6.

[6] Alexander, Burns, Manor, McRoberts, and Torriero, "Fall of Andersen."

[7] This directive was repealed in January 1982, after the SEC concluded the disclosure was of insufficient value to investors to justify its continuation.

[8] Brown and Dugan, "Andersen's Fall from Grace," Al.

[9] Alexander, Burns, Manor, McRoberts, and Torriero, "Fall of Andersen."

> remembers chatting one day with a senior auditor. The man was indignant at how the firm had changed. "I came to Arthur Andersen to be an auditor, not a salesman," he told Boyer. "When I have to start selling, I'm leaving." Boyer thought to himself, "Should I start planning your going-away party?"[10]

The new emphasis on revenue growth and profitability led some accounting partners to joke that the company's four cornerstones had become "three pebbles and a boulder."[11]

Even as the auditors' status fell and the pressure to produce financially increased, another troublesome trend manifested itself: The growing disconnection between Andersen's leadership and its top accounting experts. For decades, a small group of Andersen's most experienced technical experts—know as the Professional Standards Group (PSG)—had steered the organization through complicated questions of ethics, law, and regulation. Their final determinations on such questions were considered definitive by Andersen auditors. As the firm's ethical watchdog, the PSG was viewed as the keeper of a company culture that had set the benchmark for integrity in public accountancy. Members of the PSG worked in Andersen's Chicago headquarters, a locale which gave them immediate access to its managing partners and other senior officials. However, during the early 1990s a physical separation emerged when the partnership's new head chose to remain in New York City. Over time, organizational distance increased as well: By 2001, there were seven layers of management between Andersen's top partner and the PSG's leader.[12]

Charting a Course Alone

In December 1997 Andersen's consulting partners voted to split off entirely from Andersen Worldwide, creating a separate firm called Accenture. With the loss of its consulting unit looming, a new strategy was introduced in 1998 to help Arthur Andersen make up the revenue it was about to lose. Called "2X," it required partners to match the dollar volume of the work they managed inside their practice area with twice that volume in unrelated work. Thus, a partner responsible for $3 million in external audit fees would be expected to bring in $6 million from other services. A revised performance management system established the 2X revenue target as a critical expectation for partner evaluations.[13]

The 2X strategy emerged during a period when Andersen's structure was becoming decentralized, with power increasingly placed in the hands of local offices. Their leaders—"office managing partners"—had their own revenue targets. The PSG also was becoming more decentralized. Several members of the PSG had been dispersed from the partnership's headquarters into local offices, to improve support for Andersen auditors and clients.[14]

One response to the 2X strategy was to convince clients to outsource their internal audit function, a tactic Andersen had introduced during the early 1990s. The approach was not without its critics. Former SEC chairman Arthur Levitt warned that the practice would result in accounting firms checking their own work and would lead to a deterioration of audit quality.[15] Andersen's relationship with Enron Corporation, an audit client since 1986, provided an opportunity for an early pilot test. In 1994 Andersen signed a five-year, $18 million contract with Enron to take over the energy trader's internal auditing.[16]

Andersen and Enron

Andersen enjoyed close ties with Enron. Since 1989, roughly 90 Andersen employees had left the firm to work for Enron, including Richard Causey, Enron's chief accounting officer. Andersen and Enron employees worked together and socialized

[10] Delroy Alexander, Greg Burns, Robert Manor, Flynn McRoberts, and E. A. Torriero, "Civil War Hits Andersen," *Chicago Tribune Online Edition* 2 Sept. 2002, 26 July 2004 (www.chicagotribune.com/business/showcase/chi-0209020071sep02,1,2003981.story).

[11] Brown and Dugan, "Andersen's Fall from Grace," A6.

[12] Alexander, Burns, Manor, McRoberts, and Torriero, "Fall of Andersen."

[13] Brown and Dugan, "Andersen's Fall from Grace," A6.

[14] Brown and Dugan, "Andersen's Fall from Grace," A6.

[15] Brown and Dugan, "Andersen's Fall from Grace," A6.

[16] Delroy Alexander, Greg Burns, Robert Manor, Flynn McRoberts and E.A. Torriero, "Ties to Enron Blinded Andersen," *Chicago Tribune Online Edition* 3 Sept. 2002, 26 July 2004 (www.chicagotribune.com/business/showcase/chi-0209030210sep03,1,627722.story).

together. The 1994 outsourcing arrangement intertwined the companies even more tightly:

> [Andersen] hired Enron's entire team of 40 internal auditors, added its own people, and opened an office in Enron's Houston headquarters that was as big as some regional Arthur Andersen offices. With more than 150 people on-site, Andersen staff attended Enron meetings and helped shape new businesses, according to current and former Andersen and Enron employees.[17]

The Enron account presented Andersen with a significant opportunity. However, Enron proved to be a difficult and volatile client:

> . . . Enron's finance staff was on the phone nearly every day, demanding that Andersen auditors sign off on some transaction. "They would call you on a Friday night and say they needed an answer by Saturday," said Warren White, a former Andersen partner in the Houston office. "We were having midnight conferences with them."
>
> If Andersen accountants objected, they would get on the phone with their Enron counterparts and call Andersen's Chicago headquarters, seeking the advice of senior partners. The conference calls would stretch for hours, with Andersen staffers flipping through financial documents and policy statements, finding ways to appease Enron.
>
> The marathon sessions would pressure Andersen staffers to view accounting issues Enron's way—if only to get home. White and his co-workers knew what Enron wanted and usually sought to give it to them.
>
> "You would try to find ways to do it," White recalled. "We all knew they were the largest single client in the Houston office."
>
> When Enron didn't like the advice it got from Andersen, the company would press to get the answer it wanted.[18]

Enron eventually became so powerful that it was able to dictate which Andersen partners could oversee its account. Carl Bass, a PSG member working in Andersen's Houston office, was removed from day-to-day troubleshooting on the Enron account in early 2001 after he had objected to the accounting treatment of several Enron transactions and began to raise questions about Enron's use of special-purpose entities and partnerships. When Bass requested reinstatement, David Duncan, Andersen's lead partner on the Enron account, felt compelled to consult with Richard Causey before making the move. Causey denied the request.[19]

An Error, Shredders, and a Subpoena

Periodic client assessments undertaken within Andersen had identified the Enron engagement as one of the firm's riskiest.[20] On February 5, 2001, 14 senior partners met via teleconference to discuss whether the company should be retained as a client. Specific issues discussed included Enron's aggressive accounting practices and the conflicting responsibilities of Andrew Fastow, who served as both Enron's chief financial officer and the general manager of a set of partnerships that did business with the energy trader. The partners also considered whether the Enron account created an independence issue for the firm. During 2000, Andersen had received more than $58 million in auditing and consulting fees; and the partners noted that these revenues could grow to over $100 million. Ultimately, they decided to continue the relationship, since the "appropriate people and processes [are] in place to serve Enron and manage our engagement risk."[21] In March of 2001, the "Raptors"—a set of special-purpose entities that protected nearly $1 billion in Enron profit—faced insolvency, necessitating their restructuring. The proposed restructuring was brought to the attention of the PSG, which studied the transactions and concluded they violated accounting rules. However, Duncan and his staff overruled the PSG's finding, and approved the action.[22]

In the late spring Andersen's reputation suffered two blows. In May, the firm's leadership approved a

[17] Brown and Dugan, "Andersen's Fall from Grace," A6.

[18] Alexander, Burns, Manor, McRoberts, and Torriero, "Ties to Enron."

[19] Alexander, Burns, Manor, McRoberts, and Torriero, "Ties to Enron."

[20] Alexander, Burns, Manor, McRoberts, and Torriero, "Ties to Enron."

[21] Michael D. Jones, e-mail to David B. Duncan, 6 Feb. 2001.

[22] Peter Behr and April Witt, "Concerns Grow amid Conflicts," *Washingtonpost.com* 30 July 2002, 2 July 2004 (www.washingtonpost.com/ac2/wp-dyn/A18876-2002jul29).

$110 million payment to Sunbeam Corporation shareholders. During the early 1990s Andersen auditors had signed off on Sunbeam's financial statements even after an Andersen auditor allegedly uncovered fraudulent transactions. The payment settled shareholder litigation without accepting or denying blame. The next month Andersen agreed to pay a $7 million SEC fine for allowing another client, Waste Management, Inc., to overstate its pretax profits by over $1 billion between 1993 and 1996. Again, Andersen neither admitted nor denied blame; however, the SEC placed the firm under a cease-and-desist order, enjoining it from further complicity in accounting abuses.

In August 2001, Enron chief executive Jeffrey Skilling resigned after only six months on the job. Skilling's resignation placed Enron under a microscope. Although the company had continued to report profits throughout 2001, its share price had dropped from almost $91 to under $40 in less than a year. Chairman and former CEO Kenneth Lay took over Skilling's duties, but by late September Enron's financial infrastructure had started to unravel. Lay decided to shut down the Raptors on September 18. The decision required the company to take an after-tax charge of $544 million for the third quarter of 2001. Other write-offs inflated the total charge for the quarter to $1.01 billion after taxes.

On October 9, Andersen lawyer Nancy Temple was briefed on the Enron situation. The magnitude of Enron's special third quarter charge likely would focus attention on the Raptor partnerships and the problematic accounting that had revived them earlier in 2001. Correcting the accounting would require a restatement of Enron's first quarter earnings. This would trigger an SEC inquiry into the firm's accounting practices and disclose information that regulators could use to accuse Andersen of violating the June cease-and-desist order. On Friday, October 12, Temple e-mailed Houston staff members reminding them to destroy extraneous memorandums, drafts, and e-mails, consistent with the partnership's document retention policy. Her note set off a weekend of shredding.[23]

On October 12, Enron officials sent the Andersen staff a draft copy of its third quarter earnings announcement. The advance copy characterized the $1.01 billion loss as a one-time, "nonrecurring" charge. Andersen previously had insisted that Enron not employ the term *nonrecurring* in SEC filings. It also had privately advised Enron against using the phrase in earnings announcements because of the potential to misguide investors. Andersen partners objected to the term's use in the third quarter release because they believed some of the losses indicated weaknesses in core parts of Enron's business. Duncan notified Causey of Andersen's concerns on October 14, underscoring that the SEC had taken action against companies for similarly misleading statements. He reiterated his position a day later. Causey assured Duncan that the draft was under review. However, when the announcement was issued on October 16, "nonrecurring" appeared in its title.

That day Duncan prepared a file memorandum documenting his warnings to Causey. He sent Temple a draft of the document. Temple replied later that evening. She suggested that Duncan tone down the memo, deleting "language that might suggest we have concluded the release is misleading."[24] She also suggested that he delete references to consultations with Andersen lawyers and her name specifically. "Reference to the legal group consultation arguably is a waiver of attorney-client privileged advice," Temple stated, "and if my name is mentioned it increases the chances that I might be a witness, which I prefer to avoid."[25] Temple promised to consult with other Andersen lawyers about "whether we should do anything more to protect ourselves from potential Section 10A issues."[26] That portion of the Securities and Exchange Act required auditors to notify the audit committee of a client's board once an illegal act was uncovered. Failure to do so could result in SEC sanctions.[27]

On October 22, Enron disclosed that it was the subject of a preliminary inquiry by the SEC. The next morning, Duncan and other members of the Andersen staff listened to a tumultuous teleconference between Lay and stock analysts. After lunch Duncan called together Andersen's entire Enron team, to brief them on the developing situation. He

[23] Behr and Witt, "Concerns Grow."

[24] Nancy A. Temple, e-mail to David B. Duncan, 16 Oct. 2001.

[25] Nancy A. Temple, e-mail to David B. Duncan, 16 Oct. 2001.

[26] Nancy A. Temple, e-mail to David B. Duncan, 16 Oct. 2001.

[27] Jonathan Weil, Alexei Barrionuevo, and Cassell Bryan-Low, "Andersen Win Lifts U.S. Enron Case," *Wall Street Journal*, 17 June 2002, p. A10.

told the staff that Andersen would likely have to aid an SEC investigation into Enron. He also directed them to comply with the firm's document retention policy. The meeting set off a flurry of housecleaning in Houston and other Andersen offices where Enron-related materials resided. Within three days, approximately 30,000 e-mails and computer files had been deleted. A ton of documents was shredded, more than the quantity that typically would be discarded in a single year.[28] Questions of what should be shredded recurred throughout the exercise, which ended on November 9 when Andersen received a federal subpoena.[29]

Increased Scrutiny and a Trial

On November 8, Enron admitted that it had improperly accounted for dealings with several partnerships run by its officers. The company restated its results from 1997 onward to adjust for these errors. The restatement eliminated $586 million in profits, reduced shareholder equity by $1 billion, and added hundreds of millions in debt to its balance sheet. Four weeks later, Enron filed for bankruptcy protection from its creditors.

Scrutiny of Andersen intensified in the wake of Enron's collapse. On December 12, Joseph Berardino, Andersen Worldwide's chief executive, testified before a subcommittee of the U.S. House of Representatives investigating the energy trader's fall. In early January 2002, Andersen agreed to allow House investigators to review Enron-related information housed in Houston. However, a routine clerical check of computer files revealed a massive purge of e-mails even as the congressional team was preparing for its visit. Andersen disclosed the document destruction on January 10. It also formally notified the Justice Department and the SEC of its finding; suspended its document retention policy, telling employees to retain all Enron-related material; and waived its attorney-client privilege to all internal communications related to document purges that took place prior to November 9.

Andersen announced the firing of David Duncan on January 15. Its press release stated that "based on our actions today, it should be perfectly clear that Andersen will not tolerate unethical behavior, gross errors in judgment, or willful violations of our policies."[30] Two days later, Enron fired Andersen as its auditor.

Following the defection of several prominent clients in early February, Andersen announced an internal program of reform. The firm hired Paul Volcker, former chairman of the Federal Reserve Bank, to chair an independent oversight board. The board was vested with authority to remodel the partnership, including the power to overrule its senior management. Within a few weeks, Volcker's group issued a report that called for Andersen to drop all practice lines except external auditing. Volcker suggested that the move might serve as a model for the reform of the entire accounting profession.[31] But the oversight board never had an opportunity to implement its recommendations.

On March 7, federal prosecutors indicted Andersen on a felony charge of obstructing justice in investigations related to Enron. The indictment stated that "Andersen, through its partners and others, did knowingly, intentionally, and corruptly persuade and attempt to persuade . . . Andersen employees" to "withhold records, documents, and other objects . . . from regulatory and criminal proceedings" and "alter, destroy, mutilate, and conceal objects with the intent to impair the objects' integrity and availability for use in such official proceedings."[32] The indictment sparked a flurry of client departures. It also prompted Andersen partners in China, Russia, Australia, and New Zealand to defect to competitors. Berardino resigned under pressure on March 26.

Opening arguments in Andersen's trial were heard on May 7. The prosecution's key witness was David Duncan. Duncan had been personally indicted on an obstruction of justice charge,

[28] Alexander, Burns, Manor, McRoberts, and Torriero, "Ties to Enron."

[29] Alexander, Burns, Manor, McRoberts, and Torriero, "Ties to Enron."

[30] Delroy Alexander, Greg Burns, Robert Manor, Flynn McRoberts, and E. A. Torriero, "Repeat Offender Gets Stiff Justice." *Chicago Tribune Online Edition* 4 Sept. 2002, 26 July 2004 (www.chicagotribune.com/business/showcase/chi-0209040368sep04,17312410.story).

[31] Alexander, Burns, Manor, McRoberts, and Torriero, "Repeat Offender."

[32] *United States of America v. Arthur Andersen, LLP* (news.findlaw.com/hdocs/docs/enron/usandersen030702ind.pdf).

but agreed to cooperate with prosecutors in exchange for a possible reduced sentence. While the prosecution portrayed the partnership as a repeat offender that destroyed records to shield itself from potential regulatory punishment, Andersen's defense lawyers argued that the firm had retained all important documents and that prosecutors were misrepresenting normal company practices on the basis of insinuation and vague testimony.

On June 15, the jury found Andersen guilty of one count of obstruction of justice. The jurors had discounted evidence of massive document destruction by Andersen, focusing instead on Nancy Temple's October 16 e-mail to Duncan. They reasoned that Andersen knew Enron's characterization of the $1.01 billion charge to its third quarter earnings as "nonrecurring" was misleading. When Enron ignored its advice, Andersen altered documents to hide its knowledge from the regulators. By advising Duncan to edit his file memo at the critical juncture in time, Temple had served as a "corrupt persuader." The identification of that one incident was sufficient to convict Andersen on the charge.

By law, the SEC cannot accept corporate financial statements that have been audited by a felon. Thus, Andersen's conviction effectively put the firm out of the audit business in the United States. On July 16, Andersen notified the SEC that it would surrender its practice licenses effective August 31, 2002.

The Toll

A commentator on Andersen's trial noted that in convicting the firm all the jury did was "pull the plug" on a dying organization: Even prior to the trial's start, Andersen had been slowly disintegrating. Its U.S. workforce had dropped from 26,000 employees to 10,000 in less than six months. In April the steady flow of Andersen's international partners to competitors was matched by a similar movement within the United States, when a large block of tax partners and professionals announced plans to join rival Deloitte & Touche. On May 8, Deloitte disclosed it would hire an additional 2,000 Andersen employees, and KPMG stated it would acquire part or all of as many as 23 of Andersen Worldwide's member firms. Ernst & Young and Grant Thornton also purchased slices of the organization.

During 2001 Andersen had recorded $9.5 billion in revenues, derived from services supplied to 2,300 clients. By the end of the firm's trial, over 700 of its clients had taken their business elsewhere. As 2002 unfolded, scandals involving other Andersen audit clients—WorldCom, Global Crossing, and Qwest—also came to light. Arthur Andersen had hoped the firm which bore his name would be known for ethical integrity. In a twist of fate, it had become synonymous with failed auditing.[33]

As Andersen wound down its operations, others debated the ultimate lesson from its prosecution. At a time when increased corporate transparency was viewed as necessary to restore public trust in American business, some feared Andersen's conviction would discourage companies from becoming more forthcoming about their activities:

> Some Andersen rivals say the case has caused them to redouble efforts to audit companies scrupulously. Still, that may not be the message that many would-be corporate criminal defendants take away from the trial. One unintended result of the Andersen prosecution may be that white-collar criminal-defense attorneys urge their corporate clients to button up after discovering potential wrongdoing by their personnel. Soon after learning of last fall's widespread shredding in Houston, Andersen's top outside lawyers advised firm executives to disclose all they knew to the Justice Department. Andersen agreed to waive its attorney-client privilege to almost all internal material related to document destruction through November 9, when the firm's shredding ceased.
>
> Andersen put itself at the mercy of the government. Prosecutors then used Andersen's own documents to indict the firm, after the two sides were unable to work out a settlement under which Andersen wouldn't have to plead guilty to a crime. Ultimately, it wasn't what the firm shredded that got it convicted, but what it turned over to the government.[34]

[33] Alexander, Burns, Manor, McRoberts, and Torriero, "Civil War."

[34] Weil, Barrionuevo, and Bryan-Low, "Andersen Win," A10.

The Corporate Scandals of 2002 (C): *WorldCom, Inc.*

From 1999 until 2002, Worldcom suffered one of the largest public accounting frauds in history . . . [T] he fraud occurred as a result of knowing misconduct directed by a few senior executives centered in its Clinton, Mississippi headquarters, and implemented by personnel in its financial and accounting departments in several locations. The fraud was the consequence of the way WorldCom's Chief Executive Officer, Bernard J. Ebbers, ran the Company. Though much of this Report details the implementation of the fraud by others, he was the source of the culture, as well as much of the pressure, that gave birth to this fraud.

"Report of Investigation," Special Investigative Committee, Board of Directors of WorldCom, Inc., March 31, 2003

Company History

The company that eventually became WorldCom was founded in 1983 by Mississippi businessmen Murray Waldron and William Rector. Originally named LDDS, it was envisioned as a discount reseller of long-distance communications services. LDDS began operations the following year when it sold its first minute of long distance to the University of Southern Mississippi. Bernie Ebbers, an early investor in LDDS, was named the company's president in 1985.

Under Ebbers' leadership, LDDS experienced phenomenal growth. In 1988 the company initiated a series of acquisitions and mergers that transformed it into a regional telecommunications powerhouse and, eventually, a national one. In 1994 LDDS entered the global communications market by acquiring IDE Communications. One year later the company's name was changed to WorldCom, with Ebbers serving as chief executive officer.

The firm's growth-by-acquisition strategy continued throughout the late 1990s. To assemble an integrated package of services for its customers, WorldCom began to target data communications providers. In 1996 the company purchased the global Internet leader UUNET Technologies, Inc. This gave WorldCom a worldwide communications network and the capacity to offer businesses a comprehensive set of Internet solutions.

The scale of WorldCom's expansion was more than matched by the growth of its profitability. In 1996, WorldCom reported revenues of $5.6 billion and an operating income of $896 million—a six-fold increase over the company's 1992 profits. Ebbers won praise in the popular business press for his attentiveness to shareholder value:

> Over ten years, ending in 1996, WorldCom averaged an annual return to shareholders of 53%. Only one company, Oracle Corp., had a higher average return. WorldCom stock—now trading at a whopping 90 times earnings—gives Ebbers the cheap source of capital to do his [deals]. He also has a tidy personal stake, some 14 million shares worth about $500 million. In April [1997] Ebbers bought 1 million shares on the open market. "I'd say his interests are certainly aligned with shareholders'," says David M. Leach, head of the compensation consulting practice at Compensation Resource Group Inc.[1]

The pace of WorldCom's acquisitions and mergers made it difficult for analysts to evaluate accurately the company's financial state. This task

This case was prepared from public materials by Research Associate T. Dean Maines under the supervision of Kenneth E. Goodpaster, Koch Professor of Business Ethics, University of St. Thomas.

[1] "The New World Order," *Business Week Online* 13 Oct. 1997, 8 June 2004 (www.businessweek.com/1997/41/b3548001.htm).

was further complicated by WorldCom's extensive use of pro forma figures in its financial statements.[2]

In late 1997, Ebbers successfully engineered the merger of WorldCom and MCI, the nation's second largest long-distance carrier and a company with annual revenues more than three times those of his own firm. At the time, the $40 billion transaction was the largest merger in history. According to a company press release, the integration of the two firms created a "fully integrated communications company" that offered "a complete range of local, long distance, Internet, and international communications services."[3] It permitted WorldCom to become the first major U.S. phone company since the breakup of the old AT&T to offer both local and long-distance services.

In June 1999, WorldCom's stock hit a high of $64.50. Four months later, WorldCom and Sprint announced their intent to merge. The transaction, valued at $129 billion, aimed at adding wireless services to WorldCom's product portfolio. However, due to antitrust concerns the proposed merger failed to win the approval of either U.S. or European Union regulators. The two companies terminated the merger agreement in July 2000.

A Changing Business Environment

The complexion of the telecommunications industry changed dramatically during 2000. The sector's growth slowed, and the rates companies could charge customers dropped as competition heated up. WorldCom's fortunes began to sag in this new environment, saddled as it was with billions in debt, the legacy of its ambitious program of acquisitions and mergers. These developments were reflected in WorldCom's stock price, which by mid-2000 was trading in the mid-$40s. Ebbers restructured the company in November 2000, splitting MCI's consumer long-distance business from higher-growth services and issuing a separate tracking stock for MCI. Yet this action failed to reverse the slide: By the end of January 2001, WorldCom's share prices had dropped to the mid-$20s.

The decline of WorldCom's stock significantly affected Ebbers' personal finances. In September 1999, *Forbes'* annual listing of the 400 richest Americans had ranked Ebbers at 174, with a net worth of approximately $1.4 billion. A year later, he had fallen to 368th on the list, with net worth of $780 million. In 2001, he fell off the list completely. An accompanying profile commented on Ebbers' situation:

> WorldCom Chief Executive Bernard Ebbers has gone from telecom cowboy to corporate charity case and his once-high-flying firm is also in a downward spiral. But even though WorldCom's earnings sunk 11% in the first quarter, 25% in the second and will probably be down 30% in the third, the company still managed to bail out its overextended chief with a $75 million loan and a guarantee on another $100 million bank loan. The company Ebbers founded also floated him a $10 million "retention bonus" last year even as it slashed bonuses for the rest of its executives.[4]

In January 2002, WorldCom shares fell below $10 for first time since August 1995. On February 8, the company announced earnings of $258 million for the fourth quarter of 2001. However, it cut 2002 revenues and earnings projections, and said it expected a special second quarter charge of $15 to $20 billion to write down the value of some acquired operations. It also was revealed that the company had loaned Ebbers a total of $340 million, to cover debts he had incurred to purchase WorldCom stock. One week later, WorldCom announced that it had suspended 3 star employees and frozen commissions of 12 salespeople over an order-booking scandal.

Inquiries . . . and a Discovery

The Securities and Exchange Commission (SEC) launched an inquiry into WorldCom in early March. Company officials reported that the SEC had asked for information related to a number of items, including certain accounting practices, the loans to Ebbers, and the January order dispute. In April, the company announced that it

[2] Rebecca Blumenstein and Jared Sandberg, "WorldCom CEO Quits amid Probe of Firm's Finances," *Wall Street Journal* 30 Apr. 2002: Al. *Dow Jones Factiva*, Charles J. Keffer Library, Minneapolis, MN, 18 Feb. 2003 (global.factiva.com).

[3] WorldCom, Inc., Press Release, "WorldCom and MCI Announce $37 Billion Merger," 10 Nov. 1997, 8 June 2004 (global.mci.com/news/news2.xml?newsid=6051&mode=long&lang=en&width=530&root=/&langlinks=off).

[4] Penelope Patsuris, "Dropoffs," *Forbes.com* 27 Sept. 2001, 10 June 2004 (www.forbes.com/2001/09/27/dropoffs._print.html).

planned to lay off as many as 10 percent of its 80,000 employees, and slashed its 2002 revenue projections by an additional $1 billion. On April 24, both Fitch Ratings and Moody's Investor Services downgraded WorldCom's credit ratings. Meanwhile, investor anger about the loans to Ebbers continued to mount, fueling further divestment. Ebbers resigned from the corporation on April 29. By the end of the day, WorldCom's share price had fallen 28 percent, closing at $2.35.

On June 27, WorldCom's audit committee announced that it had discovered $3.8 billion in expenses that had been booked improperly as capital expenditures. Without the improper bookings, WorldCom would have reported a net loss for 2001 and for the first quarter of 2002. Arthur Andersen, WorldCom's external auditor, had approved the transactions. The company's internal audit organization had uncovered evidence of the accounting irregularity in March.

Initial inquiries about the transactions had been rebuffed by both Andersen and senior members of WorldCom's finance and accounting functions. The internal investigation had gained new momentum after Ebbers' resignation. It soon became apparent that during 2000 WorldCom had started to rely on problematic accounting practices to bolster its reported results. One of the company's most important day-to-day expenses as line costs, that is, fees paid to lease portions of other companies' telephone networks. Contrary to generally accepted accounting practice, line costs had been moved out of operating expense accounts and charged to capital expense accounts. In effect, WorldCom had capitalized line costs, treating them like an investment or a long-term expense. Since capital costs were not charged immediately against revenues, but depreciated over time, this approach effectively overstated WorldCom's profits. Moreover, since the critical measure WorldCom used to present its profits was EBITDA (earnings *before* interest, taxes, depreciation, and amortization), this treatment of line costs significantly boosted the company's reported financial performance.[5] It also had the effect of understating cash outflows.

[5] Jared Sandberg, Rebecca Blumenstein, and Shawn Young, "WorldCom Admits $3.8 Billion Error in Its Accounting," *Wall Street Journal* 26 June 2002: Al. *Dow Jones Factiva*, Charles J. Keffer Library, Minneapolis, MN, 18 Feb. 2003 (global.factiva.com).

WorldCom's management had hired KPMG in May as the firm's external auditor, replacing Andersen. When confronted with the internal investigation's results, Andersen advised the company that its audit reports could not be relied upon for the five quarters in question. Andersen also issued a statement accusing WorldCom's chief financial officer, Scott Sullivan, of withholding important information about line costs from its auditors.

Guilty Pleas and a New Start

In the wake of the revelation, WorldCom immediately fired Sullivan and accepted the resignation of David Myers, the firm's controller. The SEC filed a civil suit against the company on June 27, alleging that from 2001 through the first quarter of 2002 WorldCom senior management fraudulently manipulated earnings to keep them in line with Wall Street expectations. On July 21, less than one month after its audit committee's disclosure, facing $41 billion of debt and unable to raise needed capital, WorldCom filed for bankruptcy-court protection.

Sullivan and Myers were charged with securities fraud by federal prosecutors in early August. Myers pled guilty to the charges in late September. In October, Buford Yates Jr., WorldCom's former accounting director, and two of his direct reports, Betty Vinson and Troy Normand, pleaded guilty to charges of securities fraud and conspiracy.

Scott Sullivan vowed to fight the indictment against him. His trial was scheduled to begin in late March 2004. However, facing 165 years of potential jail time, Sullivan struck a deal with prosecutors that capped the length of his incarceration at 25 years. In return for the lighter sentence, Sullivan provided evidence against Ebbers. On March 3, Sullivan pleaded guilty to the charges against him just hours before Ebbers was charged with securities fraud, conspiracy to commit securities fraud, and making false filings to regulators.

Led by new chief executive Michael Capellas, WorldCom emerged from bankruptcy on April 20, 2004. The company officially restated its results for 2000 and 2001, and took a special charge that eliminated $74 billion from its pretax income for those years. Approximately $11 billion was due to fraudulent transactions that padded profits by artificially reducing expenses. The company also officially changed its name to MCI. The bankruptcy effectively wiped out the value of the stock held by former WorldCom shareholders.[6] On May 10, Capellas announced plans to eliminate 7,500 jobs during 2004.[7] The cuts would reduce MCI's workforce to 42,500 people, just over half the number of workers employed by WorldCom in early 2002.

[6] Christopher Stern, "MCI Officially Exits Bankruptcy," *Washingtonpost.com* 20 Apr. 2004, 11 June 2004 (www.washingtonpost.com/ac2/wp-dyn/A27226-2004Apr20).

[7] Christopher Stern, "MCI to Cut 7,500 Jobs, Reports $388 Million First-Quarter Loss," *Washingtonpost.com* 11May 2004, 2 July 2004 (www.washingtonpost.com/ac2/wp-dyn/A15903-2004May10).

The Corporate Scandals of 2002 (D): *Tyco International, Ltd.*

Forget Enron and WorldCom. To this day, most people have no clue what special-purpose entities are and only the vaguest notion of what sins the Andrew Fastows of the world allegedly committed. When Americans think back on the corporate scandals 25 years from now, they aren't likely to summon more than a blurry memory. What they will remember is the bald guy with the $6,000 shower curtain.

Nicholas Varchaver, "The Big Kozlowski," *Fortune*, November 18, 2002

"The Next General Electric"

Dennis Kozlowski was named chairman and chief executive officer of Tyco, Inc., in July 1992. Kozlowski had joined the organization in 1975, when it was an obscure manufacturer with annual revenues of $15 million. He transformed Tyco from an "also-ran" with annual sales of $3 billion to an expansive conglomerate with 225,000 employees and 2001 revenues in excess of $38 billion.

To build Tyco, Kozlowski directed approximately 120 acquisitions valued at over $62 billion. His appetite for acquiring firms won him the nickname "Deal-a-month Dennis" among investors and analysts. A *Business Week* article described Kozlowski's approach to the acquisition process:

> [Kozlowski] relies on a hand-picked team of six in-house M&A specialists that moves with blinding speed and uses outside investment banks sparingly. "Investment bankers will tell you it takes six months to do a deal; we often get them done in two weeks," says Irving Gutlin, a senior vice-president who until recently headed the team. Tyco screens more than 1,000 potential targets a year, most of which filter up from its operations executives. It doesn't do hostile takeovers, since that would keep it from getting a thorough look inside. Once it has a confidentiality agreement with the target company's CEO, Tyco's team pores over the books and tours operations, looking closely at what—and who—is worth keeping. That almost always means lopping off its incumbent CEO. . . . Only deals that add immediately to Tyco's bottom line go on to completion. Says Gutlin: "Dennis doesn't want to buy dreams."[1]

During the decade of high technology, Kozlowski focused on unglamorous industries, buying firms that produced industrial valves and controls, fire prevention and security systems, electronic components, garbage bags, and basic medical supplies like sutures, syringes, and incontinence diapers. Tyco's most notable purchases included Kendal International, the maker of Curad bandages and other health products; ADT, Ltd., a burglar alarm and security firm; electronics manufacturer AMP, Inc.; and the CIT Group, Inc., the largest independent U.S. commercial finance company. The company's business plan for 2001–2005 called for it to add another $50 billion worth of acquisitions, reach $100 billion in sales, and maintain 25 percent plus annual earnings growth. Kozlowski's ultimate goal was to turn Tyco into the next General Electric.[2]

Under Kozlowski, Tyco functioned as a lean, decentralized operation. Only 150 employees worked in the company's central office, located in Exeter, New Hampshire. Kozlowski practically forbade managers from sending memos. "If you're on forecast, there's no need to talk with me," he reportedly told the executives heading

This case was prepared from public materials by Research Associate T. Dean Maines under the supervision of Kenneth E. Goodpaster, Koch Professor of Business Ethics, University of St. Thomas.

[1] "The Most Aggressive CEO," *BusinessWeek*, 28 May 2001: 68. *Expanded Academic ASAP Plus*, Charles J. Keffer Library, Minneapolis, MN, 18 Feb. 2003 (web3.infotrac.galegroup.com).

[2] "The Most Aggressive CEO."

Tyco's operating units. "But if there is any bad news at all, find me wherever I am, so we can figure out what actions to take."[3] Kozlowski also took steps to limit the company's tax liabilities. As part of the 1997 ADT acquisition, he renamed the company Tyco International, Ltd., and moved its headquarters to Bermuda. By also operating in part through a Luxembourg-based subsidiary, Tyco's corporate tax rate was reduced to 20 percent, about half the typical rate.[4] In total, the firm contained over 1000 offshore subsidiaries.[5]

In December 2001, Tyco's share price reached the $60 level. This represented a 14-fold increase since Kozlowski became the firm's chief executive. The company's strong financial performance continued throughout the 2001 recession, when earnings before extraordinary charges increased 38 percent to $5.1 billion.[6]

Questions had been raised about the credibility of Tyco's results in the fall of 1999. Specifically, an analyst questioned whether the company used large accounting reserves related to acquisitions to obscure or distort its financial performance. The Securities and Exchange Commission (SEC) previously had advised companies on how such funds could be handled. Companies were allowed to book reserves for identified actions they had definite plans to execute—for example, layoffs or plant closures. The analyst suggested that instead Tyco treated its reserves as "cookie jars," drawing from them in the aftermath of an acquisition to boost earnings. In December 1999, the SEC launched an investigation into Tyco's acquisition accounting practices. The investigation was closed seven months later, without the SEC taking enforcement action.

Tyco eventually became a target for executive compensation critics. As late as 1997, Kozlowski reportedly had an annual salary of $1 million and an annual bonus limited to a maximum of $1 million. Only after 1998 was he granted stock options, although he did receive performance linked restricted shares.[7] However, since 1999 Kozlowski had been paid roughly $97 million in cash, unrestricted stock, and other compensation. He had reaped an additional $240 million by exercising stock options. A filing submitted to the SEC on December 31, 2001, outlined a board-approved retention plan for Kozlowski and Mark Swartz, Tyco's chief financial officer. The retention plan called for Kozlowski to receive 800,000 shares of restricted stock, valued at roughly $47 million. Under the plan 100,000 shares would vest each year, beginning in 2002. In the past, the company's executive compensation programs had carefully tied large stock grants, options, and cash bonuses to the achievement of aggressive financial targets. No performance hurdles were included in the retention scheme.

The Meltdown

In the first three weeks of January 2002, Tyco's share price dropped by roughly 13 percent, falling from nearly $59 to under $52. On January 22, Kozlowski announced the conglomerate would be dismantled. Tyco's plastics unit would be sold, and the remainder of the firm would be split into four publicly traded companies: financial services; securities and electronics; health care; and fire protection and flow control. The company claimed the move would "unlock tens of billions of dollars of shareholder value."[8] Kozlowski remarked to shareholders that "we are not getting paid for our results."[9] The dismantling was "designed to close . . . the gap between Tyco's market value in recent years and the value of our businesses."[10]

[3] "The Most Aggressive CEO."

[4] Mark Maremont, John Hechinger, Jerry Markon, and Gregory Zuckerman, "Tainted Chief: Kozlowski Quits under a Cloud, Worsening Worries about Tyco," *Wall Street Journal*, 4 June 2002: AI. *Dow Jones Factiva*, Charles J. Keffer Library, Minneapolis, MN, 18 Feb. 2003 (global.factiva.com).

[5] Herb Greenberg, "Still Playing the Same Old Game," *Fortune* 18 Feb. 2002: 135. *Expanded Academic ASAP Plus*, Charles J. Keffer Library, Minneapolis, MN, 18 Feb. 2003 (web3. infotrac.galegroup.com).

[6] "L. Dennis Kozlowski," *BusinessWeek* 14 Jan. 2002: 61. *Expanded Academic ASAP Plus*, Charles J. Keffer Library, Minneapolis, MN, 18 Feb. 2003 (web3.infotrac.galegroup.com).

[7] Nicholas Varchaver, "The Big Kozlowski," *Fortune* 18 Nov. 2002: 122. *Expanded Academic ASAP Plus*, Charles J. Keffer Library, Minneapolis, MN, 18 Feb. 2003 (web3.infotrac.galegroup.com).

[8] Tyco International Ltd. Press Release, "Tyco Announces Plan to Unlock Tens of Billions of Dollars of Shareholder Value," 22 Jan. 2002, 18 June 2004 (www.tyco.com/tyco/press_release_detail.asp?prid+83).

[9] "Kozlowski's Colours," *The Economist* 26 Jan. 2002. *Expanded Academic ASAP Plus*, Charles J. Keffer Library, Minneapolis, MN, 18 Feb. 2003 (web3.infotrac.galegroup.com).

[10] Tyco Press Release, "Tyco Announces Plan."

The stock's slide accelerated in the announcement's wake. It gained additional momentum when an annual proxy statement filed on January 28 disclosed that Tyco's lead independent director, Frank E. Walsh Jr., had received $20 million for helping to broker the company's 2001 acquisition of CIT Group, Inc. At the time Walsh owned stock in both CIT and Tyco. Ten million dollars of the fee had been paid directly to Walsh in cash; the remaining half was paid as a contribution to a New Jersey charitable fund of which he was a trustee. Corporate governance specialists criticized the payment as a clear conflict of interest, and noted it was particularly troubling that Walsh had voted on a deal from which he stood to profit. Tyco confirmed the fee in a written statement, which quoted Kozlowski as saying that "the board felt the fee was appropriate in light of Mr. Walsh's efforts." On January 29, Tyco's stock fell nearly 20 percent, closing at $33.65.

By February 3, Tyco shares were trading at $35. The following day, the company admitted that it had spent $8 billion on more than 700 unpublicized acquisitions over the past three years. The admission came in response to questions from analysts and investors about the doubling of Tyco's debt to $21 billion over the previous year. While Tyco had disclosed the net cost of all the transactions in its various filings, it had not revealed each individual purchase or the total number of purchases. The company maintained that issuing specific details on each small acquisition was impractical for a company its size.[11] Separately, both Standard and Poor's and Fitch downgraded their rating of Tyco's debt, a move motivated by the company's deteriorating share price and its decision to draw on existing credit lines. On February 5, Tyco's stock closed at just over $23.

Company filings in February also showed that Kozlowski and Schwartz had sold more than $500 million in Tyco stock in transactions dating back to 1999. This contradicted earlier statements made by the two executives, in which they publicly declared that they rarely, if ever, divested their shares.

On April 24, the sale of the company's plastics unit stalled because Tyco failed to provide key financial data. The next day, the company announced it was scuttling the dismantling plan, calling the strategy a mistake. However, it confirmed that the spin-off of its financial subsidiary would proceed. In response, Tyco shares lost nearly 20 percent of their value, falling from just under $26 on April 24 to $20.75 on April 25.

On Monday, June 3, Tyco announced that Dennis Kozlowski had resigned from the company for personal reasons. Three days before he had notified company directors that he was the subject of a New York State criminal investigation. Over the weekend Kozlowski and the board had agreed that it would be best for Tyco if he stepped down. Tyco investors had lost a total of $86 billion in share value during the final five months of Kozlowski's tenure. John Fort, a member of the board of directors and Kozlowski's predecessor, was named interim head.

Investigations and Indictments

On June 4, the Manhattan District Attorney's Office indicted Kozlowski on charges that he conspired to evade more than $1 million in New York sales taxes on $13.1 million in art purchases. Prosecutors alleged that Kozlowski and his art dealers had avoided New York State taxes by shipping paintings to Tyco's New Hampshire office and falsifying records:

> According to the indictment, Kozlowski and others "agreed to generate false documents, such as invoices and shipping documents, to make it appear as though the art work was to be shipped out of state and therefore not covered by New York state sales tax provisions." Tyco employees were allegedly told to sign false documents reflecting receipt of the paintings in New Hampshire, only to ship them back to New York.
>
> On Dec. 11 of [2001], the indictment says, an "art consultant employee" had a trucker "de-install" a work by John LaFarge valued at $425,000 from Kozlowski's apartment, ship it to Tyco headquarters, where it was signed for by a Tyco employee, and then ship it back to Manhattan and put it back in Kozlowski's apartment. The indictment says the work was purchased by Kozlowski's wife but that no sales tax was paid on it.
>
> In mid-December [of 2001], according to the indictment, an "art business" authorized the release of a $3.95 million Monet to Kozlowski's

[11] "Tyco Spent $8B in Deals," *CNNMoney* 4 Feb. 2002, 18 June 2004 (money.cnn.com/2002/02/04/companies/tyco).

> Manhattan apartment. The art business owner then "prepared an invoice falsely asserting that no sales tax was due because the work of art was being shipped to New Hampshire."
>
> Also in mid-December, Kozlowski allegedly purchased four more paintings valued at \$8.8 million and "asked an art consultant not to ship the four paintings and the Monet, but instead to ship empty boxes to New Hampshire." The indictment says sales tax of 8.25 percent should have been collected on all of the paintings.[12]

Prosecutors noted that six of the paintings had been bought using funds Kozlowski borrowed from Tyco under an executive loan program. The program was designed to help executives pay taxes on restricted stock awards. If Tyco had failed to disclose the loans to Kozlowski, it would be in violation of federal securities law. Furthermore, if Tyco had knowingly provided loans to Kozlowski under this program for art purchases, it could be subject to claims of improperly using corporate assets. The *Wall Street Journal* reported on June 6 that the SEC had opened a preliminary investigation into these issues.[13] One week later, the SEC reopened its investigation of Tyco's accounting practices.

On June 18, Tyco initiated lawsuits against Frank Walsh and Mark Belnick, former general counsel, for concealing payments they had received via secret agreements with Kozlowski. The suit against Walsh, who had stepped down from the board in February, stemmed from the \$20 million he received in connection with the CIT acquisition. Belnick, who had been fired on June 10, allegedly accepted over \$35 million without the knowledge or approval of the board's compensation committee.

Edward Breen, the president of Motorola, Inc., was named Tyco's new chairman and CEO on July 26. One week later Mark Swartz resigned as the company's chief financial officer, at Breen's prompting. Breen also initiated a reorganization of Tyco's board of directors.

New York State prosecutors continued their investigations throughout the summer of 2002. On September 13, they charged Kozlowski and Swartz with grand larceny, enterprise corruption, and falsifying business records. The indictment accused the pair of stealing more than \$170 million from the company and of illegally obtaining an additional \$430 million by selling stock at prices artificially inflated through the concealment of information about executive compensation and loans. Prosecutors described Kozlowski as the "boss" and Swartz as the "chief of operations" of a criminal enterprise that manipulated Tyco's stock price through false public statements and fraudulent accounting. The indictment detailed millions of dollars worth of secret loans, previously undisclosed compensation, and questionable corporate expenses. It also accused Kozlowski and Swartz of concealing their illegal actions by corrupting other key employees through lucrative payments.

If convicted on the charges, Kozlowski and Swartz faced up to 30 years in prison. Both pleaded not guilty. Prosecutors also indicted Belnick separately for allegedly falsifying business records to conceal \$14 million in interest-free loans he had received. Belnick also pleaded not guilty. In discussing the indictments, prosecutors remarked that they had chosen not to charge Tyco as a corporation because it would be unfair to punish thousands of employees for the misdeeds of a few.

Kozlowski and Swartz allegedly used the improper payments and loans to fund a lavish lifestyle, purchasing an extensive list of luxury items. These included a \$2.5 million home in Boca Raton, Florida, and \$9 million for additional property in the Boca Raton area; \$5 million for property in Nantucket, Massachusetts; \$12 million for art; an \$18 million decorating bill for Kozlowski's Manhattan duplex (allegedly a Tyco corporate apartment); \$1 million for a birthday party for Kozlowski's second wife on the Italian island of Sardinia; \$7 million for a Park Avenue apartment for Kozlowski's ex-wife; \$240,000 for jewelry; luxury cars and yachts; and charitable donations. The decorating bill for Kozlowski's New York apartment included an itemized charge of \$6,000 for a shower curtain.

The SEC filed a companion suit against Kozlowski and Swartz for their failure to disclose millions in loans from Tyco. Tyco itself filed a

[12] "Former Tyco CEO Faces Charges of Tax Dodging," *Washingtonpost.com* 5 June 2002, 11 June 2004 (www.washingtonpost.com/ac2/wp-dyn/A60713-2002 June 4).

[13] Mark Maremont, Laurie P. Cohen, and Jerry Markon, "Probe of Ex-Tyco Chief Focuses on Improper Use of Company Funds," *Wall Street Journal* 6 June 2002: Al. *Dow Jones Factiva*, Charles J. Keffer Library, Minneapolis, MN, 18 Feb. 2003 (global.factiva.com).

suit against Kozlowski, seeking the repayment of five years' salary, benefits, loans, bonuses, and payments authorized by Kozlowski to other employees. The amount included $10 million in personal expenses the former CEO had charged to the company.

On December 17, New York prosecutors charged former Tyco director Walsh with violations of securities law in connection with his role in Tyco's acquisition of CIT. According to the indictment, Walsh signed an SEC filing in April 2001 which he knew was materially misleading, in that it failed to disclose the $20 million "finder's fee" he would receive once the acquisition was completed. Prosecutors commented that Kozlowski had arranged the fee, and Kozlowski and Walsh had intentionally concealed the payment from other members of Tyco's board: While the monies had been disbursed in July 2001, Tyco directors did not learn of it until the following January. Walsh did not admit to the allegations but paid $22.5 million in restitution. The SEC permanently barred him from acting as an officer or director of a publicly held company.

On December 30, Tyco announced the outcomes of an internal investigation headed by lawyer David Boies. The review concluded that there was no evidence of "significant or systemic fraud" on the company's books. However, it noted "a number of accounting entries and treatments that were incorrect and were required to be corrected." Furthermore, Tyco's "prior management engaged in a pattern of aggressive accounting which, even when in accordance with Generally Accepted Accounting Principles, was intended to increase reported earnings above what they would have been if more conservative accounting had been employed."[14] A special charge of $382 million was announced, to rectify errors going back to 1999.

Tyco shareholders elected a completely new board of directors on March 5, 2003. On April 31, the company announced it had discovered nearly $1 billion in additional accounting irregularities. It took a special charge of approximately $1.4 billion to correct these and to reflect the use of more conservative accounting standards. "We now believe we have identified all or nearly all of the legacy issues [from the Kozlowski era]," Breen announced to investors. "We are committed to changing the culture. . . . Where we cannot change the culture, we will change the people."[15]

The criminal trial of Kozlowski and Swartz began on September 29, 2003. In October jurors viewed videotapes of Kozlowski's Fifth Avenue apartment and the now infamous Sardinian birthday party. On March 5, 2004, Judge Michael Obus threw out the charge of enterprise corruption. The charge usually was reserved for organized crime figures, and Obus previously had expressed doubt about its applicability to this case. The jury began deliberations late in March, after six months of arguments and testimony. On April 2, Judge Obus declared a mistrial, citing external efforts to pressure the jury, including threats conveyed to a juror by phone and letter.

Subsequent interviews with the jurors revealed highly contentious discussions about the innocence or guilt of the accused. The central issue was whether sufficient evidence of criminal intent had been demonstrated. "Without question, all twelve people firmly believed these guys operated in a clearly unethical fashion for years of running this company," remarked Patrick Donovan, a management consultant who served on the jury. "The question in everyone's mind: When does that lack of ethics cross the threshold of criminal intent?"[16] Jurors who spoke with the press afterwards indicated that the jury had been moving towards guilty verdicts on the various charges when the mistrial was declared.

Prosecutors underscored their intent to retry Kozlowski and Swartz in the wake of Judge Obus's ruling. A retrial date of January 18, 2005, was established in June. In the meantime, Belnick's trial on document falsification charges began in early May.

[14] Tyco International Ltd. Press Release, "Tyco Files 10-K Report on FY 2002 Financial Results," 30 Dec. 2002, 21 June 2004 (www.tyco.com/tyco/press_release_detail.asp?prid=19).

[15] Brooke A. Masters, "Tyco Finds $1.3 Billion in Accounting Errors," *Washingtonpost.com* 1 May 2003, 11 June 2004 (www.washingtonpost.com/ac2/wp-dyn/A62679-2003Apr30).

[16] Mark Maremont, Kara Scannell, and Charles Forelle, "Tyco Mistrial Scuttles Possible Guilty Verdicts for Former Executives," *Wall Street Journal*, 5 April 2004. *Dow Jones Factiva*, Charles J. Keffer Library, Minneapolis, MN, 24 Nov. 2004 (http://global.factiva.com/en/eSrch/search.asp).

An Introduction to the Sarbanes-Oxley Act of 2002

The Sarbanes-Oxley Act was signed into law by President George W. Bush on July 30, 2002. The act is named after Senator Paul E. Sarbanes (D-Maryland) and Representative Michael R. Oxley (R-Ohio), who helped shape the bill's content and guided it through Congress.

Sarbanes-Oxley was passed as a legislative response to the accounting scandals that began to surface in late 2001. This is suggested by the summary description of the House version of the bill: "An Act to protect investors by improving the accuracy and reliability of corporate disclosures made pursuant to securities laws, and for other purposes." Remarks by President Bush at the bill's signing further underscored its link to the legal and ethical failures at firms like Enron, Tyco, and WorldCom:

> America's system of free enterprise . . . is not a jungle in which only the unscrupulous survive or a financial free-for-all guided by greed. The fundamentals of a free market—buying and selling, saving and investing—require clear rules and confidence in basic fairness. . . .
>
> The only risks, the only fair risks are based on honest information. Tricking an investor into taking a risk is theft by another name. . . . Those who break the rules tarnish a great economic system that provides opportunity for all. Their actions hurt workers who committed their lives to building the company that hired them. Their actions hurt investors and retirees who placed their faith in the promise of growth and integrity. For the sake of our free economy, those who break the law, break the rules of fairness, those who are dishonest, however wealthy or successful they may be, must pay a price.[1]

The act was shaped over the course of little more than a year. The seeds of the law were sown in hearings chaired by Oxley prior to the scandals on the question of Wall Street analyst independence.[2] Hearings on legislation intended to address broader corporate misconduct began in December 2001.[3] By April 2002 the House had passed a modest reform bill sponsored by Oxley; however, a stronger bill emerged in the Senate under Sarbanes's leadership, and House members embraced its tougher stance as the list of companies caught in questionable practices lengthened.[4] The act became the occasion for legislators to adopt measures that had been floating before Congress for years. For example, Sarbanes-Oxley creates an accounting oversight board, a concept first introduced in draft legislation during the 1970s.[5]

Sarbanes-Oxley applies directly to companies that are publicly traded in the United States, that is, all corporate issuers of securities registered under the Securities and Exchange Act of 1934. It touches a number of corporate roles and practices that contributed to the scandals of 2001–02. This note briefly describes the principal provisions of the law. It emphasizes critical mandates for audit committees, public accounting firms, senior executives, corporate directors, corporate financial disclosures, securities analysts, and attorneys. It highlights sections of the act that strengthen legal safeguards for whistle-blowers and penalties for corporate misconduct. It also considers the

This note was prepared from public materials by Research Associate T. Dean Maines under the supervision of Kenneth E. Goodpaster, Koch Professor of Business Ethics, University of St. Thomas.

[1] *Weekly Compilation of Presidential Documents*, 5 Aug. 2002.

[2] Michael Schroeder, "Cleaner Living, No Easy Riches," *The Wall Street Journal* 22 July 2003: C7.

[3] Allison Fass, "One Year Later, the Impact of Sarbanes Oxley," *Forbes.com* 22 July 2003, 1 Aug. 2003 (forbes.com/2003/07/22/cz_af_0722sarbanes.html).

[4] Schroeder, C7.

[5] Fass.

implications of Sarbanes-Oxley for non-U.S. companies and privately held firms. Finally, it documents reactions to the act which emerged over the course of its first year.

An Expanded Role for the Audit Committee

Sarbanes-Oxley (SOx) expands the role of the audit committee of a company's board of directors. The act limits audit committee membership to independent directors. Under SOx, board members are considered independent if they receive no compensation from the company other than for their board duties, and they have no other affiliations with the company or its subsidiaries. In addition, the law requires a company to disclose whether its audit committee contains at least one "financial expert," as defined by the Securities and Exchange Commission (SEC). The definition identifies five competencies a committee member must possess to qualify for this status (Exhibit 1). The SEC rule recognizes these competencies can be acquired in a variety of ways; however, it suggests that they are preferably the product of experience, not merely education. If a company's audit committee does not include a qualified financial expert, SOx compels it to explain why.

SOx charges the audit committee with supervision of the company's external auditor, including (1) appointing the audit firm, (2) overseeing its activities, and (3) determining its compensation. The act empowers the audit committee to hire any external advisors or consultants needed to fulfill its responsibilities. The company is obligated to compensate the audit firm and other advisers at the level set by the committee. SOx also requires the audit committee to establish procedures to handle complaints about accounting and audit matters, including anonymous complaints from employees.

A Changing Context for Auditors

The new law has wide-ranging implications for public accounting firms. To protect investors' interests and to help rebuild public confidence, Sarbanes-Oxley established an independent, nongovernmental board to oversee public company audits. The board, called the Public Company Accounting Oversight Board (PCAOB), is responsible for establishing audit and attestation standards for auditors. All public accounting firms that prepare audit reports for corporations issuing securities in the United States are required to register with the board. The PCAOB also is charged with assessing how well public accountants comply with the act and with establishing disciplinary procedures and rules.

SOx introduced three directives intended to mitigate potential conflicts of interest for auditors. First, it prohibits auditors from providing certain services to their audit clients. These services are summarized in Exhibit 2. Second, the act prohibits audit firms from serving any company whose chief executive officer, chief financial officer, chief accounting officer, or controller was employed by the firm within the previous 12 months. Third, it requires auditors to rotate the lead partner and reviewing partner assigned to each client every five years. Nonlead auditors must be rotated every seven years.

SOx mandates specific topics on which an external auditor must report to the audit committee. These include (1) all critical company accounting policies; (2) any alternative treatments of financial information under generally accepted accounting principles (GAAP) discussed with management and their ramifications; (3) the auditor's preferred accounting treatment; and (4) any disagreements encountered with management on financial representations. Auditors also must disclose all other material written communications between management and themselves.

New Executive Responsibilities and Restrictions

Sarbanes-Oxley created new responsibilities for senior executives of publicly traded companies. Chief executive officers and chief financial officers must henceforth certify six conditions for each quarterly and annual report. These conditions are described in Exhibit 3. Executives who certify a financial report knowing that it is inaccurate can be fined up to $1 million and imprisoned for up to ten years. If an executive does this willfully—that is, to intentionally and deliberately misrepresent the company's position—the maximum penalties increase to $5 million and 20 years.

Failure to comply with federal financial reporting requirements can result in monetary forfeitures by executives. For example, if a company's reporting failure is the result of misconduct and a restatement is required, its CEO and CFO must return bonuses and other incentive-based pay they received during the 12 months following the erroneous statement's release. They also must relinquish all profits realized from sales of company securities during that same period.[6]

SOx prohibits company officers and directors, or anyone working under their supervision, from fraudulently influencing, coercing, manipulating, or misleading public or certified accountants engaged in an audit. It also prohibits officers and directors from buying, selling, or transferring securities acquired as a consequence of their employment during pension blackout periods.[7] Finally, the act forbids companies from making loans to executives and directors. An exemption is granted to consumer credit organizations, if the loans are of a type generally available to the public and the terms are market rate, that is, no more favorable than those offered to other customers.

Mandated Disclosures

Sarbanes-Oxley requires new disclosures in annual and quarterly reports. For example, it mandates disclosure of unconsolidated entities and all off–balance sheet transactions, arrangements, and obligations that have, or are reasonably likely to have, a material impact upon the firm's current or future financial condition. These disclosures must appear in a specially captioned section within "management's discussion and analysis."[8] The firm also must provide a tabular overview of certain known contractual obligations, including long-term debt, capital lease obligations, operating leases, and unconditional purchase obligations.

Companies also must clarify their use of financial measures that do not conform to GAAP requirements. These metrics, commonly described as "pro forma," increasingly have been employed by companies to place their performance in the best possible light. SOx defines a non-GAAP measure as a numerical metric of a company's historical or future financial performance, financial position, or cash flow that *excludes* amounts *included* in a comparable GAAP measure, or *includes* amounts *excluded* from a comparable GAAP measure. Metrics that fall within this definition include adjusted earnings measures or liquidity measures, for example, earnings before interest, tax, depreciation, and amortization (EBITDA). When a company publicly discloses material information that includes a non-GAAP measure, SOx requires (1) an accompanying presentation of the most directly comparable financial measure calculated and presented in accordance with GAAP and (2) a reconciliation of the differences between the non-GAAP measure and the "best-fit" GAAP measure. The act also details additional requirements and restrictions that apply when pro forma measures are utilized in SEC filings.

To complement certifications made by the chief executive and chief financial officers, a company's annual report must explicitly address its internal control structure. Specifically, the report must state management's responsibility for establishing and maintaining adequate internal controls and financial reporting procedures. It also must include an evaluation of the effectiveness of these controls as of the end of the most recent fiscal year. Furthermore, the firm's auditor must attest to assertions made by management in this evaluation.

SOx also requires publicly held corporations to disclose whether they have a "code of ethics" that applies to their chief executive officer, chief financial officer, and chief accounting officer. The SEC defines a code of ethics as a set of written standards designed to deter wrongdoing and promote:

- Ethical conduct, including the ethical handling of real or apparent conflicts of interest.
- Full, fair, accurate, timely, and understandable filings and public communications.

[6] Sarbanes-Oxley also authorizes federal courts to impose financial penalties upon corporations as well as individual executives, for the purpose of granting "any equitable relief that may be appropriate or necessary for the benefit of investors" (Section 305).

[7] A "pension blackout period" is a length of time during which the participants in a company's pension plan may neither sell shares of the company's stock present in their individual accounts, nor purchase additional shares.

[8] "Management's discussion and analysis" is a required section in annual and quarterly reports that explains major changes in the firm's income statement, capital resources, and liquidity.

- Compliance with applicable laws and regulations.
- Prompt internal reporting of code violations.
- Accountability for adherence to the code.

Companies that have adopted a code must reveal any subsequent amendments or waivers of its requirements. Companies that do not have such a code must disclose this fact and explain why one has not been adopted.

SOx also requires firms to accelerate their reporting. For example, it requires companies to report the stock transactions of directors, officers, and principal shareholders (i.e., those who own more than 10 percent of the firm) within two business days of their execution date. The previous reporting deadline for such transactions was ten days following the end of the month in which they occurred. More broadly, the act requires publicly held companies to report "on a rapid and current basis" additional information concerning material changes in the firm's financial position or operations. Such information is to be disclosed "in plain English," supplemented by trend data, quantitative information, and qualitative explanations which the SEC deems necessary for the protection of investors and the public interest.

New Obligations for Analysts and Attorneys

Sarbanes-Oxley details new responsibilities for securities analysts. Under the legislation, research analysts are now required to certify that the views expressed within their reports reflect their personal assessments. Furthermore, analysts must disclose whether they received compensation or other payments for expressing the recommendations and views detailed within their research reports. They must make a similar certification on a quarterly basis concerning views expressed in public appearances.

SOx also establishes standards for attorneys. It requires both in-house and outside counsel to report evidence of material violations of securities laws, or breaches of fiduciary duty, to the company's chief legal counsel or chief executive officer. If an appropriate response is not forthcoming, the attorney is required to bring the evidence to the audit committee of the firm's board of directors or to the full board itself.

In January 2003, the SEC extended the comment period on a controversial mandate for lawyers that appeared in the initial draft of implementation rules, the so-called "noisy withdrawal." This provision would have required attorneys to quit and inform the SEC if company directors failed to take appropriate action on their notification of a securities law violation. Critics complained that this requirement would undermine attorney-client confidentiality. While not abandoning the "noisy withdrawal" concept, the SEC proposed alternative approaches to implementation. For example, rather than requiring an individual to report his or her withdrawal, the company itself might be compelled to disclose it, or to disclose the attorney's written notice that he or she has found the company's response deficient. As of mid-2004, a final ruling on this matter had not been announced.

Strengthened Protections and Criminal Provisions

Sarbanes-Oxley strengthens legal protections for whistle-blowers while increasing penalties for fraud and other criminal behaviors. The act closes a significant loophole in the Victim and Witness Protection Act of 1982. Specifically, it prohibits companies from firing or discriminating against employees who lawfully inform their supervisors, a federal agency, or Congress about actions they reasonably believe constitute fraud. This proscription of *workplace* retaliation supplements the legal safeguards against *violent* retaliation established by the 1982 statute. Violators may be imprisoned for up to ten years and subject to fines.

SOx creates two new felonies. The first penalizes those who knowingly alter, destroy, or falsify records for the purpose of impeding federal investigations or bankruptcy proceedings with up to 20 years' imprisonment and fines. Furthermore, the act obliges public accountants to keep audit records for five years after the close of the fiscal period for which the audit was conducted. A knowing and willful violation of this requirement is punishable by imprisonment for up to five years and fines.

SOx also authorizes the SEC to bar violators of the antifraud provisions of securities laws from serving as officers or directors of public corporations. It enables the SEC to implement these exclusions as a remedy within its own administrative proceedings, supplementing the Commission's existing power to seek them in court. Past court interpretations have significantly limited the SEC's ability to obtain bars. SOx reduces the level of proof required to demonstrate that an individual is unfit to serve as an officer or director, making it easier for the Commission to impose this sanction.

Implications for Non-U.S. Companies

Sarbanes-Oxley applies to all companies that issue securities under U.S. federal securities statutes, whether headquartered within the United States or not. Thus, in addition to U.S.-based firms, approximately 1,300 foreign firms from 59 countries fall under the law's jurisdiction.[9]

Reactions from this quarter were swift. Some foreign companies that had previously contemplated offering securities in the U.S. market reconsidered in light of the conflicts they believed SOx created. For example, in October 2002 Porsche AG announced it would not list its shares on the New York Stock Exchange. A company press release identified the passage of SOx as the "critical factor" for this decision and singled out CEO and CFO certification of financial statements for criticism. Recounting the process Porsche uses to prepare, review, and approve its financial reports, the release concluded that "any special treatment of the Chairman of the Board of Management [i.e., Porsche's CEO] and the Director of Finance would be illogical because of the intricate network within the decision-making process; it would be irreconcilable with current German law."[10]

By late 2002, the SEC found itself subjected to intense lobbying by foreign companies pressing for exemptions from SOx. In remarks to an association of German firms, SEC Commissioner Paul Atkins summarized the regulatory body's obligations and its approach to conflicts between the act and the laws of other nations:

> Sarbanes-Oxley generally makes no distinction between U.S. and non-U.S. [securities] issuers. The Act does not provide any specific authority to exempt non-U.S. issuers from its reach. The Act leaves it to the SEC to determine where and how to apply the Act's provisions to foreign companies. The SEC is well aware that new U.S. requirements may come into conflict with requirements on non-U.S. issuers. As we move forward to implement Sarbanes-Oxley, we have tried and we will continue to try to balance our responsibility to comply with the Act's mandate with the need to make reasonable accommodations to our non-U.S. issuers.[11]

In January 2003 the SEC proposed rules addressing several of these conflicts. The proposal recognized that some non-U.S. corporate governance practices—in many cases prescribed by home country laws—were consistent with the act's spirit even though they violated its letter. Furthermore, the proposal suggested specific practices that the SEC could accommodate. For example, the commission signaled that it would permit nonmanagement employees of German firms to serve as audit committee members, even though they fail to meet SOx's independence test. The SEC also indicated it would allow shareholders of foreign companies to appoint outside auditors, despite the fact that the act assigns this duty to audit committees.

European responses to these rules were positive. However, by April a new flashpoint had emerged, namely, the question of whether auditors headquartered outside the United States would be required to register with the PCAOB. During a public hearing held on April 1, Charles Niemeier, the acting chair of the PCAOB, stated that "the U.S. markets now involve companies and auditors that are not in the United States. . . . We believe registration is extremely important for us to be able to fulfill our mandate."[12] European officials voiced concern about the impact on European accounting firms, particularly in light of Sarbanes-Oxley's mandate that public accountants retain audit records, a stipulation that could conflict with European Union confidentiality laws.

In late April, the PCAOB announced it would extend the registration deadline for non-U.S.

[9] Paul S. Atkins, "Liabilities of German Companies and the Members of their Executive Boards under the Sarbanes-Oxley Act of 2002," Deutsches Aktieninstitut 4 Feb. 2003 (www.sec.gov/news/speech/spch020403psa.htm).

[10] Porsche Press Release, 16 Oct 2002.

[11] Atkins, 4.

[12] Carrie Johnson, "Accounting Panel, SEC Back Registry for Foreign Auditors," Washingtonpost.com 1 Apr. 2003, 23 May 2003 (www.washingtonpost.com/ac2/wp-dyn/A62762-2003May31).

auditors to April 2004. However, this concession failed to mollify EU officials, who threatened to enact regulations for non-EU auditors. At the same time, the EU moved to strengthen its own standards for auditing and corporate governance, in reaction to both U.S. initiatives and the February 2003 scandal at Ahold, a Dutch retailer. Reflecting on these developments, Gregor Pozniak, deputy secretary general of the Federation of European Stock Exchanges, observed that "a response to recent corporate developments in the United States and Europe was necessary," and the EU action "increases the chance of mutual recognition from the United States."[13]

The Effect on Private Companies

Sarbanes-Oxley's prescriptions are reshaping corporate governance expectations. Hence, while the act does not apply directly to privately held firms, they will encounter its effects. Private companies may initially feel the law's influence through business partners who insist on compliance with specific dimensions of SOx as a condition for commencing, continuing, or expanding a relationship:

- Lenders may require the installation of independent directors and an independent audit committee prior to approving a loan.
- Insurers may require executives to certify financial statements before issuing or renewing liability coverage for the company's directors and officers.
- Prospective investors in a private security placement may insist on audited financials, assurances of auditor and audit committee independence, and disclosures of "insider transactions" before investing their funds.

The act's mandates are immediately relevant to private companies considering a public offering. Such businesses must carefully integrate the implementation of SOx's requirements into their public placement strategy. Yet compliance with the law can offer advantages even to private firms that do not intend to issue equity publicly. One corporate advisor summarized these benefits:

> By taking action now to comply voluntarily with many of these requirements, larger private companies. . . can reap rewards associated with third party approvals and improved internal controls and governance, while at the same time reducing their litigation exposure. In addition, investors and acquirers may be willing to pay a premium to invest in or buy companies with sound corporate governance practices. The administrative cost—in time and dollars—associated with undertaking such actions will in most cases be outweighed by these benefits.[14]

At a minimum, the law can provide private firms with a model for corporate governance. Thus, Martyn R. Redgrave, chief financial officer of the Minneapolis-based Carlson Companies, described his approach to its provisions:

> The standard I have applied is that if we find the rules relative to current practices would increase transparency or awareness, we are in favor of them. . . . [But] we're not going to sweep through our entire global system to do what is required of public companies. We're using it as a new benchmark against which we measure ourselves, and we have a lot of it in place.[15]

Ultimately, SOx may impact private companies through direct governmental action. State authorities could extend regulations modeled after the act directly to private firms, as well as hospitals and nonprofit organizations. Such parallel legislation was already evident in early 2003, when the legislatures of California and New Jersey passed laws limiting the services public accounting firms could sell to publicly *and* privately held clients.

Responses to Sarbanes-Oxley

Soon after Sarbanes-Oxley was signed, a number of criticisms were leveled at the act. Some critics contended that the new law was insufficiently demanding of corporate executives. Others complained that the legislation had been drafted

[13] Originally found at "EU to strengthen corporate oversight," *CNNMoney* 21 May 2003, 23 May 2003 (cnnmoney.printthis.clickability.com/pt/cpt?action=cpt&expire=&urlID=...).

[14] Andrew G. Humphrey, "The Effect of Sarbanes-Oxley on Private Companies," *Faegre & Benson LLP Legal Updates* Mar. 2003 (www.faegre.com/articles/article_838.asp).

[15] Matt Murray, "Private Companies Also Feel Pressure to Clean Up Acts," *The Wall Street Journal* 22 July 2003: B7.

and enacted too quickly to adequately address the complexities of corporate governance in a global economy. Still others focused on the specific rules developed by the SEC. Corporate advocates denounced the rules as unnecessarily costly and onerous, while investor advocates charged that the rules had grown soft under pressure from special interests, particularly the accounting and legal professions. Surveying these reactions, one commentator concluded that "[i]n the end, it's safe to say that no one came away unscathed. . . . The question now is whether corporations, accountants, [and] lawyers. . . will have time to digest these rules and regain investor trust through their actions, or whether these rules will be the source of more violations that undermine that trust."[16]

What was clear in the immediate aftermath of the law's passage is that SOx confronted business leaders with a new set of governance expectations. John Stout, a partner at the Minneapolis law firm of Fredrikson & Byron and a veteran adviser of corporate boards, summarized its impact this way: "What's being created here are some practice standards. I don't know if they're the best practice standards, but they're better practice standards."[17]

The promulgation of SOx sparked considerable corporate activity. A survey released by PricewaterhouseCoopers in March 2003 indicated that 84 percent of large U.S. multinational corporations had changed their control and compliance practices in the wake of the new law.[18] The survey also showed that executives credited SOx with providing a formalized framework for corporate governance and control. Roughly one-third of the executives surveyed view SOx as a good first step towards rebuilding public confidence in the financial markets; however, only 9 percent consider the act an adequate response to the problems of accounting and financial reporting.

A study released in April 2003 by the law firm Foley & Lardner attempted to quantify the cost of efforts aimed at meeting the requirements of the new corporate governance environment.[19] According to this report, senior managers of middle-market ("midcap") companies expected costs directly associated with being publicly traded to rise approximately 90 percent, from $1.3 to $2.5 million annually, as a result of the new mandates emanating from SOx, the SEC, and stock exchanges.[20] Costs for large midmarket and Fortune 500 companies likely would be three to five times higher in dollar terms; however, as the Foley-Lardner study noted, the resource base of the larger firms enabled them to absorb such increases more readily. One commentator bemoaned the impact of these costs upon smaller, entrepreneurial organizations:

> Unfortunately, these are dollars that will not go into research and development or increasing productivity of the workforce. This means, among other things, that public companies in this country will have to assess this radically increased cost structure in terms of the benefits provided. The benefits are going to be negligible for those companies that do not access the capital markets on a regular, perhaps even annual, basis. In other words, small, innovative, emerging growth companies that do not regularly seek equity capital through public offerings will find the cost of maintaining public status prohibitive.[21]

In contrast, some observers believed it was still too early to assess the act's strengths and weaknesses. For example, Warren Neel, the head of the University of Tennessee's Center for Corporate Governance, remarked in July 2003 that while his center is preparing to evaluate the bill's impact, it had found a "dearth of data largely because major parts of the bill's 68 sections aren't even in effect yet."[22]

Others have pointed to the limitations of *law* as a way of promoting fundamental change within

[16] Tim Reason, "Did the SEC Gut Sarbanes-Oxley?" *CFO.com* 1 Mar. 2003, 30 May 2003 (www.cfo.com/printarticle/0,5317,8843)|C,OO.html).

[17] Susan Feyder, "Veteran Advisor Makes Sense of Congress' Corporate Reform," *Minneapolis Star-Tribune* 27 July 2002: D1.

[18] PricewaterhouseCoopers LLP, "Sarbanes-Oxley Act Requires Changes in Corporate Control, Compliance, According to PricewaterhouseCoopers Survey of Senior Executives," 24 Mar 2003 (www.faegre.com/articles/article_838.asp).

[19] Lance Jon Kimmel and Steven W. Vazquez, "The Increased Financial and Non-financial Cost of Staying Public," 2003 National Directors Institute 23 Apr. 2003. Full report available upon request from Foley & Lardner, www.foleylardner.com.

[20] Eighty percent of the increase was attributable to higher costs for D&O insurance, audit fees, legal fees, board compensation and compliance personnel.

[21] Pierce A. McNally, "Too Much Cost, Too Few Benefits," *Minneapolis Star Tribune* 21 Sept. 2003: D4.

[22] Michael Schroeder, "Cleaner Living, No Easy Riches," *The Wall Street Journal* 22 July 2003: Cl.

corporations. For example, Dawn Marie Driscoll criticized SOx as an "underwhelming" initiative that failed to address the root cause of corporate misconduct:

> The reason is simple: the business scandals of the past year were caused by inattention to ethics and values. You can't legislate an ethical corporate culture, a diligent board of directors or senior executives with integrity. . . .
>
> When Enron, Tyco, WorldCom and others came to light, Congressmen acted like Captain Renault in the movie Casablanca: "shocked, shocked" that financial scandals may have resulted from legislative loopholes passed a few years earlier, from accounting reforms buried in legislative limbo and from an underfunded SEC. Unwilling to go home to the voters and say, "Capitalism is not risk-free," they needed to pass some laws that would make everyone feel better.
>
> Capitalism is not risk-free, but it must not be ethics-free. Our capital market structure is built on trust. . . . There is no law or requirement that can be passed that will mandate, "Do a good job." But economic and political leaders of integrity could have stood up and, like the little child who exposed the Emperor, said, "The folks who were responsible for those business scandals were not business leaders of integrity. There is no shortcut or quick fix to that."[23]

Frank Brown, the global leader of PricewaterhouseCoopers' Assurance and Business Advisory Services, echoed Driscoll's concern about the limited ability of law to influence a firm's moral culture. "Rules, standards, and frameworks can only do so much," he noted, "it will take demonstrated commitment to transparency, accountability, and integrity to restore public trust."[24]

[23] Dawn Marie Driscoll, "Sarbanes-Oxley: Pardon Me If I'm Underwhelmed," *Ethics Matters* Feb. 2003 (ecampus.bentley.edu/dept/cbe/newsletter/jannewsletter/SOX_Issue_1.pdf).

[24] PricewaterhouseCoopers LLP.

Conclusion

A *Forbes* article published to commemorate the first anniversary of the law's signing noted that "nobody thinks Sarbanes-Oxley will be an instant fix."[25] The law was the consequence of a "focusing moment" on corporate governance, the business scandals of 2001–02. Its standards underscore board and executive accountability for corporate conduct and financial disclosures. It also demonstrated the willingness of government to step in when the professions—in this case, the accounting and legal professions—failed to effectively regulate themselves. But while the Sarbanes-Oxley Act of 2002 represented a step toward improved corporate governance, by the summer of 2003 it remained unclear just how significant an advance it was, and whether some adjustment of its mandates was required to better balance the law's costs and benefits. It also remained unclear whether the SEC rule-making process could adequately reconcile Sarbanes-Oxley's requirements with the increasingly global nature of the capital markets.

For practitioners, the most cogent dimension of the debate over Sarbanes-Oxley was the criticism emphasizing that the scandals of 2001–02 resulted as much from *moral* failure as *legal* failure. They served as a helpful reminder that an exclusive focus upon legal compliance would ultimately prove inadequate to protecting a company from the breakdowns that undermined Enron, Tyco, and WorldCom. Laws and regulations can change behaviors by adjusting incentives and sanctions; however, they have a difficult time reaching the fundamental ethical values that operate within a firm. Hence, corporate directors and executives must complement their Sarbanes-Oxley compliance effort with work designed to create, institutionalize, and sustain a robust culture of conscience.

[25] Fass.

EXHIBIT 1 The SEC Definition of a Financial Expert

Section 407 of the Sarbanes-Oxley Act requires the audit committee of publicly traded companies to include at least one member who qualifies as a financial expert under rules promulgated by the Securities and Exchange Commission (SEC). The competencies required for this status include:

- An understanding of generally accepted accounting principles (GAAP) and financial statements.
- The ability to assess the application of GAAP in connection with accounting for estimates, accruals, and reserves.
- Experience preparing, auditing, analyzing, or evaluating financial statements that display a complexity comparable to the company's statements, or experience supervising individuals engaged in such activities.
- An understanding of internal controls and financial reporting procedures.
- An understanding of audit committee functions.

EXHIBIT 2 Nonaudit Services Prohibited by the Sarbanes-Oxley Act

Section 201 of the Sarbanes-Oxley Act prohibits public accounting firms from providing the following services to their audit clients:

- Bookkeeping, or other services related to the accounting records or financial statements of the audit client.
- Financial information systems design and implementation.
- Appraisal or valuation services, fairness opinions, or contribution-in-kind reports.
- Actuarial services.
- Internal audit outsourcing services.
- Management functions or human resources.
- Broker or dealer, investment adviser, or investment banking services.
- Legal services and expert services unrelated to the audit.
- Any other service that the Public Company Accounting Oversight Board determines, by regulation, is impermissible.

EXHIBIT 3 CEO and CFO Certifications

Section 302 of the Sarbanes-Oxley Act requires a company 's chief executive officer and chief financial officer to certify in their company's quarterly and annual reports that:

1. They have reviewed the report.
2. To the best of their knowledge, the report neither omits material facts nor contains misleading or inaccurate information.
3. To the best of their knowledge, the report fairly presents the company's financial position, including operating results and cash flows.
4. They are responsible for establishing and maintaining the company's internal controls; the internal controls have been designed, established, and maintained for the purpose of providing material information to them about the company and its subsidiaries; they have evaluated and reported on the effectiveness of these controls within 90 days of the report's filing; and they have disclosed in the report their conclusions about the controls' effectiveness.
5. They have disclosed to the audit committee and auditors all material weaknesses or deficiencies in the design or operation of the internal control system; and they have disclosed all fraud, material or not, involving any individual who plays a significant role in the internal control system.
6. They have disclosed within the report whether any changes to the internal controls that could appreciably affect their effectiveness were implemented subsequent to the date of the evaluation, including corrections of significant or material weaknesses.

A Brief Note on Corporate Ethics Officers

Because corporations and their members are interdependent, for the corporation to be strong the members need to share a preconceived notion of what is correct behavior, a "business ethic," and think of it as a positive force, not a constraint. . . . The word "ethics" turns off many and confuses more. Yet the notions of shared values and an agreed-on process for dealing with adversity and change—what many people mean when they talk about corporate culture—seem to be at the heart of the ethical issue.

—Bowen McCoy,
The Parable of the Sadhu

Introduction

A common paradigm for business through the latter part of the 20th century has been to do whatever it takes to make a profit. A 1998 study released by the American Society of Chartered Life Underwriters & Chartered Financial Consultants and the Ethics Officers Association found that 56 percent of workers surveyed had felt pressure in the workplace to act illegally or unethically. Furthermore, 48 percent of the survey's respondants admitted engaging in illicit or unethical behavior on the job during the previous year.[1]

A variation on this model suggests that managers' actions should be limited only by the demands of the market or of law. Since the mid-1970s, several laws and regulations designed to shape business conduct have been introduced. However, legal measures are not enough to prevent ethical wrongdoing. While law can change behavior by adjusting incentives and sanctions, it has a difficult time reaching the basic ethical values that operate within organizations. To help corporate leaders move beyond the prevention of illegal conduct, many organizations have created the position of the *ethics officer*. This new function is intended to assist with the task of educating managers on how to tackle issues from a balanced ethical perspective, building a corporate climate that promotes respect for law and ethical behavior.

Foreign Corrupt Practices Act (1977)

It came to light in the mid-1970s that a large number of publicly owned U.S. corporations had engaged in "illegal or 'questionable' payments to political figures both in the U.S. and abroad."[2] As a result the Foreign Corrupt Practices Act (FCPA), among other things, made it a criminal offense for an American company or its executives to bribe foreign officials and politicians (Exhibit 1).

Twenty years later, in 1997, representatives of 35 countries signed a treaty developed by the Organization for Economic Cooperation and Development (OECD) to combat bribery in international business transactions. The convention required signatories to outlaw certain forms of bribery and to develop a systematic follow-up program to ensure effective implementation. By 2003, all 35 parties to the treaty had laws in force which criminalized the bribery of foreign public officials in international business transactions.[3]

This note was prepared in 1998 by Research Assistant Hassan Valji, and revised in 2004 by Research Associate T. Dean Maines, under the supervision of Kenneth E. Goodpaster, Koch Professor of Business Ethics, University of St. Thomas.

[1] Jacquelyn Lynn, "Do the Right Thing," *Entreprenuer.com* Aug. 1998, 20 Sept. 2004 (www.entrepreneur.com/mag/article/0,1539,229088,00.html).

[2] Kenneth E. Goodpaster, Laura L. Nash, and John B. Matthews, *Policies and Persons*, 3rd ed. (New York: McGraw-Hill, 1998) 485.

[3] "Major Progress Made in Anti-bribery Campaign, Evans Says," U.S. Department of State International Information Programs 26 June 2003, 31 Aug. 2004 (usinfo.state.gov/ei/Archive/2004/Jan/07-445143.html).

The Defense Industry Initiatives (1986)

During the 1980s, "public concern about the defense industry grew as investigations of major defense contractors and reports of procurement irregularities increased."[4] In 1985, an independent Blue Ribbon Commission on Defense Management (called the Packard Commission after its chairman, David Packard) was created to conduct a broad study of defense management. An interim report, released in early 1986, recognized the limits of federal regulation and suggested that effective *self-governance* might help curb industry misconduct.

Several defense contractors responded to the preliminary recommendations by drafting six principles that became known as the Defense Industry Initiative on Business Ethics and Conduct (Exhibit 2). These principles "were intended to promote sound management practices, to ensure that companies were in compliance with complex regulations, and to restore public confidence in the defense industry."[5] In June 1986, 24 defense contractors pledged to promote ethical business conduct through the implementation of policies, procedures, and programs. The Defense Industry Initiative has since grown to 48 member firms, including virtually all of the top 25 defense contractors.

The U.S. Federal Sentencing Guidelines for Organizations (1991)

In 1987, Congress passed the Federal Sentencing Guidelines to create more uniformity in sentencing criminals. It amended the guidelines in 1991 to cover organizational offenders. The amendments, referred to as the Federal Sentencing Guidelines for Organizations, drew some of their content from the Defense Industry Initiatives. The Federal Sentencing Guidelines for Organizations were "designed so that the sanctions imposed upon organizations and their agents, taken together, will provide just punishment, adequate deterrence, and incentives for organizations to maintain internal mechanisms for preventing, detecting, and reporting criminal conduct."[6]

The guidelines allowed the imposition of reduced penalties on companies with corporate compliance programs. To qualify, such programs had to fulfill seven minimum requirements (Exhibit 3). These include assigning "high-level personnel to oversee the compliance program, such as an ethics officer, ombudsman, or compliance officer."[7]

Revised Federal Sentencing Guidelines for Organizations (2004)

In May 2004, the U.S. Sentencing Commission recommended to Congress certain modifications of the 1991 Federal Sentencing Guidelines for Organizations. The revised guidelines, which went into effect in November 2004, introduced new requirements designed to catalyze changes in corporate compliance programs.

Three changes were particularly significant. First, the revised guidelines mandated that companies periodically evaluate the effectiveness of their compliance programs. They also stipulated ongoing assessments of the risk that a compliance program might fail. A company must use the results of these risk assessments to improve its program's design or implementation.

Second, the revisions required the promotion of an organizational culture that encourages *ethical conduct* as well as observance of the law. This new provision recognized the decisive influence a firm's culture can exercise on employee behavior, as illustrated by many of the business scandals that emerged in 2001 and 2002. It also formally introduced ethics as a constitutive element in an effective compliance program.

Third, the revised guidelines underscored the responsibility of directors and senior executives for a company's compliance program. Corporate directors must be knowledgeable about the content and operation of the organization's program and must receive training appropriate to their role and responsibilities. Company executives are

[4] *1998 Annual Report, The Defense Industry Initiative on Business Ethics and Conduct*, 20 Sept. 2004 (www.dii.org/annual/1998 background.html).

[5] *1998 Annual Report*.

[6] Itamar Sittenfeld, "Federal Sentencing Guidelines for Organizations," *Internal Auditor* 53.2 (1996): 58.

[7] Paul E. Fiorelli, "Why Comply? Directors Face Heightened Personal Liability after Caremark," *Business Horizons* 41.4 (1998): 50.

responsible for ensuring the firm's compliance program is effective. This includes providing the individual charged with day-to-day responsibility for the program with adequate resources, authority, and access, including access to the board of directors or the appropriate board committee.

The Ethics Officer Role

As a position that is fairly new to the business world, there is no standard definition of the tasks an ethics officer should undertake. However, most ethics officers provide support in four major areas: (1) serving as a resource to managers and employees on questions of ethics and legal compliance; (2) monitoring the corporation's policies and procedures; (3) developing ethics training programs; and (4) assisting with deliberations on ethical concerns. In the words of Edward Petry and Fred Tietz, the ethics officer "is expected to be confessor, corporate conscience, investigator, enforcer, and teacher, all rolled into one.[8]

The Ethics Officers Association (EOA) was created in 1991 to support incumbents of this new position. From 12 charter members, the EOA has grown to include 955 companies in 34 different industries. Initially, its efforts focused on providing educational and networking opportunities. The EOA's initiatives have since expanded to include an annual conference addressing current issues facing ethics officers, as well as other opportunities for exploring ethics-related trends and practices.

[8] Edward S. Petry Jr. and Fred Tietz, "Can Ethics Officers Improve Office Ethics?" *Business and Society Review* 82 (1992): 21.

Ethics officers are not the only ethics-related careers available. Some organizations name a *compliance officer* to oversee the legal aspects of an ethics officer's role in the organization, that is, to ensure the organization is not unknowingly violating any laws or regulations. Another position is that of the *ombudsperson*, a person appointed to investigate complaints against the firm as reported by employees.

Conclusion

The ethics officer's position can be viewed as somewhat paradoxical insofar as it seems to involve being paid to "bite the hand that feeds it." However, this is a misperception that fails to appreciate the positive contribution an ethics officer can make. In many ways, the ethics officer assists with the critical task of forming the organization's "conscience."[9] The role helps foster an ethical environment, aids decision making, and supports doing the right thing even though it may not always be financially or strategically ideal.

In view of the ethics officer's role, it is vital to have access to the top of the corporation's hierarchy. Lacking this, he or she will lack the clout necessary to initiate change. Yet it also is important that the ethics officer not be identified as a member of upper management, since this could fracture communications with the rank and file. Instead, the ethics officer must be viewed as occupying a role at the center of the organization, accessible by employees at all levels and responsive to their concerns.

[9] Kenneth E. Goodpaster and John B. Matthews, Jr., "Can a Corporation Have a Conscience?" *Harvard Business Review on Corporate Responsibility* (Boston: Harvard Business School Publishing, 2003) 131–155.

EXHIBIT 1 Summary of the Foreign Corrupt Practices Act (1977)

Source: Adapted from "Summary of the U.S. Foreign Corrupt Practices Act" by Procopio, Cory, Hargreaves & Savitch LLP (www.procopio.com/publications/art_corrupt_en.html).

The Foreign Corrupt Practices Act (FCPA) represented Congress's determination that competition in overseas markets should be based on price and product quality, rather than on questionable payments to foreign political leaders.

Background

Before the enactment of the FCPA, U.S. corporations that bribed foreign officials could only be prosecuted indirectly. The SEC maintained that U.S. corporations were required to disclose such payments as part of the securities laws. In addition, prosecutors could invoke the Bank Secrecy Act, which requires the reporting of funds that are taken out of, or brought into, the United States. The Mail Fraud Act, which prohibits the use of U.S. mail or wire communications to transact a fraudulent commercial scheme, was also available to reach these bribes. The FCPA was meant to be a more direct and effective means of enforcement.

Scope

The FCPA has a two-pronged approach for (1) disclosure and (2) prohibition. The disclosure prong constitutes the first part of the act, and involves accounting and record-keeping provisions. This section requires a corporation to keep accurate accounts of all transactions it conducts. The second prong—the prohibition prong—of the FCPA forbids the bribery of foreign officials by U.S. businesses. Specifically, the act prohibits American companies and their agents from using the mail or other means of interstate commerce to make an illicit payment to a foreign official or politician to use his or her power or influence to help the American firm obtain or retain business for itself or any other person.

Persons and Entities Subject to the FCPA

The FCPA applies to all U.S. businesses and individuals by requiring adherence to the act by all issuers of securities and all domestic concerns. By law, a domestic concern is defined as:

1. Any individual who is a citizen, national, or resident of the United States.
2. Any corporation, partnership, association, joint-stock company, business trust, unincorporated organization, or sole proprietorship which has its principal place of business in the United States, or which is organized under the laws of a state of the United States or a United States territory, possession, or commonwealth.

In addition to U.S. business and individuals, the FCPA also applies to any official, director, employee, agent, or stockholder acting on behalf of such issuers or domestic concerns. A person is deemed to know that a payment to a third party will be used to bribe a foreign official if the person is aware or has a firm belief that the third party is engaging in such conduct or that such a result is substantially certain to occur.

Exceptions: Transactions Not Subject to the FCPA

There are payments that might otherwise be deemed "bribes" which are not illegal under the FCPA. Acceptable types of payments include so-called grease or facilitating payments, so long as the purpose of the payment is to expedite or to secure the performance of a "routine governmental action."

Under the act, a routine governmental action is an ordinary and commonly performed act undertaken by a foreign official. Examples include:

1. Providing permits, licenses, or other official documents to qualify a person to do business in a foreign country.
2. Processing governmental papers, such as visas and work orders.
3. Providing police protection, mail pickup and delivery, or scheduling inspections associated with contract performance or inspections related to transit of goods across a country.
4. Providing phone service, power, and water supply; loading and unloading cargo; or protecting perishable products or commodities from deterioration.
5. Actions of a similar nature.

The term does *not* include any decision by a foreign official whether, or on what terms, to award new business to or to continue business with a particular party. It also excludes any action taken by a foreign official involved in the decision-making process to encourage a decision to award new business to or continue business with a particular party.

Penalties for Violation of the FCPA

Civil violations and criminal convictions under the FCPA carry potentially severe penalties. A fine of up to $10,000 exists for civil violations as a possible sanction. Additionally, convictions of the FCPA carry criminal penalties for an individual of up to $100,000, while the maximum criminal fine for a U.S. corporation is $2 million.

EXHIBIT 2 Defense Industry Initiative (DII) on Business Ethics and Conduct

Source: Defense Industry Initiative Web site (www.dii.org/Principles.htm).

Principles

1. Each company will have and adhere to a written code of business ethics and conduct.
2. The company's code establishes the high values expected of its employees and the standards by which they must judge their own conduct and that of their organization; each company will train its employees concerning their personal responsibilities under the code.
3. Each company will create a free and open atmosphere that allows and encourages employees to report violations of its code to the company without fear of retribution for such reporting.
4. Each company has the obligation to self-govern by monitoring compliance with federal procurement laws and adopting procedures for voluntary disclosure of violations of federal procurement laws and corrective actions taken.
5. Each company has the responsibility to each of the other companies in the industry to live by standards of conduct that preserve the integrity of the defense industry.
6. Each company must have public accountability for its commitment to these principles.

EXHIBIT 3 Federal Sentencing Guidelines for Organizations (1991)

Source: Ethics and Policy Integration Centre (www.ethicaledge.com/appendix1.html).

Minimum Requirements for Corporate Compliance Programs

1. *Compliance standards and procedures.* The organization must have established compliance standards and procedures to be followed by its employees and other agents that are reasonably capable of reducing the prospect of criminal conduct.
2. *High-level personnel responsible.* Specific individual(s) within high-level personnel of the organization must have been assigned overall responsibility to oversee compliance with such standards and procedures.
3. *Due care in assignments.* The organization must have used due care not to delegate substantial discretionary authority to individuals whom the organization knew, or should have known through the exercise of due diligence, had a propensity to engage in illegal activities.
4. *Communicate standards and procedures.* The organization must have taken steps to communicate effectively its standards and procedures to all employees and other agents, e.g., by requiring participation in training programs or by disseminating publications that explain in a practical manner what is required.
5. *Establish monitoring and auditing systems and reporting system.* The organization must have taken reasonable steps to achieve compliance with its standards, e.g., by utilizing monitoring and auditing systems reasonably designed to detect criminal conduct by its employees and other agents and by having in place and publicizing a reporting system whereby employees and other agents could report criminal conduct by others within the organization without fear of retribution.
6. *Enforce standards through appropriate mechanisms.* The standards must have been consistently enforced through appropriate mechanisms, including, as appropriate, discipline of individuals responsible for the failure to detect an offensive.
7. *Respond appropriately to the offense.* After an offense has been detected, the organization must have taken all the reasonable steps to respond appropriately to the offense and to prevent further similar offenses—including any necessary modifications to its program to prevent and detect violations of law.

American Refining Group, Inc. (A)

"Harvey, I look forward to seeing the redeployment estimates."

Harvey Golubock, the president and chief operating officer of the American Refining Group, Inc., turned to see Harry Halloran standing in the doorway of his office. Halloran, the chief executive officer of the firm, was preparing to return to Philadelphia after a strategy session held at the company's Bradford refinery on August 12, 2002.

Golubock smiled. "Gee, boss, do you think you could make my job a little harder? I'm looking for a few more challenges these days."

The response elicited a laugh from Halloran. "Harvey, after what we've been through, I'd think you'd consider integrating the Rouseville operation without employee redundancies a mere *trial*, as opposed to a full-blown *challenge*. Seriously, the plan for reassigning Bradford employees is the key to making this acquisition work in a way that is consistent with what we want this company to be. Keep me updated on your progress."

"Don't worry, Harry, I will," Golubock replied. "Have a good drive home."

After Halloran had departed, Golubock sat back in his chair to gather his thoughts. The acquisition of the refinery in Rouseville, Pennsylvania, would strengthen American Refining's strategic position. But combining two refineries 80 miles apart raised a host of operational issues. Halloran had also raised the stakes during that day's strategy session by insisting the integration take place without one Bradford employee losing his or her job. In a sense, the directive was an extension of Halloran's ongoing effort to base the company's decisions and actions on a consistent set of values and principles. It was a laudable goal, and one Golubock agreed with; however, Golubock thought, values and principles only come to life through concrete plans. It wasn't clear to him that *any* plan would satisfy Halloran's expectation.

This case was prepared by Research Associate T. Dean Maines under the supervision of Kenneth E. Goodpaster, Koch Professor of Business Ethics, University of St. Thomas, as a basis for class discussion rather than to illustrate either effective or ineffective handling of an administrative situation.

Harry R. Halloran

Harry R. Halloran Jr. grew up in Philadelphia, Pennsylvania, where he attended Norwood Academy and St. Joseph's Preparatory School. He distinguished himself in competitive crew while a teenager: Rowing for the Vesper Boat Club at the age of 15, Halloran became the youngest oarsman to ever compete on a national championship team. He also participated in international competitions, rowing in Europe on a crew captained by John B. Kelly Jr., the younger brother of actress Grace Kelly.

Halloran entered the University of Pennsylvania in 1957, where he continued his rowing career. He graduated in 1961 with a bachelor of science in civil engineering, a degree that seemingly prepared him for a career with one of his family's construction companies. Instead, Halloran entered a Roman Catholic religious community, the Order of St. Augustine. Studying for the priesthood, he earned a master of theology degree from the Augustinian College of Washington, D.C.; however, he left the Augustinians in 1966, prior to ordination. Halloran taught religious and scriptural studies at St. Vincent's College in Latrobe, Pennsylvania, and was admitted to a doctoral program at Pittsburgh Theological Seminary in 1970. But rather than matriculate, Halloran accepted a position in Maine as a VISTA volunteer, serving as the manager of a rural business cooperative.

In 1972, Halloran's father, the owner and chairman of the Conduit and Foundation Company, fell ill unexpectedly. Soon after his father was hospitalized, Halloran received a phone call from one of the firm's senior managers, who lectured him on his duties to the company's 500 employees as the eldest son of the controlling shareholder. Within three weeks Halloran had returned to Philadelphia, where he became the organization's secretary and treasurer. He immediately faced a financial crisis, and successfully steered the company through it.

Halloran thereafter became increasingly involved with his family's business holdings. These holdings grew in 1975 with the purchase of American Refining Group, Inc. (ARG). Halloran was named chief executive officer of the new acquisition.

ARG and the Bradford Refinery

At the time of its purchase by the Halloran family, ARG was a start-up operation with annual revenues of approximately $4 million. The firm's principal activity was "transmix" processing. Transmix was a comingling of refined oil products, a by-product of pipeline transmission. ARG purchased transmix from pipeline operators and then further refined it, breaking the mixture into its components (gasoline, diesel fuel, and kerosene). ARG marketed these finished products at the wholesale level. ARG's transmix refining took place at facilities located near Pittsburgh, Pennsylvania, and St. Louis, Missouri. In addition, ARG had a natural gas division, which acquired drill sites in western Pennsylvania and Alabama, managed drilling operations, and captured the fuel for transmission. The company also owned and operated a chain of retail service stations in the greater Pittsburgh area.

ARG's business activities remained unchanged until the mid-1990s. In 1996, the company spun off its natural gas division as a separate organization. That same year, ARG began to investigate the purchase of a refinery in Bradford, Pennsylvania, a town of approximately 10,000 residents 70 miles southeast of Buffalo, New York. Located in an oil-rich region stretching from western New York and Pennsylvania into West Virginia and Ohio, the Bradford operation had been founded in 1881. It had the distinction of being the oldest continuously operated oil refinery in the United States.

Crude oil is a complex mixture of different components, or fractions. The refining process separated these fractions into usable products. Refineries are designed to process specific types of feedstocks, or crude oil, and the Bradford facility handled only Pennsylvania Grade crude. This class of crude contained high concentrations of waxes and paraffins. Its composition made it particularly well suited for refining into lubricating base stocks. Furthermore, the facility had its own blending and packaging operation. This gave it the capacity to mix base stocks and additives according to different formulas, to produce private label and generic lubricants. Consequently, lubrication oils—motor oils, transmission fluid, gear lubricants, hydraulic oils, metalworking oils, industrial oils, and greases —were one of Bradford's main product lines. The refinery's most recognizable product was Kendall lubricants. It also produced a range of fuels (gasoline, diesel, and boiler fuel), naphthas (lantern fuel, white gas, and mineral spirits), waxes, and other specialty products. The operation was ISO-9002 certified, the first refinery in the United States to attain this status.

The Bradford refinery was owned by Witco Corporation. When ARG began its investigation, the refinery was the second largest employer in Bradford, providing approximately 160 jobs. Given the facility's importance to the local economy, and the scarcity of other potential buyers, state and local government agencies offered grants, loans, and tax credits to encourage ARG's interest.

The Bradford facility presented numerous challenges. The primary one was the operation's financial sustainability. Roughly 30 percent of the refinery's sales came from Kendall products, and the blending and packaging facility was entirely dedicated to the Kendall line. However, in October 1996, Witco sold the Kendall brand name to Sunoco, Inc. The move induced an immediate financial crisis. Overnight, the primary customer of the facility's lubricant stocks had been eliminated, and all blending and packaging employees were laid off.

The sale of the Kendall brand name impaired the value of the Bradford operation. In the end, ARG struck an agreement with Witco to purchase the refinery's assets for one dollar, plus $17 million for the product in inventory. The agreement was signed in December 1996, and took effect on March 3, 1997.

Harvey Golubock

After negotiating the Bradford purchase agreement, Halloran knew he needed to find an experienced general manager to lead the refinery. In February 1997 he hired Harvey Golubock for this position. Golubock previously had served as Witco's Group vice president for lubricants. A New York City native, Golubock had earned a bachelor of science in chemical engineering from the City College of New York, and a master of business administration from Rutgers University. He had joined Witco in 1969 as a planning analyst, and rose to one of the company's top operating positions. Since Witco's sale of the Bradford facility was part of a divestment strategy for its entire lubricants division, Golubock welcomed ARG's offer as a new opportunity. He saw himself on a mission to save the refinery and to contribute to the broader good of Bradford by preserving and creating well-paying jobs. Golubock viewed the incentives ARG had received from Bradford and the state of Pennsylvania as a vote of confidence. He wanted to honor their trust by making the organization a source of economic vitality and community pride.

Golubock faced a number of formidable problems. First, he had to reduce the refinery's financial losses. Second, he had to find new customers or new uses for its lubricant stock production. Third, all but one of his new staff members would be tackling much larger assignments. "When control of the facility passed from Witco to ARG, all of the generals were gone," Golubock commented, "everyone needed to step up." It was unclear whether they could successfully grow into their new responsibilities. Furthermore, some members of the staff had long histories of interpersonal conflict and distrust. Fourth, Golubock had to establish personal credibility with the workforce. The Bradford employees harbored deep animosity toward Witco, a consequence of what they considered to be the company's neglect and poor management of the facility. As a former Witco executive, Golubock became the focus of their ill will. This dynamic introduced an added degree of difficulty into his job.

"The World We All Want"

In the wake of the Bradford acquisition, Harry Halloran began to devote an increasing amount of time to efforts that reached far beyond ARG. Over the course of his career, Halloran had observed that companies tended to fall somewhere between two poles. At one end of this spectrum were a few organizations whose net impact on society as a whole was unequivocally beneficial; at the opposite end were a handful of firms whose overall effect was overwhelmingly negative. Most companies fell between these two extremes. The problem Halloran began to probe was how one might measure a corporation's "total social impact."

Halloran was convinced that business leaders would find such a measurement system useful. It could function like the navigation instruments in a supertanker's wheelhouse, helping directors and executives steer their organization toward conduct that would advance the common good. To complement these internal measures, a set of external metrics might be developed that would help investors make a similar assessment, enabling them to channel capital into responsible business organizations.

Halloran's interest in corporate responsibility, along with his broader interest in questions of social development, led him to do two things. First, he created a private foundation, intended to help catalyze the emergence of "the world we all want." Halloran envisioned the foundation collaborating with other organizations to encourage the development of social conditions that would promote human flourishing, both material and moral. Second, Halloran became active within a group of executives known as the Caux Round Table.

The Caux Round Table

The Caux Round Table was a network of senior business leaders from developed and developing nations. These individuals were united by the conviction that business needed to play a larger role in creating societies that were free, fair, sustainable, and prosperous. The organization took its name from a small Swiss village, Caux sur Montreux, which overlooked the eastern tip of Lake Geneva. A grand hotel there served as the site of the Round Table's annual global dialogue.

The Caux Round Table had been launched by Frederik J. Philips, the former president of Philips Electronics. In 1986, Philips brought together executives from Japan, Europe, and United States to seek solutions to growing trade tensions between the regions. Their dialogue was characterized by mutual respect and careful listening. Participants recognized that they were motivated by common values, regardless of their country of origin. They found the discussion so helpful that they committed to return annually to address issues of mutual concern, such as company governance, corporate transparency, and responsible foreign investment and trade. By the mid-1990s, over 250 senior business leaders from 25 different countries had participated in national, regional, and global dialogues sponsored by the organization.

In 1994, the Caux Round Table promulgated a set of principles designed to help business leaders manage responsibly in a global context. The Caux Round Table *Principles for Business*[1] were fashioned in part from a document called the *Minnesota Principles*, a statement of responsible business practice developed by the Minnesota Center for Corporate Responsibility. The Principles for Business include a comprehensive set of ethical guidelines for businesses that operated internationally or across cultures. The principles were formulated so that business leaders with either an Eastern or a Western cultural perspective would find them intelligible and acceptable.

Halloran attended the Caux Round Table's 1999 global dialogue. He soon became one of the organization's most active participants and biggest donors. Meanwhile, he carefully studied the Principles for Business. He ultimately became convinced that they could serve as the platform for a "total social impact" assessment of corporate performance.

Fixing Bradford

Implementation of ARG's turnaround plan for the Bradford refinery began on Monday, March 3, 1997. The final steps in the transition from Witco to ARG had been taken over the preceding weekend. On Monday morning, Harvey Golubock cut all salaries and wages by 10 percent and introduced a strict new set of financial controls. Both moves were designed to help staunch the losses plaguing the facility.

From the start, Golubock made the development of his staff a priority. He emphasized that staff members needed to feel responsible for solving all problems that arose within the facility, even if the issue fell outside their area of immediate responsibility. "Given the challenges before the refinery, there was no room for 'us' and 'them,'" Golubock explained. "We needed to be a 'we.'" External facilitators were brought in to assist with team building, an exercise that was moderately successful in overcoming past conflicts and helping the team's members better coordinate their efforts. Most importantly, Golubock invested a significant portion of his time in coaching his direct reports, helping them to discharge their new, expanded responsibilities more effectively.

Halloran and Golubock worked together to improve the latter's credibility with the Bradford workforce. Their primary tactic was to link Golubock with Halloran, who was viewed by many employees as the facility's "savior." To create this association, Halloran spent extensive time at the refinery, interacting with employees in Golubock's presence. Halloran and Golubock consulted regularly on questions of strategy and policy, which enabled them to give consistent replies to employee questions. They also ensured that all commitments made to the workforce were enacted, since employees ultimately would judge them by what they did, rather than by what they said.

The most critical issue Golubock faced was the development of a new set of customers for the refinery's lubrication products. Immediately after ARG took control of the facility, he tried to sell lubricant stocks to other blenders and packagers. These processors all had existing supply arrangements, and there was stiff competition among new suppliers that hoped to secure a slice of the business. In such a buyer's market, the refinery could not command the favorable margins it had enjoyed when it sold its lubricant stocks to its own on-site blending and packaging operation. This impelled Golubock to try to resurrect the former capability. He pursued this goal in two ways. First, he initiated the development of a proprietary line of lubricating products. Second, he and his staff looked for opportunities to produce private-label lubricants for other companies.

ARG introduced its new proprietary lubricants in fall 1998, under the BRAD PENN brand name. A few cases of the oil were produced and seeded with selected distributors in the northeastern United States. Golubock and his team targeted the brand at the value segment of the lubricant market, to minimize the need for extensive marketing campaigns. The limited promotions

[1] The Caux Round Table Principles for Business may be found in Appendix A.

they did undertake emphasized both the quality of the Pennsylvania Grade crude from which the products were derived ("the choice of manufacturers and consumers throughout the world since its discovery in 1859") and the quality of Bradford's production processes. By underscoring the product's local roots, they appealed to the regional loyalties of distributors and consumers. So positioned, BRAD PENN lubricants slowly began to gain acceptance.

Meanwhile, Golubock and his team enjoyed some success in securing contracts to produce private-label lubricants, which brought incremental volume into the blending and packaging operation. The organization achieved a major victory in April 2000 when it won a contract to produce and market Gulf-brand lubricants for an 11-state region. This carried particular significance in light of the 1999 sale of ARG's transmix division to Buckeye Pipeline Company. With that divestiture, the refining of Pennsylvania Grade crude became the corporation's sole focus.

By mid-2000, the Bradford operation still had not yet attained sustainable profitability. However, employee morale had improved, and some important operational milestones had been achieved. For example, the rate of lubricating oil production within Bradford's blending and packaging facility had increased from zero in March 1997 to 10 million gallons per year. In addition, the refinery's financial performance had improved enough that a portion of the 1997 pay cut had been reinstated. Yet there was no room for complacency. In June 2000 a union organizing campaign received sufficient support to necessitate an election. The hourly employees ultimately voted to remain nonunion, but the election reminded Golubock's team that the turnaround was still a work in progress.

The Self-Assessment and Improvement Process

By spring 2000, Harry Halloran was ready to launch the development of a corporate assessment tool based on the Caux Round Table Principles for Business. He was convinced that the assessment process, like the principles, should be founded on the insights of business practitioners. Halloran worked with the staff of the Caux Round Table to set up a series of meetings with current and former senior executives located in Minnesota's Twin Cities. These individuals, together with the support of business scholars at the University of St. Thomas, formed the nucleus of the working group that would create what eventually became known as the *self-assessment and improvement process* (SAIP).

The SAIP was designed to facilitate a direct assessment of the alignment, or "fit," between a company's behavior and the Caux Round Table Principles for Business. The SAIP was modeled after the self-assessment methodology within the Malcolm Baldrige National Quality Program, a comprehensive and flexible process for measuring total quality. The Baldrige approach represented the best thinking available on organizational self-assessment, incorporating the insights of business leaders, academics, and learning specialists. The SAIP was conceived as a multistage process, involving data collection, scoring, feedback, and action. The process was company-led and its results were company-confidential.

The inventors structured the SAIP around the Principles for Business. A company's performance against each of the seven general principles was evaluated from seven distinct perspectives: how well the firm fulfilled the fundamental duties that flowed from a given principle, and how well it had realized the aspirations described by this principle in its relationships with customers, employees, investors, suppliers, competitors, and communities. The result was a seven-by-seven assessment matrix (Exhibit 1). Each cell within the matrix contained an assessment criterion, and a series of additional questions ("benchmarks") which amplified and elaborated the criterion.

In applying the SAIP, a company identified and evaluated its responses to these questions. For example, to appraise itself against general principle 3 ("business behavior") as it related to owners and investors, the company would reflect upon the assessment criterion and benchmarks contained in cell 3.4 (Exhibit 2). These queries required the company to review its policies and practices concerning responses to shareholder inquiries and disclosures of material risks, as well as the processes it used to help ensure auditors rendered an independent judgment on company financial statements.

The SAIP identified the maximum possible score a company could receive for each cell of the matrix. By comparing its responses to a set of quantification guidelines, the firm generated a score for its current level of performance. By totaling the scores for all 49 cells, the company generated an overall indication of its performance in relation to the Principles for Business. The scoring process helped an organization's leadership identify areas where the company's performance was relatively strong or weak. This facilitated the formulation of initiatives intended to improve the company's conduct.

It took the working group approximately two years to move from the articulation of the SAIP concept to a detailed design. However, by spring 2002, the SAIP's development had reached the point where the tool was ready for testing.

Testing the SAIP at ARG

Halloran had occasionally discussed the SAIP with members of the ARG staff, especially as he traveled to Minneapolis with increasing frequency to review its development. In early 2002, Halloran gave the company's executive team (Exhibit 3) a reason to take more than a passing interest in the process when he announced that ARG would serve as the initial test site for the SAIP.

Halloran shared copies of the SAIP's process documentation with the executive team, which then planned its implementation. The SAIP's 275 questions were distributed in April, and a deadline of approximately six weeks was established for the responses.

Executive team members and others who addressed the questions found that their assignment encompassed three distinct subtasks. First, each question had to be interpreted. Most of the SAIP's questions were straightforward; however, a handful required time and thought to discern what exactly was being asked. Second, the respondent needed to establish whether a specific question was relevant to ARG. Some of the SAIP questions were applicable only to larger firms or firms with extensive international operations. Finally, the respondent also had to determine whether he or she had the information needed to answer a query or whether additional research was necessary.

By the end of May the company's responses had been compiled into a single document. While this organizational report represented ARG's collective response to the SAIP's benchmarks, the quality of the individual responses varied considerably. Also, where two or more responses were submitted for a single question—a requirement of the SAIP with some benchmarks, to ensure that all facets of the question were addressed—no attempt had been made to integrate the multiple replies. This presented an unforeseen challenge to the team charged with scoring the organizational report. Ultimately, it took the scoring team over three months to complete the assignment.

Reactions of executive team members to the process varied. Al Doering, the company's newly appointed general counsel, found the SAIP to be valuable. The process had functioned as a comprehensive, systematic introduction to ARG's workings, providing valuable insights into the organization's strengths and weaknesses. However, Doering faulted ARG's implementation process for further burdening leaders and operations personnel already carrying significant workloads. Golubock echoed this assessment. Golubock saw value in the broad concepts and principles behind the tool and in the tool's attempt to provide a moral compass for the organization. But the process of collecting the data and scoring it was "overwhelming" for the resource-constrained organization. John Trinkl, ARG's chief financial officer, singled out the leadership team's failure to discuss adequately the company's responses to the SAIP's questions as his biggest disappointment. He observed that

> [a] lack of dialogue between senior leaders—the opportunity to compare how I would have responded to a benchmark to how others would have replied—prevented us from forming a collective understanding of the results. In short, it prevented us from drawing more and better fruit from a process in which we had invested significant time and effort.

Jeannine Schoenecker, ARG's controller, believed the SAIP had highlighted a few significant problems within the organization, including the lack of formal policies. But this was not a new revelation—the same point had emerged in other discussions.

The ARG employees involved with the SAIP had devoted hundreds of hours to the data collection and scoring phases of its implementation. As

Halloran began to consider how best to capitalize on this investment, he found his attention and the attention of the entire executive team drawn to a strategic opportunity that had the potential to secure a vital technology and drastically change ARG's operations.

Rouseville

The 18 months between July 2000 and December 2001 had proved to be a watershed period for the Bradford operation and all of ARG. The two-pronged strategy for rebuilding the refinery's blending and packaging business began to gain traction, as demand for BRAD PENN products rose and the company won new processing contracts for private-label products. As a result, in spring 2001 ARG realized its first profit since acquiring the refinery. During the course of the year, the operation slowly began to hire new workers to help meet increases in demand. The refinery eventually added 80 new hires, bringing its total workforce to approximately 220.

By early 2002, it was apparent that limitations of the Bradford plant would restrict ARG's competitiveness. Under a system developed by the American Petroleum Institute, lubricant base stocks were categorized into four groups according to their composition and performance characteristics. All of ARG's stocks fell within group I, the lowest classification. New technologies were increasing the demands placed on motor oils and other lubricants, making use of higher-quality base stocks more and more the norm. ARG's private-label customers already were starting to insist upon group II stocks for their products. However, the Bradford refinery lacked the capability to upgrade group I base stocks to grade II. This enhancement required a hydrotreater, a processing unit that removed sulfur and nitrogen impurities from oil and improved its lubricating characteristics. Halloran and Golubock saw that a failure to introduce hydrotreating would lead to customer defections and an inevitable erosion of the value of ARG's products in the marketplace.

A previous study had estimated the cost of building a hydrotreater at Bradford at $35–50 million. Given the state of ARG's balance sheet, this option was cost-prohibitive. During 2001, Golubock had arranged for nearby refineries to hydrotreat small quantities of base stock on a contract basis ("toll processing"). One of these—a refinery located 80 miles southwest of Bradford in Rouseville, Pennsylvania—was closed late that same year by its owner, Calumet Lubricants. Upon learning this, Golubock contacted Calumet to discuss how the Rouseville operation might be utilized for ARG's benefit.

Talks with Calumet focused initially on reactivating the Rouseville facility to provide toll-process hydrotreatment for ARG. The site also had the potential to solve another limitation of the Bradford facility, a bottleneck at its methyl ethyl ketone (MEK) dewaxing unit. The MEK dewaxer used solvents to remove paraffins from the base stock. This improved the lubricant's performance at low temperatures—for example, helping depress an oil's pour point, the lowest temperature at which it could still flow.

In a memorandum sent on March 12, 2002, Golubock notified Bradford employees of the company's discussions with Calumet. Golubock's memo stressed the exchanges were only preliminary. Shortly thereafter, the talks turned to the possibility of ARG purchasing the Rouseville refinery. The discussions with Calumet continued throughout the spring and summer, coinciding with ARG's implementation of the SAIP. They culminated on August 8 with ARG signing a letter of intent to purchase the facility.

A Meeting in Bradford: August 12, 2002

On August 12, Halloran convened his executive team and the senior leadership of the Bradford refinery. The purpose of the meeting was to lay out his vision for ARG's near-term future, discuss how the Rouseville acquisition fit with this vision, and plan the company's due diligence work.

Halloran began the meeting by identifying the goals he believed the company needed to attain over the next five years. This included the growth of revenues from $140 to $210 million; a nearly fourfold increase in annual profits, from $4 to $15 million; a doubling of the products ARG offered; and the ongoing enhancement of product quality and customer service. Halloran also called for ARG to increase the utilization of its blending and packaging capacity from 25 to 100 percent and to enlarge its workforce to 300 employees. He insisted the company pursue these goals within a context of responsible conduct: ARG had to address environmental issues at the Bradford site, maintain its excellent safety record, and work to be considered "extraordinarily trustworthy by all our stakeholders."

Halloran noted that completing the acquisition and integrating the Rouseville refinery would be difficult, requiring a huge commitment on the part of those attending the meeting. However, the benefits offered by the opportunity were significant. By providing ARG with hydrotreatment capability and eliminating the dewaxing bottleneck, the Rouseville acquisition would enable the company to stay even and in some cases pull ahead of its competition. It also could open up the potential for joint ventures and other partnerships that would contribute to the firm's growth.

The aim, Halloran continued, should be to complete the Rouseville integration within one year. The first step toward this goal was follow-up on the letter of intent. ARG had 120 days from its signing to perform due diligence in preparation for the negotiation of a final sales agreement. It also had to secure financing during this period. The company needed an independent assessment of the facility's buildings and equipment and, more importantly, of any environmental concerns associated with the site. Some preliminary calculations suggested that approximately \$3–7 million would be required to retrofit and restart the plant, on top of the \$3 million sale price. An investment banking firm would be engaged to help ARG obtain the capital.

To develop the required estimates, the team needed to understand the acquisition's effect on the Bradford refinery. A critical challenge, Halloran pointed out, would be to determine how to integrate profitably two operations separated by 80 miles. "Harry," John Trinkl interjected, "this might be a good time to review the preliminary cost analysis, based on our best guess of the impact at Bradford." Trinkl noted that Don Keck, the operations manager of the Bradford refinery, had identified two processes that would become redundant with the Rouseville acquisition, the MEK dewaxing unit and an extraction unit. This would also reduce maintenance requirements at the Bradford refinery, creating additional possibilities for job reductions. In total, Trinkl concluded, 39 positions within Bradford could be eliminated, yielding a total annual savings of approximately \$2 million.

Halloran thanked Trinkl for the summary. He then spoke to the estimates:

> John's comments bring up a very important point. I believe that ARG must abide by the highest standards of ethical business conduct. That is why I have introduced the Caux Round Table Principles into the organization, and why I have insisted that we utilize SAIP, as a way of looking at ourselves in a mirror. It is only by living according to standards like the Caux Principles that our stakeholders will come to see us as trustworthy in all respects.
>
> How we implement the Rouseville acquisition will serve as a litmus test for ARG on this issue. That's why I believe we need to radically change the operating assumptions behind the numbers John cited. We need to integrate Rouseville without our Bradford employees losing any jobs.

Halloran's remarks elicited an immediate reaction from Trinkl. "Harry, that's a fine aspiration, but the projections on which we based the decision to sign the letter of intent assumed cost savings from downsizing the Bradford workforce. How do you propose we meet those numbers without involuntary attrition? There are practical limits to how many redeployments we can make."

Halloran smiled at Trinkl. "John," he responded, "it is not so much what *I* propose to do, but what *we* will do. I'm challenging this team to implement the acquisition without forcing any of our current employees onto the street. The critical issue is *how we make it so*. We have taken some giant strides over the past several years toward the goal of turning Bradford into a viable, thriving enterprise. We can't step back from that goal just because of Rouseville."

"Harry," Golubock interjected, "we've done a good job growing employment at the refinery. But we need to realistically assess how we can keep Bradford workers employed. As of now, we don't have such an assessment."

"Harvey, it sounds like a plan to reassign and retrain those employees is your starting point," Halloran responded. "Look, I want to acquire Rouseville, but I want to acquire it without our Bradford employees losing their jobs. That's the kind of company I believe ARG should be. We are not about layoffs; we are about growth and providing a measure of job security. My challenge is still on the table—and I think your first step in response should be to figure out where there are opportunities for redeployment."

EXHIBIT 1 **Self-Assessment and Improvement Process—Assessment Matrix**

Source: Kenneth E. Goodpaster, T. Dean Maines, and Arnold M. Weimerskirch, "A Baldrige Process for Ethics?" *Science and Engineering Ethics* 10 (2004): 248.

Category	1 Fundamental ratios	2 Customers	3 Employees	4 Owners/ operators	5 Suppliers/ partners	6 Competitors	7 Communities
1. Responsibilities of business	1.1	1.2	1.3	1.4	1.5	1.6	1.7
2. Economic and social impact of business	2.1	2.2	2.3	2.4	2.5	2.6	2.7
3. Business behavior	3.1	3.2	3.3	3.4	3.5	3.6	3.7
4. Respect for rules	4.1	4.2	4.3	4.4	4.5	4.6	4.7
5. Support for multilateral trade	5.1	5.2	5.3	5.4	5.5	5.6	5.7
6. Respect for the environment	6.1	6.2	6.3	6.4	6.5	6.6	6.7
7. Avoidance of illicit operations	7.1	7.2	7.3	7.4	7.5	7.6	7.7

EXHIBIT 2 **Self-Assessment and Improvement Process—Selected Benchmarks, Cell 3.4**

Source: Kenneth E. Goodpaster, T. Dean Maines, and Arnold M. Weimerskirch, "A Baldrige Process for Ethics?" *Science and Engineering Ethics* 10 (2004): 249.

3.4. Owners/Investors

What level of trust has the company achieved with owners/investors? How transparent is the company to owners/investors, and how is this transparency achieved and measured?

3.4.1 What are the company's policies concerning:

- 3.4.1.1. the disclosure of information to owners/investors.
- 3.4.1.2. formal shareholder resolutions.
- 3.4.1.3. responses to inquiries, suggestions, or complaints from owners/investors. . . .

3.4.3 How does the company address the following trust and transparency issues:

- 3.4.3.1. Preparing, auditing, and disclosing financial and operating results in accordance with high quality standards of financial reporting and auditing.
- 3.4.3.2. Disclosing major share ownership and voting rights.
- 3.4.3.3. Revealing material foreseeable risk factors. . . .

3.4.5 How does the company perform an annual audit? Describe the applicable processes, including how an independent auditor is used to provide an external and objective assurance on the way in which financial statements have been prepared and audited.

3.4.6 What are the company's results with respect to third-party ratings of owner/investor relations?

EXHIBIT 3 American Refining Group, Inc., Executive Team

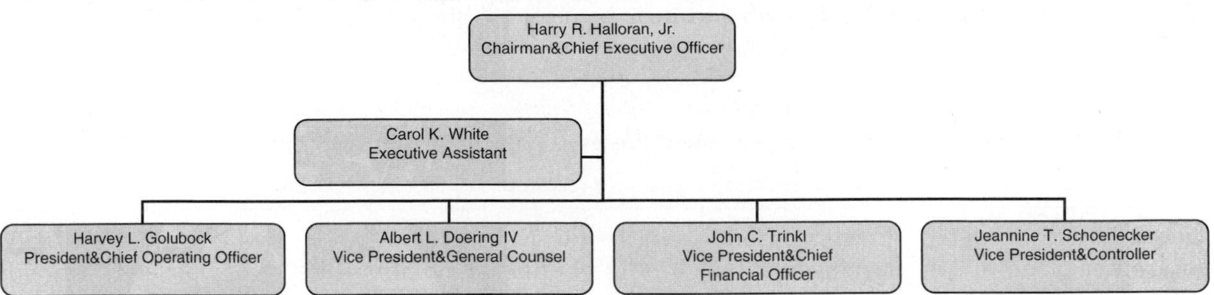

H. J. Heinz Company: *The Administration of Policy (A)*

In April 1979 James Cunningham, H. J. Heinz Company's president and chief operating officer, learned that since 1972 certain Heinz divisions had allegedly engaged in improper income transferal practices. Payments had been made to certain vendors in a particular fiscal year, then repaid or exchanged for services in the succeeding fiscal year.[1]

These allegations came out during the investigation of an unrelated antitrust matter. Apparent improprieties were discovered in the records of the Heinz USA division's relationship with one of its advertising agencies. Joseph Stangerson—senior vice president, secretary, and general counsel for Heinz—asked the advertising agency about the alleged practices. Not only had the agency personnel confirmed the allegation about Heinz USA, it indicated that similar practices had been used by Star-Kist Foods, another Heinz division. The divisions allegedly solicited improper invoices from the advertising agency in fiscal year (FY) 1974 so that they could transfer income to FY 1975. While the invoices were paid in FY 1974, the services described on the invoices were not rendered until sometime during FY 1975. Rather than capitalizing the amount as a prepaid expense, the amount was charged as an expense in FY 1974. The result was an understatement of FY 1974 income and an equivalent overstatement of FY 1975 income.

Stangerson reported the problem to John Bailey, vice chairman and chief executive officer; to Robert Kelly, senior vice president–finance and treasurer; and to Cunningham. Bailey, CEO since 1966, had presided over 13 uninterrupted years of earnings growth. He was scheduled to retire as vice chairman and CEO on July 1 and would remain as a member of the board of directors. James Cunningham, who had been president and chief operating officer since 1972, was to become chief executive officer on July 1, 1979.

Subsequent reports indicate that neither the scope of the practice nor the amounts involved were known. There was no apparent reason to believe that the amounts involved would have had a material effect on Heinz's reported earnings during the time period, including earnings for FY 1979 ending May 2. (Heinz reported financial results on the basis of a 52–53 week fiscal year ending on the Wednesday closest to April 30.) Stangerson was not prepared to say whether the alleged practices were legal or illegal. "This thing could be something terrible or it could be merely a department head using conservative accounting practices; we don't know,"[2] one Heinz senior official stated to the press.

Background

Henry J. Heinz, on founding the company in 1869 in Pittsburgh, Pennsylvania, said: "This is my goal—to bring home-cooking standards into canned foods, making them so altogether wholesome and delicious and at the same time so reasonable that people everywhere will enjoy them in abundance."[3] The company's involvement in food products never changed, and in 1979 Heinz operated some 30 companies with products reaching 150 countries. Heinz reported sales of over $2.2 billion and net income of $99.1 million in FY 1978.

After a sluggish period in the early 1960s, a reorganization was undertaken to position Heinz for growth. Under the guidance of John Bailey and James Cunningham, Heinz prospered through a major recession, government price controls, and major currency fluctuations. The 1978 annual

[1] H. J. Heinz Company, form 8-K, April 27, 1979, p. 2.

[2] "Heinz to Probe Prepayments to Suppliers by Using Outside Lawyers, Accountants," *Wall Street Journal*, April 30, 1979, p. 5.

[3] H. J. Heinz Company, annual report, 1976.

report reflected management's pride in Heinz's remarkably consistent growth:

> Fiscal 1978 went into the books as the fifteenth consecutive year of record results for Heinz. Earnings rose to another new high. Sales reached more than $2 billion only six years after we had passed the $1 billion mark for the first time in our century-long history. We are determined to maintain the financial integrity of our enterprise and support its future growth toward ever-higher levels. [Exhibit 1 presents a financial summary of fiscal years 1972–1978.]

Although Heinz was a multinational firm, domestic operations accounted for 62% of sales and 67% of earnings in FY 1978. Five major divisions operated in the United States in 1979.

Throughout the 1970s Heinz's major objective was consistent growth in earnings. While Heinz management did not consider acquisitions to be crucial to continuing growth, it looked favorably on purchase opportunities in areas where Heinz had demonstrated capabilities. Bailey and Cunningham stressed profit increases through the elimination of marginally profitable products. Increased advertising of successful traditional products and new product development efforts also contributed to Heinz's growth. Heinz's commitment to decentralized authority as an organizational principle aided the management of internal growth as well as acquisitions.

Organization

In 1979 Heinz was organized on two primary levels. The corporate world headquarters, located in Pittsburgh, consisted of the principal corporate officers and historically small staffs (management described the world headquarters as lean). World headquarters had the responsibility for "the decentralized coordination and control needed to set overall standards and ensure performance in accordance with them."[4] Some Heinz operating divisions reported directly to the president; others reported through senior vice presidents who were designated area directors (see Exhibit 2). World headquarters officers worked with division senior managers in areas such as planning, product and market development, and capital programs.

[4] H. J. Heinz Company, form 8-K, May 7, 1980, p. 7.

Heinz's divisions were largely autonomous operating companies. Division managers were directly responsible for the division's products and services, and they operated their own research and development, manufacturing, and marketing facilities. Division staff reported directly to division managers and had neither formal reporting nor dotted-line relationships with corporate staff.

World headquarters officers monitored division performance through conventional business budgets and financial reports. If reported performance was in line with corporate financial goals, little inquiry into the details of division operation was made. On the other hand, variations from planned performance drew a great deal of attention from world headquarters; then, divisions were pressured to improve results. A review was held near the end of the third fiscal quarter to discuss expected year-end results. If shortfalls were apparent, other divisions were often encouraged to improve their performance. The aim was to meet projected consolidated earnings and goals. Predictability was a watchword and surprises were to be avoided.[5] A consistent growth in earnings attended this management philosophy.

Management Incentive Plan

Designed by a prominent management consulting firm, the management incentive plan (MIP) was regarded as a prime management tool used to achieve corporate goals.[6] MIP comprised roughly 225 employees, including corporate officers, senior world headquarters personnel, and senior personnel of most divisions. Incentive compensation was awarded on the basis of an earned number of MIP points and in some cases reached 40% of total compensation.

MIP points could be earned through the achievement of personal goals. These goals were established at the beginning of each fiscal year in consultation with the participant's immediate supervisor. Points were awarded by the supervisor at the end of the year, based on goal achievement. In practice, personal goal point awards fell out on a curve, with few individuals receiving very high or very low awards.

[5] Ibid. p. 8.

[6] Ibid. pp. 10–12.

MIP points were also awarded based on net profit after tax (NPAT) goals. (On occasion, other goals such as increased inventory turnover or improved cash flow were included in MIP goals.) Corporate NPAT goals were set at the beginning of the fiscal year by the management development and compensation committee (MDC) of the board of directors. The chief executive officer, the chief operating officer, the senior vice president–finance, and the senior vice president–corporate development then set MIP goals for each division, with the aggregate of division goals usually exceeding the corporate goal. Two goals were set—a fair goal, which was consistently higher than the preceding year's NPAT, and a higher outstanding goal. The full number of MIP points was earned by achieving the outstanding goal.

Senior corporate managers were responsible for executing the system. While divisional input was not uncommon, division NPAT goals were set unilaterally and did not necessarily reflect a division's budgeted profits. Once set, goals were seldom changed during the year. The officers who set the goals awarded MIP points at the end of the fiscal year. No points were awarded to personnel in a division that failed to achieve its fair goal, and points were weighted to favor results at or near the outstanding goal. One or more bonus points might be awarded if the outstanding goal was exceeded. Corporate officers also had the authority to make adjustments or award arbitrary points in special circumstances. The basis for these adjustments was not discussed with division personnel.

MIP points for consolidated corporate performance were awarded by the MDC committee of the board. Corporate points were credited by all MIP participants except those in a division that did not achieve its fair goal. The MDC committee could also award company bonus points.

Heinz also had a long-term incentive plan based on a revolving three-year cycle. Participation was limited to senior corporate management and division presidents or managing directors for a total of 19 persons.

Corporate Ethical Policy

Heinz had an explicit corporate ethical policy that was adopted in May 1976.[7] Among other things, it stated that no division should:

1. Have any form of unrecorded assets or false entries on its books or records
2. Make or approve any payment with the intention or understanding that any part of such payment was to be used for any purpose other than that described by the documents supporting the payment
3. Make political contributions
4. Make payments or gifts to public officials or customers
5. Accept gifts or payments of more than a nominal amount

Each year the president or managing director and the chief financial officer of each division were required to sign a representation letter which, among other things, confirmed compliance with the corporate Code of Ethics.

April 1979

Heinz itself had originated the antitrust proceedings that led to the discovery of the alleged practices. In 1976 Heinz filed a private antitrust suit against the Campbell Soup Company, accusing Campbell of monopolistic practices in the canned soup market. Campbell promptly countersued, charging that Heinz monopolized the ketchup market.[8] Campbell attorneys, preparing for court action, subpoenaed Heinz documents reflecting its financial relationships with one of its advertising agencies. In April 1979, while taking a deposition from Arthur West, president of the Heinz USA division, Campbell attorneys asked about flows of funds, "certain items which can be called off-book accounts." West refused to answer, claiming Fifth Amendment protection from self-incrimination.[9] Stangerson then spoke with the advertising agency and received confirmation of the invoicing practices.

[7] Ibid. p. 12.

[8] "Heinz Slow Growth Behind Juggling Tactic?" *Advertising Age*, March 24, 1980, p. 88.

[9] "Results in Probe of Heinz Income Juggling Expected to Be Announced by Early April," *Wall Street Journal*, March 18, 1980, p. 7.

EXHIBIT 1 Financial Summary, Fiscal Years 1972–1978
($ thousands except per share data)

Source: Company records.

	1978	1977	1976	1975	1974	1973	1972
Summary of operations							
Sales	$2,150,027	$1,868,820	$1,749,691	$1,564,930	$1,349,901	$1,116,551	$1,020,958
Cost of products sold	1,439,249	1,262,260	1,228,229	1,097,093	939,565	772,525	700,530
Interest expense	18,859	16,332	22,909	31,027	21,077	13,813	11,463
Provision for income taxes	69,561	71,119	53,675	49,958	36,730	30,913	30,702
Income from continuing operations	99,171	83,816	73,960	66,567	55,520	50,082	44,679
Loss for discontinued and expropriated operations	—	—	—	—	—	3,530	2,392
Income before extraordinary items	99,171	83,816	73,960	66,567	55,520	46,552	42,287
Extraordinary items	—	—	—	—	8,800	(25,000)	—
Net income	99,171	83,816	73,960	66,567	64,320	21,552	42,287
Per common share amounts							
Income from continuing operations	4.25	3.55	3.21	2.93	2.45	2.21	1.98
Loss from discontinued and expropriated operations	—	—	—	—	—	.16	.11
Income before extraordinary items	4.25	3.55	3.21	2.93	2.45	2.05	1.87
Extraordinary items	—	—	—	—	.39	(1.10)	—
Net income	4.25	3.55	3.21	2.93	2.84	.95	1.87
Other data							
Dividends paid							
Common, per share	1.42	1.06⅔	.86⅔	.77⅓	.72⅔	.70	.67⅓
Common, total	32,143	24,260	19,671	17,502	16,427	15,814	15,718
Preferred, total	3,147	3,166	1,024	139	146	165	184
Capital expenditures	95,408	53,679	34,682	57,219	44,096	48,322	28,067
Depreciation	31,564	29,697	27,900	25,090	22,535	20,950	20,143
Shareholders' equity	702,736	655,480	598,613	502,796	447,434	399,607	394,519
Total debt	228,002	220,779	219,387	295,051	266,617	249,161	196,309
Average number of common shares outstanding	22,609,613	22,743,233	22,696,484	22,633,115	22,604,720	22,591,287	22,538,309
Book value per common share	28.96	26.27	23.79	22.04	19.61	17.50	17.26
Price range of common stock							
High	40	34⅛	38	34⅜	34⅞	30⅞	31½
Low	28¾	26½	28⅞	18	24⅞	25⅞	25⅞
Sales (%)							
Domestic	62	62	59	58	59	58	57
Foreign	38	38	41	42	41	42	43
Income (%)							
Domestic	67	78	66	71	57	53	54
Foreign	33	22	34	29	43	47	46

EXHIBIT 2 Organization Chart, April 1979

Asterisk indicates member of the board of directors.
Date in parentheses indicates year acquired.

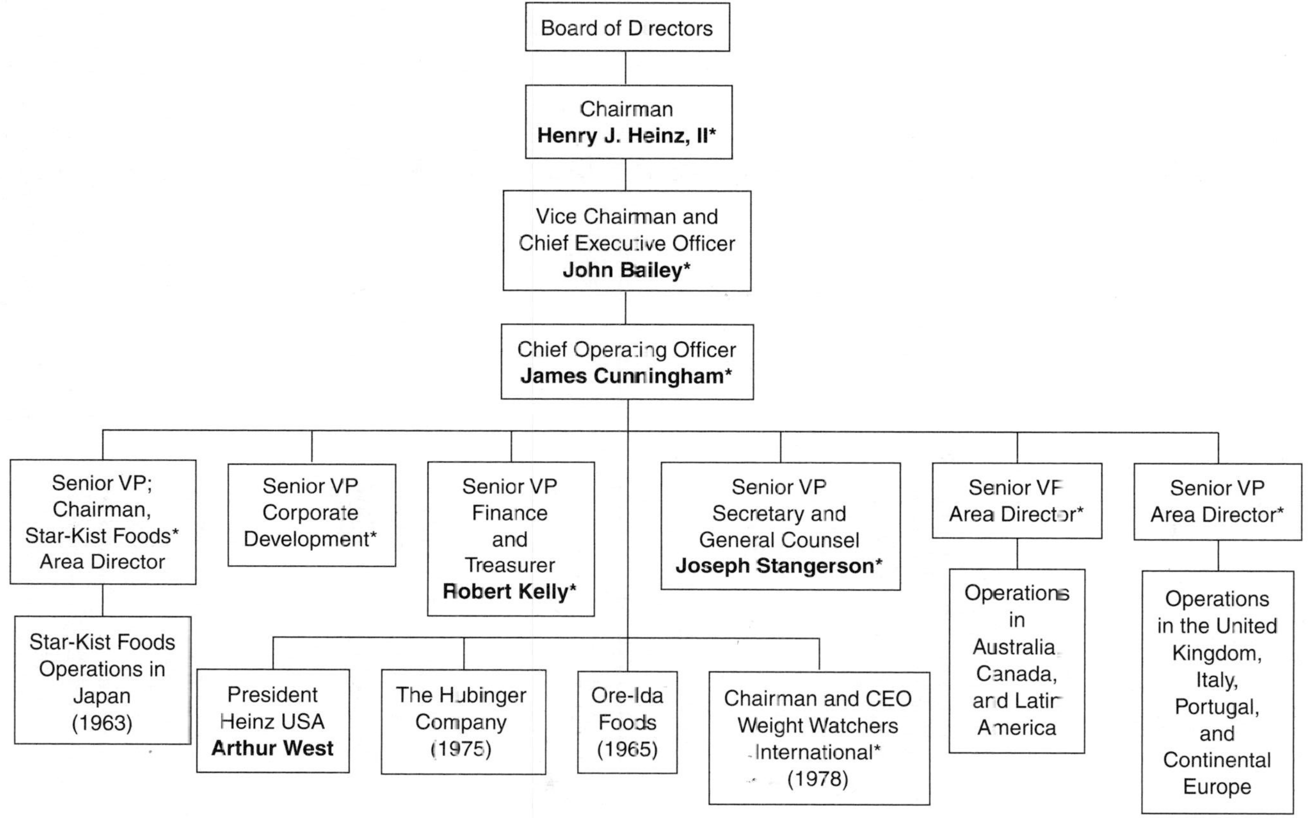

H. J. Heinz Company: *The Administration of Policy (B)*

In April 1979 Heinz's senior management learned of improper practices concerning the transfer of an undetermined amount of reported income from one fiscal year to the next. At two of the Heinz operating divisions payments had been made to vendors in one fiscal year, then repaid or exchanged for services in the succeeding fiscal year. The scope of the practice and the amounts involved were not then known.

Aware that the practice might have affected the company's reported income over the past seven fiscal years, management consulted an outside legal firm for an opinion on the seriousness of the problem. Based on that opinion, John Bailey, Heinz's chief executive officer, notified the Audit Committee of the board of directors. Composed entirely of outside directors, this committee was responsible for working with internal auditors and financial officers and with the firm's outside auditors, thus preserving the integrity of financial information published by Heinz.

The Audit Committee held a special meeting on April 26, 1979. After hearing from outside counsel and from Joseph Stangerson (Heinz's general counsel) about the practices, the committee adopted a resolution retaining an outside law firm and independent public accountants to assist in a full investigation of the matter.[1]

An attorney from Cravath, Swaine & Moore, the outside law firm, accompanied Stangerson to Washington to advise the Securities and Exchange Commission of the information available and of the investigation then under way. (An excerpt from form 8-K filed with the SEC is attached as Exhibit 1.) The two also informed the IRS of possible tax consequences of the practice.

On April 27, 1979, Heinz publicly announced its investigation. "At this stage," the formal statement said, "it isn't possible to determine the scope of the practice or the total amounts involved." It also stated that there "isn't any reason to believe there will be any material effect on the company's reported earnings for any fiscal year including the current fiscal year." While the investigation would cover the period from 1972 to 1979, Heinz would not identify the divisions or vendors involved. Stangerson stated: "We aren't prepared to say whether [the practices] were legal or illegal." He added that the company had informed the SEC and the IRS.[2]

The Investigation

The Audit Committee supervised the conduct of the investigation. Teams composed of lawyers and accountants from the two outside firms interviewed present and former company and vendor personnel about possible improprieties. The investigators focused on the following areas:

1. Practices that affected the accuracy of company accounts or the security of company assets
2. Practices in violation of the company's Code of Ethics
3. Illegal political contributions
4. Illegal, improper, or otherwise questionable payments
5. Factors contributing to the existence, continuance, or nondisclosure of any of the above

The investigating teams interviewed over 325 Heinz employees, many of them more than once. The teams also interviewed personnel employed by many of Heinz's vendors, including advertising agencies. Accounting records, correspondence, and

[1] "Report of the Audit Committee to the Board of Directors: Income Transferal and Other Practices," H. J. Heinz Company, form 8-K, May 7, 1980.

[2] "Results in Probe of Heinz Income Juggling Expected to Be Announced by Early April," *Wall Street Journal*, March 18, 1980, p. 7.

other files were examined. The board of directors at its regular May meeting asked for the cooperation of all officers and employees.[3]

On May 10, 1979, Heinz announced that a settlement had been reached in its private antitrust suit against the Campbell Soup Company. The settlement resulted in the dismissal of Heinz's action against Campbell, which had been brought in 1976, and of Campbell's counterclaim against Heinz. The court ordered the record of the suit sealed and kept secret.[4]

On June 29, 1979, Heinz disclosed a preliminary figure of $5.5 million of after-tax income associated with the income transferal practices. Stressing that this was a "very soft number," the company indicated that it was delaying release of audited results for FY 1979 (ended May 2, 1979) and that its annual meeting, scheduled for September 12, would be postponed until the investigation (which could continue well into the fall) was completed. The preliminary unaudited figures released by Heinz showed net income of $113.4 million ($4.95 per share) on sales of $2.4 billion, after the $5.5 million deduction. Press reports indicated the investigation was being broadened to include Heinz's foreign units.[5]

On September 13, 1979, it was reported that the preliminary figure had grown to $8.5 million. Heinz's statement, filed with its first quarter FY 1980 earnings report, also stated FY 1979 income as $110.4 million or $4.80 per share. Most of the $3 million growth was attributed to the discovery of improper treatment of sales in addition to the improper treatment of prepaid expenses discovered earlier.[6]

Heinz's 1979 annual report contained audited financial statements for FY 1979 and restated financial statements for FY 1978. The report contained an unqualified opinion from Peat, Marwick, Mitchell & Company, Heinz's auditors, dated November 14, 1979. In Note 2 to the 1979 financial statements, the report also contained a restatement and reconciliation of sales, net income, and earnings per share for the previous eight fiscal years. (The 1979 results are shown in Exhibit 2. The restatement of FY 1971–FY 1978 are shown in Exhibit 3.) This information was filed with the Securities and Exchange Commission on November 20, 1979.[7]

In February 1980 Heinz reorganized its top management structure (see Exhibit 4). Arthur West, formerly president of Heinz USA, was promoted to world headquarters as area director. He assumed responsibility for the Hubinger Company and Weight Watchers International, both of which had previously reported directly to James Cunningham, Heinz's president and new CEO. West was also to be responsible for Heinz's Canadian subsidiary. Heinz USA would now report through Kevin Voight, senior vice president, rather than directly to Cunningham. Unlike other area directors, West would be neither a senior vice president nor a member of the board of directors.[8]

In April 1980 Doyle Dane Bernbach, the only publicly held firm among the advertising and consulting firms included in the Audit Committee's investigation, admitted in an SEC filing that it had participated in the income-juggling practices by prebilling and issuing bills that did not accurately describe the services provided.[9]

On May 7, 1980, the Audit Committee presented its report to the Heinz board of directors. The 80-page report was filed on form 8-K with the SEC on May 9, 1980. (The remainder of this case is derived substantially from the Audit Committee's report.)

The Findings

The Audit Committee reported widespread use of improper billing, accounting, and reporting procedures at Heinz's divisions, including Heinz USA, Ore-Ida, and Star-Kist, and a number of Heinz's foreign operations. The two major areas of impropriety were:

1. *Improper recognition of expenses.* These were most often advertising and market research expenses, improperly recorded in the current fiscal period when in fact the services were performed or goods delivered in a later fiscal period. This

[3] Audit Committee Report, form 8-K, May 7, 1980, p. 4.

[4] H. J. Heinz Company, form 8-K, May 10, 1979, p. 2; *Wall Street Journal*, March 18, 1980, p. 7.

[5] "Initial Study of Some Heinz Units Finds $5.5 Million in Profit Juggling Practices," *Wall Street Journal*, July 2, 1979, p. 8.

[6] "Heinz Discloses Profit Switching at Units Was Much Broader Than First Realized," *Wall Street Journal*, September 13, 1979, p. 15.

[7] Audit Committee report, form 8-K, May 7, 1980, p. 2.

[8] "H. J. Heinz Realigns Its Senior Management in Consolidation Move," *Wall Street Journal*, February 19, 1980.

[9] "DDB Admits Heinz Role," *Advertising Age*, April 28, 1980, pp. 1, 88.

TABLE A **Increase (Decrease) of Consolidated Income before Tax, Net of Recoveries**
($ Thousands)

	Improper Recognition			Net Income before Tax		
FY	Expenses	Sales	Other Practices	Increase (decrease)	Total after Restatement	% Effects of Restatement
1972	$(513)	—	—	$(513)	$75,894	(.7)
1973	(1,814)	$(1,968)	—	(3,782)	84,777	(4.5)
1974	(4,250)	(309)	$(1,364)	(5,923)	98,173	(6.0)
1975	2,476	1,527	(615)	3,388	113,137	3.0
1976	(111)	(1,815)	877	(1,049)	128,682	(.8)
1977	(4,139)	(1,294)	268	(5,165)	160,101	(3.2)
1978	734	(2,872)	671	(1,467)	170,198	(.9)
1979	8,888	7,085	396	16,369	183,178	8.9
1980	76	(354)	(233)	(511)		

treatment resulted in an overstatement of expenses (and understatement of income) in one period and a comparable understatement of expenses (and overstatement of income) in a later fiscal period.

2. *Improper recognition of sales.* Sales were recorded in a fiscal period other than that in which those sales should have been recorded under generally accepted accounting principles.

Table A indicates the amounts involved. The accumulated effects of such practices on shareholders' equity and working capital did not exceed 2%.

The Audit Committee indicated that these income transferal practices were designed to adjust the income reported by divisions to corporate headquarters and were motivated primarily by a desire to meet the constantly increasing profit objectives set by world headquarters. While division management supported the publicly announced goal of steadily increasing profits, the committee reported that the management incentive program (MIP) under which the goals were administered created significant pressures. Aside from obvious personal financial considerations, many division-level personnel reportedly viewed the achievement of MIP goals as the key to advancement at Heinz. One manager told the committee that failure to achieve these goals constituted a "mortal sin."

The Heinz principle of decentralized authority extended to financial reporting and internal control procedures. Division financial officers were not responsible to corporate headquarters but to their division president or managing director. The MIP goal pressures provided the incentive, and autonomous control the opportunity, for adopting the improper practices being reported.

One reason for using such reporting techniques was explained to the committee:

> If this fiscal year's goal is, say, $20 million net profit after tax (NPAT), it can be anticipated that next year's goal will be, say, 15% zhigher, or $23 million NPAT. This year seems to be a good one and it is anticipated that earnings will be $24 million NPAT. But, if that figure is reported to world headquarters, it is likely that next year's goal will be about 15% higher than the $24 million NPAT, or approximately $27 million NPAT. Of course, there is no assurance that there will not be some unforeseen disaster next year. Thus, if it is possible to mislead world headquarters as to the true state of the earnings of the [division] and report only the $20 million NPAT, which is the current fiscal year's goal, and have the additional $4 million NPAT carried forward into next year, the [division] will have a good start toward achieving its expected $23 million NPAT goal next year and will not have to reach $27 million NPAT.

Explanations for accepting these practices at lower levels included job security and the desire to impress superiors.

The committee's report stated: "There is no evidence that any employee of the company sought or obtained any direct personal gain in connection with any of the transactions or practices described in this report. Nor did the investigation find any evidence that any officer or personnel at world headquarters participated in any of the income transferal practices described in this report." The report went on to describe activities at each division in greater detail.

Division Income Transfer Practices

Heinz USA

Income transfer at Heinz USA started late in FY 1974 when world headquarters realized that Heinz USA might report profits in excess of those allowed by the wage and price controls in effect at the time. World headquarters sought to have Heinz USA report lower profits, although no evidence indicates that any world headquarters personnel intended GAAP to be violated. After some commodity transactions lowered expected profits, there was a reluctance in Heinz USA to reduce its expected profits further. Nevertheless, to accomplish the further reduction, $2 million in invoices for services that would not be performed were obtained from an advertising agency and recorded as an expense in FY 1974.

Heinz USA reported FY 1974 NPAT of $4,614,000. NPAT goals for the year were $4.9 million (fair) and $5.5 million (outstanding). In calculating NPAT for MIP purposes, world headquarters allowed an adjustment of $2 million ($1 million after tax) for advertising. This adjustment resulted in Heinz USA achieving its outstanding goal for FY 1974. The division also received a bonus point. The use of improper invoices to manage reported income continued after FY 1974 at Heinz USA, although there was no evidence that world headquarters personnel knew about these transactions.

Beginning in FY 1977, additional income transfer methods were developed. Distribution centers were instructed to stop shipments for the last few days of the fiscal year to allow the recording of sales in the subsequent year. These instructions presented practical difficulties and some of the shipments were not held up. Without the authorization of division senior management, paperwork was apparently altered or misdated to record the sales as desired.

Vendors' credits were often deferred and processed in the subsequent fiscal year to assist the income management program. Detailed schedules were privately maintained that served as the basis for discussions on income management. One employee had the job of maintaining private records to ensure the recovery (in subsequent fiscal years) of amounts paid to vendors on improper invoices.

The use of improper invoices spread to the departmental level as well. Individual department managers used either prepaid billing or delayed billing, as required, to ensure complete use of their departmental budget without overspending. This practice provided protection against future budget cuts during those periods when the full budget would not otherwise have been spent. Division management actively discouraged these transactions.

Vendor cooperation was not difficult to obtain. One Heinz manager described it as "the price of doing business with us." During the period in question, 10 vendors participated in improper invoicing at Heinz USA, and 8 participated at the department level. Most vendors' fiscal years did not coincide with Heinz's.

In FY 1975 a sugar inventory write-down was used to transfer income. Sugar inventory, valued at an average cost of 37 cents per pound, was written down to 25 cents per pound. This adjustment, which amounted to an increase in FY 1975 expense of $1,390,360, was justified on the basis of an expected decline in price early in the next fiscal year. This would result in lower selling prices in FY 1976 for some division products. The lower NPAT figure that resulted was used for establishing FY 1976 goals, but when FY 1975 performance was evaluated, world headquarters adjusted Heinz USA's income up by the amount of the sugar write-down. The anticipated price decline did not occur.

At other times, inflated accruals, inventory adjustments, commodity transactions, and at least one customer rebate were used to report income other than that required by GAAP.

Ore-Ida

Improper invoices to transfer income were also used at Ore-Ida during that period, and the issue of obtaining these invoices was discussed at meetings of Ore-Ida's management board. Even though the invoices contained descriptions of services that were generic or had no correlation to the actual services to be rendered, members of the management board believed the practice was appropriate because comparable services would have been purchased at some point. During two fiscal years Ore-Ida received interest payments from an advertising agency in connection with the payment of these invoices.

Ore-Ida's management believed that members of world headquarters' management were aware of the income transfer practices, but raised no objections to them. Documents submitted to world headquarters by Ore-Ida contained references to special media billing, prebills, year-end media billing, special billing adjustments, and advertising and promotion prebilling. Some documents indicated that these items actually applied to the fiscal year following that of expense recognition. The amount of these expenses was indicated each year to world headquarters' management (in one year, the amount was understated). In FY 1974 corporate management increased Ore-Ida's income before tax by the amount of the prebilled advertising expense for MIP award purposes. Ore-Ida's management did not know if world headquarters' management appreciated the fact that this practice did not conform to GAAP.

Star-Kist

Both improper expense recognition and improper sales recognition were used to adjust reported income at Star-Kist. Improper invoices were solicited from vendors to accumulate an advertising savings account. Sales during the last month of a fiscal year were recorded during the first month of the next fiscal year by preventing selected documents from entering the sales accounting system. These practices were apparently present only in Star-Kist's marketing department.

Similar practices were also discovered at some of Heinz's foreign subsidiaries.

Other Improper Practices

Although it focused primarily on income transferal practices, the investigation uncovered a number of other practices. Again, the committee stated that no member of world headquarters' management appeared to have any knowledge of these practices, and no employee sought or obtained any personal financial gain. All of these transactions took place outside the United States. None of the countries in which the transactions took place was identified by the committee.

In one country six questionable payments totaling $80,000 were made during FY 1978 and FY 1979. Two were made to lower-level government employees in connection with alleged violations of import regulations. One was made to a lower-level government employee in connection with the settlement of a labor dispute. Municipal employees received one payment in connection with real estate assessments. Labor union officials received the remaining two payments. In January 1979 three of these payments were reported by division management to world headquarters. A brief investigation ensued and the board of directors reprimanded certain officers of the division.

Star-Kist was involved in several transactions listed in the following section of the report.

1. In one country the payment of interest to nonresidents was prohibited. Star-Kist collected interest on its loans to fishing fleets through the falsification of invoices indicating the purchase by Star-Kist of supplies for the fleets.
2. In another country Star-Kist acted as a conduit through which funds flowed to facilitate a fish purchase involving two other companies. Letters of credit requiring the approval of the exchange authorities were used.
3. In a third country Star-Kist received checks from a fish supplier and endorsed those checks to a wholly owned U.S. subsidiary of the supplier. These transactions were not recorded in Star-Kist's accounts.

The Heinz operating company in yet another country made payments for goods to individual or designated bank accounts rather than to the supplier involved. These payments were not made through the normal cash disbursement procedure; rather, the division was acting at the supplier's request.

Contributing Factors

The Audit Committee reported that only a small part of the failure to detect these practices could be attributed to weakness in Heinz's internal controls. In most cases, those controls were circumvented by or with the concurrence of division management. With the autonomy enjoyed by division management, it would have been difficult for world headquarters personnel to detect these practices.

The committee attributed part of the problem to a lack of control consciousness throughout the corporation. *Control consciousness* referred to the atmosphere in which accounting controls existed and it reflected senior management attitudes about the importance of such controls. Clearly, control consciousness was not then present in most Heinz divisions. The committee blamed world headquarters' senior management for creating an environment that was seen as endorsing poor control consciousness:

> If world headquarters' senior management had established a satisfactory control consciousness, internal accounting controls that were cost/benefit justified should have been able to survive reasonable pressures to meet or exceed the defined economic goals. In establishing this atmosphere, world headquarters' senior management apparently did not consider the effect on individuals in the [divisions] of the pressures to which they were subjected.

Other factors cited by the committee included:

- Corporate internal auditing personnel report to their respective division managers and not to the director-corporate audit
- The lack of an effective Code of Ethics compliance procedure
- The lack of standardized accounting and reporting procedures for all Heinz divisions
- The lack of an effective budget review and monitoring process
- The lack of enough competent financial personnel at world headquarters and at the divisions
- The lack of a world headquarters electronic data processing manager responsible for the control procedures of the divisions' EDP departments

Conclusions of the Audit Committee

1. The amounts involved in the income transferal practices were not material to the consolidated net income or shareholders' equity of the company in the aggregate during the investigatory period (FY 1972–FY 1978).
2. The income transferal practices were achieved primarily through circumvention of existing internal controls by division personnel who should have exercised responsibility in the enforcement of such controls. Such practices were also assisted by certain inadequacies in the internal control systems of the divisions.
3. Although world headquarters' personnel did not authorize or participate in the income transferal practices, their continuance was facilitated by the company's philosophy of decentralized management and the role played by world headquarters' financial personnel in reviewing the financial reports from divisions.
4. No individual employee obtained any direct financial benefit from the practices uncovered in the investigation.
5. Perceived or de facto pressures for achievement of MTP goals contributed to the divisions' desirability of providing a cushion against future business uncertainties.
6. The income transferal practices did not serve any valid corporate need.
7. The income transferal practices and other questionable practices described in this report [of the Audit Committee] indicate the lack of sufficient control consciousness within the corporate structure; that is, an understanding throughout the company and the divisions that responsible and ethical practices are required in connection with all transactions.
8. The entrepreneurial spirit of the divisions fostered by the philosophy of decentralized autonomy should be continued for the good of the company and its shareholders.
9. World headquarters did not have the number of competent financial personnel needed to fulfill its role.
10. The continuance of the income transferal practices was aided by the independence of division financial personnel from world headquarters.
11. The continuance of the income transferal practices was aided by the reporting relationships of the internal audit staffs within the company.
12. The administration of the MIP and the goal-setting process thereunder did not result in adequate dialogue between senior world headquarters management and managements of the divisions.
13. The board of directors and management of the company have the duty to take all steps practicable to ensure safeguarding the assets of the company and that all transactions are properly recorded on the books, records, and accounts of the company.

EXHIBIT 1 Form 8-K Excerpt, April 27, 1979

Item 5: Other Materially Important Events

On April 27, 1979, the registrant announced that it had become aware that since 1972 in certain of its divisions or subsidiaries payments have been made to certain of its vendors in a particular fiscal year, which were repaid or exchanged for services by such vendors in the succeeding fiscal year.

The registrant stated that at this stage it was not possible to determine the scope of the practice or the total amounts involved, but that there was no reason to believe there would be any material effect on the registrant's reported earnings for any fiscal year including the fiscal year ending May 2, 1979.

The Audit Committee of the registrant's board of directors has retained the law firm of Cravath, Swaine & Moore, independent outside counsel, to conduct a full inquiry of the practice. Cravath, Swaine & Moore will retain independent public accountants to assist in the investigation.

The registrant has heretofore advised the Securities and Exchange Commission and the Internal Revenue Service of the foregoing. At this time the registrant is unable to estimate the extent of any adjustments which may be necessary for tax purposes.

EXHIBIT 2 Financial Summary, 1979
($ thousands except per share data)

Source: 1979 annual report.

	1979	1978*	Change
Sales	$2,470,883	$2,159,436	14.4%
Operating income	214,735	187,062	14.8
Net income	110,430	99,946	10.5
Per common share amounts			
Net income	$4.80	$4.28	12.1%
Net income (fully diluted)	4.64	4.17	11.3
Dividends	1.85	1.42	30.3
Book value	32.29	29.33	10.1
Capital expenditures	$ 118,156	95,408	23.8%
Depreciation expense	38,317	31,564	21.4
Net property	481,688	412,334	16.8
Cash and short-term investments	$ 122,281	$ 84,044	45.5%
Working capital	401,169	453,517	(11.5)
Total debt	342,918	228,002	50.4
Shareholders' equity	778,397	711,126	9.5
Average number of common shares outstanding	22,330	22,610	
Current ratio	1.70	2.14	
Debt/invested capital	30.9%	24.7%	
Pretax return on average invested capital	20.7%	20.7%	
Return on average shareholders' equity	14.8%	14.5%	

* As restated.

EXHIBIT 3 Restated Financial Data, 1971–1978
Changes in Sales, Net Income, and Earnings per Share

Source: 1979 annual report.

In Thousands Except for per Share Amounts	1971	1972	1973	1974	1975	1976	1977	1978
Sales as previously reported	$876,451	$1,020,958	$1,116,551	$1,349,091	$1,564,930	$1,749,691	$1,868,820	$2,150,027
Net increase (decrease) resulting from restatement to correct improper treatment of sales	—	—	14,821	(1,777)	(4,747)	4,725	8,480	9,409
Sales as restated	$876,451	$1,020,958	$1,131,372	$1,347,314	$1,560,183	$1,754,416	$1,877,300	$2,159,436
Net income as previously reported	$37,668*	$42,287*	$21,552*	$64,320*	$66,567	$73,960	$83,816	$99,171
Net increase (decrease) in income before income taxes resulting from restatement:								
Correct improper treatment of sales, net of related costs	—	—	1,968	309	(1,527)	1,815	1,294	2,872
Correct improper recognition of income/expense	1,290	512	1,813	5,615	(1,861)	(684)	3,822	(1,417)
	1,290	512	3,781	5,924	(3,388)	1,131	5,116	1,455
Income tax effect	(671)	(263)	(1,566)	(2,698)	(1,254)	(604)	(2,203)	(680)
Net adjustments	619	249	2,215	3,226	2,134	527	2,913	775
Net income as restated	$38,287	$42,536	$23,767	$67,546	$64,433	$74,487	$86,729	$99,946
Income per common share amounts:								
Income from continuing operations as previously reported	$1.71	$1.98	$2.21	$2.45	$2.93	$3.21	$3.55	$4.25
Net increase (decrease) from restatement	.02	.01	.09	.14	(.09)	.03	.12	.03
Income from continuing operations as restated	1.73	1.99	2.30	2.59	2.84	3.24	3.67	4.28
Loss from discontinued and expropriated operations	.02	.11	.16	—	—	—	—	—
Income before extraordinary items	1.71	1.88	2.14	2.59	2.84	3.24	3.67	4.28
Extraordinary items	—	—	(1.10)	.39	—	—	—	—
Net income	$1.71	$1.88	$1.04	$2.98	$2.84	$3.24	$3.67	$4.28

EXHIBIT 3 Restated Financial Data, 1971–1978 (Continued)

In Thousands	Income from Continuing Operations	Loss from Discontinued and Expropriated Operations	Extraordinary Items	Net Income as Previously Reported
1971	$38,171	$ (503)	$ —	$37,668
1972	44,679	(2,392)	—	42,287
1973	50,082	(3,530)	(25,000)	21,552
1974	55,520	—	8,800	64,320

(The Following Table Presents the As-Reported and As-Restated Interim Results, Which Are Unaudited, for 1978 and 1979)

	Sales		Gross Profit		Net Income		Earnings per Share	
In thousands except per share amounts	As Reported	As Restated	As Reported	As Restated	As Reported	As Restated	As Reported	As Restated
1978								
First quarter	$ 491,469	$ 472,955	$156,538	$ 152,639	$19,645	$ 17,621	$ .83	$ .74
Second quarter	520,051	525,440	169,476	170,348	23,613	22,676	1.00	.96
Third quarter	523,640	517,738	170,621	169,001	19,901	20,208	.85	.86
Fourth quarter	614,867	643,303	214,143	221,992	36,012	39,441	1.57	1.72
Total	$2,150,027	$2,159,436	$710,778	$ 713,980	$99,171	$ 99,946	$4.25	$4.28
1979								
First quarter	$ 555,558	$ 536,301	$178,250	$ 171,330	$21,161	$ 16,783	$ .91	$ .72
Second quarter	620,230	619,627	203,708	203,964	28,204	26,026	1.23	1.13
Third quarter	575,410	566,747	202,171	199,497	23,301	21,192	1.01	.91
Fourth quarter	—	748,208†	—	267,584†	—	46,429†	—	2.04†
Total	$ —	$2,470,883†	$ —	$ 842,375†	$ —	$110,430†	$ —	$4.80†

* Net income as previously reported above includes losses from discontinued and expropriated operations and extraordinary items as shown.
† Not previously reported.

EXHIBIT 4 Organization Chart, February 1980

Asterisk indicated member of the board of directors.

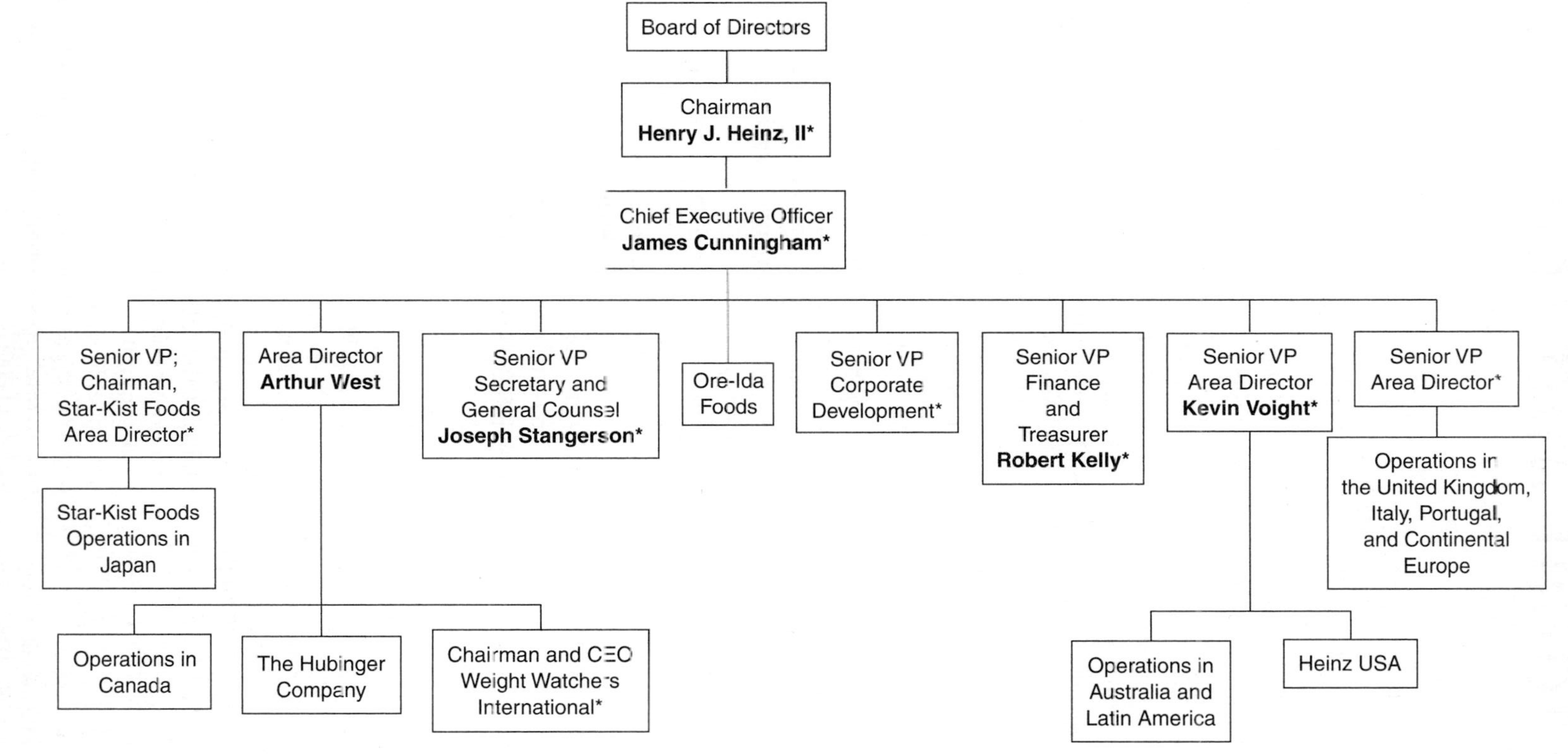

The Individual and the Corporation

In the 1830s, Alexis de Tocqueville, seeking to describe the social philosophy of the United States, put heavy emphasis on the new nation's reliance upon individualism. He said, "Individualism is a novel expression, to which a novel idea has given birth." By the latter part of the same century, the rapid industrialization of the United States had contributed to the rise of large and increasingly powerful units of economic activity. As new and more complex forms of organization developed in all sectors of life, John D. Rockefeller was led to comment, "Individualism is gone, never to return."

This case concerns one aspect of the relationship between individuals and organizations. Its focus is on the problems that arose when a senior executive of a company wrote an article for a national magazine. The case information came from (1) Donald L. Singleton; (2) annual reports of Summit Petroleum, *Look* magazine, and other published sources; and (3) Lawrence J. Mangum, a senior editor of *Look* magazine. All figures in the case are disguised. It will be evident from the material below that the case does not present the points of view of all the parties involved in the series of events described.

The Company

In the mid-1950s, a European-based oil company established a company called Summit Petroleum, Inc., in the United States. According to the new company's first annual report, Summit represented the European company's first venture in the United States. Control was assured through ownership of more than 50% of the stock of Summit. Corporate headquarters was established in a large eastern city and operating offices were set up in Dallas. The latter were later to become Summit Petroleum of Texas.

Summit began actual operations after merging with another oil company. Within a short time, the company had a refinery, substantial resources of oil and natural gas, several thousand acres of undeveloped leaseholds, and over 200 gasoline stations located in four Southwestern states.

The company continued to expand, both internally and through acquisitions, in subsequent years. The Summit trademark became increasingly well known in the Southwest and adjacent areas of the United States. By 1959, Summit had nearly 1,800 filling stations, and annual sales were approaching $70,000,000, including several billion cubic feet of natural gas. Most Summit retail gasoline stations were run by independent operators and supplied by independent jobbers, but in some cases expansion was accelerated by the lease of company-owned stations to independent operators.

By the time the 1960 annual report was issued, Summit operated in nearly 20 states and had over 2,000 filling stations. Sales had increased more than 6% over 1959, as compared to an increase in consumer demand of approximately 1% in Summit's marketing territories. The annual report stated that "The effective advertising and sales promotion programs initiated in 1958 have been responsible in large measure for expanding consumer acceptance of [Summit] products." Although total company sales dipped slightly in 1962, gasoline sales reached an all-time high. In 1963, the acquisition of another oil company almost doubled the company's facilities, gave it an entry into petrochemicals, and added more than 1,000 retail gasoline stations. Many of the latter were immediately converted to Summit colors and station signs. By the end of 1963, annual reports indicated, in brief, that net income had grown to almost $4,500,000 in the comparatively short period of Summit's life, while gross operating income was over $150,000,000.

The Individual

The *Dallas Morning News* of April 17, 1964, carried a brief story stating that Summit Petroleum of Texas had confirmed the resignation of Mr. Donald L. Singleton from the Summit organization. The story identified Mr. Singleton as the senior vice president in charge of marketing, refining, pipelines, transportation, and crude oil purchasing for Summit of Texas, and as a vice president and member of the board of directors of Summit Petroleum, Inc. Mr. Singleton had joined the Texas company in Dallas in 1957 as marketing manager. In 1958, he became vice president for marketing of all refined products. By 1962, he had become the senior vice president of the Texas firm. In addition, from 1960 through 1963, the annual reports of Summit Petroleum, Inc., listed Mr. Singleton as Vice President, Marketing, and a member of the board.

Donald Singleton was born in Santa Barbara, California, in 1922 where his father was a sales manager for an oil company in the Los Angeles area. After attending high school at St. Joseph's Academy, Singleton went to St. Mary's College and later transferred to the University of Washington. He graduated in 1943 as a foreign trade major. During his college career, Singleton served as business manager of the university's daily newspaper, belonged to the Naval ROTC, and managed a filling station. On subsequent active duty with the U.S. Navy, he saw action in the Southwest Pacific and the Philippine Islands, was wounded, and received a Bronze Star.

At the end of World War II, Singleton decided to go into business for himself. He returned to the Philippines and set up an import–export business. The business prospered, reaching an annual volume of $12 million within a 6-year period. Singleton and his wife then decided to return to the United States. Their oldest boy was ready for school, and the Singletons preferred an American school. Mr. Singleton also preferred to develop his business career in the United States. Using part of the proceeds from the sale of his import–export business, he established a firm in California that specialized in financing home builders. In addition, after a few months, he decided to enter the oil business. He set up the Singleton Oil Company, became an independent distributor for a major oil company, and phased out his finance business.

Singleton's company doubled his supplier's volume in its territory. In addition, he introduced a line of tires, batteries, and accessories (TBA). Intrigued by the possibilities of innovation in the merchandising and marketing fields, he purchased some old school buses, renovated them, and turned them into "rolling stores" for his TBA lines. In less than three years, Singleton's TBA volume in his rolling stores was $150,000.

Singleton's interest in management and innovation led him to look for an expanding company whose resources and activities would permit a greater degree of experimentation and opportunity for progression. Summit Petroleum appeared to offer such an opportunity, and in 1957 he joined Summit as marketing manager, taking a $10,000 cut in income in order to join the company.

Singleton prospered at Summit. His family and personal background in oil jobbing helped him establish good working relationships with the company's independent jobbers and retailers, and he showed a flair for merchandising, promotion, and station design. He was especially interested in design and promotion. The Summit brand attained wide publicity, both in its area and throughout the oil industry, when Singleton developed a new approach in service station design. In a busy industrial section of Dallas, Summit put up a service station that consisted of separate islands offering gasoline, service, and customer facilities. Each island was distinguished by a 30-foot concrete tower of mushroom design. The customer island had a patio and rest areas, and Summit installed air conditioning, floor-to-ceiling drapes, Oriental tile, and Florida red marble. The station received considerable attention in Dallas and was written up in a number of industry publications. Singleton had also been instrumental in the development of mobile, self-powered service stations that offered "Summit à la Carte"; the stations were written up in *Fortune*, *Business Week*, and other magazines and trade papers.

Summit's Azure Ozone (fictitious name) advertising campaign was originated by Singleton. In the early 1960s, an additive war reflected the keen competition in the oil industry, as company after company introduced special additives to gasoline to gain competitive advantage. The first additives introduced by the major oil companies attained great prominence, but later ones did not because of conflicting claims and duplication. Singleton and Summit investigated the possibilities of an additive for Summit gasoline. Singleton decided, however, that the use of an additive would be prohibitively expensive, and would be only another "me-too" type of promotion. In his opinion, the industry suffered from too much "me-too-ism" in its advertising and promotion.

As a result, Singleton developed the idea of spoofing gasoline additives as a promotional technique. Together with Summit's advertising agency, he worked out a campaign. The general idea of the promotion was that Summit gasoline had all the additives a car could possibly use. So did all the other Summit products, with the exception of the air that Summit stations put in customers' tires. Summit would, therefore, get to work immediately on the ultimate additive and under the Summit Five-Year Plan, have Azure Ozone available for tires on May 12, 1966; the time was set for 4:30 in the afternoon of that day, because some Summit trucks "don't get around until late in the afternoon." In the meantime, "to help customers through the difficult withdrawal period from regular air, Summit offered azure balloons, azure valve caps, azure asphalt, azure credit cards (for special customers), and an Azure Air Room Freshener." The latter was also promoted and sold by a Dallas department store, and achieved national publicity.

The Azure Ozone campaign was concentrated in newspaper advertisements throughout Summit's marketing area, and aided by various kinds of promotion at the service station level. For example, azure-colored asphalt aprons were installed at some stations, and various contests and promotional devices were tied to the concept.

The Azure Ozone approach was praised in trade and advertising journals, and was the least expensive major campaign ever conducted by the company. Consumers found its newness and gentle spoofing interesting. The trade recognized it as an effective promotional device, and it won a number of advertising awards. Singleton himself was in great demand as a speaker before oil industry and advertising media groups.

Thus, by the end of 1963, Summit's promotional campaigns had been extremely successful. Mr. Singleton's contributions to the company's marketing efforts had been substantial, and these and other accomplishments seemed attested to by the steady broadening of his responsibilities and his recognition by various industry journals. For example, in January 1964, *Southwest Advertising and Marketing* said:

> Probably one of the reasons for Summit's phenomenal growth is its aggressive and imaginative young senior vice president [Donald L. Singleton]. Even though he is in direct charge of the company's major operations—refining, marketing, transportation, crude oil acquisition, and other departments—[Singleton] handles the company's advertising personally. . . .

The Assassination of President Kennedy

On November 22, 1963, President John Kennedy was assassinated in Dallas. Lawrence J. Mangum (fictitious name), a senior editor of *Look* magazine, was sent from New York to cover the assassination and subsequent developments. Mangum talked to many prominent Dallas citizens, among them government, professional, and business leaders, and was struck by what seemed to him to be an attitude of defensiveness about Dallas. Attacks on the city itself had not yet begun to appear in any volume, but many of those to whom Mangum talked seemed to him to behave and speak as if the city itself were in some way guilty of the presidential assassination and the shooting of Lee Harvey Oswald.

A few days after the assassination, Mr. Mangum met the president of the advertising firm that handled Summit's account. During a discussion of events in Dallas, the agency president suggested that Mangum ought to talk with "Don Singleton, an impressive young guy from the oil industry." He described Singleton as a man who had been a registered Republican in California, an Eisenhower supporter in 1952, a Stevenson man in 1956, and a registered Democrat in Texas "because there was no point in being anything else." The advertising executive said that Singleton had something on his mind, and that it was probably quite different from what Mangum had been encountering.

Singleton's *Look* Article

Mr. Mangum was favorably impressed by Don Singleton. At a dinner meeting, he found that Singleton had strong feelings about the president's death. Singleton showed Mangum a copy of a letter that he had sent to one of the two leading papers in Dallas, setting forth what he believed should be the city's sense of shame and suggesting that the city erect a suitable memorial to the late president. The letter had not been printed, and Singleton told Mangum that he believed this was because the Dallas papers chose to print only those communications that praised the city itself while condemning acts of violence as isolated events unrelated to its general atmosphere. At the time of his initial meeting with Mangum, Singleton and the advertising agency president were preparing a newspaper advertisement for which Singleton would pay the full cost—the ad would express his feelings about the loss of the president and his dissatisfaction with his own failure to act as a responsible member of the community, and suggest that Dallas itself should erect a memorial appropriate to the memory of Mr. Kennedy.

Mr. Mangum told the casewriter that he had said to Singleton that *Look* sometimes ran articles by nonprofessional writers. He had said that the odds were against publication, but that Singleton could prepare an article if he wished to do so. Singleton's reaction was favorable, and Mangum was impressed by what seemed to be Singleton's desire to help his city reassess its attitudes and actions.

As Mr. Singleton later described his activities to the casewriter, he wrote his article during the next two weeks, spending part of his time in a Dallas hotel. Although carrying on his responsibilities at Summit of Texas, he did not tell anyone at Summit of Texas or Summit Petroleum, Inc., about the article. He considered it a personal venture and the expression of a personal viewpoint that did not concern his company or his fellow employees. He emphasized that neither in the article nor in subsequent statements did he identify the name of his company. In conversations with his wife and Mangum, Singleton had indicated an awareness that the expression of his ideas might have some repercussions. Nevertheless, he went ahead with the preparation of the article. In statements made subsequent to the publication of his article, he said that two factors had prompted him to do so. In regard to President Kennedy, he said:

> It wasn't just that I agreed with most of his policies and his plans for the future; it was his manner and his exuberance and his dignity which made our national government all the more exciting and important.

Singleton's other major reason had to do with Dallas:

> I also believe strongly that open reasoned dialogue on any subject this side of perfection is more likely to produce good results than a monolithic "everything is fine, and even if it isn't don't stir things up" attitude. Before the assassination I was willing to go along with this mystique. . . .I think we should have not only expressed regret at the assassination of President Kennedy, but at the same time should have conceded that the past ugly incidents[1] may have encouraged extremist elements here. It is only human for many outsiders to suspect our motives when they hear nothing but disclaimers that anything at all has even been amiss.

After Singleton finished his article, Mr. Mangum and his staff documented it.[2] The article was published in the March 24, 1964, issue of *Look*. Excerpts from it are reproduced below; the omissions do not detract materially from the substance of the article, and in no case do they represent excisions of the author's ideas.

> **Memo from a Dallas Citizen[3] by Donald L. Singleton**
>
> We are rich, proud Dallas, "Big D" to Texas, and we have never wanted a lesson in humility from any man. Not even from a murdered President of the United States. We have lived for three months with national tragedy, and I won't be popular for bringing this subject up now.
> But somebody must. To say nothing, more

[1] Singleton referred here to incidents involving Adlai Stevenson and Lyndon Johnson.

[2] In this context, the word "documented" refers to the process of checking on factual statements. For example, Mangum checked on the question of a Kennedy memorial in Dallas, and learned that there was strong sentiment for what he called a "modest marker" at the site of the assassination, with the bulk of the contributions going to the Kennedy Library in Boston, Massachusetts. An ad hoc commission had been established in Dallas to study the question of a fitting memorial.

[3] Reprinted from the March 24, 1964, issue of *Look* magazine.

important, to do nothing, only says to the rest of the world that, as they have read, we shrugged the whole thing off . . .

. . . The tragedy would not go away. Day after day, I drove down to the slopes in front of the Texas School Book Depository, and always, no matter when I got there, or whether it rained or snowed, groups of people stood as at a shrine among the madonnas put up by children and the fresh flowers brought by nameless citizens. It still goes on. As I write this, not so much as a street, let alone a stone monument, has been dedicated to Kennedy, but the people have built their own memorial out of their patient presence.

Now, some of our ablest citizens have begun to understand that we can't make sense out of the future until we confront the past. Kennedy's death is a fact. I hope that out of our many arguments will come a memorial that is more than a statue. If we are to learn the lessons that President Kennedy came to teach, we must build a living, searching memorial. We could, for instance, buy the Texas School Book Depository, from which the fatal shots were fired, and rebuild it for a better purpose. It would become a civic research center, under Southern Methodist University, dedicated to study of the urban evils that lead to violence and hatred. . . .

. . . I think Dallas feels shame, not guilt. Many people here are ashamed to have been caught acting like fools—as they have been doing for many months—at the moment when the nation, and their President, needed the best they could give in thought, action and coherent criticism. He came to tell us so. Leaders must be guided by learning and reason, he planned to say, "or else those who confuse rhetoric with reality and the plausible with the possible will gain the popular ascendancy with their seemingly swift and simple solutions to every world problem." He never got to deliver his address, but his death, more than his life, shocked people out of the hysterics they had worked themselves into. Big D's penance for its silly years should lead to a meaningful memorial to its dead teacher. Or his death will be, for Dallas, in vain.

You had to live here in recent years to make sense out of today's confusion. None of us can claim to be blameless. For six years I have been helping build an oil business, a successful one, but at church, civic functions and parties, I have sat on the sidelines like a foreign observer at a tribal rite. I even got so I didn't pay much attention to the "Impeach Earl Warren" stickers on the bumpers in my neighborhood. They were not, it seemed then, much more of an affectation than the genuine alligator cowboy boots and mink chaps worn by people who had every other luxurious distraction our nation can offer. . . .

. . . A Texan with a cause is formidable, and a Texan doing the work of his Lord is awesome. It was almost as if these people had set up a new religion. They put God aside, for the emergency . . .

Outsiders make the mistake of thinking that the prominent businessmen of Dallas led the Birch chapters, the National Indignation Conference and the other political equivalents of a college panty raid. Not so. The Dallas leaders, the bankers and businessmen who set up the Citizens Council, are an intelligent and dedicated group. They have given the city an efficient government, an honest (if not always efficient) police force, a low tax rate and a booming economy. But they view their leadership in a narrow sense. . . .

Then it happened. I was sitting over an eight-ounce steak at the Trade Mart, where the President was to speak. When the news came, the first reaction around my table was the one I heard over and over in the next few hours: "I hope the killer didn't come from Dallas." But Dallas was elected by Providence to stand in the hard light of tragedy.

I'll never forget the rest of that terrible day. At the first telephone booth, I called a business friend to cancel an appointment. The telephone operator was sobbing, so I comforted her. She said, "That wonderful man—why did it have to happen in Dallas?" Next, my friend's secretary said, "Oh, Mr. Singleton, I'm broken-hearted. It *must* have been somebody from out of town; nobody in Dallas would do such a thing." My friend said, "Well, they finally got what they wanted." He didn't have to explain to me—or anybody else in town—who he was talking about. I said, "Yes, but suppose it turns out to be a Communist or a Black Muslim?" His answer was loyal Dallasite: "Well, I sure as hell hope that whoever he is, he's from out of town.". . .

Basically, I suppose, the things that are wrong with Dallas are the things that are wrong with a world whose technology has raced beyond man's ability to shape it to his needs. We know how to get a man into orbit, but we can't find a good way to get to and from work. We can teach machines to think, but not our children. We have shining cities that false-front for stinking, crime-breeding slums; only a very rich society could afford so much poverty. We develop the greatest communications medium mankind has ever dreamed of, and then devote it to trivia and violence. And so on: Make up your own list. It will do, as long as it does not just pass the blame to somebody else—the UN, Washington, the Communist conspiracy, anybody. We can't pass the buck. We have work to do.

In one sense, those who say, "It could have happened anywhere," are quite right. But somehow Big D doesn't derive much comfort from that, nor is it possible. For I'm afraid the record shows all too clearly that in addition to having the world's ills, Dallas has managed to develop a few special complications. For all I know, other cities have our disease, too, but the epidemic broke out *here*. Maybe the President could have caught it anywhere, but he caught it *here*. Here is where the quarantine sign is, and I don't think it will ever really come down until we take it down ourselves.

Will we do it? The answer now is: maybe. Thousands of us are taking inventory of our civic faults. The assassination shocked us into our reappraisal, so our search for solutions should, in justice, be a memorial to the man who died here. A civic research in Kennedy's name could bring the best minds to help us, to keep up the momentum of the work. It won't happen automatically. We still have many who want the whole thing to blow away in the next dust storm.

We need help. If you who don't live here will see the difference between the guilt we don't feel and the shame many of us *do* know, we can succeed. We can bring pride, a better pride, back to Dallas, and make the School Book Depository more than a murderer's sanctuary.

One thing is sure: Thanks to the world's searchlight, we have a magnificently illuminated operating room. Never again will we be able to see our city, its good and bad, as clearly as we do now. We have the opportunity, bought by a great man's life, to treat what ails Dallas and, maybe, the "anywhere" where it didn't happen.

Aftermath

Mr. Singleton told the casewriter that shortly after the March 24 issue of *Look* was published, the president of Summit of Texas and Singleton discussed the latter's article. For a few weeks thereafter, nothing further was said on the subject. Things were less quiet on other fronts, however. Singleton said that he received over 800 letters and 500 phone calls, about 90% of which praised his position. He did not know how many other letters or calls were received elsewhere in the company, but he believed that the number was large and that the balance of their sentiment was less favorable to him. He knew that a certain number of Summit's credit cards were returned to the company.

On Monday, April 13, another conversation took place between Singleton and Summit's Texas president. The next day, Singleton signed a statement of resignation, which he told the casewriter had been presented to him.

The parent company's board meeting was scheduled for mid-April. As a board member, Singleton had had hotel and plane reservations for some time. Because he was "physically and emotionally tired and thought that a trip might help me unwind," and "just to see what would happen," Singleton went East, but did not visit the board meeting. No one from Summit got in touch with him.

On April 14, the *Dallas Morning News* stated that Summit of Texas had confirmed Singleton's resignation. In a story dated April 17, *Advertising Age* carried the information that Summit's advertising agency had resigned the Summit account, which reportedly amounted to more than $750,000 of commissionable advertising. The story quoted the agency president:

> One of the few privileges you have in the agency field is deciding whose money you want to accept. We just decided that we didn't want Summit's any longer.

The casewriter learned that some time after Singleton's departure from Summit, he and Lawrence Mangum had looked back at the events and forces that might have been involved in his situation. They considered the reactions of suppliers, jobbers, and retailers. The two men knew that some criticisms had come from these sources, but they believed these had been substantially offset by favorable comments from the same sources.

The two men also thought about the reactions of the general public and the press. The range of such reactions is reflected in Exhibits 1–3. Although most of the letters received by Singleton himself had expressed support of his position, as indicated earlier, neither he nor Mangum could be certain about the volume of letters that might have been received elsewhere in the company.

The two had not agreed as to the nature or strength of the reactions of members of the Citizens Council (referred to in the *Look* article), which is described in Exhibit 4. After Singleton's resignation became publicly known, Mangum talked to a number of prominent Dallas citizens, including several important members of the Citizens Council. All expressed regret at what happened to Singleton and emphasized that they had had nothing to do with the Singleton–Summit episode.

Singleton told the casewriter that he had been less certain than Mangum about the reactions of some of the other members of the Citizens Council. He suspected that some of them had expressed dissatisfaction to Summit about his statements. He also knew that one member of the council, in making a speech in April, had said, " . . . If Mr. Singleton would learn to know Dallas better, he would probably like it better. So much for the gratuitous defectors and journalistic buzzards that are still circling our town. Don't waste your breath lashing back."[4] In any case, Singleton had no reason to suspect any organized activity on the part of the council.

As Singleton himself looked back upon what had happened after the publication of his article, he said,

> When I resigned, . . . the impression got around that [Summit] asked for my resignation because it disagreed with what I wrote. This is not what happened and obscures the basic decision that most company men have to make, at one moment or, more likely, on the installment plan.
>
> About a month after the article, and hours after the *Dallas Morning News* took me to its editorial-page woodshed a second time, I was suddenly confronted with a company demand: I must agree never to comment publicly without formally clearing each word in advance and in writing. The issue was not *what* I said, but whether I could say anything at all.[5]

[4] Reported in the *Dallas Morning News*, April 15, 1964.
[5] This quotation from Mr. Singleton has been taken from an article entitled "Memo about a Dallas Citizen," *Look*, August 11, 1964, p. 64, copyright 1964 by Cowles Magazines and Broadcasting, Inc.

EXHIBIT 1 From Texas Press Clipping Bureau—Dallas

Borger, Texas
News Herald
(Cir. D. 9,805 S. 9,962)
March 13, 1964

Look Again

Look magazine, March 24, 1964, on page 88, gives us another one of those among us who have dared to disagree with the progress of socialists, communists, and the world government movement within our government.

The article, entitled "Memo from a Dallas Citizen," was written by [D. L. Singleton], a Dallas citizen.

Mr. [Singleton] is Senior Vice President of the [Summit] Oil Company. His address is [__________], Dallas, Texas.

So Sorry!

When reading this *Look* magazine article by a Dallas citizen, [D. L. Singleton], it is hard to escape the impression that the author would have been a lot happier had the President, John F. Kennedy, been assassinated by someone among us who had dared to exercise the privilege as an American citizen, to disagree with the establishment, the communist-serving bureaucracy in Washington, D.C., instead of being killed, *as he was*, by an admitted communist.

Such hatred as reflected in this article graphically demonstrates why we, who are opposed to socialism, communism, and the loss of our national sovereignty to a world government, should thank God that the murderer of the President was immediately apprehended and as quickly identified as a member of the communist conspiracy.

Had he escaped, it is quite obvious that such unreasonable bitterness as revealed in this article could easily have resulted in either death or imprisonment for American patriots prominent in the conservative movement.

Without the guilty party in custody, it would have been much easier to have saddled the blame upon the conservatives or right-wing element among our citizens.

But these smear writers and speakers never quit trying!

Disappointed

Since November 22, when President John F. Kennedy was assassinated and Lee Harvey Oswald, who had applied for Russian citizenship, was apprehended as the accused slayer, the news media of this country has been flooded with articles and speeches designed to saddle part of the blame, if not all of the blame, for the assassination on our conservative people, termed rightists.

(Of course, we who oppose the establishment in Washington, D.C., are often described as members of the lunatic fringe.)

These writers and speakers actually seem disappointed that one of us, instead of a communist, *had not killed* our President.

EXHIBIT 2 Letter to Singleton

March __, 1964

Dear Mr. [Singleton]:

I have just had an opportunity to read "Memo from a Dallas Citizen" which was written by you and appeared in this month's *Look* magazine. The article was timely. It is excellent. It contains factual matter, most of which are matters of record. However, I am sure you realize that this article is going to call forth. . .your condemnation, with such statements that you are a socialist or communist. Some of them may even go so far as to apply to you the dirtiest word which these extreme rightists know: namely, a Democrat regardless of the hard life one finds in Dallas.

You are well aware of the situation here. Like the members of your church not tolerating sermons that contradict their personal dogma, these [people] will not tolerate any idea that contradicts their personal ideas. For instance, the last sentence in your article implies that there is something "which ails Dallas." These citizens whom I am talking about will not admit that there is anything which ails Dallas. They are still teaching their children that our Federal Government is something to abhor and cuss, instead of pointing out to them the glories of our government.

I am very hopeful that you own your own business,. . .for you may be sure after the article they will do what they can to harm you in any way possible as their dogma and their philosophy cannot stand the light of day and you in this article are throwing a little light upon the ills of Dallas.

Congratulations again for this article, but I am afraid that it will not do Dallas much good because it will just go unheeded like the rest of the suggestions which have been made to cure the ills of Dallas. At least it is refreshing to know that men such as you live in Dallas and are willing to do whatever possible to try and make this city a better place in which to live even at the expense of having adverse criticism cast against you.

With kind regards, I am

Very sincerely,
(Name deleted)

EXHIBIT 3 Letter to President of Summit of Texas

(The following is a reproduction of a letter which was sent to the president of Summit of Texas; a carbon of the letter was sent by its author to Mr. Singleton, and this reproduction comes from Mr. Singleton's carbon.)

April __, 1964

Dear __________:

I was delighted to read in the paper this morning of the resignation from your company of [Don Singleton]. If this is really a cover-up for your discharge of him or if it was due to pressure from you, I want to congratulate you. You will undoubtedly be charged with prejudice and hate by liberal eggheads of [Don Singleton's] persuasion; and, if so, I am sure it was not an easy decision from both your company and personal standpoint.

. . . I remain astounded that an executive of a sizeable public company such as yours would be so stupid as to make such an intemperate charge against his community as did [Singleton] in a national magazine. I am even more astounded by the conclusions drawn by him as expounded in the article, as he is close enough to the community to have felt the true nature of the feeling of this city. It indicates such a prejudice against conservative view as to indicate blindness towards the good things present in Dallas, or such a shallowness of observation as to render him useless for executive position.

Finally, . . . I have heard that [Singleton] did not consult the company management prior to the release of his article. This would be reason enough for the discharge of an executive of a public company, where the article in question could cause serious repercussions to the company. Such an act is simply rank insubordination.

Unfortunately, most news media are written by liberals, who have set the standard that liberals who disagree are merely forward-looking, while conservatives who disagree are vindictive haters. Please know that you have my wholehearted support.

Sincerely,
(Name deleted)

cc: Mr. [D. L. Singleton]
[Summit]

EXHIBIT 4 The Dallas Citizens Council

The Dallas Citizens Council is a highly influential group of over 200 prominent businessmen. Membership is limited to company presidents or board chairmen, and the organization concerns itself with major problems or issues that involve the welfare of Dallas. In recent months, the Citizens Council has been the subject of much attention. For example:

> . . . Every person interviewed stated without hesitation that Dallas leadership comes primarily from the business and financial sectors of the community. Throughout the interviews, no contradictory opinion was ever expressed (p. 31) . . . .
>
> In the initial interviews, . . . respondents stressed the role of a Dallas organization called the "Civic Committee" as having "more control over what goes on here" than any other organization (p. 35). . . .
>
> The Committee as a body, they explained, meets officially only once a year, while the directors meet regularly. Whenever a serious problem arises in the city, the board may be convened quickly to decide what action should be taken.

The power of the organization was described by one of the respondents in this way:

> Why, the Board of Education would not think of proposing any bond issue, or doing anything without first clearing it with the Civic Committee. This body has the power to make or break any idea or proposal that certain groups may come up with. It is such a powerful group that nothing can succeed without its support (p. 37). . . .
>
> . . . Recent decision to combine many charity campaigns into a United Fund drive. Other problems included the financial difficulties of the symphony orchestra and of the city-owned zoo, inadequate housing for Negroes, getting a "good slate" of nominees for school board elections (and getting them elected), juvenile delinquency, school integration, and urban renewal. The range of problems in which the more influential leaders become involved seems unlimited (p. 59). . . .
>
> . . . The Civic Committee . . . functions as a mechanism for coordinating efforts of the various groups and interests within the community concerned with the particular problem at issue. . . . The leaders emphasized, however, that the board of the Civic Committee does not, itself, make decisions. Rather, it is the individual leaders who make the decisions. They use the organization as a tool for mobilizing verbal and financial support for their ideas (p. 61).*

Fortune also commented on the Citizens Council in an article that discussed the general question of business's leadership role in Dallas:†

> . . . This (Dallas) world would not have survived had it not had many positive qualities — the quality of action, of dynamism, the quality of community service and of high (if localized) morality. And it is this strange mix of the negative and positive that has come to characterize the business leaders of Dallas. Mostly self-made men, they nevertheless place public service above wealth as the supreme symbol of status; the people with the highest standing in Dallas are not necessarily the richest, but those who do the most for the community. . . .
>
> The nine most powerful men in Dallas, the inner circle of its business leadership, have many characteristics in common, including a high degree of individualism. All are directors of the unofficial but omnipotent Citizens Council, four having served as president. . . .Of the eight who are college graduates, only three took degrees outside of Texas. Collectively, the power of these men is enormous; it reaches into every phase of life in Dallas, social, political, cultural, and economic. . . .
>
> Probably not one Dallasite out of five has any real idea of the power and purpose of this twenty-seven-year-old organization. Its membership of 250 maximum is by invitation only and perpetuates the original conception that none but the chief executive officers of the city's biggest corporations—men with the power to say "yes" or "no" to a project and have it binding on the enterprises they head—be invited. . . .
>
> In addition to the work of this organization, the influence of the business leadership is brought to bear on every aspect of community life through interlocking directorates or trusteeships.

*These quotations are taken from Carol Estes Thometz, *The Decision Makers, The Power Structure of Dallas*, Southern Methodist University Press, Dallas, 1963. Mrs. Thometz's book began as a master's thesis at Brandeis University and was later expanded and revised into book form. The Citizens Council to which Singleton's article refers is presumably the book's Civic Committee.

† Richard A. Smith, "How Business Failed Dallas," *Fortune*, July 1964, p. 157.

Lex Service Group, Ltd. (A): *Developing the Guidelines*

In 1978 the British firm of Lex Service Group, Ltd. decided to shift its organization away from its current highly centralized form towards a more decentralized management structure. In the past the company had been heavily dependent on the values and decision making of its chairman and chief executive officer, Trevor Chinn—and on those of his father before him, who had been the previous CEO. Although Trevor Chinn was convinced that devolution[1] was a necessary organizational structure for Lex Service Group, Ltd., and although he had the utmost confidence in his senior managers, in reviewing the firm's devolution efforts a year later, he and Lex's senior management agreed that they needed some formal means for ensuring that the corporation maintain a cohesive character and strategy as its decision making became less dependent on Chinn's own personal judgment. Consequently, Chinn and his policy group drafted a set of twenty statements, here entitled the "Guidelines," which summarized the values and financial objectives of the company as they perceived them. The statement was then circulated to the senior managers in the firm to obtain their comments, and a final draft of the Guidelines was examined at length at a senior managers meeting in September of 1979. A short while later the revised Guidelines were adopted and the appropriate authority and role of each senior managerial level was determined within the context of that statement (for full text see Exhibit 1). The following cases represent some of the major problems which occurred in the first year of applying the Guidelines. Although some of the situations are a composite of several managers' experiences, all opinions expressed herein are direct quotations or close paraphrases of statements made by Lex senior management.

History of the Company

Lex Service Group, Ltd. was a publicly owned, diversified company with reported net revenues of approximately £500 million and retained profit of £15 million in 1979 (at the time, approximately $30 million). Although its headquarters were located in central London, the company's six decentralized business groups (in U.S. terms, divisions) were comprised of approximately 30 subsidiary companies located throughout the U.K. Lex had recently made substantial acquisitions in the United States and was planning over the next five years to expand its overseas operations until they yielded 50% of the company's profits before interest and tax.

Originally a string of parking garages and petrol stations, Lex was publicly incorporated in 1928 in London, and the company name (then Lex Garages Limited) was derived from the location of the first garage on the corner of Lexington and Brewer Streets. In 1945 Mssrs. Rosser and Norman Chinn became directors of Lex, and in 1954 Chinn Family Holdings Ltd. acquired the company's total issued share capital, which was again issued publicly in 1960. In 1980 the Chinn family owned less than 10% of the firm's shares.

Under Chinn leadership, Lex began a long series of acquisitions which continued steadily to the present time. In the 1950s and early '60s Lex's new subsidiaries bore some relationship to the historical origins of the firm: vehicle sales and servicing operations were expanded, and an exclusive franchise to import and distribute Volvo automobiles was obtained. In 1968 Trevor Chinn assumed the role of chief executive at the age of 33 upon the retirement of his father, Rosser. By 1970 Lex had become the largest British Leyland car distribution group, the second largest

[1] Originally a government term for the federal status of Scotland and Wales, "devolution" was adopted by British business to signify a partially decentralized organization.

distributor for Rolls Royce, and the largest distributor of heavy trucks in the U.K. Over the next three years Lex also moved into nonautomotive service businesses which included the acquisition of transportation and leasing firms, several hotels, and an employment agency. Following this period of rapid diversification, the company was forced to stop expansion and capital investment and to start on a process of extensive rationalization in order to survive Britain's 1973–74 economic crisis. Wishing to avoid a repeat of that experience, Lex resolved to diminish its U.K. dependency. It expanded its involvement in the deluxe hotel market by acquiring four hotels in the U.S., including the Whitehall in Chicago and the Royal Orleans, and in 1979 acquired two vehicle parts distribution concerns in California. The acquisition of a leading U.S. industrial distributor of electronic components in 1981 furthered the company's commitment to non-U.K. expansion.

From the outset of his leadership, Trevor Chinn had played a very strong role in the company's strategic and organizational decision making, particularly during the '73–'74 crisis. Chinn, however, believed that as the company became larger and more diversified, and its financial position more stable, it would be best for him to diminish his own involvement in the operational decisions of the firm. While Lex had nominally adopted a divisional, decentralized structure as early as 1970, it was not until 1978 that the company fully addressed the issue of decentralization and formally devolved into six business groups, each of which was headed by a group manager and had its own functional staff. A corporate staff was centered in London and the chairman's policy group comprised the two chief operating officers, who supervised the U.S. and U.K. groups, respectively, and the directors of finance, personnel and corporate strategy. Like Trevor Chinn, the firm's senior management was unusually young by British standards: one of the chief operating officers and several group managers were under age 40, and none was over age 50. All of them had been with the firm during its unstable strategic and organizational shifts during the '70s, and had personally witnessed the company's chaotic series of rapid hirings, firings, and promotions during that period.

When the Guidelines were proposed in 1979, none of the group managers found the statements to be extraordinarily different from his or her own way of doing business. Trevor Chinn's profound religious beliefs were well known in the corporation and had always been expressed in practical terms: in his private life he was an active Zionist and also served on several secular British public service committees, while as chairman of Lex Service Group, Ltd. he had always emphasized a concern for customer service and employee welfare. The Guidelines seemed to be a consistent—if somewhat idealized—articulation of those same beliefs, and group managers did not find it difficult to agree to comply with the twenty statements for a year's trial period. At the end of that time, it was found that, as could be expected, the Guidelines had been less easy to interpret and follow when applied to practical problems. But after a serious review of those problems at the 1980 senior managers' meeting, it was agreed to retain the Guidelines at Lex Service Group, Ltd.

EXHIBIT 1 Guidelines For Corporate Conduct

1. The company will operate a diversified range of service and distribution businesses on an international basis, aiming to develop over the next decade so that 50% of profits before interest and tax are earned outside the U.K., with no single business activity in any country contributing more than 25% of profits before interest and tax.
2. The company will be honest and responsible in its dealings with all its stakeholders, considering shareholders and employees to be of equal importance.
3. The company will operate as a management company, and as part of the process of continual improvement in management capability will seek to recruit only those managers whose intelligence, as well as qualifications or experience place them in the top quartile of their roles by national standards.
4. The company will not permit discrimination between employees or in recruitment on the grounds of sex, nationality, creed or color.
5. The company will work within the laws of any country in which it operates.
6. The company will not operate in a country where the standards of business conduct do not allow the company to meet its own values, policies, and constraints.
7. The company will offer each employee the fullest possible opportunity to develop his or her potential within the organization.
8. The company will provide all its customers with a quality of product/service which is substantially above the average for the market segment in which it is operating at a price which yields a sufficient value for money to encourage long-term customer loyalty.
9. The company aims to increase pretax earnings per share, when measured over five years,
   - At least as fast as the upper quartile of U.K. companies of comparable size.
   - Noticeably faster than the weighted average rate of inflation for the countries in which the company operates.
10. The company aims to achieve a pretax return on shareholders' funds of at least 25% per annum.
11. The company will develop an adequate supply of qualified, competent personnel to allow for a choice of internal candidates for all managerial positions.
12. The company will not close a business activity unless all the following conditions are met:
    - The scale of its performance shortfall is such that it threatens the long-term achievement of the relevant business group's objectives.
    - It is demonstrated that all possibilities for alternative developments for the business have been exhausted.
    - There is no possibility of sale of the business rather than closure within a time-scale which would protect the business group's objectives.
13. The company will:
    - Provide working and off-work* conditions which are amongst the best for relevant occupations, particularly in respect of safety, and in no circumstances will such conditions fall below statutory or nationally agreed minimum standards.
    - Offer all employees a remuneration and benefits package which reflects upper quartile practice (with special reference to the practice of high performance companies in that segment) for the appropriate industry or activity (overall industrial practice in the case of managers).
    - Be honest and open towards employees on issues that affect them, provided that the disclosure of the information involved would not be prejudicial to the interests of the business or of other employees.
    - Provide all employees with adequate training to enable them to perform their duties efficiently and the appropriate training to enable them to develop their potential.
    - Not dismiss any employee for inadequate performance unless a full disciplinary procedure at least meeting the company's standards has been followed to its conclusion. Such conclusion does not preclude a fair and mutually acceptable financial settlement.
    - Not make any employee redundant prior to the offer of any vacant position of a suitable nature in the company. If such an offer is declined, or if no such position exists, compensation must be at least equal to the company's minimum standards.
    - Not dismiss any employee who has been overpromoted prior to the offer of any vacant position at their former level for which they are suitably qualified. If such an offer is declined, or if no such position exists, compensation must be at least equal to the company's minimum standards.
    - Give any employee who transfers with a business which is purchased from Lex, and who is not offered the alternative of continued employment with Lex in a suitable position, reasonable compensation for any reduction in benefits suffered as a result of the transfer, together with a guarantee of at least Lex redundancy terms should that employee be made redundant by the purchasing company within the first year following the transfer.
    - Give every employee the right to appeal to higher management through an established grievance procedure if employees feel that their treatment by their immediate manager is unfair.
14. The company is committed to a policy of promotion from within, and will prefer an internal candidate for a vacant position whenever this is consistent with the maintenance of adequate managerial stability and the need to meet the objective of employing top quartile managers.
15. The company will be relatively high geared, in order to fund a high rate of growth and maximize returns on shareholders' funds.
16. In order to ensure that there is a very low probability of any financial pressures threatening the corporate values,

EXHIBIT 1 Guidelines For Corporate Conduct (Continued)

the company will maintain an acceptable balance between the equity base and borrowings in the light of the risks inherent in the trading activities and in the external environment.

- Net borrowings will not normally exceed 75% of shareholders' funds less goodwill and will never exceed 90%. Net borrowings will only be allowed to exceed 75% if there are clearly implementable plans to return to this ratio within the next twelve months.
- Interest charges, recalculating interest at 12%, will be covered not less than 3½ times by profit before interest and tax.
- Current assets will not be used to secure debt.

17. The amount of goodwill in the balance sheet will not exceed 25% of shareholders' funds, including goodwill.
18. Debt maturities will be spread as evenly as possible over future years and will extend as far as possible. Not more than 10% of total debt will be repayable in any of the next five years.
19. Each Business Group must be organized so as to be able to seek technological solutions towards enhancing its competitive position and meeting its own and corporate objectives and goals.
20. The performance of each business, in relation to its specified strategic plans and goals, must be measured constantly against the performance of its competitors.

*On the Lex site but away from the actual place where work is conducted.

Lex Service Group, Ltd. (B): *Closing Portsmouth Depot*

Keith Hampson,[1] group manager (in U.S. terms a divisional president) for Lex Service Group, Ltd., had just completed what he himself defined as one of the worst times in his career. Two months ago it had been finally decided that the Portsmouth Depot had to be closed or sold, and, although Lex had found a buyer who was willing to employ 50 Lex workers, and another 15 could be relocated within his own group, Keith and his personnel staff had spent the next two months working out arrangements for the other 50 employees who were slated to lose their jobs. Although the company had a firm policy that, wherever possible, alternative jobs would be offered the workers when a location was closed or sold, in this instance there were no other Lex facilities in the Portsmouth area, and few workers had been happy about the idea of relocation. Keith had just finished the last employee negotiation and it had been one of the most painful discussions of all: John Sargent, the Portsmouth facilities manager, age 57, with 30 years of service at Lex, had had to be made redundant. There simply were no comparable positions for which he would be suited in the Lex company.

It was precisely in considering seven department managers at Portsmouth who, like John, all had over 25 years with Lex and were about ten years away from retirement, that the Board of Directors had almost rejected Hampson's proposal to sell the Portsmouth Depot. Hampson had had to argue long and hard for the Portsmouth sale—preparation for that particular proposal had taken four months—and in the end he was not really certain that he had made the right decision.

Layard Motor Transport Ltd. and the Portsmouth Depot

Keith Hampson had been with Lex Service Group for 11 years, and at age 49 was one of its oldest senior managers. His business group, Layard Motor Transport Ltd., consisted of five subsidiary companies which specialized in heavy hauling. The Portsmouth Depot was one of four depots comprised by Victoria Transport Ltd., a Layard subsidiary, servicing the transport of steel in the southern half of the U.K. That particular subsidiary, which was acquired with heavy investment in 1970, was now sorely handicapped by British Steel's alarming production problems, and it had been losing its market share at the rate of about 20% in the first half of 1980. Keith Hampson felt that there were too many Victoria depots in the southern region, and that the overall number should be reduced from four to three. Portsmouth was the obvious choice: its shortfall had been worse than those of the other three depots, partially because local zoning laws restricted the hours during which the lorries could operate, and the business was smaller there than in the other three locations. With the loss of 40% of its business in 1979, Portsmouth's return on investment had dropped from 26% the previous year to 8%. Moreover, its operating costs were higher than average because previous rationalizations of Layard depots in the region had left Portsmouth with a staff level that was higher than was strictly necessary. The two depots which were closest to Portsmouth would be able to absorb the Portsmouth business easily, but Hampson could not justify financially the continued employment of the seven special category department managers with long-term service: to retain them, Layard Motors would have to place them in "nonjobs" at the other depots, which would cost the company £50,000 per annum. Hampson suspected that several might even

[1] With the exception of the chairman, the names of all Lex employees and subsidiaries are disguised.

welcome redundancy over relocation if the settlement were high enough.

The Board, however, was very reluctant to approve a closure. As Chairman Trevor Chinn put it, "We just don't have the option of putting 100 people out of work—we've got nothing to offer them instead." Some members even felt that business might pick up in a year, and that it would be better to wait for the industry to turn the corner than lose 100 experienced employees and a facility which might be needed later.

Throughout the Portsmouth discussions two statements in particular from the Guidelines had been appealed to as a basis for the Board's decision:

1. The company will not close a business activity unless all the following conditions are met:
   - The scale of its performance shortfall is such that it threatens the long-term achievement of the relevant Business Group's objectives.
   - It is demonstrated that all possibilities for alternative developments for the business have been exhausted.
   - There is no possibility of sale of the business rather than closure within a time scale which would protect the Business Group's objectives.
2. The company will be honest and responsible in its dealings with all its stakeholders, considering shareholders and employees to be of equal importance.

Before deciding to recommend a shutdown of the facilities, Hampson had tried to find a solution that would meet the financial needs of the company and still keep the Portsmouth people under Lex employment. He scouted the area and conducted an extensive study of the possibilities of undertaking a similar business at Portsmouth, but was unable to discover a viable alternative. Even if he *had* found another transport business, inherent problems at that particular location and a general shortfall of productivity in comparison with the other three depots suggested that the steel industry was not the only reason for the depot's bad return, and that a new business would not necessarily provide any better margin. But despite these problems and threatening forecasts, Keith Hampson was personally unsure whether he could honestly say that the Portsmouth Depot's performance "threatened the long-term achievement" of his Business Group's objectives, as the Guidelines prescribed. In fact, he personally believed that no single business in his group would ever be substantial enough to threaten the whole.

Joe Stearns, director of Corporate Strategy, felt otherwise:

> You may argue that no one subsidiary could threaten the company, but we could find a combination of many small events which would certainly threaten the corporate strategy if not the ultimate existence of the company. We've already decided that we need to make some dramatic changes in the businesses we've got now if we're going to generate a higher gross and higher profitability. Our whole U.S. expansion seeks to break our dependency on the U.K. economy and particularly on industries like British Steel, and now you want to keep a losing business open. It can't be done. We've got to move large numbers around, and that's going to mean either lots of redundancy, lots of closure, or being able to sell big chunks of the company and simultaneously take the even bigger risk of moving into new ventures. If you don't feel free to move in a lot of small instances in order to be able to make the larger, grander moves, then in a sense the small instances do threaten the whole.

Morey Lear, Corporate Personnel director, strongly disagreed:

> Look, these closure constraints aren't absolute. You can't pretend Keith's divestment analysis is based on a precise science—the long-term advantages of closure or continuing Portsmouth are quite unclear. But you can be sure that even the very best rationalization would still leave at least 100 people out of a job, and although we have another policy which forbids making any employee redundant prior to the offer of a vacant position of a suitable nature at Lex Service Group, you and I both know that Portsmouth people aren't going to relocate to a Newcastle just to work with us. That means, given the 12% unemployment rate in the Portsmouth area, that we will be putting those people on the dole. Besides, for every one driver Keith might look to relocate, another group manager will have six more he'd like to send to Keith.

Joe Stearns intervened:

> Aren't you really talking about two different issues? There's a long-term consideration which

> absolutely must be given the first priority, and then we can adjust the short-term decision making accordingly. Now the number one issue is whether Portsmouth fits into the long-term objectives of the company: cash generation, less dependence on the automotive and steel industries and on the U.K. economy as a whole, with substantial expansion abroad. At this point employee welfare is not really the main consideration. Once we have the financial considerations fully in line, and perhaps decide to close Portsmouth, *then* we can return to that portion of the Guidelines dealing with employee redundancy and closure constraints, and we can very well follow the spirit of the statement. But to try to justify the main decision by fooling around with the wording in the Guidelines is just silly. If Hampson's financial analysis is not a precise science, the same holds even more strongly for the relationship between employee welfare and shareholder interest. It's helpful to ensure that we don't transgress the spirit of the Guidelines, but I'm afraid Layard Motors' particular role at the moment is to generate cash. And if Portsmouth's productivity is as hopeless as it appears in Keith's analysis, then the real responsibility is to manage divestiture as humanely as possible. That's a very important role, but I'm not sure the Guidelines emphasize this part of our management philosophy strongly enough.

Although he remained quiet and heard out everyone's view, Trevor Chinn had become increasingly agitated during the discussions. The memory of the 1973–74 divestments and redundancies was still very sharp, and he blamed much of that scramble for survival on his own failure to anticipate long-term consequences during the acquisitions of the '60s. That and the sudden downturn of the British economy, the announcement of a massive increase in oil prices by OPEC, and the upsurge of Japanese competition in the steel industry had forced Lex Service Group and many other U.K. firms to make some very drastic short-term decisions. That period in the company's history had been marked by an extremely aggressive management style, and Trevor now wanted a more secure top management team which was able to consider both the long and the short term and be willing to assess these factors on their own but with less coldbloodedness than in the past.

The problem was that the company had thrived on bright young managers who were very good—perhaps even inspired—at handling the short-term implications of the corporation's strategy, and Trevor himself freely admitted to putting too much pressure on the short term in the past when things got difficult. In a sense the Guidelines had evolved out of a desire to correct this tendency, to provide greater security for employees, and better value for money for the customers through long-term stability of the businesses. Trevor was now prepared to allow for a certain amount of time and training in order to implement a truly decentralized management team which could be relied upon to consider customarily the long-term implications of its decision making, but in this case the financial and employee considerations seemed to him squarely equal, and he feared that his group managers were tending to recommend divestment of facilities in the course of which Lex would lose some very good people. He fully understood and admired the long-term strategic planning which Hampson had prepared, but he was also afraid that the short-term adaptation—a Portsmouth divestment which would cost at least 50–100 people (some with very long service) their jobs—was not consistent with the company standards as agreed upon in the Guidelines. Why wouldn't it be possible to meet the company's long-term objectives by closing more recently acquired businesses where Lex did not have such long service from its employees? Or wait out the short term and reduce headcount through natural wastage?

The Board of Directors had been unable to reach a decision, and subsequently Keith Hampson was able to find two companies in unrelated kinds of businesses which were willing to buy the Portsmouth Depot. One potential buyer had offered a substantially higher price than the other, but the lower bidder had also indicated that it was willing to keep some of the current Lex employees. The different nature of that business, however, precluded its taking on any of Layard Motors' department managers at the Portsmouth facility. Keith estimated that the sale to the lower bidder would cost Lex approximately £100,000 altogether in redundancy pay, plus employee retraining and cleaning up the Portsmouth property.

Hampson's own inclinations were to sell Portsmouth to the lower bidder on the condition that 50 of the Lex employees be offered positions with the new company, and that any redundancies among them in the first year would be accompanied by settlements equal to or better than Lex standards. While this decision was not ideal—even after relocations within Lex, approximately 50 employees at Victoria Transport would still lose their jobs—Hampson felt that if the business weren't sold now, it would be closed later, all 115 employees would be out of work, and the costs to Lex Service Group, Ltd. would be even higher. As one group manager put it, "Some employees have to suffer for the greater good. We can't have 1% of the company threatening the welfare of the other 99%."

The Chairman of the Board eventually agreed to a sale to the lower bidder, but continued to chafe at the decision. He was heard to remark as he left the meeting, "I still have my conscience: I don't like this idea that whenever the company makes a big mistake, other people—not management—end up paying. That's one of the biggest problems in business today. Well, we're going to do everything we can to be fair with those Portsmouth people, even if it costs us more than we would otherwise have to pay."

After the Board's decision to sell Portsmouth, Keith Hampson had called together all his personnel directors at Layard Motors Transport to discuss the Portsmouth sale, and to determine which 50 employees would be rehired by the purchasing company, which employees might be relocated to other Lex businesses, and which would be made redundant. Hampson felt that the Lex Guidelines clearly indicated that every employee should have the opportunity to relocate if at all possible, and that the first task of the personnel people was to hunt out all available positions within the company. After they had a better idea of how many redundancies they were actually facing, they would decide the basis on which employees would be kept or be made redundant, and the terms of the redundancy. Some of the directors had real difficulties with the relocation policy. One argued that there were so few job openings that the issue was irrelevant anyway, while another, Adam Mills, expressed his long-standing opinion that Lex Service Group, Ltd. was generally too inclined to hire and promote from within even when an employee was ill-qualified for the job.

A major problem lay with four general managers with 30 years' service who were too young to retire early but not really suited for a promotion to a higher position. (It had been decided that the three others, who were in their early 60s, would retire early with larger-than-usual pensions.) Adam Mills argued that it would be cruel to promote them beyond their competency and cited cases where line managers had been moved up and out of Layard into other parts of Lex simply because they had been "good lads," and he felt that those moves had ultimately led to their quitting Lex altogether with a great deal of mental anguish and company cost besides. Placing them in nonjobs was not the answer either. Mills had seen too many examples where jobs had been created which in the end gave little to anyone or to the company—moreover, he worried that that kind of organizational window dressing set a very bad precedent.

> We have one structure; we change it; then we say to the world, "We created this job because the change is right." Then when it doesn't work out we change it back again. Wouldn't it be better to sit down and say, "Look, we have a problem. What can we do about it together?" That way people can retain their pride and can probably end up doing something else outside the organization or within it that they can do comfortably; therefore they're happier because they're under less stress, and everybody's faced it honorably.

Hampson disagreed. He felt that the long-service people had a particular attachment to Lex that transcended their position or salary, and that they had stayed with the company in part because they liked its character and wanted to work for such a firm. Lex in turn owed them its fullest possible consideration, and Hampson argued for a first-in, last-out redundancy policy.

Walter Royce, the youngest personnel director at Layard Motor Transport, argued strongly for a meritocracy. The older managers should be judged on the same basis as everyone else. Maybe the fact that they weren't really promotable indicated that they had been falling off in their performance. To keep them and others like them would only mean a gradually worsening rate of productivity throughout the rest of Layard. It would mean four fairly important positions in the revised depots might be filled by people who were not very competent, but on whom the success or failure of three depots and the jobs of over a thousand people would be dependent. Besides, on the first-in, last-out principle, the work force kept getting older and older with each rationalization, and that only aggravated the problem. That was in part why Portsmouth was where it was currently: previous rationalizations at Victoria Transport had always favored those with long service. Walter also questioned the loyalty of these people, which Hampson had felt was implied in their continued stay at Lex: "These managers won't be heartbroken; they've stayed because we pay them such high salaries they can't afford to leave. We've bound them to Lex with golden handcuffs. I feel more sorry for the younger managers whose salaries have been so high that they're now totally priced out of the market. Where will they go?"

When Hampson had later shared this discussion over a pint with another group manager, John Price, Price had absolutely exploded.

> This whole relocation thing is a sham! It's a positive insult. Here are people who are relatively poor, who live in subsidized housing, and we'll say to them, "We've got a job for you in Newcastle. We can't give you a rented house in Newcastle, but we'll give you the company transfer payment, which is not particularly favorable if you're living in rented and going to rented accommodations. And your motorbike won't do up there, you'll have to get a car for that weather, but I'm sure you'll agree that we're trying to be fair." That just salves our conscience. Then we can say no one *had* to go. They won't relocate, they'd rather have redundancy. That way their subsidized rent is reduced and they get a lump of money besides. In my group we've offered 200 employees continuing employment at other depots and to date no one has accepted the offer. Put yourself in their position: you've got a corporate strategy that projects 50% of the company profit overseas. Would *you* relocate to the U.S.?
>
> How much time have you spent discussing relocation anyway? How much has *that* cost the company? And I suppose you're going to offer them all huge redundancy benefits. I agree with the idea of fairness, but we're positively overgenerous. We corrupt them. We offer them the alternative of a huge lump of money, bigger than they've probably ever had before, or the opportunity to move to a strange place at great cost. Which would you take? They'd be better off with a job, but they'll never take it. The only way to make money in this company is to do your job badly—at least you get a good settlement when you're made redundant.
>
> I find this whole employee concern overplayed. There's no such security for management. Aren't we employees, too? When we were hired we knew Lex was a high-performance, high-pay company, and that means when the performance is down you're out. That's all right. I can live with that, and so can most people here. What we shouldn't be doing is creating a climate where being kicked out pays well. That just encourages abuse. I had a guy who took his redundancy on the Morrisgate closure, . . . dragged his feet, expressed his sorrow, got a lot of dough from us to ease our conscience, and then he signed up with our competitor.

In spite of Price's protest, Hampson and the corporate personnel director had worked out a plan which gave about 12% of the employees a chance for relocation. An added 40% would be hired by the new buyer. When these were added to the early retirements, disciplinary dismissals, and a bit of natural wastage, about 45 people would have to be told that they were being made redundant. Hampson expected many of the employees to refuse relocation, and was prepared to offer each of them around £2,000 settlement on the average, and assist them in finding alternative jobs. Disclosing the sale of the Portsmouth Depot had not been easy.

It had been decided that because of the Guidelines on honesty to employees, the department managers would have to be told of the sale immediately. It was felt, however, that it would be detrimental to the interest of the company to tell the trade union at that time, since the regional official was on holiday and the company was hesitant to begin negotiations with an unknown union official. The morale of the department managers immediately dropped, and they had a difficult time planning the changes of personnel and transferring Portsmouth operations to the other two depots. The entire changeover had taken six weeks, and one manager had even approached Hampson with a demand for a payoff to keep quiet about the sale "so as to facilitate the shutdown."

Hampson eventually called all the Portsmouth employees together and announced the sale.

Local press, radio, and television reported the announcement, and one station tied it into a feature on the effect of Japanese steel production on Britain's steel industry. Over the following week the trade union pressed the company very hard to allow unlimited voluntary redundancy before applying LIFO (last-in, first-out). Hampson had resisted voluntary redundancy out of a fear that it might unbalance the mix of skills which the other depots required for available business. Even his desire to serve the needs of the special category long-service employees was thrown aside: the union was much more concerned about securing better compensation for shorter-service employees than it was about making special provisions for older employees with long service.

Negotiations had not been helped by a long-standing rivalry between the Victoria Transport depots at Portsmouth and Plymouth (where some of the workers were to be offered a chance to transfer), or by the timing of the union consultation. Layard was under a legislative requirement to consult with the trade union on any redundancy proposal "at the earliest opportunity . . . and in any event begin consultation . . ."; union officials expressed privately that they felt that they were being presented with a fait accompli which was not in line with the spirit of that legislation. Hampson had felt that any earlier consultation would have opened the way to negotiation, which would not only be unfair to the nonunion people, but would also introduce the possibility that Layard would be forced to make a settlement which was not in line with Lex's stated redundancy policies. Either he would be forced to propose too low a settlement and run the risk of having it accepted (in which case he would violate the minimal requirements of the Guidelines), or he would be forced to succumb to union clout and settle too high. By the end of the third meeting with the union and Portsmouth's general manager, Hampson began to wonder if Lex's redundancy policies were placing its own perceptions of what was right above the wishes of the people being made redundant and whether the company had a right to decide this issue for the workers.

A week after the announcement of the Portsmouth sale, negotiations with the union were finally settled and Hampson and the personnel director began conducting individual discussions with employees to review their situations and opportunities, juggle with staff at the other depots, and determine redundancy settlements. These discussions could not have been completed in any event in under two weeks, and production problems at another Layard business made it necessary for Hampson to take three weeks. Fifty employees were scheduled to be made redundant at an average cost of £2,000 each, and the highest settlement was £12,000 ($30,000).

The last days at Portsmouth had been absolute torture, and Hampson could not stop thinking of his conversation with John Sargent, the facilities manager who was 57 years old. John had worked 30 years at Lex, 10 of them with Keith Hampson, and had always been a quiet, dependable, and honest worker. Hampson had thought he might be able to place Sargent at the Plymouth Depot and so had delayed making a final settlement until the last minute. When the position had not become available and Hampson had told John he would have to leave Lex, John had expressed little surprise or emotion. After the redundancy terms were worked out, he simply said:

> I know you've always tried to have a concern for the employees, and I know you care about their security. And I understand from what you say that these Guidelines are an attempt to formalize that concern, but in reality, where does that get me? Sacked. Where's *my* protection? What does your statement say about *that*?

Lex Service Group, Ltd. (C): *Work Conditions at Inglesby Shipyard*

Sweating, slums, the sense of semislavery in labour, must go. We must cultivate a sense of manhood by treating men as men.
David Lloyd George

Sarah Markham[1] had every reason to be very proud of her Business Group (in U.S. terms, a division). Her Webster Hire had managed to meet the margins which she had projected a year earlier despite a recession in the British economy and a very sudden rise in the nation's unemployment rate to the extent that in August 1980, Britain's total of jobless workers had passed the 1930s' figure for the first time since the Great Depression.

Webster Hire, one of six business groups at Lex Service Group, Ltd., was primarily a fork truck hire business with a £20 million turnover and an operating profit of £2.5 million in 1979. This return was particularly impressive when one considered that many of the Webster Hire subsidiaries serviced the hardest-hit industries in the country: steel, textiles, shipbuilding, and the automotive industry. Sarah, who had been group manager for Webster for the last three years, felt that part of this performance could be attributed directly to the character of her particular business group. She had fewer unions to deal with than some of the other groups in which she had previously worked during her 12 years at Lex Service Group, Ltd., and as group manager she had sought to cultivate a spirit of employee-management cooperation in all the Webster subsidiaries. Her own door was always open, and she tried to work out as many of the normal management problems as possible at the committee meetings which she held once a month with the regional managers. They, in turn, met every month with the depot managers, and the discussions at these meetings were communicated to the employees whenever practicable. Three times a year Webster conducted a formal briefing all the way down the line regarding closure reports, productivity, and the general goals of the Webster businesses.

At Sarah's regional sessions the managers would raise and air their own difficulties of the past month and have a chance to comment on and compare conditions among the depots. Sarah felt that her own role was primarily as mediator between the broader objectives and values at Lex and the specific concerns of the Webster managers, but she also tried to develop as independent a management force as possible. During three years of such meetings a bond of trust had developed between her and her managers which ensured a general belief on both sides that everyone would work toward the general welfare of the employees and the company, and that everyone would consistently attempt to resolve problems in an open and fair way.

This ethos had developed in part out of the general values of the corporation, and partly out of Sarah's own past experience as corporate

[1] With the exception of the chairman, the names of all Lex employees and subsidiaries are disguised.

personnel director. Her knowledge of the company's business was broad, and her commitment to treating employees as individuals was the chief operating value behind what she privately called her "reasonable style." She in turn required great commitment from each employee, and had helped ensure this not only through her own management style but by instituting an extensive series of training seminars at every depot and a separate training school for the service engineers at the Webster headquarters. In 1979 the average achievement of preventive maintenance targets was 94%, and customer breakdown calls averaged 1.8 hours against the guaranteed four hours' response. Sarah made it known that she was willing to provide everything in her power to help facilitate employee performance, and last year's record-breaking productivity figures at Webster had reinforced the mutual trust and respect which the managers and employees shared.

It was precisely this same climate of trust which had enabled Webster Hire to implement rigorous cost cutting and increased productivity demands with only minimal complaints from the general managers and employees. Many traditional employee benefits such as the annual depot outing also had had to be omitted that year, but as a result of these efforts very few people had had to be made redundant at a time when unemployment levels were soaring, and the breakdown rate in 1979 had been reduced by 30% over a 50% reduction the year before.

In view of the overall cooperation which Webster people had exhibited in the last year, Sarah found the corporation's recent adoption of a general set of guidelines, which emphasized an equal consideration of employee and shareholder interests (see Exhibit 1, page 137–138, for a complete copy), to be quite consistent with her own management approach. Trevor Chinn, Chairman and CEO of Lex Service Group, Ltd., had introduced the Guidelines at the last annual senior managers' meeting, and for the most part Sarah thought that they were a reasonably accurate statement both of what she felt to be Trevor Chinn's personal beliefs and of what she herself could comfortably live with as a group manager with high performance expectations.

She was less sure, however, that a business could ever come up with a consensus of values which would be capable of adoption at all levels of the organization. One might agree to a principle in theory and still find it necessary to suspend it momentarily in an actual business situation, and the problem was that no two people would agree on which situation would justify putting the Guidelines aside for the moment. Sarah could envision her regional managers' meetings dissolving into a chaos of misunderstanding if too many people tried to stick too literally to the Guidelines' policies and constraints.

The Guidelines, she reflected, would only work if you regarded the groups as consisting of one or two top people. Sarah, for example, had jokingly entitled Terry Rockford, group personnel director, the "guardian of the group's values," and she could depend on him to interpret a situation in a way that was very consistent with the corporation's general beliefs: he would always endeavour to hit upon a "fair" solution that considered employee and shareholder interests and ultimately to give the customer value for money at the same time. Rockford also tended to favor the former in any really thorny discussion, and Sarah was constantly forced to emphasize the costs of his recommendations and their effect on the price of the service to the customer. Sarah felt comfortable in discussing these issues with her personnel director, but was not so sure that she would want to have to make explicit or defend how she viewed the balance between these interests to every one of her regional or depot managers—never mind the line employees!

Still, all in all, she thought the Guidelines were a good idea—at least as a standard to strive for—and she recalled with admiration the chairman's introduction of them. As in many meetings, Trevor Chinn had displayed a genuine concern for his employees and intellectually accepted—no, pushed—the idea of a decentralized senior management, but emotionally he was still very much a patriarch: when it came to questions of corporate values, he tended to rely heavily on his own personal beliefs. Sarah found that to be fine, and the personal tenor of the Guidelines was all to the good in that everyone had always looked to Trevor for the company's values anyway.

Trevor Chinn himself had wrestled with his role as leader in a decentralized firm during that last senior managers' meeting. In introducing the Guidelines he had said,

> I think that these are issues that are the responsibility of the chief executive. I don't believe in paternalism, but I do believe in the chief executive knowing those matters in which he must get involved, and in being prepared to make explicit statements about them. That is something that he cannot delegate. It is affected by his own attitudes and morality. He's got to think it through, and then work with his senior management in the company to come to some explicit statements that everyone can live with. But he can't leave it to somebody else because if he doesn't care about it, nobody else will. At the same time, I think it is very important not to believe that you are the only guardian of the truth. You have to keep questioning, and I expect everyone here to do the same.

Sarah wondered if she would ever as a group manager have the perspective that Trevor Chinn had, a perspective that colored his application of the Guidelines so strongly. She remembered how, when she had been at corporate headquarters as personnel director, Trevor would say, "Sarah, you've got to make sure that every employee counts. You save one life, you save the whole world—it's a Jewish concept." How would Trevor apply the Guidelines, she speculated, to Inglesby Shipyard? The position in the Guidelines seemed fairly straightforward:

> The company will provide working and off-work conditions which are amongst the best for relevant occupations, particularly in respect of safety, and in no circumstances will such conditions fall below statutory or nationally agreed minimum standards.

But when one looked at a case such as Inglesby, the proper course of action was less clear. That situation had been a bother to Sarah for three years now, and was still totally insoluble as far as she could see.

The Inglesby Site

Webster Hire had leased a small working area on the Inglesby Shipyard site in Southampton, where it contracted to supply and service 16 fork trucks for the shipyard's use. The Inglesby depot ran three shifts a day and had spare trucks ready at all times to service the shipyard's needs as fully as possible. Although Inglesby was the service base of a larger operating unit nearby which had 120 trucks, it provided close to 50% of the unit's profits before tax (= £20,000 per year). The Inglesby depot was in reality a minimal structure erected over a pounded dirt floor. It had no heating facilities, it was too small to maneuver in, and there was no place to rest. On Sarah Markham's last visit, the dirt had been ferocious and the roof leaked. Every year Sarah tried to negotiate with Inglesby Shipyard to improve the site, and every year Inglesby had refused to put any money into it at all. At one point she had considered investing Webster Hire money in the location, but a rough estimate of the costs of putting up a new depot came to £100,000. Although the Inglesby contract was extremely lucrative, that company was absolutely firm about signing with Webster Transport for no more than one year at a time, and shipbuilding was currently one of the national industries with the highest unemployment rates.

Sarah felt that without a long term contract she couldn't authorize the investment to improve the site, and yet she had always hesitated to close the whole operation down, both because of the subsequent loss of revenue and because of the three Inglesby service engineers. One of them, Joey Barton, had the longest employment of any Webster worker in the southern region. In fact, Joey had personally secured the Inglesby business for Webster Transport ten years ago, and he loved working the shipyard. Joey felt that at the smaller operation he was really running the show—which he was—while he would have been lost at the larger depot. None of the Inglesby service people had really complained about the working conditions, and Sarah had approved whatever portable facilities she could to improve the site: she had had installed a local electric heater and had instituted extra breaks in winter; an electric kettle had been set up in one corner of the depot, and they had installed a chemical toilet at the back.

But the facilities were still far below Lex standards, and ironically, Sarah Markham had always prided herself on maintaining in general the safest work places in the industry. In fact, she had almost decided to pull out of the Inglesby contract last year when there seemed no possibility of improving the depot without taking an inordinate financial risk, but there had been no comparable positions for Joey and the other two workers in the Southampton region. To ask him to take a subordinate position at one of the larger sites would be the equivalent of firing him. For Joey to accept those conditions of employment would mean the loss of his dignity and self-respect. Sarah simply would not be so absurd as to drop the job just because it did not meet company working standards.

Terry Rockford, Webster's group personnel director, knew how much the Inglesby situation bothered Sarah, but he himself had no problem with keeping the site open. He did not disguise the fact that he thought Sarah was making too big a fuss over the depot, and never failed to rib her about it when the subject came up. The last time they discussed the negotiations to renew the Inglesby contract, Terry had remarked blackly, "Yeah, you'd better close it. Joey's a heavy smoker, and most likely he'll get emphysema and sue Lex Service Group for keeping him in substandard work conditions."

Shortly after the senior managers' meeting, Terry, who had seen the Guidelines, dropped by Sarah's office and remarked, "Trevor Chinn's new personnel director wants to visit Webster's southern region next week, and I'm trying to work out a schedule. Will you be taking him for a tour of Inglesby?"

Lex Service Group, Ltd. (D): *The Reading Pallets Theft*

It was ten o'clock in the evening when Frank Heathrow's[1] wife came into his study.

"It's for you, Frank. It's the Reading police." Bewildered, Frank took the phone.

"Hello. Is this Mr. Frank Heathrow, group manager for Devon Parcel Service? Mr. Heathrow, we're sorry to bother you at this time of night, but we've just arrested a Mr. Barney Snide, who has been receiving stolen pallets and reselling them for £3–4 apiece down here in Reading. Among his suppliers were three of your employees from Devon's Reading depot. They've been selling Barney about 12 of your customers' pallets a week for £1 apiece for the last six months, and we'd like your permission to arrest them tomorrow morning at the depot."

"Are you sure these men were stealing the pallets from us?"

"Oh, yes, sir, there's absolutely no mistake. After it came to our attention that Barney was selling pallets with other company names stamped on them, we began watching his place. Six Devon Parcel Service trucks were spotted at the back of his warehouse and the drivers were seen unloading pallets from the truck. We have the names of three of them and would like to make the arrests tomorrow."

"Well, okay, go ahead, but please try to be as discreet as possible while you're at the depot. By the way, who are they?"

"Billy Simpson, Gerald Rose, and Johnny Miller, sir. Thank you very much, sir, and good night."

The Company

Devon Parcel Service was a Lex subsidiary which distributed packages in the south and west regions of England. Employing 140 workers, including 40 drivers, the main depot for sorting parcels was located in Oxford, and in 1979 reported a £650,000 profit with an 18% return on investment. Drivers in the south and west regions would pick up parcels, take them to Oxford or sometimes a local depot for sorting, and then deliver the packages to receivers in the same region. Because of its size, the Reading area had its own depot out of which 12 Devon drivers and the same number of trucks picked up, sorted, and delivered local packages. Each driver delivered approximately 120 parcels a day, and collected a hundred or more which were unloaded at the Reading depot. Drivers ran about 100 miles per day and made £125 per week on the average. The dockers at the Reading depot were paid £95 per week.

The Pallet Theft

When a large parcel or group of parcels was collected, the customer supplied a pallet (a flat wooden slat platform normally costing £4–5) on which the packages were stacked and loaded onto the truck. At the parcel service depot the packages were unloaded, sorted, and reloaded onto other trucks, and anywhere from 25–50 pallets went in and out of the depot each day. Some of the pallets were reused in deliveries, and the remainder were either returned to the customer at his own arrangement or stacked at the parcel depot. Pallets usually had the owner's name stamped on them, but in practice were employed interchangeably, and one could find an assortment of pallets stored up behind most warehouses. Apparently some of the Devon drivers, as they were loading their trucks at the Reading depot, were having the dockers pile a few extra pallets in the back of the truck for "delivery" to Barney Snide.

The morning after his telephone call from the police, Heathrow called Paul Harris, his

[1] With the exception of the chairman, the names of all Lex employees and subsidiaries are disguised.

personnel manager in Reading, to inform him of the police's intended visit that day. He briefly outlined the incident to Harris, and they agreed that the three employees should be fired. Harris, who had a reputation for being "soft" with the employees, and had run into disagreements with Heathrow on firings in the past, was particularly eager to lend his support to Heathrow's suggestion since the case was such a clear-cut incident of employee dishonesty. It was unfortunate, however, since Simpson, Rose, and Miller also happened to be by far the most productive workers at the depot.

Later that same day Heathrow casually mentioned his late-night call from the Reading police to Dave Tucker, the group personnel director.

"What did you do?" asked Dave.

"Oh, I told Harris to fire them, of course, and he agreed. We're all sorry to see them go—they're the best workers on the lot—but we can't have that sort of thing going on, can we?"

To Heathrow's surprise, Tucker got all upset.

"Wait a minute," said Tucker. "Don't you think we'd better get the whole story here? When I used to be a depot manager, those pallets were just throwaways. They stacked up behind the warehouse and they were a pain in the neck. Half the customers forget all about them or can't be bothered to take them back, and then we're stuck with them. Why, I once donated a huge pile of them to the Boy Scout's annual bonfire. You know, the one where they sell tickets to benefit handicapped children, and local businesses donate burnables and contribute toward the tickets? These Boy Scouts came 'round, and we had a huge pile of pallets that were just getting in the way, and I gave them the lot. Was I stealing from the customers? I guess I was. Arrest *me*. Besides, I'll bet you anything the depot supervisor knew all about this. Those guys probably said, 'Look, all these pallets are in the way. Would you like us to take them off your hands?' *He* knew they weren't offering out of the goodness of their hearts. Shouldn't he be fired too?"

Heathrow was stunned. "I thought you were the hard one, Tucker. You're always going on about higher work standards at the depot."

"Look, all I know is, this kind of thing goes on all the time, and probably everyone there knew about it and ignored it. Why should those three lose their jobs?"

At that point the Devon financial planner walked by and jumped into the argument. He pointed out that casual theft in the parcel industry was almost a recognized way of life, and said that he had heard that in the States a maritime union had secured adjustments in its contracts to make up for lost income when the shippers shifted over to sealed containers. The financial planner looked Heathrow in the eye and said, "If everyone knows it's going on, how can it be stealing?"

Heathrow promised to reconsider his decision. That afternoon he called the trade union and informed them of the problem. He asked them if they planned to discipline the three employees, and the union replied that it had no intention of getting involved in the incident.

Reell Precision Manufacturing, Inc.: *A Matter of Direction (A)*

If you asked people around here "What's the worst thing that could happen?" going out of business would not be the number one response. I believe they would say, to abandon the "north" that we have defined on the compass. If we were to abandon that, I know the people I work with would say, "Pull the plug on it and walk away. It's not that important to us."

—Steve Wikstrom,
VP of Manufacturing, RPM, Inc.
Quoted in Margaret Lulic,
Who We Could Be at Work,
(Minneapolis: Blue Edge Press, 1994), p. 14.

It was Friday and Steve Wikstrom, Vice President of Reell Precision Manufacturing (RPM), walked from his office down the corridor, pausing briefly at the "Meet the Owners" board that displayed snapshots of each RPM employee in order of seniority. He continued out the door into the mid-July evening, wondering whether the meetings next week would bring a satisfactory resolution. During recent weeks, a challenging leadership problem had turned into an uneasy agreement, and he knew that more of a consensus was needed. Wikstrom put his briefcase into the trunk of his car and looked around the parking lot outside the company's facility in Vadnais Heights, near St. Paul, Minnesota. There was not much traffic, a humid breeze, and signs on the horizon of a summer rainstorm. H. B. Fuller, Inc. was across the street; 3M was next door. Pretty impressive neighbors, but not likely to face *this* kind of challenge.

After the weekend, Wikstrom would meet with Robert L. Wahlstedt and Lee Johnson (the company's President and C.E.O., respectively) to plan a crucial meeting they had called for next Friday in response to a proposal from several employees. The proposal was aimed at removing from RPM's current Direction Statement references to God, religious faith, or Judeo-Christian beliefs. This was much more than rhetoric or public relations. It cut to the core of RPM's genesis and growth as a distinctive company with a distinctive culture.

Company History

RPM was officially incorporated on October 13, 1970, as a producer of wrap-spring clutches for precision applications.[1] The founders, Dale Merrick, 44, Robert Wahlstedt, 37, and Lee Johnson, 35, had been manufacturer's representatives with strong engineering backgrounds and earlier career experience at 3M. Their interest in joining forces to market and manufacture on their own, rather than selling for others, had eventually surpassed their fear of failure, but a one-year noncompete clause in their agreement with their principal OEM meant that the first year of the fledgling company's life was spent in research and development.[2]

The name of the company was chosen after its initials were settled upon ("RPM" was apt for the clutch business, and "Precision Manufacturing" was natural for the second two letters). In the words of one of the founders:

> After going through the entire "R" section of the dictionary without finding the "right" word, Lee found a German dictionary and discovered the word "Reell" (pronounced "Ray-el") which means "honest, dependable or having integrity." We easily agreed that Reell Precision Manufacturing Corporation was the perfect name to express the ideals of our new business.[3]

[1] See Exhibits 1 and 2 for product, employment, and sales information.

[2] "OEM" is an acronym for "original equipment manufacturer," supplier to manufacturer's representatives and, depending on product/industry, wholesale distributors and retailers.

[3] Company history document, p. 5.

These were not the best of economic times for starting a new venture, and the early years were very challenging. Nevertheless, the upstart company developed an improved clutch device that competed well in a market sensitive to performance, obtained a significant patent on its innovative product, and by 1972–73 found in 3M not only a former employer but a first major customer. A second major customer, Xerox, was to play a dramatic role in RPM's development as a company—both in terms of product line (the electrical clutch in the mid-to-late '70s) and JIT manufacturing methods (the mid-to-late '80s).

Shared Risk and Shared Spirituality

The three founders, besides their shared 3M "alma mater" and entrepreneurial interest in precision manufacturing, came to share many basic convictions about the value of prayer, the importance of balancing work and family responsibilities, and the need to practice Christian principles in the workplace:

> In one of the [regular] Monday morning breakfast meetings in the early '70s, Dale recognized the spiritual dimension that was growing in our relationship and our working experience together. He wondered if there could be ways to share that dimension with the other employees. At this time, there were only a few other employees. It was decided to offer an optional, weekly Bible study on company time.[4]

For nearly ten years, the Bible studies continued with almost 100% voluntary attendance, alongside a statement of purpose entitled "A Message from the Founders" which was strikingly explicit in its affirmation of Creator, Redeemer, and the need for Judeo-Christian values in the work environment (see Exhibit 3). This faith commitment on the part of the three founders (the "triad" as they were called) led to an unusual governance structure. Each of the partners resolved to be guided in important decisions only by the unanimous and prayerful agreement of the others. In effect, each had veto power, but the potential for inefficiency and discord was avoided by a strong devotion to spiritually based process: retreats, shared readings and inspirational tapes, and a conviction that aspiring to do "the will of God" was the best guarantee of avoiding self-will and conflict. When decisions on important questions looked like they would come out differently among the triad members, the questions themselves were subjected to scrutiny.

By about 1980, the company had added over a dozen new employees, some of whom were more intense about their religious opinions than had been the case before. "An example of this," Bob Wahlstedt recalled, "was a time when one person 'blew off' another's point of view because it was not based on a particular version of the Bible. And practices that not everyone was comfortable with such as praying aloud were suggested. A division developed between the more 'spiritual' and the rest." The weekly company time Bible meetings had become more divisive than unifying, and were therefore discontinued.

If the '70s were an economic stress test, the early '80s were more a personal and interpersonal stress test for the founders and their growing circle of employees. Roles and responsibilities among the members of the "triad" needed clarification, patent challenges needed patient legal defense, physical space needed to be secured by investing in a new facility, and perhaps most important of all, the company's philosophy of workplace management was transformed. Quality control problems and inefficiencies in set-up procedures had led to frustration—but also to creative suggestions for radical change. Xerox contributed support and supplier training in Statistical Process Control (SPC) and Just-in-Time manufacturing (JIT).

> The results were surprising! Not only did we achieve the expected improvement in efficiency, but the quality of production improved as well! This was the first step in a philosophical evolution from a Command-Direct-Control style of management (CDC) to a Train-Equip-Trust style (TET). . . . Previously, our assembly process required 5 weeks making, inspecting, and stocking sub and final assemblies. Now, all sub-assemblies and inspections are done in one continuous flow process by production people. The entire process takes less than 2 minutes and the finished unit is ready for shipment without further inspection when it comes off the assembly line! In fact, it is placed directly into the shipping carton. . . . People using their minds as well as their hands are more challenged and have greater job satisfaction.[5]

[4] Ibid., p. 9.

[5] Ibid., pp. 13–14.

In 1985, the triad established an Employee Stock Ownership Plan (ESOP) and by 1990, the employees owned more than 30% of RPM stock. And the company's commitment to full employment provided that even when faced with a loss, it would reduce all salaries on a percentage basis rather than implement any layoffs.

Policies toward other stakeholders were also uncommon: executive compensation did not exceed six times the lowest pay of five-year employees or ten times the pay of newcomers; vendors were paid within 30 days, even if it meant borrowing money to pay them; and contributions to charity were at 10% of pretax earnings. Employee comments about working at RPM were almost uniformly positive:[6]

- "This is a people company. The little guy gets listened to. It's easier to be happy here because there is a fundamental trust."
- "RPM has a culture of fairness—and not lip service. There's a two-decade history here of supporting people through crises as well as in good times."
- "There is a people difference here. As an African American, it was not what I was expecting. The emphasis is on personal growth. Conflict resolution is an important part of what we learn."
- "I had heard about this place several years before I was hired. It is for real here!"
- "There is a community that cares here—and it helps a person to take it home. Reinforcement."
- "The attitude around here: How can we help you to succeed?"
- "The intent around here is to balance the needs of the corporation with the needs of the person—sometimes to a fault!"

Bob Wahlstedt had made it clear that there were three very basic issues in his vision of the company: (1) the priority of family over job; (2) financial (and job) security for employees; and (3) the opportunity for each person to experience pride in what he or she does. Dick Youngblood, a business reporter for the Minneapolis *Star Tribune*, and an editorialist not known for coddling image-conscious companies, was uncharacteristically impressed with RPM's preaching and its practice, and devoted a full column to it (Exhibit 4).

Dale Merrick retired in 1991. Joining the triad as its new third member was Steve Wikstrom, 39, Vice President of Manufacturing, who had been with RPM since October 1981. By the end of 1993, RPM was earning nearly $1.4 million on sales of $13.9 million, had begun operations in Europe, and employed more than 118 people. The product line had grown beyond the original wrap-spring clutches to include constant-torque hinges for laptop computers and tubular solenoid products for valve applications (see again Exhibit 1).

Steve Wikstrom: Revising the Direction Statement

Steve Wikstrom had been hired by RPM in 1981 as Production Manager, was promoted in 1983 to Manufacturing Manager and eventually to Vice President of Manufacturing and the first nonfounder officer of the company in March of 1986. During this time, Wikstrom was an important part of RPM's transformation of operations toward using statistical process controls and Just-in-Time manufacturing techniques. He also was responsible for leading the effort to convert RPM to new, sophisticated information systems and for expanding its physical facilities by 20,000 square feet in 1989.

Early in 1989, Wikstrom initiated the writing of the first RPM "Direction Statement" with the active participation of Dale Merrick, Bob Wahlstedt, Lee Johnson, and several others. The drafting of this statement took about nine months, lasting into the fall. Wikstrom believed that the "Message from the Founders" was very useful as a welcoming message to new employees, and that it should be retained as originally written, but he also believed it was not the *corporate* or *organizational* statement needed to carry the company's culture forward into the future. "We needed a broader statement than the founders' message to say what we were about, something employees themselves could be invited to buy into on a regular basis," he said.

The regular basis included annual employee conferences, which formally included, under the heading "Additional items for discussion if

[6] Casewriter interviews with RPM employees, one on one.

desired," the "RPM Direction Statement." A review of one's job description was also part of each employee's annual conference, and each such description opened with the same first objective: "To become increasingly familiar with the company's value base and to take an active role in our pursuit of excellence."

It was the original 1989 Direction Statement that Wikstrom, now a triad member, presented again to all employees in February of 1992, with a cover memo inviting participation in revision discussions. (See Exhibit 5.) "No critical event precipitated the decision to look again at the Direction Statement. There were isolated expressions of discomfort with its wording during annual conferences. But it was mostly a matter of keeping everyone's ownership of the statement real and fresh," said Wikstrom.

"Dale had just retired. Bob and Lee would themselves be retiring in not too many years. The RPM vision could not be based simply on reverence and respect for the three founders." Company values had to be owned at least as widely as the stock, Wikstrom implied, "And it seemed important if growth and diversity had brought any measure of dissent, that it be heard and addressed."

Wikstrom was not sure what to expect in response to the triad's memo inviting revision discussions. As it turned out, the vast majority of RPM employees responded by checking the line beside "I feel the Direction Statement is fine as it is. No changes are needed at this time." A total of 17 individuals checked "I would like to have us consider making the changes indicated on the attached copy." It was to this group of 17 that an invitation was issued to meet biweekly during April and May of 1992. "As it turned out, the 17 gradually dropped back to about 14, and interest in no change was as intense as interest in change, with many shades in between," one member of the group observed.

The first several meetings (April and May) seemed to focus on revisions of a relatively noncontroversial kind,[7] perhaps while participants sensed the climate, the direction and (for some) the safety of the meeting environment. In fact, near the end of May, it began to look as if consensus had been reached and the revision was complete—so much so that Wikstrom wrote the following memo to the members of the group after a "temperature check" of each participant's level of satisfaction with the revised draft:

> May 28, 1992
>
> TO: Randy, Brad, George, Harry, Chuck, Bart, Jackie, Jon, Sharon, Louise, Jim
>
> FROM: Steve W., Lee, Bob L.
>
> The temperature check we did indicates we are at a point where we have consensus on our revisions to the Direction Statement.
>
> Our next step will be to distribute the proposed revision and ask if there is any reason not to adopt it as the current Direction Statement. Many thanks to all of you for a job well done.

A Challenge—Appearances Can Be Deceiving

More strongly felt concerns began to be voiced by three or four members of the group at an end-of-May meeting, however, about the religious references and phrases in the Direction Statement. Perhaps the immanence of closure drew out the dissenting opinions—it was "speak now or forever hold your peace." As one member of the group put it, "I wanted to participate, but not undo or break the cultural fabric here. I felt I had a right not to feel uncomfortable on the religion thing."

Bob Wahlstedt expressed his conviction at this meeting that reference to "the will of God" in the text was very important to him and to the other two founders. He added that he would be as concerned about serving as a member of the triad with someone who was uncomfortable with prayer as he would be in denying a triad position to someone who was otherwise qualified. This posed a real dilemma for him. Some members of the group objected that this could be taken to mean that religious faith might be in effect a condition of promotion, at least to the "triad" level in the company. This was not only something they had moral reservations about, it might also be

[7] E.g., Should we speak of "team members" or "co-workers"? "Shareholders" or "stockholders"? Drop "rotary" before "motion control devices" because we have nonrotary products in this category? Replace "Christian" with "Judeo-Christian"? And there were several stylistic and grammatical modifications suggested here and there.

discrimination on the basis of religion, prohibited by state and federal law. Said one member: "Bob slipped, in my opinion, in implying that he would be unable to have someone in the triad who couldn't pray with him. This is both illegal and wrong, I believe."

Others in the group disagreed forcefully, insisting that the references to God's will and Judeo-Christian values were *central* to what RPM was about from its very founding. In an effort to clear the air and to confirm or disconfirm the illegality claim, Jim Grubs, a senior manager responsible for training and development, was asked to obtain a formal legal opinion from RPM's outside law firm in Minneapolis. In early June, the legal opinion was received and transmitted to the revision committee and to the rest of the company via the employees' bulletin boards. Anyone who wished to attend the next meeting was invited to come. The opinion appeared to support the members of the committee who wished to remove religious language from the text. (See Exhibit 6.) Any thought that the Direction Statement discussions were over was clearly mistaken.

At a meeting in late June, called to discuss the implications of the legal opinion for the revision committee's task, strong and conflicting feelings were again expressed. An agreement was reluctantly reached to drop the most explicit religious references. (See Exhibit 7.) In particular the reference to "the will of God" was removed and an explicit statement to the effect that there would be "no discrimination based on religious beliefs or practices" was added. This agreement unravelled, however, in the subsequent two weeks. One member of the group dropped out shortly after the meeting, remarking in a memo to Wikstrom that his opposition to the most recent changes in the Direction Statement was

> based on my belief that if something is altered once, it will be altered again and again. In this case, eliminating the reference to striving to follow the will of God (which I consider to be a foundational type of statement), is not only wrong but sets a dangerous precedent as well. Future revisions would be much more likely to remove references to Judeo-Christian values and the Creator.

Wahlstedt was also having doubts about the wisdom of removing the "will of God" language, even though he had gone along with it at the late June meeting. Wahlstedt believed that the legal opinion resolved the question of ceilings or screens in hiring and promotions—but he was willing to risk having the religious references in the Direction Statement misinterpreted. "If we take out all references to God's will and our purposes, there would be nothing left beyond our own individual self-interest that we'd be concerned about here. . . ." In a note to Wikstrom and Lee Johnson he wrote:

> I'm having second thoughts about eliminating the reference to the "will of God.". . . Our commitment to seek the will of God is the "root" from which all the other references and all the uniqueness of RPM stems [sic]. I'm almost ready to say trim everything else back if necessary, but don't destroy the root.

By mid-July, Wahlstedt's conviction had intensified. He began to think not only in terms of the substance of the Direction Statement, but also in terms of the process. He very much wanted true consensus across the board on the revised statement, but in another note to Wikstrom he said:

> The question that is raised is *who* decides what the direction statement says or when it should change. The "power of ownership" says that a majority of the stockholders can establish and/or change the statement whenever they *choose* to exercise that power. "Precedence" says that only the *unanimous* agreement of the Triad can make such changes. Management "style" suggests that a *consensus* of co-workers can change it. I think we should stay with precedence until it is clear that another course is necessary or desirable.

The Soul of a Company

Wikstrom knew that continued discussion was wearing on everyone. Senior management, along with a majority of the revision committee members, felt that the legal opinion should *not* be taken as a prohibition against language like "the will of God" in the statement. The three or four members of the committee who wanted the language kept out were frustrated. Wikstrom hoped that closure could be achieved by the end of the month, and called a special meeting on July 21. Along with Lee Johnson and Wahlstedt, he emphasized to the group in writing that:

> The Triad does not wish to have the final say on revising the Direction Statement without the unanimous agreement of the Triad *and* the consensus of this team. It is therefore important for us to understand the meaning of the term consensus as we work together on this project. We have attached a definition of consensus decision making for your review prior to the meeting.

The "consensus" definition read as follows:

> **Consensus**
>
> Consensus is a group decision (which some members may not feel is the best decision, but which they can all live with, support, and commit themselves to not undermine), arrived at without voting, through a process whereby the issues are fully aired, all members feel they have been adequately heard, in which everyone has equal power and responsibility, and different degrees of influence by virtue of individual stubbornness or charisma are avoided so that all are satisfied with the process. The process requires the members to be emotionally present and engaged, frank in a loving, mutually respectful manner, sensitive to each other; to be selfless, dispassionate, and capable of emptying themselves, and possessing a paradoxical awareness of the preciousness of both people and time (including knowing when the solution is satisfactory, and that it is time to stop and not reopen the discussion until such time as the group determines a need for revision).

From Valley Diagnostic Medical and Surgical Clinic, Inc., Harlingen, Texas, and Foundation for Community Encouragement, Knoxville, Tennessee, 1988.

As he got into his car, Wikstrom reflected on the fact that the founders of the company, while they understood that others would need to carry their life work forward, also were convinced that the source of its excellence lay in some "politically incorrect" directions. How does one articulate the unifying spirit of an enterprise while at the same time respecting the diversity that its very success ushers in? As he looked up at the graying sky, he hoped that these rain clouds would bring vitality, not just turbulence.

EXHIBIT 1 RPM Products

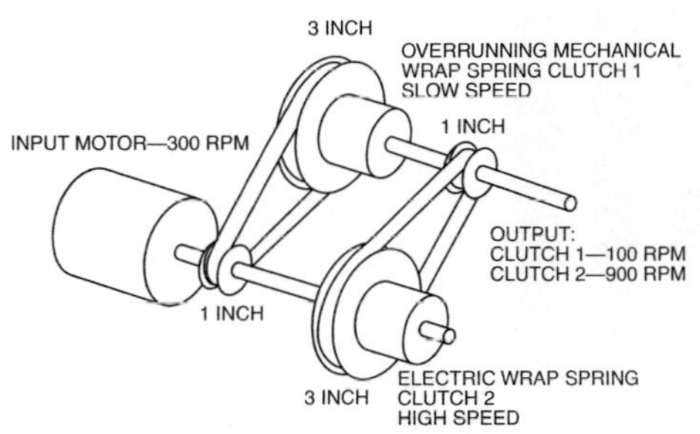

Reell clutches on two speed transmission.

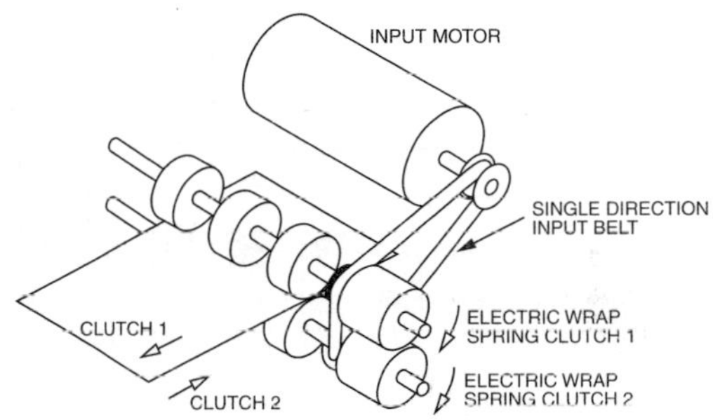

Clutches on reversing application.

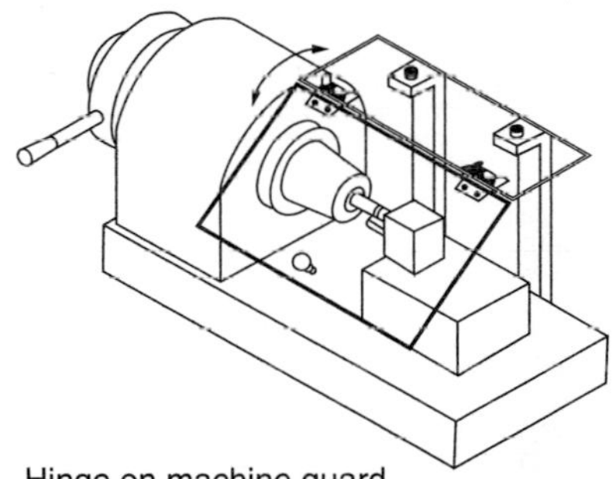

Hinge on machine guard.

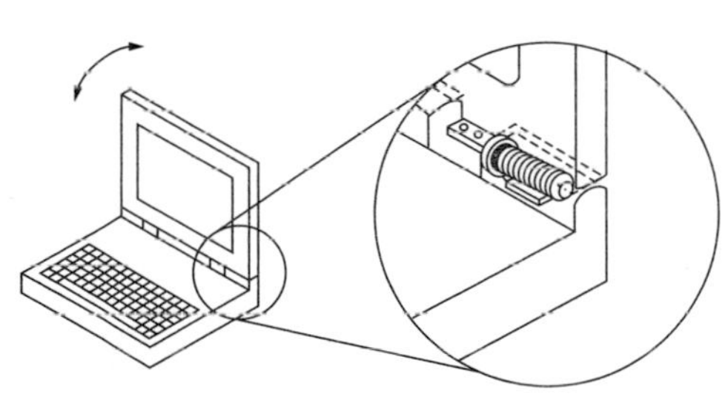

Hinge on laptop computer.

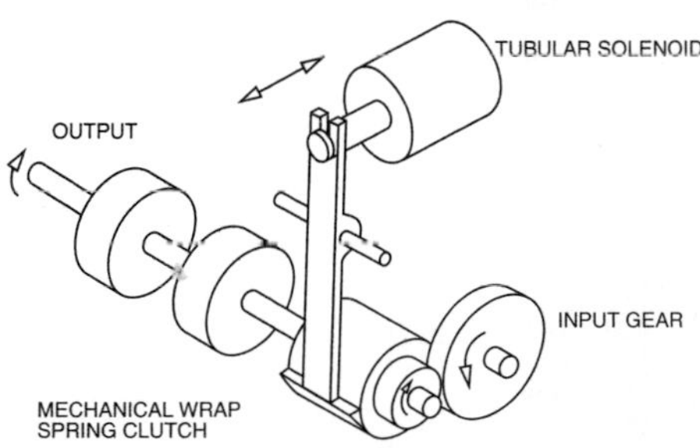

Tubular solenoid for indexing applications.

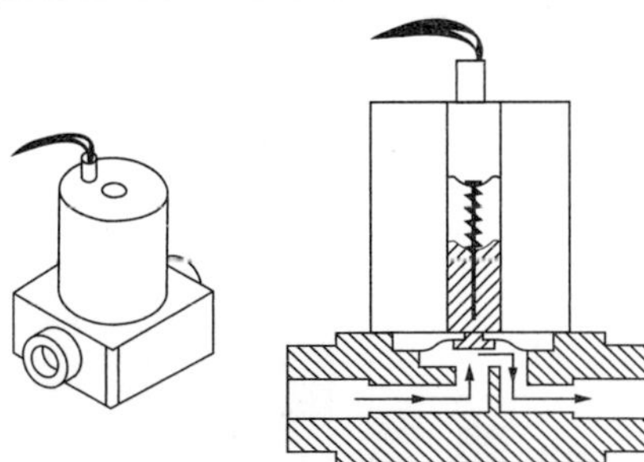

Tubular solenoid for valve applications.

EXHIBIT 2 RPM Employment and Sales Data, 1980–1993

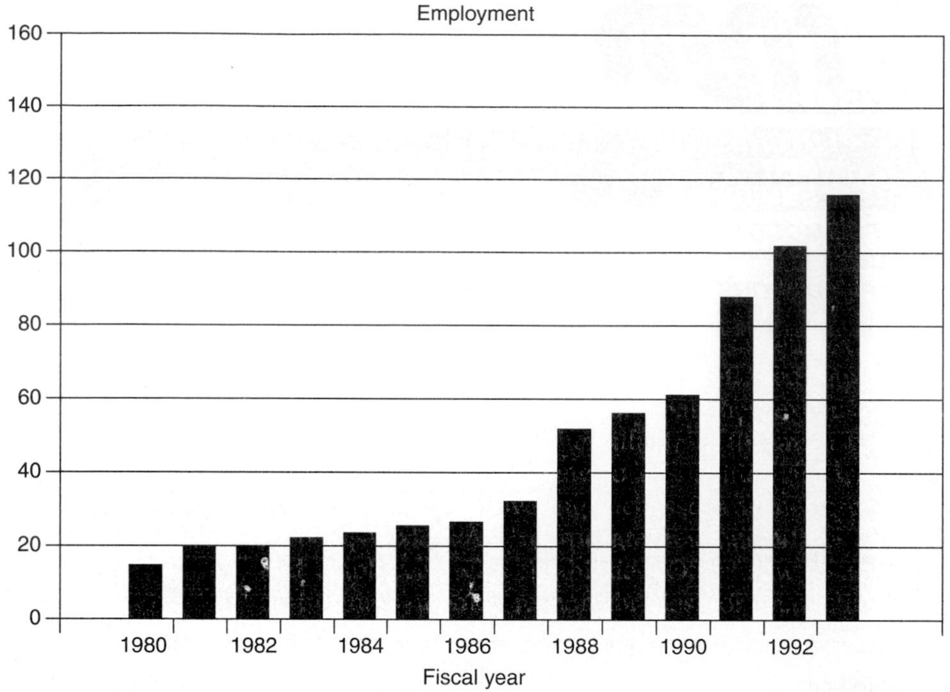

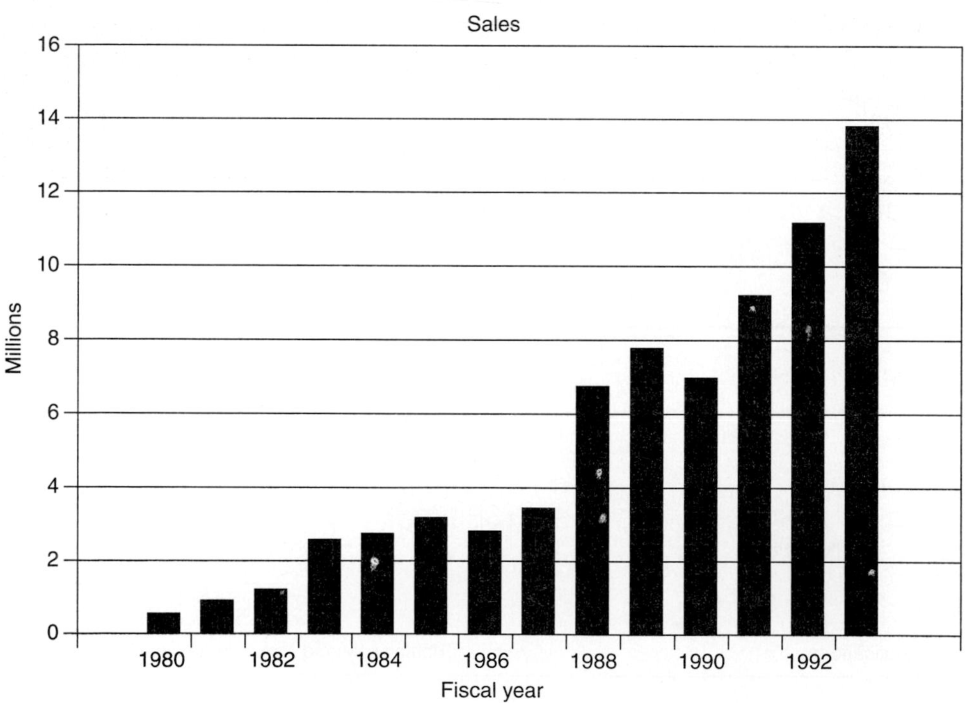

EXHIBIT 3 RPM'S Message from the Founders

A MESSAGE FROM THE FOUNDERS

WELCOME TO RPM!

The first thing we want you to know is that you are an important person. The work you have been hired to do is very necessary, but even more importantly, you are uniquely created by God with special talents and abilities. We hope that your association here will help you develop those special abilities.

The three of us, Dale Merrick, Lee Johnson, and Robert L. Wahlstedt, became acquainted through business associations between 1955–1960. This acquaintance developed into a business relationship which resulted in the incorporation of RPM in 1970. Partly as a result of this business relationship and partly through the influence of other friends, each of us found something else—a personal commitment to God, revealed in Jesus Christ. As this has grown, we have found that the operation of a business on Judeo-Christian values is not only possible, but also an invigorating and rewarding experience. It is our intent that RPM be a place where you will find no conflict between your work and your moral and ethical values.

Therefore, we have committed RPM to the following principles:

1. To follow the will of God by
   - a. Doing what is Right even when it does not seem to be profitable, expedient, or conventional.
   - b. Treating the concerns of others equally with our own concerns.
   - c. Being open to Inspirational Wisdom but acting on it only when the action is confirmed unanimously.

2. To provide everyone who works at RPM
   - a. A secure opportunity to earn a livelihood.
   - b. An opportunity for personal growth.
   - c. An opportunity to integrate Judeo-Christian values with a career.

We do not define profits as the purpose of the company, but we do recognize that reasonable profitability is necessary to continue in business and to reach our full potential. We see profits in much the same way that you could view food in your personal life. You probably do not define food or eating as the purpose of your life, but recognize that it is essential to maintain your health and strength so you can realize your real purpose.

We welcome you—and wish you a satisfying and rewarding career at RPM!!

EXHIBIT 4 Youngblood Column Abridged

Dick Youngblood, *Star Tribune*, Monday, December 28, 1992

A Firm That Means What It Says about Ethical Conduct

I've been perusing corporate mission and ethics statements for nigh unto 25 years now, and in all too many cases I've gloomily concluded that they amount to little more than boiler plate whenever the high-priced chips start hitting the table.

Most such declarations pay rhetorical homage to employees, for example—until profits are threatened and massive layoffs are ordered even as top executives continue collecting fat salaries and bonuses.

And most of the statements profess overriding esteem for customers and vendors—presumably including those who were fleeced in the savings and loan and insider trading scandals of the 1980s.

I'm delighted to report that I've stumbled across a Twin Cities company that not only has committed itself in writing to ethical treatment of employees, customers and suppliers, but has spent 20 years demonstrating in rather dramatic fashion that it actually means what it says.

Allow me to introduce you to Reell Precision Manufacturing Co. (RPM), a privately held Vadnais Heights company that, among other odd notions, places the well-being of its 100 employees and their families above unfettered profit growth. RPM makes electromechanical motors, clutches and other parts used in copiers, automatic addressing machines and similar devices.

A partnership formed by engineers Bob Wahlstedt Sr., 59, Lee Johnson, 58, and Dale Merrick, 67 and now retired, the firm has been operating since 1972 under an uncommon document titled the "RPM Direction Statement."

Consider, for example, the paragraph on the role of profits: "We recognize that profitability is necessary to continue the business, reach our full potential and fulfill our responsibilities to shareholders," the statement reads, "*but our commitments to co-workers and customers come before short-term profits.*"

Translated, that means there's never been an economic layoff, said Wahlstedt, RPM's president–and there won't be, short of a catastrophe that threatens the company's survival. "It is company policy that, before there's a layoff, we'll take profits down to zero," he said.

And if more sacrifice is required beyond that, then everyone–including founders and other officers–will be asked to accept short-term pay cuts. That happened twice in the 1970s, when 10 to 20 percent cuts were ordered for three to six months.

Or consider the stance on corporate ethics: "We are committed to do what is right *even when it does not seem to be profitable, expedient or conventional*," the RPM statement says. Thus, when a routine product-endurance test uncovered a problem with one of RPM's products last year, the customer was notified immediately and asked to return the offending items. The recall wound up costing the company upwards of $50,000, Wahstedt estimated.

What's more, "I don't believe senior management was consulted on that one," Wahlstedt said approvingly. In short, the company's ethical stance is so well instilled that the middle manager who handled the problem felt no need to cover his derrière with a superior's blessing.

The commitment to ethical dealings has had its upside, however. For example, when the buyer for a major customer tried to bully RPM into a price cut a few years back, Wahlstedt refused on the grounds that the company's pricing was honest and fair.

"The buyer said, 'If you don't reduce the price, there'll be no more business,'" recalled Wahlstedt, who responded: "Well, all I can tell you is that our last shipment will be on time." That kind of finished the conversation, he added, "but we retained the business."

Or consider the company's pledge to preserve what the directions statement terms "harmony between work and . . . family responsibilities." Wahlstedt interprets that section in remarkable fashion: "If there's a conflict between the job and the family, *we expect the employee to resolve the matter in favor of the family*."

Because of that commitment, RPM eschews the common practice of asking employees to travel on weekends to take advantage of lower air fares. "They belong at home with their families on weekends," Wahlstedt said.

For the same reason, the company also has a generous sick-leave policy, which offers employees eight annual sick days that can be taken for such nonmedical purposes as "watching your kid's baseball game," Wahlstedt said. What's more the number of unused sick days each year is doubled and placed in a bank that can build to a maximum of 60 days for use in emergencies.

Few employees take unfair advantage of the company's good will, he said. Indeed, there have been only a half-dozen dismissals in 20 years, none in the last five.

EXHIBIT 5 Memo from RPM "Triad" Inviting Participation in the Revision Discussions

February 12, 1992

Dear ______,

RPM first published the Direction Statement attached in December of 1989. At that time a team of people reached consensus that this was a good statement of our company purpose, values, and guiding principles.

The Direction Statement is a key document in the life of RPM. It presents challenges for us to strive for, identifies groups we feel are fundamental to our success, and talks about our guiding principles. It can be viewed as a Bill of Rights, a Constitution, and a License to pursue excellence.

It is now February of 1992. We want your help in determining if our Direction Statement still accurately reflects what we believe are the key ingredients for our success.

Please respond as indicated below and return this form to the box located in the reception area by February 21 or sooner. We need to have everyone respond so we are sure everyone's feelings can be considered. Thanks for your input!

______ I feel the Direction Statement is fine as is. No changes needed at this time.

______ I would like to have us consider making the changes indicated on the attached copy. (Please include the reasons why you feel any changes you propose would make the Direction Statement even better than it is today.)

LEE JOHNSON BOB L. WAHLSTEDT STEVE WIKSTROM

Our RPM Direction

RPM is a team. Its purpose is to operate a business based on the practical application of Judeo-Christian values for the mutual benefit of: *team members*, *customers*, *shareholders*, *suppliers*, and *community*.

As a team, striving to follow the will of God, we currently manufacture wrap spring clutches and other rotary motion control devices for a world market. Our goal is to continually improve our ability to meet customer needs. How we accomplish our mission is important to us. The following groups are fundamental to our success:

Team Members People are the strength of RPM. We are committed to providing a secure opportunity for each of us to earn a livelihood, an opportunity for personal growth, and an environment that allows each of us to act in ways that are compatible with Christian values.

Customers Customers are the lifeblood of RPM. Our products and services must be the best in meeting and exceeding customer expectations.

Shareholders We recognize that profitability is necessary to continue in business, reach our full potential, and fulfill our responsibilities to stockholders. We expect profits, but our commitments to team members and customers come before short-term profits.

Suppliers We will treat our suppliers as valuable partners in all our activities.

Community We will use a share of our energy and resources to meet the needs in the community around us.

The tradition of excellence at RPM has grown out of a commitment to excellence rooted in the character of our Creator. Instead of driving each other toward excellence, we strive to free each other to grow and express the excellence that is within all of us. We strive to work and make decisions based on these guiding principles:

We Will Do What Is Right We are committed to do what is right even when it does not seem to be profitable, expedient, or conventional.

We Will Do Our Best We are encouraged, trained, equipped, and freed to do and become all that we were intended to be. We have defined excellence as a commitment to continuous improvement in everything we do.

We Will Treat Others as We Would Like to Be Treated

We Will Seek Inspirational Wisdom, especially with respect to decisions having far-reaching, unpredictable consequences, but we will act only when the action is confirmed unanimously by others concerned.

EXHIBIT 6 **Memorandum and Attached Legal Opinion, June 15, 1994**

MEMO

June 15, 1992

To: Randy, Brad, George, Harry, Chuck, Bart, Jackie, Jon, Sharon, Louise, Jim

From: Steve W., Lee, Bob L.

Subject: Direction Statement

During the course of our discussions on revisions to the Direction Statement, Bob L. brought up a theoretical dilemma regarding the future possibility of being asked to be in a Triad relationship with someone who was uncomfortable with prayer.

A question was raised regarding the legal ramifications of this dilemma. Specifically, in RPM's situation, could a management promotion decision be based, in part, upon an individual's spiritual belief or practice? We asked our legal counsel to give us an opinion on this question. Attached you will find their response.

There seem to be at least two issues raised by this opinion that we need to discuss as a group. One is how to react to the opinion that it is not legal to base promotions, in part, upon an individual's spiritual development. The second is the wisdom of making changes to our Direction Statement to reduce the possibility of a successful legal challenge at some point in the future.

We feel it would be valuable to hold a meeting on Tuesday, June 23, 1992, from 10:30 to 12:00 in the training room to determine what to do. Please plan to attend.

C: All three bulletin boards.

If any co-worker not listed above wishes to attend this meeting feel free to do so.

EXHIBIT 6 **Legal Opinion from Outside Council (Name Disguised)—Continued**

LAW OFFICES

ABBOTT, BAKER, & CLARK

June 2, 1992

CONFIDENTIAL
SUBJECT TO ATTORNEY/CLIENT PRIVILEGE

Mr. Jim Grubs
Reell Precision Manufacturing Corporation
1259 Wolters Boulevard
St. Paul, MN 55110

Re:
Religious Discrimination Opinion

Dear Mr. Grubs:

You have asked me to render an opinion to RPM regarding the propriety of basing management promotion decisions, in part, upon an individual's religious beliefs. Specifically, you have indicated to me that RPM does not make any pre-employment inquiry into an individual's religious preferences or affiliations. However, throughout an individual's employment with RPM, the company may become aware of an individual's religious beliefs and practices. RPM is concerned whether, as between two equally well qualified individuals, it would constitute religious discrimination to prefer one individual over the other based upon the individual's religious values and/or religious affiliation.

Both state and federal law prohibit religious discrimination. At the state level, the Minnesota Human Rights Act prohibits a Minnesota employer from discriminating against employees with respect to "hiring, tenure, compensation, terms, upgrading, conditions, facilities, or privileges of employment ..." on the basis of religion, among other things. Title VII of the Civil Rights Act of 1964 also prohibits religious discrimination at the federal level. Because there have been several religious discrimination cases under the Minnesota Human Rights Act recently, because a Court's analysis would be similar under both state and federal law, and because a charge of discrimination is more likely to be made at the state level, this opinion will refer only to the Minnesota Human Rights Act and interpreting case law.

An exception to the Minnesota Human Rights Act's prohibition against religious discrimination exists for a religious or fraternal corporation, association, or society, which bases its qualifications on religion, where religion is considered to be a "bona fide occupational qualification for employment." The Minnesota Attorney General, in a 1956 opinion letter, concluded that a nonprofit religious organization, such as the Catholic Aid Association, was a religious organization for purposes of this statutory exception. However, the Minnesota Supreme Court has rejected a local health club's claim that it was a religious organization, exempt from the religious discrimination provisions of the Act. In this regard, the Court stated:

> When [the health club] entered into the economic arena and began trafficking in the marketplace, they have subjected themselves to the standards the legislature has prescribed not only for the benefit of prospective and existing employees, but also for the benefit of the citizens of the State as a whole in an effort to eliminate pernicious discrimination.

In my opinion, since RPM is a for profit business, it is very unlikely that it would be considered a religious or fraternal organization and exempt from the Act.

In 1985, the Minnesota Supreme Court was asked to determine if the practices of a local sports and health club constituted religious discrimination. The health club's owners indicated that they were "born again" Christians and that their fundamentalist religious convictions required them to act in accordance with the teachings of Jesus Christ and the will of God in their business as well as their personal lives.

(*continued*)

EXHIBIT 6 Legal Opinion from Outside Council (Name Disguised)—Continued

ABBOTT, BAKER, & CLARK

Mr. Jim Grubs
June 2, 1992
Page 2

The Court concluded that interviews of job applicants during which applicants were asked whether they attended church, read the Bible, were married or divorced, prayed, engaged in premarital or extra-marital sexual relations, believed in God, heaven or hell, and other questions of a religious nature, violated the Minnesota Human Rights Act.

Similarly, the Court found that the health club's refusal to promote anyone other than born again Christians to assistant manager or manager positions was illegal under the Act. The Court rejected the health club's arguments that they were justified in this policy because they felt they were forbidden by God, as set forth in the Bible, to work with "unbelievers." (See 2 Corinthians 6:14–18.)

The Court also found illegal the health club's policy of not hiring, and firing, individuals living with, but not married to, a person of the opposite sex, a young, single woman working without her father's consent, a married woman working without her husband's consent, a person whose commitment to a non-Christian religion was strong, and employees who were "antagonistic" to the Bible, which according to the health club, based upon Galations 5:19–20, includes fornicators and homosexuals.

Finally, the Court rejected the health club's claim that it was entitled to engage in the foregoing conduct based upon constitutional rights of freedom of speech, freedom of exercise of religion, and freedom of association, afforded under both the United States and Minnesota Constitutions.

One year later, in 1986, the Minnesota Appellate Court rendered a similar decision addressing one of the specific issues considered by the Minnesota Supreme Court a year earlier. In this decision, the Appellate Court concluded that a family owned farming operation engaged in illegal religious discrimination when it fired an employee because he was living with his girlfriend in a trailer located on the farm. The employer advised the employee that he would either have to marry his girlfriend, have her move out of the trailer, or leave the employer's employ, since the employee considered him to be "living in sin" based upon the employer's religious beliefs.

Based upon the Minnesota Human Rights Act, and these court decisions, I have the following recommendations. First, any individual conducting employment interviews for RPM must ensure that no questions are asked regarding an applicant's religious values and/or affiliations, whether directly or indirectly. As discussed in the health club decision, these questions may include whether or not an applicant attends church, reads the Bible, is married or divorced, prays, engages in premarital or extra-marital sexual relations, believes in God, heaven, or hell, lives with, but is not married to, a person of the opposite sex, in the case of a single woman, is working without her father's consent, or in the case of a married woman, is working without her husband's consent, and questions relating to whether or not the individual has a commitment to a non-Christian religion or is otherwise "antagonistic to the Bible."

With respect to promotion, RPM may not base a decision to promote an individual on the individual's religious values, beliefs, or affiliations. While RPM may base its promotion decisions on an individual's leadership and management capabilities, which may be a by-product of their religious beliefs, RPM may not fix its determination on individual religious values. For example, RPM must avoid any indication that its promotion decisions are based on "stronger religious beliefs," a "more Christian lifestyle," a "stronger faith," "conduct or beliefs more in line with RPM management," or similar statements. While it will obviously be difficult to separate these issues in any decision-making process, any expressed indication that the company is considering religious values in making its determination will increase the risk of liability for the company.

I have reviewed RPM's Advisor Manual and Personnel Manual in light of this issue. The Advisor Manual is fine. However, I have some concern regarding the statements contained in both the Mission Statement and Direction Statement contained in RPM's Personnel Manual. In both of these Statements, RPM very clearly expresses its preference for operating business based upon Christian values. Obviously, you have and will continue to have job applicants and employees who do not necessarily share these views. I believe that your risk of being accused of discriminatory employment practices increases

EXHIBIT 6 **Legal Opinion from Outside Council (Name Disguised)—Continued**

ABBOTT, BAKER, & CLARK

Mr. Jim Grubs
June 2, 1992
Page 3

through your references to conducting your business in accordance with Christian values in these Statements. For example, a non-Christian job applicant or employee who does not feel as though they have received the same employment opportunities as a Christian job applicant or employee, may well raise religious discrimination allegations based upon the company's Mission and Direction Statements.

Certainly no prohibition exists restricting RPM management and employees from expressing their commitment to Christian values and ideals; however, incorporating these beliefs into the company's Mission and Direction Statements verges on appearing to exclude non-Christian beliefs. While the Mission Statement indicates: "[i]t is our intention that RPM be a place where you will find no conflict between your work and your moral and ethical values ..." this may not be true for non-Christians. The interview process affords you an opportunity to determine whether or not an individual possesses the personal morals, ethics, and integrity that you seek in an employee. However, the risk I see in your Mission and Direction Statements is that you appear to exclude individuals who may possess acceptable morals, ethics, and integrity if they do not also possess Christian religious beliefs.

My recommendation to you is that you modify your Mission and Direction Statements somewhat to eliminate references to religion. You may want to substitute these references with references to cultivating an atmosphere of and conducting business in compliance with sound moral and ethical values, without regard to religion.

For example, the third paragraph of RPM's Mission Statement could be modified to provide as follows:

> Therefore, RPM is committed to the following:
>
> a. To do what is right even when it does not seem to be profitable, expedient, or conventional;
> b. To treat the concerns of others equally with our own concerns;
> c. To be open to new and innovative ways of conducting business;
> d. To provide a secure opportunity to earn a livelihood;
> e. To promote personal growth;
> f. To allow for the development of a work environment in which personal values and career can be successfully merged.

Since RPM's Mission and Direction Statements are probably two of the most personal messages contained in the Personnel Manual, I do not believe it appropriate to attempt to rewrite them for you in light of my opinion. Moreover, because of the significance of this issue for RPM, I would also be happy to further discuss any questions or concerns you may have regarding your hiring, promotion, and termination practices.

Thank you.

Very truly yours,

Adam B. Clark, Esq.

ABC:def

EXHIBIT 7 In-Process Revisions to Direction Statement, June 26, 1992

Our RPM Direction

RPM is a team dedicated to the purpose of operating a business based on the practical application of Judeo-Christian values for the mutual benefit of: *co-workers and their families, customers, shareholders, suppliers, and community*. We are committed to provide an environment where there is no conflict between work and moral/ethical values or family responsibilities and where there is no discrimination based on religious beliefs or practices.

The tradition of excellence at RPM has grown out of a commitment to excellence rooted in the character of our Creator. Instead of driving each other toward excellence, we strive to free each other to grow and express the desire for excellence that is within all of us. We strive to work and make decisions based on these guiding principles:

Do What Is Right We are committed to do what is right even when it does not seem to be profitable, expedient, or conventional.

Do Our Best In our understanding of excellence we embrace a commitment to continuous improvement in everything we do. It is our commitment to encourage, teach, equip, and free each other to do and become all that we were intended to be.

Treat Others as We Would Like to Be Treated

Seek Inspirational Wisdom, by looking outside ourselves, especially with respect to decisions having far-reaching and unpredictable consequences, but we will act only when the action is confirmed unanimously by others concerned.

We currently manufacture motion control devices for a world market. Our goal is to continually improve our ability to meet customer needs. How we accomplish our mission is important to us. The following groups are fundamental to our success:

Co-workers People are the heart of RPM. We are committed to providing a secure opportunity to earn a livelihood and pursue personal growth.

Customers Customers are the lifeblood of RPM. Our products and services must be the best in meeting and exceeding customer expectations.

Shareholders We recognize that profitability is necessary to continue in business, reach our full potential, and fulfill our responsibilities to shareholders. We expect profits, but our commitments to co-workers and customers come before short-term profits.

Suppliers We will treat our suppliers as valuable partners in all our activities.

Community We will use a share of our energy and resources to meet the needs of our local and global community.

We find that in following these principles we can experience enjoyment, happiness and peace of mind in our work and in our individual lives.

FBS Incorporated: *Ethics and Employee Investments*

Andrea Malone, director of Human Resources, put her head down on her desk and groaned. The situation had gotten out of hand. One more phone call from an employee about how to allocate retirement contributions between the various investment options and she would go insane.

FBS had switched to a defined contribution plan to simplify the organization's component of its employee retirement plan. The lower costs and the reduction in long-term liability were a definite benefit to FBS, but the phone calls were driving Andrea crazy.

Andrea Malone knew that she couldn't answer employee questions; even though she would certainly be of more help than "the person in the next cubicle," whom most people quoted as their resident expert. From the corporate perspective, the director of Human Resources was obligated to allow employees to make their own choices, thus limiting the corporation's liability in the event of misallocation. But the consequences could be significant, since the effects of misallocation could seriously hamper an employee's ability to retire at a decent standard of living. Clearly, education for the employees was necessary.

Defined Benefit Versus Defined Contribution

Traditional retirement plans offered a "defined benefit" for each employee during retirement, to the end of his or her life. Under this system, the corporation managed the retirement fund on behalf of its employees. Companies contributed money into a retirement fund for each employee based on salary and years of service. These funds had to be invested at an appropriate level to ensure that enough money was accumulated to cover the obligation to the employees.

Defined benefit plans had various drawbacks, not the least of which was risk. Risk existed because investment returns and the expected life of the employee after retirement were both actuarial estimates. If the corporation underestimated, it was responsible for any financial shortfalls due to underfunded retirement plans. In addition, since new employees were rarely eligible to participate in a pension plan for their first five years of service, many employees did not feel they had a vested interest in the organization. With the trend toward increased career mobility, this created a serious problem for both the employee and the organization.

As a result, many organizations decided to switch to a *defined contribution plan:* The organization would make contributions in tax-shielded investments and provide several investment options from which employees could choose (see Exhibit 1). The individual employee needed, therefore, to take an active role in the investment of his or her retirement program contributions. Defined contribution plans transferred the risk from the employer to the employee because the organization fulfilled its financial obligation once the employee contribution had been made. Associated with the employee's risk, of course, was the potential for higher returns than those offered by defined benefit plans. This was because defined benefit plans tended to be invested at relatively conservative levels of risk, to meet the needs of the growing retirement base. In addition, the new defined contribution plans were transferable if an employee chose to switch

This case was prepared by Research Assistant Hassan Valji under the supervision of Kenneth E. Goodpaster, Koch Professor of Business Ethics, and Professor Mary S. Daugherty, Department of Finance, University of St. Thomas, as a basis for class discussion rather than to illustrate either effective or ineffective handling of an administrative situation.

jobs from one company to another. This was truly the employee's money, to invest as he or she wished.

Many employees, however, did not understand how the change to defined contribution plans would affect them. Specifically, they did not understand the correlation between risk and return and therefore, the importance of investing at an appropriate level of risk (see Exhibit 2). Many other employees understood the importance of their choices but did not have the necessary education to make an informed allocation decision. As a result, some might retire with a capital base too small to support them through their retirement years.

Company History

FBS Incorporated was an import and export company, a part of the international distribution channel for many midsized organizations. Started in the late 1800s by the Flaherty brothers, the organization had grown from an importer of Scottish goods to a truly international organization with offices in 12 countries.

Following the trend of many organizations after World War II, FBS offered deferred wage gains to its executives to circumvent wage controls initiated by the Truman administration. Over time, these deferred wages evolved into defined benefit retirement plans. Eventually the costs and the risks associated with its defined benefit plan prompted FBS to switch to a defined contribution plan. Over the past six years, the last vestiges of the defined benefit plan had been entirely removed from the organization.

In addition to a long-term reduction in risk, FBS had found that the defined contribution plan generated immediate dollar savings. Salary reductions caused by the 300 employees' contributions to the 401(k) plan created a corresponding reduction in FBS's expenses for workers' compensation and unemployment compensation insurance by trimming the payroll subject to those taxes.[1]

What Happened Next

Andrea switched on her computer and opened the spreadsheet showing the allocation decisions of FBS employees. Many employees had simply divided the money evenly between the various plans. Scanning the list, Andrea's eyes came to rest on the name Ruth Chapman, Andrea's own secretary.

"Lord!" thought Andrea, "Ruth put all of her money into a money market fund and hasn't touched it for the past six years. Not only has she not added money to the plan, she has barely kept up with inflation!"

Continuing down the list, Andrea saw that several other individuals had also chosen the lowest level of risk for their retirement plans. Several questions crossed Andrea's mind: Will these individuals be able to afford to retire? What responsibility, if any, did FBS have for their allocation choices?

To answer the second question, Andrea made a quick call to the Profit Sharing/401(k) Council of America. She learned that FBS was responsible for a "minimal" amount of training, and this prompted her to ask what the options were when it came to 401(k) training (see Exhibit 3). The organization sent a chart showing the options, their various benefits, and the associated costs (see Exhibit 4).

Next, Andrea called the chief financial officer (CFO), Thomas Andersen, to check whether FBS had a budget for the education of its employees. Tom Andersen supported meeting the legal requirement but pointed to the need to minimize costs and not invade the privacy of the employees. "After all, we don't want to hold their hands or play Big Brother," he argued.

Conclusion

Andrea understood the obligations of FBS to its shareholders and to the law, but she was perplexed about the nature of the company's obligation to employees under the defined contribution plan. In theory, individual employees should be responsible enough to handle what was, after all, a benefit of employment at FBS. In practice, however, it was not clear whether this was a benefit or a burden.

Andrea looked over the training options again, a solution already formulating in her mind.

[1] Burton T. Bean Jr. and John J. McFaddam, *Employee Benefits*, 5th edition (*Dearborn*, 1998), P. 577.

EXHIBIT 1 Internal Revenue Code, Section 401(k)

The 401(k) is a *qualified cash* or *deferred arrangement* between the employer and the employee. Section 401(k) of the Internal Revenue Code defines a qualified cash or deferred arrangement as "any arrangement which is part of a profit-sharing or stock bonus plan."* Under such a plan, "a covered employee may elect to have the employer make payments as contributions to a trust under the plan on behalf of the employee, or to the employee directly in cash."†

There are five major advantages to 401(k) plans: (1) employees have the opportunity to choose the amount of deferral according to their individual need for savings (though there are some limitations based on income); (2) contributions occur on a pretax basis; (3) tax on the earnings is deferred until retirement; (4) contributions are convenient through systematic payroll deductions; and (5) 401(k) plans allow employees to develop asset allocations that meet their individual risk tolerances.

The 401(k) savings generate a dual tax benefit. Since the contributions are made before state and federal income taxes are applied, taxable wages for the current period are reduced, resulting in an immediate tax benefit.‡ In addition, since the contributions occur before taxation, the amount invested is a greater amount, resulting in tax-free earnings until withdrawn from the plan. This tax-deferred compounding means that even a small payroll deduction contribution can grow dramatically larger with protection from current taxes.

* Tax Code Sec. 401(k)(2)
† Tax Code Sec. 401(k)(2A)
‡ Contributions do not, however, lower amount paid for FICA.

EXHIBIT 2 The Time Value of Money

With the advent of defined contribution plans, *employees* became responsible for ensuring that their retirement savings would be sufficient.

Individuals had to consider various factors when planning for retirement:

1. Their expected cost of living in retirement.
2. Their life expectancy.
3. Their retirement date.
4. Their estimated investment returns.

The last factor was based on the concept that a dollar today is worth more than a dollar in the future. However, if one invested at a rate higher than inflation, one could improve one's financial position over time.

Returns were highly variable in the short term, especially with higher-risk investments. History suggested, however, that returns could be estimated fairly accurately over longer investment periods. In addition, people needed to remember that although their capital base would continue to earn interest in retirement, retirees often chose to reduce their risk levels, and therefore their returns would lower accordingly.

EXHIBIT 3 Employee Retirement Income Security Act, Section 404(c)

If an employer wished to reduce its potential liability for employee investment losses caused by an employee's control over his or her investment decisions in a 401(k) plan, then the employer had the option to meet minimum requirements in investment education and disclosure. These minimum standards are outlined in the Employee Retirement Income Security Act of 1974 (ERISA), Section 404(c).

To conform to ERISA 404(c), the defined contribution plan must:

- Permit participants to elect to transfer funds between investment alternatives at least quarterly.
- Offer at least three investment alternatives, each one of which is diversified and has materially different risk and return characteristics.
- Automatically provide participants with certain investment information and make additional information available on request.

An employer is under no obligation to advise the participants. However, the Department of Labor determined that "the furnishing of the following categories of information and materials to a participant and beneficiary in a participant-directed individual account pension plan will not constitute the rendering of 'investment advice'":

1. Plan information, including descriptions of investment objectives, risk and return characteristics, and historical information.
2. General financial and investment information.
3. Asset allocation models.
4. Interactive investment materials.

Even when an employer meets all the above requirements, he or she is not guaranteed compliance protection. The regulation does not have any provisions for proactive Department of Labor certification of a plan's status under 404(c).

EXHIBIT 4 Training Options

Cost	Description of Service
Do Nothing.	
$0 (No Cost)	• No education. • Information provided is limited to the basic 401(k) requirements.
Basic Investment Training: (a) Using a Mutual Fund Company	
$0 (No Cost to Company)	• Semiannual training sessions in groups of about 100. • Specific lessons on how to estimate retirement needs. • Tips on investing to achieve financial goals. • Education focused on specific funds offered by firm including risk and return goals for each fund.
Basic Investment Training: (b) Using an Independent Financial Educator	
$500 for a Half-Day Session	• Semiannual training sessions in groups of about 100. • Concept education including the time value of money and risk-and-return. • General discussions on insurance, home ownership, debt management, (college) education planning, estate planning, etc. • Specific lessons on how to estimate retirement needs. • Tips on investing to achieve financial goals.
Individualized Financial Planning: (a) Education Provided by a Planner Hired by FBS	
$300 per Plan	• Personal planner offers workshops on financial planning followed by individualized sessions at FBS's expense. • Concept education including the time value of money and risk and return. • Practical planning in all areas of financial life: retirement planning, insurance, home ownership, debt management, (college) education planning, estate planning, etc.
Individualized Financial Planning: (b) Education by a Planner Hired by Each Employee	
$500 subsicy per Employee per Year	• Employee hires a financial planner using funds provided by FBS. • Concept education including the time value of money and risk and return. • Practical planning in all areas of financial life: retirement planning, insurance, home ownership, debt management, (college) education planning, estate planning, etc. • Personal financial planners billing rates range from $75 to $200 per hour.

Note: Comprehensive financial plans take an average of ten hours to complete.

Waterbee Toy Company (A): *Should Monitoring Occur?*

On Thursday, April 17, 1998, Leila Muhammed, human resource (HR) director for the electronics division of Waterbee Toys, sat in her office and contemplated the decision facing her. The division's head of security had made a recommendation to monitor the employees' use of the Internet, and Leila had to decide whether or not to support it at the next policy meeting.

Company and Industry Background

The Waterbee Toy Company opened its doors for business in 1906 as a manufacturer of wooden water toys. The company had since grown into a three-division organization: plastics, music, and electronics. The plastics division made a full range of plastic toys: from water toys (such as ducks) to toy guns and from dolls and action figures to a variety of building blocks. The music division made low-priced musical instruments for children. Popular sales from this division included xylophones, cymbals, and minidrums.

The electronics segment was the newest and by far the fastest-growing and most competitive in the toy industry. The threat of corporate espionage in the electronics division was constant, especially since the Christmas market, which could make or break the organization's annual profit, was somewhat faddish.

> For much of our history, we sold hardware. Today we still make hardware, but customers increasingly buy the knowledge behind it. So that's how we really add value—embedding knowledge in software and services as well as products.[1]

Over the past three years, Waterbee had entered several emerging markets. Sales over that period had increased by about 10 percent per year, and staffing levels had decreased by almost 50 percent, to just over 50,000 full-time employees. As a result, people had been spending more and more time in the office.

The Decision to Allow Personal Use

Leila thought back to a decision she had made the previous month. The electronics division had decided to follow corporate headquarters' lead and allow its employees personal use of e-mail and the Internet. Traditionally, the corporate policy (see Exhibit 1) was held to the letter and use was restricted to work-related purposes. However, with e-mail becoming a widespread and everyday form of communication, corporate headquarters made the decision to allow personal use on an informal basis.

Leila's decision to follow corporate's lead hadn't been automatic. Based purely on her gut instinct, Leila felt that personal use of e-mail and Internet access should be quite limited. This gut instinct was based on several considerations. E-mail and Internet access represented some cost to the employer, and personal use equated to a utilization of company resources that was not work-related and therefore not profit-generating. In addition, while at work, employees should be focused on their jobs, she thought, not sending e-mail to their families and friends or surfing the net. Finally, the Waterbee Toy Company, as provider of the service, owned some of the liability involved with its employees' use of e-mail and the Internet. For example, if an

This case was prepared by Research Assistant Hassan Valji under the supervision of Kenneth E. Goodpaster, Koch Professor of Business Ethics, University of St. Thomas, as a basis for class discussion rather than to illustrate either effective or ineffective handling of an administrative situation. Names and locations are disguised.

[1] Waterbee's 1997 annual report.

employee sent offensive or threatening information or messages over the Internet, Waterbee, as provider of the service, might be held liable.

Nevertheless, Leila also thought there were many compelling reasons to allow informal use on a limited basis. E-mail had permeated society in the same way telephones had a hundred years ago. Asking an employee not to use e-mail for personal communication would have been akin to asking an employee not to use his or her desk telephone. In addition, e-mail was a nonintrusive form of communication and would not be as disruptive to an employee's job as a telephone call.

Moreover, Leila recognized that employees had been spending a lot more time at the office. This meant that employees had less time to deal with personal business. By allowing personal use of e-mail and the Internet during the workday, individuals were able to remain at their desks beyond regular working hours to complete Waterbee-related work.

Finally, Leila recognized that the individuals who had e-mail and Internet access at Waterbee were not hourly wage-earning employees; they were salaried employees who were paid to perform a certain job. Thus, it was somewhat irrelevant how these individuals chose to spend their time (for example, surfing the Internet for an hour in the middle of the day) provided their job was done in a satisfactory and timely manner.

Based on her considerations, the final decision to allow personal use of e-mail and the Internet seemed sound to Leila. The choice to follow corporate headquarters' lead and to leave the permission informal rather than formalizing it was less obvious, but Leila had made that decision as well. Now the question of privacy had arisen, and some of Leila's old doubts resurfaced.

Privacy Versus Security

Legally, there was no question. The log-in screen that all employees encountered before getting onto the Internet stated that privacy was not guaranteed and that Waterbee reserved the right to monitor computer use. By continuing use beyond that screen, the 2,000 employees with Internet access implicitly consented to any monitoring.

Leila considered the argument that security was making. The electronics division functioned in a highly competitive segment of the toy industry; one where corporate espionage was a constant threat, and defending intellectual property before it got to the market was a challenge that was somewhat difficult to meet. With personal use being allowed, employees now had a much larger opportunity, intentionally or unintentionally, of revealing proprietary information.

On the other hand, respecting an employee's privacy was very important for several reasons. On a social level, Leila didn't want to create a corporate atmosphere of distrust. In addition, on a purely functional level, the monitoring of employees would reduce morale and detract from employee sense of autonomy, both of which would reduce productivity.

Leila put security's formal recommendation down and leaned back in her chair. She closed her eyes and thought through the options and potential outcomes once again. By the time Leila had opened her eyes, her decision had been made. She swiveled toward her computer and began to prepare for the policy meeting.

EXHIBIT 1 Waterbee's Policy

Corporate Policy and Practice

Subject: E-Mail and Voice Mail

Policy

E-mail and voice mail are resources provided to employees to enhance the performance and productivity of Waterbee. E-mail *everyone* groups are available to facilitate reaching all members of a group or department. It is Waterbee policy to prescribe the conditions for the use of these resources.

Practice

1. E-mail and voice mail are for the primary purpose of correspondence relating to business.
2. E-mail and voice mail privacy (in accordance with Corporate Policy 105, Classification and Protection of Company Information) for employees shall be controlled, but not assured, by policies and facilities to protect against unauthorized access. Personal privacy is not assured. Access authorization techniques shall be in place.
3. Waterbee may monitor the use of e-mail and voice mail system for system performance and utilization analysis.
4. Personnel who support or maintain computer systems for e-mail and voice mail shall be considered to have limited operational access to employee e-mail and voice mail files.
5. Waterbee retains an unlimited right of access to any e-mail and voice mail data for investigation only with active participation of the Office of General Counsel and the director of Corporate Security.
6. Misconduct on the part of employees associated with the use of e-mail and voice mail shall be treated in accordance with *The Code of Ethics and Business Conduct* and the personnel policies of the relevant Waterbee location.

Note on E-Mail, Internet Use, and Privacy in the Workplace

Introduction

Over the past five years, increased use of computers, more specifically e-mail and the Internet, has vastly changed how many organizations function and communicate. E-mail and the Internet have emerged as efficient tools of both formal and informal communication and research. New technologies provide new ways to monitor productivity, how employees use their time, and everything from keystrokes per minute to Internet sites visited, to e-mail conversations. However, monitoring employees is not a new concept. Privacy issues have existed in the workplace before computers made monitoring convenient. Practices such as telephone wiretaps, checking an employee's voice messaging system, and video surveillance existed long before the computer age.

The purpose of this note is to explore the ethical issue of employee privacy in the workplace. More specifically, the focus will be on an employee's use of e-mail and Internet facilities provided by the employer. Managers, who consider the need for balance between privacy of the employee, security for the organization, and the management of company resources, may be in the strongest position to shape effective and efficient policies. Five examples of electronic communication policies are offered in Exhibit 1.

The Technology

"The Internet is a worldwide system of interconnected computers. One component of the Internet is effectively a worldwide electronic mail system. In addition, the Internet is a vast compository of information that generally can be accessed easily by an Internet user."[1] It is important to note that there is no central supercomputer and nobody controls the Internet.

Since the Internet is a free and uncontrolled entity, neither e-mail nor use of the Internet is secure. E-mail, when sent, travels through many linked servers to reach its destination. Any one server can intercept, copy, or read the contents of any message. However, most messages get split up and sent in pieces taking different paths to the destination. Typically, only two servers handle a message in its entirety: the sender and the receiver. Even "surfing the Internet" is not entirely private.[2] Individuals surfing the Internet can be tracked by the browsers that they use and by their Internet provider.

"New software will make automated monitoring of e-mail cost-effective for corporations, raising management and privacy issues. Intergralis's MIME-sweeper, a program originally used as an e-mail virus checker, disassembles all messages and attachments. In its monitoring mode, MIME-sweeper can archive or redirect messages that

This note was prepared by Research Assistant Hassan Valji under the supervision of Kenneth E. Goodpaster, Koch Professor of Business Ethics, University of St. Thomas, to accompany the Waterbee Toy Company case series.

[1] Mark S. Dichter and Michael S. Burkhardt, "Electronic Interaction in the Workplace: Monitoring, Retrieving and Storing Employee Communications in the Internet Age," *The American Employment Law Council*, 1996.

[2] "Surfing the Internet," refers to the process of casually accessing different Internet Web sites without a clear purpose.

contain encryption, viruses, or even keywords or phrases."[3]

Tracking which Internet sites are hit by an employee is an even easier task. Most browsers (including Internet Explorer and Mozilla, the two largest) keep a log of Internet sites visited and the time spent at each site.

Thus the technology is available for employers to read their employee e-mail and to track Internet use. The question is, Should they use it?

Why Is Privacy an Issue?

As a society, we consider many values to be important. Moral common sense would dictate that *respecting the privacy of others*, for the sake of their individual dignity, is one of those values. However, this duty does not come without conflict, since there are many situations in which the act of protecting a person's privacy may contradict other values that we share.

Managers, as officers of the corporation, have a duty to be concerned with how protecting an employee's privacy will impact the firm. This concern covers three general areas: (1) the security of the company's information, (2) the use of company resources, and (3) the company's liability based on its employees' use of e-mail and the Internet.

In many instances, one of these responsibilities will be compromised.

Legal Responsibilities of the Corporation

It is wise to consider the legal implications of any management action being considered. In the realm of employee privacy, as it relates to e-mail and the Internet, no specific document directly outlines what is allowed and what is not.

In the absence of a direct mandate and specific rules, the legal system defines what is right and wrong on the basis of existing laws that relate indirectly to the situation. There are several documents on several levels that may relate:

The Constitution of the United States

The Fourth Amendment to the U.S. Constitution protects an individual's right to privacy from government intrusion.[4] However, the courts have ruled that this protection does not apply to employees of private firms.

The Electronic Communications Privacy Act

The Electronic Communications Privacy Act (ECPA) was passed in 1986 to amend the Federal Wiretap Act to include electronic communications, such as e-mail. Under the ECPA, "it is unlawful to intercept telephone communications or electronic mail while in transmission and to divulge the contents of messages taken from electronic storage."[5] However, exceptions exist that give employers the right to monitor employees' e-mail:

- A *provider exception* allows the corporation (or an agent of the corporation) to intercept and disclose electronic communication, provided that it is done in the ordinary course of business.[6]
- A *business extension* or *ordinary course of business exception* allows the corporation to monitor electronic communication if (1) the monitoring is necessary to provide the service or (2) the monitoring is necessary to protect the corporation's rights and property.

[3] Mark L. Van Name and Bill Catchings, "Set Your E-Mail Privacy Policies Now," *PC Week*, October 7, 1996.

[4] "The right of the people to be secure in their persons, houses, papers, and effects, against unreasonable searches and seizures, shall not be violated, and no Warrants shall issue, but upon probable cause, supported by Oath or affirmation, and particularly describing the place to be searched, and the persons or things to be seized."

[5] Teresa Brady, "Avoid Privacy Collisions on the Information Highway," *Management Review*, September 1997.

[6] Specifically, Section 2511(2)(a)(i) of the ECPA provides: "It shall not be unlawful under this chapter for an operator of a switchboard, or an officer, employee, or agent of a provider of wire or electronic communication service, whose facilities are used in the transmission of a wire or electronic communication, to intercept, disclose, or use that communication in the normal course of his employment while engaged in any activity which is a necessary incident to the rendition of his service or to the protection of the rights or property of the provider of that service, except that a provider of wire communication service to the public shall not utilize service observing or random monitoring except for mechanical or service quality control checks."

- A *consent exception* allows the corporation to monitor electronic communication provided that consent from one of the parties has been given.[7]

The specifics, as they apply to employee privacy on the Internet, are still being decided in the court system. For the most part, management, or any individual authorized to do so by management, has been accorded the right to access employee e-mail and monitor employee use of the Internet if the company provides the service.

Ethical Responsibilities of the Corporation

Managers of a corporation have responsibilities that go beyond legal obligations. They have ethical responsibilities to their stakeholders. Balancing these responsibilities with the manager's fiduciary responsibility to the stockholders can be challenging. In this case, management of a corporation is balancing two competing responsibilities: the responsibility to respect an employee's privacy and the responsibility to protect an investor's interests. Which responsibility must prevail?

The ethical analysis of this dilemma, to protect or compromise an employee's privacy, can be performed using "a case analysis template for ethics-related cases" (see Exhibit 2). There are four basic avenues for ethical analysis: interest-, rights-, duty-, and virtue-based.

From an interest-based perspective, management acts to maximize *net expectable utility*. On one hand, there may be several benefits derived and costs avoided through monitoring employee e-mail. These include the protection of corporate information, the savings of corporate resources, and, potentially, the avoidance of legal liabilities. On the other hand, there are several benefits that may be lost and costs incurred through the compromising of an employee's privacy. These include the loss of labor-management goodwill and trust and, potentially, even legal costs.

From a rights-based perspective, management acts in order to balance stakeholder and stockholder rights. On one hand, as a society we believe that we have a right to privacy. On the other hand, management, as an agent of the corporation, has the legal right to monitor any communication that uses equipment that it pays for.

From a duty-based perspective, management must act in accordance with its fiduciary responsibilities without compromising its public trust and corporate community involvement. Management has a fiduciary duty to protect the stockholder interests and maximize long-term profitability. On the other hand, management has a duty not to compromise its public trust by violating any individual's privacy without justification.

From a virtue-based perspective, management must act in order to reinforce a virtue or positive trait of character. A manager must *trust* the employees in the corporation; on the other hand, the manager has accepted the responsibility to protect the interests of the stockholders, and not monitoring the employee's use of e-mail and the Internet might be "breaking a promise."

Conclusion

This is by no means a complete analysis of the issue that faces most managers regarding employee privacy and the problems associated with their responsibility to the corporation. It is important for the management student to recognize that there may be no single correct solution to the discord caused by conflicting responsibilities. Different managers will face a variety of nuances within the overall conflict that uniquely relates to their own organization.

Bibliography

The Privacy Pages (www.2020tech.com/maildrop/privacy.html). A center of linked web pages. All the links have an abstract so that you can consider the content before you enter the site.

Electronic Privacy Information Center (www.epic.org).

Electronic Communications Privacy Act of 1986 (cpsr.org/cpsr/privacy/communications/wiretap/electronic_commun_privacy_act.txt). The text of the Electronic Communications Privacy Act.

[7] Section 2511(d) provides: "It shall not be unlawful under this chapter for a person not acting under color of law to intercept a wire, oral, or electronic communication where such person is a party to the communication or where one of the parties to the communication has given prior consent to such interception unless such communication is intercepted for the purpose of committing any criminal or tortious act in violation of the Constitution or laws of the United States or of any State."

EXHIBIT 1 Excerpts from Company Policies

From Ceridian's "Internet and Email Use Policies"

Any use of the Internet or email to post, store, transmit, download or distribute any threatening, abusive, libelous, defamatory, obscene or otherwise objectionable materials of any kind including anything constituting or encouraging a criminal offense, giving rise to civil liability or otherwise violating any laws or that intentionally interfere with the mission or activities of Ceridian will result in disciplinary action and/or legal action against the employee to recover damages. . . .

Access to the Internet and email service is not guaranteed for all employees. An employee's manager may decide restrictions are necessary. Be aware that the company may review all messages and reserves the right to monitor all email messages and use of the Internet by its employees, consultants of the company or others that are using a Ceridian network for access or transmission of data.

From General Mills' Policy on "Electronic and Voice Communication"

General Mills does not intend to monitor utilization of voice and electronic communication. However, General Mills reserves the right to access the contents of voice and electronic communications in situations of suspected misuse of a communications system, internal compliance audits, or whenever advance notice has been provided.

From Minnegasco's "E-Mail Policy"

The e-mail system, messages and data are the exclusive property of the company and are to be used for company purposes. . . .

As property of the company, all e-mail messages and data are subject to review, disclosure and deletion as deemed necessary by the company. Sending or receiving information of a personal nature and information that may be offensive to others is strictly prohibited on the company's e-mail system.

From National City Bank's "Electronic Communication Guidelines"

The e-mail, voice mail, telephone systems, computer systems, security systems, and all digital network communications are to be used for business purposes. . . .

Use for incidental personal purposes is permissible *only within reasonable limits*. This does not include uses requiring substantial expenditures of time, uses for profit, or uses that would otherwise violate Bank guidelines with regard to employee time commitments or Bank equipment. . . .

Employees do NOT have any privacy right in any e-mail, voice mail, or telephone systems or computer generated communication or digital network communications, however created, sent, received, accessed, or stored.

From United Healthcare's Section "Information Security" of its Employee Handbook

These communication systems are to be used for company business and other company-sanctioned purposes. . . .

UHC reserves the right to inspect or review all uses of these systems.

EXHIBIT 2 A Case Analysis Template for Ethics-Related Cases

Aspects of the Moral Point of View . . .	DEONTIC (ACTION as EFFECTIVE)			ARETAIC (ACTION as EXPRESSIVE)
CASE ANALYSIS STEPS (5 D's)	*INTEREST-BASED OUTLOOK*	*RIGHTS-BASED OUTLOOK*	*DUTY-BASED OUTLOOK*	*VIRTUE-BASED OUTLOOK*
DESCRIBE	How did the situation come about? What are the key presenting issues? Who are the key individuals and groups affected by the situation, the *stakeholders?*			
	Identify interests.	Identify rights.	Identify duties.	Identify virtues.
DISCERN	What is the most significant of the "presenting issues"—the one that might lie underneath it all?			
	Are there conflicting interests with respect to this issue, and how basic are they?	Are there rights in conflict with interests or with other rights? Are some weightier than others?	Does duty come into the picture—and are there tensions with rights or interests? Can I prioritize these claims?	Is character an issue in this case—are there habits that bring us to this point or that will be reinforced later?
DISPLAY	What are the principal realistic options available to the decision maker(s) in this case, including possible branching among suboptions—leading to an array of action sequences or plans?			
DECIDE	What, finally, is my considered judgment on the best option to take from those listed above? The Moral Point of View is here joined to the Administrative or Managerial Point of View.			
DEFEND	Which of the avenues predominates in my choice of options above, and can I give good reasons for preferring the ethical priorities I have adopted in this case that are consistent with other such cases?			

Webster Health Systems (A)

It was a cold fall day in late October 1997, and Lake Michigan was pounding Chicago with an early snowfall. Cheryl Douglas, associate general counsel and ethics officer, was experiencing the usual office chaos, topped with thoughts about her long commute home. At 4:45 in the afternoon, John Mitchell, human resources director, walked into Cheryl's office with a troubled look on his face. John explained that a meeting earlier in the day with Richard Gardner, information systems manager, progressed into a heated discussion over the handling of an information systems employee. Richard wanted to terminate Patrick Cordon, an information systems desktop analyst. Richard had handed John the employee's file and claimed Patrick continued to call in sick for work and was an alcoholic. John was not comfortable terminating Patrick on those grounds and passed the file on to Cheryl for legal and ethical advice. It was not the first time that as ethics officer and associate general counsel, Cheryl had faced a situation where her two positions seemed to collide. She understood the decision was John's to make, but he understood that if he ignored her advice and legal action resulted, he would be accountable.

Company Background

Webster Health Systems was headquartered in Chicago, Illinois. Net Income for the year ending December 31, 1996, was $371 million, or $2.71 per share, compared with 1995 net income of $302 million, or $2.18 per share. Earnings per share had increased 17 percent over the previous year. Sales for the year were $6.02 billion, up 10 percent compared with $5.32 billion for 1994. Operating profit was $673.9 million, up from $570.2 million in 1994. This tremendous growth was due primarily to the quality of the company's employees and increased productivity. Webster believed that every individual was unique and valuable. The company saw every job as value added and no job as unimportant. Webster ran a highly decentralized operation with many policies and decisions delegated to each of the various divisions. Empowering the employees was essential for Webster to maintain its increased productivity. From 1990 to 1997 Webster had been successfully doing more with less. Net income had increased by 40 percent since 1990, while the number of employees had decreased by 35 percent. This productivity was due to increased technology, empowering of employees, increased work ethic, and the doubling of employee stock ownership. Employees were a tremendous asset to Webster Health Systems.

Webster owned hospitals, health plans, and clinics, and had many divisions throughout the world. Webster's corporate division, however, was located in Chicago and exemplified the character of the entire organization. With only 1,200 of the 40,507 Webster employees located in the heart of Chicago's south side, a small community atmosphere grew within the division. Webster guarded its grounds with towering buildings and heightened security. Inside the grounds was a beautiful park and play area for the day care facility. Enormous oak trees lined the walking paths, and picnic tables circled a pond. This small community, within a larger and often dangerous neighborhood, brought the employees together as a family.

The corporate division consisted of five departments. Each department was uniquely empowered but worked together within the division as parts of a team. The Information Systems (IS) department was in charge of linking information between hospitals, clinics, and the corporate division. Desktop analysts would ensure that the employees were equipped with the proper

This case was prepared by Research Assistant Aaron Macke under the supervision of Kenneth E. Goodpaster, Koch Professor of Business Ethics, University of St. Thomas, as a basis for class discussion rather than to illustrate either effective or ineffective handling of an administrative situation. Names and locations are disguised.

technology for their positions. This often meant providing hospitals with new personal computers, salespeople with laptops, corporate employees with software, and addressing other technology-related needs or questions. The IS department was vital to the success and productivity of Webster Health Systems.

Richard Gardner, 45, native of the Chicago area and educated in the computer sciences, had worked for the company for 20 years. He had become a manager in the IS department at age 35 and gradually proceeded upward on the corporate ladder. Richard had become manager of the lead area within IS in 1995, as a reward for his 18 years of devoted and quality service to Webster. He took pride in his job and the employees that worked for him.

John Mitchell, 56, director of human resources (HR), had been with the company for 30 years. John had graduated with a major in human resources from the University of Minnesota. He enjoyed helping build the small community atmosphere at Webster, because of his upbringing in a small rural Midwestern town. Employees referred to John as having a heart of gold and as an employee advocate. As director of HR, John oversaw all hiring and termination of personnel. He believed terminating an employee was the toughest decision a manager ever faced. Webster had a progressive discipline policy for the termination of an employee, and John believed in the policy (Exhibit 1). He insisted that no employee should be terminated without warning and that people deserved second chances. As a businessman and profit sharing employee, John understood the importance of balancing employee concerns with company needs. He had a record of being fair to both the company and the employee in past termination situations.

Patrick Cordon, 34, raised and married in Chicago, had been with the company for 12 years as a desktop analyst. He was hired straight from college and contributed immediately to the IS department. Patrick had a clean record and solid work performance reviews. IS managers regarded him as a good employee that did his share, but did not stand out. Coworkers of Patrick referred to him as a nice individual who provided assistance whenever needed. Patrick had worked for one manager since joining the company, until two years ago when Richard Gardner became manager of his area. The area in which Patrick worked was considered the lead area of IS, because it handled highly technical tasks. Richard and Patrick got along well and had no trouble with Richard becoming manager. (See Figure A for a partial organizational chart indicating the individuals described and their working relationships.)

Cheryl Douglas

Cheryl Douglas, 45, associate general counsel and ethics officer, was fairly new to the company. After having worked in a private law firm for 15 years, she moved to Webster in 1994. Cheryl started as a lawyer in the General Counsel's office and was quickly assigned the new position of associate general counsel and ethics officer. Cheryl welcomed the position and was enthusiastic about her job. She described her duties as "being responsible for the ethics and compliance program, which is meant to ensure that the company complies with the law. As ethics officer I am also responsible for helping employees understand the corporate culture and the way the company chooses to do business. The company chooses to go beyond what the law requires and does not simply take advantage of anything the law would allow." Cheryl's other position in the company, as associate general counsel, was to understand what the law required. She was responsible for giving advice to the company about avoiding legal problems and for helping the company work through issues when the law or company standards were involved. She had a responsibility to the company to offer the best legal advice. However, Cheryl also had an ethical responsibility to the employees and their well-being. Occasionally, Cheryl's two roles conflicted and made for difficult decisions.

Webster created the position of ethics officer as an internal mechanism for preventing, detecting, and reporting criminal activity. Cheryl once said the hallmark of an effective program was that the organization exercised due diligence in seeking to prevent and detect criminal conduct by its employees and other agents. Due diligence required at a minimum that the organization take certain required steps. As ethics officer, Cheryl was responsible for following the steps required of all organizations and implementing additional preventive measures (Exhibit 2).

FIGURE A **Partial Organization Chart, Corporate Division**

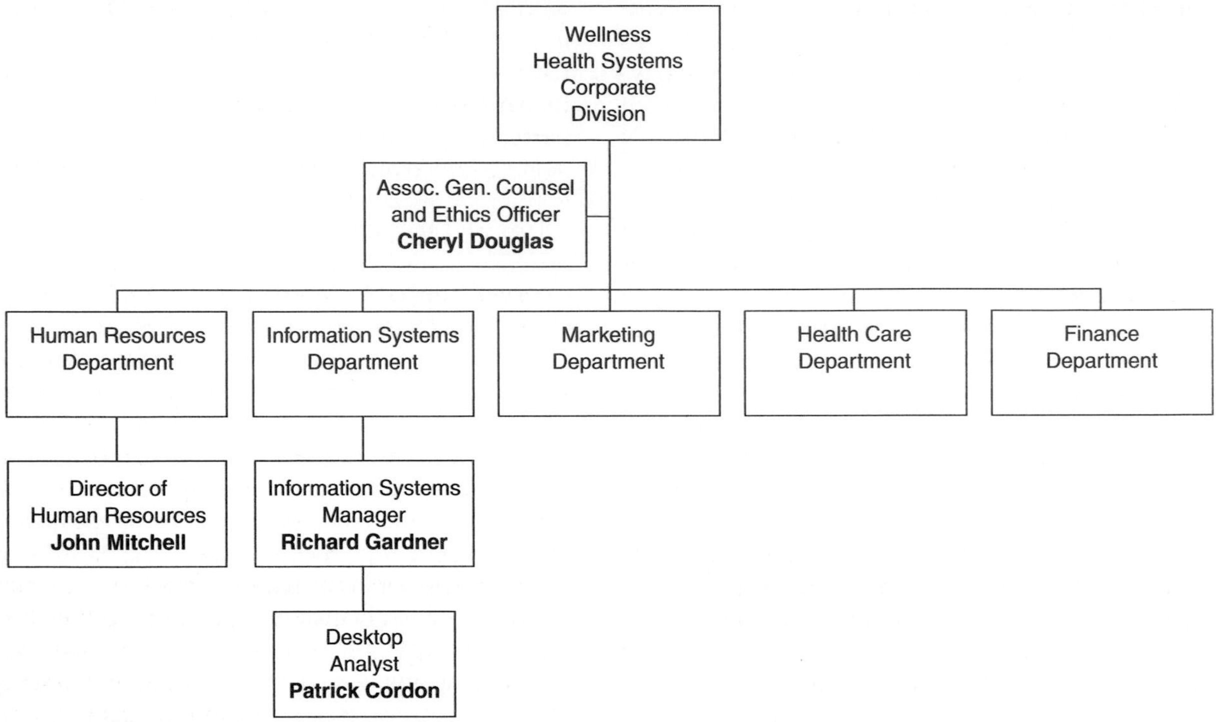

Over the past several years, lawyers had been facing new challenges. With the enactment of recent legislation, lawyers had been educating themselves on the implications for corporate policies and decision making. Cheryl had spent much of her time researching and learning about the latest talk surrounding managers and lawyers. The Americans with Disabilities Act (ADA), the Family and Medical Leave Act (FMLA), and workers' compensation (WC) had been compared metaphorically with the "Bermuda Triangle" (see the "Note on the Americans with Disabilities Act"). These three legal issues required many hours of time and occasionally caused nightmares for lawyers and companies. Prior to this October afternoon Cheryl had been preparing a slide presentation for Webster on ADA. The presentation included a working definition of ADA, who qualifies as being disabled, effects of ADA, employers' rights and employees' rights, hiring and firing guidelines, and lawsuits regarding ADA. The reason for all the time and nightmares surrounding this Bermuda Triangle was that ADA, FMLA and WC often overlapped each other.

Ethical and Legal Dilemma

The passing of the file by John to Cheryl required her to ask several informational questions. She wanted to know what caused Richard's sudden reaction to Patrick and how he felt about firing him. John proceeded to tell her what Richard said to him earlier that day. "Patrick has been calling in sick two or three times a week with every excuse imaginable. His dog has died twice, he has three dead grandmothers, he gets chronic migraine headaches, constant occurrence of stomach flu, and his car rarely starts in the morning." Richard was tired of hearing excuses and scrambling to distribute Patrick's workload at the last minute. The IS department involved highly complex work, and it was difficult to find an employee to handle Patrick's tasks. Richard felt he had let Patrick's excuses go on too long and needed to buckle down. "It looks bad to other employees, and it is not fair to them to have extra workloads," Richard had said. He did not like terminating employees, especially ones that had been around as long as Patrick had and were as talented as Patrick was. But he felt it had gone on too long, and it needed to be dealt with. In addition to the excuses, Richard had noticed the smell of alcohol on Patrick, and on several occasions other employees had mentioned to Richard how they smelled alcohol on Patrick's clothes and breath. Richard had mentioned to Patrick that he believed Patrick had an alcohol problem and that it was the reason for his calling in sick so often.

After hearing John explain Richard's comments, Cheryl asked him about his own concerns. John said that he understood why Richard was angry and why he wanted to terminate Patrick. But John did not think termination was the appropriate answer. He knew that treating and retaining an alcoholic employee was good business. Exhibits 3 and 4 contain literature about employee assistance programs and alcoholism. Patrick was a good employee and had contributed to the company. Webster had put great efforts into training Patrick and retaining him for 12 years. Termination meant lost time and money, and more expenses in hiring and training a new employee. Beyond the economic advantages of retaining Patrick, John felt that every employee was "an asset to Webster and we need to protect our assets. Webster has a community atmosphere and is ethically responsible for Patrick's health." John believed it was Webster's duty to try to get Patrick help for his alcohol problem.

Webster had an employee assistance program (EAP) in place for employees to use. The program was staffed by mental health professionals who could provide information and counseling to employees and/or family members (Exhibit 5). John believed this program was designed to provide assistance to employees like Patrick. He had seen it help other employees and return them to their former work performance levels. "This could happen to Patrick as well, if he's given a chance," said John. He hoped Cheryl would advise him to send Patrick to the EAP for help.

Cheryl knew alcoholism was a difficult subject matter to address and that it aroused a variety of emotions. She had many feelings about alcoholism and could address the issue from many angles. She knew, however, as associate general counsel, that her options were limited. By forcing or even recommending Patrick to the EAP, Webster would be legally acknowledging that it believed Patrick was disabled. That acknowledgment would open the doors for ADA and FMLA and, as Cheryl said, "might hand Patrick a lawsuit on a silver platter." The costs associated with this decision might be enormous since the outcome might not be favorable. It was not certain that Patrick was an alcoholic. He might not be addicted to alcohol but may have been abusing alcohol for other reasons. Cheryl could have recommended ignoring Patrick's potential alcohol problem and terminating him on the grounds of excessive work absences. However, she was aware that alcohol was already mentioned to Patrick as a potential reason for his absences, and she understood the ethical implications of terminating Patrick. Websters' corporate division was a close network of people, and the company needed to uphold the family atmosphere. Turning its back on an employee with a potential alcohol problem might have serious implications for morale at Webster.

It was approaching 6:00, and the chaotic day was taking its toll on Cheryl's mind. The Americans with Disabilities Act and the Family and Medical Leave Act made her decision a difficult one. She faced the dilemma of advising John to send Patrick to the EAP or advising him to ignore Richard's observations of alcohol abuse by having Richard follow the progressive discipline policy.

EXHIBIT 1 Progressive Discipline Policy

1. Talk verbally with employee about issue.
2. Put in writing the issue or discipline, and have employer and employee sign.
3. Establish a performance improvement plan.
4. Termination.

Let it be noted that each of these, with the exception of step 4, can be performed more than once. The employer can also cancel the written warning at any time that he or she feels necessary. It is customary at Webster for steps 1 and 2 to be performed several times.

EXHIBIT 2 Required Steps to Prevent and Detect Violations of the Law

Source: U.S. Sentencing Commission, *Guidelines Manual,* 8A1.2 (November 1993).

1. The organization must have established compliance standards and procedures to be followed by its employees and other agents that are reasonably capable of reducing the prospect of criminal activity.
2. Specific individual(s) within high-level personnel of the organization must have been assigned overall responsibility to oversee compliance with such standards and procedures (e.g., the ethics officer).
3. The organization must have used due care to delegate substantial discretionary authority to individuals whom the organization knew, or should have known through the exercise of due diligence, had a propensity to engage in illegal activity.
4. The organization must have taken steps to communicate effectively its standards and procedures to all employees and other agents.
5. The organization must have taken reasonable steps to achieve compliance with its standards.
6. The standards must have been consistently enforced through appropriate disciplinary mechanisms, including as appropriate, discipline of individuals responsible for the failure to detect an offense.
7. After an offense has been detected, the organization must have taken all reasonable steps to respond appropriately to the offense and to prevent further similar offenses—including any necessary modifications to its program to prevent and detect violations.

EXHIBIT 3 An Employee Assistance Program Is Good Business

Source: Alcohol and Drug Services, "What Is An Employee Assistance Program?" Copyright 1996 by Cyber Systems Inc.

What Is an Employee Assistance Program?

EAP is a management tool by which employers and/or supervisors can return employees with declining job performance to fully productive status by:

1. Identifying troubled employees; and
2. Sending them to a qualified referral source.

EAP is also a part of a company's benefits package through which an employee or family member can be referred to an appropriate source of help for any type of personal problem such as:

- Marital
- Family
- Mental health
- Emotional health
- Legal
- Financial
- Eldercare
- Substance abuse

Why Should an Employer Be Interested in an EAP?

There are two main reasons: (1) money and (2) money.

1. 25% of the salary of each troubled employee is lost due to:
   Decreased productivity
   Increased accidents
   Increased absenteeism
   Increased illness
   Increased tardiness
2. Troubled employees' health care costs can increase by as much as 15 times over the norm.

What Are the Costs of Turnover If Personal Problems Are Not Resolved?

- Replacement costs: $5,000–$17,000 (unemployment benefits, hiring expenses, training costs).
- Losses while employee is troubled but still employed.
- Possible grievance procedures.
- Loss of employee's experience.

Does EAP Work?

Success rates of EAP range from 65 to 80 percent.

EAPs return $3 to $15 for each $1 invested.

Loss reductions:

1. 50–80% decrease in absenteeism.
2. 26–69% decrease in medical care use.
3. 30–80% decrease in on-the-job accidents.
4. 33–70% decrease in sickness and accident benefits.
5. 50% decrease in disciplinary action.
6. 38–70% decrease in sick leave usage.
7. 60–80% decrease in grievances.

What Does Substance Abuse Cost the Company?

Employees with substance abuse problems have:

- 16 × normal absenteeism rate (average of 22 days per year).
- 3 × normal long-term absenteeism rate (8+ days).
- 5 × normal compensation claims.
- 3 × normal sickness benefits.
- 4 × normal accident rate.
- Work performance at 60–65% of potential.

Other statistics:

- 40% of industrial fatalities are alcohol-related.
- 47% of industrial injuries are alcohol-related.
- 20% of those injuries are disabling.

EXHIBIT 4 Facts on Alchoholism

Source: Statistics were taken from the Ala-Call Substance Abuse Hotline/New Jersey State Hotline, 1998.

Alcoholism is a major health problem in the United States, ranking with cancer and heart disease as a threat to health. Alcoholism is a progressive disease in which drinking increasingly affects a person's health, family life, social life, and job. Untreated, alcoholism results in physical incapacity, insanity, or death.

There are an estimated 10.5 million people in the country suffering from the disease of alcoholism. One out of ten people who drink becomes an alcoholic. An alcohol-related family problem strikes one of every four American homes. Individuals who are close to an alcoholic need and deserve appropriate help to recover as well.

In the workplace, 47 percent of industrial injuries and 40 percent of industrial fatalities can be linked to alcohol consumption.

Use of alcohol and other drugs is associated with the leading causes of death and injury among teenagers and young adults.

Violent behavior attributed to alcohol use accounts for approximately 49 percent of murders, 52 percent of rapes, 21 percent of suicides, and 60 percent of cases of child abuse. Of all fatal accidents on the roads, over 50 percent involve alcohol.

Alcoholism is treatable. Effective alcoholism programs show recovery rates of 65 to 80 percent. Alcoholics Anonymous (AA), for example, has an estimated world membership of more than 2 million in over 93,000 groups. Approximately 80 percent of the people sober between one and five years will remain in the AA fellowship.

EXHIBIT 5 Webster's Employee Assistance Program

Your employee assistance program (EAP) is staffed by mental health professionals who can provide information and counseling for you or a family member if there are personal or work problems.

Types of Concerns

Family and marital problems (communication difficulties, parenting, stepparenting, single parenting, divorce).

Emotional strains (grief, depression, anger, anxiety, nagging worries, loneliness).

Substance abuse (concerns for self or others regarding alcohol and/or drugs).

Work stressors (balancing work and family, harassment, fear of layoff, burnout, and organizational change).

Financial concerns.

Possible Outcomes

Assessment of the problem.
Short-term counseling with EAP.
Referral to your health plan or other appropriate resource.
Arrangement for treatment.

Confidentiality

The appointment is confidential, between you and your counselor. There are several situations where the law requires your counselor to report information to appropriate sources:

- Abuse of a child and neglect or abuse of a vulnerable adult or elderly person.
- Any serious threat of harm to you or others.

Entering EAP

Employees may voluntarily seek the services of EAP or in some cases may be referred by supervisors. However, the employee always has the final decision regarding participation in EAP.

For voluntary and confidential counseling, call the EAP to set an appointment for yourself or a family member.

Note on the Americans with Disabilities Act: *With Reference to the "Bermuda Triangle"*

Debates about workplace disabilities among managers and general counsels have been compared metaphorically with the "Bermuda Triangle." The Bermuda Triangle is the section of the North Atlantic Ocean off North America in which more than 50 ships and 20 airplanes are said to have mysteriously disappeared. The area has a vaguely triangular shape marked by the southern U.S. coast, Bermuda, and the Greater Antilles. In companies, the Americans with Disabilities Act (ADA), the Family and Medical Leave Act (FMLA), and workers' compensation (WC) are the points of this triangle. They have become for many general counsels a nightmare, because they force various legal puzzles into the organization. Managers fear the triangle, because of a lack of knowledge about how to handle the situations that arise. ADA is designed to eliminate discrimination in the workplace. The employee must be allowed to continue working, even if he or she qualifies under ADA. The employer is responsible for creating a reasonable work environment for the disabled employee. FMLA is designed to improve the connection between work and family life. The employee is allowed to take a leave of absence up to 12 weeks. This leave is unpaid, but the employee's position is reserved for him or her upon return. Workers' compensation requires that the individual leave work and receive benefits for his or her job-related injuries. Compensation typically provides salary continuation and benefits for time out of work. These laws, although sometimes conflicting, often simultaneously apply to an individual employee. The difficulty is determining which point of the triangle the employee fits under. The decision can mean an extended amount of time off, excessive compensation or benefits, and potential lawsuits. This is why ADA, FMLA, and WC are sometimes called the "Bermuda Triangle" of corporate America. Companies are losing themselves in all the legalities and litigation.

While the triangle can occasionally be troublesome to handle, it offers opportunities and benefits for many. The United States has far more disabled people on the job than ever before. Currently, half the 29 million disabled Americans aged 21 to 64 are working. Altogether, the disabled account for 14 percent of the employed population. The largest number has impairments that are hearing-, vision-, or back-related. An aging population means that the number of disabled people with jobs will grow. Medical breakthroughs are saving lives that would have been lost but leaving people with lifelong impairments. With the development of the computer age, new opportunities have been opened for disabled workers. Employers are beginning to look more seriously at this segment of the workforce. Many have found them to be loyal and productive workers, and the issue has been brought to the forefront with the passage of the Americans with Disabilities Act in 1990.[1]

This note was prepared by Research Assistant Aaron Macke under the supervision of Kenneth E. Goodpaster, Koch Professor of Business Ethics, University of St. Thomas, to aid in the discussion of the Webster Health Systems, Inc., case study.

Americans with Disabilities Act

On July 27, 1990, the Americans with Disabilities Act was signed into law by President George Bush.

[1] Paula Mergenhagen, "Enabling Disabled Workers," *American Demographics*, July 1997, pp. 36–42.

ADA gives civil rights protection to individuals with disabilities similar to those provided to individuals on the basis of race, color, sex, national origin, age, and religion.[2] ADA bans discrimination based on disability in private-sector employment, public accommodations, transportation, public services, and communications. ADA applies to employers with 15 or more employees. The term "employer" refers to private employers, state and local governments, employment agencies, labor unions, and joint labor-management committees. The term also includes "agents" of the employer (foremen, supervisors, or even agencies used to conduct background checks of applicants).

A disability is defined as (1) a physical or mental impairment that substantially limits a major life activity, (2) a record of such a disability, or (3) being regarded as having such a disability. There are also several exceptions as to who is regarded as a disabled person. "Homosexuals, exhibitionists, persons with gender identity disorders not resulting from physical impairments, compulsive gamblers, current illegal drug users, and current alcoholics who cannot perform their job duties or whose employment presents a threat to the property or safety of others" are not eligible under ADA.[3] One in ten Americans will suffer a disability from mental illness in any given year. The number of individuals between the ages of 17 and 44 with severe disabilities has increased 400 percent over the past 25 years. In the last two minutes, 104 Americans became disabled. Discrimination can cover a wide range of employment activities, including recruitment, hiring, training, promotion, rates of pay, job assignments, leaves of absence, fringe benefits, and social programs. In hiring personnel, ADA specifically prohibits discrimination against "qualified" individuals with disabilities. Individuals are qualified if they can perform the essential functions of the job with or without reasonable accommodation. Reasonable accommodation includes such things as making the workplace accessible or modifying work schedules, equipment, examinations, training materials, and policies. However, accommodations are not required if they would create an undue hardship on the financial and administrative resources of the organization.

Employers are not allowed to ask questions of job applicants that are likely to bring out information about disabilities. They can only require medical examinations after an offer of employment has been made. Employers are only allowed to ask preemployment questions related to the ability of applicants to perform specific job-related functions. Many employers complained that the guidelines for enforcement of ADA issued by the Equal Employment Opportunity Commission (EEOC) in May 1994 were too restrictive on the types of questions they could ask job applicants. The restrictions prohibited prospective employers from asking about any accommodation needed to perform the job. This made it more difficult to determine if the applicant could be employed. The reason for these restrictions was to ensure that disabilities were not considered before the employer evaluated the file of the applicant. On October 10, 1995, the EEOC issued its final guidelines for preemployment questions under ADA. The new guidelines appear to allow employers more freedom in the number and type of questions they can ask about disabilities.[4] Some of these guidelines are mentioned in the following sections.

Impairment versus Disability

Certain traits like stress, irritability, chronic lateness, or poor judgment may be linked to mental impairments. While most such impairments are not considered disabilities, they could be so classified if they substantially limit a major life activity. Major life activities include learning, thinking, concentrating, interacting with others, caring for oneself, speaking, sleeping, and performing manual tasks or working. The EEOC gives several illustrations in which impairment substantially limits a major life activity. For example, some unfriendliness with coworkers would not be sufficient to establish a substantial

[2] U.S. Department of Justice, Americans with Disabilities Act home page.

[3] Tim Barnett, Winston McVea, Jr., and Kenneth Chadwick, "Preemployment Questions under the Americans with Disabilities Act," *SAM Advanced Management Journal*, winter 1997, pp. 23–24.

[4] Tim Barnett, Winston McVea, Jr., and Kenneth Chadwick, pp. 23–24.

limitation in interacting with others. However, if an individual's relations with others are characterized on a regular basis by severe problems, hostility, social withdrawal, or failure to communicate when necessary, the EEOC guidelines indicate the individual is disabled. An individual who has difficulty concentrating would not be substantially limited if the difficulty were due to tiredness or boredom. However, if irrelevant sights, sounds, or thoughts easily and frequently distracted an employee, the individual would be considered disabled by the EEOC guidelines.[5] Examples like these make it easy to understand why the Bermuda Triangle causes so many headaches in corporate America.

Disability-Related Questions

As mentioned, employers cannot ask any questions about a disability before a conditional offer of employment has been made. Prospective employers cannot ask applicants questions about their past workers' compensation claims, since such questions would be likely to reveal information about applicant disabilities. Employers are allowed to ask questions about impairments that do not constitute disabilities. For example, if an applicant had a broken finger, an employer could ask how the injury occurred, as long as the question does not require the applicant to estimate the extent or duration of the injury. The 1995 guidelines state that employers are allowed to ask questions related to the ability of the applicant to perform the job. Employers can ask applicants if they are able to perform the essential functions of the job. If the employer does not believe the applicant has a disability, the employer can require the applicant to perform the essential job functions. However, if the employer believes the applicant does have a disability, the employer cannot ask the applicant to perform a job function unless all applicants are asked to perform the same functions.[6] For example, the manager of a construction company can require an applicant to carry wood beams, if the manager does not perceive the applicant to be disabled. However, if the manager believes the applicant has a disability, the manager cannot ask the applicant to carry wood beams unless all applicants are asked to carry the same amount of beams. This is because an individual that is perceived as having a disability is protected under ADA.

Reasonable Accommodation

The 1995 guidelines relax the restrictions on employers when asking job applicants about "reasonable accommodations." At least four situations are specified in which employers can ask questions about the reasonable accommodations an employee might need.

1. Employers can ask applicants if they need reasonable accommodation to complete the job recruiting or hiring process. If the need for reasonable accommodation is requested, the employer is required to provide reasonable accommodation or to allow the applicant merely to describe how he or she would perform the job functions.
2. Employers are allowed to ask applicants if they need reasonable accommodation to perform job functions, if applicants have obvious disabilities. For example, if an applicant is in a wheelchair, the employer could ask about what accommodations were needed in order to perform job-related tasks.
3. Prospective employers are allowed to ask questions about reasonable accommodations if the applicant voluntarily reveals a disability that is not immediately obvious. For example, if the applicant stated that he or she had a heart condition, the employer might ask about any accommodations necessary to complete the job requirements.
4. Employers are allowed to ask about reasonable accommodations if applicants state they will need accommodations to perform the job functions.

Although employers are allowed to ask about accommodations in these situations, they cannot ask about the underlying disabilities. Employers should remain cautious in seeking information about the need for reasonable accommodations, because if the applicant is not hired, the applicant could use the questions as a basis for discrimination under ADA. The EEOC could come down

[5] Robert J. Nobile, "Coping With the ADA," *HRFocus Special Report on Employment Law*, 1997, pp. s7–s8.

[6] Tim Barnett, Winston McVea, Jr., and Kenneth Chadwick, pp. 24.

hard on the employer, carefully analyzing the employer's reasons for rejecting the applicant.

Once a disability is identified and an employee requests reasonable accommodation, the employer is required to accommodate the request. "Reasonable accommodation is any modification or adjustment to a job or the work environment that will enable a qualified applicant or employee with a disability to participate in the application process or to perform essential job functions."[7]

Drug and Alcohol Problems

The illegal use of drugs is not protected under ADA, so employers are free to ask about current use of illegal drugs. Employers may hold drug addicts and alcoholics to the same qualification standards to which employers hold other employees. This is acceptable even if any unsatisfactory performance or behavior is related to the drug use or alcoholism of the employee. Alcohol testing is allowed and is considered part of an ADA medical examination. Employers are also allowed to administer drug tests to applicants even though these tests are not part of an ADA medical examination. They should be careful, however, not to ask questions about past drug addictions. Under ADA, past drug addictions are a covered disability. A prospective employer can ask an applicant if he or she ever used illegal drugs and how recently. The employer may not ask an applicant about the extent of his or her past illegal drug use or the amount of illegal drugs used. For example, if an applicant admits to marijuana use in the past, the employer may not ask him or her how much or how long it was used. These questions may lead to answers that indicate an addiction to marijuana, a covered disability. Employers are allowed to ask applicants whether they drink, but not questions designed to reveal how much an applicant drinks or whether he or she has a drinking problem. Employers are not allowed to administer sobriety tests to applicants.[8] If an employer perceives an employee to have an alcohol problem, that employee is protected under ADA. Without this perception, the employee is only entitled to medical leave if he or she is an alcoholic. Substance abuse is not a covered disability under ADA, and the employee is not required to have reasonable accommodation. This differs from the Family Medical Leave Act, in which an employee is entitled to a leave if necessary to obtain treatment for serious substance abuse. The employer needs to be careful with issues such as termination, promotions, hiring, and layoffs when ADA and FMLA apply to the situation.

The problem employers often face with alcoholic or addicted employees is that the condition may be suspected but not proven. The employer runs the risk of defaming an employee when there is no proof of the addictive condition. In dealing with an employee suspected of alcoholism, it would not be defamatory to ask the employee whether his or her absenteeism or poor work performance is caused by drinking, so long as such an inquiry is not communicated as a statement of fact to the employee or to any other person. It is acceptable to ask whether this is the problem and, if not, what is the problem, and offer the individual time off for treatment either on an in-patient or out-patient basis. The employer is advised to offer an employee with a substance abuse problem an opportunity for treatment or rehabilitation before taking any disciplinary action. If the employee refuses treatment or his or her poor performance continues after completing treatment, the employer may take disciplinary action against such an employee. However, any such action must be based on poor performance, not on the underlying condition.[9]

A Recent Court Case

In 1997 West Publishing released a case regarding an employee that alleged she was unlawfully fired.[10] The case contained many of the issues found in the Webster Health Systems situation. The employee worked for Cargill, an employer that had a strict policy regarding alcohol consumption and operation of company vehicles.

[7] Tim Barnett, Winston McVea, Jr., and Kenneth Chadwick, pp. 24–25.

[8] Tim Barnett, Winston McVea, Jr., and Kenneth Chadwick, p. 25.

[9] Minnesota Department of Trade and Economic Development, *An Employer's Guide To Employment Law Issues in Minnesota*, 1996, p. 37.

[10] *Miners v. Cargill Communications, Inc.*, 113F. 3d 820, 823 n.5 (8th Cir. 1997).

The employee was fired for violating this policy, but claimed she was terminated because of the employer's perception of her being an alcoholic.

The employee (Annie Miners) was seen by a private investigator, hired by the company, drinking at a bar with the intent of driving a company vehicle. On the next day, the president of the company informed the employee that her actions constituted grounds for termination. He offered her the opportunity to attend a chemical dependency treatment program "due to the possibility that [the employee] may be an alcoholic." He told the employee that she must accept the treatment or be fired. The employee rejected the offer, and the company immediately fired her. At no point did the employee admit to being an alcoholic.

In order to fight the termination, the employee needed to make a case of discrimination under ADA. First, she introduced evidence sufficient to establish that the company regarded her as an alcoholic. The company offered her the choice between entering a chemical-abuse treatment program or being fired, which qualified her for protection under ADA. Second, she presented evidence that she was qualified to perform the job from which she was fired. Third, Miners offered evidence that she suffered an adverse employment action. In this case, the evidence presented to establish that the employer regarded her as disabled also created an inference that her firing was motivated by unlawful discrimination.

The company said that even if it perceived the employee to be an alcoholic, its offer of treatment was an appropriate accommodation of the employee's disability. The court insisted, however, that "without actual knowledge that Miners was an alcoholic, the company could not argue that it attempted to accommodate Miners, and it certainly lacks a basis to claim that Miners' refusal of treatment warranted her termination." The court thought that the company could have rid itself of the obligation to provide reasonable accommodation if it had attempted to establish that the employee was an alcoholic and demonstrated performance problems related to her alcoholism. The company argued that ADA placed it between a rock and a hard place by forcing it to choose between facing tort liability and defending against allegations of employment discrimination.

The court concluded that Miners presented evidence to support her claim and the company should have been held accountable for its actions. The company's termination offer was not an accommodation, the court held, because the company made no attempt to confirm whether Miners was an alcoholic. The lesson learned from this case is apparently that an employer should not mention alcoholism or treatment if it wants to avoid ADA. If alcoholism had already been mentioned, as in the Webster Health Systems case, the company would have to prove chemical dependency. If the employee refuses testing or treatment, documentation must be noted and action taken on the next offense. Action may be taken immediately, but it has to be clear that the action was a result of the offense and not of the perception of alcoholism.

Human Resources

About the time the Americans with Disabilities Act became law in 1990, an employee at MICOM Communications Corp., a computer company in Simi Valley, California, suffered a series of panic attacks. The employee had what is known as panic disorder, a mental disability. The employee's supervisor did not understand the condition and felt the worker was using panic attacks as an excuse for poor performance. At times, the employee became so angry with the responses he was getting from his coworkers and supervisor that he would walk out for two to three hours at a time. The employee received poor performance reviews because of the time lost. He responded with long angry letters to management. Management began to fear the possibility of workplace violence.

The employee did mention to human resources that he had a medical problem, and he did go out for a short time on disability. He believed that when he had these attacks, he should have been given some leeway. The company's stand was that in a lean and mean industry, if a worker did not do his or her full share, it wasn't fair to others. When a larger firm bought the company and insisted on staff reductions, the employee was "downsized." After his termination, he came in once more to read his personnel file. While he sat in an unused office, leafing through the file, the HR staff worried and wondered what was coming next. They had good reason to worry. Had the employee chosen to sue the company for employment discrimination under ADA, his case probably would have been successful. The company's human resource staff had made no effort to accommodate the employee's disability. Having no clear understanding of what constituted mental disabilities was HR's first error. Having no clear accommodation strategy was its second.

In April 1997, the EEOC drafted a 40-page set of guidelines attempting to answer the most frequently asked questions about accommodating psychiatric disabilities. This document had been raising concern in HR and general counsel offices because of the debate on how far an employer must go to accommodate a person with a mental disability. What was the HR staff at MICOM supposed to do with the man having panic attacks?

It is HR's responsibility to make sure all employees are comfortable in disclosing their needs. Richard Kunnis, head of the managed care practice of Ernst and Young, has suggested that HR professionals who have felt burned by the disability assessment process may have unreasonable expectations of them. HR cannot assess all mental or even physical disabilities, because many are hidden from ordinary sight. Assessment, he insists, is not the task of the human resources office. The employer has the obligation to investigate minimally employees' concerns or complaints. The employer needs to get the facts. The employee has the obligation to self-identify as a person with a disability. This identification should be in documented form, but if not, then the employer should approach the company's health provider for a referral to an occupational psychiatrist to get an evaluation of the employee's functional limitations. HR's function is to implement accommodation, not to assess the disability. HR is a key player in the process.[11]

Beyond the Legalities

The general thrust of ADA and FMLA is to protect vulnerable employees against unfair treatment and/or dismissal. The consequences for employers can be significant and perhaps unfair also. The restrictions ADA places on companies can work against the employee, if the employer is truly trying to help. ADA was put into place, because it cannot be assumed that all companies are acting in the best interests of the employee. However, for those companies that are, ADA can be a major obstacle. For example, in a case involving an employee with a perceived alcohol problem, ADA works against the employee. For the good of the employee, the employer needs to force treatment in order for the employee to sustain his or her current position. The employee would be receiving treatment, and the employer would possibly be receiving an employee more capable of performing his or her work duties. This situation would be best for the employee and the employer. However, ADA makes it legally risky for the employer to force the employee or even recommend the employee to treatment. Once the perception of alcoholism is in evidence, the employee is legally disabled and protected under ADA. Treating the employee now becomes extremely expensive and legally risky. The employee can file a lawsuit against the company for violation of ADA, if he or she is terminated or passed over due to poor performance. Legally for the company the best thing to do is to refrain from offering treatment and to terminate the employee on other grounds. This hurts the employee and the employer, because a position is lost and retraining will need to take place.

The Bermuda Triangle

As mentioned earlier, the triangle consists of three issues facing corporate America. The Americans with Disabilities Act, the Family and Medical Leave Act (Exhibit 1), and workers' compensation (Exhibit 2). Is a worker who is injured on the job entitled to benefits under FMLA or protected by ADA? The answer is 'yes' if the employer is covered by those laws and if the injured worker "has a serious medical condition" and/or an impairment that "substantially limits a major life activity," has a "record of," or is "regarded as" having such an impairment.

While the definitions of injury or illness under WC and FMLA are not identical, many injuries may qualify for benefits under both. When covered employees request leave for an FMLA purpose, the employer should inform them of their FMLA rights and obligations. Failure to inform an employee may result in an inability to

[11] Nancy Breuer, "Must HR Diagnose Mental Disabilities?" *Workforce*, October 1997, pp. 31–35.

count the time off under FMLA. That means the worker could receive workers' compensation time off plus the full 12 weeks of FMLA leave. These subtleties can add up over time and make large differences in management decisions.

FMLA does not require an employer to return to work an employee who is medically unable to do the job, nor does it require job modification or reassignment. Since FMLA requires that a worker be restored to the same or an equivalent position upon return from leave, an employer may not compel an injured worker to accept light-duty work. Many workers' compensation programs do include this in their requirements.

Workers who claim injuries under workers' compensation can also file ADA and other discrimination claims. If an employee breaks an ankle on the job and the ankle heals normally, this generally would not be covered by ADA. However, if the ankle heals and the employee has a permanent limp that substantially limits the ability to walk, the worker might be considered a person with a disability under ADA. It is important to understand that if an impairment or condition caused by an on-the-job injury does not substantially limit an employee's ability to work but the employer *regards* the individual as having an impairment that limits the employee's ability to perform a class of jobs, such as "heavy labor," this individual may be regarded as having a disability. The individual would be protected under ADA because of this perceived disability. Thus, if the employer took action against the employee based on this perception, the employer would violate ADA (assuming the employee was otherwise qualified for the job). Employers should be aware that an employee who has a disability, as a result of an on-the-job injury, would trigger the "reasonable accommodation" provisions of ADA.[12]

Companies face decisions like these regularly in their day-to-day decision making. These issues are highly complex and have potentially significant outcomes. It is important that managers understand the legalities surrounding these decisions. The Bermuda Triangle is not a myth but a metaphor, and it is alive and creating legal problems in corporate America. Managers and lawyers are disappearing into it daily.

As the complexity and uncertainty of life in the American workplace increases and as the regulation of disabilities becomes even more stringent, the need for management education also increases. The Americans with Disabilities Act, the Family and Medical Leave Act, and workers' compensation laws pose serious challenges to managers. The only way to be an effective decision maker concerning the Bermuda Triangle is to educate oneself on the legalities of these issues.

[12] Sandra N. Hurd, "Courts Rule on Bias in Public Sector Testing," *Employment Testing-Law and Policy Reporter*, November 1998, p. 166.

EXHIBIT 1 The Family and Medical Leave Act

The Family and Medical Leave Act of 1993 allows "eligible" employees of a covered employer to take job-protected, unpaid leave. They may substitute paid leave, if the employee has earned it or accrued it, for up to 12 workweeks in any 12 month time period. An employee falls under the FMLA in one of four types of situations: (1) The birth of a child and to care for the newborn child; (2) the placement of a child with the employee for adoption or foster care; (3) the employee is needed to care for a family member with a serious health condition; and (4) the employee's own serious health condition makes the employee unable to perform the functions of his or her job. FMLA does not affect any other federal or state law that prohibits discrimination, nor does it overrule any state or local law that provides greater family or medical leave protection. It does not affect any employer's obligation to provide greater leave rights under a collective bargaining agreement or employment benefit plan. FMLA also encourages employers to provide more generous leave rights.

A person is eligible under FMLA if that person is an employee of a covered employer. A covered employer is one who employs 50 or more employees, during each of 20 or more calendar workweeks in the current or preceding year. There are three criteria for determining an eligible employee: (1) the employee has been employed by the employer for at least 12 months; (2) the employee has been employed for at least 1,250 hours of service during the 12-month period immediately preceding the commencement of the leave; and (3) the employee is employed at a worksite where 50 or more employees are employed by the employer within 75 miles of that worksite.

An employee on FMLA leave is also entitled to have health benefits maintained while on leave, as if they had continued to work. The employee generally has the right to return to the same position or an equivalent position with equivalent pay, benefits, and working conditions at the end of the leave. Taking leave cannot result in the loss of any benefit that accrued prior to the start of the leave. Under specified and limited circumstances, where leave of employment will cause substantial economic injury to an employer, the employer may refuse to reinstate certain highly paid "key" employees after returning from FMLA leave. A "key" employee is one who is a salaried eligible employee and is among the highest-paid 10 percent of employees within 75 miles of the worksite. The employer must follow several legal requirements in order to refuse pay.

The employer has a right to 30 days' advance notice from the employee when possible. The employer may also request an employee to submit certification from a health care provider to prove the leave is due to the serious condition of the employee or employee's family member. This certification may also be requested when the employee returns to work when the absence was caused by the employee's serious health condition.

FMLA is intended to allow employees to balance their work and family lives by taking reasonable unpaid leave for medical reasons, the birth or adoption of a child, and for the care of a family member. The act is intended to benefit employees as well as their employers. There is a direct correlation between stability in the family and productivity in the workplace. When workers can count on stable links to their workplace they are able to make fuller commitments to their jobs.

EXHIBIT 2 Workers' Compensation

Workers' compensation laws are designed to ensure that employees who are injured or disabled on the job are provided with fixed monetary awards, eliminating the need for litigation. These laws also provide benefits for dependents of those workers who are killed because of work-related accidents or illnesses. Some laws also protect employers and fellow workers by limiting the amount an injured employee can recover from an employer and by eliminating the liability of coworkers in most accidents. Federal and state statutes comprise the majority of laws on workers' compensation. Federal statutes are limited to federal employees.

The cost of workers' compensation benefits for employers is extremely high. The average employer in America has about 10 claims per year for every 100 employees and the average claim is $5,000. The actual numbers depend on many factors and vary from industry to industry. An average employer with 100 employees and 10 claims per year could pay $50,000 in workers' compensation premiums or claims costs. Experts estimate that the cost of lost productivity, training replacements, or retraining the injured employee is two to three times the cost of medical care and lost-time benefits.

Workers' compensation is not a law that was enacted on a particular date like ADA and FMLA. It is a set of laws and statutes that protect the employee and provide compensation. Some examples of workers' compensation acts are as follows: the Merchant Marine Act (the Jones act), which provides that employers are liable for sailors if they have been negligent, and the Longshore and Harbor Workers' Compensation Act (LHWCA), which provides workers' compensation to specified employees of private maritime employers. The office of Workers' Compensation Programs administers the act; the Black Lung Benefits Act provides for workers' compensation for miners suffering from "black lung" (pneumoconiosis). There are also workers' compensation acts for most states. Each state may have its own workers' compensation act to address issues they feel most important. For example, California's Workers' Compensation Act provides an example of a comprehensive state compensation program. It is applicable to most employers. The statute limits the liability of the employer and fellow employees. California also requires employers to obtain insurance to cover potential workers' compensation claims, and sets up a fund for claims that employers have illegally failed to insure against.

Who Pays for Workers' Compensation Benefits?

In most states, employees purchase insurance for their employees from a workers' compensation insurance company. In some states, larger employers are allowed to self-insure. When a worker is injured, his or her claim is filed with the insurance company or self-insuring employer. The company then pays medical and disability benefits according to a self-approved formula.

Are All Injuries Covered by Workers' Compensation?

Most injuries in the workplace are covered by workers' compensation. The system is designed to provide benefits to injured workers no matter whether an injury is caused by the employer's or employee's negligence. There are exceptions, however, to this general rule. Injuries caused as a result of an employee being intoxicated or using illegal drugs are not covered by workers' compensation. Coverage may also be denied in situations involving:

- Self-inflicted injuries (including those caused by a person who starts a fight).
- Injuries suffered while a worker was committing a serious crime.
- Injuries suffered while an employee was not on the job.
- Injuries suffered when an employee's conduct violated company policy.

These situations are rare and most injuries are covered under workers' compensation. It is designed to protect the employee, thus the reason for the few exceptions.

Part 3

Corporate Values: Looking Outward

In Parts 1 and 2 of this book, the cases concerned problems that focused either on individuals or on the moral environment of the firm. Nevertheless, it will already have become apparent from the discussion of several cases (such as the modules on Waterbee Toy, Inc., and Webster Health Systems) that there are other important constituencies to whom the corporation has obligations—that is, those found "outside" the boundaries of the firm. Whether those persons or groups represent themselves or are represented by a government body, it is clear that today's corporation cannot and does not operate in a social vacuum. And because the corporation can affect the lives and livelihoods of people outside, it is a kind of "moral actor" in society.

Part 3 presents a wide range of cases in which corporate behavior and policy affect the welfare of the larger society or some segment of it—from the safety of a specific product to the implied value system that choices of advertising messages and programs help to convey. We acknowledge that there are many topics that could be covered from this perspective, but we have tried to select cases of significance to various kinds of companies and industries and to different sectors of society.

We begin with a classic case, "Tennessee Coal and Iron," which looks back in time at the racial tensions in Birmingham, Alabama, during the 1960s. One of the major companies in that city considers actions it might or should take to mitigate the social effects of a highly segregated society. As the company's president considers the role of his corporation regarding segregation, he is faced with a variety of conflicting pressures from the local community, the national press, and the federal government—pressures that seem to be timeless and easily recognizable in today's business environment.

In the "Poletown Dilemma," General Motors and the city of Detroit are the institutional players. The residents of Poletown are among those affected by their decisions. How much loyalty can and should a large corporation have to its city of origin, the community it has served since its founding? Are the shareholders well served by such loyalty? Are other stakeholders? On the other hand, how much loyalty does the city owe to the corporation? To the residents who will be displaced if the corporation builds its new plant in Detroit?

In "Dayton Hudson Corporation: Conscience and Control," we witness a hostile takeover attempt with significant implications. A company (today called Target Corporation) that has an outstanding record of corporate community involvement is suddenly plunged into a major economic and political crisis as its various stakeholders become active. This case also invites careful reflection on the meaning of ownership and governance in the modern corporation, one of the major themes of Part 2.

The "Northwest Airlines: Private Sector, Public Trust" case offers a useful opportunity for comparison and contrast with the Dayton Hudson case series. Again we have a company seeking public-sector support from state government, but this time in the context of loan guarantees and implied threats of moving jobs elsewhere. What are the obligations and the opportunities of both corporate and state leaders in these so-called gray areas?

In "The Bush Foundation: A Case Study in Giving Money Away" we look at ethical issues in the context of managing a nonprofit foundation. The Bush Foundation takes great pains in the pursuit of its mission to give money away with social responsibility, with systems for review and after-the-fact grant assessment that impress many in the nonprofit field. It also has a sophisticated system for achieving a high return on its invested principal in order to sustain its mission into the future. But the question arises: Does it have a duty to invest its principal according to social criteria that may result in a lower return on the principal? And is this question so different from the question facing for-profit corporations when trade-offs are called for in connection with stakeholders like employees, customers, communities, and the environment?

In the "Note on Product Safety" and "Managing Product Safety" cases, we explore various considerations that affect the development and marketing of products. Two historic cases on very different products (the "Ford Pinto" and the "Procter & Gamble Rely Tampon") that carry potentially serious threats of injury to consumers are presented in retrospect, from both a company and a public interest point of view, to reflect the panoply of problems that managers face in deciding what to market and what liabilities may or do exist. An introductory "Note on Product Safety" accompanies these cases and furnishes information on the economic, legal, and ethical aspects of product safety problems.

The theme of product safety is then continued with the case on "Kolcraft, Hasbro, and the Playskool Travel-Lite Crib." The lives of several infants have been lost subsequent to the product's recall. Do corporate responsibilities for safety extend *beyond* ceasing production and issuing a recall? And what are the moral responsibilities of the Consumer Product Safety Commission?

Ethical aspects of marketing are the common thread in the next three cases: "Minnesota Bank, Inc. (A)" (with "A Note on Financial Privacy"), "Northwest Airlines vs. WCCO-TV: Business Ethics and the Media (A) and (B)," and "US Citizen Bank (A)" (with "A Note on the Challenge of Responsible Lending and Debt: An Introduction to Nonstandard Credit"). The first examines a company's sharing of financial data about its customers with a third party. The second looks at how news media organizations can sometimes "color" their messages with promotional imagery. The third has to do with the marketing of credit cards to college freshmen and, in general, the ethical aspects of marketing to vulnerable populations.

In the final three cases of Part 3, we shift to the theme of business ethics and the environment. "Environmental Pressures: The Pollution Problem" is a portrait of the "classic pollution case"—Reserve Mining Company's alleged deposit of iron ore tailings in the waters of Lake Superior. In tracing Reserve's strategy since the late 1940s, the reader has an opportunity to consider what he or she believes is the proper company posture regarding pollution under a variety of changing legislative requirements. The company must also deal with a complex array of government policies and political processes in order to resolve the issue.

"Ashland Oil, Inc." involves another environmental challenge. In the Ashland case, economics and ethics again meet. This time the issue is how candid the CEO should be with the media about a massive diesel fuel discharge into the Ohio River from one of this company's storage terminals.

Wrapping up the environmental theme and as a natural transition to Part 4, we consider "Exxon *Valdez:* Corporate Recklessness on Trial." Both inward- and outward-looking corporate values are at stake in this case as Exxon executives face compensatory and punitive damages for the largest oil spill in American history. Readers of this case are asked to put themselves on the jury and to consider the meaning of justice and fairness toward Exxon.

Tennessee Coal and Iron

In the early 1960s, the Tennessee Coal and Iron Division (TCI) of United States Steel Corporation (USS) was one of that corporation's largest divisions. Originally an independent company, TCI became a subsidiary of USS in 1907. It continued to grow, and added quarries, mines, reservoirs, electric power systems, and coke, wire, and many other kinds of plants and steel facilities over the years. By the beginning of World War II, TCI was by far the largest producer of primary steel and many other products in the 11-state region that it served. It moved from subsidiary to divisional status in 1953.

TCI's peak employment was in 1942, when a total of 33,000 was attained. A number of factors, e.g., decline in steel demand and a switch to imported ores, reduced the number of TCI employees to about 24,000 in 1955–57 and to 16,000 in 1964. Nearly 12,000 of these were production and maintenance employees, and about one-third of the 12,000 were black. All, or nearly all, of the production and maintenance employees were covered by a contract between USS and the United Steelworkers of America (USW). Despite the decline in its employment rolls, TCI continued to be by far the largest employer in Birmingham and the Jefferson County area of Alabama. Mr. Arthur Wiebel, President of TCI, estimated that the next largest employer was about one-third the size of TCI. Birmingham had a civilian male labor force of 78,000 and Jefferson County, of which Birmingham was the center, a civilian male labor force of about 155,000. The ratio of whites to blacks was about 2 to 1 in Jefferson County, and about 2 to 1⅓ in Birmingham itself.

In 1963, the attention of the nation was focused on racial disturbances in various parts of the South. Some of the most violent occurred in Birmingham. Bombings of black churches, incidents of personal violence, and threats of all types occurred as the drive toward racial integration kindled or kept alive old racial hatreds.

The movement toward integration was also taking place inside TCI's many plants in and around Birmingham. USS had had, orally since 1902 and in writing since 1918, a policy that employment at USS would be made available without regard to race, color, creed, or national origin. This policy, however, was affected by labor agreements, and a portion of the USS Policy Manual had, for several years, read as follows:

> Application of this policy as it relates to union-represented employees will be in accordance with applicable provisions of labor agreements.

Thus, for many years prior to the 1960s, the combined effects of seniority, contracts at individual plant and local union levels, strike threats, and local racial customs had resulted in a high degree of racial segregation within TCI's plants. It was against this backdrop that senior officials of USS, TCI, and the USW had to work to bring about a lessening of racial discrimination within TCI.

Three major events occurred to help these officials in their efforts. A Human Relations Committee was formed in 1960 by 11 major steel producers and the USW as a mechanism for exploring and solving common problems. In March 1961, President John F. Kennedy issued Executive Order 10925. The Order was intended to prevent discrimination within companies bidding or holding government contracts; it also established the Committee on Equal Employment Opportunity, and Vice President Lyndon B. Johnson was appointed chairman of the committee. Finally, there was a continuing decline in demand for TCI's products, which made it more difficult for senior employees to hold their jobs in spite of the more than 1,000 separate and rigid lines of promotion among the production and maintenance workers.

These several factors, plus months of hard and laborious work by company and union officials, bore fruit. Lines of promotion were broadened, and all claims of racial discrimination brought before the CEEO were closed out by June 1963. As a result of this, and a new 1962 contract between the USW and the 11 major steel producers that provided for sweeping changes, Hobart Taylor, Jr., executive vice chairman of the CEEO, wrote a letter to USS which included the following paragraph.

> May I thank you, too, for the example which U.S. Steel has given the rest of the managers in this country by its courageous move in Birmingham at a time of great social tension in the area. This was an important milestone toward true equal employment opportunity. You have earned the gratitude of those of us who are also working toward this important national goal.

In spite of the major accomplishments toward integration within TCI's plants and mines, however, TCI's role in the community had been an issue for some time, and was to become a major one in the summer of 1963. The remainder of this case concerns that issue.

By summer's end, 1963, officials of the United States Steel Corporation (USS) and its Tennessee Coal and Iron Division (TCI) believed that the problems of job integration among TCI's 12,000 white and black production and maintenance workers had been solved in satisfactory fashion. In addition, the physical violence that had permeated the Birmingham area in the spring and early summer of that year had greatly abated.

The tension that had preceded and accompanied the violence, however, continued to exist in the community at large. In discussing the situation, James Reston made the following comment in *The New York Times* (Sept. 22, 1963):

> The point, then, is not that Birmingham is lacking in young leaders, and not that it is lacking in biracial committees, but that the real power structure of the city—the older men who run the industries, banks and insurance companies that in turn influence the stores and big law firms—are not leading the peace effort.
>
> There are about a dozen men in this group, some of whom have worked quietly for a compromise, some of whom have tried and then withdrawn. But at no time have they all worked together. . . .

(The Reston story listed 13 prominent Birmingham businessmen and lawyers, among them "Arthur W. Weible [sic], president of the Tennessee Coal and Iron Division of United States Steel.")

> . . . There is general agreement here that these men, working together with the leaders of the local clergy of both races, could do more to produce a compromise in a month than Federal troops, Federal officials and all the national Negro organizations put together could in years.
>
> The question is who, if anybody, can get them together. They damn "The Kennedys" and concede that Senator Goldwater would carry Alabama against the President tomorrow, but even this prospect only creates a new dilemma.

On October 22, a *New York Times* reporter met with Mr. Wiebel, Mr. C. Thomas Spivey (TCI director of personnel services), and Mr. Clinton Milstead (TCI director of public relations) in Mr. Wiebel's conference room. The meeting lasted from 9:00 A.M. until 2:30 P.M., and was largely concerned with the work of TCI and union officials in bringing about job integration within TCI.

During his visit, the reporter also asked Mr. Wiebel whether TCI would use its economic power to speed integration in the community itself. According to Mr. Wiebel, the reporter suggested that TCI might put pressure on its suppliers, its bank connections, and some of its customers to aid the cause of Birmingham's blacks.

Both the question and the suggestion came as a surprise to Mr. Wiebel and his associates. In the preceding months, TCI officials had held extended conversations with union officers, representatives of the President's Committee on Equal Employment Opportunity, General Royall and Colonel Blaik, and black leaders. No question about the use of economic pressure by TCI had arisen in any discussion with these groups and no suggestions concerning its use had been made officially, although unofficially USS had been criticized in the press.

Mr. Wiebel told the reporter that there were two major reasons why TCI would not resort to economic coercion, as the area's largest employer, to try to solve Birmingham's racial problems. He pointed out that neither TCI nor USS had sufficient economic power in the area to solve the problem, and that neither had the right to tell people what they ought or ought not to do. He also stated that, if TCI were to do what the reporter suggested, charges would be made that TCI and USS were trying to run Birmingham.

Three days later, under an October 25 dateline, *The New York Times* carried a two-column story about TCI and racial integration in Birmingham. Much of the story concerned activities within TCI. Only the lead paragraphs, which discussed the issue of the division's economic influence in the community, are reproduced here:

The New York Times
October 25, 1963

The United States Steel Corporation, the largest employer in Birmingham, appears to be making significant strides in opening up Negro job opportunities in its Alabama plants.

But the nation's biggest steel maker appears to be making little effort to wield its economic influence to help solve the community's racial problems.

These conclusions emerge from talks with officials of U.S. Steel's Tennessee Coal and Iron Division here, as well as with others in both the North and South familiar with the situation.

Critics have contended that Roger M. Blough, U.S. Steel chairman, could contribute greatly toward stemming the racial strife here by simply instructing local officials to exert their power toward that end. . . . But company officials here insist they do not have that much power, and in any event they show no signs of using what power they do have on the community's racial front.

On October 29, at a press conference called to announce the results of USS operations during the preceding quarter, Mr. Roger M. Blough, Chairman of the USS Board of Directors, was asked to comment on USS policies in its TCI operation and, more particularly, on the use of its "economic influence" in the Birmingham area as a means of influencing local opinion. The portion of his response dealing with the latter issue follows:

Now, the criticism that U.S. Steel hasn't used what some people refer to as . . . economic influence, which I presume to mean some kind of economic force to bring about some kind of a change, is, I think, an improper matter upon which to criticize either Mr. Wiebel or U.S. Steel. I think I would have to take considerable time to fully explain this point, but very briefly, I'd like to say this—that I do not either believe that it would be a wise thing for U.S. Steel to be other than a good citizen in a community, or to attempt to have its ideas of what is right for the community enforced upon that community by some sort of economic means. This is repugnant to me personally, and I am sure it is repugnant to my fellow officers in U.S. Steel. I doubt very much that this in principle is a good thing for any corporation to follow. When we as individuals are citizens in a community, we can exercise what small influence we may have as citizens, but for a corporation to attempt to exert any kind of economic compulsion to achieve a particular end in the social area seems to me to be quite beyond what a corporation should do, and I will say also, quite beyond what a corporation can do.

. . . We have fulfilled our responsibility in the Birmingham area—whatever responsibility we have as a corporation or as individuals working with a corporation, because, after all, a corporation is nothing but individuals.

The October 30 issue of *The New York Times* carried a front-page story devoted primarily to Mr. Blough's comments about the Birmingham–TCI situation, and on October 31 the following editorial appeared in the paper:

Corporate Race Relations

When it comes to speaking out on business matters Roger Blough, chairman of the United States Steel Corporation, does not mince words. Mr. Blough is a firm believer in freedom of action for corporate management, a position he made clear in his battle with the Administration last year. But he also has put some severe limits on the exercise of corporate responsibility, for he rejects the suggestion that U.S. Steel, the biggest employer in Birmingham, Ala., should use its economic influence to erase racial tensions. Mr. Blough feels that U.S. Steel has fulfilled its responsibilities by following a nondiscriminatory hiring policy in Birmingham, and looks upon any other measures as both "repugnant" and "quite beyond what a corporation should do" to improve conditions.

This hands-off strategy surely underestimates the potential influence of a corporation as big as U.S. Steel, particularly at the local level. It could, without affecting its profit margins adversely or getting itself directly involved in politics, actively work with those groups in Birmingham trying to better race relations. Steel is not sold on the retail level, so U.S. Steel has not been faced with the economic pressure used against the branches of national chain stores.

Many corporations have belatedly recognized that it is in their own self-interest to promote an improvement in Negro opportunities. As one of the nation's biggest corporations, U.S. Steel and its shareholders have as great a stake in eliminating the economic imbalances associated with racial discrimination as any company. Corporate responsibility is not easy to define or to measure, but in refusing to take a stand in Birmingham, Mr. Blough appears to have a rather narrow, limited concept of his influence.

Also on October 31, the *Congressional Record* contained remarks made by Representative Ryan of the State of New York:

Mr. Speaker, yesterday's *New York Times* carried two stories—one of high corporate indifference, the other of high corporate profits. The statement of Roger Blough, Chairman of the Board of United States Steel Corp., that the corporation should not use its influence to improve racial conditions in strife-torn Birmingham is the epitome of corporate irresponsibility and callousness.

United States Steel willingly accepts all the benefits of our laws and constitution which guarantee the rights of corporations and of private property, but refuses to accept its obligation to support the same laws and constitution which also declare all men equal.

Apparently United States Steel sees [that] its only responsibility is to make profits. Public welfare is not its concern. This callous attitude is a giant step backward by a giant corporation.

It is ironic that, in the same conference, Roger Blough reported a sharp increase in third-quarter sales and earnings. Who is responsible for these profits? Roger Blough in his plush New York office did not bring this about by himself. Behind the profits are some 15,000 steelworkers in Birmingham, many of whom are black, who mine the ore, melt the steel, cut it, shape it, and by their hard labor create the product with which the profits are made. These steelworkers and their families live in a town of terror—a town with segregated schools and bigoted police where our citizens are denied their constitutional rights. United States Steel says to these workers, "Give us your labor but do not expect us to be concerned with your lives or the lives of your children."

United States Steel also says to American Society, "We will benefit from the advantages of American Society and its economic system and its laws but do not expect us to share any responsibility for improving human relations in that society."

Even a schoolboy knows that citizenship has obligations as well as privileges. If all citizens, whether private or corporate, insisted on privileges while refusing obligations, our free democratic society would disintegrate.

Mr. Speaker, power without responsibility is tyranny. United States Steel's policy of inaction is in reality a policy of action. Birmingham and other southern cities are permitted to abuse American citizens and deny to them the right to live decently because the so-called respectable and responsible people and organizations remain silent. In the case of United States Steel this unconscionable silence in Birmingham is shocking. As a giant of industry, it has a moral obligation to speak out. In Birmingham, where it is the largest employer, this corporation could use its tremendous influence to bring about substantial and constructive change.

I urge all members and all citizens to raise their voice in protest against this callous irresponsibility and indifference. It is time for United States Steel to put people ahead of profits.

President Kennedy, at a press conference on Thursday, November 1, was asked to comment on Mr. Blough's stand. The question and the President's answer follow:

Question: The United States Steel Corporation has rejected the idea that it should use economic pressure in an effort to improve race relations in Birmingham, Alabama. Do you have any comment on that position, and do you have any counsel for management and labor in general as to their social responsibility in the areas of tension of this kind?

The President: Actually Mr. Blough has been somewhat helpful in one or two cases that I can think of in Birmingham. I don't think he should narrowly interpret his responsibility for the future. That is a very influential company in Birmingham, and he wants to see that city prosper, as do we all. Obviously the Federal government cannot solve this matter. So that business has a responsibility—labor and, of course, every citizen. So I would think that particularly a company which is as influential as United States Steel in Birmingham I would hope would use its influence on the side of comity between the races.

Otherwise, the future of Birmingham, of course, is not as happy as we hope it would be. In other words, it can't be decided—this matter—in Washington. It has to be decided by citizens everywhere. Mr. Blough is an influential citizen. I am sure he will do the best he can.

On November 4, the *Congressional Record* carried the following remarks by Representative George Huddleston, Jr., of Alabama:

Mr. Huddleston: Mr. Speaker, in recent days, what I consider unjustifiable criticism has been lodged at Mr. Roger M. Blough, chairman of the board of the United States Steel Corp., as a result of comments he made in a press conference held in New York on Tuesday, October 29, in which he discussed the role of business in race relations, with particular reference to the Birmingham situation. Some misunderstanding has arisen as a result of this criticism and I feel that, in all fairness to the United States Steel Corp., Mr. Blough, and the people of Birmingham, the record should be clarified. For this purpose, I insert herewith in the *Congressional Record* a verbatim transcript of Mr. Blough's press conference of October 29.

I want to especially call the attention of the Members of Congress to Mr. Blough's comments regarding whether business should attempt to apply economic sanctions to a community in order to further so-called social or moral reforms. Mr. Blough states that such effort by business is repugnant to him and his company, and I think I speak for the overwhelming majority of the citizens of Birmingham in applauding his firm and forthright stand. For any enterprise, Government or private, to attempt to exert economic pressures on the people of any community to bring about social changes is truly repugnant to the American way of life.

We in Birmingham are proud of the contributions that United States Steel's TCI division has over the years made to the economy of our city and look forward to continued cooperation for our mutual benefit in the future.

The New York Times of Nov. 7 contained a letter from Mr. Blough:

To the editor of the New York Times:
From your Oct. 31 editorial "Corporate Race Relations" it would appear that you are under considerable misapprehension as to what I said in my press conference of the previous day concerning the policy and actions of United States Steel in Birmingham. For example, you said:

"Mr. Blough feels that U.S. Steel has fulfilled its responsibilities by following a nondiscriminatory hiring policy in Birmingham, and looks upon any other measures as both 'repugnant' and 'quite beyond what a corporation should' do to improve conditions."

Quite to the contrary, I recounted in some detail the efforts of U.S. Steel management to use its influence in Birmingham to promote better communications and better understanding between the races—not just during the recent crises but over a period of many years.

Unfortunately, the able representatives of *The Times* who attended that press conference made only casual reference to this part of my remarks in their stories. For your information therefore, and for the information of your readers, I should like to summarize the specific statements I made on this point:

The present president of our Tennessee Coal and Iron Division, Arthur Wiebel, has been working since 1946 toward developing understanding and strengthening communications between the races in Birmingham.

In 1949 he became a trustee of the Jefferson County Coordinating Council of Social Forces devoted to civic and social improvement.

. . . In 1951 an interracial committee of this council, with Mr. Wiebel as a member, was formed to improve the lot of the Negroes in many fields: health, sanitation, safety, business, housing and cultural and recreational opportunities. That same year the committee made a formal request that the Birmingham city government employ Negro policemen. That request was denied.

Mr. Wiebel worked, for example, for a Negro upper-middle-class housing project considered as attractive as any in that economic range anywhere in the nation. He helped get Negro insurance companies and investors in Birmingham to make home mortgage money available to Negroes.

From 1953 to 1961 he was a trustee of Tuskegee Institute, an outstanding Negro institution of higher learning.

As a member of the Senior Citizens Committee, last May when serious racial problems occurred in Birmingham he devoted as much time and effort as anyone there in trying to resolve this matter. More recently he has worked in cooperation with General Royall and Colonel Blaik, and was one of 44 business leaders endorsing a recent public appeal for the employment of qualified Negroes on the Birmingham police force.

. . . Mr. Wiebel has also been active in the United Fund, which supports Negro welfare activities, and in the Red Cross. He is a charter member of the Committee of a Hundred, devoted to bringing new industry to Birmingham, and in more ways than I can recount he has tried to carry out what is our overall U.S. Steel policy of being a good citizen in the community in which we live.

I also said that as individuals we can exercise what influence we may have as citizens, but for a corporation to attempt to exert any kind of economic compulsion to achieve a particular end in the social area seems to me to be quite beyond what a corporation should do, and quite beyond what a corporation can do.

To recapitulate, then, let me make our position perfectly clear:

I believe that U.S. Steel in its own plants should provide equal opportunities for all employees, and that it does so in Birmingham, as *The Times* recently reported.

I believe that U.S. Steel management people, as citizens, should use their influence persuasively to help resolve the problems of their communities wherever they may be—and that they are doing so in Birmingham.

I believe that while government—through the proper exercise of its legislative and administrative powers—may seek to compel social reforms, any attempt by a private organization like U.S. Steel to impose its views, its beliefs and its will upon the community by resorting to economic compulsion or coercion would be repugnant to our American constitutional concepts, and that appropriate steps to correct this abuse of corporate power would be universally demanded by public opinion, by Government and by *The New York Times*.

So, even if U.S. Steel possessed such economic power—which it certainly does not—I would be unalterably opposed to its use in this fashion.

We shall, however, continue to use our best efforts in Birmingham to be as helpful as possible.

Roger Blough

Chairman, Board of Directors
United States Steel Corporation
New York, Nov. 2, 1963

The matter of the possible use of economic pressure by business firms to speed the process of racial integration drew considerable attention in newspapers throughout the country. News stories, editorials, and letters from readers took various positions on Mr. Blough's stand and on President Kennedy's remarks. Several such comments follow:

Somehow Mr. Blough seems to say that the injunction "we are our brother's keepers" does not apply to corporations, or at least not to U.S. Steel. I am sure that even a most casual examination of this proposition will destroy it. Many large enterprises, including U.S. Steel, have made substantial contributions to the welfare of the community or the nation, beyond the necessities of profit and loss.

What I am afraid Mr. Blough means is that in the current effort to eliminate all the remaining vestiges of a servile history he would prefer to be neutral, at least in deed if not in thought. If we cannot be sure as to what is morally correct in this struggle, whenever will we be able to know right from wrong?

If U.S. Steel strong and great as it is, will not exert its strength for justice, what can be expected from lesser mortals? What strength U.S. Steel has in Birmingham is best known to it, but that it should be used, I have no doubt.

Carl Rachlin

General Counsel, CORE
New York, Nov. 8, 1963

Big Steel and Civil Rights
(American Metal Market, November 11, 1963)

What is the extent of the moral responsibilities of the modern, impersonal, publicly owned corporation? The question has been raised in acute fashion in Birmingham, Ala., where the city's largest single employer is the Tennessee Coal and Iron division of U.S. Steel Corp.

U.S. Steel, and Tennessee president Arthur Wiebel in particular, have been under pressure from civil rights activists to do more to promote the individual rights of Negroes in that embattled city. In response to criticism, the corporation recently disclosed that it has been moving quietly to erase some traditional barriers that have held hundreds of Negroes to low-paying jobs. U.S. Steel has merged into one line previously separate lines of promotion for Negroes and whites in its steel plants. For instance, Negroes in the open hearth shop can now rise along with whites to a job class which pays $3.83 an hour and offers a 40% incentive. Previously they had been limited to a maximum job class offering $2.78 and a 15% incentive. Moreover, in the corporation's Fairfield plant, whites are working under Negroes for the first time. The situation reportedly has caused some discontent among white workers. But U.S. Steel has been strict in the application of its policy. Workers who object are sent home. According to a corporation official, the objectors usually return quickly to the plant. Jobs, after all, are not so easy to get in the steel industry these days.

Beyond taking these forthright steps in its own operations in Birmingham, however, U.S. Steel is inclined to go no further. According to Roger M. Blough, U.S. Steel chairman, the idea that a company should "attempt to have its ideas of what is right for the community enforced upon that community by some sort of economic means" is "clearly repugnant to me personally" and "repugnant to my fellow officers" at U.S. Steel. "We have fulfilled our responsibility in the Birmingham area," Mr. Blough said at the corporation's recent third-quarter press conference. For a corporation to attempt to exert any kind of economic compulsion to achieve a particular end in the social area "seems to be quite beyond what a corporation should do, and . . . quite beyond what a corporation can do." But corporate officials who are citizens in a community "can exercise what small influence we may have as citizens," Mr. Blough said. Apparently, U.S. Steel's chairman was referring among other things to Mr. Wiebel's recent support of a move to put Negro policemen on the Birmingham police force.

A careful study of America's industrial past would probably make it difficult for Mr. Blough to support in factual detail the argument that corporations are prevented from achieving particular ends in "the social area." State and local taxes, for instance, clearly play an important social role in the community, and large corporations can wield enormous influence over tax policy. But Birmingham is a unique situation, as puzzling to politicians as it is to businessmen. Even the Federal government has been reluctant to apply economic sanctions by withholding Federal funds from states which defy Negro rights. Can U.S. Steel be expected to do more?

Indeed Big Steel has left little doubt of its sincerity in advancing civil rights in its own operations. If other businesses . . . and more particularly unions . . . were to follow the corporation's example of on-the-job reforms in the South, the civil rights problems of cities like Birmingham would be a lot closer to solution.

In the realm of morality, one positive example may be worth a dozen damaging sanctions in promoting a worthy end.

The Wall Street Journal
Monday, November 4, 1963

The Company in the Community

There are still a lot of people around who remember the old "company towns"—those communities so dominated by one business enterprise that the politics, the business and very often even the social customs of the people were ordained in the company boardroom.

Some of these company towns were run badly. But many were actually run very well, the company managements having a sincere interest in the well-being of the community. In many places the company out of necessity provided housing, streets, schools, hospitals, recreation centers, churches and a host of other things which the people would otherwise not have had. Often the resulting municipal government was a model of good management.

Yet even in the best run such communities the people always chafed. However high-minded the motives, high-handed power was rightly resented and people found intolerable the economic power that could tell the banker to whom he should lend, the shopkeeper whom he should hire, the town councillors what laws they should pass. Thus today companies make their very considerable contributions to the community in other ways—in good jobs, in gifts to local services and in lending their influence to civic progress—and, like other outmoded institutions, the "company town" has passed without mourning.

Or anyway, so it was until lately. Now in the new context of the civil rights struggle, there are voices demanding that our large corporations use exactly this sort of power to force their desired moral standards on the communities in which they live.

Specifically this has been urged by otherwise thoughtful people in the case of Birmingham. Just the other day Roger Blough of U.S. Steel had to devote the major part of a business press conference to "explaining" why the company did not use its economic power to compel that unhappy city to mend its ways.

The question here was not about U.S. Steel's own practices. Nationwide it follows a practice of nondiscrimination in employment; upwards of 10% of its employees are Negroes, including a number in clerical jobs, supervisory assignments, skilled trades and professional positions. In Birmingham itself, according to Mr. Blough, the U.S. Steel subsidiary has about 30% Negroes among its employees.

Nor is there any argument here about the duty of a company or its officers to provide moral leadership for what they believe to be right, whether in Birmingham or anywhere else.

In this instance the present president of the U.S. Steel division in Birmingham, Arthur Wiebel, has since 1946 been active in groups working for better race relations; since 1951 he has served on the integration committee formed by local citizens, white and Negro; he is a trustee of Tuskegee Institute, a Negro college; and in the latest difficulties he played an active and prominent role in the quiet citizens' group which has worked hard to improve the situation for Negroes in Birmingham.

Mr. Blough made it quite clear that he approved and encouraged this kind of leadership. But to the voices of impatience this is not enough. It is said by some that companies like U.S. Steel should not merely persuade but coerce the community into adopting the policies they believe to be right.

It is probably true, as these voices say, that a company as large as U.S. Steel could wield powerful weapons against the people of Birmingham. It could, as some clamor that it should, boycott local suppliers who did not act as U.S. Steel thinks they should; it could threaten to take away all or a part of its business if the city authorities didn't do as it wishes; it could even halt its contributions to local civic organizations, from hospitals to recreation facilities, if they did not conduct their affairs in an approved fashion.

Perhaps, although we gravely doubt it, such coercion might win some immediate point for the Negroes of Birmingham. But it would certainly do an injury to all the people of Birmingham and most of all a grievous injury to good government and society everywhere.

Mr. Blough himself put it well: "I do not believe it would be a wise thing for U.S. Steel to be other than a good citizen in a community, to attempt to have its ideas of what is right for the community enforced upon the community."

As a good citizen, business can use its influence for good, but the old-fashioned "company town" is better buried. And no one—least of all those who seek wider democracy—should wish for its resurrection.

The Poletown Dilemma

In May of 1980 executives of General Motors Corporation were facing a business environment more difficult than any since the Depression.[1] Sitting in their offices on the fourteenth floor of the company's world headquarters in Detroit, they looked out over the city which had been home to General Motors and the American automobile industry since its founding. Both the industry and Detroit were in economic trouble. Battered by recession, changing consumer tastes, and strong competition from foreign automobile manufacturers, sales and profits of the Big Three American auto makers had dropped sharply. This decline resulted in cutbacks in production and widespread layoffs of workers in the industry. Over a quarter of the Big Three's hourly work force—some 211,000 people—were laid off, as well as one-third of the work force in auto-related supplier industries.

To meet the challenge of the new environment, General Motors realized that it would have to make major changes in its operations. It had announced a $40 billion five-year capital investment program, to begin in 1980, which was designed to recondition or replace outmoded production plants. Two of the facilities targeted for replacement, the Cadillac Assembly and the Fisher Body Fleetwood plants, were located in Detroit. The decision now facing the executives was where to build the new plant which would replace these old ones.

The Structure of the Automotive Industry

History

Almost from its beginnings in the early twentieth century, the automotive industry had been highly concentrated. Ford Motor Company, the early industry leader, captured a 50.3% share of the market in 1923 while General Motors held a 20% share. General Motors pulled ahead in the late 1920s and remained the dominant manufacturer from then until the present. Together with Chrysler Corporation, the smallest of the Big Three, General Motors and Ford accounted for 80% of the market by the 1930s. By the 1950s, only American Motors remained as a minor producer to challenge the Big Three's control of the domestic automobile market.

The strategy which gave Ford its early success was an emphasis on standardization, quality, and low prices. However, the market for automobiles shifted in the 1920s toward replacement buyers. While Ford continued to compete on the basis of price, General Motors introduced a strategy of market differentiation, producing a "full line" of automobiles ranging from economy to luxury models. General Motors also recognized the importance of frequent model changeovers to further stimulate replacement purchases. In the new automobile market this strategy proved to be the most successful, and Ford's market share dropped to 25% by 1926.

The annual model changeover strategy raised high barriers to entry into the automobile manufacturing industry. It meant that high sales volume was required to pay for the cost of design and retooling of new models over a much shorter production period than previously. While this development did not produce the high concentration which already existed in the industry, it eliminated the possibility of small-scale new entrants, and presaged the decline of minor independent producers in all but specialty markets.

As an oligopolistic industry, automobile manufacturing was a cautious one. Technological innovation was not emphasized, nor was it encouraged by the dominant American consumer demand for comfort as opposed to economy and quality in the product. Alfred P. Sloan, Jr., former president (1923–1937) and chairperson (1937–1956) of General Motors and the person primarily responsible for the development of the corporation, asserted that it was "not necessary to lead in design or run the risk of untried

[1] Much of the material for this case is drawn from Bryan D. Jones, Lynn W. Bachelor, and Carter Wilson, *The Sustaining Hand* (Lawrence: University Press of Kansas, 1986); and from Joseph Auerbach, "The Poletown Dilemma," *Harvard Business Review*, May–June 1985.

experiment."[2] Fundamental changes in technology, even if they might result in more efficient or safer automobiles, presented risks which a conservative and well-positioned company was not willing to take. Until 1970 the attention of management was focused on the complex task of coordinating the production of the full line of automobiles.

General Motors

In 1980 General Motors was the largest industrial corporation in the United States. Its 1979 annual statement showed worldwide sales of $66.3 billion, of which $62 billion were in its core business of automotive products. (See Exhibit 1.) The company employed over 850,000 people worldwide. Operations were carried out in six "nameplate" divisions, each of which produced its own line of vehicles. Five of these divisions (Chevrolet, Pontiac, Cadillac, Buick, and Oldsmobile) were descendants of independent companies before the formation of General Motors. A sixth division, GMC, made trucks.

General Motors also had a number of divisions which were not dedicated to particular product lines. The Assembly Division, created in the 1960s, controlled automobile assembly in all but the five "home" plants of the car divisions which were operating when General Motors was formed. Other divisions produced automotive parts for the nameplate and the Assembly divisions. Finally, Argonaut Realty was a separate division of the company responsible for acquiring property.

The Changing Environment

Two Major Forces

In the 1970s two external forces came to prominence in the decision making of automotive industry managers. The first was government regulation which came in the wake of consumer activist Ralph Nader's investigations in the 1960s on automobile safety. The initial reaction of General Motors to Nader's investigations was extremely negative. The company hired detectives to probe Nader's past; their harassment of the consumer activist resulted in a successful lawsuit by Nader against General Motors, and a public apology by the General Motors' chairperson. However, the affair damaged the company's credibility, and encouraged the imposition of regulation on the industry.

Minimum safety standards for automobiles were enacted beginning in 1966, including fuel system safety regulations in the early 1970s. In 1968, regulations were also established for automobile exhaust emissions, and in the late 1970s, for fuel economy standards. Although these standards did produce safer, cleaner, and more efficient automobiles, the cost of complying with them added almost $2,000 to the price of an automobile. The most recent set of regulations, scheduled to go into effect in 1983, applied to pollution emitted by production plants. Most of the industry's existing facilities would not meet these standards. General Motors estimated that to bring its assembly plants into compliance with them would cost $3.5 billion.

The second external force was foreign competition. The share of foreign automobile manufacturers in the domestic market had climbed from almost zero in the 1950s to well over 20% in 1979, and was approaching 30% in 1980. When gasoline prices jumped sharply following the Arab oil embargo in 1973, and again after the cut-off of oil from Iran during its revolution in 1979, foreign manufacturers had been quicker than the Big Three to respond to the new consumer demand for smaller, more fuel-efficient automobiles. They had developed a reputation for superior quality, and had exploited cost advantages, which included lower wage rates and more efficient methods of production. One of these methods was the "just-in-time" inventory management process, which yielded savings in working capital requirements by reducing the level of materials in inventory.

Effects on General Motors

The result of these forces was a large drop in the number of cars sold by domestic auto makers, from a record high of about 9.5 million sales in the early 1970s to a projected low of under 6.5 million in 1980, the lowest level since the early 1960s. This drop in sales was accompanied by a dismal profit performance for the automobile manufacturing industry, projected for 1980 to be a return on equity of about *negative* 10%. While the industry historically was much more volatile than manufacturing generally, the magnitude of these losses was unprecedented. For General Motors, profits

[2] Cited in Jones et al., p. 58.

in 1979 were at their lowest level since the recession in 1975, and projections for 1980 indicated a loss for the year of $750 million. It would be only the second loss in the corporation's history and its first since 1921.

The executives of General Motors knew that they had to take drastic action to turn the situation around. The company decided to abandon its long-successful strategy of producing a full line of automobiles, and concentrate instead upon production of the "world car" which would satisfy the new consumer demands. The company planned to design all its new models as front-wheel drive cars, and to down-size all cars, including luxury models. Such large-scale innovation would require far more investment than a typical model changeover. The $40 billion five-year capital spending program represented a significant increase over historical spending levels of $1 billion to $3 billion per year. Replacement and reconditioning of old plants would account for two-thirds of the investment, while the remainder would pay for the new tools and equipment necessary to produce smaller, fuel-efficient, front-wheel drive automobiles.

Factors in Site Selection

There were a variety of technical, economic, and social factors which entered into the selection of a site for the new General Motors assembly plant. Wherever it was built, however, the plant construction and equipment costs would be about $500 million and there would be little difference in operating costs.

The parcel of land for the new plant had to be rectangular and approximately 500 acres in size. The plant itself would take up 3 million square feet to accommodate a state-of-the-art one-story assembly line which would wind through the building. Additional space on the site was required for a marshaling yard for the trains which would carry parts and raw materials directly into the plant. Under the new "just-in-time" inventory process which General Motors planned to use, deliveries would be coordinated with suppliers so that the parts arrived at the time they were needed for the production line. The size of the train yard was dictated by the turning radius of the train cars. Finally, space would be required for employee parking lots, a power plant, treatment and storage areas for storm water, storage of completed cars, and landscaping for the facility.

The new plant had to have access to both a long-haul railroad and freeways, to provide links with suppliers and routes to ship finished cars.

Proximity to suppliers was also important if the adoption of "just-in-time" inventory methods was to be successful. A General Motors executive at another assembly plant location commented that 99% of parts needed for assembly were available within a 300-mile radius (i.e., about a day's transit distance), 93% within 200 miles, and 83% within 100 miles. Yet in implementing "just-in-time" inventory methods, he intended to encourage suppliers to locate even closer to his plant. (See Exhibit 2 for data on General Motors plant locations.)

General Motors recognized the advantages of remaining in the immediate area around Detroit. It could employ the existing labor force from the Cadillac and Fisher Body plants, thereby avoiding the $40 million to $50 million cost to train an inexperienced work force for assembly plant jobs. The new plant would employ 6,150 workers in two shifts. Furthermore, under the collective bargaining agreement negotiated with the United Auto Workers, the company was required to provide supplemental unemployment and relocation benefits for workers idled by plant closings if the replacement plant were built more than 50 miles from the site of the closed facility. Under this contract, the expected cost of relocating workers for the new assembly plant was estimated to be $50 million to $55 million.

However, the benefits of retaining the Detroit work force were unclear. General Motors planned to equip the new assembly plant with the latest technology, including robots. The existing work force would require substantial training to unlearn old methods and to learn new ones. Some industry observers felt that training an inexperienced labor force in the new technologies would be no more difficult or expensive than retraining the existing workers, with the incremental cost estimated at $25 million to $30 million.

General Motors wanted to have the new plant ready for production of the 1983 model year cars which would begin in September of 1982. Therefore, the land for the plant would have to be available for the commencement of construction in the middle of 1981.

Detroit: The Fate of Old Cities in New Times

The Big Picture

Between 1950 and 1980, Detroit lost 35% of its population; between 1970 and 1980 alone, the loss was 21%. This change was not an isolated phenomenon, but a characteristic trend among the aging industrial cities of America. In the same 30-year period, the St. Louis population dropped by 47%; Buffalo, by 38%; and both Pittsburgh and Cleveland, by 37%.[3] In increasing numbers, Americans were forsaking large cities and the older suburbs which surrounded them, because prosperity permitted them to live where they wanted to. In a national poll in February 1985, George Gallup asked the question, "If you could live anywhere you wished, which one of these places would you prefer?" The responses were:[4]

Large city (1 million or more population)	7%
Medium city (100,000 to 1 million)	15
Small city (50,000 to 100,000)	16
Large town (10,000 to 50,000)	13
Small town (2,500 to 10,000)	23
Rural area, on a farm	17
Rural area, not on a farm	8
Don't know	1

More and more, the people living in central cities were the old and the poor, the disadvantaged and the minorities who were unable to move out. Lack of employment for them in the cities kept them in poverty.

The unemployment problem was not the result of a lack of jobs in the United States as a whole: during the decade from 1970 to 1980, total non-agricultural employment grew by nearly 20 million to 90 million. However, manufacturing employment remained almost constant in the range of 18 million to 20 million, unchanged since 1965.[5] The growth was due largely to service employment, both skilled and unskilled. Inner-city residents without skills were unable to find jobs, because the increases in unskilled employment took place in the outlying areas of increasing population.

With the departure of the middle class, the cities were becoming polarized between rich and poor. Downtown development which produced new skyscrapers, convention centers, and pedestrian malls provided jobs mainly for professionals commuting in from distant suburbs, and accommodations and attractions for tourists. Philadelphia illustrated the structural unemployment problem of the old cities:

> When the city of Philadelphia, which is a major manufacturing city, loses a hundred manufacturing jobs, seventy of those are held by municipal residents. When the city gains one hundred office jobs, only thirty are held by central city residents—thus the mismatch function.[6]

The "gentrification" of decayed city neighborhoods, resulting from prosperous young professionals moving in and rehabilitating old housing, a phenomenon praised and denounced in the media, had only a minor effect on the demographics of the cities. The number of "gentry" was far too small either to reverse the decline or to displace the bulk of the residents of poor areas.

The movement of people and industry out of inner cities and into the suburbs and beyond was spurred by government incentives. The federal government's guarantees and subsidies of home mortgages encouraged the purchase of homes in the suburbs. Express highways in metropolitan areas made it easier for people working in the city to live outside of it. Furthermore, the roads fragmented the city, cutting through and destroying neighborhoods. As the most productive people left the cities, the industries followed them. However, industrial relocation was also encouraged by tax policies such as accelerated depreciation schedules which made construction of new facilities economically more attractive than rehabilitation of old ones. State governments and local governments outside central cities also encouraged the migration, the former by locating facilities in and building roads through less-developed areas, and the latter by competing with each other in offering generous tax incentives and subsidies for new business development.

[3] George Sternlieb, *Patterns of Development* (New Brunswick, NJ: Center for Urban Policy Research, 1986), p. 110.

[4] John Herbers, *The New Heartland* (New York: Times Books, 1986), p. 188.

[5] Sternlieb, p. 102.

[6] Sternlieb, p. 91.

Businesses also preferred exurban locations for new facilities because they allowed room for landscaping and other amenities which attracted employees. In addition, they deserted central industrial areas in favor of less-developed states with lower levels of unionization, often not for lower wage rates, but for greater flexibility in work rules and job classifications.[7]

Central cities faced a grim future. Declining population meant declining tax base, at a time when infrastructure repairs and services for the poor required increasing amounts of revenue. At the same time, the movement of population to the less-developed areas shifted political power. The people living in exurban areas, isolated from the poor and the disadvantaged, believed in independence and self-help and distrusted government intervention.

Demographics

Detroit's history paralleled the experience of many old industrial cities. During the late 19th and early 20th century, Detroit was composed of separate and autonomous ethnic communities. By 1920, however, the separate hierarchies and opportunities for advancement of these communities had largely given way to a single structure for economic opportunity. In the early 1940s, Detroit's 100,000 black residents were 7.6% of the population; by 1960, blacks made up 29% of the city. Following the race riots in the summer of 1967, white migration to the suburbs increased, and the black population grew to 44% of the 1,514,000 city residents in 1970, and to 63% of 1,192,000 by 1980.

Local Economy

Economically, Detroit was suffering badly. The survey of employers taken in 1972 had indicated that firms representing 28% of Detroit area employment thought it was probable that they would leave the area within the next five years. Shift reductions and plant closings by auto makers had eliminated thousands of jobs. The closing of General Motors' Cadillac and Fisher Body Fleetwood assembly plants would add another 5,000 workers to the ranks of the unemployed, on top of the 5,000 who had already been laid off from the two plants because of production cuts.

[7] Herbers, p. 147.

City Finances

Financially, Detroit's city government was in a deteriorating position. (See Exhibit 3.) Its bonded debt had increased in recent years to nearly a billion dollars. In four out of the last five years the city's general fund expenses exceeded revenues. The tax burden was high: property taxes were over 7.5% of state-equalized value (i.e., approximately half of market value), and the city also levied a 2% income tax on residents and ½% on nonresident workers. (By contrast, property taxes in Orion Township, Michigan, where General Motors was building another new assembly plant, were only a little over 5% of state-equalized value, and there was no township income tax.)

Politics

In 1980 Coleman A. Young was the mayor of Detroit. His political roots went back to the United Auto Workers union, where he was regarded as an articulate and politically able radical. The racial discrimination which he felt at that time made him a passionate fighter for justice and equal rights for black people. From 1964 to 1973 he was a senator in the Michigan Senate, and in 1973 was elected by a narrow margin as mayor of Detroit. His first term was controversial as he implemented an affirmative action program in the city's bureaucracy and struggled with the municipal unions, especially the police union, which had opposed his election. However, in 1977 Young was reelected by a large margin, and by 1980 his approval rating in Detroit stood at 93% among the black population and 47% among the white, or 72% overall.

Young was the strongest mayor in the history of Detroit. His strength came not only from his firm support in the black community, but also from constitutional change. At the time of Young's election in 1973 a change in the city's charter expanded the powers of the mayor in financial affairs and in appointments, at the expense of the city council. Young used his strength to promote three basic goals: increasing opportunities for blacks in Detroit's bureaucracies, forming coalitions with the private sector elites of Detroit to promote economic development, and working with state and federal officials to increase intergovernmental funds for the city.

In 1980 Young had the resources of a professional city bureaucracy skilled in obtaining funds from state and federal government programs to support city services and local economic development. As an early supporter of President Jimmy Carter he had powerful allies in the administration in Washington, D.C. His director of economic development, Emmett Moten, had been an aide to Moon Landrieu, the former mayor of New Orleans who was now secretary of the Department of Housing and Urban Development. Thus, Young had the political power, the skills, and the connections to make a large-scale industrial redevelopment project in Detroit successful.

Young had made his position on Detroit plant closings and relocations clear to General Motors' chairperson Thomas A. Murphy. In September of 1979, well before the company announced plans to close its Detroit Cadillac and Fleetwood plants, the mayor had attended a meeting in Murphy's office in which Murphy announced that General Motors was relocating an assembly line from one of its Detroit plants. The announcement was in part a formality to fulfill a promise that Detroit would have a chance to bid on the next company facility. Young reacted angrily, saying:

> You knew we couldn't do that. When you ask us to do something, and you give us 24 hours, you know up front that we can't produce. When will the day be when you come to us and say, "Here are our plans; let's sit down and plan together"?[8]

Murphy, on the defensive, promised to consider Detroit seriously for the next plant.

The Search for Sites

General Motors began its site selection process in the summer of 1979. The search was carried out by a task force administered by Argonaut Realty and included representatives from real estate, plant engineering, industry-government relations, labor relations, personnel, public affairs, the corporate staff, and the Assembly Division. The focus of the search was on the area within 50 miles of Detroit, although the company knew of an out-of-state location in another part of the Midwest which met its criteria. Sites within Detroit, however, were initially rejected because of lack of rail access, or because the number of homes and businesses that had to be removed would delay the project beyond the company's construction deadlines. After nine months of searching the task force was also unable to find any sites outside of Detroit but within 50 miles of the city which met General Motors' conditions.

In April of 1980, making good on his promise to Young in September of 1979, Murphy formally invited Detroit to join with the company in an effort to locate a site within the city. Nine locations were reviewed, and each one had problems. (See Exhibit 4.) Only the Central Industrial Park site (A) met all of General Motors' requirements for site characteristics; yet it was heavily settled and would require a major residential and commercial relocation effort before a plant could be built there.

Eminent Domain

Under their power of eminent domain, governments have the right to demand that private owners sell their property to them, in return for just compensation, if the property is needed for a public purpose. A typical use of this power by governments is to acquire land for constructing new roads which would benefit the entire community; it has also been used for urban renewal projects. However, property owners could delay the acquisition through court challenges over the adequacy of compensation. Thus, even if Detroit were to exercise eminent domain to acquire the land in the Central Industrial Park site for General Motors' new assembly plant, a small number of property owners could file lawsuits against the city and effectively kill the project by delaying it beyond the company's deadlines.

Such delays had hindered urban renewal projects in the past, and in response to the problem the Michigan State Legislature had adopted Public Act 87 of 1980 in April of 1980, a statute which came to be known as the "quick take law." Under P.A. 87, cities were permitted to take title to property by eminent domain before agreeing with owners on a purchase price. Thus, court challenges over compensation for the taking of the property could not delay the start of a project. It was Emmett Moten who realized that the passage of the quick take law made the Central Industrial Park site feasible within General Motors' timetable for the construction of a new assembly plant.

[8] Cited in Jones et al., p. 73.

Profile of Central Industrial Park Site

Of all potential sites in Detroit which were studied, the Central Industrial Park site involved the largest amount of relocation. Part of the site lay within Hamtramck, an independent city completely surrounded by Detroit. Most of the Hamtramck section of the site was occupied by the old Dodge main assembly plant, which Chrysler had closed in January of 1980, eliminating 3,000 jobs. Acquisition of this property was not expected to be difficult, as Chrysler was experiencing severe financial problems and would be eager to sell. In addition, the people and government of Hamtramck strongly supported the construction of a new plant as a source of jobs for the community.

However, the Detroit portion of the site included about one-third of the Detroit district of Poletown. Nearly 3,500 people lived in this area in about 1,176 homes; the population was half black and half white, with the whites mostly of Polish descent. The Poles were all older, many of them retired or nearly so; most had been in the community for 20 to 50 years and had strong ties to it; some of them had never been outside of Poletown in their lives. A deterioration of ethnic identity in the Polish community was also a likely result of relocating the community. The commitment of these people to their neighborhood was evident in statements such as:

> The church we belong to, the bingo, my friends, everything we know is in that neighborhood. . . . I own that home free and clear, and they come along and tell you you've got to get out. I'm here to fight![9]

Sixteen churches served as focal points for the community, including eleven Protestant congregations with predominantly black membership and three Roman Catholic churches to which the Poles belonged. Two of these three churches, Immaculate Conception and St. John's, were within the project area.

Economically, the area was poor, but not destitute: 25% of Poletown families earned more than $15,000 per year. Housing was mostly detached single and two-family homes. Although in economic decline, Poletown was still a community. Abandoned property, which constituted about one-third of each block, was situated next to well-maintained homes. The area contained 150 businesses, including 28 manufacturing firms. In addition, the Poletown Area Revitalization Task Force (PARTF), a group founded in 1977 and run by local community activists, was attempting to encourage redevelopment in Poletown and had received funding grants from a number of sources, including the city of Detroit.

Opposition to the Poletown site was coordinated by the Poletown Neighborhood Council (PNC). This group was formed after the PARTF had disbanded upon announcement of plans to build a General Motors plant in Poletown, and was led by former members of the PARTF. Thomas Olechowski, a resident of Poletown and an administrative aide to a Detroit state senator, served as president; Richard Hodas, a local businessperson and community activist, was vice president. The PNC's headquarters were in the Immaculate Conception church, and many parishioners, as well as former members of the PARTF, joined the group.

In early communications with the Detroit city government and with General Motors, the PNC emphasized its willingness to negotiate and to assist in implementing the project. In return for its cooperation, however, it required that the other parties (1) recognize the PNC's role in the planning of the project, (2) treat Poletown as a single entity, including both the project and nonproject areas, (3) develop specific revitalization programs for the nonproject part of Poletown, and (4) fully disclose all facts, plans, and meetings pertaining to the project, to demonstrate the necessity to relocate several thousands of citizens from their homes.

The PNC's great weaknesses were, first, that it was supported by no more than half of the people living in the project area, primarily the Poles who had lived there for many years. Many of the other residents were relatively recent arrivals and had no particular stake in Poletown. In fact, they would welcome a chance to relocate from an area they saw as deteriorating, in return for a generous settlement payment. Second, the PNC was not supported by the larger Polish community, particularly in the predominantly Polish Hamtramck, because of their own interest in the jobs created by a new assembly plant.

[9] Cited in Jones et al., p. 145.

Acquisition Costs

The expense of acquiring and preparing the Central Industrial Park site for construction of the new plant was estimated at over $200 million. This figure included payment of $62 million to area residents for their property, $28 million for relocating residents to new homes, $35 million for demolition, and $88 million for site preparation (improvements to roads and railways, relocation of public facilities, and professional services).[10]

In sharp contrast, alternative sites in neighboring midwest states would cost $5 to 7 million for the unimproved land, plus $60 million to $80 million for site preparation. Several states were eager to attract light industry and were prepared to help General Motors secure a site. The resulting ease and speed appealed to at least several of the members of the company's site selection task force.

Labor Relations[11]

In the United States, General Motors' hourly labor force belonged to the United Auto Workers union. General Motors had fought the union's right to represent workers in its early years, and had only reluctantly agreed to negotiate with it following a sit-down strike in the middle 1930s. However, it had gradually accepted additions to the issues discussed during contract negotiations, including wages based on the corporation's "ability to pay" (1946), cost of living escalation clauses in wage contracts (1948), employee benefits (1950), and unemployment benefits (1955).

In the early 1970s, faced with growing worker dissatisfaction resulting in higher rates of absenteeism, grievances, and in some extreme cases wildcat strikes and sabotage on the assembly line, General Motors in cooperation with the UAW instituted a "Quality of Work Life" (QWL) program. The goal of the program was to increase job satisfaction by involving workers in decisions affecting their working conditions. The company hoped that the program would lead to increased productivity and quality, both necessary to compete against the high-quality and low-cost Japanese imports. "Conservatives" in both General Motors and the union distrusted the new program because it undermined management authority and softened the adversarial relationship between the company and the union. However, the leadership of both General Motors and the UAW recognized the need for cooperation to reduce costs, improve quality, and stop the soaring levels of imported cars.

In an agreement signed in 1979, General Motors in effect committed itself to automatic union recognition at all newly opened plants. The UAW no longer needed to fear the replacement of union by nonunion jobs in a relocation. However, any loss of jobs for workers in Detroit was of concern to the UAW, for the union membership wanted protection for their existing jobs. Therefore, the national union strongly supported the construction of a plant at the Central Industrial Park site, even though it meant the demolition of the neighborhood. Only the leader of a radical faction of a UAW local union whose headquarters were in the project area expressed support for the PNC.

General Motors Corporate Culture

Historically, the corporate culture of General Motors had enshrined the values of free enterprise and emphasized returns to shareholders as a primary measure of success. In his autobiography Alfred Sloan clearly expressed these values:[12]

> . . . General Motors could hardly be imagined to exist anywhere but in this country, with its very active and enterprising people; its resources, including its science and technology and its business and industrial know-how; its vast spaces, roads, and rich markets; its characteristics of change, mobility, and mass production; its great industrial expansion in this century, and its system of freedom in general and free competitive enterprise in particular. . . . If in turn we have contributed to the style of the United States as expressed in the automobile, this has been by interaction. . . .

[10] Detroit Community and Economic Development Department, *Final Environmental Impact Statement, Central Industrial Park,* December 1980, p. V-87.

[11] Much of the material in this section is taken from the Harvard Business School cases, "Contract and Consensus at General Motors, 1900–1984" (376 · 170, rev. 11/87); and "General Motors and the United Auto Workers" (481 ·142).

[12] Alfred P. Sloan, Jr., *My Years with General Motors* (New York: Doubleday, 1964), pp. xxi, xxiv, 49, 199, and 213.

> If I have expressed or implied in this book a so-called ideology, it is, I suppose, that I believe in competition as an article of faith, a means of progress, and a way of life. . . . We set out to produce not for the chosen few but for the whole consumer public on the assumption of a continuously rising standard of living. . . .
>
> . . . It is as I see it the strategic aim of a business to earn a return on capital, and if in any particular case the return in the long run is not satisfactory, the deficiency should be corrected or the activity abandoned for a more favorable one. . . .
>
> The measure of the worth of a business enterprise as a *business* . . . is not merely growth in sales or assets but return on the shareholders' investment, since it is their capital that is being risked and it is in their interests first of all that the corporation is supposed to be run in the private-enterprise scheme of things. . . .

Current Situation

The task force felt pressure to reach a decision soon. Mayor Young, suddenly aware of the possible loss of jobs, was pressing Murphy for a commitment to stay in Detroit; the neighborhood was escalating its resistance; and the Assembly Division constantly reminded the task force that a site, fully prepared for construction, was needed by mid-1981. Time was running out.

EXHIBIT 1 General Motors Corporation: Financial History
(All references to shares are to common stock only.)

Source: Moody's Industrial Manual.

	1970	1971	1972	1973	1974	1975	1976	1977	1978	1979
Sales (millions)	$18,752	$28,264	$30,435	$35,798	$31,550	$35,725	$47,181	$54,961	$63,221	$66,311
Net income (millions)	609	1,936	2,163	2,398	950	1,253	2,903	3,338	3,508	2,893
Assets (millions)	14,174	18,242	18,273	20,297	19,874	21,557	24,442	26,658	30,598	32,216
Stockholders' equity (millions)	9,854	10,805	11,683	12,567	12,531	13,082	14,385	15,767	17,570	19,179
Return on assets (%)	4%	11%	12%	12%	5%	6%	12%	13%	11%	9%
Return on stockholders' equity (%)	6	18	19	19	8	10	20	21	20	15
Earnings per share	$2.09	$6.72	$7.51	$8.34	$3.27	$4.32	$10.08	$11.62	$12.24	$10.04
Dividends per share	3.40	3.40	4.45	5.25	3.40	2.40	5.55	6.80	6.00	5.30
Share price: high	81⅜	91⅛	84¾	84⅝	55½	59⅛	78⅞	78½	66⅞	65⅞
low	59½	73⅜	71¼	44⅞	28⅞	31¼	57¾	61⅛	53¾	49⅜
Price/earnings: high	39	14	11	10	17	14	8	7	5	7
low	28	11	9	5	9	7	6	5	4	5
Times charges earned:										
Before income taxes	16	64	57	44	11	9	20	23	20	15
After income taxes	13	36	30	24	7	5	11	13	11	9
Senior debt rating	Aaa	Aaa	Aaa	Aaa	Aaa	Aaa	Aaa	Aaa	Aaa	Aaa

EXHIBIT 2 General Motors Corporation: U.S. Car and Truck/Body and Assembly Groups Plant Locations in 1979

Source: Moody's Industrial Manual.

	Fisher Body Division	Chevrolet Motor	GM Assembly	Guide	Buick Motor	Cadillac Motor Car	GMC Truck and Coach	Oldsmobile	Pontiac Motor	Total
Detroit	4	3				1				8
Other Michigan	10	12	1		1		1	1	1	27
Other East North Central	9	6	3	1	—	—	—	—	—	19
East North Central	23	21	4	1	1	1	1	1	1	54
Middle Atlantic	3	4	2							9
South Atlantic			4							4
West South Central			2	1						3
West North Central			3							3
Pacific			3							3
New England	—	—	1	—	—	—	—	—	—	1
Total	26	25	19	2	1	1	1	1	1	77

EXHIBIT 3 Detroit: Financial Statistics

Source: Moody's Municipal and Government Manual.

	1970	1971	1972	1973	1974	1975	1976	1977	1978	1979
Property tax rates per $1,000 of assessed value	$54.113	$57.060	$57.712	$53.000	$65.370	$64.518	$65.202	$71.833	$74.813	$75.079
General fund (millions):										
Revenues	368.4	391.0	456.2	555.9	542.0	527.4	524.3	608.5	657.9	685.1
Expenses	384.9	405.1	447.6	496.1	533.7	563.0	547.0	557.0	682.2	700.6
Excess (deficit)	(16.5)	(14.1)	8.6	59.8	8.3	(35.6)	(22.7)	51.5	(24.4)	(15.5)
Bond rating (general obligations)	Baa	Baa	Baa	Baa	Baa	Baa	Baa	Baa	Baa	Baa

Notes: Assessed value is based on state-equalized value, which is equal to one-half of fair value. Property tax rates include taxes payable to local government units in addition to Detroit (e.g., school districts, county government).

Income taxes of 2% and ½% are levied on the income of residents and nonresident workers, respectively.

Numbers may not total due to rounding.

EXHIBIT 4 Site Comparison

Source: City of Detroit Community and Economic Development Department, *Final Environmental Impact Statement, Central Industrial Park Project.*

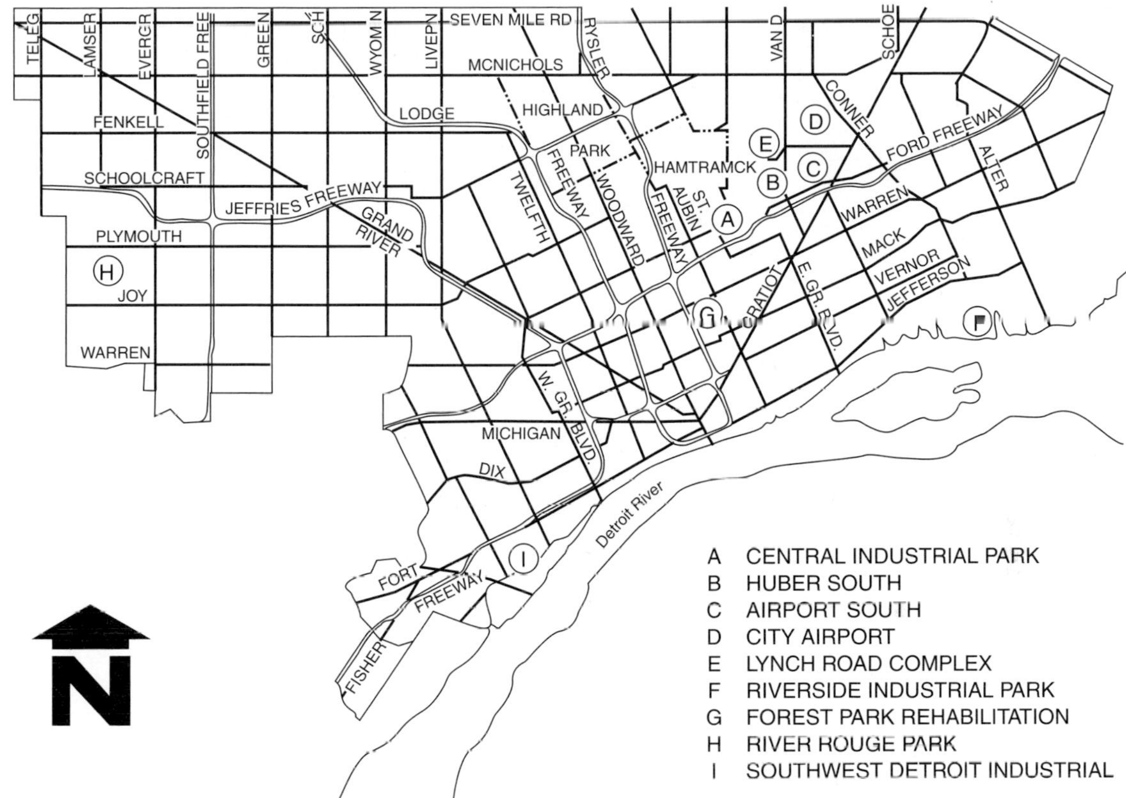

EXHIBIT 4 Site Comparison—Continued

Source: City of Detroit Community and Economic Development Department. *Final Environmental Impact Statement, Central Industrial Park Project.*

Basic Site Selection Considerations	(A) Dodge Main	(B) Huber South	(C) Airport South	(D) Airport	(E) Lynch Road	(F) Riverside Industrial	(G) Forest Park	(H) Rouge Park	(I) Southwest
Size (450–500) acres)	X*	X	X	X	X	0†	0	X	0
Configuration (¾ × 1 mile)	X	X	X	X	X	0	0	X	0
Railroad access‡	X	0	0	0	X	0	0	X	X
Freeway access	X	X	X	0	0	0	X	0	X
Readily available	X	0	0	X	0	X	0	0	0
Other related deficiencies	Relocation of numerous residential, commercial, and industrial structures.	Relocation of many commercial and residential structures and recreational services.	Relocation of numerous residential and commercial structures. Conflict with airport.	Elimination of active viable airport.	Relocation of active industrial facilities.	Riverfront land not appropriate. Recreation land displaced.	Urban renewal land for residential.	Removal of major parkland. Flood plain area.	Historical Fort Wayne impacted. School and railroad relocated.

* X—meets basic site selection criterion.

† 0—does not meet basic site selection criterion.

‡ Railroad must provide access to other GM Michigan plants that would be providing components and parts for the proposed assembly facility with a minimum time delay.

Dayton Hudson Corporation: *Conscience and Control (A)*

To those who assert that business should operate only in its own best interests, I contend that corporate social responsibility is in our best interest. It is in the interest of our survival.

—Bruce B. Dayton
Chairman, Executive Committee
Dayton Hudson Corporation
May 20, 1976

Just before lunch, the legal team reentered the meeting to share what they had been discussing. They said they had a possible "showstopper," an alternative that might permit the company to remain independent in its current form. Kenneth A. Macke, 48, CEO of the Minneapolis-based Dayton Hudson Corporation (DHC), listened intently.

Only a short time before, Macke had made it clear that he was dissatisfied with the strategies that had been discussed during the morning meeting. He had scheduled the meeting for Thursday, June 11, 1987, and opened it as a general might convene a council of war. With him were some of the senior managers of the company and a number of outside advisers, assembled to formulate a strategy for defending the company against an emerging hostile takeover threat. These advisers included representatives of Goldman Sachs (DHC's investment bankers), Kekst and Co., and the New York law firm of Wachtell, Lipton, Rosen, and Katz. One discussion focused on the financial options, while in another room DHC's legal staff and their advisers discussed legal defenses. The debate in each group ranged widely, and at one point or another, in the words of one participant, "every imaginable option" was considered.

To the financial team it was clear that every alternative entailed fighting the battle for the company's future in New York. They considered attempts to block the raider's access to needed financial resources as well as various plans to restructure the company and make it unattractive to the raider. Every participant was aware of the need for quick and decisive action.

Eight days earlier, on Wednesday, June 3, 1987, DHC's stock had increased in value by nearly $3 per share in unusually heavy trading, to close at about $50.62 (see Exhibits 1, 2). To the casual observer, this increase was puzzling, for the company had, only a few months earlier, reported its first earnings decline in sixteen years (see Exhibit 3). Since then, the stock had traded between about $42 and $45, and volume had been relatively low. Furthermore, nothing obvious had happened to account for the sudden increase in price and volume.

To the professional observer, however, the change was not so surprising. Once a favorite of Wall Street because of its consistently strong earnings, the company had fallen out of favor. In the opinion of many observers, its earnings decline was caused by the poor performance of one of its four operating companies. Furthermore, management had not kept investors and analysts well-informed about efforts to correct the problems. As a result, DHC's stock traded at a price that some analysts felt undervalued the company.

Macke was confident that DHC would rebound and post strong earnings growth within a year or two. In late May and early June,

Assistant professor Robert G. Kennedy, University of St. Thomas (St. Paul, MN), prepared this case under the supervision of Kenneth E. Goodpaster, Koch Professor of Business Ethics at the University of St. Thomas and Visiting Professor, Harvard Business School, as the basis for class discussion rather than to illustrate either effective or ineffective handling of an administrative situation. Assistant professor Randel S. Carlock, also of the University of St. Thomas, contributed to the research and editing process.

however, he watched his company's stock with growing concern. SEC regulations specified that anyone acquiring 5% or more of a company's stock must file a disclosure. No such disclosure had been filed. However, alerted by the unusual market activity, and by rumors circulating on Wall Street, Macke and his management team feared that the company might become the target of a hostile takeover attempt. By June 3 this appeared highly likely, and shortly afterward, in response to the probable threat, Macke called together a task force of senior managers that had been formed some years earlier to deal with such a situation. Included in this group were Boake Sells (president and COO), Willard Schull (CFO), James Hale (senior vice president and general counsel), Peter Hutchinson (vice president for external affairs and chairman of the Dayton Hudson Foundation), and Ann Barkelew (vice president for corporate public relations).

With the help of their Wall Street advisers the team was able to identify the likely raider as the Dart Group Corporation, a Maryland-based discounter with a recent history of unsuccessful takeover attempts. Though the Dart Group had not made a concrete proposal, nor even publicly acknowledged its interest in the company, Macke and his team were aware that they needed to act quickly if they were to protect the company from being put in play.* On Wednesday, June 10, DHC's stock was the second most heavily traded on the New York Stock Exchange. Since June 3 it had risen in value by over $4.50.

The Dayton Hudson Corporation

The Dayton Hudson Corporation described itself as "a growth company focusing exclusively on retailing." Headquartered in Minneapolis, the company operated 475 stores in 34 states at the end of 1986, employing some 120,000 people nationwide (full-time and part-time). In that year it had pretax earnings of $494.2 million on sales of $9,259.1 million.

In 1902 George Draper Dayton, a Minneapolis banker and real estate developer, entered into a partnership to operate a dry goods store in a building he owned in the downtown area of the city. The Dayton Company went on to become the most prominent retailer in Minnesota, and the Dayton family among the most important of the state's citizens. Unlike most of the state's other major employers, DHC is incorporated under Minnesota law. In 1987, DHC employed some 34,000 Minnesotans, about 20,000 of whom worked for the company part-time. That year DHC's payroll for Minnesota employees was nearly $278 million.

Through a combination of mergers, acquisitions, and retailing innovations, the company grew dramatically in the 1950s and 1960s. At one time it had interests in real estate (development and management of shopping centers) and specialty retail outlets (jewelry, books, and consumer electronics) as well as large department stores. The company was taken public in 1967, and in 1969 it merged with the J. L. Hudson Company of Detroit to form the Dayton Hudson Corporation (see Exhibit 4).

In 1962, DHC opened its first three Target stores, offering name brand merchandise at discount prices. By 1975 the Target division was DHC's largest revenue producer. In 1978 DHC acquired Mervyn's, a West Coast retailer, to become the seventh largest nonfood retailer in the United States. In 1984, the University of Southern California's School of Business Administration named DHC the best managed company in America and awarded it the Vanguard Corporation Award for its uncompromising ethical standards and unusual dynamism.

By 1987 DHC had disposed of its real estate and most of its small format, specialty retail businesses to focus exclusively on what management concluded to be the company's greatest strength: operating large retail stores.

Macke joined DHC as a merchandise trainee with Dayton's in 1961, immediately after his graduation from Drake University (Iowa). Rising through the ranks, he became president and CEO of the Target division in 1976, and chairman the following year. Under his leadership, Target grew in four years from 49 stores to 137 stores, and more than doubled its operating profit to become the top profitmaker for DHC. In 1981 Macke was

* When a company's stockholder base becomes destabilized, i.e., when a large proportion of the stock is in the hands of short-term holders (arbitrageurs, for example), the company's stock is said to be "in play." Up to this point, strictly speaking, DHC's efforts were focused on preventing the stock from being put in play.

named president of DHC. He became CEO in 1983, and chairman of the board in 1984.

Stephen Watson, chairman and CEO of the Dayton Hudson Department Store Company (a division of DHC), described Macke as a "needler," someone who "constantly needles you about areas of the business that need improvement." On the other hand, in situations where important decisions needed to be made, he was a good listener. His practice was to give a full hearing to his subordinates and advisers, and then to choose what he saw to be the best course of action. To some, Macke's management style bordered on the abrasive, but others admired his decisiveness and his commitment to DHC.

Operating Structures and Policies

DHC was composed of four operating companies and a corporate headquarters. This structure reflected DHC's fundamental management philosophy which favored decentralization. The operating companies were:

> Target: an upscale discount store chain. In 1986 Target produced 47% of DHC's revenues and 47.4% of pretax profits, with earnings of $311 million on sales of $4,355 million.
>
> Mervyn's: a highly promotional, popularly priced, value-oriented department store company. In 1986 Mervyn's produced 31% of DHC's revenues and 24.4% of pretax profits, with earnings of $160 million on sales of $2,862 million.
>
> Dayton Hudson Department Store Company (DHDSC): the largest traditional department store operation in the United States. In 1986 DHDSC produced 17% of DHC's revenues and 25.2% of pretax profits, with earnings of $166 million on sales of $1,566 million.
>
> Lechmere's: a hard goods retail store company. In 1986 Lechmere's produced 5% of DHC's revenues and 3% of pretax profits, with earnings of $19.5 million on sales of $476 million.

The operating companies made autonomous decisions about merchandising and buying, and had responsibility for profits and return on investment. They were made accountable to corporate headquarters through an annual planning cycle, considered to be crucial to DHC's management process. This annual planning cycle included a strategy and human resources review, an agreement on capital allocation, the setting of financial goals, and a performance appraisal. However, despite the apparent autonomy granted to the operating companies, Macke continued to pay close attention to details and "needle" his executives in an effort to improve performance.

Financial Policies

DHC's stated financial goal was to provide its shareholders with a superior return on their investment while maintaining a conservative financial position. More particularly, the company preferred to own assets where possible, to meet external needs with long-term debt, and to maintain a maximum debt ratio of 45% (including capital and operating leases). The majority of the company's growth was financed through internally generated funds.

In its 1986 Annual Report, DHC stated that its performance objectives were to "earn an after-tax return on beginning shareholders' equity (ROE) of 18%," to "sustain an annual growth in earnings per share (EPS) of 15%," and to "maintain a strong rating of [its] senior debt." The report also noted that "the incentive compensation of corporate management and the management of each operating company is based on return on investment, as well as growth in earnings."

These goals, however, were not extrapolated from past performance. The ROE had averaged 15.3% in the period 1975–86, and the earnings per share growth had only been above 15% five times in those twelve years (see Exhibits 5, 6).

Though DHC remained a profitable company, 1986 was a disappointing year. Revenues increased by 12% and passed the $9 billion mark, but net earnings per share dropped by 9% (see Exhibit 7). The principal reason appears to have been difficulty with the Mervyn's division, where operating profits fell by more than 34%. DHC's Annual Report for 1986 acknowledged a problem with Mervyn's and attributed the dramatic decline in profits to an organizational restructuring and to a need to reduce margins in order to remain competitive.

More specifically, Mervyn's had expanded significantly in Texas, adding buying and sales offices there in 1984 which duplicated some services performed at its California headquarters. The oil price collapse made these functions redundant and the company was forced to close that office and reorganize at considerable expense. These difficulties distracted management attention and marketing mistakes were made. Coupled with increased competition, these factors, and the efforts made to correct for them, were responsible for poor performance in 1986.

This was the second year of poor performance for Mervyn's (in 1985 operating profits had increased by only 9.7%), a sharp contrast to the previous two years, when profits had increased by 21% each year. Since the decline began when Macke became chairman, some observers raised questions about his ability to manage the corporation.

Customer Service

DHC was strongly customer-oriented. The stated merchandising objective of each of the operating companies was to fulfill the value expectations of customers more effectively than the competition. They consciously aimed to do this by providing superior value in five categories: assortment, quality, fashion, convenience and pricing. One concrete sign of this orientation was the longstanding corporate policy of accepting the return of merchandise for a full refund, no questions asked. Stories abounded, especially in Minnesota, about the lengths to which the company was willing to go to honor this policy. One customer told a story about an experience she had had in the china department.

> Not long ago a woman went to Dayton Hudson's flagship department store in Minneapolis to purchase a wedding gift in the china department. Before she could make her purchase she was annoyed to have to wait for a young woman who apparently wished to return some china. Her annoyance turned to astonishment when she heard the young woman's story. It seems that for some years the young woman's mother had been purchasing place settings and other pieces of a particular pattern and saving them for her daughter's wedding. Quite a number of pieces had been accumulated, and now the daughter was indeed to be married. However, she did not like the pattern and decided to return the entire collection to Dayton's for a refund. It turned out that the pattern had been discontinued by the manufacturer. Nevertheless, despite some understandable initial reluctance on the part of the clerk, the policy prevailed and the young woman received her refund.

What was remarkable was that people in the Twin Cities did *not* seem to find such stories unusual.

Corporate Community Involvement

In 1946 the Dayton Company became the first major American corporation to initiate a policy by which it donated 5% of its federal taxable income to nonprofit organizations. (It was a charter member of Minnesota's "5% Club," an organization founded in 1976 whose membership consisted of corporations that donated 5% of their annual taxable income.) This policy had continued without interruption, and in 1987 DHC's contributions totaled nearly $20 million (principally to arts and social action organizations). These contributions were distributed throughout the states in which DHC did business. The four states which generated the largest revenues for the company were California, Minnesota, Texas, and Michigan, but contributions were not proportioned to revenues (see Exhibit 8).

Eighty percent of DHC's contributions were made in two areas: the arts and social action,* each receiving roughly equal amounts (see Exhibit 9). The remaining community giving funds were contributed to other programs and projects that addressed responsiveness to special community needs and opportunities; and innovative partnerships with other community leaders. The company was Minnesota's largest private donor and a mainstay of many of the arts organizations in the Twin Cities. In the past, it had helped fund such activities as job creation programs, neighborhood renovations, and child care and chemical abuse programs.

Observers considered DHC's community involvement program to be distinctive in several ways. Among these was the company's commitment to maintain a professional staff, "held to standards as rigorous as any profit center within the corporation, with specific goals, objectives, and performance review." Another was the decision to commit 6% of their giving budget to emerging issues in social action and the arts. As Peter Hutchinson, chairman of the Dayton

* A very wide variety of social action projects were funded, including literacy programs, job skills training programs, development programs for minority businesses, and neighborhood renewal programs.

Hudson Foundation, commented, "Armed with an integrated view of needs and opportunities, we must . . . adapt our programs to changing circumstances. . . . Regardless of the means, our goals must be to bring programs and constituents together in a common vision and commitment for the future."

DHC's concern for social responsibility extended into other aspects of its business as well. In 1978, for example, Kenneth Dayton (then chairman and CEO of the company) was one of the principal organizers of the Minnesota Project on Corporate Responsibility. This organization sponsored seminars and other programs aimed at encouraging and strengthening a sense of social responsiveness in Minnesota corporations. James Shannon, then executive director of the General Mills Foundation, commented in a guest editorial in the *Minneapolis Star Tribune,* "In a community nationally known for its corporate support of the arts, social services, and education, the Dayton Hudson Corp. is the flagship for dozens of other publicly and privately held corporations committed to the proposition that a successful company has an obligation to be a good corporate citizen."

DHC's relations with the public were not always smooth, however. There were times when its concern for communities was questioned. In 1983, for example, Hudson's flagship store in downtown Detroit was closed. From DHC's perspective the store had become old and inefficient, and the business climate in downtown Detroit unsupportive. Mayor Coleman Young's view was different. As he told the *Detroit Free Press,* "I don't think Hudson's demonstrated any sense of responsibility or citizenship after growing in this city and off this city for almost 100 years."

The following year, 1984, Dayton's and Hudson's operations were consolidated into the Dayton Hudson Department Store Company, with a single headquarters in Minneapolis. Once again, Detroit objected, since the move resulted in the loss of about 1,000 jobs for the city, many of them well-paid management positions. Ann Barkelew, DHC's vice president for public relations, commented in the *Minneapolis Star Tribune,* "Our decision to bring the headquarters [to Minneapolis] was a business decision. The whole purpose in combining the companies was to do things better."

The Dart Group Corporation

The Dart Group Corporation's 1987 Annual Report (year ending January 31, 1987) was spartan and no-nonsense. Its only two photographs, which appeared on the first page, were of Herbert Haft, founder and chairman, and Robert Haft, president and Herbert's older son. There were no photographs of the discount retail outlets they operated or of satisfied customers, nor did other members of management or the board of directors appear. Instead, attention was focused exclusively on information about Dart's operations and finances. And not without reason, for Dart's net income more than tripled in fiscal 1987 (see Exhibit 10).

According to the Annual Report, Dart operated retail discount auto parts stores through the Trak Auto Corporation, operated retail discount bookstores through the Crown Books Corporation, and operated a financial business which dealt in bankers' acceptances. The present company was a successor to Dart Drug, a Washington, D.C., retail drugstore chain founded by Herbert Haft. Haft built a chain of stores from one store he opened in 1954 by selling most of his merchandise at discount prices. At the time the minimum price for many brand-name products was set by the manufacturer, and Haft was often in violation of fair trade laws in selling at a discount. While the practice provoked a number of supplier suits, it also attracted thousands of customers. As the suburbs of Washington grew, Dart Drug grew with them. In the 1970s, Dart pioneered the concept of a "super" drugstore that sold not only the traditional drugs and cosmetics, but beer, lawn furniture, lumber, auto parts, and almost anything else the Hafts could find.

While Robert Haft was a student at the Harvard Business School in the mid-1970s, he wrote a paper exploring the idea of selling books through discount retail outlets. By some accounts, he was motivated to set the idea in motion after listening to a Dayton Hudson executive who spoke at Harvard. Dayton Hudson operated B. Dalton Booksellers at the time and the executive claimed that a discount book chain could not be successful. Robert earned an MBA in 1977 and later established Crown Books, which sold both hardcover and paperback books at a discount. By 1986 Crown Books operated about 200 stores nationally, with 1986 earnings of $5.5 million on revenues of $154 million.

In 1984, Dart's drugstore division was sold to its employees. In the three years prior to the sale the Hafts boosted profitability by sharply cutting costs. They accomplished this in part by dramatic reductions in inventory (e.g., stocking far fewer sizes and varieties of merchandise), and customer services (e.g., declining to give cash refunds). According to a *Fortune* magazine article, they were well known among their suppliers as tough customers. They acquired a reputation of paying late and demanding discounts. Suppliers were frequently reluctant to insist on their terms and risk losing a large customer, so they often made concessions. By 1987, the independent Dart Drug Stores were struggling to survive, burdened with large interest payments and a poor reputation. In an effort to win back customers, the new owners ran ads in the *Washington Post* announcing that the stores were no longer owned or operated by the Hafts.

Attempts to Acquire Other Businesses

DHC was not the first corporation in which the Hafts took an interest. Between 1983 and 1986 they attempted to acquire Supermarkets General Corp., Jack Eckerd Drug Stores, Revco Inc., Federated Department Stores, May Department Stores and the giant supermarket chain, Safeway Stores. In each case they failed, but their failures were spectacularly profitable. They realized a $9 million profit on the sale of their Jack Eckerd stock, $40 million in their unsuccessful attempt to purchase Supermarkets General, and $97 million when they failed to take over Safeway. Not surprisingly, the value of Dart Group stock rose from $10.75 in 1982 to over $150 per share in 1987.

Target companies have seriously questioned, and seriously resisted, the Haft's attempts to acquire them. Like many other corporate raiders, the Hafts relied on "junk bonds" as part of the financial component of their proposals, and issuers like Drexel Burnham Lambert indicated that they were "highly confident" that financing could be arranged. Yet unlike many other raiders, the Hafts always targeted businesses close to their own experience. They remained in the retail industry and attempted to acquire chains, especially where their low-margin expertise might be valuable. Since they were always unsuccessful in their acquisition attempts, accusations by critics that they intended to sell off the major assets of the target companies were, while speculative, not entirely unreasonable. For their part, the Hafts insisted that they planned to operate, rather than break up, the companies they targeted.

However, even when a takeover attempt failed, the target company could face a difficult time. In 1986, the Dart Group was unsuccessful in an attempt to acquire Safeway Stores. The management of Safeway eluded the Hafts by taking the company private with a leveraged buyout. This involved taking on $4.2 billion in debt in order to purchase outstanding stock. As a result, Safeway, once the largest supermarket chain in the United States, was compelled to sell off profitable British and Australian holdings. In addition, it sold or closed 251 stores in the United States. Many of these stores were in small towns that had complained bitterly about the move. While Safeway's streamlining substantially improved profitability, it was still left with an enormous debt burden to service.

The Events Leading Up to Early June 1987

In 1986, DHC offered its B. Dalton division for sale. At that time B. Dalton, founded by one of the Dayton brothers in the 1960s, was one of the two largest and most successful retail bookselling chains in the United States. However, DHC had decided to pursue a strategy focused on the operation of large stores that offered a broad spectrum of merchandise. The typical B. Dalton store was fairly small and specialized in books and computer software. Among those seriously interested in acquiring B. Dalton was the Dart Group. Ultimately they were unsuccessful, and the division was sold to Barnes and Noble. According to one rumor, the negotiations broke down when personal hostilities flared up between senior executives of DHC and the Hafts.

Nevertheless, in their negotiations the Hafts had the opportunity to become familiar with DHC. While they recognized value in the company, they were critical of DHC's management. In a later interview with the *Minneapolis Star Tribune*, Robert Haft criticized DHC's retail strategies. "This thing is slowly going downhill," he said. According to *Business Week*, they felt that their own successful experience in managing discount retail outlets made them well suited to manage DHC properly.

In the spring of 1987, when DHC announced its first decline in earnings in sixteen years, the Hafts saw an opportunity. Though the significant drop in DHC's stock price discouraged some investors, the Hafts felt there was good reason to think that the company still had the potential for solid earnings. The Target division had acquired a number of important leases in California and was poised for expansion. With proper management, Mervyn's could certainly be turned around. Moreover, the board of directors and senior management collectively owned a very small portion of DHC's stock, far less than would be required to exercise a controlling influence.

By that same spring the legal climate was becoming less conducive to hostile takeovers. Provisions of an Indiana law that gave the state considerable power to restrict such takeovers had been upheld by the U.S. Supreme Court in April. Some Minnesota corporations (though not DHC) had lobbied hard for similar legislation in 1984, but it had failed to pass, partly because many legislators felt that it would not be upheld by the courts. The Supreme Court's decision, however, came too late to influence the 1987 session of the Minnesota legislature, which adjourned on May 18.

Another Alternative?

During the week of June 8, the Task Force met frequently and Macke remained in constant communication with the board of directors. As alternatives were generated, however, each one seemed unacceptable to management and the board.

At the meeting on June 11, Macke himself made clear his opposition to a "bust up" takeover, one that would require breaking up the corporation and selling off parts to repay the debts incurred by the takeover. He and his management team were convinced that it was best for all the corporation's constituencies—stockholders, customers, employees, and communities—that the company remain intact. As the possibilities were discussed, some were set aside rather easily. They found greenmail,* in the words of one participant, to be a "repugnant" alternative. They were also repelled by various schemes to take on debt or sell off assets, which, as another participant put it, would involve doing to themselves exactly what they feared the Hafts would do. Nor were they convinced that the financial defenses would be successful. They realized that if they chose to fight a financial battle, the action would take place in New York, where they had less influence. On the other hand, they had considerable influence in Minnesota, but it was not clear how to bring that influence to bear.

As Macke listened to the legal team, he anticipated the direction of their proposal. Would this alternative take advantage of DHC's strengths and preserve the integrity of the company? Or would it be flawed like all the others?

* "Greenmail" is a payment made to a raider, and not to other stockholders, by a target company in exchange for the raider's stock, where the price paid is higher than the market value of the stock.

EXHIBIT 1 **Closing Price of Common Stock, May–June 1987**

Source: Standard & Poor's *Daily Stock Price Record*, New York Stock Exchange, 1987.

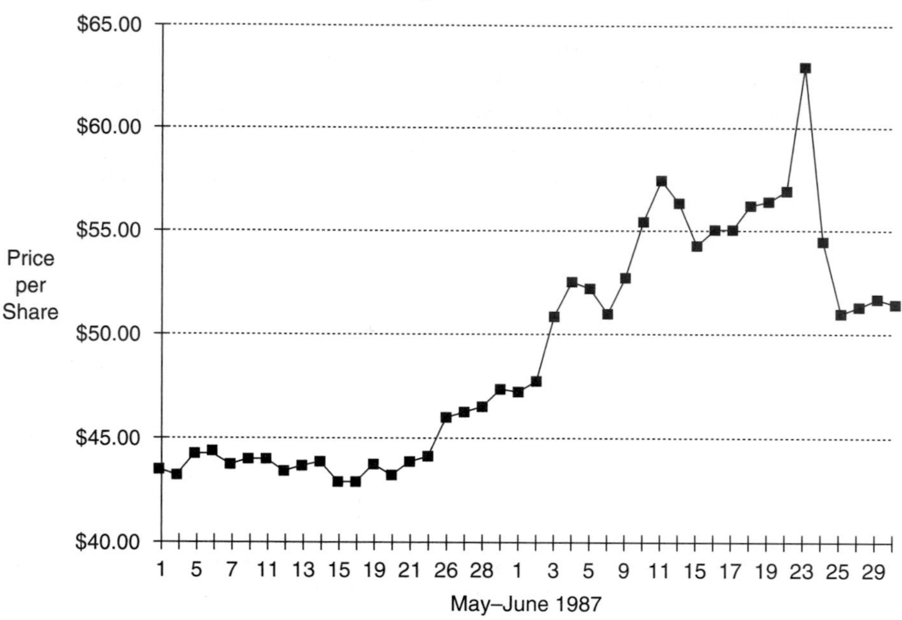

EXHIBIT 2 **Volume of Common Stock Traded, May–June 1987**

Source: Standard & Poor's *Daily Stock Price Record*, New York Stock Exchange, 1987.

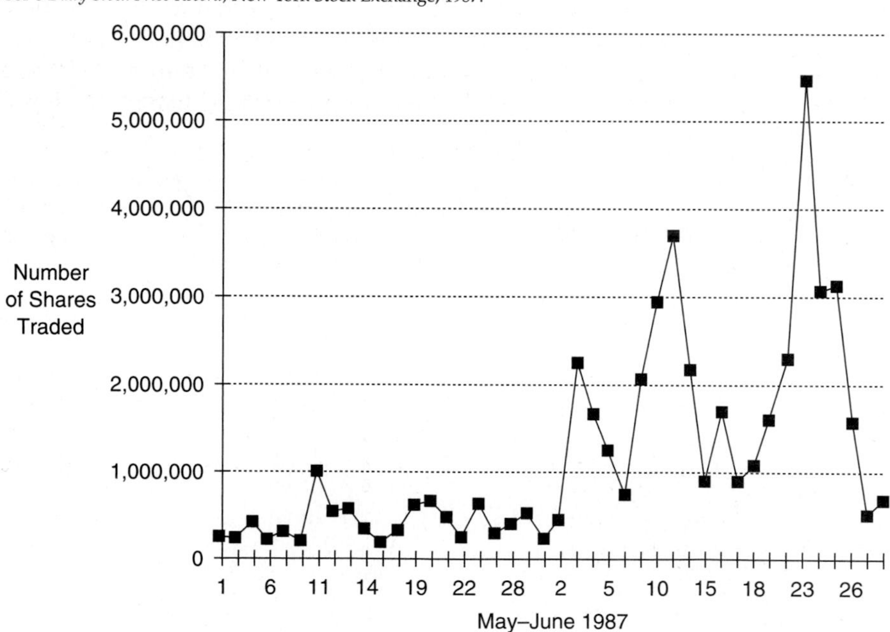

EXHIBIT 3 Earnings per Share, 1970–1986

Source: Dayton Hudson Corporation Annual Reports, 1979, 1986.

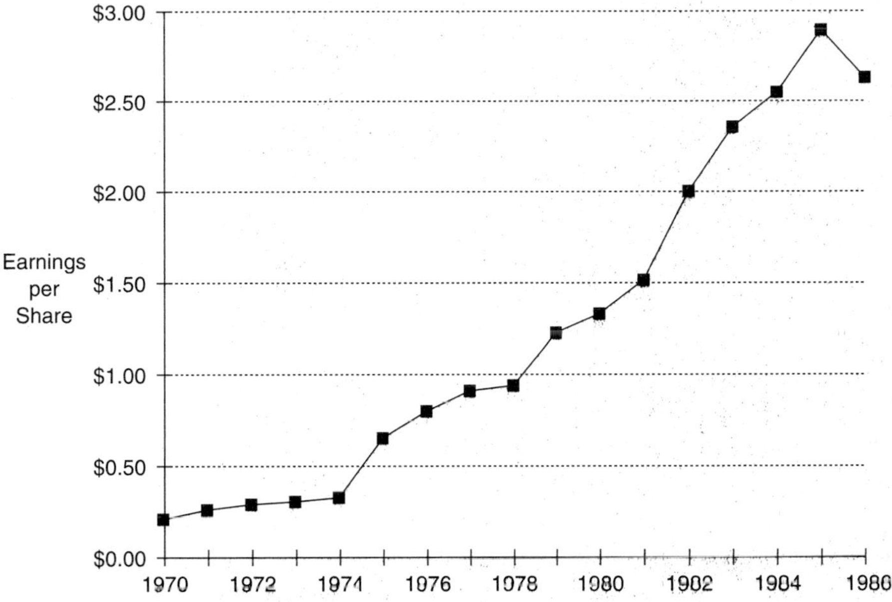

EXHIBIT 4 Highlights from Company History

Source: Dayton Hudson Information Booklet, Dayton Hudson Public Relations.

1881 The J. L. Hudson Company founded in Detroit.

1902 The Dayton Company, later to become Dayton Corporation, founded in Minneapolis.

1956 The Dayton Company opens Southdale, the world's first fully enclosed two-level shopping center in suburban Minneapolis.

1962 The Dayton Company enters low-margin merchandising with the opening of three Target stores.

1966 The Dayton Company enters specialty book retailing through the creation of B. Dalton Booksellers.

1967 Dayton Corporation has first public offering of common stock.

1968 Department store expansion to the West through merger with Lipmans in Oregon and Diamond's in Arizona. Acquisition of Pickwick Book Shops in Los Angeles, later to be combined with B. Dalton.

1969 Merger of the Dayton Corporation and the J. L. Hudson Company to form Dayton Hudson Corporation, then the nation's 14th largest general merchandise retailer. Listing of Dayton Hudson common stock on the New York Stock Exchange.

1971 Revenues top the $1-billion mark.

1973 Corporation becomes nation's 11th largest general merchandise retailer.

1975 Target becomes corporation's top revenue producer.

1977 Corporation passes the $2-billion mark in annual revenues.

1978 Merger with Mervyn's. Corporation becomes the country's seventh largest general merchandise retailer. Dayton Hudson discontinues real estate line of business. The sale of nine regional shopping centers brings more than $300 million.

1979 Corporation passes $3-billion mark in annual revenues.

1980 Corporation purchases Ayr-Way, Indianapolis-based chain of 40 low-margin stores. Ayr-Way stores are converted to Target stores. Dayton Hudson passes $4-billion mark in annual revenues.

1981 Target passes $2-billion mark in annual revenues. Mervyn's reaches $1 billion.

1982 Sale of Dayton Hudson Jewelers. Corporation reaches $5 billion in annual revenues.

1983 Dayton Hudson moves up to fifth largest general merchandise retailer, opens 1,000th store and passes $6-billion mark in revenues.

1984 Hudson's and Dayton's combined to form Dayton Hudson Department Store Company, the largest individual department store company in the nation. Annual revenues reach $8 billion.

1986 B. Dalton Booksellers sold. Target negotiates major West Coast real estate transaction.

1987 Dayton Hudson receives and rejects unsolicited merger proposal from Dart Group Corporation.

EXHIBIT 5 **Return on Beginning Equity (ROE), 1971–1986**

Source: Dayton Hudson Corporation Annual Reports, 1979, 1986.

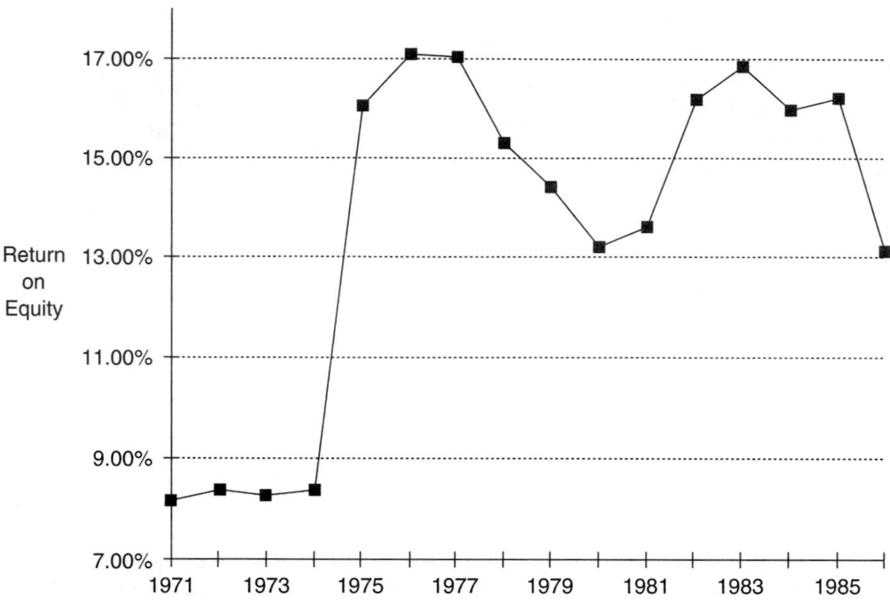

EXHIBIT 6 **Earnings per Share Growth Rates, 1971–1986**

Source: Calculated from Dayton Hudson Corporation Annual Reports, 1979, 1986.

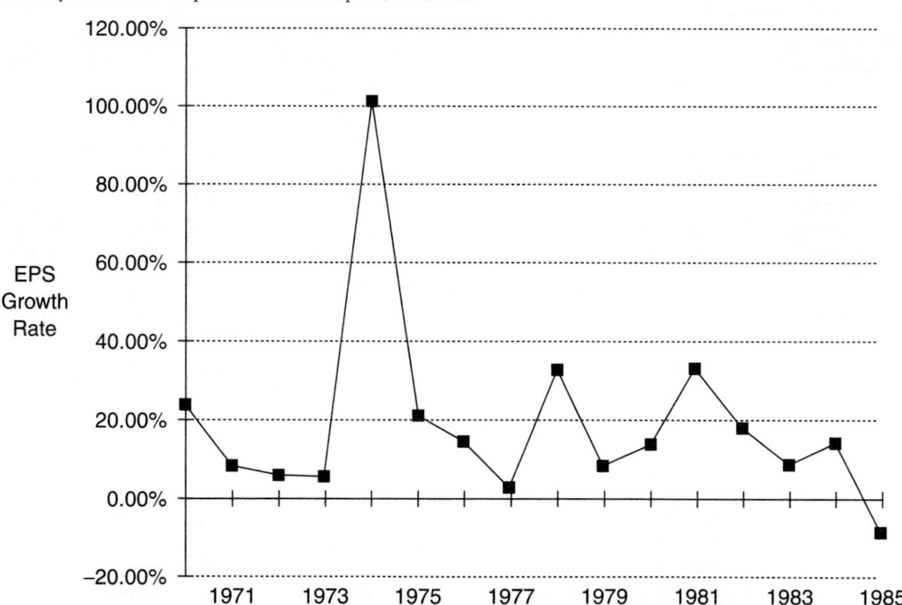

EXHIBIT 7 Consolidated Results of Operations

Source: Dayton Hudson Corporation Annual Report, 1986.

Dayton Hudson Corporation and Subsidiaries (millions of dollars, except per-share data)	1986	1985	1984
Revenues	$9,259.1	$8,255.3	$7,519.2
Costs and expenses:			
Cost of retail sales, buying and occupancy	$6,705.2	$5,908.3	$5,392.1
Selling, publicity and administrative	$1,538.1	1,365.9	1,234.4
Depreciation	182.7	158.2	144.9
Rental expense	73.1	69.0	69.5
Interest expense, net	117.5	99.8	97.7
Taxes other than income taxes	148.3	136.3	127.1
	$8,764.9	$7,737.5	$7,065.7
Earnings from continuing operations before income taxes and extraordinary charge	$494.2	$517.8	$453.5
Provision for income taxes	239.2	237.3	207.9
Net earnings from continuing operations before extraordinary charge	$255.0	$280.5	$245.6
Net earnings from discontinued operations:			
Earnings from operations	2.1	3.1	13.7
Gain on sale of B. Dalton	85.2	—	—
Net earnings before extraordinary charge	$342.3	$283.6	$259.3
Extraordinary charge from purchase and redemption of debt. Net of tax benefit	(32.3)	—	—
Consolidated net earnings	$310.0	$283.6	$259.3
Net earnings per share			
Continuing operations	$2.62	$2.89	$2.54
Discontinued operations:			
Earnings from operations	.02	.03	.14
Gain on sale of B. Dalton	.88	—	—
Earnings before extraordinary charge	3.52	2.92	2.68
Extraordinary charge	(.33)	—	—
Consolidated	$3.19	$2.92	$2.68

EXHIBIT 8 Corporate Overview

Source: DHC Community Involvement Annual Report, 1987.

DAYTON HUDSON CORPORATION

WHO WE ARE

Operating Companies	1987 Revenues	Stores	States
TARGET	**$5.3 Billion**	**317**	**24**
MERVYN'S	**$3.2 Billion**	**199**	**13**
DH	**$1.6 Billion**	**37**	**7**
LECHMERE	**$636 Million**	**24**	**8**

Dayton Hudson Corporation is a growth company focused exclusively on retailing.

The Corporation's principal strategy is to provide exceptional value to the American consumer through multiple retail formats.

Our customers know us as: Target, an upscale discount store chain; Mervyn's, a highly promotional, popular-priced, value-oriented department store company; Dayton Hudson Department Store Company, emphasizing fashion leadership, quality merchandise, broad selections and customer service; and Lechmere, a hardlines retail company.

WHERE WE DO BUSINESS

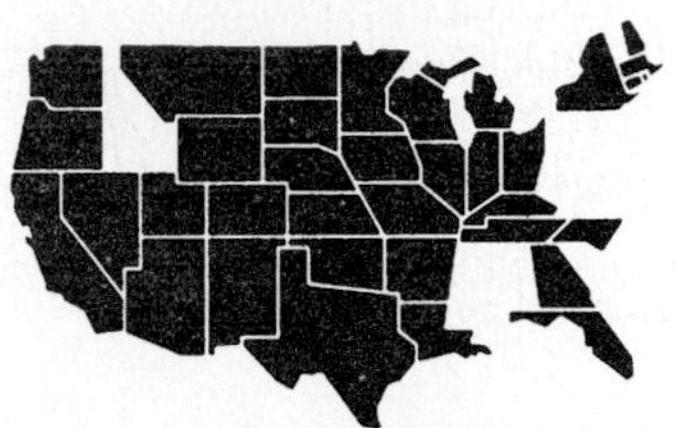

Arizona
Arkansas
California
Colorado
Connecticut
Florida
Georgia
Illinois
Indiana
Iowa
Kansas
Kentucky
Louisiana
Massachusetts
Michigan
Minnesota
Missouri
Montana
Nebraska
Nevada
New Hampshire
New Mexico
New York
North Carolina
North Dakota
Ohio
Oklahoma
Oregon
Rhode Island
South Dakota
Tennessee
Texas
Utah
Washington
Wisconsin
Wyoming

ECONOMIC IMPACT IN TEN LARGEST STATES

States	Companies	Revenues	Payroll	Giving Funds
Arizona	**T/M**	**$ 397,470,000**	**$ 33,651,000**	**$ 180,000**
California	**T/M**	**3,163,750,000**	**406,313,000**	**2,728,000**
Colorado	**T/M**	**411,610,000**	**38,033,000**	**496,000**
Indiana	**T/D**	**466,140,000**	**45,679,000**	**518,000**
Iowa	**T**	**271,350,000**	**20,365,000**	**275,000**
Massachusetts	**L**	**358,700,000**	**44,103,000**	**224,000**
Michigan	**D/M/T**	**879,950,000**	**118,087,000**	**1,881,000**
Minnesota	**T/D/F**	**1,357,940,000**	**277,884,000**	**9,253,000**
Texas	**T/M**	**1,189,210,000**	**113,708,000**	**1,165,000**
Wisconsin	**T/D**	**218,330,000**	**17,632,000**	**242,000**
All other states	**T/M/D/L**	**1,962,900,000**	**183,511,000**	**2,419,000**
Total		**$10,677,350,000**	**$1,298,966,000**	**$19,381,000**

T Target/**M** Mervyn's/**D** Dayton Hudson Department Store Company/**L** Lechmere/**F** Dayton Hudson Foundation

EXHIBIT 9 Corporate Giving

Source: DHC Community Involvement Annual Report.

1987 Community Involvement Report
Financial Highlights

We concentrate our community involvement on programs that offer the potential for achieving results and demonstrating leadership.

We do 80 percent of our giving in two focus areas where we believe we can have significant impact: Social Action and the Arts. The other 20 percent of our giving responds to special community needs and opportunities.

Social Action

Forty percent of community giving funds are contributed to programs and projects that result in: **a** the economic and social progress of individuals; and/or **b** the development of community and neighborhood strategies that respond effectively to critical community social and economic concerns.

Arts

Forty percent of community giving funds are contributed to programs and projects that result in: **a** artistic excellence and stronger artistic leadership in communities; and/or **b** increased access to and use of the arts as a means of community expression.

Social Action	$ 8,658,275
Arts	$ 7,738,094
Miscellaneous	$ 2,984,141
Total 1987 Giving	$19,380,510

Miscellaneous

Twenty percent of community giving funds are contributed to programs and projects outside Social Action and the Arts that result in: **a** our responsiveness to special community needs and opportunities; and/or **b** innovative partnerships with other community leaders.

EXHIBIT 10 **Dart Group Corporation and Subsidiaries: Consolidated States of Income**

Source: Dart Group Corporation Annual Report, 1987.

	Years ended January 31		
	1987	1986	1985
Sales	$338,008,000	$97,833,000	$73,834,000
Income from bankers' acceptances (Dart Group Financial Corporation)	10,563,000	7,315,000	—
Other interest and other income	18,830,000	14,201,000	16,391,000
	$367,401,000	$119,349,000	$90,225,000
Expenses:			
Cost of sales, store occupancy and warehousing	$271,119,000	$75,540,000	$54,388,000
Selling and administrative	62,165,000	22,271,000	17,300,000
Depreciation and amortization	4,978,000	1,189,000	666,000
Interest	36,357,000	12,738,000	522,000
	$374,619,000	$111,738,000	$72,876,000
Income (loss) before unusual items, income taxes, equity in loss of affiliates, preacquisition minority interest in losses of purchased subsidiary, minority interest, discontinued operations and extraordinary item	$(7,218,000)	$7,611,000	$17,349,000
Unusual items	78,294,000	13,275,000	—
Income before income taxes, equity in loss of affiliates, preacquisition minority interest in losses of purchased subsidiary, minority interest, discontinued operations and extraordinary item	71,976,000	20,886,000	17,349,000
Income taxes	28,423,000	9,648,000	7,917,000
Income before equity in loss of affiliates, preacquisition minority interest in losses of purchased subsidiary, minority interest, discontinued operations and extraordinary item	42,653,000	11,238,000	9,432,000
Equity in loss of affiliates	—	(1,098,000)	(2,027,000)
Preacquisition minority interest in losses of purchased subsidiary	519,000	—	—
Minority interest in income of consolidated subsidiaries and partnerships	(7,187,000)	(270,000)	(1,093,000)
Income from continuing operations before extraordinary item	35,985,000	9,870,000	6,312,000
Discontinued operations:			
Income from operations of discontinued division (net of taxes of $1,010,000 for the year January 31, 1985)	—	—	1,010,000
Gain on sale of discontinued division (net taxes of $39,000,000)	—	—	75,000,000
Extraordinary item:			
Loss on reacquisition of debentures, net of income tax benefit of $5,212,000	(5,258,000)	—	—
Net income	$30,727,000	$9,870,000	$82,322,000
Earnings per common share and common share equivalent:			
Income from continuing operations before extraordinary item	$19.24	$5.28	$3.46
Discontinued operations	—	—	.55
Gain on sale of discontinued division	—	—	41.14
Extraordinary item:			
Loss of reacquisition of debentures	(2.81)	—	—
Net income	$16.43	$5.28	$45.15
Weighted average common share and common share equivalent outstanding	1,870,000	1,868,000	1,823,000

Dayton Hudson Corporation: *Conscience and Control (B)*

On Thursday, June 11, while Macke and his management team were meeting with their advisers, Wendy McDowall was beginning a well-earned fishing vacation. Director of Government Affairs for DHC, she had finished several grueling months as the company's chief lobbyist at the Minnesota legislature. The 1987 session, which adjourned May 18, had been more difficult than most and everyone involved was relieved to see it end. By this morning Wendy had been at a cabin on the North Shore of Lake Superior for only a day or two. As she sipped a cup of coffee she turned on the radio and was stunned by the news she heard. DHC's stock had been the second most actively traded issue the day before. Although she did not know quite what she could do to help, she quickly decided that she could not continue fishing while her company was in danger. Within the hour she was in her car speeding back to Minneapolis.

That afternoon, after listening to discussion about alternative defenses, Macke had made it clear to his team that the responsibility for the decision would be his. Later that evening, after consulting with the board of directors, he decided to approach the governor regarding a special session of the legislature to strengthen Minnesota's corporate takeover statute. It seemed to be the alternative that took best advantage of the company's strengths, all things considered, and the one most likely to succeed. But many obstacles still lay in the path.

Friday, June 12

D. J. Leary remembered the afternoon very well. Friday afternoons during summer in the Twin Cities were usually not busy times, certainly not good times to do business. People leave the cities by the tens of thousands, clogging the northbound highways, heading for a weekend "at the lake."

Leary himself was leaving the office a bit early, around 4:00 P.M. He had pulled off his tie and settled into the seat of his car, waiting for the air conditioner to take effect, when his car phone beeped. Wendy McDowall was calling from DHC's corporate headquarters to ask Leary to come by as soon as possible. She needed to talk with him about something too sensitive to discuss over the phone.

Something serious was obviously happening. Leary, a former aide to Minnesota's premier politician, Hubert Humphrey, and a prominent legislative lobbyist and public relations consultant, hurried to McDowall's office. When he arrived she told him that the company was "in play," and that she had been asked to help plan a strategy for approaching the legislature in a special session, one called by the governor just for this purpose. She asked Leary if he would join the team being formed to work on the project, specifically to help develop a media strategy.

Leary was stunned. One of the most difficult sessions in recent memory had just concluded. How could anyone ask the governor to call a special session now? Special sessions were notoriously unpopular in Minnesota, not least among the legislators themselves. But Leary agreed to consider the problem, and over the weekend he began to put together the pieces of a plan. On Monday he reported back with some thoughts about how it could be done.

Wednesday, June 17

The pieces of DHC's action plan were falling into place, and a large implementation team had been gathered under the direction of the Task Force members. As a beginning step, Robert Hentges, an attorney with a local firm advising DHC about the legislative option, called Gerry Nelson, communications director for Minnesota's Democratic governor, Rudy Perpich. Hentges' message was cryptic. First, he inquired about Perpich's schedule for the next day. Then, Nelson recalled, "He said there might be some people who have to see [the governor] on an urgent matter." Nelson said that something could be arranged and as he put his phone down, he puzzled about what might be brewing.

Thursday, June 18

At 9:30 in the morning Hentges called Terry Montgomery, Governor Perpich's chief of staff. Telling Montgomery that Macke had an urgent matter to discuss with the governor that day, he said, "He'll meet any place, any time!" Montgomery rearranged Perpich's schedule and set a meeting for 3:00 P.M. in Macke's office.

When Montgomery and Perpich met with Macke that afternoon, they were told that DHC had become the target of the Dart Group, and that millions of shares of stock were changing hands. Macke outlined the options identified by the Task Force and explained why he had decided on seeking a change in Minnesota's takeover statute. He asked Perpich to call a special session of the legislature as soon as possible to enact the changes. That same afternoon, Boake Sells, DHC's president and COO, called Minnesota Attorney General Skip Humphrey to tell him about their plan. Humphrey called in his office's expert in takeover law to prepare him to examine DHC's proposal. In a third meeting, Ann Barkelew and Leary met with Gerry Nelson to discuss the media aspects of the plan.

Perpich was taken completely by surprise and agreed merely to explore the possibility with legislative leaders. That evening, during a birthday party held for him at a downtown Minneapolis hotel, Perpich slipped away to consult with a handful of legislators. They were willing to consider a special session under the circumstances, but insisted that hearings be held to explore the matter first. For his part, Perpich refused to call a special session unless legislative leaders supported the idea and could agree on a limited agenda and specific provisions for a new takeover bill.

But Perpich's efforts to keep DHC's request private were in vain. By that evening the information had leaked out and Perpich was besieged by reporters at the birthday party. As a result, he scheduled a press conference to be carried live at 10:30 P.M., immediately following the local television news broadcasts.

Both the media and DHC people were caught off guard by the governor's abrupt decision to call a news conference. Macke was expected to be present, but he was at home on a sticky summer evening, getting ready to go to bed. Peter Hutchinson, DHC's vice president for external affairs, called Macke with the news. He dressed as quickly as he could and dashed back downtown from his suburban home to join Perpich. He arrived just in time.

Moments after Macke arrived, Perpich told reporters and a live television audience that DHC had asked for a special session. He went on to say that he had agreed to consider it.

Friday, June 19

Commerce Commissioner Mike Hatch canceled his morning schedule to prepare for an 11:00 A.M. meeting with Perpich. Some years earlier, Hatch had written a law review article on Minnesota's takeover statute and was quite familiar with the issues. His principal concerns were to protect shareholders and to see restrictions imposed on golden parachutes and greenmail. When he met with Perpich and his staff to explain his position, DHC's attorneys, who had been working for nearly ten days on a detailed plan to amend the statute, had not yet delivered their proposal.

In downtown Minneapolis the phones were ringing frantically at DHC's corporate headquarters. Some of the most urgent calls were directed to the Dayton Hudson Foundation, and to its chairman, Peter Hutchinson. As vice president for external affairs, Hutchinson had been heavily involved in the activities of the previous weeks. Many of the callers represented arts and social action organizations that received major funding from DHC. They wanted to know what was going to happen if the Dart Group succeeded. Hutchinson and his staff quickly realized that too many calls were coming in to be handled effectively, so they scheduled an informational meeting for 1:30 P.M. that afternoon at the Children's Theater in Minneapolis. DHC routinely used that auditorium for its shareholder meetings and for other company events.

Shortly after noon, DHC's formal proposal was delivered to Perpich at the Capitol. Soon afterward, the acting Speaker of the House, Robert Vanasek, shared the proposal with Rep. Wayne Simoneau, the author of the 1984 takeover bill that DHC declined to support. Vanasek asked Simoneau if he would sponsor the bill in the House. Simoneau was delighted to see that some of the provisions paralleled those in his earlier bill and agreed to be the sponsor.

At about the time that Simoneau became sponsor of DHC's proposal, Macke and Leary were meeting with the editorial board of the *Minneapolis Star Tribune.* Leary recognized the crucial value of favorable editorials in the upcoming Sunday editions, with their statewide circulation and influence. They explained the situation and asked for help in getting their message across to readers. Later, they also met with the editorial board of the *St. Paul Pioneer Press Dispatch.*

Shortly after 1:00 P.M., Peter Hutchinson arrived at the Children's Theater auditorium. He was uncharacteristically nervous and what he saw on the way in did not put him at ease. He and his staff had contacted scores of people about the meeting, but barely a hundred seats were filled and the auditorium looked empty. Hutchinson went backstage to prepare. When he walked out a few minutes later he was shocked and amazed to see that the auditorium was full.

People called by DHC had spontaneously called others and word of the meeting had spread throughout the community. Even people from organizations who had never received funding from DHC had come. Television crews, who had not been called by DHC, began to set up their lights and microphones. Neither Hutchinson nor his staff were prepared for a response like this.

Not knowing quite what to say, he began the meeting by explaining why DHC had called it. "Since so many of you have called in with questions, we felt it was the best way to communicate with you," he said, "and to tell you what is going on." He then outlined the events of the previous weeks. He told them what a hostile takeover was, what the company's position was, and what steps they were taking. No one could know, he said, what would happen if the Hafts were successful. After about ten minutes he stopped and asked if there were any questions.

Someone raised the question that was on everyone's mind, "What can we do to help?" Hutchinson replied that they had not called the meeting to recommend tactics but merely to provide information. Silence fell over the auditorium. Suddenly, a woman sitting on the left side stood up. "I'll tell you what you can do," she shouted. "Call the governor! His number is 296-0093." "I have a pocketful of quarters, and a list of legislators" shouted another person, "Let's call right now!" For the next twenty minutes audience members made suggestions to one another. Then the meeting broke up as people spilled out of the auditorium determined to do something.

While Hutchinson was meeting with the people from the community at the Children's Theater, DHC's attorneys were conferring with the state's attorneys. Later that afternoon, Perpich's office requested an evaluation of DHC's proposal from the Attorney General's office. Meanwhile, Wendy McDowall was beginning to implement the plan that she and Leary had devised earlier in the week. Having divided the legislature into three groups of descending importance, she began her lobbying efforts.

DHC found that the governor's announcement the previous evening had set off a string of reactions that management had not anticipated and could barely control. Store managers began to call headquarters asking for directions. They wanted to know what they should tell employees to do. Senior management was preoccupied with other pressing tasks, so at first they told employees to do nothing. But when managers insisted that their employees were determined to do something, Macke sent a letter to all of them explaining the situation and suggesting that they communicate with their legislators (see Exhibit 1). That evening employees began doing just that.

Saturday, June 20

The strategy that DHC laid out with respect to the legislators was simple in theory, but was complicated to execute in such a short time. Their aim was to help legislators understand clearly what was at stake and to help them become comfortable with the idea of a special session *and* with amending the statute. To accomplish this they did five things.

First, they hired some of the most experienced professional lobbyists in the state to ensure that every legislator would be contacted personally. Second, they commissioned an opinion poll to discover the reaction of citizens to DHC's plight and the proposed special session. Third, they prepared an information packet for each legislator. By coincidence, the June 22, 1987, issue of *Fortune* magazine carried an article on the Hafts entitled "The Most Feared Family in Retailing." The article, which was included in an information packet, described the Hafts' businesses and detailed their efforts to acquire a national retailer, with a special sidebar about the damage done to Safeway.

Fourth, they made strenuous efforts to contact newspapers in rural Minnesota and urge them to publish editorials supporting the special session. Fifth, they planned to send DHC executives to every community in the state where DHC had a store and where there was an important media instrument.

Some tactics, however, were rejected. DHC's advertising department had been asked earlier in the week to develop some ideas for advertisements that could be placed in newspapers to inform the public and gather support. On the afternoon of the 20th, management discussed what to do with the proposed ads. A couple of years earlier, Dayton's department stores had offered a small, white stuffed bear as a Christmas premium to customers. The response to "Santabear" had been overwhelming and the company had become closely associated with the toy, especially in Minnesota (see Exhibit 2). Some of the ads attempted to capture attention by suggesting that Santabear was at risk. After considerable debate a decision was made not to use the ads. Management was concerned that they might be perceived as too manipulative.

Sunday, June 21

Lobbying efforts were put on hold for Father's Day. In the afternoon, Commerce Commissioner Hatch drove to Montevideo, a rural town not far from the Twin Cities, to attend a parade. He asked people there what they thought about calling a special session to address DHC's problem. For the most part they were not enthusiastic about the plan.

In the evening, two lawyers from the Attorney General's office completed a memo evaluating DHC's proposed bill. They concluded that it probably did not violate the state constitution.

Monday, June 22

Early in the morning, Steve Watson, president of the Dayton Hudson Department Store Company, and Leary boarded the company plane to fly around the state implementing their plan to make media appearances and meet with legislators. By evening they had visited four different cities.

In the afternoon, Hatch reviewed options with Perpich. They could (a) call the special session and try to pass the proposal, (b) modify the proposal and recommend only those provisions that had been tested in the courts, (c) promote strong provisions restraining greenmail and golden parachutes, or (d) do nothing at all. In the evening, Hatch attended a fund raiser in St. Cloud, in the heart of Minnesota's farming community. Once again he asked people about the plan to call a special session. Once again he received a negative response. People in attendance wanted to know when a special session would be called to help farmers in danger of losing their land.

Tuesday, June 23

In the morning, the results of the opinion poll commissioned over the weekend were released. A large majority of citizens, 85%, favored the special session and the proposed toughening of the takeover statute. At the Capitol, a joint meeting of the House Judiciary and Commerce committees convened. Macke was the first to testify, but, as the *Minneapolis Star Tribune* reported, his performance was anything but smooth. Out of his element and disconcerted by recent developments, he seemed nervous and abrupt. He told the committees that he not only believed in a free market, but also in a fair market. "During the last three weeks," he said, "30 percent of our stock was traded. This means that 30 percent of our stock is owned by people who have held it for less than three weeks." Later, an attorney representing DHC reported, "In 10 minutes or less, more than 3 percent of the stock changed hands this morning."

But the most startling moment came when Macke announced that another attempt to acquire the company had begun that morning.

A $6.8 billion offer had been made by a Cincinnati stock analyst thought to be representing a wealthy Ohio family. In a matter of hours, the paper value of the company increased by nearly a billion dollars. By the afternoon, however, the offer was shown to be bogus and the stock analyst was found to have had a history of mental illness. The incident graphically underscored the volatility of the circumstances in which the company found itself, and drove home the urgency of the situation to the legislators.

Also that morning a variety of demands began to surface for additional agenda items, threatening to force the special session out of control. By afternoon, it became clear that compromises were necessary and that DHC needed to make some concessions in its proposed amendments.

No decision was reached by the committees that night, except to postpone a recommendation for the governor until the following day. Macke and his team closed the day not knowing what recommendation to expect.

EXHIBIT 1 **Macke's Memo to Employees**

Source: Dayton Hudson Department Store Company—Public Relations.

DAYTON HUDSON CORPORATION

777 Nicollet Mall
Minneapolis, Minnesota 55402-2055
612/370-6948

June 19, 1987

Dear Dayton Hudson Corporation Employee:

I'm sure that you are aware that for the past several weeks there has been very heavy trading in Dayton Hudson common stock.

We want you to know that we believe it is in the long-term interests of our shareholders, employees, customers and communities for Dayton Hudson to remain independent in its present form. To support this belief, we have taken two recent actions. First, we met with Minnesota Governor Rudy Perpich yesterday to express our concern over the growing problem of hostile takeovers. And second, we are communicating today with an aggressive buyer of our stock that we are not interested in being acquired.

We applaud Governor Perpich in considering a special session of the legislature to enact tougher corporate anti-takeover laws. The proposed legislation will strengthen our existing laws to protect Minnesota companies from the disruptive and irreparable damage to a corporation's shareholders, employees, customers and communities that frequently results from stock market raids and other abusive tactics.

The new legislation will provide Minnesota companies with protection from threatened takeovers and restructuring similar to the protection offered to corporations in certain other states. It is also consistent with a recent decision of the U.S. Supreme Court and the present mood of many other state legislatures.

We need everyone's help in this matter. If you have friends, family or other relatives who live in Minnesota, ask them to contact their Governor and legislators to support this special legislation.

Working together we can keep Dayton Hudson a healthy and independent company.

Sincerely yours,

Kenneth A. Macke
Chairman and Chief Executive Officer

EXHIBIT 2 Santabear

Source: Dayton Hudson Corporation, Public Relations Department.

Dayton Hudson Corporation: *Conscience and Control (C)*

The joint House committees agreed on Wednesday, June 24, to recommend a special session to the governor, and endorsed a bill quite similar to what DHC proposed. But the hearings on the Senate side ran into trouble. Commerce Commissioner Hatch was determined to see that provisions were contained in the bill that made golden parachutes illegal and strongly discouraged greenmail. He threatened to recommend against a special session if he failed to receive support on these issues. "If you don't include them," he told the Senate hearing, "it's just big business crawling into bed with big government." DHC, however, opposed the greenmail provision. After considerable discussion, all sides agreed to language severely restricting both golden parachutes and greenmail. Senate leaders then decided to join the House in recommending a special session.

Legislative leaders met with Perpich in the afternoon and agreed on a very limited agenda for the special session. However, disagreement between the House and Senate versions of the bill surfaced. Perpich refused to call the special session until everyone agreed on one bill, and insisted that agreement be reached in time for an announcement on the 10:00 P.M. news.

Negotiations involving legislators from both houses and DHC lawyers began at 7:30 in the evening, and two hours later the House members left the meeting in frustration when they could not reach agreement over the question of a "sunset" provision.* Communication resumed, however, and minutes before the 10:00 P.M. deadline, agreement was reached by phone. Perpich announced the special session on television and ordered the legislature to convene at 2:00 P.M. the following day.

* A sunset provision causes a statute to expire after a specified date unless the legislature enacts an extension.

The Provisions of the Bill

In 1986, the Indiana legislature passed the Control Share Acquisitions Act (CSAA). As suggested in the "A" case, this statute placed restrictions on attempts to acquire a controlling interest in a company without approval of the board of directors, but only applied to those Indiana corporations that elected to be covered. Shortly after it went into effect, a company that was the apparent target of a hostile takeover chose to be protected by the act. The bidder immediately sued and a lower court found in its favor, as did the court of appeals. However, in April 1987, the U.S. Supreme Court reversed the decision and upheld the statute. Indiana's CSAA subsequently became the model for DHC's proposal, as well as for similar legislation in other states.

The bill proposed in the Minnesota legislature aimed to protect companies by addressing the problem of tender offers. It required approval of the majority of disinterested shareholders before a bidder could gain voting rights for a controlling share of the stock. It also required the approval of a majority of the disinterested members of the board of directors (i.e., those who were neither managers nor representatives of bidders) before the bidder could enter any business combination with the target. Furthermore, and perhaps most importantly, it prohibited the sale of a target company's assets to pay debts incurred in financing a hostile takeover for a period of five years.

One of the most controversial provisions of the Minnesota bill, however, was the stipulation that the board of directors of a target company could legitimately take into consideration the interests of a wide range of groups in exercising their "business judgment." In discharging their duties, directors were authorized to consider "the interests of the corporation's employees, customers, suppliers, and creditors, the economy of the state and nation, community and societal considerations, and the long-term as well as short-term interests of the corporation and its shareholders including the possibility that these interests may be best served by the continued independence of the corporation."

Finally, the bill introduced measures which virtually prohibited golden parachutes and the payment of greenmail, but the greenmail provision was not scheduled to become effective until some months afterward.

Thursday, June 25

The debate on the floor of the House was broadcast in the afternoon over Minnesota Public Radio. Several representatives rose to oppose the bill. They argued that it would not only violate the rights of shareholders but that it was also an unjustified government interference with the freedom of the market. Members clearly felt pressured by the emergency atmosphere of a special session.

At DHC headquarters, management and staff members were glued to their radios. The longer the debate went on, the more worried they became. During one of the speeches, Wendy McDowall, DHC's director of Government Affairs, called the office to get a message and spoke to Inez, one of the secretaries:

"Wendy, have you been listening to the debate? Do you think many of the House members feel that way?"

"No, Inez, I haven't been listening just now. In fact, I haven't gone to the House chamber this afternoon."

"You didn't go over there! But Wendy, it sounds like we're going to lose. Everybody here is getting pretty discouraged."

"Inez, turn off your radio! It's going to be all right."

And indeed it was. Despite the rhetoric of the opposing speeches, the bill passed by an overwhelming margin: 120–5 in the House and 57–0 in the Senate. Perpich made the 10:00 P.M. news as he signed the bill into law. (See Exhibits 1, 2 for a sampling of editorial responses to the legislation.)

Friday, June 26

Macke sent a letter to DHC's employees in Minnesota thanking them for their support. He also urged them to write their legislators once more to express their appreciation, and he invited them to corporate headquarters that day to sign a banner to be given to the governor (see Exhibit 3).

DHC's corporate headquarters occupied several floors of the IDS Center, the tallest building in downtown Minneapolis. On the first floor of that building was a large enclosed courtyard and it was there that DHC held an enormous ice cream social for anyone who cared to come. A life-sized Santabear worked the crowd and hundreds of DHC employees stopped by to sign the giant banner that read simply, "Thanks, Minnesota." (See Exhibit 4 for an ad with the same theme that appeared in newspapers throughout Minnesota.)

EXHIBIT 1 Dayton Hudson

Irwin L. Jacobs,* Letter to *City Business,* July 15, 1987

Dayton Hudson certainly enhanced its "can-do" reputation in the business world when it "took over" the state of Minnesota one afternoon last week and had a well-tailored and highly polished and manicured management-entrenching law passed by *its* governor and *its* Legislature. The law will hereafter be known as the "Dayton Hudson Protective Act of 1987."

It is not difficult to believe the Legislature would pass a bill that will further regulate a market. The history of our Legislature is much the same as that of other state legislatures: "If it moves, let's tax it and regulate it" and "Let's try and get a competitive advantage in Minnesota over South Dakota, or Wisconsin, or Tennessee, etc."

Also, the attitude of the governor—a long-time minion of Control Data Corp. and William Norris—was certainly never in question.

However, the Dayton's executive group that lobbied and fought for the new antitakeover bill is indeed a mystery. Doesn't the group have golden parachutes, poison pills, and every other known protective device in place? The executive group crying over the prospect of the Dart Group Corp. coming in with an unsolicited tender offer for Dayton Hudson is much like Chicken Little crying over the falling sky. Where is the so-called imminent offer? Don't fear, "Imminent Suitor"—there is still time, thanks to the Dayton Hudson Protective Act of 1987, which allows greenmail payments until March of 1988.

It is little wonder that the Legislature welcomed Dayton's with open arms. The IOU's now will most certainly abound; the Dayton's executives can count on receiving campaign solicitations from state legislators for the next decade. Isn't it also true that Dayton's lobbying position on many crucial business issues in the future will be greatly compromised because of its rash rush to seek legislative protection from the Dart bullies?

My position on the tendency of large corporations to get bloated, inefficient, and unimaginative like government bureaucracies is certainly no secret. Dayton's now certainly can fall within the definition of a "corporacracy," as a minion of the state of Minnesota. The management has deserted its principal constituency—Dayton's shareholders—in favor of its suppliers, charities, state legislators, employees, and customers. Maybe Dayton's management can convince the state during a regular session of the Legislature to tender for its stock; then it would be completely free from any attempt at a takeover from other states.

Dayton's, the governor, and the state Legislature deserve each other. Dayton's shareholders deserve better, and they should now sell their stock and find a corporation to invest in that has not abandoned its shareholders. Or there is another solution: *a proxy fight to throw the rascals out.*

* Irwin L. Jacobs was a Minneapolis-based entrepreneur engaged in corporate acquisition.

EXHIBIT 2 **Excerpts from "Dayton Hudson Reaps Benefit of its Good Image"**
James Shannon,* *Minneapolis Star Tribune,* July 5, 1987.

. . . The onus and the bonus of [its] impressive corporate image came into sharp focus in Minnesota two weeks ago when Dayton Hudson announced that it might be the target of a takeover by the Dart Group of Maryland, which had then acquired a significant stake in Dayton Hudson stock. What the Dayton Hudson managers, the governor of Minnesota and the Legislature have done since June 18 to impede a hostile takeover of Dayton Hudson is an illustration of how community good will toward a publicly held corporation can be translated into political muscle.

On June 19 at the Children's Theater in Minneapolis, Peter Hutchinson, chairman of the Dayton Hudson Foundation, addressed an emergency meeting of more than 500 community leaders to explain the elements and the dangers of a possible takeover. At that meeting Gleason Glover, president of the Urban League of Minneapolis, urged people to write the governor and their legislators to endorse the calling of a special session of the Legislature and the passage of legislation designed to impede or prevent the hostile takeover of Minnesota-based corporations. Several legislators have said since then that no single issue has ever generated as much mail or as many phone calls to their offices as the threat of a hostile takeover of Dayton Hudson.

On June 22 the House Judiciary Committee met to hear testimony on whether to have a special session; the Senate Judiciary Committee met on June 23 for the same purpose. On June 24 Gov. Rudy Perpich called for a special session; on the 25th both houses convened. In three hours they enacted a new anti-takeover statute modeled on an Indiana law that in April was found constitutional by the U.S. Supreme Court.

The takeover threat seems to have eased. The Dart Group still has not commented publicly on its plans. But given the new Minnesota statute, which would deny a raider the chance to break up a company like Dayton Hudson and sell off pieces of it to pay for his takeover debt, the Dart Group or any other future raider eyeing a Minnesota target company will need lots of money in hand to pay for its purchase before it puts the desired company "in play."

The new Minnesota statute is not a panacea. But it has bought precious time for all companies incorporated in Minnesota. Granted, this new law was occasioned by the threat to Dayton Hudson, but its benefits flow to every publicly held Minnesota corporation.

A key element is that the directors of a target company may now take into consideration the benefit or the harm to the community from a takeover. Heretofore directors of such companies have felt legally compelled to consider only the financial benefit or loss that their shareholders would sustain in a takeover. It is doubtful, at least to this writer, whether any company in the nation was in a better position than Dayton Hudson, because of its good public image, to orchestrate such a campaign for urgently needed legislative protection for community values in this age of whirlwind and disastrous takeovers.

There is an abundance of legal precedent, in our statutes and in court decisions, defending the rights of shareholders in takeover battles. The new Minnesota statute breaks new ground in saying that there are also community values that directors, judges, and raiders should evaluate in deciding when a takeover serves the common weal. Caveat raider.

* James Shannon was Executive Director of the General Mills Foundation.

EXHIBIT 3 Macke's Memo to Employees

Source: Dayton Hudson Corporation, Public Relations Department.

DAYTON HUDSON CORPORATION

777 Nicollet Mall
Minneapolis, Minnesota 55402-2055
612/370-6948

June 26, 1987

Dear Dayton Hudson Corporation Employee,

With your help, Minnesota has achieved something we believe is unprecedented: we have taken important steps to deter corporate raiders from hostile takeovers of Minnesota businesses.

On Wednesday, Governor Rudy Perpich called a special legislative session. Yesterday, the Minnesota legislature took action to toughen the state's anti-takeover laws.

While there are no absolute guarantees that Dayton Hudson cannot be taken over (nor do we believe, philosophically, there should be), we believe that the new law will prevent many abusive tactics used by raiders, including "bust-up" hostile takeovers.

For that, we have many of you to thank. You were great! With thousands of letters and phone calls, you let the Governor and the legislature know, in no uncertain terms, what was at stake.

Because this state has taken historic action, I'd like to ask you to help us say "Thanks, Minnesota" by writing your state representative and state senator one more time. Tell them how much you appreciate what they have done, and what this legislation means for Minnesota's entire quality-of-life, because it helps preserve this as a "headquarters state."

Also, if your work schedule permits, come sign the giant "Thanks, Minnesota" banner in the IDS Crystal Court between 11:30 a.m. and 1 p.m. today. Once signed it will be displayed on Nicollet Mall.

I'd like to make one additional request: Say "Thanks, Minnesota" in the way you do better than anybody I know—by serving our customers the very best way you know how.

Let's redouble our efforts to make Dayton Hudson the best retailer in the country—one that provides exceptional value to its customers, employees, communities, and its long-term shareholders.

That is the best way—indeed, the only way—to ensure that Dayton Hudson continues to be a growing, dynamic, and independent company.

Again, thank you for your extraordinary teamwork. I am honored and proud to be able to say, "I'm part of the Dayton Hudson family of companies."

Sincerely,

Kenneth A. Macke
Chairman and Chief Executive Officer

EXHIBIT 4 Thanks, Minnesota

Source: Dayton Hudson Department Store Company—Public Relations.

There's no place like home.

Thanks, Minnesota

DAYTON HUDSON CORPORATION

TARGET MERVYN'S DAYTON HUDSON DEPARTMENT STORES LECHMERE BRANDEN'S PRIMENET

Northwest Airlines: *Private Sector, Public Trust (A)*

On December 16, 1991, Minnesota State Senate Majority Leader Roger Moe conferred with his assistant before the meeting began. They could hear hundreds of Northwest Airlines employees chanting outside the hearing room. Moe looked over two pages of speech notes, and put one in each pocket. Moe took his seat and proceeded to call the meeting to order. He was still undecided about which speech he would use.

The previous May, in an eleventh-hour vote, the Minnesota House and Senate had approved a controversial $838 million incentive package for Northwest Airlines by a two-thirds margin. Through state and local tax breaks, and over $700 million in bond issues, Northwest sought financing for Northern Minnesota maintenance bases to service its growing fleet of Airbus jets, and an unrestricted loan from the Metropolitan Airports Commission (MAC). As chairman of the joint Legislative Commission on Planning and Fiscal Policy (LCPFP), Moe had conducted 15 Commission meetings over the last few months since the regular legislative session ended.

As a safety net, the legislation passed in May authorized the eighteen-member LCPFP to hire financial analysts on behalf of the state to make a "due diligence" review of Northwest's finances and to determine Minnesota's risk before going forward with the bond sale.[1] Unless a majority of the LCPFP was satisfied with the terms of the deal, the economic package would not proceed. At the last meeting, the Legislative Commission had approved, based on the analysts' reports, the $350 million portion of the package that financed a MAC-owned aircraft maintenance base and engine repair facility in Duluth and Hibbing, Minnesota. The bases would provide the specialized service Airbus jets required and would employ over 1,500 skilled people in an economically depressed region of the state. An intense controversy remained, however, about the $320 million unrestricted loan Northwest wanted from MAC-issued bonds. Without loan approval, the entire deal would fall through.

Lobbyists had clogged the Capitol in St. Paul over the last several weeks, presenting opposition to the Northwest bonding bill from an ad hoc citizen committee and Minnesota companies of all sizes, and support for Northwest from its labor unions, and city officials from Duluth and Hibbing, the two cities which would directly benefit from the maintenance facilities.

Senator Moe was a key swing vote. Yet undecided, he reflected on the complex events which led up to this high-profile debate.

Background

The 1980s had been good to Minnesota-based Northwest Airlines, and its Delaware-chartered parent company, NWA, Inc. Steve Rothmeier, Chief Executive Officer of the airline since 1985 and CEO and Chairman of NWA, Inc., since August 1986, inherited a company in a sound financial position. Rothmeier, like his predecessors Donald Nyrop and Joe Lapensky, came from a tight-fisted

This case was prepared by Research Assistant Beth Goodpaster, under the supervision of Professor Thomas Holloran, as the basis for class discussion rather than to illustrate either effective or ineffective handling of an administrative situation. Names of some individuals have been disguised.

Acknowledgments: We would like to thank David Beal of the *St. Paul Pioneer Press*, Jeff Hamiel of the Metropolitan Airports Commission, and Commissioner Peter Gillette of the Department of Trade and Economic Development, for their generous help in putting this case together.

[1] Two independent consulting firms were hired. The "due diligence" process involved an examination of Northwest's financial books, an evaluation of the airline's position in the industry, and an assessment of the risks and implications of the transaction with the state, if the financing were to be approved. The decision of the LCPFP was to be based on this review.

management mindset that kept a sharp eye on the balance sheet and maintained an adamant resistance to carrying a significant debt load.

Rothmeier led Northwest's successful 1986 acquisition of Republic Airlines, also based in the Twin Cities. Initially facing transition challenges, the merged airline operations would yield longer-term positive impacts: domestic route expansion, a strong "hub and spoke" system which included the Twin Cities, Memphis, and Detroit,[2] and a diverse (though older and noisier) fleet of short-haul and long-haul aircraft. Despite the difficulties in melding the different payscales and seniority rights of the two airlines' 37,000 employees, analysts viewed the marriage of Republic and Northwest as a "match made in heaven."

Giving priority to structuring an acquisition transaction in the quickly consolidating airline industry, management was slow to give post-merger attention to employee relations, labor union leadership and customer service, a reputation which led Northwest to earn the public nickname,"Northworst." Ridiculed in the press for inept baggage handling, regularly tardy arrivals, and frustrating ticket reservation mishaps, Northwest was ultimately reprimanded by the Minnesota Attorney General, Hubert H. Humphrey III, in November 1987. The U.S. Department of Transportation had listed NWA as the recipient of the largest number of consumer complaints of all U.S. airlines in consecutive months since August 1987.

Despite Northwest's dubious public relations image, Rothmeier's fiscally conservative strategy gave the company such good financial standing in the late eighties that deregulation (held responsible by some for widespread airline industry disintegration) left Northwest unscathed. With a comparatively low stock price and debt-to-equity ratio (1.3 to 1 in the last quarter of 1987), beneficial options on a $4 billion modern fleet of European Airbus Industry jets on order, plans to build the nation's only Airbus maintenance facility, control of coveted Pacific air routes, and undervalued real estate assets in Japan, Northwest was a tempting target for a takeover.

Takeover Contest

In January 1989, Northwest's stock had increased to over $60 per share, up from $40 in September 1988. The reality of a potential hostile takeover of the airline emerged when Marvin Davis, a billionaire from California, acquired 3% of Northwest's common stock. Though Davis did not make an offer, discussions of his believed intent to do a leveraged buyout and sell off the assets of the company (as had been the case with numerous takeovers) dominated the Northwest boardroom and the Minnesota press.

Davis had a reputation as a brutal businessman in the oil industry and the real estate market—labor groups feared the work climate would worsen, state agencies feared the economic and community repercussions of such a sale, and residents living near the airport were concerned that instead of investing in newer, quieter engine equipment, Davis would merely funnel money to reduce acquisition debt.

Since NWA, Inc. was chartered in Delaware, leadership at Northwest initially examined measures permitted by Delaware corporate law to ward off a hostile takeover. Rothmeier did not respond to Minnesota politicians who thought there was an opportunity to offer Dayton-Hudson-style help.[3] Rothmeier approached employees for a concessions-for-ownership arrangement that would have prevented Davis from acquiring enough stock to complete a hostile takeover. Labor turned down the offer.

Ultimately Rothmeier and the board rejected traditional means to fight off unwanted suitors. Northwest's board decided to form an acquisition committee made up of outside directors in April 1989 to open up a controlled bidding process. The board laid ground rules for the bidding process which forced Davis to "walk with the pack," rather than continue an unfriendly pursuit. With

[2] Deregulation of airlines, legislated in 1978, inadvertently invented flight origination patterns which centered a dominant carrier in one or more major urban areas. Its domestic routes radiated from these hubs where plane-change connections were made. The pattern resembled the hub and spokes of a wheel.

[3] The Minnesota Legislature had a special session in 1987 to prevent the hostile takeover of Minnesota-chartered Dayton Hudson Corporation. The legislature passed a bill which placed severe restrictions on hostile takeovers. At the time, Dayton Hudson was trying to fend off such an acquisition. (For more information, see "Dayton Hudson Corporation: Conscience and Control," pp. 221–47.)

an agreement to make only friendly overtures, bidders gained access to the company's financial books. Davis communicated his intent to offer $2.72 billion, or $90 per share, for the airline. Others submitted bids, including one organized by Rothmeier, all of which valued the company at over $90 per share. Rothmeier and the board rejected all the offers and set a deadline for another round of bids.

In June, the Northwest board agreed to sell for $121 per share to a group led by Al Checchi, who was viewed by board members as the lesser of several evils. Seen as the "white knight," Checchi promised that there would be neither layoffs nor sale of assets other than real estate property in Japan valued at $500 million. The sale closed in August and newly formed Wings Holdings, Inc. became the parent company of the now privatized Northwest.

Los Angeles resident Checchi had extensive experience in the hotel business at Marriott, where, as part of an executive triumvirate which included Gary Wilson and Fred Malek, he was instrumental in turning the hotel chain's dismal performance into full-blown growth in the late seventies and early eighties. They dramatically increased Marriott's level of catering and hotel service marketed to business customers, financed large numbers of acquisitions with debt and limited partnerships, and arranged for long-term operations fees to be paid to Marriott. The company tripled its earnings by the time Checchi left Marriott in 1983. According to one financial journal, however, Marriott was later saddled with so little equity and so much debt that it had no defenses against the collapse of the real estate market. Meanwhile, Checchi had forged a partnership with the Bass family of Texas to finance the expansion to the Walt Disney Corporation.

Checchi convinced bankers that a $3.65 billion loan to provide funds to leverage his purchase of Northwest was a safe bet, despite his inexperience in the airline operations business. His projections for $850 million in earnings over the next few years took into account the effects of an economic recession, he said. The bank leverage allowed Checchi and Wilson, his partner and mentor from Marriott/Disney days, to invest only $40 million of personal assets in the $4 billion acquisition. (Checchi and Wilson would subsequently recoup much of their initial investment from $10 million annual management fees which Checchi negotiated for his lightly staffed consulting group, Checchi and Associates.) Checchi also forged equity partnerships for the acquisition with KLM Royal Dutch Airlines, Bankers Trust Co., Blum and Associates, and Elders Finance Group to bring the total equity investment to $700 million. (See Exhibit 1.) Checchi's purchase of Northwest is known as the last of the 1980s wave of leveraged buyouts.

Winner Takes All

The airline industry is well-known for its volatile and cyclical responses to market pressures, most commonly attracting institutional investors, who include stock in airlines to diversify a portfolio. There was a great deal of uncertainty about the terms of Checchi's privatizing purchase of Northwest, particularly due to the expected economic recession and the predicted slow recovery. The wisdom of carrying large debt in the airline business was questioned in the press, by labor union officials, and by some financial analysts. The high leverage in the Northwest deal also caused some discomfort among public officials such as Congressman James Oberstar of Chisholm, Minnesota, the influential chairman of the House Subcommittee on Aviation. Transportation Secretary Samuel Skinner also indicated skepticism and announced that he would carefully review the Northwest buyout proposal. Although government regulators could not block the purchase of the airline, they could order more stringent financial reporting and place limits on foreign ownership.

"The amount of debt is not the least bit excessive . . . it's almost laughable that this is being brought up as a concern," Checchi responded. Checchi's outspoken confidence and optimism for his company's place in the industry recalled to some airline analysts Rothmeier's quip from years ago: "The airline industry is the only business in the world where once-in-a-lifetime economic catastrophes occur every two years."

After making several trips to Washington, D.C., Checchi ultimately reassured the skeptics. Checchi put together a management team which included himself, his partner and former Northwest board member Wilson, and Marriott executive Frank Malek. The transition was complicated in part when Rothmeier, and three other top executives, unexpectedly resigned after four months with the Checchi-owned Northwest. The final management lineup included Checchi and Wilson as co-chairmen and Malek as President. After Rothmeier's exit, Checchi and Malek assumed Chief Executive responsibilities until they hired Fred Rentschler who then left after six months. John Dasburg (also of Marriott), after a year as Chief Financial Officer at Northwest, became the new ownership's fourth CEO replacing Rentschler in November 1990.

Messages from management to the community included Checchi's intent to make significant improvements in customer service and employee satisfaction, goals which tapped his skills from the hospitality industry. Checchi pledged a "new era" of passenger service and employee good will. In early press statements, Checchi asserted, "Employees in the service business are absolutely your most important assets. Job enrichment is a priority."

Indeed, evidence of improvements in labor relations and customer service emerged during the first year of Checchi leadership. Consumers had noticed. Checchi personally and publicly ushered in his "new era" of improved operations. His open, personable style contrasted with Rothmeier's stern reputation. Checchi stressed in his public statements that he would concentrate on building a better work climate for employees and become the number one airline for service. He announced a $422 million spending program to institute the service changes. Early on, Checchi took steps to demonstrate his commitment to a "cooperation over confrontation" ethic toward employees. Employees found Checchi much more open and accessible, and appreciated his lively personality. He liberalized employee flight pass policies, removed nepotism rules at the airline, and eased restrictions on rehiring former employees. During 1990, he increased Northwest's payroll by 5,000, bringing the company's worldwide total to 42,000 employees. (Northwest was the largest private employer in the state of Minnesota.) Checchi and his team maintained a visible presence within the daily workings of the airline and in the community, despite their commutes from California residences. Checchi's managerial role was unusual for an owner, and later was a difficult hat to take off.

Partly to quell anxiety over Northwest's 4:1 debt-to-equity ratio, another early priority of the Checchi team was extending a hand to local politicians. Checchi offered a board seat to former Vice President Walter Mondale, a well-regarded Minnesota Democrat. In a private meeting in Washington, D.C., Congressman Oberstar asked Checchi to locate a planned maintenance base in Minnesota for the Airbus jets Northwest was scheduled to acquire; Oberstar said he "sensed a tilt" from Checchi in Minnesota's direction. On September 23, 1989, Checchi made a high-profile appearance at Minnesota's annual state Democratic party fundraiser, the Humphrey Day Dinner. The NWA team maintained connections to the Republican party as well, since company president Malek had served in the Nixon Administration and was a close friend of President Bush.

Expansion was also on Checchi's mind. He initiated investments to expand Northwest's presence on the East coast. He purchased gates at Washington National Airport from insolvent Eastern Airlines, and expressed an interest in creating an Atlanta hub. Checchi also would have won for Northwest the operations of the New York–Boston–Washington, D.C., Trump shuttle, had the deal not fallen through at the last minute due to labor representation questions.

In the first year under new ownership, the acquisition debt was whittled to under $2 billion. This was achieved by transferring takeover debt to higher interest sale-leaseback agreements on jets. Since previous strategy at the airline had favored purchased rather than leased equipment, Checchi was able to raise capital by selling the planes, and then continuing to operate the aircraft under lease agreements. (The disadvantage in arranging leasebacks instead of maintaining purchased aircraft, some observers noted, was the payments due to the lessor did not stop, even if the company's cash flow did.) Northwest also refinanced its Tokyo real estate, and secured new long-term loans from its equipment suppliers. Critics maintained that although Northwest's acquisition debt column looked different, the airline's overall debt service burden had not changed.

High-Pressure Market Atmosphere

The airline industry as a whole faced turbulent times in late 1990 and early 1991. An economic recession was emerging nationwide, and it hit the airlines especially hard. The Iraqi invasion of Kuwait in August 1990 marked the beginning of further economic hardship for airlines. Fuel prices doubled. Passenger traffic dropped off drastically due to fears of terrorism during the Gulf War. In response to these unforeseen obstacles, airlines began widespread costcutting.

Northwest Airlines, unlike other carriers, suffered the economic crisis with the added burden of a potentially devastating debt load. Northwest had obtained a $500 million loan from its suppliers, Airbus and General Electric, to restructure its debt in the fall of 1990. United, Delta, American, and US Air had the advantage of being publicly held, buffered by a large block of shareholder equity. American and Delta in particular had healthy balance sheets, benefiting from stock offerings made earlier in the year. The Gulf War shook out struggling Eastern and Pan Am Airlines, and sent Midway and TWA seeking bankruptcy protection.

Northwest got mixed reviews. Forecasters thought the company would survive the shakeout, but some of its bonds were placed on a Standard & Poor's creditwatch list in February 1991. Moody's Investors Service downgraded parts of NWA debt to the level of junk bonds in March. To conserve cash, Northwest froze hiring, eliminated low-yield flights, and deferred new programs including the $422 million service improvement program. Employees were asked to take voluntary leaves of absence, while the number of flights was reduced by 2 percent.

The financial challenges of the Airbus maintenance base construction became evident. Northwest also was experiencing persistent cost overruns in airport development underway at its Detroit hub. The costs associated with meeting federal regulations calling for a transition to modern, quieter "Stage III" jets soon after the year 2000 were seen as prohibitive. Of all the U.S. carriers, Northwest had the largest percentage of older, noisier, Stage II aircraft in its fleet.

Al Checchi joined other airline executives, including Hollis Harris, the president of bankrupt Continental Airlines, in asking Congress to relax the statutory Stage III jet replacement timeline and to provide financial assistance to the carriers. They proposed to Congress that airlines be authorized to keep the money from the federal 10% ticket tax (earmarked for airport improvements), and repay it to the government as a loan. Members of the Congress raised their eyebrows. Skeptics wondered why Northwest needed financial help when it had money to buy routes and landing slots for expansion in Washington, D.C.

Turning to States' Governments

The initial siting process for an Airbus maintenance base was begun before Checchi's leveraged buyout of the airline. CEO Rothmeier had indicated in September 1988 that due to the state's unfavorable business climate, and the unfriendly relations between Minnesota and Rothmeier's Northwest, the Airbus base would not likely be built in Minnesota. In addition, Rothmeier said the airline would not ask for direct subsidies in an economic package: "It's not our style . . . we're not going in with our hat in our hand." With new ownership, however, Minnesota regained a spot on Northwest's short list of financial assistance possibilities.

After the Northwest takeover was finalized in late 1989, talk of building Airbus maintenance facilities for NWA's fleet-on-order was set on the back burner for the next year. During the early part of 1991, the idea returned to the forefront of Northwest's public discussions. Northwest's current stock of 32 Airbus jets would need a scheduled overhaul in the spring of 1993; there was just enough time for maintenance base construction.

Management approached the Metropolitan Airports Commission (MAC) indicating that Northwest would build the bases at the Twin Cities airport if MAC would finance the construction. The Commission, a public corporation created by the Minnesota Legislature in 1943 to manage the state's airport facilities in the metropolitan area, was used to getting such proposals from Northwest. It was general practice for MAC to undertake (and underwrite) airport facilities construction for airlines' use. MAC worked out a $33 million proposal which would make the Airbus base possible for Northwest through low-interest bond issues, averted sales and property taxes, and tax breaks for each job created. Once the company received MAC's bid, however, NWA announced it would look more seriously at a nationwide pool of bids on the maintenance facilities. It became a competition.

Prompted by Congressman Oberstar, the city of Duluth, Minnesota, developed an independent bid for the maintenance base financed in part by city-owned water and utility revenues. Duluth offered two benefits that the Twin Cities airport could not: increased airport noise was a non-issue in the relatively underpopulated site, and the base and influx of needed jobs would be situated in the middle of Congressman Oberstar's district.

Since other airlines were not making expansion moves, economic development packages of tax breaks, construction financing and existing maintenance buildings vied for Northwest's favor. Estimates of new job creation from the project varied from 1,500 to 2,000 high-paying positions totaling a $100 million payroll. Detroit reportedly offered Northwest incentives in connection with plans for the new $1 billion passenger terminal at Detroit Metropolitan Airport. Northwest indicated that in addition to the Twin Cities and Duluth in Minnesota; Atlanta; Milwaukee; Kansas City; Memphis; Lake Charles, Louisiana; and Portland, Oregon, had also submitted bids. Northwest never disclosed to Minnesota decision makers the terms of the bids it claimed to have.

In February, it became evident to newly elected Governor Carlson that in order to distinguish a Minnesota bid from other states' proposals, the state needed to pool resources. In April, a jointly sponsored bid linked the finances of St. Louis County, the cities of Duluth and Hibbing, the state of Minnesota, and the Metropolitan Airports Commission. The maintenance base would be sited in Duluth, and the engine overhaul facility would locate in Hibbing. MAC would hold title to the property and oversee construction. MAC, while continuing to favor the Twin Cities' bid for the base since the site would remain in MAC's seven-county jurisdiction, decided to back the Duluth–Hibbing proposal as a second-best option. The Northern Minnesota bid was seen to offer what other states could not, and to keep Minnesota in the running for the economic stimulus the project was expected to deliver. The Governor, MAC, Oberstar, and city and county officials from the Duluth and Hibbing area joined forces to convince Northwest. (See Exhibit 2.)

The terms of Minnesota's bid presented to Northwest included a $350 million state revenue bond issue to finance construction. The MAC would own the buildings and lease them back to Northwest. The city of Duluth would offer a $47.6 million direct subsidy, and the Iron Range Resource Recovery Board (IRRRB) would provide a $10 million direct subsidy for the Hibbing facility. The package included $50 million in future income tax breaks by qualifying the Northern Minnesota sites as enterprise zones. Northwest would get a $5,000 tax credit per job created and a waiver for construction related property and sales taxes. (See Exhibit 3.) The proposal was part of the state's economic development philosophy which sought to increase the size of its "economic pie," retaining and creating jobs in Minnesota companies as a means of augmenting its tax base. To avoid raising taxes while continuing to provide an increasing number of government services, Governor Carlson's administration endeavored to keep the expansion of a hometown company at home.

No Place (to Make Deals) Like Home

By early May, the Minnesota bid for the bases had been put together—and put to the public. Governor Carlson, Representative Oberstar, and city officials vied for a nod from Northwest. Ever the deal maker, Checchi met with the governor to better the financing package. With Representative Oberstar's zealous support, Checchi was able to secure Carlson's commitment to sweeten the state's appeal to Northwest.

Checchi characterized the state's original offer as "generous, comprehensive, professional, and quite attractive," but sought the addition of other provisions—foremost, legislative approval of a $320 million unrestricted loan from MAC. With the stagnant economy and a declining credit rating, Northwest had not been able to get an infusion of money from private sources. Without putting it in writing, Northwest also indicated interest in raising an additional $200 million private placement from the State Investment Board, which managed state employees' pension funds. E. Peter Gillette, Commissioner of the Minnesota Department of Trade and Economic Development, worked closely with the governor, Oberstar, and MAC to respond to this new counterproposal. This group agreed that the new package, which necessitated full legislative approval, would guarantee Minnesota a first-place bid. MAC Executive Director Jeff Hamiel noted that this was not the first mention of a loan for Northwest—the airline had approached MAC earlier that year for a $500 million loan for "future investment," separate from any base financing. MAC had turned down the airline's request. With Oberstar's help, Hamiel speculated, the loan request now locked elbows with the base construction.

Though it was only three weeks before the end of the 1991 legislative session, the Northwest bonding bill became the center of attention, and began its sometimes tumultuous journey through the committee process at the Capitol. Checchi told a group of state senators that the company needed to look for ways to expand at a time when airlines were falling by the wayside. He said that the search for cash and the incentive package to build the bases were not inextricably linked, but nonetheless, Northwest needed money to aggressively expand and be one of the survivors. "It's in our long-term interest to be an acquirer," he said, "we must play offense." Checchi noted that previous leadership at Northwest had intended to locate the new job-creating facilities elsewhere, but that he would "bend over backwards" to locate in Minnesota. "It's our home, too," he said.

At the same time, Northwest had not rejected purported proposals and packages from other cities and states. Checchi refused to characterize the offers he claimed to have from six or seven other communities, or to say whether those also involved state subsidies: "We have alternatives, from other jurisdictions, that many people think from an economic point of view would be superior." In a letter to employees, CEO Dasburg restated the company's desire to build in Minnesota, but asked Minnesotans "to acknowledge our right and obligation to structure a transaction that makes the most strategic sense for the company. We will locate these facilities where our needs are best met, whether it be in Minnesota or in another state."

Public Image: Wolf or Waif?

The debate in the legislature over the Northwest Airlines bill was Minnesota's most controversial of the session and the most frequently reported story of 1991. The inclusion of the unrestricted $390 million MAC loan to Northwest ($320 million plus a $70 million reserve) in the proposed legislation added a complexity to the debate that caused some to question NWA's motives, financial soundness, and the precedent set if the state made such large-scale economic commitments to a private corporation.

Lobbying efforts redoubled with the revised two-part legislative package. The total value of the deal was $838 million. (See Exhibit 4.) MAC lent its support to the loan which would be secured by $200 million in collateral for the mortgage on a pilot training center that Northwest owned. The remaining collateral would be arranged by a pledge of routes and adjusted leaseback agreements on various gates, hangars, and concourses at the Minneapolis/St. Paul International Airport. The bonds issued by MAC had an AAA bond rating; default on loan repayment was backed by MAC's taxing authority on the seven-county metropolitan area residents. MAC acknowledged that this type of capital infusion loan by a public entity was unprecedented in the airline industry, but maintained that the airline was too important to the state to risk losing by doing nothing.

Despite the blessings of state and airport commission officials, advocates of the Northwest deal faced an uphill battle against public opinion. NWA's financial condition was scrutinized and criticized. NWA officers assured doubters that the package was not a "bailout," and that the airline's future was sound. The year's losses were explained in terms of transitory industry circumstances beyond anyone's control. To illustrate its healthy prospects and that cash was needed for growth rather than rescue, Northwest emphasized its commitment to purchase 60 Airbus aircraft over the next three years, and its untapped $600 million revolving line of credit. "Our company's future does not hinge on state involvement," asserted CEO Dasburg.

Advocates of the Northwest bonding and loan bill pointed to the employment the new maintenance bases could bring to the region, and the safeguards and financial review requirements written into the legislation to spread out and protect taxpayers' investment. Should the deal not be approved, they argued, Minnesota incurred the risk of losing the economic benefits to the business and labor community provided by Northwest's Twin Cities hub. It was acknowledged that Minneapolis–St. Paul was a geographically "unnatural" hub, far north of typically travelled routes. The many economic and trade benefits of hosting the hub were a lucky rather than strategic consequence of Northwest's historical tie to the Twin Cities. Though Northwest Airlines never indicated that it would move its operations to another out-of-state hub during the legislative proceedings, there was widespread concern that if Northwest found another more strategic location to begin to establish a presence, a slow drain of operations from Minnesota would be inevitable.

The bill's House sponsor, Democratic Representative Wayne Simoneau, acknowledged that the proposed Northwest/State of Minnesota relationship would be unique, but lobbied his colleagues to support an assured influx of 2,000 new directly related jobs, and up to 10,000 ancillary jobs, for the Iron Range region.

An ad hoc committee of individual citizens formed to oppose the Northwest deal. Bruce Hendry, corporate bankruptcy expert, was the lead spokesperson for the group. This group and its legislator allies pointed to the risks from the leveraged buyout in 1989 that would now be borne by taxpayers. Hendry was concerned about the airline's economic peril and consequences for the state in case of a Northwest default (e.g., the difficulty of releasing a large maintenance facility in Northern Minnesota). Opponents of the Northwest financing suggested alternative ways to spend economic development money from the state, such as for small business support. And the propriety of NWA linking the maintenance base financing to the MAC loan was questioned. If banks won't lend to Northwest Airlines, they said, why should the Metropolitan Airports Commission or the State of Minnesota do the deal? In addition, many members of the Minnesota business community resented Northwest's pursuit of preferential treatment from state government.

Debate on Giving Northwest Credit

The financing package had to pass through eight policy committees in the state legislature before coming to a full floor vote. A two-thirds majority of the full legislature was needed to approve bonding authorization. An early quote from Commissioner Gillette, who strongly supported the bonding and loan package, was used to fuel arguments on both sides of the issue: "This is not a bankable deal," he said. His comment which followed was rarely quoted: "But bankers don't have to worry about public policy."

People began to wonder if the loan was not bankable because Northwest was a lost cause. What if NWA went bankrupt? Where would that leave the state of Minnesota? Was Northwest's collateral valuable? Given the risk, shouldn't the state or MAC get equity for this investment? What if Northwest picked up and moved its headquarters elsewhere, no matter what the legislature did? Would the Twin Cities suffer the major economic turmoil of 18,000 laid-off workers and become an inaccessible hub has-been?

Legislators, such as Republican Representative Don Frerichs, raised the issue of fairness, stressing that government's role was to establish a beneficial business climate for all. He suggested that lowering workers' compensation costs to the state's employers was within the Legislature's purview, whereas becoming the "First State Bank of Minnesota" was not. He and others shared the view that Minnesota was sophomorically embracing the "too big to fail" philosophy and deferring to political pressure from Washington, D.C. "Economic development has changed dramatically . . . [state government] now has to pick winners and losers," Frerichs stated. "We were here two years ago talking about Dayton Hudson, and now it's the expansion of Northwest Airlines. . . . We help the big people, and the little person can't compete," he said. According to one small business development expert, the money invested in the Northwest deal, if invested in assistance programs for small- and medium-sized businesses instead, would create 16,000 well paying jobs.

The bill passed all the committees by the last week of the session. Ten minutes before the session would officially end, floor votes in both the Senate and House tentatively declared Northwest a winner. The legislature approved the package as a matter for the Legislative Commission on Planning and Fiscal Policy to consider after due diligence reviews were conducted. Since the Legislative Commission would have the final say, the battle over the financing package heated up even more.

The Last Hurdle

Meetings of the LCPFP, chaired by Senator Moe, commenced that summer. Legislators soon found out that, in the first seven months of 1991, Northwest had had losses of $263.9 million. The company's debt-to-equity ratio was 30 to 1.[4] (See Exhibit 5.) The consultants projected income over the next several years at a much lower level than Northwest had presented to the legislature. They characterized the financing deal as one with "significant risk . . . and highly dependent on achievement of a number of assumptions." The consulting firms still considered the risk manageable, particularly if the MAC agreed to loan the airline $270 million, rather than the requested $320 million. After discussions with Northwest, MAC followed the consultants' advice.

The airline's negotiators became frustrated with the deliberative public policy process. Northwest temporarily broke off the slow-going negotiations with MAC when the lower loan amount was offered. Northwest officials asserted to MAC that the airline required the original $320 million loan, and no less. The company then reportedly resumed unofficial talks with the campaigning Governor of Louisiana about siting the Airbus bases in Lake Charles, Louisiana. "Negotiations are active, hot, but not yet concluded," Louisiana Governor Buddy Roemmer said. "I think Northwest has decided to leave Minnesota."

Congressman Oberstar, whose interest was to revive the deteriorating talks to secure the aircraft facilities for his district, took on the role of mediator. Within a couple of weeks, the airline's negotiators came back to the table. MAC offered $45 million from its construction fund to supplement the $270 million loan, stressing to Northwest that MAC's bonding capability could be strained no further. All parties agreed to the revised funding, which then went before the LCPFP.

Northwest had hoped for financing approval by the end of September 1991. Discovery of Northwest's worsening financial status stoked the coals of the legislative fire, however, and the commission meetings continued on into December. To make the financing bill acceptable to more legislators, and to ease fears about Northwest's future intentions, amendments were offered by Commission members which attached strings to the bond approval: Northwest would be required to keep its corporate headquarters and hub in the Twin Cities and to guarantee 1,500 new jobs for Minnesotans. After hard-hitting media analysis of the airline's proposal to seek investments from state pensioners, John Dasburg sent a letter to Senator Moe, informing him that Northwest had decided not to approach the State Investment Board for $200 million beyond the legislative package. House Speaker Robert Vanasek said that final approval of the Northwest deal would be "a strong sign to the largest private employer in Minnesota that we want them to remain a vital force . . . and to grow and expand in Minnesota."

At a climactic point in the debate, the media became the stage for fiery attacks from people on both sides of the issue. Over Thanksgiving weekend, the group of citizens and individual businesses opposing the financing deal took out full page ads in the local papers that depicted Al Checchi as the wolf at Minnesota taxpayers' door. (See Exhibit 6.) Equally stinging were the response ads that Northwest ran on television and in print. (See Exhibit 7.) The political stakes of the decision had been raised.

Proponents characterized the decision as a vote for jobs. Opponents couched the decision as a vote for taxpayers. Many legislators serving on the Legislative Commission had firm positions from the start. For those who had not yet committed, the political risk calculators were working overtime. Senator Don Samuelson, a declared "yes" vote, stated, "If the package is approved and successful, most folks won't remember what we [decided]. If it fails, everyone will."

Picking a Pocket

After final testimony and questions, Moe indicated that each legislator would have a chance to make a brief statement before casting his or her vote. Thus, members tried one last time to lobby colleagues with speeches pro and con. Cheers and boos could be heard from outside the hearing room as each statement was given. The last person to speak before the vote, Moe reached for the notes in his right pocket.

[4] Debt is defined as short-term and long-term debt, capital leases and land mortgages. Equity is defined as preferred stock and common stockholders' equity.

EXHIBIT 1 **1989 Acquisition Equity Stakes**

Al Checchi, Gary Wilson, and Fred Malek	$ 40 million (7 board seats)
Bankers Trust Co.	75 million (1 board seat)
KLM Royal Dutch Airlines	400 million (3 board seats)
Blum and Associates	100 million (2 board seats)
Elders Finance Group	85 million (2 board seats)
Total Equity	$700 million

EXHIBIT 2 **Locations of Duluth, Hibbing, and Twin Cities, MN**

EXHIBIT 3 **Northwest Airlines' Base Financing Package**

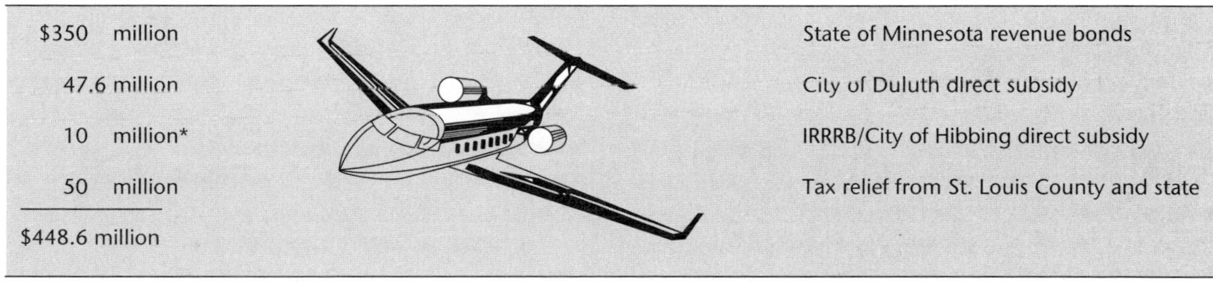

$350 million	State of Minnesota revenue bonds
47.6 million	City of Duluth direct subsidy
10 million*	IRRRB/City of Hibbing direct subsidy
50 million	Tax relief from St. Louis County and state
$448.6 million	

* $1 million per year for 10 years.

EXHIBIT 4 **Revised Northwest Airlines' Financing Package**

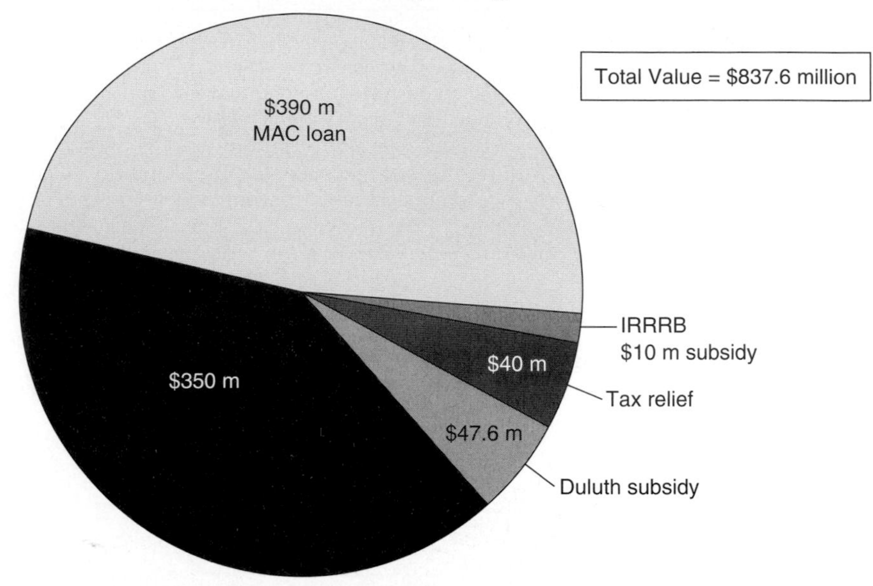

EXHIBIT 5 **Northwest Airlines**

Debt to Equity Comparison with and without Acquisition-Related Debt

Source: Price Waterhouse, Northwest Airlines.

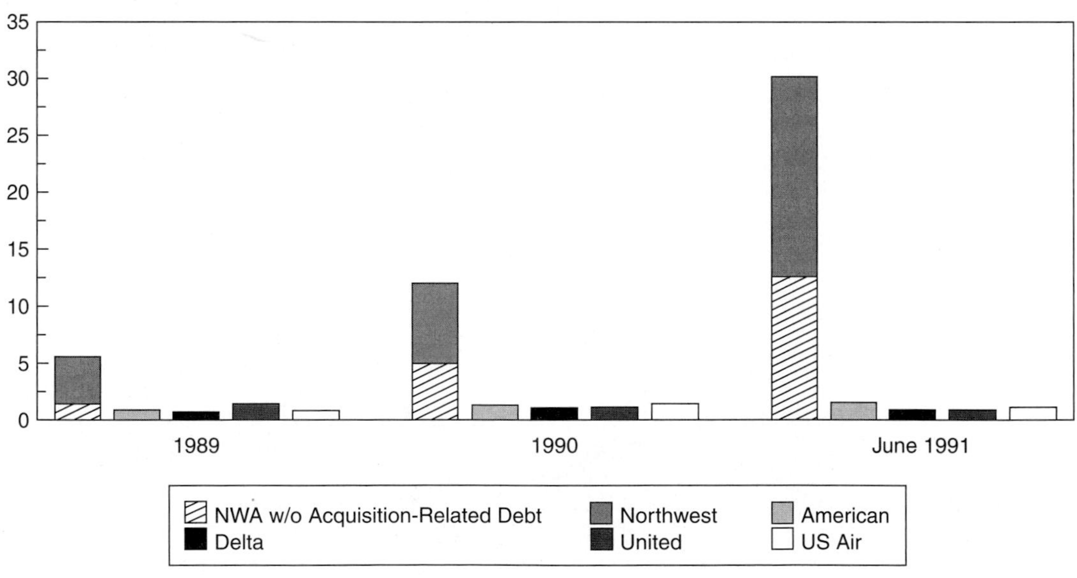

1) Debt is defined as short-term and long-term debt, capital leases and land mortgages
2) Equity is defined as preferred stock and common stockholders' equity

EXHIBIT 6

THE WOLF IS AT YOUR DOOR.

AND HIS NAME IS AL.

Now that Al Checchi has devoured Northwest Airlines, he's back for more. But this time Al is about to tear $800 out of **your** wallet. That's your family's share of Governor Arne Carlson's $838 million dollar loan and "Jobs" program for Northwest Airlines. But it's really a bailout.

IN 1989, AL CHECCHI TOOK THE MOST SUCCESSFUL AIRLINE IN AMERICA AND BLED IT DRY. NOW HE WANTS YOU TO PAY FOR IT.

For 39 years, Northwest made money. In 2½ years under Al Checchi, Northwest has lost $752 million dollars.* Do you really think it'll stop there?

Minnesota is about to hand a private company hundreds of millions of your tax dollars **with no strings attached.** That means you have no say over how Al gets to spend your money.

Supposedly, this money will create jobs. But for whom? How many jet aircraft mechanics live in Northern Minnesota? None of the best jobs in this deal are being created for the people of Duluth or Hibbing.

What's more, Northwest has refused to put up a single plane as collateral for this loan. So how will you get your money if this deal goes bad?

Fact is, Northwest is close to the edge. If the airline goes bankrupt, it'll be Al Checchi's fault, not yours. And it should be his money lost, not yours. In a bankruptcy, Al and his current creditors would feel the pain. Employees and the flying public would hardly be affected. **The airline would stay here and continue to fly,** which is what we all want.

You can stop this insane giveaway with just a phone call. Call any of the numbers of the public officials listed here. Or write. Tell them what you think. Just say, **"NO WAY, AL."**

*Source: ARVAI Group Report to the State of Minnesota, Department of Finance, September 1991.

Roger Moe, Chair (S)
208 State Capitol
St. Paul, MN 55155
612-296-2577

Bill Schreiber (H)
247 State Office Bldg.
St. Paul, MN 55155
612-296-4128

Jim Gustafson (S)
115 State Office Bldg.
St. Paul, MN 55155
612-296-4314

Ember D. Reichgott (S)
301 State Capitol
St. Paul, MN 55155
612-296-2889

Dave Bishop (H)
357 State Office Bldg.
St. Paul, MN 55155
612-296-0573

Wayne Simoneau (H)
365 State Office Bldg.
St. Paul, MN 55155
612-296-4331

Linda Berglin (S)
G-9 State Capitol
St. Paul, MN 55155
612-296-4261

(S) Senate Fax: **612-296-6511**

IF YOU, AS A TAXPAYER, ARE OUTRAGED AT THIS TRANSACTION, LET US KNOW.

Mail to: **Citizens Committee to Stop the NWA Loan**
P.O. Box 581996
Minneapolis, MN 55458-1996

Add my name to the list of those opposed.

NAME: ______________________

ADDRESS: ______________________

____

I would like to contribute $ ______________

Make check payable to: Stop NWA Loan

I would like to help, call me at: ______________

[illegible]

TO VOICE YOUR VIEWS AT THE LEGISLATIVE HEARINGS STARTING DEC. 2, CALL ROGER MOE'S OFFICE AT 296-2577. THE COMMITTEE TO STOP THE NWA LOAN CAN BE REACHED AT 1-800-NO WAY AL (800-669-2925).

Douglas J. Johnson (S)
205 State Capitol
St. Paul, MN 55155
612-296-8881

Paul Ogren (H)
443 State Office Bldg.
St. Paul, MN 55155
612-296-7808

Terry Dempsey (H)
267 State Office Bldg.
St. Paul, MN 55155
612-296-9303

Robert Vanasek (H)
463 State Office Bldg.
St. Paul, MN 55155
612-296-4229

Dee Long (H)
459 State Office Bldg.
St. Paul, MN 55155
612-296-0171

Ken Nelson (H)
267 State Office Bldg.
St. Paul, MN 55155
612-296-4244

Governor Arne Carlson
State Capitol, Rm. 130
75 Constitution Ave.
St. Paul, MN 55155
612-296-3391

(H) House Fax: **612-296-1563**

EXHIBIT 7

This is your captain speaking...

And your first and second officers. You know us, the Northwest pilots. We're your friends and neighbors; you've flown with us for years.

Pilots deal with facts - altitude, temperature, speed. And we want you to know the facts about Northwest Airlines.

Fact #1: Northwest isn't losing money because of Al Checchi. The entire industry is in serious trouble. The combined losses of 1990 and 1991 have wiped out the profits all commercial airlines have made since the day they carried the first paying passenger over 60 years ago.

Fact #2: Northwest is nowhere near bankruptcy, as a recent ad implied. However, if Northwest Airlines did go bankrupt, not only Checchi but thousands of Minnesotans would be hurt. Northwest employees would be out of work, and the airline would stop flying. The cost of unemployment benefits, welfare payments, and other assistance to those out-of-work employees would be far more expensive than the loan for the maintenance base.

Fact #3: Minnesota residents need Northwest Airlines. Northwest provides direct transportation from Minnesota to all parts of the world. It's your airline as well as ours.

Fact #4: The maintenance base will create new jobs for mechanics and thousands of other tax-paying Minnesotans. Just what we need now that our country is in a recession.

These are turbulent times for airlines. Many have already gone bankrupt or ceased operations. Very few U.S. airlines will survive deregulation. We want Northwest Airlines to be one of the survivors, and we believe you do too.

Urge your legislator to vote "YES" for the NWA Air Base.

Roger Moe, Chair (S)
208 State Capitol
St. Paul, MN 55155
612-296-2577

Bill Schreiber (H)
247 State Office Bldg.
St. Paul, MN 55155
612-296-4128

Jim Gustafson (S)
115 State Office Bldg.
St. Paul, MN 55155
612-296-4314

Ember D. Reichgott (S)
301 State Capitol
St. Paul, MN 55155
612-296-2889

Dave Bishop (H)
357 State Office Bldg.
St. Paul, MN 55155
612-296-0573

Wayne Simoneau (H)
365 State Office Bldg.
St. Paul, MN 55155
612-296-4331

Linda Berglin (S)
G-9 State Capitol
St. Paul, MN 55155
612-296-4261

Douglas J. Johnson (S)
205 State Capitol
St. Paul, MN 55155
612-296-8881

Paul Ogren (H)
443 State Office Bldg.
St. Paul, MN 55155
612-296-7808

Terry Dempsey (H)
267 State Office Bldg.
St. Paul, MN 55155
612-296-9303

Robert Vanasek
463 State Office Bldg.
St. Paul, MN 55155
612-296-4229

Dee Long (H)
459 State Office Bldg.
St. Paul, MN 55155
612-296-0171

Ken Nelson (H)
267 State Office Bldg.
St. Paul, MN 55155
612-296-4244

Governor Arne Carlson
State Capitol, Rm. 130
75 Constitution Ave.
St. Paul, MN 55155
612-296-3391

Paid for by the more than 5000 Northwest members of the Air Line Pilots Association.

We thank you for your concern and support.

The Bush Foundation: *A Case Study in Giving Money Away (A)*

At the first of the 1993 Bush Foundation biennial board retreats, John Ireland, a director of the philanthropic, nonprofit foundation, announced that the Investment Committee would meet the following month, on April 16, to evaluate and revise its investment decisions. As chairman of that committee, he briefly outlined the scope of its upcoming meeting, and urged directors who did not serve on the committee to forward any suggestions for the agenda to him. Gwendolyn Anderson, the newest member appointed to The Bush Foundation board of directors, chose to bring up an issue for the Investment Committee to consider. Formerly a commissioner of the state Department of Health, Anderson also was a member of the University of Minnesota Board of Regents. Her academic and policy expertise was valued by the Bush board, especially since health care services were becoming a prioritized area in the Foundation's grantmaking.

On April 8, Ireland received a memo from Anderson. She had attached an article regarding recent pressure on Stanford University to remove tobacco stocks from its endowment investment portfolio. Given recent scientific reports in the media, tobacco use was the number-one underlying cause of death in the United States. She wondered whether The Bush Foundation also owned stock in tobacco companies and, if so, whether it was feasible and prudent to divest. Anderson's memo to the Investment Committee explained her concerns, summarized her initial research in the matter, and proposed a course of action for the coming year.

Ireland, in his personal investments, avoided the stocks of tobacco companies, although he did invest in mutual funds, which included tobacco stocks. He was uncertain how this would apply on an institutional investment level. If The Bush Foundation did have tobacco holdings, did this undermine the foundation's mission as an education, community development, and health services grantmaking institution? Or was the return on such investments more important in order to sustain the long term health of the $460 million endowment? Ireland put the issue on the Investment Committee's agenda for discussion. As always, new board members brought important questions for the Foundation to examine. "Social investing" had the potential to be an issue the Foundation would struggle with long into the future.

Foundation History

Archibald G. Bush, an early 3M executive, and his wife Edyth Bassler Bush, incorporated the Foundation in 1953 as a tax-exempt nonprofit corporation to promote charitable, scientific, literary, and educational efforts. On Mr. Bush's death sizable additional funds flowed into the corporation. In 1992, the corporation had an endowment of approximately $460 million and made annual grants of approximately $20 million.

The corporation was governed by 15 directors elected by the board as vacancies occurred. Directors could serve until age 70 and (for directors elected after 1990) not more than 12 years. The board selected a chair and appointed members to Grants, Investment, Nominating, and Audit Committees. The Grants and Investment

This case was prepared by Professor Thomas Holloran with Research Assistant Beth Goodpaster as the basis for class discussion rather than to illustrate either effective or ineffective handling of an administrative situation. The situation as described is hypothetical, but is based on actual issues.

Committees met quarterly. The other committees met as required.

A belief that diversity leads to quality in governance led to director selection from a variety of occupations—city council chair, paint company CEO, child psychiatrist, small business owner, college president, federal judge, museum director, professor, financial services executive, banker, and partner in a large accounting firm. Seven of the directors were women and four were people of color. The directors received a small stipend and were covered by a director and officers' liability policy.

The Executive Director was selected by the board. Humphrey Doermann, executive director since the early seventies, was prominent in national foundation activities having served as president of the National Council of Foundations.

Periodically, through the use of outside consultants, the board endeavored to judge the effectiveness of its governance. Recently, the executive director and the chair of the board met individually with each of the directors to explore individual perceptions of strengths and weaknesses and areas where improvements can be made. Biennially, the board met in retreat to re-evaluate its priorities and processes.

Grantmaking Process

While almost all of the grants were made for activities in Minnesota, North Dakota, and South Dakota, exceptions were made for grants to historically black and Native American colleges. During the last two decades, The Bush Foundation had concentrated its grants in the areas of education, humanities and the arts, community and social welfare, health, and leadership development. (See Exhibit 1.) The most noticeable change in Bush Foundation grantmaking during this time was the rise in the number of applications and of grants in health and human services. The Foundation in 1991 approved 85 such grants, totaling $6.1 million. (For other grant statistics, see Exhibit 2.)

Applications for grants were submitted in writing and reviewed by staff. If the request was for a large amount or for a unique purpose, the advice of an outside consultant was sought. The staff (which did not have authority to make grants) recommended either approval, approval with modification, or denial, with a written analysis to the Grants Committee of the board. The Grants Committee after discussion with staff made its recommendation for action by the full board. Periodically, a postreview was conducted on grants made and major grants denied in an effort to better understand the impact of the Foundation and to improve the proposed review process.

While awards were customarily made to not-for-profit grantees, approximately 10% of funds granted have gone to individuals (called "Bush Fellows") to continue personal education and development. Bush Fellows were selected by advisory panels from the community. Between 1965 and 1992, a total of 1,847 grants have been made (see Exhibit 3).

Investment Strategies

Federal tax law required that to maintain its tax-exempt status, a charitable foundation must distribute annually to charitable activities not less than 5% of the market value of its endowment. Thus, unless earned return is 5% plus the rate of inflation, the foundation would gradually spend itself out of existence.

Bush and many other endowment funds measured financial performance on total return. That is, they aggregated dividends, interest, and increase in market value of assets to determine investment performance.

Prior to 1984, Bush retained three balanced fund managers. These were managers who had discretion over the selection of asset category (stocks, bonds, or cash), as well as individual security selection within each category from funds allocated to the managers.

Dissatisfaction with performance led to the hiring of an investment consulting firm. As a result of its findings the board fired the three managers, set more specific goals regarding expected returns, embarked on a discipline of much closer performance measurement and allocated the funds among managers specialized in the management of particular asset categories.

The intent was to produce a total return of at least 5% plus inflation with a minimum level of risk. Risk was defined as a function of volatility. The greater the volatility of an asset category, the higher the risk. Acceptable minimum and maximum allocation percentages were set for each asset category. Minimum levels of total return and public indices for performance measurement were selected. After competitive interviews, managers were retained for each category. (The construction of the portfolio by asset and by manager is described in Exhibit 4.)

Critical to control of performance was frequent monitoring as well as a willingness to change managers who were performing poorly. Quarterly, an investment consultant prepared an extensive analysis of performance. Each manager was measured against return objectives as well as rated by percentile against the performance of a large group of managers of similar assets. The comparisons were done for the last quarter, year to date, last year, last five years, and for the period starting with the inception of the revised investment program in 1984. Any significant changes in manager personnel were noted. Since the beginning of the new system and through September 30, 1993, the total fund had had an annualized return of 13.91%. (See Exhibit 5.)

Social Investing

Gwendolyn Anderson knew that as a director of a charitable foundation she was acting in a fiduciary capacity and her standard of performance had to be that of a reasonable person acting in a like capacity. Over the years, foundation directors had used their discretion in the nature and amounts of grants approved, in the structuring of the investment portfolio and in myriad decisions that affected the organization and compensation of staff.[1] But where were the outer limits of "reasonability" with respect to ethical investing? Socially "screened" investments were more common than just a decade ago, when about $40 billion resided in such portfolios. Together, institutional and individual investors in 1993 had screened portfolios worth $700 billion, representing a wide diversity of social concerns and investment priorities.

Generally, she found, there were three approaches described by social investing experts. She outlined each in her memo to Ireland:

- *Avoidance.* You don't invest in companies whose products or services you find repugnant thereby not benefiting from activities you do not condone.
- *Positive.* You seek investments that enhance the quality of life, e.g., companies with needed goods and services, good employee relations, and an eye on the needs of the community.
- *Activist.* You take the avoidance and positive approaches a step further, see your role as an agent of change, and try to organize others or act as vocal shareholder-critics.

Anderson recommended that the board seek advice from an investment consulting firm that had extensive experience in social investing, and urged the board to consider seriously a divestiture from tobacco stocks.

Formulating a Response

Ireland understood that these approaches could and perhaps should govern his personal investing. But he was puzzled about how these concepts should govern his actions as a director of a foundation. From his discussion at quarterly review sessions with portfolio managers, he believed that by prohibiting certain investments, one limited choice and potentially diminished return. And he realized that from time to time Bush invested in index funds such as the S & P 100 fund or a foreign fund, and in these instances there was no way to remove a single security or class of securities. He saw himself as a decisive person, yet he felt ambivalence on this one.

The next day, time in the library revealed to Ireland those companies in the S & P 500 that produced tobacco products and the percentage of their revenues derived from tobacco.

American Brands	58%
Philip Morris	42%
Sara Lee Corp.	<5% (European sales only)
UST Incorporated	85%

Ireland also looked at a brief percentage performance comparison indicated as of March 31, 1993.

[1] The board had a conflict of interest policy embodied in its bylaws that represented discretion of another kind in matters of portfolio management: "The foundation shall not enter into any transaction with nor contribute to an organization with respect to which a director has any interest, pecuniary or otherwise, unless such interest is disclosed and the interested director refrains from discussion and voting on the matter" (Article XI, Bylaws, paraphrased).

	Year to Date	Last 12 Months	Since January 1990
S & P Index	4.4%	15.2%	42.0%
Tobacco Free S & P Index	4.9	16.6	40.4

Ireland recalled his own service in the 1980s on the board of a private college that agreed to remove from its endowment the stocks of companies who did business in South Africa. The action was taken only after angry confrontation with faculty and students. Now, with a changed government in South Africa, the companies who chose to relinquish their business there or be divested were being encouraged to reinvest. Many of these companies suggested that reinvestment would be very difficult since the market share they abandoned had been taken by well-entrenched German and Japanese companies.

He had other concerns as well. The Foundation had made deliberate, thoughtful steps to ensure the highest quality among its balanced fund managers. Since social investing was a relatively novel idea, could he expect difficulties in evaluation of managers' investment performance? If Bush avoided tobacco stocks, would this have any impact on tobacco consumption? If Bush embarked on "social investing," what categories of investment would other trustees want to avoid? How small would the Foundation's "universe of investment funds" become? Should he try to persuade the investment committee to prohibit Bush's portfolio managers from purchasing shares in companies with products they thought injurious to health? He found it difficult to reconcile his responsibilities as a trustee—which he believed to be to maximize investment return to the ultimate benefit of grant recipients—with a personal objection to the societal impact of tobacco.

Ireland looked forward to hearing other committee members' responses to Anderson's memo. He anticipated an animated discussion at the Investment Committee meeting.

EXHIBIT 1

Distribution of 1992 Grants

This chart shows the distribution of 1992 Foundation grant appropriations by program area. The Bush Board does not have any prior policies which determine the amount to be spent in one program area in a given year, except in the Fellowship Programs.

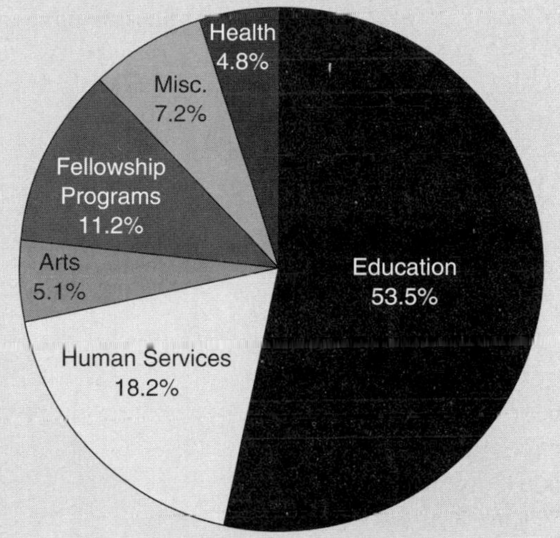

Grants Classified by Purpose 1988–1992

This table shows summaries of current and past year grants classified by purpose for which funds were granted. In each cell, the dollar figure represents the total amount granted, the figure next below in parentheses shows the number of grants made, and the bottom figure shows the percentage of all grant dollars awarded during that fiscal period.

Program	1990	1991	1992	3-Year Total
Arts & Humanities	$ 2,986,240 (22) 17.1%	$ 2,028,700 (17) 10.0%	$ 1,028,550 (17) 5.1%	$ 6,043,490 (56) 10.5%
Education	$ 7,261,296 (54) 41.7%	$ 8,774,258 (44) 43.5%	$10,781,966 (53) 53.5%	$26,817,520 (151) 46.5%
Health	$ 675,156 (8) 3.9%	$ 1,208,273 (13) 6.0%	$ 960,470 (11) 4.8%	$ 2,843,899 (32) 4.9%
Human Services	$ 3,428,105 (66) 19.7%	$ 4,940,388 (72) 24.5%	$ 3,660,514 (48) 18.2%	$12,029,007 (186) 20.8%
Miscellaneous	$ 990,075 (17) 5.7%	$ 1,140,841 (12) 5.6%	$ 1,463,244 (19) 7.2%	$ 3,594,160 (48) 6.2%
Fellowship Program stipends	$ 2,076,000 (3) 11.9%	$ 2,090,000 (3) 10.4%	$ 2,252,700 (3) 11.2%	$ 6,418,700 (9) 11.1%
Total	$17,416,812 (170) 100%	$20,182,460 (161) 100%	$20,147,474 (151) 100%	$57,746,776 (482) 100%

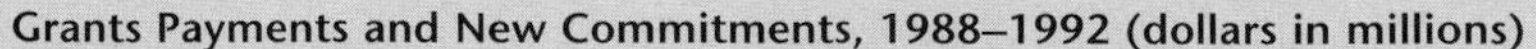

EXHIBIT 2 **Grants Statistics**

Grants Payments and New Commitments, 1988–1992 (dollars in millions)

Grant payments are those made in the year indicated on current and past grants. New commitments are the total of board-approved grants each year, less cancellations. These obligations will be paid in either the current year or in later years.

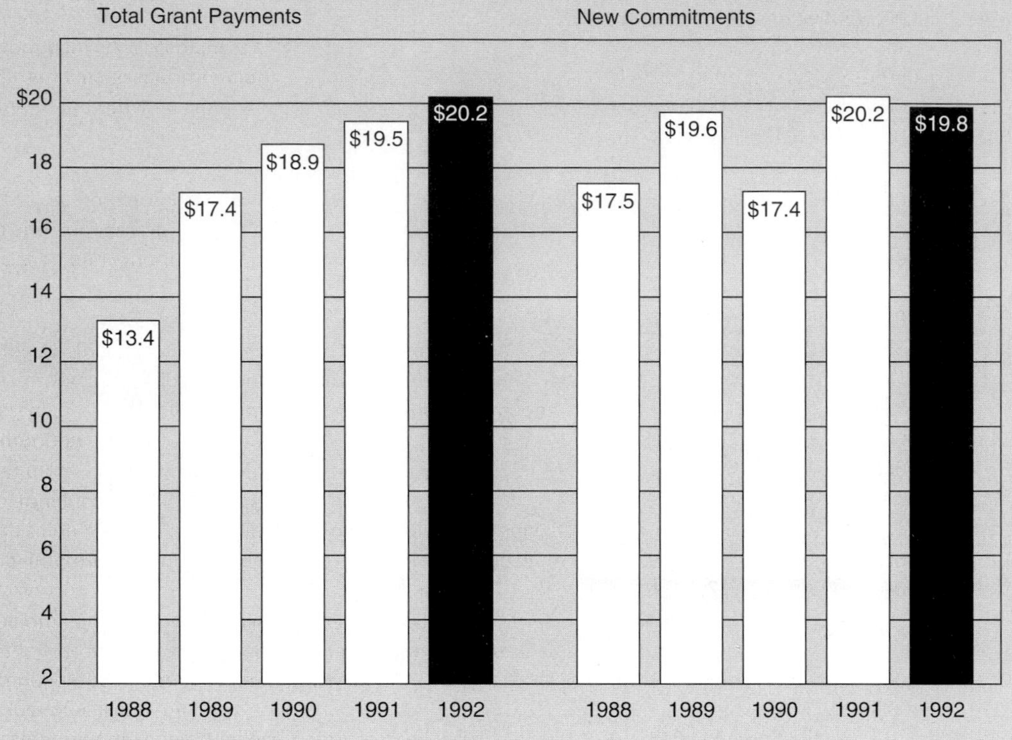

EXHIBIT 2 Grants Statistics—Continued

Classification of 1992 Grants

These tables show summaries of 1992 grant appropriations, classified by size, duration, and location. The Bush board does not have any prior policies, however, which give automatic preference to any particular grant size, duration, or location within the Foundation's primary geographic region.

Classification	Number of Grants Approved
Size (in dollars):	
0– 9,999	3
10,000– 24,999	20
25,000– 49,999	27
50,000– 99,999	43
100,000– 199,999	32
200,000– 499,999	19
500,000– 999,999	6
1,000,000–2,000,000	1
Total	151
Duration:	
1 year	80
2 years	35
3 years	34
4 years	2
Total	151
Geographic location:	
Twin Cities	73
Other Minnesota	19
Total Minnesota	92
North Dakota	22
South Dakota	20
Other	17
Total	151

EXHIBIT 3

Program	Year Established	Number of Awards
Bush Leadership Fellows Program	1965	919
Bush Public Schools Superintendents Program	1975	393
Bush Artist Fellows Program	1976	207
Bush Medical Fellows Program	1979	133
Bush Principals Program	1985	195
Total Fellowship Awards		1,847

EXHIBIT 4 **The Bush Foundation**
Portfolio Construction

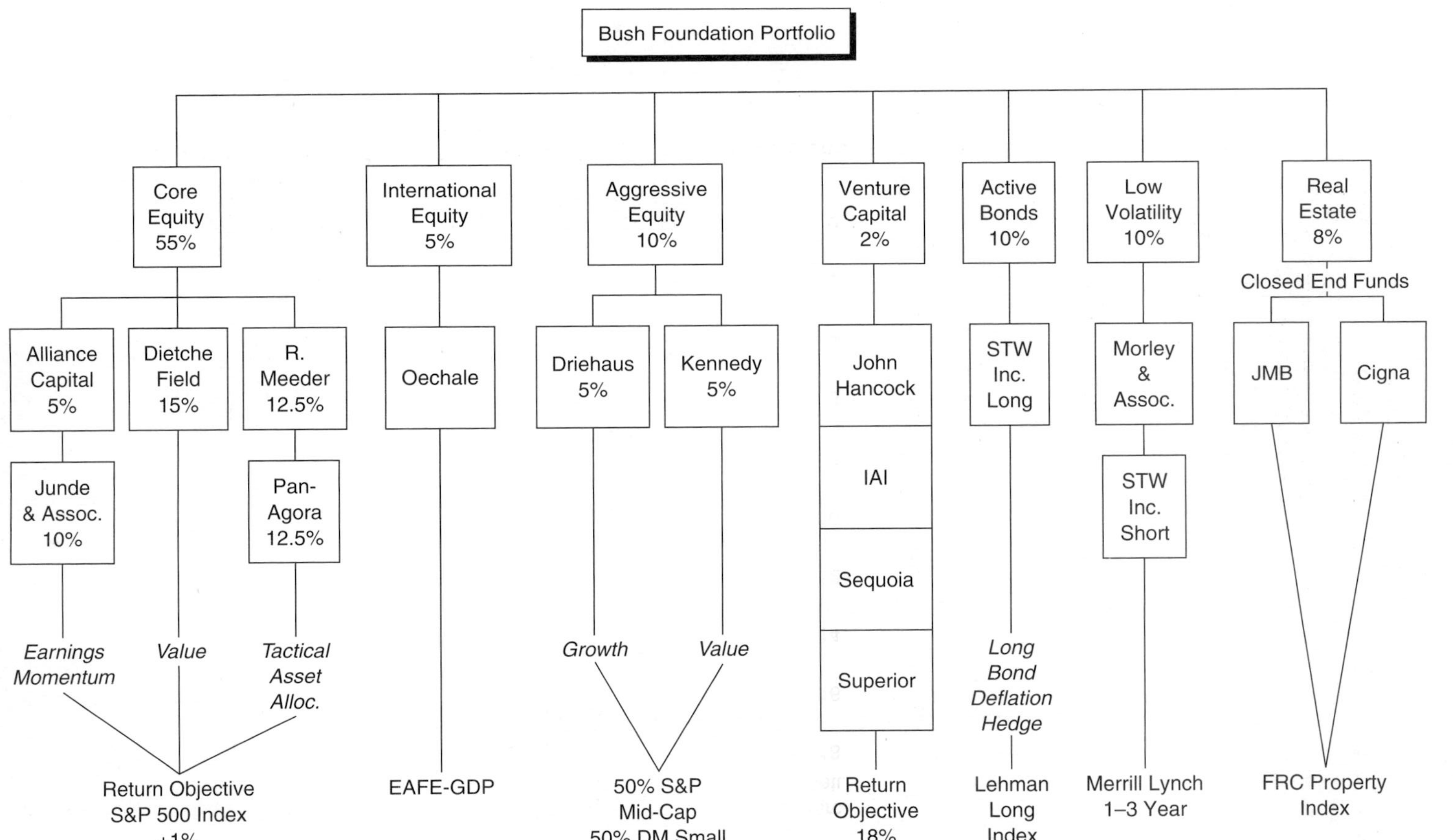

EXHIBIT 5 **Total Fund**
Performance to Objectives

Source: Bush Foundation. Copyright 1993 DeMarche Associates, Inc.

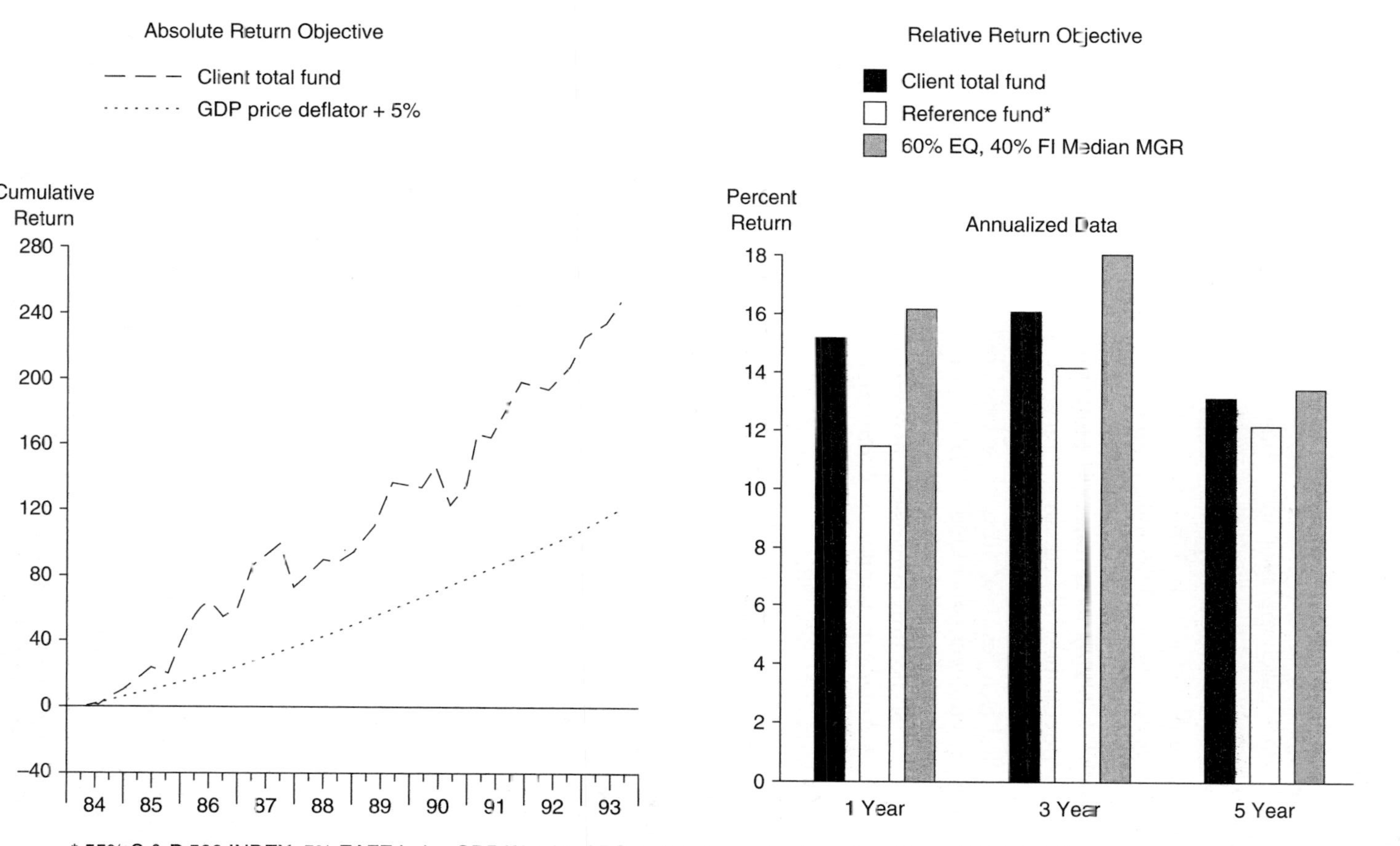

* 55% S & P 500 INDEX, 5% EAFE Index GDP Weighted PC, 30% Lehman Brothers Govt/Corp, 10% NCREIF—FRC Property Index

Note on Product Safety

General managers readily admit today that we have entered an era of increased emphasis on safety in the design, production, and distribution of products. The problem of business's responsibility for its products and services is large in scope. According to government statistics, 20 million Americans are injured annually as a consequence of incidents involving consumer products, with 30 thousand of those killed. In addition, each year 5 million Americans are injured and 30 thousand killed as a result of automobile accidents. One safety engineer concluded: "The odds against escaping an injury at home, at work, or at the steering wheel are thus surprisingly low for the average American family of four—an injury every four years or so."[1]

Since the birth of the Industrial Revolution, a product-oriented philosophy has dictated that principles of efficiency should guide the design of industrial and consumer goods. This efficiency was reflected in lower operating expenses and lower per unit costs for finished goods. Obvious safety problems—ones impinging directly on the bottom line—were faced and many were solved. As the revolution matured, this product orientation gave way to a market orientation that "literally bombarded twentieth-century man with delights that an earlier age would have considered both miraculous and beyond the economic grasp of common people."[2] Consumers quickly grew accustomed to an economy that delivered innovative products capable of improving the buyer's lifestyle. Eventually, a conditioned public began to insist on infallibility in its products as well as availability.

The emphasis on product safety has been growing since World War II. Consumerism—a social movement that sought to augment the rights and powers of buyers in relation to sellers—was born of a paradoxical market situation.[3] Although business had tried to pay full attention to the needs, wants, and satisfactions of its market, consumers began to raise their voices, exclaiming that business did not *care* about them. The problem in part for the general manager is philosophical: What constitutes a safe society, and what is a *safe* product for that society? While answers to such questions can be elusive, ignoring the spirit of such questions can lead to severe consequences not only for consumers but also for business and its managers.

Managing product safety requires that general management consider its economic, legal, and ethical responsibilities. As Figure A illustrates, these responsibilities are not mutually exclusive, nor are they arrayed on a continuum with economic concerns on one end and social concerns on the other. Rather, they are nested domains—the economic within the legal and both of these within the ethical.

Economic Responsibilities

Business is expected to deliver desired goods and services at a profit. Although consumers usually accept some degree of risk with products they find necessary, most buyers assume that companies will be prudent in the design, production, and distribution of their products. While business can employ specialists (risk managers, insurers, lawyers) to weigh product risks against rewards (consumer benefit), it is the general manager who is held accountable. But the competitive dynamics of the "invisible hand" can often create tensions for general managers in the area of product safety.

Legal Responsibilities

Society expects business to operate within the laws and regulations society has laid down. Courts have moved toward a doctrine of strict

[1] John Kolb and Steven S. Ross, *Product Safety and Liability* (New York: McGraw-Hill, 1980), p. 4.

[2] Ibid., p. 1.

[3] Philip Kotler, "What Consumerism Means for Marketers," *Harvard Business Review* (May–June 1972), p. 49.

FIGURE A **General Management's Responsibilities**

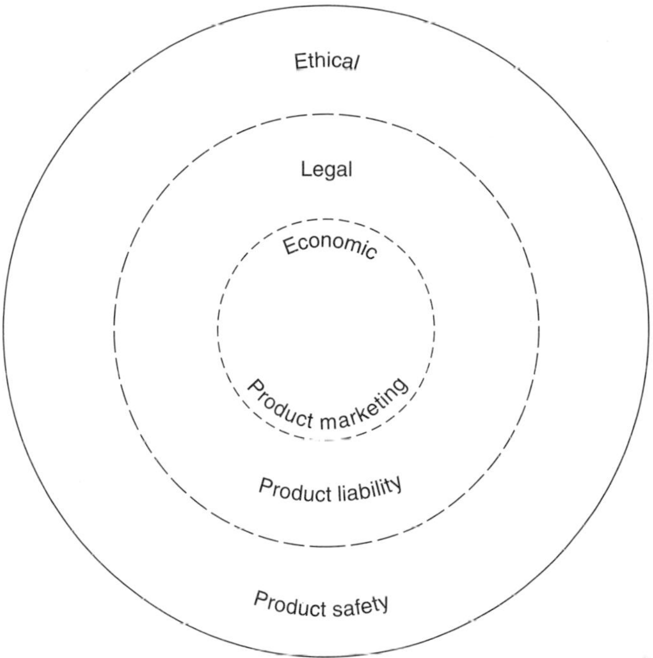

liability, holding manufacturers responsible for any product defects that result in injury. Plaintiffs no longer need to prove manufacturer negligence to win a personal injury case. Increasingly, the courts and the regulatory agencies are placing the blame for corporate lawbreaking on the top manager, who is being held personally responsible and even jailed. The doctrine of "vicarious liability" holds that it is irrelevant whether the executive was directly involved in the illegal activity or whether he or she was simply informed of such activity. A "responsible manager" cannot always count on a corporate shield of protection. Nevertheless, this sue syndrome and the increasing frequency and size of court-ordered awards result in skyrocketing premiums for product liability insurance. *Caveat venditor* (let the seller beware) is replacing the old adage *caveat emptor* (let the buyer beware) as a watchword for business. Public policy, through the promulgation of numerous regulations, codifies many of management's responsibilities for product safety. In a world of rapidly emerging technologies, however, the "hand of government" does not always provide relevant guidance to the general manager.

Ethical Responsibilities

Society has expectations of business that transcend economic and legal requirements. Ethical responsibilities are difficult to define and consequently difficult for business to deal with. When the economic and political systems fail to provide guidance on product safety, however, the "hand of management" must fill the void.

Corporations have increasingly recognized the importance of social issues to their performance and success. At the same time, awareness of management's multidimensional responsibilities has not always been translated into meaningful action. A first step for managers who must deal with product safety controversies is to develop a philosophy to guide their future actions. As Figure B illustrates, companies that have been involved in product safety controversies can pass through several phases of social response.

Lacking adequate information and time for a complete analysis of the situation, managers must rapidly formulate some kind of public *reaction* in response to allegations that one of its products is not safe. If both the company and its critics believe there is time to discuss the safety

FIGURE B Corporate Social Response Phases

Source: Adapted from Archie B. Carroll, "A Three-Dimensional Conceptual Model of Corporate Performance," *Academy of Management Review*, Vol. 4, no. 4, 1977, p. 502.

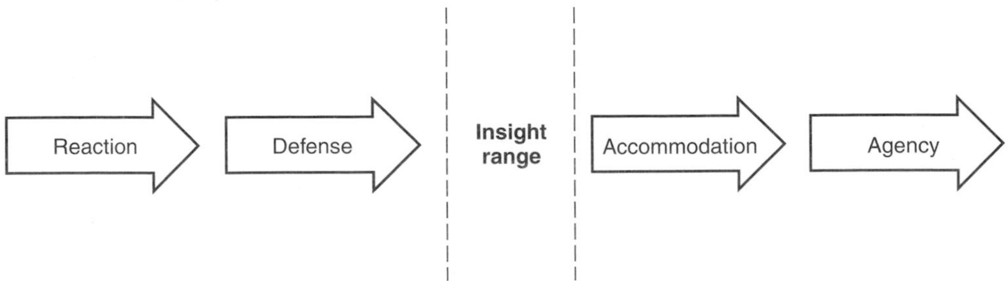

controversy, a more thorough resolution is likely. This is seldom the case, however, especially when the public perceives a clear and present danger. When overwhelmed by public scrutiny and media attention, many business organizations—believing they have been unfairly attacked—will recoil in *defense.* The product safety crisis still remains in the public eye, however, thus further tarnishing the company's reputation. The *insight range* represents the most agonizing moment in the controversy. At this point, the company's stakes can be enormous and may involve its very survival. Management must remodel the situation in light of pressing external forces. *Accommodation* might consist of two different options: the company, still believing in its product, should refute the charges, if it can, that its product is not safe; otherwise, it must postpone its defense and withdraw the product to ameliorate public anxiety. *Agency* will involve actively researching the causes of the safety problem and then an education program to comfort or warn the public about the safety of the product in question.

A comprehensive understanding of the behavior of companies entangled in product safety controversies can help other general managers assess their own responsibilities and options. A company's social response strategy, if properly selected, can help it anticipate and confront difficult situations. Its reputation and future prosperity may hinge on its ability to gain insight into, and deal with, such crises.

The practical and philosophical issues raised in product safety controversies are profound. From a practical viewpoint, the management student is challenged to evaluate and compare specific responses to each product safety controversy. From a philosophical viewpoint, it is worth noting that the challenges involve more than product and safety considerations. In many ways, these issues cut to the core of the relationship between organizations and society. Goods and services of all kinds affect the physical and mental health of people both inside and outside the corporation. Safety is an issue that has both highly visible and subtle influences on the well-being of the community. The relationship among economic, legal, and ethical reasoning in the mind of an agent (either an individual or an organization) can become stressful as a particular controversy unfolds. Understanding how each crisis is handled sheds light on the values and beliefs that guide individuals and organizations involved in business activity. Although risk is inevitable in a society that considers innovation its economic bread and butter, the educated executive will be pressed to carefully balance the rewards of technology with the responsibilities of general management.

Managing Product Safety: *The Ford Pinto*

On Tuesday August 9, 1977, Herbert L. Misch, vice president of environmental and safety engineering at Ford Motor Company, picked up a copy of the magazine *Mother Jones* featuring an article entitled "Pinto Madness." This exclusive story would surely stir up a public controversy over the safety of the company's successful subcompact car, the Ford Pinto.

This self-styled radical magazine had cited Ford "secret documents" which, according to the author, proved the company had known for eight years that the Pinto was a "firetrap." The article claimed that preproduction rear-end crash tests had revealed the dangerous nature of the design and placement of the car's fuel tank. According to the author's investigation, Ford was so anxious to get the car on the market that it decided design changes would not be made—they would "take too much time and cost too much money." The article went on to charge that Ford had used "some blatant lies" to delay enactment of a government safety standard that would have forced the company to change the Pinto's "fire-prone" gas tank. The article concluded: "By conservative estimates, Pinto crashes have caused 500 burn deaths to people who would not have been seriously injured if the car had not burst into flames."[1]

Nothing in Ford's records supported the contentions made in the article. Nevertheless, Misch knew that the overall effect of this *Mother Jones* article—one that relied heavily on the testimony of a former Ford engineer—could be highly damaging to the company. It would sharpen consumer criticism of the U.S. auto industry in general and Ford in particular. Misch and his associates at Ford were angered by the allegations and were ready to denounce the article as "unfair and distorted."[2] They knew, however, that it would not be an easy task to counter such sensational charges with their own statistical analyses of accident reports.

Ford believed that the source of this trouble, like so much of the criticism leveled at the auto industry, was external to its operation. The development of a large consumer movement, along with the enactment of the National Traffic and Motor Vehicle Safety Act of 1966, had revolutionized the car business. In the view of *Mother Jones*, the industry had been considered the "last great unregulated business" in the United States.[3] The industry now had to answer to many more people than just auto buyers. The multitude of often conflicting regulations had, according to auto executives, placed unreasonable burdens on domestic automakers. An exasperated company chairman, Henry Ford II, lamented, "It's the mess in which we live."[4]

The company had dealt with all of the major federal regulatory agencies in earlier controversies, some of which had involved the beleaguered Pinto. The National Highway Traffic Safety Administration (NHTSA)—a regulatory agency in the Department of Transportation—was considered the industry's chief antagonist. NHTSA investigations had led to previous Pinto recalls because of problems with engine fires and fuel-line hose construction. The appointment of Joan Claybrook—a Ralph Nader lobbyist—as NHTSA administrator had been strongly, but unsuccessfully, opposed by the auto industry. Claybrook was expected to press hard for increased safety and miles-per-gallon (MPG) features.

[1] Mark Dowie, "Pinto Madness," *Mother Jones*, September/October 1977, p. 18.

[2] "Ford Is Recalling Some 1.5 Million Pintos, Bobcats," *Wall Street Journal*, 12 June 1978, p. 2.

[3] Dowie, p. 23.

[4] Walter Guzzardi, Jr., "Ford: The Road Ahead," *Fortune*, September 11, 1978, p. 39.

The Environmental Protection Agency (EPA)—a regulatory agency reporting directly to the U.S. president—had pressed the industry to reduce auto emissions in an effort to clean up air pollution. In 1973, after an internal audit, Ford volunteered it had withheld information from the EPA concerning unauthorized maintenance performed on emission test cars. The agency subsequently levied a $7 million fine on Ford. In one incident, a small number of Pintos had been recalled because of a flaw in the car's air pollution control equipment. The Federal Trade Commission (FTC)—a regulatory agency reporting directly to the U.S. Congress—had decided to become more involved in oversight activities in the industry. The FTC was mostly concerned that product performance features be candidly disclosed. It had charged that gas mileage claims made by Ford's Lincoln-Mercury division were inaccurate and exaggerated.

While relations between the government and the auto industry were often adversarial, each side realized that self-interest lay in maintaining a workable peace. Auto companies would often settle disputes by agreeing to a recall without admitting fault and without a flurry of negative publicity. The government preferred such voluntary actions because court battles were usually time-consuming and rarely resulted in an efficient resolution of a product controversy.

Another group that served as an industry watchdog was the Center for Auto Safety, a privately funded consumer advocate organization founded by Ralph Nader in 1970. The center had noticed in its records a larger-than-expected number of accident reports involving burn deaths in the Ford Pinto. In this, as in other cases, it forwarded the information to NHTSA in an effort to force the agency's hand in confronting the automobile companies. The center's director, Clarence M. Ditlow, who often pressed for auto recalls, had claimed that "the number of recalls and the (number of) cars involved would be high for several more years."[5] In the minds of some industry observers, the center had targeted the Pinto for special attention.

Ford was determined to fight hard for the Pinto. Since it was put into production in 1970, the subcompact had become one of the company's best selling cars and had allowed Ford to fight off some of the foreign competition. Furthermore, company executives knew that its next-generation small car would not be ready for introduction until 1980.

Competitive Environment

The American automobile industry's fortune had historically been tied to the pattern of the nation's economic cycle. Three or four good years were inexorably followed by one or two poor years. There had been a shakeout of the weakest companies over the years, leaving four major U.S. automakers. In 1977 General Motors (46.4% market share), Ford (22.3%), Chrysler (11.1%), and American Motors (1.8%) shared the $100-plus-billion U.S. auto market. Imports, consisting mostly of subcompact cars, had captured 18.4% of this market. Car sales were made primarily through manufacturers' franchised dealers located across the country.[6]

Competition among the four U.S. firms was intense. Pricing, performance features, consumer financing, and advertising had always been important competitive weapons. With the arrival of stiffer foreign competition, however, pricing became an even more critical selling feature. Moreover, in the aftermath of the Arab oil embargo, good fuel economy became especially important, a trend that had favored foreign producers because they had adapted to high fuel costs in their home markets.

For domestic car companies profit margins on all vehicles had declined in the early 1970s, mostly reflecting poor recovery from inflation-related cost increases. Pricing was limited first by price controls, then by the 1974–1975 recession. According to industry experts, domestic labor costs had served significantly to disadvantage American automakers. Small car margins continued to decline after the recession as a result of reduced demand for small cars in general, heightened competition from imports, and cost increases to achieve safety, damageability, and emission requirements. Large cars, still in demand, fared much better.

Though auto companies were very secretive about new car designs and technologies, there

[5] "Detroit Stunned by Recall Blitz," *New York Times*, 12 March 1978, Sec. 3, p. 1.

[6] "You're Damned If You Do . . . ," *Forbes*, January 9, 1978, p. 35.

were otherwise very few secrets in the car business. Auto company engineers could, and often would, tear apart a competitor's new car to glean details about a new design or production technique. If one firm changed its price structure or its financing rate, the competition would be able to adjust its strategy quickly. Because of its dominance in the American market, General Motors was considered the market leader and usually dictated the sales strategies for its smaller rivals.

Ford Motor Company was founded in 1903 and had been a family-owned and family-managed business until stock was first sold publicly in 1956. Family members still retained 40% of the voting power in the company, which ranked third (in sales) on the 1977 *Fortune* 500 list of the largest U.S. industrial corporations.

Much like its principal competitor, GM, Ford produced a complete range of cars and trucks. The company had scored some notable successes, however, in cultivating market segments ill-served by General Motors. Ford gained an early edge on its rival by producing the first American-made compact car, the Falcon, in 1960. Its luxury cars, the Thunderbird and Cougar, were also considered attractive by the American car buyer. The Mustang, designed and introduced in 1964 by Lee Iacocca (who later became Ford president), gained wide favor as the "sports car for the masses."[7]

Despite the successes of these specialty cars, Ford did not gain any ground on General Motors during the 1960s. Furthermore, some Ford executives believed that imports were posing a threat to Ford's traditionally strong position in the small car market. Though the company was ready with new compact cars (the Maverick was introduced in 1969), it still did not have a subcompact to counter the import challenge effectively.

In June 1967 Ford management became embroiled in a protracted internal debate over the company's position on subcompacts. When it was over, Lee Iacocca had become Ford's president and the Pinto was born. Iacocca directed that the Pinto was to be in showrooms with 1971 models. Formal planning started immediately and the journey to production took less time than the prevailing industry average. In September 1970 the Pinto was introduced as a "carefree little American car," and it gained quick acceptance by the market.[8] After six years of production over 2 million Pintos had been sold, making it one of the company's all-time best-selling automobiles.

Between 1970 and 1977, the Pinto helped stabilize Ford's market position. The 1973–1974 Arab oil embargo hit Ford's major competitors (GM and Chrysler) particularly hard because neither had a large offering of small cars. The following year, Congress set mandatory fuel economy targets that encouraged auto makers to sell smaller cars. GM quickly responded with a massive downsizing program that helped it become more small car oriented. Chrysler, in bleak financial straits, belatedly followed with its own small car program. Ford undertook a program to convert its Wayne, Michigan, assembly plant from production of full-size cars to compact cars, completing this transition in only 51 days. By 1975 subcompact and compact cars glutted the market, however, as consumers shunned small cars. Burdened with high inventory levels, the industry began to offer rebates on most small cars. The Pinto, however, continued to outsell most competitive offerings in its size category. Consequently, Ford management decided to focus its new product development on a replacement for the compact-sized Maverick which had been introduced two years before the Pinto. The Pinto would have to hold the consumer's interest until the company was ready to make the investment in the next generation subcompact.

By mid-1977 the outlook for the auto industry was uncertain in the opinion of most industry analysts. While some predicted the coming year would bring record sales, others worried that shrinking consumer credit would reduce car buying. Apart from sales volume, several industry observers believed Detroit's profits would be hurt by declining margins and a "less rich" sales mix that included more small cars. Each company was scrambling to ensure that its fleet averaged the legally mandated 18 miles per gallon in 1978. This meant selling more models that were smaller and fuel-efficient but were also less profitable. Faced

[7] Mark B. Fuller and Malcolm S. Salter, "Ford Motor Company (A)" (Boston, MA: Harvard Business School, 1982), p. 4.

[8] Lee Patrick Strobel, *Reckless Homicide?* (South Bend, IN: 1980), p. 82.

with intensified competition, most auto makers were placing a premium on innovative design and engineering.

Product Safety Controversy (1970–1977)

To meet the competition from imported subcompacts, Ford accelerated the Pinto planning process. In June 1967 Ford commenced the design and development process; production of the Pinto began on August 10, 1970. Ford achieved this 38-month development time, 5 months under the average time of 43 months, by assembling a special team of engineers who directed their efforts entirely to the Pinto. Unlike the development cycles for most new car lines, Pinto start-up planning was simplified and included only a two-door sedan (hatchback and station wagons were added in later years). Pinto engineers were constrained by Iacocca's goal, known as "the limits of 2,000"—the Pinto was not to weigh an ounce over 2,000 pounds and not to cost a cent over $2,000.[9] These limits, according to former Ford engineers, were strictly enforced. Even at this price and weight, the Pinto would still cost and weigh more than some imported subcompacts.

An early question during the car's design stage was where to safely put the gas tank. Although engineers were familiar with ways to move the gas tank away from the rear of the car—Ford had a patent for a saddle-type tank that could fit above and mostly forward of the car's rear axle—they opted for a strap-on tank arrangement located under the rear floorpan and behind the rear axle. At that time almost every American-made car had the fuel tank located in the same place. Late in the design process, however, an engineering study determined that "the safest place for a fuel tank is directly above the rear axle."[10] It was later determined by senior company engineers that such a design, while moving the tank farther away from a rear-end collision, actually increased the threat of ignition in the passenger compartment. The over-the-axle location of the fuel tank would also require a circuitous filler pipe more likely to be dislodged in an accident. Raising the height of the fuel tank by putting it above the axle would also raise the car's center of gravity, thereby diminishing its handling capabilities. In the opinion of Ford's senior engineers, this would undermine the car's general safety. Practical considerations also dictated the traditional location. The fuel tank could not be placed over the axle, for example, if a station wagon or a hatchback option was going to be offered. The over-axle location would also greatly reduce storage space and would make servicing more difficult.

When the Pinto was in the blueprint stage, the federal government had no standards concerning how safe a car must be from gas leakage in rear-end crashes. In January 1969, NHTSA proposed its first rear-end fuel system integrity standard, called Standard 301. The original standard required that a stationary vehicle should leak less than one ounce of fuel per minute after being hit by a 4,000 pound barrier moving at 20 mph. Ford supported such a standard in writing and voluntarily adopted the 20 mph standard as an internal design objective for its entire line of cars. In mid-1969 the company began a series of crash tests with preproduction Pinto prototypes, as well as with other car lines, in an attempt to meet this objective. Four tests were conducted on vehicles modified to simulate the Pinto's rear-end design. In three of these tests, the leakage slightly exceeded the one-ounce-per-minute standard. In the other test, massive fuel leakage occurred because an improperly welded fuel tank split at the seams.[11] After these tests Ford altered the Pinto's fuel tank design and was able to incorporate these changes before production began. The first Pinto rolled off the assembly line on August 10, 1970. A month later the subcompact was introduced to the American consumer boasting a price tag of $1,919—about $170 less than GM's subcompact and within $80 of the best-selling Volkswagen Beetle.[12]

The 20 mph moving-barrier standard proposed by the government was never adopted. Just days after the manufacture of the first Pinto, NHTSA announced a proposal requiring all vehicles to

[9] "Ford Ignored Pinto Fire Peril, Secret Memos Show," *Chicago Tribune*, 13 October 1979, Sec. 2, p. 12.

[10] Strobel, p. 80.

[11] Ford Motor Company Crash Tests 1137, 1138, 1214; memorandum, H. P. Freers to T. J. Feaheny, January 31, 1969.

[12] Strobel, p. 82.

meet a 20 mph fixed-barrier standard within 18 months. In a fixed-barrier test, the vehicle is towed backwards into a fixed barrier at the specified speed. NHTSA also indicated that its long-term objective for rear-end crashes included a 30 mph fixed-barrier standard. This new proposal caught automakers by surprise and provoked universal industry opposition. Ford estimated that a 20 mph fixed-barrier test could, because of the laws of kinetic energy, be nearly twice as severe as a 20 mph moving-barrier test. Many auto engineers were quick to point out the unrealistic nature of fixed-barrier tests: in the real world, vehicles are not driven backwards into walls. Moreover, data available to Ford indicated that 85% of rear-end collisions occurred at speeds equivalent to or less than a 20 mph moving-barrier standard.[13] In addition, the available information indicated that only .45% of injury-producing accidents involved fire.[14] Preventing injuries from fires caused by rear-end impacts at very high speeds was beyond practical technology, according to many auto executives. Protection against fire at such high speeds would be of little benefit, it was argued, since the force of impact alone was likely to be fatal.

Ford considered it unlikely that the government would adopt fixed-barrier standards. Nevertheless, the company began to test its vehicles against this proposed requirement to determine what would have to be done to meet NHTSA's proposals. Subsequent fixed-barrier tests conducted with standard Pintos at 20 and 30 mph resulted in excessive leakage. To meet the more stringent fixed-barrier standards, a major tear up of all cars would be required to modify vehicle design. Because of the significant costs involved and doubts about the viability of the fixed-barrier standard, Ford management decided to continue with its own internal 20 mph moving-barrier standard. Engineering work on developing ways to meet a 30 mph moving-barrier standard—which Ford believed NHTSA would eventually adopt—continued.

In early 1971 a junior company engineer began to explore various ways to make the company's smaller cars capable of meeting the 30 mph moving-barrier standard. A 30-page study, called the "Pricor Report," listed several specific recommendations for how to make the car substantially safer from fuel leakage and fire in rear-end crashes. An over-the-axle gas tank, a repositioned spare tire, installation of body rails, a redesigned filler pipe, and an "inner-tank" rubber bladder were among major options for improving the Pinto's overall performance.[15] The first four suggestions were ruled out on the grounds that they would require extensive vehicle design changes. The rubber bladder—a tank liner with an estimated variable cost of $5.80—was seriously considered. On the basis of a crash test in which a bladder was hand placed inside a Pinto tank, a company engineer concluded that the bladder tank "provided a substantial improvement in crashworthiness."[16] In cold weather, however, the bladders became stiff, making gas filling very difficult. And in very hot climates, the bladders failed under test conditions.

In August 1973, NHTSA announced a proposal for a 30 mph moving-barrier, rear-end fuel system integrity standard, effective September 1976 for all 1977 models. A prolonged debate ensued between government officials and industry executives over the appropriate test technique. NHTSA was a proponent of car-to-car testing, arguing that this was a closer approximation to actual accident situations. Auto representatives maintained that a standard moving barrier (which was towed along a track to the point of impact) was much more appropriate because it was repeatable and, therefore, a more reliable measurement of crashworthiness.

At the same time that NHTSA proposed the rear-end crash standard, it also adopted a fuel system integrity standard applicable to rollover accidents. Although Ford did not oppose the rear-end standard, it vigorously fought the rollover standard. Under provisions of the rollover test, minimal gasoline leakage would be permitted when a car was turned upside down in an accident.

[13] Fuel System Integrity Program, Percent of Rear Accidents Occurring at or below Equivalent Fixed (Movable) Barrier Speeds, Car Product Planning, March 14, 1971. (Accident data file from Accident Crash Injury Research [ACIR] Project at Cornell Aeronautical Laboratory.)

[14] "Observations on Fire in Automobile Accidents," Cornell Aeronautical Laboratory, Inc., February 1965.

[15] A. J. Pricor, "197X Mustang/Maverick Program: Fuel Tank Integrity," Ford Motor Company.

[16] "Ford 157 Report—Bladder Fuel Tank Test," Ford Motor Company.

This presented automakers with obvious problems as leakage would occur from the carburetor, fuel vents, and the gas cap air hole when a car was upside down; yet each of these openings was necessary for the normal functioning of the fuel intake. After extensive study Ford determined that the rollover requirement might be met by installing an $11 valve on each of its 12.5 million cars and trucks then on the road. Among the materials submitted was a cost-benefit analysis prepared according to NHTSA criteria and using government figures ($200,000 per death; $67,000 per injury). The values reflected only the economic loss to society resulting from injuries and deaths, because the government had no estimate to place on human pain and suffering. The analysis, done by Ford personnel with no design responsibilities, presented the case that the $137 million in cost far outweighed the dollar values assigned for the loss of 180 burn deaths, 180 serious burn injuries, and 2,100 burned vehicles.[17] The rollover standard was eventually adopted with some minor modifications. The cost-benefit analysis on rollover accidents became the basis for countless media claims that Ford delayed *rear-end* fuel system integrity standards because "its internal cost-benefit analysis, which places a dollar value on human life, said it wasn't profitable to make the changes sooner."

The first notable public criticism of the Pinto's fuel tank design came in late 1973. Byron Bloch, an independent consultant in automobile safety design, warned a Department of Transportation conference that the Pinto's fuel system design was "very vulnerable . . . to even minor damage."[18] On a national television program, Bloch held up a model of a Pinto and pointed out what he saw as its fuel system hazards. When Ford announced it was recalling the Pinto for minor repairs, Bloch urged the government to require a recall that would improve the car's resistance to fires in rear-end crashes. Early in 1974 the Center for Auto Safety pressed NHTSA to investigate the fuel system integrity of the Ford Pinto and the Chevrolet Vega. The center cited concerns expressed by attorneys engaged in liability lawsuits, as well as its own research findings, in calling for a defect investigation. NHTSA reviewed these complaints and determined that there was no demonstrable safety problem.

NHTSA, still a relatively new federal agency in the mid-1970s, was seriously hampered in most of its investigatory work by a lack of relevant and meaningful statistical information. In early 1975 a study commissioned by the Insurance Institute for Highway Safety concluded that the number of fire-related incidents involving vehicles was growing more rapidly than the number of other incidents of fire. The study noted a striking difference between Ford's 20% national representation among domestic passenger cars and its 35% frequency in surveyed collision-ruptured fuel tanks.[19] The study's author cautioned, however, that it was not possible to draw definitive conclusions about causal relationships; nor was it possible to identify differences between car models. This study, and others like it, came at a time of growing public concern over motor vehicle fires. Between 1974 and 1976 consumer groups and Congress exerted considerable political pressure on NHTSA to finally implement all provisions of the fuel system integrity standard. In 1977 Standard 301 was fully enacted.

On August 10, 1977, the allegations contained in the *Mother Jones* article were first made public at a news conference in Washington, D.C. The charges against Ford appeared to have been based on quotes attributed to either past or present company engineers, along with a digest of confidential company memoranda. Ford executives took a dim view of the magazine, but they knew its editors had obtained some key sensitive documents that could easily be misinterpreted by the public. As far as the company knew, no government investigation was being conducted that concerned the Pinto's fuel system.

Postscript

On September 26, 1977, Ford officials publicly responded to the *Mother Jones* article—which had appeared seven weeks earlier—by issuing a news release aimed at refuting the magazine's allegations. The news release claimed: "There is no

[17] "Fatalities Associated with Crash Induced Fuel Leakage and Fires," E. S. Grush and C. S. Saundby, Ford Motor Company, September 19, 1973.

[18] Strobel, p. 145.

[19] Eugene M. Trisko, "Results of the 1973 National Survey of Motor Vehicle Fires," *Fire Journal* (March 1975), p. 23.

serious fire hazard in the fuel system of the Ford Pinto, nor are any Pinto models exceptionally vulnerable to rear-impact collision fires. [NHTSA] statistics establish that Ford Pinto is involved in fewer fire-associated collisions than might be expected considering the total number of Pintos in operation." Ford cited government figures for the period 1975–1976 for which comprehensive information was available. These figures showed that Pintos were involved in about 1.9% of fire-accompanied passenger car fatalities in 1975–1976, years in which Pintos made up an average of about 1.9% of passenger cars. Ford explained that early experiments with its rubber bladder gas tank were conducted to see if the company could meet its own ambitious performance requirements. "The truth is that in every model year the Pinto has been tested and met or surpassed the federal fuel system integrity standards applicable to it."[20]

The company acknowledged that later model Pintos had an improved fuel system design, but argued that "it simply is unreasonable and unfair to contend that a car is somehow unsafe if it does not meet standards proposed for future years or embody the technological improvements that are introduced in later model years." The company denied that it had purposely delayed Standard 301 and said it had only "opposed . . . certain excessive testing requirements."[21]

In September 1977, NHTSA opened an investigation into the Pinto's fuel tank system and ran an engineering analysis of the pre-1977 Pinto. As reported by the *Wall Street Journal,* the agency found that "the fuel tank's location and the structural parts around it permitted easy crushing or puncturing of the tank in a crash. Officials also found that the short fuel tank filler pipe could easily pull away from the tank." There was "a real potential for trouble," said one government official.[22]

Ford's management was angered by NHTSA's inquiry and believed the basis for its examination to be unfounded. In a 1974 investigation of complaints, NHTSA had determined that no action concerning Pinto fuel system integrity was necessary. Indeed, by NHTSA's own admission, its action was in response to the enormous flood of mail demanding that it do something about the Pinto. The company was further incensed when the agency acknowledged that its accident statistics were "notoriously incomplete." NHTSA had only begun to develop a comprehensive accident reporting system.

By early 1978 the Pinto controversy began to attract national attention. The Center for Auto Safety had called for a national campaign to force Ford to recall the country's 2 million-odd Pintos and retrofit a safety bladder into the gas tank of *all* Pintos. The car's image was further tarnished by recalls due to piston scuffing and steering failures.

In February 1978 a California jury handed down a verdict that assessed $125 million in punitive damages against Ford in a case involving the rupture and explosion of the fuel tank on a 1972 Pinto. One person had died in the fiery Pinto crash, and the surviving passenger had undergone 60 different operations in the six years since the accident. It was testimony by Harley Copp, a former Ford senior engineer, that apparently convinced the court the Pinto was, in the words of one juror, "a lousy and unsafe product."[23] The massive amount of money awarded by the jury, easily the highest for such a suit in American history, led to heightened media interest in the Pinto issue. A judge later reduced punitive damages to $3.5 million.

During the same month as the California verdict, NHTSA conducted experimental crash tests of the Pinto as part of its ongoing investigation. A total of 11 rear-end crash tests of 1971–1976 Pintos were staged at speeds between 30 and 35 mph. Two cars tested at 35 mph caught fire, and the other tests at 30 mph resulted in "significant leakage."[24] When NHTSA similarly tested GM's Chevrolet Vega, a larger and slightly heavier vehicle than the Pinto, minimal gasoline leakage was reported. Ford management believed these tests were unfair and inappropriate. Some of the tests were more severe

[20] Ford Motor Company News Release (Dearborn, Michigan: Ford Motor Company, September 26, 1977), p. 1.

[21] Ibid. p. 1.

[22] "Car Trouble: Government Pressure Propels Auto Recalls toward a New High," *Wall Street Journal*, 16 August 1978, p. 1.

[23] "Why the Pinto Jury Felt Ford Deserved $125 Million Penalty," *Wall Street Journal*, 14 February 1978, p. 1.

[24] National Highway Traffic Safety Administration, *Report of Defects Investigation* (Washington, DC: NHTSA, May 1978), p. 11.

than the government required even for later model vehicles, and this was apparently the first time the agency had ever used car-to-car crash tests to determine if there was a safety defect.

In March 1978 Pinto owners in Alabama and California filed class action suits, demanding that Ford recall all Pintos built from 1971 through 1976 and modify their fuel systems. The California civil complaint alleged that Ford "persistently and willfully failed and refused to remedy the design defect in the fuel tank." Around this time the head of the American Trial Lawyers Association, in an unprecedented step, had appealed to the company to "recall all of the cars in question."[25] Later that same month, NHTSA notified Ford that its 1976 Pintos had not passed a 30-mph *front-end* barrier test. This test result, which revealed occasional fuel leakage in the engine compartment, led to a recall of 300,000 Pintos.

On May 9, 1978, NHTSA announced that it had made an "initial determination" that a safety defect existed in the fuel systems of Ford Pintos for the 1971 through 1976 model years. This finding had been reached after eight months of analysis, testing, and review of pertinent company records. The government claimed that it was aware of 38 cases in which rear-end collisions of Pintos had resulted in fuel tank damage, leakage, and/or ensuing fires. Of those 38 cases, it said, there were 27 fatalities among occupants and 24 instances in which individuals suffered nonfatal burns. In its four-paragraph letter to Ford's President Iacocca, NHTSA informed the company that it could respond to the initial findings at a public hearing scheduled for mid-June.[26] During late May and early June, Ford officials met with NHTSA to discuss privately the government's findings and to consider possible remedies. A few days before the hearing date, the decision was made to recall the cars.

On June 9, 1978, after years of vigorously defending the safety of the Pinto's fuel system, Ford management announced the recall of 1.5 million of its subcompacts. In a press release issued on the day of the recall announcement, Ford management insisted "that it does not agree with the agency's initial determination . . . that an unreasonable risk to safety is involved in the design of [the Pinto], and that it believes it can be demonstrated that the actual performance of the vehicles is comparable to that of other subcompact and compact cars manufactured during the same periods." The company did concede that "NHTSA had identified areas in which the risk of fuel leakage could be reduced significantly on a practical basis." Accordingly, Ford decided to offer the modifications to "end public concern that had resulted from criticism of the fuel system in these vehicles."[27] The company agreed to notify all Pinto owners that it was ready to replace the fuel filler pipe and install a polyethylene shield across the front of the fuel tank. Ford estimated this offer could cost the company as much as $20 million after taxes. During the previous year Ford had earned a total of $1.5 billion after taxes.[28]

NHTSA administrator Joan Claybrook said the government wanted to work out a voluntary agreement with Ford to avoid a long-drawn-out court battle. In response to Ford's recall, the government closed its investigation without making a final determination.

In Detroit, Michigan, Ford Chairman Henry Ford II said: "The lawyers would shoot me for saying this, but I think there's some cause for concern about the [Pinto]. I don't even listen to the cost figures—we've got to fix it."[29]

[25] "Class Action Suit Seeks Recall of 1971–76 Pintos," *Wall Street Journal*, 7 March 1978, p. 34.

[26] "U.S. Agency Suggests Ford Pintos Have a Fuel System Safety Defect," *New York Times*, 9 May 1978, p. 22.

[27] "Ford Orders Recall of 1.5 Million Pintos for Safety Changes," *New York Times*, 10 June 1978, p. 1.

[28] "Ford Is Recalling Some 1.5 Million Pintos, Bobcats," *Wall Street Journal*, 12 June 1978, p. 2.

[29] Guzzardi, p. 42.

Managing Product Safety: *The Procter and Gamble Rely Tampon*

On Thursday, September 18, 1980, Mr. Edward G. Harness, chairman of Procter & Gamble (P&G) leafed through a stack of newspaper clips that highlighted the health hazards associated with the company's Rely tampon. One newspaper carried the headline "RELY CAUSES 25 DEATHS" with an article citing conclusions from a just-released government report. The fact that another newspaper had just told the world that P&G had quietly halted production of Rely—which many people would take to indicate that the company knew something it wasn't telling—only made things more complicated. These articles would heighten the public controversy that had suddenly surrounded the safety of tampon usage since the beginning of the summer.

Harness and his associates at P&G believed that recent news accounts and allegations linking the Rely tampon to toxic shock syndrome (TSS)—a recently discovered disease that could result in death—were often inaccurate and misleading. Furthermore, P&G executives felt this adverse publicity would only serve to alarm unduly an estimated 50 million American women that regularly used various brands of tampons. P&G had investigated TSS since the Center for Disease Control (CDC) first linked the rare disease to tampon use in a June 1980 study. This original CDC report had not implicated any particular brand of tampon with TSS.

In the September 1980 study, however, the Center said that "among women who develop the disease, the use of tampons generally and Rely in particular is more common than among comparable groups of healthy women."[1] CDC investigators had interviewed 50 women. Seventy percent reported using Rely tampons, about twice the percentage of users in a control group of 150 healthy women. The report did *not* conclude that Rely (or any other tampon) *caused* TSS; it simply concluded that there was a "statistical association"[2] between the tampon and the disease.

P&G executives knew that they faced a major crisis. The allegations about Rely were the most serious charges against one of its products that the company had ever encountered in its 143-year history. The company had a reputation for reliability and was noted for its conscientious product testing. Now, in September 1980, the company found its recently introduced Rely tampon under a barrage of criticism. Some company executives were concerned that P&G was being tied to a "bad product" and worried that the publicity might blemish its other brands.

P&G had maintained a cooperative relationship with the Center for Disease Control—a *research* agency of the U.S. Department of Health and Human Services—since the time tampon use and TSS were first linked. The disease itself had been identified only two years earlier and little was known about its causes or symptoms. Intensive research efforts by tampon makers and CDC had so far failed to yield any new information beyond that established by the medical community. When one scientist publicly theorized—prior to concluding his investigation—that superabsorbent tampons, such as Rely, might be the trouble source, P&G

[1] Center for Disease Control, *Morbidity and Mortality Report*, Atlanta, Georgia, May 23, 1980, p. 230.

[2] Ibid.

executives expressed anger and dismay about the premature conclusion.[3] Despite an occasional disagreement, the company and the Center worked well together and kept each other fully informed of their research on TSS.

The Food and Drug Administration (FDA)—a *regulatory* agency in the U.S. Department of Health and Human Services—became involved with TSS research in midsummer 1980. P&G had dealt with the FDA on previous occasions in skirmishes over ingredients in peanut butter, detergent, and deodorant products. Since the FDA had authority to issue consumer warnings and/or product recalls, its relationship with P&G had been somewhat adversarial. Nevertheless, P&G and the FDA freely exchanged information pertaining to Rely tampons and TSS. The relationship had been chilled recently by FDA media tactics. Knowing P&G to be highly sensitive about bad publicity, the FDA aggressively used the media, some P&G insiders believed, to drive Rely off the market. The FDA claimed that it was critical to keep the public fully informed about "developments involving such an important health and safety issue."[4]

Despite the spate of public attention and the presence of a number of product liability lawsuits, P&G was "determined to fight for a brand, to keep an important brand from being hurt by insufficient data in the hands of a bureaucracy."[5]

Competitive Environment

Menstrual products had become a $1 billion-a-year industry by mid-1980. Sales were evenly divided between tampons and sanitary napkins. The tampon business included five major competitors: Tampax (20.3% market share), Playtex (10.9%), P&G (8.4%), Johnson & Johnson (4.4%), and Kimberly Clark (2.9%).[6] The sanitary napkin business was dominated by Johnson & Johnson (29.0% market share) and Kimberly Clark (21.4%).[7] Menstrual products were usually sold in drug and grocery stores.

Competition in this industry was only a recent phenomenon. In 1936, Tampax pioneered the first commercially successful tampon and for the next 30 years it had the business to itself. By the 1960s, changing lifestyles converted more and more women to the advantages of internally worn protection and Tampax's business grew at an astonishing rate, return on equity reaching 40% in one year. The success of Tampax invited competition from some of the larger consumer goods companies. The marketing muscle of these bigger companies was released when a television advertising ban on menstrual products was lifted in 1972. Playtex quickly entered the market by introducing a new deodorant tampon and Johnson & Johnson soon followed with its own unique tampon design. Meanwhile, Procter & Gamble was preparing for its first product introduction in this market arena.

Procter & Gamble was founded as a partnership in 1837 and was initially engaged in the manufacture and sale of soap and candles in Cincinnati. From its very beginning, the company gained a reputation for being a "good listener"[8] that was responsive to consumer needs. The company, which ranked 23 (in sales) on the 1980 *Fortune* 500 list of largest U.S. industrial corporations, believed that close communication with consumers accounted for its success. The company's sales came from laundry cleansing, personal care, and food products.

The company first began work on menstrual products in the early 1950s but apparently did not succeed in developing a satisfactory product at that time. Following a 1957 acquisition of Charmin Paper Company, P&G researchers succeeded in overcoming the absorbency problems that had previously proved intractable. The research was first applied to such products as toilet tissue, paper towels, and disposable diapers, all of which were introduced successfully. By 1968, P&G was convinced it had come up with

[3] "Procter & Gamble Tampon Is Withdrawn from Stores Because of Toxic-Shock Link," *Wall Street Journal*, September 23, 1980, p. 2.

[4] "The FDA and Rely," *Wall Street Journal*, November 11, 1980, p. 24.

[5] "Killing a Product: Taking Rely Off the Market Cost Procter & Gamble a Week of Agonizing," *Wall Street Journal*, November 3, 1980, p. 16.

[6] "Tampon Use Stays Strong Despite Scare, Though Some Women Alter Their Habits," *Wall Street Journal*, October 31, 1980, p. 31.

[7] Ibid.

[8] "Good Listener: At Procter & Gamble, Success Is Largely Due to Heeding Consumer," *Wall Street Journal*, April 29, 1980, p. 1.

"a revolutionary kind of tampon."[9] That design, which would later become Rely, consisted of a unique construction of superabsorbent cellulose material and foam rubber. It resulted in quick acceptance of the product by women who tried it.

In January 1974, Rely was test marketed for the first time and was vigorously promoted as being twice as absorbent as any other tampon then available. Rely surprised even P&G by quickly achieving a 30% market share in its trial cities. Early success was only briefly interrupted in 1975 by health-related publicity in the Rochester, N.Y., test market. P&G had conducted safety tests of the materials and clinical tests of the tampon by itself. At the time Rely was introduced, there were not any regulatory procedures in the law that pertained to government testing of medical devices such as tampons. Although P&G denied that Rely caused health problems—no specific health hazards had been cited—the company eventually reformulated Rely by removing polyurethane to quiet consumer complaints. Slowly, test market by test market, P&G expanded its distribution of Rely and gained skill in marketing the product.

Regional marketing began in August 1978. Rely's success was not lost on competitors, who had entered the "absorbency sweepstakes" by adding synthetic fibers to their own products. The competition became particularly intense in 1979. P&G filed a trademark suit against Johnson and Johnson's new superabsorbent tampon. The giant medical products company countered this action by claiming that P&G had "gone to great lengths to disrupt the test-marketing of its (Johnson and Johnson's) new tampon." (P&G's response: "It turned out, obviously, to be more a defensive effort than a business-building effort.")[10]

In February 1980, Rely finally went into national distribution and quickly captured a substantial share of the U.S. tampon market. To convince women to try Rely, P&G had mailed 60 million sample packages to reach 80% of the nation's households and had spent almost $10 million on advertising the product.[11] Even though Rely was gaining widespread attention, it still accounted for less than 1% of company sales.

Rely's success had cut deeply into the sales of its competitors. Tampax, the leading manufacturer, lost 8.2% of its market share and others suffered even larger proportional losses in their shares.[12] The competitive struggle further intensified with news that the tampon industry's unit sales growth had slowed. Two factors were cited to explain this phenomenon. Women were apparently finding that they did not have to change superabsorbent tampons as frequently and sanitary napkin makers had introduced a thinner and more absorbent product that had gained widespread acceptance. Faced with lower sales volume, many of the menstrual-products companies were rethinking their product and promotional strategies.

Product Safety Controversy (1980)

The first known report concerning TSS was issued by a group of Denver pediatricians on November 25, 1978. In an article in a prestigious British medical publication, they reported finding common symptoms in a group of seven children (3 boys and 4 girls), which they postulated were caused by a new toxin produced by a *staphylococcus aureus* bacterium. No mention was made of menstruation or tampon use.

Searches of the medical literature, prompted by the appearance of this syndrome, uncovered a 1927 journal article that described a disease that resembled TSS but was also similar to scarlet fever. A 1942 medical report detailed a case of "clinical syndrome" indistinguishable from that of scarlet fever.[13] This disease, however, had not been specifically identified or named until the 1978 Denver study was released.

The next report of the disease came 15 months later. A March 28, 1980, letter to the editor of an American medical journal reported a disease characterized by high fever and fluid loss in three

[9] Pamela Sherrid, "Tampons after the Shock Wave," *Fortune*, August 10, 1981, p. 14.

[10] "Procter & Gamble Isn't Ready to Give Up on Tampon Market Despite Rely's Recall," *Wall Street Journal*, November 5, 1980, p. 3.

[11] "Tampon Alert Jeopardizes P&G's Rely," *Wall Street Journal*, September 19, 1980, p. 31.

[12] "Toxic Shock and Tampax," *New York Times*, October 1, 1980, p. D8.

[13] "Mystery of Toxic Shock Cases Is Unfolding at Disease Center," *New York Times*, October 9, 1980, p. C6.

menstruating women. The letter suggested that herpes virus was a possible causative agent. There was no mention of tampon involvement.

A May 23, 1980, report from the Center for Disease Control (CDC) listed the symptoms of toxic shock syndrome (TSS). Most cases had occurred in women under 25 and had begun during the menstrual period. There were, however, some reports of TSS in men and children. As in earlier reports, no mention was made of tampons. In early June, at a hearing before Senator Edward Kennedy's Senate Committee on Labor and Human Resources, CDC described the symptoms of TSS and stated that "the cause was unknown."[14]

Procter & Gamble and other tampon makers first became involved with the CDC's investigative efforts in mid-June. On June 13, CDC contacted P&G to obtain data concerning tampon usage. CDC was organizing a new study of TSS cases involving menstruating women and was apparently exploring possible links to tampon use. In its telephone call to P&G, the CDC doctor mentioned speculation by a newspaper reporter that tampons might be associated with TSS, but indicated that there were "no data to suggest this."[15] P&G cooperation was pledged and CDC agreed to keep the company informed.

CDC telephoned P&G on June 19 and alluded to an apparent link between TSS in menstruating women and tampon use. A total of 93 women who had the disease were included in three studies, which were conducted by CDC and two state health agencies. All but one of the women regularly used tampons.

Representatives of all tampon manufacturers met with CDC on June 25–26, 1980, to discuss the preliminary research findings. At that meeting, each of the tampon makers turned over product and market share data to the Center's researchers. P&G had been puzzled as to why CDC officials had specifically mentioned Rely (and no other brand) in their questioning at the meeting.

In a June 27 press release, CDC reported the apparent link between tampon use and TSS. It carefully noted, however, that "for the vast majority of women, the risk attributable to tampon use is so low that it seems unwarranted to recommend that use of tampons be discontinued."[16] CDC also noted that while 50 million American women used tampons, TSS was believed to occur in only about 3 of every 100,000 menstruating women. About 6% of those cases resulted in fatalities. Since 1978, according to the press release, 128 cases of toxic shock syndrome had been reported, with 10 resulting in death. A CDC spokesman reminded the public that the study had not implicated any particular brand of tampon.

According to the Center, TSS was characterized by high fever, vomiting, diarrhea, a sunburn-like rash and a rapid drop in blood pressure, which frequently resulted in shock. A CDC epidemiologist said they had not determined exactly how tampon use was related to the disease. If *staphylococcus aureus* was the cause, said CDC, "the use of tampons might favor growth of the bacterium in the vagina or absorption of the toxin from the vagina or uterus—but these possibilities have not been investigated."[17] Future tests were to be conducted in consultation with the Food and Drug Administration (FDA).

At this point, P&G began to collect information about the disease and any possible link between tampon usage in general and Rely in particular. P&G was prevented from obtaining access to patient lists used in the CDC study because of provisions in federal privacy laws. The company was able, however, to collect information from state health departments and individual physicians. This study found no correlation between any specific tampon brand and the toxic shock syndrome.

In July 1980, an FDA bulletin reported CDC's findings and also said that "no particular brand of tampons is associated with high risk."[18] The surgeon general said that women who have not had TSS "need not change their pattern of tampon use . . ."[19]

[14] U.S. Congress, Senate Committee on Labor and Human Resources, *Hearings Before a Senate Subcommittee on Health and Scientific Research*, Washington, DC, June 6, 1980, p. 11.

[15] Procter & Gamble, "Current Knowledge Concerning TSS," Cincinnati, Ohio, 1980.

[16] Center for Disease Control, *Morbidity and Mortality Report*, Atlanta, Georgia, June 27, 1980, p. 2.

[17] "Tampons Are Linked to a Rare Disease," *New York Times*, June 28, 1980, p. 17.

[18] FDA, *FDA Drug Bulletin*, Washington, DC, July 1980, p. 11.

[19] Ibid.

During the summer months, P&G microbiologists continued testing the Rely tampon and each of its ingredients with particular reference to the growth of bacteria. Initial results from the program showed that the superabsorbent material in Rely did not encourage TSS and may have actually inhibited bacterial growth. During this time, the company also arranged to convene an outside advisory group, which included eminent scientists from around the country.

By the end of August, the Center for Disease Control had confirmed 213 cases of TSS across the country, of which 16 had been fatal. Public speculation about the cause of the disease began to focus on the superabsorbent tampons, such as Rely. One TSS victim filed a $5 million lawsuit against P&G. Other tampon-TSS suits quickly followed—three of every four TSS liability claims involved P&G's Rely tampon.

On Monday, September 15, CDC telephoned P&G's executive offices in Cincinnati, Ohio, to report that Rely was more frequently associated with TSS than any other tampon. CDC officials cited results from a just completed two-month survey of TSS victims. In the sample of 42 women who had suffered TSS, 71% had used Rely.[20] The results of CDC's second study prompted the scheduling of a meeting in Washington between P&G, the FDA and CDC officials. P&G prepared for this meeting by quickly assembling a task force that included the vice president of the paper products division, a physician on P&G's staff, and members of the research and legal departments.

On Tuesday, September 16, thirteen P&G representatives met face to face with twelve FDA representatives and three CDC officials to exchange and review available data. P&G arrived ready to take issue with many parts of the CDC study. Company representatives argued that extensive news coverage of TSS may have biased the survey's results. They also challenged the study's interviewing techniques and claimed that CDC's data were "too limited and fragmentary for any conclusions to be drawn."[21] P&G was determined to fight for its product and felt it was being unfairly singled out for media attention.

According to one government representative, the FDA entered the meeting "very concerned about the data, . . . thinking that unless the company had a justification for keeping the product on the market, we would ask that it be withdrawn."[22] The FDA was convinced that Rely's superabsorbent ingredients were partly to blame for the incidence of TSS. They knew, however, that "P&G was not likely to roll over easily."[23] But, anticipating they might have to make some concessions, P&G managers had prepared a warning label that they were willing to put on their packages. The FDA's cool reception made it clear that warning labels would not be enough. The meeting ended with the government allowing P&G one week to study the CDC's findings and respond.

On Wednesday, September 17, P&G decided to halt production in the two plants that produced the Rely tampon. One P&G executive would later say that production was stopped because "it seemed likely that at the very least warning labels would be required on tampon packages, so we didn't want to fill more and more packages without labels."[24] At that time, the company had a one-month inventory of tampons on hand in its warehouses.

On Thursday, September 18, P&G was at a critical juncture in the Rely crisis. Media attention on its tampon was threatening to overwhelm the company. Earlier in the day, CDC released updated statistics on TSS and claimed 25 deaths had occurred since the syndrome was first identified. P&G was further jolted by the news that several of its major retailers had already pulled Rely off their shelves.

Without the abundance of information it normally compiled to make important marketing decisions, P&G had "excruciatingly little data" upon which to base its next move. Four days remained until the company would have to reappear in front of FDA and CDC investigators. P&G could continue its defense of Rely or it could begin to seek some kind of accommodation with the government.

[20] Center for Disease Control, *Morbidity and Mortality Report*, Atlanta, Georgia, September 19, 1980, p. 1.

[21] "P&G's Rely Tampon Found Implicated in Rare Disease by U.S. Disease Center," *Wall Street Journal*, September 18, 1980, p. 6.

[22] "Killing a Product," p. 16.

[23] Ibid.

[24] Ibid.

Postscript

On Friday, September 19, the case for Rely weakened as the Utah Health Department reported results of its own study that seemed to confirm CDC's earlier linkage of Rely to TSS. As the weekend approached, P&G convened its previously recruited group of independent physicians, microbiologists, and epidemiologists to review all the studies that had linked Rely with TSS. This outside scientific advisory group reported that although the studies were inconclusive and fragmentary, and did not establish a scientific basis for a decision, they could not assure P&G that the data of the latest study could be safely ignored. One P&G executive later recalled that, "looking at the numbers, we couldn't tell if the TSS was already a major disease, with reported cases just a bare indicator, or whether it was still a small-scale disease but was spreading."[25] As Mr. Harness remembered, "that was the turning point. . . . I knew what we had to do."[26]

On Monday, September 22, P&G announced that the company had suspended sale of Rely tampons. In a press release, the company said, "We are taking this action to remove Rely and the company from the controversy surrounding a new disease called toxic shock syndrome (TSS). This is being done despite the fact that we know of no defect in the Rely tampon and despite evidence that the withdrawal of Rely will not eliminate the occurrence of TSS. . . ."[27]

P&G estimated the voluntary suspension of sales would cost it $75 million after taxes. This would dampen earnings growth but would not place the company in severe financial difficulty. During the previous year, P&G had earned a total of $512 million after taxes.

The FDA viewed P&G's decision as a "preemptive strike" and, as such, a smart move. But at the September 23 meeting with the company, the FDA told the P&G delegation "it had to do more—much, much more."[28] P&G was concerned that the government might still ask the company to admit violation of safety standards. Such an admission would severely damage the company's defense in numerous product-liability suits being filed across the country. P&G did not want the word "recall" used because it might imply safety violations. P&G and the FDA hashed out the details of the voluntary action for three days before finally reaching an agreement.

On Friday, September 26, P&G signed a consent agreement with the government. Under terms of the agreement P&G denied any violation of federal law or any product defect, but agreed to buy back any unused product the customer still had, including $10 million in introductory, promotional free samples. The company pledged its research expertise to CDC and agreed to finance and direct a large educational program about the disease. The company developed an informational advertising program of unprecedented scope that warned women not to use Rely and cautioned them on the use of other tampons. By deploying 3,000 members of its sales force, P&G removed Rely from retail stores within two weeks of the September 22 announcement.

Food and Drug Administration Commissioner Jere Goyan said, "The recent tampon recall showed how government and industry can act together in the public's interest and should reassure consumers about federal regulations."[29]

In Cincinnati, Ohio, P&G's Chairman Edward G. Harness said, "The company agreed to the withdrawal not because it believed the tampon was defective, but because we did not know enough about TSS to act, and yet we knew too much not to act. We did the right thing in suspending the brand."[30]

[25] Ibid.

[26] Ibid.

[27] Procter & Gamble, Press Release, Cincinnati, Ohio: Procter & Gamble Company, September 22, 1980, p. 1.

[28] "Killing a Product," p. 16.

[29] "FDA Official Praises Tampon Recall," *Cincinnati Enquirer*, October 3, 1980, p. C11.

[30] Elizabeth Gatewood and Archie Carroll, "The Anatomy of Corporate Social Response," *Business Horizons* 24 (September/October 1980), p. 12.

The Playskool Travel-Lite Crib (A)

Prologue

Sanfred Koltun sat in his office in the Chicago headquarters of his company, Kolcraft Enterprises, reading a letter. Addressed to Bernard Greenberg, president of Kolcraft, the February 1, 1993, letter had been passed around to the company's handful of top executives. He would get their perspectives on the situation. But Koltun knew that, as owner and CEO, he would be the one to determine the company's actions. It had been that way since his father started the company in 1942.

The three-and-a-half page letter was from Marc J. Schoem, director of the division of corrective actions for the U.S. Consumer Product Safety Commission (CPSC). Schoem's office, his letter explained, was responsible for making a preliminary determination about "whether a defect is present in a product and, if so, whether that defect rises to the level of a substantial risk of injury to children."

"The CPSC has received reports of two infant fatalities resulting from the collapse of 'Playskool' brand portable cribs manufactured and distributed by Kolcraft," Schoem wrote. "In both cases it appears the infant was entrapped when the crib collapsed while the infant was in the crib." Schoem then requested a "full report": Kolcraft would have to provide, among other materials, "copies of all test reports, analyses, and evaluations, including premarket tests and reports of tests and any analyses related to the locking mechanism and/or potential for collapse of product." The CPSC also requested copies of all engineering drawings, any consumer or dealer complaints, lawsuits, assembly instructions in all their forms, and two samples of the Travel-Lite crib. Finally, Schoem noted, Kolcraft had a "continuing obligation to supplement or correct its 'full report'" as new information about the product or incidents related to it became known.[1]

Schoem closed his letter with the request that Kolcraft respond within ten working days.

History of Kolcraft

Kolcraft Enterprises was started in Chicago in 1942 as a manufacturer of baby pads, a foam product commonly used in high chairs, play pens, and bassinets. In 1950 Kolcraft began manufacturing mattresses for use in baby cribs. Sanfred Koltun, the founder's son, graduated with a bachelor's degree from The University of Chicago in 1954 and an M.B.A. from the same school in 1955. He then joined the company, which at that time employed about 30 people.[2]

By the early 1980s, Kolcraft diversified into the manufacture of various juvenile seats, including car seats and booster seats. Koltun opened a 25,000-square-foot facility in North Carolina making what are generically known as play pens, a metal and masonite folding device

Written by David Zivan, Senior Editor, *Chicago* magazine.
Funded by the James S. Kemper Ethics in Business Grant to the Graduate School of Business at the University of Chicago, under the direction of Professor Linda Ginzel.

Please write: Professor Linda Ginzel, Graduate School of Business, The University of Chicago, 1101 East 58th Street, Chicago, IL 60637, USA. Or email linda.ginzel@gsb.uchicago.edu.

[1] Marc Schoem, letter to Bernard Greenberg, 2/1/93. From tab 7, *Linda Ginzel, as independent administrator of the estate of Daniel Keysar, deceased, and on behalf of Boaz Keysar, Ely Keysar, and Linda Ginzel, next of kin, plaintiff, v. Kolcraft Enterprises, Inc., a Delaware Corporation, and Hasbro, Inc., a Rhode Island Corporation, defendants*, #98L7063, pending in the Circuit Court of Cook County, County Department, Law Division.

[2] Deposition of Sanfred Koltun, 4/19/2000, pp. 6–8.

typically measuring 36 by 36 inches with mesh sides. Children would nap and play in these common household products. Kolcraft eventually expanded to include operations in Pennsylvania, Georgia, and California.[3] By the late 1980s, the company had hundreds of employees, with headquarters in Chicago and a separate manufacturing and engineering facility in Bedford Park, Illinois.[4] Though dwarfed by major corporations like Mattel's Fisher-Price and Hasbro's Playskool, Kolcraft eventually grew to become the seventh largest juvenile products manufacturer, with revenues around $30 million.[5]

Kolcraft maintained a small executive suite with Sanfred Koltun as CEO. Kolcraft's flow of information was informal, with meetings taking place frequently in a centrally located conference room at the headquarters.[6] Although the managers of various divisions controlled the day-to-day operations of their projects, Sanfred Koltun had the final word in all important decisions of the company.

In 1979, Kolcraft hired Edward Johnson, a graduate of a technical high school where he received training in draft work. Johnson had worked as a design draftsman for a lighting company, served four years in the Air Force, and worked for seven years at J.E. Industrial Molding as a designer in custom blow molding, a process that made plastic products with a cushion of air inside. He designed Kolcraft's first car seat, which was sold in the Sears retailing chain, and by 1987 he had been named engineering head of Kolcraft. Johnson worked mainly on car seats and other seat products like high chairs until his first design of a portable crib, in 1989.[7]

In 1987, Kolcraft hired Bernard Greenberg as a vice president. A graduate of New York University, Greenberg had worked at Macy's for six years as a buyer, then spent a number of years with various manufacturers of juvenile products, eventually serving as president of Century, a juvenile product manufacturer which was a division of Gerber baby products. Greenberg became president of Kolcraft around 1990.

Development of the Playskool Travel-Lite

In the mid-1980s, the U.S. juvenile product market saw a substantial influx of imported goods, primarily from Asia, including a new product—portable play yards, or portable cribs as they came to be known. Rectangular in shape, the traveling cribs often folded into a carrying bag. Sanfred Koltun believed that Kolcraft could manufacture a similar, better product.

In the first half of 1989, Edward Johnson drew up some preliminary sketches for a portable, collapsible crib. Johnson's design featured two hollow plastic sides that would serve as the exterior shell of the crib when it was folded for transport. The other two sides would be made of mesh supported by two collapsible top rails with a hinge in the middle. The solid floor would also fold at the center.

That spring, Sanfred Koltun gave the go-ahead to create a mock-up of the portable crib. "His comment from the very beginning was like it was the best thing he'd ever seen," Johnson remembered later. "It was unique because there was nothing out there with a carrying case. Nothing that was that structurally sound. Nothing that looked as nice as that."[8] Johnson's painted wood model of the crib was well received by Kolcraft's marketing department, and the company decided to try to get the portable crib ready for the annual Juvenile Products Manufacturers Association (JPMA) trade show, scheduled for mid-September in Dallas.

Initial prototype models of the crib were heavier than Johnson had hoped—close to 19 pounds, as opposed to the 10 or 11 he had originally planned. Nevertheless, the company's optimism for the product continued. According to Johnson, the engineering department generated an "unbelievably thick" file on the Travel-Lite while trying to make the product achieve the portability that had been a major selling point of its competitors.[9]

A Travel-Lite prototype was made and sat in the break room across from Johnson's office in

[3] Deposition of Bernard Greenberg, 9/30/99, pp. 8, 20.

[4] Illinois Manufacturers Directory, 1988–92.

[5] E. Marla Felcher, *It's No Accident: How Corporations Sell Dangerous Baby Products*, Common Courage Press, 2001, p. 83.

[6] Deposition of Edward Johnson, 5/13/99, p. 14.

[7] Johnson, pp. 3–9, 29.

[8] Johnson, pp. 31–32.

[9] Johnson, p. 20.

Bedford Park. Soon Johnson found himself demonstrating the crib to other Kolcraft employees. "We constantly were taking this thing down and putting it back up, kicking it around, because it was a unique product and everybody was . . . excited about it," Johnson remembered. "Whenever someone walked into the room, they'd come in to me and say, 'what is this?' and I'd have to go through and explain it. And every time they asked, I'd tear it down and put it back up again. This thing [was] going up and down all the time."[10]

A prototype model of the portable crib received a generally favorable reception from retail buyers at Sears, K-Mart, JC Penney, Walmart, Montgomery Ward's, Service Merchandise, and Target. Several buyers noted that they would like to see the crib be a little lighter. Some also noted that they had difficulty turning the crib's locking mechanism, which consisted of round plastic knobs or dials located at the end of each top rail. "Some of the buyers told us they just could not turn the lock," said Greenberg, who visited the engineering offices once a week to check on the project's progress. "And [Johnson] kept on working on it."[11]

The final design featured a nub on the outside portion of the dial that would slide into an indent on the inside portion. Once the crib was standing up, users would turn the knobs to the "lock" position (eventually designated by decals) and then hear a small "click" (Exhibit 1). "When we put it back to the buyers, they liked it a lot," Greenberg said. "They thought it was a very good idea."[12]

The crib would be ready for the trade show in Dallas.

Licensing the Travel-Lite

Sanfred Koltun believed that affiliating with a recognized brand name would be beneficial for Kolcraft. "I thought in terms of customers," he said. "I wanted to get [our product] on the floor of juvenile departments in retail stores."[13] In 1989, as Bernard Greenberg would later put it, Sanfred Koltun "went after the Playskool name," and by that summer Koltun had negotiated a licensing deal with Hasbro.[14] Koltun hired Ernst Kaufmann, a 32-year veteran of Sears, to handle the merchandising of the new line, which Kolcraft would license under the Playskool brand name.

Playskool, well known in the juvenile products market for its reputation as a maker of high-quality toys, was a property of the Hasbro company. Founded in the 1920s by Polish immigrant Henry Hassenfeld and publicly traded since 1968, Hasbro was in the 1980s one of the fastest-growing companies in the nation, with successful brands, such as Raggedy Ann and G.I. Joe, and revenues surpassing $2 billion. In 1983, Hasbro had hired John Gildea to be its director of licensing. Gildea had been employed by the owners of Hanna Barbera, where he had negotiated licensing contracts for such properties as the Flintstones, Scooby Doo, and Huckleberry Hound. Prior to 1983, licensing had not been a separate department at Hasbro, and top management at the company had directed the new department to find high-quality manufacturing partners who would uphold Playskool's reputation in the marketplace. Through the mid-1980s, Gildea hired account executives to handle such properties as G.I. Joe, My Little Pony, and Mr. Potato Head.

By the end of the decade, Hasbro had begun licensing the Playskool name—a brand associated, as Gildea put it, with "quality, fun products."[15] In an interview with *Children's Business*,[16] Gildea outlined the emerging benefits of the company's licensing business:

> The non-toy products are Playskool line extensions that we don't happen to make. Our strategy is twofold. We gain incremental exposure of the Playskool name, [creating] brand awareness at a very early age that will pay dividends down the line. Secondly, and not insignificantly, it brings income. Licensing allows us to concentrate on our core business and also take advantage of the corporate name in appropriate products.

Both benefits looked relatively easy to achieve, and may have seemed necessary, as one of Hasbro's

[10] Johnson, pp. 14–15.

[11] Greenberg, p. 82.

[12] Greenberg, p. 85.

[13] S. Koltun, pp. 73–75.

[14] Greenberg, p. 26.

[15] Deposition of John Gildea, 8/26/99, p. 11.

[16] Gregory J. Colman, "What's Playskool's Name Doing on a Pair of Sneakers?" *Children's Business*, February 1991, p. 61.

main competitors, Fisher-Price, had already begun making products outside its traditional lines.[17]

In the original agreement, Kolcraft would manufacture and distribute mattresses, play pens, and car seats with Hasbro's Playskool name attached. The agreement stipulated, among other provisions, that

> the licensee shall, prior to the date of the first distribution of the licensed articles, submit to the licensor a test plan which lists all the applicable acts and standards and contains a certification by the licensee that no other acts or standards apply to the licensed articles. . . . Test plan shall describe in detail the procedures used to test the licensed articles, and licensee shall submit certificates in writing that the licensed articles conform to the applicable acts and standards. Upon request by the licensor, licensee shall provide licensor with specific test data or laboratory reports.[18]

Kaufmann helped with the final terms of the licensing agreement, and came up with one amendment: adding the new portable crib to the deal.[19] "When you develop your company into new products, the competition is way ahead of you," said Greenberg. "If you develop a product that is similar to the competition, especially in price, you need something to put on it to give more flavor to it, so to speak."[20]

Going to the Show

Kolcraft's display at the JPMA trade show in Dallas featured a separate area for its Playskool products, staffed by Kaufmann. The Travel-Lite received a warm reception, and a press release by the JPMA, dated September 15, 1989, named the Travel-Lite one of the top new products at the trade show:

> At a press conference today, the Juvenile Products Manufacturers Association (JPMA) announced the winners of the "Ten Most Innovative Products Contest."
>
> A panel of independent judges . . . were instructed to judge on: creativity, originality, function, convenience, safety, innovative design, fashion, style, and overall appearance and use of the product.

Later, the crib even got some national press attention in the "What's New in Design" section of the December 4, 1989, edition of *Adweek* magazine (Exhibit 2).

Final Preparations

On September 28, 1989, Hasbro's David Schwartz, who handled the Kolcraft account for the company, wrote a letter to Ernst Kaufmann, reminding him of Kolcraft's obligations under the licensing agreement. "Pursuant to the terms of the contract between Hasbro and Kolcraft Enterprises, please be aware that Kolcraft must adhere to the terms set forth in Paragraph 7 (quality of merchandise), stating that: 'The licensee warrants that the licensed articles will be designed, produced, sold, and distributed in accordance with all applicable U.S. laws.'"[21] Schwartz then specifically asked for documents he had not yet received: "I would also request test plans and results for the Playskool travel crib . . . when they have been obtained."[22] While Hasbro had its own quality assurance department, it did not perform tests on the Travel-Lite.[23]

On December 1, 1989, Kaufmann answered Schwartz with a letter, noting various government and industry testing standards that had been applied to the other juvenile products about to come to market under the Playskool name. For the portable crib, he noted only that the product would come with a one-year limited warranty. "My intention was to show that we had a quality product," Kaufmann said later. "[One] that we were willing to put a warranty behind."[24]

In subsequent conversations with Kaufmann, Schwartz again requested test plans for the Travel-Lite.[25] Kaufmann answered with a December 21, 1989, letter,[26] which in its entirety read as follows:

> Dear Mr. Schwartz:
>
> Please be advised that there are no government or industry test standards applicable to the Playskool portable crib.

[17] Details of this expansion also included in *Children's Business*, February 1991.

[18] Gildea, pp. 54–55.

[19] Deposition of Ernst Kaufmann, 6/29/99, p. 16.

[20] Greenberg, p. 27.

[21] Deposition of Laura Millhollin, 3/29/00, p. 47.

[22] Kaufmann, p. 74.

[23] Deposition of Malcolm Denniss, 8/27/99, pp. 18–22.

[24] Kaufmann, p. 76.

[25] Deposition of David Schwartz, 3/17/00, pp. 62–66.

[26] From appendix to #98L7063, tab 17.

> We have therefore taken all reasonable measures to assure that this portable crib is an acceptable consumer product.
>
> Very truly yours,
> [signed] Ernst Kaufmann

Schwartz filed the letter.

Going to Market

Kolcraft began producing and shipping the Travel-Lite in January 1990. Both the crib and its packaging featured prominent placement of the Playskool name, and it was available in retail chains such as Toys 'R' Us, K-Mart, JC Penney, and Walmart. An instruction sheet for setting up the crib was affixed to the floor of the crib, underneath the mattress—"a standard production step," Johnson noted. "It's in the specifications for [conventional] play yards. . . . All the other play yards have them."[27]

Sanfred Koltun was by now a proud grandfather. On family visits, his grandson would spend time in a Travel-Lite. "I was very happy with it," Koltun said.[28]

In June 1991, Edward Johnson received a patent for the Travel-Lite design. His petition noted that "the present invention relates to collapsible or foldable structures; and more particularly, to a collapsible structure suitable for use as a portable play yard." Other play yards, the patent application contended, were difficult to fold, whereas Johnson's design for the Travel-Lite was "easy to fold and transport."[29]

Sanfred Koltun would later attribute the poor sales of the Travel-Lite to the fact that the crib was more expensive than similar imported items, causing discount retailers like K-Mart and Walmart to shy away from the product. The design team felt that the product had simply become too heavy. "As far as the buyers go, [the] unit [was] too heavy," Johnson said. "I don't think it was the consumer. The buyers kept asking for more and more—more padding, things like that. And eventually, enough buyers said, 'no.' "[30]

[27] Johnson, p. 94.

[28] S. Koltun, p. 61.

[29] Report of Shelly Waters Deppa, Safety Behavior Analysis, Inc., 11/16/2000, p. 3.

[30] Johnson, pp. 43–44.

Kolcraft ended up selling only about 11,600 of the cribs, models 77101 and 77103, and shipments stopped in April 1992.[31]

The First Deaths

On July 3, 1991, an 11-month-old boy in California died of strangulation while in a Travel-Lite crib.[32] The child's neck was caught in the "V" created when the crib's top rails collapsed (Exhibit 3). The CPSC investigated the incident, and produced a report by the end of the year.

That spring, the report was mailed to Hasbro, which forwarded it to Kolcraft. In June 1992, Kolcraft responded with a letter to the CPSC which stated in part:

> The CPSC report on the July 3, 1991 incident involving a small child notes that the travel crib is subject to the voluntary standards of the juvenile products manufacturing industry. We note that there is no such standard applicable to travel cribs. The ASTM standard for play yards, ASTM F 406 does not apply to this product, which is a wholly different structural entity. Nor does the CPSC standard for non-full-size cribs, 16 CFR Part 1509, apply to travel cribs of this design."

The letter also noted that nothing in the report "suggests at this point that the Travel-Lite portable crib is defective in any way or presents a substantial hazard."[33]

On November 30, 1992, a nine-month-old girl in Arkansas died when her Travel-Lite collapsed, strangling her in the "V." A ten-month-old girl in California was killed in the same manner in another Travel-Lite on January 5, 1993.

The CPSC had only heard about two of the deaths when Marc J. Schoem wrote his February 1, 1993, letter to Kolcraft, requesting a full report on the Travel-Lite. Sanfred Koltun was shocked at the news. "I was appalled when I heard about the deaths," he said. "I just couldn't believe people were so careless."[34]

[31] Jonathan Eig, "How Danny Died," *Chicago* magazine, November 1998.

[32] Mitch Lipka, "Deaths of Six Babies Expose Fatal Flaws of System," *Sun-Sentinel, South Florida*, November 28–30, 1999.

[33] Mitch Lipka, ibid.

[34] S. Koltun, pp. 62–63.

EXHIBIT 1 **Travel-Lite Crib with View of Two Side Knobs**

EXHIBIT 2 Travel-Lite Crib in *Adweek* Magazine

December 4, 1989 ADWEEK'S MARKETING WEEK Page 53

In the always-hot market for portable everything, Kolcraft Enterprises Inc. of Chicago is tickling the offspring of mobile cellular-phone users and other travelers with a portable crib. The No. 5 juvenile-products manufacturer, under a licensing agreement with Playskool, has designed a 19-pound all-in-one unit that folds up into its own carrying case.

The crib's nylon walls unfold, and the frame locks in place to hold an infant up to 24 months old. In the closed position, the crib case measures 29-by-5½-inches—the size of a large typewriter. Transparent walls made out of mosquito netting let guardians keep an eye on the baby, and vice versa. The $89 travel crib is expected to hit the market in March.

The Trav'l Light is one of three products that Kolcraft licensed from Playskool this year. The company is also making a Playskool car seat and stationary-crib mattress that will ship to major retailers during the winter.

It looks like an unassuming hassock fan, but the No-Rad Radon Removal System is a patented combination of air ventilator, filter and ion generator. It's the latest product designed in recent years to quell consumer fears about cancer-causing radon.

Backed by findings by Harvard University researchers, Ion Systems Inc. says its $350 gadget can reduce radon decay particles in a room by as much as 90%. Homeowners spend thousands of dollars on reconstruction to seal, pressurize and ventilate their houses against radon.

No-Rad is positioned as a serious but inexpensive option. Its 360-degree air vents are supposed to improve effectiveness, and the neutral gray case is designed to fit into almost any home. It weighs 19 pounds.

Designer Nolan Miller—whose fashions graced the primetime soap queens on *Dynasty*—has created a signature gown for The Black Velvet Lady. The spokeswoman for the No. 3 brand of Canadian whiskey will wear the plush dress in ads and promotions.

For years Heublein Inc. used professional models as the Black Velvet Lady. But three years ago it launched annual beauty contests to boost brand awareness with younger women. This year's regional contests had more than 5,000 participants. And in these markets, sales jumped 10% during the promotion.

EXHIBIT 3 Travel-Lite Crib in Collapsed Position

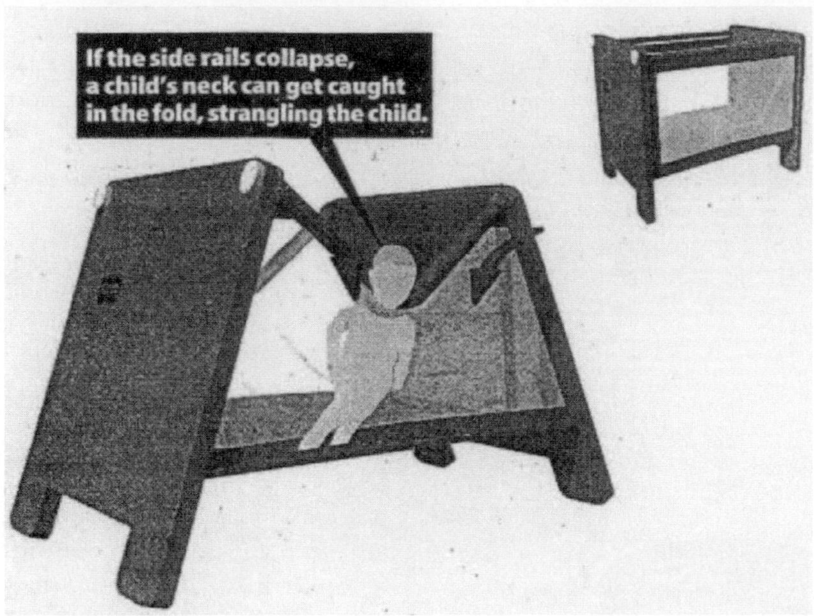

The Playskool Travel-Lite Crib (B)

Starting the Recall

The Travel-Lite had been off store shelves for almost a year when Kolcraft received the February 1, 1993, letter from the CPSC. And although the crib carried a limited one-year warranty, the product had not included a mail-in warranty registration card for consumers. By February 1993, the earliest users of the crib would have long outgrown it, and in many cases the original purchasers would have discarded, stored, sold, or given away their cribs.

Sanfred Koltun met with Bernard Greenberg and John Staas, an attorney and Kolcraft's vice president of operations, to discuss the situation. Kolcraft retained a law firm in Washington, D.C., and on February 12 drafted a response to the CPSC. In it, they proposed notification procedures, including contacting retailers with a letter and a poster informing them of a potential problem with the Travel-Lite, and providing a toll-free number for consumers to call. A copy of the poster Kolcraft designed for display in retail locations was passed to Hasbro, and on February 18, staff at Hasbro approved the poster.[1] On Friday the 19th, Kolcraft sent retailers a letter and an accompanying 8½- by 11-inch poster, which included a drawing of the Travel-Lite.

Written by David Zivan, Senior Editor, *Chicago* magazine. Funded by the James S. Kemper Ethics in Business Grant to the Graduate School of Business at the University of Chicago, under the direction of Professor Linda Ginzel.

Please write: Professor Linda Ginzel, Graduate School of Business, The University of Chicago, 1101 East 58th Street, Chicago, IL 60637, USA. Or email linda.ginzel@gsb.uchicago.edu.

[1] Deposition of Malcolm Denniss, 8/27/99, p. 64.

Also on February 19, Kolcraft's lawyers in Washington received notice that the compliance staff at the CPSC had made a preliminary determination that the Playskool Travel-Lite crib presented "a substantial risk of injury to children as defined by section 15(a) of the Federal Hazardous Substances Act (FHSA), 15 U.S.C. δ 2064(a). Specifically, there have been three reports to the Commission of infant fatalities resulting from the product folding up during use."[2] On February 22, 1993, the CPSC received from Kolcraft a copy of the letter and poster the company had mailed to retailers the previous Friday. On February 24, 1993, William J. Moore, Jr., an attorney in the office of compliance and enforcement of the CPSC, wrote a letter to Kolcraft's attorneys in Washington, D.C. His letter stated, in part:

> We take serious exception with your proposal to print the pediatrician poster in black and white. The poster will be competing with many other pieces of information . . . . The staff was very troubled to learn that the retailer letter and accompanying poster you provided to us on Monday, February 22, 1993, had already been sent to the retailers the previous Friday. The staff had been asking to review the proposed retailer notice for several days. Your February 12 letter promised to provide these documents to us by February 16. We stood willing and able to give quick guidance for producing effective notice documents.
>
> The 8½ × 11 inch, black and white, thin stock "poster" sent to retailers had many serious shortcomings, in our view. It did not even have the Playskool name on the crib.

[2] *Linda Ginzel, as independent administrator of the estate of Daniel Keysar, deceased, and on behalf of Boaz Keysar, Ely Keysar, and Linda Ginzel, next of kin, plaintiff, v. Kolcraft Enterprises, Inc., a Delaware Corporation, and Hasbro, Inc., a Rhode Island Corporation, defendants,* #98L7063, pending in the Circuit Court of Cook County, County Department, Law Division. From appendix, tab 7.

Moore added that his staff "wishes to work with Kolcraft to make this an effective . . . recall and to prevent further tragedy."[3]

In a conference call on March 1, Kolcraft's attorneys in Washington tried to reassure the CPSC that Kolcraft and their firm were responding quickly and responsibly. Kolcraft had by then agreed to send a notice to approximately 26,000 pediatricians on a list maintained by the American Academy of Pediatrics. In addition, it would send a revised letter to Sears and to smaller retailers. The JC Penney's chain would be able to notify its catalog customers directly from its database. Kolcraft's attorneys expressed concern with the tone of Moore's letter and asked that it be purged from the case file, a suggestion that the CPSC rejected.[4]

After confidential negotiations between Kolcraft attorneys and the CPSC, the CPSC on March 10 issued a press release announcing the product recall (Exhibit 1). Hasbro was not involved.

Six weeks after its request for a full report, the CPSC was still attempting to acquire testing data on the Travel-Lite and status reports on the progression of the recall.[5] On March 19, 1993, John Staas wrote a memo to Kolcraft's file,[6] with a subject line: "Testing information requested by CPSC."

It read in part: Using the ASTM play yard standard as a model, Kolcraft measured and maintained the following performance features on the Travel-Lite crib:

1. Caps, sleeves, etc. secured to stay on with 15 lbf force or more.
2. Uniformly spaced components.
3. Side height of 20 inches.
4. Side strength and deflection of top rails and supporting methods to withstand 50 lbf static load.
5. Floor strength to withstand 50 cycle 30 ft. load.
6. Holes sized to avoid finger entrapment.
7. Mesh openings to avoid finger and toe entrapment and snaring of buttons.
8. Twelve-gauge vinyl used on the top rails.

Staas mentioned reaching compliance with regulations on sharp points and edges, and flame-retardant standards, and added that:

> Kolcraft designers conducted use and abuse tests on these cribs, consisting of repeated cycles of leaning, pushing, sitting on and throwing the crib, and turning it on its sides. Kolcraft also tested the folding mechanism to determine if it could be inadvertently folded or lowered by a child while the crib was in use. Kolcraft used CPSC 16 CFR δ 1500.53(e)(3) as its standard to test the folding mechanisms.
>
> CPSC use and abuse standard 16 CFR δ 1500.53(e)(3) prescribes a standard of 4 inch-pound torque to measure the susceptibility of a product to the twisting motion of a child 36 to 96 months of age. The Travel-Lite top rails were designed and measured to require four times the force of the CPSC regulation. Kolcraft's measurements using a torque wrench indicated that 15–20 inch-pounds was approximately the range needed to activate the folding mechanism.

Kolcraft was able to produce no records on the testing of such a twisting motion. Later, Edward Johnson said he could not recall which of the tests his department performed had received written notations and which had been informal.[7] In addition to a person simply turning the dials at either end of the crib, as intended, the crib could also fold closed if the collapsible top rails were turned firmly enough (i.e., 15–20 inch-pounds, as noted by Kolcraft) to dislodge the nub holding them in place.

On July 12, 1995, a ten-month-old boy in Indianapolis was strangled in the "V" of his collapsed Travel-Lite. He was the fourth known victim of the crib.

By June 1996, of the 11,600 sold, 2,736 Travel-Lites could be accounted for. Noting that the returns had stopped and that there had been no recent injury or death reports, the CPSC closed its case. The status of 76 percent of the cribs remained unknown.[8]

[3] From appendix to #98L7063, tab 7.

[4] From telephone notes in appendix to #98L7063, tab 7.

[5] March 16, 1993, documents from appendix to #98L7063, tab 7.

[6] From appendix to #98L7063, tab 6.

[7] Deposition of Edward Johnson, 5/13/99, pp. 20–26.

[8] Mitch Lipka, "Deaths of Six Babies Expose Fatal Flaws of System," *Sun-Sentinel, South Florida*, November 28–30, 1999.

After the Recall

On May 12, 1998, during naptime at his childcare provider, 16-month-old Danny Keysar was found unconscious in the "V" of a Travel-Lite. He was rushed to the emergency room but could not be revived. He was the fifth reported death in a Travel-Lite (Exhibit 2).

On August 19, 1998, a ten-month-old New Jersey boy was found dead, strangled in the "V" of his Travel-Lite. He was the sixth victim (Exhibit 3).

EXHIBIT 1 **News from CPSC: U.S. Consumer Product Safety Commission**

Office of Information and Public Affairs **Washington, DC 20207**

FOR IMMEDIATE RELEASE
March 10, 1993
Release # 93-043

CONTACT:
(301) 504-0580

Playskool Travel-Lite Portable Cribs Recalled By Kolcraft—Suffocation Risk Cited

PRODUCT: 11,638 Playskool Travel-Lite Portable Cribs, models 77101 and 77103 manufactured by Kolcraft Enterprises, Inc.

PROBLEM: If the side rails of the portable crib fold during use, an infant can become entrapped and suffocate. Three deaths have been reported.

WHAT TO DO: Stop using and call Kolcraft at 1-800-453-7673 for instructions on how to obtain a refund.

WASHINGTON, DC—Kolcraft Enterprises, Inc., Chicago, IL, is voluntarily recalling 11,638 Playskool Travel-Lite portable cribs, models 77101 and 77103. The cribs were manufactured by Kolcraft under license from Playskool and sold nationally from 1990 to 1992. This recall is being conducted in cooperation with the U.S. Consumer Product Safety Commission (CPSC). The Commission has received three reports of infant deaths due to suffocation in these cribs. In each case an infant allegedly was found entrapped in a folded crib.

The incidents reported to CPSC suggest that if the side rails of the crib fold during use, an infant may become entrapped in the "V" where the side rails fold. While it is still unclear exactly why the crib side rails folded, Kolcraft is recalling all Travel-Lite cribs in an effort to prevent any further risk of injury to infants using these cribs.

The Playskool Travel-Lite portable crib has two nylon mesh sides and two blue solid plastic ends. "Playskool" appears in white letters on a red background on each end. The crib folds in the center for storage and handling.

Consumers who have a Playskool Travel-Lite portable crib should immediately stop using it and call Kolcraft toll-free at 1-800-453-7673 for instructions on how to obtain a refund. The toll-free line is open between 9:00 a.m. and 4:00 p.m. Eastern time.

Send the link for this page to a friend! The U.S. Consumer Product Safety Commission protects the public from unreasonable risks of injury or death from 15,000 types of consumer products under the agency's jurisdiction. To report a dangerous product or a product-related injury, call CPSC's hotline at (800) 638-2772 or CPSC's teletypewriter at (800) 638-8270, or visit CPSC's web site at www.cpsc.gov/talk.html. Consumers can obtain this release and recall information at CPSC's web site at www.cpsc.gov.

EXHIBIT 2 News from CPSC: U.S. Consumer Product Safety Commission

Office of Information and Public Affairs **Washington, DC 20207**

FOR IMMEDIATE RELEASE CPSC Consumer Hotline: (800) 638-2772
June 18, 1998 CPSC Media Contact: Nychelle Fleming, (301) 504-0580 Ext. 1192
Release # 98-128

CPSC Urges Search for Previously Recalled Portable Cribs and Play Yards

WASHINGTON, D.C. - The U.S. Consumer Product Safety Commission (CPSC) is urging consumers to search for and stop using previously recalled child products, in particular the "Playskool Travel-Lite" portable crib, which was manufactured by Kolcraft from 1990 through 1992 and recalled in 1993. In May of 1998, a Chicago toddler died after a Playskool Travel-Lite portable crib collapsed.

Manufacturers of portable cribs and play yards are joining in the effort to warn consumers and childcare providers to stop using the more than 1.5 million portable cribs and play yards that have been recalled in past years. Top rail hinges must be turned to set up the cribs and play yards. These top rails can collapse, entrapping children and suffocating them. Twelve children have died from suffocation in collapsed play yards and portable cribs manufactured by various firms. Current production play yards have top rails that automatically lock into place when the play yards are fully set up.

"A death caused by a previously recalled product is a tragedy," said CPSC Chairman Ann Brown. "We urge consumers to make an all out effort to search their homes and daycare centers for these portable cribs and play yards and stop using them."

The Playskool Travel-Lite portable cribs have two nylon mesh sides and two blue solid plastic ends. "Playskool" appears in white letters on a red background on each end. The portable crib folds in the center for storage and handling. Stores nationwide sold 11,600 of the products from 1990 through 1992.

Kolcraft has gone to great lengths to renew their recall efforts. Kolcraft is offering a $60 refund to consumers for the return of the Travel-Lite portable cribs. They also are notifying pediatricians and childcare providers about the recall. Consumers should call Kolcraft at (800) 453-7673 for instructions on disposing of the products and receiving the refund.

A number of portable cribs and play yards manufactured by other companies also have been recalled because of the risk of suffocation posed by collapsing top rails. Consumers and childcare providers should check for the following recalled play yards and portable cribs. If these products are found, consumers should call the company.

Date Recalled	Product and Firm	Numbers/Dates Sold	Remedy
6/25/97	**Evenflo "Happy Camper," "Happy Cabana," and "Kiddie Camper"** Portable Play Yards	1.2 million units sold between 1990 and 1997	Free hinge covers. Call firm 800-447-9178
11/21/96	**Century "Fold-N-Go Models 10-710 and 10-810"** Portable Play Yards	212,000 units sold between 1993 and 1996	Free repair. Call firm 800-541-0264
11/21/96	**Draco "All Our Kids"** (models 742 and 762) Portable Cribs/Play Yards	13,000 units sold between 1992 and 1995	Stop use and destroy (Firm out of business)
1/1/95	**Baby Trend "Home and Roam" and "Baby Express,"** Portable Cribs/PlayPens, **manufactured before 1995**	100,000 units sold between 1992 and 1994	Free repair. Call firm. 800-328-7363

CPSC is asking the help of consumers, childcare providers and child welfare associations to help spread the word about the search for these portable cribs and play yards in an effort to avoid another tragic incident.

"CPSC gets recalled products off store shelves, but we can't go into consumers' homes and remove the products," said Brown. "That's why we want to get this message out and have consumers act immediately to prevent another tragedy."

Before using used nursery equipment, even if it has been used for a sibling, consumers should check the recalled product lists, available 24-hours-a-day, through the CPSC hotline at (800) 638-2772 or through the CPSC web site at www.cpsc.gov.

EXHIBIT 3 News from CPSC: U.S. Consumer Product Safety Commission

Office of Information and Public Affairs **Washington, DC 20207**

FOR IMMEDIATE RELEASE
August 21, 1998
Release # 98-156

CPSC Consumer Hotline: (800) 638-2772
CPSC Media Contact: Nychelle Fleming, (301) 504-0580 Ext. 1192

In Wake of Another Death, CPSC Again Urges Search for Previously Recalled Portable Cribs and Play Yards

WASHINGTON, D.C. - The U.S. Consumer Product Safety Commission (CPSC) again is urging consumers to immediately search for and stop using previously recalled child products, in particular the "Playskool Travel-Lite" portable crib, which was manufactured by Kolcraft from 1990 through 1992 and recalled in 1993. According to the Asbury Park Press newspaper, a 10-month-old New Jersey infant died on Wednesday after becoming trapped in a collapsed Playskool Travel-Lite portable crib. CPSC issued this same warning in June, following the death of a 17-month-old Chicago toddler in the Playskool Travel-Lite portable crib. A $60 bounty is being offered for the return of each Travel-Lite crib.

Manufacturers of portable cribs and play yards have joined in the effort to warn consumers and childcare providers to stop using the more than 1.5 million portable cribs and play yards that have been recalled in past years. Top rail hinges must be turned to set up the cribs and play yards. These top rails can collapse, entrapping children and suffocating them. Thirteen children have died from suffocation in collapsed play yards and portable cribs manufactured by various firms. Current production play yards have top rails that automatically lock into place when the play yards are fully set up.

CPSC has been actively publicizing these previous recalls. Each recall has been distributed to media outlets nationwide and state and local health organizations. CPSC has included these products in the past two years' national recall roundup campaigns. The Commission has held multiple press conferences and broadcast video news releases by satellite so that local television stations can report these stories by showing the product and demonstrating the collapsing side rails. Chairman Brown has announced these play yard recalls on network morning shows, which reach millions of viewers.

"Once again, we urge consumers to immediately search their homes and daycare centers for these portable cribs and play yards and stop using them," said CPSC Chairman Ann Brown. "We are asking the news media to help us get word of these dangerous products out to consumers so that another tragedy is prevented. The media plays a critical role in reaching consumers. We can't go into everyone's home, but newspapers, and radio and television stations can. I ask every newspaper and every radio and television station to run weekly recall announcements so that consumers can find out if products in their home are being recalled. The news media should be their reliable source for product recall information."

The Playskool Travel-Lite portable cribs have two nylon mesh sides and two blue solid plastic ends.

"Playskool" appears in white letters on a red background on each end. The portable crib folds in the center for storage and handling. Stores nationwide sold 11,600 of the products from 1990 through 1992.

Kolcraft has gone to great lengths to renew their recall efforts. Kolcraft is offering $60 to consumers for the return of each Travel-Lite portable crib. They also sent new recall notices to pediatricians, childcare providers and consumer magazines. Consumers with Playskool Travel-Lite cribs should call Kolcraft at (800) 453-7673 for instructions on receiving the refund and disposing of the products.

EXHIBIT 3 News from CPSC: U.S. Consumer Product Safety Commission—Continued

The following table lists the portable cribs and play yards, manufactured by various companies, that have been recalled because of similar hazards. Consumers and childcare providers should check for the following recalled play yards and portable cribs. If these products are found, consumers should call the company listed below.

Date Recalled	Product and Firm	Number/Dates Sold	Remedy
6/25/97	Evenflo "Happy Camper," "Happy Cabana," and "Kiddie Camper" Portable Play Yards	1.2 million units sold between 1990 and 1997	Free hinge covers Call firm 800-447-9178
11/21/96	Century "Fold-N-Go Models 10-710 and 10-810" Portable Play Yards	212,000 units sold between 1993 and 1996	Free repair Call firm 800-541-0264
11/21/96	Draco "All Our Kids" (models 742 and 762) Portable Cribs/Play Yards	13,000 units sold between 1992 and 1995	Stop use and destroy (Firm out of business)
1/1/95	Baby Trend "Home and Roam" and "Baby Express," Portable Cribs/Play Pens, manufactured before 1995	100,000 units sold between 1992 and 1994	Free repair Call firm 800-328-7363
2/17/93	Kolcraft "Playskool Travel-Lite" Portable Cribs	11,600 units sold between 1990 and 1992	$60 refund Call firm 800-453-7673

Consumers can also view video clips showing how the top rails of some of these recalled portable cribs and play yards can collapse.

Before using used nursery equipment, even if it has been used for a sibling, consumers should check the recalled product lists. Consumers can get information about recalled products in the following ways:

- Call the CPSC hotline, available 24-hours-a-day, at (800) 638-2772.
- Check the CPSC web site at www.cpsc.gov.
- Receive recall notices automatically by FAX, e-mail or regular mail free of charge by calling the CPSC hotline or writing to CPSC, Washington, DC 20207.
- Return product registration or warranty cards so manufacturers can reach you directly if there is a recall.

Send the link for this page to a friend! The U.S. Consumer Product Safety Commission protects the public from unreasonable risks of injury or death from 15,000 types of consumer products under the agency's jurisdiction. To report a dangerous product or a product-related injury, call CPSC's hotline at (800) 638-2772 or CPSC's teletypewriter at (800) 638-8270, or visit CPSC's web site at www.cpsc.gov/talk.html. Consumers can obtain this release and recall information at CPSC's web site at www.cpsc.gov.

The Playskool Travel-Lite Crib (C)

In the early 1990s, Thomas Koltun was being groomed to take over Kolcraft Enterprises, his father's Chicago-based company. A manufacturer of juvenile products, Kolcraft had been started by Thomas's grandfather in 1942, and had grown to become the seventh largest company in the industry, with several hundred employees and annual revenues above $30 million.[1] After completing his MBA at the Kellogg School of Management at Northwestern University, Thomas had worked for three years in New York as a product manager with Colgate-Palmolive. He joined Kolcraft in 1990 as director of marketing and in 1994 was named vice president of marketing.

When Koltun joined the company, his father Sanfred, CEO of Kolcraft, had recently entered into a licensing agreement with Rhode Island–based Hasbro, which would allow Kolcraft the use of Hasbro's Playskool brand name. Under the agreement, Kolcraft would manufacture and distribute mattresses, play pens, car seats, and a new product, a portable crib, which came to be called the Playskool Travel-Lite.

Kolcraft had initially been optimistic about the crib, introduced in January 1990. The company believed that the well-known Playskool name would bring consumer attention to the product. It also believed that the portability of the crib—it could fit into the trunk of a car—would provide a useful solution for various situations parents would encounter. But the crib did not sell well, and by April 1992, when it stopped shipping, only about 11,600 of the cribs, models 77101 and 77103, had been sold.

In March 1993, the Travel-Lite was recalled by the Consumer Product Safety Commission (CPSC). Three infants had been strangled in the cribs when its top rails collapsed, and the agency determined that the crib posed "a substantial risk of injury to children as defined by section 15(a) of the Federal Hazardous Substances Act (FHSA), 15 U.S.C. δ 2064(a)."[2] Kolcraft conducted a recall by sending posters to pediatricians and retailers, and the CPSC issued press releases to the media. The company offered a $60 bounty to consumers who returned the cribs, which had been sold at retail usually for $89.

Thomas Koltun had assisted with the company's trade catalog presentation of the Travel-Lite in 1991, but had otherwise not been much involved in its marketing or licensing. He believed that the failure of the Travel-Lite in the marketplace arose from strong competition from other manufacturers' cribs, which were several pounds lighter. Regardless, by the time the decision came to stop making the Travel-Lite, he was already looking past the product toward the company's future. "I was involved somewhat," he put it simply. "The product wasn't selling, so it was time to move on to another product."[3]

Written by David Zivan, Senior Editor, *Chicago* magazine. Funded by the James S. Kemper Ethics in Business Grant to the Graduate School of Business at the University of Chicago, under the direction of Professor Linda Ginzel.

Please write: Professor Linda Ginzel, Graduate School of Business, The University of Chicago, 1101 East 58th Street, Chicago, IL 60637, USA. Or email linda.ginzel@gsb.uchicago.edu.

[1] E. Marla Felcher, *It's No Accident: How Corporations Sell Dangerous Baby Products*, Common Courage Press, 2001, p. 83.

[2] *Linda Ginzel, as independent administrator of the estate of Daniel Keysar, deceased, and on behalf of Boaz Keysar, Ely Keysar, and Linda Ginzel, next of kin, plaintiff, v. Kolcraft Enterprises, Inc., a Delaware Corporation, and Hasbro, Inc., a Rhode Island Corporation, defendants,* #98L7063, pending in the Circuit Court of Cook County, County Department, Law Division. From appendix, tab 7.

[3] Deposition of Thomas Koltun, 5/31/2000, p. 8.

Further Travel-Lite History

On July 12, 1995, while the recall of the Travel-Lite was still active, a ten-month-old boy in Indianapolis was strangled in the "V" of his collapsed Travel-Lite. He was the fourth known victim of the crib.

By June 1996, of the 11,600 sold, 2,736 Travel-Lites could be accounted for. Noting that the returns had stopped, and that there had been no recent injury or death reports, the CPSC closed its case. The status of 76 percent of the cribs remained unknown.[4]

Kids in Danger—And a Lawsuit

In mid-1995, a Travel-Lite crib found its way into a childcare home in Chicago—the third owner of that particular Travel-Lite. The provider set up, used, and took down the crib each day she was open for business, from the time she received it until May 1998. During naptime on May 12, 1998, 16-month-old Danny Keysar was found unconscious in the "V" of his Travel-Lite. He was rushed to the emergency room but could not be revived. He was the fifth reported death in a Travel-Lite.

Danny Keysar was the son of Linda Ginzel and Boaz Keysar, professors at the University of Chicago. At first, Danny's death seemed to his parents to be a freak accident, a cruel tragedy with no explanation. But through news reports and the investigations of friends, Linda and Boaz learned that four children had previously been killed in Travel-Lite cribs. They also learned that the crib had been recalled five years earlier.

Ginzel and Keysar felt they had to take action, and created a nonprofit organization, Kids in Danger (KID), whose mission would be to promote the development of safer children's products, advocate for legislative and regulatory strategy for children's product safety, and educate the public, especially parents and caregivers, about dangerous children's products. The organization started a Web site, www.KidsInDanger.org, and their efforts to bring the tragedy into the open resulted in substantial press attention.

On May 14, 1998, Thomas Koltun—now president of Kolcraft—drafted his company's public response to the death of Danny Keysar and noted that he was "deeply saddened" by the tragedy. Kolcraft, he wrote, had "always been concerned with the safety of children."[5]

Later that month, Koltun received a phone call from Malcolm Denniss,[6] a Hasbro executive who has been called the company's "safety czar." Though the licensing agreement was no longer in effect, Kolcraft and Hasbro still communicated on matters related to the Travel-Lite. Denniss inquired about Kolcraft's activities in relation to the recent events, and Koltun described the press release he was drafting, with help from a public relations firm. Koltun agreed that he would keep Denniss informed of Kolcraft's actions.[7]

On June 18, 1998—the same day the CPSC issued a press release headlined, "CPSC Urges Search for Previously Recalled Portable Cribs and Play Yards"—Linda Ginzel and Boaz Keysar filed suit against Kolcraft and Hasbro and sought damages for their negligence in bringing the Travel-Lite to market. The suit alleged that not only was the product unreasonably dangerous but also Kolcraft and Hasbro had failed to properly warn the public about its danger. Hasbro was also responsible, Ginzel and Keysar contended, because by receiving licensing fees and allowing its Playskool brand name to be used prominently on the product, it was, to the public, the "apparent manufacturer" of the product.[8]

News of the lawsuit was featured on the Reuters and UPI newswires and received national press coverage. The *Chicago Tribune* ran a short feature story, including a photo of the Travel-Lite that had killed Danny Keysar, shown in the collapsed position by Dan Webb, one of the plaintiff's co-counsels and a former U.S. attorney.[9]

Filing a motion to have itself removed from the lawsuit, Hasbro contended that the responsibility was solely Kolcraft's and referred calls regarding the Travel-Lite case to Kolcraft.[10]

On August 19, 1998, a ten-month-old New Jersey boy was found dead, strangled in the "V" of his Travel-Lite. He was the sixth victim.

[4] Mitch Lipka, "Deaths of Six Babies Expose Fatal Flaws of System," *Sun-Sentinel, South Florida*, November 28–30, 1999.

[5] T. Koltun, p. 56.

[6] Deposition of Malcolm Denniss, 8/27/99, pp. 45–47.

[7] Denniss, pp. 47–48.

[8] Case materials from #98L7063.

[9] Jon Bigness, "Suit Filed over Faulty Playpen," *Chicago Tribune*, June 19, 1998.

[10] Mitch Lipka, ibid.

Acknowledgments

The author wishes to thank a number of individuals who gave generously of their time and expertise during the creation of this case.

Numerous faculty members, PhD candidates, and MBA students from the Graduate School of Business at the University of Chicago attended several brown bag seminars to critique drafts of the case study. Their input was extremely helpful, as was the help of various experts from around the nation. I thank all those listed here and apologize to those whose names do not appear: Robert Adler, Holly Burt, Jonathan Eig, Howard Haas, Josh Klayman, Richard Larrick, Harold J. Leavitt, Carmen Marti, Cade Massey, David Messick, Sharon Peck, Megan Rostan, Caroline Schoenberger, George Wu, and Jeff Zivan.

Mary Abowd provided extensive research and expert fact checking on the entire case, and Patricia LaMalfa served as a tireless editor and proofreader.

Attorneys Stephen Senderowitz, Bradford Springer, Patrick Stanton, and Bryan Sup of Schwartz, Cooper, Greenberger & Krauss generously provided expert legal advice.

Marla Felcher's *It's No Accident: How Corporations Sell Dangerous Baby Products* is a tour de force of investigative reporting in the area of juvenile product safety, and her work was a valuable resource and an inspiration.

Tom Hellie, executive director of the Kemper Foundation, not only helped put this case in the public domain but also provided insight and encouragement.

Finally, my heartfelt thanks to Linda Ginzel and Boaz Keysar, who have shown great patience during the case's composition—and more courage than any of us should ever have to muster.

Minnesota Bank (A)

Minnesota Bank President Dale Roberts stopped to check her e-mail before heading out for the day. She was tempted to skip over the message from Michael Worth, head of the bank's Middle Market Division (MMD), until the next morning. Roberts double-clicked. Two rooms down, her assistant could hear, "Say *what*? You're *giving* them *what*?"

The e-mail from Worth had been short and casual: "Great news Dale! An agreement in the works with ACME Leasing will ensure the bank meets its income goal. We provide customer information—it takes care of everything else!" The message referred to a plan on which a group within the MMD division had been working. The Group was one of several areas that reported to Worth, and had been charged with enhancing bank income. It was expected to approach this mission entrepreneurially. The bank's marketing strategy recently had shifted from a business-to-customer (B2C) emphasis to a business-to-business (B2B) focus.

Minnesota Bank

Minnesota Bank had been around long enough to build customer trust. Incorporated in 1946, the bank had initially served the needs of individual customers and a few midsize companies within a five-state area. Headquarters were located in Rochester, Minnesota, and assets for 1998 were $2.7 billion, up 4.1 percent from the previous year. The bank had 415 employees.

This case was prepared by Research Assistant Linda Swenson under the supervision of Kenneth E. Goodpaster, Koch Professor of Business Ethics, and William A. Estrem, PhD, associate professor, University of St. Thomas, as a basis for class discussion rather than to illustrate either effective or ineffective handling of an administrative situation. The circumstances described in this case are reported with some modifications from the perspectives of Dale Roberts and Helen Smith, and do not necessarily reflect the perceptions of others involved. Names of persons, institutions, and locations have been disguised.

"In the mid-80s, it was typical for companies to write business plans and then put them on the shelf where they wouldn't interfere with day-to-day life. That was Minnesota Bank's initial attitude about its privacy policy," bank attorney Helen Smith recalled. "We adopted a privacy policy when we launched our bank Web site in spring 1999. The OCC was saying, 'Get a policy or we'll make one for you.'[1] We all made and distributed them. Then we went about our business. We didn't let it impact or interfere with our operations. Institutionally we had approved the decision to adopt the statement and had posted it. However we had not embedded it in the culture."

The Group's Deal with ACME

The bank had an established set of channels through which projects normally passed for approval. The Group didn't always follow this route strictly but its approach hadn't been cause for concern before. "We didn't advertise our business services," bank attorney Helen Smith explained. "Our business development was based on referral. We had strong relationships with lawyers and accountants. The Group had the authority to strengthen those relationships and to accept referrals from this cadre. In turn, the bank would refer to them customers who needed legal or financial services. However, the Group did not have carte blanche to build a referral relationship with XYZ law firm with whom we had not done business before."

After considering Worth's e-mail, Roberts asked Smith to educate the Group and other areas of the bank on the matter of privacy. "When I informed the Group that the ACME deal could potentially pose a problem," Smith recalled, "department members felt very put upon over what they perceived as unreasonable restraints hampering their ability to do a deal. They'd made promises. They were being held accountable to produce income, and yet here were these big

[1] The Comptroller of the Currency (OCC) charters, regulates and supervises national banks.

barricades that were keeping them from doing what they were expected to do.

"The Group had developed a relationship with ACME, seemingly unaware of privacy issues and how their deal might affect the bank and its customers." Smith recalled. "There had been no background check—a prerequisite if the bank had been considering a lending relationship with ACME. The Group members were convinced the people at ACME were great guys. Group managers had been to ACME's telemarketing site and had listened to ACME representatives. The company's soundness just wasn't an issue. It was this kind of emotional response—they hadn't done due diligence, which would have determined whether ACME had any problems. I asked if they had checked on Better Business Bureau for complaints. None of this had been done."

A lot was at stake for key people within the Group. The proposed deal was that Minnesota Bank would receive a 10 percent commission for every transaction resulting from information it provided, beginning with ACME's first lease to a customer and continuing for every subsequent lease to that customer thereafter. Worth had estimated that ACME's potential first-year earnings from the Minnesota Bank customer list could range from $1 million to $5 million. The payoff for the Group and managers, in addition to career growth, would be a healthy 15 to 25 percent bonus tacked onto their $60,000 to $100,000 salaries if (1) the bank met its income goal and (2) the Group or manager met his or her individual income production goal.

The Group managers believed they had found a way of achieving an income boost for the bank and themselves: Many of the bank's business customers would benefit from access to leasing services. Smith recalled, "They went out and found an alliance partner and were marching straight down the road to literally hand over the bank, provide the financials, provide the names of potential clients, provide all the information and say, 'Here it is folks. Somewhere in here there certainly are some potentials.' "[2]

[2] The Group's agreement with ACME called for the bank to screen business customers for financial viability as potential customers of leasing services. The bank would provide its internal analysis—its credit write-ups—to ACME for customers who expressed interest in learning more about leasing. These customers would not be informed their financial information was being forwarded to ACME.

Roberts's View

"We were aware of the industry practice of posting privacy statements," Smith said. "Unlike the statements of other institutions. Minnesota Bank didn't distinguish between individual consumers and businesses. Its privacy statement referred simply to customers. Dale insisted that individual consumers and businesses had an equal right to privacy and confidentiality."

Over time, rules on customer information became more complicated. Roberts explained, "In today's financial arena, a bank buys the services of a securities brokerage firm, or a brokerage and insurance company get together. Suddenly customers need financial services, and the bank can refer them to one or more of its affiliates. Does the bank share its customer information with everyone? Does it tell the customer it shared the information? To an institution whose bread and butter depends on their database, sharing that data is one issue, but selling to an outside company is another."

In Robert's view, if people wanted one-stop financial services, they had to give up some privacy. "I think everyone would agree that it's improper to provide detailed information about customers' financial circumstances. However, we may not all agree that it would be improper to make a referral based on that knowledge."

Roberts's personal need for privacy had motivated her to sign onto a national opt-out database.[3] When she applied for a mortgage, several unauthorized credit checks showed up on the required credit report. A major credit card company to whom she had never applied had conducted one of these inquiries. "I copied the report and sent it to the company informing them this action was in violation of the law," she said. "If I want to upgrade my credit card, the carrier has my implied consent that they can go in and check my credit. But I didn't have a card with this carrier. Therefore they were not entitled and they can't preapprove me by going in and looking at my credit bureau status."

[3] Customers may "opt out" of having their information shared with affiliates or outside third parties by writing to the bank or returning signed opt-out forms provided by the bank. Consumer advocates support banning banks' disclosure of customers' financial data to anyone without written permission—a so-called opt-in provision.

The Leasing Option

When Minnesota Bank's business customers applied for loans, they provided information about the kinds of business they were in and what kind of property and capital equipment they used. "We could see whether they used or could benefit from using leasing services," Roberts explained. "We knew whether they were candidates for leasing cars, furniture, computers and other equipment." Companies could realize tax benefits and achieve a significantly lower cost of financial by leasing equipment instead of buying it.

"If you know that the companies that are your customers would benefit from leasing and you'd like to earn income from it, you could form a leasing company or you could form an alliance with a company that specializes in leasing and provide a referral," Roberts said. "How do you get paid? You haven't sold the information, but you've provided information that will earn you a commission if there is a sale."

Terms of the Group's Deal with ACME

The deal as originally set forth by the Group called for Minnesota Bank to provide ACME[4] with the names, financial information, and assessment of financial capacity on 1,000 companies—the bank's write-up and periodic assessment (as often as quarterly) of how the company was doing, including editorial comments.[5] ACME planned to use the list to target potential clients for current and continued direct marketing. No agreement on confidentiality had been signed with ACME. No limits had been set on how the information might be used.

Banks often would release company credit information to other financial institutions if a transaction was in progress.[6] "Financial institutions routinely provide vendors credit ratings to determine whether to extend credit to companies," Smith explained. "To make the banking system work for businesses, the exchange of credit information is much freer on businesses than on individuals. But the deal with ACME had nothing to do with facilitating transactions between financial institutions."

CEO Contemplates: Modify the Deal or Drop the Idea

In Roberts's view, a financial institution's greatest asset was its list of customers and their financial information. "If we don't protect that, we're out of business. Then there's the reputation of the bank. We believe our customers should be able to rely, without reservation, on how we deal with them and the commitments we make. And one of those promises is that we will keep their financial information confidential."

The privacy issue was always in the background, but the competitive issue was just as significant. Should we strike a deal with ACME, Roberts considered, and if so, what should the terms be? How would it affect the bank and its customers? And how would they break the news? If the bank decided against the deal, what would be the repercussions internally and for the future?

4 The ACME Leasing Company had been founded to provide leasing services to distributors used by its own parent company; it had no prior affiliation with Minnesota Bank.

5 Selected companies came from those customers on the 20 percent side of the 20/80 rule: 20 percent of bank customers produce 80 percent of their profits.

6 Information about individual consumers could not be released unless the consumer had consented.

Note on Financial Privacy

According to a fall 1999 *Wall Street Journal*/NBC News poll, 29 percent of polled Americans ranked loss of personal privacy at the top of a list of eight concerns that might worry them most in the new century.[1] That same year at least seven major banking companies named senior-level executives to hone and supervise privacy policies.[2]

One trade publication warned that the banking, medical and insurance subsidiaries of emerging financial services companies were creating the fear "that detrimental information from one subsidiary will affect consumers' eligibility for service from another and [consumers] won't even know it."[3] Reports of the surreptitious collection of consumer data by Internet marketers and questionable distribution of personal data by other companies also heightened consumer concern over privacy.[4]

Worry about misuse of consumer information also extended into the federal arena. In 1999 public protest quashed the proposed "know-your-customer" rule, which would have required banks to go beyond reporting suspicious activity (indicative of possible money laundering) to divulge the source of customer deposits. Not since the 1970 Bank Secrecy Act, designed to assist criminal investigations into income tax evasion and laundering illegal drug money, had there been as strong a move to gather information on bank customers. Why the move toward regulation?

Regulation

The central Federal Reserve Bank oversees some categories of banks, including those organized in a holding company structure. Other agencies that oversee banks include the Securities and Exchange Commission, the Office of the Comptroller of the Currency, the Treasury Department division that regulates national banks, the Office of Thrift Supervision, and the National Credit Union Administration.

The Federal Trade Commission writes the rules for businesses other than banks and securities firms, including insurance companies and agents, travel agencies, mortgage companies, credit bureaus, and department stores that issue credit cards.

Government Intervention

In his June 1999 statement before a congressional subcommittee, Comptroller of the Currency John D. Hawke, Jr cited the Truth-in-Lending, Truth-in-Savings, and Fair Credit Reporting laws as expensive compliance headaches that the banking industry could have prevented. He warned banks, "Treat customers better or face onerous new laws and regulations." Hawke contended "[practices] that are at least seamy, if not downright unfair and deceptive . . . virtually cry out for government scrutiny [and] the persistent failure of the industry itself to address abusive conduct creates a fertile seedbed for legislation."[5]

Addressing a U.S. House subcommittee in July 1999, Federal Reserve System Board of Governors Member Edward Gramlich provided the judicial system's perspective on who owns customer information:

This note was prepared by Research Assistant Linda K. Swenson under the supervision of Kenneth E. Goodpaster, Koch Professor of Business Ethics, and William A. Estrem, PhD, Associate Professor, University of St. Thomas, to accompany the Minnesota Bank case series.

[1] Glenn R. Simpson, "E-Commerce Firms Start to Rethink Opposition to Privacy Regulation as Abuses, Anger Rise," *The Wall Street Journal*, Jan. 6, 2000, p. A24. Dow Jones Reuters Interactive.

[2] Lisa Fickenscher, "Big Banks Put Senior-Level Execs on Privacy Watch," *American Banker*, July 12, 1999, p. 1. Dow Jones Reuters Interactive.

[3] Orla O'Sullivan, "The Darker Side of Database Marketing," *US Banker*, May 1999. Dow Jones Reuters Interactive.

[4] Glenn R. Simpson, op. cit.

[5] "Comptroller Threatens Crackdown on Privacy Issue," *American Banker*, June 8, 1999, p. 1. Dow Jones Reuters Interactive.

> The courts have considered customer lists to be intellectual property protectable as trade secrets for most of this century. . . . The Supreme Court has flatly characterized documents relating to a customer's account as "the business records of banks" to which the customer "can assert neither ownership nor possession." Although ownership of property, including intellectual property, ordinarily includes the power to use or transfer the property, a number of state courts have limited banks' ownership rights in customer information, recognizing the value of the privacy of financial transactions to individuals.[6]

Recent Legislation

Supporters of the 1999 Gramm-Leach-Bliley Act, also known as *The Financial Services Modernization Act*, or *HR10*, contended it would save customers $15 billion a year out of the estimated $350 billion Americans spend annually on banking, brokerage, and insurance fees and commissions. (See Exhibit 1.) HR10 was also projected to improve choice and convenience and to stimulate competition. Opponents of the legislation maintained it would jeopardize consumer financial privacy and raise prices.[7]

HR10 mandates that any company having even a slight financial relationship with customers must disclose to them what it does with their account information. Companies have to explain privacy procedures to customers when they apply for services, or at least once a year, and each time privacy policies change. If companies sell, exchange, or provide nonaffiliated companies with access to customers' private data, they have to disclose that fact and offer customers the right to opt out of their data sharing.[8]

Gramm-Leach-Bliley: The Financial Services Modernization Act, HR10

- Allows banks, securities firms, and insurance companies to merge and sell each other's products.
- Bars companies outside the financial industry from merging with banks, brokerages, or insurers.
- Makes it a federal crime to misrepresent oneself to obtain someone's private financial data.
- Gives supremacy to state laws that grant consumers greater privacy protections than the federal bill.

Regulators decided that basic information such as customers' names, addresses, and telephone numbers is nonpublic when taken from sources such as customer lists. Nonpublic information, names, and addresses and personal financial data such as account balances cannot be shared with outside telemarketers if customers expressly ask their banks, brokerages, or insurance companies not to do so.[9]

A privacy amendment to HR10 prohibits the sharing of medical information across entities incorporating both financial and medical businesses.[10]

Compliance

Banks' costs and regulatory burdens were expected to increase under Gramm-Leach-Bliley. Institutions had to make more disclosures, track which customers asked for greater privacy protection, and weigh which information to disclose. They also faced added burdens during examinations: Regulators would look for compliance with privacy rules as well as existing laws.[11]

A low-end option privacy policy would apply to every customer through all channels. A high-end option would allow customers to specify how different types of information about them should be treated under different scenarios. The industry watchdog Banking Industry Technology Secretariat

[6] Edward M. Gramlich, "Statements to the Congress," *Federal Reserve Bulletin*, Washington, September 1999 pp. 624–626. Dow Jones Reuters Interactive (*Statement before the Subcommittee on Financial Institutions and Consumer Credit* of the *Committee on Banking and Financial Services, U.S. House of Representatives*).

[7] Marcy Gordon, "Clinton Signs Banking Overhaul Law. Congress: It Will Open the Way for Financial 'Supermarkets' That Sell Loans, Investments and Insurance," *The Orange County Register*, November 13, 1999. Dow Jones Reuters Interactive.

[8] Kenneth Harney, "Privacy Regulations Will Bring Options and Mail Companies Will Have to Disclose Their Policies Regarding Sharing Consumer Financial Data, *Star-Tribune*, February 12, 2000. Dow Jones Reuters Interactive.

[9] Marcy Gordon, "Regulators Propose New Rules to Protect Financial Data," *Associated Press Newswires* Financial/Business, February 3, 2000. Dow Jones Reuters Interactive.

[10] Orla O'Sullivan, op. cit.

[11] "Watching the Customer: New Rules on Banking and Privacy," *St. Paul Pioneer Press*, February 6, 2000, p. 1D. Newslibrary.com, *St. Paul Pioneer Press*.

(BITS) estimated that the cost to a $70 billion–asset bank for these options would range from $7 to $20 million—for a $400 billion–asset bank, the cost of implementing such privacy policies would range from $19 to $89 million.[12]

The Climate That Spawned New Regulation: US Bancorp Lawsuit in Minnesota

In June 1999, Minnesota Attorney General Mike Hatch filed a suit against *US Bancorp* and alleged it had violated the Fair Credit Reporting Act and the Electronic Fund Transfer Act, and had engaged in consumer fraud and deceptive advertising. US Bancorp was alleged to have provided a telemarketer with customers' Social Security numbers, account balances, names, addresses, checking and credit card numbers, average account balances, finance charges, and credit limits.[13] The bank responded with a $3 million out-of-court settlement and an agreement that allowed customers to bar the bank from sharing information.[14]

US Bancorp CFO Susan Lester later remarked, "We can't afford to have even a small percentage of our customers distrustful of us or unhappy with the way we have treated them. Privacy is important to us and to our customers. That is why we have spent a lot of time, effort and money in the last year to make sure customers understand our position." The corporation mailed its data privacy policy to its 6.5 million customers.[15]

Hatch intensified his fight for consumer privacy in December 1999, urging the Minnesota Department of Health to stop collecting information from individuals' medical records. Minnesota law required that certain information be forwarded to the Health Department with names attached in code. The information was used to research health trends and quality of care. That same month Hatch also sued *Minnesota Public Radio* (MPR) and alleged that the nonprofit network illegally misled members over its sharing of donor lists with other fund-raising groups.[16]

Hatch's concern about consumer privacy extended to placing limits on the release of driver's license information.[17] Although the Driver's Privacy Protection Act of 1994 barred states from disclosing such personal information without drivers' consent, it was difficult to administer. The law permitted exceptions for matters of motor vehicle and driver safety, theft, and manufacturers' product recalls. South Carolina, backed by a dozen other states, challenged the law as an unconstitutional encroachment on its business. The U.S. Court of Appeals for the Fourth Circuit agreed, saying the law wrongly forced states to administer a federal regulation and violated federalism principles.

In January 2000, however, the Supreme Court reversed the circuit court's decision and explained that the privacy statute was not telling states to pass specific legislation or to regulate their citizens in particular ways. The ruling meant that states *could* be barred from disclosing the personal information drivers provided to obtain a license. Prior to that decision, states were making millions of dollars a year selling the information, including Social Security numbers, medical information and photographs.[18]

[12] Orla O'Sullivan, op. cit.

[13] "Suit Accuses US Bancorp of Peddling Data Privacy: Minnesota Alleges That the Company Broke Consumer Protection Laws in Selling Information to a Telemarketer," *Los Angeles Times*, June 10, 1999. Dow Jones Reuters Interactive.

[14] Scott Carlson, "Minnesota Official Sues Connecticut-Based Telemarketer over Data Use," *Saint Paul Pioneer Press*, July 20, 1999. Dow Jones Reuters Interactive.

[15] Martin Moylan, "Going Public about Privacy," *Saint Paul Pioneer Press*, April 23, 2000, p. 1C.

[16] Conrad deFiebre and Noel Holston, "Attorney General Sues MPR over Donor Lists. Hatch Says the Nonprofit Network Misleads Members about How Often It Shares Names with Other Groups," *Star-Tribune*, December 29, 1999. Dow Jones Reuters Interactive.

[17] Conrad deFiebre, "Hatch Persists for Consumer Privacy: Legislative Priorities Laid Out by the State Attorney General Include Limiting Access to Driver's License, Medical Records," *Star-Tribune*, December 23, 1999. Dow Jones Reuters Interactive.

[18] Joan Biskupic, "Court Backs Privacy for Data on Drivers," *The Washington Post*, January 13, 2000. Dow Jones Reuters Interactive.

Federal Databases and Function Creep

In the late 1990s, Congress authorized the establishment of a myriad federal databases that could be used for purposes that ranged from tracking children's birth defects and vaccinations to monitoring new hires and promotions. New proposals sought to use the databases to track student loan defaults and unemployment compensation fraud. The easy availability of information caused concern among privacy advocates. One observed, "Once all data is compiled it is very tempting to use it for other things." This phenomenon is known as "function creep."[19]

Outrage over the attempted use of IRS records to punish perceived Nixon administration enemies during the Watergate scandal provided the impetus for the 1974 Federal Privacy Act. This law established a Code of Fair Information Practices that allowed individuals to discover, correct, and control dissemination of sensitive personal information in the government's possession. It also limited circulation of identifiable personal information and prohibited the government from selling or renting a name and address unless authorized. An amendment, the Computer Matching and Privacy Protection Act of 1988, regulated (with exceptions) the matching of federal, state, and local records.[20]

Privacy Guidelines outside the United States: OECD Guidelines and the European Union Privacy Directive

In 1980, the Organization for Economic Cooperation and Development (OECD)—primarily industrialized countries, including Australia, Canada, western European nations, Japan, and the United States—adopted a set of guidelines that included safeguards against unauthorized access, use, and modification of data. The guidelines gave individuals the right to know who was collecting data, for what purpose, where the data originated, and who would receive it. These rules also gave individuals the right to opt out of receiving direct marketing material.

The privacy directive passed by the European Union (EU) in October 1998 prohibited the transfer of consumer information across national borders unless consumers had been given a chance to opt out. Information was not to be relayed to any non-EU country that failed to meet EU privacy standards. Opt-in requirements also sometimes limited the sharing of customer information per the EU directive. And according to one banker, only about 30 percent of consumers who are offered the opportunity will opt in.[21]

Privacy on the Internet

Consumer advocates lobbied the federal government in November 1999, asking it to ban Internet customer profiling. Agreements like the proposed merger between an online advertising network (*DoubleClick*) and an offline market customer researcher (*Abacus Direct*), it was feared, would increase the likelihood of corporate abuse of customer data.

The proposed merger would link the profiles obtained from Internet advertisements with consumer catalog transaction histories. [22]

Concern about abuse of consumer information obtained online is being addressed by organizations such as TRUSTe. Web sites that adhere to the nonprofit's core tenets on data gathering and dissemination and agree to dispute resolution by an independent third party can display the TRUSTe Privacy Seal. The program is available to all, regardless of location or citizenship. TRUSTe may refer a case to government authorities such as the Federal Trade Commission but revocation of its seal is its greatest leverage.[23]

[19] Paul Barton, "Some Fear That Federal Databases Threaten Privacy," *Gannett News Service*, December 6, 1999. Dow Jones Reuters Interactive.

[20] "Protecting Privacy and Securing Data," a whitepaper from IBM's Institute for Advanced Commerce presented at the May 1999 symposium "Privacy in a Networked World" (www.ibm.com/iac).

[21] Orla O'Sullivan, op. cit.

[22] Evan Hansen, "Rights Groups Urge Government to Protect Privacy," *CNET News.com*, November 5, 1999.

[23] www.truste.org.

As the U.S. Congress adjourned before the elections in November 2000, the privacy legislation under consideration was postponed until a new administration took office. It was clear however that new federal legislation was inevitable, given the lack of reliance on industry self-regulation.

TRUSTe's Core Tenets Include

Notice: Web Sites displaying the TRUSTe seal must post clear notice of what personally identifiable information is gathered and with whom it is shared. This disclosure must be easy to read and accessible by one mouse click from the home page.

Choice: Users must have the ability, through opt-in or opt-out functions, to choose whether to allow secondary uses of that personal information. In effect users must be able to prevent the Web site from selling, sharing, renting, or disseminating their personally identifiable information.

Access: Users must have reasonable access to information maintained about them by a Web site to correct any inaccuracies in the data collected.

Security: The Web site must provide reasonable security to protect the data that is collected.

Source: www.truste.org.

EXHIBIT 1 Federal Privacy Legislation

The 1970 *Fair Credit Reporting Act* (FCRA) regulates disclosure of personal information by consumer credit reporting services, requiring such services to adopt "reasonable procedures" to ensure the accuracy of personal information contained in their credit reports. This law entitles consumers to know what information is held on them and to have it corrected if wrong. FCRA prohibits banks from sharing customers' credit information among affiliates, unless customers agree to such usage. The law allows information to be released to third-party inquirers when the reporting agency believes information will be used for credit, employment, or insurance evaluations or other "legitimate business needs" affecting the consumer.

The *Bank Secrecy Act* of 1970 was crafted to thwart money laundering during the federal government's war on drugs. This law requires financial institutions to report cash transactions of more than $10,000 to the IRS. The act's constitutionality was challenged by banks that balked at the expense of maintaining customer records but was upheld. A 1974 trade journal article presented the court's perspective: "banks are not bystanders with respect to transactions involving drawees and drawers of their negotiable instruments but are parties to the instruments with a substantial stake in their continued availability and acceptance."

The 1974 *Federal Privacy Act* established a Code of Fair Information Practices applying to government records. This allows individuals to discover, correct, and control dissemination of sensitive personal information in the government's possession. The act also limits circulation of identifiable personal information and prohibits the government from selling or renting a name and address unless authorized.

The *Electronic Fund Transfer Act* of 1978 requires a financial institution holding certain accounts to inform consumers of the circumstances under which information will be made available to affiliates and third parties. Sharing this kind of information for marketing is disallowed, but banks may share "experience information" for underwriting; that is, a bank could tell a mortgage subsidiary that an applicant had a bad payment history without getting that customer's permission.*

The *Right to Financial Privacy Act* of 1978 prohibits the government from getting access to banks' customer records without a good reason and appropriate process.

The *Privacy Protection Act* of 1980 protects materials intended for publication from police searches and seizures without a warrant. Some hold that this protection extends to materials intended for publication online.

In 1988, *The Computer Matching and Privacy Protection Act*, an amendment to the Federal Privacy Act, was passed to regulate matching of federal, state, and local records.

In 1994 *the Driver's Privacy Protection Act* was passed to bar states from disclosing personal information without drivers' consent. Exceptions exist for matters of motor vehicle and driver safety, theft, and manufacturers' product recalls. The law was challenged by states for whom information sales had become a lucrative income but upheld by the U.S. Supreme Court in January 2000.

In the late 1990s Congress authorized the establishment of a multitude of federal databases that could be used for everything from tracking children's birth defects and vaccinations to monitoring new hires and promotions.

The 1999 *Children and Privacy Act* requires sites targeting children under age 13 to post data collection practices and in most cases also to get "verifiable parental consent" before gathering children's personal information or sharing it with a third party. Sites also have to give parents access to their children's personal information and allow them to prevent further use of the data.

In 1999 *Gramm-Leach-Bliley*, or the Financial Services Modernization, Act, HR10, was passed, allowing banks, investment firms, and insurance companies to sell one another's products. This law says that if a state passes tougher privacy rules, the state laws prevail.

* "Bank Secrecy Act," *The Magazine of Bank Administration*, July 1974.

Northwest Airlines vs. WCCO-TV: *Business Ethics and the Media* (A)

April is the cruelest month.

—T.S. Eliot

Her green Irish eyes flashing in fury, Marta Laughlin exclaimed to her colleague Kathleen Peach, "That's just great! They wait until the day before their response deadline and then ask for an extension!" Kathy, too, was disappointed at WCCO-TV's action and wondered out loud whether this latest development would mean a loss of momentum for Northwest's complaint before the News Council—or was a sign of weakness in the opposition. "What's ironic is that it's probably *both*," she said to Marta.

It was Thursday, August 8, 1996, and they had just been informed that morning by their boss, Jon Austin, Northwest's managing director of corporate communications, of the latest development in the formal complaint process. WCCO-TV had just requested a postponement for its response to the Northwest Airlines complaint and for the hearing before the News Council that was scheduled for August 15.

The safety and workplace practices of Northwest Airlines (NWA) had been attacked in a series of investigative reports by WCCO-TV, the Minneapolis–St. Paul subsidiary of CBS. The reports aired on April 29 and 30, during the television ratings period. NWA President and CEO John Dasburg decided soon afterward to challenge the station in the court of public opinion by directing NWA Corporate Communications Managing Director Jon Austin to file a complaint with the Minnesota News Council (MNC). The council, a unique-in-the-nation nonprofit organization, provided individuals and organizations that felt they had been damaged by a news story with an opportunity to hold accountable the originating news organization. (See Exhibit 1 for partial NWA organization chart.)

This case was prepared by Professor Kenneth E. Goodpaster, Koch Endowed Chair in Business Ethics, as a basis for class discussion rather than to illustrate either effective or ineffective handling of an administrative situation.

Marta Laughlin

Marta Laughlin became senior manager of media relations at Northwest Airlines in 1993 at age 26. She was responsible for all elements of the external communications function, including working with local and national media, acting as principal corporate spokesperson in Minnesota, and developing corporate messages and strategies.

A native of Downers Grove, Illinois, Laughlin was an avid runner and earned many competitive honors, including being named in college to the NCAA all-American track and cross-country teams. In 1988, she had graduated summa cum laude from the University of St. Thomas in St. Paul, Minnesota, with a BA in journalism/public relations and a minor in business administration. From 1989 to 1993 Laughlin was the communications specialist for Northwest Airlines pilots as represented by the Air Line Pilots Association, International (ALPA).

Kathy Peach

Kathy Peach became manager of media relations at Northwest Airlines in February 1996 at age 45. Prior to joining Northwest, she served as account manager for Shandwick, an international public relations agency. From 1992 to 1996, she directed the activities of Shandwick agencies in Europe and Asia on behalf of Northwest Airlines, as well as managing various projects for clients including First Bank System, Pillsbury, Honeywell, and Cray Research. On a *pro bono* basis, she served on the executive committee of the Children's Defense Fund, which developed and for three years directed the annual "Beat the Odds" award and scholarship program for inner-city youth.

A mother of two teenage daughters when she joined Northwest, Peach was a native of Minneapolis and held a JD from William Mitchell College of Law, a BA in communications from Augsburg College, and an associate of applied science in medical technology degree from the College of St. Catherine.

The Minnesota News Council

The 24-person Minnesota News Council was made up of half media professionals and half public members and was chaired by Minnesota Supreme Court Justice Paul Anderson as a nonvoting member. Its mission: "To promote fairness in the news media by helping the public hold news organizations accountable for stories they publish or broadcast; by encouraging the public to demand high standards and responsibility in the exercise of free expression; and by helping the media avoid lapses that lead to complaints."

The British Press Council had been the original model for the mission and structure of the MNC when it was fashioned in 1970. The first chair of the MNC, Justice C. Donald Peterson of the Minnesota Supreme Court, declared the council's independence at its first meeting in 1971, remarking that it would not be a "kept spaniel" of the news business.

The MNC had no authority to require a retraction, correction, or apology from news organizations, but the outcome of its hearings received extensive media coverage that was valuable in upholding the reputations of individuals and organizations whose complaints were found convincing. The MNC's open invitation to the public was as follows:

> If you feel harmed by a news story and you want the News Council to hear your complaint, and you waive your right to sue, you can get a public hearing that allows you to hold the news outlet accountable. . . . The News Council does not accept government support. It does not have, and does not want, authority to impose sanctions. It does offer a forum for moral suasion, and a lot of good has come from public hearings. Regardless of the vote, minds and policies have changed for the better.

The 1996 MNC budget of $185,000 covered program operations and the employment of a full-time executive director and 2 three-quarter-time assistants. Thirty percent of the MNC's contributions came from the media, 30 percent from nonmedia companies, 28 percent from foundations, and 12 percent from associations and individuals. An endowment fund, started in 1993, grew to $110,000 by 1996. Both NWA and WCCO were among the major financial sponsors of the MNC.

About 8 percent of complaints reached a public hearing, twice as many were settled before a hearing, and the remainder were dropped by complainants. Half the complaints heard by the MNC had been decided for the complainant, half for the news outlet. Members were elected by the council to three-year renewable terms. An executive committee guided the work of the staff and of the council members. The MNC's service was free to the public and the media.

WCCO-TV Background

WCCO-TV (Channel 4) was a well-known institution in Minnesota life, competitive with its arch-rival KSTP-TV (Channel 5). WCCO had been innovative over its broadcast lifetime, which extended back to 1946. Its newscasts became nationally known for creative and controversial ideas over the years, such as an extended 45-minute newscast, the establishment of one of the first documentary units, a "family sensitive" 5:00 P.M. newscast (which attempted to leave out some violent content at that hour), and the cutting away from parent network's "CBS Evening News." The station won a number of national journalism awards and had produced some critically acclaimed documentaries. In 1980, "at the urging of reporter Don Shelby, [news director Ron] Handberg launched an investigative-reporting team [the *I-Team*], one of the first such broadcast units in the country."[1]

During the 1980s and into the 1990s, television news, generally, and WCCO-TV news, in particular, underwent significant change in response to a turbulent environment by comparison with its early years. As one pair of observers put it:

> By the 1970s economic and political pressures on the station's once-stable ownership, as well as the rise of competition, left the station in a state of flux. WCCO responded to the changes by increasing its emphasis on in-depth television journalism in the early 1980s. By the end of the decade, however, market forces took their toll on the owners, and social forces affected the viewers, who were less interested in documentaries and more interested in where to find good day care for their children. By the 1990s marketing played the central role in the development of a news product at WCCO-TV.[2]

In 1992, when CBS acquired WCCO-TV, the news operation was competing well in local markets, and by 1996, the power of Nielsen ratings and the need to maintain viewer attention had never been greater. "Sweeps weeks," during which ratings were measured with special care for setting advertising prices, were scheduled (among other times) in late April.

Northwest Airlines Background

With its world headquarters in Minneapolis–St. Paul, Northwest Airlines is the world's fourth largest airline and the oldest carrier in the United States with continuous name identification. It began operations in October 1926, flying mail between Minneapolis–St. Paul and Chicago. Passenger service began the following year. In July 1947, NWA pioneered the "great circle" route to Asia and has operated across the Pacific longer than any other airline.

The 1980s had been good to the airline and its Delaware-chartered parent company, NWA Inc. Steve Rothmeier, then CEO and chairman, inherited a company in sound financial condition. Rothmeier led Northwest's successful 1986 acquisition of Republic Airlines, also based in the Twin Cities. The merged airline operations would yield longer-term positive impacts: domestic route expansion; a strong "hub and spoke" system which included the Twin Cities, Memphis, and Detroit; and a diverse (though older and noisier) fleet of short- and long-haul aircraft. So despite difficulties in melding the different pay scales and seniority rights of the two airlines' 37,000 employees, analysts viewed the marriage of Republic and Northwest as a "match made in heaven."[3]

In the quickly consolidating airline industry of the late eighties, management was slow to give postmerger attention to employee relations, labor union leadership, and customer service, a reputation which earned Northwest the public nickname, "Northworst." The U.S. Department of Transportation had listed NWA as the recipient of the largest number of consumer complaints of all U.S. airlines in consecutive months since August 1987. But despite its poor public relations image, Rothmeier's fiscally conservative strategy gave the company such a strong balance sheet that deregulation left the company unscathed. Northwest was a tempting target for a takeover.

When Marvin Davis, a billionaire from California, acquired 3 percent of Northwest's common stock in 1989, Rothmeier did not respond to Minnesota politicians who thought there was an opportunity to offer Dayton Hudson–style help.[4] Ultimately he and the board rejected traditional methods of fighting off unwanted suitors, formed an acquisition committee made up of outside directors, and opened up a controlled bidding process. Davis communicated his intent to offer $2.72 billion, or $90 per share, for the airline. Others submitted friendly bids, all of which were higher.

[1] This section draws upon the chapter "News Leader: WCCO-TV, Minneapolis" by Mark Neuzil and David Nimmer, Chapter 14 in Murray & Godfrey, eds., *Television in America* (Ames, IA: Iowa State University Press, 1997), pp. 245–67.

[2] Ibid., p. 267.

[3] Information in this section draws upon the case study "Northwest Airlines: Private Sector—Public Trust" by Research Associate Beth Goodpaster under the supervision of Professor Thomas Holloran, University of St. Thomas (1994).

[4] The Minnesota legislature had a special session in 1987 to prevent the hostile takeover of Minnesota-chartered Dayton Hudson Corporation. The legislature passed a bill which placed severe restrictions on hostile takeovers. At the time, Dayton Hudson was trying to fend off such an acquisition. (See the "Dayton Hudson Corporation: Conscience and Control," readings, presented earlier in this part.)

In June 1989, the Northwest board agreed to sell for $121 per share to Wings Holdings, Inc., a group of investors led by Al Checchi and Gary Wilson. The acquisition was completed in August 1989, and Wings became the parent company of the now-privatized Northwest. The purchase of Northwest was often referred to as the last of the 1980's wave of leveraged buyouts.

By 1996, NWA had gone public with its stock again and along with American, United and Delta was among the "big four" U.S. carriers. It employed 47,000 people and served more than 400 cities in over 80 countries. NWA managed a fleet of 400 aircraft (with 65 on the way) and operated more than 1,700 flights daily.

Spring and Summer 1996

At their regular Monday morning staff meeting on April 22, 1996, Marta and Kathy read with dismay the three "bristling" fax transmissions that had just passed the previous Friday between Jacquee Petchel, senior producer at WCCO-TV, and their boss, Jon Austin. Petchel had requested an interview with NWA President and CEO John Dasburg before April 25 and indicated that WCCO-TV intended to run a story on alleged FAA safety violations and certain "personnel issues and complaints" at NWA (see Exhibit 2).

Austin had replied immediately to Petchel and asked for more specific information about the basis of the intended program and the name of the reporter who would be doing the story. The fax memo also indicated that Northwest executives would be away during the next week for the annual meeting in New York (see Exhibit 3). Petchel's same-day "reply to the reply" communicated the planned date of the first broadcast (April 29), the reporter (WCCO news anchor Don Shelby), and a list of former or current employees whose names were mentioned in court complaints against the company (see Exhibit 4). Monday and Tuesday, Jon and Marta spent a great deal of time poring over the FAA complaints they thought WCCO might use in the *I-Team* reports. At this point WCCO had shared no specifics about which cases would be included. "There were hundreds of cases involved in the FAA settlement," said Marta, "and our task was to become as familiar with them as possible."

Marta continued the communication with Jacquee Petchel while Austin accompanied NWA executives to New York. In Austin's absence, she recalled, "I began working with NWA maintenance and legal staff to research the background of these cases. Our public responses would be developed in conjunction with NWA senior management after my research was completed." Knowing that April 29 was the beginning of television sweeps week, the NWA staff suspected the upcoming story would be aimed at attracting the largest possible audience, which might mean going for the sensational and attempting to engage their most visible top executive, John Dasburg, in an on-air battle of "sound bites."

On Wednesday, April 24, the first promotional TV ad for the *I-Team* report on safety at Northwest Airlines confirmed their suspicions. The promotional ads were highly inflammatory and accusatory, without providing any factual foundation. A letter of warning to WCCO-TV General Manager John Culliton from NWA's legal counsel was sent the next day (see Exhibit 5), and Marta called Petchel on the telephone to indicate that it sounded as if the story had already been written without NWA input. She invited Petchel, Don Shelby, and their WCCO crew to meet with company officials and employees the next morning, Friday, April 26.

"When the WCCO team arrived on Friday, they were met by at least 20 NWA people familiar with the FAA cases," Marta said. "We attempted damage control by educating Petchel and Shelby on the meaning and nature of the FAA complaints. It was also at this meeting that Shelby told us that the series piece had nothing to do with sweeps. We complained about the promo (and played a video of it for the crowd), pointing out the doctored photo of a Northwest airplane with its nose pointed headlong toward the bottom of the screen (see Exhibit 6), and asked that it be modified. Shelby agreed with us but the ad continued to run."

On Sunday, April 28, the Minneapolis *Star Tribune* ran a relatively positive, 4,000-word story that had been in preparation for months on NWA's safety and maintenance practices, scooping somewhat the anticipated WCCO-TV broadcast. John Dasburg and his senior managers had made a strategic decision that John Kern, the company's chief safety officer and a member of Dasburg's executive management team, was in the best position to represent NWA on the safety violation allegations. On Monday morning, April 29, Marta arranged an on-camera interview with Kern. "The meeting on Friday had helped prep him for the cameras on Monday," she remarked. Thirty Northwest employees were sitting off-camera listening, watching, and commenting audibly when the news team betrayed ignorance of industry language or practices.

That night on the 10:00 o'clock news, the first of the two-part report aired. The next day, after full-page advertisements by the NWA mechanic's union ran in both the *Star Tribune* (see Exhibit 7) and the St. Paul *Pioneer Press*, and after more than 400 negative calls flooded Don Shelby's voice mail and 1,400 more calls were received by the station switchboard, the second part of the *I-Team* report was aired.[5]

For nearly three weeks, Jon, Marta, and Kathy worked on damage control and religiously reported each new development and the continuing media interest to senior management. Numerous discussions with Chris Clouser, Northwest senior vice president–administration, and a Dasburg direct report, helped determine what steps the company would take next.

"The options were essentially (1) to let it drop, something we all knew would leave our employees feeling 'let down,' (2) to take WCCO to a court of law for what might have been a three or four-year tangle, or (3) to use the News Council approach," said Kathy Peach. "The legal route, besides being costly and time-consuming, would have taken away much of the public exposure we felt was necessary to answer the allegations made by WCCO-TV." And Marta Laughlin added, "Dropping the whole thing would let stand a direct assault on what NWA stood for. Every employee knew our first guiding principle—never compromise safety."

During this time, on May 16, the News Council held a fund-raiser at Orchestra Hall in downtown Minneapolis headlined by Mike Wallace, famed and feared anchor of the CBS news documentary program *60 Minutes*. Wallace praised the role of the council and suggested that it should be the model for a national news council. Jon Austin had heard Wallace's remarks that evening, and sensed the possibility that if NWA did make a formal complaint, the hearing could end up on *60 Minutes*.

John Dasburg, with the consent of NWA's board of directors, approved the decision to take the News Council option, and on May 21, 1996, Austin filed the official complaint ("short form") with the MNC (see Exhibit 8). A day later, WCCO-TV aired a follow-up installment on its Northwest story, described in a NWA press release as an attempt to "redeem itself for its earlier embarrassing mistakes." This third program was not included in the NWA complaint to the MNC, though WCCO asked later for the News Council to consider it.[6]

On June 13, Jon Austin shared with Marta and Kathy the letter he received from WCCO's Culliton, indicating that he had heard from the News Council about NWA's complaint and threatening to use "additional information" that would "paint a more negative picture of the airline's safety practices" if the company persisted in the complaint process. Culliton made it clear that NWA was in for charges of defamation if the News Council sustained the complaint.[7] He added that WCCO would not discuss the promotions to the *I-Team* story before the MNC, something the Northwest team considered very important to its case (see Exhibit 9).

Marta and Kathy acknowledged that Culliton's sabre-rattling had some effect behind closed doors. "It made us wonder," they remembered, "What else does WCCO have? We checked again with our legal and safety departments to make sure we hadn't overlooked anything." The issue had been joined, however, and the confrontation was anticipated by both sides. Jon with help from Marta and Kathy, began to develop the more extensive narrative that would support their complaint, a document that would need to be prepared before the date of the hearing, once it was set. Two weeks later, at the end of June, John Culliton announced that he would leave WCCO to manage the CBS affiliate in Los Angeles.

On July 25, 1996, Jon Austin petitioned the News Council formally to include the promotions leading up to WCCO's *I-Team* stories (see

[5] For a well-written chronology of these events, see Mary Lahr Schier, "Dogfight!" in *Twin Cities Business Monthly* (February 1997), pp. 36–41

[6] Ibid., p. 39.

[7] For a legal interpretation of *defamation* when the contending parties are corporations, see Exhibit 12.

News Council's Biggest Hearing Ever Involves Northwest Airlines Complaint against WCCO-TV

WCCO-TV reported in May that Northwest Airlines management was pressuring mechanics to return airplanes to service faster than safety guidelines would dictate, so that the airline could maintain its outstanding on-time departure rating and use it as a tool in selling tickets.

Northwest challenged the station's conclusion and filed a complaint with the News Council. The airline also complained that the station's promotional announcements for the investigative series were sensational and inflammatory, using the image of an airplane heading downward at a precipitous angle.

If the two sides cannot resolve their differences, a public hearing will be held at noon on Thursday, August 15, in the Lutheran Brotherhood Auditorium, 625 4th Ave. S., in downtown Minneapolis. Everyone is welcome.

Source: MNC's publication *Newsworthy*.

Exhibit 10). He also heard back from the MNC that the formal hearing was scheduled for August 15, three weeks away (see excerpt above from MNC's publication *Newsworthy*). The final "long version" of the NWA complaint, incorporating reference to the promotions, was submitted to the News Council a week later, on August 2 (see Exhibit 11). "Sending the long version off was a big moment," Kathy recalled. "We knew that the information in that document would play a major role in educating the council and persuading them to find in favor of NWA's position. But there was no overconfidence on our part about winning this thing."

Back to August 8, 1996

The mood in Marta's and Kathy's NWA offices after the postponement of the News Council's hearing, scheduled for August 15, was a mixture of outrage, fear, and exhaustion—as if a hard-working sailing crew suddenly felt a strong tailwind do a silent full stop. Discussion was constant—even intense—but time was now the enemy. The further April receded into the background of public memory, the harder it would be to maintain the complaint's momentum.

Austin knew John Dasburg and the other senior managers were confident about NWA's position, but the delays in getting the hearing scheduled seemed to be threatening Austin's resolve to press on. "The day-to-day stress of managing communications for the world's fourth-largest airline and worry about his wife's difficult pregnancy (their third child was due in November) in addition to the News Council complaint was taking a toll on him," said Kathy. "His energy, humor and easygoing manner just weren't the same. I think he was beginning to view 'settling' with WCCO as an appealing option."

"We'd done a "mock hearing" with the help of our PR agency, Shandwick," said Marta. "It was clear that Jon needed more preparation and that may have made him feel less enthused about going forward."

EXHIBIT 1

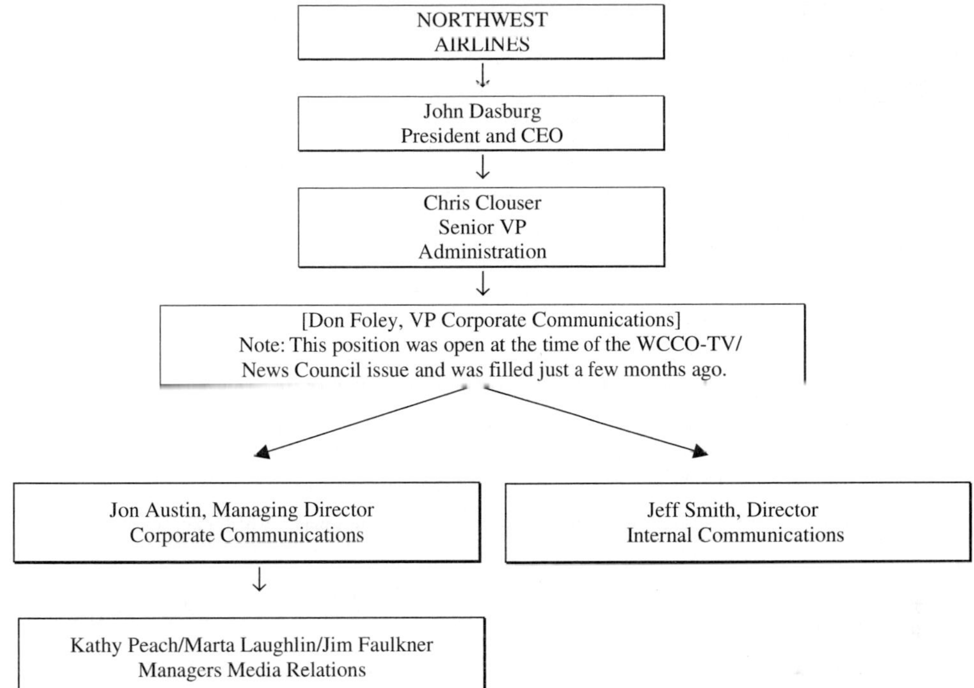
NORTHWEST AIRLINES
John Dasburg
President and CEO
Chris Clouser
Senior VP
Administration
[Don Foley, VP Corporate Communications]
Note: This position was open at the time of the WCCO-TV/
News Council issue and was filled just a few months ago.
Jon Austin, Managing Director
Corporate Communications
Jeff Smith, Director
Internal Communications
Kathy Peach/Marta Laughlin/Jim Faulkner
Managers Media Relations

EXHIBIT 2

WCCO-TV
CBS Television Stations
A Division of CBS Inc.
Eleventh on the Mall
Minneapolis, Minnesota 55403
(612) 339-4444

April 19, 1996

Transmitted by fax

Dear Mr. Austin,

We have recently received information from the Federal Aviation Administration regarding the matter of Northwest Airlines, Inc. alleged violations of Title 14 C.F.R. Parts 25, 39, 91, 32 and 121 and consent order. We are requesting an interview at this time with John Dasburg and other persons you deem important to discuss this matter and the supporting documentation.

As you know, there are dozens of support documents related to this mater, which I am confident you have in your possession.

As well, we are interested in discussing several matters involving personnel issues and complaints filed by current and former Northwest Airlines employees.

It's our intention to broadcast a story on these matters within the next two weeks and we want to give you every chance in advance to provide input on these records. Therefore, I respectfully request you to schedule an interview sometime before April 25.

Thank you in advance for your help.

Sincerely,

Jacquee Petchel
Senior Producer

EXHIBIT 3

Northwest Airlines Inc.
5101 Northwest Drive
St. Paul MN 55111-3034

April 19, 1996

Ms. Jacquee Petchel
Senior Producer
WCCO-TV
90 South 11th Street
Minneapolis, MN 55403

BY FAX: 330-2767

Dear Ms. Petchel:

Thank you for your letter. Before we make a decision on how to respond to your request for an interview, we would appreciate the following additional information:

- The scope and date of your FOIA request to the FAA (i.e., what documents and information were requested).
- The material provided by the FAA (or any other agency) in response to your FOIA request and the date on which it was provided. (Case numbers and descriptions will suffice.)
- The specific "alleged violations" referred to in paragraph 1.
- The specific "personnel issues and complaints" referred to in paragraph 3 of your letter.
- The name of the WCCO reporter who would conduct any interview and do reporting for the story.

In addition, we would appreciate any other information you would care to provide on this subject that would enable us to better prepare a response and to decide which officials of Northwest, if any, should participate in an interview.

Finally, with our annual meeting scheduled for the end of next week, neither I nor any of the appropriate Northwest executives will be able to accommodate your request for an interview before the 25th of this month. Please let me know if you would consider dates toward the end of the following week as a timeframe for a possible interview.

Sincerely,

Jon Austin
Managing Director
Corporate Communications

EXHIBIT 4

WCCO-TV

CBS Television Stations
A Division of CBS Inc.
Eleventh on the Mall
Minneapolis, Minnesota 55403
(612) 339-4444

April 19, 1996

Dear Mr. Austin:

This is a follow-up note to our conversation this afternoon. Just to reiterate, we intend to broadcast a story, based on the information we've received, on April 29 so that you will have a reasonable amount of time to respond. As I explained, by TV news standards, this is an unusually long period of notice since we would have liked to broadcast this story even sooner than that. However, considering the complexities of the issues involved, we think it's only fair to give you more time to prepare.

The cases, derived from court complaints that I referred to, involve the following former or current employees:

Alan Mitzel
Carol Ann Hochhalter
Debra Forsell
Todd Digatono
Sandy Eissenger
Gwendolyn Adjua Adams
Robert Benson
Denise J. Martinez (State of Michigan)

To answer your question earlier this afternoon, Don Shelby will be working with me, along with another producer, Beth Pearlman.

Thanks again for your prompt response.

Sincerely,

Jacquee Petchel
Senior Producer

EXHIBIT 5

DORSEY & WHITNEY LLP

Minneapolis Washington D C London Brussels Hong Kong Des Moines Rochester Costa Mesa	Pillsbury Center South 220 South Sixth Street Minneapolis, Minnesota 55402-1498 Telephone (612) 340 2600 FAX. (612) 340-2863 Thomas Tinkham (612) 340-2829	New York Denver Seattle Fargo Billings Missoula Great Falls

April 25, 1996

Mr. John Culliton
General Manager
WCCO TV
90 South 11th Street
Minneapolis, MN 55403

BY FACSIMILE

Dear Mr. Culliton:

This Firm represents Northwest Airlines and has been asked to review a story that WCCO is apparently contemplating airing during the current "sweeps" period.

Apparently, based on some old and routine issues between Northwest and the FAA, your producer intends to suggest in a story that there are maintenance or safety problems at Northwest Airlines. While that story line might make a tantalizing promotion for the sweeps period, there are no such problems and to suggest there are would be false.

I also understand that WCCO has been talking with two former and disgruntled employees of Northwest Airlines. These individuals have their own disputes with the Company and cannot be relied upon to paint an accurate or complete picture of the Company's maintenance practices.

The facts are that Northwest maintenance practices are the highest in the industry. Its record for safe practices is second to none. The FAA itself has recognized Northwest maintenance practices as superior.

In short, Northwest's reputation for safe flights and superior maintenance of its aircraft is long held and well deserved. If you do a story that states or suggests that Northwest's practices are other than appropriate, the story will be false and will be extremely damaging to Northwest. It will also undermine the appropriate confidence that the traveling public in this area has with regard to Northwest. Should you proceed with such a story in spite of the facts of this matter, Northwest will vigorously and appropriately respond.

Yours truly,

Thomas Tinkham

TT/cs

Bcc Mr. Christopher E. Clouser

EXHIBIT 6

Source: Northwest Airlines files.

EXHIBIT 7 An Open Letter to the People of Minnesota

Air Transport
District 143
2000 Eagan Woods Drive, Suite 220
St. Paul, Minnesota 55121-1152
612-688-2640 fax-688-7229

1946-1996
International Association of Machinists and Aerospace Workers AFL-CIO

April 30, 1996

For the last week, Minneapolis television station WCCO-TV has been making some very serious accusations about Northwest Airlines' maintenance and employment practices; accusations which don't hold up when you know a little about the issues and about the people WCCO has been relying on for their information.

As President of District 143 of the International Association of Machinists, I represent 26,000 men and women who work at Northwest, including 15,000 mechanics and other safety professionals. We maintain the aircraft and engines that carry more than 120,000 Northwest passengers every day. Safety is our highest priority. WCCO's reporting in this area is a slap in the face of each of our members and everyone who works at Northwest. You—our customers, friends, neighbors and family—should know more about our safety record than the half truths and distortions that WCCO is willing to tell you; we want you to know the real facts about what we do.

FACT: Northwest Airlines is one of the safest carriers in the world, a fact backed up by statistics from the Federal Aviation Administration. During its most recent FAA safety inspection, for example, Northwest scored significantly better than the industry as a whole in every category.

FACT: Northwest's exceptional record on safety is the result of the professionalism, integrity and commitment of all our IAM members. We are highly trained, skilled and licensed by the FAA. Our responsibility is to ensure that every plane departing a Northwest gate or hangar is ready for flight and maintained to the highest levels of safety.

FACT: We work with the FAA's inspectors and with Northwest's management every day as part of a consistent, reliable safety system. Every job is done to exacting standards set by the FAA, the manufacturers and Northwest. Every job is inspected; every procedure is reviewed. The result is a high standard of safety that is always improving.

Frankly, I am angry—and our members are angry—at the reckless way WCCO has chosen to report on these important issues. Their allegations are an insult to every Northwest mechanic, to every inspector and to everyone who works at Northwest Airlines. The public deserves better and we deserve better, than their one-sided attack based on ignorance, distortions and sensationalism. The 26,000 men and women of District 143 think you should know all the facts. And the fact is safety is never compromised.

Thank you.

Marvin E. Sandrin

Marvin E. Sandrin
President/Directing General Chairman

EXHIBIT 8

COMPLAINT FORM

Date: 5/21/96

Complainant Name & Address
Northwest Airlines
5101 Northwest Drive
St Paul, MN 55111

Media Name & Address
WCCO-TV
30 South 9th Street
Minneapolis, MN 55403

Phone/Fax: (day) 612-727-4284 (evening) 612-926-5172

Type of complainant: ____ private individual ____ private organization
____ public figure ✓ public organization ____ public official
____ political candidate ____ government agency

Type of medium: ✓ TV newspaper ____ daily ____ other
____ radio ____ weekly
____ wire service ____ community
____ magazine ____ college

Complaining about:
✓ news story ____ editorial/commentary ____ letters to the editor
____ political ad ____ other (specify) ________

Dates of media coverage (enclose copies if available): 4/22- 4/30/96

Was the story, in whole or in part, factually inaccurate? ✓ yes ____ no
(If yes, please state specific inaccuracies)

Was the story: ✓ incomplete ✓ inflammatory ✓ sensationalized
✓ misleading ____ in poor taste ✓ biased
____ racist/sexist or other form of stereotyping ✓ otherwise unfair

Were there ethical lapses? (check all that apply)
✓ Did it harm your reputation or that of your company?
____ Was there a conflict of interest for the reporter or the news organization in this story?
____ Did the reporter misrepresent him/herself or his/her motive?
____ Was your confidentiality betrayed or did the reporter or editor break a promise?
____ Did the news organization invade your privacy?
* ✓ Did the news organization fail to contact you when preparing a story about you?
____ Did the news outlet deny access to the news or editorial pages?
✓ Was there a misleading impression created by the layout, graphics, headlines or other elements of the page or story?
____ Other, please explain: ________

* see attachment regarding promotions related to story

Have you discussed your complaint with the news outlet named? ____ yes ✓ no
With whom (name, position and date) ________

What action or response would resolve your complaint? A correction of the errors committed therein of comparable size and prominence as the original segments, plus an apology to the people of Northwest.

Please summarize your complaint in narrative form, including specific inaccuracies or statements to which you object. You may write on the back of this sheet or attach another sheet.
Please contact: Jon Austin, Managing Director, Northwest Airlines

EXHIBIT 8—Continued

On April 29 and 30, WCCO-TV aired a two-part "I-Team" report into the maintenance and employment practices of Northwest Airlines. The segments were based on the anonymous allegations of several individuals who claimed to be current and former Northwest employees, on the on-the-record allegations of former employees who are each pursuing legal claims for monetary settlements against the Company, and on documents obtained from the FAA under a Freedom of Information Act request.

Through images, words and narrative choices, WCCO-TV unfairly and inaccurately portrayed Northwest Airlines as rife with on-going maintenance problems and unsafe operating conditions and as a hostile workplace for women. In addition to the factual errors committed therein, WCCO-TV also failed to provide any appropriate context for the viewer to interpret the allegations represented, including but not limited to, accident rates or other indices of safety for the airline industry, the scope of Northwest's operations relative to the number of incidents cited, comparisons of fines paid by Northwest and other airlines (even though the segment producers were in possession of such information prior to broadcast). Further, WCCO-TV failed to present any comment from the regulators or from independent third-party experts that might have provided confirmation or rebuttal for the allegations.

The result damaged Northwest's reputation and business prospects, was harmful to morale among the Company's workforce and recklessly provoked feelings or concern and anxiety about air travel using Northwest Airlines. WCCO-TV, as an experienced and well-funded news organization, had it in its power to produce an accurate and useful report for its viewers on the subject of safe air travel, but instead chose to sensationalize and misrepresent its findings in order to produce higher ratings for its newscast during a sweeps period.

Finally, Northwest seeks to include in this complaint not just the segments themselves, but the promotional spots produced to publicize the segments and to attract viewers. Produced and aired before the Company had even heard (much less responded to) the allegations against it, the promotional pieces were highly inflammatory and accusatory. The Company believes that the tone and substance of the promotional pieces constituted trial and conviction on the subject of Northwest's maintenance and employment practices, again, without the benefit of hearing from the accused.

EXHIBIT 8—Concluded

Please read this form carefully before you sign it. If you do not understand it, consult an attorney before signing it. If the News Council hears your complaint, you may have an attorney accompany you but not speak for you.

Waiver of Claims

I understand that if the Minnesota News Council hears my complaint against WCCO-TV (name of news outlet), I may present matters that otherwise could be the basis of a claim before a court or a government agency.

I also understand that the news organization will be asked to appear voluntarily and may present information and defenses that otherwise could be evidence in a court or agency proceeding.

In consideration of the Minnesota News Council's agreement to consider my grievance and of the WCCO-TV's (news outlet) agreement to abide by the procedures of the Minnesota News Council in responding to my grievance, I hereby waive any and all claims or demands that I may now have or may hereafter have, of any kind of nature, before a government agency or before a court of law, including defamation actions arising out of or pertaining to the subject matter of my grievance against any person or corporation, including WCCO-TV (news outlet) and its employees and agents, or against any and all persons presenting information to the Minnesota News Council or against the Minnesota News Council, its members and employees for statements made during the proceedings or from the content of its decision or report.

If the Minnesota News Council or one of its committees finds this complaint unsuitable for adjudication, this waiver will cease to be binding.

(signature) 5/20/96 (date)

Minnesota News Council • 12 S. 6th Street, Suite 1122 • Mpls. MN 55402 • 341-9357 • fax 341-9358

EXHIBIT 9

WCCO-TV
CBS Television Stations
A Division of CBS Inc.
Eleventh on the Mall
Minneapolis, Minnesota 55403-2450
(612) 330 2600

Dear Jon, June 13, 1996

We have received your complaint to the Minnesota News Council regarding stories which aired on April 29th and 30th.

Before we proceed, we wanted to offer you an opportunity to adapt or dismiss your complaint in light of our ensuing report on your company which aired May 22nd.

In that report, both the National Transportation Safety Board and the leader of the IAM, the union which represents 18 thousand Northwest mechanics, stated clearly and decisively that the main thrust of our initial reports were, indeed, correct. The comments from Marv Sandrin, from the IAM, bear particular significance in that he had initially led a public crusade against the stories highlighted by a full-page advertisement in the Star Tribune and the St. Paul Pioneer Press.

While the emotions created by the initial stories ran high, it is now clear that most observers see accuracy, merit and fairness in our reporting.

If you would prefer to leave this in the public limelight by taking it before the News Council, please be aware that we will include the May 22nd story in our presentation. We will also feel compelled to include additional information. It will paint a more negative picture of the airline s safety practices on both a domestic and international level. The fact we have additional information which has not yet aired will help support our case that we showed sensitivity and restraint. It will, however, create even more public scrutiny of the airline s safety practices.

Nonetheless, if you are unswayed by these points, then let us add a more definitive level to the discussion. We will not discuss promotion before the News Council. While it would make for good debate, we do not believe it is the News Council s role to evaluate promotion. We are not beyond scrutiny on anything we do, but we would be no more willing to discuss promotion before the News Council than we would be to discuss news content before the Advertising Council. However, we ARE prepared to put our reporting before the News Council. We ARE prepared to put our product, practices and people to the test.

Lastly, your request for an apology brings forth a similar request from WCCO-TV. Should the News Council sustain the complaint, the station will ask the News Council to order Northwest Airlines to air and publish a full public apology to WCCO-TV for the airline s derogatory and defamatory statements aired and published in the wake of the I-Team reports.

Sincerely,

(John Culliton)

Jon Austin
Director of Corporate Communications
Northwest Airlines, Inc.
Department Number 1300
5101 Northwest Drive
St. Paul, MN 55111-3034

c.c. Gary Gilson, Minnesota News Council

EXHIBIT 10

Northwest Airlines, Inc. 612-726-2331
5101 Northwest Drive
St. Paul, MN 55111-3034

July 25, 1996

Mr. Gary Gilson
Executive Director
Minnesota News Council
822 Marquette Avenue
Suite 200
Minneapolis, MN 55402

BY FAX: 341-9358

Dear Gary:

Thank you for the opportunity to petition the Complaint Committee on the question of whether to include the WCCO-TV promotional pieces aired prior to their April 29 and 30 newscasts. I would hope that the committee would rule in favor of such a motion based on the Council's mission to promote fairness in the news media as well as responsible reporting and editing. In support of my position, I offer the following points for the committee's consideration:

1. **The promotions were approved by the news departments.** By his own admission, WCCO-TV News Director Ted Canova signed off on the promotions before they began airing and anchor Don Shelby admits he and others in the newsroom reviewed the script (*WCCO-TV, Northwest Airlines tangle needs Minnesota News Council airing,* St. Paul Pioneer Press 5/30/96). John Culliton, until recently the station's general manager, stated that newsroom personnel have veto power over the promotional pieces (*Airlines vs. WCCO could be big deal,* Minneapolis Star Tribune, 5/26/96). Clearly, the newsroom can and should control the content of these promotions and their failure to do so in this case does not excuse them from their responsibilities in this area.

2. **The promotions were created from the same raw footage that formed the basis of the April 29 and 30 broadcasts.** WCCO-TV did not send its promotions department out to gather footage to promote the news department. Instead, the news department's own work product, including identical shots used later in the broadcasts, formed the raw material for the promotions. As a result, the promotions closely resembled the newscast material.

3. **The promotions were unfair, biased and accusatory.** The promotions began airing as early as Wednesday, April 24, and contained wholesale accusations of improper maintenance ("They asked me to look the other way a lot," said Tony Digatano), of illegality ("Find out why the Feds moved in," said the voiceover), hostility toward women ("The environment is hostile," said Debra Forsell) and implied violence on the part of Northwest and its people ("I was scared to go to anyone," said Carol Ann Hocholter). Accompanying these accusations were images showing an aircraft flying toward the ground at an extreme attitude achieved only in accidents, shots of maintenance operations (photographed almost exclusively at night even though time of day is not particularly relevant to the package but does effectively convey a sinister, furtive atmosphere), and extreme close-ups of chainlink and barbed wire fences (implying a prison-like atmosphere or unpleasant secrets kept inside). The promotion concludes with, "Is Northwest compromising your safety? Don Shelby and the I-Team returns Monday at 10 on 4 News." And a shot of Don Shelby looking worried and pensive outside of the airport fence. The clear impression of the promotion is that widespread problems existed inside Northwest and that the viewer would learn of them during the Monday newscast.

EXHIBIT 10—Continued

These promotions ran for five days without rebuttal from the Company. One can only wonder how many people were exposed to these and similar promotions on local radio stations without hearing Northwest's response, a response which was finally aired, in edited form, on the evening of April 29 as part of WCCO's 10 p.m. broadcast. The tone and substance of the promotional pieces constituted trial and conviction on the subject of Northwest' maintenance and employment practices, again, without the benefit of hearing from the accused.

4. **It is common practice in today's broadcast newsrooms, including WCCO-TV, to consider stories in terms of "news packages" which include not only the actual newscast itself but other elements as well, including how can the story best be promoted.** Souces within WCCO's own newsroom have confirmed to me that stories are rejected simply because they would be difficult to effectively promote to key demographic groups. Addressing this blurring between journalism and marketing would be an important contribution to the public discourse on the limits of acceptable journalistic behavior.

In summary, the pieces were clearly within the responsibility and authority of the WCCO-TV newsroom to direct and control, the material of the promotions was almost entirely the product of the newsroom and the promotions were grossly unfair, biased and accusatory toward Northwest. To exclude them from consideration by the Council would send a message to news organizations in Minnesota that this sort of irresponsibility can continue unchecked and accountability for the results rests with no one.

I urge the committee to examine this area of journalism.

Thank you.

Sincerely,

Jon Austin
Managing Director
Corporate Communications

EXHIBIT 11

In the Matter of Northwest Airlines v. WCCO-TV
Before the Minnesota News Council
August 15, 1996

Excerpts from Statement of Complaint and its Appendix B

Introduction

Sometime this spring, WCCO-TV decided to frighten its viewers during the May ratings period with a story that portrayed Northwest Airlines as rife with shoddy maintenance and as a workplace where those who spoke up or "rocked the boat"—even on important safety questions—suffered retaliation and harassment and were even murdered.

The question Northwest brings before the council is, in essence, "Was WCCO-TV justified in its efforts?" Based on the arguments herein, we submit that the answer should be a resounding and decisive "No." The people of Northwest believe that WCCO-TV failed to deliver on the premise of its story, that its package violated the standards of journalism and was:

- Promoted in a manner that amounted to a trial and conviction of Northwest without affording the Company the opportunity to respond.
- Poorly sourced in that it relied on the testimony of persons of questionable motives, knowledge and relevance. Similarly, documents obtained from the FAA were hastily reviewed, poorly understood and consistently mischaracterized.
- Lacking in context and objective analysis as to Northwest's safety and employment record, both in absolute terms and in relation to other airlines.
- Factually incorrect in numerous instances, and
- Needlessly sensational in tone and lacking in balance.

WCCO-TV's failure to uphold the standards of its profession recklessly and wrongly damaged Northwest's reputation and business prospects, harmed the morale of the Company's workforce, and caused unjustified concern and anxiety among the public about travel on Northwest Airlines.

Through its choice of images, words and narrative, its improper juxtaposition of unrelated facts and events, its failure to provide any appropriate context and its failure to present any comment from the regulators or from independent third-party experts, WCCO-TV painted a distorted, untruthful picture of Northwest Airlines and the men and women who work there.

We urge the council to rebuke, in the strongest possible terms, WCCO-TV for these lapses of journalistic standards.

[*22 pages on sources, errors of omission, tone, and factual errors*]

Conclusion

At the end of Part II, Mr. Shelby asked the camera, "What would you have us do?" Having examined the WCCO-TV product, we would ask the same question of Mr. Shelby and his colleagues:

Should we have ignored WCCO-TV's five-day attack on our reputation because the news room authorized a promotion that made no pretense of balance or objectivity? Let go without protest the station's compromised sources, its lack of context and factual errors, the gratuitous tone of danger that pervades each scene? Should we have dismissed the I-Team's efforts to unjustly portray Northwest as a hostile workplace as "just hype" associated with sweeps weeks?

We couldn't. We couldn't because Northwest is an extremely safe airline and it was unjustly portrayed otherwise. We couldn't because the people who fly our planes, the men and women who maintain and repair them, the agents at our ticket counters and on the telephone, the employees working in offices and on the tarmac were maligned by WCCO-TV for no better reason than ratings. We couldn't because WCCO-TV was wrong and it needs to be told it was wrong.

WCCO-TV failed in this instance to fulfill its journalistic mission. We ask that the news council join with us in sending WCCO-TV that message in the strongest possible language.

[*Appendix B of the full complaint follows.*]

EXHIBIT 11—Continued

Appendix B

Recent articles in the *Minneapolis Star Tribune*, the *Chicago Tribune* and the *Wall Street Journal* all contained important and relevant quantitative data on airline operations.

- *Minneapolis Star Tribune*, April 28, 1996

Pilot violations: Here are data on major airline pilots who were fined or had their certificates suspended or revoked for violations of FAA regulations. Violations might include deviating from assigned routes, operating an aircraft recklessly, failing to follow an aircraft controller's instructions or flying in restricted airspace.

	1991	1992	1993	1994	1995	Totals
American	2	1	1	0	0	2
America West	1	2	2	0	0	5
Continental	0	2	7	4	0	13
Delta	4	1	3	3	0	11
Northwest	2	6	0	1	0	9
Southwest	0	0	0	0	0	0
Trans World	0	0	2	0	0	2
United	6	4	1	0	1	12
USAir	1	6	3	2	0	12

Source: Federal Aviation Administration

Enforcement actions (EIRs): Here is a breakdown of flight standards cases lodged against each of the major airlines from 1990 through 1994. The cases stemmed largely from alleged failures to follow proper FAA safety procedures ranging from maintenance of aircraft to ensuring that passengers' carry-on bags are properly stowed. The number of cases has declined in recent years since the FAA shifted policies to ease penalties when airlines voluntarily disclose infractions.

	1990	1991	1992	1993	1994	Totals
American	222	151	125	94	99	691
America West	33	36	13	20	14	116
Continental	4,039	1,120	750	342	32	6,283
Delta	26	43	60	42	132	303
Northwest	47	37	36	28	37	185
Southwest	142	187	68	32	32	461
Trans World	15	28	9	9	10	71
United	26	38	37	49	12	162
USAir	33	38	75	52	23	221

Source: Federal Aviation Administration

Near midair collisions: A near midair collision is reported when two planes come within 500 feet of each other or a pilot feels they were in danger of colliding.

	1990	1991	1992	1993	1994	1995 (to 6/30)
American	17	17	8	13	10	2
America West	6	6	4	2	5	2
Continental	7	5	1	1	8	4
Delta	11	6	14	10	8	2
Northwest	4	2	0	3	10	4
Southwest	3	7	6	6	5	1
TWA	2	0	2	3	1	0
United	25	17	13	10	11	8
USAir	10	8	9	3	4	1

Source: Federal Aviation Administration, Global Aviation Associates, Ltd.

EXHIBIT 11—Continued

	Departures 1/90 3/96	Accident rate	Serious accidents	Total accidents	Pilot deviations	Runway incursions
Alaska	769,396	0.130	1	0	15	0
Northwest	3,370,474	0.178	1	5	65	4
USAir	5,659,155	0.212	5	12	147	9
TWA	1,743,675	0.229	2	4	45	4
Southwest	2,931,385	0.235	0	7	42	4
America West	1,233,395	0.243	0	3	11	0
Delta	5,785,803	0.311	3	18	148	0
Continental	3,053,288	0.328	5	10	194	7
American	5,472,678	0.385	4	20	196	6
United	4,543,516	0.418	4	19	109	7

Source: *Chicago Tribune*, May 19, 1996.

All Accidents, 1992 to 1995

	Rate per 100,000 departures
USAir	0.17
Northwest	0.18
American	0.22
Delta	0.36
Continental	0.36
TWA	0.36
United	0.43

Source: *Wall Street Journal*, July 24, 1996.

Fatal accidents, 1975–1995: Of 85 fatal accidents involving U.S. airlines over the past 20 years, Northwest Airlines passenger planes have been involved in two, both at the Detroit airport. Six of the nine airlines that carry the most passengers today account for 26 of these accidents. Three carriers have had no fatalities.

	Number of Accidents	Number of Fatalities
America West	0	0
Southwest	0	0
Trans World	0	0
Continental	3	31
Delta	3	150
United	6	161
Northwest	2	164
USAir	8	236
American	4	469

Sources: National Transportation Safety Board, Global Aviation Associates.

EXHIBIT 11—Concluded

Pilot deviations: Pilot deviations may be reported when a plane strays from its assigned course or altitude, travels at the wrong speed, or is operated in a reckless manner.

	1990	1991	1992	1993	1994	1995 (to 6/30)
American	25	37	46	43	19	11
America West	5	1	3	0	3	0
Continental	20	16	14	18	9	4
Delta	21	34	23	26	19	10
Northwest	15	11	12	9	7	3
Southwest	6	3	7	4	5	90
Trans World	12	11	9	7	3	1
United	17	33	22	19	9	9
USAir	49	40	26	17	16	3

Source: Federal Aviation Administration, Global Aviation Associates, Ltd.

EXHIBIT 12 Legal Aspects of Defamation

Source: John T. Wendt, Esq., University of St. Thomas.

Legal actions in defamation are difficult to pursue, and even more so, actions for corporate defamation. The difficulty stems from (a) burden of proof and (b) the calculation of damages. Basically defamation is taking from someone's reputation or injuring a person's character, fame, or reputation by false and malicious statements. It can include both libel (in writing) and slander (defamation in spoken form). The basic requirements for a prima facie case for defamation include:

- Defamatory language by the defendant, namely language which tends to adversely affect plaintiff's reputation.
- The defamatory language must be "concerning the plaintiff"; in other words, it must identify the plaintiff to a reasonable reader, viewer, or listener.
- There must be a publication of the defamatory language by the defendant to a third party.
- And the plaintiff must have suffered damage to his, her, or its reputation.

Because defamation as a field of tort law was developed long before modern broadcasting could ever have been considered, the law of defamation over the airways is still new. When defamatory material has been broadcast, even though it is spoken, the prevalent opinion is that it is libel, at least when a written script was used, but some courts have embraced a new tort of "defamacast."

There has always been tension between the First Amendment right of free speech and defamation. In the landmark case of *New York Times v. Sullivan* (386 U.S. 254, 1964) the *New York Times* published a paid ad, signed by a number of prominent individuals complaining of the conduct of the police in dealing with racial disturbances in Montgomery, Alabama. Police Commissioner Sullivan brought an action for libel alleging that he was defamed. The U.S. Supreme Court held that the First Amendment conferred a "qualified privilege" on the defendants, which was not limited just to comment or opinion, but which extended to false statements of fact, provided that they were made without malice, that is, without knowledge that the statements were false or recklessness as to their truth or falsity.

With private individuals there has been less concern for freedom of speech and the press, and in a claim for defamation in a private matter, plaintiffs do not have to prove malice. However, this "qualified privilege" given to the defendants has been extended to private individuals *on matters of public concern*. The scope of this constitutional privilege is evolving, but it appears that there is still a need to show "actual malice."

A corporation may be defamed by language which has a tendency to injure its business reputation, as by deterring persons from dealing with it. And anyone who publishes defamatory matter concerning a corporation is subject to liability. Thus a corporation may maintain an action for defamatory words that discredit it and tend to cause loss to it in the conduct of its business. But the loss attributable to the alleged defamatory words can be hard to quantify and hence damages hard to establish.

If the plaintiff can prove that the defendant was negligent in ascertaining the truth of what it published, but cannot prove malice, damages are limited to the "actual injury" suffered by the plaintiff. If the plaintiff can overcome the obstacles and prove malice, and can show that the publication was made with knowledge of its falsity or with a reckless disregard of the truth, then the plaintiff can recover "presumed" or compensatory damages and even punitive damages (over and above compensation in some cases.)

Northwest Airlines vs. WCCO-TV: *Business Ethics and the Media (B)*

Northwest Airlines vs. WCCO-TV
Hearing Rescheduled

Source: *NewsNotes from the News Council* (September 1996).

> Northwest Airlines' complaint against WCCO-TV will come before the News Council at a public hearing on Friday, October 18, at 1:30 P.M. in the Lutheran Brotherhood Auditorium, 625 4th Ave. S., in downtown Minneapolis.
>
> The questions the News Council will consider are: Did WCCO make its case on a alleged deficiencies in airline maintenance and safety procedures? Did the *I-Team* series use sensationalistic techniques? And should promotional announcements for news stories be held to the same journalistic standards as the stories themselves? . . .
>
> The News Council expects heavy media coverage of the hearing. The public is invited.

In the weeks following WCCO-TV's request for an extension to submit their response to the NWA complaint (and therefore postponement of the scheduled August 15 hearing before the Minnesota News Council), NWA senior management and the corporate communications staff continued to discuss the pros and cons of continuing the complaint process to the hearing. John Dasburg had expressed full confidence in the corporate communications group's ability to present NWA's argument to the News Council. But the scheduling delays threatened to slow the company's momentum, making it tempting to "declare victory and go home."

"Apparently, rescheduling the hearing from August to September wasn't going to work," Kathy recalled. "It meant our earliest opportunity for the hearing would be sometime around mid-October, which seemed a very long time away. We kept reminding ourselves that John Dasburg, our mechanics, and all of the Northwest people were counting on us to represent our position on these safety violation allegations. We didn't want to walk away from this fight."

"In early September, though, things started happening," Marta remembered. "Gary Gilson of the News Council finally received and sent us copies of the WCCO-TV response to NWA's complaint." (See Exhibit 1 for excerpts from the full text of the WCCO reply to the complaint.) "After reading their 60-page document," Kathy added, "our first reaction was a huge sigh of relief: Was this it? Was this their argument? In our minds we'd created a dragon that in reality didn't seem to exist." Marta felt new momentum. "I was strengthened in my resolve and fully convinced we were right and had to move forward."

On September 24, Gary Gilson officially set the hearing date at October 18 and articulated for the first time the specific questions the council would deliberate and vote upon (see Exhibit 2).

NWA had prevailed in its late-July petition to the News Council to include consideration of WCCO's promotions of its *I-Team* reports. The second question in Gilson's agenda for the hearing was, "Should promotional announcements for news be held to the same standard as news?"

"Not long after that the rumors started about Mike Wallace doing a *60 Minutes* segment on the hearing," said Marta, "and that concerned us.

This case was prepared by professor Kenneth E. Goodpaster, Koch Endowed Chair in Business Ethics, as a basis for class discussion rather than to illustrate either effective or ineffective handling of an administrative situation.

What if the News Council didn't find in our favor?" By mid-October, the rumors about *60 Minutes* had been confirmed. Wallace and camera crew would attend the hearing. This development virtually guaranteed that the outcome would at some point be broadcast before a national audience on one of the most widely watched television news programs in the country. Whether or not NWA prevailed at the hearing, the risk of moving ahead now included the likelihood that some portion of the inflammatory WCCO report would reach viewers all over the United States.

"The closer we came to the hearing date, the more unlikely it became that Austin and Culliton would resolve the differences needed to reach a settlement," said Kathy. "Austin sincerely wanted to avoid the hearing, which he saw as the last resort, so the tension increased with each passing day. For two weeks prior to October 18, the frequency of calls and faxes between Culliton and Austin was high. Jon reminded us regularly that if WCCO responses warranted settling, it would be in NWA's best interest to do so." And Marta recalled, "They did come close at one point—Jon thought it was a matter of 'five magic words'—but 'CCO wouldn't acknowledge using unreliable sources'."

Kathy summarized the feelings in the department during the days immediately preceding the hearing. "Don Shelby reports the news for a living, and he'd been doing it for many years, so we knew he'd carry a lot of credibility. We were confident our case was solid, but we were less certain that it could be effectively communicated to the Council members, especially since some of our supporting data tended to be rather technical and could be confusing to people outside the airline industry."

"We knew we'd communicated the issues effectively and that we were going to win a decision once the question period of the hearing began," agreed Marta and Kathy. "The Council members were directing the majority of questions at WCCO, and you could just tell by their tone that WCCO was being challenged."

EXHIBIT 1

WCCO-TV
Response to Northwest Airlines Complaint
Minnesota News Council

Introduction

At the heart of good journalism is a commitment to the truth, no matter how negative that truth may seem to some. We at WCCO-TV take our responsibility to tell the truth more seriously than we take anything else. To say otherwise, ever, is simply wrong.

The complaint on the part of Northwest Airlines takes WCCO-TV and its stories to task for many things. And yet, few of the allegations, if any, deal with the most critical question of all: were the core assertions in WCCO-TV's reports true? In fact, the airline's rambling complaint barely touches on the issue of truth, focusing instead on a series of meaningless allegations, riddled with sarcasm, that attack style and choice of specific words.

We ask the Council to look beyond Northwest's rhetoric and ask itself the tough question that Northwest's PR man Jon Austin so aptly poses in the complaint: "Was WCCO-TV justified in its efforts?" Indeed, to give Mr. Austin credit, that is the key question before the Council. And the answer, we assert, is a simple yes.

As discussed below, our reports focused on three important issues:

- Northwest was fined $725,000 for violations of FAA safety regulations over a period of years, violations which included a significant number of maintenance failures that compromised passenger safety
- Employees said they felt pressure to get planes out "on time" and believed this pressure caused them and other employees to make inadequate repairs in some cases
- Employees said they feared retaliation for reporting maintenance problems

We stand by our reporting on each of these issues, and we submit that Northwest's complaint provides no evidence that we were incorrect. Northwest Airlines does not claim that WCCO was wrong in its underlying contention that mechanics, from time to time, are put into a position of conducting work in violation of safety standards, FAA regulations, manufacturers manuals and Northwest Airlines' own policies. And Northwest's contentions that employees did not believe pressure caused maintenance errors and that they did not fear retaliation for reporting problems fly in the face of the evidence.

The real thrust of Northwest's complaint seems to be that the very act of focusing on maintenance problems at Northwest is evidence of bad faith. This is simply not the case. Hundreds of thousands of travelers put themselves in the hands of the aviation industry, including Northwest Airlines, every day. We trust that industry to fly us and our loved ones all over the world. We trust the airlines will follow the guidelines, regulations and manuals of the Federal Aviation Administration, aircraft manufacturers and the airlines themselves.

In short, we trust them with our lives. We know from time to time, that trust is broken and rules are violated. One need only watch the news over the last six months to know that the aviation industry and its regulators do, at times, merit scrutiny. While it may not be welcomed by the industry, it is the job of the journalist, and this television station, to report the shortcomings of the airline industry, with the hope that such stories bring attention to critical issues resulting in changes that create a safer industry.

What person wouldn't want to know as much as they possibly could about the airline they fly? And for our viewers, overwhelmingly the airline they fly is Northwest. We believe that no airline, including Northwest, should be making judgments about what the public should and should not hear, see or read about their maintenance records.

Northwest Airlines fails to seriously challenge the critical findings of our report, and instead says we decided to "frighten" viewers and is quick to criticize us for the "tone" of the broadcasts. But here again, Northwest is off the mark. Our motive was never to "frighten" viewers. We made no reference to past horror stories at Northwest Airlines, specifically the gruesome disaster of Flight 255 in 1987, from which one lone child survived. We did not revisit our stories of some years ago about Northwest Airlines and MELs, which resulted in a substantial fine against Northwest, when, among others, a passenger and flight attendant died in the tail cone of the plane because the emergency exit wouldn't open as they tried to escape. We did not rely at all on the *U.S. News and World Report* article of May 1996 that concluded that Northwest Airlines had more problems per 100,000 departures than any of the other major airlines.

EXHIBIT 1—Continued

And we made no reference to the recent Valujet disaster, which might have increased interest in our reports. The truth is, we took great steps not to capitalize on fear. Rather than do so, we carefully took the time at the beginning and end of each story to point out Northwest's overall record of safety.

In fact, WCCO-TV stated Northwest Airlines was one of the safest airlines in the country, despite the fact that other noted investigations had found otherwise. The Council must understand that the airline industry does not have one standard by which safety is judged, and that by some standards, Northwest is viewed as an unsafe airline . . . . "Accidents alone don't paint a meaningful picture of an airline's safety," a source says. In fact, that report asserts that problems per 100,000 departures is a more meaningful measure. Northwest, in that instance appears to be the worst.

But WCCO reported what it believed to be the truth, that Northwest Airlines is one of the safest airlines in the country. In our third report, in which our earlier allegations are supported as true by the National Safety Transportation Board, industry experts and a union official, we stated that "you can fly no safer airline than Northwest." We also reported that Northwest had won awards for safety, a fact told to us by a Northwest official in the presence of dozens of Northwest managers and union officials, but which Northwest now denies to be the case. In short, the suggestion that our reports were designed to instill fear of flying Northwest—rather than to inform the public of important facts regarding Northwest's airplane maintenance—has no merit whatsoever. . . .

[*7 pages between introduction (above) and conclusion (below)*]

Conclusion

In conclusion, WCCO-TV asks the Minnesota News Council to consider the single most important fact: Northwest Airlines, throughout its entire complaint, does not offer any substantial evidence that the essence of the WCCO-TV report was inaccurate. We ask you to read Northwest's complaint and judge it against our reports, and are confident you will find that Northwest has utterly failed to refute the important facts contained in them that the flying public should know.

We also ask you to remember that the U.S. Senate Select Committee on Government Oversight has recently taken testimony that questions whether the FAA and the airline industry are properly ensuring safety, whether the FAA can both protect and promote aviation interests, and whether the cozy relationship between the airlines and FAA has jeopardized our safety. In light of the evidence that the FAA has been unwilling or unable to properly police the airlines, it is even more important that journalists fulfill their obligation to present serious allegations of problems in the industry to the public.

Finally, we refer you to the conclusion of Northwest's complaint. It asks whether Northwest should have ignored WCCO-TV's purported attack on its reputation, stating, "We couldn't because the people who fly our planes, the men and women who maintain and repair them, the agents at our ticket counters and on the telephone, the employees working in offices and on the tarmac were maligned by WCCO-TV for no better reason than ratings." Where in that paragraph does Northwest even mention its passengers? These were not reports meant to malign Northwest and its employees. They were, however, very much meant to provide important information to the traveling public, the people who trust Northwest every day. We never told the public it was unsafe to fly Northwest. But we do contend this, and we do so strongly: maintenance problems that may bear on the safety of passengers can and should be reported.

EXHIBIT 2 **Minnesota News Council**

September 24, 1996

To the Participants in the Public Hearing
on the Complaint of Northwest Airlines against WCCO-TV

Jon Austin, Northwest Airlines
John Culliton, WCCO-TV

Gentlemen:

The News Council will convene at 1:30 P. M. on Friday, October 18 in the Lutheran brotherhood Auditorium, at 625 4th Avenue South, Minneapolis.

You have chosen to resolve your dispute before this impartial body, whose activities both of you help to sponsor, and we are happy to serve you. This letter contains the specific questions the Council will deliberate and vote upon.

First question: **"Did WCCO-TV paint a distorted, untruthful picture of Northwest Airlines?"** The language comes from the next-to-last paragraph on page 1, in the introduction to the complaint:

> "Through its choices of images, words and narrative, its improper juxtaposition of unrelated facts and events, its failure to provide any appropriate context and its failure to present any comment from the regulators or from independent third-party experts, WCCO-TV painted a distorted, untruthful picture of Northwest Airlines and the men and women who work there."

We'll approach this question through the bulleted items in the second paragraph on the same page, identifying what Northwest sees as violations of journalistic standards. Northwest charges that the station used poor sources and mischaracterized documents; failed to analyze data fairly and to put its findings into context; made numerous factual errors, and presented its series in a needlessly sensational and unbalanced manner.

Please note that the bulleted items we have just listed exclude promotional spots. We'll deal with that subject by asking a second question: **"Should promotional announcements for news be held to the same standards as news?**

Both parties will be invited to express their views on that question to the News Council, which will then deliberate and reach a determination.

If the Council decides that promos should not be held to the same standards as news, there will be no further discussion, and the hearing will be adjourned, with only the first question (on the series itself) having been decided.

EXHIBIT 2—Continued

If the Council decides that promos should be held to the same standards as news, then we will consider a third question: **"Did WCCO-TV's promos paint a distorted, untruthful picture of Northwest Airlines?"** Both parties will be invited to state their views, as in the earlier questions, and the Council will be deliberate and reach a determination.

A few words about the hearing process: It is informal, but orderly. Our chair, Justice Paul Anderson, presides, but does not vote except to break a tie. You each will get 10 minutes for opening remarks, then members will ask you questions designed to clarify the issues. Finally, you will be invited to stay at the table, but to refrain from speaking further as the members openly deliberate in order to reach a determination.

Since Council members will have read the complaint and response carefully and will have seen the videotape, you should use your 10 minutes of presentation, not to read or repeat your submitted materials, but to argue their merits.

Please call me with any comments or questions. We look forward to seeing you on October 18, and we appreciate your trust in the News Council process.

Best wishes,

Gary Gilson
Executive Director

U.S. Citizen Bank (A)

Entering her New Orleans office after a late Friday meeting, Michelle Jeffries discovered a note bearing the distinctive scrawl of Howard Fine, president of U.S. Citizen Bank's Card Services division:

> Michelle: Here's the latest installment in our ongoing drama. Please see me regarding the attached. What do you think? How should we respond? Also, I'd like an update on developments around the first letter. —Howie, 1/19/01

Clipped to Fine's note was a letter from the U.S. General Accounting Office, (GAO) the investigative arm of the United States Congress (Exhibit 1). This was the second request for information on college students and credit cards the bank had received from the GAO within the last three months. The first had arrived in mid-October, and had been forwarded to Howard Fine's attention by Leonard Jonas, president and chief executive officer of U.S. Citizen Bank. Its opening provided a succinct statement of the GAO's interests:

> At the request of three members of Congress the General Accounting Office is conducting a study of credit cards and college students. We are asking your financial institution to participate in this study by providing relevant data and discussing issues related to credit cards and college students, such as targeted marketing, performance on these accounts, and educational efforts directed at them. . . . Such information would help inform any public debate about college students and their credit cards.

The October letter had been accompanied by an extensive set of data requests (Exhibit 2). The requests had raised concerns at U.S. Citizen about the privacy of proprietary information. They also posed a significant data retrieval and programming challenge.

The Consumer Bankers Association, a financial services industry group, was now working with a university-based research institute to formulate an alternative proposal that would provide useful information to the GAO while allaying the confidentiality and technical concerns of card issues.[1] U.S. Citizen was involved in a process, with Michelle as its representative.

As vice president for Niche Credit Markets, Michelle was responsible for marketing U.S. Citizen credit cards to college students and consumers in other specialized markets. These segments were dynamic, and presented significant challenges and opportunities, aspects that had attracted Michelle to the job. The student segment had received increased attention lately from the media, academics, consumer organizations, and public policymakers. The October letter from the GAO had made this clear:

> In recent years the media have presented anecdotal reports of college students who have mismanaged their credit cards. Although sound surveys of college student credit use have been conducted, we think that an analysis of card data maintained by card issuers would help determine whether or not college students manage their cards any differently than other card users and the extent to which college student credit card debt may or may not be a problem.

This case was prepared by Research Associate T. Dean Maines under the supervision of Kenneth E. Goodpaster, Koch Professor of Business Ethics, University of St. Thomas, as a basis for class discussion rather than to illustrate either effective or ineffective handling of an administrative situation. Names of persons, institutions, and locations have been disguised.

[1] The specific analyses proposed by the GAO would yield highly sensitive information about a card issuer's portfolio of student and nonstudent credit card accounts. The GAO also had requested two-years' worth of data. Since most card issuers archive information more frequently than every 24 months, complying with this request would entail merging data from two or more archives. Finally, the varied nature of the data requests would require card issuers to access several different databases, thus compounding the difficulty and cost of assembling the two-year history.

Michelle quickly scanned the GAO's new letter. It acknowledged the ongoing discussions about the October data requests and solicited additional information:

> Whether or not our negotiations concerning access to account data are successful, we still want to offer you the opportunity to share information with us about how your firm markets credit cards to college students, how it informs students about the risks of borrowing, how it identifies good credit risks, how it manages accounts, and any other information you deem important . . . . We have enclosed a list of questions based on the issues Congress asked us to study . . . . we believe a summary based on written responses to these questions from credit card firms would be an important contribution to our report.

The GAO letter identified ten specific questions, covering such topics as the terms associated with student credit cards, underwriting and solicitation practices, and consumer education efforts. It also asked companies to identify interventions that might assist college students who have trouble managing debt and offered a pledge of confidentiality. If U.S. Citizen chose to address these questions, its reply was due by February 13.

Michelle looked up briefly from the letter. Although the GAO had promised confidentiality, she was concerned that vital competitive data might be leaked by a zealous staffer or congressional aide. It also remained unclear how many card providers ultimately would participate in the GAO's study. If the bank chose to contribute information, it might find itself one of only two or three companies willing to "go public," a move that could bring unnecessary scrutiny. On the other hand, by submitting a reply, U.S. Citizen might be able to influence the developing debate about student credit cards, as well as any new federal legislation or regulations directed at this market.

As Michelle began to collect her thoughts about how U.S. Citizen should respond to the GAO, she noticed a second message on her desk. It was a note regarding a call from Sandy Dawkins, a manager within U.S. Citizen's Government and Media Relations department. It indicated that Sandy had left Michelle a voice mail about an "upcoming television special on student credit cards."

U.S. Citizen Bank

U.S. Citizen Bank was founded in Philadelphia in 1885. During its first 60 years, the bank had focused exclusively on serving customers in metropolitan Philadelphia and southeastern Pennsylvania. The post-World War II economic expansion and new leadership at the bank combined to catalyze its emergence as a financial services powerhouse. The firm's growth resulted largely from the acquisition of many small banks and financial institutions, first along the Atlantic seaboard and then throughout the east. By 1998, U.S. Citizen had become one of the ten largest banks in the United States, with assets totaling $110 billion (Exhibit 3). Its operations included approximately 3,000 branches in 17 states. Furthermore, U.S. Citizen was recognized nationally for its diversified services. In addition to traditional banking services, it offered mortgages, credit cards, and investment, brokerage, and insurance services.

During the late 1990s, mergers in the financial services sector proceeded at a furious pace, including many so-called megamergers. The most prominent of these deals fused Citicorp, a bank holding company, with the Travelers Group, an insurance conglomerate. Such mergers sought to take advantage of economies of scale, and were prompted in part by a belief that consumers increasingly desired "one-stop shopping" for financial services. Consistent with this trend, U.S. Citizen deviated from its "many and small" acquisition strategy in 1998 to negotiate a friendly takeover of Louisiana Purchase Bank (LPB). Founded in 1900, LPB was headquartered in New Orleans. Its 2,100 branches were spread across 15 states in the southern United States, with large customer populations in New Orleans, Atlanta, Memphis, Birmingham, Houston, and Dallas. At the time of its purchase, LPB held assets of $81 billion (Exhibit 4).

The U.S. Citizen name and its Philadelphia headquarters were retained for the new firm. However, the profile of the new bank was vastly different from either of its predecessors. The merged entity enjoyed a widely expanded territory, stretching across two-thirds of the continental United States. It also benefited from a set of complementary competencies: While the "old" U.S. Citizen Bank was famous for its high-profile commercial lending services, LPB had a reputation for innovation, pioneering a plethora of new consumer financial products. LPB also had an organizational culture that emphasized creative problem solving in response to customer needs. The leadership of the merged organization hoped this focus on innovation would leaven the more staid and conservative approach traditionally favored inside U.S. Citizen. It also agreed upon a set of guiding values for the new bank, and invested significant resources in communicating them to employees at all levels (Exhibit 5).

Michelle Jeffries

The oldest of four children from a middle-class family, Michelle Jeffries had grown up in Glendive, Montana, a town of 6,000 near the South Dakota border. Ranching, mining, and tourism provided most of Glendive's economic lifeblood, and Michelle's father had worked as an agricultural loan officer in a community bank. The mores of the town mirrored the traditional values of the "old West," emphasizing honesty, fairness, industriousness, and self-reliance. Michelle graduated from Glendive High School in the late 1970s, and matriculated at the University of Montana in Missoula. There she studied economics, earning a minor in information systems and undertaking special research on financial institutions. She also worked part-time as a teller in a local Missoula savings and loan, frequently putting in as many as 20 hours a week to support herself. After graduating magna cum laude, Michelle applied for and won a position in LPB's management training program.

Michelle's intelligence, work ethic, and unassuming personality distinguished her from colleagues in her training class. Upon completion of the yearlong program, she received offers from all the divisions in which she had completed rotations. Michelle chose retail banking, and was named assistant manager of a branch bank in Casper, Wyoming. Within 18 months, she was promoted to manager of a branch in Dallas. After two years of superb performance in this role, Michelle was offered a New Orleans–based position in operations management. The assignment required her to design, launch, and manage a 24-hour telephone customer service operation, one of the first in the financial services industry. Although the job presented a wide range of technical and managerial challenges, Michelle persevered and developed a call center that met or exceeded all performance requirements. This achievement earned Michelle a promotion in early 1993 to the Strategic Management organization within LPB's Card Services division.

Origins of the LPB Student Card

Michelle joined Card Services at a challenging juncture. During the 1970s, many banks considered their credit cards "loss leaders." That is, while the cards helped attract new clients and cement customer loyalty, they generated marginal profits at best and more often substantial losses. This picture changed dramatically as a result of a complex set of factors: regulatory reforms and judicial rulings in the late 1970s and early 1980s; changing popular attitudes toward debt; a decrease in the real cost of consumer credit; and the economic expansion of the mid- to late 1980s. By the end of the 1980s, credit cards were contributing substantially to the profitability of financial institutions. Nevertheless, during the early 1990s, cards began to take on the attributes of a commodity, driving down pricing and profit margins. Furthermore, the primary market for credit cards, middle- and working-class families, was saturated. Thus, card issuers increasingly sought out new, untapped growth segments into which their business might expand.

College students represented one such segment. Four characteristics of the student market made it particularly attractive. First, the annual enrollment process replenished this segment with a new population of potential customers each fall. Second, the number of American college students was expected to grow at an accelerated rate between 1997 and 2010 as a result of the "baby boom echo" (Exhibit 6). Third, with proper pricing, short-term returns from a new-to-credit market were good. Fourth, the earnings potential of college graduates made them good long-term prospective customers. The College Board, an association of over 3,800 institutions of higher learning, estimated that over a lifetime the difference in earnings potential between a high school graduate and the holder of a bachelor's degree exceeded $1 million.

The following card specific projections exemplified the potential. Of the 15 million college students, 80 percent were likely to have a checking account in their own name. Roughly 90 percent of students with a credit card in their own name were likely to have a checking account. Of all college students, 60 percent were likely to obtain and use a credit card. Even if students only carried a small balance each month ($100–$150), total receivables could easily reach or exceed $1 billion.

The opportunity represented by an extended business relationship with such clients more than offset the short-term risks presented by students' limited financial resources and inexperience with credit. Furthermore, card usage patterns encouraged issuers to attract student customers and retain them. As the president of one marketing firm remarked, "Students remember who issued them their first card or cards."[2] Another marketing executive noted that an industry rule of thumb suggested student customers would use their "card of choice" at the time of graduation for an average of 12 years.[3]

Spurred by student requests at its branch offices and the market potential, LPB introduced its first student credit card in 1989. The LPB Student *Visa* was priced to mitigate the risks associated with new-to-credit customers while supporting growth in this new segment. It featured a fixed annual percentage rate (APR) of 18.5 percent, with an annual fee of $15.[4] By comparison, LPB's standard unsecured Visa carried an APR of 11–15 percent and a $25 annual fee. The credit line of the student Visa was limited to $700. Marketing of the card was relatively low key, usually restricted to the placement of applications in branch office brochure racks. A few branches near colleges marketed the card directly on campus.

In 1996, two initiatives were introduced to help increase student sales. First, information systems supporting LPB branches were enhanced with a new prequalification feature. Bankers opening a student *checking account* would be notified automatically if their customer met underwriting criteria that would qualify him or her for a student credit card. Bankers could then advise the customer of this opportunity, giving the branch a chance to sell two products simultaneously. Second, the first "Fall Student Campaign" was launched in August. The campaign was designed to increase student ATM checking and credit card accounts and enhance awareness of the LPB brand on campuses within the firm's territory. It emphasized LPB as a leader in "convenience banking," offering students a choice between a checking account and a student-oriented package that could include checking, an ATM card, and/or a student Visa. The effort also utilized merchandise to encourage applications. For example, a student would receive a T-shirt or coffee mug for opening a student account either on campus or in a branch office.

Competition within the student market stiffened throughout the 1990s, as issuers of general purpose credit cards—Visa, MasterCard, Discover, and American Express—struggled to gain an advantage within this important growth segment. By 1997, forty of the top fifty U.S. credit card providers pitched their products to college students.[5] Competitors in this segment tended to fall into one of two categories: "monoline issuers" and banks. For the former—companies like Capital One and MBNA—credit cards represented their exclusive or primary line of business. The latter ranged from small credit unions to larger regional banks such as Bank of America, Chase, Fleet, and Wells Fargo. Card pricing generally followed one of two approaches, applying either a *fixed* or a *variable* APR to card balances. A few card issuers practiced a form of differential pricing, supplying a card with either a variable or fixed price depending upon the applicant's prior credit history. Variable APRs typically were pegged to changes in the prime rate, the interest rate charged by banks to their most creditworthy customers.[6] Card issuers also offered incentives to make their cards more attractive to students, including annual fee waivers, low introductory interest rates, cash rebates, and airline mileage

[2] Trudy Ring, "Issuers Face a Visit to the Dean's Office," *Credit Card Management* 10 (October 1997): p. 2 of 5.

[3] Ring, p. 2 of 5.

[4] The annual percentage rate is the interest applied to a credit card's monthly balance, expressed as an annual figure.

[5] Ring, p. 2 of 5.

[6] In July 1997 the prime rate was 8.5 percent. By mid-1999 it had dipped to 8.0 percent.

programs. As a result, student credit cards displayed a wide range of prices and features (Exhibit 7).

Evolution of the Student Card at LPB

Working from the results of a strategic marketing study, LPB decided in early 1997 to dedicate resources to emerging customer segments. Michelle was named vice president–niche credit markets in March of that year. With her appointment, the development of LPB's student card program accelerated rapidly. This evolution affected the product's features, pricing, and marketing and included the introduction of educational assistance for student customers.

Features, Pricing, and Marketing

The pricing of the LPB Student Visa was modified in mid-1997. First, Michelle changed its APR from a flat 18.5 percent to a variable rate of prime plus 9.99 percent, with a "floor" of 18.5 percent. Second, behavior fees—the fees assessed for late payments and for charges exceeding the card's credit line—were increased from $20 to $30 per incident. The motivation for this move was twofold. LPB's entire card division had lagged industry levels on behavior fees. Raising these charges for the student Visa helped ensure a competitively priced product in the new-to-credit market. Furthermore, the increases addressed the enhanced risk endemic to this market by (1) offering customers additional incentives to avoid undesirable behaviors and (2) providing income to cover higher levels of operational expenses typically associated with the management of delinquent accounts (e.g., increased customer service calls, collection costs, and account charge-offs).[7] In combination, these pricing actions provided Michelle and her team some latitude to introduce additional features that could make the student Visa more desirable to potential customers.

In June 1998 LPB made an important decision concerning how it would present the student Visa card within the marketplace. Previously the card's positioning had been left largely to branch discretion: Managers would determine the best way to sell the card within their territories—for example, as a discrete product, or in conjunction with one or more other LPB products—and then implement sales plans utilizing this approach. LPB now introduced a comprehensive strategy that positioned the student Visa as one element within an integrated set of financial services tailored to student needs. Called "BankSuite," the bundle included a student checking account with university-branded checks, an ATM/check card, the student Visa, and free online banking.

In effect, the BankSuite strategy represented a decision that LPB would not compete with rivals that marketed cards as discrete financial instruments. Such organizations typically used price as their primary source of market advantage. More positively, the BankSuite approach recognized that the bank's competitive advantage lay in providing an integrated set of financial services that addressed the short-term needs of student customers, enabling the bank to build relationships that could continue beyond graduation. This strategy was supported by data suggesting that student cardholders who used other LPB services were better customers, with lower rates of delinquent payments and account charge-offs. The 1998 "Fall Student Campaign" was used to introduce BankSuite. It was a vastly expanded effort compared with the 1996 sales effort, featuring newspaper advertising, radio spots, dedicated "tabling" efforts at selected universities, and posters throughout LPB's branch system.[8]

Concern about the retention of current accounts led to the introduction of a credit line increase program in December 1998. Student cardholders became eligible for the program after one year and only after meeting qualifying criteria tied to their past credit performance, for examples, strong credit bureau scores, minimal cash advances, payments that consistently exceeded the required minimum, and a credit line utilization rate of 85 percent or less. A line increase of $500 would be granted every 12 months thereafter, provided the student continued to meet the designated criteria.

[7] An account "charge-off" is a write-down of the account's full balance as uncollectible.

[8] "Tabling" is a marketing technique in which credit card issuers (or their representatives) staff a table at a campus location and solicit card applications from students. It may include the use of incentives—for example, free merchandise—to motivate students to apply.

Notification of the increase was given via a message on the monthly card statement.

Education

Building on past experience with new-to-credit clients, Michelle and her team recognized that helping students understand the importance of good credit management would create better customers and enhance portfolio performance through reduced operating expenses. Thus, in January 1998, they inaugurated a credit education program for students. By mid-1999, the program encompassed three components:

- *Periodic reminders.* Customers with account activity received a "tip of the month" on their billing statement (Exhibit 8), as well as a quarterly newsletter, "Credit Management 101".
- *Brochures.* Credit education pamphlets were placed in all LPB branches and included in the initial issuance package for each new student credit card. The pamphlets covered credit basics, key terminology used on LPB billing statements, and helpful rules for managing credit.
- *Online education.* A short seminar on credit management tailored to student needs was introduced on LPB's Web site. The seminar focused on developing the skills necessary to build and maintain a good credit history.

Over time, this program functioned as a "proving ground" for LPB and, postmerger, U.S. Citizen: New educational efforts would be tested with the student population, and effective ones expanded to other customers with minimal credit experience. For example, Michelle's team implemented a "Welcome Call" pilot in early 2000. The program featured a phone call to a small sample of new student card customers and offered the bank's top four tips for managing credit cards. Educational efforts for students and all new-to-credit customers were reviewed annually, to identify improvement opportunities in existing programs and new credit education initiatives.

Merger Implications for the U.S. Citizen Student Portfolio

When the LPB acquisition was announced in late 1998, the leadership of the merged firm stated that it would take a "systematic approach" to determining how the operations of the two organizations would be integrated. As plans progressed, it became clear that most of LPB's Card Services would remain intact. Personnel from U.S. Citizen's smaller card operation would largely be incorporated into LPB's structure, with managers from both organizations assuming leadership roles. Howard Fine, a former senior vice president at U.S. Citizen, was named head of the merged card operation, while Michelle's boss, Joan Michaels, was given responsibility for its marketing arm. Risk assessment was placed under the leadership of Perry Moyle, who had led the same function within the "old" U.S. Citizen. Most personnel in the merged Card Services organization would be based in New Orleans; however, a few functions, including risk assessment, would be located in Hagerstown, Maryland, the former home of U.S. Citizen's card division.

The student credit card portfolio that resulted from U.S. Citizen's acquisition of LPB established the merged organization as one of the top ten student card issuers within the United States. The combined student portfolio contained approximately 594,000 accounts, roughly 4 percent of the national student market and 6 percent of the student market within U.S. Citizen's 30-state territory. U.S. Citizen earned income on essentially 60 percent of these accounts, the cardholders who were active (completed a transaction or carried a balance) each month. At the beginning of 1999, the average U.S. Citizen student cardholder maintained a revolving balance of $627, about $100 more than the national mean for this consumer segment. Consolidated income statements for the past five years revealed a healthy degree of positive portfolio performance. Its pretax net income margin during this period had ranged around 6 percent, compared to nonstudent portfolios that generated 4 percent.

Operations proceeded apace in 1999 within the new Card Services division, with veterans from both predecessor firms striving to forge effective working relationships. However, the student card portfolio quickly became a flash point. The "old" U.S. Citizen had been involved in the student market but only in a limited manner. Most of its student cardholders had been college seniors. The performance of its student portfolio had tracked closely with the performance of its standard Visa product: Accounts 60 days or more past due typically constituted only 4 percent of the total student portfolio, and on average only 6 percent of this portfolio had been written off as uncollectible. In contrast, LPB student cardholders were spread evenly across all four college classes, between 5 and 10 percent of student accounts were delinquent by 60 days or more, and typically 9–11 percent of the portfolio was written off annually as uncollectible. These differences troubled Perry Moyle, who ordered a complete review of the LPB portion of the combined student portfolio.

The risk assessment study consumed most of Michelle's energy and attention through the first half of 1999. She frequently found herself in the position of defending past decisions which ran counter to the more conservative culture of the old U.S. Citizen. She quickly discovered that it had been a culture in which risk assessment had reigned supreme, with marketing loath to challenge its judgment. After months of argument, a pained consensus was reached. The merged organization would remain in the student credit card segment, and would market to all student classes. However, a modified version of the more restrictive, old U.S. Citizen underwriting criteria would be used to evaluate new student applications. Two factors had proved decisive in the debate: the demand from old U.S. Citizen branches for the BankSuite product and the tremendous financial opportunity represented by the student card market over the next five to ten years.

Emerging Public Concerns

Prior to 1999, public relations issues associated with the student credit cards were minor. By the beginning of 2000, however, a number of organizations and public officials were expressing concern and dismay about the targeting of college students by card issuers. These concerns were fueled in part by an enhanced awareness of the growth of personal debt within the United States, and ensuing debate about the impact of this debt upon the nation's economy.

During the 1980s and 1990s, the percentage of consumer debt attributable to credit cards had grown rapidly. In 1980, credit card debt represented 15.8 percent of all outstanding consumer debt; by 1995, this proportion had increased to 40.4 percent.[9] Furthermore, the level of credit card debt assumed by individual households increasingly outstripped their financial resources. One study found that in 1983, roughly 4 percent of all U.S. households had credit card debt greater than their monthly incomes, and 1 percent had more than twice their monthly incomes. By 1995, these statistics had risen to 16 percent and 8 percent, respectively.[10] Reports in the popular press fleshed out such figures by highlighting financial and family tragedies created by credit card debt across the demographic and economic spectrum.

As the 1990s progressed, college students reported increased credit card solicitations on campus—for example, through tabling within student unions and at university events, card applications inserted in bookstore bags, applications received in the mail, Internet promotions, and telemarketing. The solicitations could be quite aggressive. One student union administrator complained that credit card vendors sometimes created a "carnival atmosphere," complete with loud music, games, and gifts for students who completed an application. The "party environment" and incentives effectively masked the responsibilities of owning a credit card, especially when there was no discussion of the consequences of misuse.[11]

At the same time, some credit card issuers were forging stronger ties to colleges through sponsorship arrangements. For example, First USA, the credit card division of Bank One Corp, agreed in 1999 to pay the University of Tennessee $16 million over seven years for the right to serve as the sole marketer of the university's Visa "affinity card" to the university's students and alumni.[12] In addition to the $16 million fee, the

[9] Robert D. Manning, *Credit Card Nation: The Consequences of America's Addiction to Credit* (New York: Basic Books, 2000) p. 13.

[10] Edward J. Bird, Paul A. Hagstrom, and Robert Wild, "Credit Card Debts of the Poor: High and Rising." Unpublished paper, Department of Public Policy, University of Rochester, 1998.

[11] United States General Accounting Office, *College Students and Credit Cards* (Washington DC: U.S. Government Printing Office, 2001), p. 27.

[12] A college affinity card is a credit card that is typically adorned with a school's official seal, logo, or sports mascot. Marketing of the card may be limited to the school's alumni, or alumni and students.

university also would receive 0.5 percent of every transaction charge, a benefit valued at $4 million annually.[13] Similar deals totaling over $9 million were struck by First USA's rival, MBNA, with Georgetown, Michigan State, the University of Hawaii, and the University of Ottawa.[14] Critics suggested that such arrangements permitted universities to profit at the expense of students. Administrators at state-supported schools countered that these contracts helped make up shortfalls in public funding.

A broad picture of credit card use by full-time students at four-year colleges and universities could be constructed from data compiled by Student Monitor, a market research firm.[15] At the close of the 1990s college students were obtaining their first credit card at an increasingly early age: Over 67 percent of freshman entering college in fall 2000 reported receiving their first card in their own name prior to enrolling. On average, college students had 1.6 general-purpose credit cards. The average credit limit on each card was $2,322. Thirty-six percent of the students polled indicated they had received a credit line increase within the past year. Sixty-five percent of student cardholders paid off their balance each month; those who did not carried an average monthly balance of $531. In spring 2000, only 16 percent of the students reported balances in excess of $1,000.[16] However, 53 percent of the students polled believed they did not receive adequate credit education from the issuer of their first card. The top three reasons cited for obtaining a credit card were the desire to establish a credit history, convenience, and emergency protection.

In 2000 Robert Manning, a professor at the University of Houston, published *Credit Card Nation: The Consequences of America's Addiction to Credit*. Combining macroeconomic research with data from first-person interviews, Manning's book painted a bleak portrait of credit cards' impact. One chapter was devoted to problems resulting from the growing presence of credit cards and card issuers at U.S. colleges and universities. In his summary, Manning noted two disturbing trends:

> Since the mid-1970s, rapidly escalating college costs and declining financial aid and real wages have forced students increasingly to rely on credit cards to help pay for their college educations. This has led to a new trend in which credit card debts are being revolved—paid off with federal student loans or even with private debt consolidation. For growing numbers of students, credit cards are becoming a savior for financing their education . . . . For others, consumer credit initially offers freedom but may become a financial shackle by the end of their college career. The most unfortunate may find that their only option for regaining personal control in the just-do-it culture of credit dependency is to withdraw from school and work full-time in order to pay off their debts. Indeed, official dropout rates (attributed to low grades) include growing numbers of students who are unable to cope with the stress of both their debts and the part-time jobs they must take to service those debts. For others, the reality of their credit card indebtedness may not be realized until after graduation when prospective employers question their past financial recklessness or when they must accept a sharp decline in their standard of living.
>
> A key factor in college marketing campaigns is that adolescence and early adulthood are the formative periods for shaping consumer attitudes [and] consumer tastes for specific products and corporate brand loyalty. . . . Not surprisingly, the social pressures of college—especially for students from modest-income families—constitute an ideal setting for manipulating parental authority conflicts and status anxiety among young, impressionable students. The ability to acquire credit cards, without parental consent, is exacerbating family tensions over unapproved behavior (drinking, sex, drugs, body piercing, tattoos, holiday trips, expensive clothes). In fact, many students with credit cards provided by their parents are acquiring their own in order to conceal their social, sexual, and consumption activities. Hence, student credit cards are contributing to heightened family tensions as well as shielding potential financial responsibility from the purview of parents or guardians.[17]

[13] Marsha Vickers, "Big Cards on Campus," *BusinessWeek*, 20 September 1999, p. 136.

[14] Vickers, p. 136.

[15] Student Monitor LLC, "Financial Services Study" (CD-ROM), Spring 2001, Ridgewood, NJ, 2001.

[16] Student Monitor LLC, "Financial Services Study," Spring 2000, cited in U.S. General Accounting Office, *College Students and Credit Cards*, p. 22.

[17] Manning, pp. 191–92.

Many universities undertook initiatives to address the situation. For example, a number of them imposed bans or restrictions upon credit card solicitations. In some cases, institutional regulations covered activities campuswide; in others, rules were more selective. For example, a student union might prohibit credit card solicitations, while a campus bookstore would permit them.[18] Some universities also responded by augmenting their financial education programs, integrating segments on debt management into freshman orientation and offering access to credit counseling services.[19] Still, administrators remained concerned that credit card debt played a major role in prompting some students to withdraw from school. Asked about the impact of credit cards upon student performance, an Indiana University official replied, "Credit cards are terrible things. We lose more students to credit card debt than to academic failure."[20] Data also indicated that bankruptcy filings for individuals 25 or younger had increased 51 percent between 1991 and 1999.[21]

As the 1990s drew to a close, public policymakers took increased notice of the issue. In 1999, fifteen bills addressing the marketing and management of student credit cards were introduced or enacted in the legislatures of nine states. Twelve more bills were introduced or enacted in ten states during 2000. In October 1999, legislation was introduced in the U.S. House of Representatives that sought to amend the Consumer Credit Protection Act to prevent credit card issuers from taking "unfair advantage" of full-time, traditional-aged college students. Support for this legislation eventually led Representatives Louise E. Slaughter (D-NY), John J. Duncan Jr. (R-TN), and Paul E. Kanjorski (D-PA) to request a formal GAO study of college students and credit cards. While it remained unclear what new legal or regulatory restrictions ultimately might be introduced, it was quite possible that future college students would be barred from obtaining credit cards prior to age 21 unless their applications were cosigned.

[18] United States General Accounting Office, pp. 25–26.

[19] United States General Accounting Office, pp. 31–32.

[20] Quoted in "HR 184, The College Student Credit Card Protection Act: Why We Need This Legislation" (www.house.gov/slaughter/leg-record/leg184.htm).

[21] United States General Accounting Office, p. 14.

A Cloud on the Horizon

Michelle settled back in her chair as she reviewed the thoughts she had drafted concerning U.S. Citizen's response to the GAO's new list of questions. Taking a break to mull over a troubling point, she picked up her phone to check her voice mail message from Sandy Dawkins:

> *Hi Michelle, this is Sandy. I'm calling from Reagan National. As you know, we caught wind in December of a planned* Sixty Minutes II *segment on student credit cards. I thought the segment was still in production, but it looks like it will air next Tuesday, January 23. I don't know much about its contents, but my contact suggested that it more or less puts student card issuers in the same league as tobacco companies. We should talk ASAP. I'm flying back to New Orleans tonight, but won't be in until late. Please give me a call tomorrow. You have my home number*

"Great," Michelle thought to herself, "I weather the internal tornado of the merger just in time for a real PR blizzard to kick up outside." She made a mental note to warn Howard Fine and Joan Michaels about the segment after calling Sandy on Saturday morning.

EXHIBIT 1 **January 2001 Letter from the General Accounting Office**

Source: Company files.

General Accounting Office
Washington, DC 20548

January 18, 2001

Mr. Howard Fine
President – Card Services
U.S. Citizen Bank
6159 St. Philip Street
New Orleans, LA 70195

Dear Mr. Fine,

As you know, at the request of three members of Congress, GAO is in the process of developing one or more reports on college students and credit cards. In October 2000, we wrote to your firm requesting data on college students and other credit card accounts. We continue to negotiate with several card issuers concerning access to this account data. Our work at universities and other research is substantially complete, and we plan on reporting this work in May 2001.

Whether or not negotiations concerning access to account data are successful, we still want to offer you the opportunity to share information with us about how your firm markets credit cards to college students, how it informs students about the risks of borrowing, how it identifies good credit risks, how it manages accounts, and any other information you deem important.

We have enclosed a list of questions based on the issues Congress asked us to study. Representatives of several credit card firms have already discussed responses with us informally, and one provided written documentation. We believe that a summary based on written responses to these questions from credit card firms would be an important contribution to our report. In keeping with our policies, we will not identify individual respondents in our report. Our pledge of confidentiality, and that of our requestors, will apply.

In order to provide a balanced report to the Congress, we feel it is essential to include some general information from credit card issuers in the May report. We are requesting that you provide a written response to the enclosed questions by February 13. Please reply to the address above or fax to 202-512-3642. You can contact Davi D'Agostino or Katie Harris at 202-512-8678 with any questions.

Sincerely yours,

Thomas J. McCool
Managing Director, Financial Markets and Community Investment

EXHIBIT 1—Continued

GAO Study on College Students and Credit Card Debt
Questions for Credit Card Issuers

1. How do the terms (e.g., interest rates, late fees, initial credit limit, and other fees) for any credit cards you market specifically to students compare to those for non-students? (It may be helpful to provide application forms for your products, if you have not done so previously.) What factors are considered in deciding to raise a student's credit limit?
2. What underwriting standards do you apply to college student applications? How important are employment history, salary, credit report, credit needs, and ability to pay? What other issues do you consider? What are your underwriting standards for other customers with characteristics similar to those of college students, e.g., income, credit history? How does the risk adjusted performance of student portfolios compare with non-student portfolios?
3. What means of solicitation do you use to attract college student applications (direct mail, on-campus marketing, etc.)? What is most productive for your firm?
4. What disclosure guidelines does your organization follow when soliciting college students? Do they differ from non-students?
5. Describe some typical arrangements your firm has with universities regarding solicitation for or issuance of your credit card to students or alumni. For example: guidelines for on and off campus solicitations, credit limits, formulas for increasing and decreasing credit limits, interest rate changes, late payment fees, payments between the card issuer and the universities.
6. Do you use subcontractors for marketing to college students? If so, what policies or procedures do you set for them regarding campus solicitation, disclosure of card terms, any efforts to ensure students' understanding of terms and their responsibilities? Do you allow subcontractors to use campus groups to solicit?
7. If aggregate transaction data is available for your college student customers, what were the top categories of spending during the most recent 12-month period available?
8. What consumer education efforts aimed at college students do you sponsor or participate in? (If you have not done so previously, it would be helpful to provide sample copies of materials.)
9. What financial literacy issues are particularly important for college students? How do your educational efforts for students differ from those of non-students?
10. What kinds of intervention could be taken to assist college students who have trouble managing debt? Who should take those actions? What actions does your firm take?

EXHIBIT 2 Sample Data Requests from October 2000 General Accounting Office Letter

Source: Company files.

I. Target Populations to Be Sampled

We would like a sample to be drawn from two different groups of credit card accounts. The first group is to be drawn from those who identify themselves as college students at the time of application or issuance . . . . The second group—a comparison group—is to be drawn from all other credit card holders who had open accounts for at least one statement during the study period except those defined as college students.

II. Study Period

The study period would be October 1, 1998, through September 30, 2000. . . .

III. Data Needs

The following are the raw data that GAO needs to perform its analysis—basically the data submitted on the card application and the information that card holders receive monthly. . . . In addition to this data, we need to know the total number of college student accounts and non-college student accounts. . . . We need a value for each and every data field—not summary statistics.

Initial Application Information: Applicant income; sources of income—for example, full-time or part-time job, summer job, allowance/parents, savings, loan, stipend, spouse, grant/scholarship; length of time in current job; date of birth; age at application; college class; housing—own, rent, parents, dorm; permanent/school address; time at current address; status—part-time or full-time; institution type—4 year/2 year; credit score.

Type of Card: Card type; solicitation/marketing source; credit limit; grace period; interest rate; late payment fee.

Card Usage for Each Statement Period in Study: total charges; total amount charged by category—mail and phone, food, restaurants, education, discount stores, department stores, book/newspapers, specialty retail, apparel, gas/automotive.

Card Payment during Each Statement Period: Days in billing cycle; previous balance; total charged in statement period; cash advances; minimum payment required; total new balance; available credit; amount over credit limit; amount paid in statement period; finance charges; late payment fee; over limit fee; late payments—1–29 days; 30–89 days; 90+ days; amount written-off; interest rate.

IV Analysis Plan

Some of the questions we pian to address are:

1. What are the demographic characteristics of college student cardholders?
2. How much do college students charge on their cards and how many pay off their balance each month and how many carry a balance . . . ?
3. How often are college students on time or late in making their monthly payments?
4. How do college students acquire their credit cards? Is there any connection between the way a college student acquires a card and the amount of debt they incur?
5. What underwriting standards do issuers apply to college students?
6. What interest rates and late fees are college students charged?
7. Do college students use their credit cards to pay necessary school expenses?

We will ask you to calculate descriptive statistics such as ranges, means, and other frequency counts to answer the above questions. When you have provided us with specific data formats we can specify what particular statistics we need. We will need some correlations run on several variables. . . .

We will calculate statistics separately for each issuer. However, individual issuer statistics will not be reported if there is any possibility the identify of the issuer would be revealed. . . . We will be seeking your input on how to display our results in a fair and informative manner that safeguards the identify of the card issuer.

EXHIBIT 3 **1998 U.S. Citizen Bank Consolidated Balance Sheet ($ in billions)**

Source: Illustrative data.

Assets	
Cash & due from banks	$16.0
Federal funds sold and securities under resale agreement	2.1
Securities available for sale	19.1
Loans	60.2
Allowance for losses	(1.2)
Loans, net	58.8
Premises and equipment	2.0
Interest receivable	2.0
Other	10.0
Total assets	*$110.0*
Liabilities	
Deposits	$69.3
Federal funds borrowed	4.3
Short-term notes and borrowings	8.0
Long-term debt	11.0
Guaranteed preferred beneficial interests in company's subordinated debentures	0.9
Accrued expenses and other liabilities	5.5
Total Liabilities	*$99.0*
Stockholders' Equity	
Stockholders' equity and retained earnings	*$11.0*
Total liabilities and stockholders' equity	*$110.0*

EXHIBIT 4 **1998 Louisiana Purchase Bank Consolidated Balance Sheet ($ in billions)**

Source: Illustrative data.

Assets		
	Cash & due from banks	$9.7
	Federal funds sold and securities under resale agreement	0.9
	Securities available for sale	14.0
	Loans	48.1
	Allowance for losses	(1.4)
	Loans, net	46.7
	Premises and equipment	0.8
	Interest receivable	0.7
	Other	8.2
	Total Assets	*$81.0*
Liabilities		
	Deposits	$50.2
	Federal funds borrowed	3.6
	Short-term notes and borrowings	5.9
	Long-term debt	4.3
	Guaranteed preferred beneficial interests in company's subordinated debentures	0.8
	Accrued expenses and other liabilities	6.5
	Total Liabilities	*$71.3*
Stockholders' Equity		
	Stockholders' equity and retained earnings	*$9.7*
	Total Liabilities and Stockholders' Equity	*$81.0*

EXHIBIT 5 Core Values of Postmerger U.S. Citizen Bank

Source: Illustrative data.

The Values of U.S. Citizen Bank

We want every U.S. Citizen employee to know our values so well that if we threw out all our policy manuals, we could still make decisions based on an understanding of what ultimately matters to this organization. Our core values are:

Ethics. We maintain the highest standards of conduct in our interactions with customers, fellow employees, shareholders, and our communities:

- We value and reward open, honest, two-way communication.
- Each of us is accountable for our decisions and conduct.
- We only make promises we intend to keep, and we do what we say we will.
- If things change, we let those affected know.
- We avoid any actual and perceived conflicts of interest.
- We always treat others the way we would want to be treated.

Customer satisfaction. We consider the customer in all we do:

- We exceed the expectations of internal and external customers, surprising and delighting them.
- We do what is right for the customer.
- We look for new, creative ways to meet customer needs.
- We always talk and act with the customer in mind.
- We build long-term relationships with our customers.
- We always treat customers with respect and care.

Leadership and personal accountability. Every employee contributes to the success of U.S. Citizen. This means:

- We run the business like we own it.
- We take prudent risks.
- We lead by example.
- We make decisions locally, close to the customer.
- We know the numbers.
- We make decisions with our stakeholders in mind.
- We always respect one another and care for one another.

Diversity. We respect differences among employees, our customers, and within our communities:

- We behave in a way that supports our core values.
- We capitalize on the different perspectives and competencies present in the organization to develop innovative solutions for our customers.
- We support the diversity of employees, customers, and communities.
- We leverage diversity as a competitive advantage.

EXHIBIT 6 Total Fall Enrollment in Degree-Granting Institutions, 1970 to 2010 (in thousands)

Source: U.S. Department of Education.

1970	1980	1990	1997	1998	1999	2000	2001	2002	2003	2004	2010
8,581	12,097	13,819	14,345	14,549	14,860	15,135	15,370	15,610	15,853	16,099	17,490

Note: Figures for years after 1998 are forecasts.

EXHIBIT 7 Comparative Student Card Characteristics, July 2001

Source: CardTrak Student Card Report, company files.

Card	Pricing (APR)*	Annual Fee	Annual Fee Waive	Card Type	Rewards Program
Fixed APR					
MBNA Student Card	15.99%	$20	No	Visa/MasterCard	
First Interstate Bank Student Card	16.80%	$15	Yes	Visa	
Discover Classic Student Card	17.99%	$ 0		Discover	
First Union Collegiate Card	18.00%	$20	Yes	Visa/MasterCard	
Capital One College Card	19.80%	$ 0		Visa	
Variable APR					
First Tennessee Bank Student Card	9.65% (P+2.9, 10.9 max.)	$ 0		Visa	
Commerce Bank Student Card	12.65% (P+5.9)	$ 0		Visa	
Fifth Third Bank	13.65% (P+6.9)	$18	Yes	Visa	
Bank of America Student Visa	13.74% (P+6.99)	$ 0		Visa	
American Express Optima Student Card	14.74% (P+7.99, 14.49 min.)	$ 0		American Express	
Fleet BankBoston	15.40% (P+8.65)	$21	No	Visa/MasterCard	
Associates National Bank Student Cards	16.24% (P+9.49)	$ 0		Visa/MasterCard	Rebate
Washington Mutual Student Card	16.24% (P+9.49)	$ 0		Visa	
First USA /United College Plus Student Card	16.65% (P+9.9)	$ 0		Visa/MasterCard	Air Miles
Wachovia Bank Student Card	16.65% (P+9.9)	$ 0		Visa/MasterCard	
First USA Student Card	16.74% (P+9.99)	$ 0		Visa	
U.S. Citizen Student Card	**18.5% (P+9.99, 18.5 min.)**	$15	No	Visa	
Associates National Bank Phillips 66 Card	18.65% (P+11.90)	$ 0		MasterCard	Rebate
Associates National Bank Verizon	18.65% (P+11.90)	$ 0		Visa	Rebate
Wells Fargo Student Card	19.8% (P+11.55, 19.8 min.)	$18	Yes	Visa	Rebate
Credit Based					
Fidelity National Bank Student Card	P+2.9–10.9	$ 0		Visa	
First National Student Card	13.9%†	$ 0		Visa/MasterCard	
Citibank Student Cards	16.74% (P+9.99)†	$ 0		MasterCard	Rebate
HSBC Bank Student Card	18.90%	$ 0		Visa/MasterCard	

* *P* = prima rate.

† Average.

EXHIBIT 8 Sample "Tips of the Month"

Source: Illustrative data.

January: Be conservative when starting a new budget. Estimate income on the low side and expenses on the high side. Developing a good budget will help you obtain the personal possessions you want and need.

February: A good credit rating can be the best asset you own! Payment history is a critical factor in determining your rating. Don't wait to make your payment. If you're short of cash, make at least the minimum payment.

April: You should review the Account Summaries portion of your statement each month. If your New Balance divided by your Credit Limit is equal to or greater than 85%, then you may need to curtail spending. Going over limit on a regular basis can be costly, embarrassing, and can affect your credit rating.

August: It's Back-to-School time. Your U.S. Citizen Card is there to help! Save your receipts and review your statement each month. If you're unsure of a purchase, compare the amounts to your receipt. And remember, finance charges can add up fast, so budget to make at least a 5% payment each month.

October: Wondering how to improve your credit rating? Here are three points to keep in mind:

- Make payments on time—and above all don't get 60 days past due.
- Keep your New Balance to Credit Limit at 85% or less.
- The total amount of monthly minimum payments should normally be no more than 10% of your monthly income.

Through prudent use, your U.S. Citizen Student Visa can help you build a healthy credit rating!

The Challenge of Responsible Lending and Debt: *An Introduction to Nonstandard Credit*

Nonstandard lending encompassed a wide spectrum of credit instruments. These instruments—usually credit cards or some form of consumer loan—were marketed to borrowers who failed to qualify for credit at more favorable (lower) interest rates. Such customers were considered a "higher risk" from a lender's perspective, for a variety of reasons: a lack of experience managing credit, a previous bankruptcy, or limited financial resources. This note introduces nonstandard lending, examining a few of the forms this credit has taken within the marketplace.

Subprime and Predatory Lending

Ambiguity in terminology requires distinctions to be drawn between nonstandard lending and practices popularly associated with it. For example, nonstandard lending has frequently been equated with *subprime lending*. In a January 2001 letter to financial institutions, the Federal Deposit Insurance Corporation defined subprime lending programs as those targeting "borrowers with weakened credit histories typically characterized by payment delinquencies, previous charge-offs, judgments or bankruptcies," or "questionable repayment capacity evidenced by low credit scores or high debt-burden ratios."[1] On this understanding, subprime lending has been considered one *type* of nonstandard credit. That is, a subset of nonstandard lending programs have qualified as subprime practices, but not *all have*. For example, some programs aimed at new-to-credit customers have fallen outside the subprime domain.

Similarly, some consumer advocates have equated all nonstandard lending with *predatory lending*. At a 2000 hearing on predatory mortgages, Congressman James Leach (R-Iowa), then chairman of the House Committee on Banking and Financial Services, identified some distinguishing marks of predatory practices:

- Predatory lending is typified by a *lack of transparency*. Predatory loans frequently are accompanied by incomplete, confusing, or untimely term disclosures that hide special charges or high rates of penalty interest.
- Predatory lending usually entails *deception*—for example, misleading sales claims or marketing practices.
- Predatory lenders *inappropriately target customers or inadequately assess a borrower's repayment capacity*.[2]

This note was prepared from public materials by Research Associate T. Dean Maines under the supervision of Kenneth E. Goodpaster, Koch Professor of Business Ethics, University of St. Thomas.

[1] Federal Deposit Insurance Corporation, "Federal Banking Regulatory Agencies Jointly Issue Expanded Examination Guidance for Subprime Lending Programs," January 31, 2001 (www.fdic.gov/news/news/financial/2001/fil0109.html).

[2] U.S. House of Representatives Committee on Banking and Financial Services, Hearing on Predatory Lending Practices, May 24, 2000 (commdocs.house.gov/committees/bank/hba64810.000/hba64810_0.htm).

The Minnesota Attorney General's Office has noted that predatory lenders play on consumers' lack of financial sophistication.[3] For example, they may present an applicant with a favorable schedule of monthly installments that masks a large, unaffordable final "balloon" payment. Predatory loans may "lock" customers into high-cost arrangements through excessive prepayment penalties or interest rates. Also, they may charge for features that purportedly work for the customer's benefit but do the opposite in fact (e.g., expensive credit insurance).

Characteristics such as these can help inform judgments as to whether particular nonstandard lending practices or loans are predatory. Consumer advocates, regulatory officials, industry representatives, and business executives alike have decried abusive lending, even if they have differed in their assessments of specific practices. They also have agreed upon the *benefit* provided by nonstandard lending, namely, the extension of credit to individuals and groups who otherwise would not receive it.

The Growth of American Consumer Debt

Consumer debt has usually been divided into four categories. *Installment debt* is debt incurred for household, family, or personal expenditures and repaid at regular intervals over a specified time period. A car loan is an example of installment debt. *Revolving debt* results from the use of credit cards and related credit plans. *Mortgage debt* is debt incurred for the purchase of a residence. *Home equity loans* are related to mortgage debt. These typically have taken the form of a revolving credit line that enables homeowners to borrow against the equity in their homes on an "as needed" basis.

American consumer debt has risen rapidly over the past two decades. From 1980 to 1992, total home mortgage debt and consumer installment debt rose by more than 400 percent in unadjusted dollars, from $1.4 trillion to $5.7 trillion.[4] Household debt of all kinds continued to increase rapidly during the 1990s. Research by the Federal Reserve Bank of Cleveland indicated that mortgage debt grew more than 50 percent between 1990 and March 1996, while credit card debt increased 127 percent over the first seven years of the decade.[5] By 2001, total household liabilities were estimated at $7.9 trillion.[6]

A number of factors have contributed to the growth of consumer debt. Four are commonly cited. First, American attitudes toward debt have liberalized. Interviews conducted with three generations of one family help to dramatize this shift. An 86-year-old grandfather characterized his approach to credit as, "If you don't have the cash, you just don't buy." In contrast, his 29-year-old granddaughter insisted, "Just because I don't have the cash for something doesn't mean I shouldn't buy it. . . I'm living in a style I want to become accustomed to."[7] Second, increased employment and income volatility has fostered greater credit dependency. More and more families now utilize debt to fund *needs* as well as *wants*. Third, the number of American homeowners has soared, as well as the size of the average mortgage.[8] Fourth, regulatory reforms and judicial rulings during the late 1970s and early 1980s have permitted consumer interest rates to remain at historically high levels, even as the real cost of credit to lenders has dropped. These high rates have helped accelerate the compounding of consumer liabilities.

Nonstandard lending has taken root within this environment of growing consumer debt. The volume of nonstandard lending has increased significantly since 1990.[9] According to one analysis, the subprime component of

[3] Minnesota Attorney General's Office, "Know Your Rights," July 2001 (www.ag.state.mn.us/consumer/kyr/kyr_5Fjuly01.htm).

[4] Teresa A. Sullivan, Elizabeth Warren, and Jay Lawrence Westbrook, *The Fragile Middle Class: Americans in Debt* (New Haven: Yale University Press, 2000) p. 18.

[5] Federal Reserve Bank of Cleveland, "December Economic Trends: Consumer Debt," December 1996 (www.clev.frb.org/research/et96/1296/condeb.htm).

[6] David Leonhardt, "A Blasphemy Spreads: Debts Are OK," *New York Times on the Web*, January 19, 2002 (www.nytimes.com/2002/01/19/arts/19DEBT.html) p. 2 of 4.

[7] Daniel McGinn, "Maxed Out," *Newsweek*, August 27, 2001, p. 34.

[8] Leonhardt, p. 3 of 4.

[9] Ron Feldman and Jason Schmidt, "Why All Concerns about Subprime Lending Are Not Created Equal," *Fedgazette*, July 1999 (www.minneapolisfed.org/pubs/fedgaz/99-07/banking.html) p. 1 of 5.

nonstandard credit was the most rapidly expanding segment of consumer lending.[10]

Forms of Nonstandard Credit

The growth of nonstandard lending has been fueled both by consumers' needs or desires for credit and the willingness of financial institutions to extend credit to higher-risk customers. To balance the enhanced risk, nonstandard lenders have offered credit at relatively higher rates of interest and/or fees (application fees, late payment fees, etc.). The market's attractiveness to lenders stemmed from two features. First, subprime consumers have been willing to accept higher interest rates in return for credit access. Second, these customers have paid off their debts more slowly, permitting interest income to mount. The lender must allocate some portion of this additional interest and fee income to cover higher levels of operational expenses. These expenses have arisen from the management of marginal accounts, for example, increased customer service calls, collection costs, and losses associated with uncollectible loan balances. The remainder of this note examines some forms nonstandard credit can take.

Student Credit Cards

From 1979 to 1998, median U.S. household income rose only 6.9 percent, from $36,259 to $38,885 (measured in 1998 dollars).[11] Yet the total cost of attending a four-year college rose nearly 38 percent between 1986 and 1998, according to the Institute of Higher Education.[12] Students have sought to close this gap through a variety of "traditional" means: scholarships, summer employment, work/study jobs, and (increasingly) various subsidized and unsubsidized loans. Since the late 1980s, students have used credit cards as an additional source of college funds. These cards also enable students to build a credit history prior to entering the workforce full-time.

By the end of the 1980s, the traditional market for credit cards—middle- and working-class families—was becoming saturated. The college market presented card issuers with an opportunity for profitable growth, in both the short and long term.

In the short term, the nearly 14 million undergraduates enrolled in 1990 would only need to maintain a small card balance to generate tremendous receivables. In the long term, the strong earning potential of college graduates made them highly desirable customers.

Over the course of the 1990s, student credit cards became an accepted part of campus life. Student cards are major, general-purpose credit cards—Visa, MasterCard, Discover, and American Express. While a few student cards have annual interest rates below 10 percent, most charge between 13 and 20 percent. Many student cards featured variable pricing, which links their interest rates to fluctuations in the prime lending rate. Typically, student cards have not charged annual fees; those that have frequently waived them under specific conditions—for example, for the student's first year as a cardholder. Like all major standard and nonstandard credit cards, student cards also assessed fees for late payments and for charges that exceed a cardholder's credit line.

While information on initial credit limits was difficult to obtain, market data published in 2001 suggested that the average credit limit on a student charge card was approximately $2,300.[13] This market data also indicated that just over one-third of student cardholders received a credit line increase sometime during the previous 12 months.[14]

Citibank and Capital One were the leading issuers of student cards. Also in the top five were MBNA, small credit unions, and Bank of America. Some companies had entered into contracts with colleges and universities that gave them the exclusive right to market special "affinity cards" to the school's alumni and/or students. These cards typically were adorned with the school's official seal, logo, or sports mascot. Some portion of the proceeds that resulted from the card's use was paid back to the university, in addition to a contract fee.

[10] Sullivan, Warren, and Westbrook, p. 24.

[11] Robert D. Manning, *Credit Card Nation: The Consequences of America's Addiction to Credit* (New York: Basic Books, 2000), p. 164.

[12] Manning, p. 165.

[13] Student Monitor LLC, "Financial Services Study" (CD-ROM), Ridgewood, NJ, 2001, p. 64.

[14] Student Monitor LLC, p. 66.

Subprime Credit Cards

Subprime credit cards offered an individual with a poor credit history the chance to obtain a major credit card with an unsecured credit line. Specific features of these cards varied widely from issuer to issuer. Annual interest rates were as low as 15 percent, but could rise to 30 percent or more. Rates between 22 and 25 percent were typical. Terms for these cards usually included penalty interest rates. These became active if a customer displayed a pattern of late payments. For example, the interest rate on one subprime MasterCard increased from 21.5 to 29.5 percent if the cardholder paid late twice in any six-month period.

Initial credit lines were modest, often starting at $500. Subprime issuers usually rewarded a record of prompt payment by increasing the cardholder's credit line. Some cards required an annual fee, which could vary from $25 to $100. Issuers could charge a fee for processing card applications. Subprime cards also could offer customer "perks" similar to those associated with standard cards—for example, rebate programs, frequent flyer miles, online account access, or automatic bill payment.

Some card issuers catered exclusively or primarily to the subprime segment (e.g., Metris). Other major card issuers offered products specifically tailored to this niche. The importance of the subprime credit card market was indicated by the fact that both Capital One and Providian, two of the top ten card issuers in the United States, were very active within the segment. Industry analysts expected issuers to market more aggressively to subprime customers as credit assessment tools become increasingly sophisticated.[15] Others noted that while this segment has proved "remarkably profitable," its resilience had yet to be tested by a sustained recession.[16]

Secured Credit Cards

A secured card was a major credit card that was tied to a collateral account. The cardholder placed money into the account, which functioned as a security deposit on card purchases. The card's initial credit line reflected the amount on deposit. If the cardholder failed to pay, the issuer would deduct the outstanding balance (plus interest and fees) from the collateral account. Merchants typically could not distinguish secured cards from standard credit cards.

As a history of reliable repayment was established, the issuer could extend credit in a multiple of the security deposit. For example, a $600 deposit could be doubled or tripled to produce a credit line of $1,200 or $1,800. Eventually, the cardholder could be "mainstreamed" to a regular card. This usually required a minimum of one year of prompt payments.

Secured cards provided an avenue for borrowers with impaired credit histories to rebuild their records. New-to-credit customers also could use them to establish a credit history. Secured cards typically required an annual fee and featured an interest rate between 19 and 26 percent.[17] Some secured card issuers also charged special application and processing fees. The borrower's security deposit usually earned interest, although the rate varied from issuer to issuer. A 1997 market study estimated the number of potential consumers for this product at 25 million.[18]

Secured card issuers did not necessarily provide information to credit bureaus. Thus, individuals who wanted to use a secured card to improve their credit record needed to determine an issuer's reporting practices.

Subprime Installment Loans and Mortgages

Subprime debt has been offered through such instruments as auto loans, finance contracts for furniture or major appliance purchases, personal credit lines, mortgages (original purchase or refinancing), and home equity loans or credit lines. A study published in 1999 by the Federal Reserve Bank of Minneapolis indicated the rapid rate at which the markets for these instruments were growing. For example, estimates suggested that between 1988 and 1998 the market for subprime auto loans grew from $15 billion to $65 billion. The total subprime mortgage market expanded by nearly 50 percent between 1995

[15] Lucy Lazarony, "People with So-so Credit Can Find More Choices and Better Card Deals," *Bankrate*, June 5, 2000 (www.bankrate.com/brm/news/cc/20000605.asp?), p. 3 of 6.

[16] Sullivan, Warren, and Westbrook, p. 24.

[17] Manning, p. 346, n. 37.

[18] "Juiced-Up Cards," *CardTrak Online*, September 1997 (www.cardweb.com/cardtrak/pastissues/ctsept97.html), p. 1 of 4.

and 1998, from $290 billion to $415 billion.[19] An *Economic Letter* issued in 2001 by the Federal Reserve Bank of San Francisco reported that subprime mortgage originations grew from 5 percent of all mortgage originations in 1994 to over 13 percent by 2000, totaling $140 billion.[20]

The Minneapolis Reserve study noted the risks taken by some subprime lenders, as evidenced by "unfavorable delinquency trends," a rash of business failures within the subprime mortgage industry in 1998–1999, and the bankruptcy of at least 11 subprime auto lenders.[21] Federally insured banks were becoming more active in these markets, either through in-house efforts or the acquisition of subprime specialists.[22] A highly visible example of the latter strategy was Citigroup's purchase in 2000 of Associates First Capital, a leading subprime lender.

Like subprime credit cards, subprime loans and mortgages were characterized by relatively higher rates of interest and/or fees. Some subprime auto lenders, for example, charged their riskiest customers annual percentage rates of 20 percent or more.[23] During 1998–2001, the subprime mortgage rate exceeded the prime mortgage rate by an average of 3.7 percentage points.[24]

Most subprime mortgage loans were home equity loans.[25] These loans were a point of conflict between the subprime industry and consumer advocates. The latter contended that fees associated with many subprime home equity loans—for example, application fees and loan origination fees—constituted as much as 10–20 percent of a loan's value, as opposed to 3–5 percent for conventional loans. These fees allegedly "stripped" homeowners of the equity they had built in their homes.[26] Advocates also claimed that other predatory practices were regularly associated with subprime home loans: deceptive marketing, incomplete disclosure, fraud, excessive penalty fees, and so on. In recent years, cities, states, and federal regulators have enacted restrictions upon subprime mortgage lenders and brought their loans under greater scrutiny.[27] The hope has been that such actions would help weed out predatory lenders from the subprime industry. Industry representatives have expressed concern that the new regulations would effectively reduce the availability of credit for consumers whose borrowing opportunities were already limited.

Payday Loans

A "payday loan" enabled a customer to borrow $100–$400 against his or her next paycheck. For example, a borrower might need $200 on April 1, two weeks prior to her next payday. She would present the payday lender a check for $240, payable on April 15. The check total represented the principal borrowed, plus a "service premium" (here, $40). In return, the borrower received the required cash ($200) when she needed it.

Critics of the payday loan industry objected to their "usurious" lending rates. In this illustration, for example, the effective annual interest rate was 520 percent. A survey by the Consumer Federation of America found that the effective annual rates on payday loans ranged from 390 to 871 percent.[28] Defenders countered that the short-term nature of these loans made such calculations misleading, the equivalent of comparing the cost of a per-mile cross-country cab ride with a plane fare. They also noted that the service fee was generally cheaper than the charge for a bounced check or a late payment.[29]

Another charge leveled against payday lenders was that their loans were designed to keep

[19] Feldman and Schmidt, p. 2 of 5.

[20] Elizabeth Laderman, "Subprime Mortgage Lending and the Capital Markets," *Federal Reserve Bank of San Francisco Economic Letter* 2001-38, December 28, 2001 (www.frbsf.org/publications/economics/letter/2001/el2001-38.html), p. 1 of 3.

[21] Feldman and Schmidt, p. 3 of 5.

[22] Feldman and Schmidt, p. 2 of 5.

[23] Feldman and Schmidt, p. 1 of 5.

[24] Laderman, p. 2 of 3.

[25] Laderman, p. 1 of 3.

[26] Coalition for Responsible Lending, "Executive Summary: The Case against Predatory Lending", originally found at: (www.responsiblelending.org/), p. 2 of 5.

[27] Holden Lewis, "Fed Tightens Rules on Subprime Lending," *Bankrate*, December 20, 2001 (www.bankrate.com/brm/new/mtg/20011220a.asp), p. 1 of 5.

[28] Public Interest Research Group and Consumer Federation of America, *Show Me the Money! A Survey of Payday Lenders and Review of Payday Lender Legislation Lobbying in State Legislatures* (Washington, DC: PIRG, 2000, p. 1.

[29] Ramesh Ponnura and John J. Miller, "Payday Mayday," *National Review Online*, June 6, 2000 (www.nationalreview.com/daily/nrprint060600.html).

consumers in perpetual debt. A 1999 study of 47 licensed payday lenders by the Indiana Department of Financial Institutions found that the average customer took out 10 loans per year, and 77 percent were rollovers of previous loans.[30] However, a study published in 2001 by Georgetown University's Credit Research Center found that payday borrowers typically took only one to four loans annually, and about half the borrowers rolled over previous loans, usually for less than three months.[31]

The payday loan industry grew rapidly during the 1990s, expanding from approximately 300 outlets to over 10,000 by the end of the decade.[32] They included national chains, established check cashing locations, convenience stores, gas stations, and pawn shops. Payday loans also were available on the Internet or through faxed offers.[33] Projections made in 1999 suggested that payday lending would be a $6 billion industry by 2003.[34]

Rent to Own

Rent-to-own dealers provided immediate access to household goods (furniture, electronics, and appliances) for a relatively low weekly or monthly payment. Typically, they did not require a down payment or credit check. Consumers entered into a self-renewing weekly or monthly lease. The lease included the option to purchase the merchandise by (1) continuing to pay rent for some time period (usually 12 to 24 months) or (2) early payment of some specified portion of the remaining, unpaid lease. The offered terms were attractive to consumers who could not obtain credit, afford a cash purchase, and were unable or unwilling to wait until they could save the funds necessary to buy an item outright. Rent-to-own agreements also offered flexibility. Merchandise could be returned at any time without obligation for future payments or any negative impact on the consumer's credit rating.

[30] Cited in PIRG/CFA, p. 8.

[31] "New Data on Payday Advance Lenders," *AFSA Spotlight on Financial Services*, July 2001 (www.spotlightonfinance.com/issues/July01/Stories/story11.htm), p. 2 of 3.

[32] Manning, p. 205.

[33] PIRG/CFA, p. 8.

[34] PIRG/CFA, p. 8.

An industry association estimated that 7,500 rent-to-own stores served nearly 3 million customers and took in $4.4 billion in revenues during 1998. However, an April 2000 Federal Trade Commission report identified a number of concerns about rent-to-own practices:[35]

- Total charges for merchandise, which could be 200–300 percent of retail prices or more.
- Mistreatment of customers during overdue payment collections.
- The repossession of merchandise after customers have paid substantial amounts toward purchasing them.
- The provision of inadequate information about the terms and conditions of leasing agreements and purchase options.
- Inadequate disclosure of whether merchandise was new or used.

Conclusion

Over the past decade, nonstandard lending has emerged as a prominent feature within the landscape of the American economy. By tailoring their pricing and underwriting practices to higher-risk borrowers, nonstandard lenders have provided these customers with funds they otherwise would not have had access to and the opportunity to build a sound credit history that might eventually have helped them achieve standard or prime status. Although the ethical analysis of nonstandard lending programs could be a complex affair, two general considerations were integral to such an evaluation: (1) the specific *terms* attached to the credit by the lender and (2) the *context* within which these terms were offered—for example, the transparency of the transaction, the consumer's level of financial fluency, the overall fit of the proffered credit with the consumer's needs, and the consumer's prima facia responsibility to honor terms he or she had accepted.

[35] James M. Lacko, Signe-Mary McKernan, and Manoj Hastak, "Survey of Rent-to-Own Customers (Federal Trade Commission Bureau of Economics Staff Report, Executive Summary)," (http://www.ftc.gov/reports/renttoown/rtosummary.htm) 3 of 6.

Environmental Pressures: *The Pollution Problem*

A prominent politician commented in 1970 that "ecology has become the political substitute for the word 'mother.'"[1] Since the publication of Rachel Carson's *Silent Spring* in 1962, ecology had become a political issue of increasing salience. By 1970, environmental protection had carved out a niche in the federal bureaucracy with 26 quasi-government bodies, 14 interagency committees, and 90 separate federal programs dealing with the environment. Federal spending on maintaining or improving the quality of the environment had risen from less than $5 million in the mid-fifties to several hundred million dollars by 1970.

More significant than federal spending were the new regulations and standards legislated for industry. It had been estimated that business would have to spend approximately $22 billion to meet the air and water pollution standards in effect as of January 1, 1973.[2] Industries which would have to spend the most were:

Total Investment Required	
Electric utilities	$ 3.9 billion
Petroleum	2.7 billion
Chemicals	2.3 billion
Iron and steel	1.7 billion
All manufacturing	16.1 billion
All business	22.3 billion

This case focuses on the effects of government pollution regulations and their enforcement on one alleged industrial polluter, Reserve Mining Company. This company's situation was chosen because of the importance of the issues to the parties involved and the accessibility of relevant information. It is not intended to illustrate "right" or "wrong," "wise" or "unwise" actions by any of the parties involved. That is for the reader to consider, bearing in mind that the information herein was drawn from a variety of published material as well as almost 20,000 pages of public court records. A great deal of material was of necessity omitted, and this case represents the casewriter's attempt to present fairly, in a highly condensed form, some of the major issues involved in a long and complex controversy.

Because the issues were still in litigation at the time of the writing of the case, neither the plaintiffs nor the defendants were given the opportunity to modify the selection of material presented herein, all of which was drawn from publicly available sources.

[1] Jesse Unruh as quoted in *Newsweek*, January 26, 1970, p. 31.

[2] *Business Week*, May 19, 1973, p. 78.

Reserve Mining Company

The Situation in April 1974

On April 20, 1974, Judge Miles Lord of the Federal District Court in Minneapolis handed down a decision ordering the Reserve Mining Company to halt the discharge of taconite tailings (or wastes) into Lake Superior. The company's plant, the largest in the world, was ordered to close down for an indefinite period of time.

This order climaxed the biggest pollution case ever, "The Classic Pollution Case," according to *Time* magazine. The trial had lasted 8½ months, and had generated almost 20,000 pages of testimony and more than 800 exhibits. The stakes involved dwarfed all previous environmental cases. The Reserve plant produced about 10,000,000 tons of iron ore annually (15% of total United States ore production), valued at close to $150 million. It supplied between half and three-quarters of the ore needs of its parent companies, Republic and Armco Steel, which were two of the country's five largest steel companies. Three thousand jobs were directly at stake, and an estimated 8,000 more were indirectly involved. It was alleged that Reserve's daily discharge of 67,000 tons of taconite tailings threatened the ecological balance of the world's largest freshwater body, and in addition created a significant health hazard to the communities which drew their drinking water from the lake.

Two days after Judge Lord's decision, an Appeals Court granted a 70-day stay on the order. The plant was allowed to reopen, but Reserve and its parent firms were given 25 days in which to present plans for abatement of the discharges into the lake.

Reserve's Early History

Reserve Mining Company was organized on March 24, 1939, with ownership divided among Armco Steel, Wheeling Steel, Montreal Mining Co., and Cleveland Cliffs Iron Co. Later that year, the company obtained leases on land near Babbitt, Minnesota, in the Mesabi Range. The land contained a deposit of magnetic taconite 9 miles long, an average of 2,800 feet wide, and as thick as 175 feet, with an estimated two billion tons of ore.

Although about 95% of the Mesabi Range iron formation was taconite, it was not commercially mined until the 1950s. High-grade ores (up to 70% iron oxides compared with 30% or less for taconite), were more economical to mine, as they could be shipped directly to steel mills without processing.

The Babbitt property was considered a long-term investment, to be mined if and when taconite became competitive with direct shipment ores. Steel production expanded greatly during World War II, and by the late forties the high-grade ores in the Mesabi Range were largely gone. The economy of northern Minnesota declined sharply, unemployment soared, and the Mesabi Range appeared to be becoming another Appalachia.

In 1942, however, Reserve personnel and Dr. E. W. Davis, Director of the Mines Experiment Station at the University of Minnesota, had begun research into processes for transforming taconite into usable form. By 1947 their work had yielded results: a method of refining and concentrating taconite into small pellets of iron ore, usable as blast furnace feed. The decision was made to build a beneficiation[3] plant to process taconite mined at Babbitt. The estimated reserves were enough to yield up to 650 million tons of ore, sufficient to keep the plant in operation for 75 years. Since the beneficiation process required large amounts of water, a plant site was selected at Silver Bay, on the north shore of Lake Superior.

In 1950 Republic Steel purchased 42½% ownership of Reserve, and the following year, Armco and Republic acquired the remaining interest, bringing their shares up to 50% each.

In late 1955, five years after construction began, the Reserve Mining Company plant at Silver Bay was completed, and by the middle of 1956, a million tons of iron ore had been produced.

The new plant played a key role in revitalizing the economy of northeastern Minnesota. Congressman John Blatnik, who represented the area, said:

> Reserve Mining was not just another industry in Silver Bay, Minnesota. It was the forerunner of a dramatic revolution in the entire economy of northeastern Minnesota and a pacesetter for the iron ore industry. Reserve Mining Company initiated the taconite industry with an investment that eventually totalled $350 million.[4]

By 1972, total investment in taconite plants and facilities in the Mesabi Range had amounted to well over a billion dollars.

The Silver Bay plant was hailed as a technological breakthrough of major importance to the American economy. Estimates of future sources of iron ore showed taconite filling the gap caused by depletion of available direct shipping iron ore. *Engineering and Mining Journal,* in a 1956 article, commented:

> The Reserve taconite project is one of the most impressive in mining history, not only because of its size, but also because of the numerous technical headaches involved in large-scale mining, concentrating, and pelletizing concentrates from one of the hardest, toughest, abrasive ores known to man.[5]

[3] The process of extracting usable ore from taconite.

[4] *National Journal Reports,* March 2, 1974, p. 310.

[5] *Engineering and Mining Journal,* December 1956, p. 75.

The Reserve plant employed the world's largest crusher and the world's strongest conveyor belt. It required construction of a 47-mile railroad (to haul the ore from Babbitt to Silver Bay) with specially constructed railroad cars, which allowed rotation of 180 degrees without uncoupling, to facilitate unloading, and included numerous other innovations in material handling and processing.

Processing Taconite

The process used by Reserve was essentially the same as that developed by Dr. Davis in the forties. First, at the mine in Babbitt, rocks and earth were stripped away to expose the taconite. Jet piercers, invented for this purpose, used a 4,250°F flame to drill 40-foot-deep holes in the hard rock. Explosives were loaded into the holes and detonated to break the taconite into pieces. The rocks were hauled by truck to crushing plants where they were reduced to pieces 4 inches or less in diameter, and then loaded on rail cars to be carried the 47 miles to Silver Bay.

At Silver Bay another crushing plant further reduced the taconite to less than ¾-inch size. The taconite was then conveyed to the concentrator plant, where beneficiation or separation of the mineral was performed in three stages of grinding and five steps of separation. In this process, the taconite was reduced to a powder finer than flour. Large magnets were used to separate particles rich in iron oxide from those that were lean or barren. The latter were called "tailings." Hydraulic separation, a process in which heavier iron-rich particles were permitted to sink in a pool of water while lighter, low-iron-content particles overflowed as tailings, was also employed. The grinding and separation steps were performed with the solid material suspended in water. Finally, the tailings from each step of separation were joined together and transported down a system of troughs and discharged into Lake Superior. When the discharge entered the lake, it was a slurry (mixture of water and suspended solids) of approximately 1.5% solids. In the lake, the slurry formed a "heavy density current" (the solid material suspended in water made it heavier than the surrounding water) which flowed to the bottom of the lake. Over the years, the coarser tailings discharged from the troughs had settled offshore and formed a delta.

The iron ore concentrate from which the tailings had been separated was conveyed to a pelletizing plant where it was rolled into ⅜-inch pellets and hardened by heating to 2,350°F. Approximately 3 tons of taconite were required to produce 1 ton of pellets.

Importance of Water

Water was vital in taconite processing. Edward Furness, the President of Reserve, explained the importance of water to the company's operations as follows:

> A substantial part of the success of Reserve's taconite operations is the availability of large quantities of water. The grinding and the following magnetic separation stages—where the magnetic iron ore is recovered from the waste sand—is done with the material suspended in water. It requires 50 tons of water to make 1 ton of finished iron ore concentrate—about 12,000 gallons! We use about 350,000 gallons of water a minute.
>
> On the subject of water use in taconite processing, let me point out one thing—water is used, but it is not lost. The separation process uses no heat; therefore, there is no evaporation except what would occur naturally. Thus, after the water is used and the tailings settle out, the water again becomes part of the existing water supply.
>
> Reserve's earliest studies showed that it wasn't possible to conduct its concentration process at Babbitt, the site of our mine. There simply was no water available in Babbitt. The only solution, engineering studies made clear, was to locate the processing plant at Silver Bay and bring the crude taconite there by rail from Babbitt.
>
> It's very expensive to haul that crude rock down to Silver Bay. We had to build a 47-mile, double-tracked railroad through muskeg and rock—the worst kind of terrain. And, since we mine 3 tons of taconite for every ton of pellets we make, two-thirds of all the material we haul is unusable.
>
> After thorough study, then, engineers agreed that the only possible site for our processing plant was on the north shore of Lake Superior at what is now Silver Bay. The site was suitable both because of the existence of nearby islands to which breakwaters could be built forming a harbor and, directly offshore from the plant, there is a very deep area of Lake Superior.

> This deep area—a great depression extending for many miles parallel to the shore—is 600 to 900 feet deep. Its proportions are immense; up to 8 miles wide, 59 miles long, big enough to hold our entire Babbitt ore body without raising the bottom more than a few feet. It is here our tailings settle. From a conservation standpoint, Reserve's use of Lake Superior is sound. There is no waste water and no injury to water. Reserve's method of disposal of the sand left over from processing taconite incorporates harmless, permanent deep-water deposition of an inert material—tailings.[6]

Permits for the Plant

Certain federal and state permits were required to either withdraw water from or discharge into a public body of water. In 1947 Reserve applied to the Minnesota Department of Conservation and the Water Pollution Control Commission for permits to use Lake Superior water and discharge taconite tailings into the lake. Hearings were held, and in December 1947, Reserve received the desired permits, subject to certain conditions. In 1956 the permit was amended, increasing allowable water usage from 130,000 gallons per minute (GPM) to 260,000 GPM. In 1960, it was further increased to 502,000 GPM.

In 1947 Reserve also applied to the Army Corps of Engineers for a permit. They routinely issued thousands of permits a year, applying the sole criterion of whether the discharge would obstruct navigation. This permit was granted and periodically revised and renewed until 1960, when Reserve was given an indefinite extension.

The Corps of Engineers permit became a problem to Reserve in 1966, however, when President Johnson issued an executive order providing that the Secretary of the Interior give assistance to other departments in carrying out their responsibilities under the Federal Water Pollution Control Act. The next year, this policy became operational as the regulations of the Corps were altered so that in granting permits consideration would be given to the "effects of permitted activities on the public interest, including effects upon water quality, recreation, fish and wildlife, pollution, our natural resources, as well as effects on navigation."[7] Indefinitely extended permits such as Reserve's were to be periodically reexamined, applying the new criteria.

Stoddard Report

Thus in November 1967, revalidation proceedings were begun for Reserve's permit and Charles Stoddard, the Interior Department's Regional Coordinator, was assigned the task of compiling and consolidating the various reports which could pertain to Reserve's impact on the environment. Studies and reports from the Bureau of Commercial Fisheries, the Bureau of Mines, the Bureau of Sport Fisheries and Wildlife, the Federal Water Pollution Control Administration, the Minnesota Department of Conservation, the Minnesota Pollution Control Agency (PCA), and the Reserve Mining Company were among those considered.

In December 1968, after about a year of preparation, the Stoddard Report was completed but not officially released. Its conclusions [some of which are included in Appendix A] and the recommendation that Reserve be required to dispose its tailings on land after three years posed a serious problem to Reserve. The report, written for Interior Department officials and the Corps of Engineers, was leaked to the press, and soon became embroiled in controversy. Reserve attacked the report, claiming that it contained serious errors and jeopardized thousands of jobs. It was alleged that pressure was applied on the Johnson Administration and that the Interior Department reacted by claiming the report was only preliminary, classifying it as "unofficial" (thus keeping it out of circulation) and rewriting the conclusions and recommendations.[8] An "official" report issued later recommended continuing surveillance of Reserve, but little action to halt the discharge.

Enforcement Conference

On January 16, 1969, Secretary of the Interior Udall called for an Enforcement Conference on the pollution of Lake Superior. Under the terms

[6] Digest of Statements presented by Reserve Mining Co. to Conference on Pollution of the Interstate Waters of the Lake Superior Basin—May 13, 14, 15, 1969, pp. 2–3.

[7] Stanley Ulrich et al., *Superior Polluter* (Duluth: Save Lake Superior Association and Northern Environmental Council, 1972), p. 30.

[8] David Zwick et al., *Water Wasteland*, Ralph Nader's Study Group report on water pollution (New York: Grossman, 1971), pp. 144–49. Ulrich, pp. 40–43.

of the Federal Water Pollution Control Act, the Secretary of the Interior could initiate enforcement proceedings if it was believed that the health and welfare of persons in one state were endangered by pollution originating in another state. The first step in this process was an Enforcement Conference, to be followed by public hearings and court action if the pollution persisted.

The first session of the Enforcement Conference began in mid-1969 and lasted for several months. It provided a forum for politicians, company officials, and environmentalists. Technical consultants for Reserve and the environmentalists gave conflicting testimony, and the final recommendation called for

> . . . further engineering and economic studies relating to possible ways and means of reducing to the maximum practicable extent the discharge of tailings to Lake Superior and . . . a report on progress to the Minnesota PCA and the conference within six months of the date of release of these recommendations.[9]

In December 1969, Reserve filed a suit against the Minnesota PCA seeking exemption from a state water pollution regulation (WPC-15) as it related to their disposition of tailings. Two months later, the state filed a countersuit to force compliance with the regulation. The effect of these suits was to force a delay in hearings scheduled to consider alleged permit violations by Reserve. The hearings, requested by the Sierra Club,[10] could have led to immediate revocation of Reserve's dumping permit.

The trial was held at the Lake County District Court, only 20 miles from Silver Bay. As in the past, contradictory evidence was presented by each side. In December 1970, the District Court found that WPC-15 was not applicable to Reserve, but Reserve was ordered to alter its method of disposition so that the tailings would be confined to a small section of the lake. The PCA appealed the District Court ruling to the State Supreme Court. In August 1972, a decision was handed down ordering Reserve to apply to the PCA for a variance from WPC-15, reestablishing the legal position which had existed three years earlier.

Meanwhile, the focus had shifted back to the Federal Government. A second session of the Enforcement Conference was convened during 1970. Most notable of its findings was that there was interstate pollution, thereby conferring jurisdiction on the conference. In April 1971, a third session was held. A Reserve proposal to pipe tailings to the bottom of the lake was rejected, and the EPA served notice on Reserve that it was in violation of established federal water quality standards. The company was given 180 days to submit an acceptable plan for tailings disposal. This laid the foundation for future court action.

"The Classic Pollution Case"

In January 1972, EPA chief Ruckelshaus asked the Justice Department to take Reserve to court to force abatement of its discharge. The government suit, filed a month later, claimed Reserve violated Minnesota water quality standards and the Refuse Act of 1899, created a public nuisance, had an invalid permit to discharge, and polluted the waters of other states.

The trial promised to be important, complex, and lengthy. Intervenors entered the case on both sides, and the final lineup pitted the Justice Department; the states of Minnesota, Wisconsin, and Michigan; the Minnesota PCA; the cities of Duluth, Minnesota, and Superior, Wisconsin; and five environmentalist groups against Reserve, Armco, Republic Steel, and 11 towns, counties, and civic associations in northeastern Minnesota. Highly technical determinations had to be made, especially regarding the taconite tailings and their ecological impact. The two sides were at odds over basic questions such as the quantity of tailings being discharged, their movement in the lake, the amount which remained suspended, and their size. The plaintiffs charged that the Reserve discharge adversely affected the lake by:

1. Increasing turbidity and reducing water clarity by 25% or more over an area of more than 600 square miles
2. Causing a "green water" phenomenon in which sections of the lake reflected a muddy green color

[9] Ulrich, p. 87.

[10] A nationwide environmental and educational organization with more than 140,000 members.

3. Assisting algae growth and accelerating a process which has severely damaged the other Great Lakes (eutrophication)
4. Being ingested by fish, altering their feeding habits, and killing trout sac fry

The most significant controversy centered on the movement of the tailings once they entered the lake. Reserve contended that the slurry which flowed off the delta in front of the plant formed a "heavy density current" which flowed down to the lake bottom, where the tailings were deposited. The environmentalists did not dispute the existence of this current, but claimed that a variety of phenomena caused a significant portion of the tailings to become suspended and dispersed over more than 2,000 square miles of the lake. To support their position, Reserve presented an inventory allegedly accounting for 99.6% of their tailings within a small area directly offshore from the plant. Environmentalists then pointed out that even if the Reserve inventory were accepted, over one million tons of tailings were still unaccounted for.

Consequences of a Shutdown

To some observers it appeared that the esthetic benefits of keeping Lake Superior pure would have to be weighed against the economic hardship which would be created by closing, or forcing on-land disposal. But Verna Mize,[11] a leading opponent of Reserve, pointed to the economic impact of the company's discharge:

> You can't put a price tag on one of the world's largest and cleanest bodies of fresh water, the one lake responsible for flushing the other already polluted Great Lakes. If you want to argue dollars, Lake Superior was conservatively estimated to be worth $1.3 trillion for pure drinking water alone. We may soon know whether that value has been reduced to zero.[12]

On the other hand, if Reserve were to shut down, it appeared the consequences would be far more tangible and immediate.

There would clearly be an economic effect on the economy of northeastern Minnesota. Reserve had 3,000 employees on its payroll. In 1973 Reserve had purchased $44,000,000 of supplies from 530 Minnesota businesses. It had been estimated that indirectly each Minnesota mining job supported about nine people; thus 27,000 people could be affected.

Reserve contributed a significant portion of the revenues for six taxing districts. A total of $6,500,000 in state and local taxes was paid in 1973. Hardest hit by the loss of revenues would be the towns of Babbitt (80% of revenues from Reserve) and Silver Bay (64%) and Lake County (57%). Babbitt and Silver Bay had issued bonds secured by revenues from Reserve, and these probably would go into default. The threat of a Reserve shutdown had already made financing difficult for Silver Bay; a recent attempted bond issue was withdrawn when there were no bidders to underwrite it.

The towns of Babbitt, Silver Bay, Ely, and Two Harbors were those most dependent on Reserve. More than 70% of the company's employees resided in these towns. Their relative dependence on Reserve is shown in Table A.

Silver Bay and Babbitt had been carved out of the wilderness and built entirely by Reserve in the early fifties. In 1974, they remained "company towns."

[11] A housewife and secretary from Potomac, Maryland (and a former Michigan resident), who had lobbied in Washington against Reserve for seven years.

[12] *National Journal Reports*, March 2, 1974, p. 312.

TABLE A Dependence on Reserve

	Number of Reserve Employees (8/73)	Estimated Population Directly Dependent on Reserve (@ 4 per Employee)	Estimated Total Population
Silver Bay	930	3,720	3,800
Babbitt	665	2,660	3,076
Ely	500	2,000	4,904
Two Harbors	249	996	4,437

Silver Bay's dependence on Reserve had been stated with obvious pride in a Chamber of Commerce brochure:

> The area's industry is Reserve Mining Company. Due to its tremendous tonnage of taconite pellets, Reserve has earned for the village the slogan "Taconite Capital of the World." To produce this tonnage, the village affords a population of 3,800 people.

In the center of town, a 7-foot figure of a taconite man stood on a pedestal of taconite ore. Most local merchants provided visitors with free sample packets of taconite ore and pellets, and the Chamber of Commerce actively distributed bumper stickers proclaiming "Silver Bay—Taconite Capital of the World." . . . Even the altar and baptismal font of the Catholic church were made of taconite. Few would disagree with the mayor, who said the loss of Reserve "would effectively terminate the village."[13]

The people who lived in Silver Bay had come in two migrations, one associated with the opening of the plant in the mid-fifties and the other with its later expansion. Their homes were built by Reserve and sold to them with little or no down payments. Their children attended one of three schools built by Reserve at a cost of over $6,000,000. The threat of a Reserve shutdown had shaken the community, however:

> The problem of their homes is the thorn that keeps awakening in the workers the dimensions of their possible fate. If the company goes, the town goes. No one believes there will be any buyers for the wood frame residences that line the streets of Silver Bay.[14]

Babbitt was haunted by a similar episode in its past. In the early twenties, the Mesabi Iron Company had attempted a pioneering venture in mining taconite. A town was constructed at Babbitt and 300 workers were employed there until 1924. Unable to compete with direct shipping ore, Mesabi abandoned the mine and the town. In 1954, when Reserve arrived, there was only one family remaining. Four miles from the abandoned town, Reserve built the new Babbitt. The houses at first were rented to employees, but had since been sold on what were believed to be excellent terms. By all accounts, Reserve had been a good benefactor, and Babbitt residents were grateful.

> They like the company. They don't think of it as patronizing; they think it's just good to its workers. When the men talk of Iron Range jobs, they say Reserve is the best employer of the bunch. The key reason is few layoffs—and perhaps more important, they like Babbitt and its environment of lakes and forest. Talk with a Babbitt resident for all of three minutes, and he'll start the pitch about Babbitt being a great place to raise kids and to hunt and fish.[15]

The effects of a Reserve shutdown would extend beyond Minnesota. There were reports that parent firms Republic and Armco could be forced to shut down some operations at least temporarily. Senior officials of the Steelworkers Union (USW) estimated that as many as 50,000 jobs could be affected. Reserve's stockpile of 3,000,000 tons of taconite would be sufficient to keep the furnaces operating for only four months. Republic obtained 55% of its ore supply from Reserve, and four of its six domestic mills relied primarily on Reserve ore. Armco would likely be hit harder, as 75% of its ore came from Reserve. Alternative sources of that magnitude were not believed to be presently available. The University of Minnesota's School of Mineral and Metallurgical Engineering, in 1970, saw the following consequences of a Reserve shutdown:

> A loss of such tonnage would have severe impact on the abilities of the steel producers (particularly Armco and Republic) to meet their demands. It would force the reopening of abandoned mines that are incapable of providing the high-grade pellet feed so essential to the economic operation of blast furnaces today. More likely the companies would attempt to purchase on the world market where the supply is already short, tending to increase prices and causing a further deterioration in our balance of payments. A compounding factor is the real and present possibility of long strikes or expropriation of foreign producing mines, causing further disruptions. The loss of some 10 million tons of Canadian production in 1969 due to strikes is a case in point.[16]

[13] *U.S.A. et al. v. Reserve Mining Co. et. al.*, U.S. District Court, District of Minnesota, Fifth Dist. Civil Action, No. 5—72, Civ. 19, Offer of Proof, pp. 12–13.

[14] *Minneapolis Star*, April 22, 1974, p. 4A.

[15] *Minneapolis Tribune*, May 5, 1974, p. 13B.

[16] *U.S.A. et al. v. Reserve Mining Co. et al.*, Defendant Reserve Mining Co.'s Opening Statement, p. 12.

The Outlook in Early 1973

In early 1973, despite the magnitude of the stakes involved, the upcoming trial appeared to some observers to be just another step in the long history of unsuccessful attempts to halt Reserve's alleged pollution. Previous suits and hearings had bogged down in contradictory and inconclusive testimony, and had resulted in weak court orders and calls for further study. The case against Reserve did not appear to warrant immediate action, and the economic consequences of a shutdown all but ruled out that path. In 1973, one environmentalist commented:

> How much more time will Reserve Mining gain to continue its dumping? Five years have gone by since Charles Stoddard organized Interior's study, and nearly four years have passed since that first Enforcement Conference in Duluth. If the Federal Court finds against the firm, there are always appeals.[17]

Another predicted that "the case could drag on for years in the courts."[18]

The Asbestos Issue

On June 15, 1973, a totally new factor was introduced into the controversy. The EPA released a report revealing that high concentrations of asbestos fibers, which were alleged to be from Reserve's discharge, were present in the drinking water of four Minnesota communities which depended on Lake Superior for their supply. Asbestos was believed to be a cancer-producing agent (carcinogen) when inhaled. Ingestion of asbestos had not been studied extensively, but it also was believed to cause cancer.

The EPA warning recommended that "while there is no conclusive evidence to show the present drinking water supply is unfit for human consumption, prudence dictates an [alternative] source of drinking water be found for young children."[19] The rationale for suggesting the alternative source for only young people was that even if the water were dangerous, the damage had already been done to those people who had drunk the contaminated water for years.

The asbestos fibers were believed to have originated in Reserve's ore body at Babbitt. It was claimed that at least 25% of the ore consisted of minerals closely related to asbestos, and an undetermined portion of those were identical to amosite asbestos,[20] that which was believed to cause cancer. It was also alleged that in processing the ore at Silver Bay, Reserve emitted asbestos fibers into the air, as well as discharging them into the lake in their tailings.

Although the EPA warning dealt only with the contamination of drinking water, it also served to focus attention on the potential hazards from emission of asbestos into the air.

Reaction to the EPA Warning

Reserve reacted immediately to the EPA warning. Mr. Edward Schmid, assistant to the president, stated:

> We know of no indications to support the charge that there is any present or future hazard to drinking water supplies due to tailings. It is unfortunate that this unfounded charge has been made public without testing its validity. . . . (There is no) more substance to this charge than there was to similar claims involving arsenic and mercury in Reserve's tailings which created mild sensations before they were disproved and abandoned.[21]

In Duluth, the largest city affected, residents were scared by the EPA warning. Bottled water sales took off. In the words of one merchant, it was "selling to beat hell and people don't care about price."[22] State and local officials, working with the EPA, attempted to locate available alternative water supplies. Thirty EPA staff members were brought in from other states to set up water monitoring operations with the PCA. Meanwhile, well water from the Superior, Wisconsin, municipal system was trucked into Duluth, bottled, and sold through food stores.

Political leaders looked to the Federal Government and Reserve to bear the costs. Within a month

[17] *Audubon magazine*, March 1973, p. 121.

[18] *Minneapolis Tribune*, June 16, 1973, p. 1A.

[19] Ibid.

[20] Most of the other ore in the Mesabi Range was believed to be free of asbestos.

[21] *Minneapolis Tribune*, June 16, 1973, p. 1A.

[22] *Minneapolis Tribune*, June 19, 1973, p. 1A.

- The Army Corps of Engineers brought in portable filtration units to test their effectiveness in removing the tiny asbestos fibers.
- Duluth received a $100,000 federal grant to purchase bottled water for low-income families.
- The mayor of Duluth proposed a city water filtration system to be paid for mainly with federal funds.
- A state senator urged that Reserve be forced either to close or to provide pure drinking water to the affected communities for at least 18 months.

In Silver Bay, where asbestos allegedly contaminated both the air and the water, there was little visible reaction. Most of the bottled water sold continued to go into car batteries and irons, as the average person dismissed the EPA warning. One woman commented, "We've lived here for 16 years. Our children are perfectly healthy. If I worried about this with all these kids, I wouldn't be here today. . . . I just don't believe there's any danger."[23] An accountant for Reserve complained that "since 1965, everybody has been gunning for us. Let's get these people off our backs. . . . They're just trying to take our jobs away."[24]

Asbestos soon became the subject of local jokes. Dr. Selikoff, the asbestos expert who had expressed strong concern for the health hazard, became "Dr. Silly Cough." Asbestos was adopted as a synonym for water, and people spoke of a Silver Bay man who died recently, and when they tried to cremate him, his body wouldn't burn. Clearly, in this town where Reserve's plant and offices were located, people felt there were more serious things to be concerned about than a little asbestos in the air and water.

The Trial

On August 1, 1973, the trial began in the Federal District Court in Minneapolis. The dominant issue had now become the potential health hazard created by Reserve's discharge. During the course of the trial evidence was taken from nearly all of the world's experts on asbestos. Judge Miles Lord, who presided, commented that "the scope and depth of the review of the literature and scientific knowledge in this area which was presented to this court [have] not been approached either in the field of science, or in law."[25] Weeks of testimony by experts representing both sides were often contradictory. Judge Lord relentlessly cross-examined the experts, and finally reached the following conclusions:

1. There probably would be a consensus of opinion that there is a level of exposure below which there is no detectable increase in asbestos-related diseases—a so-called threshold. Unfortunately, no one can state with any authority what this level of exposure is.
2. The state of the art at present is so limited, as indicated by the various studies in this case, that man's ability to quantify the amount of particles in the air and water is subject to substantial error. Hence, we are faced with a situation where too much exposure to these particles results in fatal disease, and yet nobody knows how much is too much.
3. The asbestosis and various cancers associated with asbestos exposure are generally irreversible and often fatal.
4. There is a significant burden of amphibole (asbestos) fibers from Reserve's discharge in the air of Silver Bay, a burden that is commensurate with the burden that was found in areas in which there had been a proven health hazard.
5. The evidence in this case clearly indicates that the ingestion of amphibole, or asbestos fibers, creates a hazard to human health. . . . When asbestos workers inhale asbestos, approximately 50% of what they inhale is coughed up or brought by ciliary action into the back of the throat and then travels to the stomach. Furthermore, once fibers are ingested, they have the ability to pass through membranes and find their way to various parts of the body.
6. It is virtually uncontradicted that there is an extensive latency period before asbestos-related diseases are manifested. Generally, it is not until 20 or 30 years have elapsed from the initial date of exposure to a population that there is a detectable increase in disease. The Reserve plant has been in operation for only 17 years, and it was only in 1960, after a major plant expansion, that present levels of taconite discharge were achieved. Because of these factors, it would be highly unlikely that the public health effects from the

[23] Ibid.

[24] Ibid., p. 4A.

[25] *U.S.A. et al. v. Reserve Mining Co. et al.*, Supplemental Memorandum, p. 53.

> discharge would be noticed for some years to come. . . . It should be pointed out that Duluth residents do not at this time enjoy a fortunate position with respect to the cancer experience for the entire state of Minnesota. There is at this time a statistically significant excess of rectal cancer with an increasing trend. . . . Consistent with past experience of populations exposed to asbestos, the actual health effects of Reserve's discharge on the people in Duluth will not be known for many years.[26]

In ordering the plant closed, Judge Lord concluded:

> The court has no other alternative but to order an immediate halt to the discharge which threatens the lives of thousands. In that defendants have no plan to make the necessary modifications, there is no reason to delay any further the issuance of the injunction.[27]

Alternative Methods of Disposal

During the course of the controversy over Reserve's pollution the company and its opponents had proposed numerous alternatives to reduce or eliminate the environmental damage resulting from the tailings discharge.

Reserve's Deep Pipe Plan

In 1971 Reserve had proposed extending a pipe from the Silver Bay plant to the bottom of Lake Superior. The taconite tailings would thus be discharged directly into the lower depths. It was claimed that this "deep pipe" would ensure that the tailings would fall harmlessly to the bottom. Originally, capital costs were estimated to be $14 million, with $2.4 million added to annual operating costs. By 1972, the estimates had nearly doubled to $27 million of capital costs and $4.7 million in annual operating costs, or about 3% of the value of ore shipped.

Numerous disadvantages to the "deep pipe" concept were raised. It increased operating costs but produced no improvement in plant efficiency or product quality. There was little chance that it would eliminate pressure from the environmentalists, since the tailings were still entering the lake, and future legislation could make this "solution" obsolete.

EPA Proposals

The EPA, recognizing the need for alternatives other than simply closing the plant down, commissioned independent studies of Reserve's options.

The most important of these was an International Engineering Company analysis (IECO Plan) of the costs and feasibility of constructing a new concentrator, tailings disposal pond, and related facilities at Babbitt. This alternative would involve moving beneficiating operations from Silver Bay to Babbitt, but leaving the pelletizing plant in Silver Bay. This plan was strongly endorsed by the state and by the environmentalists, who saw several advantages in this setup. The health hazard would be removed far from Lake Superior. The area had a favorable topography, dam construction materials were close by, and there was ample room for expansion of the tailings disposal pond. In addition, savings would probably be realized in transportation costs, as the tonnage hauled to Silver Bay would be reduced by two-thirds because concentrated ore rather than taconite would be carried. There was also the possibility of improvements in pellet quality which could not be achieved if tailings were pumped into the lake. By decreasing silica content of the pellets, the parent companies could recognize savings in coke costs and blast furnace lining wear. The silica reduction would increase the iron content of the pellets, resulting in further savings by increasing the amount of iron obtained from one operation of the blast furnace. Total capital costs were estimated at $188 million–$211 million.

Reserve's Palisades Plan

In April 1974 Reserve advanced a new proposal which provided for total on-land disposal in the Palisades Creek area near Silver Bay. Reserve Chairman William Verity made the following offer:

> Reserve and its shareholders are prepared to authorize commencement of engineering on April 22, 1974, and to recommend to the respective Boards of Directors the construction of facilities which would eliminate the discharge of taconite tailings to Lake Superior and place those tailings in a total on-land system in the Palisades Creek area as modified near Silver Bay. . . . The new

[26] *U.S.A. et al. v. Reserve Mining Co. et al.*, Supplemental Memorandum, pp. 53–74.

[27] *U.S.A. et al. v. Reserve Mining Co. et al.*, Memorandum and Order, p. 12.

> facilities will be so designed as to provide for some improvement in the finished pellets in an effort to make the pellets competitive and improve Reserve's posture among similar producers.
>
> The Palisades Creek total tailings plan is estimated to cost approximately $172,000,000. The expenditure of such sums would substantially reduce the rate of return on the Reserve investment. This additional large investment would not result in any economic benefit to the shareholders, even taking into consideration product improvement. Integral parts of this offer are the following would-be conditions:
>
> 1. Continued operation during construction is required so as to be in a position to generate the coarse tailings essential for dam building.
> 2. Appropriate permits to be issued by all affected regulatory agencies ensuring that the operation of Reserve will be permitted to continue for the anticipated mine life.
> 3. A satisfactory court resolution of the alleged health hazard issues, thus permitting a reasonable operating lifetime for the properties and helping make possible the financing of the project.
> 4. Inasmuch as the existing facilities were constructed and operated in accordance with state and federal permits, it is believed that any change now required constitutes a violation of Reserve's rights to so operate for the life of the permits. Under these circumstances, we believe it appropriate that governmental financial assistance be extended as may be legally available, including assistance with industrial revenue bonds and a satisfactory mechanism be established for assistance in pledges for repayment of bonds. Consistent with the foregoing, it is the intent that the new facilities would be financed and paid for by Reserve with, however, assistance in bonding requirements so as to secure a lower interest rate on the substantial indebtedness.[28]

Reaction to Palisades Plan

The state rejected Verity's offer, and continued to reject modifications of the Palisades concept, for the following reasons:

1. The site of the tailings basin was only a few miles from Lake Superior. It was possible that asbestos particles could flow from there into the lake.
2. The dams would be visible from North Shore scenic and recreational areas. One dam would be 7,000 feet long and 450 feet high or more than twice as long as, and only 100 feet lower than, the Grand Coulee Dam.
3. The dam, constructed from earthen materials, would present a potential hazard to the people and area below it.
4. Any plan must provide for use of asbestos-free ore during the switch-over to land disposal.

Judge Lord also found the plan unacceptable. He stated:

> The chief executive officers of both Armco and Republic have proposed a plan for an on-land disposal site in the Palisades Creek area adjacent to the Silver Bay plant. Although this particular plan was in existence for several years, it was not brought forward until the latest stages of this proceeding. The plan, which has been rejected by the plaintiffs because it is not environmentally sound, is totally unacceptable to the court because of the conditions imposed with it. In the first place implementation of the proposal fails to effectively deal with the problem caused by the discharge of amphibole fibers into the air. Secondly, the plan contemplates that the discharge into the water will continue for five more years. In light of the very real threat to public health caused by the existing discharge, this time period for abatement is totally unacceptable. Third, it is suggested that the court order all appropriate state and federal agencies to grant permits that would immunize Reserve's operations from ever complying with future environmental regulations as they might be promulgated. The court seriously doubts that it has the power for such an order and states flatly that if it had the power it would not grant such an order. Reserve in this case has argued that certain state and federal permits granted years ago sanction their noncompliance with existing regulations and should preclude the court from abating the discharge of human carcinogens into the air and water. Such a claim is preposterous and the court will have no part in perpetuating such claims. The proposal is further conditioned on obtaining compensation from the federal and state governments. The court has previously discussed the lack of necessity for such a subsidy and finds the suggestion absurd. Finally, the proposal was conditioned upon favorable findings by the court as to the public

[28] *U.S.A. et al. v. Reserve Mining Co. et al.*, Transcript, pp. 19,075–19,078.

> health issues. The court finds this condition to be shocking and unbecoming in a court of law. To suggest that this or any other court would make a finding of fact without regard to the weight of the evidence is to ask that judge to violate the oath of his office and to disregard the responsibility that he has not only to the people but also to himself.
>
> Defendants have the economic and engineering capability to carry out an on-land disposal system that satisfies the health and environmental considerations raised. For reasons unknown to this court, they have chosen not to implement such a plan.[29]

Reserve Strategy

Both the plaintiffs and the court were interested in Reserve's strategy for dealing with the pollution issue. Midway through the trial, the court subpoenaed internal company documents. Boxes of reports and correspondence, including confidential memoranda and handwritten notes, were made available to the judge and plaintiffs. Some of these entered into the public domain by being quoted or offered as exhibits in the trial. The documents available to the public and accounts by various observers can be used to sketch a tentative picture of Reserve's responses at various times. Because the issues were still in litigation as of the writing of the case, the casewriter did not discuss Reserve's strategy with company officials.

Political

The Stoddard Report, completed in December 1968, appeared to have posed the first serious threat to Reserve.[30] It was alleged that when company officials heard about the report and its recommendation that Reserve be forced to switch to on-land disposal within three years, their response was to contact Congressman John Blatnik, whose district included Reserve's operations.

[29] *U.S.A. et al. v. Reserve Mining Co. et al.*, Memorandum and Order, pp. 10–11.

[30] This account of the events that transpired was drawn primarily from two sources: *Superior Polluter*, a book published by two environmentalist groups, and *Water Wasteland*, written by a Ralph Nader task force. No information was available on the authors of *Superior Polluter*. David Zwick, the editor of *Water Wasteland*, was a third-year law student and graduate student in Public Policy at Harvard University. The members of the task force were mainly graduate students.

It should be noted that other Nader reports had drawn both praise and criticism and had been quite controversial.

It was claimed that Blatnik was a good friend of Reserve President Edward Furness, and that he had worked closely with company officials to obtain passage of a 1964 amendment to the Minnesota Constitution which provided for favorable tax treatment of the taconite industry. An aide to Blatnik had commented that the congressmen and Reserve people "have a real support." The report prepared by Ralph Nader's task force described their view of Reserve's actions in response to the Stoddard Report:

> It was only natural when the Stoddard Report came out on December 31, 1968, with its recommendation that Reserve's dumping permit be terminated in three years, that Ed Schmid, Assistant to the President of Reserve Mining for Public Relations, should telephone Blatnik's Washington office immediately to express his outrage at the findings. Schmid's call signaled the beginning of an all-out attempt by Reserve to quash or at least discredit Stoddard's work. . . . Another government official contacted by Reserve was Max Edwards, the Assistant Secretary of Interior for Water Research and Pollution Control . . . Edwards was leaving government to become an industrial pollution control consultant and presumably wouldn't have minded lining up a future customer—Reserve Mining.
>
> Edwards went right to work. He ordered all Interior copies of the Stoddard Report held in his office for "review" and refused to release the study or its findings to inquiring newsmen. . . . When asked by newsmen about the Stoddard study, Edwards described it as not an official document and full of inaccuracies. . . . Congressman Blatnik, who had been in touch with Assistant Secretary Edwards (for fact-finding) as well as Udall, echoed for the press what Edwards was saying about the report. The study, according to Blatnik, had no official status, was only a preliminary report . . . (and) was completely false.[31]

The Federal Enforcement Conference on the Pollution of Lake Superior became the next hurdle for Reserve. In April 1969, a month before the conference began, Harry Holiday, Executive Vice President of Armco, wrote a memorandum which appears to lay out an organizational structure to deal with Reserve's pollution problems. Seven committees were set up "to ensure proper

[31] Zwick, pp. 144–49.

coordination and decisive action in the various areas of concern regarding the Reserve tailing disposal problem." One of the seven, the Public Affairs Committee, was instructed to

> meet immediately to determine (1) the identity of those individuals in federal, state, or local governments who should be contacted, (2) the identity of those individuals who should make the contacts, and (3) the type of information that should be supplied. . . . Preparation for and carrying out of the presentation for the May 13 conference has priority in the activities of all committees, but it should be clearly understood that the tailings disposal problem will be a continuing one. Such being the case, all committees will be prepared to continue their efforts in the indefinite future.[32]

According to the Nader report, by the time the Enforcement Conference opened in May 1969, Max Edwards, the first public official to criticize the report, was out of government and on retainer as a consultant to Reserve Mining. The Nader report continued:

> The government was still walking a shaky tightrope between Congressman Blatnik and Lake Superior. The political sensitivity of the proceedings was underscored by Secretary Hickel's unusual choice for conference chairman. Assistant Secretary of Interior Carl Klein headed the gathering, the first time in 46 federal enforcement actions that FWQA's Murray Stein had not been in charge. If Klein's performance at the conference is any indication, he had been brought there for one reason: to repudiate the Stoddard Report. The Assistant Secretary stayed only one day, just long enough to run through what appeared to be a well-rehearsed routine with Congressman Blatnik.
>
> *Mr. Blatnik:* . . . I ask you for a brief comment at this point, Mr. Secretary. Do you or any of your administrators or officials under your jurisdiction to your knowledge, know of any federal report that has been suppressed?
>
> *Mr. Klein:* Congressman Blatnik, you give me a chance to lay the ghost to rest . . . the official report and the only official report of the Department of the Interior . . . was issued about a week ago. There has been no attempt at suppression by any congressman or any other federal official. There is in existence a report put out by an individual who used to be employed by the Department of the Interior shortly before he left and that is his report, despite the fact it bears the words "Department of Interior." *The Department of the Interior did not authorize it* and is not bound by the report. The only report that was put out officially by the Department of the Interior is this one put out a week ago.[33]

In October 1969, after the first session of the Enforcement Conference had been completed, Armco's manager of Air and Water Pollution Control, in a memo to Harry Holiday, laid out the action alternatives to be considered:

> With a limited amount of time to evaluate this problem, it appears there are several alternatives that must be weighed and considered. Some of these are:
>
> a. The recommendations made at the conference are not "official" until they have been approved and issued by the Secretary of the Interior.
> By vigorous political activity, primarily in Washington, D.C., it may be possible to amend or modify the "conclusions" and "recommendations."
>
> b. While I do not claim to have a detailed knowledge of the legal aspects involved, it appears to me that the federal case of "interstate pollution" is very weak. The facts presented both in May and September 1969 have not demonstrated a significant danger to the "health and welfare."
> I would assume that if we (Reserve–Armco–Republic) were to fight this issue in the courts that the "public image" would suffer somewhat from the "robber baron" concept. Nevertheless, I believe this approach must be carefully studied.
>
> c. A careful study should be made of the present processing techniques to determine if the production of "superfine tailings" can be reduced by changes in processing—even perhaps if it involves a decrease in product quality. This may be a way to satisfy, at least temporarily, the recommendations of the conference.
>
> d. The engineering committee can prepare a "broad brush"–type concept of several alternative ideas to present at the next meeting of the conference, which will probably be in

[32] *U.S.A. et al. v. Reserve Mining Co. et al.*, Exhibit, Memorandum from Harry Holiday, April 24, 1969.

[33] Zwick, pp. 144–49.

> April or May 1970. I would suggest that if this is the desired approach that we present several schemes that have been studied but without indicating that we have sufficient detailed knowledge to recommend any given scheme or that we are prepared to designate a timetable for completion. We should indicate to the conference members to realize the magnitude of the problem, the complexities involved, and the tremendous impact on the economy of the region.
>
> I suggest that we should also offer some "pilot" schemes that we believe may have merit in reducing the problem. By this technique we may be able to gain a few years' time.
>
> e. Another obvious alternative that is available to management is to close down the existing facilities, which eliminates the reported water pollution problem. If the Federal Government will assume a major part of the cost (equity) involved in this decision it may have some merit for consideration. After all, they were involved in the original hearings that granted the permits which led to the establishment of this particular process.[34]

Lobbying efforts in Washington were conducted by Reserve, Armco, and Republic in late 1971. In April, the Federal Enforcement Conference had rejected the "deep pipe" plan and federal action against Reserve appeared likely. Top officers from Armco and Republic went to Washington to sell key congressmen on the "deep pipe" plan, although it had been claimed that this plan had already been found impractical. In court testimony, Mr. William Verity, Armco President, explained:

> We felt it would be very advisable to inform various people as to the problem at Reserve Mining, and so a presentation was prepared to take this information to various people who might have an interest in the Reserve Mining situation. So that this was a joint effort by Republic and Armco to do as good a job as we could in describing the underwater system and why we felt this system of deposition was the best. . . . There [were] Senator Muskie, Senator Humphrey, various congressmen like Mr. Blatnik and others who were very interested in this problem. There [were] a great number of people which we felt were entitled to know our view on the situation. . . . They were mostly in charge of the various committees of the Senate. We did meet with Republicans. We showed this to Mr. Taft, Jennings Randolph. . . . I can't recall the whole list, but we presented this to quite a few different people.[35]

The plaintiffs and the court were also interested in the political activities and relationships of the companies and their executives with the Nixon Administration. Portions of the trial proceedings relating to this are shown in Appendix B.

During several days of intense questioning, no evidence of illegal activity emerged.

Charges of Delay

Reserve was accused of attempting to delay resolution of the pollution problems and the associated investments as long as possible. One alleged tactic was to continue to offer variations of the "deep pipe" plan after an internal Engineering Task Force had advised against it. In June 1972, this internal task force had reported:

> Information recently obtained from the Colorado School of Mines study indicates that the required pipe flow velocity and related line pressure loss and pipe wear will be far greater than assumed initially. This may make it impossible to move the tailings the distance required underwater from a delta pumping station. A second question is raised by the extreme difficulty anticipated in replacing and extending pipe under all weather conditions in the open and unprotected reaches of Lake Superior. . . . For these reasons, the Engineering Task Force does not recommend pursuing this concept any further.[36]

Although environmentalists, state officials, and the EPA had opposed the "deep pipe" concept from the start, and the Task Force had found it infeasible, Reserve repeatedly revised and resubmitted it until February 1974, when it was finally abandoned.

The value of the numerous exhibits and data supplied by Reserve was openly questioned by Judge Lord. At a point near the end of the trial,

[34] *U.S.A. et al. v. Reserve Mining Co. et al.*, State of Minnesota, Exhibit 74.

[35] *U.S.A. et al. v. Reserve Mining Co. et al.*, Transcript, pp. 18,879–18,882.

[36] *U.S.A. et al. v. Reserve Mining Co. et al.*, U.S. Exhibit 430.

he asked Reserve for cost estimates which were "not padded" and then added:

> I might suggest to you that the reason that I make this statement that I just made about padding figures, and so forth, is based on the nine months of experience in looking at Reserve's exhibits, which have, by and large, not been worth the paper they're written on. And I determine that, well, the profits are at the rate of sixty thousand dollars a day. Every time they can keep the judge looking at an exhibit all day, it's worth sixty thousand dollars, even though the exhibit is useless in its final analysis.[37]

In April 1974, as the trial was drawing to a conclusion, Judge Lord recounted Reserve's alleged tactics of delay:

> When the case was started, Mr. Sheran asked me if I could help to negotiate a settlement of this case. I started to negotiate toward a settlement of this case. And my first utterances were "Is there any plan? Can you bring any sort of skeleton plan forward which would provide for on-land disposal?"
>
> Mr. Fride (a lawyer for Reserve) said, "No, judge, that's not fair to me. You have prejudged the matter by even asking the question. We have an underwater disposal plan which we—the so-called 'deep pipe,'—we want you to consider that."
>
> All discussions—I withdrew from discussions then, waiting anxiously to hear about the underwater pipe. About six months later, the underwater pipe was brought forward. That's six months later and ten million dollars' profit later and fifty billion fibers later down the throats of the children in Duluth, after I applied every bit of judiciousness and dedication and study and patience that I could to the problems created here, I found that the six months that I had spent—not the total six months, but a good portion of it—the six months I had spent waiting to hear about "deep pipe," and the week or two that we spent hearing about it were just another presentation by Armco and Republic to delay that which I now found you then knew to be the inevitable day when that discharge would be taken out of the lake.
>
> We've now gone on about four months past that time. We had a judge named Eckman who about three years ago in a state trial, who heard all the ecology said, "This must come out of the lake. We must change the charge." They were then talking to him. They were feeding him the "deep pipe."
>
> All of this delay—now you're talking—when we talk about the time from Judge Eckman's trial forward, the total profits to Reserve are somewhere in the vicinity of fifty to sixty million dollars. The total damage to the people of Duluth I cannot equate.
>
> Now, as soon as I saw that "deep pipe" was no longer an alternative method of disposal, when I myself decided it was a joke, I then ordered you into negotiations. The negotiations have gone on.
>
> What you're arguing about is a question of some twenty or thirty million dollars. No matter what I write here, if I appeal—you appeal it, you can have your cake and eat it, too. You can have the time within which to make another twenty million dollars and pay in your profits the cost that you will here argue about.
>
> The cost to the people of Duluth I cannot calculate. I don't wish to alarm anybody. All I can say is I don't know. Dr. Brown, whom I retained as a court witness at the suggestion of Reserve, says it should come out. He can't calculate it.
>
> Now, what I want to ask you is there any prospect that you—and I know what the pressures are here and you know what they are. The court here is faced with the prospect of a stranded population, hostages of the Reserve Mining Company, with a whole economic segment standing almost in arms ready to march on the State Capitol or the Federal Government in Washington. They're doing it because Armco and Republic have seen fit to hold out for the last dollar of profit and to the last point of time.
>
> If I indicate to you that you have turnaround time, you will immediately take the indication to the Court of Appeals and say the judge found there was no health hazard. He gave us turnaround time. We want the time for the Court of Appeals to minutely examine this record of some eighteen thousand pages, several thousand exhibits, with all the briefing that goes with it, the people of Duluth for another year will have that unwelcomed addition to their diet. Your own internal documents indicate the game you have been playing with the court.[38]

[37] *U.S.A. et al. v. Reserve Mining Co. et al.*, Transcript, p. 19,387.

[38] *U.S.A. et al. v. Reserve Mining Co. et al.*, Transcript, pp. 19,069–19,072.

Appeals Court Decision

After Judge Lord's order closing the plant, Reserve immediately appealed to the U.S. Court of Appeals for a stay of the ruling. Two days later, on April 22, 1974, a 70-day stay was granted and the Reserve plant reopened. The Appeals Court, in its limited review, stated:

> We have reviewed the testimony on the health issue. . . . While not called upon at this stage to reach any final conclusion, our review suggests that this evidence does not support a finding of substantial danger and that, indeed, the testimony indicates that such a finding should not be made. . . . We believe that Judge Lord carried his analysis one step beyond the evidence. Since testimony clearly established that an assessment of the risk was made impossible by the absence of medical knowledge, Judge Lord apparently took the position that all uncertainties should be resolved in favor of health safety.[39]

The Court also instructed Reserve and the plaintiffs to attempt to reach a settlement within the 70-day period. Otherwise, the Appeals Court would review the status of the stay order based on plans, comments, and recommendations of Reserve, the plaintiffs, and Judge Lord, and decide to either continue it, or let the plant close down.

[39] *Reserve Mining Co. et al., v. U.S.A. et al.*, U.S. Court of Appeals, Eighth Circuit, No. 74-1291, pp. 9, 24

Appendix A

Stoddard Report, Excerpted Conclusions

The following [are some of the] conclusions derived from the investigations and analysis of findings of the Interior Taconite Study Group on the effects of taconite waste disposal in Lake Superior:

- Slightly less than half of the tailings waste discharged between 1956 and 1967 was deposited on the delta above the deep trough in Lake Superior; evidence indicates that some of the remainder moves downshore with lake currents.
- Turbidity is commonly three to five times greater in the area near and southwest of the plant. Turbidity values in bottom water over the tailings deposit are ten to sixty times greater than at the surface.
- Tailings suspended in the water cause "green water" for distances at least 18 miles southwest from the point of discharge.
- Tailings are dispersed on the lake bottom at least 10 miles offshore and 18 miles southwest of the plant.
- Net lake current velocities are sufficient to keep micron-size particles in suspension for long periods and carry them long distances and to carry such particles across State boundaries.
- Federal–state water quality standards for iron, lead, and copper are violated as a result of tailings discharge.
- The water quality criteria recommended by the National Technical Advisory Committee for zinc and cadmium for aquatic life production are exceeded.
- The widely accepted criteria of 0.01mg/l of phosphorus to limit algal growth is exceeded.
- Bottom fauna, especially one species important as a fish food, show progressive reduction in numbers southwest of the plant.
- In laboratory tests, tailings less than 0.45 microns stimulated additional algal growth in Lake Superior waters.
- Taconite tailings discharged from the effluent were found to be lethal to rainbow trout sac fry in a few days.

Source: An alleged copy of the original (but unofficial and unreleased) Stoddard Report provided to the casewriter by Northern Environmental Council. The above conclusions are reproduced here because of their impact at the time of their circulation. Some of the above conclusions still remain unsubstantiated and have been dropped from subsequent actions against Reserve, and thus their validity is open to question.

Appendix B

Political Activities of Companies and Executives, Selected Excerpts

Testimony indicated that William Verity had served on the National Industrial Pollution Control Commission Subcouncil on Steel and had been chairman of a region of the Ohio Republican Finance Group. Along with other Armco executives he had taken a $10,000 table at a "Victory Dinner" for the 1972 Nixon campaign.

It was also brought out that both Armco and Republic encouraged employees to make political contributions. In fact, the two companies had adopted similar plans which allowed employees to have a portion of their salary withheld and put into a trust. When the employee decided to make a political contribution, he notified the trust and a check was sent to the individual or party specified.

Mr. Verity's relationship with the Nixon Administration was also of particular interest to the plaintiffs and Judge Lord. The following exchange took place during the trial:

Q.: Did you call anyone on the telephone at the Department of Justice between September 1, 1971, and October 5, 1971?

Verity: Not to my recollection.

Q.: Did you call anyone at the Department of Justice on the telephone between October 5, 1971, and March 1, 1972?

Verity: Not to my recollection.

Q.: Did you meet with any official of the Justice Department during the period October 5, 1971, to March 1, 1972?

Verity: Not to my recollection.

Judge Lord: Now, let us stop here. We will take a recess. You have answered the last four questions not to your recollection, which are in effect nonanswers. You should, in matters as important as this, be able to have a yes or no answer. You think that over.

We will recess for ten minutes.

(Recess)

Judge Lord: You see, Mr. Verity, one of the problems that I have here is that in your work as president of the company apparently you have such a remarkable memory that it is not necessary for you to take any notes or memoranda, because none are in existence, as you say, so you must be doing your work by memory. Now, what has happened to that memory this morning?

Mr. White (defense lawyer): I am sorry, Your Honor, I am not clear on just what the question is.

Judge Lord: He doesn't remember any meetings and he has no records of them. You see, ordinarily a corporate president would get memoranda from his underlings, he would get summaries, he would get notes, he would have notes of meetings and summaries of meetings, and position papers. Now, absent the existence of those papers you must assume that in order for the corporation to stay on the black side, that the people have remarkable memories. Now, when you ask him about what happened, he doesn't remember. How does this work? If you have neither a memory nor a piece of paper, what happens to the company?

Mr. White: Your Honor, I respectfully submit that if there are memoranda relative to that, they would be in the documents of some five boxes that we have presented.

Judge Lord: Well, that may be. Let me ask a question about that. Do you keep a diary? Does your secretary keep a diary for you?

Verity: I keep an appointment book, if that is what you are referring to.

Judge Lord: All right. Is your appointment book a part of the papers that have been sent here this morning?

Verity: No, sir.

Judge Lord: Well, you may examine further.*

Mr. Verity's appointment book was finally produced and gave a picture of his relationship with administration officials. For example, between February 7, 1974, and April 23, 1974, he attended dinners for Alexander Haig and Secretary of Commerce Dent, met with Dent and attended a White House dinner for the Russian Trade Delegation.

* *U.S.A. et al. v. Reserve Mining Co. et al.*, Transcript, pp. 18, 891–93.

Mr. Verity claimed that Reserve was not discussed with members of the Committee to Re-Elect the President, although he did discuss it with Interior Secretary Morton.

> The purpose of the conversation was to tell him that it appeared that there might be a requirement to do something on land and that this would be such a financial burden to the company that we were wondering if it was possible under any legal or government grant to get help to finance whatever might be required.[†]

[†] *U.S.A. et al. v. Reserve Mining Co. et al.*, Transcript, p. 18, 902.

Ashland Oil, Inc.: *Trouble at Floreffe*

On Saturday, January 2, 1988, at 5:02 P.M., a 4-million-gallon storage tank at the Floreffe terminal outside of Pittsburgh, Pennsylvania, collapsed while being filled, releasing a 3.9-million-gallon wave of diesel fuel. As the fuel gushed, it slammed into an empty tank nearby and surged over containment dikes onto the surrounding properties, creating the first major oil pollution accident for Ashland Oil, Inc. (AOI), in its 64-year history. By nightfall, nearly three-quarters of a million gallons of oil had spilled into the Monongahela River, threatening the drinking water supply of communities in Pennsylvania, Ohio, and West Virginia, as well as the safety of nearby residents.

Over the next three days nearly 200 people participated in the clean-up, including AOI employees; the Coast Guard and its Gulf Coast emergency strike force; O. H. Materials Co. of Ohio, a professional hazardous material clean-up company hired by AOI; the Red Cross; and the Audubon Society.

On Tuesday, January 5, at 10:00 A.M., John Hall, CEO and chairman of the board of AOI, as well as other officers and executives boarded two of six corporate Cessna aircraft to address the media in Pittsburgh at a press conference scheduled for 2:00 P.M. that afternoon. Accompanying Hall were Robert Yancey, Jr., president of Ashland Petroleum Company (APC); H. M. Zachem, senior vice president, External Affairs; and J. Dan Lacy, vice president, Corporate Communications, AOI. For security reasons Charles J. Luellen, president, AOI, flew to Pittsburgh on a separate plane. With him were Richard W. Spears, senior vice president, Human Resources and Law; and metallurgist Vern Ragle. (See Exhibits 1 and 2 for organizational charts.) During the past three days the circumstances surrounding the spill had gone from bad to worse. Initial reports, which indicated no oil had entered the river, had soon proved false, and a number of discrepancies concerning the construction of the tank were making headlines in the local and national press. As Hall entered the aircraft he reflected on the events that had transpired over the last few days and thought about how he should respond to the issues that would confront him at Floreffe. The news conference would be the first time Hall had spoken publicly on the disaster, and he knew his every word would be intensely scrutinized.

Company Background

Ashland Oil, Inc., with revenues exceeding $7 billion in FY 1987, was the sixtieth largest company in the country and the nation's largest independent oil refiner. The company employed over 42,000 people worldwide and had refining capacity of 346,000 barrels of oil per day. Key oil supplies came from the Middle East and Nigeria, where Ashland Oil had a long-term production contract. To reduce its dependence on the volatile refining industry, AOI had diversified into other energy-related activities such as petroleum product transportation and marketing, chemicals, coal, engineering and highway construction services, as well as oil and gas exploration and production operations. Oil refining remained the backbone of the business, however, with Ashland Petroleum Company (APC) representing about 30% of sales in 1987. (See Exhibit 3 for sales and profit information of key business units.)

Sales of $7,189,000,000 in 1987 reflected a modest decline from sales of $7,283,000,000 in 1986. However, margins and profitability were even more volatile. A severe crude oil margin squeeze in 1987 caused APC's record-high operating income of $252 million in 1986 to drop to only $10 million. Record profits occurred in 1986 because crude oil prices declined, widening the gap between crude oil and product prices. In 1987, however, the table turned. As APC's refineries and other refineries throughout the industry built product inventories, OPEC returned to its official pricing system, increasing crude oil prices. Unable to pass through the price increases due to its high inventory levels, APC margins suffered serious erosion. In fact, Ashland's average margin on a barrel of oil dropped by $2.17.

Ashland Oil, Inc., produced a range of petroleum products which it sold primarily to resellers and consumers in the East, South, and Upper Midwest. In addition to its refining business, key business units included: SuperAmerica, a chain of more than 450 combined gasoline and convenience stores; Valvoline, the number three marketer of branded motor oil and related automotive chemicals such as coolants and rust preventatives, and an operator of 100 quick-lube outlets; Ashland Chemical, a growing division in chemical distribution and specialty chemical products; Engineering and Construction Division, whose APAC group was a leading highway contractor in the South and Southwest; as well as several other coal, oil, and gas interests.

The SuperAmerica stores and Valvoline Division represented cornerstones of AOI's strategy, which relied on key distribution channels and specialty products as well as large volume fuel production to provide earnings strength and stability. In addition to its SuperAmerica outlets, Ashland sold gasoline products to over 1,500 other company or dealer-operated outlets. As part of its terminal/distribution infrastructure, Ashland Oil operated the largest private tank barge fleet on the inland waterways and had recently expanded this system by acquiring terminal locations at Cincinnati, Ohio, and Midland, Pennsylvania. At the time of the spill, Ashland operated 32 terminals in nine states. At these terminals the various products resulting from the oil refining process—like diesel fuel—were stored in holding tanks, awaiting further distribution.

Recent Events

Ashland Oil grew from a relatively small $448 million company in 1965 to a $9.5 billion conglomerate in 1981, enabling the company to compete more effectively with major oil companies. Growth was achieved primarily through acquisitions under the "wheeling and dealing"[1] guidance of former chief executive Orin Atkins. As one former officer described him, "For a number of years, Atkins was just God around [the] company."[2] However, some executives felt that Atkins' aggressive acquisition strategy and loose deal-making style strained other corporate resources. As a result, some business units were sold when new management took power in the early 1980s.

Ashland's rapid growth and diversification were not without a few adverse moments in the public eye. Ashland received its first public reprimand in 1975, when the Securities and Exchange Commission (SEC) fined AOI for making $717,000 in illegal political contributions. Ashland, along with several other companies, was also cited by the Justice Department for rigging construction bids in the Southeast.

From 1979–1981, senior executives became divided over a series of questionable payments to Middle Eastern middlemen, some of whom were foreign government officials. (The Foreign Corrupt Practices Act barred U.S. firms from bribing foreign officials.) While Ashland wasn't publicly reprimanded, the eventual shake-up changed the management team at Ashland and brought in John Hall as CEO. These difficulties aside, Ashland Oil fended off a takeover bid by the Canadian-based Belzberg family in 1986. The Belzbergs were later charged with violating federal disclosure laws.

As management entered the latter part of the decade, it was optimistic over the core strengths and capabilities of the firm, feeling it was well positioned to deal with the uncertainties and instability inherent in global petroleum and financial markets. It also embarked on a large-scale technology systems program to improve the quality, safety, and efficiency of its operations and renewed its commitment to employee involvement and innovation programs.

[1] Zachary Schiller, "Ashland Just Can't Seem to Leave Its Checkered Past Behind," *BusinessWeek*, October 31, 1988, p. 122.

[2] Ibid., p. 123.

The Floreffe Spill

Saturday

Within seconds, storage tank No. 1338 ripped open after being filled to 45 feet, 10¼ inches with diesel fuel at 5:02 P.M., January 2, 1988. Immediately Ashland personnel shut off all pumps, called the National Response Center as required by the Clean Water Act, and turned off all electrical power in the terminal.

In a second call from the Floreffe terminal manager to the National Response Center, at about 7:00 P.M., the agency informed him that the U.S. Coast Guard and the U.S. Environmental Protection Agency (EPA) had also been notified of the accident. By this time, local authorities including the Floreffe fire department, Jefferson Borough police, and various hazardous materials teams had already arrived on the scene.

By late evening, the confusion, darkness, and lack of electrical power made it difficult to assess the full scope of the spill. However, fire officials at the scene eventually discovered that the spilled oil had crossed Ashland property lines onto nearby Highway 837 and surrounding wetlands, as well as flowed onto the adjoining property of Duquesne Light Company. Upon entering the utility property, the oil seeped into an open storm sewer, which then carried over 700,000 gallons of oil undetected into the Monongahela River.

Clean-up of the spill began around 9:00 P.M. when the Coast Guard and hazardous materials removal experts stretched booms, absorbent pads, and air-filled fire hoses across the river to contain and absorb the oil. Since oil is lighter than water, officials hoped to skim the oil off the river's surface. To help clean-up efforts the Coast Guard closed river traffic on the Monongahela from the spill site to the Lock and Dam No. 2 in Braddock, a few miles downstream. By 10:00 P.M. the West Pennsylvania Water Co. and the West View Water Co., the nearest water companies downstream of the spill, were notified of the accident.

Clean-up efforts were halted later Saturday night due to unusually swift river currents (moving at twice their normal speed), and subzero temperatures. To avoid any injuries the Coast Guard recalled clean-up crews from the river until daylight the next morning.

As these activities transpired, AOI management tried to assess the severity of the situation. Bob West, director of Surface Transportation and Facilities at Floreffe, walked down to the dock where oil had been pumped from barges to the storage tanks to determine if any oil had spilled into the river. Shining his flashlight onto the river to detect any sheen that would indicate oil on the surface and checking the aroma in the air, he decided no oil had reached the river. At 6:30 P.M. he communicated this information initially to his boss Bob Keifer, group vice president, Supply and Transportation for APC. However, unbeknownst to West, oil was pouring into the river at the rate of 250 gallons per minute from a storm drain on the adjacent utility property. In addition, as the oil moved downstream through the series of locks and dams it began emulsifying. By 8:30 P.M. Keifer received a second telephone call from West confirming that oil was definitely in the river. At that time Bob Yancey, Jr., Richard Thomas, then vice president and division counsel of APC, and Roger Schrum, manager of corporate media relations, at corporate headquarters in Ashland, Kentucky, were informed of the spill. At headquarters, management began forming a crisis team to fly to Floreffe first thing Sunday morning. The task force included Thomas, Schrum, Keifer, as well as an environmental engineer, a metallurgist, and the project engineer who had constructed the tank.

By 11:00 P.M. Saturday night, Ashland employees living near Pittsburgh had set up a command post at the spill site to delegate action and organize activities. But with the EPA, fire department, Coast Guard, and the Pennsylvania Department of Environmental Resources (DER) as well as other agencies trying to direct activities, the situation was more chaotic than organized.

During the night (around 1:00 A.M.) emergency personnel believed that an undisclosed amount of gasoline had leaked from a pipeline connected to a storage tank near the spill area. Unsure of the amount of gasoline spilled and concerned over the resulting risk of fire and explosion, local emergency personnel evacuated 1,200 people from communities surrounding the Floreffe terminal. The evacuation order was eventually lifted by 12 noon once authorities plugged the leak and closed the sewer drain from which the oil was leaking.

Ashland's Response

Sunday Morning

On the way to Floreffe, the crisis management team asked their pilot to fly over the Floreffe terminal facility so they could get a better view of the spill. Roger Schrum recalled that as the pilot made several passes over the facility, everyone in the plane fell deadly silent.

> We could see the spill in the river. We could see the collapsed tank. Our first impression was, "Oh, my God! This is absolutely beyond what we ever dreamed had happened." We thought maybe the tank was still upright, and had just split or something. The tank was ripped open and thrown back a hundred yards from where it had been sitting. [See Exhibit 4 for a picture of the collapsed tank.]

The AOI crisis management team was greeted by police when it arrived at the terminal gates and escorted to the volunteer fire station being used as the command center. According to Schrum:

> There were literally hundreds of emergency people all over the place. Some were sleeping; some were doing television interviews, complete bedlam. . . . I got ushered into a meeting with the head of Allegheny County's disaster emergency service. I was worried for a while. We had a lot of police around us, and I thought they were going to arrest us or something. Police were literally circling us. Finally, they let us into the terminal. We had one or two hours to understand the nature of the situation before waves of press and politicians began showing up.

About noon, U.S. Senator Arlen Specter arrived from Philadelphia with an entourage of press and cameramen to examine the spill site. Diesel fuel was in pools waist deep. Concerned about safety, Schrum offered to guide Senator Specter on a tour of the facility and discussed what had occurred. Schrum then offered to join the senator in a meeting with the press following the tour. During the half-hour tour, the senator met with AOI personnel, the EPA representative, and the Coast Guard representative. Similar situations occurred with Lt. Governor Mark Singel, who flew in by helicopter, and local Congressman Doug Walgren. Meanwhile, AOI employees continued the clean-up effort, siphoning the oil from the retention dike to prevent groundwater contamination.

Later that afternoon, the first of an ongoing series of joint news conferences took place. The news conference panel, moderated by a representative of the EPA, included representatives from AOI and all other participating agencies. These panel-like news conferences continued to be held twice daily over the next several days.

Initially, authorities felt that the residential and commercial water supplies would not be adversely affected, since the river intakes were from 16 to 20 feet below the river's surface. With the oil floating on top, it was not expected to enter the water supply system.

2:00 P.M.

When John Hall was first informed of the spill at about 9:00 Sunday morning, he knew he had a major environmental problem on his hands. However, he believed the immediate logistical problems could be controlled by on-site AOI personnel. As a result, he decided not to go to the site. Rather, Hall spent early Sunday morning in his office with Charles Luellen keeping in touch with his people at the site via speaker phone, gathering information, and authorizing expenditures to hasten clean-up activities. His immediate goal was to determine an overall company response that would minimize the spill's impact.

At Floreffe, however, the situation continued to worsen. Authorities estimated that the slick was nearly 33 miles long and moving downriver at 10 to 20 miles per hour. Emergency crews continued to place containment booms around the perimeter of the spill to control the floating oil. Vacuum trucks, pumper trucks, and skimming barges stationed offshore attempted to skim the oil off the water as the slick moved downriver. However, as the fuel oil emulsified with water, it flowed past the booms, making containment and clean-up extremely difficult.

Hall soon learned that the Western Pennsylvania Water Co., which supplied part of suburban Pittsburgh, had shut down one of its facilities whose water intake was downriver from the spill. Suddenly the problem took on a whole new dimension: water shortages. To prevent a threat to the water supply of greater Pittsburgh, Hall directed AOI to pay for a temporary pipe to be laid across the affected area to secure fresh water from the Allegheny River. (The Allegheny and Monongahela Rivers merged downriver from the terminal, forming the Ohio River. See Exhibit 5 for map.) To expedite clean-up, Hall authorized flying in the Coast Guard Strike Force on TC5A planes. Attention at Floreffe focused more sharply on working with various agencies to offset water shortages.

That evening Hall telephoned Governor Casey of Pennsylvania and Governor Moore of West Virginia to apologize for the situation and to assure them that the company was making every possible effort to improve it.

Monday Morning 6:30 A.M.

Hall arrived at his office a half hour earlier than usual. Believing the crisis management team at the terminal and other Ashland management at headquarters were controlling problems associated with the spill, Hall took advantage of his three-hour Monday morning meeting with his top executives to discuss other business issues in addition to the spill. However, by midmorning the situation had seriously escalated.

At a Monday morning news conference at the terminal, the national press began increasing its coverage and investigation of the spill. The media expanded its original story from the details of the collapsed tank and began investigating the potential water crisis and issues related to the tank construction, quality, and testing. The press began quizzing AOI representatives on such matters as the age of the tank, whether it had been properly tested before it was filled, and whether the company had received a proper permit allowing its construction.

Unable to respond immediately, Ashland representatives began investigating these issues. Sources at Floreffe indicated that Ashland had indeed followed proper procedures. At the time, the project engineer and his staff produced a document at the spill site as proof of a permit for the tank. Other crew members stated that the tank was newly constructed in 1986 and that it had been tested before it was filled.

By early afternoon, however, as the press questions continued, it became clear to the media, Ashland management, and Hall that the information AOI provided was inaccurate. One member of the press contacted the local Fire Marshal's office where a written permit would have been filed. No permit or request for a permit was on file for the tank in question. Further investigation revealed that the documentation provided by Ashland personnel was actually a statement from a different agency acknowledging that construction was underway.

Another member of the press, armed with a copy of American Petroleum Industry (API) standard 650 (the industry guideline for proper testing of oil tanks), began asking whether the tank had been properly tested by the hydrostatic (water) method specified by API 650. (Hydrostatic testing was a process that required new tanks be filled with water in order to settle their foundations and test their welds for strength.)

2:00 P.M.

As Hall dug deeper into the situation discrepancies became greater. He found that the tank had not been hydrostatically tested as directed by API 650, but was tested by an alternative method. Oil was sprayed on the welds inside the tank and then vacuum suction was applied from the outside to determine if any oil could be pulled through possible leaks in the welds. Additionally, the tank had been filled with only three feet of water to settle the foundation. Apparently, this alternative testing method, while specified by API 650, was intended for desolate locations where water was scarce.

As to the age of the tank, Hall learned that it was indeed newly constructed, but that it had been rebuilt from 40-year-old steel, which was moved from a tank at the Cleveland terminal. Reconstructing tanks from used steel was not uncommon within the industry, since steel did not deteriorate with age, but to Hall this had the ring of a bad decision.

As Hall forced a deeper investigation into the issues the press was probing, he continued to uncover "bad facts." Apparently, employees closely involved with construction of the collapsed tank had wrongly communicated to management that AOI had received a construction permit for the tank. What became clear was that while an application for a permit had been made, construction started based on verbal communication only. Furthermore, the permit application did not mention that the tank would be constructed of used steel.

Meanwhile, 15,000 residents of Pittsburgh were without water and authorities asked the remainder of the city to ration water supplies. That evening, Hall watched TV network news anchors describe to the nation the effects of Ashland's oil spill.

The print press also continued to push the tank construction issue. News stories reported discrepancies between what AOI was claiming as fact and what other sources were claiming as fact. For example:

> Ashland spokesmen, in discussing the accident, made no mention of the tank's age until asked by *The Pittsburgh Press*. . . . "The tank's supposed to be brand new. That's what we were told . . . [on] Sunday," [claimed Jacobs, Allegheny County Fire Marshal, in a live interview]. . . . Jacobs [added that] the age of the tank was likely to become a factor in a joint local, state, and federal investigation into what caused the tank to burst Saturday night.[3]

As the climate intensified, the growing sentiment among Ashland's crisis management team was that Hall needed to come to Floreffe.

Later that night Hall himself began thinking he should go to the site to survey the situation, see how things were going, and be visible there.

> By this time we had part of the city of Pittsburgh with no water. We've got everybody downriver wondering whether they will have water or not. We don't know if it will cause the water problems for Ashland, Kentucky, next week. We have the press all over us, we don't have a permit for the tank. It's old steel. What's the long-term environmental impact going to be? Who's going to pay for all this? What's the financial impact on the company going to be? All of this is brewing.

Repercussions from the financial community also concerned Hall. Monday morning, AOI stock fell one point to 57¾ "amid nervous speculation about Ashland's financial liability resulting from . . . [the] massive oil spill."[4] News sources quoted William Hyler of Oppenheimer and Co. as saying, "Whenever you hear about a spill, investors get a little scared."[5] To protect against speculators taking advantage of the adverse circumstances and buying undervalued AOI stock, management initiated an immediate buy-back strategy through an existing board resolution.

To get an outside impression of the situation, that night Hall telephoned a close personal friend, a fellow CEO who lived in Pittsburgh. After asking him what he was hearing about the accident, Hall's friend replied, "It's pretty damn bad. . . . Ashland is not getting its story through." That conversation convinced Hall to go to Pittsburgh.

Candor vs. Liability

Monday Evening—Pittsburgh

Members of the crisis management team met with AOI's outside legal counsel in Pittsburgh. They knew that legal action would result from the spill, but tensions heightened amid growing concern that communicating inaccurate information—although unknowingly—could have legal implications as well. To minimize future litigation, AOI lawyers advised caution and prudence in responses to future questions by the press. They advised Ashland to respond to inquiries by replying that the company was trying to investigate the matter as quickly as possible and that the firm would cooperate with all authorities.

Tuesday Morning—Ashland

Hall announced he was going to make a public statement at the accident site. Dan Lacy initially made arrangements to hold the news conference at 11:00 A.M. at the Pittsburgh press club. However, Lacy later learned that Governor Casey planned to give his assessment of the accident in another news conference in downtown Pittsburgh at noon. Knowing that competing news conferences would not work in AOI's favor, Lacy postponed the news conference until 2:00 P.M.

Drafting the company's statement became the next challenge. Many people contributed

[3] Dennis B. Roddy "Failed Storage Tank Was Used in Ohio," *The Pittsburgh Press*, January 4, 1988.

[4] Reuters News Service, January 4, 1988.

[5] Ibid.

ideas and concerns for the statement including Hall, Lacy, Luellen, Yancey, and Spears. As Lacy related:

> That statement was very important on a lot of different levels. Obviously there were legal ramifications but additionally we knew that this was the first time the Boss had spoken directly. So what he said was critical. The tone was critical and we felt the statement would position all future actions for the company. We also wanted it to come across as factual as possible. We knew it would be the basis for a lot of responses to press inquiries during the next few days. So it was important from a communications point of view as well.

When Spears learned from Luellen that the tank had been built without a written permit, he knew that whether or not it turned out to be a violation of law, the press and the public would interpret it as such. As a result, Spears believed Hall needed to address the issue. On the other hand, Spears was keenly aware that an openly admissive statement by Hall could have far-reaching legal implications.

Paramount on Spears' mind was the risk of jeopardizing the attorney–client privilege. The privilege protected clients, and of course lawyers, from revealing conversations, documents or other forms of communication from open courtroom proceedings in both civil and criminal cases. Trial and practice lawyers zealously guarded the privilege. Once an issue, which might be privileged, was revealed, every matter associated with it was open to inquiry. If Hall, as CEO and spokesman for the company, publicly admitted any wrongdoing, including whether AOI had a permit, he could open the issue to further public scrutiny and possibly risk the privilege. The client privilege in this situation applied to AOI as a corporation as well as to individuals in the company.

Spears was also aware of other issues that might hover over the company. Class action lawsuits were likely, as well as possible criminal exposure. The increasingly nasty situation regarding the lack of a permit and reconstruction of the tank out of 40-year-old steel could also leave individuals open to criminal indictment. Ashland's legal staff was deeply concerned that whatever was said in the press conference would have legal—if not criminal—repercussions.

The Trip to Pittsburgh

Tuesday 10:00

After spending the morning discussing the latest developments with staff, Hall drafted a public statement for the afternoon news conference. But, from the time Hall wrote the draft until he addressed the media, the statement was in perpetual change. As Lacy recalled,

> I remember taking with me Scotch tape, scissors, and a black marker. On the flight up to Pittsburgh, on the way to the terminal so Mr. Hall could survey the damage and speak to our team, and in the car on the way to the press conference, I was cutting and pasting and changing it.

Throughout the flight, the pros and cons of the various responses to issues resulting from the spill were debated. To prepare Hall for any questions the press might ask, Yancey and Lacy frequently played devil's advocates, ferreting out any angles they had not considered.

Once everyone reached Floreffe, they received word that Governor Casey's news conference had been postponed until 2:00 P.M. In response, Lacy rescheduled Hall's press conference for 4:00 P.M.

As Hall toured the terminal he expressed genuine thanks to everyone who had been working 18-hour days in cold, wet, and miserable conditions to clean up the spill. During the entire week temperatures never reached above 10 degrees and the wind chill factor frequently pushed temperatures below zero. As the Ashland team surveyed the terminal, they met with EPA officials from Philadelphia and various emergency clean-up crews. They attempted to get current on new developments, particularly the water shortages, and to demonstrate the company's responsiveness to do whatever they could to improve the situation. One representative from a local agency informed Luellen that in the next day or so they would need towboats and barges to go upriver to bring fresh water to communities whose water supplies were in danger of contamination. Concerned that time was of the essence, Luellen ordered the vessels to be sent immediately.

Climbing into the car that would take him and his group to the press conference, Hall pondered the situation confronting him. Regardless of which course he took in his statement—publicly admitting "wrongdoing" or being somewhat circumspect on issues like the permit and the used steel—he was in for tough questioning by the press. Furthermore, he would undoubtedly be queried on the wisdom of the actions the company had taken so far. He himself was unsure about this. Should others who had been more closely associated with the clean-up also participate in the press conference? The trip from the terminal to the press conference site was short, and Hall knew he had to resolve his mind finally on these points before he met reporters.

EXHIBIT 1 Ashland Oil, Inc.—January 2, 1988

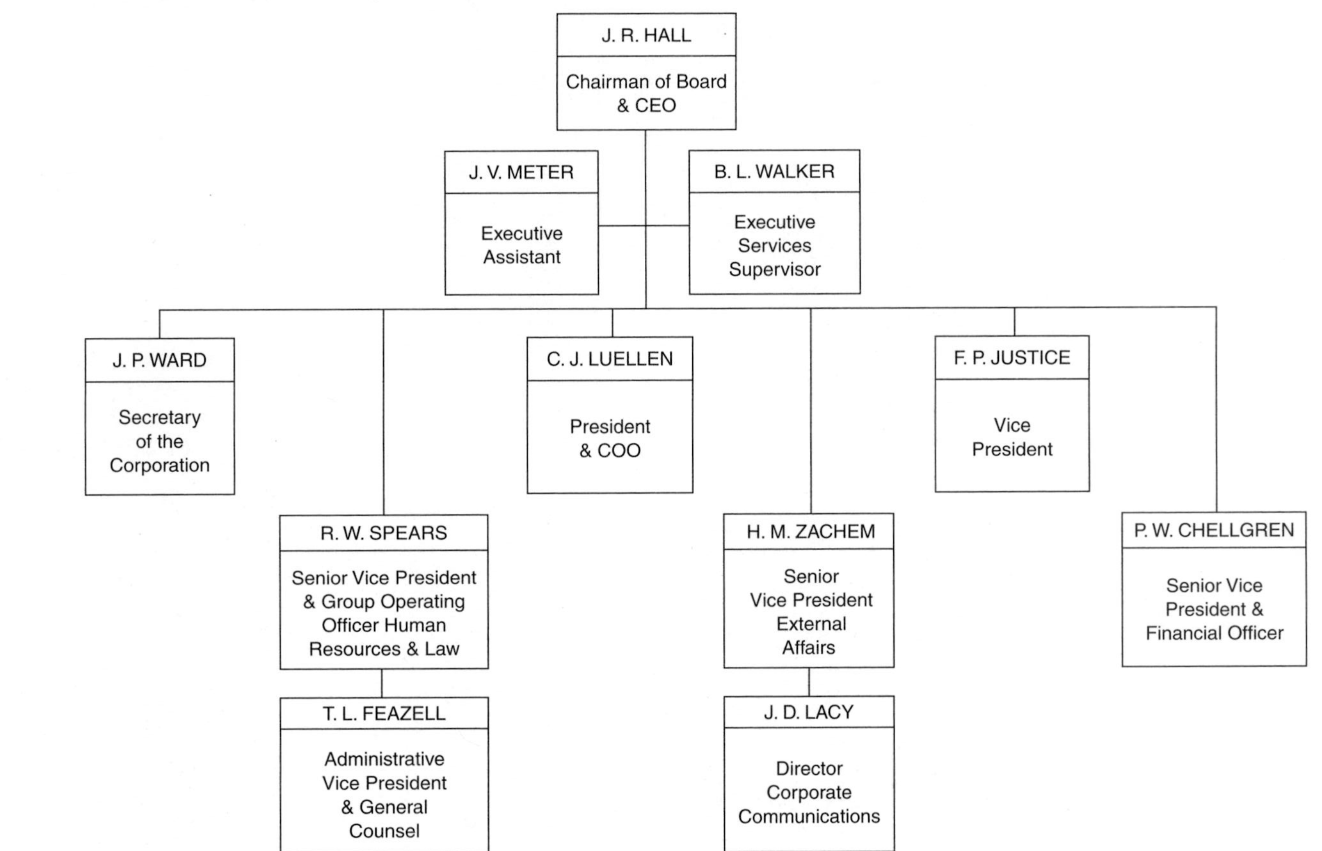

EXHIBIT 2 Ashland Petroleum Company—January 2, 1988

R. E. YANCEY, JR.
President

E. H. MONK
Manager Administration

A. V. PEPPARD
Group VP Manufacturing

R. B. KEIFER, JR.
Group VP Supply & Transportation

C. R. LOVORN
Group VP Marketing

D. C. WELLER
Group VP COS & Transportation

R. H. COMPTON
Administrative Vice President

R. P. THOMAS
Vice President Law

M. J. DUFFY
Director Environmental Affairs

E. W. STAMPER
Administrative Vice President

EXHIBIT 3 Ashland Oil, Inc.—Key Business Units

Source: 1987 company annual report.

Fiscal Year Revenue and Income (in millions)	1987	1986
Petroleum:		
Sales and operating revenues	$2,919	$3,366
Operating income	10	252
SuperAmerica	1,364	1,365
	16	37
Valvoline	552	529
	48	37
Chemical	1,643	1,477
	90	71
Coal	199	190
	31	14
Engineer construction	1,317	1,185
	72	86
Exploration	248	232
	1	(23)
Intersegment sales:		
Ashland Petroleum	(813)	(851)
Exploration	(213)	(184)
Other	(27)	(26)

EXHIBIT 4 Collapsed Storage Tank No. 1338

EXHIBIT 5 Map of Spill Area

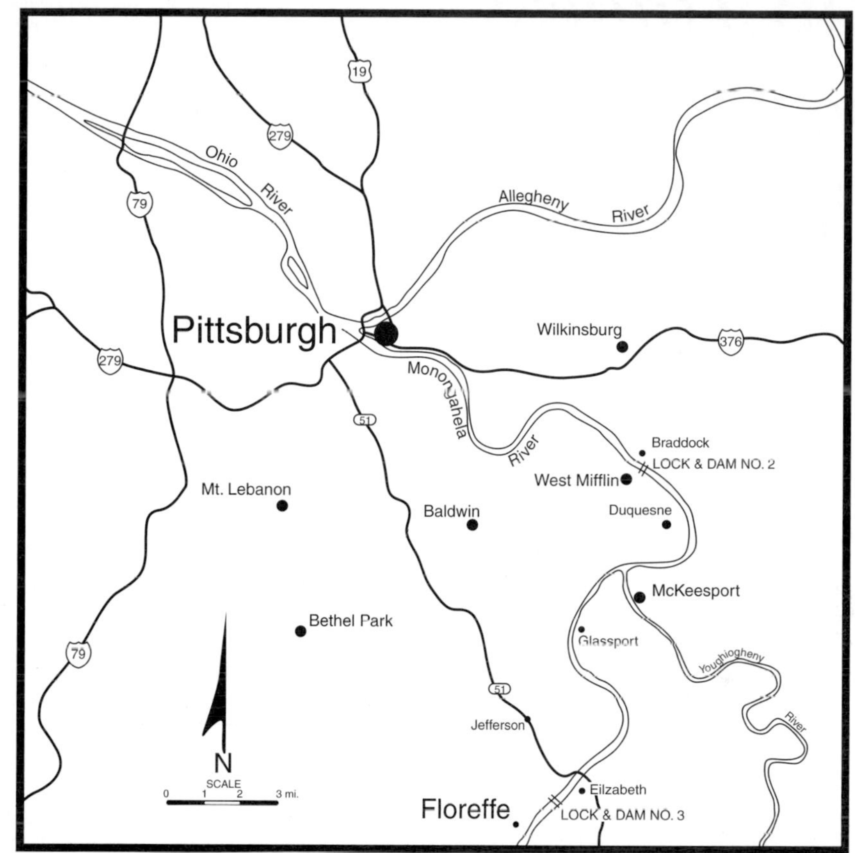

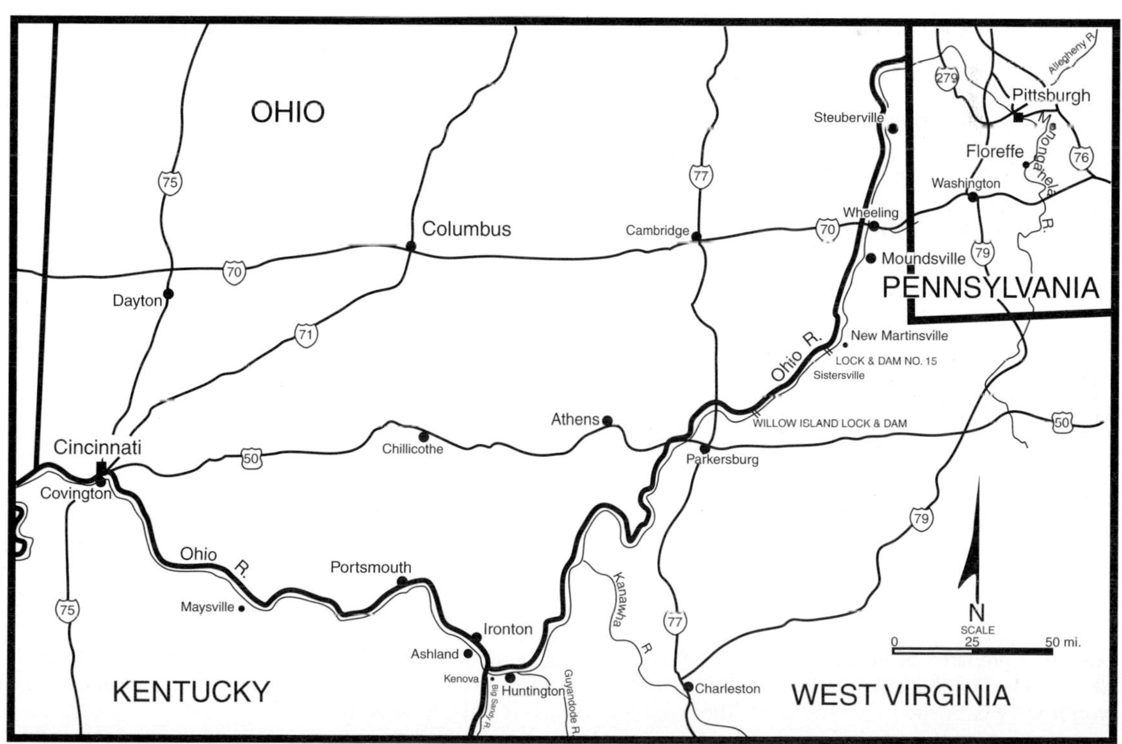

Exxon *Valdez*: *Corporate Recklessness on Trial*

United States District Court for the District of Alaska, August 29, 1994, In Re Exxon Valdez
Instructions to Jury from
Judge H. Russell Holland

Members of the Jury:

. . . In your decisions on issues of fact, a corporation is entitled to the same fair trial at your hands as a private individual. All persons, including corporations, partnerships, unincorporated associations, and other organizations, stand equal before the law, and are to be dealt with by the judge and jury as equals in a court of justice. . . .

You are permitted to draw, from facts which you find have been proved by the evidence in this phase of the trial, such reasonable inferences as seem justified in light of your experience. Inferences are deductions or conclusions which reason and common sense lead the jury to draw from the facts which have been established by the evidence in the case. . . .

An award of punitive damages may be made only if you find that plaintiffs have shown by a preponderance of the evidence that an award is proper, applying the instructions that I will give you. . . . Punitive damages are not favored in the law, and are never awarded as a right, no matter how egregious the defendant's conduct. This means that you have discretion to award or not to award punitive damages in accordance with these instructions. . . .

The purposes for which punitive damages are awarded are:
1. to punish a wrongdoer for extraordinary misconduct; and
2. to warn defendants and others and deter them from doing the same.

It is for you to decide as to each of defendant Hazlewood and the Exxon defendants whether or not plaintiffs have established that:
1. an award of punitive damages would serve the purposes of punishment and deterrence; and
2. if so, what amount is necessary and appropriate to achieve those purposes.

The amount of punitive damages that is necessary to punish a defendant is the penalty that is necessary to express society's disapproval of conduct that society condemns. The amount of punitive damages that is necessary to deter a defendant and others is the amount of money you find will induce a defendant and others not to repeat the conduct that you have found to be wrongful. . . .

This case was prepared by Research Assistant Beth Goodpaster, under the supervision of Professor Thomas Holloran, as the basis for class discussion rather than to illustrate either effective or ineffective handling of an administrative situation.

Defendant: Exxon Corporation

On September 16, 1994, Exxon stock was trading at $58.75 per share. Phase III of the trial, which would determine how much Exxon must pay in punitive damages to the commercial fisherman of Prince William Sound, was coming to an end. The jury had been deliberating now for 13 days. In June, the same jury had delivered its first verdict in Phase I of the trial: Exxon and Captain Hazelwood had been reckless in causing the *Valdez* supertanker to spill almost 11 million gallons of oil into the Sound when it hit Bligh Reef on March 24, 1989. Phase II, which focused on determining the amount of compensatory damages Exxon owed the Alaskan commercial fishermen, ended in August after tedious testimony by scientific and economic experts hired by both sides. The jury directed Exxon to pay $286.8 million—one-third the amount plaintiffs argued they had lost from the spill.

The jury's determination of recklessness in Phase I made Phase III necessary to decide whether Exxon must also pay punitive damages to the plaintiffs. Had the jury found instead that it had only been negligence (the failure to use reasonable care) which caused the *Valdez* spill, the company would only have been liable for the actual damages determined in Phase II. Recklessness, however, defined as "conduct which requires a conscious choice of action with some knowledge that the action is risky and could cause danger to others," opened the door to as much as $15 billion in punitive damages.[1]

Now, after over four months of trial, jurors had before them arguments from Exxon that the company had paid enough for the damage it caused from the 1989 *Valdez* spill. Exxon had paid $2.1 billion in cleanup, settled claims with the State of Alaska and the federal government for $1.25 billion, agreed to pay $20 million to native subsistence fishermen, and voluntarily paid out $300 million to 11,000 fishermen immediately after the spill. The $286.8 million in compensatory damages awarded in Phase II was added to the total. "I think it is common sense that any business that has suffered over a $3 billion payout will do everything in its power to avoid having a similar occurrence," said Patrick Lynch, one of Exxon's lead trial lawyers.[2]

On the other side, lead attorney for the class action plaintiffs, Brian O'Neill, argued that punitive damages were required since "the culture of [the Exxon] company has gone so sour we need to . . . shock them into some kind of corporate personality change."[3] O'Neill, a partner in the Minneapolis firm Faegre & Benson, further argued that in order for a company as big as Exxon to feel the financial sting of punitive damages, the jury would have to break some records. O'Neill urged the jurors to use two numbers—the $20 billion increase in the value of Exxon's stock since 1989 and the $5 billion in annual profits the company averaged over the last several years—as parameters for their verdict.[4] Any verdict within this range would be a first in American legal history. (See Exhibit 1.)

1. Events Leading to the Trial

History of Exxon Corporation

Exxon was incorporated in 1882 as Standard Oil of New Jersey, part of the 19th century Rockefeller empire. By that time, Rockefeller and his 30 Standard Oil companies already controlled 80 percent of the nation's refineries and 90 percent of the oil pipelines in the United States.[5] To avoid state laws which restricted the activity of a corporation to its home state, Rockefeller reorganized in 1882 and concentrated the assets of all his oil companies in the New York entity, Standard Oil Trust, the first trust in U.S. business history. Standard Oil of New Jersey—which would rename itself Exxon in 1972—was created as a regional corporation to handle the trust's activities in surrounding states. The 1890 Sherman Antitrust Act was passed largely in response to Standard's oil monopoly. Once the Standard Oil Trust was dissolved, Standard Oil of New Jersey became the dominant Standard company.

Over 100 years later, Exxon still stands at the top of corporate America, ranked number three in

[1] Phillips, "Exxon Wallet in Jury Hands." [Full citations are listed in Works Consulted.]

[2] Schneider, "Exxon Is Ordered to Pay. . . ."

[3] Schneider, "With 2 *Valdez* Oil-Spill Trials Down, Big One Is Coming Up."

[4] Barker, "The Exxon Trial: A Do-It-Yourself Jury."

[5] *International Directory of Company Histories*, p. 427.

the *Fortune* 500 for 1994, and is the 26th largest corporation in the world. Exxon Corporation continues to be known for its shield against the price volatility of oil: an integrated balance between "upstream" production of crude oil and natural gas, and "downstream" products like gasoline and chemicals. Most of Exxon's current top executives established their careers in the company from work on the "upstream" side of operations, however, drawing from backgrounds in engineering rather than business. Though Exxon made several unsuccessful diversification maneuvers in the early 1980s—including losing ventures in office equipment, the purchase of Reliance Electric Company, coal holdings, and shale oil—it refocussed operations by the late 1980s on areas where it was more experienced and profitable.

With reductions in oil prices and with Lawrence Rawl's transition to CEO in 1986 and 1987, Exxon cut costs significantly to make the sprawling company more efficient. As part of Rawl's "lean and mean" philosophy, Exxon centralized overseas operations, reorganized its chemical business, closed many of its gas stations, sold off the company's nuclear businesses, and cut about 80,000 jobs from its peak 182,000 employees a few years before. One oil industry consultant stated that Exxon "has got about the strongest balance sheet in the industry." (See Exhibit 2.)

Mixing Alcohol, Water, and Oil

At 12:04 A.M. on March 24, 1989, when the *Valdez* ran aground, Captain Joseph Hazelwood was not on the ship's bridge. Hazelwood had turned over navigation out of the Sound to third mate George Cousins although Cousins was not licensed to navigate in closed waters. According to Cousins, this was a relatively common practice aboard Exxon oil tankers.[6] To avoid potentially dangerous ice floes, Hazelwood had ordered the tanker off course, which with reduced speed and precise navigation could have avoided the ice and Bligh Reef. In violation of regulations, the *Valdez* crew failed to notify the Coast Guard that the ship was out of the radar tracking area. According to some reports, the ship was then set on autopilot, something Coast Guard regulations and Exxon policy said should be done only in the open sea.[7] At 11:53 P.M. Hazelwood left Cousins alone on the bridge; though he took the ship off autopilot, Cousins for unknown reasons failed to execute a turn toward the customary course. Traveling at nearly 12 knots, the supertanker crashed into the reef several minutes later, tearing eight gashes in the hull, some estimated to be 15 feet wide.[8] Eleven million gallons of the 50.4 million gallons on board poured into the pristine waters of Prince William Sound.

A blood test taken 10 hours after the accident revealed that Captain Hazelwood had a blood-alcohol level of .061%, 50% above the maximum .04% allowable under Coast Guard regulations. At the time of the grounding, the captain could have been five times more inebriated than the legal limit.[9] Coast Guard regulations prohibited officers from drinking any alcoholic beverages four hours before sailing. Witnesses testified, however, that Hazelwood had been drinking in local bars as late as 1½ hours before the tanker left port. Hazelwood later admitted having several vodka drinks before the *Valdez* left port, but denied that he was impaired by the alcohol.

Hazelwood had a reputation as a first-rate officer, "the best pilot in Exxon's fleet."[10] The captain also had a reputation, however, for his "dark moods" and alcohol consumption—problems which led Hazelwood to enter treatment in April 1985. Exxon knew of Hazelwood's 28-day treatment and allowed him leave to attend AA meetings. Frank Iarossi, the president of the Exxon Shipping Company, stated after the *Valdez* disaster that once Hazelwood had been reinstated in 1987 he was the "most closely scrutinized employee" at Exxon.

[6] Egan, "Elements of Tanker Disaster."

[7] Ibid.

[8] During Phase I of the Exxon trial in Alaska, the president of Atlantic Richfield Corp., another major Alaska oil-trade participant, said his company's general policy for dealing with Prince William Sound ice was to keep vessels docked in port or traveling at speeds no more than 5 knots. (Rosen, "Exxon Ex-CEO Retracts Statements. . . .")

[9] In 1990, Captain Hazelwood was tried and acquitted in Alaska for operating the ship under the influence of alcohol. Questions about the Coast Guard's alcohol testing procedures created uncertainty as to Hazelwood's degree of impairment, if any.

[10] Behar, "Joe's Bad Trip."

Though there was no documentation, there was anecdotal evidence among some Exxon employees that Hazelwood continued to drink excessively on board and off ship after treatment. Indeed, as Exxon management found out after the *Valdez* accident, at the time of the grounding, Captain Hazelwood's automobile operating license in New York had been revoked for drunk driving since the previous fall. Hazelwood's license had been suspended for drunk driving violations three times since 1984.[11]

The National Transportation Safety Board investigated the spill and found that, (a) Exxon had a policy of manning its vessels with reduced crews, (b) the Coast Guard should not have allowed ships to leave port with inadequate crews, and (c) the officers on the *Valdez* had worked more hours without rest than were permitted by Coast Guard regulations. In addition, the board faulted Exxon for lack of a program to respond to drug and alcohol abuse and the Coast Guard for unpreparedness in postaccident drug and alcohol testing.

Immediately following the accident, Exxon executives explained the disaster as a result of Hazelwood's drunkenness. Five years later at trial, however, Exxon officials testified that their conclusions about Hazelwood were mistaken, and that the captain had not been impaired by alcohol the night of the *Valdez* grounding.

Separating Oil from Water

The Alyeska Pipeline Service Company, a consortium of seven oil companies including Exxon, had as its mission to manage the pipeline which carried oil from the Alaskan North Slope to Valdez.[12] Alyeska handled the first stage of cleanup emergencies. Alyeska had estimated that a spill of the *Valdez* magnitude could happen only once every 241 years.[13] The Alaska spill was by no means unprecedented, however. Though the *Valdez* spill was the largest oil spill in U.S. waters, recent history showed significantly larger spills had occurred worldwide. (See Exhibit 3.) Although Alyeska had dismissed its oil spill response team in 1981, the only unit set up exclusively to clean up spills in Prince William Sound, the company claimed that it could have equipment on the scene of any major spill within five hours.[14] When the *Valdez* hit Bligh Reef, however, Alyeska's only response barge was in dry dock awaiting repair. It contained none of the necessary spill cleanup equipment and arrived at the reef more than 14 hours after the accident.[15]

Within 48 hours of the spill, Exxon and Alyeska had made very little headway in retrieving the spilled oil. Cleanup was delayed due to disagreements between company and government officials about the effectiveness and environmental impact of chemical dispersants, which were designed to break down the oil on the water's surface, and whether the requisite approval would be given to use the dispersants.[16] Exxon and Alyeska's response was seen as slow and disorganized. Finger-pointing played out in the media with Exxon blaming governmental bureaucracy and oversensitive environmentalists for holding up cleanup efforts and government officials blaming Exxon and Alyeska for misrepresenting their ability to deal with a spill of this size. One commentator noted that "more than anything else, the running aground of the tanker *Valdez* underscores the fact that crises in business are inevitable and companies must have rehearsed crisis management plans in place well before disaster strikes. While Exxon had a crisis management plan that boasted that an oil spill could be contained within five hours, the critical flaw in the plan was that it was untested."[17]

In the summers of 1989 and 1990, Exxon spent $2.1 billion on cleanup operations in Alaska. According to scientists gathered at Anchorage for the 1993 Exxon *Valdez* Oil Spill Symposium, Exxon's cleanup process netted 14 percent of the oil spilled. Twenty percent evaporated from the

[11] Davidson, *In the Wake of the Exxon* Valdez *Oil Spill*, p. 65.

[12] Goodpaster, with Delahunt, "Exxon Corporation: Trouble at Valdez." See "Trouble at Valdez" for more detailed information about the events of the grounding, early attempts at cleanup, as well as background information on oil industry organizations in Alaska.

[13] Egan, "Elements of Tanker Disaster."

[14] Eliminating the oil spill response team was a cost-cutting measure approved by the Alaska Department of Environmental Conservation.

[15] Davidson, *In the Wake of the Exxon Valdez Oil Spill*, p. 28.

[16] Ultimately, Exxon obtained approval for use of chemical dispersants on Sunday, March 26, but the company encountered weather problems which interfered with the dispersants' effectiveness. By Tuesday, when the weather was better, the oil spill had spread too far to use the dispersants, according to company officials.

[17] Fink, "Learning from Exxon."

water's surface; 12 percent sank to the bottom of the sea. As of late 1992, the remaining 50 percent had broken down, much of it into components and chemicals remaining on beaches and in the water. In the end, the spill contaminated 1,567 miles of shoreline. An estimated 300,000 to 645,000 birds (including bald eagles) and 1,000 to 5,000 sea otters were killed.[18] The spilled oil and summer cleanup operations destroyed the 1989 salmon and herring harvest, and may have affected prices for fish caught in subsequent seasons.[19]

Misreading an Angry Public

Exxon struggled to clean up not just the oil, but also its public image. Since 1987, Lawrence G. Rawl, chairman and CEO of the Exxon Corporation, had a very "private" public image and rarely spoke to the media. The company was described as "low profile," "inward looking" and strong economically. When the *Valdez* disaster hit, a company which routinely shunned the spotlight was forced to accept its place in the public eye. Exxon was criticized for being unprepared, moving slowly, communicating poorly, displaying arrogance rather than contrition, and failing to show leadership. Such criticisms brought on a debate over the proper way for large corporations to manage crises. One corporate spokesperson noted that the early stages of a crisis are particularly important: "If you aren't geared up and ready to inform the public, you will be judged guilty until proven innocent."[20]

Some faulted Rawl for not traveling to Valdez soon after the spill. Instead, lower-level executives were dispatched to Alaska, and conflicting statements issued from multiple company spokespeople. One *Wall Street Journal* commentary stated that the "top officer's presence in an emergency can be an important symbol . . . telling the whole world that 'we take this as a most serious concern.' Mr. Rawl's low profile as well as the company's other communications problems in dealing with the spill may have hurt Exxon's credibility."[21] Others argued that overconcern with symbolism (and media photo opportunities) is not the best way to manage a crisis, because although there are times when a chief executive's presence is needed at the scene of a crisis, there are also compelling reasons to remain at headquarters, take charge of communications, and exercise leadership from there. The criticism persisted, however, that Rawl did neither. Making no public statement until almost a week after the event, and not visiting the site until three weeks after the spill, he let rumors mix with facts in the remote town of Valdez.

Annual shareholder meetings following the spill (which coincided with environmental groups' Earth Day demonstrations and activities) became a public image tug-of-war between Exxon's top executives and critics of the company. On April 25, 1990, numerous shareholders proposed resolutions aimed at the company's environmental protection policies. All proposals were defeated. One proposal called for an environmental audit to measure progress toward achieving the goals of the Valdez Principles, a 10-point environmental agenda for corporations. Another proposal pressed Exxon to use tankers with double-hulls, which would reduce oil spill damage if such tankers ran aground.[22] "[F]ear of pending litigation was a major factor in the board's refusal to endorse any of the proposals, Rawl and some other directors said . . . [civil suits have] made the company's senior managers leery of taking any stand that could be used against them."[23] The "tight-lipped" approach to communicating with the media and the public was typical of the Exxon personality, but led to criticism of the company, perceived by the public as arrogant and uncaring.[24] Attorneys for Alaskan fishermen

[18] Gottschalk, *Crisis Response: Inside Stories on Managing Image under Siege*, p. 201.

[19] At trial, plaintiffs and Exxon would hotly dispute whether the oil spill could be linked to depressed prices for fish after the Exxon cleanup was finished at the end of 1990.

[20] Pitt and Groskaufmanis, "When Bad Things Happen to Good Companies."

[21] Sullivan and Bennett, "Critics Fault Chief Executive of Exxon."

[22] Use of double-hulled tankers is now required by federal law, passed by Congress in 1990, in response to the *Valdez* disaster.

[23] Sullivan and Solomon, "Environmentalists Claim Gains at Exxon Meeting."

[24] Exxon's approach also prevented the company from receiving much credit for actions it had taken, such as creating a new Vice President for Environment and Safety, and for revamping alcohol policies to prevent employees with a history of substance abuse to be assigned to safety-sensitive positions.

ensured that this public view of Exxon lingered in each phase of the jury trial in 1994.

Settling with the Government

On February 27, 1990, a grand jury indicted Exxon on three misdemeanor charges and two felony charges for violating environmental and safety laws. The State of Alaska and the U.S. government also filed civil claims against the company for costs associated with oil cleanup. At the 1991 shareholders meeting, Exxon had hoped to report not only that net profits had surged 75 percent in the first quarter of the year, but also that a $1 billion settlement with the U.S. and Alaska governments had been approved by the federal district judge in Alaska.[25] However, Exxon's remarkable profit margin was overshadowed by Judge Holland's rejection of the proposed settlement. Holland said, "The fines send the wrong message, which suggests spills are a cost of business [that] can be absorbed."[26]

In the fall of 1991, the same judge ended up approving a similar settlement agreement which required more money to go to environmental restoration and upped the criminal fine $25 million. The judge cited Exxon's significant cleanup expenditures and the agreement's improved terms regarding environmental restitution as reasons for approval. The settlement avoided a complicated and expensive trial for all parties.

Meanwhile, a civil lawsuit brought by thousands of Alaskans was brewing. The lawsuit charged Captain Joseph Hazelwood, Alyeska Pipeline Company, and Exxon with recklessly causing the *Valdez* oil spill, destroying the livelihoods of commercial and native subsistence fishermen, and others who depended on the fisheries. A group of 15 law firms represented over 14,000 plaintiffs in the *Valdez* lawsuit, and over the course of five years sank nearly $100 million in litigation costs. Many were skeptical that the case would actually go to trial, since such big cases usually wind up getting settled. In fact, the plaintiffs did settle with defendant Alyeska in 1992 for $98 million, money which funded the next two years of trial preparation against the remaining defendants. As it became clear that the class action lawsuit would indeed have its day in court, Exxon's stock plummeted to its 12-month low of 56.1 per share.

II. Alaskan Class Action Suit Goes to Trial

21st Century Courtroom

The courtroom for the *Valdez* trial had been outfitted with a sophisticated computer system to create what Brian O'Neill called the first "paperless trial" in legal history. Both plaintiffs' and defendants' counsel displayed thousands of documents, depositions, and exhibits—barcoded, catalogued, and instantly retrieved from CD-ROM—on large screen monitors in the courtroom. The multimedia system was capable of displaying animation, graphics, photographs and full-motion video as well. The plaintiffs and defendants split the $100,000 cost of the equipment setup. Observers remarked that the courtroom resembled the set of a network news station.

Credited with saving enormous amounts of court time by eliminating paper shuffling, the computer system also afforded attorneys the opportunity to present their exhibits interactively: circling an important part of a document on screen using a light pen, enlarging portions of a page, or simultaneously showing two documents side by side to the jury. Most helpful to the plaintiffs' side, according to O'Neill, was the ability to use "video cross-examination" when Exxon executives took the stand, effectively splicing video clips of public statements Exxon made to the media immediately after the spill with displays of contrasting statements made in depositions or in trial testimony. "I know of no antidote to video cross-examination," O'Neill said.

O'Neill also made extensive use of jury consultants and psychologists to design exhibits, to

[25] In exchange for Exxon's guilty plea, the settlement would have fixed criminal fines at $100 million for violation of various environmental laws and $900 million in civil damages related to spill cleanup. The tentative agreement required judicial approval, however.

[26] At a news conference the previous month announcing the proposed agreement, Rawl had said, "the settlement will have no noticeable effect on our earnings for 1991. The company has provided for after-tax losses of $1.68 billion for the spill." All but the $100 million criminal fine would have been tax deductible, as were $2.2 billion in prior cleanup costs. (Barrett, "Environmentalists Cautiously Praise $1 Billion Exxon *Valdez* Settlement.")

craft opening and closing arguments, and to select "winning themes" to sway the Alaskan jury. He tested arguments for and against Exxon in mock trials with mock jurors. When it came to selecting the actual jurors, O'Neill knew he wanted "to avoid tort reformers," particularly since typical juries are already skeptical about punitive damages claims. "Ordinary citizens don't like to make their neighbors rich, and they are cheap with defendants' money," O'Neill said.

Phase I

In Phase I, the jury needed to answer two questions: were Captain Joe Hazelwood's actions in the *Valdez* disaster reckless? And was Exxon reckless in allowing Hazelwood to command a supertanker given his recent history of alcohol abuse? Exxon had admitted negligence and the need to pay some amount of compensatory damages to fishermen.[27] Exxon contended, however, that alcohol had not been a factor in the grounding of the *Valdez*—the sole cause was the human error of Gregory Cousins, the ship's third mate who failed to follow Captain Hazelwood's command and turn the ship back to the proper channel. Hazelwood testified that though he had had several vodka drinks before setting sail, he was not impaired at the time of the *Valdez* grounding, and he would sometimes consume large amounts of alcohol at one time without feeling drunk.

Patrick Lynch, Exxon's co-counsel, compared the grounding of the *Valdez* to a car accident where the driver fails to make a right turn: "what happened here is similar to what happens in an intersection accident. A third mate on the bridge, fully qualified, failed to make a turn. If that same conduct had resulted in an accident in an intersection, I don't think the people would call the driver reckless."[28]

James Neal, also a member of Exxon's defense team, emphasized that Exxon had monitored Hazelwood after his 1985 treatment for bouts of depression and alcohol abuse.[29] Exxon testified that the company would not have put Hazelwood in command of the supertanker if it had believed he had a drinking problem. Exxon had several witnesses who claimed that they followed up hints that Hazelwood was drinking, but who had come up with no evidence that he was drinking on the job. "If Hazelwood had returned to drinking during his time away from the job, that did not violate any company policies . . . the only thing he did wrong, was leaving the bridge of the ship at a critical moment," Neal said.[30] Hazelwood acknowledged that he should have been on the bridge at that juncture in the Sound, and another pilot testified that it was unusual for a captain to go below at that point in the crossing.

Lawyers for the plaintiffs pointed to the absence of a "paper trail" documenting any monitoring of Captain Hazelwood between 1985 and 1989. Hazelwood testified that though Exxon was aware of his 1985 treatment, the company had permitted him to return to sea without monitoring.[31] Exxon had a drug and alcohol testing policy for a number of years, but employees—including Hazelwood—stated that they had never been checked.

Iarossi, president of the shipping subsidiary, stated that the Exxon Shipping Company relied on Exxon's medical department staff for employee monitoring, but the medical department denied that it had such responsibility. Testimony followed from Exxon employees in both the medical department and the human resources department showing that (within the company) managers did not know whose responsibility it was to administer substance abuse monitoring or aftercare for employees. Iarossi also explained a conflict he had with the human resources department when Hazelwood was re-assigned to captain's duty after his alcohol treatment: might the company be liable for discrimination against Hazelwood if they refused to allow him a job based on his past drinking problems?

[27] Exxon prevailed in repeated pretrial motions to limit the class of plaintiffs in the lawsuit; cannery workers and other businesses that claimed they had been harmed by the spill were barred from the proceedings. (Schneider, "With 2 *Valdez* Oil-Spill Trials Down. . . .")

[28] Schneider, "Jury Finds Exxon Acted Recklessly. . . ."

[29] Neal is known for his successful defense of Ford Motor Company in the celebrated Ford Pinto case, as well as assisting in the Watergate prosecutions of President Nixon's aides H. R. Haldeman and John Ehrlichman.

[30] Phillips, "Exxon Wallet in Jury Hands."

[31] Associated Press, "Skipper of Exxon *Valdez* Testifies. . . ."

Plaintiffs argued that the disastrous grounding of the *Valdez* was reckless and an inevitable consequence of a course of conduct pursued by Exxon: failing to adequately monitor an alcoholic employee who had significant responsibilities in a safety-sensitive position. "The grounding of the Exxon *Valdez* was an accident waiting to happen. Exxon corporate policies made this disaster inevitable. Maybe not this rock, this day, but another rock, another day," O'Neill said.

O'Neill described Exxon's lack of a developed, consistent, or institutionalized substance abuse policy as symptomatic of a company which showed lack of care for its employees, a company out of touch with modern American personnel needs. O'Neill asked the jury to discredit Exxon's senior executives' defenses because of the discrepancies between what spokespeople said immediately after the spill and what they were saying in the courtroom. The contrasts between Exxon's trial defense statements and 1989 statements stood out most starkly during the testimony of former CEO Lawrence Rawl.[32] After the 1989 accident in Valdez, Rawl testified before Congress and stated to the media that it had been a "gross error" for the company to allow Hazelwood to skipper the *Valdez* because of the Captain's drinking problems. During trial Rawl testified that he had been misled by news reports, Coast Guard reports, and statements by the company's own lawyers, and that he now believed that Hazelwood had not been impaired.

O'Neill maintained that Exxon's senior corporate executives had failed to account for the risks of hauling millions of gallons of oil in a supertanker commanded by a skipper they knew was prone to bouts of drinking. After four days of deliberation, the jury brought in reckless verdicts for both Hazelwood and Exxon. The jury concluded that Exxon was reckless when it permitted a captain with a history of alcohol abuse to command a supertanker, and also found Hazelwood reckless when he drank heavily before the spill occurred and left the bridge in the hands of an unqualified officer.

After the verdict, Exxon's CEO Lee Raymond issued a statement that the company was "disappointed with the jury's finding that Exxon's conduct was reckless and that this recklessness was a legal cause of the accidental grounding of the *Valdez*." He stated that the oil spill was a "tragic accident which impacted the lives of many Alaskans. For that we are truly sorry." Exxon's stock dropped another $2.50 per share after the Phase I verdict came in, a drop valued at $3.5 billion.

Phase II

Plaintiffs demanded $895 million in the next phase of the trial to compensate fishermen fully for their actual damages due to the 1989 spill. They based the amount on the loss of fishing for the summer of 1989 as well as on decreased prices for fish caught in 1990 and 1991 due to public perceptions of tainted fish, especially in their biggest market—Japan. Exxon's experts testified that low fish prices were based instead on market availability, and the company maintained that the spill caused only $113 million in additional damage to the fishermen. Exxon pointed also to the $300 million that Exxon paid to fishermen in 1989 "upon a showing of no more than a fishing license and the last year's tax return."[33]

Jurors were asked to sift through enormous amounts of technical, scientific, and economic information: from the life stages of herring and salmon to ocean temperatures to the price volatility of fishing permits and the workings of wholesale fish markets. The jury took 23 days to deliberate. On August 11, 1994, the jurors largely rejected plaintiffs' claims of lost profits in the seasons after 1989, but awarded $286.8 million for damages suffered immediately after the spill. Before the verdict, Exxon settled with native Alaskans who sued for loss of the tribe's subsistence fishing harvests for $20 million.

Phase III

Much was at stake in the punitive damages stage of the trial. Plaintiffs sought $15 billion as punishment based on the jury's findings of recklessness in Phase I. Exxon argued that the company had already atoned for the consequences of the oil spill given the $3.4 billion it had spent for the *Valdez* disaster. "Exxon's behavior after the accident was exemplary. We took extraordinary steps

[32] Rawl's scheduled retirement took place at the end of 1992. Lee Raymond, who was president of Exxon at the time of the spill, assumed Rawl's position as CEO and Chair.

[33] Behar, "Exxon Strikes Back."

to clean up, to compensate people, and to correct and improve operating practices," said Patrick Lynch, Exxon co-counsel.[34] SeaRiver Maritime (formerly Exxon Shipping Co.) testified that since the disaster, the company boosted crew sizes, started recording work hours to guard against crew fatigue, strengthened drug and alcohol policies, and adopted stricter rules about travel through ice and other marine conditions.[35] Exxon maintained that punitive damages were not warranted.

O'Neill concentrated on Exxon's assets to persuade jurors to feel comfortable using big numbers when it came to calculating a punitive award. Since the spill, the value of Exxon's stock had risen $20 billion and profits had averaged $5 billion per year. A footnote in Exxon's 1993 annual report stated: "It is believed the final outcome [of litigation] will not have a materially adverse effect upon operations or financial condition." O'Neill asked for a symbolic $1 judgment against Hazelwood, stating that the captain had suffered enough.

O'Neill placed the ultimate responsibility for the oil spill at the feet of Exxon's senior corporate executives, whom he blamed for setting the tone for a corporate culture gone bad. He portrayed the company as one which was not genuinely contrite nor understanding of the damage Alaskans suffered from the spill. O'Neill argued that punitive damages were needed to force the company to accept responsibility for its actions.

When questioned on the witness stand, CEO Lee Raymond and Augustus Elmer, president of SeaRiver Maritime, refused to admit that recklessness caused the grounding of the *Valdez*, referring to the incident instead as a "tragic accident."[36] When asked whether Exxon as a company was sorry for the spill, Exxon's repeated response was "I believe that Larry Rawl as chairman issued an apology."

In his closing argument, O'Neill played video clips of Exxon testimony the jury had heard in the trial. The tape focused on conflicting statements about whose responsibility monitoring Hazelwood should have been and on Exxon executives' reluctance to make statements of apology in the courtroom. He added to the tape public statements Exxon executives had made in 1989 about Hazelwood's alcohol history and his intoxication at the time of the oil spill. O'Neill used the popular bestseller, *All I Really Need to Know I Learned in Kindergarten*, to hammer home to the jury his theory of the case: "When you made a mess at school, you had to clean it up. If you did it deliberately, or recklessly, you'd be punished by having to stay after school. Exxon's cleanup operations in Valdez were only the first step."

Amidst the uncertainty of the trial's outcome, analysts and investors on Wall Street speculated about the potential effect of a damages award on Exxon. The *Wall Street Journal* quoted one analyst at Bear Stearns & Co. who said that while punitive damages at the upper end would impair Exxon's stock price, earnings, and dividend policy, the company was so large that even a $15 billion penalty wouldn't be big enough to cripple it: "Given Exxon's financial strength, it's almost impossible to dream up a number high enough to damage its economic viability."[37]

Charge to the Jury

Throughout the deliberations, the jurors frequently consulted Judge Holland's instructions. The instructions continued:

> In determining the amount of punitive damages to award, if any, you may consider, among other factors:
>
> a. the degree of reprehensibility of the defendants' conduct,
>
> b. the magnitude of the harm likely to result from the defendants' conduct, as well as the magnitude of the harm that has actually occurred, and
>
> c. the financial condition of the defendants.

[34] Schneider, "Jury Finds Exxon Acted Recklessly. . . ."

[35] Rosen, "Exxon Chairman Talks of Chagrin over Oil Spill."

[36] Rosen, "Exxon Chairman Talks of Chagrin over Oil Spill." At one point, Raymond responded to O'Neill, "Why is it relevant that I say Exxon was reckless?" O'Neill offered the explanation that "anyone familiar with a 12-step program knows that it's a prerequisite to recovery to admit the scope of the problem." Although Raymond testified that he had played a role in revamping Exxon's alcohol and drug policies after the accident, he asked, "what's a 12-step program?" O'Neill referred to this exchange with the Exxon executive as further demonstrating that the company was out-of-touch with modern American norms in a way that could only have led to a disaster such as the *Valdez* oil spill.

[37] Solomon, "Jury to Consider Whether Exxon Acted Recklessly. . . ."

You may also consider, as mitigating factors:

a. the existence of prior criminal sanctions or civil awards against the defendants for the same conduct, and

b. the extent to which a defendant has taken steps to remedy the consequences of his or its conduct or prevent repetition of that conduct.

In evaluating the degree of reprehensibility of a defendant's conduct, you may take into account the nature of the conduct, the duration of the conduct, and defendant's awareness that the conduct was occurring . . . you may consider not just the fact that a corporation may have legal liability for the acts of its employees, but also whether corporate policy makers actually participated in or ratified the conduct that was wrongful, and whether the conduct that was wrongful was carried out by lower-level employees and was contrary to corporate policies.

. . . If you find that a number of Exxon defendants' employees participated in or failed to prevent the wrongful conduct and that those employees held positions involving significant duties and responsibilities within the corporation, then, in judging the reprehensibility of the Exxon defendants' conduct, you may take these factors into consideration in increasing any award of punitive damages that you might otherwise find proper. . . .

Your verdict must be unanimous. . . . Each of you must decide the case for yourself, but only after an impartial consideration of the evidence in the case with your fellow jurors. . . ."[38]

[38] Special thanks to Brian O'Neill, of the Faegre & Benson law firm, for taking the time to share his thoughts and expertise with us in the preparation of this case. Also, thanks to Kathy McCune at Faegre & Benson for responding to our requests for information and documents so promptly.

Works Consulted

Associated Press. "Skipper of Exxon *Valdez* Testifies in Oil-Spill Lawsuit." *New York Times*, May 13, 1994, Sec. A, p. 14, Col. 3.

Barker, Emily. "The Exxon Trial: A Do-It-Yourself Jury." *The American Lawyer*, November 1994, p. 68.

Barrett, Paul M. "Environmentalists Cautiously Praise $1 Billion Exxon *Valdez* Settlement." *Wall Street Journal*, March 14, 1991, Sec. A, p. 4, Col. 2.

Behar, Richard. "Exxon Strikes Back." *Time*, March 26, 1990, p. 62.

Behar, Richard. "Joe's Bad Trip." *Time*, July 24, 1989, p. 42.

Davidson, Art. *In the Wake of the Exxon* Valdez *Oil Spill*. San Francisco: Sierra Club Books, 1990.

Egan, Timothy. "Elements of Tanker Disaster: Drinking, Fatigue, Complacency." *New York Times*, May 22, 1989, Section B, p. 7, Col. 1.

Fink, Steven. "Learning from Exxon: Prepare for Crisis, It's Part of Business." *New York Times*, April 30, 1989, Sec. 3, p. 3, Col. 1.

Goodpaster, Kenneth, with Anne Delahunt. "Exxon Corporation: Trouble at Valdez." Harvard Business School case 9-390-024, 1989.

Gottschalk, Jack, ed. *Crisis Response: Inside Stories on Managing Image under Siege*. "The Exxon *Valdez* Paradox." Detroit: Gale Research, 1993, pp. 185–213.

International Directory of Company Histories. Vol. IV, Chicago: St. James Press, 1991, pp. 425–429.

Phillips, Natalie. "Exxon Wallet in Jury Hands." *Anchorage Daily News*, June 7, 1994, p. B1.

Pitt, Harvey, and Karl Groskaufmanis. "When Bad Things Happen to Good Companies: A Crisis Management Primer." *Cardozo Law Review*, Yeshiva University, Vol. 15, 1994, p. 951.

Rosen, Yereth. "Exxon Ex-CEO Retracts Statements about Captain." *Reuters World Service*, May 18, 1994.

Rosen, Yereth. "Exxon Chairman Talks of Chagrin over Oil Spill. *Reuter Business Report*, August 26, 1994.

Schneider, Keith. "Exxon Is Ordered to Pay $5 Billion for Alaska Spill." *New York Times*, September 17, 1994, Sec. A, p. 1, Col. 3.

Schneider, Keith. "Jury Finds Exxon Acted Recklessly in *Valdez* Oil Spill." *New York Times*, June 14, 1994, Sec. A, p. 1, Col. 6.

Schneider, Keith. "With 2 *Valdez* Oil-Spill Trials Down, Big One Is Coming Up." *New York Times*, August 14, 1994, Sec. 1, p. 34, Col. 1.

Solomon, Caleb. "Jury to Consider Whether Exxon Acted Recklessly in *Valdez* Spill." *Wall Street Journal*, June 7, 1994, Sec. B, p. 2, Col. 3.

Sullivan, Allanna, and Amanda Bennett. "Critics Fault Chief Executive of Exxon." *Wall Street Journal*, March 31, 1989, Sec. 2, p. 1, Col. 3.

Sullivan, Allanna, and Caleb Solomon. "Environmentalists Claim Gains at Exxon Meeting." *Wall Street Journal*, April 26, 1990, Sec. B, p. 1, Col. 5.

EXHIBIT 1 Record Jury Verdicts

Source: "Exxon Must Pay Award of $5 Billion in Oil Spill," *St. Paul Pioneer Press*, Saturday, Sept. 17, 1994, p. 1.

Top Judgments or Settlements against U.S. Companies

Texaco, Inc.

Pennzoil wins a $10.3 billion judgment in 1985 after a jury finds that Texaco wrongly interfered with Pennzoil's agreement to buy a part of Getty Oil before Texaco bought Getty itself. In December 1987, Pennzoil agrees to accept $3 billion in cash from Texaco to drop the judgment.

A. H. Robins

Robins' bankruptcy reorganization plan in 1988 establishes $2.5 billion fund to cover claims against its Dalkon Shield birth control device.

Union Carbide Corp.

In 1989 Union Carbide agrees to a $470 million settlement in connection with the 1984 gas leak at the company's pesticide plant in Bhopal, India.

EXHIBIT 2(A) General Company Overview

Source: Standard and Poor's, 03/23/95.

Business Description

Net crude oil and natural gas liquids production in 1993 averaged 1,667,000 bbl. a day, of which 33% was from the U.S. Natural gas available for sale was 5,825 million cubic feet a day (30% U.S.). Refinery runs were 3,269,000 b/d in 1993 (26% U.S., 12% Canada, 42% Europe, and 20% other foreign), and petroleum product sales amounted to 4,925,000 b/d (8% aviation fuels; 37% gasolines; 32% heating, kerosene, and diesel fuels; 11% heavy fuels; and 12% specialty products).

Net proved reserves at the end of 1993 stood at 6,250 million bbl. of crude oil (6,478 million bbl. at 1992 year end) and 42,251 Bcf of natural gas (41,413 Bcf). Capital and exploration expenditures for 1994 are planned between $8–$9 billion. In 1993, spending was $8.2 billion.

In May 1994, a civil lawsuit was initiated against the company regarding the 1989 *Valdez* oil spill in Alaska. In March 1989, the Exxon Valdez tanker ran aground off the port of *Valdez*, Alaska, spilling about 260,000 bbl. of crude oil (11 million gallons). EXXON spent $2.5 billion ($1.33 a share) on the cleanup in 1989.

5-Year Financial Trends

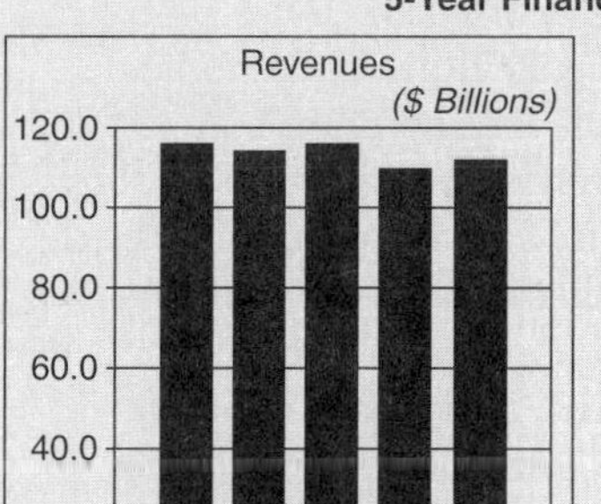

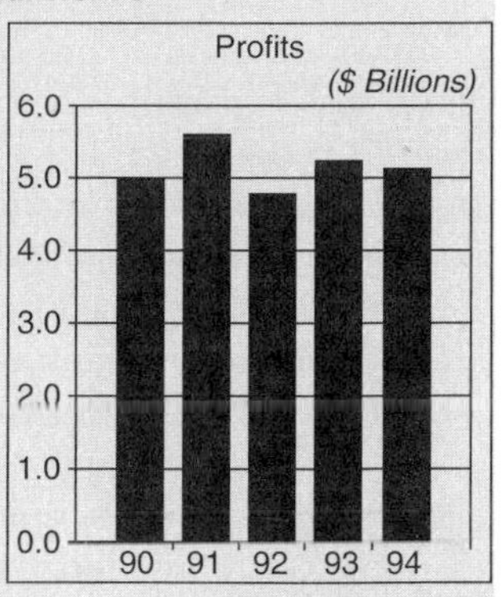

(Source: 10-K)

Recent Quarterly Trends

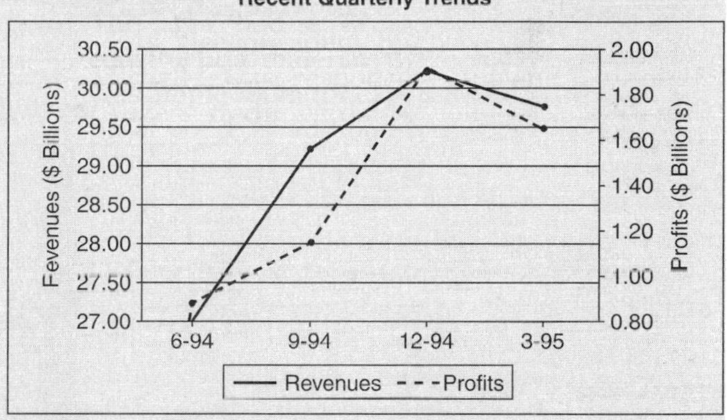

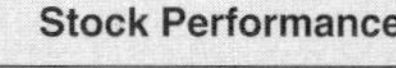

(Source: 10-Q)

Stock Performance

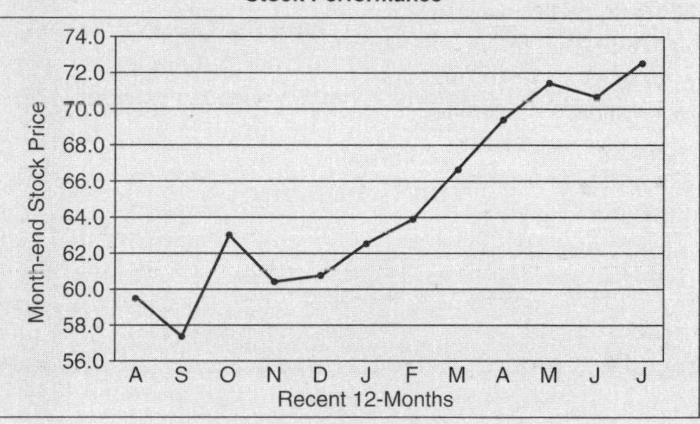

(Source: Media General Financial Services)

Segment Sales (in millions)

Source: 10-K, 12/31/94.

Segment	Sales
Petroleum	$100,409
Chemicals	9,544

EXHIBIT 2(B)  **Financial Statement Analysis**

Financial Statements (in millions of dollars)					
	12/31/94	**12/31/93**	**12/31/92**	**12/31/91**	**12/31/90**
Income Statement:					
Net sales revenues	112128.00	109532.00	115672.00	115068.00	115794.00
Cost of goods sold	58558.00	58235.00	61479.00	60334.00	62741.00
Selling, general & administrative	40885.00	38461.00	41457.00	40925.00	37945.00
Depreciation & amortization	5015.00	4884.00	5044.00	4824.00	5545.00
Interest expense	773.00	681.00	784.00	810.00	1300.00
Provision for income taxes	2704.00	2772.00	2477.00	2918.00	3170.00
Net income	5100.00	5280.00	4770.00	5600.00	5010.00
Balance sheet—Assets:					
Cash	1157.00	983.00	898.00	1496.00	1332.00
Receivables (net)	8073.00	6860.00	8079.00	8540.00	9574.00
Inventories	5541.00	5472.00	5807.00	6081.00	6386.00
Notes receivable	N/A	N/A	N/A	N/A	N/A
Total current assets	16460.00	14859.00	16424.00	17012.00	18336.00
Property, plant & equipment	63425.00	61962.00	61799.00	63864.00	62688.00
Intangibles	N/A	N/A	N/A	N/A	N/A
Total assets	87862.00	84145.00	85030.00	87560.00	87707.00
Balance sheet—Liabilities & equity:					
Accounts payable	13391.00	12122.00	12645.00	14079.00	15611.00
Current L-T debt	N/A	N/A	N/A	N/A	N/A
Accrued expenses	N/A	N/A	N/A	N/A	N/A
Total current liabilities	19493.00	18590.00	19663.00	20854.00	24025.00
Long-term debt	8831.00	8506.00	8637.00	8582.00	7687.00
Capital leases	N/A	N/A	N/A	N/A	N/A
Total liabilities	48279.00	46958.00	48279.00	49666.00	51702.00
Preferred stock	554.00	668.00	770.00	867.00	955.00
Common equity	37415.00	34792.00	33776.00	34927.00	33055.00
Retained earnings	50821.00	49365.00	47697.00	46483.00	44286.00
Total liabilities & equity	87862.00	84145.00	85030.00	87560.00	87707.00
Cash flow statement:					
Cash from operations	9851.00	11503.00	9611.00	10942.00	10646.00
Cash from investments	–5422.00	–6101.00	–7033.00	–6220.00	–5169.00
Cash from financing	–4234.00	–5280.00	–3123.00	–4557.00	–6033.00
Effect of exchange rates on cash	–21.00	–37.00	–53.00	–1.00	23.00
Net change in cash	174.00	85.00	–598.00	164.00	–533.00
Cash at start of year	983.00	898.00	1496.00	1332.00	1865.00
Cash at year end	1157.00	983.00	898.00	1496.00	1332.00

EXHIBIT 2(B) **Financial Statement Analysis—Continued**

Source: 10-K.

	Financial (in millions of dollars)				
	12/31/94	12/31/93	12/31/92	12/31/91	12/31/90
Profitability:					
Net profit margin	0.05	0.05	0.04	N/A	N/A
Return on assets	0.06	0.06	0.06	N/A	N/A
Return on equity	0.15	0.17	0.16	N/A	N/A
Sales per employee (000s)	1303	1203	1217	N/A	N/A
Liquidity ratios:					
Quick ratio	0.51	0.46	0.49	N/A	N/A
Current ratio	0.84	0.80	0.84	N/A	N/A
Receivables turnover	13.89	15.97	14.32	N/A	N/A
Inventory turnover	20.24	20.02	19.92	N/A	N/A
Leverage ratios:					
Total assets/equity	2.35	2.42	2.52	N/A	N/A
Long-term debt/equity	0.24	0.24	0.26	N/A	N/A
Total liabilities/total assets	0.55	0.56	0.57	N/A	N/A

All financial statement figures include restatements filed by the company with the Securities and Exchange Commission.

EXHIBIT 2(C)

Industry Group Comparison

Source: *Media General Financial Services,* 07/07/95.
To obtain company profiles on any of the industry group companies listed above, please call 1-800-989-4636.

Industry Group: Oil Refining and Marketing — Group Size: 54 Companies

The companies listed below derive the majority of their revenues from the oil refining and marketing industry. Only U.S. public companies are included in this industry group comparison.

	Last 4-Qtrs. Rev. ($mil)	Rank	Last 4-Qtrs. Rev. Growth Rate	Rank	5-Year Rev. Growth Rate	Rank	Last 4-Qtrs. Profit Margin	Rank	Last 4-Qtrs. % Chg. in Spending*	Rank
Group average	11,553.5		16.4%		7.0%		(9.6%)		9.0%	
The Top 25										
Exxon Corp.	110,051.0	1	8.4%	25	2.5%	15	5.1%	9	3.1%	22
Royal Dutch Pete	79,173.7	2	6.5%	29	1.9%	16	4.8%	12	2.7%	25
Mobil Corp.	63,407.0	3	8.5%	23	1.5%	18	2.9%	21	1.4%	28
Shell Transport	52,782.4	4	53.0%	7	(1.2)%	27	4.8%	13	47.6%	6
British Petro	50,667.0	5	(2.0)%	43	(1.7)%	30	4.8%	11	(.3)%	31
Elf Aquitaine Cap.	37,130.4	6	6.4%	30	NC	49	.8%	36	13.0%	13
Texaco	34,134.0	7	4.4%	38	(2.8)%	35	3.0%	20	(6.0)%	35
Chevron Corp.	33,739.0	8	8.5%	24	(.4)%	22	4.9%	10	(56.4)%	51
Amoco Corp.	27,788.0	9	11.3%	20	.2%	21	6.9%	4	20.4%	9
Atlantic Richfield	16,207.0	10	(3.4)%	46	(1.1)%	25	6.7%	5	37.1%	8
Repsol S.A. ADR	15,140.0	11	(8.8)%	50	15.0%	8	3.7%	16	(25.3)%	46
Phillips Petrol	12,534.0	12	2.7%	39	(1.1)%	26	3.7%	15	(19.9)%	42
Ashland Inc.	10,864.0	13	16.7%	13	4.5%	11	1.0%	32	2.8%	24
Sun Co.	9,258.0	14	31.9%	11	(8.5)%	39	.6%	41	8.7%	19
Imperial oil	7,891.2	15	8.8%	22	(4.5)%	36	4.5%	14	NC	52
Unocal Corp.	6,968.0	16	4.8%	37	(8.7)%	40	2.1%	26	19.7%	10
Amerada Hess Corp.	6,722.6	17	9.4%	21	.4%	19	.2%	43	(2.0)%	32
Tosco Corp.	6,566.5	18	41.6%	9	27.7%	4	.6%	40	44.5%	7
Lyondell Petroch	4,210.0	19	16.7%	14	(9.4)%	42	7.8%	3	5.4%	21
Fina Inc.	3,506.8	20	5.0%	35	(.5)%	23	3.2%	19	(25.3)%	45
MAPCO	3,113.2	21	14.6%	17	3.3%	13	2.1%	25	(6.5)%	36
Kerr-McGee	3,016.0	22	(8.6)%	49	(.8)%	24	3.5%	17	85.8%	44
Horsham Corp.	2,757.1	23	22.3%	12	.2%	20	6.4%	6	(23.2)%	4
Dia Shamrock Inc.	2,699.2	24	7.2%	27	1.6%	17	2.6%	22	17.7%	11
Pennzoil Co.	2,576.2	25	5.2%	34	3.8%	12	(11.3)%	50	1.4%	29

* Change in spending includes only selling, general, and administrative expenses.

EXHIBIT 3 Record Oil Spills

Source: "Disabled Tanker Off Shetlands Forms Oil Slick," *The Wall Street Journal*, January 7, 1993, Sec. A, p. 10.

July 19, 1979
300,000 tons spilled.
Collision off Trinidad and Tobago of the *Atlantic Empress* and *Aegean Captain*.

August 6, 1983
250,000 tons spilled.
Fire aboard the *Castilio de Bellver*, off Cape Town, Africa.

March 16, 1978
223,000 tons spilled.
Tanker *Amoco Cadiz* ran aground off the coast of northwest France.

March 18, 1967
119,000 tons spilled.
The *Torrey Canyon* grounded off the coast of Lands' End, England.

December 19, 1972
115,000 tons spilled.
Sea Star involved in a collision in the Gulf of Oman.

May 12, 1976
100,000 tons spilled.
Urquiola runs aground near La Coruna, Spain.

February 25, 1977
99,000 tons spilled.
Fire aboard the *Hawaiian Patriot* in the northern Pacific Ocean.

Note: In shipping, oil normally is measured by ton. A ton of crude oil is roughly equal to 300 gallons but the exact number of gallons varies according to the type of oil. The Exxon *Valdez* lost less than 40,000 tons.

Part 4

Corporate Values: International Business

As we have seen in the cases studied so far, solutions to problems that have ethical dimensions do not come easily. In Part 4, we encounter a series of cases, indeed complex, that deal with the globalization of business activity.

Part of the complexity of ethical issues in this arena stems from the fact that "other" countries may have customs and values which *are* or *seem to be* different from one's home country—and the distinction between "are" and "seem to be" can be critical. For the businessperson, understanding and assessing whether and how these cultural and ethical conflicts should be taken into account are often very difficult.

Philosophers sometimes have difficulty with cross-cultural differences. There is debate as to whether the differences are real and, if so, how important they are and how they can be dealt with in moral thinking. One well-known British philosopher, Philippa Foot, described this situation in a thoughtful observation: "Granted that it is wrong to assume identity of aim between people of different cultures; nevertheless there is a great deal that all men have in common."* While this is undoubtedly true, the generality of the statement stands in sharp contrast to the highly specific decisions which business executives are forced to make against the twin backdrops of the real or presumed differences in ethical standards between countries and the constraints of the law.

In the "Changmai Corporation" case, two Western expatriates are faced with questions about their own and their company's integrity in connection with what amounts to extortion. But they are also confronted with the temptation to overlook serious environmental and workplace safety issues in the name of "cultural differences" in Northern Thailand.

* Philippa Foot, *Moral Relativism* (Lawrence, KS: University of Kansas, 1979), Lindley Lecture.

"Safety First?" presents an American manager in Jakarta with what appears to be a cultural difference that calls for ethical criticism. It raises the question, "When is such criticism a form of ethical imperialism and when is it simply refusing to acknowledge one's responsibilities when the host country practices are less strict?"

In "The Evaluation," the challenge comes to a Swiss multinational manager trying to be fair about performance evaluation. When is insisting on cross-cultural consistency a matter of ethical principle and when is it a cop out? The stakes could be high in this case, since the risk is losing some very good people in Thailand and Singapore. The applicability of the lessons of this case will be appreciated by many contemporary global corporations.

"Dow Corning Corporation: Business Conduct and Global Values" and "Dow Corning Corporation: The Breast Implant Controversy (A)" provide a natural segue from the domestic stakeholder issues in Part 3 to the challenges of international business. The main issue in the first Dow Corning case is how to formulate and implement a consistent corporate value system on a worldwide basis—even when different business practices prevail in different geographical areas. It is not widely known that Dow Corning was a pioneer in this effort several decades ago. But the case also includes the themes we have traced throughout: personal values and corporate values looking inward and outward. The second Dow Corning case, on the breast implant controversy, presents a puzzle to the thoughtful reader about product responsibility in a litigious environment, and it demonstrates both the power and the vulnerability of the modern global corporation.

The question of standards of conduct in differing cultural contexts is addressed in a fresh way by the general manager of a Mexican maquiladora in "Managing Boundaries: ADC Telecommunications in Mexico (A)." To what extent (if any) do international corporations based in developed countries have special obligations to employees or the communities of their operations in developing countries?

Turning to the northern rather than the southern border of the United States, "Ethics, Power, and the Cree Nations (A)" presents another challenge for international business: Do the social and environmental practices of key suppliers enter into the moral legitimacy of sourcing contracts across national boundaries? A Minnesota utility—seeking to advance its mission of providing safe, adequate, reliable electrical service—must confront the protests of Native North Americans in Canada as it purchases hydropower from the Province of Manitoba.

Electricity is also a key factor in "Medtronic in China (A)," although in a very different way. The company's leadership is faced with an unexpected challenge as it completes its newly constructed pacemaker plant in Shanghai and asks to be connected to the local power grid. When is a payment a "questionable" payment—and what can a company do when the stakes are very high?

Ethics and communication seem to come into conflict in "Business E-Ethics: Yahoo! On Trial (A)." Are Internet service providers and search engines responsible for the content that their commercial Web site subscribers offer? What if the content is Nazi-related items and the legal protests come from French citizens whose painful memories about World War II are alive to this day?

The energy sector is again a factor in "The Oil Industry and Climate Change" case series; only this time it is oil industry executives who must confront the challenge of climate change and the Kyoto Protocol. Is there an analogy—ethically speaking—between the response of the tobacco industry to health hazard claims and the response of the oil industry to the threat of global warming?

"Monsanto and Genetically Modified Organisms" is a case with many important dimensions, including emerging issues in the political and regulatory environment of international business, the power of public opinion, the importance of stakeholder relationships, U.S.-EU trade relations, and the World Trade Organization's international product standards. Its lessons are many for globalizing corporations.

"Soccer Balls Made for Children by Children?" discusses child labor through the lens of the Atlanta Agreement, an initiative designed to eliminate child labor in Pakistan's soccer ball industry. Both public policy and corporate policy issues are present in this case, raising questions about whether child labor is a "necessary evil" in economic development and how corporations should responsibly address this practice in dealing with their suppliers.

In the "Mobil in Aceh, Indonesia (A)" case, the leadership of Mobil Oil Indonesia is charged by several nongovernmental organizations with environmental and human rights abuses in its joint venture with Pertamina, the state-owned oil company. When a company's leaders are convinced that the allegations against them are false, misleading, and damaging to their reputation, how should they respond in a highly charged social environment? Again the challenge is managing effectively across cultures and over great distances.

Changmai Corporation

David McLeod has been general manager of the All-Asia Paper Co. (AAP), part of the Changmai Corporation, for just two months. Previously, he had spent four years running a large and long-established pulp mill in South Africa. Bored by a job that had fallen into well-ordered routine, McLeod had eagerly responded to the challenge presented to him by Changmai's director of personnel, Barney Li, to take over as head of the five-year-old AAP pulp mill, one of the biggest in SE Asia, and double production within a year.

As Li explained, the ethnic Chinese owner of the Changmai group, Tommy Goh, was dissatisfied by the performance of the mill, then headed by a Malaysian expatriate and producing on average 21,500 tons of pulp per month. The mill contained state-of-the-art equipment which, Goh felt, was not being used to full capacity. He was therefore looking for an experienced western manager to introduce a more professional approach and increase production. Time was of the essence as Goh's instinct, which had never failed him yet, told him that the volatile paper industry was about to undergo one of its periodic surges. When this happened, Goh wanted to be able to take full advantage of the rise in pulp prices. Currently, the mill's production costs ran at U.S. $200 per ton of kraft pulp, for which the selling price was U.S. $350 per ton. If, as Goh anticipated, the price climbed again to its previous high of U.S. $700 per ton, he stood to make a real killing.

McLeod, a highly qualified engineer, had a wide experience gained in some of the most sophisticated pulp mills in the world. A Scotsman by birth, he had begun his career in Scandinavia before moving on to Canada, the U.S., and finally South Africa. For him, the opportunity to work in Asia was an added attraction. When he finally met Goh, in a hotel room in Hong Kong, he was impressed both by the man and by his knowledge of the industry.

At age 45, the entrepreneurial Goh was head of a diversified empire. Building new businesses was his life's blood so although rich and successful he remained restless, always searching for the next big opportunity. Closest to him, apart from two family members working in the Changmai group, were those dating from his early days in the tough world of street trading, where he made his first million by the age of 24. These people bore Goh unstinting loyalty.

Goh was a forceful personality, whose enthusiasm for what the mill could achieve made McLeod eager to get to work. His new boss, McLeod decided, was a man of some vision, clearly used to making fast decisions and seeing them implemented immediately. In meetings, Goh's impatience was signalled by the way he constantly checked his Rolex wrist watch, and barked orders to the young, smartly suited aide who relayed his chief's commands into a mobile phone. McLeod was surprised, therefore, when Goh invited him to lunch and then took him to a small, back street restaurant that looked only one level up from a street stall, though the food was excellent. The incongruity of Goh, his aide, and himself in such a setting while outside Roni, the waiting driver, leaned against the BMW eating a bowl of noodles, had struck McLeod forcefully. It was a memorable introduction to the cultural dissonances of this new world.

Goh's latest project was to build a rayon mill on the AAP site. Although the later chemical processes were different, pulp and rayon used the same wood and shared the initial production stages, so the synergies were obvious. To build the rayon mill, Goh had entered into a 50-50 joint venture with a Chicago-based U.S. company whose representative, Dan Bailey, was permanently on site. McLeod was pleased to learn that he would find a fellow westerner at AAP. Most of the workers on the site, said Li, were locals led by expatriate managers, mainly from the region.

This case was written by Charlotte Butler, Research Associate, and Henri-Claude de Bettignies, Professor at INSEAD. It is intended to be used as a basis for class discussion rather than to illustrate effective or ineffective handling of a situation.

Fired by his meeting with Goh, McLeod had gone to AAP full of energy and enthusiasm. His first sight of the mill was a rude shock. To his experienced eye, the five-year-old infant looked more like a battered old lady. On closer inspection it was clear that although the mill was indeed equipped with the most modern technology, its maintenance had been dangerously neglected. A dozen urgent repairs leapt to McLeod's eye following his first tour of the mill, and every succeeding day he discovered more. In the first few months, McLeod worked 18 hours a day, often being called out in the middle of the night to deal with some urgent breakdown. The local employees he found willing, but completely untrained. Safety precautions were rudimentary, and McLeod was undecided about whether or not to try and impose Western standards. However, in a preliminary effort to raise standards he had regularly toured the site and pointed out the most glaring breaches of safety regulations to the offending superintendents.

Until today McLeod had felt that, with effort and organization, he could get the mill into shape and reach Goh's target. Then, at ten o'clock that morning, he had received a visit from Mr. Lai, a government official from the Ministry of Safety and Environmental Control. McLeod knew that Lai had been inspecting the site for the past three days and had anticipated a reprimand from him as, judged by Western environmental standards, the mill had several defects. On the other hand, thought McLeod, no accidents had occurred while Lai was on site which was a good sign, and perhaps an indication that his emphasis on obeying safety rules was having an effect. So he was relieved when a beaming Mr. Lai said how pleased he was with his inspection and invited McLeod to walk with him down to the river into which waste water from the mill was emptied after passing through the two-level treatment plant, Goh had been very proud of this feature of the mill which, he had told McLeod, made environmental standards at AAP "the equal of those prevailing in Oregon." After primary treatment in a settling basin, the water passed through to a lagoon for secondary, bacteriological treatment in accordance with government standards. Only after two days of treatment in the lagoon was the water let out into the river.

As they walked along the muddy bank and discussed Lai's findings, only minor infringements were mentioned, from which McLeod inferred that local enforcement of environmental regulations was indeed less stringent than in the West. "So all in all," Lai concluded, "I would say that I could put in a favorable A1 report on environmental standards at the mill," he paused, "except, of course, for the unfortunate incident last year, when I understand that the lagoon dam collapsed and untreated waste water poured into the river, just at this bend. I hear that several shacks were washed away, and that the river was poisoned. The villagers have told me how angry they were when they found dead fish floating in the river. They say that the compensation they were given was very small, hardly anything, and that they greatly fear a repeat of this shocking incident.

"Just imagine, Mr. McLeod, if one of the local newspapers decided to write about their fears, about how the poor villagers and their simple fishing life were threatened by a rich and powerful company. Such publicity would be most unwelcome to AAP, not to mention Mr. Goh. It might even harm his plans for future projects involving government concessions. How angry he would be in such a case—and I hear that his anger can be terrible indeed for those around him. You would have my very great sympathy." And the smooth brown face of Mr. Lai had looked anxiously up at McLeod, apparently in genuine concern.

"My other small concern," continued Mr. Lai, "is the mill's long-term safety record. Really, I am sorry to see that so many grave accidents have occurred; two deaths by falling from a height, and another from being caught and mangled by machinery in motion. Then there are several reports of serious burns and blisters to people working in the lime kiln, an operator blinded in one eye after iron chips flew out of the spinning tank and another who lost an arm when he slipped onto the roller conveyor. Plus many other small accidents such as people being struck by falling objects or stepping onto nails with their bare feet. When you add up the number, Mr. McLeod, the safety record does not look very harmonious.

"But do not look so worried, Mr. McLeod," continued Lai. "I am sure we can find a solution if we put our heads together. I am returning to my hotel room in the village now, to write my report. It is my last task before I go on leave for a week. My wife has won money on a lottery ticket and is going to use it to make a pilgrimage to Lourdes. As Christians, it has always been our dearest wish to visit Lourdes together one day. It would have meant so much to us. But sad to say this will not be. I cannot accompany her as the lottery money will only pay for one person. So I must stay at home and look after our children." Lai sighed. "For someone like me on the salary of a humble government official, to visit Lourdes with my wife must remain just a dream. I was only just thinking to myself how wonderful it would be if I had a fairy godfather who could wave his wand, and make my dream come true."

McLeod felt sweat trickle down his back, not wholly because of the humid heat of the morning. The collapse of the lagoon dam, which had happened long before his arrival, he knew about. According to Goh, the contractors building the dam had cheated by using poor quality cement. As a result, the dam had burst after a season of exceptionally heavy rains, with the consequences as recounted by Lai. However, Goh had assured McLeod that since then the lagoon had been rebuilt using the best quality materials, and thoroughly tested. There was absolutely no possibility of such an incident being repeated. With so many other things on his mind, it had not occurred to McLeod to associate this past problem with the present official inspection. However, as McLeod was only too well aware, if the incident was resurrected by Lai and the gossip he had picked up repeated into the wrong ears, then the effects could be catastrophic both for AAP and the Changmai group. Inevitably, Goh had business rivals who would be only too pleased to have a reason to attack him.

As for the safety record, McLeod wondered where Lai had got his information, as not all the examples he gave were familiar to him. McLeod had been strictly monitoring the accident figures since his arrival and although there had been the usual crop of minor injuries inevitably associated with high tech machinery and an unskilled workforce, nothing major had occurred. Again, Lai must be using past history for, as McLeod knew, in the early years of operations the mill's safety record had been very poor. As he tried vainly to think of a suitable reply, Lai turned to leave.

"You know where to find me," said Lai. "I will return to the Ministry tomorrow at nine thirty with my report, which I'm sure will be positive now we have had this little chat. I must say, I will be glad to get back to my family. We are quite worried about my eldest son. He has recently graduated from a small technical college in the south of England. It was a great sacrifice to send him, but we hoped that it would open up many opportunities for him. He is now a qualified mechanical engineer, but so far, has not been able to find a job that suited his talents. You know, it has occurred to me while touring this mill that here would be an ideal opening for my son. He would be very interested to work with your Control Distribution System. Computers have always fascinated him, and I'm sure he could very quickly learn to manage the system. What a good start it would be for him. Perhaps you have a suitable vacancy? If so, let me know tomorrow. Good day, Mr. McLeod."

With a final beaming smile, Lai got into the company car that had been arranged for his use during his stay, and was driven off. His mind whirling, McLeod drove back to the office. This was the last thing he had expected. As he thought about what had passed, his shock was replaced by anger. How dare Lai try to blackmail him in this way. He would never give in to such demands. The thought of an inexperienced, unqualified person meddling in the computerized Control Distribution Center, one of the mill's most advanced features, made his hair stand on end. It was AAP's nerve centre, monitoring operations in all parts of the mill. Any breakdown there would be disastrous. Then he remembered Lai's comments about the damage that would be caused by a negative report that dug up the old scandal of the lagoon and hinted that history might repeat itself, or that highlighted AAP's early safety record, and the effects of all this on the villagers and on Goh. What was he going to do?

Just then, his thoughts were interrupted by a knock and his secretary, Anna, rushed into the room. "Quick," she said, "accident in the chemical area. Many people hurt." Grabbing his hard hat, McLeod rushed from the room and drove over to the plant where a crowd was gathering. He cursed. The chemical plant had been one of the worst maintained areas, and he had been renovating it as fast as he could.

The supervisor, Mr. Budi, met him. "It's not as bad as we first thought," said Budi, "there was a loose valve and some of the chlorine leaked. But one of the workers panicked and started shouting, and then everyone began rushing about yelling it was 'another Bhopal.' Only one person has been hurt because of the leak—he inhaled the gas and so burned his throat. His hands and eyes also need medical attention. Two others were trampled in the rush to get out, but I think that the guards are getting things under control." McLeod looked out the window. The security guards were trying to disperse the crowd, with some success. "Luckily, it's nearly lunch time," continued Budi. "That should help." McLeod inspected the leak. As Budi said, it was minor. But given the lack of training among the staff and the reluctance to wear safety clothing, any incident could fast become a full scale disaster. "I'll go and see the injured men in the clinic," said McLeod, "and then get back to the office. Let me know if you need me."

Back in his office, McLeod added "safety drill" to the long list of jobs he had to tackle in the very near future. He knew he should phone Goh and tell him what had happened, but he didn't yet feel strong enough. On impulse, he decided to go over to see Dan Bailey on the rayon site. He needed to talk to someone, a fellow westerner. As he drove up, however, he saw that Dan, too, was having problems. He was arguing with a man McLeod recognized as one of the local contractors whose gang was part of the construction team. As McLeod arrived, the contractor shrugged and walked off.

"What's up, Dan?" said McLeod, seeing the anger in Dan's face. "We've just had another man killed in a fall from the scaffolding," Bailey replied. "That makes ten since we started eight months ago. The man wasn't wearing boots, safety harness, or a hard hat. I've told the contractors over and over again that they must provide the right equipment, it's even written into their contract. But they say 'Yes, boss' and do nothing. They say they can't afford to, as Goh has negotiated such a tight contract. I spoke to Goh about it, but he says the workers don't belong to him, and that he cannot be held responsible for what the contractors do in his plant. His main concern is to get the mill finished fast and start production. Everyone squeezes everyone else, corners get cut and as usual, it's the poor bastards at the bottom who pay for it. Have you seen the way they are living? There is no more room in the dormitories, so some containers have been temporarily converted by putting in wooden bunks. They have no running water, no electricity, they work up to their knees in mud in bare feet, and no one thinks anything of it. What a country!"

McLeod nodded in agreement, "The working conditions were the first thing that shocked me when I came to the site. I mentioned it to Goh, but he got really mad and told me the West had a nerve to try and interfere with other countries. He said to me, 'Look at your own history and see how you treated your workers in the past. Did any outsider tell you it was wicked? Look at conditions in your cities today—the drugs and violence, the crime and the homelessness—and then decide if you have a right to preach to others. I can't stand this Western pressure for labor rights in Asia, and your arguments about "social dumping." It's the same in China, where the Americans are always moaning about human rights. To us, trying to impose Western values seems just a dirty trick to protect your inefficient businesses. Don't condemn us before you take the beam out of your own eye.'" McLeod paused, "Goh must have learned that at mission school," he said with a smile. Then he went on to describe his encounter with Mr. Lai.

Dan's reply was not comforting, "Sounds like you've got no choice, old buddy," he said. "It just shows you how the attitude towards the enforcement of environmental standards, which is being monitored by powerful pressure groups, differs from the way safety legislation, which does not attract the same level of interest in the outside world, is more or less ignored. But if you think you've got problems, listen to this." Bailey lowered his voice, "You know that our CEO, Howard Hartford, is visiting from Chicago on his annual tour of our operations in the region. I spent yesterday morning with him in a meeting with Goh—it was quite a combat. Anyway, that evening, as I was leaving the office, Benny Burdiman, who's heading procurement for the rayon project, poked his head round the door, apologized for disturbing me and asked me to sign a form so he could go to town next day and clear the new power boiler we've been expecting through customs. The form, from accounts, was a bill for 'R.S. Tax: U.S. $35,000.' I was puzzled, as I thought everything had been paid for. I remembered authorizing a check for the vendors a week ago. I hadn't a clue what this was for."

Bailey continued, "Well, you know what Benny is like. He has been with Goh from the beginning and is the sharpest negotiator in the region. He treated me like I was a backward child, and explained that the boiler was now in a bonded warehouse at the port. To get it, he had to give the director of customs a little present. He said it was quite normal, and that U.S. $35,000 was the going rate. Apparently 'R.S. Tax' is a local joke—it stands for 'Reliable service tax.' Accounts keeps a special budget to pay it. 'You'll get used to it,' Benny said. Wanted me to sign at once but I said now hold on, I'll have to think about this. Let me get back to you tomorrow."

"So what did you do?" asked McLeod. "I dumped it straight in the CEO's lap," said Bailey, with some satisfaction. "You know how outspoken he has always been in the press about the decline of moral values in business. Well, I told him the whole story last night over dinner and said that obviously, in the light of the circular he sent around to all operations six months ago stating the company's commitment to conducting business around the world (in a totally clean way and in the best traditions of U.S. ethical business practice, backed by the threat of legal prosecution and instant dismissal for anyone contravening these standards, etc., etc.), there was no way I could do what Benny wanted. Then I also reminded him how vital the boiler was for the plant, and how far we already are behind schedule, and how there are half a dozen other important items to be delivered in the very near future. He looked quite dazed."

"So what did he decide?" asked McLeod. "Haven't heard from him yet," said Bailey. "But he promised to call me before he left this evening." McLeod turned to go, "See you in the bar after work then, Dan. Can't wait to hear how it ends." He returned to the office and to his relief, the rest of the afternoon passed without incident. Standing at the guest house bar later he reviewed his day; a near riot and an attempt to blackmail him. Not quite what he had anticipated on taking the job. Still pondering his problems, McLeod took his drink over to a quiet corner, but within a few minutes, he was joined by Hari Tung, Financial Director of the Changmai Corp., and a Frenchman, Thierry Dupont.

Born locally, Harvard-trained Hari Tung was a very smart young man who worked closely with Goh. Thierry Dupont, who worked for a French multinational, was one of the many vendors to the rayon project, on site to check the machinery his company had supplied. He was holding a bottle of champagne. "Come, my friends," said Thierry, "celebrate with me. I just heard that I have won a *very* lucrative contract for my firm with, let's say, a large conglomerate in a country not far from here. And you know what? I got it because of my 'corruption skills.' I outbid and outdid German and U.S. (even Japanese) competition to get it. It was hard work requiring a lot of creativity, but it was worth it and tonight, I am so proud."

"Proud!" exclaimed McLeod, "You can't be serious! You are corrupt, and you have corrupted someone else. What is there to be proud of in that?"

"My friend," said Thierry, "thanks to this contract, my company back home will have work for the next two years. With 13 percent unemployment in France, anyone who creates jobs is a hero. In my opinion, corruption is a small price to pay to give work to Europeans. And of course, there will be a nice little promotion in it for me. Now, stop making a fuss and have a drink."

"But David has a point," said Hari in his perfect English. "By your actions you are corrupting others. And if you think about it, that is not the only way that you in the west are helping to corrupt the people of this region. It is something that I and my friends, who are the fathers of young children, often argue about. Look at the Western values the young are absorbing while watching your films, full of sex and violence. What sort of heroes are they going to copy? I have always been glad to be part of a culture with such a strong sense of family. Take Mr. Goh, whose family is extended to include all those who work for him. They know that the next generation will also find a place with him and so, secure in their 'iron rice bowl,' they work together for the good of the group, not for the individual as I have seen people do in the west. But this sense of community is beginning to break down, and we Asians are allowing it to happen."

Hari continued, "Although we welcome the transfer of Western technological progress, we do not feel the same about your moral standards. As we see it, Western values are poisoning the local people who in the end, we fear, will be as morally bankrupt as people in your part of the world. You cannot stop the poison spreading. In every hotel, there is CNN showing the same images, encouraging the same materialist attitudes of want, want, want. Global products for global consumers, they claim. But where will it all end? Imagine, if each and every one of the 1.2 billion Chinese were to consume as much as Americans, it would mean 'good-bye planet earth.' It could not support that degree of consumption and the pollution that would go with it. And we would all be responsible."

"What absolute rubbish," said Thierry. "It will never happen. Come on, let's talk about something more cheerful. Leave morality to the professors. While there's business to be done and a buck to be made, why should we worry?"

Safety First?

With a weary sigh, Walter P. Elliot sank into an armchair at the end of a long day's work and settled down to read a dog-eared copy of the *Jakarta Times*. The newspaper was several days old, having been delivered to the steel mill in a remote part of Kalimantan where Wally worked after a tortuous journey by boat and truck. As usual, Walter turned first to the sports section to check on the progress of his football team back home in Chicago. As he turned the pages, a special pullout section caught his eye. The banner headline proclaimed "Indonesians—be proud of yourselves. We have nothing to learn from the West," and below it was a photograph of a mill similar to the one where Wally was employed, captioned "Built by locals, for locals—but at what terrible cost?" His interest aroused, Wally began to read the editorial that accompanied the photograph.

> *The picture shown below recently appeared in an American journal which discussed the issue of safety on building and working sites in Indonesia. To our mind, the article was both patronizing and pompous, and represented the all too common colonial attitude still prevailing among many Westerners towards the developing countries in Asia. The article claimed to be based on a letter sent in by an expatriate manager, an American, who had recently been involved in the construction of a steel mill in Kalimantan. Typically taking a high moral tone, the expatriate dwelt at length on the lack of safety precautions evident on the site where he worked, and lamented the high incidence of death among local workers that had occurred during the two year construction period.*
>
> *In emotive words, the expat described barefoot workers, clad only in torn jeans and T-shirts, working in deep muddy trenches pulling cables and heavy machinery, operating welding equipment or working on unstable scaffolding high above the ground. None of them, the author sanctimoniously pointed out, wore safety shoes, helmets or masks. In such circumstances, he claimed, the accident and the death rates were unacceptably high—such a cost in human life would not be tolerated in Detroit or Birmingham, why should it be so in Jakarta or Medan? The article concluded that Indonesia must act quickly to raise the safety standards on building sites throughout the country. Those responsible for building the new hotels, shopping plaza and factories must bring in consultants and safety experts from the U.S. or Europe, and make every effort to approach the Western ideal of safety.*
>
> *Yet again, we are sorry to say, we find an example of a foreigner who has come to our country, looked at what we are doing and judged us to be lacking. Today, the issue is safety. Tomorrow, it might be human rights or environmental damage. In every case, the presumption of these Westerners is quite astounding. Just imagine what would be the response if one of us were to go to New York, and take a photo of a victim of a drug overdose in a shop doorway, or of a wounded and dying victim blasted to pieces by a shotgun in a liquor store robbery. And what if we then published those pictures in a newspaper, with a headline questioning the values of a society that allowed such things to happen, and advised Americans to call in Indonesian experts to help to improve their way of living? Such actions would rightly be judged as interference and sharply rebuffed. So why do Westerners constantly seek to preach to us about what happens in our country, and insist on the superiority of their way of doing things? We could take any book of the history of the industrial revolution in the West, and point to far worse examples of unsafe working conditions; children being forced to climb chimneys or crawling under moving machinery to change bobbins in the cotton mills of Lancashire, or miners working in perilous conditions underground in any mine from Pittsburgh to Siberia. It took the Westerners a long time to reach their present safety standards, in fact it took decades, during which time no outsider condemned them publicly for "wicked practices." Let the West have the grace to accord us the same freedom, to develop in our own way and at our own pace.*

The article continued to develop its themes further, but Wally did not read on. The editorial had set him thinking about his own experiences

This case was written by Charlotte Butler, Research Associate, and Henri-Claude de Bettignies, Professor at INSEAD.
It is intended to be used as a basis for class discussion rather than to illustrate effective or ineffective handling of a situation.

during his two years at the mill. He had been in charge of the power plant, and could still vividly recall his first sight of Hendra, one of his best foremen, swaying above him, his bare toes curled over the edge of a piece of scaffolding 35 meters above the ground. Hendra had been hammering in rivets, using a homemade hammer and hardly able to see where the blows were going. Around his waist had been a safety harness, but it had been unhooked.

Wally remembered when he first came to work in Kalimantan, how shocked he had been at the working practices he observed. One day, after finding a welder working without goggles, the cable of the equipment trailing behind through pools of water, he had protested about the safety standards to Iwan, the company's human resources manager. Iwan had explained that the company itself was deeply concerned with safety issues and had a full manual in the personnel office covering all safety rules and regulations. Policies and procedures had been fully defined, and every supervisor had been told where to find them. But, Iwan pointed out, in the pressure of finishing the mill on target these rules could not always be adhered to and so "there is a tolerance."

In any case, Iwan had continued, most of the deaths and most serious accidents occurred among the gangs—which included both men and women—of contract workers for whom the company was not responsible. At meetings, said Iwan, he himself had frequently remonstrated with the contractor supervisors about the lack of safety clothing, for it had been agreed that the contractors would set up a safety department and provide the proper equipment for its contract workers. The contractors always promised to obey the rules but once back at work, nothing changed. When challenged again, the contractors would claim that they had financial problems, that they could not provide shoes for everyone, indeed could not afford to do so because they had not been paid on time by the company.

Concerned that his teams, at least, should be properly equipped, Wally had personally handed out safety shoes, hard hats, besides goggles to the welders. He had delivered a long lecture on the subject of safety, and was determined that there should be no serious accidents among his teams. However, within a few days he had been dismayed to note that several men were not wearing their hats and shoes. On inquiry, he discovered that either the men had sold the hats or had given them to their children to play with, and that none of the shoes fit the slender feet of the local workers. "Shoes are more dangerous, boss," Hendra had explained to him. "They are heavy and we are not used to wearing them, so we are afraid we will fall." The goggles had also been rejected. His welders said that they made their heads ache.

Within a short time, Wally too had been swept up in the mad pressure to get the mill up and running by the target date, and his preoccupation with safety had begun to seem less urgent. With a chuckle, he recalled how once he himself had hung upside down from some scaffolding when trying to carry out a difficult emergency repair. Back home, he would never have dreamt of doing such a thing, whereas here it seemed the natural thing to do. As his friend Dan, in charge of maintenance, had observed, "Safety is a way of life. You can't expect everyone to think of safety if he has never been wakened to it. It's a long-term process of education and training." Wally also recalled the comment of a newly arrived expat, who had the same reaction as himself to such wilful disregard for elementary safety precautions: "It's amazing. Every second guy is doing something wrong. But considering the risks, they don't often hurt themselves. Under the circumstances, I think they are doing pretty well."

Another Scandinavian expatriate worker, however, had not been so generous. As Wally recalled, the man had argued that such disregard symbolized the fact that human life was held cheap out in the East, and that a dead or crippled worker was not worth worrying about. After all, with a population of 178 million and growing, what was the significance of the lives of a few local workers who lived in huts with corrugated iron roofs, and whose living standard would never rise beyond the level of poverty? Wally had felt compelled to challenge the Scandinavian about the implications of this view. Was he saying that the life of a Wall Street banker was worth more than that of an Indonesian construction worker? In which case, where did a housewife, or an automobile worker come in the scale of things? Just how did one put a value on a human life?

Wally remembered this conversation and others in the same vein as he looked again at the picture in the newspaper. It was such arguments that had troubled him throughout his time in Indonesia, now drawing to an end, and which had prompted his letter to the American journal. He had not realized what a storm he would cause. Both sides seemed equally convinced that their view was right. What, he wondered, would other readers think?

The Evaluation

"Why?" To Richard Evans, Managing Director (MD) of the Siam Chemicals Company (SCC), the single word, written in the margin of the company evaluation form, seemed to stare accusingly up at him. The form was densely written, filled out with comments under all the headings that made up the annual assessment process, yet for him, this one word obliterated all the carefully thought out phrases he had composed. For that single word represented a spontaneous and quite uncharacteristic outburst from the subject of the evaluation, Mr. Somsak, one of his Thai business managers. For Richard Evans it meant that he would now have to make a critical decision which could affect both his authority in the company, and the future standards by which his local managers would be judged.

The ringing of the phone interrupted his thoughts. He picked it up and his secretary, Wilai, put through James Brown, a colleague based in the Singapore office of their mutual parent company, Chimique Helvétique Ltd. (CHL), a Swiss chemicals group headquartered in Basle.

"Dick," James' voice echoed down the line. "I just got a copy of Somsak's evaluation. I was absolutely amazed when I read it. I gave the guy an 'A' but you've only given him an overall 'C.' What's going on? As you know, he's worked with me for the last three years in the polymers side of the business. I know he reports to you as his direct line manager for his activities as a senior manager in SCC, but I am his boss when it comes to his operating performance and his work for us has been outstanding. He has way surpassed all his commercial and financial objectives—moved more product and at higher prices. We consider him exceptional. So what are you trying to do to the guy? Make him quit? You know how sensitive the Thai locals are to the slightest hint of a negative remark, let alone anything as direct and public as this. I told him when we had our assessment interview how pleased I was with his performance. Now, when he sees this he's going to be devastated. This is just a slap in the face. You know the problem we had when you first took over. This will finish things off, for sure. What's going on?"

Evans did indeed remember the problem. He had flown out from Geneva to take over as MD of the company with very little preparation or briefing. Newly promoted to his present grade it was his first time in Asia, and the cultural shock had been enormous. He still remembered those first weeks with a shudder. It had been a nightmare of trying to note all the advice his predecessor, who had stayed on for a few days, was giving him, to absorb the details of the company's businesses in the local market and master the details of its past and current performance, then meeting his exclusively local staff and, at the same time as all this, settling in his unhappy family.

Richard, an Englishman, had joined CHL five years ago, having been recruited from the British chemicals group he had joined straight after graduating. He and his wife, Mary, had welcomed the move to Switzerland and spent four happy years in Basle, their three children well settled in the international school and all of them enjoying the novelty of being able to spend weekends skiing in the mountains. To be then so suddenly uprooted and put down in a strange new world where they spoke not a word of the language or had any notion of its customs, was a terrible and unwelcome shock, especially to his wife. In Bangkok, there were no pavements along which she could take the baby out in its pram, shopping for food was a major expedition and, with the elder children leaving at 7 A.M. for the long bus journey to school, she was thrown on her own resources for the 12, 13, or even 14 hours a day her husband was absent. Coping with their new life imposed a considerable strain on all of them.

It was on one of those exhausting and confusing first days that Somsak, considered one of the

This case was written by Charlotte Butler, Research Associate, and Henri-Claude de Bettignies, Professor of Organizational Behavior at INSEAD. It is intended to be used as a basis for class discussion rather than to illustrate effective or ineffective handling of a situation.

senior and longer established mainstays of the company after three years in the job, had resigned. It had happened after a meeting during which Somsak had mentioned that he did not always find the CHL matrix system easy to understand. Thai people, he explained to Richard, found the concept of two bosses impossible to reconcile with their strong sense of hierarchy. They preferred to know exactly who was their senior manager, the man whose approval they should seek. Richard had seized on the opportunity to demonstrate his qualities as the new MD by, as he saw it, helping Somsak function better within the system. In what he considered a constructive way, one that had always previously been successful in dealing with European managers, he had tried to coach Somsak in how to approach his dual responsibilities more effectively. He had been stunned when Somsak had reacted with the words, "I realize from what you have said that I am not doing a good job. I am not suitable for my post and so the only thing I can do is to resign." Only the strenuous efforts of Somsak's other boss, Brown, to whom he owed a strong sense of allegiance, had persuaded Somsak to stay.

In the 18 months since this early setback, Evans had undergone an intensive and often tough course in cross-cultural management. His experiences had led him to conclude that some issues were not important enough to bring out in the open and risk undermining the harmony of the company and that more often than not, discretion was indeed the better part of valor. However, the evaluation issue was one that he judged would have to be tackled head-on. Unfortunately, it seemed likely that the first casualty of this intention would be Somsak.

During the last 18 months, Somsak had maintained a very polite and correct but by no means warm attitude towards his MD. For his part, Evans had come to appreciate that Somsak was a hard-working and meticulous manager. He was willing to work every hour of the day, was highly intelligent, and spoke excellent English, having dealt with European companies for many years. Richard had made every effort to convey his appreciation of Somsak's efforts and recently, had been heartened by signs of a more trusting, comfortable relationship between them. Now, the evaluation question threatened all the gains Richard had so painstakingly made.

The annual evaluation process was imposed on all the CHL group's subsidiaries and had been in use in Thailand ever since the company's foundation, seven years ago. The same format was used companywide for all management grades, while employees in supervisory grades and below were evaluated by a much simpler, numerical form. The process was designed to measure an individual's input and output, competencies and results. (See Exhibit 1.) The basis for performance appraisal was a set of six to seven key, previously agreed objectives, to be achieved by a certain point in time. Objectives could be weighted to show their relative importance, and all were judged according to a grading system ranging from A to E.

The actual process was carried out during two, one-to-one interviews. During the first, a manager's past year's performance was reviewed. The senior manager would encourage the subordinate to talk about his or her performance, go through last year's objectives, and assess how well they had been achieved. In Europe, individuals did this without hesitation, enjoying the opportunity to debate their performance as equals and quick to argue their cases forcefully if they disagreed at any point.

Such frankness was impossible in Thailand where, as it quickly became clear to Richard, his managers expected to be told how well they had done. It was not for them to make any judgment about their performance; what else was the boss there for? They were not disposed to talk about themselves at all. Moreover, the discomfort with any hint of criticism made the whole meeting a minefield. So instead of a dialogue, Richard found himself spending an hour in which he did most of the talking. He tried in vain to provoke some response, posing open, detached questions such as what did they want out of their job, were they happy or not. The reply was always polite, brief, and invariably noncontroversial except for any issue concerning their staff or the overall business performance. Their perceived role as middlemen for their staff would prompt them to talk about pay and whether or not it was up to market rates, or about parity between jobs. But to talk about *themselves* was something they resolutely refused to do.

A second meeting set objectives for the coming year. In the West, managers usually set their own objectives, and Evans had some success in instituting this revolutionary procedure with some of his direct reports. But it was a difficult process, more characterized by verbal suggestions from himself that his managers would go away and write up. If their English was poor, they would return and ask him to do the write-up for them.

Richard knew that his local managers found the very idea of sitting down with the boss to appraise their performance a threatening and alien concept. Even the most senior, who had a good command of English and had been with the company for some time, found it difficult to meet Richard for their own assessment, and also to carry out the process with their own staff.

The most contentious part concerned the overall performance rating. The group used a standard A–E grading in which, according to a normal distribution, an "A" grade would apply only to the top 3–4 percent of outstanding managers. These would not necessarily be the most senior, but those who had displayed real leadership qualities, for example, those who had developed a new way of doing things, and whose performance was above and beyond the average.

A "B" grade was awarded to those whose performance was judged to be excellent in all respects, and who had added to the overall improvement of the company (perhaps by serving on one of the committees for safety or an action team). A "C" grade, into which category 60–70 percent of managers usually fell, implied a good, standard performance with all requirements fulfilled. A "D" grade implied that there was scope for improvement and an "E" grade that there was a real problem.

Looking through the record of previous evaluations, it was clear to Richard that his predecessors had decided it was better not to rock the boat by insisting on European standards. More than 90 percent of managers had been awarded an "A" grade, although some MDs had tried to indicate nuances by giving A−, A+, A++, etc. Richard also suspected that in interviews with their subordinates, his managers had similarly glossed over any potentially controversial issues. A query he had once made about an "A" grade awarded to someone who was clearly not pulling his weight had been met with the assurance, "Oh, it's OK, we all work around him."

His suspicions were confirmed when he checked the previous year's results. Then, 95 percent of those evaluated had been given an "A" grade, with a very few reluctantly given "B" grades. In part, he had come to realize, the local attitude was associated with the Thai school marking system where a "B" meant "could try harder" and a "C" meant trouble. Only an "A" grade, therefore, was psychologically acceptable.

This year, however, Richard had decided that he would tackle the issue directly by imposing the norm for the performance rating, and so align SCC with standards in the rest of the group. He himself would make sure that the norm was respected in his own direct reports and, where there were discrepancies in those of other managers, he himself would change the grades.

In part, he was motivated by wider strategic considerations. SCC had been established in Thailand for eight years. The last three years had seen rapid growth and good results. The company was considering implanting itself in other parts of the region, and would expect its successful Thai offshoot, staffed by experienced people familiar with the parent company's organization and trained to the high standards of safety and quality that were a key part of its culture, to provide managers for the new subsidiaries.

This project coincided with a move, initiated by the group human resources director, to identify an international cadre of managers that could be moved between countries in support of CHL's global ambitions. However, this required a common standard in grading job performance and career potential between different parts of the group. Richard therefore decided that this year, he would implement the system as intended by headquarters, and award grades so that anyone looking at the results would be able to make judgments about an individual's potential based on a common language.

Not greatly to his surprise, the whole process had brought nothing but trouble. Faced with this latest problem, Richard was almost tempted to give up and award everyone the "A" grade they were accustomed to and the same salary increase. However, he knew this would only be a short-term respite that would not be good for SCC in the long run. It would not give recognition for an exceptional performance and so effective SCC managers would probably vote with their feet, confident that in the hectic Thai job market they could walk into another probably better-paid job the same or, at the latest, the next day.

With this in mind, Richard had to decide what to do about Somsak. In his own mind, an overall "C" grade was the correct judgment. For despite his outstanding work for his Singapore boss, Somsak had failed to meet three out of the four objectives Richard had set for him in his wider role as a senior manager in SCC. These had been concerned with building up communications between his polymers business and the rest of the company, and supporting the key safety and quality assurance initiatives.

In the last year, Somsak had put a huge effort into building up his own team but ironically, instead of building bridges he had only succeeded in forming an isolated clique whose behavior was having a divisive effect on the rest of SCC. The team acted like a family centered on Somsak. While the shared strong identity and bonds made them all work well for each other, it meant they rejected all those outside the group. Consequently, working relations between the polymers team and the rest of the company were very strained. Again, this mirrored Thai society, where the family formed the core that owed no allegiance to anyone outside it. All the energy expended on fostering the inner circle was countered by an attitude of total selfishness toward everyone else.

During the interview, Richard had spent considerable time talking with Somsak about the evaluation process in a bid to explain what he was trying to achieve by introducing the new approach. Going through the four objectives and where he felt they had not been achieved, he had explained that his notion of leadership in a senior manager like Somsak was to help lead the company by building bridges. He had also emphasized that in the wider CHL group, "C" was considered a good grade.

Later, after much heart searching, Richard had given Somsak a "C" grade overall, not the "A" grade he had so obviously expected. In reaching this decision, Richard felt he had made a big effort to be fair. He believed that he now understood some of the conflict that Somsak felt, the permanent tension caused by trying to please two bosses and the consequences of failure in terms of loss of face. So he ignored the things Somsak had not done and gave him credit for those that he had. After working together for the past 18 months, he felt that he was finally able to communicate with Somsak and that therefore Somsak would understand and accept the decision in the spirit in which it was meant.

The reaction had been far worse than his expectations. A visibly hurt and uncomprehending Somsak had asked, "But where did I go wrong?" As far as he was concerned, he had worked incredibly hard for 12 months and at the end, had been awarded a disgraceful "C" grade. He had returned that day and given back the form on which he had written his single comment. His injured pride and sense of injustice were affecting his whole team, and Richard could see only problems ahead.

As he looked through the report one more time, Richard Evans knew he had to make an important decision. Should he compromise his principles and upgrade Somsak, or stick to his guns and risk losing him? Sticking to his principles, it was clear, would make life difficult with his Singapore colleague who would resent the loss of such an effective manager. And after all, he wondered, was it fair to inflict Western standards on Asian managers who worked hard, and did everything right according to their own cultural norms? Whatever the outcome, Richard was determined to find some way of avoiding a recurrence next year, which raised the question of how.

"Dick? Are you there?" asked the voice on the other end of the line.

EXHIBIT 1 **Chimique Helvétique Ltd.**

Executive Performance Review

Name | Job Title

Division | Company

Age | Years in Service | Years on the Job

1. EXECUTIVE PERFORMANCE REVIEW

a. Review is to be done by the Reviewer and discussed with the Employee.
b. Complete Sections 2, 3, 4, 5, and 6 before completing this Section.
c. Highlight most noteworthy areas of performance after taking into consideration achievements against objectives, work-related dimensions, and external/other factors. Indicate both achievements and areas for improvement.

OVERALL PERFORMANCE RATING

A	Excellent	Reviewer's Name	
B	Superior		
C	Competent	Reviewer's Position	
D	Marginal		
E	Poor	Reviewer's Signature	Date

RATING DEFINITIONS

To arrive at the overall rating, an 80:20 weighting between objectives and work related dimensions is recommended.

Excellent	(A)	______	Performance that consistently delivers very high quality results, far exceeding expectations.
Superior	(B)	______	A high-quality performance where results exceed expectations.
Competent	(C)	______	Satisfactory performance that effectively meets expectations.
Marginal	(D)	______	Performance that often falls short of expectations.
Poor	(E)	______	Totally unsatisfactory performance that does not meet expectations.

Dow Corning Corporation: *Business Conduct and Global Values*

In the early 1970s, both the aftermath of Watergate and disclosures by the Lockheed Corporation that it had spent millions bribing Japanese officials produced a mood of cynicism regarding large organizations, especially multinational corporations. It was expected that Congress would enact legislation prohibiting the use of bribes to obtain business (which it eventually did with the passage of the Foreign Corrupt Practices Act in 1977; see Exhibit 1). In response to this mood, the IRS asked the heads of U.S. corporations to answer eleven questions concerning bribes, gifts, slush funds, and "grease payments."

Considering how to answer these questions forced Jack Ludington, the CEO of Dow Corning Corporation (DCC), to think about the company's way of doing business. Ludington believed the company already deserved high marks for corporate responsibility, but he thought that more could be done. Ludington was keenly aware of how quickly DCC had expanded overseas and the problems of doing business in other cultures. In the early 1960s, less than 3% of its employees were in foreign operations; by the 1970s, about one-third of its workforce was based in other countries.

Ludington was confident that his corporate managers would not intentionally do anything questionable and would even blow the whistle if they learned of any actual wrongdoing within the company. But with so many new employees from other cultures, where values and ways of doing business were different, he wanted to feel confident that everyone would live up to the same high ethical standards.

In March 1976 Dow Corning's board of directors appointed a three-person Audit and Social Responsibility Committee (ASRC) to oversee certain aspects of the company's internal as well as external activities. In May of that year four senior managers were appointed by Ludington to the first corporate Business Conduct Committee (BCC), which would report to the ASRC.

The Business Conduct Committee was charged with the following tasks:

- Learning more about how the company really operated outside this country.
- Developing guidelines that would be the basis for communicating legal and ethical standards of business conduct around the world.
- Developing a workable process for monitoring and reporting the company's business practices.[1]
- Recommending ways to correct questionable practices as they became known.

In order to prepare a code of conduct, the BCC studied codes of other companies and learned of efforts to develop an international code by such groups as the International Chamber of Commerce and the Organization for Economic Cooperation and Development (OECD). The committee also examined existing and proposed legislation and surveyed area managers to learn what issues they thought a code should cover.

[1] Dow Corning considered the pros and cons of the commonly used sign-off procedure whereby employees, on a selected level of management, annually attest in writing that they have not participated in illegal or unethical practices during the preceding year. In view of its decision to use face-to-face audits, Dow Corning decided against the use of sign-offs.

The Company

Dow Corning Corporation was founded in 1943 as a 50/50 joint venture of Dow Chemical Company and Corning Glass Works. The corporation's charter was to develop, manufacture, and market silicone-based products. Silicones were made by combining the element silicon with organic compounds. They could be formulated to possess unique physical characteristics, such as electrical insulating properties, maintenance of physical properties at extreme temperatures, water repellency, resistance to aging, lubricating characteristics, and chemical and physiological inertness. Because of these properties, silicone-based products had a multitude of uses. In 1984, DCC sold over 2,000 different silicone products to more than 40,000 customers in every major industry, including automobiles, health care, construction, aerospace, pharmaceuticals, cosmetics, petroleum, electronics, and textiles.

Dow Corning was a multinational company with headquarters in Midland, Michigan. In 1983, it employed 6,000 people and had twelve manufacturing locations in the U.S. and thirteen abroad, with offices in thirty-five countries. Approximately 50% of sales came from foreign operations, primarily Europe and the Pacific. DCC depended on distributors for over one-third of its total business.

In 1983 DCC had a record $763 million in sales, up 15% over 1982, and had net income of $68 million, a 30% improvement over the previous year. The company was ranked 355th in sales among *Fortune* 500 companies and 183rd in net income. Exhibit 2 shows the company's 1983 consolidated balance sheets and statements of income and retained earnings.

DCC was technology-driven and, in 1983, invested $57 million in R&D (7% of sales). The company held well over 4,000 silicone patents, and one out of ten employees was involved in new product development.

Initially, Dow Corning's expertise in silicones had made it the sole producer of many products. Within the past fifteen years, however, competition at home and abroad had increased dramatically, and DCC's market share for many products declined. Companies competed on the basis of product quality, performance, price, and technical service and delivery, and there were now thirteen major competitors worldwide.

In 1967, DCC reorganized from a conventional divisionalized structure into a global matrix form of organization, which the company called "multidimensional." Along one dimension were the different businesses, defined by product lines. Along a second dimension were the traditional functions, such as marketing, R&D, and manufacturing. The third dimension comprised the five geographic areas of the U.S., Europe, the Pacific, Canada, and InterAmerica (Latin America and South America). Exhibit 3 illustrates the multidimensional structure.

While retaining the basic matrix structure, in 1981 DCC reduced its businesses to five: Fluids, Resins, and Process Industries; Elastomers and Engineering Industries; Basic Materials Business; Health Care; and New Ventures. In that year Dow Corning recommitted its efforts to strengthen its ties to the marketplace and to concentrate on value-added growth.

For each business, there was a business board, with a manager responsible for the profits for that business as the only full-time member. The other members of the board were representatives from the various functions. Thus, dual-authority relationships existed for professional personnel. Functional staff reported directly to their functional group heads, such as the vice president–sales and marketing, but also had a dotted line relationship to a business manager.

The effect of this structure was to decentralize authority and push decision making as far down as practical. The structure put a premium on communication, planning, teamwork, and trust. DCC believed the structure was particularly valuable in providing flexibility to respond to a rapidly changing and competitive environment.

DCC's culture therefore was open, informal, and relaxed; there was little emphasis on official status or a traditional organizational chart with clear-cut reporting relationships. Exhibit 3, however, does indicate some of the reporting relationships in 1984 when the formal designation of a U.S. area was eliminated, and the executive vice president became responsible for business in the U.S. and for maintaining the balance between U.S. resources and the other areas.

Writing the Code of Business Conduct

Not everyone was enthusiastic about developing a corporate code of conduct in 1976. In a lengthy memo to Ludington, the Pacific area manager expressed the views that DCC was "clean" and that a code should only be for internal use. He also pinpointed some issues in the Pacific area that should be addressed in such a code. Portions of that memo are included as Exhibit 4.

Once the corporate code was drafted, it was sent to area managers with instructions that they develop their own codes, paying particular attention to their unique concerns. The only constraint was that area codes not conflict with the corporate code.

Writing the several area codes was a lengthy process and involved many revisions, with contributors often debating whether or not a phrase captured exactly what was meant and whether it was liable to misinterpretation. A recurring dilemma was producing a code general enough to be relevant to a variety of cultures and business practices and, at the same time, specific enough to be a useful guide for action.

In 1977, DCC published its first corporate code, *A Matter of Integrity* (see Exhibit 5) along with five separate area codes for the Pacific, Latin America, Canada, Europe, and the U.S. It was distributed to employees accompanied by a letter from Ludington encouraging them to read it. Emphasizing that one of DCC's "most valued assets is our reputation for quality and integrity," he stated: "Our aim should be to continually build commitment to the highest standards possible throughout the organization. . . . I personally believe the integrity of Dow Corning's people is exceedingly high. As of now, we can all consider our business conduct to be as subject to accountability as anything we do." Ludington closed with "If you have any questions, please let me know."

DCC revised the code in 1981. This time there was one corporate code and each area manager wrote a message on a panel of the code brochure which would be distributed in his area. In keeping with what was now the company's goal of reviewing the code every two years, it was again revised in 1983, and sent to all employees, accompanied by a letter from Ludington emphasizing the company's commitment (see Exhibit 6).

Communicating the Code and Monitoring Compliance

To communicate the code to employees and to monitor compliance, the Business Conduct Committee began conducting annual audits in 1977. In that year audits were held at the area level in Mexico City, Toronto, Brussels, Hong Kong, Tokyo, and Midland. In 1979, seventeen audits were held worldwide, and they began to include regional personnel, one or two levels below area management. It was thought that this would allow input from those closest to day-to-day operations. Since 1979, approximately twenty audits per year have been conducted by the BCC.

Prior to each audit, a worksheet containing a list of questions or issues was sent to the managers at the audit site in order to guide—but not restrict—the discussions. Exhibit 7 contains the worksheets sent to managers in preparation for the 1980 audits. (Not all questions and issues listed on the worksheets pertained to every location audited.) Audits included five to fifteen people and lasted five to eight hours. At least one representative of the Business Conduct Committee was present and sometimes two or more. A written record of each audit was kept in the files of the BCC at corporate headquarters. Each year, the committee summarized the results of all of the year's audits in a report to the Audit and Social Responsibility Committee of the Board of Directors. The annual report on business conduct was also presented to Dow Corning's global management at a regular meeting in August.

Each summer, the BCC discussed the results of the previous year's audits (it operated on a split year which ended in June), and with suggestions from area and regional managers, decided where and when audits would be held for the year ahead. In the fall, the auditing process began anew.

A typical audit opened with a summary of objectives; a review of the BCC's activities; a discussion of "gray areas" of business practices, such as what constitutes a questionable payment;

and a briefing by the committee on issues related to the code of conduct, such as interpretations of the FCPA, progress on international codes, etc. The remainder of the meeting was then spent discussing such topics as competitor, government, and customer relations; distributor practices; pricing; entertainment; questionable payments; conflicts of interest; importing procedures; employee concerns; purchasing practices; and product and environmental stewardship.

Since its inception, the BCC had asked Dow Corning managers in key locations to keep a file of code-related incidents. By 1980, a more systematic approach was developed to document such incidents. A copy of the Business Conduct Reporting Procedures is included as Exhibit 8. This form helped assure that (1) only relevant incidents were kept on file, and (2) that a uniform method was used by Dow Corning worldwide.

The company used the audits to clarify questions of interpretation regarding the code of conduct and to get suggestions for revisions. For example, in 1981 the code had stated: "We will also respect information belonging to others, and will not condone any attempt to secure proprietary information belonging to others." At one U.S. audit, it was learned that a salesman had been offered a competitor's price list by a customer. Not being sure if this was allowed by the code, he refused it. Learning that an opportunity was lost to obtain valuable competitive information in a legal way, the vice president–sales and marketing suggested changing the code. The 1984 code read: "We will respect proprietary information belonging to others."

In reflecting on his seven-year tenure as a member of the Business Conduct Committee, John Swanson, manager–business communications, observed that audits were generally spirited and informal. He believed the key to their success was face-to-face interaction and that committee members were supportive, open-minded, and listened a lot. He did point out, though, that at first there was some anxiety because people did not know what to expect and many employees, even those in top management, were not sure how serious the company was about its increased emphasis on corporate responsibility and ethics. Jerry Griffin, DCC's treasurer in 1977, admitted wondering early on whether or not it was just going to be a short-lived response to media issues.

Although audits were the most significant way in which the message and commitment to the code was communicated to employees, several other channels were used. The code was framed and hung in conspicuous places in all offices around the world. DCC also used videotapes of the annual reviews of audits as well as videotaped discussions of current audit topics by BCC members in order to keep employees informed. These videotapes were often sent ahead to sites where audits were being held for the first time. Business conduct updates were occasionally included in the six annual management reports to employees. In addition, two of the company's training programs included modules on the code. And in the semiannual employee opinion survey, there was a section on business ethics. The survey indicated that employee attitudes toward the company's ethical posture had improved every year since the code was developed.

The U.S. Business Ethics Committee

While the scope of the corporate BCC was global, the president of the U.S. area appointed a separate U.S. Business Ethics Committee in 1978. At first, this committee did audits also, but in 1979 it functioned more like an ombudsman, studying various issues brought to its attention by employees. For example, in 1982 the committee responded to employee concerns over the privacy of personnel records. Working with the Personnel Policy Committee, it reviewed the recordkeeping process and formulated guidelines for what should be in company files and when these files should be purged. Some of the issues that the U.S. Business Ethics Committee was examining in 1983–84 were the company's forced ranking performance review system, how to deal with the older employee, sexual harassment, and restrictions on accepting gifts and gratuities by salesmen.

The BCC and the U.S. Business Ethics Committee had been different in that the BCC was responsible for making policy, revising the code, and monitoring compliance, whereas the U.S. committee responded primarily to issues as they "bubbled up" from the ranks. Relationships between the two committees had been informal, and they met only as needed.

Beginning in 1982, the BCC began conducting an increasing number of audits within the United States. By mid-1984, it was determined that there was no need for a separate U.S. committee and it was disbanded.

The Future

In discussing the future, Swanson pointed to both general and specific concerns. He wondered about the effect of the anticipated amendment to the FCPA, for example. How would less stringent legal requirements impact future revision of the company's code of conduct? Another concern was an increasingly competitive marketplace and its potential effect on Dow Corning's process of monitoring global business conduct.

Speaking of future code revisions, Swanson said, "We stress to our people that the code of conduct is a 'living' statement, one that can change as accepted business practices change. A few statements in the code probably will not change: (a) All relations with employees will be guided by our belief that the dignity of the individual is primary and, (b) Dow Corning will be responsible for the impact of its technology upon the environment. Other positions are subject to continuing review. The recognition (not endorsement) of facilitating payments in our current code is one example."

The BCC also planned to look more closely at health care business practices. DCC had only recently decided to expand into this market and believed there were some questionable but common practices here. For example, it was well known that medical suppliers sometimes entertained doctors in a more lavish manner than was customary in the industrial segment of Dow Corning's business. The committee wanted to make recommendations as to what DCC's policy should be with regard to these practices.

Other items on the agenda were transborder data flow, developing duty classification guidelines, discriminatory practices, the security of the company's information systems, examining purchasing practices, and whether or not foreign subsidiaries and joint ventures should be expected to abide by the code of conduct. Swanson was also certain that Dow Corning's current strong concern over the protection of proprietary information would continue to receive high priority as competition for markets increased.

EXHIBIT 1 Background on the Foreign Corrupt Practices Act

In response to disclosures in 1976 that 450 U.S. companies reported over $300 million in questionable payments, on December 19, 1977, Congress passed the Foreign Corrupt Practices Act (FCPA). The FCPA covered all issuers of securities subject to the jurisdiction of the SEC under the Securities Exchange Act of 1934 and any other "domestic concerns." Put simply, the intent of the act was to prohibit the use of bribes to obtain business. Using some of the key language of the act, the following summarizes the major provisions: The FCPA prohibited the offer or payment of anything of value, directly or indirectly, to foreign officials, political parties, or candidates for foreign political office for the purpose of influencing an act or decision of such person(s) or to induce such person(s) to influence or affect an act of a government, or instrumentality thereof, where such influencing is intended for the purpose of retaining or obtaining business for the U.S. concern.

Companies and their managers were also liable if they knew or had reason to know that their agents used the payments received from the U.S. concern to pay a foreign official for a prohibited purpose. The law also applied to a foreign subsidiary of a U.S. company if it was using the subsidiary as a conduit for illegal payments.

Violations of the act carried fines of up to $1,000,000 for companies and up to $10,000 or five years in prison for individuals. If an individual was fined, his/her company could not pay the fine for the employee.

The act intended to exclude facilitating or "grease payments" by distinguishing "foreign officials," who acted in an official capacity, from those whose duties were "essentially ministerial or clerical." Payments to the latter were legal, although such transactions had to be recorded according to the act's accounting standards.

Although the U.S. business community praised the overall intent of the FCPA, there was widespread criticism of it on the grounds that portions of the act were ambiguous and unduly restrictive. Much criticism was directed at the section which held a company liable if it "had reason to know" an agent was making questionable payments. It was claimed that "reason to know" was too vague and that U.S. companies should not be held liable for an agent's actions, particularly if those actions were legal in the agent's country.

Many in the business community claimed that the FCPA had resulted in significant and widespread loss of business for U.S. companies. Others, however, disputed this. For a discussion of this debate, see "The Foreign Corrupt Practices Act: A Reconsideration," 1981, HBS Case Services 9 · 382 · 032.

EXHIBIT 2 Dow Corning Corporation and Subsidiary Companies

Consolidated Balance Sheets
(thousands of dollars)

	December 31	
	1983	**1982**
Assets:		
Current assets	$364,163	$322,512
Property, plant and equipment	479,178	492,372
Other assets	22,620	23,663
Total assets	$865,961	$838,547

	December 31	
	1983	**1982**
Liabilities and stockholders' equity:		
Current liabilities	$154,046	$133,622
Long-term debt	125,734	153,907
Deferred credits and other liabilities	109,941	97,040
Minority interest in subsidiary companies	13,759	11,955
Stockholders' equity	462,481	442,023
Total liabilities and equities	$865,961	$838,547

Consolidated Statements of Income and Retained Earnings
(thousands of dollars)

	Year ended December 31	
	1983	**1982**
Net sales	$763,063	$662,755
Interests, royalties, and other income	15,939	8,811
Net revenues	779,002	671,566
Costs and expenses	664,264	587,896
Income from operations	114,738	83,670
Provision for income taxes	44,405	29,062
Minority interests' share in income	1,933	1,823
Net income	68,400	52,785
Net income per share (in dollars)	$ 27.36	$ 21.11

(continued)

EXHIBIT 2 Dow Corning Corporation and Subsidiary Companies—Continued

Source: Dow Corning Corporation Form 10k for fiscal year ended December 31, 1983.

Industry Segment and Foreign Operations
(thousands of dollars)

The company's operations are classified as a single industry segment. The following table summarizes information regarding the company's geographical operations for the year ended December 31, 1983.

Year Ended December 31, 1983

	United States	Europe	Pacific	Other	Eliminations	Consolidated
Sales to customers	$390,152	$182,696	$137,267	$52,948	$	$763,063
Transfers between geographic areas	101,314	4,409	254	—	(105,977)	—
Total sales	$492,466	$187,105	$137,521	$52,948	($105,977)	$763,063
Operating profit	$133,934	$ 9,915	$ 18,002	$ 7,200	($ 7,515)	$161,536
General corporate expense						(44,374)
Interest expense, net						(2,424)
Income from operations						$114,738
Identifiable assets	$474,415	$195,025	$156,290	$34,628	($102,684)	$757,674
Corporate assets						108,287
Total assets						865,961

EXHIBIT 3 The Multidimensional Organization

Source: "How the Multidimensional Structure Works at Dow Corning," *Harvard Business Review*, January–February 1974, p. 57.

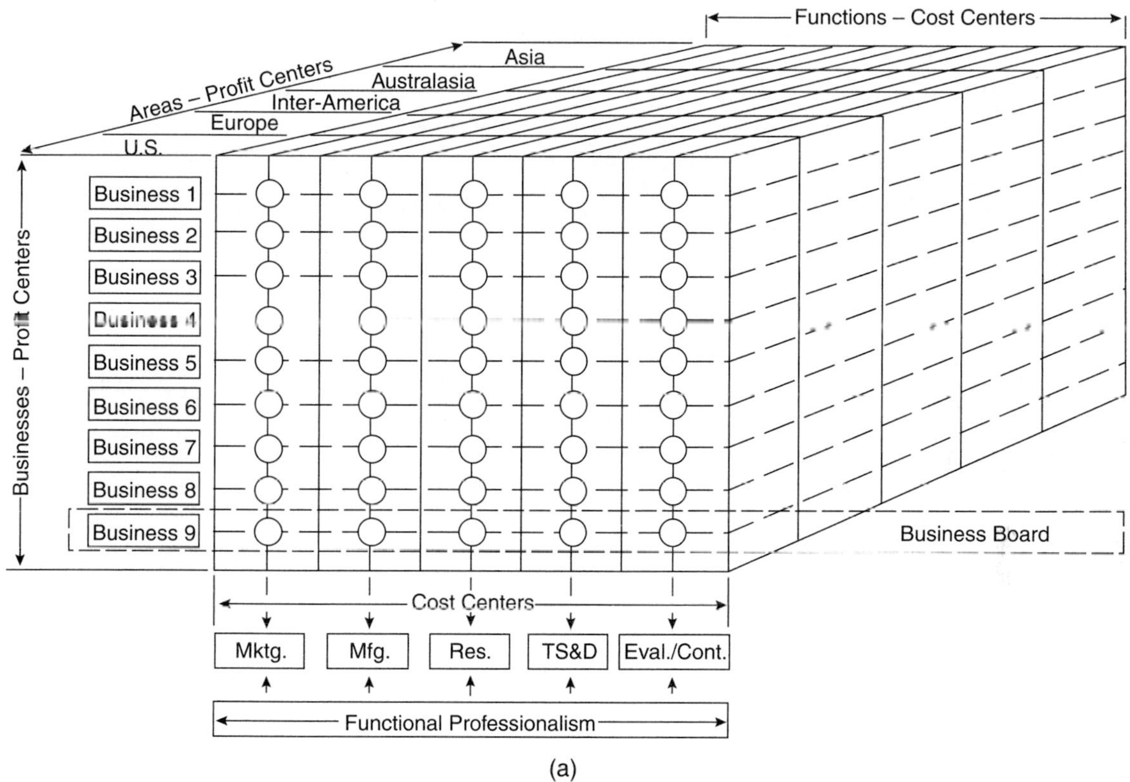

(a)

EXHIBIT 3 The Multidimensional Organization—Continued

Source: Dow Corning Corporation, 1984.

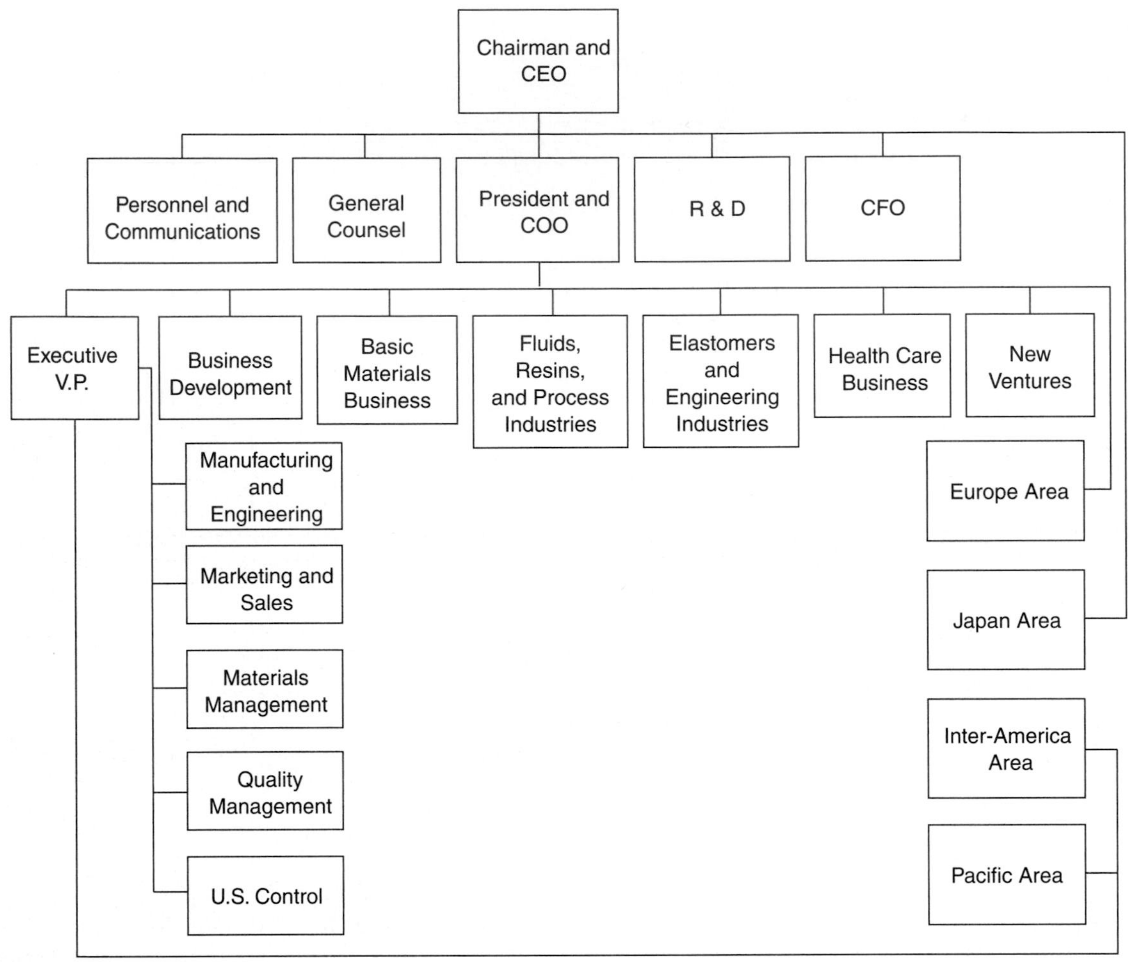

(b)

EXHIBIT 4 Memo from Pacific Area Manager

April 1, 1976

To: J.S. Ludington

From: [Pacific area manager]

Subject: **Corporate Code of Business Conduct**

First of all let me say that I don't think Dow Corning has a problem and that our house doesn't need putting in order. Therefore, we need to agree on the purpose of any code and that purpose must arise from some need. What is the need if we already believe (as I do) that we are morally, legally, and ethically correct in all aspects of our business conduct?

I think the need arises from inflation by the news media (and some social-conscious mongers) of some malpractices by some companies—often MNCs [multinational corporations]—over the past several years. The fact that such stories have so much credibility to the general public, besides a sad commentary on the abuse of their power by the media, also means that public denials or public statements of corporate codes are bound to misfire and be considered self-serving. Thus I believe the purpose of any code should be primarily internal—a means of listing those company standards which represent the minimum acceptable performance in conducting business. Every member of management then has the responsibility to see that his subordinates understand the code and are working properly within it. The outside world will become convinced only by consistent demonstration, in practice, of the agreed principles.

So I am fully in favor of a Dow Corning Code of Business Conduct to be used as an internal management and operating tool. Such a code must not only embrace parochial Dow Corning and U.S. moral, legal, and social requirements, but must also have pertinence and value in the rest of the world. If we are to do business successfully in such diverse places as U.S.A., Latin America, Japan, Italy, Korea, and India, we have also to operate in accordance with each local country's set of laws, customs, and prerogatives.

Now to the Asian Area. We do have some problem areas, of course, and some downright conflicts. I'll try to indicate some of the issues where I think we'll need to modify or expand the general principles in a Code of Conduct.

Equal Pay

The aggressive "equality of the sexes lobby" in the U.S. might lead Dow Corning to declare adherence to the principle of equal pay. In most, if not all, Asian countries, such a concept is laughable at the present time. Thus we would need to write something like: "Dow Corning will pay its employees fairly and competitively in each country and in accordance with legal and social practices."

Sex Discrimination

Again, I'm sure our corporate code would want to point out that our policy is to have none. But in many countries in Asia, the roles of male and female are still severely and vehemently separated. I'm sure there are places where we would not be allowed to promote a woman rather than a man or to have a female manager or supervisor. So we would need a qualifying clause here too.

Job Security

The two-way commitment between company and employee varies enormously from the one extreme of the lifelong contract in Japan to the laissez-faire attitude existing in Hong Kong and other places. Therefore, we would need to be very careful that any policy statement did not overcommit the company or place an unwarranted restriction on the employee. We'd need to say something like: "It is Dow Corning's policy to establish a stable and lasting employment situation for its employees consistent with the need for the company to meet its overall business and social objectives and with the need for the employee to develop his full career potential."

(continued)

EXHIBIT 4 Memo from Pacific Area Manager—Continued

Bribery and Special Payments

As you know, various forms of commissions, finder's fees, or whatever you want to call them, are the norm in several countries out here and such payments are considered normal business expenses. This situation is not going to change overnight because it has been going on for many years and is endemic in the system. We are careful not to get directly involved but we know that it goes on and will continue. Therefore our statement should be pretty general, something like: "Dow Corning will not pay bribes, illegal political contributions, or any form of nonstandard commission or business expense, in an attempt to influence customers to do business with Dow Corning."

Pricing

In view of the laws in the U.S., we may decide to say something pretty specific about fair pricing. But if such a policy is applied rigidly here, it may deny us necessary flexibility. We need something like: "Dow Corning will price its goods in the marketplace according to the value of the goods as determined by the market forces. It will not seek to offer unfair and unilateral advantages to some customers on a selective basis."

EXHIBIT 5 Corporate Code of Business Conduct, 1977

A Matter of Integrity

Dow Corning believes in private enterprise. We will seek to establish an atmosphere of trust and respect between business and members of society, an atmosphere where business and the public understand, accept, and recognize the values and needs of each other.

To establish and promote this atmosphere of mutual trust and respect, Dow Corning accepts as our responsibility a recognition, evaluation, and sensitivity to social needs. We will meet this responsibility by utilizing our technological and management skills to develop products and services that will further the development of society.

The watchword of Dow Corning worldwide activities is integrity. We recognize that due to local differences in custom and law, business practice differs throughout the world. We believe that business is best conducted and society best served within each country when business practice is based on the universal principles of honesty and integrity.

We recognize that our social responsibilities must be maintained at the high standards which lead to respect and trust by society. A clear definition of our social responsibilities should be an integral part of our corporate objectives and be clearly communicated to every employee.

Statement of General Conduct

We shall not tolerate payments in any illegal or questionable form, or nonstandard commissions or other compensation, given or received, that may influence business decisions.

We shall not make any political contribution nor participate in partisan political activity as a company, recognizing however the rights of employees to participate in legal political processes as private citizens.

We shall be knowledgeable of local laws and customs and operate within them. On the other hand, when we are not being treated legally or ethically we will pursue whatever legitimate recourses are available to us.

Responsibilities to Our Employees

Relations with employees are based on the understanding that attracting and retaining talented and dedicated employees is vital to the accomplishment of financial and social objectives.

Our responsibilities to our employees are:

To manage our activities in such a way as to provide security and opportunities for our productive employees.

To hire, train, evaluate, and advance on the basis of individual ability, contribution, potential, interest, and company needs without distinction as to nationality, sex, age, color, or religion.

To compensate in accordance with local, national, or industry practice.

To provide a safe and healthy work environment that at least meets the applicable government laws and regulations.

To provide a work environment that encourages individual self-fulfillment, open communication, and free interchange of information and ideas.

Responsibilities to Host Countries in Which We Operate

Activities in host countries are based on the premise that we can and wish to contribute to the economic objectives of the host government while concurrently meeting our corporate objectives.

Our responsibilities to host countries are:

To preserve and, where possible, enhance the environment through elimination or control of pollution.

To conserve natural resources.

To design and modify facilities which meet or exceed current and anticipated environmental and safety laws and regulations.

To hire, train, and qualify host country nationals for positions of responsibility consistent with their demonstrated capabilities.

To pay our required share of taxes and duties but resist inequitable or double taxation between countries.

To resolve any government relations problems or conflicts among overlapping jurisdictions through prompt, direct, and open discussions with responsible government officials.

To follow responsible monetary and credit practices and conduct foreign exchange operations not for speculative purposes, but in accordance with normal business requirements and to protect our exposure fluctuations.

To encourage the flow of our technology across borders to the extent needed and appropriate in our local operations and markets, and to receive adequate compensation and protection of this technology.

EXHIBIT 6 Corporate Code of Business Conduct, 1983

To Dow Corning Employees:

At the top of the list of our corporate objectives is this statement: "Dow Corning's actions shall be guided by its Corporate Code of Business Conduct." Dow Corning places an exceedingly high value on corporate integrity. A sense of fair play, honesty and ethical business practice has always been the foundation of Dow Corning's operating philosophy.

Since 1976 we have extended our efforts to formalize Dow Corning's approach to business conduct. The Code itself is regularly reviewed and updated; a top level Corporate Committee monitors and audits our worldwide compliance with Code principles; we report on business conduct practices annually to the Audit and Social Responsibility Committee of the Board of Directors.

Our intent goes beyond compliance with the law, although that is quite fundamental. Throughout the organization we are developing a sense, or attitude, of personal integrity among our employees. Each employee plays a part in maintaining the integrity of the organization in all its business activities.

I assure you the management of Dow Corning places top priority on fair, legal and ethical business conduct. As an employee of Dow Corning, I ask that you continue to share this key commitment.

Sincerely,

John S. Ludington
Chairman and Chief Executive Officer

Dow Corning
Area Headquarters

United States
Midland Center
P.O. Box 1767
Midland, MI 48640

Europe
154 Chaussee de la Hulpe
1170 Brussels, Belgium

Inter-America
Midland Center
P.O. Box 1767
Midland, MI 48640

Pacific
21 Tattersall Road
Blacktown
New South Waies 2148
Australia

Japan
15-1, Nishi Shimbashi 1-chome
Minato-Ku, Tokyo, 105, Japan

DOW CORNING

Dow Corning Corporation
Midland, Michigan 48640 U.S.A.

EXHIBIT 6 Corporate Code of Business Conduct, 1983—Continued

Our Standards of Business Conduct

Fair, legal and ethical business practice has been the cornerstone of Dow Corning's operating philosophy since the company was founded in 1943. We believe that business is best conducted and society best served when business practice is based on the principles of honesty and integrity.

The Code of Business Conduct provides guidelines, but can not cover every situation you may encounter. Should you become aware of — or involved in — a questionable practice, bring it to the attention of your supervisor or a member of the Business Conduct Committee at any time.

Dow Corning's Responsibilities to Employees:

All relations with employees will be guided by our belief that the dignity of the individual is primary.

Opportunity without bias will be afforded each employee in relation to demonstrated ability, initiative and potential.

Business decisions will be consistent with our intent to provide long-term stability and opportunity to all productive employees.

Qualified citizens of countries where we do business will be hired and trained for available positions consistent with their capabilities.

The work environment will encourage individual self-fulfillment, the maximization of skills and talents, open communication and the free exchange of information and ideas.

A safe, clean and pleasant work environment that at minimum meets all applicable laws and regulations will be provided.

The privacy of an individual's personal records will be respected; employees may participate in a review of their personnel records upon request.

Employee's Responsibilities to Dow Corning:

Employees will regard proprietary information as a valuable corporate asset and will avoid the unauthorized disclosure of Dow Corning's business activities, future plans, technology or other proprietary information. We will respect proprietary information belonging to others.

Employees must be free of conflicting interests which could inhibit or detract from their on-the-job performance or with Dow Corning's business interests.

Employees will not engage in bribery, price fixing, kickbacks, collusion, or any practice which might give the appearance of being illegal or unethical.

Employees will avoid discussions with competitors that could be construed as unfair competition or the restriction of free trade. Relations with our competitors will be limited to buyer-seller agreements, licensing agreements or matters of general concern to the industry or society. All such discussions will be documented.

Relations with Customers, Distributors, Suppliers:

Dow Corning will provide on time products and services that meet the requirements of our customers. We will provide information and support necessary to maximize the use and effectiveness of our products.

Dow Corning expects and encourages its agents, representatives and distributors to conduct business in a legal and ethical manner.

The purchase of supplies, materials and services will be based on quality, price, service, ability to supply and the vendor's adherence to legal and ethical business practices. Fees paid for business services must be reasonable and in line with customary local rates.

Conservation, Environmental and Product Stewardship Practices:

Dow Corning will be responsible for the impact of its technology upon the environment. We will protect the natural environment by continually seeking reasonable ways to eliminate or minimize discharges of potentially harmful waste materials.

All waste will be recycled when possible and economical. Non-recyclable waste will be disposed of in accordance with applicable standards.

New facilities will be designed to optimize the efficient use of natural resources and to conserve energy. Existing facilities will be modified to meet current and anticipated environmental laws and regulations.

We will continually strive to assure that our products and services are safe, efficacious and accurately represented in our literature, advertising and package identification.

Product characteristics, including toxicity and potential hazards, will be made known to those who produce, package, transport, use and dispose of Dow Corning products.

International Business Guidelines:

Dow Corning endeavors to be a productive and cooperative corporate citizen wherever we do business. We recognize, however, that laws, business practices and customs differ from country to country and may occasionally inhibit rather than foster open competition. Such practices could include boycotts, information requests, tax systems, duty classification procedures, labor standards and property protection, among others. If there is a conflict with U.S. law or a Dow Corning standard of business conduct, we will seek reasonable ways to resolve the difference. Failing resolution, Dow Corning will remove itself from the particular business situation.

Dow Corning personnel will not authorize or give payments or gifts to government employees or their beneficiaries in order to obtain or retain business. We will strongly discourage facilitating payments to expeditite the performance of routine services. Where the practice is common and there is no reasonable alternative, a minimum payment may be considered. Such payments will be accurately documented and recorded.

No payment, contribution or service will be offered by Dow Corning to a political party or a candidate, even in countries where such payments are legal.

While encouraging the transborder transfer of technology necessary to support its subsidiaries and joint ventures, Dow Corning expects to receive fair compensation for, and protection of, its technology.

Dow Corning will strive to establish intercompany prices at a level that would prevail in arm's length transactions. The intent of this approach to pricing is to assure each country a fair valuation of goods and services transferred.

Financial Responsibilities:

Dow Corning funds will be used only for purposes that are legal and ethical. All transactions will be properly and accurately recorded.

Dow Corning will maintain a system of internal accounting controls and assure that all involved employees are fully apprised of that system.

Dow Corning encourages the free flow of funds for investment, borrowing, dividending and the return of capital throughout the world.

We Are Committed . . .

. . . to the letter and spirit of this Code of Business Conduct. The character and conduct of Dow Corning Corporation depend on the actions of its employees. As a Dow Corning employee, you are expected to know these standards and live up to them.

EXHIBIT 7 Worksheets—Code of Business Conduct Audits

"Issues" to be Emphasized in Audits at Area or Regional Headquarters

I. Customers, Distributors, and Competitors

a. Dow Corning encourages competition in the open market and will avoid all association with competitors that could be construed as unfair competition or the restriction of free trade. Competitor relations will be limited to buyer-seller agreements, licensing agreements, or matters of general concern to the industry or society. *Dow Corning personnel do not participate in discussions on the pricing of our products with our competitors.*

b. *No bribe, payoff, rebate, kickback, or other form of remuneration will be given to secure or retain business. This applies to all Dow Corning officers and employees as well as agents, consultants, distributors, or any third party authorized to represent Dow Corning.* It precludes the use of agreements, arrangements, or devices intended to compensate government employees (including agencies and commissions) or shareholders of private customers for decisions or actions that would give Dow Corning Corporation an unfair competitive advantage.

1. Has Dow Corning ever found it necessary to provide "grease payments" in order to get products evaluated or qualified as an approved source in government facilities or in commercial operations?
2. Have we ever used any distributor or agents to make questionable payments or accept kickbacks on behalf of Dow Corning or any of our employees?
3. Do the improper payments that are reported in the local papers generally occur in (1) public companies, (2) private companies, (3) government-managed manufacturing, or (4) government agencies?

c. Dow Corning does not use reciprocity in any form in obtaining orders from our customers.

d. Dow Corning personnel are being practical and judicious in their offering or accepting of gifts and entertainment in their relationships with customers, distributors, suppliers, and government employees.

1. Are there any examples of business that Dow Corning has lost because of our refusing to provide "gifts" or other incentives to government officials or various personnel at our customer's facilities?
2. Payment of travel expenses for government officials, consultants, or employees of customers or prospective customers who visit a facility of Dow Corning, or a Dow Corning–sponsored event, is permissible under certain conditions. First, there must be a legitimate business reason for the trip. Second, the expenses must be reasonable and properly recorded and accounted for by Dow Corning.

e. Dow Corning employees are not involved by investment, consulting, or employment in any situations that could be considered a conflict of interest.

1. Do any of our employees have any ownership or financial interest in any of our distributors?
2. In any other organization that supplies services to Dow Corning?

f. Procedures have been established in all areas to provide *appropriate controls* on any requests for terms beyond 30 days to 60 days.

1. What use is made of special arrangements involving items such as extended terms, rebates, discounts, allowances, etc.?

g. Dow Corning distributors, sales representatives, and agents have received copies of our Code of Business Conduct. They have acknowledged that they have read the code, understand it, and will abide by it. In addition, our 1981 contracts with distributors, agents, and representatives require adherence to the Dow Corning Code of Business Conduct.

1. What do distributors think about our Code of Business Conduct Program? Do they fully understand our Business Conduct brochures?
2. Have our salesmen been able to conduct the Business Conduct discussions with our distributors in such a manner as to actually strengthen our ties and relationship with them?
3. Do we find it necessary to employ any distributors with questionable character or integrity or those who are highly political?
4. Has Dow Corning been forced to terminate any distributors because of their "Business Conduct" practices?
5. Do you believe that our distributors are in "regular" contact with their competitors? If so, why?
6. Are any customers invoiced by our distributors at a price higher than the "established local market" price? Are these invoiced amounts over market price rebated to anyone?
7. Have we received any customer lists or other proprietary information from our distributors? How is this information protected?
8. Are our distributors asking for or expecting any "gifts" or special arrangements?
9. Have we paid any expediting fees or travel expenses for our distributors?
10. Have any of our employees been exposed to extensive entertainment by any of our distributors? Are our employees able to remain

(continued)

EXHIBIT 7 Worksheets—Code of Business Conduct Audits—Continued

objective in their dealings with competitive distributors?

11. Are any of our distributors involved in any programs that will involve the relabeling or repackaging of our products? Have they been authorized by Dow Corning to do this? Do their repackaging and relabeling meet Dow Corning's standards?

h. Sales representatives should only be compensated in the country in which they operate and in the currency or currencies in which they are doing business.

i. Product characteristics, including toxicity and potential hazards, are being made known to customers and distributors who use, package, transport, or dispose of Dow Corning products.

1. Is Dow Corning able to provide adequate "Emergency Response" in the event that a major spill or other crisis develops in the transportation or use of our product?

j. Dow Corning personnel—with considered judgment and guidance from their country and/or regional manager—document all definite, illegal, or improper incidents involving customers, distributors, government representatives, suppliers, or consultants.

k. The changes that Dow Corning has initiated in order to comply with the Code of Business Conduct have added some expense; also, a few significant orders may have been lost. However, the overall program is definitely leading to a stronger, healthier relationship with our customers, distributors, and employees.

II. Host Country Relationships

a. Qualified citizens of countries where we have facilities will be hired and trained for available positions consistent with their capabilities.

b. Dow Corning will provide a work environment that encourages individual self-fulfillment, the maximization of skills and talents, open communication, and the free exchange of information and ideas.

c. Dow Corning will establish a safe, clean, and pleasant working environment that at a minimum meets all applicable laws and regulations.

d. Dow Corning will abide by the applicable United States laws in all its worldwide operations. Dow Corning will also obey the laws of those countries where we do business. If there is a conflict, Dow Corning must follow the dictates of the U.S. law. Have any problems resulted from this position? How have they been resolved?

e. Dow Corning appreciates that *business practices and customs* differ from country to country and occasionally tend to inhibit, rather than foster, open communication. When a host country practice restricts free trade or conflicts *with a Dow Corning policy or guideline, we will seek reasonable ways to resolve the difference*. Lacking appropriate resolutions, *Dow Corning will remove itself from the particular business situation.*

1. In what countries will we experience major conflicts with the "Dow Corning policies"?
2. Which specific "Dow Corning policies" conflict with local practices?
3. Can these differences be resolved or will Dow Corning be forced to discontinue seeking specific pieces of business in certain countries?

f. *No funds or services of the Dow Corning Corporation, its subsidiaries, and joint ventures will be contributed to political parties, politicians, or office holders—even in countries where such payments are legal.* However, employees may make individual political contributions through legal and company-approved programs, e.g., a Political Action Committee in the United States.

1. In what countries is it difficult for Dow Corning to do business without making political contributions?
2. What percentage of the silicone business could be affected?

g. Dow Corning employees do make necessary "expediting payments" for the company, but they are not considered to be excessive or improper in consideration of the services being performed. Accurate records of such payments are kept.

1. How are the "expediting payments" being documented?
2. Is the need for "expediting payments" increasing or decreasing?

h. Dow Corning is maintaining a comprehensive system of internal accounting controls and is taking steps to assure that all employees having access to our funds or other resources are fully aware of the existence of these controls.

1. Do you feel our financial controls are adequate to prevent funds being accumulated to make improper payments?
2. If you do not feel our controls are adequate, how would it be possible to work around them?
3. Are any of Dow Corning's procedures exposing any of our employees to inappropriate temptations?

i. Dow Corning will *not make any payments, other than approved payrolls and documented petty cash, in currency*. No payments shall be made into numbered bank accounts or any other Dow Corning account by any means that is not clearly identifiable. Any form of payment that could be viewed suspiciously is to be avoided.

(continued)

EXHIBIT 7 Worksheets—Code of Business Conduct Audits—Continued

j. *The use of "false" invoices or other misleading or fictitious documentation for any purpose is prohibited.* This applies to the invention of any false entities such as sales, purchases, services, loans, and other financial arrangements.

k. Dow Corning does not provide any inaccurate or incomplete memos, pro-forma invoices, or other documents that could assist distributors or customers in arranging for lower duties on indent shipments of our products.

   1. Do our distributors pay the appropriate import duty on their indent shipments?
   2. Do you believe it should be a Dow Corning concern if the distributor "arranges" for a lower, questionable duty on his indent shipments, provided Dow Corning support is not used in making the arrangement?

l. Dow Corning does not support or participate in any boycotts involving the selling or distribution of our products.

Additional Issues

1. Are we *inappropriately* favoring any customers or distributors with allocated products, large samples, low prices, bargain off-spec material, credit terms and allowances, or excessive gifts and entertainment?
2. Are "Competitive Activity Reports" being completed and filed on specific customers to support our selling below book price? Do we frequently review these situations to determine if below book prices are still being offered at this account by the competition?
3. How much notice do local companies expect and offer on price increases when inflation is running 10 percent to 20 percent?
4. Have we been approached by individuals affiliated with competitors, distributors, sales agents, or any other contacts with offers to purchase proprietary information—such as customer lists, technical information, etc.? Have others been approached?
5. Is Dow Corning putting adequate emphasis on the protection of our employees from international or national terrorism and local crime?
6. Do any of our business practices expose our personnel to any improper temptations (i.e., cash collections without proper controls)?
7. Of the countries within this area or region, list those in which you believe the majority (80 percent) of U.S. companies could operate within the general guidelines of the Dow Corning Code of Business Conduct.
8. Also list the countries that you believe would fall far short of this target.
9. In what cities are your people experiencing requests for grease money in amounts that definitely exceed the usual requests for tips or "expediting payments"?
10. What is the status of the Code of Business Conduct file? Does it need to be cleaned up? Does it contain sufficient information to adequately describe questionable experiences and their resolution?
11. Do you believe the region's business conduct standards have been improved significantly, slightly, or not at all by the programs of the past four years?
12. What comments have you heard from companies that use "a sign off procedure" with their regional management rather than a business conduct audit? What do you think of this approach?
13. What have you heard about the practices other U.S.–based companies are following in their business conduct audits?
14. Do you have any suggestions to make the Dow Corning Business Conduct Program more productive?
15. What is the most significant weakness in the Dow Corning Code of Business Conduct program?
16. What type of questionable business conduct do we miss in our present business conduct audit program? What additional specific questions should be asked?

EXHIBIT 8 Business Conduct Reporting Procedures

Purpose

The nine questions listed below were developed to facilitate the accurate and uniform reporting of improper and illegal situations in which Dow Corning personnel could be implicated. A reportable situation could involve customers, distributors, government officials, suppliers, consultants or Dow Corning employees. Examples of reportable incidents could include: conflicts of interest; requests for questionable payments or kickbacks; misleading or deceptive product classifications intended to affect import duties. The Corporate Code of Business Conduct describes several additional situations that, if violated, would be reportable incidents.

Reporting

The resolution of a business conduct problem is expedited when the details of the incident, and the subsequent action(s), are immediately reported and recorded. *The question should include only that information believed to be accurate*. The reporting steps are as follows:

1. Complete the questionnaire as completely as possible.
2. Send the questionnaire to the department manager or regional manager for review, judgment, and, if possible, resolution.
3. If the manager determines that area headquarters' attention is required, copies should be sent to the area manager and to the chairman, Business Conduct Committee.

Disposition

Business conduct files in regional offices should be purged every six months and completely cleaned at the end of 12 months. Area headquarters will retain a business conduct file containing reports of incidents for the current year. That file should be destroyed in December of the following year.

Documentation of Illegal, Unethical, and/or Questionable Business Practices

1. List name(s) and title(s) of individual(s) and their organization(s) who offered, or were a party to, the questionable business practice or proposition.
2. Specify by name, title, and organization others outside Dow Corning who were directly or indirectly involved.
3. List other Dow Corning employees who have first-hand knowledge of the proposition or who have helped you resolve the proposition.
4. If the questionable business practice could possibly damage Dow Corning or its reputation—or involve us in any way—but was not presented directly to Dow Corning, please explain how you learned about it (i.e., distributor and customer, distributor and government agent, etc.).
5. Briefly describe the proposition itself and what, in your opinion, it was expected to accomplish.
6. What form of remuneration was to be used: cash, gifts, entertainment, extraordinarily high fees or payments, reciprocity, other?
7. Describe actions taken or being considered to resolve the situation by you and/or others.
8. Did our response or action have any effect, positive or negative, on Dow Corning's operations (i.e., customer relations, sales, relationship with distributor, relationship with a supplier, etc.)?
9. What suggestions do you have that might prevent, or reduce, the possibility of this type of questionable business practice occurring another time from a different source?

Dow Corning Corporation: *The Breast Implant Controversy*

John E. Swanson rescheduled two meetings and stayed in his office the entire afternoon of June 10, 1991. Two floors above him, a meeting of Dow Corning's Board of Directors was in session. Board meetings were usually two or three hours long. This one had taken the entire afternoon. Would the directors agree to temporarily suspend sales of silicone breast implants pending further safety studies, as he had recommended? Or would they continue sales to avoid any suggestion of a safety problem until more information was available?

Two weeks before the Directors' meeting, Swanson was stunned by a *Business Week* article entitled, "BREAST IMPLANTS: WHAT DID THE INDUSTRY KNOW, AND WHEN?" The article alleged that Dow Corning Corporation (DCC) had known of animal studies linking silicone breast implants to illness for over a decade and had covered it up. (See Exhibit 1.) Dow Corning, the leading manufacturer of silicone implants, was explicitly charged in the article with hiding the damaging results of a series of internal tests for years. Further, the article said that Dow Corning was aware that the implants could bleed or even rupture but had not informed the public. Swanson, the only permanent member of the corporation's Business Conduct Committee, was essentially Dow Corning's point man on ethical issues, and he was chagrined by his ignorance of these charges. After 26 years with the company, Swanson thought he knew where all the potential problems were.

Dow Corning had a hard-won reputation as an ethical company and was proud of its product quality. Swanson recognized the potentially damaging nature of the *Business Week* charges, so with the company's integrity hanging in the balance, he felt he had no choice but to recommend that Dow Corning temporarily suspend sales until a thorough review was performed. He doubted, however, that the directors would want to make any move that could imply guilt or needlessly alarm the thousands of women who had implants. Dow Corning had long taken the position that no science existed showing significant danger to women with silicone implants. To suspend production now could send a signal saying exactly the opposite.

As the meeting went on behind closed doors, Swanson shook his head at the way events had steamrolled. He believed management was entering a labyrinth of its own making, and he was not sure it knew the way out. When the doors opened and the Board meeting adjourned, he would know what the first steps would be. Until then, he remained in the dark, trying to understand how the company had gotten to this point.

Company Background

The Dow Corning Corporation (DCC) was founded in 1943 as a 50/50 joint venture of Dow Chemical Company and Corning Glass Works. The corporation's charter was to develop, manufacture, and market silicone-based products. Silicones were made by combining the element silicon with organic compounds. They could be formulated to possess unique physical characteristics, such as electrical insulating properties, maintenance of physical properties at extreme temperatures, water repellence, resistance to

This case was prepared by Research Assistant Charles Sellers, under the supervision of Professor Kenneth E. Goodpaster, University of St. Thomas, and Professor Norman E. Bowie, University of Minnesota, as the basis for class discussion rather than to illustrate either effective or ineffective handling of an administrative situation. Special cooperation in researching and preparing the case was provided by John E. Swanson, principal consultant, Applied Business Ethics, and by spokespersons for Dow Corning Corporation.

aging, lubricating characteristics, and chemical and physiological inertness. Because of these properties, silicone-based products had a multitude of uses. By 1993, DCC sold over 5,000 different silicone products to more than 45,000 customers in every major industry, including construction, engineering, personal care, household, automotive, chemicals and coatings, semiconductors, and health care.

In 1993, Dow Corning was a multinational company with headquarters in Midland, Michigan. Over half of its business took place outside the United States, and only 13 of its 35 manufacturing locations were inside the U.S. It employed over 8,000 people and had over two billion dollars in annual sales. Prior to 1993, the company ranked with the top two hundred and fifty companies in the country for annual sales and near the top one hundred for profits according to *Fortune* magazine. In 1993, the company's *Fortune* 500 profit ranking had slipped to 465th. When dividends were last paid in to the parent companies in 1991, each received $77.5 million.[1]

Initially, Dow Corning's expertise in silicones had made it the sole manufacturer of many products. The company invested heavily in research and development and was especially proud of its progress in pioneering new uses for silicones. By the 1970s, however, competition tightened and DCC started to lose market share in some product lines. In response, the company took two major steps. First, in 1977 it acquired the Wright Manufacturing Company, a small company concentrating on metal orthopedic implants. Through this acquisition, Dow Corning expanded its base in the health care industry and Wright expanded its product mix and expertise in applied science. Over several years, the new subsidiary, called Dow Corning/Wright, assumed most of the responsibility for silicone breast implants, although the implants were still manufactured at a Dow Corning medical facility in Hemlock, Michigan.

Second, Dow Corning tried to decentralize authority and push decision making as far down as possible. Management believed this provided the necessary flexibility to respond to a rapidly changing, competitive environment.

[1] Figures from casewriter's interview with John Swanson.

Introducing the Code of Business Conduct[2]

DCC's culture was relatively open, informal, and relaxed through the 1970s. There was little emphasis on official status, and no traditional organizational chart with clear-cut, hierarchical reporting relationships. Instead, the company had adopted its own multidimensional, matrix-style organization.[3] With the ascension of John S. (Jack) Ludington as DCC's CEO in 1975, the company saw a need to develop a formal code of business conduct. As the corporation became more and more of an international entity, it was critical to make sure everyone operated under the same guidelines. In effect, it sought to construct a safety net that would catch or, ideally, prevent ethical mistakes while preserving its fluid decision-making structure.

Dow Corning had always enjoyed a degree of loyalty among its employees that was rare in the business world,[4] and some thought a formal code of conduct unnecessary. However, in the wake of Watergate and disclosures that the Lockheed Corporation had spent millions bribing Japanese officials, multinational corporations were viewed cynically by the public. It came as no surprise when in 1977 Congress adopted the Foreign Corrupt Practices Act (FCPA). To head off any possible regulatory requirements and to ensure ethical internal and external business practices, CEO Jack Ludington appointed four senior managers to DCC's first Business Conduct Committee (BCC) in May 1976. John Swanson helped Ludington develop the committee's mission and became the sole permanent member. The Business Conduct Committee was charged with the following tasks:

> Learning more about how the company really operated outside the country.

[2] Much of this section is derived from HBS case 9 · 385 · 018, "Dow Corning: Business Conduct and Global Values" (1984, revised 1989).

[3] The company's matrix-style organization was described in a 1979 *Harvard Business Review* article titled "How the Multi-dimensional Organization Works at Dow Corning."

[4] Andrew W. Singer, "In Breast Implants Scandal, Where Was Dow Corning's Concern for Women?" *Ethikos*, May/June 1994. Singer notes overall employee pride in DCC's ethics from 1976 through the 1992 controversy.

Developing guidelines that would be the basis for communicating legal and ethical standards of business conduct around the world.

Developing a workable process for auditing and reporting the company's business practices.

Recommending ways to correct questionable practices as they became known.

In 1977, DCC published its first corporate code, *A Matter of Integrity*, along with five separate codes for each of the corporation's geographic regions, i.e., Europe, Asia, Latin America, Canada, and the U.S. It was distributed to employees accompanied by a letter from Ludington encouraging them to read it. Emphasizing that one of DCC's "most valued assets is our reputation for quality and integrity," he stated: "Our aim should be to continually build commitment to the highest standards possible throughout the organization." The Code has been revised several times since 1977 to reflect Dow Corning's changing concerns, but the basic text has remained the same.

Implementing the Code and Monitoring Compliance

By 1979, 17 audits had been held worldwide, and they began to include regional personnel one or two levels below area management. Records of all audits were kept at corporate headquarters, and each summer, the Business Conduct Committee discussed the results of the previous year's audits before starting another round of interviews in the fall.

A typical audit opened with a summary of objectives; a review of the BCC's activities, a discussion of "gray areas" of business practice; and a briefing by the committee on issues related to the code of conduct, such as interpretations of the FCPA, progress on international codes, etc. The remainder of the meeting was then spent discussing such topics as competitor, government, and customer relations; distributor practices; conflicts of interest; employee concerns; and product and environmental stewardship. The audits were generally spirited and informal, especially after employees understood that the company was serious about its increased emphasis on ethics and corporate responsibility.

Other Steps Taken to Ensure Ethical Behavior

Audits were the most significant way in which the message and commitment to the code was communicated to employees, but several other channels were also used. The code was framed and hung in conspicuous places in the company's offices and plants around the world. DCC also used videotapes of current audit topics by BCC members in order to keep employees informed. And the results were positive: beginning with the code's inception in 1976, a semiannual employee survey registered a steady improvement in attitudes toward the company's emphasis on ethics.

While the scope of the corporate BCC was global, the president of the U.S. area appointed a separate U.S. Business Ethics Committee in 1978. At first, this committee did audits also, but by 1979 it started to function more like an ombudsman, studying various issues brought to its attention by employees. For example, in 1982 the committee responded to employee concerns over the privacy of personnel records. Working with the Personnel Policy Committee, it reviewed the recordkeeping process and formulated guidelines for what should be in company files and when these files should be purged.

The BCC and the U.S. Business Ethics Committee developed different identities: the BCC was responsible for making policy, revising the code, and monitoring compliance, whereas the U.S. committee responded primarily to issues as they "bubbled up" from the ranks. Relationships between the two committees had been informal, and they met only as needed. Beginning in 1982, however, the BCC began conducting an increasing number of audits within the United States. By mid 1984, it was determined that there was no need for a separate U.S. Committee and it was disbanded.

Entering the Implant Manufacturing Business

Liquid silicone injections for breast augmentation first caught on in Beverly Hills in the early 1960s after Japanese doctors developed a silicone fluid with one percent olive oil in the 1950s.[5] Dow Corning first marketed its silicone breast implants in 1964, following two years of clinical experience with the device led by physicians from Baylor University. Some research had been done during the 1950s indicating that silicones, especially of a high grade, were relatively inert, but at this time there were no test protocols or data available for breast implants regarding cancer or immune system disease.[6]

In addition to the 1950s studies, in 1962 DCC initiated research on the long-term stability of implanted silicone materials. According to the company, these results, completed in 1961, "confirmed that implanted silicone elastomers had superior stability compared with other implanted materials. These findings, combined with the positive clinical experience with breast implants, led Dow Corning to commercialize breast implants in 1964."[7] As demand grew, DCC gained a reputation as a company with high-grade silicone breast implants.

As it increased production, however, the company also got into a brush with the law, pleading *nolo contendere* (i.e., no contest) to a charge of illegally transporting silicone fluids across state lines for direct medical purposes. By pleading *nolo contendere*, the company did not admit guilt but did accept a fine. Dow Corning maintained that it was transporting silicone solely for industrial applications, and that it was medical practitioners who were illegally converting the company's industrial-grade silicone into "medical-grade" material. Some were profiting by injecting liquid silicone directly into women's breasts. Dow Corning was adamantly against these practices, but deemed it wiser to settle by pleading no contest than to fight a lengthy court battle.[8]

In the 1960s and 1970s, Dow Corning biologists and chemists started to explore additional medical applications for a variety of different silicones including some of those used in breast implants. The results were conflicting. Most of the silicones tested produced no effects, according to DCC, including the fluids used in breast implants. However, a low molecular silicone that appears in trace amounts in the breast implants acted as an adjuvant when tested with a foreign material called an antigen.[9] Adjuvants were generally used to increase the efficacy of vaccines by stimulating the immune system.[10]

Dr. Don Bennett, an expert in drug metabolism and head of the in-house DCC research team studying the effects of silicone on the immune system, recalled in connection with this research that the chemists were "sold on the idea of inertness" while the biologists "were almost an embarrassment" to the company because they found active silicones. In an interview with *New York Times* reporter Sandra Blakeslee, Bennett offered an explanation of the contradictory interpretations of the two research groups. "Compounds that are chemically inert, like silicone, are not necessarily biologically inert. And Dow Corning, the chemical company, paid more heed to its chemists than to its biologists."[11]

[5] From a speech by Dr. Norman Anderson, a plaintiffs' expert witness in litigation against DCC, at the Command Trust Conference, November 7, 1992.

[6] According to John Swanson, in 1962 when the first silicone breast implant was performed, "Dow Corning had no safety department or toxicological laboratory. Dow Chemical had one of the best in the world. Dow Corning's materials—later used in breast implants—were tested by Dow Chemical. Evidence presented in a Reno, NV, trial against Dow Chemical in October 1995 persuaded the jury that Dow Chemical did early testing for DCC and found health-related problems with silicones. Dow Corning had a close working relationship with Dow Chemical through the 40s, 50s, and 60s. Dow Corning did not have its own toxicology laboratory until the early 1970s." Courts in Michigan, New York, and California have dismissed all cases against Dow Chemical.

[7] Source: Case supervisors' interviews and correspondence with DCC spokespersons.

[8] Source: Casewriter's interview with John Swanson.

[9] According to John Byrne in his book on the controversy, *Informed Consent* (McGraw-Hill, 1996), "The 10-month study on guinea pigs found that one version of silicone fluid used in breast implants increased immune response tenfold when compared to implants filled with saline solution," p. 176.

[10] Based on these studies, DCC decided not to pursue adjuvant medical products such as anti-viral compounds because the results were not promising enough to be commercially viable. Other research, however, confirmed the value of silicones in medical applications like artificial hearts, pacemakers, and kidney dialysis, devices that were starting to revolutionize medicine. Source: Case supervisors' correspondence with DCC spokesperson.

[11] "Chemists typically think that biology will take care of itself," Dr. Bennett said. Source: Sandra Blakeslee, "Implant Maker Had Conflicting Findings on Silicone," *New York Times*, May 9, 1994.

Dow Corning continued scientific experiments on silicones, implanting the devices into dogs during 1968. After six months, DCC researchers announced they had not seen any response in the tissue around the implant. The implications seemed clear: either the silicone was not leaking out of the implant envelope, or if it was, there were no adverse reactions. The study affirmed the conventional wisdom at Dow Corning that silicones were inert. A 1973 article in *Medical Instrumentation* would attest to the success of the dog study and bring more attention to Dow Corning's silicone breast implant business.[12]

With these studies behind them, Dow Corning published its first version of "Facts . . . About Your New Look" in 1972. This pamphlet was distributed to plastic surgeons to support their discussions with their patients about the risks and benefits of breast implant surgery. The pamphlet was written in a question and answer format and included a statement that said fibrous capsules can cause "excessive firmness and/or discomfort" sometimes requiring surgical correction. The brochure also stated, "Based upon laboratory findings, together with human experience to date, one would expect that the Mammary Prosthesis would last for a natural lifetime. However, since no Mammary Prosthesis has been implanted for a full life span, it is impossible to give an unequivocal answer."

In the 1970s, Dow Corning decided to bring a new implant model to the market in two phases.[13] First, it introduced a new thinner-walled implant in the early 1970s, but retained the same silicone gel. The company spent the next several years safety testing a new "responsive" gel before bringing the second phase of the new model to the market in late 1975. Animal tests on the new gel were done on different species using varying ranges of viscosity. By September 1975, DCC was manufacturing between six and seven thousand a month.

[12] Silas Braley and Gordon Robertson, *Medical Instrumentation*, 1973.

[13] A DCC spokesperson described this new effort to the case supervisors as a "response to physicians wanting a more natural feeling implant, one that more closely resembled breast tissue." John Swanson's description of the effort was "to bolster its eroding market share in the booming and increasingly competitive breast implant market."

A Mammary Task Force was created early in 1975 to complete the final manufacturing and other tasks needed to bring the second phase of the new model to market. During this time, rejections occurred in the manufacturing start-up—"working out the flaws in the system before releasing the new model for general commercial use," according to the company. Some of the samples produced led to some concerns among team members that the new model of implants had more silicone fluid bleeding through the envelope than previous models. "In response to the sometimes colorful memos expressing this concern," a company spokesperson observed, "the company tested the samples and found that the level of bleed was no different between the old and the new models."

Entering the Regulation Era

Relationship with the FDA

In 1976, the Food and Drug Administration (FDA) was empowered by the Medical Device Amendment Act to regulate implants and other devices. In addition, the Amendment allowed the FDA to require long-term studies on product safety and effectiveness by implant manufacturers, including Dow Corning. In the past, the FDA and organizations like Dow Corning had generally had more informal relations that did not involve legal mandates. The Medical Device Amendment Act was the first specific delineation of powers, and it sparked the agency to become more active in the industry. With this act, the FDA became more public and more vocal in its requests for more information.

Dow Corning agreed that further studies were needed and participated in conferences with the FDA on the need for safety in manufacturing. DCC assured the FDA that internal studies were being performed and that more long-term studies would occur in the near future. Dow Corning's reputation as an ethical company and a general atmosphere of trust combined for a "hands off" attitude from the FDA. The agency was satisfied by DCC's intentions and saw no need to clamp down on the company.

While Dow Corning continued to research silicones for a variety of purposes, including breast implant materials, revenues from breast implants were small, less than one percent of sales.[14] The majority of Dow Corning products involved industrial applications of silicones; much of its research concentrated on those applications. During this period, according to the company, the primary concern regarding breast implants had to do with cancer. Results of animal and clinical research on that issue, rather than effects on the immune system, were communicated to the FDA.[15]

Dow Corning prided itself on the caliber of scientists it hired and was generally more willing to believe the results of its inside testing than FDA-generated reports or those from outside labs. As the FDA requested more specific tests from 1976 through 1983, the company consistently reported that its tests indicated no link between silicone and risk of disease. In 1983, an FDA advisory panel strongly recommended that manufacturers be required to prepare safety and effectiveness data specific to cancer, reproductive effects, silicone migration, and foreign body reactions.

Entering the Litigation Era

The Maria Stern Case and Its Effects

In 1982, a woman named Maria Stern, represented by lawyer Nancy Hersh, brought suit against Dow Corning. At the time, Stern was suffering from debilitating fatigue and arthritis that her doctor believed was caused by her silicone gel breast implants.

Hersh suspected there was information in Dow Corning's archives that it had not released, possibly information that the company did not even know existed. Hoping for something tangible, she sent an associate, Dan Bolton, to make a legal request (i.e., *discovery*) to sort through the company's files. What he found became the basis of the case. Several memos written by employees involved with the silicone breast implant business gave the impression of numerous complaints and warnings that had gone unheeded. They also implied that requests for additional research had been ignored.[16]

In 1984, the case went to court. Stern was the first plantiff to have had silicone implants, develop an autoimmune disease, and then have the disease subside when the implants were removed. This evidence, though circumstantial, persuaded the jury.[17] Hersh produced company documentation stating previously unreleased results from the 1968 dog study. Although, as Dow Corning maintained, there had been no localized reaction after six months, after two years one dog was dead and two had severe chronic inflammation. In addition, some dogs had spots on their spleens while others suffered from a thyroid disease (thyroiditis), and many of their autoimmune systems were affected. None of the dogs in the control group developed any disease.

Dow Corning vehemently denied that there was a connection between the presence of autoimmune diseases in the dogs and Stern's autoimmune disease. The report from the outside laboratory which conducted the dog study stated that the death of the dog at 48 weeks "was not associated with implant material."[18] However, the

[14] Karen Zagor, "Getting the Chemistry Wrong," *Financial Times*, March 25, 1992.

[15] Source: Case supervisors' interviews and correspondence with DCC. A company spokesperson added that "The question as to whether a relationship existed between implants and immune system disease did not begin appearing in medical case reports involving women with implants until the early 1980s. Prior to that, the association had only been mentioned in a case report involving injected silicone contaminated with other substances."

[16] "What was lacking from the files," according to a DCC spokesperson, "were documents that indicated how the company had actually responded to these issues, as well as how it had *encouraged* doctors to report problems with the products." John Swanson disagreed in an interview with the casewriter in January 1995: "As a cultural matter, the younger scientists learned it was corporate heresy to protest too loudly; while some of the older scientists said little or resigned quietly. Silicone was inert, period."

[17] A DCC spokesperson argued that such circumstantial evidence is inconclusive since some women with symptoms have reported *no change* when implants were removed and that others reported a *temporary* change followed by a return of the symptoms.

[18] Dow Corning also said that the study's investigators "noted signs of distemper in the dog colony and that the dog in question had vomited immediately before death. The most severe chronic inflammation reported in the study involved silicone elastomer, not a mammary gel implant, which was placed in the muscle tissue where irritating movement would be more pronounced than at other sites. Sites in the dog study implanted with miniature silicone gel implants had only a mild reaction. In addition, the gel implants used in this study were covered with a dacron patch, a material known to produce inflammation based on previous research. Finally, all organ weights and histopathology among the dogs in the study were within the normal range, and no control group was included for comparison." Source: Case supervisors' interviews and correspondence with DCC spokesperson.

jury did not agree and awarded Stern $1.5 million in punitive damages and $211 thousand for product liability damages. DCC was accused of fraud and negligence, and was chastised by the judge for hiding the results of the dog study and other internal memoranda.[19]

Dow Corning was successful, however, in asking the court to seal the records of the case from public disclosure and in obtaining a court order to keep key witnesses from sharing their testimony. After the decision, company management agreed to perform more studies but maintained that past science had never established or proven a link between the presence of silicone in the human system and an overexcited autoimmune response.[20] DCC justified sealing the records, a not uncommon practice in these kinds of cases, on the basis of the large amount of proprietary information that was revealed in the course of the case. Were the records to become public, the company claimed, it could lose manufacturing secrets and market share.

In 1985, Dow Corning revised and expanded the package insert that accompanied its breast implant products.[21] The new insert contained a 17-point list of possible adverse reactions and complications, among them:

> 3. *Sensitization.* There have been reports of suspected immunological sensitization or hyperimmune system response to silicone mammary implants. Symptoms claimed by the patients included localized inflammation and irritation at the implant area, fluid accumulation, rash, general malaise, severe joint pain, swelling of joints, weight loss, . . . Such claims suggest there may be a relationship between the silicone mammary implant and the reported symptoms.
>
> Materials from which this prosthesis is fabricated have been shown in animal laboratory tests to have minimal sensitization potential. However, claims from clinical use of the silicone prosthesis in humans suggest that immunological responses or sensitization to a mammary prosthesis can occur.

More Studies, More Suits

During 1986, internal pressures grew as well. Following a Business Conduct Committee audit of Dow Corning/Wright, two members of the committee were given an assignment to examine how Dow Corning/Wright was using the results of research in introducing new products. This report was scheduled to come out in 1987, but it is unknown whether it gained wide distribution in the company. In 1988, another Business Conduct audit was completed by John Swanson in which recommendations were made and questions asked about the extent to which information about implants was being made available to the end user. The audit included questions of efficacy and safety, noting that there was no standard among supplier companies on the amount of information distributed to surgeons and patients. The audit made no specific recommendations, however, nor did it, as Swanson later admitted, contain a disciplinary tone. "In retrospect," he said, "I wish the statement had been written much more forcefully."[22] (See Exhibit 2.)

By 1987, a two-year study on rats was finished. The results, according to Dow Corning scientists, were conflicting. Tumors *were* noticed with some frequency at the site of the implant. However, an expert panel commissioned by Dow Corning was unable to state definitively that this would presage a similar cancer risk in humans. Instead, they noticed that the kinds of tumors the rats had were of the solid state variety, a kind not noticed in humans. While the results were disconcerting, the scientists ultimately stated that the risk, if any, was minimal and they called for more experimental work.

More anecdotal reports filtered in, both in medical journals and from concerned women. In

[19] Kim S. Hirsch, "Breast-Implant Lawsuits Start to Build Momentum," *Chicago Tribune*, January 19, 1993.

[20] According to John Swanson in a January 1995 interview with the casewriter, the Stern case was regarded within the company as something not to be discussed.

[21] Prior to 1985, the inserts had addressed complications like the formation of a capsule around the implants, the risks inherent in surgery, and the potential for implant rupture due to surgical procedures to trauma. (Source: Casewriter's interviews and correspondence with DCC spokesperson.) By June 1991, the insert indicated that "Many case reports suggest systemic illness with joint pain, myositis (a rare muscle disease), fever and swollen lymph nodes being most frequently mentioned . . ." But the company was careful to note in the same pamphlet that any connection between silicone and immune system diseases "remains to be established."

[22] From casewriter's interview with John Swanson.

1988, Sidney Wolfe of Public Citizen's Health Group, a nonprofit legal organization based in Washington, D.C., filed a letter with the FDA asking for an investigation of Dow Corning's records. Public Citizen believed these records would show silicone gel to be carcinogenic. Public Citizen contended that the public needed to know any potential dangers of silicone implants. Wolfe demanded public release of at least part of the information. Dow Corning challenged the request on the grounds that the records contained a large amount of proprietary information crucial to sales. The company won, keeping its records private. By November, Dow Corning distributed a press release to doctors reflecting the FDA advisory panel's published comments that the solid state phenomenon did not apply to humans.

In 1988, Dow Corning was selling thousands of implants a month when the FDA acted on its own 1983 recommendations and ordered manufacturers to provide safety and effectiveness information. Up until now the FDA and manufacturers of implants had enjoyed a fairly warm relationship. In the face of an increasing number of health complaints, however, that relationship started to change.

Later in 1988, the FDA was concerned enough to classify silicone breast implants as "Class III" devices. Dow Corning and other manufacturers agreed to provide the information to the FDA, including materials previously submitted. As required by law, the Agency kept the manufacturers' submitted material confidential to protect competitive and proprietary information.

In conjunction with the Class III designation, the FDA set a 30-month comment period on the rules it had published regarding the safety data it would require of manufacturers. The Class III designation also involved a warning by the FDA that any manufacturer who could not provide such data would have its products barred. July 1991 was the deadline for implant manufacturers to provide safety data on silicone gel implants for approval by the FDA.

In November of 1990, U.S. District Court Judge Stanley Sporkin ruled on an appeal of Public Citizen's 1988 request for more information from the FDA. Sporkin ruled that the FDA should make public data as far back as the 1960s. He then criticized Dow Corning for keeping the information private and specifically scolded the company for barring the release of testimony by witnesses familiar with animal testing procedures. Dow Corning appealed the ruling.

Rylee and Hopkins: Internal and External Warning Signs

When Dow Corning acquired Wright Manufacturing in 1977, Robert Rylee was Wright's President and CEO. After the acquisition, he continued to head the company, now known as Dow Corning/Wright. By the mid-1980s, Rylee was appointed General Manager of Dow Corning's Health Care Businesses. By 1987, he was named a Dow Corning Corporate Vice President. Rylee's main strength lay not in the chemical industry but in his contacts in the health care industry, especially among doctors and surgeons. He had also become well known to members of the Society of Plastic and Reconstructive Surgeons (ASPRS). Rylee became DCC's spokesperson on health care matters, including silicone breast implants.

In December of 1990, Rylee was preparing to speak in front of the House Human Resources and Intergovernmental Relations Subcommittee on behalf of the company. A staff group met at DCC's headquarters to review some of the testimony Rylee would give. To help prepare him, members of the group had, among other things, drawn together results of a 1988 survey by the National Center for Health Statistics (NCHS) which pertained to breast implants.

The completed study would not be published until three years later in 1993. It was designed to estimate the number of women who had breast implants and to obtain an understanding of complication rates. Analysis of the survey data showed that among the 143 women with implants who were interviewed, 25.9% had "some type of problem" associated with them; that 13% of surveyed women had a replacement within 5 years; that 17% had a replacement within 10 years; that device defect, failure, or malfunction was reported for 11% of surveyed women; and that "defect or malfunction" was given as the reason for replacement in 30% of replaced devices.[23]

A summary of the raw data from the NCHS survey was passed around to those attending, including Dr. Charles Dillon, Corporate Medical Director, and Mary Ann Woodbury, an epidemiologist reporting to Dr. Dillon. Woodbury had been responsible for compiling the NCHS survey data and had issued a report in which she both summarized the data and listed the limitations of the survey.

Several days later, on December 20, John Swanson received a memo from Dr. Dillon about events that occurred after the meeting adjourned. (See Exhibit 3.) Specifically, Dr. Dillon believed that one of the senior litigation attorneys at DCC had approached Mary Ann Woodbury and had asked her to destroy all copies of the NCHS survey report she had circulated at the meeting as well as all overheads on mammary devices. This request, according to Dillon's memo, had come from Rylee, who believed that the wording of Ms. Woodbury's report could be harmful in terms of earlier and current litigation. Dillon, concerned for the integrity of the department and its research, felt that this was an ethical breach and asked Swanson to have the Business Conduct Committee look into the situation.

Swanson contacted Richard A. Hazelton, then chairman of the committee, and drew up an agenda for the proposed January 9, 1991, meeting. Hazleton, in turn, contacted another committee member to join him in conducting the January meeting. To ensure that issues could be resolved candidly and quickly, the normal procedure in these matters was to convene one or two committee members to listen to the issues and make a recommendation. While Swanson recalls that Hazleton specifically asked him not to attend the session, Hazleton does not recall such a conversation. During this time (1990), Hazleton had no knowledge of Swanson's views on implants nor was he aware that Swanson's wife had implants. According to DCC, committee meetings on ethical issues had previously occurred both with and without Swanson's attendance. But according to Swanson, "Since Dillon's original memo was addressed to me, it was highly unusual that I would not attend the subsequent meeting."

At the January 9 meeting, the events of the December 12 meeting were reviewed by each of the direct participants, i.e., Dillon, Rylee, Woodbury, and attorney Theiss. During the course of the discussion, Ms. Woodbury indicated that she had not been asked to destroy any documents, nor had this been requested of her by either Rylee or Theiss. Instead, she had been asked to collect copies of her report.[24]

As a result of the meeting, all parties agreed that there had been a considerable amount of misunderstanding involved in the incident. A policy was subsequently developed in case similar situations occurred in the future. The main provisions of the policy were, in Swanson's words:

1. Employees can't force the withdrawal or retrieval of documents authored by others.
2. Employees must bring disagreements to relevant management when they can't agree among themselves.
3. When documents might relate to litigation, they can't be withdrawn or retrieved without prior discussion with the legal department.

[23] Subsequent research on complications conducted by The Mayo Clinic and published in 1997 in the *New England Journal of Medicine* reviewed the records of 749 women with implants. Complications requiring surgery occurred in 24% of the women, with the leading cause being local complications involving capsular contraction (17.5%) followed by implant rupture (5.7%). (Dow Corning reported one percent of its implants as having ruptured.) In March 1992, DCC revised its *Patient Information Pamphlet* to read as follows: "Because silicone breast implants have not existed for a patient's life cycle, no definitive data on life expectancy can be stated. It has been suggested that a reasonable life span may be ten years, but this has not been substantiated by scientific data." Sources: Case supervisor interviews with John Swanson; correspondence and interviews with DCC spokesperson; "National Survey of Self Reported Breast Implants: 1988 Estimates," *Journal of Long-Term Effects of Medical Implants* 3, no. 1 (1993), 81–89; and "Complications Leading in Surgery after Breast Implantation," *New England Journal of Medicine* 336, no. 10 (1997), pp. 677–82.

[24] According to DCC, the concern leading to this request "was that the wording of Ms. Woodbury's report could be misconstrued to mean that the NCHS survey was a reliable estimate of women with implants or of complications, even though both Ms. Woodbury and Dr. Dillon believed otherwise." John Byrne, in *Informed Consent*, pp. 132–35, offers a different interpretation of these events, especially regarding the company's concerns about the Woodbury report.

At approximately the same time as these meetings were being held, Dow Corning's legal department was watching the rise of another suit reminiscent of the 1984 Maria Stern fight. After appealing the Stern case, DCC had finally settled out of court in 1987 for an undisclosed amount, with all witnesses' comments placed under a protective seal. Although they had kept the Stern case out of the public eye, DCC was not anxious to get involved in another lengthy case. Unfortunately, the new case showed all the signs of a protracted legal battle.

Mariann Hopkins, a woman in her mid-forties, had first discovered a lump in her breast in 1973. She underwent a double mastectomy and then had reconstructive surgery that included two silicone gel implants in 1976. They ruptured soon after her operation and spilled silicone throughout her body, including her lymph system. She subsequently experienced mixed connective tissue disease and immune system disorders.

Hopkins filed suit in December of 1988, years after the initial ruptures. The lateness of the filing date, DCC contended, put Hopkins outside the statute of limitations on the matter. She should have filed years earlier, company attorneys argued, in order for her case to have had any validity. Dow Corning also asserted that Hopkins' symptoms had been present for over two years before she received the implants. Moreover, DCC still held that there was no scientific evidence linking silicone gel with mixed connective tissue disease or immune system disorders. Therefore, according to the company, no matter when Ms. Hopkins developed the disease, it still was not related to the presence of silicone in her system. Dow Corning wanted the case dismissed. The regulatory maze was complicated and pressure-filled enough without the spotlight of a highly publicized court case. Instead, it was headed for a jury.

In The Public Eye

Business Week Appears

Even as the Dow Corning leadership watched its legal problems build, the company could not have foreseen the *Business Week* article. (See again Exhibit 1.) At the time of the article, June 1991, between 1.5 million and 2 million women had silicone breast implants. The article put forward detailed allegations by plaintiffs' attorneys that Dow Corning and other companies in the industry had misled women by hiding the results of damaging experiments. Just as importantly, it questioned the core ethical values of Dow Corning, and the reputation the company had built over years. John Swanson believed in the work of the Business Conduct Committee. To have the company's integrity challenged in a magazine like *Business Week* was something Swanson knew could not be ignored.

With this in mind, Swanson sent an electronic mail message to George Callaghan, the Corporate Comptroller and chair of the BCC. In it he recommended no actual steps, but he did make a case for fundamentally "re-examining" Dow Corning's position on being in the implant business. (See Exhibit 4.) Although the business represented only one percent of sales, the implants were just the kind of product that could ignite public opinion against all of Dow Corning.

Swanson went further, meeting with the vice president in charge of managing the breast implant controversy, J. Kermit Campbell. Although they agreed that the best thing to do might be to suspend sales pending further review, Campbell had reservations based on the legal implications of such a move. He indicated, however, that he would try to raise the issue at the next Board meeting. What would happen then was hard to predict. The last thing Dow Corning wanted was to provide more ammunition for possible future plaintiffs, and the company did not want to do anything that would imply any guilt or negligence on its part. A suspension would seem to imply both.

Nevertheless, Swanson prepared a draft press release that announced suspension of sales. (See Exhibit 5.) He made it clear in the draft that this was in no way an admission of guilt, merely a statement of caution and concern for customers.

That was over a week ago. Now Swanson waited. The meeting had lasted the entire afternoon. Could the Board afford to question publicly the safety of two million women who had DCC implants? What kind of hysteria would this kind of an announcement generate? Could they ride out another trial as well as this article? John Swanson thought he knew what the right thing to do was. His only question was, would they do it?

EXHIBIT 1 Breast Implants: What Did the Industry Know, and When?

Documents Obtained by *Business Week* Suggest Implant Makers May Have Seen the Dangers Long Ago

When lawyers square off in a San Francisco courtroom on June 25, there will be more at issue than the question of whether Dow Corning Corp. knowingly sold Mariann Hopkins a defective silicone breast implant. In a way, an entire industry will be on trial.

After three decades on the market—and sales to roughly 2 million women—breast implants are facing a legal assault that some lawyers are comparing to the multibillion-dollar litigation over the Dalkon Shield contraceptive. Plaintiffs' attorneys say hundreds of women have filed suit so far. The suits allege that the implants deteriorated—with disastrous results. Among the claims: that silicone can leach throughout the body, wreaking havoc on the immune system. In March, a New York jury awarded $4.5 million to a woman who asserted that a 1983 silicone implant with a polyurethane-foam covering caused her breast cancer. An appeal is pending.

Concern about potential health risks has spurred the government to begin to regulate what is now the third-most popular form of cosmetic surgery after nose and liposuction operations. In April, the Food & Drug Administration told implant manufacturers to prove their products are safe—a step an agency advisory panel had recommended nearly a decade ago. A week later came reports of an ongoing FDA study linking the foam-covered implants to a cancer-causing agent. That led the implant's maker, Bristol–Myers Squibb Co., to suspend shipments of its product.

Foot-Dragging

An investigation by *Business Week* has uncovered evidence that the industry has been aware for at least a decade of animal studies linking implants to cancer and other illnesses. Women were not told of these risks until years later. "The manufacturers and surgeons have been performing experimental surgery on humans," Thomas D. Talcott told a congressional panel in December. A Dow Corning materials engineer for 24 years, Talcott quit his job in 1976 in a dispute over the implants' safety. He now testifies for women who sue.

Dow Corning and other implant manufacturers dispute allegations that their products are unsafe and say several medical studies support them. "Our objective is to produce the best possible product in terms of safety and efficacy," says Robert T. Rylee II, Dow Corning's health care general manager.

The controversy has caught the attention of lawmakers. In an April 26 letter to FDA Commissioner David A. Kessler, Representative Ted Weiss (D–N.Y.), chairman of a human resources and intergovernmental relations subcommittee studying the implant issue, criticized the agency for dragging its feet. "FDA documents indicate that for more than 10 years, FDA scientists expressed concerns about the safety of silicone breast implants that were frequently ignored by FDA officials," wrote Weiss. The agency agrees "it's taken a long time, but FDA had higher priority devices to deal with," says Elizabeth D. Jacobson, deputy director at the agency's Center for Devices & Radiological Health.

Eager Lawyers

The companies, especially Dow Corning, are responding to safety questions and lawsuits with a full-court press to keep their internal memos and studies from reaching the public. When the manufacturers settle suits, often for a few thousand dollars, they demand that court orders keep the pacts and any information provided in the cases under seal. The court orders also forbid medical experts who have studied the companies' data to discuss them publicly.

Company officials say secrecy is crucial to guard proprietary data that could benefit competitors. But there is another reason. Says Dow Corning's Rylee: "We don't want to be overeducating plaintiffs' lawyers."

Implant makers are confident that they can weather the legal storm—unlike other manufacturers assaulted with product-liability suits. "Notwithstanding the claims and allegations," says Cincinnati lawyer Frank C. Woodside III, who is coordinating Dow Corning's legal strategy, "the vast majority of lawsuits are ones in which the damages are not very high."

That could soon change. The women who are suing implant makers have powerful allies: organized trial lawyers and consumer-rights crusader Ralph Nader. Emboldened by some court victories and the FDA's recent call for safety data, they smell blood. In May, they huddled in Washington to share notes and to coordinate their attack. "I doubt whether a tiny fraction of those injured have sued," says Sidney M. Wolfe, director of Nader's Public Citizen Health Research Group.

Women who pay surgeons $450 million a year for implants also are gaining momentum from some emerging evidence. Court records in a pending Michigan case show several references to Dow Corning documents concerning silicone-gel "bleed," or leakage, from the membrane-covered implants. Currently under a protective order, the documents go back to the mid-1970s—a decade before the company first acknowledged the phenomenon in its package inserts. And in 1976, James Rudy, then president of Heyer–Schulte Corp., an implant maker in Goleta, Calif., wrote a "Dear Doctor" letter to inform physicians that implants could rupture.

The companies may not be able to keep such material private much longer. In November, U.S. District Court Judge Stanley Sporkin in Washington ordered the FDA to make public hundreds of animal studies dating back to the 1960s that Dow Corning had given the agency. The company had provided the data under a confidentiality procedure Sporkin criticized as an FDA ruse to avoid the Freedom of Information Act. Dow Corning is appealing that ruling.

(continued)

EXHIBIT 1 Breast Implants: What Did the Industry Know, and When?—Continued

Inconclusive Results

The types of studies under contention include internal Dow Corning research conducted in the mid-1970s that revealed tumors in laboratory animals exposed to silicone gels. According to a 1988 FDA memo summarizing the data, Dow Corning convened a review panel that determined the presence of malignant tumors in up to 80% of the test animals. The figure was so high that the panel considered the study suspect and eventually deemed it inconclusive. A decade later, another Dow study found that tumors could be induced in rats when foreign agents, such as silicone implants, were put into them. Dow Corning, and some FDA officials who reviewed the studies, contend that while silicone can cause cancer in rats, there is no proof it would in humans. But the FDA summary concluded that "there is considerable reason to suspect that silicone can do so" (page 94).

One group of lay citizens who reviewed many of Dow Corning's internal documents didn't buy the company's arguments. A San Francisco federal court jury concluded in 1984 that the company had committed fraud in marketing its implant as safe. The jurors awarded Maria Stern of Nevada $1.5 million in punitive damages. After Dow appealed, the case was settled for an undisclosed sum, and much of the file is under a protective order. Many of the same issues will soon reemerge in the Mariann Hopkins trial. Hopkins, 47, who is represented by Stern's Redwood City (Calif.) Lawyer, Dan C. Bolton, claims that her 1976 Dow Corning implants ruptured, damaging her immune system.

In a post-trial ruling in the Stern case that is public, U.S. District Judge Marilyn Hall Patel found that the evidence showed Dow Corning's implant was inherently defective. The company's own studies, the judge wrote, "cast considerable doubt on the safety of the product" that was not disclosed to patients. The judge also upheld the jury's finding that Dow Corning had committed fraud and said the jury could conclude that Dow's actions "were highly reprehensible." Dow Corning's Rylee says the company "totally disagrees" with the verdict in the Stern case, terming it "a highly charged, emotional piece of litigation." Rylee says that all of the early Dow Corning studies have been redone and now show that implants have "no adverse effect."

Following the Stern case, Dow Corning changed its product literature to include a warning that surgeons were to pass along to patients. A 1985 package insert mentions the possibility of immune-system sensitivity and possible silicone migration following rupture. That could blunt post-1985 legal claims that Dow Corning had inadequately disclosed potential risks. But a 1987 Dow Corning "position statement" discounted the immune-system problem, saying it is linked to silicone of lesser purity than is used in the company's implants. Still, the company began a program to replace ruptured implants and those removed because patients complained of adverse reactions.

No Correlation

Dow Corning officials do not dispute that silicone can leak from the implants, but they say it is harmless: "Typically, the reaction is benign," says Rylee. "It's picked up by the lymph system, transported around, and either excreted or stored." Industry officials argue that no medical proof exists to link silicone with immune-system ailments. And they point to a 1982 medical study that showed no correlation between implants and breast cancer.

Silicone isn't the only potential problem with implants. Bristol–Myers withdrew its implant in April following FDA confirmation of a study that linked the foam used to coat the device with a cancer-causing agent known as 2-toluene diamine (TDA). But then the agency seemed to backtrack, issuing a press statement on April 17 that praised Bristol–Myers for its actions and played down the cancer risk of TDA, a substance produced when the polyurethane foam disintegrates. The statement was issued despite an internal agency memo, dated two weeks earlier, that found the foam, used primarily in automobile air and oil filters, inappropriate for use in breast implants. The agency had long known the hazards of TDA. In the 1970s, it banned TDA's use in hair dyes, citing risks of birth defects.

Bristol–Myers will not comment on any pending litigation but plans to resume sales of the product when the FDA finishes its review. Medical literature "contains no reported cases of human cancer associated with polyurethane foam," says a Bristol–Myers spokesman.

Leading the public furor over breast implants is Sybil Goldrich, who had implants in 1983 following a bilateral mastectomy for breast cancer. Complications ensued, and she eventually had four different sets of implants before abandoning them. Since then, Goldrich has been plagued by medical problems she and her doctors attribute to the implants. She had to have her ovaries and uterus removed, and doctors later discovered that silicone had migrated to her liver. Goldrich, who is a co-leader of a national advocacy group of breast-implant patients, is suing Dow Corning and another implant maker in Los Angeles for damages. "There is no way to detoxify from this chemical," she says. The companies dispute the claim.

Tougher Rules

Goldrich and others wonder why the FDA hasn't moved faster. But when implants were first marketed in the U.S. in the early 1960s, such medical devices were unregulated. Only in 1976 did Congress give the FDA powers over devices. Two years later, an FDA advisory panel—staffed heavily with plastic surgeons—recommended implants be classified so that manufacturers could sell them without having to prove they were safe. FDA staffers disagreed and pressed for a more restrictive category.

In 1982, the agency proposed the stiffer classification, noting concerns about gel migration and unknown

(continued)

EXHIBIT 1 Breast Implants: What Did the Industry Know, and When?—Continued

long-term toxic effects from silicone. The industry and surgeons contested this but lost. Still, it wasn't until April of this year that the rule change proposed a decade earlier requiring proof of safety became law. Companies have until July to submit evidence of their products' safety or withdraw them.

For the implant manufacturers, the strategy of keeping quiet about their products' potential problems may not work much longer. If Sporkin's ruling forcing the release of the Dow Corning studies is upheld, and if the jury in the Mariann Hopkins case concludes Dow Corning knew of problems long before it let on to consumers, then the litigation floodgates will open wider. With women such as Hopkins claiming implant-related illnesses that take years to develop, manufacturers could be on the defensive for a long time.

By Tim Smart in Washington

EXHIBIT 2 Excerpts from Business Conduct Committee Audit, 10/19/88

In DC/W's business, the limits to which information about implants is taken is, or could be, a Code related issue. Should communications about the safety and efficacy of products (implants) be taken directly to the end user/patient? Can we satisfy the Code of Conduct position of taking responsibility for the impact of our technology by providing information to doctors/physicians and relying upon them to pass along appropriate information to their patients? There is no standard accepted among supplier companies.

The subject of DC/W's responsibility needs to be continually tested and debated.

Additional Topics

- *Substance Abuse*. Interest expressed in any corporate programs (rehabs and educational). Mentioned that K. Yerrick (Human Resources) has appointed a team to look into this and develop an approach that considers today's problems.
- *Aids*. Corporate position being developed under lead of Dr. Chuck Dillon.
- *Honesty/Candor* among employees. Good discussion of the importance of living up to commitments we make internally, among ourselves. If we fail to do this, can we realistically expect to conduct our external affairs properly and ethically?

Only a few Code items were not covered during this meeting, but the most important ones were. Throughout the review, the point was made that Dow Corning is developing a "cultural sensitivity" for not only trans-national practices, but also for varying business practices from industry to industry. When a subsidiary company has a concern about compliance with a particular part of the Code, we ask that it be brought to the attention of the committee. There can be discussion about a great many Code statements. There are, however, several guidelines that are very firm, i.e., dignity of the individual, opportunity without bias, bribery/price fixing, et al.; environmental integrity, to name a few.

The point is that there can and should be continuing discussion about business practices and our relative behavior. DC/W and its management team are encouraged to perpetuate this dialogue.

Dan, thanks for your participation and that of the DC/W staff.

DCC 080021560

10–19–88. .IS
ne:3

EXHIBIT 3 Memo from Dillon to Swanson

Source: MDL repository of discovered documents.

December 20, 1990

TO: John Swanson CO2100
DC Corporate Ethics Committee

FROM: Chuck Dillon CO1120
Corporate Medical Director

cc: Ken Yerrick CO1116 Jim Jenkins CO1222
Director, Human Resources General Counsel

RE: Ethics Committee Review

I am writing to report a recent incident and to request a formal review by the DC Corporate Committee on Ethics. I make this request because I feel that this episode represents a violation of corporate, professional, and commonly accepted business ethics.

The specific incident occurred on Friday, December 14th at 5:15 P.M. Greg Thiess, a senior litigation attorney in the corporate legal department, approached Mary Ann Woodbury, a research scientist on my staff, in her DC-1 office. He asked that she destroy all copies of a memo she circulated two days previously. The memo contained a data analysis of a recent National Center for Health Statistics Survey of Surgical Device complication rates, and the overheads for a presentation to the Reed Committee on mammary implant issues that summarized the overall scope and current status of epidemiology projects for the Health Care Business's Mammary implant products.

Mary Ann asked me to join them in her office and Greg repeated his request to both of us. Greg stated to us that he was acting at the specific request of Robert T. Rylee II, Vice President and General Manager of the Health Care Business, who was very angry with the memos, and that he had spoken to Mr. Rylee on this subject earlier by telephone. He also stated that from his personal viewpoint, the information contained in the memos would compromise projects that he was then working on in Dow Corning product liability litigation and be adverse to the company if publicly revealed. I directed Mary Ann not comply with the request and stated to Greg that to do so would in my opinion be unethical conduct.

I feel that this is a serious example of misconduct requiring formal review. I am concerned that these documents may be sought out and destroyed. Also, I am concerned that the incident, if not amended, may lead to others that would threaten the integrity of my department, its employees, their ability to provide valid scientific evaluations to management, as well as their careers in the company. I therefore ask the committee's review of this matter.

EXHIBIT 4 E-Mail from Swanson to George Callaghan

Source: MDL repository of discovered documents.

FROM: JESWANSO—MIDVM01 Date and time 06/04/91 09:11:30
TO: GPCALLAG—MIDVM01

NOTE FROM: J.E. Swanson—4612
Internal Communications C02100
SUBJECT: 6/10 *Business Week* Article

If you haven't yet read or heard about the BW article on silicone implants, you soon will. If there was question—and I believe there was in some quarters—about whether or not DC's position vis-à-vis the production, marketing, and safety testing of silicone mammary implants is a "business" issue or an ethical issue, the BW article clearly moves it toward the latter.

You and I have talked about this before, George, and I believe you know how I feel. I'm not sure the Business Conduct Committee will have any involvement in this, or for that matter be asked to be part of any ensuing discussion. The sad reality is that the BW article casts a cloud over the company's hard earned reputation as an organization dedicated to integrity. There is no reason to believe that the momentum around the implant issue will not transfer to other segments of Dow Corning's core businesses.

The position of the Health Care Business on behalf of the corporation as expressed by RTR in the article does not portray DC favorably. The time may have come for influence leaders in this company to come to grips with the total issue and re-examine our position. When a respected business publication that is well read by much of our customer base takes the stand that it has, isn't it time that we began to look a little harder at our own position? Some 20 years ago, Dow's intransigence about napalm gave the company a public image that took hundreds of millions of dollars and a total change in attitude to reverse. It's a lesson worth studying.

George, I'm not suggesting specific "next steps" or "action." But as the chairman of the Business Conduct Committee, I think you should be well apprised of as many sides of this issue as possible.

Regards,

John

EXHIBIT 5 E-mail to J. Kermit Campbell

Source: MDL repository of discovered documents.

FROM: JESWANSO-MIDVM01
TO: JKCAMPBE-MIDVM01

NOTE FROM: J.E. Swanson-4612
Internal Communications C02100
SUBJECT: Position on Breast Implants

Kerm, I appreciated the opportunity to talk about DC's choices re this whole issue. We still have the opportunity to take a responsible leadership position which would be consistent with Dow Corning's traditional philosophy.

Here is a statement intended to start the process of getting us out of this business:

Dow Corning Wright to Suspend Production of Mammary Implants

Dow Corning Corporation announced that a subsidiary company, Dow Corning Wright, will temporarily suspend the production and sale of silicone mammary implants until research on certain biosafety issues has been concluded. Since entering the market in 1963, Dow Corning has continuously studied the health and safety effects of these devices. "We believe our breast implants are safe and pose no significant health risk," said J. Kermit Campbell, Dow Corning Group Vice President, USA. "But we also recognize that questions about the safety of silicone implants exist and we are placing a high priority on finding scientifically sound answers to these questions."

****

A couple of internal points to keep in mind when discussing the above:

1) We should understand that the probability of ever actually concluding research on biosafety issues is remote.
2) Because the statement refers to "certain biosafety issues," we should be prepared to name a few specific studies, in general terms, that we intend to conduct.
3) The statement implies that the reason for suspending production and sales of implants is the increasing attention from the media and special interest groups. There is no need to refer specifically to external sources.

Let me know if any of this is unclear or provokes a question. I've tried to keep it simple, straightforward

Regards,

John

Managing Boundaries: *ADC Telecommunications in Mexico (A)*

Mario Dena glanced at his watch as he picked up the two folders from his desk and slipped them into his briefcase. It was 10:00 A.M., May 25, 1999. The outside temperature had already reached a sweltering 98°F in Juárez, Mexico. Dena was vice president of manufacturing at ADC de Juárez, a maquiladora owned by ADC Telecommunications.[1] He hurried to the van that would whisk him across the border checkpoint in time to catch his flight from El Paso, Texas, to Minneapolis, Minnesota. He was scheduled to meet key members of ADC's Broadband Connectivity Group (BCG) at ADC's Twin Cities headquarters the next day.

The folders contained presentation materials with which Dena would try to convince the BCG members to approve construction of an on-site child care center and a water treatment facility. Few of the nearly 250 maquilas in Juárez (employing 200,000 people) had incorporated such facilities, improvements heretofore seen as the responsibility of the public sector.

If approved, the child care center and water treatment facility would be built on the site of Loon II, ADC's second wholly owned operation in Juárez. The city was not far from ADC's shipping point, Santa Teresa, New Mexico (just 11 miles west of El Paso, Texas). Construction of Loon II, which would be located 2½ miles from ADC de Juárez (Loon I), was to begin four months later in October 1999, and the plant was scheduled to be in operation by August 2000.

Dena's Perspective

Dena and other members of the ADC de Juárez management team showed signs of a mind-set common in Central and South America and Mexico. ADC de Juárez controller Ricardo Villarreal was the plant's liaison with government agencies. ADC had provided support for various community projects. One such effort to construct housing was underway in 1999. Several scholars have described this attitude:

> In the maquila, paternalism is expected—management's role is to take care of the workers. Managers and supervisors are expected to be the authority—their status is respected, and in return the worker's status is also respected. From this perspective, workers become a manager's 'extended family,' the manager is the patron (pah'trone) or father figure. . . . When maquila assembly workers were asked what they would change if they were supervisors, responses included encouraging workers to share problems so that supervisors could make necessary or appropriate changes to solve them; helping the workers actually do their jobs; creating a more sociable

This case was prepared by Research Assistant Linda Swenson under the supervision of Professor Kenneth E. Goodpaster, Koch Endowed Chair in Business Ethics, University of St. Thomas, as a basis for class discussion rather than to illustrate either effective or ineffective handling of an administrative situation.

[1] The term *maquiladora* originated in colonial Mexico. The *maquila* was the portion of the finished product a miller would keep for grinding another's grain. Manufacturing plants in Mexico known as maquiladoras or maquilas imported components duty-free and assembled them for export. Favorable tariff provisions allowed U.S. companies to ship product parts across the border, assemble them in maquilas, and then import them back to the United States duty-free except for the value-added in labor.

FIGURE 1

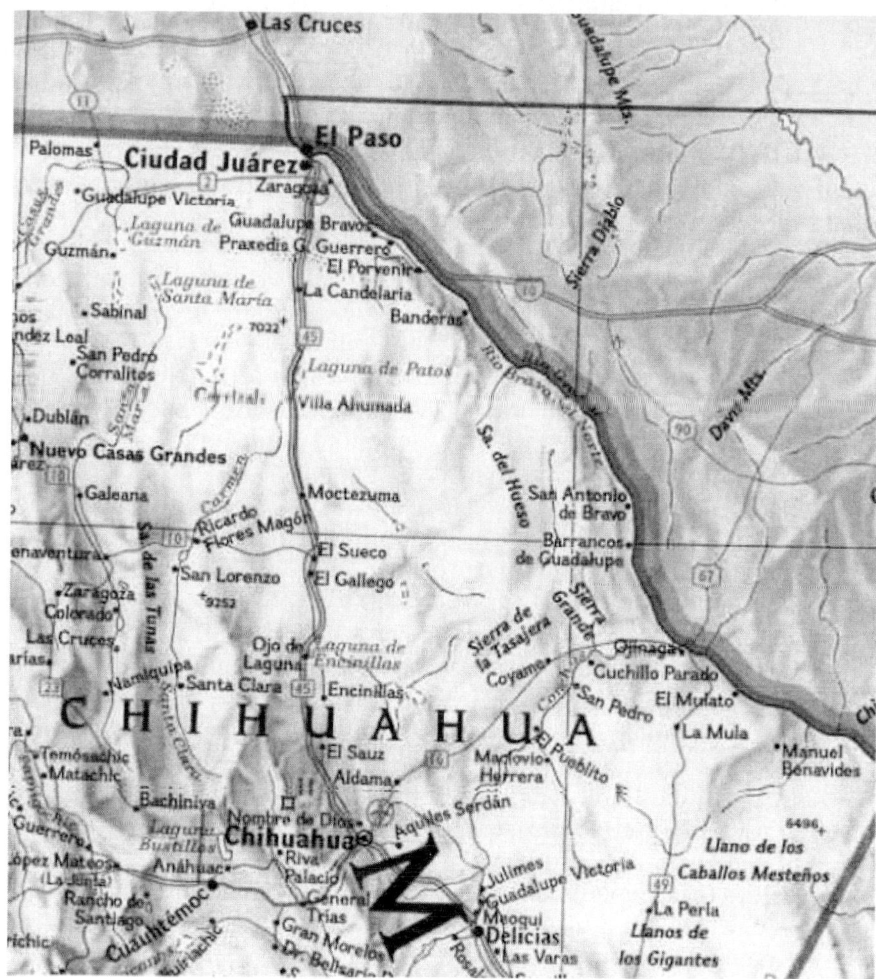

work environment; holding social events; not making workers nervous; and allowing workers to work at their own pace.[2]

ADC Vice President of Manufacturing Richard Ness observed that Dena had internalized some of this attitude:

> I've known Mario for years. He cares a lot about employees, the city of Juárez and the Mexican people. He wants to do everything he possibly can to improve pay and conditions. He's very emotional about it. I'm sure the issue of whether ADC would approve the water treatment plant and child care center was very important to him. I'm sure he felt conflicted about what would be good for ADC, what would be good for his people, and how much he should try to push through headquarters.

But concern about staying within budget was also an issue for Dena. Previous experience had taught Dena (and the other managers ADC had hired) that a focus on cost was essential. Frequently, for example, workers would not be hired until absolutely necessary. Capital expenditures were carefully scrutinized. Prior to announcing earnings for the quarter ended January 31, 1998, ADC issued two press releases indicating that it would have disappointing earnings. When announced earnings failed to meet Wall Street expectations, the company's

[2] Mary Teagarden, Mark Butler, and Mary Ann Von Glinow, "Mexico's Maquiladora Industry: Where Strategic Human Resource Management Makes a Difference," *Organizational Dynamics*, winter 1992.

stock tumbled to \$16¾ per share from the previous year's \$30⅛.[3] CEO William Cadogan endeavored to reassure shareholders that the company would sharply curtail capital and operating expenditures.

ADC had put Dena in charge of setting up and managing ADC de Juárez. He previously had managed more than 3,000 employees in facilities at four locations in Mexico and had 25 years of experience in the maquilas. He was working for Elamex S.A. de C.V. in 1984 when ADC selected that shelter operation as its contract manufacturer.[4] From the beginning, Dena had reported to Peter Hemp, vice president and general manager of BCG's Copper and Wireless Division, when Hemp was ADC's director of manufacturing. Dena later moved to ADC de Juárez when ADC exercised an option to transfer labor from Elamex.

ADC de Juárez practiced a total quality management (TQM) philosophy, and employees were empowered to maximize their contribution to quality improvement. Dena told employees their work was as essential to the success of ADC as to the well-being of their families. He encouraged employees to try to enjoy their jobs as they worked toward new opportunities. The company offered free elementary, junior high school, and high school courses at the plant on Saturdays.[5] (See Exhibit 1 for other employee benefits at ADC de Juárez.)

Over the years, Dena had adopted guiding principles that helped him clarify issues and make decisions. These included:

- Face realities, especially if unpleasant.
- Consider boundaries and precedents.
- Reinvest in employees.

Early in 1999, these principles led Dena to do a survey to provide information on employee satisfaction. "I had measures of customer service, the number of defects per million of products, and costs per hour. I wanted indicators of employee comfort. Such surveys are uncommon in the maquilas."

The idea for the survey followed a long stretch of overtime. "The employees had received overtime pay," Dena said. "But money wasn't everything—they had families. We needed to consider their role in their families and in society. So I invited some employees to form a committee and put together a survey."

Dena said he had been told before administering the survey, "Don't do it. You'll find snakes, scorpions, and centipedes!" He recalled thinking, "If you have these things, you'd better clean them out! We asked employees how they felt about the environment—the temperature, the noise, how they were being treated, about the amount and quality of food in the cafeteria, the amount of time they have for lunch, and how pleased they were with service provided by Human Resources, the infirmary, and the social workers. I wanted to use the survey results as a benchmark."

Results of the first survey motivated Dena to hire a supervisor to ensure cafeteria workers treated employees with courtesy. The company also modified bus routes and began requiring drivers to wear badges so employees could identify reckless drivers. "We set schedules with tolerances. We wanted employees to arrive happy, not upset because they'd had a scary bus ride." Dena planned to repeat the survey every 10–12 weeks.

Company History: ADC Telecommunications Inc.

ADC sprang from the drawing board of a young Minneapolis engineer, Ralph Allison, as Audio Development Company in 1935. Allison's first product was an electronic device designed to test hearing. By 1949 the company had expanded and was developing products that included jacks and plugs.

In 1961 ADC merged with Magnetic Controls Company, a manufacturer of power supplies and magnetic amplifiers. When AT&T was deregulated in 1983, its seven Regional Bell Operating Companies (RBOCs) established themselves as independent entities, expanding

[3] Share price from ADC Telecommunications Inc., 1998 Annual Report.

[4] Elamex delivered finished assemblies to manufacturers in the consumer, telecommunications, computer, industrial, medical, and automotive industries. "S.A. de C.V." means "Sociedad Anónima de Capital Variable," or corporation with variable capital. (www.corporatewindow.com/fprofiles/elamffp.html).

[5] As of July 1999, from this program, 5 ADC-Juárez employees had graduated from elementary courses, 23 employees were attending junior high school courses, and 17 employees had graduated from high school courses.

the U.S. telecommunications market by 90 percent. Over time, these RBOCs became ADC's key customer base.[6]

In 1970, Charles Denny, Jr., a Honeywell executive, joined the company as president. A strong, charismatic leader, Denny built on ADC's growing sales of jacks and plugs. In the early 1970s, ADC introduced prewired, "connectorized jackfields," wired assemblies, and test equipment for telephone companies. By 1974, the company was on solid financial ground.

In 1987, William Cadogan joined ADC as vice president of private networks, moving the company to a more sophisticated communication technology. In 1991, Denny retired and Cadogan became CEO. He promised that the company would expand international sales and fiber-optic expertise. Denny stayed on as board chairman. In 1994, Cadogan succeeded Denny as chairman of the board as the Internet started to boom.

ADC's 1998 annual report described the company as "a leading global supplier of voice, video and data systems and solutions for telephone, cable television, Internet, broadcast, wireless and private communications networks." (See Exhibit 2 for comparative stock performance.) Customers needed broader bandwidths for these services, and company growth focused on "unlocking the capacity of the 'local loop' . . . the last mile of the communications network from the local service providers' offices through network equipment that connected to the end user's residence or business." (See Figure 2.)

ADC de Juárez operated under the aegis of the Broadband Connectivity Group (BCG), one of four divisions from which ADC offered hardware and software systems and integrated solutions.[7] (See Figure 3.) BCG products were sold to both public and private global service providers, including RBOCs, other telephone companies, long-distance carriers, private network providers and original equipment manufacturers. Products included network access/connection devices for twisted-pair and coaxial networks and for fiber-optic networks, modular fiber-optic cable routing systems, outside plant cabinets and other enclosures, and wireless infrastructure equipment.

During the fiscal years ended October 31, 1996, 1997, and 1998, net sales of BCG products increased 36.7, 34.7, and 19.6 percent, respectively, over prior years.[8] (See Exhibit 3.)

[6] www.adc.com/aboutadc/history.

[7] ADC Telecommunications Inc., 1998 Annual Report.

[8] Ibid.

FIGURE 2 **ADC'S Mission: Broadband, Multiservice Networks in the Last Mile**

Source: ADC, Telecommunications, Inc. Reprinted with permission.

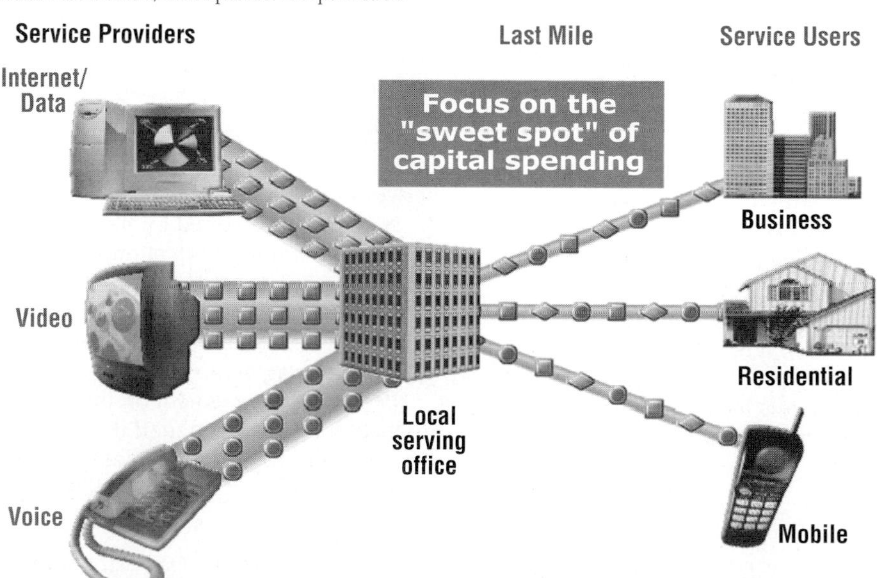

FIGURE 3 ADC Corporate Structure

Source: ADC Telecommunications, Inc. Reprinted with permission.

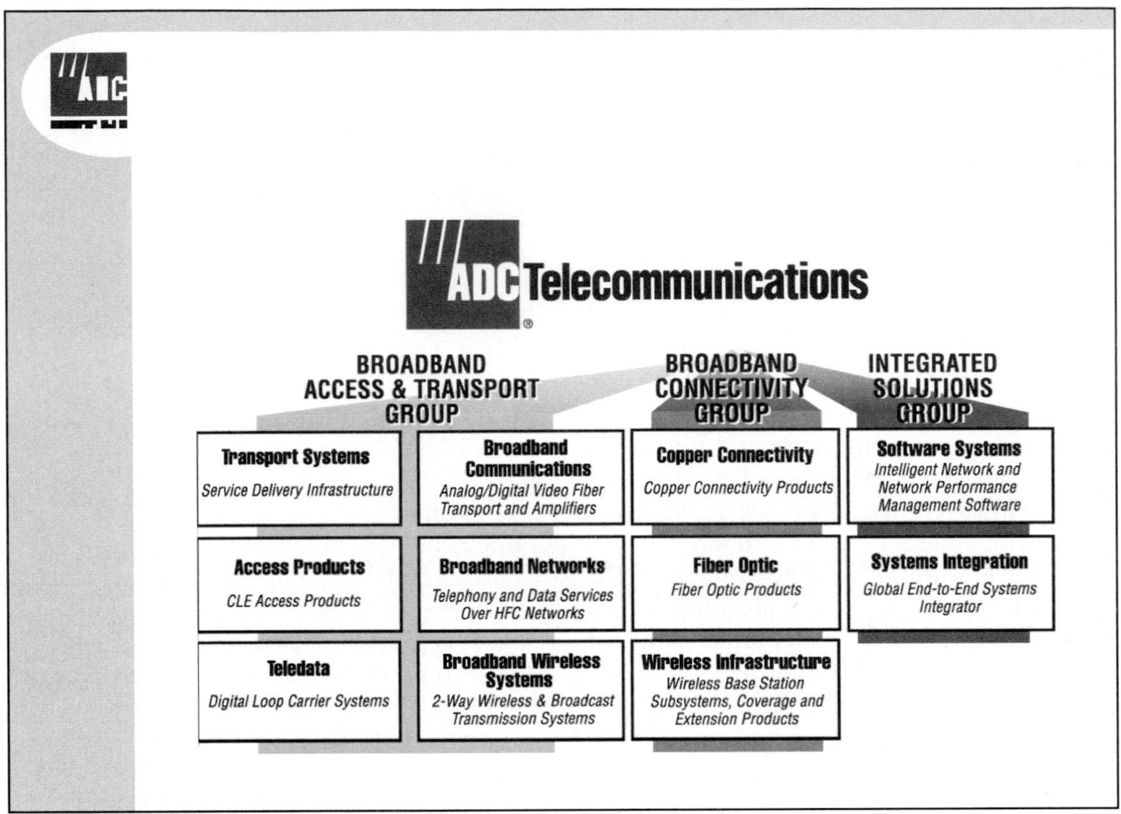

NAFTA and the Maquila Phenomenon

In 1965 Mexico "relaxed restrictive foreign investment policies," establishing the *Border Industrialization Program* (BIP) and creating the climate in which maquilas could take hold along the U.S.-Mexico border.[9]

> The goals for the BIP [were] to increase Mexico's level of industrialization, especially in the border region; to create new jobs; to raise the domestic income level; to facilitate absorption of technology and skills (technology transfer); and to attract much-needed foreign exchange. In turn, the program [would provide] foreign investors an array of benefits including cost saving, especially regarding labor, energy and rent; 100 percent foreign ownership, if desired; and proximity to U.S. markets and suppliers.[10]

But the maquiladora phenomenon expanded considerably in the wake of the 1994 *North American Free Trade Agreement* (NAFTA), which was designed to

> [g]radually eliminate most tariffs and other trade barriers on products and services passing between the United States, Canada and Mexico . . . NAFTA was inspired by the success of the European Community in eliminating tariffs in order to stimulate trade among its members. A Canadian-U.S. free-trade agreement was concluded in 1988, and NAFTA basically extended this agreement's provisions to Mexico. . . . Preliminary agreement on the pact was reached in August 1992, and it was ratified by the three countries' national legislatures in 1993 and went into effect on Jan. 1, 1994."[11]

[9] Mary Teagarden, Mark Butler, and Mary Ann Von Glinow, "Mexico's Maquiladora Industry: Where Strategic Human Resource Management Makes a Difference," *Organizational Dynamics*, winter 1992.

[10] Ibid.

[11] *Encyclopedia Britannica Online*, "North American Free Trade Agreement."

In December 1994, the United States intervened to restore confidence in Mexico's economy by backing an international credit arrangement with guarantees after a collapse of the Mexican peso. The subsequent drop in Mexico's living standards, currency values, and labor costs was compelling enough to persuade a number of U.S. companies that they should move operations to Mexico.[12] One report put the hourly minimum wage pay in maquilas along the border (including productivity bonuses, subsidized meals and transportation, savings plans, and other benefits) between $1 and $1.20 per hour.[13]

NAFTA proponents enthused that more jobs, better wages, and improved conditions would result from increased industry along the U.S.-Mexico border. But the campaign rhetoric of Ross Perot, the 1996 U.S. presidential Reform Party candidate, presented a very different view. Perot often referred to a "giant sucking sound" coming from south of the U.S. border. This phrase became emblematic of the fear that U.S. jobs and industry would be lost to Mexico because of NAFTA.

Other NAFTA critics complained that the ability of U.S. labor to gain concessions from industry would be hurt by companies' readiness to threaten a move to Mexico and that working conditions in the maquilas would drag down conditions in the United States and Canada.[14]

ADC Goes to Mexico

Peter Hemp had headed offshore operations for a year and a half when, in late 1983, he was charged with evaluating shelter operations along the U.S.-Mexico border. He visited plants from Tijuana to Brownsville, considering road systems, water, power grids, zoning, plans for expansion, safety records, factory cleanliness, staff-employee relationships, attention to quality, available labor, turnover, and ratio of engineers, supervisors, and laborers.

[12] *Encyclopedia Brittanica Online*, "Year in Review 1995: World Affairs: The Economy."

[13] "Juárez, Mexico Infrastructure Fact Book and Industrial Overview" (www.elpaso-juarez.com/juarez.htm).

[14] "NAFTA's Broken Promises: The Border Betrayed," NAFTA: Report on Environmental Issues. (www.citizen.org/pctrade/nafta/reports/enviro96.htm).

One operation—Elamex S.A. de C.V.—was a standout. Elamex provided facilities and workers to a wide variety of companies. Its operations ran the gamut from sorting coupons to packaging medical products in a clean room. The "have-labor-will-sell" operation was located in Juárez in the state of Chihuahua, Mexico, and practically a straight shot south on Interstate 35 from ADC's headquarters in Minneapolis and across the border from El Paso, Texas.

In May 1984, six months after ADC had selected Elamex as its shelter operation, Hemp began reporting to Lynn Davis, then director of international operations. Davis later recalled.

> When the question of whether to continue subcontracting in Minnesota came up, we had several discussions about where we were going to grow. We looked at the merits of remaining in the Midwest and Minnesota versus moving some operations offshore, considering China, India, Singapore, Malaysia, Puerto Rico, Ireland, and Mexico. We had to choose between adding low-level jobs in Minnesota, or creating high-level jobs in Minnesota by locating low-level jobs offshore. We were convinced that offshore operations would make our product more competitive, so we could sell more, then hire more engineers, accountants, and salespeople and keep things moving in that direction.

Because rapid delivery was one of the company's competitive advantages, slow-moving ocean freighters were out of the question, and air freight would have been prohibitive due to the weight of product to be manufactured. The best option for offshore operations quickly became Mexico.

Of all the maquilas evaluated by ADC, Elamex had the highest cost per labor hour, but the company was clearly superior to others. Engineers at Elamex were trained in modern statistical techniques. Elamex employees were provided two meals a day and transportation to and from centralized sites near their homes. They played on adjacent softball and soccer fields. "We weren't going to lower our expectations of quality or customer service to proceed with the offshore venture," Davis said.

> We would be putting ADC's highest-volume, most profitable products into this operation, so we wanted to minimize any risk by choosing the best maquila available. To ensure product

> quality we decided to pay by the hour instead of the unit. ADC was Elamex's only subcontractor to pay by the hour and to provide compensation beyond wages and salary. We let efficiency evolve naturally, setting the production rate so employees wouldn't feel compelled to work faster in order to earn more.

It took time for ADC to convince Elamex to change pay policies, but eventually starting pay increased, and a grading system was put in place to reward workers in technical jobs such as jack adjusters, and quality and inventory workers. ADC also began paying employees year-end bonuses based on team performance, an uncommon practice in the maquilas.

Despite ADC's no-layoff policy, Minnesota employees were not happy about the decision to move the manual assembly of switch jacks to Mexico in 1984. "We were pure Minnesota when we started this project," Davis recalled.

> People didn't think we could manufacture these products as well anywhere else. Our response was to involve ADC employees in the outcome. I firmly believe if you have a problem, you should reach out and ask those involved to own the solution. If you do that, they're going to make it work. So we relied a bit on the egos of lead operators and supervisors, sending them to Juárez to train workers at Elamex. Once they saw the industriousness and pure will to succeed of the Mexican people, they were converted.

In 10 weeks the Elamex plant would begin shipping product back to Minnesota. Remarkably, the first 5 million units produced at the Juárez plant were defect-free.

Growth of ADC in Mexico: Juárez, Delicias, and Juárez Again

Dena had hired Sergio Trabulsi in 1985 to help migrate production from the United States to Mexico. An electromechanical operations manager at ADC de Juárez, Trabulsi supervised three foremen.[15] "Over time headquarters began to trust us with new processes," Trabulsi said. "We would observe, replicate a setup and make adjustments to improve the process, always with the blessing of ADC." (See Exhibit 4 for reporting relationships.)

Through the 1980s, ADC's operations at Elamex were limited to mechanical assembly. In September 1994 the plant began to manufacture fiber-optic patch cord. "We had so much confidence in the workers at Elamex, we decided by June 1995 to do the electronics 'first builds' in Mexico," Davis said.

In November of that year, ADC contracted with Elamex to manage a *second* shelter operation for a facility ADC had built in Delicias (see Figure 1 on page 465). The Delicias plant began with 25 direct and 5 indirect employees.[16] By the end of 1996 it employed 301 direct and 32 indirect employees; and by May 1999 the numbers had reached 790 direct and 104 indirect employees.

Into its contract with Elamex, ADC had built the provision that if and when ADC decided to become an independent facility, Elamex would facilitate the transfer of labor to the ADC facility. In December 1996, Davis informed the CEO of Elamex that ADC wished to exercise this option and would invite all 1,300 Elamex employees under ADC's management to transfer to the new plant it would build in Juárez.

Although ADC's move was a big loss for Elamex, the transition went smoothly. Within 18 months (by June 1998) ADC de Juárez was open for production.

ADC's cost per fully loaded hour at Elamex had been two thirds of what it was in Minnesota. But the company saved another 15 percent in operating costs by moving from Elamex to ADC de Juárez. This move also allowed ADC to set policies, pay scales and benefits, hire employees and project its philosophy.

Dena and other managers had been asked by ADC to work on plans for a wholly owned facility before the decision to proceed with the plan was approved. To keep their work confidential, the Elamex team came up with the code name "Loon" for the ADC de Juárez project.

[15] At ADC de Juárez workers categorized as direct labor reported to group leaders, who reported to production supervisors, who reported to a foreman or superintendent, who then reported to Dena.

[16] Direct labor comprised people who actually touched the product. The indirect labor force was made up of inspectors, warehouse personnel, and production and quality control supervisors.

Employees who opted to transfer from Elamex to ADC de Juárez would keep seniority and get a pay hike.[17] With this plan ADC hoped to keep 70 percent of the direct labor force and 90 percent of the indirect labor force.[18] Amazingly, all but one of the 810 people under ADC direct management moved to ADC de Juárez. In June 1998, when the doors opened at the 157,000-square-foot facility, plans were already being made for a 53,000 square-foot-addition.[19] By August 1, ADC would also assume management (from Elamex) of its Delicias facility.

ADC was doing its best to keep up with the "explosive" demand for bandwidth, which was growing at the rate of up to 100 percent per year.[20] Product turnaround time also had to be cut in response to customer demand: 57 percent of orders required a two-day shipment.

In March 1999, Dena was managing 1,600 employees at ADC de Juárez, and plans were underway for Loon II.[21] The cost of constructing an on-site child care center and water treatment facility at Loon II would be close to $2 million—an estimated 10 percent of the budget for the new building.

Attending to Turnover

Turnover was a serious problem for maquilas along the border. One report cited the average monthly rate at 10 to 15 percent.[22] In Dena's experience, most employee departures occurred within 10 days of hire. "At Elamex we didn't pay enough attention to turnover," he said. "Instead of looking for the cause and fixing the problems, we learned to manage them."

In the early 1990s, ADC researched turnover in the maquilas of Chihuahua's other cities, discovering the rate in Delicias to be significantly lower than in border cities. Delicias, a city of 125,000 set amid agricultural communities and located 300 miles from Juárez, was experiencing a severe drought (as were many cities in Mexico), so unemployment was high. When agricultural conditions improved, turnover remained at 2 to 3 percent.[23] In contrast to a more transient workforce that migrated from the south to work in maquilas along the border, most of the workforce in Delicias lived and had grown up there or in surrounding communities. By early 1999, turnover at ADC de Juárez was holding at 8 percent per month.

Dena's File Folders

File 1: The On-Site Child Care Center

In addition to disbursing retirement benefits, the Social Security System in Mexico ran the country's child care centers, clinics, and hospitals. But the agency could meet only 5 percent of the demand for child care and had begun approaching maquilas, proposing that they help meet this need. Representatives of the Social Security System for the state of Chihuahua had visited Dena in early February 1999 about constructing an on-site child care center.

Mario knew that many ADC de Juárez employees depended on a grandparent or other family member for child care. Some employees traded child care with neighbors who worked a different shift. But even the *minimal* fee charged by some child care centers was a hardship for these workers. The fortunate few who could get their children into a government-sponsored center had to adhere to strict drop-off and pickup times—meaning that overtime was not an option for them. He reasoned that an in-house child care center would give employees more flexibility. More importantly, he believed, it would help

[17] One woman, who had worked for ADC 11 years, had been absent only one day—when her granddaughter was born; another had worked for the company 15 years.

[18] See footnote 16.

[19] ADC de Juárez was larger than the combined space of all BCG assembly operations.

[20] ADC Telecommunications Inc., 1998 Annual Report.

[21] In some respects, it would have been cost-effective for ADC to locate new processes in its ADC de Juárez facility. "In Juárez, some companies employ 5,000 people under one roof. About 20 percent or more of the maquilas are unionized," Dena explained. But locating different processes in separate facilities, i.e., keeping electronics separate from mechanical processes, helped ensure that should a strike occur in one plant, ADC's other operations could keep running.

[22] Fawcett et al., "The Realities of Operating in Mexico: An Exploration of Manufacturing and Logistics Issues," *International Journal of Physical Distribution and Logistics Management*, March 1995, p. 49.

[23] In addition to the rate of turnover in Delicias, the level of service, literacy, availability, skills, and the required transportation radius figured importantly in selecting this site.

workers' children to become better citizens. They would receive nutritious meals and information on hygiene, conduct, and culture.

Mexico's Social Security System, the state of Chihuahua, and the city of Juárez would fund the dieticians, doctors, nurses, and employee training, as well as infrastructure such as kitchen equipment, that would be needed for a child care center. ADC's part of the project would be to buy the land, build the facility, and pay associated taxes. The projected cost of a facility equipped to serve 96 children initially and 200 children eventually: $1.1 million. (See Exhibit 5.) The center would offer 24-hour child care (all three shifts).

File 2: The Water Treatment Facility

In 1999, when northern Mexico was suffering possibly its worst drought in history, Dena knew the Loon II facility would include an area for stamping and painting, a process which used large quantities of water.[24] "I debated what to do about this," Dena recalled. "Water was a huge concern for the city of Juárez, yet nearly all the other maquilas in Juárez used city water for manufacturing processes, and we could have done the same.[25] Nevertheless, I didn't feel comfortable using this much city water for manufacturing. ADC would be paying for the water of course, but this wasn't the only issue. The community was suffering a water shortage. When should the community's need take precedence over the needs of industry?"

Dena recently had met with a city representative about a permit for water use. With its own water treatment facility, Loon II would require only 5 gallons per minute of city water for the sheet metal stamping and powder paint process. City water was priced with conservation in mind: the more water used, the higher the rate per cubic meter. With its own water treatment plant ADC de Juárez would pay a projected 6 pesos per cubic meter but twice that if it had to purchase all the water needed for its operations.

It would cost ADC an estimated $535,000 to construct a water treatment facility with the capacity to process 100 gallons of water per minute, an amount difficult to justify in the company's customary ways. The Loon II facility could use up to 80 percent of the processed water for landscaping and janitorial needs. Surplus water might be used to irrigate public parks. (See Exhibit 5.)

Managing Boundaries

When one of his employees lacked the funds to make funeral arrangements for a relative, Dena got approval to provide 1,500 pesos (about $150) for this purpose, making this benefit available to all employees for immediate family members. But not everything received upper management's blessing. When Dena first asked headquarters to reduce the number of hours employees worked each day on the first shift from 9½ to 9 hours, the company did nothing at first. Dena persisted and eventually—most maquilas already had reduced the first shift to 9 hours—ADC approved the change.

ADC de Juárez paid a competitive wage—at the midpoint or slightly above that of other maquilas. Asked by Mario the night before the meeting how he thought the two project proposals would be received, BCG's Richard Ness had responded, "We're not a charity organization. We're running a business. We need to remain as competitive as possible. The city of Juárez didn't ask us to build a water treatment facility, and it isn't essential to operate Loon II. On the other hand, we do have an obligation to improve working conditions, the environment, and the community when we can."

As he took his seat on the airplane in El Paso, Dena reflected, "Business has to include negotiation. You give me this, and I'll give you that. Before I ask for something, I must prove we are running this business successfully. We also have to keep shareholders happy. And to keep the business growing, we need to reinvest in ADC de Juárez, the employees, and the community."

[24] According to a report by Charles Turner, professor of civil engineering at the University of Texas, El Paso, "the sustainable limit of water usage in the region may have already been surpassed, with very little cushion for the present population, and virtually no room for future growth. . . . [However] the population of Juárez continues to increase while its water resource base is decreasing" (twri.tamu.edu/twripubs/WtrSavrs/v1n2/article-8.html).

[25] With a population of more than 1.2 million, Juárez is the largest city in the state of Chihuahua and the fourth largest city in Mexico. "Juárez, Mexico Infrastructure Fact Book and Industrial Overview" (www.elpaso-juarez.com/juarez.htm).

EXHIBIT 1 Other Employee Benefits at ADC de Juárez

- Vacation—6 days plus 2 each subsequent year up to 120 days/year.
- Maternity Allowance—1,500 pesos (about $150) if employee or wife gives birth at a private hospital.
- Three days with pay for a marriage or the funeral of a direct family member.
- Weekly perfect attendance bonus.
- Showers.
- 10 percent of salary or wages in nontaxed food coupons.
- Life insurance.
- Free legal advice.
- On-site infirmary for workers and their families.
- Eye exam plus 80 percent of the cost of glasses.
- Company credit union savings and loan program.
- Scholarships for higher education.
- Christmas bonus—a minimum of 15 days of pay after one year.
- Soccer field.
- Savings plan—ADC matches employee contributions up to 10 percent of salary/wages and pays interest.*

* "Workers deposit 11.5 percent of their salaries in their *Afore* accounts and the government and employers deposit an additional 2 percent. The *Afores* invest the money in financial markets and the gains accrue directly to each account." Brendan Case, "Mexico's Pension Reform Sparks Saving, Investing," *Knight-Ridder Tribune Business News: The Dallas Morning News*, June 6, 1999.

EXHIBIT 2 ADC Comparative Stock Performance

The graph compares the cumulative total shareholder return on the common stock of the company for the last five fiscal years with the cumulative total return on the S&P 500 index and the S&P communication equipment index over the same period (assuming the investment of $100 in the company's common stock, the S&P 500 index, and the S&P communication equipment index on October 31, 1993, and reinvestment of all dividends).

The company changed from the Telco index to the S&P communication equipment index in fiscal 1998, because the Telco index was discontinued by Investor's Business Daily. Because the Telco index is no longer published, the company's total shareholder return for the last five fiscal years cannot be compared to the Telco index.

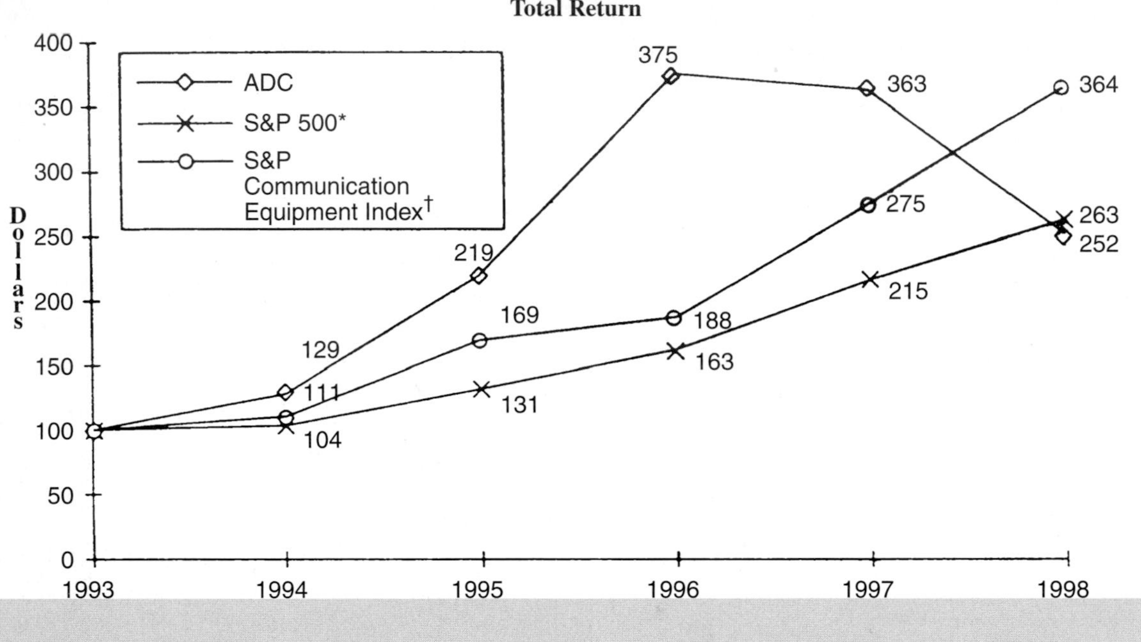

* Total return calculations for the S&P 500 index were performed by Standard & Poor's Compustat.

† Total return calculations for the S&P communication equipment index (consisting of communications equipment manufacturers in competition with the company) were performed by Standard & Poor's Compustat.

EXHIBIT 3 ADC Telecommunications Summary of Operations, 1984–1999

	For the Years Ended October 31 Dollars in Thousands, Except Per Share Amount														
	1984	1985	1986	1987	1988	1989	1990	1991	1992	1993	1994	1995	1996	1997	1998
Net sales	$87,595	$124,883	$143,677	$ 166,863	$ 179,852	$196,388	$259,802	$293,839	$316,496	$366,118	$448,735	$586,222	$828,009	$1,164,450	$1,379,678
Cost of product sold	51,456	69,515	73,908	87,981	97,427	107,764	133,802	148,614	155,074	178,572	221,448	302,094	438,847	621,811	736,537
Gross profit	36,139	55,368	69,769	78,882	82,425	88,624	126,000	145,225	161,422	187,546	227,287	284,128	389,162	542,639	643,141
Expenses:															
Development and product engineering	7,721	11,844	12,982	15,473	17,401	17,360	25,462	32,315	36,063	40,988	48,974	66,460	90,038	122,638	137,912
Selling and administration	21,209	28,910	35,032	38,927	40,921	48,580	62,793	74,369	82,966	93,311	110,799	130,297	160,705	221,624	263,007
Goodwill amortization						267.00	920.00	1,953	2,720	2,798	3,135	3,133	5,235	10,013	11,656
Nonrecurring charges									3,800			3,914		22,700	
Total expenses	28,930	40,754	48,014	54,400	58,322	66,207	89,175	108,637	125,549	137,097	162,908	203,804	255,978	376,975	417,575
Operating income	7,209	14,614	21,755	24,482	24,103	22,417	36,825	36,588	35,873	50,449	64,379	80,324	133,184	165,664	225,566
Interest expense				(460)	(450)	(493)	(615)	(1803)	(1912)	(285)	(151)	(275)	(402)	(393)	NAV
Interest income				1,223	2,306	3,324	1,870	1,695	970.00	468.00	1,309	7,078	10,906	7,369	NAV
Other income (expense), net	(2,743)	(1,710)	(795)	193.00	(1028)	997.00	92.00	(75)	(205)	(895)	(1,216)	(898)	(7,025)	(2,583)	NAV
Income before income taxes and extraordinary item	4,466	12,904	20,960	25,438	24,931	26,245	38,172	36,405	34,726	49,737	64,321	86,229	136,663	170,057	225,734
Provision for income taxes	1,223	5,033	8,992	10,175	7,978	9,842	15,269	14,380	13,700	18,101	23,800	31,043	49,200	61,220	79,007
Income before extraordinary item				15,263	16,953	16,403	22,903	22,025	21,026	31,636	40,521	55,186	87,463	108,837	146,727
Extraordinary item, net of income taxes											(1450)				
Net income	$ 3,700	$ 7,871	$ 11,968	$ 15,263	$ 16,953	$ 16,403	$ 22,903	$ 22,025	$ 21,026	$ 31,636	$ 39,071	$ 55,186	$ 87,463	$ 108,837	$ 146,727
Average common shares outstanding	$8,598,056	8,593,460	8,604,488	103,552	104,376	105,336	106,120	106,952	108,352	109,996	111,220	117,094	128,314	131,673	134,327
Earnings per share															
Income before extraordinary item	$ 0.43	$ 0.92	$ 1.39	$ 0.15	$ 0.16	$ 0.16	$ 0.22	$ 0.21	$ 0.19	$ 0.29	$ 0.36	$ 0.47	$ 0.68	$ 0.83	$1.08
Net income	$ 0.43	$ 0.92	$ 1.39	$ 0.15	$ 0.16	$ 0.16	$ 0.22	$ 0.21	$ 0.19	$ 0.29	$ 0.35	$ 0.47	$ 0.68	$ 0.83	$1.08
Return on sales indices															
Gross profit/expenses:				47%	46%	45%	48%	49%	51%	51%	51%	48%	47%	47%	NAV
Operating income				15%	13%	11%	14%	12%	11%	14%	14%	14%	16%	14%	NAV
Net income				9%	9%	8%	9%	7%	7%	9%	9%	9%	11%	9%	NAV
International sales				$ 20,659	$ 26,115	$ 31,277	$ 41,623	$ 37,960	$ 49,347	$ 58,919	$ 67,113	$ 106,416	$172,212	$ 247,409	$ 278,154

NAV = Figures not available.

EXHIBIT 4 **Some ADC Reporting Relationships**

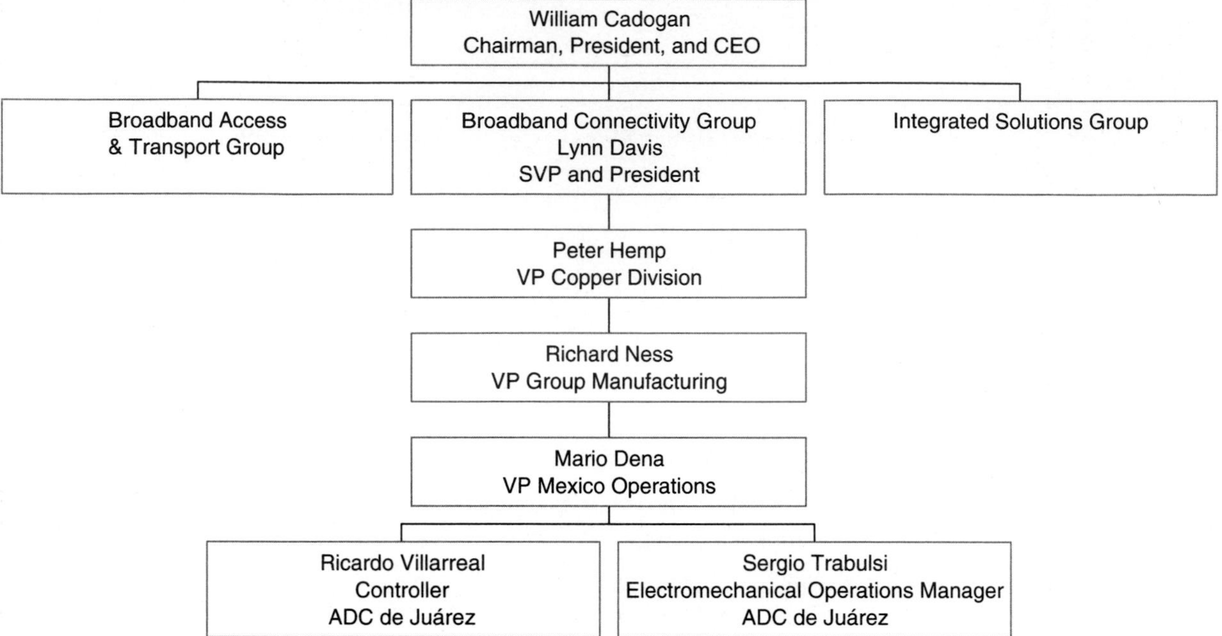

EXHIBIT 5 **Mario Dena's PowerPoint Presentation: Selected Slides**

México Operations
Capacity Assessment
1999- 2003

- Loon Plan
  - Original
  - Actual situation
  - Projection
- Delicias Plan
  - Original
  - Actual situation
  - Projection
- Mexico Operations
  - Growth projection
  - Building requirements
  - Sites-Buy Vs. Lease

México Operations

- Growth Projection

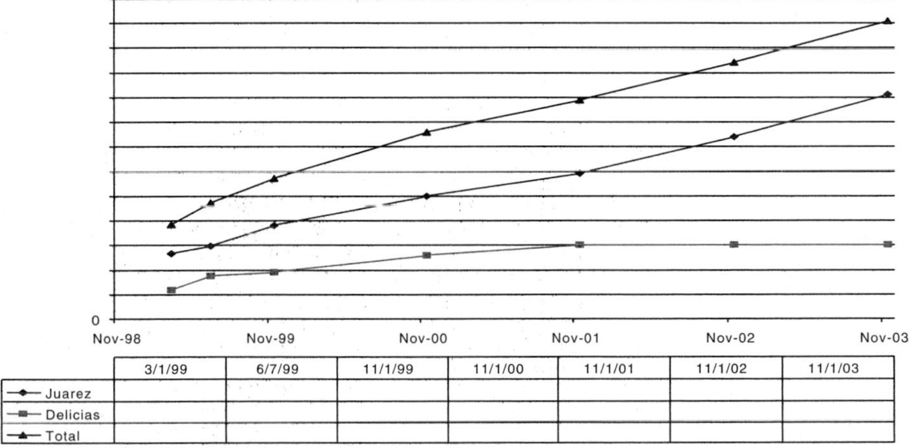

	3/1/99	6/7/99	11/1/99	11/1/00	11/1/01	11/1/02	11/1/03
Juarez							
Delicias							
Total							

MD/6.17.99 3

EXHIBIT 5 Mario Dena's PowerPoint Presentation: Selected Slides—Continued

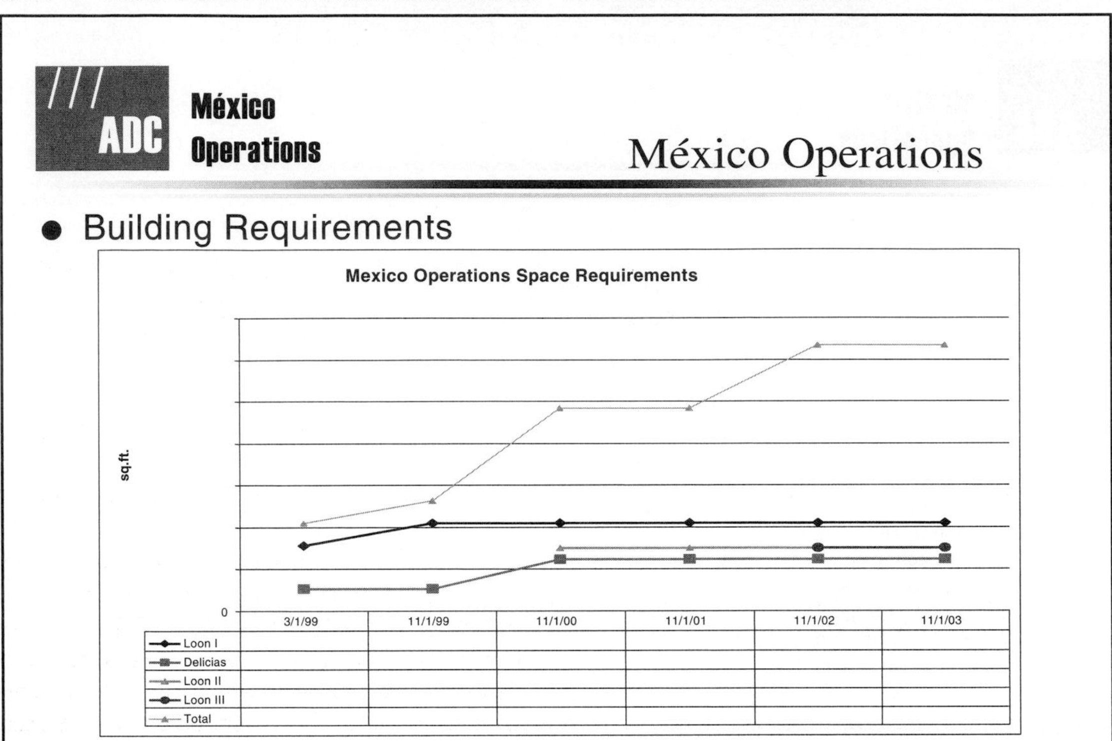

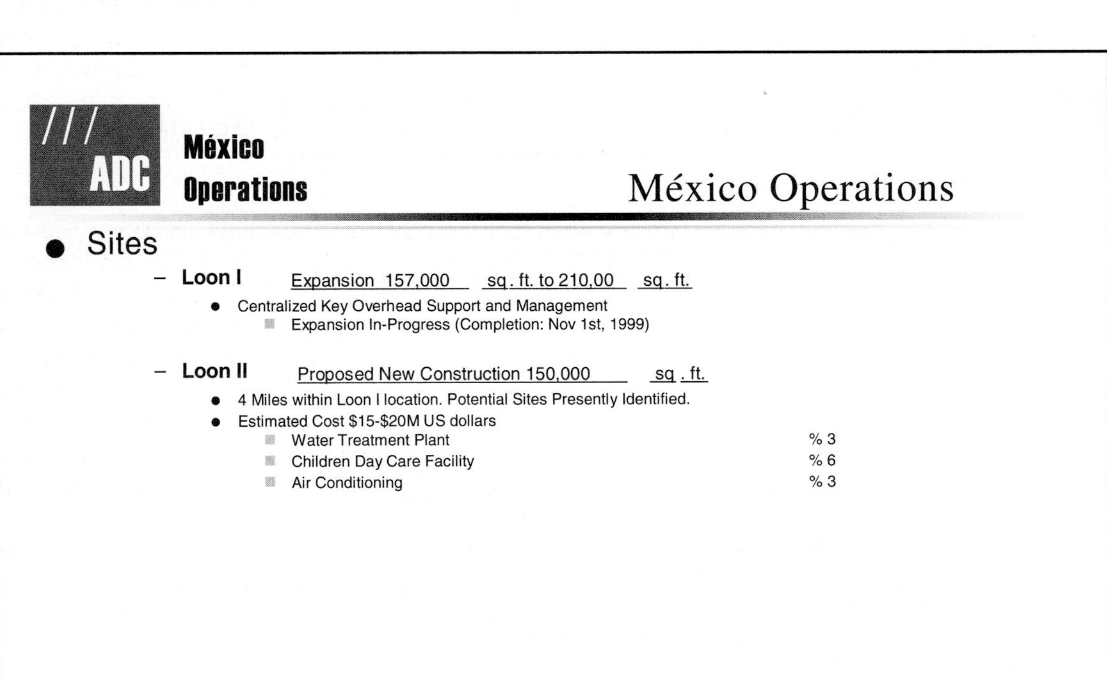

Ethics, Power, and the Cree Nations (A)

Minnesota Public Utilities (PUC) Commission Chair Greg Scott looked up momentarily from his papers to consider the large assembly of witnesses, reporters, and concerned citizens gathered in the commission's hearing chamber this November 30. Many were taking advantage of the brief break in the PUC's proceedings to stretch their legs and confer with colleagues; others sat quietly in their seats, reviewing the notes they had jotted while listening to the testimony offered by various parties. Regaining his focus, Scott glanced at the agenda on the briefing papers before him.

Minnesota Public Utilities Commission
Staff Briefing Papers

Meeting Date:	Nov. 30, 2000
Company:	Northern States Power Co.
Docket No.	E-002/M-99-888
	In the Matter of the Petition of Northern States Power Co. for Review of its 1999 All Source Request for Proposals
Issue(s):	Should the Commission initiate an investigation into the socioeconomic costs associated with large-scale hydro generation projects?
	If so, should the Commission allow the competitive bidding process to proceed, or should it stay consideration of the Manitoba Hydro bid until the investigation is completed?
	Should the other two final selections (Black Hills Corp. and Northern Alternative Energy) be allowed to proceed?

Emotions were running high. Scott recalled the passionate testimony of the Pimicikamak Cree Nation (PCN) chief and the PCN's other representatives, all of whom had urged the PUC to consider the socioeconomic effects of further hydro development in Manitoba. He also remembered the frustration that had welled in the voices of those representing NSP, Manitoba Hydro, and other Cree First Nations.

The PUC's commissioners had been appointed by the governor to six-year, staggered terms, with Scott designated as chair. The Minnesota Legislature required the PUC to ensure that utilities provided safe, adequate, reliable service at fair, reasonable rates. Electric service in Minnesota was provided by 50 cooperative electric utilities, 124 municipal electric utilities, and 5 investor-owned utilities. The PUC was charged with regulating rate changes; constructing power plants, transmission lines, and other large energy facilities; and establishing rates and conditions of service for cogenerators and small power producers.

During the 1990s, the PUC had gone from policing electric rates to overseeing sourcing arrangements. This put Scott and the other commissioners in the position of deciding whether to approve the combination of energy sources selected by NSP. The company's most recent request for proposals (RFP) had resulted in a selection that included the renewal of a 500-megawatt contract with Manitoba Hydro, a Crown corporation owned by the Province of Manitoba, Canada.

The PCN had launched a highly visible public relations campaign that had vilified Manitoba Hydro for the extensive environmental damage

This case was prepared by Research Assistants Linda Swenson and T. Dean Maines under the supervision of Kenneth E. Goodpaster, Koch Professor in Business Ethics, University of St. Thomas, as a basis for class discussion rather than to illustrate either effective or ineffective handling of an administrative situation. The chief institutions in this case and their representatives are outlined in the appendix.

caused by major hydro projects in the 1960s and early 1970s. Because of its prolonged and expensive arbitration process, the Northern Flood Agreement (NFA), the formal agreement that was to have brought about resolution and healing, had been a disappointment to the Cree. Four of the five First Nations eventually signed independent agreements with Manitoba Hydro, and the governments of Manitoba and Canada. The PCN alone was steadfast in its resolve to use the NFA's provisions to address the impact of hydroelectric development upon its lives and the environment—a struggle for "survival, dignity, a sustainable and healthy environment, inclusion in the benefits of the Canadian economy, and respect for our rights."[1] Meanwhile, NSP was facing the challenge of supplying a growing demand for electricity in a climate where deregulation was creating power shortages in California.

In August 2000, the PCN filed motions to compel the release of documentation relevant to Manitoba Hydro's bid and to extend the comment period. The PCN contended that by law the Minnesota PUC must evaluate resource options and plans on its ability to (1) maintain or improve the adequacy and reliability of utility service, (2) keep customers' bills and utility rates as low as practicable, and (3) minimize adverse socioeconomic and environmental effects. PCN representatives had objected to NSP's RFP process, claiming that Manitoba Hydro was being given an unfair advantage that ultimately would result in higher electric rates for Minnesotans. The PCN contended that Manitoba Hydro's bid should have included the cost of "externalities" for the facility the utility planned to build west of Winnipeg near Brandon, Manitoba.[2] The PCN's request for information asked:

- For each year of the contract, what percentage of the operation's power (500 megawatts) would be supplied from the Brandon gas turbine electricity generating facility?
- What percentage of that power would be supplied from the Brandon facility during a drought?

Scott recalled exchanges between PCN hydrologic consultant Robert McCullough and a Manitoba Hydro representative:

> McCullough: If they have the Brandon facility in place, they don't have to take the precaution of keeping Lake Winnipeg above minimum levels. River and lake levels will be operated to follow short term margins . . . the river will simply become an economic quantity. . . .
>
> Manitoba Hydro representative: What's being proposed at Brandon is a 225-megawatt peaking plant. A single-cycle plant designed to run at about 10 percent capacity factor.

Peaking resources were designed to operate relatively few hours. Peaking plants characteristically involve relatively low capital costs but high operating costs. Most of the demand for electric power was being met by baseload resources, which carried high capital investments but low operating costs.

McCullough argued that if Manitoba Hydro had the Brandon facility as a backup, it wouldn't be compelled to keep water levels as high or as stable. "There are no external environmental controls. There is no EPA. The PCN have to live with the stench of rotting vegetation on days when those rivers are pulled down to the minimum," he told the commission.

In September 2000, the commission stated it was not persuaded that an order compelling the release of the requested information was warranted. Yet throughout spring, summer, and fall 2000, the PUC had received communications related to NSP's selection of Manitoba Hydro as a bid winner. The North American Water Office had requested an investigation, and the Clean Water Action Alliance and the Minnesota Public Interest Research Group had recommended the PUC not approve the contract between NSP and Manitoba Hydro. Furthermore, Minnesotans for an Energy Efficient Economy and the Izaak Walton League of America had petitioned for a stay in the PUC's consideration of proposed contract. Their petition argued that the PUC must investigate and report upon the environmental and socioeconomic

[1] John Miswagon, "We Won't Be Beaten Up in Silence," *Toronto Globe and Mail*, 6 March 2000, A13.

[2] In 1997, the Minnesota Public Utilities Commission had ruled that environmental costs must be taken into account for purchases of electric power if the facilities were located 200 miles or less from the Minnesota border.

impact of large-scale hydroelectric generating facilities to fulfill its statutory duties. Such research would create a standard the PUC could then utilize to judge whether the agreement between Manitoba Hydro and NSP was in the public interest. The Izaak Walton League also argued that NSP's process for evaluating bids systematically discriminated against wind power.

Greg Scott took a deep breath. The situation confronting the commission was complex. Whatever decision the PUC reached, it would almost certainly alienate and anger at least one of the parties. With that prospect before him, Scott called the hearing back to order.

The Pimicikamak Cree

The Pimicikamak Cree Nation makes its home in and around Cross Lake, Manitoba, on the Nelson River at the northern edges of Lake Winnipeg. (See Exhibit 1.) Manitoba Hydro, and the governments of Manitoba and Canada, undertook construction of the Lake Winnipeg Regulation, Churchill River Diversion and Nelson River Project in the late 1960s and early 1970s.[3] This involved the diversion of entire river systems and the conscription of Lake Winnipeg as a reservoir. The project proceeded without baseline environmental or socioeconomic impact assessments. When it was completed, vast acreages of traditional lands had been flooded, contaminated, or otherwise rendered inaccessible.

PCN Chief John Miswagon elaborated, "When Manitoba Hydro arrived more than 30 years ago, it did not inform us of its plans, and did not ask for Cree consent. To this day we do not know how many species have been lost, how many habitats destroyed, or how many traditional campsites and burial grounds lie underwater, or disappeared during construction. We have lost burial sites, the entire fisheries of whitefish and sturgeon, our ability to travel safely on the waterways, and much of our ability to sustain ourselves from the land."[4]

Like other aboriginal societies, the culture and economy of the PCN was tied to the land it inhabited. Some have argued that the irreversibility of the hydro projects along with a process of social degradation combined to undermine the prospect for the Cree to return to a land-based or traditional form of hunting, trapping, and fishing. In addition many of the Cree communities had lost the traditional base of knowledge required for long-term cultural restoration. According to Ronald Niezen, a former professor of anthropology at Harvard who studied the effects of megahydro developments on Cree populations in Quebec and Manitoba:

> Dams and resettlement projects mean not only a loss of home and the identity that comes from a sense of place; they can obliterate generations of practical culture and knowledge. Further, if compensation for this trauma is delayed, withheld, inadequate or poorly distributed . . . [it] leaves painful memories, exacerbates loss and feelings of impotence, fuels distress and discontent, and can haunt a project with a rankling sense of grievance.

Chief Miswagon commented: "How has electricity benefited us? We don't have to haul water or wood. The result is a static lifestyle, high blood pressure, and heart attacks. There's nothing for people to do. Old people who used to be out fishing, hunting, trapping, and gathering now sit around and drink. We've already had richness. What we've lost will never be the same. You can't put a dollar value on a healthy lifestyle or dignity."

Jenpeg, the first dam at the north end of Lake Winnipeg, is located 5 miles south of Cross Lake, a community with a population of 5,670.[5] Construction of Jenpeg began in 1972 and was completed in 1975. Cross Lake resident Kenny Miswaggon (no relation to the chief) recalled, "People today still remember the Hydro engineer who visited Cross Lake and held up a pencil to illustrate that water levels would fluctuate only six to eight inches." As one publication reported, however, "the effects have been significant: eight to ten foot . . . fluctuations both above and below normal. . . . High water levels also have entered previously undisturbed soil, contaminating the river with the toxin methyl mercury. . . . The river is dangerous in winter because it is kept at an unnatural level, making the ice thin in places once

[3] Manitoba Hydro operated as an arm of the provincial government.

[4] From Pimicikamak Chief John Miswagon's presentation at the Environmental Justice and Energy Policy in the Upper Midwest Conference, April 15, 2000.

[5] *Pimicikamak* is the native word for Cross Lake.

considered safe. Even in summer the river is a threat. There has been at least one boating death that many directly attribute to a low water level and the ever-changing landscape beneath its surface."[6]

The hydroelectric system used "load following," a process that imposed a pattern of water releases aligned with electric system requirements. These could vary radically from the natural, pre-hydroelectric development pattern. While natural water flows typically were highest in spring, the flow downstream of a hydro reservoir was low in the spring because this was a low-demand period for electricity. The result was major alterations to the natural pattern of seasonal water flows and the flooding of terrestrial habitat.

Kenny Miswaggon explained, "Stagnant water has created a proliferation of aquatic weeds. Water deoxygenation creates fish kills. The local ecology has changed. The water smells. As recently as the late 1960s and early 1970s our people were self-sustaining, proud and happy. We lived and traveled on the water, and obtained our food from the water. Even in our sacred teaching, water is life. Everything has changed. Everyone from the eldest to the youngest has been affected."

The Northern Flood Agreement

By 1974, the five Cree bands living along the Nelson and Churchill rivers had organized themselves into the Northern Flood Committee.[7] The committee was comprised of the elected First Nation chiefs, and began to meet formally with the federal and provincial governments. On December 16, 1977, the governments of Canada and Manitoba, Manitoba Hydro, and the Northern Flood Committee signed the Northern Flood Agreement (NFA). Chief Miswagon explained, "The Northern Flood Agreement was designed as a compensation package for loss of livelihood—loss of fishing, hunting, trapping and gathering medicines."

The NFA recognized that not all adverse effects of the Lake Winnipeg Regulation and Churchill River Diversion Hydro Project could be determined with certainty in 1977. Thus it called for the establishment of an arbitrator to whom any person adversely affected by the project might submit a claim.

Despite the hoped-for resolution, however, the NFA was a bitter disappointment for many. The Royal Commission on Aboriginal Peoples noted that the history of the NFA had been marked by little or no action in the implementation of NFA obligations and a long, drawn out process of arbitration. By 1990, the five Cree Nations were frustrated with the failure of Manitoba Hydro, the government of Canada, and the province of Manitoba to cooperate and fully implement the NFA. The communities were poverty-stricken, people were suffering, and they were pressuring community leaders to do something.

The Cree Nations Divide on Resolution

Four of the five communities eventually entered into Master Implementation Agreements (MIAs). (See Exhibit 2.) The Split Lake, York Factory, Nelson House, and Norway House Cree Nations opted for a kind of "revenue-sharing" based upon the development of additional hydro capacity along the Nelson. Given the inability to maintain a traditional way of life, Split Lake representatives said that the community's future viability required a determined effort in the area of economic development. In 1995, however, the PCN had rejected such an agreement on the advice of its elders.

Chief Miswagon explained, "The Northern Flood Agreement (NFA) was drawn up with the wisdom of farsighted elders. This government said the NFA would last for the lifetime of the project. Manitoba Hydro's offer of $6 million (Canadian) a year for 20 years came nowhere close to our $27 million dollar annual budget. Our elders would not have agreed to terminate the NFA in 20 years. The social and environmental damage will continue to affect us generation after generation. We will be living with this forever.

"The ideal situation would be a moratorium on dam construction and implementation of as much of the NFA as possible—the land exchange, employment, and training and education aspects of the agreement. The NFA promised that most if not all Jenpeg employees would be our people.

[6] Eli Johnson, "Trail of NSP's Hydro Power Leads to Destruction in Cree country," *The Circle* 21(2000), p.7.

[7] This included the Cree communities of Norway House, Split Lake, Cross Lake, Nelson House, and York Factory.

There are 55 to 60 jobs at the Jenpeg Dam. Only four of our people work there. Hydro has a $2 million contract to fly people in from Winnipeg to work at Jenpeg. All the linemen should be our people. We need to work toward this. We lost a living. We need to explore and maximize all opportunities."

The Pimicikamak Cree and the Minnesota Public Utilities Commission

In April 2000, Chief Miswagon outlined the plight of the Pimicikamak Cree Nation to approximately 200 attendees at a conference in Minneapolis. Miswagon told the group that the hydroelectric power NSP purchased from Manitoba Hydro was perpetuating the consequences of "diverted rivers, flooded forests, decimated fisheries, eroded burial grounds and ruined trapping routes."[8] The cumulative effect, Miswagon said, has been to deprive his community of 5,500 people of their pride and livelihood, which has been replaced largely by an "underlying common denominator of hopelessness."[9] Miswagon then referred to the seven suicides at Cross Lake the previous year.

Cross Lake's efforts to prevent the expansion of Manitoba Hydro's generation and transmission capacity eventually developed into a public information campaign. That November Chief Miswagon addressed the Minnesota PUC, advocating the expanded use of renewable energy sources.

During a series of hearings in 1999 and 2000, the PCN told the Minnesota PUC that Manitoba Hydro had remedied none of the environmental, social, and economic damage created by the hydroelectric projects and that the NFA treaty of 1977 had not solved the PCN's concerns. The PCN also questioned whether Manitoba Hydro could meet energy commitments to customers if river flows in Manitoba were lower than average. If it could not, PCN explained, Hydro's plan was to purchase energy from the United States to meet the shortfall. PCN argued that NSP's approach to evaluating power purchases from Manitoba Hydro was inadequate given the complex and evolving nature of the wholesale electricity markets. In order to evaluate the environmental and socioeconomic impacts of NSP's electric power purchases from Manitoba Hydro, the PCN contended, the PUC would need to consider how the energy was obtained.

The PCN explained that elsewhere, hydro operations were being modified to mitigate impacts through adoption of a water release regime more like naturally occurring patterns. However, Manitoba Hydro's long-term contracts with NSP required it to schedule deliveries that maximized the use of electricity. "Manitoba Hydro is typically a large net exporter, but it does import substantial amounts of electricity, especially in drought years. Its large storage reservoirs give it great flexibility in scheduling imports and exports. It can purchase electricity off-peak when prices are low, and sell it on-peak when prices are high. With the advent of open access to transmission and more vibrant wholesale power markets, Manitoba Hydro has strong economic incentives to use its hydro system to benefit from these peak/off-peak price differentials. These types of transactions will exacerbate the large fluctuations in water flows and the associated environmental and socioeconomic impacts."[10]

PCN contended that NSP's bid process had been unfair: NSP had introduced short-term purchases into an RFP process intended for long term resources, favoring bidders who could supply short-term power, especially Manitoba Hydro, a large utility with existing resources and an ongoing relationship with NSP; NSP had disregarded reliability issues related to purchases from Hydro; and NSP had disregarded the severe environmental and socioeconomic impacts associated with Hydro's hydroelectric projects, as well as the possible impacts if Manitoba Hydro relied on thermal generation.

In February 1999, the PUC had stated that the question of environmental costs normally would not have come before it in this case, since "in its Order setting environmental cost values, the Commission, for practical reasons, limited its application to facilities within 200 miles of the Minnesota border." NSP had attributed no externality costs to Manitoba Hydro imports, both

[8] Tom Meersman, "Link between Energy Issues, Human Rights Explored," *Minneapolis Star Tribune*, 17 April 2000, B2.

[9] Ibid.

[10] Minnesota Public Utilities Commission Staff Briefing Papers for November 30, 2000, meeting.

because Hydro generation facilities were assumed to be more than 200 miles from Minnesota and these imports were assumed to be from plants that produced no air emissions. The PCN contended that Hydro could engage in "electricity laundering." That is, it could buy cheap electricity generated by coal-fired power plants within 200 miles of Minnesota and then resell it to NSP without the high-externality penalty such power would incur if it were sold directly to the utility. The PUC declined to require further investigation of the issues, directing NSP to monitor them as part of its ongoing review of resources.

On April 1, 2000, Manitoba Hydro announced the construction of a new 260-megawatt simple-cycle gas turbine at its Brandon Station, adjacent to the coal-fired generation plant already located at that site, within 200 miles of Minnesota. The Brandon gas turbine project was being built to support increased exports of electricity to the United States. The PCN told the commission that much of NSP's proposed purchase could be supplied with thermal generation, and that the emissions associated with this gas and coal-fired generation would be as high as, or higher than, the emissions from NSP's proxy resource, that is, a new gas-fired generation subject to stringent pollution control requirements.

In a May 2000 newsletter article, Manitoba Hydro said that it "relies heavily on the power generated by its two thermal stations at Brandon and Selkirk in drought situations." Hydro also could import electricity from utilities in Saskatchewan, Ontario, and the United States. This allowed the firm to take advantage of export opportunities, even in low water years, buying additional low-cost energy overnight, storing water and then using the water to generate electricity that can be sold during daytime hours at high prices created by the summer air-conditioning loads in the United States.[11]

Manitoba Hydro[12]

By 2000, Manitoba Hydro had more than 5000 megawatts of hydroelectric generating capacity and more than $7 billion in assets. It was Manitoba's major distributor of electricity and natural gas, and the fourth largest electrical utility in Canada.

About 30 percent of Manitoba Hydro's revenue came from its approximately $300 million in sales of power annually to the United States. About 90 percent of these sales were to Minnesota.[13] Three of Manitoba Hydro's long-term export trade agreements with American utilities involved seasonal diversity exchanges—exporting energy in the summer and importing it in the winter. The trading partnership between Manitoba and Minnesota allowed utilities to forego the construction of additional generating stations, therefore reducing revenue requirements, which, in turn, reduced rate increases. Coordination of facility operations also distributed maintenance outages so that system performance could be optimized.

Hydropower had been considered environmentally friendly, and was referred to as a renewable energy source. It allowed a fast response to demands for energy and energy storage (in the form of water) for short periods.

Construction of the Lake Winnipeg Regulation (LWR) and Churchill River Diversion Projects in the late 1960s and early 1970s made possible the large-scale export of electric power.[14] In 1970, a 230-kilovolt power transmission line was built between Canada and the United States, stretching from Winnipeg, Manitoba to Grand Forks, North Dakota. This enabled Manitoba Hydro to contract a power exchange with Minnkota Power Cooperative of Grand Forks, Otter Tail Power of Fergus Falls, Minnesota, and NSP. Construction of a second 230 kV line in 1976 connected Minnesota Power and Light of Duluth to the international border in southeastern Manitoba. In 1980, a 500-kilovolt line was built to bring hydro-generated electric power to the United Power Association of Elk River, Minnesota, and additional power to Minnesota Power & Light and NSP.

[11] "Energy Outlook—Waiting for Rain" (www.hydro.mb.ca/whats_newsworthy/insights_may2000.html).

[12] Unless otherwise noted, information for this section was compiled from http://www.hydro.mb.ca/exports_minnesota/exports.html.

[13] Manitoba Hydro reply before the Minnesota Public Utilities Commission in the matter of Northern States Power Company's petition for review of its 1999 all source RFP, MPUC Docket No. E-002/M-99-888.

[14] When this major hydroelectric development began, it was subject to authorizations from both federal and provincial Canadian governments, in accordance with existing legislation.

The Impact of Lake Winnipeg Regulation on Cross Lake

The massive LWR project had brought electric power to the Cree at the same rates charged to residents of southern Manitoba. The LWR was designed to ensure that releases from Lake Winnipeg could be increased during the winter and that water could be stored from one year to the next in the event of low runoff conditions. To accomplish this, the lake's discharge capacity was increased by the construction of three channels and Jenpeg, a 168-megawatt power-generating facility and control structure that permitted the flow releases from Lake Winnipeg to be controlled.[15]

Pre-LWR water elevations had followed a seasonal pattern with highs occurring in the late summer (August) and lows in the spring (April). Following LWR, average water level highs occurred in January and average lows occurred in June. During open water season, the total volume of water in Cross Lake decreased by an average of 53 percent. In Hydro's view, the most drastic change for the Cross Lake community had been these seasonal and monthly fluctuations of water levels. Hydro noted that the aftereffects of the LWR had required no resettlement of Cross Lake homes.[16]

In 1991, Manitoba Hydro constructed a $9.5 million rock weir, or dam, across one of Cross Lake's four outlet channels to maintain higher summer water levels and moderate the drastic spring and autumn water level fluctuations. Mid-North Development Corp. of Cross Lake and Vector Construction (Winnipeg) were awarded a $7.8 million contract for construction of the weir and channel excavation on Cross Lake. More than 90 percent of the workforce was comprised of northern aboriginal residents, including 40 Cross Lake residents.[17] Manitoba Hydro later implemented an aboriginal preplacement training program, in the mechanical, electrical, and station operator trades.

Prior to LWR, Cross Lake residents used the lake for a range of recreational activities; traditionally, their leisure pursuits were not "town-centered." Changes in the lake's level due to hydroelectric development now made many of these avocations problematic. An interim claim settlement in the mid-1980s had provided for a 500-seat indoor arena complex and ongoing funds for its operation and maintenance. Other compensation covered construction of seasonal ice trails and portages. In addition, Hydro undertook a long-term fish-restocking program to return the Cross Lake fish population to predevelopment levels.

On the whole, in Manitoba Hydro's view, the northern ecosystem had "adapted" to hydroelectric projects and transmission lines; it had "remained a multi-use environment, and in impacted areas, a process of recovery was well underway."

In a February 1999 newsletter, Manitoba Hydro reported that it had spent or committed over Can.$376 million on comprehensive community settlements, resource sector or remedial work settlements, and settlements with individuals to remedy problems and offset losses. The newsletter added that "four of the five First Nation signatories to the NFA have elected to enter into arrangements with the governments of Canada, Manitoba, as well as Manitoba Hydro, which allow a community approval process to determine how the NFA can best be implemented. Agreements have been put in place, which transfer land and put money in trust for present and future NFA initiatives. The arrangements only cover those issues known and understood at the time of their signing and allow that anything unforeseen and unforeseeable or future development are legitimate topics for further discussion."[18]

Among the claims submitted by Cross Lake, 12 involved personal injury, including six deaths. Manitoba Hydro became involved in ongoing programs such as the annual creation of ice trails and open water navigation routes in the Cross Lake resource area, to provide passage for resource harvest and recreation use. It established

[15] http://www.hydro.mb.ca/exports_minnesota/impacts.html.

[16] The Cross Lake reserve lands—located adjacent to Cross Lake, downstream and north of the Jenpeg control structure—covered approximately 20,233 acres. The Cross Lake Resource Area corresponded to the traditional hunting and fishing area used by the Pimicikamak Cree Nation.

[17] In fiscal years 1995–1997, Manitoba Hydro awarded 188 contracts worth about $49 million to northern aboriginal businesses.

[18] www.hydro.mb.ca/whats_newsworthy/insights_feb1999.html.

programs for cleanup of debris in the water and the maintenance of docks and portages. Manitoba Hydro also established an office and staff in the community.[19]

Manitoba Hydro's Testimony to the Minnesota PUC

On April 6, 2000, NSP named Manitoba Hydro to a short list of energy providers. NSP planned to renew a major 10-year contract with Manitoba Hydro set to expire in 2005. (See Exhibit 3.) While the Pimicikamak Cree Nation had appeared before the Minnesota PUC to object to NSP's bidding process, representatives of Manitoba Hydro urged the commissioners to allow the selection process to proceed. In Hydro's view, the arguments and proposals, particularly the valuation of environmental and socioeconomic costs, could be addressed in a future proceeding but were not sufficient reason to interrupt the current process. The independent auditor, the Department of Commerce, and the Office of Attorney General had reviewed the bidding process and selections. All had stated that they saw no unfairness or impropriety and had recommended that the commission allow the process to move forward.

The primary point of disagreement between Manitoba Hydro, the governments of Canada and Manitoba, and the PCN was their divergence on the "spirit and intent of the Northern Flood Agreement." The former parties saw it as a process that "was intended to provide a way to deal with the adverse effects of the LWR/CRD hydro project on the participating communities." The NFA provided a mechanism for determining the economic value of claims or damages resulting from the project and making one-time cash payments. In turn, this compensation provided relief to the governmental parties, including Manitoba Hydro, from all future claims. Manitoba Hydro contended that "regardless as to the treaty status of the NFA (which is not agreed to by the Government parties or Manitoba Hydro) the view of Canada, Manitoba and Manitoba Hydro is that the NFA was not intended to be a funding arrangement to meet all of the needs of these five First Nations forever."[20]

Northern States Power[21]

Northern States Power Co. (NSP), headquartered in Minneapolis, Minnesota, was a major U.S. utility with growing domestic and overseas operations. NSP and its wholly owned subsidiary, Northern States Power Co.–Wisconsin, operated generation, transmission and distribution facilities that provided electricity to about 1.4 million customers in Minnesota, Wisconsin, North Dakota, South Dakota, and Michigan.

NSP's utility rates were subject to the approval of the Federal Energy Regulatory Commission (FERC) and state regulatory commissions in Minnesota, North Dakota, South Dakota, Wisconsin, Arizona, and Michigan. Utility rates were gauged to recover plant investment, operating costs, and an allowed return on investment. Because comprehensive rate requests were infrequent in Minnesota, NSP's primary jurisdiction, changes in operating costs could affect NSP's financial results.[22]

In the late 1960s and early 1970s NSP was listening seriously to Manitoba Hydro's talk of developing hydro resources on Canada's Nelson and Churchill rivers. NSP Manager of Regulatory Administration Jim Alders explained, "Demand

[19] http://www.hydrolmb.ca/exports_minnesota/implementation.html.

[20] Interviews were conducted in Winnipeg and Cross Lake with officials from Manitoba Hydro and with the leadership of the Cross Lake community in November 1999. Other discussions were conducted at a conference held in April 2000 at the University of St. Thomas entitled "Energy Policy and Environmental Justice in the Upper Midwest." (Background Paper #3: 3-4)

[21] On August 18, 2000, NSP merged with New Century Energies of Denver to become Xcel Energy, Inc. The Minnesota Public Utilities Commission approved the deal, including a commitment by NSP to $50 million in rate cuts and rate freezes until 2005 for electric customers. References to NSP after the merger date should be understood to mean Xcel Energy.

[22] NSP's earnings also could be significantly altered by weather. Very hot summers and very cold winters could increase electric and gas sales, but also could increase expenses that might not be fully recoverable. Conversely, unseasonably mild weather would reduce electric and gas sales. For example, in 1999 weather increased earnings by an estimated 8 cents per share. Similarly, in 1998 weather increased earnings by an estimated 11 cents per share, and in 1997 by an estimated 6 cents per share.

for electricity was projected to keep growing at about 6 or 7 percent per year in the mid-1970s and NSP was looking for ways to meet that demand. Hydropower was considered a favorable alternative to coal and NSP planners saw it as a way to diversify the mix of its power supply." NSP's initial agreements with Manitoba Hydro called for selling power to Hydro during the Crown corporation's peak demand periods (winter) and buying power from Hydro during NSP's peak demand periods (summer). By 2000, NSP's summer peak demand for power had reached 8,000 megawatts, including 5,000 megawatts for Minnesota's Twin Cities area alone.

The electric power industry changed dramatically during the 1990s. The Energy Policy Act of 1992 promoted the creation of wholesale nonutility power generators and authorized FERC to require utilities to provide wholesale transmission services to third parties. This legislation also allowed utilities and nonregulated companies to build, own, and operate power plants nationally and internationally without being subject to previous restrictions. Alders explained, "With this law, the federal government established a competitive wholesale market for power, saying in essence, that anyone could get into the energy market at the wholesale level."

In 1996, FERC issued orders creating competition in the electric utility industry, giving competing wholesale suppliers the ability to transmit electricity through another utility's transmission system. Some states began allowing retail customers to choose their electric power supplier, and other states were considering retail access proposals. The Minnesota Legislature decided to study the issue further before taking any action.

A New Power Acquisition Process

Until 1995, NSP generated, transmitted, and distributed electric power. That year NSP's approach to capacity management changed from building power plants to seeking energy through a competitive bidding process. The company began issuing RFPs to obtain bids from independent power suppliers and other utilities.

NSP's 1998 Resource Plan had identified the need for an additional 2,400 megawatts over the 1998–2012 planning period. An existing contract with Manitoba Hydro would expire in 2005, leaving a 500-megawatt power gap—the equivalent of a large new coal- or gas-fired power plant. In addition, despite efforts to encourage conservation, NSP expected a growth in demand of about 100 megawatts a year.

The Public Utilities Commission approved NSP's forecast and bidding schedule in which the company had addressed electric power needs for the first half (1998–2005) of the planning period. On August 2, 1999, NSP issued an all-source RFP for 1,200 megawatts in 2003–2005 and subsequently notified bidders that it was interested in considering in-service early options for 2001–2003. The company decided to consider all options available for a short-term supply because the region's higher-than-forecast peaks in summer 1999 had sharply increased wholesale prices for electricity.

NSP received proposals from nine bidders and analyzed them using the Electric Generation Expansion Analysis System (EGEAS) production model.[23] The company subsequently named all nine bidders to its initial shortlist, but later eliminated two of these on the basis of additional information. In its RFP, NSP had described bid characteristics that could add value, including low cost, minimal environmental impact, and viability.[24]

Role Shift for the PUC

As NSP shifted its strategy from building power plants to sourcing capacity, the Minnesota PUC's role underwent a similar change. Rather than serving primarily as a watchdog on rates, the PUC had become an overseer of sourcing plans. Prior to the mid-1990s the PUC had no authority to grant precontract approval or disapproval. "When NSP requested a rate increase, the PUC would look at our expenses and capital investments and determine which decisions were prudent and which were not," Alders explained. "This put the PUC in the position of making judgments about the wisdom of management's

[23] EGEAS used various assumptions about market prices and operating characteristics of generation, comparing bids to a hypothetical new NSP generating unit.

[24] Viability was assessed through demonstrable reliability, replacement cost guarantees, and dispatch control and coordination.

decisions after the fact and it put NSP in the uncomfortable position of being at risk of failing to cover expenses until it received approval for a rate increase. If NSP entered into a multimillion-dollar purchase contract and two years later requested a rate increase to recover its costs, the PUC could say the contract was not prudent and not allow NSP to recover its costs in the price of its product. That was an impetus for the development of resource plans."

The period during which the public could comment on NSP's resource plans became the venue for debating the role of nuclear power and various energy policy issues. It was during such debates that the growing disenchantment with hydropower first surfaced. "Environmental groups contended that we should be relying on small hydro and wind, solar and biomass," Alders said. The PCN also brought its concerns to this forum, voicing its objections to NSP's RFP process and its contention that Manitoba Hydro's bid should have included the cost of "externalities" for the Brandon peaking facility.

Alders explained that "the capital costs of a peaking plant are relatively low but operating costs are high; peaking resources are designed to operate relatively few hours. Conversely, the bulk of demand for electric power is met by baseload resources, which require high capital costs but low operating costs. If peak levels of electricity are needed only a few hours a year, it makes sense to get this with a reduced capital expenditure. Manitoba Hydro would have no incentive to build a peaking resource and use it to meet high demand. It would be a lot more costly in a competitive marketplace and someone else would be able to beat that price."

One commissioner, LeRoy Koppendrayer, failed to see the merit in the PCN's argument:

> Koppendrayer: We're talking about this in terms of reliability to the Minnesota consumer. If I'm looking at emissions as a concern and I can't use coal, I can't increase nuclear, and hydro is a problem with the environment, and now I can't use gas because I have to be concerned with the Brandon plant, how in the devil are we going to keep the lights on? . . . [A] drought . . . [would] draw this system down to levels that are dangerous to the environment and the only thing left . . . is windmills. And when that severe drought hits the wind might not blow either. Then we're in the dark.
>
> Mr. McCullough, you're going . . . to ask me as a commissioner to tell the Canadian government and the Manitoba provincial government, "You aren't managing your natural resources correctly." I as a commissioner . . . dealing with reliability of public utilities issues and concerns of the consumer am not going to be the position of saying, "Look, Manitoba, we don't believe you know what you're doing with your natural resources." I'm never going to go there. . . . I'm not going to tell Manitoba what the level of the lake should be behind a dam.
>
> McCullough: In no sense do I believe you should be ordering Manitoba around. But I do feel there should be a level playing field.
>
> PUC Chair Scott: You want me to focus on the fairness of the bidding process and that's what this is about but it's not what this is exclusively about. There is another element to the statute here and these folks are entitled to argue about socioeconomic costs.

Selection of Vendors and Delivery Parameters

After reviewing possible combinations and risks, NSP decided that it should purchase 350 megawatts for 2000–2004 and another 500 megawatts for 2004–2005. Purchase of the remaining 1,200 megawatts would be deferred. The balance was delicate. Taking less than 850 megawatts from this RFP might jeopardize lower-cost energy for 2004–2005, while taking more could result in a mismatch of need and time.

NSP explained that the state of the market, a reasoned risk assessment, and the resource planning process provided a sufficient record to support the selection of its three finalists as energy suppliers at a reasonable price in 2001–2004. Black Hills Corp. of Rapid City, South Dakota (25–45 megawatts) could provide a competitive baseload product with an early in-service value (2001–2003) and a unique location relative to the western interconnect. Manitoba Hydro (500 megawatts) offered price advantages and a renewable resource to supply intermediate needs in 2004–2005. Northern Alternative Energy Inc., Minneapolis, Minnesota (350 megawatts) could provide a peaking project with an early 2001 in-service date, coupled with 50 megawatts of wind generation, which would help manage environmental cost risks. NAE also offered dispersed site flexibility for both peaking and wind resources. Each of these bids provided a competitive product on a stand-alone basis and as part of a combination.

NSP's View of Its Role in the Dispute between Hydro and the PCN

"NSP does not consider itself as a mediator in this situation," Alders said. "There are details and history that can only be overcome through the interactions of Manitoba Hydro, the First Nations, and the provincial and national governments of Canada. NSP has encouraged Hydro and Cross Lake to get to 'yes.'

"Regardless of how this is decided, socio-economic impacts will not change. If the power is not sold elsewhere, the way the river runs through the Cross Lake resource area will not be significantly different. There will still be fluctuations because Manitoba Hydro needs to meet the electrical needs of the province. Given all the dynamics, as a purchaser of that power I ask myself, can I bring any value to that complex set of negotiations? I keep coming up with 'no.' As a practical matter there's very little I can do other than to publicly encourage the parties to reach an agreement. Not to buy that power is detrimental to our customers and shareholders.

"It is our obligation to meet our customers' demand for electricity as cost effectively and as environmentally sensitively as we can. The issue before the Public Utilities Commission is whether or not to extend one of these many contracts we have with Manitoba Hydro. If we don't extend the Manitoba Hydro contract out of the 99 bidding process, what is the outcome? We see absolutely no change in the way Manitoba Hydro operates its system as a result of that decision. The United States has a robust, federally mandated, wholesale market for electricity. If we don't buy power from Manitoba Hydro, does that mean it won't be produced? No. It means someone else will purchase that power.

"We're no longer in the catbird seat because of geographic location," Alders said. "If we don't purchase Hydro's power we have to make our transmission system available to whomever does and to Manitoba Hydro as the seller."

The November 30 Meeting of the Minnesota PUC

Greg Scott called the Public Utilities Commission's November 30, 2000, hearing to order at 10 A.M. Jerry Primrose, Chief of the Nelson House Cree Nation (NCN), was one of the parties scheduled to testify before the PUC:

> There is no need for the Minnesota Public Utilities Commission to embark on an investigation of the socioeconomic costs associated with hydro developments in Manitoba. There are adequate processes in our country for dealing with these matters and they are being dealt with. Should you embark on such an investigation, it could have an adverse impact on potential development opportunities for our people. . . .
>
> In the late 1970s [our] people could not hunt and fish the way they used to in part from Hydro and also due in part to the anti-fur lobby. Because our way of life was lost we experienced suicides. An increase in alcohol consumption added to the social chaos. Outside influences that modern day society offered did not help either.
>
> The 1977 Northern Flood Agreement (NFA) gave hope to our people. The governments of Canada and Manitoba, and Manitoba Hydro promised things would improve. Nelson House had an unemployment rate of more than 90 percent. But the parties to the NFA could not agree on the scope of promises and people became very frustrated. They lost trust in Manitoba Hydro and the governments of Canada and Manitoba. They had nothing to look forward to except a welfare economy. . . .
>
> By the fall of 1992 we felt we had to try another approach. We entered into negotiations for a Comprehensive Implementation Agreement for our community alone. We no longer wanted to collaborate. . . . We finally started making inroads when the community took charge. . . .

We began looking after our own best interests.

A recent opinion survey clearly demonstrates the people's satisfaction with the programs we have and the businesses that are being developed with compensation from this implementation agreement. Of the 64 percent of NCN members on- and off-Reserve who voted in the December 1996 referendum, the overall approval rate was 77 percent, with an on-Reserve approval rate of 80 percent. While we did not get everything we wanted, we believe the agreement is fair and has benefited our community. We have to move forward and become economically self-sufficient. We want our children and our children's children to live in prosperity and happiness. We must break the cycle of poverty. We believe this agreement allows us to take steps forward to self-sufficiency and self respect.

Our community was not bought-out. The community made the decision, based on negotiations and information provided by our local negotiation team and our legal counsel. I have tried to listen respectfully to PCN's story, about the social devastation that Manitoba Hydro has caused on PCN, the suicides, the hopelessness, the despair. As leader of my community, I must speak out. All of the socioeconomic difficulties facing the Cree in Manitoba or any other Canadian Aboriginal peoples cannot be blamed on specific entities or, in this case, Manitoba Hydro. The issues are very complex—suicides occur in other communities including my own. Yet the Nelson House was the most severely impacted of the five NFA communities. A recent opinion survey indicated that overall our membership is quite positive about our future. By the path that we have followed by developing a positive, cooperative relationship with the governments and Manitoba Hydro we have created a mood of optimism, not desolation or despair. . . .

We have been impacted socially and economically in the last 25 years since the Churchill River Diversion. Socioeconomic conditions have improved tremendously since we signed the implementation agreement in 1996. The potential agreement being discussed will continue to enhance our socioeconomic opportunities. We are not being exploited by big corporations. The exploitation of our people is coming from groups that continue to suppress economic opportunities for my people.[25]

The Decision

After listening to the testimony of Chief Primrose, Chairman Scott called for a brief recess. Sitting back in his chair, Scott collected his thoughts. The decision before the committee was thorny and multifaceted, involving everything from "keeping the lights on" in Minnesota to justice for the people of the Cree First Nations. A series of options was forming in his mind. Picking up his pencil, Scott sketched five alternatives:

1. Take no action. Allow the bid process to continue without further investigation.

2. Approve NSP's selection of the final vendors, reject all requests for investigations and public hearings, and reject all requests to stay the decision on the selection of Manitoba Hydro.

3. Stay consideration of the Manitoba Hydro bid, allow the NAE and Black Hills projects to continue and:
   a. Initiate an investigation into the socioeconomic costs of large-scale hydroelectric generation.
   b. Initiate an investigation and hold public hearings on the reliability of the Manitoba Hydro bid.

4. Stay consideration of all bids and initiate an investigation into the socioeconomic effects of all generation methods.

5. Allow the bid process to continue. Initiate an investigation into:
   a. The socioeconomic effects of large-scale hydroelectric generation.
   b. The socioeconomic effects of all generation methods.

[25] Hearing handout of the Nelson Cree Nation Comments, Minnesota Public Utilities Commission Hearing, November 30, 2000.

EXHIBIT 1 Northern Flood Agreement (NFA) Cree Nations Affected by Manitoba Hydro

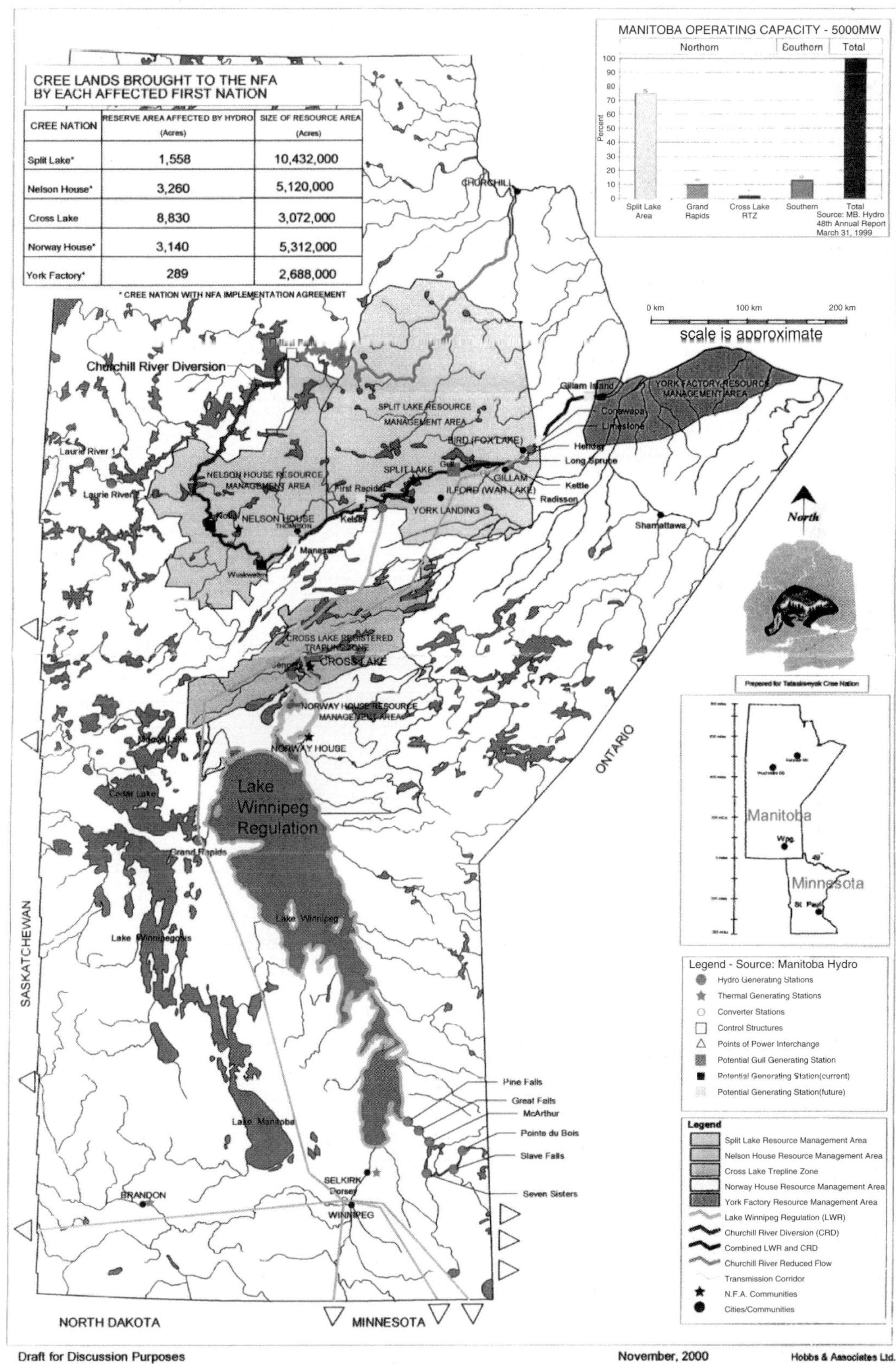

CREE LANDS BROUGHT TO THE NFA BY EACH AFFECTED FIRST NATION

CREE NATION	RESERVE AREA AFFECTED BY HYDRO (Acres)	SIZE OF RESOURCE AREA (Acres)
Split Lake*	1,558	10,432,000
Nelson House*	3,260	5,120,000
Cross Lake	8,830	3,072,000
Norway House*	3,140	5,312,000
York Factory*	289	2,688,000

* CREE NATION WITH NFA IMPLEMENTATION AGREEMENT

EXHIBIT 2 Master Implementation Agreements: Provisions and Chronology

Source: July 1999 Letter to Manitoba Aboriginal Rights Coalition from Regional Director General, Manitoba Region, Indian and Northern Affairs Canada

Cree Nation	Date of Agreement	Settlement Proceeds	Land Component
Split Lake	June 1992	$47.4 million	34,100 acres to reserve 2,800 acres fee simple+
York Factory	December 1995	$25.2 million	19,000 acres to reserve fee simple land in Churchill
Nelson House	January 1996	$64.9 million	60,000 acres to reserve 5 acres fee simple
Norway House	December 1997	$78.9 million	55,000 acres to reserve 2,000 acres fee simple

1986 The NFA First Nations receive $7.8 million to complete the design of the proposed water and sewer systems and to construct four water treatment plants.

1988 Canada and the Northern Flood Committee announce an $88.5 million settlement to ensure the continuous availability of a potable water supply on the five reserves. A multiyear implementation agreement provides for water and sewer services along with required housing upgrading, new housing, and improvements.

1992 *Split Lake* signs settlement agreement.

1995 Negotiations with Cross Lake are suspended.
York House signs settlement agreement.

1996 *Nelson House* signs settlement agreement.
Negotiations with Cross Lake resume.

1997 *Norway House* Master Implementation Agreement takes effect.

1998 Canada, Manitoba, and Manitoba Hydro sign an MOU and commit to establishing a working group to address outstanding NFA obligations in partnership with the *Cross Lake First Nation.*

+ "Lands being made available in fee simple title for the use and benefit of community members." Taken from "Chronology of Events, Northern Flood Agreement."

EXHIBIT 3 Contracts between NSP and Manitoba Hydro

Source: Northern State Power Company, 1999 Annual Report.

Power Agreements	Years	Megawatts
Participation power purchase	2000–2005	500
Seasonal diversity exchanges		
Summer exchanges from MH	2000–2014	150
	2000–2016	200
Winter exchanges to MH	2000–2014	150
	2000–2015	200
	2015–2017	400
	2018	200

Appendix

Chief Institutions and their Representatives

Institution	Page*
Manitoba Hydro	479
Minnesota Public Utilities Commission (PUC)	479
Koppendrayer, LeRoy (member)	488
Scott, Greg (chair)	479
Nelson House Cree Nation	482
Primrose, Jerry (chief)	489
Northern States Power (NSP)	486
Alders, Jim (manager–regulatory administration)	486
Norway House Cree Nation	482
Pimicikamak Cree Nation (PCN)	481
McCullough, Robert (hydrologic consultant)	480
Miswagon, John (chief)	481
Miswaggon, Kenny (Cross Lake resident)	481
Split Lake Cree Nation	482
York Factory Cree Nation	482

* Page number indicates first occurrence of the organization's (or person's) name within the case.

Medtronic in China (A)

Before he walked out of the meeting, an angry Ron Meyer blurted, "Gentlemen, this is bullshit! You've got my deal and what I will pay for. I want to know right away if this isn't going through because I need to contact 300 cardiologists who are planning to attend our open house in a few months and tell them that because Shanghai PuDong can't give us electrical power, we can't host the Chinese Society for Pacing and ElectroPhysiology!"

It was 9 P.M., June 6, 1997, in Shanghai, China. (See Exhibit 1.) Meyer, vice president, Bradycardia Pacing at Medtronic Inc., had been in negotiations with officials of the Shanghai Eastern Power Supply Bureau—PuDong Office (hereinafter "Power Bureau") since 2 P.M. The meeting was a continuation of one begun two days earlier, and it had been conducted entirely in Chinese. Melvin Le, operating manager of the new facility Medtronic was building in ZhangJiang (pronounced *Zhong Jong*) Hi-Tech Park, was Meyer's liaison and interpreter.

The matter in question was the method and cost of connecting Medtronic's new facility to permanent power. Medtronic originally understood that it would connect to permanent power from overhead power poles near its facility. Throughout this meeting, however, Jiang Qian (pronounced *Jong Chyen*), vice director for the Power Bureau, insisted that the electric utility now planned to install an underground "ring" system which it expected Medtronic to fund to the tune of $200,000.

Meyer had told the Power Bureau early on that he liked the idea of a ring system, if it could be constructed in the same time frame that it would take to install overhead power. He had budgeted $50,000 for cable and installation, and had agreed to pay Medtronic's fair share. But he was not going to make a questionable, undocumented, and overbudget payment to construct the ring system for the entire block. He'd had enough.

This case was prepared by Research Assistant Linda Swenson under the supervision of Professor Kenneth E. Goodpaster, Koch Endowed Chair in Business Ethics, University of St. Thomas, as a basis for class discussion rather than to illustrate either effective or ineffective handling of an administrative situation.

Company Background

Medtronic, the world's leading medical technology company in implantable and invasive therapies, employed nearly 14,000 people in 1997.[1] It developed, manufactured, and sold products to alleviate heart arrhythmia and neurological disorders. The creation of devices such as pacemakers, defibrillators, angioplasty balloon catheters, guidewires and guiding catheters, heart valves, neurological implantables, stent grafts, and infusion and perfusion systems had helped the company to improve the lives of millions of people throughout the world. (See Exhibit 2.) Headquartered in Minneapolis, Minnesota, the company's products and services were used in treating 1.5 million people each year in more than 120 countries.

Earl Bakken, a graduate student in electrical engineering at the University of Minnesota, had founded the company in 1949. Bakken's development of the world's first wearable pacemaker, an external device, launched the company and provided its mission: "To contribute to human welfare by application of biomedical engineering in the research, design, manufacture and sale of instruments or appliances that alleviate pain, restore health and extend life."

Medtronic's revenues for its fiscal year ending in 1997 were $2.4 billion and its after-tax profits $530 million. (See Exhibit 3.) Among industrial companies in the United States, it ranked 80th in market value and 168th in profits. Approximately 20 percent of its after-tax profits were paid as a common stock dividend. For the previous

[1] Medtronic Inc., 1997 Annual Shareholders Report. By 2004, Medtronic had over 30,000 employees.

10 years, its average annual rate of return to its investors had been 35 percent.[2]

Looking toward China

One of Medtronic's primary goals in the early 90s had been to "expand globally in established and developing markets."[3] This strategy included moving operations closer to physicians and patients. The company had set sales objectives in Europe, Australia, Latin America, India, China, and Asia, as well as North America.

Medtronic had been distributing in China for 20 years through a Hong Kong company that handled customs and then sold to a regional subdistributor. From there, pacemakers were channeled to hospitals, doctors, and patients. Medtronic essentially lost control of distribution once product arrived at the China gate. This started executives thinking in the direction of establishing a greater and more direct presence in China, even though they had been cautioned by others with experience that Medtronic was "too ethical to operate in China."

Medtronic had made an earlier attempt to establish an entity in China beginning in 1988. It was to be a joint venture, but after nearly four years of effort and the failure of the Chinese partner to meet its agreed-upon commitments, Medtronic withdrew from the partnership.

Two years later, however, in September 1994, the company would begin negotiations with the Chinese government to open a wholly owned foreign enterprise (WOFE) rather than another joint venture, which Chinese government officials would have preferred.

Bobby Griffin's Vision

Bobby Griffin, Medtronic executive vice president and president of the Pacing Business, was a key influence in the company's renewed initiative in China. "I felt tremendous pressure to find markets and technologies to grow the business in other parts of the world. Ninety-seven percent of Medtronic's products were being sold to twenty-seven percent of the world," Griffin later recalled. "I'd read books on China and *BusinessWeek* articles about the success of General Electric and other companies that had gone into China with scaled-down products. These nuggets encouraged my thinking."[4]

Griffin interviewed Chinese physicians who wanted a highly reliable, basic pacing device that would allow them to serve more people in need. Every year in China, only 4,000 cardiac patients were implanted with pacemakers—a small minority of the patients who needed them. "These doctors were motivated not by greed but by their desire to help and heal their patients," Griffin explained. "Their relationships with their patients in the hospitals were touching. Instead of talking down to them from a standing position, they would get down on one knee and whisper in the patient's ear."

"It was clear that a certain class of people in China could afford almost anything, while most could afford no treatment at all," Griffin said. "Yet more people in China could afford pacing than the populations of Germany and France combined. Of the millions of people living in the coastal cities of China, those in the middle class had $2,000 in disposable income. Ten thousand television sets were being sold every week. In accord with Maslow's hierarchy of needs, after reaching their first $1,000 of disposable income, people start spending on health care."

As Griffin's plane lifted off one afternoon from the Hong Kong airport in 1994, he recalled, "I looked down at the beehive of activity below and the gestalt hit me. Because of the Clinton administration's health care goals, medical device companies would have to lower prices anyway. If we could build a product we could sell in China for $1,000 and still make our margins, we could serve many more people all over the world with reliable products and still make a profit. I made up my mind to set an audacious goal. I'd shoot for a *radical* cost reduction in product."

Back at corporate headquarters, after a "You're crazy, Griffin!" reaction, Medtronic's head of development agreed to support the project. This meant that a team of as many as 25 people could be assembled, full- or part-time, for the project. Medtronic's marketing organization liked the

[2] *Business Week*, March 30, 1998, p. 155. Return includes dividends and market appreciation.

[3] *Medtronic Vision Statement*, 1994.

[4] William H. Overholt, *The Rise of China: How Economic Reform is Creating a New Superpower*, (W. W. Norton), *1993.* "A bullish report on China's explosively growing economy", (*Kirkus Reviews*), 1993.

idea because the company could lead with an inexpensive product that would leverage sales of higher-end products.

In July 1994, Ron Meyer returned to Medtronic headquarters in Minneapolis as vice president of Bradycardia Pacing, and Bobby Griffin asked him to work on the effort to get Medtronic into China. Meyer had previously worked for Griffin managing Promeon, the company's vertically integrated battery manufacturing division. As one of the six who started the division, he had overseen the building of its first facility. Meyer's charge was to oversee not only the development of a new product but also the building of a plant to produce the new product in China.

Developing the Champion Pacing System

The company's strategic decision in 1994 to expand production into developing markets and Bobby Griffin's audacious vision of the way to go about it coincided with development of what was to be called the "Champion" pacemaker, a simplified version of the company's existing pacing systems that would meet specifications of cardiologists in China and India.[5]

Mechanical engineering design manager Bill Hooper had been supporting the Champion pacing system through Quest, a special program within the company that funded the work of engineers who wanted to develop projects that wouldn't otherwise receive funding. "Sometimes," Hooper observed, "the vision starts putting everything into place. My dream was to see patients in less developed countries restored to full life in ways that had been available for years in more developed countries. The second dream was about making it possible to build the product in China."

A pacemaker consisted of a small metal "can" that housed the circuitry and the battery power supply. Connected to the lead, an insulated wire carried the electric impulse from the pacemaker to the heart and relayed information about the heart's natural activity back to the pacemaker. The Champion pacing system contained these basic features (see Exhibit 4) and was of the endocardial type—the lead would be implanted through a vein (see Figure A).[6] The battery for the Champion system would last nine years.

Hooper and electrical engineer Larry Hudziak took advantage of sophisticated technology already in place and simplified it. "We wanted to

[5] The name "Champion" came out of a worldwide look at the branding strategy, i.e., name acceptability in India, Pakistan, China, Singapore, and Malaysia.

[6] When speaking generically of pacemaker implants, a small percentage are implanted using the epicardial implant technique (See Figure B.)

FIGURE A Endocardial Implant

FIGURE B Epicardial Implant

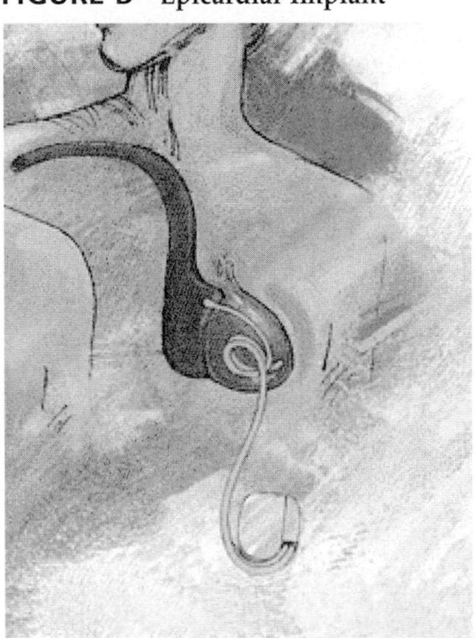

reduce the cost to make it affordable in the China market. By using a proven pacing lead technology for the coil, insulator, electrode, and tine, we were able to save substantially. We simplified the connection end, that is, the end next to the pacemaker. One of the most critical parts of the device, the lead wire, would flex whenever patients breathed, their hearts beat, or they moved. We chose a lead that had the best reliability of anything we make," Hooper explained.

The Champion design did not include more complex, state-of-the-art features like dual-chamber stimulation, activity sensors, or steroid-eluding leads. The doctors Bobby Griffin and others had met with in China and India considered these features unnecessary, preferring high quality, low cost, longevity, and ease of use. The design team worked hard to reduce the cost of the Champion pacemaker, which could translate into a lower selling price.

The Path toward Building

"In September 1994," Hooper recalls, "Ron sat me down and said, 'We need to construct a building, and we have no employees in China. Do you think we can do this?' " Hooper was one of Medtronic's most knowledgeable mechanical systems designers. His specialty was packaging all the intricacies of the pacemaker into the device. But he also knew how to design facilities to cut costs. Meyer explained, "The expense of a specially designed facility and equipment can be a burden when you have to allocate that cost to each product. We weren't going to be producing huge volumes."

When the China project was in the planning stage, Meyer also consulted with a specialist on Chinese culture. "Particular ways of relating became extremely important in China," Meyer explained. It was important to consider the business practices signified by the terms *guanxi* (pronounced *gwonche*), *mianzi*, and *renqing*. *Guanxi* meant "relationship"; *mianzi* meant "saving face"—never challenging someone openly so they have no way of gracefully backing down; and *renqing* meant "the ability to feel and express emotions," considered essential to communication. "Building relationships and being sensitive to *mianzi* and *renqing* would be crucial to our success," Meyer said. "The Chinese know who you know," Meyer noted. "It often happened that something I'd said in Beijing got back to me through government connections in other places."

Personal Sacrifice

From September 1994 through February 1995, Meyer, Hooper, and Hudziak developed plans for the Champion product and for establishing a presence in China with approval from Medtronic upper management. Over a three-year period, Hooper would make 19 trips, Meyer 26. They each were gone two to three weeks at a time. Meyer worked with the Asia Pacific sales team for a full year, setting up the WFOE, finding a site, and negotiating a business license. The WFOE license was approved December 29, 1995. Eventually a Shanghai facility was recommended by the team and strongly supported by Medtronic Chairman and CEO Bill George and President and Chief Operating Officer Art Collins.

Meyer and Hooper would take turns maintaining a near-constant presence in Shanghai while the facility was under construction. They reported to each other via e-mail and phone calls. "The routine was grueling," Hooper recalls. "Check into the hotel, unpack, head out to buy water and walk for exercise, then back to your room. It was such a drill."

Hooper recalled that these were tough times for both of them: "We both had families. When I was doing algebra with my daughter on the phone in the middle of the night from China, I could remind myself, 'I'm here because of Medtronic's mission and my part in fulfilling that mission.' If I hadn't had that, I would have given up."

Building a Plant in Shanghai

Vice Mayor Zhou Qi Zheng (pronounced *Jow Chi Jeng*) was in charge of the PuDong area among his duties as one of the vice mayors of the province of Shanghai. Medtronic executives first met Zhou before the press conference that announced Medtronic's plans to open a plant in Shanghai. It was a formal meeting in which the vice mayor was representing Shanghai and Medtronic Vice Chairman Glen Nelson was representing Medtronic. During conversation, the vice mayor mentioned he had a brother in Minnesota who taught at Carleton College. Nelson later established contact with the Carleton professor.

Art Collins had met Zhou at the groundbreaking ceremony. When Zhou visited his brother in spring 1997 to give a joint talk at one of Minnesota's international trade organizations, he stopped at Medtronic headquarters because of the effort Medtronic had made to contact his brother.

In early November 1995, ZhangJiang Hi-Tech Park in Shanghai was selected as the plant site. (See Exhibit 5.) At a November 4 press conference announcing Medtronic's plans, Wu Cheng Liu, former general manager of the industrial park, stood and said he expected his organization, the Shanghai Foreign Investment Commission, to help Medtronic through the process of getting a business license before December 31.[7] That a Chinese official would make this kind of a commitment was extraordinary, Meyer later observed.

The response of Wu's group was immediate. When Meyer visited the Shanghai Investment Commission the day after the press conference, he was given a PERT chart that told him, day by day, what had to be done to meet the December 31 deadline.

During the process of site selection, Medtronic had narrowed the field to Beijing, Tianjin, and Shanghai. ZhangJiang was one of two sites being considered in Shanghai. Wu was head of the park at this juncture. Because Medtronic was a *Fortune* 500 company, it was important for Wu to secure the company's commitment to locate in ZhangJiang. Wu was promoted to executive vice chairman of the Shanghai Foreign Investment Commission shortly after Medtronic signed the contract with the park. This was fortuitous, because Medtronic would need the help of this organization to establish a business plan and get approvals for licensure.

Between early November and the end of December, Medtronic completed the business plan and feasibility study necessary for licensure. "It's not uncommon for this process to take six months to a year to accomplish. To write an entire business plan and be granted a license in China and get all the approvals in 60 days—I don't think it had been done before," Meyer said.

[7] A change in tax laws effective January 1, 1996, would have cost the company significant import duties if it did not make the December 31 deadline for completing the business license.

In December 1995 and early 1996, representatives of six large Hong Kong construction companies flew to Minneapolis to bring their bid proposals to headquarters for a six-hour meeting. Medtronic eventually signed a contract with Parsons Brinkerhoff-Asia (PBA) in April 1996. Groundbreaking was set for July that year on the 1.4-acre site. The floor space of the new building would be 20,000 square feet, and the facility would employ 80 people, including management, sales, marketing, operations, and logistics. All labor and general contracting had to be performed by a Chinese company, but PBA oversaw construction, which began in late September 1996. From January through July 1996, between trips to China, Hooper continued to work on the Champion product in Minneapolis.

On any given day 75 workers who had come from all over China would be at work on the site. The concrete superstructure of the building was completed and the roof finished in time for Lunar New Year (late January 1997). Work on the electrical, mechanical, and air-conditioning systems began and continued throughout spring 1997.

By early May 1997, Medtronic's Spring Lake Park, Minnesota, facility had produced 2,500 Champion pacing systems. By June 15, the equipment used to produce these units was dismantled and airfreighted to China for installation in the new Shanghai facility. Since Chinese regulations on the import of capital goods were about to change, the equipment needed to clear customs by June 30. Otherwise it would be subject to a 40 percent import duty—about $250,000.

The equipment arrived in Shanghai June 15 and cleared customs June 25. On June 29, Hooper guided a semitrailer cab that led three flatbeds of crated equipment through the streets of Shanghai to the PuDong area. "The building wasn't ready. We unloaded equipment into unfinished rooms and hallways," Hooper recalled. "Workers were using the crates as scaffolding. The concrete driveway wasn't poured so one of the semitrucks sank in the mud. It was gut-wrenching."

The electrical cable carrying temporary power was too small for both the lights and the air-conditioning. Water heaters, welders, and ovens couldn't run simultaneously. The contractor agreed to put a generator on site. Hooper decided they couldn't test the equipment until final power was hooked up. The plant's grand opening was scheduled for October 22, 1997.

Medtronic sponsored the Chinese Society for Pacing and ElectroPhysiology. This group comprised about half of Medtronic's customer base in China and had been invited to the new plant's grand opening. The organization had rescheduled its own annual meeting to coordinate with the Medtronic Shanghai grand opening in October. Collins and Zhou also would attend the opening.

The Power Bureau's Unexpected Request for $200,000

Meyer had examined Medtronic's contract with ZhangJiang Hi-Tech Park and saw that the industrial park's commitment regarding electric utilities was unclear. "The contract mentioned 'conduit'[8] so I kept asking whether this meant the park would be bringing in underground power," Meyer recalls. "I never got a straight answer." One early June 1997 evening, Meyer got a hint of things to come when a young Hi-Tech Park project manager said to him after a beer, "Have a care, Ron, there's no cable in those conduits."

"We had planned to pay for cable," Meyer said, "but I still assumed we would be hooked up to overhead power." Two other facilities on the block were hooked up in this way.

An underground double-ring system was designed with cable that came off both of the rings, so that if one side was shut off for maintenance, businesses could hook up to the other side—electrical power was always available. This system was also commonly used in U.S. industrial parks.

Ron Meyer received a voice mail and an e-mail from his Shanghai facility operations manager, Melvin Le, about a problem with the Power Bureau on June 3, 1997. The next afternoon, Meyer, Le, and PBA met with Jiang Qian of the Power Bureau. Jiang was both young and new to his position at the Power Bureau. The meeting was conducted entirely in Chinese. Le translated for Meyer. Jiang started the conversation with, "We can't bring in overhead power."

Meyer: "Why not?"
Jiang: "Because we're building a new underground ring system."
Meyer: "But the overhead power is running right by us. There's a power pole on our property. Why are we going underground?"
Jiang: "That's the way we want to do it now."

"I didn't have a problem with the Power Bureau wanting to install an underground ring system," Meyer said. "But it had estimated the cost to be $200,000 to $225,000 (including $70,000 for cable). PBA had budgeted $50,000 for electrical power. The electrical utility provided no documentation for the fee request and no estimated time of installation."

"Early on when we talked to people about facility construction challenges, they told us it wasn't uncommon for new construction projects to have to renegotiate their positions with utilities—that infrastructure was funded in this way. We had been warned that near the end of the construction process when things got critical, one of the utilities could do this," Hooper explained. "We didn't know which one. The gas company might say, 'We can't hook up from here,' or the electrical utility might say, 'We need to bring your power in from a substation that isn't built yet.' You could be across the street from a substation, and they could say, 'You can't use that substation; you have to build your own.' "

"Coming from the United States, you have a different frame of reference about how utilities work and that affects how you plan," Meyer said. "In China, the industrial park steps out of it and says, 'This is between you and the power company.' So you never know who's on first."

So the June 4 meeting went on into the night. "At the second meeting on June 6, we started rehashing the issue at about 2 P.M.," Meyer recalls. "By that evening, the negotiation process, which had been conducted entirely in Chinese, was starting to wear on me. Finally I asked Melvin Le where we were. We were nowhere. By about 9 P.M., I'd had enough and I blew up."

As he left the meeting after the blowup, Meyer considered the disparity between the Chinese and American way of handling disputes and wondered if he'd made an irreparable mistake. Had his show of anger hurt Medtronic's chances of reaching an agreement with the Power Bureau?

[8] The tube that holds the cable.

He considered his options. He could stay the course and see what happened. He could try to work on the situation behind the scenes now that he had expressed his position at the Power Bureau. He could pay what he considered to be an extortionate request for money. He could slow down the project, preparing his superiors for a delay of the grand opening ceremony. Maybe he could discuss the worst-case scenario: that this plant was a mistake to begin with. And maybe there were other options.

Meyer's notes following the second meeting revealed his skepticism and discouragement:

> *I'm not sure I have any information that is accurate or useful. Shanghai Eastern Power Supply simply wants more money and they've got the power.*

To add to Meyer's frustration, time spent negotiating with the Power Bureau was to have been devoted to developing a sales plan for the Champion pacing system. The sales policies in China would define how Medtronic would deal with corrupt business practices—usually the toughest issue facing foreign companies in China.

"Many companies would consider a problem like Medtronic's issue with the Power Bureau enough reason to pull their business out of China," Hooper said. On one visit to Hong Kong before a site had been identified, there had been some strategizing about what would be a big enough issue to justify such an action.

EXHIBIT 1 **Shanghai, China**

Source: Map: Reprinted with permission © 2004 Lonely Planet Publications Pty Ltd. All rights reserved.

Shanghai China is one of the world's largest seaports and a major industrial and commercial centre of China. The city is located on the coast of the East China Sea between the mouth of the Yangtze River to the north and the bays of Hangchow and Yü-pan to the south. The municipality covers . . . 2,383 square miles, which includes the city itself, surrounding suburbs and an agricultural hinterland; it is also China's most populous urban area.

Shanghai was the first Chinese port to be opened to Western trade. . . . The city has also undergone extensive physical changes with the establishment of industrial suburbs and housing complexes, the improvement of public works and the provision of parks and other recreational facilities. Shanghai has attempted to eradicate the economic and psychological legacies of its exploited past through physical and social transformation to support its major role in the modernization of China.

The city's maritime location fosters a mild climate characterized by minimal seasonal contrast. The average annual temperature is about 58°F . . . the July maximum averages about 80°F . . . and the average January minimum is about 37°F . . . . About 45 inches . . . of precipitation fall annually, with the heaviest rainfall in June and the lightest in December.[9]

[9] Reprinted with permission from Encyclopedia Brittanica, © 2004 by Encyclopedia Brittanica, Inc. Text source: *Encyclopedia Brittanica Online* http://www.brittanica.com/eb/article?tocld=24135.

EXHIBIT 2 Glossary of Terms for Medical Devices

Angioplasty balloon catheter – A device for dilatation of a blood vessel by means of a balloon catheter inserted through the skin.

Defibrillator – Electronic device that applies an electric shock to restore the rhythm of a fibrillating heart.

Guidewires and guiding catheters – Devices to assist the physician to correctly locate angioplasty balloon catheters.

Heart valves – Devices to replace defective or diseased heart valves made from either metal, plastic, or porcine natural heart valves.

Infusion and perfusion systems – Devices used to complete external blood circuits; used during surgery in which the heart is stopped.

Neurological implantables – Devices to stimulate nerves by electrical impulses to block pain sensation, and devices to infuse drug compounds to block pain sensation and reduce muscle spasticity.

Pacemaker – A device designed to stimulate the heart muscle by electrical impulses.

Stent graft – A tubular device expanded within a blood vessel to clear blockages or support weak sections.

EXHIBIT 3 **Medtronic Financial Highlights 1985-1997**

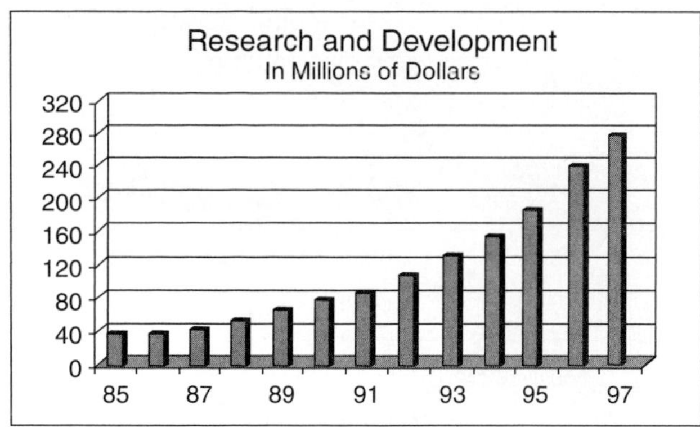

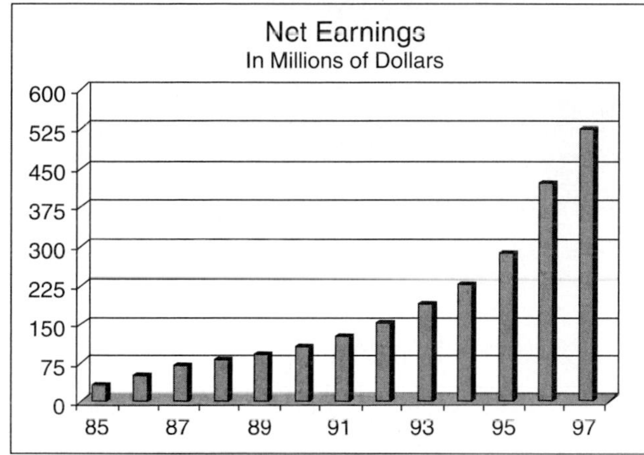

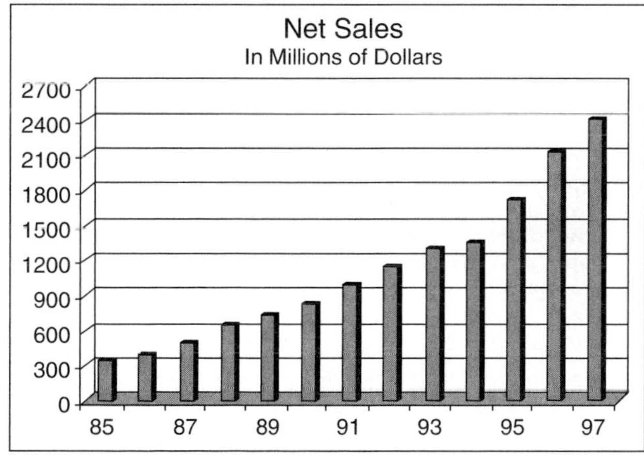

EXHIBIT 4 The Champion Pacing System

Features of the Champion Pacing System:

- Single chamber ventricular pacing provides dependable pacing therapy for bradycardia
- Medtronic proven Target Tip lead offers highly reliable pacing and sensing performance
- Pacing parameters pre-set to accommodate most patients' needs
- Unique magnet allows fast and accurate program pacing parameters (rate and output)
- New "tool-less" connector simplifies implant procedures
- The Champion Pacing System which includes both pacemaker and Target Tip lead makes pacing affordable for more patients

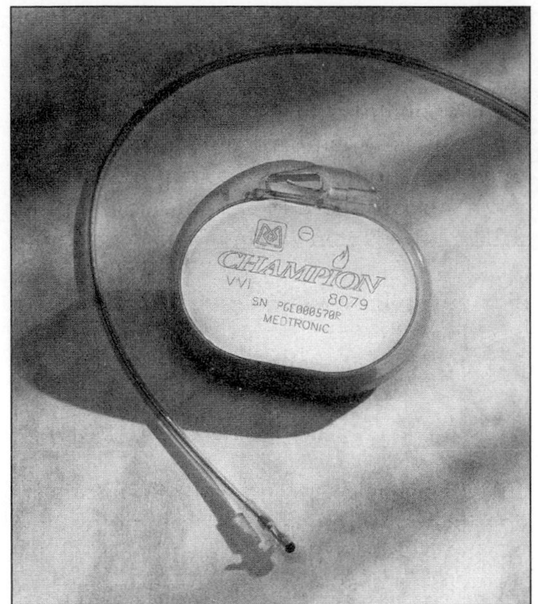

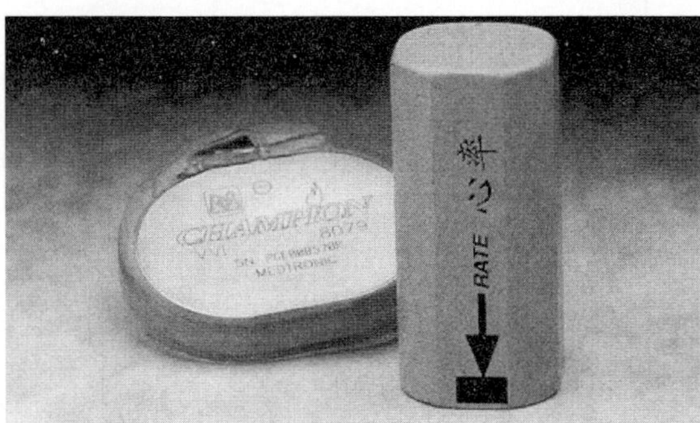

The unique programming magnet is the only device needed to adjust parameters in the Champion Pacing System.

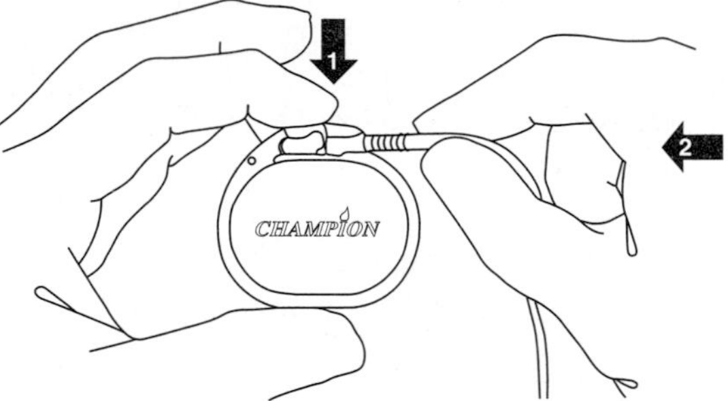

The Champion "tool-less" connector makes implant procedures easier. Apply pressure to the top of the connector spring clip to align opening (1) while pushing the lead pin into the connector port (2).

EXHIBIT 5 ZhangJiang Hi-Tech Park, Shanghai, China

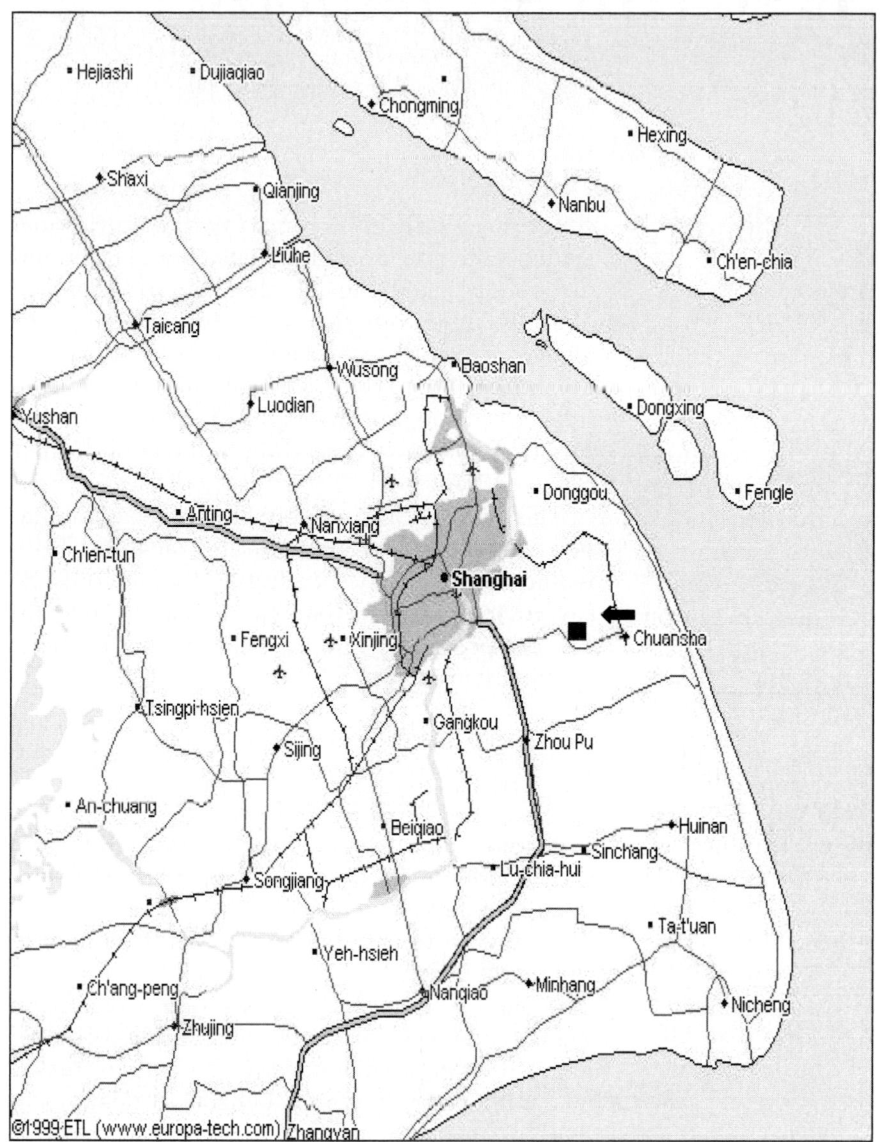

Business E-Ethics: *Yahoo! on Trial (A)*

Introduction: Calling Jerry Yang

On a fine day in June 2000, Jerry Yang, the cofounder of Yahoo, arrived in the Paris offices of his company's French subsidiary. The previous evening, fresh from a conference in London sponsored by *Fortune* magazine where he was among the star speakers, he had joined in the inaugural bash for Yahoo France's new building in an elegant quarter of Paris. Upholstered in Yahoo's purple and orange team colors, with a soda machine offering free drinks and five-point yellow stars bearing the names of new employees on the walls, the place evokes a magically perfect American high school, except that the youthful employees work very fast, long, and hard.

As Yang settled in, a reporter for one of France's major newspapers, *Libération*, called to request an interview on a painfully sensitive subject. Since April, French antiracist groups had been suing to block access by French net surfers to Yahoo.com's site, on the grounds that Yahoo provided the opportunity to buy Nazi objects online, which is illegal in France. Yahoo had lost the first round in May, when the court issued a preliminary ruling in accord with the plaintiffs' demands. The next hearing was scheduled for mid-July.

Yahoo France's employees, at least one of whom had been pressured by her family to leave the company over the issue, urged Yang to meet the reporter. Though his operational responsibilities are limited, the creator of the online portal concept is still the company's inspirational leader, with the title of "Chief Yahoo!" He and his colleagues believed that the freedom of not only Yahoo but also of the Internet might be affected by this case. They saw themselves as defending the right of internauts everywhere to free expression, and the right of Internet companies to do business according to the laws of their home nations.

The decision was quickly made: The combination of *Libération*'s prominence and Yang's celebrity would assure a wide hearing. But what could he say to the reporter that would clearly explain Yahoo's position on the case and its implications for the Internet?

An Activist Sounds the Alert: February 2000

The events that preceded the reporter's call were set in motion by Marc Knobel, 39, a Parisian, doctor of history, and a researcher who earns his living by tracking hate groups for the Simon Wiesenthal Center in Los Angeles, California. Ever since his Jewish ancestors were driven from the Ukraine by Czarist pogroms, recalled Knobel in a bitter euphemism, "My family has tasted fascism in every flavor."[1] He had lost relatives in the Nazi extermination camps, where 6 million European Jews were systematically murdered in the Shoah, or Holocaust, before the fall of the Third Reich in 1945. For Knobel, the atrocities of genocides never ended: They continued in Rwanda, Bosnia, and anyplace else where a given people decides to annihilate another.

Since 1997, when he began conducting his research online, he had become convinced that the Internet was changing the landscape of hate for the worse. American extremists who

This case was prepared by Dr. Mark Hunter, Senior Research Fellow at INSEAD, under the supervision of Marc Le Menestrel, Assistant Professor of Economics and Business at University Pompeu Fabra and Visiting Professor at INSEAD, and Henri-Claude de Bettignies, Professor of Asian Business at INSEAD and Visiting Professor at Stanford University. It is intended to be used as a basis for class discussion rather than to illustrate either effective or ineffective handling of an administrative situation.

[1] Marc Knobel's quotes are drawn from an interview, February 6, 2001, and from follow-up telephone calls, unless otherwise indicated.

previously risked arrest when they carried their propaganda to countries like France or Germany could now distribute their wares safely over the Web. Said Knobel:

> The Internet didn't invent anything. These groups existed, they distributed their propaganda, forged bonds among themselves, met with each other. That hasn't changed. But before Internet, they were largely confined to specific geographical zones. What's new is the very great ease which allows me today to connect to the Web pages and sites created by these groups, and to see what they distribute, who they are, what they're doing, and to have access to their very essence.

Ironically, he acknowledged that this shift had greatly facilitated the work of researchers like himself. And yet, said Knobel, "I would prefer, frankly, to never see a site that was created by the extreme right. Every time we leave open ground to the extreme right, it moves in." One of his lawyer friends, Stéphane Lilti, agreed: "The day we shut them down, and there are less of them, it's a victory."[2]

One day in February 2000, an American acquaintance called Knobel to ask: "Are you aware that on Yahoo, they're selling Nazi stuff?"

Knobel's first reaction was disbelief. Yahoo, for him, stood for "the great community of internauts where you find everything right away, and even better, for free. A wonderful new world." He opened Yahoo.com's home page, clicked on the link to auctions, typed the word "nazi" into the search window, and discovered 800 items for sale. He kept clicking until, he recalled, "I came across a box of Zyklon-B." This was the poison gas used to kill his people at Auschwitz and other Nazi extermination camps.

The item was identified as a "museum-quality replica." Noted Greg Wrenn, Yahoo's associate general counsel for international affairs: "The vendors didn't say, 'Throw this at your Jewish neighbor and scare him.' Nothing to indicate they were offered by Nazi supporters."[3] But for Knobel, the object in itself was intolerable.

Knobel understood that it wasn't Yahoo but visitors to the site, who sold and bought these things, and that Yahoo earned no commissions or fees from auctions. Still Knobel felt betrayed by Yahoo's "nice image."

His goal was now to stop these sales. In conjunction with Stéphane Lilti, he decided that the first step would be a campaign in the Paris press. If that failed, they would turn to the French courts. Unlike the United States, where the First Amendment to the Constitution broadly protects free speech, French law sets numerous limits on public discourse (see Exhibit 2), but he doubted it would come to that.

> I thought I could make Yahoo understand that it's no big problem if they take these things off the site. They'd get the idea; they'd contact me. I said to myself, "They're Americans; they'll understand that the French see this differently, that it isn't good to sell this stuff. It's their responsibility, and it's in their power to do something." And I said to myself—not to them—"Maybe they will. I'll give them two months."

Early Warnings in the Press: February 17–April 5, 2000

Knobel convinced the Union of Jewish French Students (UEJF) and the international League against Racism and Anti-Semitism (LICRA), where he sat on the executive board, to join his cause. Lilti tried to recruit other lawyers, with no success. "It isn't very smart for a lawyer specialized in the Internet to attack Yahoo," he commented ironically. "It doesn't help him get clients."

Their press campaign took off on Feb. 17, 2000, in the weekly *Paris-Match*, which announced its "discovery" of Nazi goods on the Internet—"nearly 500 on Yahoo!, and over 3,500 on eBay," noted the reporters. An illustration of a Waffen SS, a member of the Nazi party's armed forces, was captioned: "On Yahoo! Auctions: A mouse pad glorifying the SS troops."

The article ended with a quote from Knobel: "It's up to Internet companies to regulate themselves. If not, we'll launch a boycott."[4] The LICRA did just that two days later.

During an interview with the leading French newsweekly *L'Express*, Knobel suggested asking

[2] Interviewed by telephone, March 13, 2001.

[3] Interviewed by telephone, March 29, 2001.

[4] François Labrouillère and Laurent Léger, "Quand Yahoo et eBay deviennent les supermarchés des souvenirs nazis," *Paris-Match*, February 17, 2000.

Yahoo's advertisers what they thought about the Nazi goods. The reporter followed his advice:

> Questioned and informed by *L'Express*, the companies Ford and Visa declared themselves stupefied to discover that their banners are displayed on the same page as the SS. "We aren't indifferent," said Ford, "but what can we do? The laws governing the Web are so complex." The London-based managers of Visa, however, claimed they had demanded that Yahoo! stop this "abusive use" [of Visa's ads].[5]

L'Express also quoted a spokesperson for Yahoo France: "To censor [Nazi goods] would create a dangerous precedent. But we respect a certain morality: there are no live animals sold at auction."

"If they can do that, why not purge their site of Nazis?" thought Knobel. And why, he and Lilti wondered, had Yahoo made no attempt to contact them? In March, the LICRA wrote to Yahoo Inc., but received no reply.

However, the article in *L'Express* had been read with foreboding at Yahoo France, whose general director, Philippe Guillanton, remembered thinking: "This feels like a complicated affair." He contacted Yahoo Inc., which replied that the company received "five letters like that every day." Looking back, he said, "We could have called the LICRA to say, 'Listen, there's a problem, but it's not something we control, can we talk about it?' " But very soon the opportunity would be lost.

As the press campaign lost momentum, Knobel and Lilti prepared a legal assault. In France, the display for sale of Nazi objects is a crime under Article 645 of the Penal Code. Lilti had successfully used that law to obtain the conviction of French "revisionist" Robert Faurisson, whose denials of the Holocaust, illegal in France, had been published on a Swedish Web site. "The court ruled that when the content is received in France, French law applies," noted Lilti.[6] He added, "I never take on a case without knowing that I'll get a good result. With Yahoo, we were going to annoy them badly, if not worse."

On April 5, 2000, Yahoo France received a registered letter from the LICRA. Postmarked April 3, it warned that if the auctions of Nazi objects did not cease within eight days, charges would be filed. Thus Yahoo had less than a week to resolve the problem before it went to the courts. Lilti, who was preparing a similar lawsuit for the UEJF, gave Yahoo no advance warning whatsoever.

The Rise of the Online Auction Business: 1998–2000

Online auctions are among the fastest-growing and most profitable sectors of e-commerce. As early as 1998, B2C auction sites attracted 1.2 million purchasers in the United States, according to Jupiter Communications. Jupiter predicted that by 2002, online B2C auctions in the United States would total \$3.2 billion in annual sales and draw 6.5 million customers for goods ranging from toys to technology.[7]

The C2C sector—an outgrowth of the online forums that first created a mass public for the Internet—was rising even faster, led by eBay, QXL, and iBazar. Within a single year, eBay's revenues, mainly derived from a variable fee on transactions, practically doubled, from \$150 million through the first nine months of 1999 to \$297 million for the same period in 2000. In the latter period, gross profit was \$225 million and net income reached \$39 million.[8] In January 2001, Forrester Research reported that online auctions in Europe had passed the billion-euro landmark, and would attain 8.8 billion euros by 2005, with 62 percent of transactions taking place in C2C sites.[9]

Advertising revenues are also crucial to auction sites, especially Yahoo, which earned no direct commissions or fees on its auction services in 2000, and gained 90 percent of its revenues

[5] Cédric Gouverneur, "Internet: Comment éliminer les sites nazis?" *L'Express* No. 2541, March 16, 2000, p. 40.

[6] For the judgment, see Tribunal de Grande Instance de Paris, 13 novembre 1988, Faurisson c/ Ministère public.

[7] "Jupiter: Online Retailers Must Embrace Auctions as New Platform for Discounts," press release, New York: January 25, 1999 (through www.jup.com).

[8] Figures are taken from eBay's quarterly reports (form 10-Q) to the Securities and Exchange Commission.

[9] Hellen K. Omwando et al., "Europe's Online Auction Prize: SME's," Forrester Research, Inc. January 2001, pp. 1, 2, 6. The report quotes a competitor of eBay who estimates that 10 percent of the site's inventory, and 80 percent of its gross auction value, is accounted for by businesses posing as consumers (p. 4). The masquerade is presumably designed to profit from the fad for C2C auctions.

from advertising.[10] Among 25 auction sites surveyed by Forrester, advertising generated an average 22 percent of revenues, second only to commissions. Auctions help to sell ad banners: The average visit on eBay lasts 50 minutes, compared to 20 minutes for conventional online retailers.[11]

By spring 2000, daily auction listings on Yahoo.com totaled some 2.5 million items. On any given day, a search of the auction site using the keyword "Nazi" would turn up some 1,000 objects, ranging from anti-Nazi films and books to the Zyklon-B replica that revolted Knobel.

Protests against Hate for Sale on the Web: August 1999–February 2000

The appearance of objects of Nazi provenance in online auctions was predictable, given the experience of brick-and-mortar auctioneers. In 1985, the attorney general of the State of New York opened an investigation into Sotheby's sale of rare books that had formerly belonged to the Hebrew Theological Seminary of Berlin, destroyed by the Nazis. The vendor claimed that he had been given title to the works in exchange for smuggling them out of Germany in 1943, at the height of the Holocaust. Sotheby's settled the case.[12] Christie's sold a painting publicly listed as stolen by the Nazis from the Schloss collection of Old Masters in France, at the company's New York showroom in 1989. The buyer later returned the work to France, where he was indicted and convicted on charges of receiving stolen goods.[13]

Related conflicts arose on the Internet at the end of the 1990s. Online booksellers Barnesandnoble.com and Amazon.com stopped selling Adolf Hitler's *Mein Kampf* to German customers in August 1999, after the Simon Wiesenthal Center notified the German Ministry of Justice that the companies might be violating the Federal Republic's laws against hate literature. Nonetheless, reported the online magazine *Salon,* "While German extremists can't buy their books from the Internet's biggest vendors, they can find them if they dig a little deeper."[14] (See Exhibit 3 for a historical review of European struggles with "left and right")

Three months later the center attacked what it called "eBay's current policy of marketing Nazi memorabilia," adding that it intended to ask German leaders to "review existing anti-Nazi laws and possible legal actions." Executives at eBay argued that its German subsidiary "adheres to German law and does not allow the posting of Nazi items" and that they were "hesitant to perform the role of censor." One eBay manager complained, "They [the Wiesenthal Center] are worried about crazies having and buying these things, but the way to alert the crazies is to act like that." He compared the center, known for its pursuit of war criminals, to "a Nazi Gestapo force [that wants to] police everything that goes on the market."[15]

In February 2000, eBay came under fire from a New York–based antihate group, BiasHELP, which asked the auctioneer to remove all listings of items related to the Ku Klux Klan, infamous for its lynchings of Afro-Americans since the late 19th century. The group suggested that "the incredible size and reach of [eBay's] audience creates special responsibilities." A reporter for Auctionwatch.com noted that "the request puts eBay in a no-win situation, especially considering the family image the site works hard to present." Richard Bondira, president of the Indiana Historical Society and an expert on the Klan, commented that "selling original collectibles has nothing to do with bias, it's a piece of history."[16]

[10] According to its quarterly SEC filings, Yahoo Inc. earned $799 million through the first nine months of 2000, of which $722.8 million came from advertising.

[11] Omwando, op. cit., pp. 3, 4.

[12] For a detailed account of this incident, see Mark Hunter, *Le Destin de Suzanne: La véritable affaire Canson*, Paris: Fayard, 1995, pp. 63–65. It is worth noting that until the attorney general of New York, Robert Abrams, filed suit against Sotheby's, the identity of the vendor of the books was kept secret by the company, in accord with the auction industry's traditional practice and privilege of "client confidentiality." The anonymity of buyers and sellers is likewise assured by online auction sites.

[13] See Mark Hunter, "Nazi Theft Still Haunts the Art World," *Wall Street Journal Europe*, March 27, 1996, p. 7.

[14] Craig Offman, "Hate Books Still for Sale on the Web," Salon.com, August 17, 1999.

[15] Ed Ritchie, "No Tolerance for Nazi Items," Auctionwatch.com, December 1, 1999.

[16] Ed Ritchie, "BiasHELP Wants Klan Items Banned from eBay," Auctionwatch.com, February 3, 2000.

But the next day, eBay announced that its site "will not become a platform for those who promote hatred toward their fellow man." Kevin Purslove, vice president of communications, denied that the protests had been a "catalyst" but admitted: "It's fair to say they were one component that helped us come to a decision on this." The company's new policy attempted to balance the interests of legitimate collectors against the concerns of protestors:

> Relics of groups such as the KKK or Nazi Germany may be listed on eBay, provided that they are at least 50 years old, and the listing is not used as a platform to glorify or promote the organization or its values. . . . eBay will judiciously disallow listings or items that promote hatred, violence or racial intolerance, including items that promote organizations with such views. eBay will review listings that are brought to its attention by the community, and will look at the entire listing to determine whether it falls within this rule.

The Public and Governments Intervene against Hate on the Web: January–February 2000

Meanwhile, the issue of Internet hate steadily widened. In January 2000, the United Kingdom's Internet Watch Foundation (IWF), an industry self-regulatory group established in 1996, announced that it was extending its authority to hate materials on the Internet. Under an agreement with the British government, the IWF investigated complaints received on its hotline, to determine if pages on a given site contained illegal hate content. If so, the IWF would ask the service provider to take down the site. Providers that complied were guaranteed immunity from criminal prosecution, though not from civil actions. (See Exhibit 1.)

For British civil liberties activists like Chris Ellison, founder of Internet Freedom, the IWF's goal was to "extend their ability to censor," at a moment when the Blair government sought to improve its "politically correct" image.[17] But for IWF Chairman Roger Darlington, self-regulation, not censorship, was the issue: "We have no formal legal powers—Parliament hasn't legislated this. The strength [of the IWF] is that the industry is more sensitive to a body it set up, and it works faster than a public body. The weakness is that [its actions] could still be challenged in the courts."[18]

Government leaders in other countries were calling for stricter regulation. On January 27, 2000, German Chancellor Gerhard Schroeder, inaugurating the first International Forum on the Holocaust in Stockholm, asked for international cooperation to keep neo-Nazis off the Internet.[19]

The debate over misuse of the Internet was particularly intense in France, where a new "Law on the Liberty of Communication" was under debate in the National Assembly. The law held Internet service providers responsible for illegal content that transited by their servers, exactly as printers could be held responsible under French law if the authors and publishers of a defamatory printed work could not be located. A leading free-access provider, altern.org, had already paid ruinous damages after French model Estelle Hallyday discovered her photographs on an unauthorized site that used altern.org's server and sued. Noting that access providers were increasingly accused of promoting "defamation, pedophilia, violations of authors' rights, and incitation to racial hatred," *Libération* remarked that they "are trapped, at once guarantors of the freedom of expression and subject to the pressure of plaintiffs."[20]

Yahoo Inc. likewise felt the rising heat. On February 23, 2000, the Anti-Defamation League (ADL), an American nonprofit group founded in 1913, charged Yahoo with hosting an entire category of "White Pride and Racialism" clubs. Noting that Yahoo's "Terms of Service" agreement prohibited users from posting content of a "racially, ethnically or otherwise objectionable" nature, the ADL demanded that Yahoo cease to "ignore its own policy and us." Two days later, the ADL triumphantly reported that Yahoo had "apologized for not addressing the violations sooner" and had encouraged the ADL's Internet Monitoring Unit to report such abuses.

[17] Lakshmi Chaudry, "British ISPs Crack Down on Hate," Libertarian Alliance, January 25, 2000 (www.codoh.com).

[18] Interview, March 30, 2001.

[19] Kim Gamel, "Forum: Keep Neo-Nazis from Web," Associated Press, January 27, 2000.

[20] Florent Latrive, "Les hébergeurs priés de sévir," *Libération*, April 7, 2000 (www.liberation.com).

Yahoo's response reflected an emerging consensus among leaders of the new economy to deal with offensive materials largely through a policy of "notice and take down." While refusing to act as a censor by establishing broad preemptive standards, Yahoo, like eBay and members of the Internet Watch Foundation, removed materials that generated significant protests from users or spokespeople for legitimate causes. Thus Internet companies could hope to avoid heavy-handed government regulation that might harm their industry.

In Darlington's opinion, notice and take down is an insufficient solution: "It will work for defamatory libel and copyright issues, but it will not solve all the problems of the Internet." But Greg Wrenn, Yahoo's international affairs counsel, contends that it is the best available means of keeping illegal or offensive content off the Web:

> A couple of issues come into this—first, what's the policy, what are the criteria? A second issue is, how is the policy enforced? It's not self-executing. You either have to monitor and catch it, or do creative things with tools, automatic systems. [But] when you have 180 million active visitors—Geocities [a Yahoo subsidiary] has 15 million pages added per month—there's no way a company can have enough people to read all that stuff before it goes on. . . . Or, you can do notice and take down. That's a do-able system, in terms of reality. We'll always have to rely on users for that, to spot things they think are inappropriate.

Prior to Knobel's press campaign, Wrenn had contacted Inktomi, which provides Yahoo France with Web page search results, to ensure that the subcontractor would remove sites considered illegal in France from its index. "It's an automatic system—they'd find French-language sites and index them," explained Wrenn. "They don't do human reviews." The group at the origin of the complaint, which was successfully resolved, was the LICRA.

Yahoo Stands Accused: April 2000

Even before the nominal six-day delay expired, Yahoo France was served with notice that it and Yahoo Inc. were being sued on April 8, 2000. Under a special procedure called the *reféré*, which allows a judge to ordain immediate preventive measures against a defendant without a full trial, the plaintiffs demanded that Yahoo be fined 100,000 euros ($90,000) for each day that the sales of Nazi objects continued. The UEJF further demanded that Yahoo Inc. "suppress, on any listings accessible from French territory," all links to negationist Web sites, and eliminate from its Geocities.com subsidiary two sites, including one in French, that offered the text of *Mein Kampf*.

Greg Wrenn immediately faxed LICRA President Patrick Gaubert:

> Yahoo! applauds the mission of your organization and in no way does Yahoo! endorse anti-Semitism or racism of any sort. In fact, as you may recall, Yahoo! France has cooperated extensively this year with LICRA regarding your concerns about Nazi-related sites. . . . Within the bounds of the law of the 23 different countries in which our international properties are located, we promote freedom of expression and choice and Yahoo! believes it should not act as a political censor . . . in the U.S., the removal of such items would be considered censorship and treated by many as more offensive than the isolated postings themselves.

Explained Guillanton, "The reaction of the Americans was, 'We can't censor what goes on the site. We're not content providers.' " He and his Paris team wondered if Americans could appreciate the horrors of Nazism to the same extent as a nation that was occupied by the Nazis from 1940–44. It was a reasonable question, said Yahoo Inc.'s international communications director, Scott Morris, whose mother is French: "From the cultural perspective, we didn't all understand how sensitive things would get when the word 'Nazi' was mentioned. In France, World War Two is yesterday. But for Greg Wrenn, who served as liaison between Paris and Santa Clara, the weight of the Nazi question was evident:

> We were developing our strategy on the assumption the boat was going to sink. We went through the issues with our French counsel, and we did not start out thinking we had great cards. . . . We were American, that was one strike. The second was Nazi-related content. It's such an emotional issue in France. I knew that, from knowing the history of the Second World War. You could also see from the complaints

> we get—the users that complain most about Nazi-related material come from France and Germany.

Both of Yahoo's teams were fully committed to a vision of the Internet, which Guillanton defined:

> We don't work the same way as a traditional medium. We're not a minority of specialists who create content for a passive majority. In most cases, we put tools at the disposition of people so they can communicate; they're the stars. So groups form around little centers of interest, like sports cars, and in certain cases, around opinions like these. . . . Sure, Internet is a medium where a minority can fabricate content for a greater number, but what's most interesting is that the greater number can publish what they want.

Consequently, said Guillanton, "The Internet forces everyone to have a more skeptical approach, to be wary. There's a lot of crap, and the Internet forces you to put it aside. The tool imposes this revolution." He believed that the ultimate effect was to expose neo-Nazis, not to promote them: "[Our adversaries] say that Internet banalizes these groups. But it banalizes them so much that they're merely banal; they aren't dangerous anymore. What counts is that people have the right to form their own opinions."

"We're not talking about free speech; we're talking about commerce," countered Lilti. "The first thing I did was to read Yahoo's contractual conditions, which allow them to clean up their site." He added, "We knew that the ADL had challenged them." If Yahoo Inc. could concede the point of an American association, why not in France?

The reason was simple, from Wrenn's standpoint: "We can work around local groups and mores. What we can't do is make different countries happy with content on every site." But Yahoo's adversaries were no longer willing to discuss the issues out of court.

The Initial Response of the Media and the Market: April 11–May 15, 2000

The first dispatches on the case were filed by Reuters and the Agence France Presse (AFP) on April 11. The AFP, France's leading press service, reported that an "American giant" was accused of "banalizing Nazism," doubly attacking the Yahoo brand name. French online media, notably Transfert.net, devoted extensive coverage to the affair.

Outside France, coverage was nonexistent, with the sole exception of a major Israeli newspaper, the *Jerusalem Post*. In an April 17 story on "Weaving the Web in Paris," *BusinessWeek* found it more interesting that in France, unlike Silicon Valley, "the locals smoke cigarettes in Internet cafés." Likewise, when CNN's Internet-savvy "New Show" discussed the international strategies of Yahoo and eBay on April 25, the Paris affair never came up. Only scattered online media, like ZDNet News, picked up the Reuters coverage, while other leading online news sources, like *Hotwired*, remained silent. Like the English-language media, market analysts in London and New York apparently saw no significance in the case, which did not appear in a single analyst's report through the spring.

Yahoo Inc. indirectly contributed to the silence by following its established policy of refusing to comment about ongoing judicial proceedings. At Yahoo France, Guillanton took an optimistic view of the decision to come: "We thought the judge might order us not to put links to Yahoo.com, which would be fine for us, since we do everything possible to keep surfers on Yahoo.fr, to increase the value of the audience."

Yahoo Makes Its Case: May 15, 2000

For Yahoo Inc., simply showing up in a French court could be interpreted as admitting its competence over the case. However, said Wrenn, "The company felt strongly, on a PR basis, that a response was needed—to explain what the content was for, and why Yahoo didn't take down the items when they were identified." Most crucially, Yahoo Inc. felt obligated to defend the position that content originating in the United States should be governed by U.S. law. Said Wrenn, "It was clear from the beginning that there was a principle on regulation we had to deal with. We would've been thrilled if it was another company. But we felt, 'We can't let this go. We can't afford, and the industry can't afford, to lose.' "

At the first hearing in the *Tribunal de Grande Instance de Paris* on May 15, defending counsel Christophe Pecnard argued that "Internet users who go to Yahoo.com undertake a virtual voyage to the U.S.," and so no offense could be said to take place in France. Even if the contrary were true, it would be technically impossible for Yahoo to block all access to its sites from France, noted Pecnard. He declared, "The plaintiff has picked the wrong enemy, and finds himself, unjustly and in spite of himself, putting Internet on trial instead of neo-Nazi propaganda."

Pecnard emphasized that the company "deeply deplores having to oppose, for the legitimate cause of its own defense, the ideas of the plaintiffs. . . . Yahoo Inc. has never, in any way, subscribed to the ignoble ideas of Nazism or neo-Nazism in any form." Nor, Pecnard noted, had Yahoo been offered the opportunity, as it still desired, to engage in a constructive dialogue with the coalition out of court.[21]

Lilti counterattacked that "Yahoo Inc. has not seen fit, since the delivery of the lawsuit, to remedy the problems that were denounced, which it maintains in full awareness." He noted that "the First Amendment to the U.S. Constitution cannot forbid Yahoo Inc. to apply restrictions to the liberty of expression that are freely consented by its users," and which allowed Yahoo to take down offensive content. As for the tribunal's competence, said Lilti, "American jurisdictions systematically retain the application of the law of the country of reception—when the U.S. is concerned."[22]

The Judge and the Ruling: May 22, 2000

Jean-Jacques Gomez, who presided over the case, resented the fact that his personality became a subject for the French media—and a matter of deep concern to plaintiffs and defendants alike. Like many French judges, he became a magistrate because he could not afford to open a private law office, which made the Republic his benefactor as well as his employer. Though he noted that a higher court could overturn any of his opinions, he believed that as a judge, he could influence society: "When you read a judgment," he said, "sometimes you remember one sentence on a great principle, and that's an encouragement to follow the principle." He deliberately sought to maintain "a down-to-earth mentality, what they used to call a 'peasant' mentality. Why get philosophical when you can do things simply?"[23]

He had studied the Internet assiduously since Web cases started arriving in his courtroom in 1996, and was proud that on one occasion a reporter who accused him of ignorance was forced to admit that Gomez knew more than a little about the subject. He had concluded that the Internet was promoting lies:

> From 1996 to 1999, people said that if you regulate the Internet, you'll kill it. My answer resides in a very simple example: If you want to upload an application on the Web that enables someone to get my credit card number, I don't agree. . . . Some people try to make internauts believe that the Web is totally free, without any obligation—and we all know it's not true. In real life, my freedom stops where the freedom of others begins. On the Internet, it's the same thing.

Lilti was concerned that Gomez might refuse to rule on the case, by sending it on to a full trial: "We said to ourselves, 'A judge can get scared.' " Only a trial, argued Pecnard—and not the urgent procedure of the *référé*, which is designed to stop disruptions of public order while awaiting trial—could determine the responsibility under French law of an American company "that acts in conformity with the judicial norms of its home country for an activity on the Internet."[24] As it happened, four years earlier Gomez had cut short a *référé* involving the Internet, on the grounds that the case demanded fuller debate.

Now, two points concerned him: Did French law apply to the case? If so, did his court possess the means to apply it?

On May 22, Judge Gomez answered yes to the first question: "In permitting the visualization in France of [Nazi] objects and the eventual

[21] Christophe Pecnard's quotes are drawn from "Conclusions pour la Société Yahoo! Inc., A Monsieur le Président du Tribunal de Grande Instance de Paris," Audience de référé du 15 mai 2000, pp. 4, 6, 7, 10.

[22] "Conclusions en réplique de L'Union des étudiants juif de France, A Monsieur le Président du Tribunal de Grande Instance de Paris," Audience de référé du 15 mai 2000 (www.juriscom.net).

[23] Interview, March 2, 2001.

[24] "Conclusions pour la Société Yahoo! Inc.," op. cit.

participation of a French internaut in such a sale, Yahoo Inc. commits a fault on French territory." True, said the judge, "the unintentional character [of Yahoo's 'fault'] is evident." For the judge, the sales were "an offense to the collective memory of a nation profoundly wounded by the atrocities committed in the name of the Nazi criminal enterprise . . . and especially to its Jewish citizens."

Could the ruling be applied? Yes, declared Judge Gomez: "[T]he genuine difficulties encountered by Yahoo do not constitute insurmountable obstacles."

His decision went far beyond Lilti's demands: Yahoo Inc. must now "take all measures of a nature to dissuade and to render impossible all consultation on Yahoo.com of the online sale of Nazi objects and of any other site or service that constitutes an apology for Nazism or a contestation of Nazi crimes." A date of July 24 was set for Yahoo's presentation of those still undefined "measures."[25]

For Wrenn, satisfying such a broad and categorical order was an unthinkable task. "We knew it was impossible to do it, and we knew we'd have to come back and say that." Gomez ordered Yahoo to pay the costs of the hearing, including the legal fees of the plaintiffs' lawyers, plus $1,390 in provisional damages to the LICRA and the UEJF. The ruling turned the case into an international affair. For the first time, leading English-language media like the *New York Times* and *Los Angeles Times* covered the story.[26] The LICRA declared that the judge had "rendered a service to the Internet," which was turning into an "outlaw zone."[27] There was no apparent impact on Yahoo's share price, which dipped from 126 to 118 on May 23, rebounded to 122 the following day, and rose to 144 on June 7.

However, damage to the brand was inevitable, particularly in Europe. As Wrenn said, "We're a global brand, not just a U.S. brand. And a lot of people just kept seeing 'Yahoo-Nazi.' " Within the industry, Yahoo found no defenders. Rivals like eBay profited from Yahoo's troubles to promote their own auctions, while content providers, said Wrenn, "were not publicly behind us, because of the Nazi issue—they were saying, 'it's a good fight, Yahoo! Go to it! We're quietly behind you.'"

For Guillanton, there was a sense of personal loss, after four years of around-the-clock work to create a thoroughly French version of Yahoo:

> One of our greatest successes in France was to have managed to insert ourselves perfectly into the local tissue. The site is very "Frenchy." Up until this affair, when we asked focus groups questions about our identity, one in four people thought we were a subsidiary of France Telecom, one in four thought we were American, and the other half didn't know. . . . It was terrible to be attacked [as American] when we were really pioneers of localization.

By the time Jerry Yang arrived in France in June, Yahoo's management had realized that silence was no longer a viable tactic. "There was a moral issue," said Wrenn:

> We needed people to understand that we didn't do this thoughtlessly. We realized we were getting beat up. LICRA and the others were very good—they didn't want a settlement; they wanted press and publicity for the issue. So we had to get more aggressive about doing interviews and getting the word out.

The Chief Yahoo Prepares his Case

As Jerry Yang prepares to meet his interviewer, he is aware of a major constraint: the possible effects his statements may have on his company's and his shareholders' fortunes. It is time to explain clearly that trying to prevent French users from going on Yahoo's site in the United States is technically unrealistic. And he is concerned by the risk that regulating the U.S. site on the basis of French law could open the door to Internet regulation by restrictive—and highly politicized—national laws.

On another level—symbolic but no less real—Yahoo and Jerry Yang represent crucial promises of the Internet, as a vehicle of free expression and an engine of the new economy. He must carry the

[25] Tribunal de Grande Instance de Paris, UEJF et LICRA c. Yahoo! Inc. et Yahoo! France, Ordonnance de référé, 22 mai 2000 (www.juriscom.net).

[26] Associated Press, "French Court Says Yahoo Broke Racial Law," *New York Times*, May 23, 2000, Section C, p. 27, and Bloomberg News, "Yahoo Launches Stock Purchase Plan," *Los Angeles Times*, May 23, 2000, Part C, p. 3. Coverage of the French case constituted the second half of an article focused mainly to Yahoo's stock market strategy, a clear indication of the priorities of American readers.

[27] Associated Press, op. cit.

issue to a higher level: If individuals cannot express themselves on the Internet, and are denied the opportunity to form bonds of their choice across national and social borders, the attraction of the Web—for users as for investors—will inevitably decline.

In one sense, Jerry must choose what kind of leader he wants to be today.

- How should he address the business, technical, legal, cultural, and possibly philosphical questions of the journalist?
- Which principles make these answers legitimate? Which principles are violated?
- What consequences might be expected from these answers? What are the risks associated with them?
- What are the dilemmas that can no longer be avoided? Might they have been avoided, and if so, how?

EXHIBIT 1 An Interview with Roger Darlington, Chairman of the Internet Watch Foundation

The Internet Watch Foundation (IWF) was founded in the United Kingdom in 1996, at the initiative of the U.K.'s Internet service providers (ISPs). In four years of operation, it has served to remove 28,000 illegal images from the U.K.'s Internet sites.

Mark Hunter: First, should the Internet be regulated?

Roger Darlington: The short answer, in the broadest sense, is that it does have to be regulated—but it's so different from traditional media, we have to do it in distinct ways. It's not like the telecommunications networks, though some ISPs argue that they're just common carriers. Hosting a Web site is not the same as carrying phone conversations. On the other hand, it's not like a newspaper, where the publisher can be expected to review content in advance. The Internet falls in between.

The second major difference is that we're talking about a global medium, accessible to 400 million people, and every user can put their own site online. It isn't possible for one government to regulate it. But I don't think many ISPs realize that it's no longer the same net. The origins of the net are free speech, free expression. Now it's a mass medium. A different consumer base, different concerns.

MH: How did the IWF begin?

RD: What's peculiarly British is that this is an industry initiative to create a self-regulating formula. In the U.K., in 1996, the Metropolitan Police indicated a concern for the growing amount of child porn on the net. In the U.K., possession of child porn is a criminal offense, and so is having an image on your screen or server. The police said, "If you don't get your act together, we'll prosecute." They listed a number of newsgroups they thought should be closed down. The ISPs wanted to avoid prosecution and also the Draconian approach of closing newsgroups. The U.K. government favors self-regulation, where that is seen to work.

MH: How does it work?

RD: Through a hotline. ISPs say they can't proactively monitor all the contents. I agree. There are 2 billion Web sites, and no way providers can know what they're hosting. So people report, they phone or write, or almost invariably, e-mail us through the IWF site. Our staff is trained by the police; they know the law. If it's illegal, we see where it's hosted. If it's in the U.K., we notify the provider, who takes it down. Formally, it's a recommendation. But in effect, it's an order. If they don't take it down, they don't stand a chance in court.

We have no formal legal powers. In theory, we could be challenged in the courts. It's possible that someone who posted content that we'd recommended be removed could say it's not illegal, and sue. But it hasn't happened. It [the IWF] *has* combated child porn, and avoided prosecutions.

MH: You are now extending operations to hate literature. Why?

RD: The American view is that words themselves aren't illegal—only actions. The European view is that words of a particular kind can of themselves lead to consequences—so words like denial of the Holocaust can be illegal. U.K. laws don't make Holocaust denial illegal—but incitement to racial violence *is* illegal. The overwhelming majority of race hate material is in the U.S.—partly because there *is* a lot of race hate, and partly because of the First Amendment. In the U.K., they've been careful to stay just this side of the law. Our judgment is that it's unlikely the Attorney General would prosecute, or that prosecution would succeed.

But the issue is real. People in the past who propagated race hate had physical constraints. A printer wouldn't print it; a bookshop wouldn't put it on the shelf. There's no doubt the Internet has provided a cost-free way to publish and distribute it anonymously. In my view, we've seen an increase in race hate material on the net. Not just in the U.S., but in France and

(continued)

EXHIBIT 1 An Interview with Roger Darlington, Chairman of the Internet Watch Foundation—Continued

Germany, which had horrific experiences of the outcome of such views, and in countries that are havens of tolerance, like Switzerland.

MH: Is there a better way to get it off the net?

RD: Even if the IWF got it all off the net in the U.K., it would still be in the U.S. If we persuaded all the ISPs in the U.S. not to host it, it would *still* be hosted somewhere. Some of these people host their own material on their own servers. A server isn't expensive. And they can put it on all sorts of uninhabited islands—this is already happening—or on a ship or a satellite. A second set of problems is techniques; peer to peer [P2P] that mean you won't be able to locale geographically where this material is. So it can't happen. We have to operate on that assumption. We won't eliminate it, but we'll contain it.

Governments have to set a legal framework: What's illegal offline should be illegal online. ISPs have obligations, especially with material focused on children, to take a special interest in the content. Parents have an obligation to use the filtering software. And society as a whole has to raise the level of knowledge and understanding—so we recognize that all sources of information are not equally valid. I'm in favor of self-labeling on Web sites, so the content is electronically marked. Porn sites don't *want* children to access them—it causes problems, and the kids have no money. Once you have labeling, then filtering software can act more effectively.

MH: Will the measures ordained by the French courts against Yahoo work?

RD: No. The problem was sales of Nazi memorabilia. The court's solution won't solve that. And I wouldn't trust my government—and I voted for it—to decide what I can see on the net.

MH: Are you afraid that your model will be perverted toward censorship?

RD: The IWF model has already been distorted by Saudi Arabia, where the government makes clear to ISPs what is or isn't acceptable. But sooner or later we'll see that governments which try to control the net will fail. The Internet is designed to withstand nuclear attack—and to find a way around obstacles.

EXHIBIT 2 Free Speech in the United States and France

Two different conceptions of free speech were in explicit conflict during the Yahoo case. In the United States, the right of "free speech" is predicated on the notion that in an open marketplace of ideas, the best will sooner or later drive out the worst. In France, as in most European countries, public speech is regulated on the assumption that certain ideas can destroy society, and with it all pretense of a democratic debate.

Contrary to popular belief (especially among Americans), even in the United States free speech is not an ironclad right. What's true is that it is at the heart of the historic Bill of Rights, in the First Amendment to the Constitution: "Congress shall make no law respecting an establishment of religion, or prohibiting the free exercise thereof; or abridging the freedom of speech, or of the press; or the right of the people peaceably to assemble, and to petition the Government for a redress of grievances."

Thus in theory, any and all religious, political, or personal speech cannot be subjected to legal interdiction. However, the U.S. courts, which have the sole right to interpret the Constitution, have never established a final or comprehensive definition of which speech should be protected by that guarantee. Thus the right of free speech is constantly evolving.

Political speech of a rare virulence, including barely masked appeals to violence or racial hatred, is indeed legal under current jurisprudence. In April 2001 the Supreme Court upheld the right of an antiabortion Web site to publish a "hit list" of doctors who perform abortions, and to mark their photographs with a red cross when they died—or were murdered, which had in fact occurred.

The Court's basic test for the legality of such materials was formulated in the late 19th century: One does not have the right to scream "fire" as a joke in a crowded theater. Thus, speech that is specifically aimed at producing harm to others is not protected. But celebrating the murder of one's enemies, and publicizing the names of others whose disappearance would be welcomed, is legal.

It often occurs that the American public enacts restrictions on its own—sometimes with the active assistance of prosecutors, who at the state and local levels are elected officials, and thus highly alert to public opinion. At the height of the Vietnam War, publishers of "alternative" newspapers were regularly arrested or harassed by police, and beaten up by pro-war citizens. In the 1970s, the expansion of the pornography industry into mainstream distribution venues (such as convenience stores) met with violent reactions from feminist groups such as the Preying Mantis Women's Brigade of Santa Cruz, California, which initiated a national campaign of attacks on newsstands. In the 1980s, the Reagan administration co-opted feminists into a national antipornography campaign that resulted in the prosecution in several states of not only producers of porn films but also their actors.

(continued)

EXHIBIT 2 Free Speech in the United States and France—Continued

Among the first and most successful Web sites and forums, as the Internet expanded in the mid-1990s, were those offering pornography. Responding to public concern over the issue, President Bill Clinton signed the Communications Decency Act of 1996, which outlawed "indecent" communications online. The Supreme Court unanimously struck down the law, agreeing with a lower court that the Internet constitutes "the most participatory form of mass speech yet developed," and was thus entitled to "the highest protection from government intrusion."

An indirect result of the Court's decision was the explosive growth of the market in "blocking" software, which enables parents to set limits on materials that can be accessed by their children from a home computer. The American Civil Liberties Union, the most important defender of free speech in the United States, went repeatedly to court to stop the use of these applications in public libraries. Ironically, among the victims of blocking software was the American Family Association (AFA), an archconservative group that found itself blacklisted by the popular software CyberPatrol because of the AFA's outspoken hostility to homosexuals.

In France, the Declaration of the Rights of the Man and Citizen—a crucial summation of the principles behind the Revolution of 1789—guarantees the right of free speech, "except in cases foreseen by the law," which are in practice fairly numerous. The importance of "public order" frequently takes precedence, in the French penal and civil codes, over the rights of individuals to express themselves. For example, it is illegal to discuss the private lives of public figures, or to insult the president, or foreign heads of states. It is also illegal to publish materials or to make public declarations that constitute an "apology" for Nazi crimes, including the denial of the Jewish genocide, or an incitement to racial hatred. While it is legal in the United States for Nazis to demonstrate in Jewish neighborhoods, in France the organizers of the demonstration could be convicted of various crimes, and their group banned (as happened to several extreme right groups in the 1970s).

Conversely, the French government did little to stop the explosion of so-called pink—that is, pornographic—services on the Minitel, the telematic predecessor of the Internet in the 1980s. Observers noted that the Minitel represented a major commercial gamble for then government-owned France Telecom, and that pornography did a great deal to build its public.

In 2000, as the Yahoo affair was generating headlines, the Socialist government of France pushed through a "Law on the Freedom of Communication," requiring service providers to demand the identities of publishers of Web pages using their servers. Service providers who did not comply with this requirement could be prosecuted for crimes (such as defamation) committed by the publishers, in the event the latter could not be found and brought to trial. A similar provision already applies to printers of defamatory books whose authors or publishers cannot be located. However, after concerted protests from the Internet industry and criticism from the Constitutional Council, France's Parliament enacted a glaring loophole: While service providers must collect identifying information from Web page authors, they are not required to verify it, and cannot be held responsible in place of the authors if it turns out to be false.

EXHIBIT 3 The Rise, Fall, and Rise of the Extreme Right in Europe

Source: Adapted from Mark Hunter, *Un Américain au Front: Enquête au sein du Front National* (Paris: Stock, 1998).

The concept of Left and Right was born with the French Revolution of 1789, in which anti- and pro-monarchy representatives to the National Convention sat on opposite sides of the assembly hall. France remained the battleground of these forces through successive empires, monarchies, and three republics. It was here that the extreme right began to take its modern form, through the Dreyfus Affair at the end of the 19th century—a case in which a Jewish army officer was falsely accused and convicted of espionage, with the approbation of anti-Semites and Catholic royalist intellectuals like Charles Maurras, who invented the label "nationalist" for his allies.

Following World War I, the triumphant emergence of Benito Mussolini's Fascists in Italy established a new paradigm of the extreme right: a union of the state, industry, and an elite, based on an ideology that proposed a total unity of the nation and the individual (hence the term *totalitarianism*). In this schema, as in Sovietism, the rights of the nation completely dominate those of the citizen. It was during this period that the first major antiracist citizens' groups, such as the LICRA in France (founded in 1927), began to mobilize. Throughout the 1980s and 1990s, such citizens' groups took the lead in combating the resurgence of the extreme right. Their activities included prosecuting violations of French antiracist laws, training activists, and compiling extensive documentation on the extreme right. In Germany, as depression and hyperinflation ravaged the population, Adolf Hitler launched the National Socialist (Nazi) party at the end of the decade. Condemned to prison for the abortive "Beer Hall Putsch," he composed a master plan, *Mein Kampf*, which became a best-seller. It called for the subjugation of Germany's Jews and the conquest of Europe. It later became the blueprint of the Third Reich.

(continued)

EXHIBIT 3 The Rise, Fall, and Rise of the Extreme Right in Europe—Continued

In 1933, after a determined program of assassination and other crimes directed at opponents within and outside the Nazi party, Hitler became chancellor of Germany, and began the military buildup that led to Word War II. By the mid-1930s, fascist movements were underway in Spain, where the *Generalissimo* Francesco Franco (aided by Italy and Germany) emerged victorious from a brutal civil war, and in France, where the left-wing government of the Popular Front was nearly overturned by street battles with extreme right movements.

Following the Nazi conquest of France in 1940, nearly all these movements were absorbed into the Pétain government, also called the Vichy State, which abrogated the Republic and voluntarily "collaborated" with the Nazi "occupant." In 1942, the Nazis launched their "Final Solution" to the "Jewish question"—a program of mass extermination, involving the deportation and murder of 6 million Jews (and an equal number of other ethnicities, such as Gypsies, and political opponents) in concentration camps, of which the most infamous is Auschwitz. The surviving Jews gave this catastrophe the name of *Shoah*, or Holocaust. It is generally conceded that while other genocides have occurred and continue to occur, the singularity of the Shoah resides in the industrial organization of the massacre of a people.

After the defeat of Nazi Germany in 1945, fascists were hunted down, imprisoned, and executed throughout the former Third Reich, and their political parties were banned in France and Germany. Only in the 1970s, when Italian neo-fascists materially aided the founding of a French party, the National Front (FN), were the conditions for a continentwide resurgence of the extreme right established. They included a new cadre of young militants and a new body of ideological doctrine, organized on the principle of "national identity" and the tactics of populism.

By the end of the 1980s the FN was represented in the European Parliament and municipal and regional councils across France—and, more important, had created a body of doctrine and militant practice which it exported to similar populist movements like Germany's Republikaners, the Vlaams Blok in Belgium, and the Austrian Freedom Party (FPO) of Jorg Haider. The increasing success of these movements was based on two key factors: permanent militant activity in public spheres (such as markets, cafés and bars, and even soccer stadiums), which had been abandoned by media-savvy traditional parties, and increasingly professional images. Where its mainstream opponents thought in terms of demographics, like marketing executives, the extreme right thought like an infantry division, in terms of seizing and holding territory.

Even Le Pen's scandalous 1987 declaration that the Holocaust was a mere "detail of the Second World War" and his party's subsequent "demonization" did not stop its rise. Since 1985, when the epochal "Single Act" started to open Europe's national borders to the free flow of persons, goods, and services, the European Union had mainly benefited big business, at the expense of the working class and small businesses. At the beginning of the 1990s, unemployment reached 3 million in France and 4 million in Germany, while the providential social benefits put in place after the Second World War were abrogated from the top down, in order to meet the stringent budgetary criteria of the European Monetary Union. Simultaneously, taxes reached historic levels—in Germany, 45 percent of the GDP, and 44.7 percent in France. As corruption wracked Europe's political elites in one country after another, the extreme right found a sympathetic hearing for other aspects of its programs—and notably, the idea that immigrants were responsible for the continent's hard economic times. It was a direct (and in Haider's case, explicit) adaptation of Hitler's argument that Jews were taking away Germans' jobs. The revived extreme right also provided a safe harbor for the unrepentant veterans and nostalgics of Hitlerism, who, behind the cover of legal parties, developed far more explicitly totalitarian, anti-Semitic and racist doctrines.

These neo-Nazi forces were among the first political elements in Europe to understand and exploit the potential of the Internet. The Web offered literally hundreds of groups an opportunity to export their news and doctrines—in particular, the denial of the Holocaust—and to establish regular contact with movements as widespread as the American Militias, the neo-Pagans of Nouvelle Résistance, and the Russian "brown-and-red" nationalists who flourished after the collapse of the Soviet state. Ironically, the Web also enabled enemies of the extreme right to track its movements with unprecedented ease. But that was cold comfort to those who had never forgotten that the ravings of a would-be dictator could lead, within a decade, to the slaughter of millions.

Should Business Influence the Science and Politics of Global Environmental Change? The Oil Industry and Climate Change (A)

Henri Twist, vice president for strategic affairs of OILCO is rushing toward his office, somewhat worried. In half an hour a special meeting of the executive committee will convene to address the climate change issue. He is about to propose a strategic line that would amount to a radical shift in OILCO's strategy—and for that matter in a direction never taken by any other major oil and gas corporation. Meanwhile, Maria Goodfellow, vice president for financial affairs is waiting in the meeting room, reviewing her notes, while Colin Haddock vice president for production and operations is still stuck in a traffic jam.

OILCO is among the ten largest oil and gas corporations in the world. Annual revenue is of the order of U.S.$90 billion. It employs 85,000 persons worldwide. Its key business areas are oil and natural gas exploration, production, refining and distribution, and chemicals production. These activities amount respectively to 85% and 10% of its turnover. In OILCO's total oil equivalent production 67% is oil and 33% is natural gas.

At 9 A.M. on January 29, 1997, the committee convenes. Paul Hardy, CEO of OILCO, addresses his colleagues: "In less than a year, next December, some 150 nations will meet in Kyoto to finalize negotiations of a protocol to strengthen their commitments under the 1992 United Nations Framework Convention on Climate Change. This political process may lead to legally binding commitments from industrialized countries to reduce their greenhouse gas emissions—and in particular CO_2 emissions—in the midterm future. As a major international oil and gas corporation, these new constraints on gas emissions may profoundly affect our activities, so we have to decide on our strategy toward the science and politics of climate change."[1]

As Colin Haddock enters the room breathlessly, Maria Goodfellow starts her presentation: "Ladies and gentlemen, my conviction is that we have to stick to our path and fight by all means against any action by governments to reduce greenhouse gas emissions. Obviously it is in our interest to prevent the adoption of any mandatory policy that would constrain our activities. We have to keep pursuing the goal of exposing the weaknesses of climate science and explaining

This case was prepared by Dr. Sybille van den Hove, Research Fellow at INSEAD, under the supervision of Marc Le Menestrel, Assistant Professor of Economics and Business at University Pompeu Fabra and Visiting Professor at INSEAD and Henri-Claude de Bettignies, Professor of Asian Business at INSEAD and Visiting Professor at Stanford University. It is intended to be used as a basis for class discussion rather than to illustrate either effective or ineffective handling of an administrative situation.

The authors gratefully thank the interviewees for their time and openness and Prof. Daniel Esty for his helpful comments on an earlier draft of this case. The authors are solely responsible for the content.

[1] See Exhibits 1 and 2 for a short briefing on the climate change issue and the international negotiation process.

to policymakers that they cannot act on the basis of such an exceptionally uncertain science. Let us win the debate on science so that the climate change issue loses its unjustified credibility and popularity. By keeping open the discussion on the existence of a problem, we will avoid discussion of what to do about it, hence preventing unnecessary action."

"We should endeavor to inform the public on objective grounds. Both on its understanding of the science—we have to show the public how uncertain climate science is—and on its understanding of the costs in terms of individual well-being associated with action. Finally, we have to act upon the political process and find powerful allies amongst policymakers. Whatever happens, we should make sure that the environmental problems associated with fossil fuels (if any) are understood in terms of consumption rather than production."

"What are your main arguments to support this position?" Hardy asks.

"Well, as you said Paul, climate change policy represents a threat to our business, so we have to act. If governments decide to act on greenhouse gas emissions, then this represents a regulatory risk to us. More than anything, we must avoid more command and control regulations—in particular supranational regulations—of our activities. A binding treaty in Kyoto could create a bad precedent of 'world regulation.'" As she notices several nods of approval at this in the room, she projects a slide and continues.[2] "In the case of climate change, the situation is that there is no scientific evidence of human influence on the climate system; the best the UN IPCC scientists can agree on is a *suggestion* of a human influence on climate, while they stress that '*there are still many uncertainties*.' So, obviously, there is no scientific proof as such.

"Then why should we—and the citizens of developed countries—make sacrifices on a doubtful basis? And sacrifices they are: the Protocol, as it is discussed today, has powerful negative implications in economic, investment, trade competitiveness, and employment terms. We make a positive contribution to the political debate by pointing to those implications, and we must be heard on this: what is good for us is good for the economy. We do not want to become hostages of the green lobby. We are strong enough on science, technology, and economic analysis; we have enough credibility as researchers and analysts to fight their science."

"But what if scientists reduce uncertainties and show a more obvious link between human emissions of greenhouse gases and global warming?" asks Julia Orwell, the human resources director.

"If human-induced climate change turns out to be a reality, then what we need, as a fossil fuel company, is time. By fighting against climate policy now, we will gain precious time. As this century has shown, technology will provide a solution soon enough. Now is not the right time for a drift away from fossil fuels. In the past, we have lost a lot of money already trying to go into the renewable energies business, so let's not make the same mistake twice. Renewables are a completely different business. We know about extraction, refining, and fuel distribution technologies, while photovoltaics are based on semiconductor technology, and wind power draws on turbines and electronics. These are not part of our know-how, so again: now is not the right time (if ever there is a right time, for I personally believe that this whole global warming stuff is just green doomsaying). In addition, industry has already made huge efforts in energy efficiency. It is really in other sectors (such as in agriculture for instance) that the real reduction potentials lie, but, as always, industry will be the easy target for policymakers. The problem is the oil use, not its production. Let's be serious, if we show strong determination, governments are not in a position to impose this on us."

"This is quite convincing, but how do you suggest we implement this strategy?" asks Hardy.

[2] On the slide are the following statements: "Our ability to quantify the human influence on global climate is *currently limited* because the expected signal is still emerging from the noise of natural variability, and because *there are uncertainties in key factors*. These include the magnitude and patterns of long-term natural variability and the time-evolving pattern of forcing by, and response to, changes in concentrations of greenhouse gases and aerosols, and land surface changes. Nevertheless, the balance of evidence *suggests* that there is a discernible human influence on global climate" (IPCC, 1996, p. 22, my emphasis). "*There are still many uncertainties*. Many factors currently limit our ability to project and detect future climate change. In particular, to reduce uncertainties further work is needed" (ibid., p. 24).

"Well, first of all we have to contest their science with our own—which is more objective. We have a good tool at hand to help us: the Global Climate Coalition, of which we are already a member. It is an organization of business trade associations whose aim is to coordinate business participation in the scientific and policy debate on the global climate change issue.[3] Its membership includes many companies from the fossil fuel industry—coal, oil, and gas—and the automobile industry, but also other sectors of industry, agriculture, and transportation. Up to now, it has effectively combated action in climate policy. We should support and orient the GCC strategy in order to reach our goals.

"On the scientific front, we have to sponsor scientists who have a strongly skeptical stance on the climate change issue. We have to help them gain visibility and media access, so that they will weaken the mainstream science of climate change in the eyes of the public and of policymakers. This will reposition global warming as theory rather than fact.

"In parallel, we should finance and support the development of economic models that predict extremely high costs of action. In this manner, we alert public opinion and policymakers on the sacrifices that will be imposed on their well-being solely on the basis of alarmist speculation. We also need to show them that investing in renewable energy technology development for climate change reasons will take away investment resources from other public policy areas such as health and education. Doing this, we highlight the uncertainty of climate science and the certainty of the required economic sacrifices. In particular, we can point to the danger of migration of industries overseas, which would result in losses of jobs here and, by the way, would not reduce global emissions.

"On the political front, we should target legislative decision makers and negotiators in the U.S. We can also target some traditional U.S. allies that have heavy stakes in the issue, such as Australia for instance. We can use our lobbying networks for the U.S. administration and Congress. We can enhance and target our financial contributions to U.S. congressmen. This is where the key is, because any treaty will have to be ratified by the Senate to enter into force. We can easily have the Republican-dominated Senate on our side. But we should not forget to target developing countries' governments, so that they oppose the protocol. Developing countries are a major growing market for fossil fuels in the future. We can show them that the protocol, as discussed these days, will impede their economic development which unavoidably will require fossil fuels. There exists already some significant division between developing and developed countries in the treaty negotiations, and this indicates that the whole process can be blocked.

"To summarize, scientific evidence is extremely weak. There is actually no definitive proof that climate change is happening, or that it is human-induced, or even that it must be considered as a threat. We have to prevent action for as long as possible. Thank you." She slowly puts her notes and slides away.

"All right" says Hardy, "before we discuss this presentation, I suggest that we hear two more views by Colin Haddock and Henri Twist. Colin, if you please."

"Contrary to the views of Maria, I believe that we should reorient somewhat our strategy by becoming less active in the fight against action and by adopting a more low-key attitude. We should refrain from influencing the science, and, at this stage, neither should we influence the international political process. And I will show you why. Obviously, the science of climate change is still the object of violent debate between those who claim that the whole issue is not relevant and those who consider that human-induced climate change is one of the most critical global environmental threats today. We have no direct role to play at this stage, except for losing energy, time, money, and—maybe most important—credibility. In fact, as of today, our efforts to combat climate science and to counter the political impetus have resulted in worsening public opinion on the attitude of oil companies in this debate. As shown by several opinion polls in different countries, the oil industry's environmental credibility is among the lowest of all industry sectors. So we really should not take the risk of worsening our public image. The science is still too uncertain; we should not try to influence it; neither should we endeavor to influence a political process that is

[3] See Exhibit 3 for background information on the GCC.

clearly tentative and unfinished. We should step back and let both processes take their course. Meanwhile, we start thinking about how we could react in the future.

"Moreover, we all know that international political agreements do not have much enforcement power, and, in any case, we know that the U.S. Senate will never ratify any significant agreement taken in Kyoto. Without the U.S., nothing will happen; the EU won't go ahead alone. There really is no reason to be alarmed now since whatever environmentalists say, and whatever the international decisions on climate change, for a very long time, energy from fossil fuels—in particular oil and gas—will be needed, and the demand for it will continue to grow, simply because there is no alternative. In the worst case, should we end up with some kind of constraining climate policy, it would more or less impose the same constraints on us and on our competitors, so we will always manage to stay ahead.

"Now is not the right time to act; we can always act later, depending on the evolution of the science and of the regulatory context. Finally, I can only agree with Maria on the fact that our past experience with renewables has not been convincing. So let's not fall into the trap again. I don't think I need to go into more details here."

"But Colin," asks Julia Orwell, "if we just sit back and wait, how will we manage the growing public pressure?"

"I am not at all convinced that public pressure is actually growing on this issue," answers Haddock. "Certainly environmental NGOs' pressure is increasing—and they do all they can to make us believe that it corresponds to public pressure. They are undoubtedly vocal on climate change; they urge governments of the world to adopt a precautionary principle approach and act immediately, even though scientific uncertainties are still very high. They also focus on equity issues between developed and developing countries, arguing that the former are responsible for today's levels of atmospheric greenhouse gas concentrations, and, as such, should be the first to reduce their emissions. They have gained quite a bit of expertise on climate change, actually. But the public is not so united behind them, if only because the issue is long term and much harder to grasp than many other environmental questions. To me, on this file, NGOs have adopted a top-down approach rather than a more participatory kind of bottom-up stance.

"Going back to my proposition now, to sum up, I propose that we adopt the following tactics: first, we refrain from taking a position publicly; second, we participate passively in the political process by sitting back and watching; third, we remain within our current industry trade associations but without aiming at driving their strategies; and fourth—and this is crucial—we gather as much information and knowledge on this issue as possible."

"Thank you, Colin, you've been very concise and to the point, as usual. Now Henri, what is your view?" says Hardy.

"Well, let me warn you that it will take me a little bit more time to expose my views, for the simple reason that I am suggesting a radically new course," begins Twist.

"Don't worry, Henri, we are ready for that too," answers Colin Haddock jokingly.

Henri Twist takes a deep breath and starts: "My proposal is to construct a dynamic strategy and become proactive in the industrial reorientation that emission reduction policies will imply. Let us publicly acknowledge the role of fossil fuels in the buildup of greenhouse gas concentrations in the atmosphere and the need to address the problem of global warming." As Twist says this, he notices a discernible stir in the audience, but he goes on: "Let us decide on a series of actions by OILCO to curb our own emissions and to develop alternative energy sources. By doing the latter, let us position ourselves not as a fossil fuel or a petroleum company but as an energy company. We have to be future-oriented and become the leaders in the next energy economy. And let us use our proactive position to influence governments, so that in both international and national policy they favor flexible market mechanisms rather than command and control regulations and taxes. To sum up, we have to reposition ourselves as part of the solution rather than part of the problem." He pauses.

"Well, Henri," Hardy says, "now I see why you will need time, this is . . . provocative. Please, tell us what would justify this strategy."

"First of all—and we have to face it—the risk of climate change has been assessed as very serious by the IPCC, which, as you all know, is an international panel of some 2,500 scientists that has been working on the issue since its 1988 creation by the United Nations and the World Meteorological Organization.[4] It is not credible for us to contest the science. We have to go from a discussion about the science to a discussion of the impacts on our business. Climate change policy represents a threat to our business so we cannot ignore the problem. We have to act because what we are potentially facing here is an important shift in our business environment and operating conditions. We have to be ready to adapt to this shift. Let's face reality: fossil fuels will not remain the dominant energy source forever. We want to manage the transition instead of having it managed for us from outside. If we are in a carbon-constrained world, then carbon is a cost, and it is good business practice to take costs seriously.

"Climate change is the most complex environmental issue that has ever been addressed. Attempts at addressing it will have powerful implications for the world economy—bad and good. It is an issue that will shape policy for decades to come. Markets could soon be influenced, as products with high carbon content such as coal and oil lose favor. We cannot afford not to have a constructive strategy on the biggest environmental issue of the coming century. In our business we have a tradition of long-term thinking; climate change is a long-term issue, but we can, and should, start acting on it today. As I see it, being strategic and proactive, in a dynamic sense, will help us do better business in a world that has become highly complex and dynamic.

"The prospect is that public attitudes and demands will progressively shift under the perceived reality of the risk, and my point is that, in the medium and long term, those companies able to anticipate the major changes required from the industry will benefit. We want to stay in business; we want to remain a growth industry. If we fail to address the climate change challenge and find solutions, we will survive but decline into dull utilities, selling yesterday's product. Moreover, as Colin pointed out, we all know that fossil fuels will still be needed for a long time, whatever the outcomes of the Kyoto talks. So recognizing that there is a problem won't make us lose our core business for a long while. To the contrary, what we have to aim at is to grab a larger share of the future shrinking oil market cake. And once we are ahead of the curve in moving to new cost-effective energy sources, we may benefit from a possible acceleration of the political and scientific process.

"Meanwhile, this strategy will give us a commercial advantage over our competitors. We all know that there really is not much difference between our products and theirs. By doing this, we differentiate ourselves in the minds of consumers: it is good marketing. This brings me back to public pressure. We know, from our own experience and from that of our competitors, that the public is requiring more and more environmental consciousness from corporations. Civil society has now gained enormous pressuring power through the development of information and communication technologies. The examples of Shell's public exposure in Nigeria or on the Brent Spar speak for themselves. We are in no less danger of exposure than they are. A proactive stance not only will give us a good image with the public, consumers, and the media, but also with the authorities. To put it briefly: it is good marketing and good lobbying practice to show a green face. But I would go a step further: we should not only *appear* as being proactive, but we should really *act* proactively, in diversifying our investments for instance. Recent studies show that social responsibility—and in particular environmental responsibility—is more and more becoming a corporate imperative.[5] Adopting the strategy I propose is a way of accepting our corporate social responsibility and of maintaining a social license to operate.[6] It will impact on our image and reputation—as I tried to make clear.

"Another of our objectives, internally, is to have employees who are committed to the company. To this aim, we have to act as a responsible company. A proactive strategy will motivate our employees and unleash creativity. Our employees don't leave their values at the door when they come to work. Furthermore, a good reputation will help us recruit and retain the most talented people whose services we need

[4] See Exhibit 1.

[5] See for instance the Burson-Marsteller report "The Responsible Century?" available at (www.BM.com).

[6] The expression is from Daniel Esty. See Esty & Gentry (1997).

to do the best possible business. We should not overlook the extraordinary motivating power of a constructive environmental stance.

"But this strategy is also justified in terms that are more immediately pragmatic. Such justifications might turn out to be decisive, should the board be asked to endorse my proposal. Let me summarise them briefly. By following this path, we will position ourselves as the leading oil and gas corporation on the issue. Being the leader will help us in our contacts with governments. It will allow us to influence the negotiations and policies in a way that is beneficial to us. Our biggest fear is that climate policy will result in command and control policies. This is just another reason to hurry up. We need to participate in the development of policies that will influence our future, rather than have that policy imposed on us. We will also be in a better position to influence decisions on the rules for market mechanisms, and we can ensure that they are effective, simply because we will be in the game when the rules regarding emissions reduction are written.

"Another important factor, to which our lawyers are pointing with more and more insistence, is the future of liability laws for our products. They could significantly evolve in the next 10 to 15 years, and that would mean that we could be sued on the impact of our products on the climate. In such a case, showing that we were early starters will greatly help us in court. Neither should we disregard potential credits for early starters; if, as one hears in the U.S. administration hallways, companies will be granted credit for early action, then it makes good business sense to be proactive.

"As far as our competitors go, our breaking ranks with the industry will surely annoy them at first, but I am convinced that our move will induce them to follow our steps. However, when they do so, they will always appear as followers. The question is not primarily whether climate change constraints will impose a cost on us, but whether such cost will be higher for our competitors. If such is the case, then it can be good for us.

"I have emphasized the strategic and pragmatic justifications of this strategy, but there is also an ethical dimension."

"I am not sure we should waste any time on this," says Maria Goodfellow. "Our ethical responsibility is to make profit, and I doubt that one could secure this objective with your approach. I do not think that a company can afford to focus so strongly on an environmental issue such as this one, and still make money. We just have to delay action as much as possible."

"Who says that my strategy does not allow us to delay political action?" answers Twist. "Given the public opinion and political climate (if I may say), we will gain more time and will more efficiently delay political action by acknowledging the problem and then acting slowly, than through openly obstructive denial."

"You should have been a lawyer, Henri," Paul Hardy says sighing, "but please, go on with the tactics you propose."

"We should start with a well-publicized recognition of IPCC science and conclusions and an acknowledgment of the need for curbing international CO_2 (and other greenhouse gas) emissions. We accompany this statement by a set of internal measures that OILCO will implement to reduce its process emissions. These measures are actions that we start taking now, before Kyoto, and in some sense, independently of Kyoto's eventual outcome."

"So you begin by announcing things that we have not yet achieved," interrupts Ms. Goodfellow.

Twist continues: "I suggest that we decide on a CO_2 emissions reduction target and timetable for the entire group. To achieve this goal, we set up an internal emissions trading system. This will help us lower the costs of reaching our target, by allowing the reductions to be made wherever they are cheapest. It would be a powerful means to gain knowledge on the potential and practicalities of tradable permits, as well as the necessary managerial skills to efficiently participate in a world emissions market. This knowledge, in turn, will enhance our legitimacy as participants in the international negotiations that will eventually determine rules for the international market of emissions permits in case of the entry into force of a protocol containing legally binding emission reduction commitments. Finally, we should not overlook the fact that our emissions reduction target—if intelligently achieved—could lower our operating costs in the midterm, simply because it will force us to be more energy efficient.

"Also, we could start testing the other flexibility instrument discussed today: *joint implementation*.[7] We could work on joint implementation and carbon offset schemes around the world, again to gain expertise.

[7] See Exhibit 1.

"Finally, we could increase our investment in renewable energies, in particular in solar energy. This would be a first step toward a transformation of OILCO from a fossil fuel company to an energy company. And even if we start by a small investment as compared to our core business, it would constitute a strong signal that we are 'going green' so to speak. In parallel, we could fund more research on low carbon technologies. We don't know what the future dominant fuels and technologies will be."

"I saw it coming," says Haddock, "you are now asking for a bigger budget line."

"Please go on," says the CEO.

"Meanwhile, at the societal level, we should reinforce our relationship with the various stakeholders in this debate. In particular, we could collaborate with well-disposed environmental NGOs. We could even organize our own stakeholder consultations, which could both enhance our knowledge of their demands and our public image. Also, around the international negotiation process, the trend is toward more and more participatory approaches whereby stakeholders are involved. We should make sure we take part in those, again for both public relations and efficiency reasons. We have to show our willingness to engage in dialogue, and to be part of the solution. Finally, we should enhance our communication of the company's action on this issue, in a huge public relations endeavor. Thank you for your attention," he says, going back to his chair.

"You have done an impressive job," says Hardy. "How come you are proposing such a strategy?"

"I am here to serve the company, Paul, but my role is also to participate in the development of the society I am living in. We can accomplish a lot by combining the two."

"Well now, let us make the best of all this," says Paul Hardy.

Questions to Students

You are Paul Hardy. Now that you've heard all the proposals, you have to make up your mind and devise a consistent strategy that you will have to get approved first by the board and then by the market. You need to:

1. Consider what has not been said during this debate: the underlying ethical dimensions, the moral principles involved, and their potential impact.
2. Define the "position" you would take, and why you would take it.
3. Construct your strategy with elements taken from one or several of the proposed strategies. Identify implementation tactics.
4. Prepare your arguments to promote and defend your position within and outside the company.

References

Agrawala, S., & Andresen, S. (1999) "Indispensability and Indefensibility? The United States in Climate Treaty Negotiations," *Global Governance* 5, pp. 457–482.

Esty, D., & Gentry, B. (1997) "Foreign Investment, Globalisation, and the Environment," in T. Jones, ed., *Globalisation and Environment*, Organization for Economic Cooperation and Development, Paris.

Grubb, M., Vrolijk, C., & Brack, D. (1999) *The Kyoto Protocol*, RIIA and Earthscan Publications, London.

Harris, P. (1998) "Understanding America's Climate Change Policy: Realpolitik, Pluralism, and Ethical Norms," *OCEES Research Paper*, Oxford Centre for the Environment, Ethics & Society, 15.

Houghton, J., Meira Filho, L., Callander, B., Harris, N., Kattenberg, A., & Maskell, K. (eds.) (1996) *Climate Change 1995, The Science of Climate Change*, Contribution of Working Group I to the Second Assessment Report of the Intergovernmental Panel on Climate Change, Cambridge University Press, Cambridge.

IPCC—Intergovernmental Panel on Climate Change. (1996) *Climate Change 1995: Intergovernmental Panel on Climate Change Second Assessment Report*, Summary for Policy-Makers (www.ipcc.ch).

IPCC. (2001) "IPCC Working Group I Third Assessment Report. Summary for Policymakers" (www.meto.gov.uk/sec5/CR_div/ipcc/wgl/WGI-SPM.pdf, February 2001).

Jehl, D. (2001) "Bush Defends Emissions Stance," *The New York Times*, March 15, 2001.

Jehl, D., & Revkin, A. (2001) "Bush in Reversal. Won't Seek Cuts in Emissions of Carbon Dioxide," *The New York Times*, March 14, 2001.

Oberthür, S., & Ott, H. (1999) *The Kyoto Protocol. International Climate Policy for the 21st Century*, Springer, Berlin.

Pianin, E., & Goldstein, A. (2001) "Bush Drops a Call for Emissions Cuts. Energy Firms Opposed Carbon Dioxide Pledge," *The Washington Post*, March 14, 2001.

UNEP—United Nations Environment Programme. (1999) "Climate Change Information Kit: UNEP's Information Unit for Conventions" (www.unfccc.de).

UNFCCC—United Nations Framework Convention on Climate Change. (1992) "United Nations Framework Convention on Climate Change" (www.unfccc.de).

UNFCCC. (1997) The Kyoto Protocol to the Convention on Climate Change (www.unfccc.de).

UNFCCC. (2000) "A Guide to the Climate Change Process," UNFCCC Secretariat (www.unfcc.de).

van den Hove, S. (2000) *Approches participatives pour les Problèmes d'Environnement. Caractérisations, justifications, et illustrations par le cas du changement climatique*, PhD dissertation, Université de Versailles Saint-Quentin-en-Yvelines, France.

Vrolijk, C. (2001) "Meeting Report: President Bush Might Have Done Kyoto a Favour; Report of a Discussion Meeting Organised by the Royal Institute for International Affairs entitled *"Is Kyoto Dead?"* Chatham House, London, 25 April 2001 (www.riia.org/Research/eep/eep.html, April 2001).

EXHIBIT 1 Background Information on Climate Change

The Greenhouse Effect[a]

The earth's climate is driven by a continuous flow of energy from the sun. This energy arrives mainly in the form of visible light. About 30% is immediately scattered back into space, but most of the 70% which is absorbed passes down through the atmosphere to warm the earth's surface. The earth must send this energy back out into space in the form of infrared radiation. "Greenhouse gases" in the atmosphere block infrared radiation from escaping directly from the surface to space. Infrared radiation cannot pass straight through the air like visible light. Instead, most departing energy is carried away from the surface by air currents and clouds, eventually escaping to space from altitudes above the thickest layers of the greenhouse gas blanket (Figure 1).

The main greenhouse gases are water vapor, carbon dioxide, ozone, methane, nitrous oxide, and the chlorofluorocarbons (CFCs). Apart from CFCs, all of these gases occur naturally. Together, they make up less than 1% of the atmosphere. This is enough to produce a "natural greenhouse effect" that keeps the planet some 30°C warmer than it would otherwise be—essential for life as we know it.

[a] Excerpts from UNEP (1999) "Climate Change Information Kit" (www.unfcc.de).

FIGURE 1: Schematic Presentation of Earth's Radiation and Energy Balance (fluxes in W m^{-2})

Source: Houghton et al. (1996, p. 58).

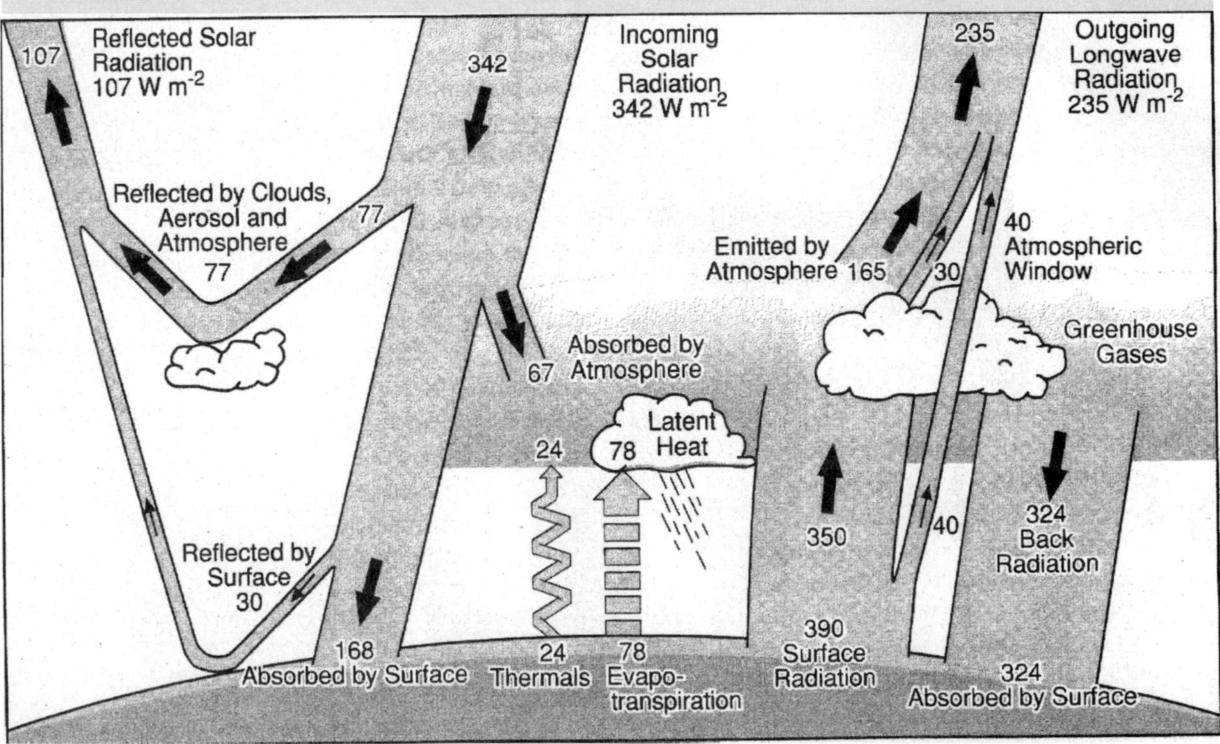

EXHIBIT 1 Background Information on Climate Change—Continued

Levels of all key greenhouse gases (with the possible exception of water vapor) are rising as a direct result of human activity (see Exhibit 2). Emissions of carbon dioxide (mainly from burning coal, oil, and natural gas), methane and nitrous oxide (due to agriculture and changes in land use), ozone (generated by the fumes in automobile exhausts), and CFCs (manufactured by industry) are changing how the atmosphere absorbs energy. Water vapor levels may also be rising because of a "positive feedback." This is all happening at an unprecedented speed. The result is known as the "enhanced greenhouse effect."

The climate system must adjust to rising greenhouse gas levels to keep the global "energy budget" in balance. In the long term, the earth must get rid of energy at the same rate at which it receives energy from the sun. Since a thicker blanket of greenhouse gases helps to reduce energy loss to space, the climate must change somehow to restore the balance between incoming and outgoing energy.

This adjustment will include a "global warming" of the earth's surface and lower atmosphere. But this is only part of the story. Warming up is the simplest way for the climate to get rid of the extra energy. Even a small rise in temperature will be accompanied by many other changes: in cloud cover and wind patterns, for example. Some of these changes may act to enhance the warming (positive feedbacks), others to counteract it (negative feedbacks).

The Science of Climate Change[b]

While the world's climate has always varied naturally, the vast majority of scientists now believe that rising concentrations of greenhouse gases in the earth's atmosphere, resulting from economic and demographic growth since the industrial revolution, are overriding this natural variability and leading to irreversible climate change. In 1995, the Second Assessment Report of the Intergovernmental Panel on Climate Change (IPCC) confirmed that "the balance of evidence suggests that there is a discernible human influence on global climate." The report projected that global mean surface temperatures would increase by between 1 and 3.5°C by 2100, the fastest rate of change since the end of the last ice age, and that global mean sea levels would rise by between 15 and 95 cm by 2100, flooding many low-lying coastal areas. Changes in rainfall patterns are also predicted, increasing the threat of drought, floods, or intense storms in many regions.

The climate system is complex, and scientists still need to improve their understanding of the extent, timing, and impacts of climate change. However, what we know already alerts us to the potentially dramatic negative impacts of climate change on human health, food security, economic activity, water resources, and physical infrastructure. Farming could be seriously disrupted, leading to falling crop yields in many regions. Tropical diseases are expected to spread; the geographical zone of potential malaria transmission, for example, could increase from around 45% of the world population today to approximately 60% by the latter half of this century. Sea level rise and changing weather patterns could also trigger large-scale migration from more seriously affected areas. While no one will be able to escape from climate change, it is the poorer people and countries who are most vulnerable to its negative impacts.

The United Nations Framework Convention on Climate Change

In the late 1980s, under the combined pressure of scientists and environmental NGOs, the issue of climate change appeared on the international political agenda. The creation of the IPCC by the United Nations Environment Programme and the World Meteorological Organization resulted in the publication in 1990 of a first assessment report which found human-induced rises of greenhouse gas concentrations in the atmosphere and the consequent risk of significant climatic changes. This report launched an international negotiation process which resulted in the signature by 154 nations of the United Nations Framework Convention on Climate Change (UNFCCC), in Rio in 1992. The ultimate objective of the convention is the "stabilization of greenhouse gas concentrations in the atmosphere at a level that would prevent dangerous anthropogenic interference with the climate system."[c] Two important principles underlie the convention: the principle of equity and that of "common but differentiated responsibility" of countries. As a consequence, the treaty divides its parties into two groups: Annex 1 parties are industrialised countries and non-Annex 1 parties are developing countries. It does not contain legally binding emissions reduction, only a commitment by Annex 1 parties to adopt policies and measures to mitigate climate change, and a loosely stated objective of returning to 1990 emission levels by the year 2000.

The Kyoto Protocol

In 1995, parties to the UNFCCC decided that the commitments under the convention were inadequate and agreed to start the negotiation of a protocol that would contain quantified limitation and reduction objectives for Annex 1 parties. Schematically, there are three main groups around the negotiation table: the European Union and its allies, the United States and its allies, and the developing countries (grouped under the so-called Group of 77 plus China). The EU, which probably has the greenest environmental constituency and has a clear interest in both reducing its importations of fossil

(continued)

[b] UNFCCC Secretariat, "A Guide to the Climate Change Process" (www.unfcc.de).

[c] UNFCCC, Article 2 (www.unfccc.de).

EXHIBIT 1 Background Information on Climate Change—Continued

fuels and taking leadership in the development of environmentally friendly energy technologies, has always adopted the more proactive position, pushing for high reduction targets and a great deal of domestic effort (in the form of policies and measures) to achieve them. The United States is the world champion both in terms of total greenhouse gas emissions (about 20% of the world's CO_2 emissions in 1990) and in terms of per capita emissions (about 20 tons of CO_2 per habitant in 1990 as compared to less than 9 tons for the EU and 0.7 tons for India).[d] The tradition of cheap energy, the power of industrial lobbies (in particular the fossil fuels, electricity, and automobile lobbies), and the cultural aversion to policies that are perceived as restricting one's individual freedom, render the U.S. particularly reluctant to international and national climate change mitigation measures. For this reason, the U.S. from the start called for maximum geographical flexibility in the implementation of emission reductions and unconstrained use of market instruments, in particular emissions trading.

After more than two years of negotiations, the parties adopted the Kyoto Protocol in December 1997. The protocol contains a legally binding commitment from Annex 1 parties (industrialised countries) to collectively reduce their yearly emissions of a basket of six greenhouse gases (CO_2, CH_4, N_2O, HFC, PFCs, and HF_6)[e] by 5% in the period 2008–2012 as compared to 1990. This commitment is differentiated according to the countries' circumstances and negotiation power. For instance, the U.S. goes for a 7% reduction, the EU for 8% reduction—but this is further differentiated within the so-called EU bubble where for instance Germany committed to a 21% reduction and Greece goes for a 25% increase. Japan commits to 6% reduction, and the Russian Federation is allowed the status quo with 0%.[f]

Geographical flexibility is provided for through the introduction of three economic instruments, the so-called flexibility mechanisms: international emissions trading among Annex 1 parties; joint implementation (i.e., the acquisition by an Annex 1 country of emission reduction units resulting from projects aimed at reducing emissions of greenhouse gases in another Annex 1 country), and the clean development mechanism (i.e., the transfer to an Annex 1 country of certified emission reductions resulting from project activities in non-Annex 1 countries). These mechanisms "are designed to help Annex I parties reduce the costs of meeting their emissions targets by achieving or acquiring reductions more cheaply in other countries than at home. The clean development mechanism also aims to assist developing countries in achieving sustainable development by promoting environmentally friendly investment in their economies from industrialized country governments and businesses."[g]

However, the parties in Kyoto could only go so far as to agree on the principle of such mechanisms, but could not define precisely the corresponding operational rules. This was left to further negotiations.

To enter into force, the protocol needs to be ratified (not just signed) by at least 55 parties, incorporating developed countries (from Annex 1) which together accounted for 55% of total Annex 1 CO_2 emissions in 1990. At the time, the U.S. accounted for 36% of these emissions, and Russia for more than 17%.[h] In the U.S., the Senate has to ratify international commitments by a two-thirds majority vote. And the prospect for ratification is rather meager.[i]

Post-Kyoto Developments

In November 2000, the parties to the climate convention convened in The Hague for the third time since Kyoto. The expectancies were high since the objective was to come to an agreement on the rules for the flexibility mechanism, compliance, and enforcement and the role that sinks of greenhouse gases (e.g., forests which, under certain conditions, may be net absorbers of carbon) would be allowed to play in the implementation of the parties' commitments. The meeting failed, and the parties decided to reconvene in summer 2001 to pursue their work.

In January 2001, IPCC Working Group One, charged with studying the science of climate change, adopted the summary for policymakers for its contribution to IPCC's third assessment report. Its main conclusions include the following statements:[j]

- An increasing body of observations gives a collective picture of a warming world and other changes in the climate system.
- Emissions of greenhouse gases and aerosols due to human activities continue to alter the atmosphere in ways that are expected to affect the climate.
- Confidence in the ability of models to project future climate has increased.

[d] Source: Oberthür and Ott (1999).

[e] See Exhibit 2 for information on these gases.

[f] Note that this apparent status quo in reality comes down to a license for increasing Russian emissions, since Russia's emissions at the time of Kyoto were about 30% lower than in 1990, due to the dramatic collapse the economy.

[g] UNFCCC, "A Guide to the Climate Change Process" (www.unfcc.de).

[h] See UNFCCC (1997) and Grubb et al. (1999, p. 253–54).

[i] On the U.S. and international climate policy see Harris (1998), Agrawala and Andresen (1999), and Vrolijk (2001).

[j] IPCC (2001).

EXHIBIT 1 Background Information on Climate Change—Continued

- There is new and stronger evidence that most of the warming observed over the last 50 years is attributable to human activities.
- Human influences will continue to change atmospheric composition throughout the 21st century.
- Global average temperature and sea level are projected to rise under all IPCC SRES scenarios.

On March 13, 2001, in a letter addressed to four Republican Senators, U.S. President George W. Bush reversed his campaign promise that his administration would regulate CO_2 emissions from power plants and strongly reaffirmed his opposition to the Kyoto Protocol, calling it an "unfair and ineffective means of addressing global climate change concerns."[k] The president's move followed a powerful pressure campaign from congressional and industry leaders—in particular form the electricity, coal, and oil sectors.[l]

[k] Letter from President Bush to Senators Hagel, Helms, Craig and Roberts, March 13, 2001 (www.whitehouse.gov/news/releases/2001/03/20010314.html, April 2001).

[l] See coverage in the *New York Times* and *Washington Post*: Jehl & Revkin (2001), Jehl (2001), Pianin & Goldstein (2001).

EXHIBIT 2 Sources of Anthropogenic Greenhouse Gas Emissions

Source: Adapted from Oberthur and Ott (1999) and van den Hove (2000).

Greenhouse Gas (GHG)	Main Anthropogenic Sources	Shares in Emissions in Industrialised Countries in the 1990s	Share of GHG Emissions of Industrialised Countries in Early 1990s
Carbon dioxide (CO_2)	Fossil fuel combustion (coal, oil, natural gas)	>95%	ca. 82%
	Industrial processes: production of cement, aluminium, steel, ammonia, and hydrogen		
	Deforestation, desertification, and agriculture	2–3%	
Methane (CH_4)	Fossil fuel production, distribution, and combustion (coal and oil extraction; oil refining; natural gas flaring)	ca. 30%	ca. 12%
	Landfills	ca. 30%	
	Agriculture: rice fields; livestock (bovines & ovines)	ca. 30%	
	Production of steel, ammonia, and hydrogen; biomass combustion	Not available	
Nitrous oxide (N_2O)	Agriculture (nitrogen-based fertilizers)	40%	ca. 4%
	Fossil fuel combustion	20–25%	
	Industrial processes: nitrous and adipic acid production for the nylon industry	ca. 30%	
Halogenated hydrocarbons (CFCs, HCFCs, HFCs)*	Cooling processes (refrigerants)	not available	not available
	Industrial processes: solvents, industrial foams		
	Insulation		
Perfluorocarbons (PFCs)	Industrial processes: aluminium production, solvents (semiconductors)	not available	not available
Sulphur hexafluoride (SF_6)	Industrial processes: solvents, magnesium production, electric industry	not available	not available

* CFCs and HCFCs are both ozone depleting substances and greenhouse gases. They are being phased out under the 1987 Montreal Protocol on Substances that Deplete the Ozone Layer; hence they are not addressed in the Kyoto Protocol.

EXHIBIT 3 Background Information on the American Petroleum Institute and the Global Climate Coalition

In the U.S., many lobby groups participate in the debate on climate change to defend the interests of those they represent. This exhibit gives some background information on the American Petroleum Institute (API) and the Global Climate Coalition (GCC), both very important groups for the oil industry.

The American Petroleum Institute

The American Petroleum Institute is the most important U.S. trade association for the petroleum industry. "It is a forum for all parts of the oil and natural gas industry to pursue priority public policy objectives and advance the interests of the industry in a legally appropriate manner. . . . Today, the most pressing issues revolve about public perceptions and government policies toward our industry—many of which have international dimensions. Speaking with one voice on these issues has become as essential as having interchangeable parts in the field. API speaks for the petroleum industry before Congress, state legislatures, the executive branch of government, and the news media. It negotiates with regulatory agencies and represents the industry in legal proceedings. It participates in coalitions that help shape public policy on issues such as global climate change, access and alternative fuels. And it strives to enhance credibility on the environmental, health and safety issues that are central to the public's perception of the industry and its products. . . . API is the petroleum industry's 'think tank.' It sponsors research, tied to the organization's priorities, that runs the gamut from economic analysis to toxicological testing, to public opinion polling."[a]

API opposes the Kyoto Protocol. Today, the underlying argument for this position goes as follows: "The ultimate question is how the world should deal with a highly uncertain problem like climate change. Should we turn to international bureaucracies and global mandates or should we rely on the energy, creativity, and flexibility of the private sector, the free market system, and public-private collaboration? Companies in the private sector know that if science ultimately shows the problem to be serious, then controls on emissions will become inevitable. They have strong incentives to respond to the risk of climate change because many of their investments have long economic lives. And companies are responding, in multiple ways. A program of mandates by an international bureaucracy would entail the worst characteristics of central planning and industrial policy. To oppose this is hardly to advocate 'no action;' it is, rather, to recognize that our decision as to which mechanisms of action to rely upon will have significant consequences for the efficacy and cost of the effort."[b]

The Global Climate Coalition

The Global Climate Coalition was created in 1989 by a group of organizations and companies willing to have a single organization to coordinate their action on the climate change issue. Its members included trade association and private companies from the fossil fuel, mining, transportation, and heavy manufacturing sectors, as well as from agriculture and forestry. Says former chairman of the GCC and vice president of the API, William O'Keefe: "In the beginning it was an information exchange and sharing tool. But in this country, if business wants to have a voice in a policy issue, it is typical to create a coalition. It is better to have unity to make one's voice heard."[c] The API was a board member of the GCC from the start. "At the time," recalls O'Keefe, "climate change was one of the many issues that we [API] were following. But in 1993, it became clear that this issue would grow in importance and potential impact for the oil industry, so the API asked me to become more involved in the GCC."[d] Other board members included American Forest & Paper, Exxon, Chevron, Mobil, National Mining Association, and General Motors.[e] Until October 2000, the GCC's objective as stated on its Web site was "to coordinate business participation in the scientific and policy debate on the global climate change issue."[f]

The GCC has been one of the most influential U.S. lobbying front groups on the climate issue. Its strategy was aiming at impeding action on climate change by influencing public opinion and policymakers. This was done by several means. First, mostly in the earlier years, by questioning the IPCC science in which climate policy is grounded: "Existing scientific evidence does not support actions aimed solely at reducing or stabilizing greenhouse gas emissions. GCC does support actions to reduce greenhouse gas emissions or to increase greenhouse gas sinks that are justified for other economic or environmental reasons."[g] Second, by questioning the economics of proposed national and international policy actions: "Unrealistic targets and timetables, such as those called for under the Kyoto Protocol, are not achievable without severely harming the U.S. economy and all American families, workers, seniors and children. A new approach to climate policy is

[a] API (www.api.org/about/aboutindex.htm, February 2001).

[b] API (www.api.org/globalclimate/apipos2.htm, February 2001).

[c] Interview with William O'Keefe, January 2001.

[d] Ibid.

[e] Board members in 1998 (Ozone action, www.ozone.org/page16.html, January 2001).

[f] (www.globalclimate.org/oldsite/mission.htm, February 2001). On the new GCC Web site, this objective is restated without reference to participation in the scientific debate: "to coordinate business participation in the international policy debate on the issue of global climate change and global warming" (www.globalclimate.org/aboutus.htm, February 2001).

[g] (www.globalclimate.org/oldsite/mission.htm).

EXHIBIT 3 Background Information on the American Petroleum Institute and the Global Climate Coalition—Continued

needed."[h] Third, by rejecting the Kyoto Protocol as inadequate: "The issue is what constitutes responsible action and the Kyoto Protocol is not responsible action. It is a flawed agreement and cannot be salvaged with bilateral Band-Aids or further negotiations in Bonn, Buenos Aires or elsewhere. It is not a global agreement and will not work. Thus, we recommend that the President not sign and that the Congress not approve the Kyoto Protocol."[i]

In 1996, BP was the first major corporation to withdraw from the coalition. It was followed in 1998 by Dow Chemicals and Shell, and in 1999 by Ford. In 2000, Daimler-Chrysler, Texaco, and General Motors also left. In March 2000, the GCC was restructured and, since then, only accepts trade associations as members.

[h] GCC Position Summary (www.globalclimate.org/aboutus/possummary.htm, February 2001).

i Statement by Mrs. Constance Holmes, chair of the GCC before the U.S. House Committee on Science, February 4, 1998 (www.house.gov/science/holmes_02-4.htm, February 2001).

Should Business Influence the Science and Politics of Global Environmental Change? The Oil Industry and Climate Change (B): *Climate Change Strategies of Three Multinational Oil Corporations*

The Kyoto Protocol is a climate policy derived from a debate that for too long has been driven by ideological rhetoric, pseudo facts, staged media events and scathing attacks on those who raise legitimate doubts.

William O'Keefe[1]

If, at the cost of corporate pocket change, industrial giants can control the publicly perceived reality of the condition of the planet and the state of our scientific knowledge, what would they do if their survival were truly put at risk?

Ross Gelbspan[2]

Introduction

This case B contains a synthetic presentation of historical developments of the climate change strategies of three multinational oil corporations: ExxonMobil, TotalFinaElf, and BP Amoco. It looks at the 1990s with an emphasis on the period around the Kyoto Conference (1997–1998). The three companies we concentrate on—Exxon, Elf, and BP—have merged with competitors in the late 1990s to form respectively ExxonMobil, BP Amoco, and TotalFinaElf. In this document, we refer to their names at the date considered.

This case was prepared by Dr. Sybille van den Hove, Research Fellow at INSEAD, under the supervision of Marc Le Menestrel, Assistant Professor of Economics and Business at University Pompeu Fabra and Visiting Professor at INSEAD and Henri-Claude de Bettignies, Professor of Asian Business at INSEAD and Visiting Professor at Stanford University. It is intended to be used as a basis for class discussion rather than to illustrate either effective or ineffective handling of an administrative situation.

The authors gratefully thank the interviewees for their time and openness and Prof. Daniel Esty for his helpful comments on an earlier draft of this case. The authors are solely responsible for the content.

The material used to explore those corporations' strategies consists of (1) publicly available documents from the companies; (2) public statements by corporate officials; (3) interviews with individuals within these corporations and with other stakeholders and analysts; (4) newspaper articles; and (5) information provided by various NGOs.

[1] O'Keefe (1998b).

[2] Gelbspan (1995), p. 36.

ExxonMobil

> Although the science of climate change is uncertain, there's no doubt about the considerable economic harm to society that would result from reducing fuel availability to consumers by adopting the Kyoto Protocol or other mandatory measures that would significantly increase the cost of energy. Most economists tell us that such a step would damage our economy and almost certainly require large increases in taxes on gas and oil. It could also entail enormous transfers of wealth to other countries.
>
> ExxonMobil CEO and Chairman Lee Raymond[3]

Ever since climate change became a subject of public and policy concern, ExxonMobil has been the most active major oil and gas corporation in the debate. "Since the 1980s, we started thinking about climate change as a potentially important issue," says Brian Flannery, the science strategy and programs manager for ExxonMobil's Safety, Health, and Environment Division. "This was in the context of major long-term investment projects. The issue held business meaning as a regulatory risk driven by public policy."[4] Since the Rio Summit in 1992, the company's strategic line has been to oppose mandatory restrictions to curb greenhouse gas emissions.

ExxonMobil describes itself as "a science- and technology-based company,"[5] making decisions on the basis of hard facts. "Our public policy positions are based on scientific, economic, and technical analysis. And this, even if it is not politically easy. It is very different from BP Amoco and Shell who have other drivers that are mainly of a political nature," says Flannery.[6] Vidal characterizes ExxonMobil as "a strongly legalist corporation, recognizing only public authorities and institutional interlocutors."[7] Says Flannery: "We do not acknowledge the notion of social responsibility as defined by some NGOs. NGOs are not the sole arbiters. We comply with the laws of countries. We maintain and enforce a strict code of ethical conduct for all employees. Consumer behavior and preferences are powerful indicators of what society wants."[8] In this context, the company has always striven to participate in the debate with a discourse presented as purely scientific, economic, and technological.

The core arguments of many opponents to mandatory emissions restrictions to address the issue of climate change can be summarized by the following progression of statements: climate change is not happening; the science of climate change is uncertain; climate change is not human-induced; climate change will not necessarily be bad; the timing of proposed action is not adequate; and the policies under discussion (at national and international levels) are not the good way to tackle the issue. Not all arguments have been pushed by all opponents, nor have they been put forward at the same time, as the latter imply implicit recognition of a problem. In the early days of the debate, Exxon was mainly contesting the science, based on its complexity and associated uncertainties. Its strategy of preventing political action on climate change was chiefly implemented through efforts denying the existence of a problem. The objective was to convince the public and policymakers, chiefly in the U.S., that human-induced climate change was not an issue requiring mandatory restrictions on greenhouse gas emissions. As time went by, efforts were also directed at addressing the economic impacts of the policy proposals under examination, which were viewed by ExxonMobil as unacceptably costly and threatening to the U.S. and world economies. The uncertain science was deemed insufficient to justify the supposedly certain and massive economic costs that would ensue. In parallel came more and more arguments against the diplomatic foundations of the Kyoto Protocol that ExxonMobil believes are fundamentally flawed.

Instrumental to the implementation of Exxon's strategy was its participation in industry and lobby groups. Exxon is a prominent member of the American Petroleum Institute

[3] Excerpt from ExxonMobil (2001).

[4] Interview with Dr. Brian Flannery, The Hague, November 2000.

[5] Lee Raymond, CEO and chairman of ExxonMobil; excerpt from ExxonMobil (2001).

[6] Interview with Dr. Brian Flannery, The Hague, November 2000.

[7] Vidal (2000, p. 4).

[8] Interview with Dr. Brian Flannery, The Hague, November 2000.

(API), the major U.S. petroleum industry trade association, and was, from the date of its creation in 1989, a board member of the Global Climate Coalition (GCC).[9] "At the time, and until Kyoto," says Rafe Pomerance, former deputy assistant secretary for environment and development at the U.S. State Department, "the trade associations were the key players [on the U.S. scene] and the companies were on a lower level. The American Petroleum Institute and the Global Climate Coalition were very hostile to action on climate change. . . . They were key to defeating President Clinton's 1993 BTU tax proposal, through lobbying the Congress.[10] I think they put together a U.S.$7 or 8 million campaign. The BTU tax was a climate move in the mind of Clinton, but he did not play it as a climate measure, for political reasons. This was a key moment."[11, 12] The strategy of the GCC and the API to fight against mandatory climate policy at U.S. and international levels rested on two main pillars: "raising questions about and undercutting the prevailing scientific wisdom"[13] on climate change in order to cast doubts in the mind of the public and policymakers on the existence of a problem, and attacking the policy proposals on economical grounds.

On the science, these groups criticized the 1995 IPCC review process that led to the drafting of the summary for policymakers on the grounds that it was politicized and biased. In June 1996 for instance, the George Marshall Institute,[14] the API, and the GCC personally attacked one of the lead authors of the IPCC, Dr. Benjamin Santer. It started with an op-ed article by Dr. F. Seitz in the *Wall Street Journal*, charging Santer with having made unauthorized and politically inspired changes to Chapter 8 of the IPCC second assessment report, hence with being responsible for "disturbing corruption of the peer-review process."[15] Chapter 8, because it addresses the question of attribution of climate change to human activities, is key to the overall IPCC conclusion of the plausible existence of a discernible human influence on global climate. Many IPCC leading figures replied by supporting Santer and pointed to his faithful work.[16] Exxon was also directly very critical of the summary for policymakers: "[T]he executive summary of the [IPCC] report, the part most people read, was heavily influenced by government officials and others who are not scientists. The summary, which was not peer-reviewed, states that 'the balance of evidence suggests a discernible human influence on climate.' You'll note that this is a very carefully worded statement, recognizing that the jury is still out, especially on any quantifiable connection to human actions. The conclusion does not refer to global warming from increases in greenhouse gases. Indeed, many scientists say that a great deal of uncertainty still needs to be resolved."[17] Other criticisms of mainstream climate change have been articulated through the more or less direct funding of individual scientists holding the contrary view—the so-called climate skeptics—and by amplification of their access to the media and policymakers.

Economic arguments against mandatory climate policy included the threat of losses of jobs

[9] See Exhibit 3 from "The Oil Industry and Climate Change (A)" for background information on the American Petroleum Institute and the Global Climate Coalition.

[10] One can read on API's Web site, under the title "How API Adds Value," "When our members' interests are under attack, API acts as the industry's crisis communications manager. When a BTU energy tax was proposed in 1993, API created an effective coalition to stop the tax in its tracks" (www.api.org/about/valueadd.htm, February 2001).

[11] Interview with Rafe Pomerance, Amsterdam, November 2000.

[12] On the BTU tax and interest group politics, see Agrawala & Andresen (1999, p. 470).

[13] This quote is extracted from an API internal memo leaked to the *New York Times* in April 1998. The memo also states: "Unless 'climate change' becomes a non-issue, meaning that the Kyoto proposal is defeated and there are no further initiatives to thwart the threat of climate change, there may be no moment when we can declare victory for our efforts." See Cushman (1998) (www.corpwatch.org/trac/feature/climate/culprits/bigoil.html, January 2001).

[14] An ultraconservative U.S. institute aiming to provide "rigorous, unbiased technical analysis of scientific issues with impact on public policy" (www.marshall.org, February 2001) and chaired by Dr. Seitz, who for years has been among the most active "climate skeptics"—scientists who strongly disagree with mainstream climate science as embodied by the IPCC process—in the U.S.

[15] Seitz (1996).

[16] See Stevens (1996).

[17] Flannery (1999, pp. 5–6). To back these remarks Flannery also refers to an article by R. Kerr, published in *Science* in May 1997: "Climate Change: Greenhouse Forecasting Still Cloudy" (Kerr 1997).

and of competitiveness in the U.S., of higher gasoline prices, and of overall huge negative impacts on the U.S. economy. "Our view is that the [Kyoto] Treaty has powerful implications in economics, investment, trade competitiveness, and employment terms," says Flannery from ExxonMobil.[18] These arguments are grounded in a series of economic models, some of which have been funded by ExxonMobil or the American Petroleum Institute, directly or indirectly, with the aim of providing models that are more realistic and more transparent in their assumptions. Influential among these are studies by the U.S. Energy Information Administration—an agency within the Department of Energy charged with providing advice to Congress on these matters. Also widely used are studies by the Wharton Econometric Forecasting Associates[19] and by the Charles River Associates, for which the API provided funding.[20] These models have in turn been criticized on the grounds of inaccurate assumptions, such as a restricted set of policy options, noninclusion of the negative impacts of climatic changes, flaws in modeling procedures, noninclusion of secondary benefits of climate policy in terms of health, environment, and technological development, noninclusion of savings from improved energy efficiency, and so on.[21] Exxon is also said to have been a contributor to the works of an Australian government forecasting agency—the Australian Bureau of Agriculture and Resources Economics—which put together a controversial economic model predicting huge job and economic losses to achieve emissions reduction targets.[22]

In the year before the Kyoto conference, the Global Climate Coalition concentrated its efforts on fighting to prevent significant climate policy outcomes from the negotiations. The tactics consisted of ensuring that any binding commitment on targets and timetables coming out of Kyoto would not be ratified by the U.S. Senate. To this end, the GCC pursued its efforts aimed at raising doubts about the integrity of the mainstream science of climate change in the eyes of the American public and policymakers, by pointing to the uncertainties and gaps in scientific knowledge and to what the GCC saw as distortions of the science and of the conclusions made on its basis. Meanwhile, the GCC put together a vast advertisement campaign in the U.S. against any international agreement that would aim at emissions reduction. The main theme of the campaign was, "The UN Climate Treaty isn't Global . . . and it won't work." As William O'Keefe, former vice president of API and chairman of the GCC describes it: "We only had one public relations campaign, prior to Kyoto. It cost $12 million. The GCC participated, but did not have the money to finance it alone. This campaign was very effective. The reason why, is that fairness is very important to the American people. And the Treaty, by not being global, is not fair. Another important thing is the economic impacts on them. This campaign did galvanize public opinion and helped the passing of the [Byrd-Hagel] Senate resolution. But it did not prevent [Vice President] Al Gore from going to Kyoto and agreeing to something that President Clinton had said just 60 days before that he would not do."[23]

On the Congress front, the GCC was instrumental to reinforcing the value of a Senate resolution in July 1997—known as the Byrd-Hagel resolution—which states: "The United States should not be a signatory to any protocol to, or other agreement regarding, the United Nations Framework Convention on Climate Change of 1992, at negotiations in Kyoto in December 1997, or thereafter, which would: (a) mandate new commitments to limit or reduce greenhouse gas emissions for the Annex I Parties, unless the protocol or other agreement also mandates new specific scheduled commitments to limit or reduce greenhouse gas emissions for Developing Country Parties within the same compliance period, or (b) would result in serious harm to the economy of the United States."[24] O'Keefe, then chairman of the GCC, recalls: "We had regular meetings with members of the Congress to discuss our positions and views. In

[18] Interview with Dr. Brian Flannery, The Hague, November 2000.

[19] This company is not related to the business school.

[20] O'Keefe (1998a).

[21] See Krause (1997) and Cool the planet (1999).

[22] Hamilton (1998a) and Rampton & Burton (1998).

[23] Interview with Mr. William O'Keefe, January 2001.

[24] U.S. Senate Resolution 98, 105th Congress, 1st Session (www.senate.gov, January 2001).

1997, at the request of Senator Byrd, a democrat, and Senator Hagel, a republican, we communicated a lot with members of the Congress to get them to support their resolution. It ended as a 95-0 vote, so it was really a bipartisan one."[25]

In effect, this resolution lowers the chances of ratification of the protocol by the U.S. Senate. And it significantly delays (and could even prevent) the entry into force of the protocol which is almost impossible without U.S. ratification.[26] It also damaged U.S. diplomatic credibility during the Kyoto talks since it evidenced the lack of consensus among the legislative and executive branches of the U.S. government.[27]

This was not the only influence of U.S. industry opponents—including ExxonMobil—on the U.S. political process. From 1990 to 2000, the oil and gas industry contributed more than $122 million in political donations—through so-called PAC contributions to federal candidates, soft money contributions to national parties, and individual contributions.[28] Exxon alone is reported to have officially contributed some $2.9 million in political donations at federal level from 1991 to 1998 (see Exhibit 1). As Pomerance, from the State Department, puts it: "This created a political climate that made things difficult [for the administration]. . . . The oil industry has also had a strong influence by de-legitimizing the science and by using the Congress as a voice for their own agenda. For instance, the Congress may put riders on Appropriations bills—bills that allow the executive branch to spend money. As an example, the Congress used [this means] so that we could not spend money on the implementation of the Kyoto Protocol."[29]

By inducing the Senate to require immediate reduction commitments from developing countries, Exxon and its allies in the GCC have been successful in reopening the debate on developing countries' participation, pointing to the future rise in their emissions, and contesting the underlying principles of the Climate Convention: the common but differentiated responsibilities of countries (in particular the historical responsibility of developed countries) and the principle of equity. It is on the basis of such principles that the treaty calls for developed countries to demonstrate that they are taking the lead in modifying long-term trends in human-induced greenhouse gas emissions.[30] Meanwhile, in a speech before the World Petroleum Congress in Beijing in October 1997, Exxon's CEO, Lee Raymond, was urging developing countries to resist climate policies: "Before we make choices about global climate policies, we need an open debate on the science, an analysis of the risks, and a careful consideration of the costs and benefits. So far this has not taken place and until it has, I hope that the governments of this region will work with us to resist policies that could strangle economic growth."[31]

Around the end of 1998 Exxon's strategy implementation appeared to evolve to a more moderate stance, where climate change started to be characterized as a legitimate, potential long-term risk, albeit in prudent terms. While at the beginning of 1998, one could read on Exxon's Web site: "It appears that climate variability is still too large and complex a subject for current measurements and projections to be able to determine whether reliable links exist between human activity and future global warming,"[32] in 1999, Flannery was writing: "Exxon does not believe that uncertainty is an excuse for doing nothing. We acknowledge that global climate change is a legitimate concern and we are taking

[25] Interview with William O'Keefe, January 2001.

[26] There are at least two reasons for this. First, other developed countries are not keen to go along without the U.S., in particular for competitiveness reasons. Second, the rule for entry into force in the protocol requires it to be ratified by at least 55 parties, incorporating developed countries (so-called Annex 1 parties) which in total accounted for 55% of total Annex 1 CO_2 emissions in 1990. At the time, the U.S. accounted for 36% of these emissions, and Russia for more than 17%. (See UNFCC, 1997, and Grubb et al., 1999, p. 253–54).

[27] Note that the signature and ratification of a protocol imposing mandatory emissions reductions was also strongly opposed by organized labor and farm groups, which were also active in influencing the U.S. Congress.

[28] Exhibit 1 has definitions, references, and details on those numbers.

[29] Interview with Rafe Pomerance, Amsterdam, November 2000.

[30] See the text of the Climate Change Convention, in particular the preamble and articles 3 and 4 (www.unfccc.de).

[31] Cited by Hamilton (1998a, p. 46). The speech is no longer available from ExxonMobil's Web page. See also the comments on this speech in *BusinessWeek* (Raeburn, 1997).

[32] Excerpt from Exxon Web site, 1998, cited by Hamilton (1998a).

steps now that we believe will lead in the right direction."[33] In a 2000 op-ed ad, the company was further stating: "Science has given us enough information to know that climate changes may pose long-term risks. Natural variability and human activity may lead to climate change that could be significant and perhaps both positive and negative."[34] Against this milder position on the existence of the problem and the need for action, ExxonMobil's focus shifted toward the acceptable means to tackle the issue, which—ExxonMobil believes—is technology development induced by market forces, not mandatory measures. "As one of the world's leading science and technology organizations, ExxonMobil is confident that technology will reduce the potential risks posed by climate change."[35]

Not surprisingly, environmental NGOs are denouncing ExxonMobil's strategy on the climate issue loudly and strive to bring to light the hidden public relations, lobbying, and other tactics of ExxonMobil and of the lobby groups in which it is influential.[36] So do other stakeholders who have come directly under ExxonMobil's—or its allies'—charges, such as, in particular, mainstream climate scientists. Arguments go back and forth between ExxonMobil and other oil corporations which have opted for more active positions on climate change.

Some analyze ExxonMobil's position in light of the dominant corporate culture. For Björn Stigson, president of the World Business Council for Sustainable Development: "ExxonMobil does not believe in sustainable development. They have another view of the world. But we do not know what they are really doing internally."[37] The corporate culture is itself seen as strongly influenced by the political context of the company's country of origin. "The confrontational tradition of U.S. lawmaking and the power the oil industry has in the ratification process—in coalition with other interest groups—thus stand out as crucial determinants for ExxonMobil's [regulatory] risk assessment and hence the perceived long-term viability of their strategy choice on the climate issue."[38] ExxonMobil indeed does not seem to feel the urge to green its image, as some of its competitors have done in recent years. As noted by the *Financial Times*, ExxonMobil did not take the opportunity of its merger with Mobil to "recast its image." To the contrary, "ExxonMobil reintroduced itself to customers and clients with studied plain-speaking as 'the world's premier petroleum and petrochemical company.' . . . The U.S. company, which is now the world's largest publicly traded oil group and an industry icon of capital productivity, would rather let the numbers behind its enviable financial performance speak for themselves."[39]

How effective has ExxonMobil's strategy on the climate change issue been from a business standpoint? First, ExxonMobil—together with its partners in U.S. lobby groups—has been instrumental to the hindrance of U.S. ratification of the Kyoto Protocol. Without U.S. ratification, the chances of entry into force of the protocol are meager.[40] In terms of delaying international and national actions on climate change, there is no doubt that ExxonMobil's strategy succeeded. When asked whether there was any sign that ExxonMobil's position on climate change was affecting its business, Flannery clearly responded with a short and definite no.[41] Overall, ExxonMobil gained valuable time during which no climate change policy will come as a constraint on its activities. This makes good sense for ExxonMobil's executives who believe that "if there indeed is a climate problem, it is a long-term problem for which we have plenty of time to develop appropriate responses."[42]

Another indicator of ExxonMobil's self-confidence on the climate issue is the way it repeatedly fought back—and defeated—shareholder proposals initiated by environmental and other civic groups that were challenging the

[33] Flannery (1999), p. 9.

[34] "Unsettled Science," ExxonMobil (2000).

[35] "The Promise of Technology," ExxonMobil (2000).

[36] See Hamilton (1998a and b); Greenpeace (www.greenpeace.org/~climate/industry/); Corporate Watch (www.corpwatch.org/trac/climate); The Heat Is On (heatisonline.org); Ozone Action (www.ozone.org/warming.html).

[37] Interview with Björn Stigson, Geneva, December 2000.

[38] Skjaerseth and Skodvin (2000, p. 27).

[39] Durgin (2000).

[40] See note 26.

[41] Interview with Dr. Brian Flannery, The Hague, November 2000.

[42] B. Flannery and G. Ehlig, March 2000, cited by Skjaerseth and Skodvin (2000, p. 10).

company's climate change strategy.[43] However, the mere fact that shareholders—at least the most strongly pro-environment among them—are starting to raise the issue at annual meetings could indicate that ExxonMobil's strategy will, at some point, need to be significantly revised. Noticeable in this regard is the framing of the issue in terms of liability: "Shareholders at both companies [5.4% at Exxon and 5.18% at Mobil] voted on a global warming resolution that asked the company to report what actions they are taking to address global warming and what potential liabilities shareholders may face as a result of inadequate actions," states the NGOs' press release.[44] ExxonMobil is apparently ready for that too: "Exxon's actions and position on climate change have evolved over the years. They will continue to be responsive to emerging scientific and technical understanding in the future. Exxon has been in business for over 100 years, and we intend to remain a profitable, responsible supplier of energy through the next century. As the climate change debate progresses, so too will our actions."[45, 46]

Will ExxonMobil's successful gaining of time be damaging from an ecological standpoint? Only the future will tell.

TotalFinaElf

> The Elf Aquitaine Group is ready to commit to a reduction of 15% of its [CO_2] emissions in 2010.
>
> Elf Aquitaine CEO, Philippe Jaffré[47]

In 1985, the issue of global warming was raised at a meeting of the executive committee of Elf Aquitaine for the first time. Bernard Tramier, director for environment and safety, who had come up with the question was asked to monitor the scientific and political evolution of the issue. An additional person was charged with the detailed follow-up.

On November 24, 1997, only a few days before the meeting of the Conference of the Parties to the Climate Convention in Kyoto, the CEO of Elf Aquitaine, Philippe Jaffré, in an interview with the French newspaper *Le Monde* announced, "The Elf Aquitaine Group is ready to commit to a reduction of 15% of its [CO_2] emissions in 2010."[48] According to the CEO, this decision was based on an acknowledgment that "the consensus within the scientific community appears to be stronger and stronger in affirming that a climatic warming is happening. A number of facts are not disputable. First there is a rise in greenhouse gas concentrations, in particular carbon dioxide (CO_2). Second, these gases have an effect on the climate. What is not measured is the extent of this effect and the potential for natural regulation via the carbon cycle."[49] To Jaffré, however, it is a long-term problem which "leaves us time to react."[50] He called for the application of the precautionary principle, which "for a business leader means that he needs to consider how he can reduce his [company's] emissions and how these reductions could be financed." However this announcement did not constitute a firm commitment. It was presented as an agreement to comply with the 15% emissions reduction goal that constituted the negotiation position of the European Union. It was conditional on equal commitments from other nations: "We can adopt the global emissions reduction objective proposed by the European Union only if all nations of the world do the same."[51] The other condition put forward by Jaffré was the necessity for geographical flexibility in fulfilling its commitment: "Concerning Elf Aquitaine, it seems possible to reduce our total world emissions by 15% in 2010. But such a reduction is only possible if we account for our activities in the entire world. We could not achieve this result solely for our European activities."[52]

The Kyoto conference passed, and Elf did not publicly go much further on the issue. As stated by Bernard Tramier, now senior vice president–environment and industrial safety for

[43] See Durgin (2000); Ozone Action (1999); and the Campaign ExxonMobil NGO Web site (www.campaignexxonmobil.org).

[44] Ozone Action (1999).

[45] Flannery (1999).

[46] On the history of oil corporations, see Yergin (1991).

[47] Interview with Philippe Jaffré, *Le Monde*, 24 November 1997, our translation.

[48] Ibid.

[49] Ibid.

[50] Ibid.

[51] Ibid.

[52] Ibid.

the merged TotalFinaElf Group: "It was a commitment taken before Kyoto; it is more difficult for us to comply with it after [what happened in] Kyoto."[53] The protocol adopted in Kyoto has not yet entered into force, and the commitment of the EU is a reduction of 8% of emissions for six gases in the period 2008–2012 as compared to 1990 levels. Furthermore, the years after Kyoto have seen the merger of Elf with TotalFina. "Among the three companies united in the new group, only Elf had a quantitative reduction commitment," says Tramier. "Today, our position is that we are going to reduce our emissions, but we do not yet know by how much. It will depend on the rules of the game—in particular on accounting rules—that will be imposed on us. We will spend a certain amount of money to reduce our emissions, but the result in reduction terms will depend on where we will do the reductions, and how they will be accounted for."[54]

Concerning its influence on the scientific debate over climate change, Elf was always very clear: "When we are confronted with an issue that raises fears . . . our attitude is scientific: it is that of the 'Cartesian doubt.' We then turn to the scientific community in which we have confidence."[55] And Tramier confirms: "None of the three companies of the TotalFinaElf group has ever contested the principle of climate change."[56] As for the U.S. lobby groups, he recalls: "We have never been members of the Global Climate Coalition. Note that, in terms of publicity, some have achieved great benefits by conspicuously leaving this coalition. We are indeed members of the American Petroleum Institute, but this is completely different because API is the fossil fuel industry trade association, and membership is normal when one operates, even on a small scale, in the U.S."[57]

On the political process, TotalFinaElf does not acknowledge much influence either. In France, says Tramier, "the possibility [to participate] was not offered much to us by the authorities. . . . At the international level, before the merger none of the three companies carried much weight. The game was led by the big groups. We were more or less midway between two extreme positions (ExxonMobil on one side, BP Amoco and Shell on the other) and for this, were sometimes considered as the voice of reason."[58] TotalFinaElf did not make much use of industry groups to participate in the political process at the European level. "We have underestimated their influence. But this is changing. We realize that we need to be more present in this process of influencing the politics. But this is more for reasons of competition among companies than to influence the political process itself. . . . What we need to do is to influence the process in order to have a simple and efficient system as an outcome."[59]

Clearly, with the exception of the 1997 emissions reduction announcement—which turned out to be a mere announcement and not a commitment—TotalFinaElf has publicly taken a low-key position on the climate change issue. It concentrated on gathering information and knowledge, waiting to see where the international negotiations would lead. With the merger, although company documents now acknowledge the necessity of "effectively taking into account the concept [of sustainable development] in all [the group's] activities,"[60] the publicly displayed strategy on climate change is not yet very elaborate. The group's documents state: "TotalFinaElf adheres to the conclusions of the Kyoto Conference on climate change and will participate in the necessary efforts to reach greenhouse gas emissions reduction objectives which have been agreed to by the nations, and this without waiting for the elimination of scientific uncertainties."[61] One can read that the group participates in simulation exercises on flexibility mechanisms. It also plans to reduce its own emissions, although, given uncertainties on the evolution of the world's energy consumption, on the rules of flexibility mechanisms, on financial incentives, and on the inclusion on carbon sinks, "a quantitative commitment cannot be taken today with sufficient accuracy and

[53] Interview with Bernard Tramier, Paris, January 2001.

[54] Ibid.

[55] Interview of Philippe Jaffré, *Le Monde*, 24 November 1997, our translation.

[56] Interview with Bernard Tramier, Paris, January 2001.

[57] Ibid.

[58] Ibid.

[59] Ibid.

[60] Introduction by CEO T. Desmarest in TotalFinaElf (2001), our translation.

[61] TotalFinaElf (2001), our translation.

credibility."[62] Moreover, the group aims at offering products that are more efficient in terms of their greenhouse gas emissions to consumers and at participating in the development of new energy resources.

From a business standpoint, Elf's (and subsequently TotalFinaElf's) strategy on climate change has been generally positive. Given the developments on the political scene, both at international and national levels, which have been fairly slow since the Kyoto Conference, there was no urgency for the company to take a strong public position on the issue. Even the *Erika* oil spill in December 1999 did not induce a major shift in the group's environmental position, in contrast with the Brent Spar issue at Shell. As noted by Denis Goguel, director for ethics of TotalFinaElf, the *Erika* accident "has been negative for our image but we have not seen any measurable decrease in sales."[63] TotalFinaElf is advancing step by step in the construction of its climate change strategy and its overall environmental strategy. The group prefers not to communicate beforehand on its future positions and actions. As Tramier said: "If there is so little information on our actions on the climate change issue as compared to some of our competitors, it is because we are acting. We do not consider climate change as a communication issue. We take it seriously, it is part of our business, but we do not think that it is necessary to make a lot of fuss about it."[64]

BP Amoco

> We must now focus on what can and what should be done, not because we can be certain climate change is happening, but because the possibility can't be ignored. If we are all to take responsibility for the future of our planet, then it falls to us to begin to take precautionary action now.
>
> BP Chief Executive, John Browne[65]

Until BP's withdrawal from the Global Climate Coalition in 1996 and, more visibly, until BP Chief Executive Officer John Browne's landmark speech at Stanford University in May 1997, BP's strategy regarding climate change did not differ significantly from that of all the other major oil and gas corporations. As a member of both the Global Climate Coalition and the American Petroleum Institute, BP was participating in the efforts of these groups to negate the existence of the problem, to influence public opinion, and to prevent any political action on the issue.[66]

The radical shift in strategy that BP operated a few months before Kyoto came as a surprise to many observers, but also to competitors in the oil and gas industry. BP's new strategy was based on a recognition of the scientific assessment of the existence of a serious risk of human-induced climate change by the Intergovernmental Panel on Climate Change.[67] As Browne put it, in Stanford: "[T]here is now an effective consensus among the world's leading scientists and serious and well-informed people outside the scientific community that there is a discernible human influence on the climate, and a link between the concentration of carbon dioxide and the increase in temperature."[68] However, he also pointed to the remaining "large elements of uncertainties."[69] From this premise, he proposed a conclusion that action was needed, which was rooted in the precautionary principle: "The time to consider the policy dimensions of climate change is not when the link between greenhouse gases and climate change is conclusively proven but when the possibility cannot be discounted and is taken seriously by the society of which we are part."[70] The framework in which he placed his analysis is the recognition of a need for "a rethinking of corporate responsibility."

BP became a member of the Pew Center on Global Climate Change's Business Environmental Leadership Council, a coalition of companies which agree that "businesses can and should take concrete steps now in the U.S. and abroad to assess opportunities for emission reductions,

[62] Ibid.

[63] Interview with Denis Goguel, Paris, January 2001.

[64] Interview with Bernard Tramier, Paris, January 2001.

[65] Excerpt from Browne (1997).

[66] See Exhibit 3, from "The Oil Industry and Climate Change (A)," for background information on the API and GCC.

[67] See Exhibit 1 from "The Oil Industry and Climate Change (A)."

[68] Browne (1997).

[69] Ibid.

[70] Ibid.

establish and meet emission reduction objectives, and invest in new, more efficient products, practices and technologies."[71]

Through 1997 and 1998, BP progressively made public a multiaction plan on climate change based on increased research and development, addressing BP's own operations, and developing the solar energy business. As of 2001, BP's climate change action plan is composed of six main areas.[72] First, reducing the company's emissions. BP set an internal greenhouse gases reduction target of 10 percent from a 1990 baseline over the period to 2010. This is combined with the development and implementation, in collaboration with the NGO Environment Defense Fund (EDF), of an internal emissions trading system: the Pilot Emissions Trading System (PETS).[73] Second, the company focuses on energy conservation, through continuous improvement of its use of energy, and by encouraging customers, suppliers, and partners to conserve energy. Third, it fosters the introduction of new energy technologies by growing investment in the solar business and by collaboration to create energy-efficient new technologies. Fourth, it promotes the use of flexible market instruments, including emissions trading, joint implementation (JI) and the clean development mechanism (CDM), to demonstrate the potential of these market-based concepts to reduce greenhouse gas emissions cost effectively.[74] Fifth, it seeks active participation in the climate change policy debate, by investigating innovative ways of reducing greenhouse gas emissions, and contributing to the design of new national and international institutions and processes. Sixth, BP continues its investments in—and support of—science, technology, and policy research.

According to Klaus Kohlhase, senior environmental adviser to BP Amoco, this strategy has several drivers: (1) pressure from governments, "the Kyoto Protocol and subsequent governmental action has had a major impact on EU industry"; (2) the need to attract and retain customers in a potentially shrinking oil market in the future; (3) the willingness to enhance company's reputation, (4) the people inside the company, and finally, (5) unions, who are slowly becoming drivers, "Unions will become more and more active on the issue as it is their responsibility to represent the social side."[75]

Many insist on the leadership dimension of BP's strategic repositioning. "What is driving change in a particular situation?" asks Björn Stigson, the president of the World Business Council for Sustainable Development, before replying: "It is very fuzzy. Often it comes down to individuals and people like John Browne for instance. People don't understand how much it comes down to individuals. If you are a CEO, you have to decide; you cannot avoid it. It seems that Browne has decided for sustainable development and that so far, for BP, it has served them well."[76] Even William O'Keefe, former chairman of the Global Climate Coalition insists on the leadership aspect: "Browne has shown leadership," he says; "this is what leadership is about."[77]

Another major driver has been the growing importance of the notion of corporate social responsibility. Since the mid-90s a combination of studies and surveys has pointed to the need for multinational corporations to pay more attention to the social and environmental responsibility dimensions of their actions.[78] For the oil industry, it has combined with various public relations disasters such as, in particular, Shell's involvement in human rights issue in Nigeria, Total's involvement in Burma, or Shell's Brent Spar

[71] Pew Center on Global Climate Change (www.pewclimate.org/belc/index.cfm, February 2001).

[72] Browne (1998); BP Amoco (www.bp.com/alive/index.asp?page=/alive/performance/health_safety_and_environment_performance/issues/climate_change, February 2001).

[73] See BP Amoco (1999).

[74] See Exhibit 1, in "The Oil Industry and Climate Change (A)," for a brief description of these instruments.

[75] Interview with Klaus Kohlhase, The Hague, November 2000.

[76] Interview with Björn Stigson, Geneva, December 2000. A BP executive, Lee Edwards also refers to "a true leadership act on the part of [John Browne]," cited in Reinhardt and Richman (2000), who provide an excellent and extensive case study on BP Amoco and climate change.

[77] Interview with William O'Keefe, January 2001.

[78] See for instance the Burson Marsteller opinion leader survey: "The Responsible Century?" (summary available from www.bm.com/insights/corpresp.html), or the "Millenium Poll on Corporate Social Responsibility," conducted by Environics International Ltd. (summary available from www.environics.net/eil).

crisis.[79] BP took the issue of social responsibility seriously[80] and used it to frame its active climate change positioning. "It is important to see that our position is argued in an ethical sense, but as businesspersons. We are responsible to our shareholders, our employees, the local populations, and the environment. This constitutes an enlargement of responsibility," says Kohlhase.[81]

But some analysts temper the social responsibility issue: "I think that they [BP and Shell] are overdoing their explanation of how socially responsible they are. When you ask them if they are funding their statements with money, they are shrinking, not delivering," says Hermann Ott, acting head of the Climate Policy Division of the Wuppertal Institute for Climate, Environment and Energy.[82] While Benito Müller, senior research fellow at the Oxford Institute for Energy Studies, regards the question as one of time frame: "Why would a corporation acknowledge a social responsibility?" he asks. "Because in the long run it could be more profitable. The question is, What is the firm in for? If it is thinking short term, then there exists no good argument for social responsibility."[83]

To Ott, there is another substantial incentive: "An important question [in this debate] relates to what the product liability laws [on oil products] are going to be like 10–15 years from now. Some of the oil companies are aware of the risk. BP definitely, their strategy is a containment strategy, for image and reputation . . . maybe for more. In court, they could be acquitted because they could show early action. This is an important driver of their strategy."[84]

Some critics remain skeptical and interpret BP Amoco's strategy as a pure communication and public relations strategy, devoid of substantial and concrete commitment. Not surprisingly, many environmental NGOs point to a contradiction between BP Amoco's rhetoric and the reality of its actions. Says Kirsty Hamilton, climate campaigner with Greenpeace International: "There is a discrepancy between the discourse and actions of oil companies, in different areas. First, investments: compare an investment of $20 million per year in solar energy to over $4 billion in exploration and production expenditures in 1998. Second, advocacy: it is now considered good marketing practice to show a green face, and also good lobbying practice. And third, advertising: they advertise being green, and at the same time join [antiaction] lobby groups."[85, 86] O'Keefe underlines his understanding of the nature of BP Amoco's strategy: "Doing this move, [Browne] created an image of BP that differentiated it from his competitors, and this was good marketing. . . . But if you look at what they are doing, apart from BP's internal emissions trading scheme, there is no significant difference between what ExxonMobil and what BP Amoco are doing, in terms of money invested, research, etc."[87]

Brian Flannery of ExxonMobil, discussing the actions of some competitors, notes that some significant actions taken had little or nothing to do with climate change but were already in the pipeline for other reasons. He asks, "Is this good public relations? Is this good ethical business?"[88] Flannery also expresses doubts regarding the depth of competitors' commitment to emissions reductions: "We will be watching our competitors to see as a result of their commitments and procedures whether, on the one hand, they forgo

[79] On the Brent Spar, see Neale (1997) and Grolin (1998). Note that the two almost simultaneous crises for Shell—Nigeria and the Brent Spar—seem to have been instrumental in initiating a huge corporate reorganization process based on more transparency, corporate responsibility and later, sustainable development.

[80] BP first complemented its "Annual Report and Accounts" by environmental reports, then in 1999, by a combined environmental and social report. Finally, in 2000, it proposed a combined financial, environmental, and social report (www.bpamoco.com/alive).

[81] Interview with Klaus Kohlhase, The Hague, November 2000.

[82] Interview with Dr. Hermann Ott, The Hague, November 2000.

[83] Interview with Dr. Benito Müller, The Hague, November 2000.

[84] Interview with Dr. Hermann Ott, The Hague, November 2000.

[85] Details of sources for these figures are given in Hamilton (1998a, p. 30).

[86] Interview with Kirsty Hamilton, The Hague, November 2000. As of today, BP America is still a member of the API. However, BP has prohibited the API from using BP membership funds for anticlimate work (ICCR, 2000).

[87] Interview with William O'Keefe, January 2001.

[88] Interview with Dr. Brian Flannery, The Hague, November 2000.

an economically attractive project that would significantly increase their emissions or whether they make a large investment that is uneconomic to reduce their emissions. So far we have not seen sufficient examples of those outcomes."[89] Another reason for caution on BP Amoco's strategy is the fact that the company continued its contribution to the US political process after 1997, albeit in smaller amounts (see Exhibit 1).

Will BP Amoco deliver on its strategy and yield positive results in ecological terms? Active strategies encompass at least one built-in incentive for corporations to act on what they say. As pointed out by Müller: "They do care about their image, and this induces them to act as they say. When there are proactive companies, the role of NGOs and consumers becomes that of watch-dog elements."[90] This role is made more effective by the rapid development of information and communication technologies, which give more power to civil society through stronger connections and the possibility of by-passing governments and putting direct pressure on corporations to behave in a more socially acceptable manner.

As for the effectiveness of BP Amoco's climate change strategy in terms of business results, it is probably too early to judge, since it is a long-term positioning strategy. In particular, effects on competitiveness are hard to detect as of today. The question is, Is it losing something now? The answer is no, BP Amoco does not seem to have experienced negative impacts from its strategy. It probably costs it a bit in terms of money and efforts, but BP Amoco people do not comment on this. BP Amoco did experience positive effects in terms of image. However, this could backfire if at some point the public and stakeholders feel that the company does not live up to its promises. On another important level, BP Amoco clearly improved its legitimacy as a participant in the political process, at least in European circles, and probably worldwide. Overall, in the words of Kohlhase: "It is important to understand the importance of the process here: every year now, climate change is a topic for the board at BP Amoco. . . . We have been learning a lot, and we are improving our understanding of the options. These last two aspects put us in a good position to face the issue."[91]

Another test for BP Amoco's good faith on its active climate strategy is going to be the evolution of its position now that the Bush administration—with all its ties to the oil business—is in power in the U.S.

[89] Brian Flannery, cited in "Hardliner ExxonMobil Opposed to Kyoto Treaty," *The Earth Times*, 15 November 2000.

[90] Interview with Dr. Benito Müller, The Hague, November 2000.

[91] Interview with Klaus Kohlhase, The Hague, November 2000.

References

Agrawala, S., and Andresen, S. (1999) "Indispensability and Indefensibility? The United States in Climate Treaty Negotiations," *Global Governance* 5, pp. 457–482.

BP Amoco. (1999) "Greenhouse Gas Emissions Trading in BP Amoco," November 1999 (www.bp.com/alive_assets/downloads/100000000034161/climatechange.pdf, February 2001).

Browne, J. (1997) Speech delivered at Stanford University, California, May 19, 1997 (www.bp.com/pressoffice/, January 2001).

Browne, J. (1998) Address to the conference "Climate after Kyoto. Implications for Energy," Royal Institute for International Affairs, London, February 5–6, 1998.

Burson-Marsteller. (2000) "The Responsible Century? Summary of an International Opinion Leaders Survey on Corporate Social Responsibility" (www.bm.com/insights/corpresp.html).

Common Cause. (1999) "Some Like It Hot: As Global Temperature Rise Contributions Flow to Parties & Candidates," Common Cause Report (commoncause.org/publications/hot, February 2001).

Cool the Planet. (1999) "Summary of Activities Global Climate Coalition: 1996–1999" (cool.policy.net/proactive/newsroom/release.vtml?id=17382).

Cushman, J. (1998) "Industrial Group Plans to Fight Climate Treaty," *New York Times*, 26 April 1998.

Durgin, H. (2000) "Giant That Sees No Evil," *Financial Times*, 11 August 2000.

ExxonMobil. (2000) "Global Climate Change Op-Ed Series" (www.exxonmobil.com/news/publications/c_global_climate_change/c_oped.pdf, February 2001).

ExxonMobil. (2001) "Global Climate Change," ExxonMobil Publication (www.exxonmobil.com/news/publications/c_global_climatechange/c_index.html, February 2001).

Flannery, B. (1999), "Global Climate Change: Speeches to the European Affiliates of Exxon Corporation," *International Association for Energy Economics Newsletter,* Third Quarter, pp. 4–10.

Gelbspan, R. (1995) "The Heat Is On: The Warming of the World's Climate Sparks a Blaze of Denial," *Harper's Magazine,* September 1995.

Gelbspan, R. (1998) "Putting the Globe at Risk," *The Nation,* 30 November 1998.

Grolin, J. (1998) "Corporate Legitimacy in Risk Society: The Case of Brent Spar," *Business Strategy and the Environment,* vol. 7, pp. 213–222.

Grubb, M., Vrolijk, C., and Brack, D. (1999) *The Kyoto Protocol,* RIIA and Earthscan Publications, London.

Hamilton, K. (1998a) "The Oil Industry and Climate Change: A Greenpeace Briefing," Greenpeace International (www.greenpeace.org/~climate/industry/reports/).

Hamilton, K. (1998b) "Oiling the Machine: Fossil Fuel Dollars Funnelled into the US Political Process," Greenpeace International (www.greenpeace.org/~climate/industry/reports/machine.html).

ICCR—Interfaith Center on Corporate Responsibility. (2000) "A Brief Survey of Oil Company Responses to Global Warming" (www.campaignexxonmobil.org/learn/oilco_response_table.shtml, February 2001).

Kerr, R. (1997) "Climate Change: Greenhouse Forecasting Still Cloudy," *Science,* May 16, 1997, p. 1040.

Krause, F. (1997) "The Costs and Benefits of Cutting U.S. Carbon Emissions: A Critical Survey of Economic Arguments and Studies Used in the Media Campaigns of U.S. Status Quo Stakeholders," paper presented at the GLOBE Conference Targeting Kyoto and Beyond, Bonn, October 1997.

Neale, A. (1997) "Organisational Learning in Contested Environments: Lessons from Brent Spar," *Business Strategy and the Environment,* vol. 6, pp. 93–103.

O'Keefe, W. (1998a) "Kyoto's Mounting Costs," *The Journal of Commerce,* 6 July 1998.

O'Keefe, W. (1998b) Testimony of William F. O'Keefe, executive vice president of the American Petroleum Institute, at the House Government Reform and Oversight Subcommittee on National Economic Growth, Natural Resources and Regulatory Affairs, 16 September 1998.

Ozone Action. (1999) "Exxon's Avowed Anti-environmental Position Dominates Merger Talks," press release, 27 May 1999 (www.ozone.org/mr052799.html, February 2001).

Raeburn, P. (1997) "Global Warming: Is There Still Room for Doubt?" *BusinessWeek,* 3 November 1997.

Rampton, S., and Burton, B. (1998) "The PR Plot to Overheat the Earth," *Earth Island Journal,* spring 1998.

Reinhardt, F., and Richman, E. (2000) "Global Climate Change and BP Amoco," Harvard Business School Case 9-700-106 (www.hbsp.harvard.edu).

Seitz, F. (1996) "A Major Deception on Global Warming," *The Wall Street Journal,* 12 June 1996.

Skjaerseth, J., and Skodvin, T. (2000) "Climate Change and the Oil Industry: Common Problem, Different Strategies," paper presented at the Sixth Session of the Conference of the Parties to the Climate Convention, The Hague, 23 November, 2000.

Stevens, W. (1996) "A Hot Center of Debate on Global Warming," *The New York Times,* 6 August 1996.

TotalFinaElf (2001) "Profil Environnement," TotalFinaElf brochure.

UNFCCC—United Nations Framework Convention on Climate Change. (1992) "United Nations Framework Convention on Climate Change" (www.unfccc.de).

UNFCCC. (1997) "The Kyoto Protocol to the Convention on Climate Change" (www.unfccc.de).

Vidal, E. (2000) Pétrole et environnement: le défi vert de l'or noir, *Impact Entreprises,* no. 20, juillet–août 2000, CFIE.

Yergin, D. (1991) *The Prize. The Epic Quest for Oil, Money and Power,* Simon & Schuster.

EXHIBIT B-1 Oil and Gas Industry Contributions to U.S. Political Process

U.S. Political Donations Of Some Oil and Gas Corporations, in U.S.$

	Year				
Company	**1991/2**	**1993/4**	**1995/6**	**1997/8**	**1999/2000**
Amoco	332,200	371,400	479,866	493,000	
ARCO	1,245,706	936,154	1,232,662	743,477	(est.)957,570*
BP America	117,400†	107,450†	374,829	316,766	
Exxon	499,110	733,953	816,329	847,125	
Mobil	295,278	293,650	346,712	503,731	
Exxon + Mobil	794,388‡	1,027,603‡	1,163,041‡	1,350,856‡	1,206,305
BP + Amoco	449,600‡	478,850‡	854,695‡	809,766‡	(est.)338,344‡
BP + Amoco + ARCO					1,295,914

* Data for individual contributions were not readily available: these have been estimated by the authors, on the basis of CRP data, to be approximately $175,000.

‡ This figure, given by the CRP, includes numbers for ARCO: $957,570 ($671,275 soft-money donations and $111,295 PAC contributions, plus an estimation by the author of $175,000 in individual donations).

Source: All numbers are from the Center for Responsive Politics (www.opensecrets.org), based on data from the Federal Election Commission with the exception of those marked with a † which are from Greenpeace (1998b) and only cover PACs and soft money (see "Methodology" below). Numbers marked with a ‡ are computed from other data in the table.

Methodology[a]

The numbers are based on contributions from PACs, soft-money donors, and individuals giving $200 or more. Political action committees (PACs) are political committees organized for the purpose of raising and spending money to elect and defeat candidates. Most PACs represent business, labor, or ideological interests. In the broadest sense, *soft money* encompasses any contributions not regulated by federal election laws. The exemption was made to encourage "party-building" activities which benefit the political parties, in general, but not specific candidates. In reality, though, this has emerged as the parties' primary means of raising tens of millions of dollars from wealthy contributors during the fall presidential campaigns, when direct contributions to candidates are prohibited. They are also used to support congressional candidates in key battleground states during off-year elections.

In many cases, the organizations themselves did not donate; rather the money came from the organization's PAC, its individual members, employees, or owners, and those individuals' immediate families. Organization totals include subsidiaries and affiliates.

All numbers attributed to a particular industry can be assumed to be conservative. Tens of millions of dollars of contributions in each election cycle are not classified by industry at all—either because the original data is incomplete or too vague to categorize, or because of limitations on the Center for Responsive Politics' ability to fully research the millions of individual contributions given over the years.

As a general rule, PAC contributions are almost 100% categorized by industry; soft money in the current election cycle is more than 90% coded. In earlier cycles, the proportion is lower. Individual contributions to candidates and parties are the most difficult to classify—both because of the huge number of contributions, and because the data is based on employer/occupation data that is often incomplete. In most cycles, approximately 70% of the contributions there have been categorized, based on the occupation/employer reported by the donor.

[a] This section is a compilation from various pages on the Centre for Responsive Politics' Web site (www.opensecrets.org).

EXHIBIT B-1 Oil and Gas Industry Contributions to U.S. Political Process—Continued

Oil and Gas Industry: Long-Term Contribution Trends

Election Cycle	Rank* ($)	Total Contributions	Contributions from Individuals ($)	Contributions from PACs ($)	Soft Money Contributions ($)	Donations to Democrats ($)	Donations to Republicans ($)	% to Dems	% to Repubs
2000†	9	29,733,766	9,679,680	6,594,952	13,459,134	6,057,031	23,199,731	20%	78%
1998	7	21,677,051	6,372,834	6,542,204	8,762,013	4,864,258	16,732,696	22%	77%
1996	7	24,847,230	8,663,250	6,284,593	9,899,387	5,533,584	18,933,949	22%	76%
1994	7	16,616,090	5,956,078	6,313,539	4,346,473	6,040,075	10,564,520	36%	64%
1992	7	20,189,649	8,779,085	6,255,621	5,154,943	6,656,495	13,423,902	33%	66%
1990	8	9,046,667	3,324,994	5,721,673	0	3,621,114	5,424,153	40%	60%
Total	**7**	**122,110,453**	**42,775,921**	**37,712,582**	**41,621,950**	**32,772,557**	**88,278,951**	**27%**	**72%**

* These numbers show how the industry ranks in total campaign giving as compared to more than 80 other industries. Rankings are shown only for industries (such as the automotive industry)—not for widely encompassing "sectors" (such as transportation) or more detailed "categories" (like car dealers).

† So far. Availability of electronic records by the Federal Election Commission is typically two months delayed during the busy election season, since most campaigns still file their reports on paper rather than by computer.

Methodology

The numbers in this table are based on contributions to federal candidates and political parties from PACs, soft-money donors, and individuals giving U.S.$200 or more, as reported to the Federal Election Commission. While election cycles are shown in charts as 1996, 1998, 2000, etc., they actually represent two-year periods. For example, the 2000 election cycle runs from January 1, 1999, to December 31, 2000. Data for the last election cycle were released by the Federal Election Commission on Tuesday, January 2, 2001. Soft-money contributions were not publicly disclosed until the 1991–92 election cycle.

Monsanto and Genetically Modified Organisms

In 1997, Monsanto CEO Robert B. Shapiro laid out, in an interview published by the *Harvard Business Review*, an ambitious vision in which innovation and corporate responsibility blended harmoniously to create shareholder and customer value in an environmentally sustainable way. "The market," he explained, "is going to want sustainable systems, and if Monsanto provides them, we will do quite well for ourselves and our shareowners. Sustainable development is going to be one of the organizing principles around which Monsanto and a lot of other institutions will probably define themselves in the years to come."[1] Shapiro saw the application of biotechnology to agriculture as part of a broader technological revolution in which information, whether coded in DNA or in computer chips, would greatly reduce our reliance on material inputs, in particular nonrenewable ones. His ideas, which, for some, set him apart as one of a few visionary CEOs, created tremendous excitement in and outside of the company.

Yet, only two years later, everything seemed to be falling apart for the company and its CEO. In Europe, a virulent anti-GMO campaign was raging, run by an odd coalition of consumers, environmentalists, and farmers; and of all the companies that were active in agricultural biotechnology, Monsanto was particularly vilified. On the policy front, a major transatlantic trade conflict was looming, as the EU's restrictive regulatory regime for GMOs was effectively shutting American exporters out of the European market. This combination of bad-mouthing and trade restrictions damaged Monsanto so much that, with its stock market capitalization down by a third and sitting over valuable intellectual property, the company was becoming, by 1999, an attractive takeover target. Had Monsanto failed to take heed of European cultural sensitivities? Had it fallen victim to a broad conspiracy aimed at keeping U.S.-made biotechnology products out of the EU market? Had it simply stuck its neck out too visibly in an environment that was turning increasingly hostile to large, American-based multinational companies?

The Life Science Company Concept

When molecular biology labs ignited the "biotech revolution" in the mid-1980s, the industry was ready to seize the opportunity. Plagued with cyclical sales, intense price competition, low growth, and mounting environmental challenges, the chemical industry's giants were on the lookout for new value-creating strategies. The news from R&D labs triggered a gold rush, with key players redeploying assets through an unprecedented wave of divestitures, mergers, and integration. Du Pont sold Conoco, its oil subsidiary, which used to bring in half of its $45 billion annual revenue; Novartis sold its processed food subsidiaries, Wasa bread and Biscottes Roland, while Monsanto got rid of Nutrasweet—producer of aspartame—and Canderel. The spinoffs generated some of the cash that was to be invested in biotechnologies. But the required R&D investments were so large that, in addition, midsize European players like Rhône-Poulenc or Hoechst had to merge

This case was written by Sara McDonald, Assistant, under the supervision of Olivier Cadot, Professor of Economics and International Business at the University of Lausanne and Senior Research Fellow at INSEAD; H. Landis Gabel, Otto Fellow of Environmental Recourse Management, and Daniel Traça, Assistant Professor of Economics, both at INSEAD. It is intended to be used as a basis for class discussion rather than to illustrate either effective or ineffective handling of an administrative situation.

[1] Joan Magretta, "Growth through Global Sustainability: An Interview with Monsanto's CEO, Robert B. Shapiro," *Harvard Business Review*, January–February 1997, p. 84.

(together, Rhône-Poulenc and Hoechst formed Aventis, a finely balanced Franco-German company with headquarters strategically located in Strasbourg). If the R&D effort was considerable, the rewards were commensurate, and numerous synergies were expected between the health and agricultural applications of molecular biology if managed as an interconnected system. With a strong presence in both health and agrochemicals, Monsanto was well placed to leverage those synergies. Its pharmaceutical subsidiary Searle had been particularly successful in recent years with its 1998 launch of a series of new drugs for arthritis treatment, one of which was second only to Pfizer's celebrated Viagra in terms of total prescriptions (Viagra was not for arthritis).[2]

In addition to horizontal mergers, forward and backward integration was taking place along new lines. The most aggressive forward-integration strategy was pursued by Monsanto, which, under Shapiro's leadership, took over DeKalb (a seed producer), the international operations of Cargill (a seed trader), and a number of other companies[3] for a total bill approaching $8 billion.[4] According to Shapiro's vision, a "life sciences company" could benefit from synergies between some of its traditional crop-protection activities, herbicides and pesticides, and the new genetically engineered products (see Exhibit 1). Among Monsanto's most valuable products was its best-seller herbicide Roundup, whose patent in the U.S., the last country where it was protected, was to expire in 2000. The company expected tough price competition after the patent's expiration; in the worst case, Roundup's U.S. price could creep down to the low levels at which it was sold in Asia, a fraction of its current U.S. price. Thus it was clear to Monsanto management that growth in Roundup revenues, if any, would have to come from increased volumes rather than prices.[5] How could this be achieved? This was where genetically engineered seeds could play a role. Roundup was a broad-spectrum herbicide, which could be sprayed only before sowing, since it would otherwise kill the crop itself. Seeds modified to be resistant to Roundup could allow farmers to spray Roundup not only before sowing but also after. Thus, a marketing strategy involving joint sales of Roundup-resistant seeds (so-called Roundup-Ready), priced at a relatively high level in order to recoup the investment in R&D, and Roundup, priced relatively low so as to undercut the competition, could extend the useful life of the herbicide well beyond its patent's expiration.

One problem with this strategy was that many farmers traditionally "brown-bagged" seeds, that is, saved them for replanting the following year or for sale to other farmers. Monsanto's pricing policy, which would encourage them to do so, could become self-defeating, unless seeds could be genetically engineered so as not to be reusable. As it turned out, the U.S. Department of Agriculture (USDA) had for several years supported private and university research on genetic seed sterilization techniques aimed at reducing the risk of unwanted escape into the environment,[6] and in March 1998, a U.S. company, Delta and Pine Land, won a series of joint patents with the Agricultural Research Service on one such technique. The technique, officially named Technology Protection System but better known under the nickname "Terminator,"[7] could be what Monsanto needed. Although the company's senior management was not entirely convinced of the viability of this particular technology,[8] plans were made to acquire Delta and Pine Land.

Cultural Revolution at Monsanto

Under CEO Shapiro, Monsanto did not just refocus; it went through a cultural revolution. Shortly after taking over in 1995, Shapiro

[2] Monsanto, "Delivering on the Life Sciences Strategy," Annual Report 1998, pp. 1, 8.

[3] Pierre-Benoit Joly and Stéphane Lemarié, "Industry Consolidation, Public Attitude and the Future of Plant Biotechnology in Europe," *Agbioforum* 1, 1998, pp. 1–2.

[4] Richard Ernsberger Jr et al., "High-Tech Harvests," *Newsweek*, July 13, 1998, p. 42.

[5] "Monsanto Company: The Coming of Age of Biotechnology," HBS case 9-596-034, 1996.

[6] Rick Weiss, "Gene Police Raise Farmers' Fears," *The Washington Post*, February 3, 1999.

[7] "Terminator" was a nickname successfully tagged on the sterilization gene by Rural Advancement Fund International, a Canadian NGO campaigning against GMOs.

[8] Robert Shapiro, speech delivered at the conference on "Trade and the Environment: Conflict or Compatibility?" INSEAD, June 2000.

convened 500 of the company's employees from around the world to a "Global Forum" addressing five themes: strategies for achieving aggressive growth and for becoming truly global; operational excellence; encouraging entrepreneurship within the corporation; and sustainable development.[9] Sporting a sweater-vest decorated with little quilted cats,[10] he laid out his vision of the company—flexible, forward-looking, and environmentally responsible.[11] Once heavily hierarchical, the new company was to emphasize "openness, innovation, and initiative and the ability to act quickly and decisively,"[12] and this would be achieved through a sweeping reorganization of the firm into a flatter and leaner structure.

Shapiro's speech at the Global Forum riveted the crowd, and at a dinner in Chicago's Field Museum that evening, one enamoured employee even hung her name tag around his neck.[13] Encouraging open debate and insisting on employees calling him Bob, his relaxed style stood in stark contrast to the company's traditional ways. Together with his bold vision (which was also remote from anything the company had been familiar with) his new leadership style won him the unconditional loyalty of a group of people, sarcastically referred to by others as "Friends of Bob." Outsiders, who charged that there were few voices in his inner circle providing a reality check, dismissed Shapiro's style as "New Age management." But he viewed it simply as a way of "setting the metronome at a higher speed to compete."[14]

Monsanto's corporate-culture revolution was not limited to style, and had in fact started before Shapiro was appointed CEO. As early as 1990, Monsanto had become the first *Fortune* 500 company to publish a full-fledged annual environment report, and in 1994 it had started to seek the advice of environmental thinkers like Amory Lovins or Herman Daly. The "company enviros love to hate," which once produced such poisonous products as PCBs or Agent Orange, a defoliant used massively during the Vietnam War and containing dioxin, was now at the forefront of Business for Social Responsibility (BSR), a San Francisco–based progressive industry association. Monsanto's corporate communication was in line with its new culture. The company's new motto, "Food, Health, and Hope," conveyed the message that biotechnologies held the promise of better health and improved nutrition for the 850 million malnourished people in the developing world.

By 1998, Monsanto's strategy was a resounding success. Reductions in Roundup's price led to tremendous sales increases because of the high elasticity of demand: in Canada, a 33% price cut over a six-year period (1992–98) led to a 287% sales increase; in Brazil and Argentina, price cuts between 50% and 60% led, respectively, to 647% and 28-fold sales increases. An augmentation in herbicide use, together with "conservation" (i.e., reduced) tillage, was touted by the company to reduce soil erosion and CO_2 emissions, thus benefiting the environment. Of the 28 million hectares of genetically modified crops planted worldwide, Monsanto varieties accounted for over 70%.[15]

Once a stodgy chemicals producer, in 1995 Monsanto repositioned itself with investors as a biotech stock. The markets' reaction was enthusiastic, with the company's total capitalization soaring to $38 billion in 1998 from under $10 billion in 1994, well ahead not only of the S&P 500 (see Exhibit 2) but also of direct competitors.

GMOs: The Health and Environmental Issues

But not everyone shared in Bob Shapiro's vision. In the U.K., widespread distrust of official science after the mad-cow disease epidemic made consumer confidence particularly vulnerable to health alarms. In 1998, Dr. Arpad Pusztai, a researcher at the Rowett Institute in Aberdeen,

[9] Carl Frankel, "Monsanto Breaks the Mold," *Tomorrow*, May–June 1999.

[10] Scott Kilman and Thomas Burton, "Farm and Pharma: Monsanto Boss's Vision 'Life Sciences' Firm Now Confronts Reality;" *The Wall Street Journal Europe*, December 21,1999.

[11] Joan Magretta, "Growth through Global Sustainability: An Interview with Monsanto's CEO, Robert B. Shapiro," *Harvard Business Review*, January–February 1997.

[12] Monsanto, ibid., p. 1.

[13] Scott Kilman and Thomas Burton, ibid.

[14] David Barboza, "At Monsanto, Can Openness Last? Casual Style Could Become a Casualty of Talks with Du Pont," *International Herald Tribune*, May 4, 1999, p. 1.

[15] Robert Service, "Chemical Industry Rushes toward Greener Pastures," *Science* 282, October 23, 1998, p. 608.

triggered a bitter controversy by claiming that rats who were fed genetically modified potatoes suffered, after 10 days of the diet, lower levels of lymphocytes and degraded intestine walls compared to a control group. A few days after Pusztai disclosed the results of his study on British TV, the Rowett Institute suspended him, declaring that "[t]he institute regrets the release of misleading information about issues of such importance to the public and the scientific community." As justification for dismissing Dr. Pusztai, the institute stated that publicizing controversial results, especially in such a sensitive area, before submitting them to peer review violated a basic rule of academic conduct. A two-page note in which Pusztai and a co-author described the experiment was published in October 1999 by *The Lancet*[16] after being reviewed by six referees, but with a warning from the journal's editor that publication was not to be construed as giving a seal of approval to the authors' results. Other scientists were highly critical, with the Royal Society declaring the study "flawed in many aspects of design, execution and analysis," and adding that "no conclusions should be drawn" from it.

Other health hazards were widely mentioned in the press. The use of antibiotic-resistance marker genes in genetic manipulations was feared to induce the development of antibiotic-resistant bacteria, which could reduce the effectiveness of antibiotics in therapeutic uses against various infections. According to some scientists, these concerns were off the mark, as modern techniques allowed the separation of DNA containing the gene of interest (e.g., the one coding a protein toxic for pests) from DNA containing the antibiotic-resistant gene. Transgenic plants currently on the market were the offspring of plants that had been produced using an old technique which did not allow for such separation. But the problem, if indeed there was one, could be rapidly overcome. Moreover, they pointed out that a large proportion of the bacteria present in human digestive tracts was already resistant to the antibiotics in question and to a host of other ones, for that matter.[17]

Even as the evidence that GMOs represented a direct hazard to human health remained inconclusive, controversy erupted over their environmental effects. In what was perhaps the most publicized issue, the monarch butterfly, to which many Americans are sentimentally attached, was said to be at risk from exposure to genetically modified crops. In a Cornell University study published in *Nature*,[18] monarch larvae were fed milkweed leaves sprayed with transgenic (bt) corn pollen. The larvae were found to develop more slowly and had a significantly higher mortality rate than a control group: after only four days, 44% of those exposed to transgenic pollen had died, against none in the control group. Seizing on the issue, Greenpeace activists staged colorful demonstrations with protesters dressed like butterflies. Some scientists, however, expressed doubts on the severity of the problem, questioning whether corn pollen travels in sufficient quantities to accumulate substantially on milkweed, which grows on field edges. Some also said that, contrary to the paper's assertion that "corn fields shed pollen for 8–10 days between late June and mid-August, which is during the time when Monarch larvae are feeding" (p. 214), the periods in fact do not really coincide.[19] European scientists added that, out of three transgenic corn varieties authorized in Europe in 1999, only one had the bt toxin present in its pollen; thus, if the monarch issue was really a serious one, simply banning the variety in question would take care of the problem. Finally, nobody seemed to notice that some of the insecticides sprayed on corn in conventional agriculture were also toxic to butterflies.

In spite of scientific doubt, the campaign against GMOs went on unabated—at times run by organizations that were simultaneously stressing the importance of scientific evidence in the global warming debate. Private citizens began

[16] W. B. Ewen and A. Pusztai, "Effect of Diets Containing Genetically Modified Potatoes Expressing Galanthus Nivalis Lectin on Rat Small Intestine," *The Lancet* 354, October 16, 1999, pp. 1353–54.

[17] See Francine Casse, "Le mais et la résistance aux antibiotiques," *La Recherche* 327, Janvier 2000, pp. 35–39.

[18] J. E. Losey, L. S. Rayor, and M. E. Carter, "Transgenic Pollen Harms Monarch Larvae," *Nature* 399, 1999, pp. 214–215.

[19] Andrew Chesson and Philip James, "Les aliments avec OGM sont-ils sans danger?" *La Recherche* 327, Janvier 2000, pp. 27–35.

taking legal action against biotech companies and regulatory bodies in several countries, and experimental GM crops were uprooted by angry demonstrators in Germany, the Netherlands, Ireland, and France. In the U.K., shipments of genetically modified products from the U.S. in fall 1997 provoked an outcry that Sir John Gummer, U.K. Minister of Agriculture, tried to control by issuing bland statements, such as "[t]here is no reason to believe that genetic modification of maize will give rise to adverse effects on human health from its use in human food." Of course, the fact that he had earlier given similar reassurances regarding mad cow disease did little to enhance his credibility.[20] Monsanto itself attempted to stem the tide of hostility with an ad campaign featuring environmental-friendly slogans like "we believe food should be grown with less pesticides" or "worrying about starving future generations won't feed them. Food biotechnology will." The campaign posters listed phone numbers or Web addresses of anti-GMO associations, as a way of conveying the company's readiness for dialogue. The effort proved fruitless; perhaps even counterproductive, some argued, because by raising Monsanto's profile, the campaign was making a target of the company. Surfing on public anxieties whipped up by alarmist tabloid reports and by Prince Charles's crusade against GMOs, in 1998–99 British supermarket chains, starting with Iceland, all adopted "GMO-free" slogans. In March 1999, Sainsbury's, Marks&Spencer, Carrefour, and Superquinn set up a consortium to buy jointly non-GM foods. In the end, while the U.K. had been considered by biotech companies, for a variety of reasons, to be a potentially friendly market for GMOs, it became clear that the "battle of the aisles" had been fought and lost in British supermarkets.[21]

EU Resistance

Biotechnologies encountered difficulties on other fronts as well, as European governments and the EU Commission appeared to multiply hurdles to the import of U.S.-made transgenic products. The EU's regulatory regime was based on two pieces of legislation: Directive 90/220 concerning the release of genetically modified organisms, adopted by the European Council in April 1990, which covered essentially genetically modified crops and their environmental risks, and Regulation 258/97 concerning novel foods, adopted in January 1997, which concerned essentially foodstuffs containing GMOs and their risks for food safety. The "90/220" process was a complicated mixture of subsidiarity[22] and centralized decision making. Producers or importers of GMOs like GM seeds were required to notify the regulatory authority of the relevant member state (Article 11), which could either withhold approval or issue a favorable opinion. In the latter case, other member states would be allowed to raise objections (Article 13); if none objected, the file would come back to the original member state for final "written consent." In case of objections, member-state regulatory authorities would try to reach a consensus; failing to do so, the commission would take over and conduct a scientific review at the end of which a committee of member-state representatives would rule at the qualified (two-thirds) majority. If no qualified majority emerged, the commission itself would draft a decision and submit it to the European Council. If the council failed to reach a decision (again at the qualified majority), the final word would go back to the commission (Article 21), and, if positive, the file would return to the original member state for official approval.[23] Then, according to the mutual recognition principle, the product could be marketed in all member states, including those that had objected. Regulation 258/97 set up a fairly similar procedures for foodstuffs, but in contrast with the original version of Directive 90/220 it also

[20] David Levy, "Oceans Apart? Comparing Business Responses to the Environment in Europe and North America," mimeo, 2000.

[21] Vivian Moses, "GM Foods: What Went Wrong," *Wall Street Journal Europe*, March 15, 2000.

[22] *Subsidiarity* is a Euro-jargon term meaning that the European Commission should be involved only in matters in which it has a clear comparative advantage over member states, i.e., basically, in matters involving cross-border externalities.

[23] The summary description is taken from Sebastian Princen, "Genetically Modified Foods and Food Products," mimeo, September 2000. See also *EC Council Directive 90/220/EEC of 23 April 1990 on the Deliberate Release into the Environment of Genetically Modified Organisms*, OJ L 117, 8 May 1990, pp. 15–27.

contained a labeling requirement (a labeling requirement was also appended to 90/220 in 1997).

Notwithstanding its complication, the EU's regulatory process relied on principles and methods of scientific risk assessment that were not fundamentally different from those used in the U.S. by the Department of Agriculture, the EPA, and the FDA.[24] However the philosophy of the European and American regulatory regimes differed in a key way. The latter were based on the premise that GMOs were not fundamentally different *products* from conventional seeds and foodstuffs and, as such, did not require a separate regulatory regime. The former, by contrast, held that GMOs were different from other agrifood products because, although their physical attributes might be similar, they were produced by different production processes, and as such required specific regulation. Thus, U.S. and EU regulations were based on different premises. Philosophical differences in the regulatory processes were probably not the most important source of friction. In 1999, the assistant USTR also charged that:

> In practice, the 90/220 process has proven to be susceptible to political interference, non-transparent and virtually endless in duration. Scientific reviews that take months in the US are measured in years under 90/220. Member states have increasingly acted outside of the 90/220 procedures, most recently just last month when the original sponsoring member state for two GMO varieties of cotton failed to vote in favor of final EU approval because of concerns outside the 90/220 process.[25]

In February 1998, with only 18 products approved since 1991, the EU had proposed to amend its 1990 directive to make the approval process speedier and more transparent; however, there was little improvement in the eyes of American exporters. The new system, adopted by the European Parliament in April 2000,[26] was seen to be as unpredictable and arbitrary, if not more so, than the old one. As one American grain exporter put it, "[w]e are being asked to jump from the Empire State Building and check mid-way if the parachute is opening."

As if the EU's procedures weren't slow enough, some member countries were raising additional barriers. In 1998, France blocked the import of GM maize varieties that had been cleared by the EU Commission. The following year, Austria and Luxembourg also banned a Brussels-approved product. France was targeted by a commission procedure; however, Austria's and Luxembourg's action, coming at a time where the commission was weakened by a corruption scandal, went unchallenged. U.S. Agriculture Undersecretary Schumacher Jr. complained that the Europeans' bureaucratic delays cost the U.S. $200 million in 1998 alone.[27] In 1999, political pressure heightened to a point where the commission found itself unable to clear any new genetically engineered product and, on June 26, suspended all new GMO approval procedures.[28]

Even some Europeans recognized that "European Union rules for approving genetically modified products are absurdly cumbersome and, in some cases, offend basic rules of democracy."[29] But from the U.S. standpoint, these rules were not only absurd: they also violated international law. Product-approval rules and labeling requirements were covered by two key WTO agreements, namely one on Technical Barriers to Trade (TBT) and one on Sanitary and Phytosanitary Standards (SPS) (see Exhibit 3). These agreements were meant to ensure that product standards were not used as hidden barriers to trade. If there was little doubt in the U.S. that EU rules violated the spirit if not the letter of these agreements, whether consultations or even an official complaint at the WTO would solve the matter within a reasonable time frame was another question. The record of EU compliance with the decisions of GATT and WTO panels in another key dispute, on bananas, did not make Americans overly optimistic in this matter. Moreover, public sentiment on the issue ran so strong in Europe that a U.S. victory at the

[24] Princen, op. cit, p. 20.

[25] Statement by James Murphy, assistant U.S. trade representative for agricultural affairs before the U.S. House Agriculture Committee, Subcommittee on Risk Management, Research and Specialty Crops (www.useu.be/archive/biotech34.html).

[26] See details at www.europarl.eu.int or www.europa.eu.int/eur-lex.

[27] *Newsweek*, July 13, 1998.

[28] *Sept Jours Europe* 7, April 25, 2000, supplement, p. 1.

[29] *Financial Times*, June 13, 1999.

WTO would run the risk of undermining the WTO itself.

Charges that the EU was deliberately using technical regulations to restrict access to its market would make sense if the EU was lagging in biotechnology and could consequently be suspected of resorting to "infant-industry" protection. After all, infant-industry protection, albeit in a different form (loans and subsidies rather than restrictions on market access) had paid off in other areas such as civil aeronautics,[30] where Europe had also been trailing the U.S. As heavy-handed industrial policy *á la* Airbus was increasingly difficult to reconcile with WTO rules, the EU could be expected to use instead indirect ways of favoring domestic producers at the expense of foreign ones, such as imposing discriminatory health regulations.

Europe's Competitive Position

Did Europe have a competitiveness problem? The EU's performance in high-tech sectors had been lackluster in the past two decades, but pharmaceuticals had been one of the few remaining strongholds—that is, until the biotech revolution hit the industry. A 1997 study commissioned by the industry association, Europabio,[31] suggested that in the new and growing biotech sector, Europe suffered from a growing competitiveness gap relative to the U.S. Exhibit 4 shows rough indicators of the size of the "specialist biotechnology" sector (typically small R&D-intensive firms, with a few larger ones such as Chiron, Amgen, Genentech, or Genzyme) in Europe and the U.S. In the agricultural biotech sector, the gap between Europe and the U.S. was striking when considering indicators such as the number of field trials (67% in the U.S., against 22% in Europe) or areas planted with genetically modified crops (3.5 million acres, against virtually zero in Europe). This could be argued to be the consequence, rather than the cause, of stringent regulations; however, the same gap appeared in the drug sector, where public hostility was not an issue. For instance, 70% of the gene therapy drugs that were developed in 1995 were American, whereas only 22% were European. Patenting activity showed similar trends: between 1981 and 1995, 40% of the human DNA sequence patents were granted to American firms, against 24% to European firms. A count of the automated DNA sequencers in current use showed that 60% of them were located in North America, versus only 25% in Europe.

In sum, it was hard to escape the conclusion that Europe was off to a slow start in biotechnology, pretty much as it had been slow to embark on the information-technology revolution. Having a clear first-mover advantage in the industry, and suffering a severe trade deficit in other sectors, the U.S. was accordingly keen to press ahead and prevent the erection of barriers to its exports. In the words of a Department of Agriculture official,

> U.S. multinational companies are among the leading developers of genetically modified crop varieties—especially export crops such as corn, soybeans, and cotton—and U.S. producers of these crops are adopting this new technology at a rapid rate. The acceptance of GMOs in the world market is critical for the future prosperity of U.S. producers of corn, soybeans, and cotton, and for the companies that provide the technology, because of these crops' dependence on exports.[32]

The Labeling Controversy

Cumbersome product-approval regulations weren't the only U.S. concern. Labeling requirements were spreading quickly around the world, in particular in Japan, Australia, New Zealand, and the EU, where they were part of the new version of 90/220. The U.S. government deemed these labeling requirements discriminatory and detrimental to the interests of U.S. exporters:

> We are . . . very concerned, as are many U.S. exporters, about EU regulations adopted this past September which require the labeling of foods containing GMO corn or soybeans. These regulations focus on how a food was produced rather than on whether the use of biotechnology has changed its quality, safety or nutritional composition.
>
> The costs to producers and consumers of labeling regulations that are confusing, based on

[30] "Reinventing Airbus", INSEAD case [ref.], 1999.

[31] "Benchmarking the Competitiveness of Biotechnology in Europe," Europabio, June 1997.

[32] USDA (www.usda.gov/biotechnology/research).

> questionable science, impractical, and time consuming will be immense as will be the potential for ongoing trade disputes and disruption. Again, we have communicated our position clearly and directly to EU officials and also within the WTO, where we have presented detailed written comments to the Committee on Technical Barriers to Trade.[33]

A former FDA official and adviser to the U.S. delegation to the Codex Alimentarius Commission, another international body, was even less friendly to the labeling schemes, writing that:

> Among the most egregious [requirements] is something called "traceability," an array of technical, labeling and record-keeping mechanisms to keep track of a plant "from dirt to dinner plate," so that consumers will know whom to sue if they get diarrhoea from GM prunes. . . . The prospect of unscientific, overly burdensome Codex standards for GM foods is ominous, because members of the WTO will, in principle, be required to follow them, and they will provide cover for unfair trade practices.[34]

The Japanese labeling scheme had officially nothing to do with safety, as the Japanese government was a supporter of GMOs, but was only "a matter of giving consumers choice. That is how it should be seen."[35] But as a lobbyist for a major soybean processor put it, "once you get a mandatory labeling scheme in place, it will be damn hard to make a positive claim about your product."

Meanwhile, the Europeans claimed good faith and rejected all accusations of red tape and hidden trade barriers. Instead, they argued, their procedures simply reflected the "precautionary principle" according to which a product should be cleared for public use only after all doubts about its safety for human health and the environment have been dispelled.

In contrast with this cautious approach, the Europeans claimed, the U.S. was trying to ram through potentially hazardous products without adequately consulting or even informing consumers. A somewhat cavalier American attitude was illustrated by U.S. obstructionism in international negotiations aimed at drafting a biosafety protocol to regulate the movement of living modified organisms (LMOs) having the potential to harm biodiversity. After failing to ratify the Rio Convention and consequently losing its voting right in the Biosafety Convention, the U.S. nevertheless used its observer status to lead a small group of countries opposing any agreement, the so-called Miami group. It was only in January 2000 that, feeling increasingly isolated,[36] the U.S. administration dropped its opposition to an agreement officially recognizing the "precautionary principle" and giving the host country the power to restrict the import of LMOs.

The labeling issue also illustrated, from the European point of view, the lack of respect that the U.S. administration and producers of GMOs had for the consumers' rights to know what they were eating. In fact, as labeling schemes spread worldwide in spite of U.S. discontent, Agriculture Secretary Dan Glickman recognized that "[a]t the end of the day, many observers, including me, believe that some type of informational labeling is likely to happen."[37]

Monsanto in the Eye of the Storm

While U.S. official efforts to promote the biotech industry abroad were losing steam, other clouds were appearing in the industry's sky. In July 1999, a study released by the USDA suggested that the effectiveness of GM crops in raising yields, a key argument for the promoters of GMOs, wasn't quite as impressive as initially claimed. Beyond the obvious fact that "expected benefits appear to have outweighed expected costs, as evidenced by the rapid adoption rates," the study found that yield increases attributable to the use of herbicide-resistant crops were, for many varieties, "statistically insignificant." Only in the case of pest-resistant crops (so-called bt cotton and bt corn) did the study find statistically significant

[33] James Murphy Jr, assistant USTR for agricultural affairs, Speech to the House Agriculture Committee, March 4, 1999.

[34] Henry Miller, "Anti-biotech Sentiment Has Its Own Risks," Science Viewpoint, *Financial Times*, March 22, 2000.

[35] Michiyo Nakamoto, "Japan's Food Labels Decision May Fuel Trade Friction," *Financial Times*, September 6, 1999, p. 10.

[36] "Talks on Modified Food Put US on Defensive", no byline, *International Herald Tribune*, January 25, 2000.

[37] Kurt Kleiner, "Soft Words, Big Sticks," *The New Scientist*, July 24, 1999, p. 12.

increases in yields, at least in areas with high infestations levels.[38]

By 1999, mounting doubts over the marketability of GM crops led traders to offer a premium for non-GM crops.[39] As a result of this, after several years of explosive growth the total U.S. crop area planted with GM seeds was expected to decline in 2000.[40] In a further blow to its corporate strategy, Monsanto's plan to buy Delta and Pine Land ran into difficulties with the U.S. Department of Justice. In October 1999, bowing to intense public and media pressure, Shapiro announced in an open letter to the Rockefeller Foundation that Monsanto was renouncing the use of Delta and Pine Land's "Terminator" (seed sterility) technology.

Partly as a result of the difficulties and contradictions met by Monsanto in developing its "life science company" model, by 1999 it found itself embroiled in a web of lawsuits. Some of these had the potential to seriously affect its bottom line, like Delta and Pine Land's action for $1 billion after the failed takeover.[41] Some others, initiated by the company itself, contributed to its public relations disaster. In order to protect its intellectual property, and having officially renounced the use of seed-sterility technology, Monsanto had to deter farmers from brown-bagging GM seeds, which unfortunately involved suing some of them. In the U.S., the company opened more than 475 seed piracy cases, generated from over 1,800 leads. According to Monsanto's Kate Marshall, more then 250 of these cases were under active investigation by five full-time and a number of part-time investigators, and by Pinkerton, a private detective firm.[42] However the lawsuits could go both ways. In 1999, a shipment of U.S. corn that was certified organic was found by a European importer to contain GMOs, and the contamination was attributed to cross-pollinization on a Texas farm.[43] This type of incident could lead to countless lawsuits against farmers using GM seeds. In anticipation of such lawsuits, a bill was introduced in 1999 in the Nebraska state legislature making GM seed companies liable for damages awarded against farmers in cross-pollinization cases.[44] How far could the liabilities go? As if all this wasn't enough, in late 1999 a number of NGOs and farmers organizations launched a multicountry antitrust lawsuit against Monsanto. The action was not considered likely to be successful; however, it reflected growing unease with the potential abuse of dominant positions by the huge life-sciences companies in their relations with farmers.

All this was taking its toll on Monsanto's stock market performance. With a capitalization down to $22 billion, and with the drug Celebrex alone estimated by analysts to be worth at least $23 billion, the group's agri-biotech activities were valued by markets at less than zero.[45] Indeed, as if their agri-biotech activities were becoming a liability, competitors were busy spinning them off and focusing on the less controversial pharmaceuticals business. Finally, in fall 1999, Monsanto announced a "merger of equals" with Pharmacia & Upjohn, after which Robert Shapiro would become nonexecutive chairman. The adventure looked all but over.

In his 1998 letter to shareowners, Shapiro had conceded that "[changes] happened at a fast pace. Could we have stretched the process over a few more years? Certainly, that would have been attractive from many standpoints. It would have reduced the strains on our balance sheet and our people. It would have reduced the likelihood of making mistakes, both in reaching decisions and in implementing them. And it would have given our shareowners more time to understand the changes that were happening and the reasons for those changes." Shareowners and employees were probably not the only ones who could have done with a little more time to understand what the new Monsanto was up to. Kate Fish, the

[38] Agra Europe, July 9, 1999, EP/6.

[39] "GMOs: Thanks but No Thanks," Deutsche Banc Alex Brown, 1999.

[40] Scott Kilman, "US Becomes Increasingly Wary of Genetically Modified Crops," *Wall Street Journal Europe*, April 3, 2000.

[41] Shereen El Feki, "Agriculture and Technology: A Survey," *The Economist*, March 25, 2000, p. 5.

[42] Ariane Kissam, "Fact Sheet on Genetic Engineering" in *Agriculture Farmers' Declaration on Genetic Engineering in Agriculture*, National Family Farm Coalition, Washington, D.C. (www.inmotionmagazine.com/geff6.html).

[43] Megan Ladage, "The Front Line for Biotech," *Grocery Headquarter* 5, May 1999, p. 45.

[44] David Stipp, "Is Monsanto's Biotech Worth Less than a Hill of Beans?" *Fortune*, February 21, 2000, p. 21.

[45] David Stipp, op. cit., p. 80.

company's director of public policy, admitted a few months later that "[w]e're beginning to recognize that a global company can't afford to ignore the long-term downstream consequences of its actions."[46] But then, quoting Shapiro again, "Whether we've been too aggressive or not aggressive enough, . . . whether we've bitten off more than we can chew or been too timid—these questions always arise for companies that choose to lead in fast changing markets."[47]

[46] Carl Frankel, op. cit., p. 63.

[47] Robert Shapiro, "Delivering on the Life Sciences Strategy," letter to shareowners, Monsanto, Annual Report 1998, p. 4.

Questions

- What were the Europeans' key concerns with regard to GMOs? What answers did Monsanto have to offer to alleviate these concerns?
- Why did the anti-GMO campaign focus on Monsanto? Did the company have an image problem? Was the integrated "life science company" concept flawed?
- Did the EU deny market access to U.S. companies for strategic reasons? Without prejudging of an eventual panel ruling on the matter, do you feel that EU restrictions on the commercialization of GMOs were broadly compatible with WTO rules as shown in Exhibit 3? Would you advise the U.S. government to lodge a formal complaint at the WTO?

EXHIBIT 1 The Life Sciences Company Concept

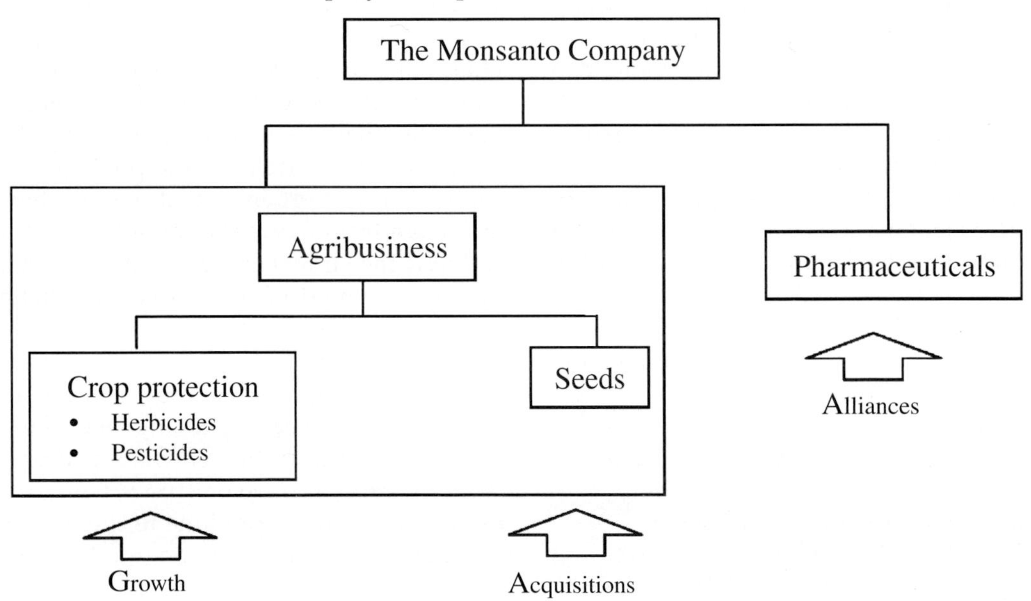

EXHIBIT 2 **Monsanto's Stock Market Valuation**

Source: Datastream.

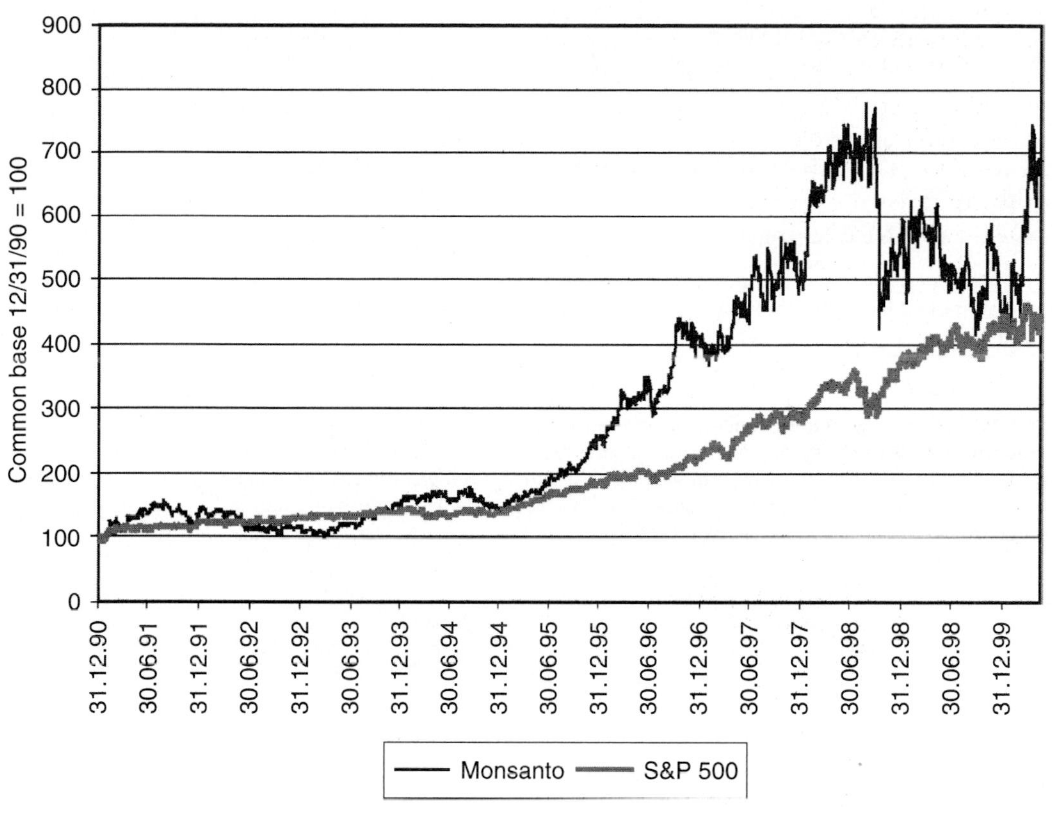

EXHIBIT 3

WTO Agreement on Technical Barriers To Trade, Article 2.2

"Parties shall ensure that technical regulations and standards are not prepared, adopted or applied with a view to or with the effect of creating obstacles to international trade. For this purpose, technical regulations shall not be more trade-restrictive than necessary to fulfil a legitimate objective, taking account of the risks non-fulfillment would create. Such legitimate objectives are, inter alia: national security requirements; the prevention of deceptive practices; protection of human health or safety, animal or plant life or health, or the environment. In assessing such risks, relevant elements of consideration are, inter alia: available scientific and technical information, related processing technology or intended end-uses of products."

WTO Agreement on Sanitary and Phytosanitary Measures, Article 2.2

"Members shall ensure that any sanitary or phytosanitary measure is applied only to the extent necessary to protect human, animal or plant life or health, is based on scientific principles and is not maintained without sufficient evidence, except as provided for in paragraph 7 of Article 5."

Article 5.7

"In cases where relevant scientific evidence is insufficient, a Member may provisionally adopt sanitary or phytosanitary measures on the basis of available pertinent information, including that from the relevant international organizations as well as from sanitary or phytosanitary measures applied by other members. In such circumstances, Members shall seek to obtain the additional information necessary for a more objective assessment of risk and review the sanitary or phytosanitary measure accordingly within a reasonable period of time."

Article 5.8

"When a Member has reason to believe that a specific sanitary or phytosanitary measure introduced or maintained by another member is constraining, or has the potential to constrain, its exports, and the measure is not based on the relevant international standards, guidelines or recommendations, or such standards, guidelines or recommendations do not exist, an explanation of the reasons for such sanitary or phytosanitary measure may be requested and shall be provided by the Member maintaining the measure."

EXHIBIT 4 Size Indicators in the Biotech Sector, 1996

Source: "Benchmarking the Competitiveness of Biotechnology in Europe," Europabio, 1997, p. 31.

Indicator	Europe	U.S.A.
Turnover (€ m.)	1,700	11,700
R&D expenditure (€ m.)	1,500	6,300
Number of companies	700	1,300
Number of publicly quoted companies	50	300
Number of employees	27,500	118,000

Soccer Balls Made for Children by Children? *Child Labor in Pakistan*

Background: The Rise of Sialkot

Located in the Punjab province near the disputed border of Kashmir, the site of the first of many wars between Pakistan and India, over the few decades following independence from British rule, Sialkot lost virtually all the non-Muslim entrepreneurs and managers who had run the few industries in the area. Most of the workers left behind were manual laborers, skilled in the manufacture of sporting goods, such as boxing gloves, cricket bats, and tennis rackets. According to local entrepreneur Zaka-ud-Din:

> In 1947, all trade [in Sialkot] was in Hindu hands. The people who took over from them were not professionals, and, with their lack of organizational skills, it took government incentives to keep them going. They manufactured the cheapest things you could buy, with very low quality.

However, a new class of entrepreneurs rose in Sialkot, many with the help of foreign manufacturers, who offered both new technologies and management training. As subcontractors making components for assembly by name-brand groups in Europe, Japan, and the U.S., Pakistani entrepreneurs moved into more profitable, finished product lines. According to Zaka-ud-Din:

> I saw that there was a need for real entrepreneurs. People wanted higher quality goods. At first we were [soccer ball] stitchers for others, and then gradually we came to want to make the entire product ourselves. We became better organized and hired more educated staff. . . . I myself was trained in the FRG [Federal Republic of Germany] and later in Japan.

From its humble beginnings in the mid-1960s, Zaka-ud-Din's business grew into a multimillion dollar business employing hundreds of workers in both central factories and home-based cottage industries.

By the mid-1990s, Sialkot had become a major hub for the highest-quality sporting goods and hardened-steel surgical equipment, together accounting for approximately 25,000 jobs in the Punjab province. Their products were highly customized, requiring great skill and training, which so far no outside competitor had been able to profitably mechanize. These industries made Punjab one of Pakistan's richest provinces, with a growing middle class and one of the country's highest literacy rates. Unlike many of Pakistan's provinces with poorly integrated local economies, little if any infrastructure, and people living in mud huts, Sialkot's surrounding villages were built largely in brick and enjoyed a certain level of infrastructure, frequently including schools and running water. With 300,000 residents, Sialkot City had an international hotel as well as a neighborhood of walled, luxury family compounds of poured concrete and tinted glass. Of course, Sialkot's development was all relative: traditional sectors like wheat farming, brick kilns, and leather tanneries operating alongside export-oriented industries still accounted for at least 80% of local economic activity and far more in terms of manpower employment. The local infrastructure was rather poorly maintained and foul-smelling pools of industrial chemical wastes

This case was written by Robert Crawford, Research Associate, under the supervision of Olivier Cadot, Professor of Economics at Lausanne University, and Daniel Traça, Assistant Professor of Economic and Political Sciences, INSEAD. It is intended to be used as a basis for class discussion rather than to illustrate either effective or ineffective handling of an administrative situation.

were common next to offices and residential areas in the middle of the city. More importantly, many laws on the books, including prohibitions on child labor, went simply without enforcement.

In 1995–96, exports of soccer balls brought in revenues of 1.3 billion in Pakistani rupees (PRs)—on average 35 million balls were exported to the U.S. and Europe per year—while surgical equipment brought in PRs1.5 billion.[1] Because demand tended to fluctuate wildly, depending on where the World Cup tournament was held or, in the case of surgical instruments, the state of the world economy, Sialkot entrepreneurs preferred a flexible workforce that they could engage as needed; in 1994, the U.S.-based World Cup games resulted in an enormous boost in demand for soccer balls, raising export revenues to PRs3.2 billion that year.[2] As a consequence of this and of the unusually high level of product customization, the niche that Sialkot's export sectors came to occupy remained extremely labor intensive, depending less on industrial investments than on specialized manual laborers, experts in stitching and metal filing by hand. This could be a dangerous choice: while competitors began to incorporate carbon fibers and other high-tech materials in tennis rackets, Sialkot's sports manufacturers chose to stick with traditional wood frames and labor-intensive techniques; eventually, manufacturers in Taiwan and other newly industrialized countries took over the entire industry.

Child Labor in History and Today

Although child labor is, by all accounts, common in the developing world, estimates vary widely, if for no other reason because the definition of "child labor" is by itself a matter of debate. A child employed in a factory or a mine is undoubtedly "working." So is a child begging in the streets with his parents. But what about a boy herding cattle on his parents' farm in the morning before school? What about a girl helping with household chores while her mother is working outside the home? The answer depends on what is included in the definition of "child labor." Using a standard definition—"economically active individuals under 15"—the ILO has produced on the basis of a sample of 124 member countries an estimate of 78.5 million children working. By its own reckoning, however, this number is likely to be a gross underestimate, the reality being probably closer to 200 million. More than actual numbers, it is "participation rates" which best capture the incidence of child labor, as they measure the proportion of an age cohort being employed. Table 1 shows participation-rate data collected by a number of microstudies (in which researchers actually went to the fields and counted people):

However, not all "economically active" children work full-time; on average, about half are secondary workers who contribute to family income by after-school or seasonal labor.[3] The vast majority of child laborers are unpaid family members, who work in the informal sector, either in agriculture or related activities as well as an increasing number in small urban production units. A very small number of child laborers—perhaps less than 2%—work in "export" sectors, such as carpet weavers or as manufacturers of sports equipment, leather goods, and surgical instruments.[4]

While no one knows the precise number of child laborers in Pakistan, analysts estimate that there are 3.6 million, almost half of whom work more than 35 hours per week, and many over 56 hours per week. Only about a third are wage earners, the remainder being mainly family helpers, particularly in rural areas. Nearly 400,000 (11% of the total) work in manufacturing industries; somewhere in the region of 50,000 work in the export sectors, which include soccer balls, carpets, surgical instruments, and leather goods. Around 2 million (60%) of Pakistan's child laborers are in the Punjab alone.

Child labor is a perennially divisive issue. It is by no means a new phenomenon: indeed, children working in the factories and mines were one of the most detestable by-products of the

[1] At that time, PRs traded at approximately 30 to the U.S. dollar.

[2] "The Sialkot Story: Making Villages 'Child Labor Free,' " *Economic Review*, April 1997, p. 33. No byline.

[3] "Unicef Report Demands End to Most Intolerable Forms of Child Labor," *M2 Presswire*, 10 Dec. 1996. No byline.

[4] See "Child Labor: How the Challenge Is Being Met," *International Labor Review*, summer 1997, pp. 233–257. No byline.

TABLE 1

Source: Christian Grootaert and Ravi Kanbur, "Child Labor: An Economic Perspective," *International Labor Review* 134, 1995, p. 190.

Study	Age Cohorts	Participation Rates (%)
Rural Egypt, 1975	6–11	17
	12–14	43
Ivory Coast, 1986	*Urban*	
	Boys	5
	Girls	6
	Rural	
	Boys	55
	Girls	54
Philippines, Bicol region, 1983	*Market work*	
	7–12	22
	13–17	44
	Home work	
	7–12	49
	13–17	68
Pakistan, 1990	Boys	31
	Girls	7
5 villages in rural Pakistan, 1990	Boys	19–25
	Girls	22–32
One district in rural Maharashtra, India, 1993	*Wage work*	
	Boys	9
	Girls	6
	Family farm or business	
	Boys	24
	Girls	16
	Household work	
	Boys	34
	Girls	65

early Industrial Revolution. Even to this day, historians disagree about its proper interpretation. For some writers, especially in the tradition of Chicago school economist Gary Becker,[5] putting children to work should be construed as a rational household decision given the available alternatives and should therefore be excluded from the realm of normative or ethical judgments. This view is neatly summarized by Nardinelli (1990):[6]

> According to [Becker's] model, the household can be thought of as attempting to maximize its output of consumption commodities (p. 59). . . . In the short run, I would argue, the movement of child labor out of the home and into the factory made little difference to the family economy. The principal effect was to raise family income. If it is assumed that work at home and work in the market are close substitutes, the division between the two is purely a matter of relative productivities. There is no particular reason to attach great importance to the particular division chosen by any family (p. 60). . . . Before the coming of the factory age, employment as an agricultural servant or the beginning of apprenticeship meant leaving home to live with the employer. With factory employment, children continued to live at home after entering the labor market. One of the short-term effects of child labor in factories was therefore to keep children living at home longer than under previous types of child employment (p. 61).

[5] See Gary Becker, *The Economic Approach to Human Behavior*, The University of Chicago Press, 1976; or *A Treatise on the Family*, Harvard University Press, 1981.

[6] Clark Nardinelli, *Child Labor and the Industrial Revolution*, University of Indiana Press, 1990.

Unsurprisingly, a starkly different view was expressed in the 19th century by Karl Marx, who viewed child labor as inherently exploitative:

> [To] purchase the labor-power of a family of four workers may, perhaps, cost more than it formerly did to purchase the labor-power of the head of the family, but, in return, four days' labor takes the place of one, and their price falls in proportion to the excess of the surplus-labor of four over the surplus-labor of one.[7]

Irrespective of whether child labor was exploitative (as Marx suggested) or not (as liberal and, later, neoclassical economists argued), what accounted for its ultimate elimination is also a matter of debate: Was it legislation or technical progress? Both certainly contributed to its phasing out in most of Europe and the U.S. over the period extending roughly from the 1833 Factory Act to the First World War. A careful study of the elimination of child labor in U.S. canneries during the so-called Progressive Era (1880–1920)[8] indicated that child labor laws were in some cases welcomed by employers for whom children in a modern factory were a source of trouble:

> [Canners] are almost unanimous in the opinion that this law has done them a great good, for without fear of arousing the displeasure of parents, little children can at present be kept out of the cannery. . . . Many canners do not hesitate to seek the assistance of the inspector in dealing with the troublesome parents who insist on bringing into the work room children under the legal working age.[9]

In those cases, mothers insisted on bringing children to the factories primarily because of the lack of child care facilities. However, in other factories—typically less mechanized rural ones—labor inspectors checking compliance with child labor laws were less than welcome:

> On approaching a particular [rural] cannery, a worker at the front door was seen to give a "high sign," and the children darted to the rear exit. Since it is the duty of the inspector to know conditions as they really are, and not as the employer would have them represented, the inspector ran to the rear door on the outside of the cannery in time to catch the youngsters tumbling forth, with bags tied around them, skinning knives still in their hands and greatly bespattered with tomato juice and skins. The parents of these children were sought out and their responsibilities in the matter explained. By this time, the employer, greatly excited, appeared on the scene. Nothing uncomplimentary to the inspector remained unsaid.[10]

Many of the issues relating to child labor during the Industrial Revolution remain relevant to this day. How exploitative is child labor in modern emerging economies? Would social legislation patterned after Britain's Factory Acts effectively eliminate it? How much would it penalize poorer economies for whom cheap labor is a key source of competitiveness? In other words, could it retard economic development, in effect penalizing the very people it would seek to help by perpetuating the poverty that causes child labor?

Social engineers and activists take a different view. They argue that child labor is a violation of fundamental human rights, as is the case with slavery and prison labor. Children deserve time for play, personal development, and a "childhood," which together represent the surest route to equitable and sustainable economic development.[11] Many activists in Pakistan and many outside observers seem to share this view. According to Zahid Siddiqi, a founder of the nongovernmental organization Sudhaar, child labor in Pakistan created a kind of underground market for parents willing to exploit their families: "The more children they put to work," he said, "the more money they can get. Lots of their fathers even stop working themselves. Why should they work when they can get five or six of their own children working for them? This has to stop."

[7] Karl Marx, *Capital*, vol. 1, p. 395; quoted in Nardinelli, op. cit., p. 67.

[8] Martin Brown, Jens Christiansen, and Peter Philips, "The Decline of Child Labor in the US Fruit and Vegetable Canning Industry: Law or Economics?" *Business History Review* 66, pp. 723–738.

[9] Maryland, Bureau of Statistics and Information, 24th Annual Report, Baltimore, 1915, p. 210; quoted in Brown, Christiansen, and Philips, op. cit., p. 727.

[10] Maryland, Bureau of Industrial Statistics and Information, 24th Annual Report, Baltimore, 1915, p. 210; quoted in Brown, Christiansen, and Philips, op. cit., p. 726.

[11] See ILO, *Report VI: Child Labor*, International Labor Conference, 86th Session, 1998.

Approaches to Child Labor in International Law

Efforts to establish international norms began early in the 20th century. In 1919, the Treaty of Versailles created the International Labor Organization (ILO) in an "endeavor to secure and maintain fair and humane conditions of labor." Since then, the ILO promulgated over 180 multilateral conventions to establish international standards in virtually every area of employment and labor relations laws.[12] Convention 138, adopted in 1973 (although an earlier text, Convention 5, had been adopted at the time of the ILO's foundation), prohibits the employment of children under 15 or before the end of the mandatory school age, whichever comes latest. If the work is "dangerous or immoral," the minimum age is 18. Farm work is exempted from the general minimum-age rule. Other exceptions include a minimum age of 13 when the work is "not prejudicial" to educational attainment, and a waiver for poor countries which can set a minimum employment age of 14 (12 for light work and 16 for dangerous work). Finally, child labor is acceptable if it is an integral part of training.[13]

For many years, Convention 138 provided a legal basis for international scrutiny of child labor practices in member countries. However, because the ILO does not mandate that its members adopt all of its conventions, member countries have tended to pick ILO conventions *á la carte,* and it so happens that, of the "basic rights" conventions, 138 is the one that has—by far—the smallest adoption rate. Only 46 countries have signed it, and Pakistan isn't among them, though neither are the U.S., the U.K., Switzerland, Canada, Japan, New Zealand, and Australia; their common objection to signing it is that the convention is too inflexible to accommodate local idiosyncrasies. Of course, nonsignatory countries cannot be legally forced to comply.

A new ILO Convention (182), unanimously adopted in June 1999, is intended to complement existing ILO conventions and is designed specifically to eliminate the "worst forms of child labor." The signatories accept to implement provisions that include:

- Precise definitions of what constitutes the "worst forms of child labor," including all forms of slavery, prostitution, pornography, illicit trafficking activities, and hazardous forms of labor.
- The design and implementation of programs to eliminate these labor activities.
- The establishment or designation by signatories of appropriate mechanisms to monitor compliance.
- Adoption of all necessary measures to enforce compliance.

Unfortunately, because the new convention is administered exclusively by the national institutions of each signatory, it too may prove ineffective: no one can force the signatories to implement it in good faith.[14]

For want of an effective enforcement mechanism for ILO conventions, the idea has been floated on numerous occasions that "core labor standards" (covering basic principles, such as the prohibition of child labor) should be appended to trade agreements and hence made enforceable by the WTO. The advantage of the WTO over the ILO is that multilateral trade agreements signed at rounds of trade talks are binding for all signatories and enforceable under WTO dispute-settlement mechanism. But the WTO route also raises numerous problems. For one thing, one of the basic principles underpinning the multilateral trading system is the "like product" treatment enshrined in Article III of the organization's basic charter. According to this principle, effectively identical goods ("like" products) cannot be treated differently by the importing country on the basis of how they are produced. For instance, if one soccer ball is produced using child labor and the other is not, trade sanctions against the first would be deemed discriminatory and in violation of Article III. The only exceptions, under Article XX, are prison labor and health concerns—but Article XX refers to the health of consumers, not of producers.

[12] Steve Charnovitz, "Environmental and Labor Standards in Trade," *The World Economy,* vol. 15, no. 3, pp. 339–340.

[13] Mascus, op. cit., p. 53.

[14] See Bob Davis, "Clinton Backs Effort to Curb Child Labor," *Asian Wall Street Journal,* 17 June 1999; Ranabir Ray Choudhury, "ILO Convention on Child Labor Adopted Unanimously," *Businessline,* 19 June 1999.

At a deeper level, many economists, in and outside of the WTO's secretariat, fear that including labor standards in trade agreements would open a Pandora's box. According to a high-level WTO official: "We view the social sanctions issue as a slippery slope—once you admit the legitimacy of using [the WTO's arbitration process] for political purposes, there's no telling where it will all end. . . .The WTO just isn't equipped for that kind of thing and would get overwhelmed by cases if it tried to." To this effect, at the WTO's 1996 summit, the organization accepted the banning of child labor as "nonbinding," but it designated the ILO as "best equipped" to handle issues of workers' rights. Of course, WTO signatories in less developed countries vehemently denounce any attempt by rich countries to include labor standards in trade agreements as a thinly disguised protectionist ploy.

Indeed, whereas some of the "social protectionism" has been driven by good intentions, a lot of it appeared self-serving. For example, a 1992 proposal by U.S. Senator Tom Harkin—the Child Labor Deterrence Act—sought to ban the import into America of goods produced by children under 14 years of age. Although similar legislation was supported by President Clinton and other members of the U.S. Congress,[15] Harkin's links to organized labor raised suspicions that the senator was more interested in protecting American jobs, particularly in textiles, than he was in child rights. In the same vein, Richard Gephardt, an influential leader in the U.S. House of Representatives, once declared that:

> The repression of political rights is inevitably combined with the denial of economic rights . . . we can't compete against workers who have no rights to demand a higher wage in return for their hard work and increased productivity. We can't compete with slave labor. . . . We demand that efforts to expand coverage of the World Trade Organization include human rights, for they are inextricably intertwined with any true strategy of global prosperity.[16]

Harkin's bill was later passed in the form of an amendment to the 1997 Treasury spending bill, but the agent of enforcement—the U.S. Customs Service—was ill-equipped to carry out its mandate; additional funds for the service, while promised, were slow in coming. The ultimate effect of the bill was minimal.[17] It did, however, scare people in Sialkot: regarding the senator's visit to the area in the mid-1990s, one Pakistani observer said, "Harkin was very harsh. He created more awareness here and generated more criticism abroad. We were beginning to work on the problem and visits like his changed the atmosphere. . . . The [U.S.] Congress started trying to make special laws, sanctions [against child labor] on a regional basis and against Pakistan." There was even discussion in the U.S. about a campaign to force the withdrawal of Pakistan's most favored nation status,[18] but a proposal that drastic did not go very far. Indeed, the links of the trade-sanctions advocates with protectionist lobbies severely undermined the credibility of their campaigns.

New International Activism

Starting in the 1960s, consumers began to play a larger and larger role in economic affairs, moving from safety concerns at home to corporate ethics and citizenship abroad. New-style consumer activists like Ralph Nader, founder of the Public Citizen in Washington, DC, led lobbying campaigns for safer cars and a cleaner environment. By recruiting young idealists whom they trained to run their crusades, these activists operated largely through the provision of information and the results of their investigations to the media. It was the outrage of the average consumer, who participated in demonstrations or wrote letters to their U.S. congressmen, that advanced the new policies.[19] In the 1980s, wealthier consumer activists began to take a different tack: employing the clout of socially responsible pension funds, often run by "cash czars" who scrutinized the actions of the companies in their portfolios from the standpoint of both financial

[15] John Berlau, "The Paradox of Child-Labor Reform," *Insight in the News*, 24 November 1997, p. 20.

[16] See "Free Trade, Fair People: China's Free Trade Status," Vital *Speeches of the Day*, 15 July 1997, pp. 581–585.

[17] "USA Trade: Customs Walks Tightrope on New Child Labor Law," *Journal of Commerce*, as cited by EIU Views Wire, 15 October 1997. No byline.

[18] Shahidul Alam, "Thank You, Mr. Harkin, Sir!" *New Internationalist*, July 1997.

[19] See Karen Croft, "Citizen Nader," *Salon Magazine*, Great Careers #11, 1999.

returns and ethics. According to New York comptroller Carl McCall, who oversaw one of the largest public pension funds in the U.S., "When you own one million shares of stock, you don't have to picket." If he saw something he didn't like, such as a discrimination scandal at Texaco, McCall was able to pick up the phone and ask corporate executives about it.[20]

It was not long before consumer activists turned to global concerns. With the rise of the Internet as a tool to disseminate information, a new style of international muckraker and activist emerged in the late 1980s. For the first time, independent agents and local observers had the means to find and publicize, cheaply and instantaneously, the global issues that concerned them. If for whatever reason an issue caught on, it could generate enormous interest worldwide, either as coordinated campaigns or spontaneous outpourings of protest and donations.[21] In the mid-1990s, a number of television news magazines visited Bangladesh and Pakistan to report on alleged cases of bonded child labor, a kind of modern slavery through the debt obligations of their parents. While consumers remained unwilling to pay higher prices for goods produced by "socially responsible" methods—they preferred known brands, price, and quality—their perceptions of "exploitive" multinationals were beginning to change for the worse.[22] Fearing that these perceptions would affect their bottom line, many marketers of craft products from the third world began to refuse imports of goods produced by children and other victims of human rights abuses.[23]

In 1996, a sweatshop-related discovery helped to catapult the issue of child labor into the international spotlight: a line of clothing sponsored by U.S. television personality Kathy Lee Gifford, reporters found, relied on children who were paid only U.S.$0.30 per hour in Honduran sweatshops. Entering an arena that had long been the concern of a few politicians and professionals in international organizations, suddenly scores of activists became concerned about working children. Armies of reporters, some of them celebrities in their own right, joined the cause, scouring the third world for examples of abuse and exploitation of children; their harrowing tales of brushes with mysterious thugs, some clad like local policemen, lent them credibility and élan. In addition to stories of slave labor and cruel punishments—one famous reporter claimed to have found children "branded, beaten, blinded as punishment for wanting to go home"[24]—alarming estimates began to surface. A movement to end child labor coalesced around soccer ball manufacturers in the "Foul Ball" campaign.[25]

Zaka-ud-Din and M. Yunas Ratra (managing director of a sporting goods company that bore his name) remembered vividly when the spotlight fell on them as soccer ball manufacturers in Sialkot. "An American friend, who was a business associate and customer, called me at home," Zaka-ud-Din recalled. "He told me he was watching the news on television, and asked me whether it was true that I used children to stitch soccer balls. I was surprised by his question because I had never looked into it. . . . All we did was subcontract out kits that were taken to villages and stitched. We didn't know who stitched them."

These campaigns could backfire. As a result of a high-profile public opinion campaign in the U.S. and in fear of trade sanctions, garment factory owners in Bangladesh had turned out approximately 50,000 working children into the street, virtually overnight. Unfortunately, rather than return to school, instead many of the children lost status within their families, becoming an insupportable burden—in a country where 65% of the children were malnourished, their earnings had been desperately needed. As a result, the number of homeless children increased, while many others were forced into more hazardous occupations, such as brick baking,

[20] Eileen P. Gunn, "The Money Men," *Fortune*, 4 August 1997, p. 74.

[21] Deborah Spar, "The Spotlight and the Bottom Line," *Foreign Affairs*, March–April 1998, pp. 7–12.

[22] Ibid. p. 9.

[23] "USA Trade: Customs Walks Tightrope on New Child Labor Law," *Journal of Commerce*, as cited by *EIU Views Wire*, 15 October 1997. No byline.

[24] See Sydney Shanberg, "Six Cents an Hour: On the Playgrounds of America, Every Kid's Goal Is to Score. In Pakistan, Where Children Stitch Soccer Balls for Six Cents an Hour, the Goal Is to Survive," *Life*, June 1996, p. 38.

[25] "USA Trade: Customs Walks Tightrope on New Child Labor Law," *Journal of Commerce*, as cited by *EIU Views Wire*, 15 Oct. 1997. No byline.

street scavenging, and even prostitution.[26] Because the industry brought in U.S.$1.24 billion in 1995–96, which accounted for 62% of Bangladesh's export earnings, the government became involved in negotiations; it eventually secured an agreement with UNICEF and the ILO for over U.S.$250,000 in aid per year, to be matched by the local garment industry.[27] According to businessman Zaka-ud-Din, who had traveled to investigate the situation in Bangladesh while deciding what to do about the soccer ball industry, "Only about two-thirds of the children [who had lost jobs] went back to school." He said, "It created so much hardship. In any program we created, the children would have to be given something to do."

Multinational Corporations: Seeking the Lowest Possible Costs

Having been thrust into the international spotlight by accusations of exploitation and hypocrisy regarding child labor, a number of sporting goods multinationals imposed their own policies in Sialkot. Reebok, one of America's premier designer-marketers of sporting goods, took the vanguard, lobbying its sports industry association to abolish child labor and undertaking its own extensive investigations at approximately 40 Reebok subcontractor factories in the third world. According to Douglas Cahn, Reebok's vice president for human rights, [B]ecause we wanted to move quickly, we proceeded on our own . . . in a tripartite approach: (1) bring stitching out of the home and into larger factories; (2) set up a vigorous monitoring system; (3) start remediation programs in education." The fourth element consisted of labeling Reebok's finished balls, to be purchased from a local contractor who had built a new child-free factory, as "child labor free."

The brand manufacturers' interest in labor issues in poor countries was indeed something new. As competition between sporting goods manufacturers had become increasingly global in recent years, outside pressure had become extremely intense on Sialkot subcontractors to keep prices as low as possible. Cheap labor, it turned out, was the key to this strategy, as multinational corporations actively sought to find the lowest-priced producer-contractors for labor-intensive goods, frequently playing them against one another in bidding wars.[28] To compete with Adidas in the mid-1960s, for example, Nike had begun to import shoes manufactured from a low-wage country of that time, Japan. As the yen and wages in Japan rose during the next decade, Nike switched to Taiwan and Korea, where the labor force remained relatively inexpensive. Nike's latest moves, in the early 1990s, were to Indonesia, China, and other countries in Asia, where workers were paid very low wages.[29] Such constant relocation was, of course, nothing reprehensible in itself, but critics charged that its effect was to pitch workers of poor countries against one another in a "race to the bottom." Moreover, historical evidence, as well as economic reasoning, suggested that low wages for adult workers were very much at the root of the child labor problem, since poverty was the primary reason why parents allowed their children to work.

So better adult wages would clearly have to be part of any solution to the child labor problem. For instance, a Save the Children report[30] suggested raising the daily wage of an average adult stitcher from the current range of PRs75–100 (roughly U.S.$2.50 to U.S.$3.00) to the wage of construction workers, that is, PRs120 (U.S.$4.00). But what would be the effect of such a wage hike on the prosperity of the industries in Sialkot? Whereas Sialkot's position in the market for soccer balls was well established—especially in the tournament-grade segment of the market, where it controlled 80% market share worldwide—how would this position withstand the shock of restrictive labor laws? How much loyalty would the brand manufacturers have for their Sialkot

[26] Owen Bowcott, "Save the Children: The World Wrings Its Hands over Child Labor, but What Has It Done to Stop It?" *The Guardian*, 11 October 1997.

[27] Tabibul Islam, "Bangladesh Labor: Garment Industry Claims No Child Workers," *Inter Press Service*, 19 November 1996.

[28] Adam Schwarz, "Low-Tech and Labor Driven," *Far Eastern Economic Review*, 2 April 1992, p. 53.

[29] Philip Knight, "Global Manufacturing: The Nike Story Is Just Good Business," address delivered to the National Press Club, 12 May 1998. See Also Bill Saporito, "Can Nike Get Unstuck?" *Time*, 30 March 1998, pp. 48–53.

[30] "Stitching Footballs: Voices of Children in Sialkot, Pakistan," Save the Children, 1997.

subcontractors if their costs rose because of a wage hike or child labor ban? On the one hand, at about U.S.$1.00 per ball the stitching cost was but a tiny fraction of the wholesale price of a high-quality soccer ball, which could fetch as high as U.S.$75 on the U.S. market.[31] So the impact of a wage rise on the balance sheet of the big brand manufacturers was unlikely to be significant. However, on the other hand, Nike and other brand name sports MNCs had given little hint that they would be willing to consider raising their purchase prices for soccer balls in exchange for social progress. There was no question about their eagerness to put a "child labor free" label on their products; but how much were they willing to pay for it?

NGOs: Trying to Find Innovative Solutions

NGOs have progressively entered areas traditionally reserved for governments, starting with environmental policies in the early 1990s and moving into economic development and workers' rights. Stepping into the role that many local governments could no longer afford, NGOs were increasingly serving as providers of basic services, for example, health care, education, and banking; they were becoming community organizers with greater expertise than the intergovernmental organizations mandated in the same issue areas.[32] For example, Sudhaar, a Pakistani NGO founded in 1994 and funded by the ILO and other groups, began to set up educational facilities for children in leather tanneries; according to observers, it was so successful that a number of foreign NGOs and intergovernmental organizations encouraged it to expand into other areas as an instrument of change.[33]

During the soccer ball controversy, NGOs took on a larger role in Sialkot. Under the leadership of David Husselby, program director of the Save the Children Fund UK (SCF) office in Islamabad, SCF first came to Sialkot in July 1996. Though his organization was wary of allying itself with the private sector, Husselby sensed an opportunity and hired a handful of researchers in Sialkot, many of whom worked for local NGOs such as Sudhaar, to investigate child labor in the soccer ball manufacturing industry. "The industry really wanted to quickly announce a program to end child labor," Husselby said. "But SCF wanted to give children a chance to talk first, to find out how they felt" about the sudden attention that child labor was generating. SCF's final report cleared up a number of misconceptions that apparently had been perpetuated by shoddy and exaggerated reporting. "I found that the reporting of some journalists was hard to stand by or support," Husselby said.

SCF served as a catalyst to facilitate communication between hitherto hostile groups. The SCCI and the ILO, for example, at first regarded each other with suspicion: while the ILO feared it was becoming coopted by private-sector "enemies," the SCCI distrusted the labor union affiliation of the UN organization. Soon, the U.S. government also became interested, promising funding and attracting the participation of both UNICEF and the ILO. Even the Pakistani government joined the Sialkot "Partnership to End Child Labor," as it came to be called, with the Department of Education and the National Rural Support Program, a publicly funded NGO. With a view to launching the project at the next "Super Show," an annual sports trade fair in the U.S. scheduled for February 1997, members of the Sialkot partnership negotiated to draft goals for the project.[34]

The Atlanta Agreement

The Atlanta Agreement was unveiled at the 1997 "Super Show," in a media blitz of high drama and expectation. Brand manufacturers in the Sporting Goods Manufacturers Association of the U.S. pledged to "eliminate child labor"—workers under 14 years of age—from the stitching and production of soccer balls, as did the members of the SCCI, within two years. In a major departure from its role as a local observer and funder of

[31] Tahir Ikram, "Child Labor a Painful System," *Reuters*, 13 December 1996.

[32] See Jessica T. Mathews, "Power Shift," *Foreign Affairs*, January–February 1997, pp. 50–66.

[33] "Sudhaar—A Profile," *Brochure*, 1998.

[34] David Husselbee, "How Close Is too Close? International NGOs as Development Partners with the Corporate Sector," presentation to the Conference of Business for Social Responsibility, November 1997.

small-scale initiatives, the ILO stepped forward to monitor the agreement, acting as a kind of guarantor of the integrity of the process.

The agreement,[35] which was formulated to avoid the problems experienced by child laborers in Bangladesh, juggled a number of provisions and requirements:

- Stitching centers were to be established, which would bring the work out of the household and into official manufacturing facilities.
- Workers were to be systematically registered in corporate records for the first time, an additional mechanism for verification of worker age.
- In order to create alternative activities and employment for displaced workers, programs would be created for purposes of both education for children and wider economic development.
- A system of rewards, warnings, and penalties was set up to encourage company compliance.
- Members of the World Federation of the Sporting Goods Industry would favor vendors who did not use child labor. For its part, SCCI undertook a commitment to expand the elimination of child labor to additional industries.

Financial support for the agreement came from a wide variety of sources. The U.S. Department of Labor promised to supply U.S.$500,000 for the first two years of the program. SCCI members would provide U.S.$360,000 to finance independent monitors. UNICEF would provide U.S.$200,000. Finally, the Soccer Industry Council of America (the industry association of brand sporting goods manufacturers) would add U.S.$100,000. The bulk of foreign contributions was targeted for education and prevention programs for the children and other affected workers.[36] Financed largely by SCCI monitoring funds, the ILO had hired 15 staff monitors to work in teams of two, traveling on motorbikes for random, unannounced visits to the stitching centers. According to Antero Vahapassi, the ILO official in charge of the initiative, "This is the first program in which the ILO is getting its hands dirty in the details of implementation. We cannot afford to fail. It is a very bold step for us."

As soon as money for the partnership began to flow into Sialkot, an astonishing variety of NGO programs blossomed. Engaging the energies of many talented policy entrepreneurs, NGOs set up initiatives in consciousness raising, community mobilization for economic development, and the improvement of educational facilities. Sudhaar began to fund improvements in existing schools and set up nonformal supplementary schools in the hope of reintegrating working children into the school system for at least a few hours a day: 154 nonformal education centers were set up for child laborers, many of them in villages that had had no schools.[37] Nighat un Nisa, a team leader for the National Rural Support Program (or NRSP, a Pakistani government–supported NGO), set up community credit unions. In an effort to create alternative sources of income and employment, particularly in rural areas far from Sialkot, she was counseling village leaders in business and credit management. She was particularly interested in enticing women to work, and was actively seeking ideas that would allow them to contribute to household income, which, she believed, would make them more confident and active. The women, she said, "are easily motivated. . . . Once child labor is eliminated, some means will have to be found or created to make up for the financial shortfall. Some family incomes will be cut in half. Everyone's participation is vital." But in spite of their long-run potential, these initiatives were unlikely to make up for the immediate income shortfall due to the child labor ban.

SCCI members fulfilled their promises on schedule: as of November, 1998, 50% of their manufacturing took place in the approximately 500 new stitching centers they had set up; 36 manufacturers—about half of the manufacturers in Sialkot—participated under SCCI auspices, which represented 65–70% of total annual production of export-quality balls. But all this did not come for free. According to Naeem Javed, managing director of the Sublime Group of

[35] Memo from Sublime Corp.

[36] U.S. Dept. of Labor, "Labor Department to Fund Elimination of Child Labor in Soccer Ball Industry," ILAB Press Release, 13 February 1997.

[37] See "Elimination of Child Labor in the Soccer Ball Industry in Sialkot," *ILO Mid-Term Review*, November 1998, paragraphs 8–18.

Companies, in the new centers "each ball costs about PRs15 more to produce; we used to be able to do it for PRs30–35, but now it costs us PRs50–55." Because Sublime enjoyed a solid relationship with Adidas for the high-quality ball market, it did not lose its business, but it did need to produce more to keep the same profit. This was of course deeply resented by Sialkot employers. "We all talk about ethics and fair trade," Ratra said. "But when I ask my buyers to share the cost, they refuse." By and large, SCCI member profits were down by a significant margin. While the exact figures were confidential, one executive of a major firm confided that his cumulative gross profit had fallen from 18% of revenues to about 10% since the program began. The drop in profits, which differed from company to company, was due primarily to the costs of opening and running larger stitching centers, that is, providing the infrastructure that home-based cottage industries had long allowed them to avoid. Local contractors footed the entire bill for these. As a result, soccer ball manufacturers were struggling to improve their efficiency—reducing rejection rates by a factor of almost 90%, investing in whatever labor-saving technologies they could find, and training their labor force. In addition, to maintain profits with the higher overhead costs of their stitching centers, the larger firms were increasing the scale of production. For less efficient small- and medium-sized producers, the bottom line was squeezed to a new low. "It is becoming a matter of survival," Ratra said. "For now we [the larger firms] are keeping our heads above water." But many others were likely to be pushed out of business by an industrywide consolidation in the next few years.

The initiative also had an unforeseen impact on Punjabi women. By taking labor out of the home environment to outside stitching centers, the new manufacturing arrangement would effectively prevent them from working for a variety of reasons. First, there were the prohibitions of religion, which in Pakistan coexisted with caste: according to increasingly influential Islamic law and custom, women were not allowed to mingle with men who were not in their immediate families, which included working alongside men; caste restrictions added to the complexity of women's work opportunities, effectively eliminating many "higher" caste women from traveling outside their villages. Second, despite the relative wealth of Punjab province, the state of local infrastructure often hindered women from traveling. Bus services for women effectively ended at 4 P.M., which meant that they could not be at home to "take care" of their husbands when they returned from work, as dictated by regional custom. Preventing women from working would compound the income-loss problem created by the elimination of child labor, as the male household head would then become the sole wage earner.

The decline in numbers of working women also threatened to reverse recent gains in their social status. According to Ms. un Nisa:

> If [women] have income, they begin to feel empowered within the family. Before, they could do housework, care for children and livestock and that was about all. Now they can earn their dowry on their own, buy clothes. . . . A female that contributes income to the family is more confident and can talk and discuss things. [The opportunities for women in faraway, isolated villages were extremely limited.] We are headed for a real crisis.

Other participants also worried that, while a lot was occurring at present, there was a danger that little, if anything, lasting would be established. "No one has an overview of what everyone is doing," one official complained. "There is a lot of duplication in the same village. It is a mess and may be making communities more dependent on outside [actors]." Moreover, he feared that international attention was fickle and likely to shift to some other fashionable cause, perhaps soon. "We are beating the drum, getting people together, raising awareness," he said. "It is very positive that the business community has finally admitted that child labor exists. But if we stop, everything will probably disappear. We are building no permanent structures." Another former government official was even more pessimistic and openly questioned whether the entire initiative was becoming a tool of corporate propaganda. The NGOs, he said, "are trying very hard to infiltrate the feudal power structure in Pakistan. But they don't want the international community to know how badly the odds are stacked against them. The stories of [government-sanctioned] violence and Mafia thugs are very real. So they have to appear optimistic. Their jobs depend on international funds."

Was the Atlanta Agreement a success? Have the Sialkot children gained? In the words of Fawad Usman Khan, a founder of Sudhaar,

> [I]f it were up to me, I would take all child laborers out of the more hazardous professions and put them *into* the soccer ball industry—there are no chemicals, they are well paid, and the hours are flexible. The children can work at home in their spare time, mixing it with housework or after school. I am very worried that the children taken out will end up in more dangerous occupations. This is an easy sector when compared to carpets or leather tanneries.

Have Pakistani women, whose position is most vulnerable, gained in the new arrangement? If the Atlanta Agreement was indeed a success, does it provide a model that can be emulated elsewhere, say in the carpet industry? Is it likely to have ripple effects in other industries?

Mobil in Aceh, Indonesia (A)

> Mobil and Arun are the largest oil and gas companies in Indonesia and should therefore be of benefit to the people of Aceh local to their area of operation. However, it is in fact the case that these companies have brought misfortune to the people of Aceh, not only because the detrimental impact of their presence has never been seriously addressed, but moreover because of their implication in human rights abuses which have caused the suffering of the people of Aceh. The implication of these two companies in human rights violations is in the form of their involvement with military operations in Aceh.[1]

In December 1998, Ron Wilson, chief executive of Mobil Oil Indonesia (MOI) considered how he should respond to allegations made by a group of nongovernmental organizations (NGOs) that Mobil had been complicit in serious human rights abuses in Aceh, Indonesia (Exhibit 1). MOI, established in 1968, was a 30–55 joint venture between Mobil and the Indonesian oil company, Pertamina. Based in Lhokseumawe, MOI was responsible for setting and managing the terms of the various contracts with Pertamina and the Indonesian government, and for establishing and managing the exploration and exploitation operations. Certainly, no one had ever thought managing the Indonesian operations was going to be easy—as a location, Aceh was far from convenient. But could anyone have imagined just how challenging managing operations in Aceh would be?

Liana Downey prepared this case under the supervision of Professor Henri-Claude de Bettignies as the basis for class discussion rather than to illustrate either effective or ineffective handling of an administrative situation.

[1] Carolyn Marr, "Translation of Press Release Issued on 10 October 1998 by a Number of Indonesian NGOs in Respect of Mobil Activities in Aceh, Indonesia," *NGOs Implicate Mobil in Indonesia*, December 3, 1998, (csf.colorado.edu/mail/elan/dec98/0022.html, September 9, 2002).

The Aceh Region—Overview and History to 1976

Aceh, located in the northwest of Sumatra Island (Exhibit 2), was the westernmost point of the Indonesian Archipelago. Aceh's population, estimated at 4,074,900[2] in 1998 represented 2 percent of the population of Indonesia.[3] Aceh comprised nine ethnic groups, and six of Indonesia's 365 languages were spoken in Aceh. Many historians believed that Aceh played an important role in converting much of the Indonesian population to Islam sometime around the eighth century. Throughout the 15th century, Aceh was home to a prosperous trading port, and linguists believed common Malay, the national language of Indonesia, originated with Acehnese traders.

Despite the apparent cultural and religious connections with the rest of Indonesia, Aceh had a long history of rebellion and often exhibited a fierce determination to be independent. Beginning in 1641, the British and Dutch attempted to dominate Aceh. Although the Dutch eventually wrestled the island of Sumatra from the British via the Treaty of London in 1824 and subsequently dominated much of what is now Indonesia, they were unable to dominate Aceh.

In 1871 the Dutch and British signed the "Sumatra Treaty" authorizing the Dutch to invade Aceh. In 1873, the Dutch declared war on Aceh and embarked on the longest war in Dutch history, costing more than 10,000 lives. After years of persistence on the part of the Dutch, the sultan of Aceh surrendered in 1903, thus ending the centuries-old sultanate system. The Dutch appointed a governor to rule Aceh and installed district chiefs which were know locally as *uleebalang*. These appointments deepened

[2] *The Jakarta Post.com*, "Aceh: Facts and Figures," (www.thejakartapost.com/special/os_7_facts.asp, September 18, 2002).

[3] "Indonesia: General Data of the Country," University of Utrecht Library: Population Statistics, (www.library.uu.nl/wesp/populstat/Asia/indonesg.htm, September 26, 2002).

conflicts with the *ulema*[4] who considered the Dutch administration *kaphee*, the unbeliever according to Islamic teaching. Despite the Dutch victory, guerilla activity continued for years. Some historians suggest the Aceh War did not really end until 1942, when the Dutch surrendered to Japan.[5]

In 1945, when the rest of Indonesia declared independence from Japan, Aceh made the decision to become part of the new Indonesian republic. Initially, many Acehnese were strong supporters of the central government. In October 1945, four *ulema* from Aceh made the following declaration:[6]

> The very destructive second World War has just ended. . . . and the Republic of Indonesia has been established under the leadership of our respected, great leader Ir. Soekarno. . . . All of our people have united, standing behind the great leader Ir. Soekarno to await orders as to what they must do.[7]

In addition to declarations of moral support, Aceh supplied cash donations and two aircraft, and purchased bonds issued by the newly formed central government. Not all Acehnese were in agreement however, and in 1945, the "Cumbok Incident," a battle ensued between the *uleebalang* led by Cumbok and supporters of the Indonesian government.

Despite the initial enthusiasm, Aceh leaders became increasingly dissatisfied with the central government over the next eight years. A series of conflicts rocked Aceh, reflecting a number of changes in the Indonesian system. In 1950, one such change was Indonesia's acceptance into the United Nations and transformation from the Federal Republic of Indonesia to the Republic of Indonesia. This resulted in the newly formed Aceh Province being "dissolved." Finally, on September 20, 1953, the short period of political cooperation came to an end, when Daud Beureueh, the governor of Aceh until the change of status in 1950, declared Aceh's independence from Indonesia.

Years of conflict and rebellion followed until 1959 when Aceh was decreed a "special territory" within the Republic of Indonesia and granted a high degree of autonomy in educational, religious and cultural matters. Observers welcomed the move, believing that Aceh's status of special territory would lead to greater prosperity and help bring Aceh into the Indonesian mainstream. In practice, this autonomy was never fully realized,[8] and the desire among some Acehnese for an independent Islamic state remained strongly entrenched. In support of this desire, on December 4, 1976, Teungku Hasan M. di Tiro founded the Free Aceh Movement (*Gerakan Aceh Merdeka*, or GAM).[9]

The Indonesian Oil Industry

In 1967, Indonesia's new president, Suharto, was establishing a set of statewide systems to manage interests throughout the Indonesian Archipelago. In 1968 the president passed Oil Law 44, effectively nationalizing oil production. This law decreed that "oil and gas mining is conducted only by the State, and only a State enterprise is authorized to engage in oil and gas mining on behalf of the State."[10] Over the next decade, most foreign corporations gradually sold back their assets in marketing, refining, and shipping to the central Indonesian government.[11]

Fortunately for companies such as Mobil, the law allowed foreign companies to obtain exploration and producing concessions provided

[4] Muslim proponents of sacred law and theology.

[5] "Aceh: The History of Aceh," *The Jakarta Post.com*, September 10, 2002, (www.thejakartapost.com/special/os_7_history.asp, September 10, 2002).

[6] According to the *Jakarta Post*, "On October 15, 1945, four of the most respected ulema in Aceh—Teungku Hadji Hasan Kroeeng Kale, Teungku M. Daoed Beureueh, Teungku Hadji Dja'far Sidik Lamdjabat and Teungku Hadji Ahmad Hasballah Indrapoeri—issued an announcement in the name of all ulema in Aceh, calling on all Acehnese to help defend the new Indonesia. The announcement was endorsed by Aceh regent Teungku Nja' Arif and the chairman of the National Committee, Toeankoe Mahmoed. In the announcement, the four ulema declared war in defense of Indonesia against foreign aggression *sabil* war, or war in the way of God." Ibid.

[7] Ibid.

[8] Stephen R. Shalom, "Exxon-Mobil in Aceh," *Znet Daily Commentaries*, June 26, 2001, (www.zmag.org/sustainers/content/2001-06/26shalom.htm, September 9, 2002).

[9] *The Jakarta Post.com*, op. cit.

[10] Vaughan, R., *Mobil Oil Indonesia: 100 Years and Generations to Go*, Mobil Oil Indonesia, Inc., Hong Kong, 1998, pp. 69–70.

[11] Vaughan, loc. cit.

they were in partnership with the state. By 1968 there was only one state organization with responsibility for oil and mining—Pertamina.[12]

Mobil Oil Indonesia

Mobil's association with the region extended back over a century, when Socony, a predecessor of Mobil Oil, established relations with Indonesia in 1894. Socony, also known as the Standard Oil Company of New York, sold products into Indonesia through its Singapore office. Socony had established itself quickly throughout the region, opening up offices in Singapore, Japan, and China in the period from 1893 to 1895. In 1898, confident with the results of their recent expansion into Asia, Socony opened a marketing office in the area that was to become Jakarta. In 1931, Socony underwent a major merger, combining its operations with Vacuum Oil. In 1933, Vacuum Oil in turn merged its assets in Indonesia with Standard Oil of New Jersey (known as Esso, and already a major producer of oil in Indonesia). In 1959 Socony Mobil was organized to form two major divisions: Mobil Oil Co. in the U.S. and Canada; and for the rest of the world, Mobil International Oil Co.[13]

In the years leading up to the opening of operations in Aceh, Mobil was already a large global corporation, looking ever outward for new energy reserves. In 1968 Mobil became one of the first organizations not already exploring in Indonesia to take advantage of the opportunities afforded under the production-sharing contract arrangement made possible by Oil Law 44. MOI was formed as a 30-55 joint venture with the Indonesian oil company Pertamina on December 6, 1968. The Japanese Indonesia LNG Company (representing the buyers) held the remaining 15 percent. The terms of their production-sharing contract called for Mobil to explore the "B" block in Aceh Province in northern Sumatra.[14]

Based in Lhokseumawe, MOI was responsible for setting and managing the terms of the various contracts with Pertamina and the Indonesian government, and for establishing and managing the exploration and exploitation operations. In 1970 Mobil Oil added exploration rights on about 900,000 acres bringing its total net interest in Indonesia to more than 13 million acres.[15]

The Development Phase: 1971 to 1978

Mobil in Aceh

While the primary negotiations had taken place with the central government, the Acehnese were also extremely interested in the proceedings. Muzakir Walad, then governor of Aceh Province, recalled being challenged to

> open Aceh to the international world. . . . General Dr. Ibnu Sutowo, then President Director of Pertamina, and General T. Hamzah, Supreme Military Commander from Aceh, questioned me as to whether I dared to "modernize" Aceh and welcome a world-class investor into the Province. I said that I would, provided I get concurrence and support from the social and religious leaders of Aceh.[16]

In commemoration of Mobil's 100 years in Indonesia, author Ray Vaughan recorded the initial experience of Sudhyarto (Sudy) Suwardi, the geologist in charge of drilling the A-1 well at Arun, near Lhok Sukon:

> Sudy [recalled] "the road to the site was not very good, and we ran into a major rain storm. The Land Rover was stuck in the mud and we had to stay the night until the morning came and we could move about in dryer weather.". . . At the time, the local Acehnese people were not very happy to have exploration going on in their area and were hostile to outsiders. . . . Nevertheless, despite the lack of a warm welcome, Sudy stayed with the task at hand.[17]

In October 1971, Mobil had already drilled 14 unsuccessful wells in the block, and Sudy was still looking for more when:

[12] Initially, three organizations were established to oversee all of Indonesia's oil operations, but by 1968, only two were still in operation—Pertami & Permina and in that year, President Suharto combined them to form Pertamina.

[13] Vaughan, op. cit., pp. 43–60.

[14] Vaughan, op. cit., p. 73.

[15] "Mobil Corporation Annual Report, 1970," New York, 1970, p. 6.

[16] Vaughan, op. cit., p. 73.

[17] Vaughan, op. cit., p. 74.

> He saw what appeared to be a "kick" in the log. . . . The decision was made to do an open-hole drill test. . . . Graves [the man in charge of exploration] remembers, "It was the shortest drill stem test in Mobil history . . . that well unloaded in about 60 seconds and started blowing gas like you wouldn't believe." After testing these wells under controlled conditions, they knew they had a huge find. It was a discovery that would eventually develop into a field with reserves of 14 trillion cubic feet of gas and 950 million barrels of condensate—a field that would be, for its time, the largest producing natural gas field in the world.[18]

Good News For Indonesia

If the men on site were pleased, and Mobil by implication, state-owned Pertamina, and the Indonesian central government were delighted. Under the production-sharing agreement, the majority of revenue from the sales of gas would go to the Indonesian government. As a result, Dr. Ibnu, the director of Pertamina, predicted that "the new agreement would enable Indonesia to pay off all of its debts—then more than $6 billion."[19]

Pertamina and Mobil Oil Indonesia

In 1973, Mobil continued discussions with Pertamina regarding plans to construct a gas liquefying plant.[20] Mobil also signed a production-sharing agreement with Pertamina covering 5 million acres in other parts of Indonesia.

By 1977 the relationship with Pertamina was well and truly established. Each day, 600 million cubic feet of gas were being produced and recycled for the production of condensate.[21] Mobil was responsible for developing the gas field, recovering the condensate, and also for acting as a consultant to the Pertamina-owned PT Arun plant. In that same year, Mobil declared the Arun natural gas field one of the world's largest, stating that it expected it to contribute importantly to future earnings and predicting "unusually high per-well production rates."[22] The first shipments of condensate were delivered to Washington in 1977, and to Japan in 1978.

Early Challenges

Getting to this stage had been difficult. The negotiation of the terms had involved a large number of parties, with Indonesia pressing to get the projects on stream as soon as possible, and all parties pushing to get the best deals possible. On behalf of Mobil, Vaughan perhaps understated the situation when he said negotiations produced some tension.[23]

Building the plants in the middle of rice paddy land was a tremendous challenge. Paul Hellman, president and general manager of MOI from 1977 to 1981, remembered:

> In the beginning it was nothing more than rice paddies and a farming area on the edge of a rain forest. There were no roads and a very small narrow gauge railroad track meandered through the fields. There were large areas under cultivation and the people and the villages were located on higher ground. In that particular kind of culture, probably the most complicated thing mechanically was a bicycle. And here comes a foreign oil company and state-of-the-art technology and equipment, construction facilities and people. We knew we were alien to the Acehnese and their environment; these people had never seen anything like this.[24]

Given the challenges of constructing such a huge field in this area, Mobil employees were proud of their accomplishments. Mobil suggested that the development of the massive Arun field could be deemed "a modern miracle of technology."[25]

Disaster Strikes

On June 4, 1978, one of the Arun wells blew out of control, resulting in a fire that lasted for almost three months. In his book *Mobil Oil in Indonesia*, Robert Vaughan described Mobil's response: the company brought in Mobil people from around the world in an effort to control the well and

[18] Vaughan, op. cit., pp. 74, 77.

[19] Vaughan, op. cit., pp. 82–83.

[20] The proposal was to build a plant to turn gas into liquefied natural gas (LNG), a convenient form for transportation and exporting.

[21] Vaughan, op. cit., p. 91.

[22] "Mobil Corporation Annual Report, 1977," New York, 1977, p. 9.

[23] Vaughan, op. cit., p. 16.

[24] Vaughan, op. cit., p. 101.

[25] Vaughan, op. cit., p. 83.

Pertamina evacuated people from a number of small villages around the field.

Again

Friends of the Earth Indonesia (*Wahana Lingkungan Hidup Indonesia*, or WAHLI), together with several Sumatran NGOs described Mobil's response to catastrophic events differently: "Another incident which was of concern to the local people was the explosion of an oil well in 1979, which was located in Cluster II. As a result of the explosion, the inhabitants of Nibong Baroh village who lived next to the well had to move to another area for a period of six months."[26] The groups claimed that "such incidents were never addressed by Mobil Oil, and moreover the impression given by the company is that they just ignore problems until the local people give up."[27]

Maintenance Phase 1978 to 1998

In addition to building a state-of-the-art production facility, Mobil worked hard to ensure that the safety and comfort of its expatriate employees were provided for. Most expatriate employees were housed in the company-built neighborhood called Bukit Indah. Mark Mitchell, writing from Lhokseumawe on behalf of the Campaign ExxonMobil,[28] described life in Aceh for Mobil employees as follows:

> It is a fenced-off and fortified oasis of ranch-style homes and green lawns, a place where kids ride bikes, carefree, on tree-lined streets. There are swimming pools, tennis courts and a nearby golf course. Weekends bring barbecues or softball games. And in the evenings, residents watch satellite TV, the latest episode of Friends sometimes interrupted by the faint chatter of machine-gun fire—a sound that causes unease, but only a little, like a clap of thunder from a faraway rainstorm.[29]

[26] Marr, loc. cit.

[27] Marr, loc. cit.

[28] Campaign ExxonMobil described itself as a "religious shareholder based campaign to compel ExxonMobil (EM) to take a responsible position on global warming" (www.campaignexxonmobil.org/learn/about.shtml, September 19, 2002).

[29] M. Mitchell and J. Tedjasukmana, "The Unmaking of a President," *Jakarta Times*, Lhoksumawe, Campaign ExxonMobil—Can We Save the Tiger from ExxonMobil? August 6, 2001.

The Claims

From 1978 to 1998, Mobil faced numerous accusations regarding its presence in Aceh. It was claimed that Mobil's operations were harmful to the environment, that the company made negligible contributions to the local economy, and even more seriously, that Mobil had been complicit in human rights abuses. (See Exhibit 3 for a timeline of events.)

Perspectives of Aceh Activists and MOI on the Community, the Environment, and Human Rights

The Community

Aceh Activists

Down to Earth, an international NGO, stated that Mobil's activities, while highly profitable, benefited both Mobil and the central government much more than the local economy.

Many Acehnese argued that there was too much federal support for Mobil and recalled situations where housing developments were vacated to accommodate construction workers and Mobil employees. In the late 1980s, the Acehnese lamented the disparity between the province of Aceh's production (11 percent of Indonesia's total exports) and reinvestment in the province by Indonesia's government. Within Indonesia, Aceh held the richest supplies of natural resources, including oil, timber, and minerals in significant quantities and roughly a third of the country's liquefied natural gas. In 1998, the revenue generated from oil and gas comprised 30 percent of Indonesia's total revenue.[30] Aceh was exporting over U.S.$2 billion of goods, most of which were from the Arun gas fields. However, despite the apparent wealth of the region, at least 40 percent of the Acehnese villages could be considered "poor" by

[30] Jay Soloman, "Fueling Fears: Mobil Sees Gas Plant Become Rallying Point for Indonesian Rebels—Ties to Jakarta and Military Make Firm Easy Target for Aceh Secessionists—Muslim Women in the Ranks," *The Wall Street Journal*, September 7, 2000, p. A1.

governmental standards.[31] As well, local people claimed that they had been forced off their land with only minimal compensation.[32]

Mobil Oil Indonesia

The company stated: "Wherever we operate around the world, Mobil wants to be viewed as a responsible member of the business community and the communities in which our people live and work. To that end, Mobil Oil Indonesia . . . has involved itself deeply in the needs and aspirations of the people of Indonesia."[33]

Mobil highlighted its contributions to the local community: two civic mission clinics in the Lhok Sukon area that served the needs of more than 100,000 people from surrounding villages.[34] Mobil claimed that their services had "wiped out neonatal tetanus and death from measles in the Arun field area—living proof that industrialization brings some major benefits."[35] The company drilled fresh water wells, "built and repaired roads and bridges and helped in the construction of a number of schools and mosques."[36]

The Environment

Aceh Activists

According to watchdog NGOs, examples of environmental detriment included the oil cluster explosion and a 1983 incident when Mobil Oil's Cluster I discharge flooded and contaminated local paddy fields and shrimp farms. There were further claims that MOI was regularly discharging industrial waste into public drainage channels, an act that led to the destruction of dozens of hectares of shrimp and fish ponds owned by 240 Acehnese farmers.[37] Locals' attempts to take MOI to court in Indonesia over such incidents were documented in press releases by various Sumatra NGOs. The Acehnese were never victorious.

Mobil Oil Indonesia

Mobil claimed it "wanted as little change as possible" in the local environment. Mobil did not have global environmental standards, but instead required compliance with local environmental rules and regulations to safeguard environmental and public health. In some countries, such as Indonesia, where environmental requirements were still being developed when the field was discovered, Mobil's policy called for the affiliate to develop its own standards.[38] With respect to the Arun field, Mobil Oil claimed "it established aggressive environmental standards for air, water and solid waste and regular inspection programs to prevent spills and other potential accidents. . . . At Mobil, safety performance is every bit as important as our operating performance."[39]

Human Rights

Political Context

The Indonesian government's response to the 1976 formation of the Free Aceh Movement, or GAM (*Gerakan Aceh Merdek*), was harsh. Mass arrests of GAM members in the late 1970s forced many of their activities underground for years. In 1988, the Mobil liquified petroleum gas (LPG) plant at Arun went on stream. A year later, in 1989, according the *Jakarta Post*:

> The group, now also calling itself the Aceh-Sumatra National Liberation Front (ASNLF), came out of hibernation and renewed its quest for independence, often through attacks on police and military installations. The government responded to GAM's campaign of violence with its own campaign of violence, declaring Aceh a Military Operation Zone (DOM).[40]

Human Rights Watch claimed:

> The Indonesian army's response was disproportionate to the threat. Using indiscriminate force, the army killed more than a thousand civilians, often leaving their mutilated bodies by the side

[31] "Aceh: A Province in Distress," *The Jakarta Post*, (www.thejakartapost.com/special/os_7_facts.asp), and "Mobil Oil and human rights abuse in Aceh," *Down to Earth*, November 1998 (dte.gn.apc.org/39mob.htm September 18, 2002).

[32] Ibid.

[33] Vaughan, op. cit., p. 107.

[34] Vaughan, op. cit., p. 108.

[35] Vaughan, loc. cit.

[36] Vaughan, loc. cit.

[37] Jeremy Schnack, "The Acehnese Resistance Movement and Exxon Mobil," *Inventory of Conflict and Environment Case Studies*, American University of Washington, number 85, May 2001, (www.american.edu/projects/mandala/TED/ice/aceh/htm, September 18, 2002).

[38] Vaughan, op. cit., pp. 104–105.

[39] Vaughan, op. cit., pp. 105, 107.

[40] "Aceh: A Province in Distress," op. cit.

> of roads or rivers. Many more were arrested, tortured and arbitrarily detained for months, sometimes years. Hundreds of Acehnese disappeared.[41]

In May 1998, in the wake of widespread allegations of corruption, Suharto was forced to resign as Indonesia's president. His successor, Habibie, publicly apologized for past abuses, including those in Aceh.[42] Under Habibie's guidance, the Indonesian Human Rights Commission (*Komas* HAM) was established to investigate human rights abuses. In Aceh alone, the commission gathered evidence of the death of 781 people at the hands of the military, 163 disappearances, 368 cases of torture, and came across at least 3,000 cases of women widowed because their husbands had been killed or had disappeared in the region.[43]

By mid-1998, locals and human rights activists were becoming increasingly vocal in their claim that the imposition of the military operation zone (DOM) only worsened the situation in Aceh and had led to massive human rights violations by military and police personnel. In response the DOM was lifted in August 1998. Unfortunately the resultant euphoria was short-lived, and violence increased.

Aceh Activists

Terry Collingsworth, general counsel of the DC-based International Labor Rights Fund, said: "ExxonMobil understood from the day it decided to bring its project in Aceh, that the army units, Tentara Nasional Indonesia, assigned to protect company wells, were notoriously brutal in their treatment of Indonesia's ethnic minorities."[44] The five major claims made by Friends of the Earth (WAHLI) and the other Sumatran NGO's were itemized on the press release shown in Exhibit 1.

Furthermore, WAHLI and other local NGOs claimed the support Mobil received from the federal government made it difficult for many Acehnese to speak on the record. They claimed that Mobil and P.T. Arun "so dominate the economy in Aceh, [the Acehnese] feared they would not be able to find good jobs or win more contracts if their names were used" in addition to the fear of military reprisal.[45]

Mobil Oil Indonesia

The corporation flatly denied the allegations and claimed to have no knowledge of human rights abuse. "I can frankly say that we have no knowledge of that happening," said Neil Duffin, executive vice-president for production and exploration of Mobil Oil Indonesia.[46] The company said it would have protested such abuse and would have referred issues involving potential criminal conduct to appropriate authorities. Pertamina's public relations general manager, A. Sidick Nitikusuma, concurred: "Incidents connected to human rights violations were beyond Pertamina and MOI's authority and knowledge."[47]

Mobil did admit to loaning excavators to the army and supplying troops with food and fuel on occasion over the course of three decades, while insisting that they were for peaceful purposes. Mobil denied allowing the army to use its buildings. In fact, most of the buildings were under Pertamina's ownership. Duffin said that Mobil was told that any equipment used was "for projects beneficial to the community," such as building roads. Mobil claimed to have no control over wrong use of its equipment.[48]

Summary

Despite the denial made by Duffin, the furor surrounding Mobil's activities in Indonesia did not cease. Was Duffin's response all that was

[41] "Indonesia: Civilians Targeted In Aceh: A Human Rights Watch Press Backgrounder," *Human Rights Watch, Indonesia Page*, (no date), (www.hrw.org/press/2000/05/aceh05-back.htm, September 18, 2002).

[42] Ibid., and: Yenni Kwok, "Words Ring Hollow for Aceh and Papua," *CNN.com*, August 20, 2001 (www.cnn.com/2001/WORLD/asiapcf/southeast/08/20/indo.aceh/, September 18, 2002).

[43] Lisa Macdonald, "Mobil Linked to Atrocities in Aceh," (no date), (www.greenleft.org.au/back/1999/347/347p14c.htm, September 18, 2002).

[44] International Labor Rights Organization Press Release, "ExxonMobil Sued in U.S. Court for Human Rights Abuses in Indonesia," June 21, 2001, (www.laborrights.org/press/exxonmobil062101.htm, October 23, 2002).

[45] Michael Shari, Pete Engardio, and Sheri Prasso, "What Did Mobil Know?" *Business Week*, December 28, 1998, p. 68.

[46] Shari, Engardio, and Prasso, loc. cit.

[47] Shari, Engardio, and Prasso, loc. cit.

[48] Shari, Engardio, and Prasso, loc. cit.

needed, or did these problems run deeper? It certainly did not seem as though many in the Acehnese community saw Mobil in the way the company wished to be viewed—as a responsible member of the business community. Wilson pondered how he was going to manage a deluge of bad publicity, both locally and internationally.

Case Study Questions

1. What do you think MOI did well in its development phase? Would you do anything differently?
2. What stakeholders do you think were important in the 1970s? Has this changed at all in the 80s and 90s? If so, how?
3. How relevant, if at all, do you think the political situation in Aceh is to Mobil?
4. Is there anything that gives you concern for the future of operations in Indonesia?
5. It is December 1998, and you are the CEO of Mobil Oil Indonesia. How do you respond to the five claims made by Sumatra NGOs and WAHLI (Exhibit 1)?
   a. How will you handle your relationship with the Jakarta government?
   b. How will you handle international media relations?
   c. How do you handle relations with NGOs?

EXHIBIT 1 Press Release By Sumatra NGOs and WAHLI

Source: Marr, loc. cit.

Mobil Oil and PT Arun Must Be Held Accountable for Human Rights Violations in Aceh

Mobil and Arun are the largest oil and gas companies in Indonesia and should therefore be of benefit to the people of Aceh local to their area of operation. However, it is in fact the case that these companies have brought misfortune to the people of Aceh, not only because the detrimental impact of their presence has never been seriously addressed, but moreover because of their implication in human rights abuses which have caused the suffering of the people of Aceh.

The implication of these two companies in human rights violations is in the form of their involvement with military operations in Aceh. These can be documented as follows:

1. Mobil Oil provided specific facilities in the shape of building and contents for military Post 13. Information gathered from victims of human rights abuses indicated that a number of them were interrogated in Post 13 before being moved to other locations.
2. Mobil Oil provided heavy equipment such as escavators [*sic*] in order that the military could dig mass graves for its victims at Sentang Hill and Tengkorak (Skull) Hill.
3. Mobil Oil road was used in order to transport the victims of human rights violations in order to be buried on "Skull" Hill.
4. Mobil Oil did not take issue with nor take responsibility for the number of its own employee [*sic*] who were kidnapped and disappeared by the military when at work.
5. PT Arun, some shares of which are owned by Mobil Oil, built Camp Rancong which was used by Kopassus in order to torture and murder victims of human rights abuses.

Because of the evidence above, we make the following demands:

1. That the United States Government take firm action against Mobil Oil in order to uphold human rights.
2. Mobil Oil and Arun must be made accountable to the people of Aceh. They should apologise to the international community, the people of Indonesia and the people of Aceh in particular. They should offer just compensation and rehabilitation to the victims of human rights abuses, as perpetrated by the military and with the support of both Mobil Oil and Arun.
3. That Amnesty International and Human Rights Watch Asia should carry out their own investigation into the financial affairs of Mobil Oil, particularly in respect of their relationship with the military and its operations.
4. Urge oil and gas-consuming countries to boycott oil and gas products of both these companies should Mobil Oil and Arun shirk from their responsibilities.

(continued)

EXHIBIT 1 Press Release By Sumatra NGOs and WAHLI—Continued

Banda Aceh
10 October 1998

—Chalid Muhammad (Indonesia Friends of the Earth)
Maimul Fidar (Coalition of Human Rights NGOs) Risman A Rachman (WALHI Aceh)
Dikson Aritonang (WALHI Bengkulu)
Rachmadi (WALHI West Sumatra)
Hariansyah (WALHI South Sulawesi)
Chairul Hasni (YAPDA Lhokseumawe)
Yusuf Ismail Pase (LPLH Aceh)
Zulfikar MS (Committee for Missing Persons)
Afrizal Tjoetra (Forum LSM Aceh – NGO Forum)
Sanusi M Syarif (YRBI Aceh)
M Zul Frima Putra (YBA Aceh)
Rully Syumanda (YGHL South Aceh)
Kamaludin (KPA Leuser Unsyiah)
Juli R Miansyak (KPA STIK Pante Kulu)
Aiyub Syah (YBAI)
Rahmadsyah Putra (Metalk Unsiyah)*

* Signatory organizations included WALHI (Wahana Lingkungan Hidup Indonesia), a member of Friends of the Earth International (global federation of autonomous environmental organizations), campaigned on environmental and social issues (www.walhi.or.id/ and www.foei.org/); YAPDA (Yayasan Putra Dewantara), founded in 1993 and concerned with wrongdoings by Indonesian governments and corporations (www.lp3es.or.id/direktori/data/aceh/aceh_024.htm); LPLH (Lembaga Pembelaan Lingkungan Hidup Aceh), founded in 1992 to improve Aceh's welfare using environmental advocacy and mediation (www.lp3es.or.id/direktori/data/aceh/aceh_007.htm); YRBI (Yayasan Rumpun Bambu Indonesia), founded in 1995 to improve the quality of life of Indonesian people in their relation to God and the environment (www.lp3es.or.id/direktori/data/aceh/aceh_025.htm). (All Web sites accessed September 18, 2002).

EXHIBIT 2 Indonesia and Aceh

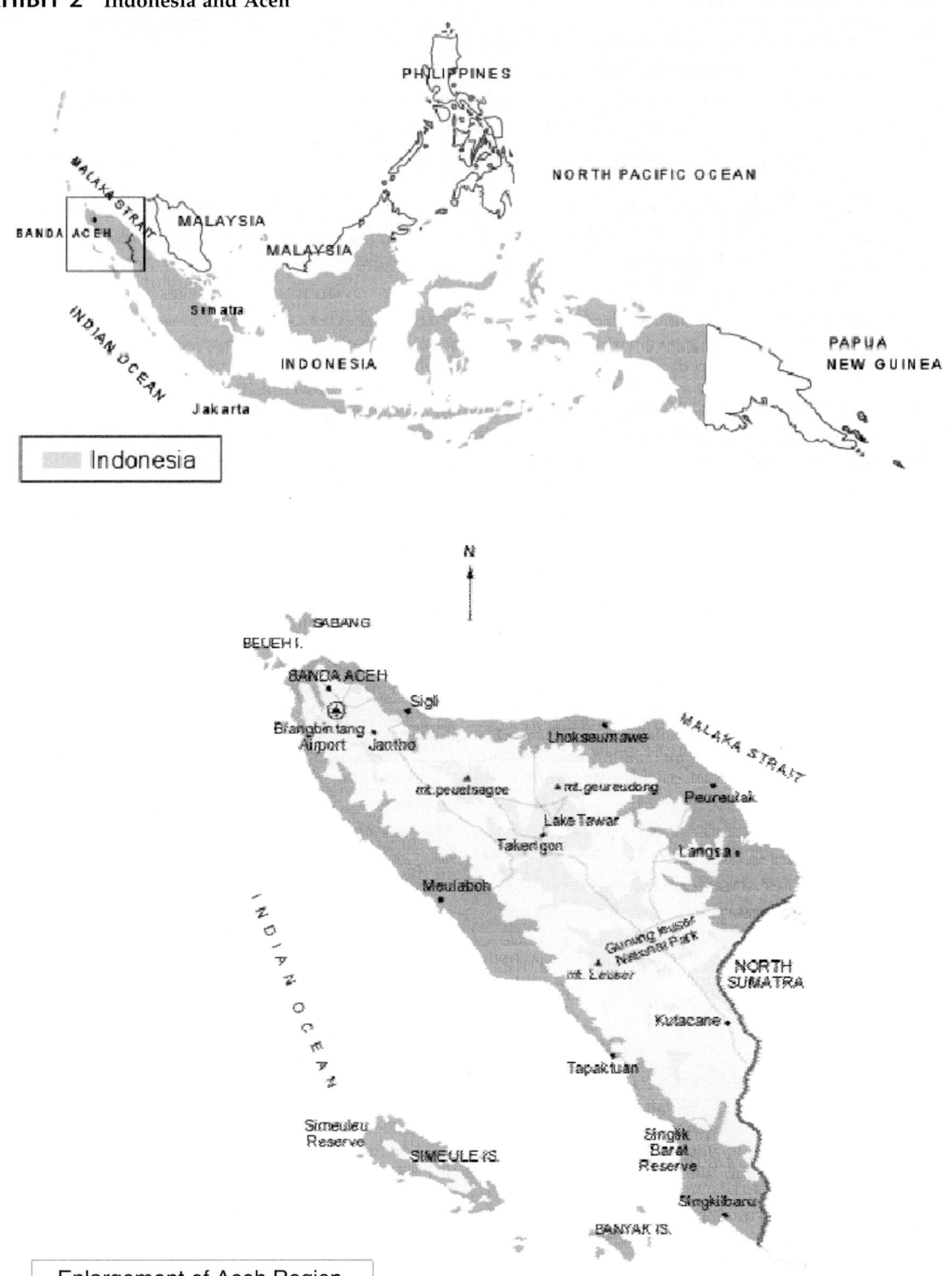

Enlargement of Aceh Region

EXHIBIT 3 Timeline of Events

1898	Socony opens up marketing office in Indonesia.
1931	Vacuum Oil merges assets with Standard Oil of New Jersey (Esso).
1959	Socony Mobil reorganizes as Mobil Oil Co. & Mobil International Co. Aceh decreed as "Special Territory."
1967	Suharto assumes presidency, replacing Sukarno after almost 50 years in power.
1968	Oil Law 44 is passed, nationalizing oil production in Indonesia. MOI established as a 30-55 joint venture with Pertamina.
1970	Mobil Oil adds exploration rights on an additional 900,000 acres in Indonesia, bringing its total net interest in Indonesia to more than 13 million acres.
1971	Mobil discovers Arun gas reserve.
1973	LNG plant is planned with Pertamina.
1976	Free Aceh Movement (GAM) founded.
1978	An Arun Oil well fire starts, and takes three months to extinguish. First exports to Japan take place.
1979	Oil well explodes.
1983	Mobil Oil Cluster 1 discharge contaminates local paddy fields and shrimp farms.
1988	LPG Plant at Arun goes on stream.
1989	Aceh-Sumatra National Liberation Front (GAM's successor) surfaced and renewed the quest for independence.
	Government of Indonesia declares Aceh a military operation zone (DOM).
Early 1990s	Arun field produced nearly a quarter of Mobil's global revenue.
1998	Suharto forced to resign.
	Habibie succeeds Suharto, publicly apologizes for abuses in Aceh.
	Indonesian Human Rights Commission established.
	DOM lifted in August.
	Friends of the Earth Indonesia (WAHLI) and other NGOs claim that Mobil has been complicit in human rights abuses.

Appendix 

Bridging East and West in Management Ethics: *Kyosei* and the Moral Point of View

Abstract

In this article, I examine two broad ideals or "umbrella" concepts in management ethics, one Eastern and one Western, with an eye toward explaining their fundamental similarities. Beyond questions of meaning and conceptual analysis, however, are questions of implementation. Institutionalizing an ethical orientation—Eastern or Western—is the theme of the last part of the article. Different approaches to institutionalization are discussed and a strategy is suggested for making the "umbrella" concepts part of the operating systems of organizations.

My objective in this discussion is to highlight what I believe is a conceptual bridge between Eastern and Western ethical thinking, with a view to facilitating a second bridge—between these basic ideals and their application in organizational decision making. I will begin with the Japanese concept of *kyosei* and then examine the Western idea of the *moral point of view,* before turning to application questions.

The Concept of *Kyosei*

The Chairman of Canon, Inc., Ryuzaburo Kaku, has proposed a unifying concept that he believes can serve as a core for the development of business ethics as we enter the 21st Century. The concept is *Kyosei*—symbolized by the two Kanji

Author, Kenneth E. Goodpaster, reprinted with permission from the *Journal of Human Values,* Indian Institute of Management, Calcutta, 2, No. 2 (July–December 1996).

characters *kyo* (working together) and *sei* (life) 共生. *Kyosei* can best be defined using several excerpts from Mr. Kaku's recent speeches:

- "What must be done to ensure happiness for humankind is an eternal question. *Kyosei* is the answer to this question."
- "*Kyosei* provides the concept of living together as we learn to tolerate diverse cultures and to accept their differences."
- "The relations between *kyosei* and the common good may be likened to necessary and sufficient conditions in mathematics. In other words, the common good is a necessary condition to make the world better, whereas *kyosei* is the sufficient condition."
- "From another perspective, we may say that *kyosei* is an objective for making people truly happy and that the common good is the means of achieving it."
- "I believe the most acceptable phrase in English is: 'living and working together for the common good.'"

These observations about *kyosei* illustrate the subtle complexity of the concept. Consider the strands of meaning presented. One connotation of *kyosei* is the notion of a social *goal*—true happiness or the common good. Another connotation is a kind of respect or tolerance for cultural differences and diversity (*fairness*). Yet a third strand of meaning is a valuing of *community,* illustrated in the references to "living and working *together.*"[1]

Kyosei takes us beyond conventional business thinking (markets and laws) to a comprehensive aspiration for happiness, justice, and cooperation. In practice, we must assume, this means tempering individual, organizational, and even national self-interest by concern for more embracing "common goods" and tempering the assertion of narrower entitlements by a concern for more basic rights (e.g., liberty and equality) in a just society. Market forces and government regulations are important disciplines for corporate decision making—but they are not enough.

We should notice, however, that *kyosei* is an integrative concept in *two* ways. Firstly, it seeks to integrate the three strands of meaning mentioned above. But secondly, it has application across several *levels* of analysis as well—to global society as a whole, to the more local (national, regional) society surrounding the corporation, to the organization itself as a micro society, or even to subgroups within the organization. Like the triad of "prosperity, justice, and community," *kyosei* ramifies and can manifest itself on levels ranging from humanity as a whole to "wherever two or three are gathered together." As an imperative for business philosophy, *kyosei* represents what Kaku describes as a fourth stage of evolution, beyond the first three stages of pure self-interest, concern for employees, and concern for relatively local stakeholders, respectively.[2]

[1] As characterized by Kaku, *kyosei* includes the core values of: (1) social well-being or prosperity, (2) respect for diversity or justice, and (3) community. It calls not only for working toward prosperity, but also the fair distribution of resources in a society, and the realization of community or social cohesion.

[2] Kaku's fourth stage corresponds rather directly to the "Type 3" mindset described in Kenneth E. Goodpaster's "Ethical Imperatives and Corporate Leadership," reprinted in *Ethics in Practice*, Kenneth Andrews, ed., (Cambridge, MA: Harvard Business School Press, 1991), pp. 212–22.

Kyosei and the Moral Point of View

Western moral philosophy in the modern period can be seen as a search for the meaning and justification of *morality,* the *moral point of view.* Harvard philosopher Josiah Royce described the foundation of the moral point of view—what he called *the moral insight*—in his book *The Religious Aspect of Philosophy* (1905):

> The moral insight is the realization of one's neighbor, in the full sense of the word realization; the resolution to treat him unselfishly. But this resolution expresses and belongs to the moment of insight. Passion may cloud the insight after no very long time. It is as impossible for us to avoid the illusion of selfishness in our daily lives, as to escape seeing through the illusion at the moment of insight. We see the reality of our neighbor, that is, we determine to treat him as we do ourselves. But then we go back to daily action, and we feel the heat of hereditary passions, and we straightway forget what we have seen. Our neighbor becomes obscured. He is once more a foreign power. He is unreal. We are again deluded and selfish. This conflict goes on and will go on as long as we live after the manner of men. Moments of insight, with their accompanying resolutions; long stretches of delusion and selfishness: That is our life.

This quotation reminds us that a theme of Western moral philosophy has been an emotional and intellectual escape from the "illusion" of egocentrism or selfishness. Indeed, one way to read modern ethical theory in the West is as a series of challenges to the basic proposition that the governing force in human conduct is self-interest.

Eighteenth-century British philosopher Thomas Hobbes argued in *Leviathan* that self-interest was both motivationally and ethically the supreme principle of conduct—and that because of this principle, men come together to form a powerful state to protect themselves from the "war of all against all." Without such a sovereign power, the life of man would be "solitary, poor, nasty, brutish, and short."

Three major challenges to this ethical principle have been presented over the last few centuries—each mindful that the motivational significance of self-interest is not to be understated, but each convinced also that it is not overriding. The driving force behind these challenges has been a conviction that the dictates of conscience in human life ask more of us than the dictates of the other principles in question. One consequence of these philosophical debates has been a "shaping" of the Western idea of the *moral point of view.* As we shall see, the resulting contours of this "shaping" relate directly to the idea of *kyosei.*

The first challenge to self-interest came from those who argued that *interests* were indeed the correct touchstones of morality, but that the *self*—even in the longer run—provided too narrow a measure of which interests to care about. This challenge has taken several forms, depending on the extension of the class of ethically significant interests. The interests might extend to the family or the clan or the tribe, leaving "outsiders" out of consideration. Some defended the nation state or the region as the boundary of significant interests. The utilitarians in the 19th century went further—insisting that *all* human beings, not just some, be considered. Indeed, some went further still—to include all *sentient* beings, creatures capable of experiencing pleasure or pain. The main point to be made in this connection is that one of the dynamics of moral theory consisted in expanding the class of *interests* to be considered in decision making.

But there was another dynamic at work simultaneously, as the "interest-based" philosophers were having their debates over expansion. This dynamic challenged the adequacy of interests themselves—no matter how narrowly or widely conceived—as the foundation for ethical thought. Oversimplifying somewhat, and attributing this challenge to German philosopher Immanuel Kant, we can say that the second wave of criticism focused on the dignity of the individual person and the rights and liberties to which that dignity gave rise.

Simply basing one's ethical choices on interests—*even universal interests*—these critics argued, might permit the greater good of the many to excuse atrocities directed at the few. Some basic principle of justice or fairness was required in order to assert the legitimate claims of the individual person against the will of the many, even in democratic societies.

Such thinking gave rise in the American constitutional debate to the "Bill of Rights" as a protection against certain possible abuses of majority power. The core insight of this second wave of moral theorizing was that *expansion of interests considered* was not sufficient to capture the moral point of view. A second dynamic was called for—what we might call the impulse to *expand the claims of the individual* in the face of the claims of the majority.

A third wave of criticism was born of the first two waves by calling into question what both of them had in common—a strong focus on the individual (either by way of interests or by way of rights) as the principal bearer of value.[3] In the work of philosophers F. H. Bradley (British) and Josiah Royce (American) at the turn of the 20th century, we see a clear emphasis on the community as a whole, rather than the individual, as the locus of value. Bradley built his ethical theory on "*My Station and Its Duties*," while Royce made *loyalty* the central principle of his moral philosophy.[4]

Expanding the *interests considered* was the impulse of the "interest-based" moralists and expanding the *rights protected* was the impulse of the "rights-based" moralists. The new wave of ethical critique had as its source an impulse toward expanding the *communities served,* toward shared communal goods which are more than sums of the individual fortunes that participate in them. It was "duty-based."[5]

This third wave, it should be mentioned, was a critique not only of interests and rights as the sole bases of ethical thought—it was a caution about the adequacy of "stakeholder" thinking in general. Since contemporary business ethics is often characterized as "stakeholder" ethics, this point might lead us to explore the territory "beyond" stakeholder thinking.[6]

[3] To be sure, interest-based and rights-based ethical thinking sought to extend and universalize beyond attention solely to the self, but in the end, ethical reflection was *atomic* in its approach to making ethical decisions. Morality was a function solely of the benefits or harms to the interests and rights of individuals.

[4] Royce was introduced above in connection with the "moral insight." Bradley, writing in 1876, made his point in the language of community: "To the assertion . . . that selves are 'individual' in the sense of exclusive of other selves, we oppose the (equally justified) assertion that this is a mere fancy. We say that, out of theory, no such individual men exist; and we will try to show from fact that what we call an individual man is what he is because of and by virtue of community, and that communities are thus not mere names but something real. . . ."

[5] We might recall in this context John F. Kennedy's inaugural address: "ask not what your country can do for you, My fellow Americans, ask what you can do for your country." Even though it is clothed in somewhat nationalistic garments, this exhortation goes beyond interests and rights.

[6] Note that this is also a Western source of what we saw earlier in the *kyosei* concept as another kind of integration—ethical attention to nested *levels* of community.

What can we learn from this brief review of the search for *meaning* and *justification* in Western ethics? Two things, I believe. First, that definition has proved itself to be *elusive*—perhaps as some have argued[7]—impossible. Second, that the impulse of ethical reflection, even if it is not easy to define, is toward *expansion or inclusiveness along several dimensions: interests, rights, communities.*

Bridging Ideals: Congruence between East and West

Recalling the three strands of meaning that we found in the Japanese concept of *kyosei* (the pursuit of happiness or prosperity, the concern for justice or fairness, and the affirmation of community), it is clear that the Western search for the *moral point of view* includes very similar elements in its history. This congruence in the "deep structure" of the two concepts makes the metaphor of a bridge seem appropriate. It is implausible to suggest that Eastern and Western ethical ideas are so culturally alien that ethical dialogue is impossible—that traffic between them cannot lead to practical consensus.

It may be that as Eastern moral thought seeks to recover the individual in its traditional affirmation of the common good or the social whole, Western moral thought seeks to recover the social whole in its traditional affirmation of the individual. The basis for bridge-building lies precisely in this complementarity.[8]

As we reflect on the meaning of *kyosei* in the context of global business organizations, we might benefit from noticing the patterns in the West that have preceded it on the scene—and we might be mindful of some of the *partial* interpretations that might be substituted for it. For if *kyosei* is understood to mean an expanded attention to *interests,* then it will need to confront those who would charge that it is inattentive to *rights.* If it is understood to mean an expansion of attention to rights, then it will need to confront those who would charge that it is inattentive to larger duties of loyalty to a whole community.

As I understand it, *kyosei* (like the *moral point of view*) is not to be identified with any one of these logics of moral thinking—but with some kind of balanced blend of all three. I find these attractive ideals—but ideals that make precise *definition* a problem and, therefore, rigorous *application* difficult.[9]

A Different Bridge: From Ethical Ideals to Action

Concurrent with the pursuit of meaning and justification in ethics (Eastern and Western), there has been a second pursuit to find ways of taking moral ideals and values from the realm of *aspiration* to the realms of *policy, practice, and behavior.* Whatever the outcome of the philosophical dialogue over the basic ideals of human conduct, there has always been this second challenge of bringing ideals (whatever they may be) into action.

[7] For example, British philosopher G. E. Moore in his classic work *Principia Ethica.*

[8] Such an interpretation of the Eastern and Western ethical mindsets certainly fits with this author's experience in helping negotiate the operating philosophy behind the Caux Round Table Principles for Business. "*Kyosei*" from the Japanese side was eventually joined with personal "*dignity*" from the European side to form the foundation of the principles.

[9] I believe I understood Mr. Kaku to be suggesting this interpretation in October 1994 in Washington, DC, at a conference sponsored by the Center for Strategic and International Studies (CSIS).

Some examples of arenas within which the ideals of *kyosei* and the *moral point of view* might be expected to manifest themselves in the decision making of the organization are:

- Unemployment and retraining of employees whose jobs are made redundant by technological and competitive pressures.
- Environmental impacts of corporate production including pollution, conservation of resources, and preservation of biological species.
- Work and family issues, including the impact of work demands on marriage relationships, the education of children, physical and mental health, and social harmony.
- The efficiency of wealth production alongside the justice of wealth distribution in local, national, regional, and international communities.
- The use of advertising messages to mislead or misinform potential customers who are vulnerable in various ways, especially in less developed countries.

Historically, there have been several strategies for building a bridge from ideals to action—but let us here focus on three: *dictation, surrogation,* and *institutionalization.*[10]

The first strategy consists of an authority figure dictating a set of rules—along with some guidelines for interpretation. Fascism is one extreme example of such a view—but so is the "dictatorship of the proletariat" in Marx, at least in Communist practice. Penalties for disobedience or noncompliance are enforced firmly, and behavior (often because of fear) is influenced. In effect, the bridge between ethics and practice becomes the will of the one in power, the will of the strongest.[11]

A second strategy consists in identifying *systemic substitutes* for our moral ideals (*kyosei* or the *moral point of view*) different from the will of any individual authority figure. Adam Smith looked for such a substitute in what he called the "invisible hand" of the free market system. Locke and Rousseau found a substitute in the "visible hand" of the government—whether in the executive, legislative, or judicial branches.

What all of these strategies have in common is reliance upon a *process,* either economic or political, to act as a *surrogate* for the realization of our moral principles and ideals. It is as if they do not trust the leadership of organizations or the insights of ordinary people with the capacity to build the bridge to action. Or to shift the metaphor—it is as if they insist that flying the airplane of morality cannot be trusted to the captain. It must be governed by a surrogate captain—an autopilot.

The third strategy I will call *institutionalization.* It is the one I believe is the most acceptable. There are two types: *macro*-institutionalization and *micro*-institutionalization. *Macro*-institutionalization means creating support systems

[10] Philip Selznick, in his classic book on leadership, wrote in 1959 that: "There is a close relation between 'infusion with value' and 'self-maintenance.' As an organization acquires a self, a distinctive identity, it becomes an institution. This involves the taking on of values, ways of acting and believing that are deemed important for their own sake. From then on self-maintenance becomes more than bare organizational survival; it becomes a struggle to preserve the uniqueness of the group in the fact of new problems and altered circumstances." (*Leadership in Administration*, 1959, pp. 21–22).

[11] The cover story in *Business Week* (October 9, 1995) was entitled "Blind Ambition," and it described the problems currently being faced by Bausch & Lombe because its Chief Executive Officer dictated commands without checking out their concrete implications in the world of work. In many ways, this story parallels that of the H. J. Heinz company written a decade or more ago. Both involve fixation, rationalization, and eventual indifference to the lives of subordinates caught in this kind of trap.

between and among organizations willing to self-impose *kyosei* or *moral* principles. Association among such organizations may be essential if the risks of unilateral adoption of such ideals are to be minimized. The Caux Round Table Principles for Business (Exhibit 1) and the support system implicit among organizations endorsing these principles are an example of macro-institutionalization in action.[12]

By *micro*-institutionalization, I mean the creation of an organizational analogue to personal discipline and learning. I mean a sequence of activities designed

- To articulate a corporate philosophy.
- To assign special responsibility for transforming it into action.
- To educate employees about its meaning.
- To audit operations with attention to conflicts between the corporate philosophy and other organizational incentives that undermine it.
- To report on difficult cases to the corporate leadership.
- So that finally re-integration and clear communication can be restored.

The essential nature of this process is that it involves ethical "flying," consciously, not simply by using automatic pilot. This approach acknowledges the authority of leadership, the importance of market signals, and the validity of governmental regulation—but it goes further. It seeks to carry ideals into action and to sustain their presence as guiding influences by creating an organizational cycle of communication—*articulating, educating, listening, reflecting,* and, if necessary, *revising* espoused values in view of the realities of the decision-making environment.

These measures foster *living conversation* between employees and executives. And if we reflect on the ideals of *kyosei* and the *moral point of view*—living and working together for the common good—we may be persuaded that the best way to apply ideals lies not in dictation or surrogation, but in institutionalization. The challenge for corporations that would build this bridge is to undertake alliances (externally) and foster moral conversation (internally). These are the principal defenses against competitive forces (outside) and hypocrisy (inside) that might lead a company to abandon its ethical ideals.

In summary, *kyosei* and the *moral point of view* offer broad ethical ideals that are congruent with one another in their deep structure. Each seems to be anchored in three avenues of ethical reflection: interest-based, rights-based, and duty-based thinking. Each also finds application on multiple levels, e.g., family, group, organization, state, region, and globe. When we bridge from these ideals to *action,* the most promising path lies not in dictating or relying on surrogates, but in what we have called *institutionalization* (internal as well as external). Let us hope that this broad foundation for dialogue between Eastern and Western thought can lead to improved business and government behavior in the 21st century.

Minneapolis, Minnesota
December 1, 1995

[12] The work of the Caux Round Table—in particular its development of the Principles for Business—is an important step in the direction of identifying arenas in which corporate ideals most need to be carried into action. The Caux Round Table Principles consist of a Preamble followed by seven general principles and six more specific stakeholder principles. See Exhibit 1 for a summary of their content.

EXHIBIT 1 Summary of the Caux Round Table Principles for Business

The Caux Principles

Business Behavior for a Better World

Introduction. This document has been developed by the Caux Round Table, an international group of business executives from Japan, Europe, and the United States who meet each year in Caux, Switzerland, and who believe that the world business community should play an important role in improving economic and social conditions. As a statement of aspirations, it is not meant to mirror reality but to express a world standard against which corporate performance can be held accountable. In the end, members seek to begin a process that identifies shared values and reconciles differing values so we may move toward developing a shared perspective on business behavior that is acceptable to and honored by all.

These principles are rooted in two basic ethical ideals: the Japanese concept of "kyosei" and the more Western concept of "human dignity." "Kyosei" means living and working together for the common good—in a way that enables cooperation and mutual prosperity to coexist with healthy and fair competition. "Human dignity" refers to the sacredness or value of each human person as an end, not simply as a means to others' purposes or even—in the case of basic human rights—majority prescription. The intermediate General Principles in Section 2 help to clarify the spirit of "kyosei" and "human dignity," while the more specific Stakeholder Principles in Section 3 represent a practical way to apply the ideals of kyosei and human dignity.

Business behavior can affect relationships among nations and the prosperity and well-being of us all. Business is often the first contact between nations and, by the way in which it causes social and economic changes, has a significant impact on the level of fear as well as confidence felt by people worldwide. Members of the Caux Round Table place their first emphasis on putting one's own house in order, seeking what is right not who is right.

Section 1. Preamble

The mobility of employment and capital is making business increasingly global in its transactions and its effects. Laws and market forces in such a context are necessary but insufficient guides for conduct. Responsibility for a corporation's actions and policies and respect for the dignity and interests of its stakeholders are fundamental. And shared values, including a commitment to shared prosperity, are as important for a global community as for communities of smaller scale. For all of the above reasons, and because business can be a powerful agent of positive social change, we offer the following principles as a foundation for dialogue and action by business leaders in search of corporate responsibility. In so doing, we affirm the legitimacy and centrality of moral values in economic decision making because, without them, stable business relationships and a sustainable world community are impossible.

Section 2. General Principles

Principle 1. The Responsibilities of Corporations: Beyond Shareholders toward Stakeholders

The role of a corporation is to create wealth and employment and to provide marketable products and services to consumers at a reasonable price commensurate with quality. To play this role, the corporation must maintain its own economic health and viability, but its own survival is not an end in itself. The corporation also has a role to play in improving the lives of all of its customers, employees, and shareholders by sharing with them the wealth it has created. Suppliers and competitors as well should expect businesses to honor their obligations in a spirit of honesty and fairness. And as responsible citizens of the local, national, regional, and global communities in which they operate, corporations share a part in shaping the future of those communities.

Principle 2. The Economic and Social Impact of Corporations: Toward Innovation, Justice, and World Community

Corporations established in foreign countries to develop, produce, or sell should also contribute to the social advancement of those countries by creating jobs and helping to raise their purchasing power. They should also give attention to and contribute to human rights, education, welfare, vitalization of communities in the countries in which they operate. Moreover, through

(continued)

EXHIBIT 1 Summary of the Caux Round Table Principles for Business—Continued

innovation, effective and prudent use of resources, and free and fair competition, corporations should contribute to the economic and social development of the world community at large, not only the countries in which they operate. New technology, production, products, marketing, and communication are all means to this broader contribution.

Principle 3. Corporate Behavior: Beyond the Letter of Law toward a Spirit of Trust

With the exception of legitimate trade secrets, a corporation should recognize that sincerity, candor, truthfulness, the keeping of promises, and transparency contribute not only to the credit and stability of business activities but also the smoothness and efficiency of business transactions, particularly on the international level.

Principle 4. Respect for Rules: Beyond Trade Friction toward Cooperation

To avoid trade frictions and promote freer trade, equal business opportunity, and fair and equitable treatment for all participants, corporations should respect international and domestic rules. In addition, they should recognize that their own behavior, although legal, may still have adverse consequences.

Principle 5. Support for Multilateral Trade: Beyond Isolation toward World Community

Corporations should support the multilateral trade system of GATT/World Trade Organization and similar international agreements. They should cooperate in efforts to promote the judicious liberalization of trade and to relax those domestic measures that unreasonably hinder global commerce.

Principle 6. Respect for the Environment: Beyond Protection toward Enhancement

A corporation should protect, and where possible, improve the environment, promote sustainable development, and prevent the wasteful use of natural resources.

Principle 7. Avoidance of Illicit Operations: Beyond Profit toward Peace

A corporation should not participate in or condone bribery, money laundering, and other corrupt practices. It should not trade in arms or materials used for terrorist activities, drug traffic, or other organized crime.

Section 3. Stakeholder Principles

Customers We believe in treating all customers with dignity and that our customers are not only those who directly purchase our products and services but also those who acquire them through authorized market channels. In cases where those who use our products and services do not purchase them directly from us, we will make our best effort to select marketing and assembly/manufacturing channels that accept and follow the standards of business conduct articulated here. We have a responsibility:

- To provide our customers with the highest quality products and services consistent with their requirements.
- To treat our customers fairly in all aspects of our business transactions, including a high level of service and remedies for customer dissatisfaction.
- To make every effort to ensure that the health and safety (including environmental quality) of our customers will be sustained or enhanced by our products or services.
- To avoid disrespect for human dignity in products offered, marketing, and advertising.
- To respect the integrity of the cultures of our customers.

Employees We believe in the dignity of every employee and we therefore have a responsibility:

- To provide jobs and compensation that improve and uplift workers' circumstances in life.
- To provide working conditions that respect employees' health and dignity.
- To be honest in communications with employees and open in sharing information, limited only by legal and competitive constraints.
- To be accessible to employee input, ideas, complaints, and requests.
- To engage in good faith negotiations when conflict arises.

(continued)

EXHIBIT 1 Summary of the Caux Round Table Principles for Business—Continued

- To avoid discriminatory practices and to guarantee equal treatment and opportunity in areas such as gender, age, race, and religion.
- To promote in the corporation itself the employment of handicapped and other disadvantaged people in places of work where they can be genuinely useful.
- To protect employees from avoidable injury and illness in the workplace.
- To be sensitive to the serious unemployment problems frequently associated with business decisions and to work with governments and other agencies in addressing these dislocations.

Owners/Investors We believe in honoring the trust our investors place in us. We therefore have a responsibility:

- To apply professional and diligent management in order to secure a fair and competitive return on our owners' investment.
- To disclose relevant information to owners/investors subject only to legal and competitive constraints.
- To conserve and protect the owners/investors' assets.
- To respect owners/investors' requests, suggestions, complaints, and formal resolutions.

Suppliers We begin with the conviction that our relationship with suppliers and subcontractors, like a partnership, must be based on mutual respect. As a result, we have a responsibility:

- To seek fairness in all our activities including pricing, licensing, and rights to sell.
- To ensure that our business activities are free from coercion and unnecessary litigation, thus promoting fair competition.
- To foster long-term stability in the supplier relationship in return for value, quality, and reliability.
- To share information with suppliers and integrate them into our planning processes in order to achieve stable relationships.
- To pay suppliers on time and in accordance with agreed terms of trade.
- To seek, encourage, and prefer suppliers and subcontractors whose employment practices respect human dignity.

Competitors We believe that fair economic competition is one of the basic requirements for increasing the wealth of nations and ultimately for making possible the just distribution of goods and services. We therefore have responsibilities:

- To foster open markets for trade and investment.
- To promote competitive behavior that is socially and environmentally beneficial and demonstrates mutual respect among competitors.
- To refrain from either seeking or participating in questionable payments or favors to secure competitive advantages.
- To respect both material and intellectual property rights.
- To refuse to acquire commercial information by dishonest or unethical means, such as industrial espionage.

Communities We believe that as global corporate citizens we can contribute, even to a small extent, to such forces of reform and human rights as are at work in the communities in which we operate. We therefore have responsibilities in the communities in which we do business:

- To respect human rights and democratic institutions, and to promote them wherever practical.
- To recognize government's legitimate obligation to the society at large and to support public policies and practices that promote human development through harmonious relations between business and other segments of society.
- To collaborate in countries and areas which struggle in their economic development with those forces which are dedicated to raising standards of health, education, and workplace safety.
- To promote and stimulate sustainable development.

(continued)

EXHIBIT 1 Summary of the Caux Round Table Principles for Business—Concluded

- To play a lead role in preserving the physical environment and conserving the earth's resources.
- To support peace, security, and diversity in local communities.
- To respect the integrity of local cultures.
- To be a good citizen by supporting the communities in which it operates; this can be done through charitable donations, educational and cultural contributions, and employee participation in community and civic affairs.

Table below Illustrates the Ideals and Applications Discussed Above.

	KYOSEI and the MORAL POINT OF VIEW	*Meaning and Justification of Ethical Ideals*		
	共生	*Interest-based (Prosperity)*	*Rights-based (Fairness)*	*Duty-based (Community)*
Applying Ethical Principles	Dictation			
	Surrogation			
	Institutionalization *Macro…* and *Micro…*			

Appendix B

A Baldrige Process for Ethics?

Abstract

In this appendix we describe and explore a management tool called the Caux Round Table Self-Assessment and Improvement Process (SAIP). Based upon the Caux Round Table Principles for Business—a stakeholder-based, transcultural statement of business values—the SAIP assists executives with the task of shaping their firm's conscience through an organizational self-appraisal process. This process is modeled after the self-assessment methodology pioneered by the Malcolm Baldrige National Quality Award Program.

After briefly describing the SAIP, we address three topics. First, we examine similarities and differences between the Baldrige approach to corporate self-assessment and the self-assessment process utilized within the SAIP. Second, we report initial findings from two beta tests of the tool. These illustrate both the SAIP's ability to help organizations strengthen their commitment to ethically responsible conduct, and some of the tool's limitations. Third, we briefly analyze various dimensions of the business scandals of 2001–2002 (Enron, WorldCom, Tyco, etc.) in light of the ethical requirements articulated with the SAIP. This analysis suggests that the SAIP can help link the current concerns of stakeholders—for example, investors and the general public—to organizational practice, by providing companies with a practical way to incorporate critical lessons from these unfortunate events.

Introduction: Preventing the Collapse of Towers

> As an organization acquires a self, a distinctive identity, it becomes an institution. This involves the taking on of values, ways of acting and believing that are deemed important for their own sake. From then on self-maintenance becomes more than bare organizational survival; it becomes a struggle to preserve the uniqueness of the group in the face of new problems and altered circumstances.
>
> —Philip Selznick, *Leadership in Administration*[1]

This appendix was written by Kenneth E. Goodpaster, T. Dean Maines, and Arnold M. Weimerskirch, University of St. Thomas, Minneapolis, Minnesota, U.S.A. An earlier version of this appendix was presented at the "Ethics and Social Responsibility in Engineering and Technology" meeting, New Orleans, 2003.

For Americans, everything seemed to change in fall 2001. Why? In part at least, because our country was living in illusion, not unlike the prisoners in Plato's *Allegory of the Cave.* We were shocked on September 11 to discover that there were realities in our world far different from the shadows cast on our walls. Realities that threatened not only *individual lives*—but our entire *way of life.*

The Enron/Arthur Andersen scandal, which we can date from October and November of 2001, *also* revealed that we Americans were living in an illusion, only this time an illusion related to shadowy financial reporting—misrepresentation to concerned parties (employees, shareholders, etc.) of the realities on which their financial security was based.

The collapse of the financial towers of Enron and Andersen is parallel to the collapse of the World Trade Center towers—both revealed our vulnerability in the face of certain kinds of fanaticism. And both called forth from American public institutions an aggressive response. In the case of 9/11, it was Afghanistan and eventually Iraq. In the case of Enron and Andersen (and WorldCom and Tyco and Adelphia and many others), it was the *Sarbanes-Oxley Act of 2002* and the U.S. Department of Justice.

Many have remarked about the limitations of law when it comes to effecting changes in corporate cultures. Laws can change behavior by adjusting incentives and sanctions for those covered by them, but laws have a difficult time reaching basic ethical values—what we might call corporate *consciences.*

Why? Because the essence of corporate conscience is not in the end a matter of external *compliance;* it is a matter of internal self-assessment and improvement. It is a matter of what we as persons and corporations as organizations *stand for.*

Discussing the collapse of Enron, Warren Bennis, professor of management at the University of Southern California, wrote in the *New York Times* that:

> Mr. Lay's failing is not simply his myopia or cupidity or incompetence. It is his inability to create a company culture open to reality, one that does not discourage managers from delivering bad news. No organization can be honest with the public if it is not honest with itself.[2]

There are three key imperatives for leaders who would avoid Mr. Lay's legacy and create or maintain an organizational conscience: (1) orienting, (2) institutionalizing, and (3) sustaining ethical values.[3] These imperatives deal with placing and maintaining moral considerations in a position of authority alongside considerations of profitability and competitive strategy in the corporate mindset.

Orienting is about guiding the group toward a shared vision and a shared set of values to achieve it. The objective is to discern the dominant ethical values of the company and to subject them to critical scrutiny. Then a decision is made either to maintain those values or to adjust them as the company moves forward.

Once corporate leadership has clarified the direction it wants to take, the process of *institutionalizing* becomes paramount. How can the company's shared ethical values be made part of the operating consciousness of the company? How can they gain the attention and the allegiance of middle management and other employees?[a]

Sustaining ethical values has to do with passing on the spirit of this effort to future leaders of the organization and to the social system as a whole.

[a] The answers lie in three areas: decisive *actions*, a statement of *standards* with regular *audits*, and appropriate *incentives*.

While these imperatives fall within the purview of company leaders, they are of direct concern to all members of the firm. Leaders who successfully address these tasks engender an organizational culture that supports and propagates ethical conduct. Such a culture promotes the moral flourishing of individual employees as they pursue their professional vocations—for example, enabling engineers to act with both *technical proficiency* and *moral integrity.*

Perhaps the most difficult of these three imperatives is the second. As most engineers can appreciate, *institutionalizing* an ideal, or rendering it *operational,* calls for a thorough understanding of current practices, along with the ability to articulate and measure the degree to which current practices fall short of aspirations.

Ethics as a Business Imperative

Why should corporate leaders concern themselves with institutionalizing corporate conscience? Certainly the scandals at Enron and Andersen have heightened awareness of the need for ethical business conduct. At a minimum, they have led to a clearer recognition of the concrete misfortunes unethical behavior can bring. Not the least of these misfortunes is a tarnished corporate reputation, which can impair a company's long-term sustainability to the detriment of all its stakeholders. A number of studies suggest the vital role corporate reputation plays in the eyes of customers and investors. *The Millennium Poll on Corporate Social Responsibility*—a 1999 survey conducted with 25,000 individuals in 23 countries—revealed that one in five consumers had either rewarded or punished companies in the previous year based on their perceived social performance.[4] A 2001 study by the public relations firm Hill and Knowlton found that nearly 80% of Americans consider reputation when buying a company's product.[5] The Hill and Knowlton study also showed that more than 70% of investors consider reputation when purchasing stocks. The *2002 PricewaterhouseCoopers Sustainability Survey Report* noted that:

> [t]he mantra in today's business world is honesty in accounting, a natural and appropriate response to the scandals at Enron, WorldCom, and a growing list of top tier U.S. companies. Tomorrow, however, we will be expected to go a giant step further—creating corporations that are sustainable, as well as accountable . . . [C]ompanies that fail to become sustainable—that ignore the risks associated with ethics, governance, and the "triple bottom line" of economic, environmental, and social issues—are courting disaster. In today's world of immense and instant market reaction, an action or inaction that undermines the integrity, ethics, or reputation of a company can lead to immediate and dire financial consequences.[6]

The results of the *2002 Sustainability Survey* indicate that senior executives are beginning to recognize the connection between ethical behavior and corporate viability. Ninety percent of those surveyed indicated that their company had adopted "sustainable practices"—defined as a "business approach to create long-term shareholder value by embracing opportunities and managing risks deriving from economic, environmental, and social developments"—in order to enhance corporate reputation. Seventy-five percent indicated that they had done so as a way of developing a competitive advantage. Customer demand, revenue growth, shareholder demand, and access to capital also figured prominently in responses (see Exhibit 1).

EXHIBIT 1 **Top Ten Reasons Companies Are Becoming More Socially Responsible**

Source: Reproduced with permission from PriceWaterhouseCoopers *2002 Sustainability Survey Report*.

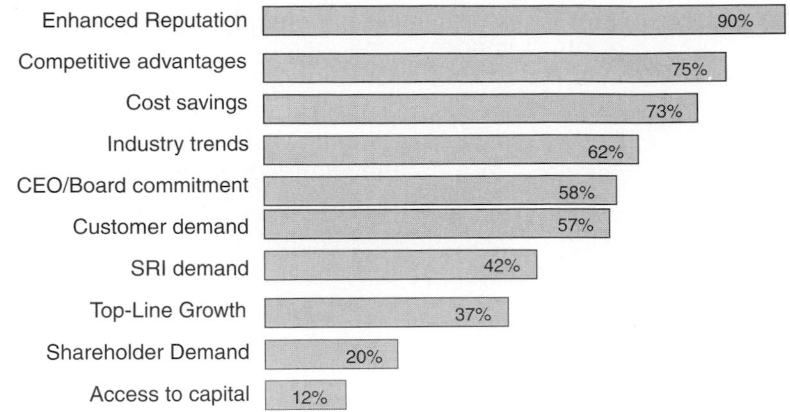

Studies such as these support the conviction that institutionalizing corporate conscience is increasingly a mandatory task for senior leaders. A failure to integrate ethical values into decisions and actions taken at all levels of an organization potentially puts the entire enterprise at risk, jeopardizing relationships with stakeholders whose cooperation is required for long-term business success.

From Aspirations to Operational Assessments and Improvements

The Caux Round Table *Principles for Business* were officially launched in July 1994. They emerged from discussions among Japanese, European, and American executives, and were fashioned in part from a document called the *Minnesota Principles.*[b] The Caux Principles articulate a comprehensive set of ethical norms that could be embraced by a business operating internationally in diverse cultural environments. For this reason, the framers of the Caux Principles had to formulate them so that both Eastern and Western mindsets could find them intelligible and acceptable.

The Caux Principles rest upon two basic ethical ideals—human dignity and the Japanese concept of *kyosei.* The former values each person as an end and implies that one's worth can never can be reduced to his or her utility as a means to someone else's purpose. The ideal of *kyosei* was defined by Ryuzaburo Kaku, the late chairman of Canon, Inc., as "living and working together for the good of all."[7] *Kyosei* is a concept that tempers individual, organizational, and even national self-interest with concern for more embracing "common goods."[8]

The Caux Principles express these two ideals in a format that progresses toward greater specificity. The document's Preamble establishes the vital need for corporate conscience in the modern business world. Then follow seven General Principles which clarify how the values of human dignity and kyosei inform business practice within a global context. The third and final section of the Caux Principles utilizes a stakeholder framework to supplement the general norms with more specific guidelines. These Stakeholder Principles specify how the ideals

[b] The Caux Round Table Principles for Business may be viewed on the Caux Round Table's Web site (www.cauxroundtable.org). In language and form, the Minnesota Principles provided the substantial basis for the Caux Principles. To obtain a copy of the *Minnesota* Principles, contact the Center for Ethical Business Cultures (www.cebcglobal.org).

FIGURE 1
Progressive Articulation of the Caux Round Table Principles for Business

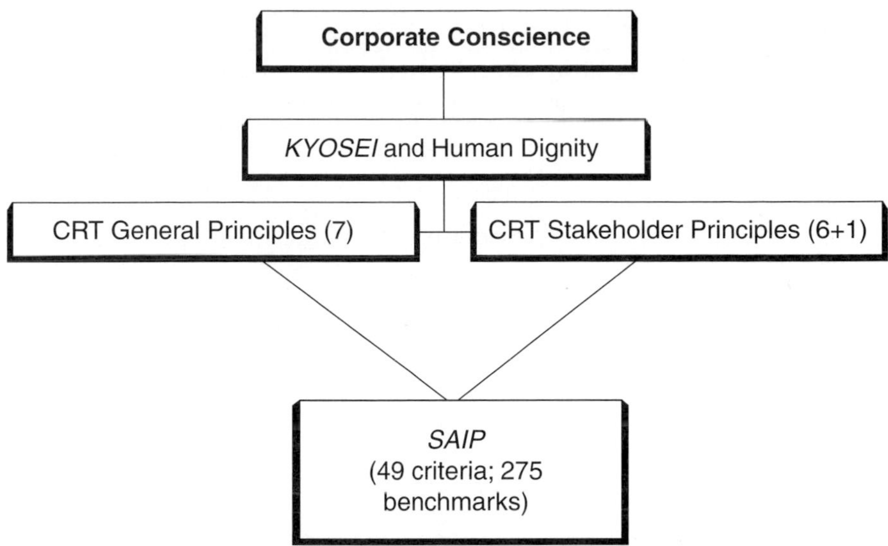

of human dignity and *kyosei* engage a company's relationships with customers, employees, investors, suppliers, competitors, and communities.

The Caux Principles help define the phrase "principled business leadership." Their progressive articulation continues with the Self-Assessment and Improvement Process (SAIP), which facilitates a more direct assessment of the fit between the *Principles* and a company's operations (see Figure l).[c] The SAIP enables managers to identify behavior inconsistent with the principles, detect current and emerging corporate responsibility concerns, and launch targeted improvement initiatives. It equips senior executives to address the growing expectation of responsible business conduct through a confidential, systematic self-appraisal.

Applying the SAIP is a multistage process, involving data collection, scoring, feedback, and action. The process is company-led and company-controlled. It also is company-confidential, at least during the early stages of its application. There is extensive process documentation to accompany the SAIP, and the tool may be applied to corporations either *in toto* or in part (e.g., certain divisions or business units).[d]

The SAIP is structured around the Caux Principles. A company's performance against each of the seven General Principles is evaluated from seven distinct perspectives: How well the firm has fulfilled the fundamental duties that flow from a principle, and how well it has realized the aspirations articulated by that principle in its relations with six stakeholder groups. The result is a 7-by-7 matrix of assessment criteria (see Figure 2).

To illustrate the use of the SAIP, let us consider a company's self-assessment regarding the general principle "Business Behavior" and a specific stakeholder

[c] The SAIP was developed by a working group of practitioners and academics, including Harry R. Halloran, American Refining Group; T. Dean Maines, University of St. Thomas; Charles M. Denny, ADC, Inc. (retired); Kenneth E. Goodpaster, University of St. Thomas; Timothy T. Greene, The Enlightened World Foundation; Lee M. Kennedy, 3M; Clinton O. Larson, Honeywell, Inc. (retired); Arnold M. Weimerskirch, Honeywell, Inc. (retired); Stephen B. Young, Caux Round Table.

[d] The SAIP is currently being translated and adapted for use in Japan and Germany. The goal is to have 50 U.S. corporations utilizing the SAIP within one year after the completion of beta testing.

FIGURE 2 The SAIP Matrix

Category	1 Fundamental duties	2 Customers	3 Employees	4 Owners/ operators	5 Suppliers/ partners	6 Competitors	7 Communities
1. Responsibilities of business	1.1	1.2	1.3	1.4	1.5	1.6	1.7
2. Economic and social impact of business	2.1	2.2	2.3	2.4	2.5	2.6	2.7
3. Business behavior	3.1	3.2	3.3	3.4	3.5	3.6	3.7
4. Respect for rules	4.1	4.2	4.3	4.4	4.5	4.6	4.7
5. Support for multilateral trade	5.1	5.2	5.3	5.4	5.5	5.6	5.7
6. Respect for the environment	6.1	6.2	6.3	6.4	6.5	6.6	6.7
7. Avoidance of illicit operations	7.1	7.2	7.3	7.4	7.5	7.6	7.7

Note: The SAIP matrix translates the 7 general CRT principles and the 7 stakeholder principles into 49 assessment categories, containing criteria and more detailed benchmarks.

group, owners and investors. To perform this appraisal, the company must reflect upon the assessment criterion contained in cell 3.4, which addresses the challenge of developing trust with shareholders through truthfulness and transparency. Criterion 3.4 is shown in Exhibit 2, together with some of the specific questions ("benchmarks") that amplify and elaborate it. For example, the benchmarks require the company to consider its established policies and practices for responding to shareholder inquiries, the way it addresses the issue of revealing foreseeable material risks, and the process it uses to ensure that auditors render an independent judgment on its financial statements. In short, criterion 3.4 and its benchmarks prompt a company to evaluate its standards for disclosures to shareholders, and the processes it employs to ensure these standards are consistently met.

The *SAIP* identifies the maximum possible score a company can receive for its performance against these interrogatories. By comparing its responses against a set of quantification guidelines, the firm can generate a score that characterizes its current performance level for each cell of the assessment matrix. By totaling the scores for all 49 cells, the company can generate an overall indication of its performance against the requirements of the Caux Principles for Business.

The scoring process highlights areas where company performance is relatively strong or weak. This information can help the organization formulate initiatives intended to improve the company's conduct. In addition, sharing this information with critical stakeholders can improve the company's credibility.

EXHIBIT 2 **Cell 3.4: Criterion and Selected Benchmarks for SAIP Long Form**

3.4. Owners/Investors

What level of trust has the company achieved with owners/investors? How transparent is the company to owners/investors, and how is this transparency achieved and measured?

3.4.1 What are the company's policies concerning:
3.4.1.1. the disclosure of information to owners/investors;
3.4.1.2. formal shareholder resolutions;
3.4.1.3. responses to inquiries, suggestions, or complaints from owners/investors. . . .

3.4.3 How does the company address the following trust and transparency issues:
3.4.3.1. Preparing, auditing, and disclosing financial and operating results in accordance with high quality standards of financial reporting and auditing;
3.4.3.2. Disclosing major share ownership and voting rights;
3.4.3.3. Revealing material foreseeable risk factors. . . .

3.4.5 How does the company perform an annual audit? Describe the applicable processes, including how an independent auditor is used to provide an external and objective assurance on the way in which financial statements have been prepared and audited?

3.4.6 What are the company's results with respect to third-party ratings of owner/investor relations?

What *results* might a company hope for from the SAIP? At a minimum, it means that company performance is being evaluated against a global standard for ethical business conduct. In the process, it also serves as an assessment of compliance for U.S. companies bound by the federal sentencing guidelines. The SAIP helps to identify company strengths and to detect problems and emerging issues (an "early warning system"). It also clarifies improvement opportunities based on systematic, credible data.

As to *rewards,* the SAIP promises several: (1) improved management awareness and control; (2) enhanced congruence between stated values and behavior; (3) reduced risk of noncompliance; (4) improved communication and credibility with multiple stakeholders; (5) increased likelihood of positive evaluations from third-party monitoring organizations (for example, non-governmental organizations and socially responsible investment funds); (6) enhanced reputation among peer companies; and (7) improved revenues and profits.

Building on Baldrige—A Second Pillar

The authors have developed the SAIP for measuring the degree to which an organization has *institutionalized* its ethical values. We have seen that the SAIP rests upon the Caux Round Table Principles as a kind of pillar. But there is a second pillar of equal importance. The SAIP utilizes the concepts behind the *Malcolm Baldrige National Quality Program.* The program has had a profound impact on American businesses. Its success in revolutionizing American industry led to the program's extension into education and healthcare, where it is exerting a similar positive influence. The inventors of the SAIP have attempted to build on this legacy by applying the Baldrige self-assessment model within the arena of business ethics.

The Baldrige Criteria for Performance Excellence have been described as a large open-book test on business management—"Everything you've always wanted to know about business management, but didn't have time to ask." They serve as:

- A focused business excellence model.
- A realistic basis for self-assessment.
- A comprehensive communications vehicle.
- A mechanism for continual improvement.
- A framework for learning.

Consistently applied, the Baldrige Criteria provide a model for assessing the current state of business performance and a roadmap to performance excellence.

Similarly, the SAIP can be viewed as a large open-book test on business ethics, encompassing all the corporate social responsibility questions business leaders now feel compelled to ask—a kind *of corporate* examination of conscience. The goal of the SAIP is an ethical reengineering of the corporation in the same sense that the Baldrige Criteria helped reengineer corporate performance.

Comparison of the Baldrige Model and the SAIP

Principles

Both the SAIP and the Baldrige Criteria are nonintrusive and aspirational. They focus on common *results* rather than common procedures. For example, the SAIP does not specify the exact methods, procedures, or processes that should be used to assure a culture of trust, as these may well depend upon business and organizational specifics. However, the SAIP and the Baldrige Program both articulate a set of foundational beliefs and behaviors that are characteristic of exemplary organizations. In the case of the SAIP, these are the Caux Round Table Principles; the Baldrige refers to them as *core values* (see Exhibit 3).

EXHIBIT 3 Comparison of the Baldrige Core Values and the Caux Round Table Principles

Core Values behind the Baldrige Process	CRT Principles behind the SAIP
Visionary leadership	Beyond shareholders toward stakeholders*
Customer-driven excellence	Toward innovation, justice, and world community
Organizational and personal learning	Beyond the letter of the law toward a spirit of trust
Valuing employees and partners	Respect for rules
Agility	Support for multilateral trade
Focus on the future	Respect for the environment
Managing for innovation	Avoidance of illicit operations
Management by fact	
Social responsibility	
Focus on results and creating value	
Systems perspective	

* A set of principles is included that covers relations with customers, employees, owners/investors, suppliers, competitors, and communities.

Measurement

An important feature of the SAIP is its introduction of measurement and quantification into the ethics conversation. Specifically, it quantifies the degree to which a culture of trust has been institutionalized in an organization. The scoring system, based on 1,000 points, evaluates approach, deployment, and results. In the Baldrige Program, companies are similarly evaluated on a 1,000-point scale. Leading Baldrige companies score approximately 700 points; no company has ever approached 1,000 points. Although a data base has yet to be built, an SAIP score of 700 points might represent "best in class." It should be noted that a score of less that 1,000 points would not imply that an organization is unethical, but rather than a culture of trust has yet to be completely institutionalized throughout the organization—a possible but daunting achievement.

SAIP assessment is done by a unique consensus process. Consensus is a powerful win-win process which is somewhat difficult to understand. We learn at an early age that we get our way through the power of persuasion, with the objective of winning over our opponent. This win-lose system stresses articulation over understanding. It frequently leads to gridlock. To break the gridlock, we resort to compromise. In a compromise, neither side completely achieves its objectives and a lose-lose situation results.

The consensus process requires that all team members agree with and support the decisions made. This is critical in a field such as ethics, which has "degrees of goodness." We would probably all agree, for example, that employers should pay a fair wage, but what constitutes a fair wage might be a subject for considerable discussion. The consensus process drives that discussion to a conclusion with which everyone can agree. Frequently, consensus decisions require some generalization in order to reach agreement. Such generalizations uncover areas where more research is needed and hence motivate further learning.

Differences

The inventors patterned the SAIP after the Baldrige assessment process in order to leverage the power of the Baldrige model. At the same time, they recognized that there are some fundamental differences between a performance excellence system and an ethics assessment. The inventors recognized three significant differences and designed the SAIP to accommodate those differences. They are:

1. *An organization's ethics assessment is likely to be regarded as more proprietary than its performance excellence system.* All the Baldrige Award winners have had their performance excellence systems evaluated by teams of external examiners. While the examiners themselves are pledged not to divulge any information about the organizations they assess, the Baldrige Award winners themselves have been very generous in sharing their knowledge and practices in a public manner. Organizations may not be as willing to expose or share their ethics assessments. The SAIP scoring will largely be done internally by members of the organization. Accordingly, the inventors have tailored the scoring system to facilitate organizational learning rather than scoring precision.
2. *Ethics results are likely to be more difficult to quantify than other business results.* Any Baldrige application contains several pages of graphs showing performance levels, trends, targets and benchmarks. Earnings per share and similar business results are stated as exact numbers and are regarded as more precise than perhaps they really are. While some ethics results are quantifiable—e.g., health- and safety-related incidents—many will not be. The question then becomes,

"What constitutes evidence in the SAIP?" To help resolve this problem, the inventors have accepted other kinds of data as empirical indicators of responsible conduct—for example, public recognition. Public recognition would include awards for outstanding community citizenship, positive reviews by rating agencies, and similar acknowledgments of exemplary behavior.

3. *The SAIP is designed around a discrete set of principles and stakeholders, while the Baldrige process is an integrated system for business performance.* In accommodating this difference, the inventors incorporated a subtle change in scoring methodology. The Baldrige assessment contains seven evaluation categories, six of which are scored on approach and deployment. Category 7 reports the results which derive from the approaches deployed in the first six categories. By contrast, the SAIP (in its unabridged form) evaluates approach, deployment, and results for each of the 49 cells within the assessment matrix. This assures that there is actual verification of an organization's progress in institutionalizing a culture of responsible conduct and trust.

Beta Test Lessons

If the SAIP is to effectively shape and institutionalize corporate conscience, it must be easily employed by companies. To assess how well the SAIP fares against this requirement, beta tests of the tool have been initiated at two firms. The first test began in mid-2002; the second was launched in early 2003.

Both beta test companies are privately held. In both cases, the firm's participation in the beta test process was instigated by its chief executive officer, who viewed the SAIP as an opportunity to evaluate and strengthen the organization's commitment to responsible conduct. Both chief executives also have played a critical role in the tool's implementation. However, similarities between the companies end there. The two organizations participate in different sectors of the economy: One is an energy company that produces a range of refined fuels and lubricants for the domestic U.S. market, while the other is a U.S.-based firm that provides consulting services to schools, communities, and public agencies primarily located within the developing world. The energy firm recorded revenues in excess of $130 million in 2001. It employs roughly 300 individuals, with most working at a single site. The consulting operation is little more than one-quarter the size of its beta test counterpart, recording 2001 revenues of $35 million. Its 200 employees are located in 12 countries.

As of June 2003, the beta tests remained in progress. However, the results to that point led to three preliminary conclusions about the SAIP's usefulness and effectiveness. In turn, these conclusions have influenced the tool's ongoing development.

Lesson 1

Implementation of the SAIP is time- and labor-intensive. The version of the SAIP used in the beta tests contains 275 benchmarks. Both companies faced the challenge of responding to all of these benchmarks, and then scoring each individual response. For small- to medium-sized organizations, which typically face tight staffing constraints, such a task can be overwhelming. This is particularly true if the firm must simultaneously confront other challenges, for example, weathering an economic downturn, investigating a potential acquisition, or undertaking a critical, highly visible consulting engagement—actual situations encountered by our two pilot companies. The practical effect of undertaking the SAIP within such an environment was to further tax already heavily burdened employees. Consequently, both organizations were compelled to revise their original timetable for implementing the SAIP.

The SAIP's inventors discussed a streamlined version of the tool about a year prior to inaugurating the first beta test. The experiences of the two beta test companies decisively confirmed the need for such a design. Efforts to develop an abridged SAIP have led to two important products: a set of "gateway" assessment criteria, and an implementation model that recognizes a spectrum of ways to utilize the SAIP.

To understand the gateway criteria, one must recall that in the most detailed version of the SAIP each criterion is associated with an average of five to six benchmarks. The benchmarks explicate the criterion by further detailing its requirements. They inject a degree of specificity into the self-assessment process that helps guard against vague or overly general responses. But this specificity comes at a price, namely, the time that must be invested to develop and evaluate detailed replies. The gateway criteria limit the time necessary to perform the self-assessment by capturing within a single query much of the content expressed by the benchmarks. Use of the gateway criteria compels a company to consider this critical content, while reducing the number of responses it must formulate and score from 275 to 49.

Early in the SAIP's development, its inventors recognized the flexibility latent in the tool. The drafting of the gateway criteria, however, enabled them to better articulate the range of implementation options available to users of the tool. Figure 3 illustrates three different levels or stages at which a company could engage the SAIP. These stages are distinguished by several factors, including:

- *Who* is performing the assessment.

FIGURE 3 **Three Stages of Engagement with the SAIP: (I) The Executive and Board Survey, (II) the Senior Management Survey, and (III) the Long-Form SAIP (Each stage utilizes a more elaborate rendering of the criteria and benchmarks than the one preceding.)**

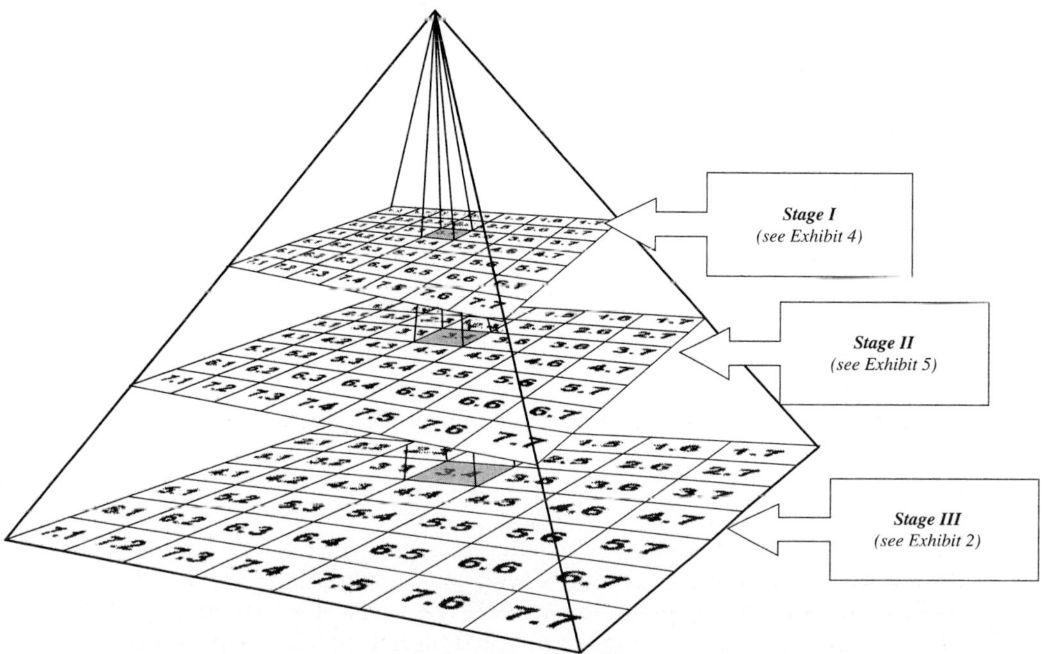

- The *criteria* employed within the assessment process.
- *The performance dimensions* that serve as the assessment's primary focus.
- The *length of time* necessary to complete the assessment.
- The expected *outcomes*.

The Stage I assessment represents the most rudimentary application of the SAIP. At this stage, the assessment is performed by the CEO and/or the company's board of directors. A version of the tool called the SAIP *Executive and Board Survey* is used. The *Executive and Board Survey* employs the gateway criteria. However, at this stage the self-assessment is limited to a single performance dimension: it asks executives to evaluate the *approach* taken by their company to each of the 49 criteria (see Exhibit 4). The *Executive and Board Survey* is designed to be completed in approximately 90 minutes. Assessors are not required to collect data as part of the Stage I appraisal; rather, they are asked to assign a score based on their present understanding of the firm's operations. Hence, the outcome at this level is "systematic speculation" about how the organization addresses critical ethical aspirations. Such speculation is obviously imprecise, but the process of working through the survey generates greater awareness of corporate responsibility issues. In short, the Stage I assessment raises questions which prompt chief executives and board members to undertake a more detailed evaluation of the company's practices.

Stage II employs a version of the SAIP called the *Senior Management Survey*. The requirements of the Stage II assessment differ from those of Stage I in four ways. First, more perspectives are engaged in Stage II: As suggested by its name, the Senior Management Survey is designed to be completed by the organization's chief operating officer and his or her leadership team. Ideally, this would take place in a working session of four to eight hours. Second, while the gateway criteria are utilized in Stage II, a second performance dimension is introduced. That is, the assessors must consider not only the *approach* the company takes to each criterion, but also *deployment*, that is, the extent to which the approach is utilized across the company's various divisions, functions, or subsidiaries (see Exhibit 5). Third, data is introduced in Stage II to confirm (or refute) the assessors' perceptions of the company's corporate responsibility efforts. Evidence that typically would be considered includes statements of corporate values, documented

EXHIBIT 4 Cell 3.4: Executive and Board Survey Gateway Criterion (SAIP Stage I)

3.4 Owners/Investors

How does the company elicit the trust of owners/investors (e.g., through responsible disclosures, timely and complete responses to shareholder/investor inquiries, governance policies, comprehensive and accurate external audits, etc.)?

EXHIBIT 5 Cell 3.4: Senior Management Survey Gateway Criterion (SAIP Stage II)

3.4 Owners/Investors

How, and to what extent, does the company elicit the trust of owners/investors (e.g., through responsible disclosures, timely and complete responses to shareholder/investor inquiries, governance policies, comprehensive and accurate external audits, etc.)?

policies and practices, procedural statements, and other forms of written guidance. Fourth, the outcomes in Stage II move beyond enhanced awareness towards more tangible benefits. For example, the company receives an initial score for its efforts on a 1,000-point scale. It also preliminarily identifies improvement opportunities that might be addressed by specific programmatic initiatives.

At Stage III the company encounters the complete or ("long-form") version of the SAIP. The most important difference between Stage II and Stage III is that in the latter a company utilizes the unabridged assessment criteria—including the 275 explanatory benchmarks—rather than the gateway criteria. The growth in the assessment task is accompanied by a corresponding expansion of the time required to complete the self-appraisal. Depending upon their circumstances, companies can expect to take between 3 and 12 months to complete the process. Furthermore, the self-assessment in Stage III touches upon *results* as well as *approach* and *deployment* (see Exhibit 2). Thus, the data the assessors must consider will extend beyond statements of policy and practice to actual outcomes of the company's corporate responsibility efforts, both qualitative and quantitative. The outcomes at Stage III include a score on a 1,000-point scale, an identified set of improvement opportunities, and (most importantly) a detailed plan to address these opportunities through specific initiatives and actions. Thus, the ultimate result at Stage III is an enhancement of the company's performance, a consequence of implementing actions suggested by the SAIP's outcomes.

Lesson 2

Full implementation of the SAIP requires more than just collecting data, developing responses to benchmarks, and scoring these responses. It requires the organization's leadership to reflect on these outcomes and accurately judge their implications. Thus, dialogue and discernment play a vital role in the application of the SAIP. They catalyze the process by which outcomes from its self-assessment segment are translated into actions that advance the institutionalization of corporate conscience. At best, a failure to subject the self-assessment's outcomes to discussion and managerial judgment amounts to a missed opportunity. On this point, the comments of the chief financial officer of a beta test company are instructive. At an informal midcourse review of the company's implementation efforts, this executive observed that:

> [a] lack of dialogue between senior leaders—the opportunity to compare how I would have responded to a benchmark to how others would have replied—prevented us from forming a collective understanding of the results. In short, it prevented us from drawing more and better fruit from a process in which we had invested significant time and effort.[e]

At worst, a failure to engage in this activity undermines the SAIP's purpose. Mechanically applying the results of self-assessment, without subjecting them to the demands of *prudence*—understood not as narrow self-interest, but as the capacity to judge the best way to achieve the moral good within a set of concrete circumstances—reduces the SAIP to a surrogate for ethical decision making within the organization. In short, this misapplication turns the tool into a substitute for corporate ethical reflection. The SAIP is intended to assist, not replace, the ethical deliberation of executives. It is designed to facilitate the institutionalization of corporate conscience, not its outsourcing.

[e] Personal communication, March 27, 2003.

Lesson 3

The SAIP's criteria and benchmarks are useful not only for designing programmatic initiatives intended to strengthen corporate conscience, but also for shaping strategic decisions. This point was underscored by the experience of the energy company during its beta test. Immediately after completing the data collection stage of the SAIP, the firm confronted the opportunity to acquire a valuable piece of technology. The acquisition would take place through the purchase of a second refinery. Buying the refinery would necessitate rationalizing operations across both sites, as the technology in question could not be relocated to the company's original production facility. A likely outcome of this action would have been the layoff of approximately 20 to 30 employees.

However, the company's CEO challenged his staff to address this task differently—that is, "without the loss of a single job." The decision to issue this challenge resulted from his review of SAIP criteria and benchmarks relevant to the company's situation. While the SAIP does not mandate a "no-layoff policy," the chief executive's approach to this decision illustrates an important point: The assessment questions contained within the SAIP can help to illuminate ethical dimensions of the strategic decisions facing a company. By highlighting these dimensions, the criteria and benchmarks help decision makers identify the ethical implications of the various options they may be considering—implications that otherwise might have been overlooked. The recognition of these ethical dimensions offers executives a chance to better shape their decisions to honor the legitimate moral claims of the individuals and groups affected by them.

Conclusion

In this paper, we began with a reflection on the collapse of towers—both the World Trade Center towers and the Enron-Andersen towers. Restoring the damages associated with these collapses will take time and enormous effort. In the case of the Enron-Andersen restoration, the economic confidence of a whole society is at stake, and it is imperative that concrete measures be taken to assure not only legal compliance in the future, but something deeper: corporate conscience. In our opinion, the SAIP, built as it is on the pillars of the Caux Principles and the Baldrige Process, offers a pathway to the restoration that we seek. It represents a comprehensive, tested measure of the degree to which a company has institutionalized fundamental ethical values. Charles M. Denny, former CEO of ADC Telecommunications, Inc., summarized the matter eloquently:

> The only way a director can totally understand the behavior of a company is to shake it from top to bottom, by means of a thorough and systematic assessment like the SAIP. Performing just such an assessment is critical if directors are to assure themselves that the company for which they are responsible is performing as they believe it should.[9]

No tool, including the SAIP, can guarantee responsible corporate conduct. But it seems reasonable to suggest that honest, forthright application of the SAIP could help uncover behavior and tendencies like those which undermined Enron, Andersen, and other companies. It would be difficult to respond with honesty and integrity to the questions in Exhibit 2 (Cell 3.4 of the SAIP) about financial disclosure, auditing, material risk factors, and auditor objectivity while still engaging in the behaviors that gave rise to the scandals.

The pursuit of corporate conscience suggests that engineering and ethics perhaps have more to offer each other than one may have thought. The Hungarian engineer Theodore von Karman purportedly said, "Scientists discover the world that exists; engineers create the world that never was." To which we could add, "ethicists seek the world that ought to be." At graduation ceremonies each year, engineering students at the University of St. Thomas recite the "Obligation of the Engineer," an adaptation of the "Faith of the Engineer" prepared by the *Engineers' Council for Professional Development.* In part, it says:

> As an engineer, I pledge to practice integrity and fair dealing, tolerance and respect, and to uphold devotion to the standards and the dignity of my profession, conscious always that my skill carries with it the obligation to serve humanity by making best use of the Earth's precious wealth.

The fulfillment of this pledge depends not just on the moral character of the *individual* engineer, but also the moral climate of the organization wherein he or she practices. In short, a robust corporate conscience helps create an organizational context that enables engineers to employ their *technical skill* with *moral integrity.*

Conversely, if scientists seek to understand what is and ethicists seek what ought to be, then engineers—by showing how to create a world that never was—can help build a bridge from the former to the latter. We believe the Caux Round Table *Self-Assessment and Improvement Process* is an example of such a bridge, a tool that uses the quality engineering concepts behind the Baldrige Process to foster corporate cultures supportive of behaviors which "ought to be." Should we not expect corporate executives and boards of directors to create such cultures? We think so.

References

1. Selznick, P. (1957) *Leadership in Administration: A Sociological Interpretation*. Harper & Row, New York.
2. Bennis, W. (2002, January 17). A corporate fear of too much truth. *New York Times*, p. D11.
3. Goodpaster, K. E. (1989) Ethical imperatives and corporate leadership, in K. Andrews, ed., *Ethics in Practice*. Harvard Business School Press, Boston: 212–228.
4. Environics, Ltd. (1999) Millennium Poll on Corporate Social Responsibility. Retrieved May 15, 2003, from www.pwcglobal.com/extweb/ncpressrelease.nsf/0/07eab72b718eelee852567fc005ee5df/$FILE/Millennium_Exec.A4.pdf.
5. Hill and Knowlton, Inc. (2001) Corporate Citizen Watch Survey. Retrieved May 15, 2003, from www.hillandknowlton.com/common/file.php/pg/dodo/hnk_global/binaries/7/HK%202001%20Corp%20Citizen%20Watch.pdf.
6. PricewaterhouseCoopers, LLP. (2002) Sustainability Survey Report. Retrieved May 15, 2003, from www.pwcglobal.com/extweb/ncsurvres.nsf/0cc1191c627d157d8525650600609c03/9ff9d50e5171b38b85256c400056c1c8/$FILE/Sustainability%20Final.pdf.
7. Kaku, R. (1997) The path of kyosei. *Harvard Business Review* 75(4): 55–63.
8. Goodpaster, K.E. (2006) Bridging east and west in management ethics: Kyosei and the moral point of view, in K.E. Goodpaster, L.L. Nash, & H.C. de Bettignies, eds., *Business Ethics: Policies and Persons*. McGraw-Hill, New York: 583–593.
9. Goodpaster, K.E., Maines, T.D., & Weimerskirch, A.M. (2003, December 1). Ethical re-engineering. *Minneapolis Star-Tribune*, p. D3.

Appendix C

Self-Assessment and Improvement Process: Executive Survey

Instructions

This survey is designed to help you perform a preliminary assessment of how your company addresses issues of corporate responsibility. It is based on the principle that capable processes yield results which consistently meet desired specifications.

More specifically, it invites you to examine the **approach** your company takes to forty-nine criteria for responsible conduct, and to consider how well **developed** this approach is. By "approach," we mean *the method, process, or practice your company uses to address a specific criterion.* The forty-nine criteria are derived from the Caux Round Table *Principles for Business,* a comprehensive standard for ethical business behavior.

STEP 1. For each criterion, please rate the level of development attained by your company's approach on a ten point scale. Please mark your rating in the blank adjacent to the criterion.

0--------1--------2--------3--------4--------5--------6--------7--------8--------9--------10

No Approach	Moderate Development	Excellent Development

Please base your rating on the following questions:

- Does your company have a process or a practice that addresses the criterion's requirements?
- Is the process documented?
- Is the process effective? Does it achieve its intended purpose?
- Does your company have a way to evaluate and improve the process over time?

To the extent your answer to each of these is affirmative, your company's approach will qualify for a higher rating on the scale.

These following guideposts may be helpful to your evaluation:

0 points	No process or practice
2–3 points	Some evidence of a policy or practice. Documentation may be outdated or rudimentary at best.
5 points	A documented policy or practice exists, with some evidence of its effectiveness.
7–8 points	A documented policy or practice exists. There is evidence that this approach has proven largely effective over time. The organization has examined and modified the approach to enhance its effectiveness, although a formal improvement mechanism has not been established.
10 points	The company has implemented a proven, documented approach that is supported by a systematic improvement methodology.

Do not attempt to be overly precise in your rating. Simply assign a score that indicates your assessment of your company's approach in light of the four questions and the guideposts, given your present knowledge of your firm's activities.

Note: **You may encounter criteria that are inapplicable to your company, due to the current nature of your firm's operations. In such cases, do not rate your company against that criterion. Simply mark "N/A" in the adjacent blank.**

STEP 2. Once you have completed your ratings, transfer them to the *Executive Summary Scorecard.* **Total both rows and columns.** This will enable you to see how your company fares against both the Caux Round Table's seven General *Principles for Business* (rows) and the more specific Stakeholder *Principles* (columns).

Please note that the maximum possible score for your company will be reduced by 10 points for each inapplicable criterion. For example, if you encounter two inapplicable criteria, the maximum total score your company could attain is 490 minus (2 X 10), or 470 points.

Stakeholder: Fundamental Duties

Score (0–10)

Criterion 1.1 *Principle: Beyond Shareholders towards Stakeholders*

How does the company manage its fundamental duty to provide products and/or services that promote the common good and human dignity?

|-------|-------|-------|-------|-------|-------|-------|-------|-------|-------|

0 5 10

Lesser Quality — Greater Quality ______

Criterion 2.1 *Principle: Economic/Social Impact of Business*

How does the company promote economic and social advancement in the countries in which it develops, produces, or sells?

|-------|-------|-------|-------|-------|-------|-------|-------|-------|-------|

0 5 10

No Approach — Moderate Development — Excellent Development ______

Criterion 3.1 *Principle: Business Behavior*

How does the company achieve trust with its stakeholders (e.g., through honesty, transparency, candor, promise-keeping, and reliability)?

|-------|-------|-------|-------|-------|-------|-------|-------|-------|-------|

0 5 10

No Approach — Moderate Development — Excellent Development ______

Criterion 4.1 *Principle: Respect for Rules*

How does the company manage compliance with the letter and spirit of national and international rules?

|-------|-------|-------|-------|-------|-------|-------|-------|-------|-------|

0 5 10

No Approach — Moderate Development — Excellent Development ______

Criterion 5.1 *Principle: Support for Multilateral Trade*

How does the company support international agreements on multilateral trade and promote the liberalization of trade (e.g., by supporting fair trade policies and discouraging protectionism)?

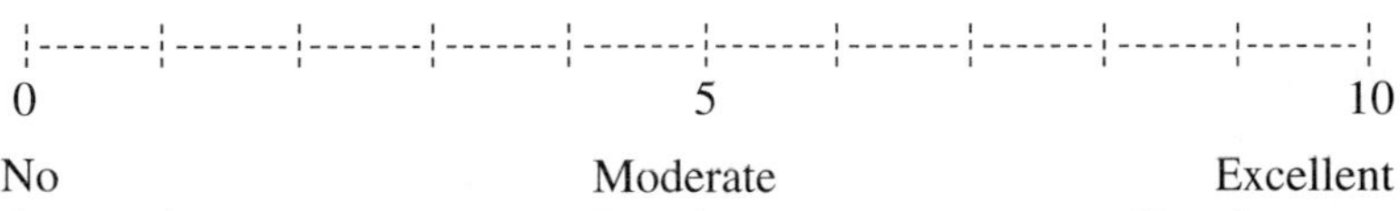

0	5	10
No Approach	Moderate Development	Excellent Development

______

Criterion 6.1 *Principle: Respect for the Environment*

How does the company manage and assure the environmental sustainability of its operations, products, and services?

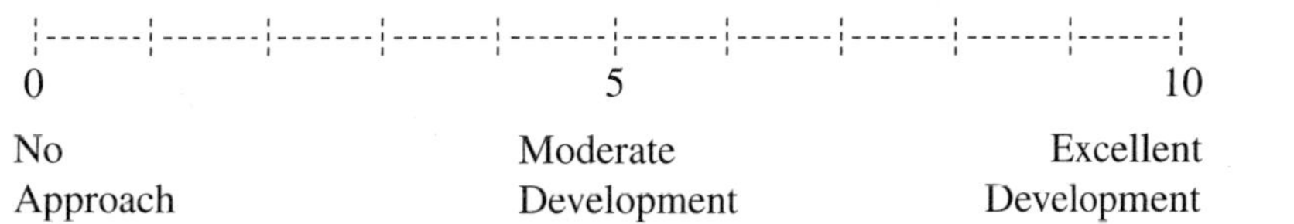

0	5	10
No Approach	Moderate Development	Excellent Development

______

Criterion 7.1 *Principle: Avoidance of Illicit Operations*

How does the company take action, by itself or collaboratively, to prevent illicit and corrupt activities (e.g., money laundering, drug trafficking, organized crime, etc.)?

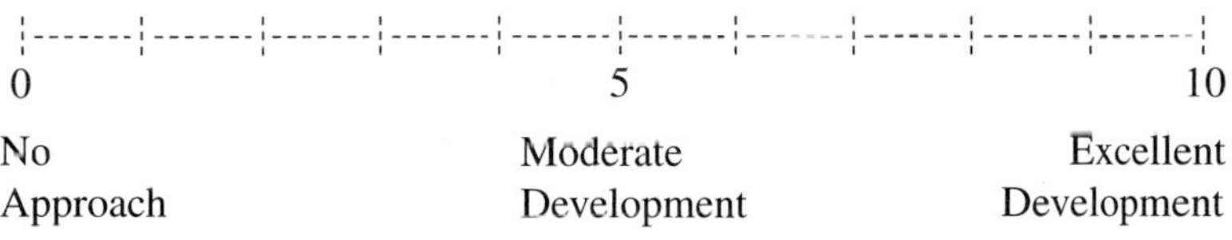

0	5	10
No Approach	Moderate Development	Excellent Development

______

Total Score (maximum possible points = 70) ______

Stakeholder: Customers

Score (0–10)

Criterion 1.2 *Principle: Beyond Shareholders towards Stakeholders*

How does the company provide quality products and services which maximize their value to the customer while assuring respect for human dignity?

|-------|-------|-------|-------|-------|-------|-------|-------|-------|-------|

0	5	10
No Approach	Moderate Development	Excellent Development

Score: ______

Criterion 2.2 *Principle: Economic/Social Impact of Business*

How does the company assure protection for its customers, and demonstrate respect for their cultures in its marketing and communications?

|-------|-------|-------|-------|-------|-------|-------|-------|-------|-------|

0	5	10
No Approach	Moderate Development	Excellent Development

Score: ______

Criterion 3.2 *Principle: Business Behavior*

How does the company elicit the trust of customers (e.g., through responsible advertising, warranty fulfillment, etc.)?

|-------|-------|-------|-------|-------|-------|-------|-------|-------|-------|

0	5	10
No Approach	Moderate Development	Excellent Development

Score: ______

Criterion 4.2 *Principle: Respect for Rules*

How does the company manage compliance with the letter and spirit of national and international customer-related rules?

|-------|-------|-------|-------|-------|-------|-------|-------|-------|-------|

0	5	10
No Approach	Moderate Development	Excellent Development

Score: ______

Criterion 5.2 *Principle: Support for Multilateral Trade*

How does the company support its customers throughout the world, and improve the cost and quality of its good/services through international trade?

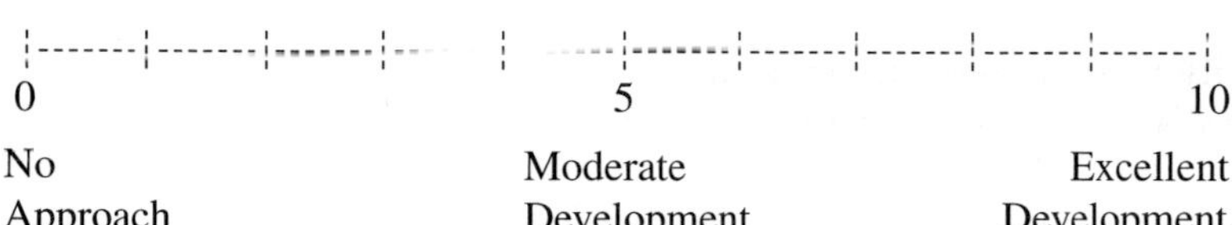

No Approach	Moderate Development	Excellent Development	_______

Criterion 6.2 *Principle: Respect for the Environment*

How does the company manage customer-related environmental issues (e.g., health and safety, "green design," recycling, etc.)?

No Approach	Moderate Development	Excellent Development	_______

Criterion 7.2 *Principle: Avoidance of Illicit Operations*

How does the company take action to prevent such illicit activities as deceptive sales practices and sales to inappropriate customers?

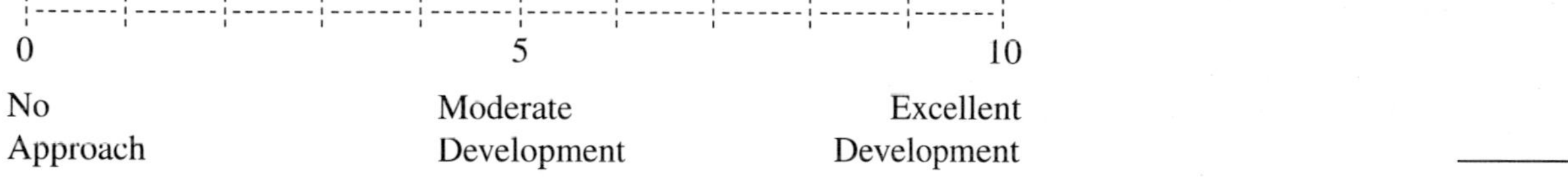

Total Score (maximum possible points = 70) _______

Stakeholder: Employees

Score (0–10)

Criterion 1.3 *Principle: Beyond Shareholders towards Stakeholders*

How does the company recognize employee interests and take steps to improve employees' lives, individually and collectively?

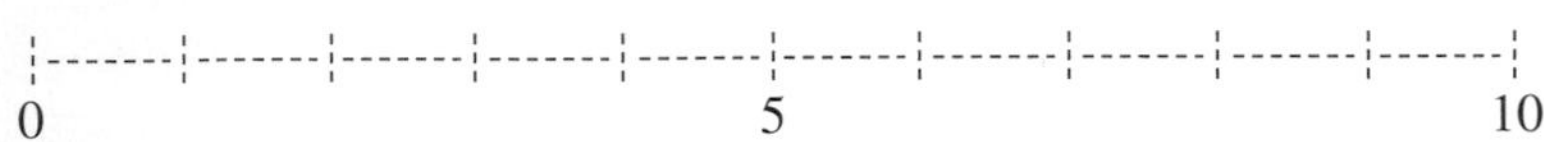

0 5 10

No Approach | Moderate Development | Excellent Development ______

Criterion 2.3 *Principle: Economic/Social Impact of Business*

How does the company create employment and employability, and honor human rights within its operations?

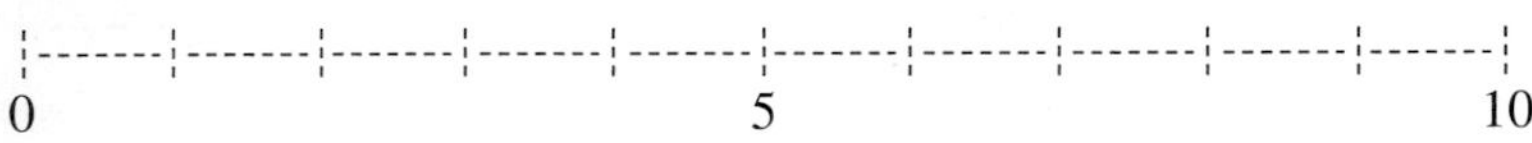

0 5 10

No Approach | Moderate Development | Excellent Development ______

Criterion 3.3 *Principle: Business Behavior*

How does the company elicit employee trust (e.g., through effective communication and dialogue, credible evaluation systems, etc.)?

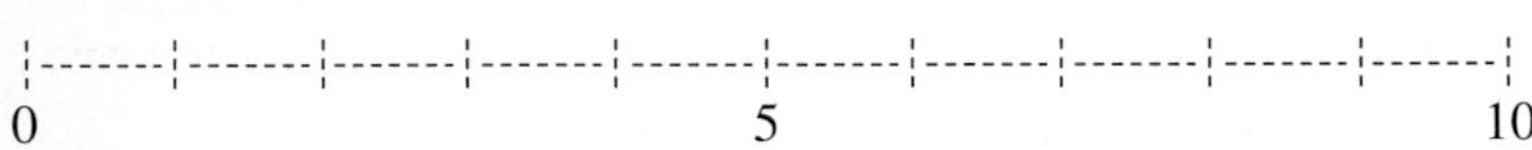

0 5 10

No Approach | Moderate Development | Excellent Development ______

Criterion 4.3 *Principle: Respect for Rules*

How does the company manage compliance with the letter and spirit of national and international employee-related rules?

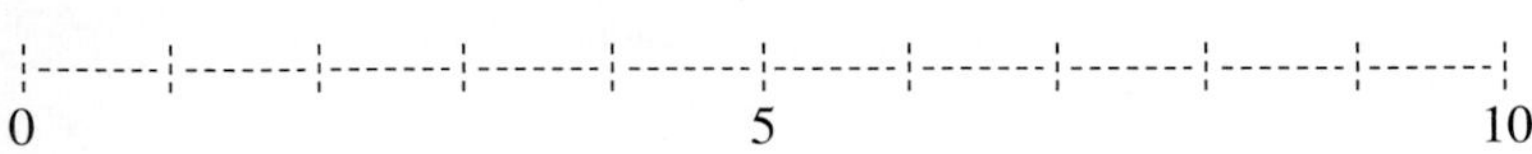

0 5 10

No Approach | Moderate Development | Excellent Development ______

Criterion 5.3 *Principle: Support for Multilateral Trade*

How does the company develop its human capital globally while attending to employee needs domestically?

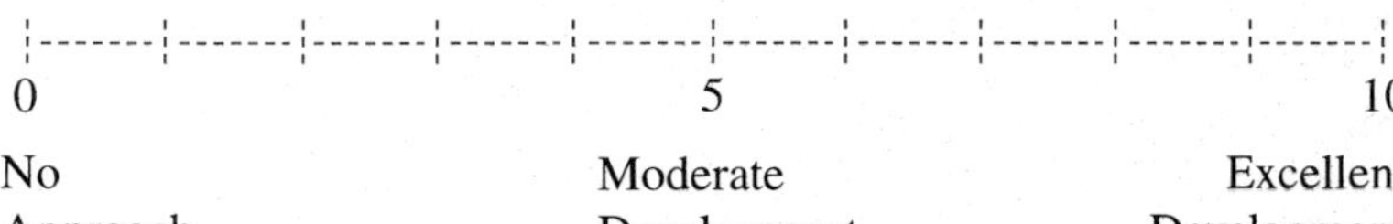

____

Criterion 6.3 *Principle: Respect for the Environment*

How do employee policies and practices help prevent environmental damage and promote sustainability?

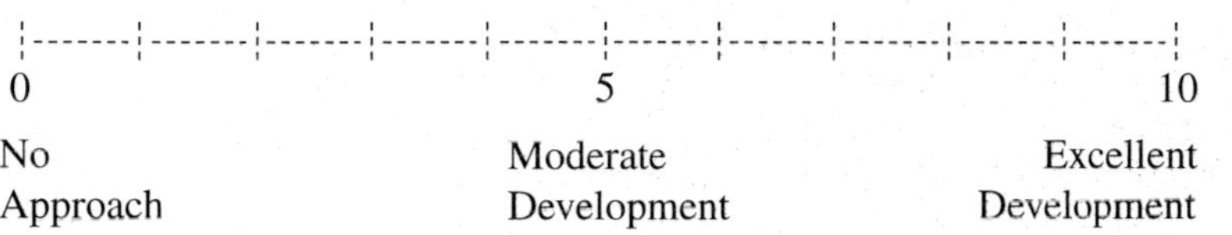

____

Criterion 7.3 *Principle: Avoidance of Illicit Operations*

How does the company take action to prevent illicit activities by employees (e.g., offering /accepting bribes, violating licensing or copyright restrictions, etc.)?

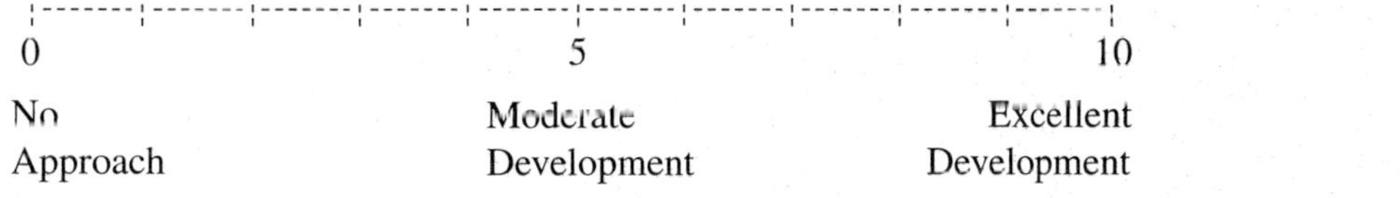

____

Total Score (maximum possible points = 70) _______

Stakeholder: Owners/Investors

Score (0–10)

Criterion 1.4 *Principle: Beyond Shareholders towards Stakeholders*

How does the company's governance structure assure the health and viability of the business, and respond to the concerns of current owners/investors and other stakeholders?

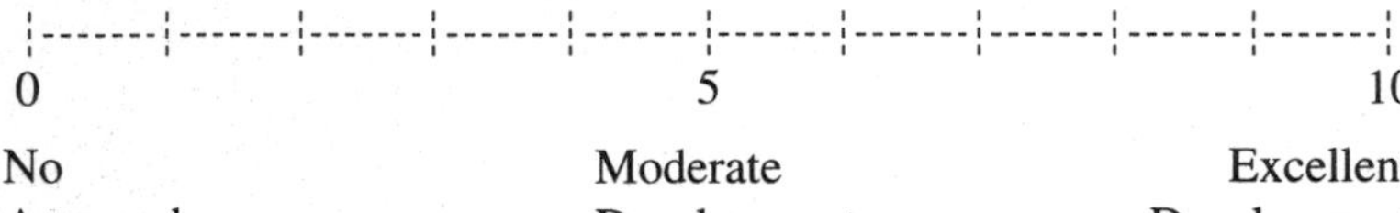

0 5 10

No Approach | Moderate Development | Excellent Development ______

Criterion 2.4 *Principle: Economic/Social Impact of Business*

How does the company use its resources to enhance the economic and social value of its products/services (e.g., through the development of new products/services, new applications for existing products, new production processes, etc.)?

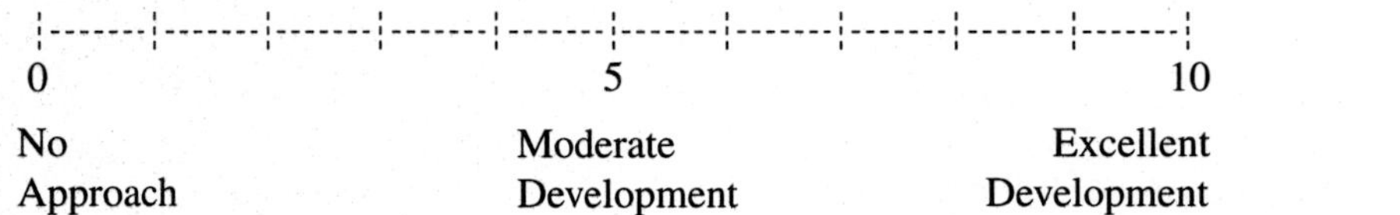

0 5 10

No Approach | Moderate Development | Excellent Development ______

Criterion 3.4 *Principle: Business Behavior*

How does the company elicit the trust of owners/investors (e.g., through responsible disclosures, timely and complete responses to shareholder/investor inquiries, governance policies and practices, etc.) ?

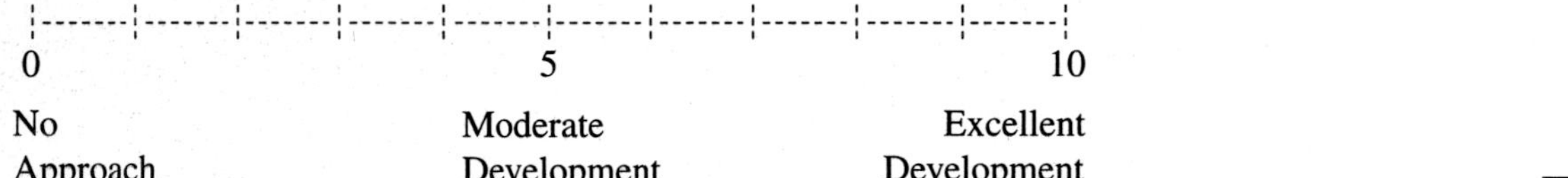

0 5 10

No Approach | Moderate Development | Excellent Development ______

Criterion 4.4 *Principle: Respect for Rules*

How does the company manage compliance with the letter and spirit of national and international owner/investor-related rules?

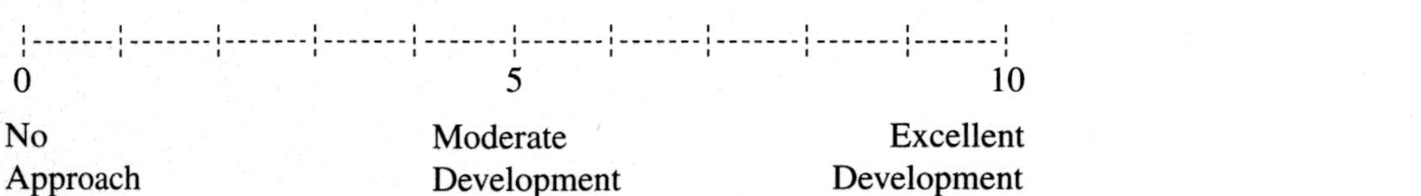

0 5 10

No Approach | Moderate Development | Excellent Development ______

Criterion 5.4 *Principle: Support for Multilateral Trade*

How does the company avail itself of international business opportunities for the benefit of owners/investors?

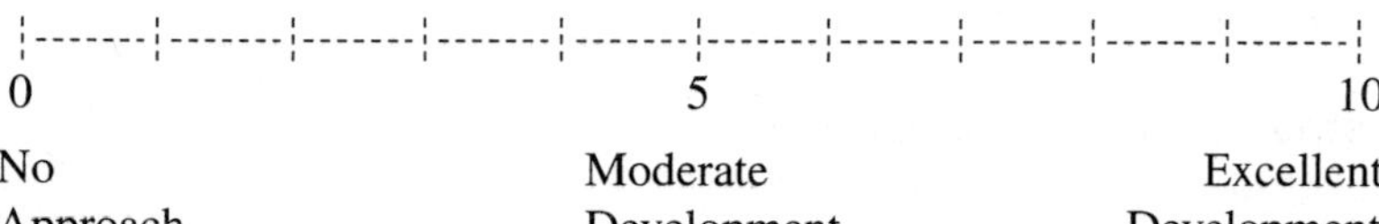

No Approach	Moderate Development	Excellent Development	______

Criterion 6.4 *Principle: Respect for the Environment*

How does the company manage environmental issues that impact owners/investors (e.g., health and safety risks, legacy issues, litigation and financial risks, etc.)?

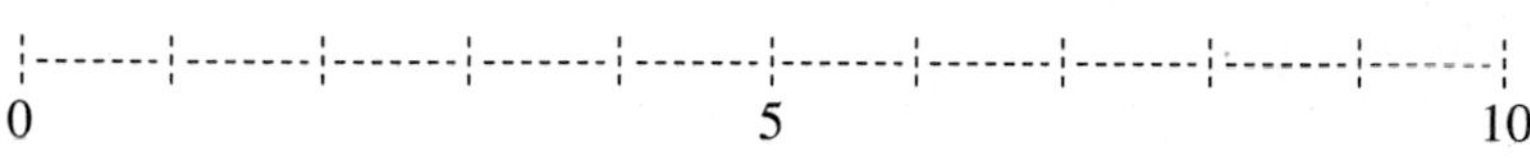

No Approach	Moderate Development	Excellent Development	______

Criterion 7.4 *Principle: Avoidance of Illicit Operations*

How does the company take action to prevent such illicit activities as insider trading and fraudulent reporting?

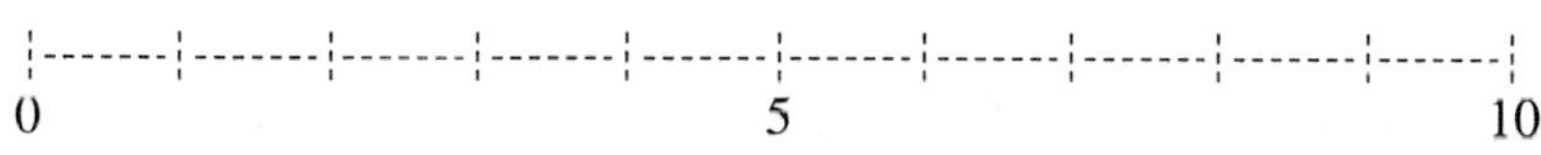

No Approach	Moderate Development	Excellent Development	______

Total Score (maximum possible points = 70) ______

Stakeholder: Supplier/Partners

Score (0–10)

Criterion 1.5 *Principle: Beyond Shareholders towards Stakeholders*

How does the company assure the practice of honesty and fairness in supplier/partner relationships (e.g., including, but not limited to, issues of pricing, technology licensing, right to sell, etc.)?

______

Criterion 2.5 *Principle: Economic/Social Impact of Business*

How does the company assure stable supplier/partner relationships, and the prudent and innovative utilization of resources by supplier/partners?

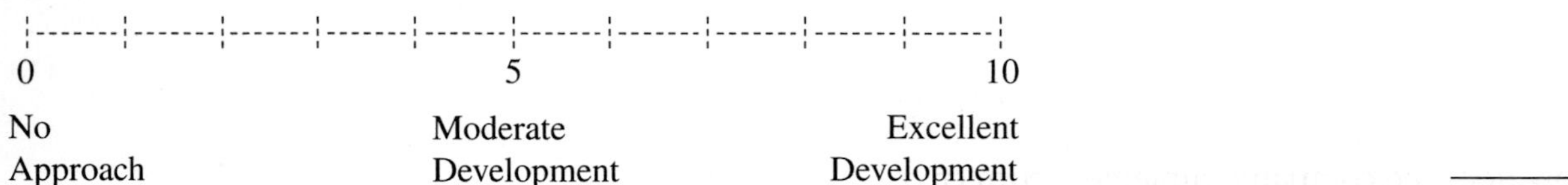

Criterion 3.5 *Principle: Business Behavior*

How does the company achieve trust with supplier/partners (e.g., through integrity in the bid evaluation process, protection of proprietary innovations, etc.)?

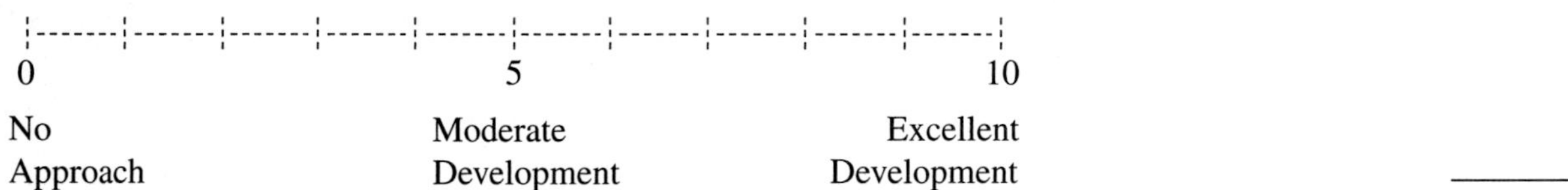

Criterion 4.5 *Principle: Respect for Rules*

How does the company manage compliance with the letter and spirit of national and international supplier/partner-related rules?

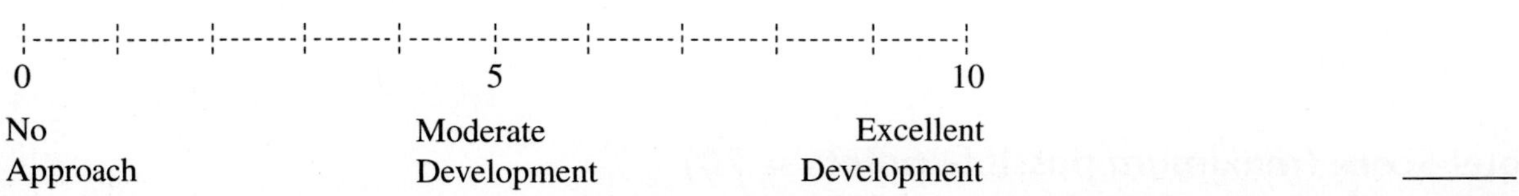

Criterion 5.5 *Principle: Support for Multilateral Trade*

How does the company seek and utilize international suppliers, in both its domestic and non-domestic operations?

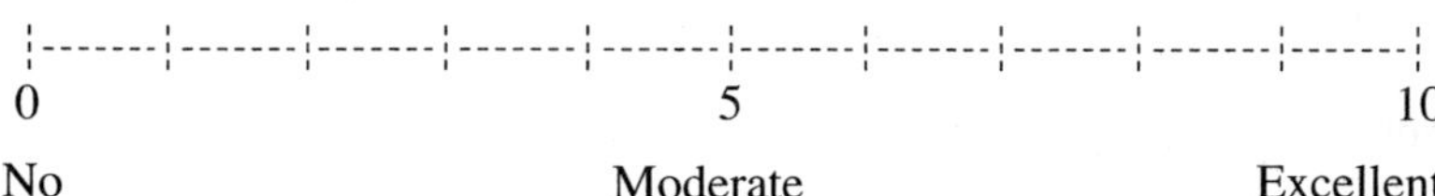

0	5	10
No Approach	Moderate Development	Excellent Development

______

Criterion 6.5 *Principle: Respect for the Environment*

How does the company manage environmental performance standards on a comparable basis throughout its supply chain?

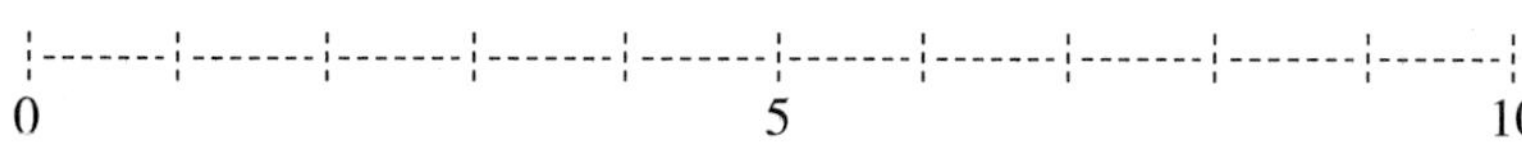

0	5	10
No Approach	Moderate Development	Excellent Development

______

Criterion 7.5 *Principle: Avoidance of Illicit Operations*

How does the company implement corrective action when it uncovers illicit activities by a supplier/partner?

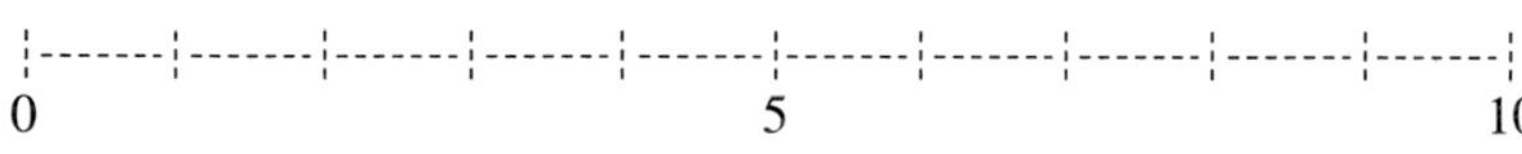

0	5	10
No Approach	Moderate Development	Excellent Development

______

Total Score (maximum possible points = 70) ______

Stakeholder: Competitors

Score (0–10)

Criterion 1.6 *Principle: Beyond Shareholders towards Stakeholders*

How does the company assure honesty and fairness in its relationships with competitors?

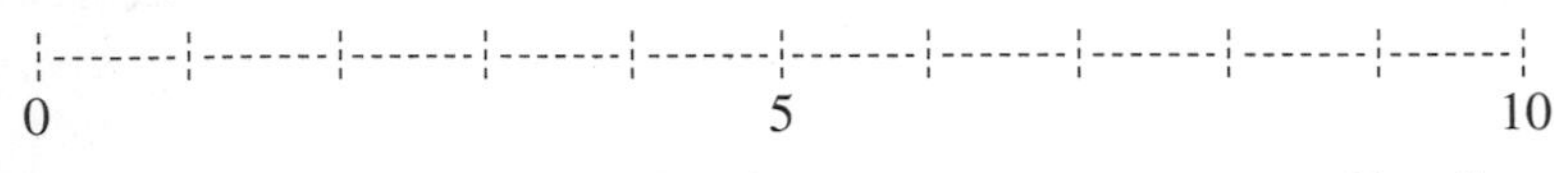

No Approach | Moderate Development | Excellent Development ______

Criterion 2.6 *Principle: Economic/Social Impact of Business*

How does the company promote free and fair competition in its home market and in other countries in which it operates?

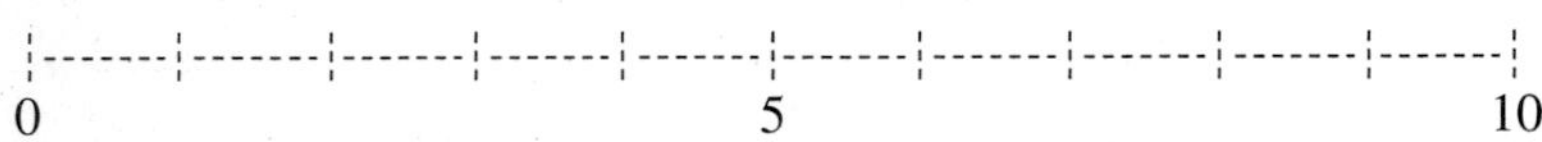

No Approach | Moderate Development | Excellent Development ______

Criterion 3.6 *Principle: Business Behavior*

How does the company achieve trust with competitors (e.g., by demonstrating respect for confidential competitor information, preventing the acquisition of commercial information by unethical means, etc.)?

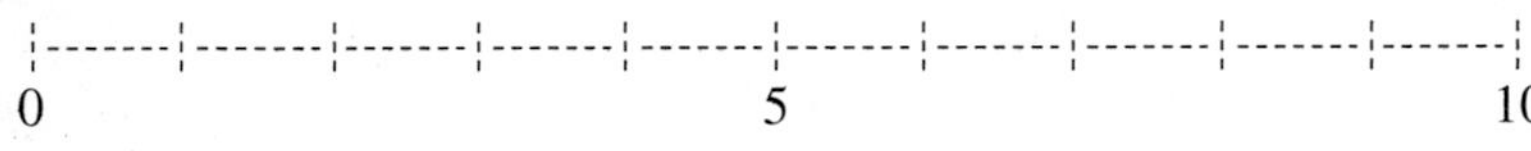

No Approach | Moderate Development | Excellent Development ______

Criterion 4.6 *Principle: Respect for Rules*

How does the company manage compliance with the letter and spirit of national and international competitor-related rules?

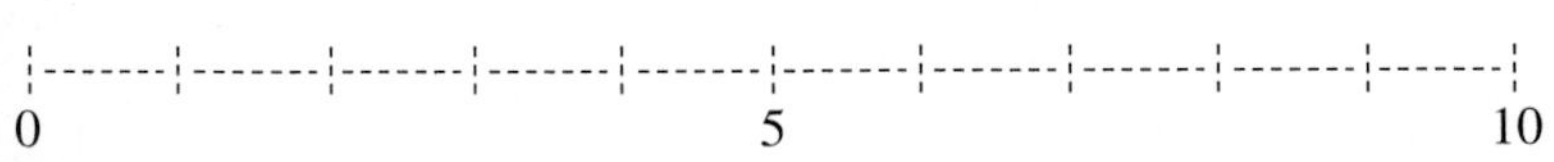

No Approach | Moderate Development | Excellent Development ______

Criterion 5.6 *Principle: Support for Multilateral Trade*

How does the company take action to generally promote the opening of new markets to free and fair trade?

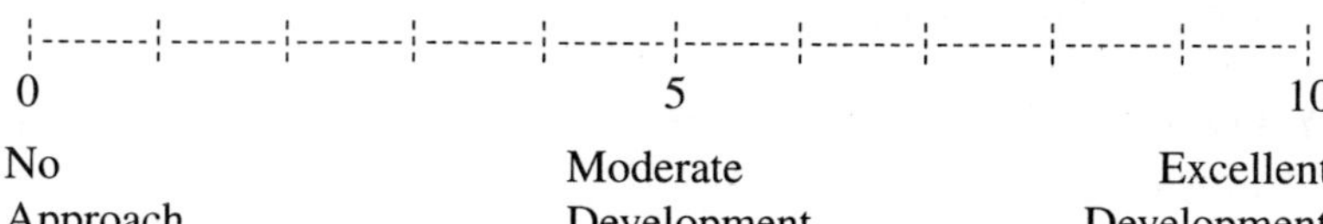

No Approach | Moderate Development | Excellent Development ______

Criterion 6.6 *Principle: Respect for the Environment*

How does the company participate in the development of industry-wide standards for environmental management, promoting both performance measurement and compliance?

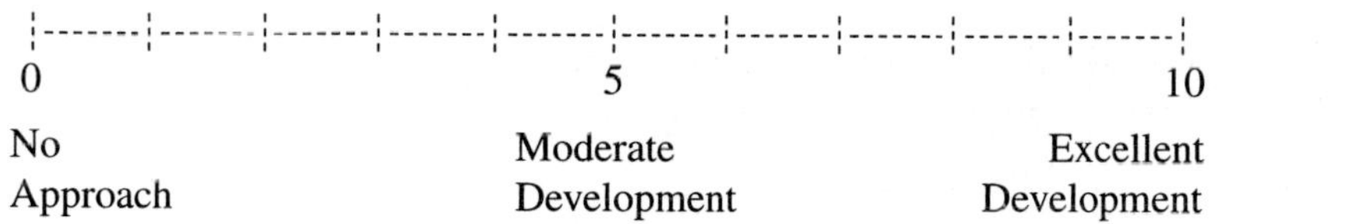

No Approach | Moderate Development | Excellent Development ______

Criterion 7.6 *Principle: Avoidance of Illicit Operations*

How does the company take action to prevent illicit competitive activities (e.g., illegal payments to secure a competitive advantage, collusion with competitors, etc.)?

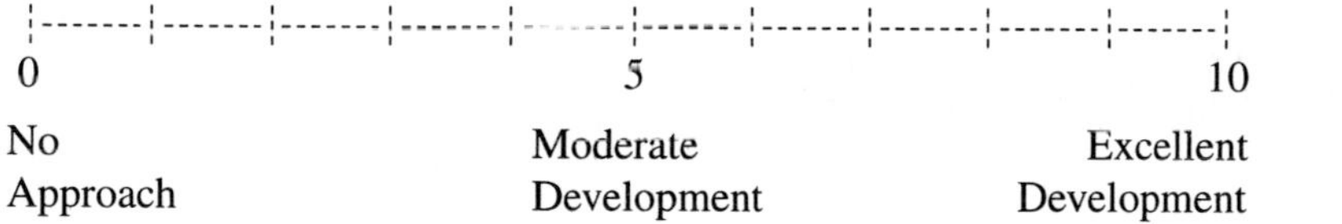

No Approach | Moderate Development | Excellent Development ______

Total Score (maximum possible points = 70) ______

Stakeholder: Communities

Score (0–10)

Criterion 1.7 *Principle: Beyond Shareholders towards Stakeholders*

How does the company demonstrate respect for the integrity of local cultures and for democratic institutions?

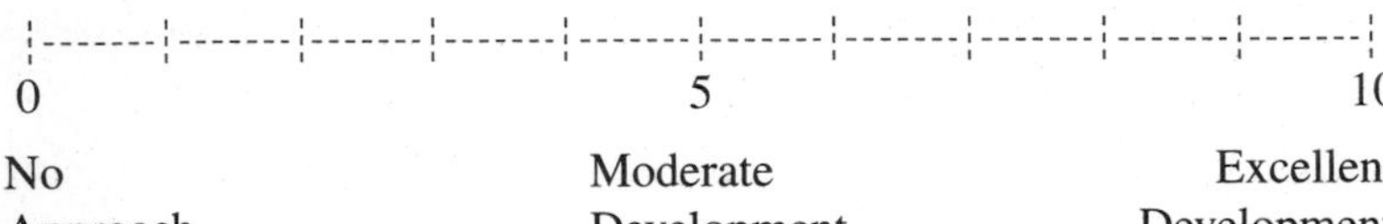

0 — 5 — 10

No Approach — Moderate Development — Excellent Development ______

Criterion 2.7 *Principle: Economic/Social Impact of Business*

How does the company contribute to the social and economic advancement of the communities in which it operates (e.g., promoting human rights, employability, the community 's economic vitalization, etc.)?

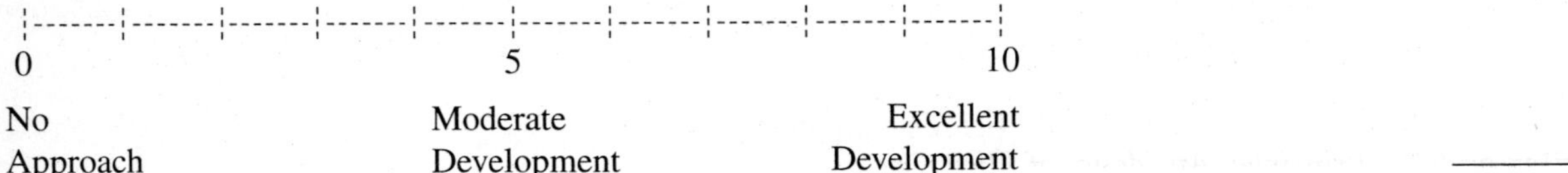

0 — 5 — 10

No Approach — Moderate Development — Excellent Development ______

Criterion 3.7 *Principle: Business Behavior*

How does the company identify important constituencies within its communities, eliciting trust from them (e.g., through effective dialogue, responsible disclosures, etc.)?

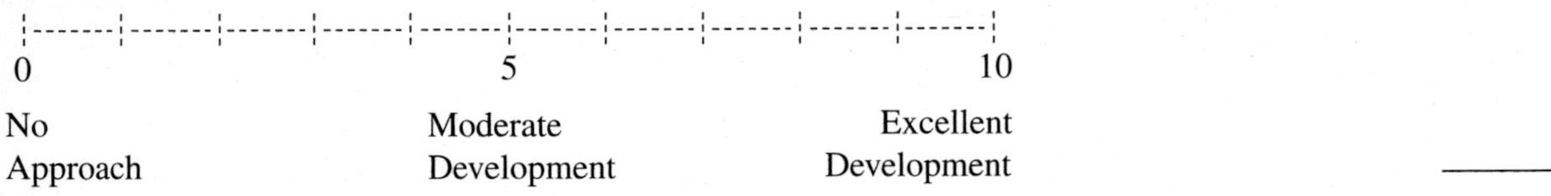

0 — 5 — 10

No Approach — Moderate Development — Excellent Development ______

Criterion 4.7 *Principle: Respect for Rules*

How does the company manage compliance with the letter and spirit of national and international community-related rules (e.g., the Worker Adjustment and Retraining Notification Act)?

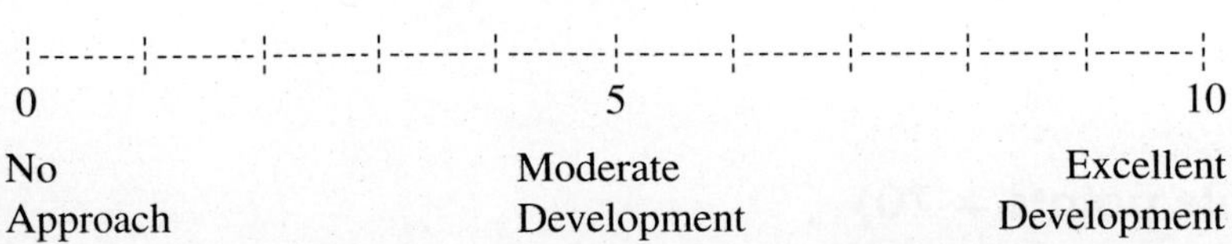

0 — 5 — 10

No Approach — Moderate Development — Excellent Development ______

Criterion 5.7 *Principle: Support for Multilateral Trade*

How does the company manage the impact of international trade upon its communities (e.g., issues related to increased or decreased employment levels, capital mobility and labor immobility, etc.)?

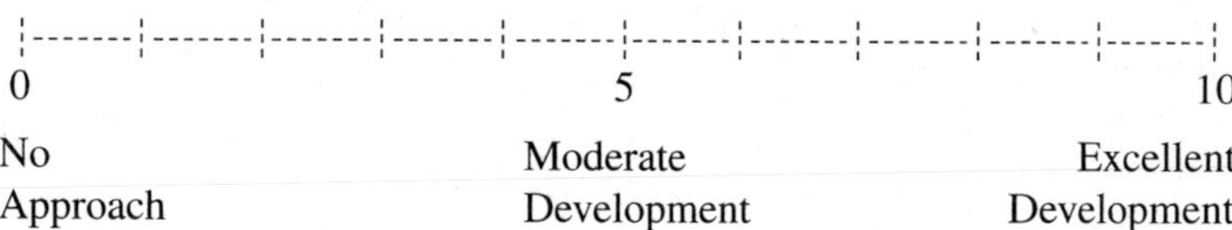

______

Criterion 6.7 *Principle: Respect for the Environment*

How does the company manage community-related environmental impacts (e.g., land management, water contamination, air pollution, noise pollution, etc.)?

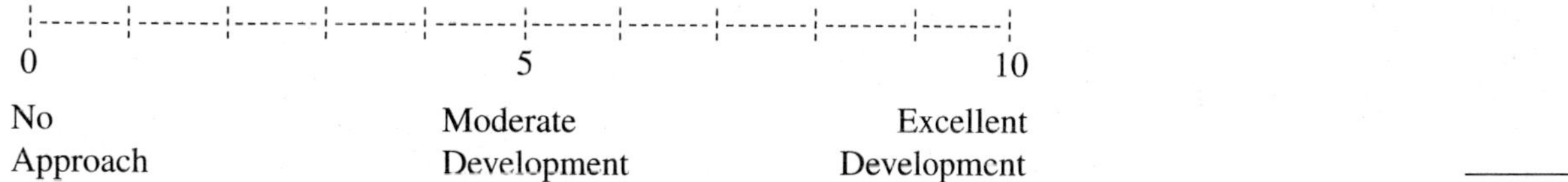

______

Criterion 7.7 *Principle: Avoidance of Illicit Operations*

How does the company take action to prevent such illicit activities as illegal campaign contributions and the avoidance of legitimate taxation?

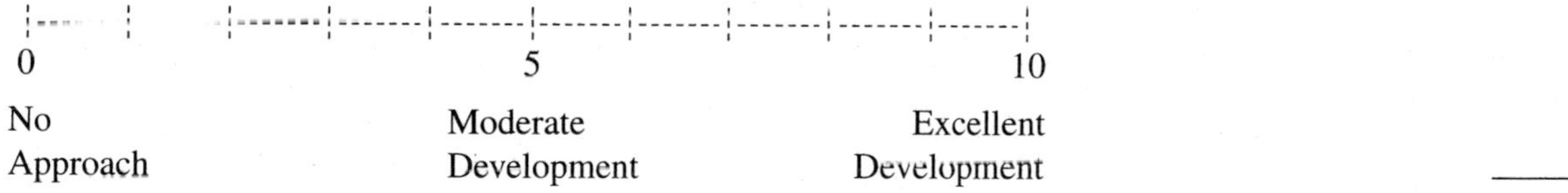

______

Total Score (maximum possible points = 70) ______

For More Information

If you are interested in learning more about the *Self-Assessment and Improvement Process,* or in exploring the possibility of utilizing the tool within your company, the following individuals can provide you with additional information:

Kenneth E. Goodpaster
Professor and Holder of the
Koch Chair in Business Ethics,
University of St. Thomas
Telephone: 651-962-4212
E-mail: kegoodpaster@stthomas.edu

T. Dean Maines
Project Director, Caux Round Table,
and Research Associate,
University of St. Thomas
Telephone: 651-962-4261
E-mail: tdmaines@stthomas.edu

Self-Assessment and Improvement Process—Executive Survey Scorecard

Company Name: ______________________

Stakeholders	**1. Fundamental Duties**		**2. Customers**		**3. Employees**		**4. Owners/ Investors**		**5. Suppliers/ Partners**		**6. Competitors**		**7. Community**		**Performance by Principle**	
Principles	Max. Pts.	Score	Max. Pts.	Score	Max. Pts.	Score	Max. Pts.	Score	Max. Pts.	Score	Max. Pts.	Score	Max. Pts.	Score	*Max. total points*	*Total score*
1. Responsibilities of Businesses	*1.1* 10		*1.2* 10		*1.3* 10		*1.4* 10		*1.5* 10		*1.6* 10		*1.7* 10		70	
2. Economic/ Social Impact of Business	*2.1* 10		*2.2* 10		*2.3* 10		*2.4* 10		*2.5* 10		*2.6* 10		*2.7* 10		70	
3. Business Behavior	*3.1* 10		*3.2* 10		*3.3* 10		*3.4* 10		*3.5* 10		*3.6* 10		*3.7* 10		70	
4. Respect for Rules	*4.1* 10		*4.2* 10		*4.3* 10		*4.4* 10		*4.5* 10		*4.6* 10		*4.7* 10		70	
5. Support for Multilateral Trade	*5.1* 10		*5.2* 10		*5.3* 10		*5.4* 10		*5.5* 10		*5.6* 10		*5.7* 10		70	
6. Respect for Environment	*6.1* 10		*6.2* 10		*6.3* 10		*6.4* 10		*6.5* 10		*6.6* 10		*6.7* 10		70	
7. Avoidance of Illicit Operations	*7.1* 10		*7.2* 10		*7.3* 10		*7.4* 10		*7.5* 10		*7.6* 10		*7.7* 10		70	
Performance By Stakeholder	70*	*Total score*	70*	*Total score*	70*	*Total score*	70*	*Total score*	70*	*Total score*	70*	*Total score*	70*	*Total score*	490	

* Maximum total points.

Alphabetical List of Case Studies